Ancient Egyptian Materials and Technology

This is a study of the procurement and processing of raw materials employed by the ancient Egyptians over the five millennia of the Predynastic and Pharaonic periods (*c.* 5500–332 BC). During this time, there were not only variations in the preferred materials for particular types of artefacts, but also gradual processes of technological change, and the industries of the Chalcolithic period were complemented and sometimes superseded by the innovations of the Bronze and Iron Ages. Among the topics covered are stone quarrying, the building of temples and pyramids, techniques for preserving meat, fish and poultry, the making of glass and faience, the baking of bread, the brewing of beers, the preparation of soils and perfumes and the mummification of humans and animals. Each chapter has been written by one or more specialists, drawing not only on conventional Egyptological skills but also on expertise in the natural sciences as applied to archaeological data.

Paul Nicholson is senior lecturer in Archaeology at Cardiff University. His publications include *Egyptian Faience and Glass* (1993), and (with Ian Shaw) *The British Museum Dictionary of Ancient Egypt* (1995). **Ian Shaw** is a lecturer at the Institute of Archaeology, University College London. He is the author of *Egyptian Warfare and Weapons* (1991) and *Timeline of the Ancient World* (1993), and editor (with Robert Jameson) of *A Dictionary of Archaeology* (1999).

Ancient Egyptian Materials and Technology

Edited by

Paul T. Nicholson
and Ian Shaw

CAMBRIDGE UNIVERSITY PRESS
Cambridge, New York, Melbourne, Madrid, Cape Town, Singapore, São Paulo, Delhi

Cambridge University Press
The Edinburgh Building, Cambridge, CB2 8RU, UK

Published in the United States of America by Cambridge University Press, New York

www.cambridge.org
Information on this title: www.cambridge.org/9780521452571

First published 2000
Fifth printing 2009

Printed in the United Kingdom at the University Press, Cambridge

A catalogue record for this publication is available from the British Library

Library of Congress Cataloguing in Publication data

Ancient Egyptian Materials and Technology / edited by Paul T.
Nicholson and Ian Shaw.
p. cm.
Includes index.
ISBN 0 521 45257 0 (hardback)
1. Building materials – Egypt. 2. Technology – Egypt. 3. Egypt –
civilization – To 332 BC. 4. Raw materials – Egypt. I. Nicholson,
Paul T. II. Shaw, Ian, 1961– .
TA402.5.E3A53 1999
620.1'1'0932 – dc21 98–3434 CIP

ISBN 978-0-521-45257-1 hardback

Contents

Figures

Tables

Contributors

BARBARA ASTON, Daly City, California
NEIL BOULTON, Department of Archaeological Sciences, University of Bradford
JANINE D. BOURRIAU, The McDonald Institute for Archaeological Research, University of Cambridge
ROSALIE DAVID, The Manchester Museum, University of Manchester
JOANN FLETCHER, Manchester, UK
ROWENA GALE, Royal Botanic Gardens at Kew
PETER GASSON, Royal Botanic Gardens at Kew
JAMES HARRELL, Department of Geology, University of Toledo, Ohio
JULIAN HENDERSON, Department of Archaeology, University of Nottingham
NIGEL HEPPER, Richmond, Surrey
CARL HERON, Department of Archaeological Sciences, University of Bradford
SALIMA IKRAM, American University in Cairo
BARRY KEMP, The McDonald Institute for Archaeological Research, University of Cambridge
GEOFFREY KILLEN, St Ives, Cambridgeshire
OLGA KRZYSZKOWSKA, Institute of Classical Studies, University of London
BRIDGET LEACH, Department of Conservation, British Museum
LORNA LEE, Department of Conservation, British Museum
ROBERT MORKOT, DCAE, University of Exeter
MARY ANNE MURRAY, Institute of Archaeology, University College London
RICHARD NEWMAN, Research Laboratory, Museum of Fine Arts, Boston, Massachusetts
PAUL T. NICHOLSON, School of History and Archaeology, Cardiff University
JACK OGDEN, Cambridge
EDGAR PELTENBURG, Department of Archaeology, University of Edinburgh
JACKE PHILLIPS, The McDonald Institute for Archaeological Research, University of Cambridge
STEPHEN QUIRKE, Petrie Museum, University College, London
PAMELA ROSE, The McDonald Institute for Archaeological Research, University of Cambridge
DELWEN SAMUEL, Institute of Archaeology, University College London
MARGARET SERPICO, Wainwright Fellow, London
IAN SHAW, Institute of Archaeology, University College London
JOHN TAIT, Institute of Archaeology, University College London
CAROL VAN DRIEL-MURRAY, Instituut voor Pre- en Protohistorische Archeologie, Amsterdam
GILLIAN VOGELSANG-EASTWOOD, Department of Egyptology, University of Leiden
WILHEMINA WENDRICH, University of Leiden
RAYMOND WHITE, London

Note

It should be noted that the order of authors given at the start of each chapter does not necessarily indicate seniority of authorship. Where authors have collaborated extensively on chapters and it is not possible to identify particular sections, the authors generally appear in alphabetical order. Where sections are readily identifiable, the authors usually appear in order of their individual contributions, and these are further marked in the text.

Acknowledgements

We would like to thank Sal and Barbie Garfi for their redrawing and inking of most of the line-drawings and Ian Dennis for his work on supplementary illustrations. Nigel Hepper kindly allowed us to reproduce many of his botanical drawings. We are also indebted to Stuart Laidlaw and the Photographic Department of the Institute of Archaeology, University College London, for producing many of the photographs throughout the book. We would like to thank the Committee of the Egypt Exploration Society, the Trustees of the British Museum, London and the Trustees of the Metropolitan Museum of Art, New York for their generous permission to use a number of line-drawings and photographs from their publications. We are grateful to numerous other colleagues and institutes for permission to use other illustrations and those are credited in the list of figures. We are extremely grateful to the Humanities Research Board of the British Academy for a grant covering the cost of preparation and inking of line-drawings. We are indebted to New Hall, Cambridge University, the Institute of Archaeology, University College London (Shaw), the Department of Archaeology, University of Sheffield, and the School of History and Archaeology, Cardiff University (Nicholson) for their support during the time that the book was being produced. We are grateful to Jane Collins of the School of History and Archaeology for her assistance in printing out the typescript. We would particularly like to thank Professor Keith Branigan of the University of Sheffield, and his wife Mrs N. Branigan and Dr Caroline M. Jackson, for their assistance in holding a seminar for the contributors at the Department of Archaeology in January, 1994. We are most grateful to Dr Jessica Kuper, Archaeology and Anthropology Editor at CUP, for her patience and advice during the commissioning and preparation of the book. Finally, we would like to thank the contributors for taking part in the project and for their unstinting efforts over several years.

Paul T. Nicholson and Ian Shaw
August, 1999

Abbreviations

AGSE *Annals of the Geological Survey of Egypt*
AIHV Association Internationale pour l'Histoire du Verre
AJA *American Journal of Archaeology*
AO *Archiv für Orientforschung*
ARCE The American Research Center in Egypt
ASAE *Annales du Service des Antiquités de l'Egypte, Cairo*
a.s.l. above sea level
BAR *British Archaeological Reports*
BES *Bulletin of the Egyptological Seminar*
BIE *Bulletin de l'Institut d'Egypte, Cairo*
BIFAO *Bulletin de l'Institut Français d'Archéologie Orientale*
BL *Bulletin de Liaison*
BM British Museum
BMFA *Bulletin of the Museum of Fine Arts, Boston*
BMMA *Bulletin of the Metropolitan Museum of Art*
BMP British Museum Press
BMQ *British Museum Quarterly*
BSA *Bulletin of Sumerian Agriculture*
BSAE British School of Archaeology in Egypt
BSFE *Bulletin de la Société Française d'Egyptologie*
CAJ *Cambridge Archaeological Journal*
CBA Council for British Archaeology
CCE *Cahiers de la Céramique Egyptienne*
CdE *Chronique d'Egypte*
CNRS Centre National de la Recherche Scientifique (France)
CNWS Centre for Non-Western Studies, Leiden
CRIPEL *Cahiers de Recherche de l'Institut de Papyrologie et Egyptologie de Lille*
CSJ *Cairo Scientific Journal*
CUP Cambridge University Press
DAIK Deutsches Archäologisches Instituts, Abteilung Kairo
DE *Discussions in Egyptology*
DOG Deutsche Orient-Gesellschaft
EA *Egyptian Archaeology*
EEF Egypt Exploration Fund
EES Egypt Exploration Society
ERA Egyptian Research Account
ET *Etudes et Travaux*
FAO Food and Agriculture Organisation
GM *Göttinger Miszellen*
GSE Geological Survey of Egypt
HMSO Her Majesty's Stationery Office
IEJ *Israel Exploration Journal*
IFAO Institut Français d'Archéologie Orientale
JAOS *Journal of the American Oriental Society*
JARCE *Journal of the American Research Center in Egypt, Boston*
JAS *Journal of Archaeological Science*
JEA *Journal of Egyptian Archaeology*
JNES *Journal of Near Eastern Studies*
Kêmi *Kêmi: Revue de Philologie et d'Archéologie Egyptiennes et Coptes, Paris*
Kew Museum of the Royal Botanic Gardens at Kew
KPI Kegan Paul International
LÄ *Lexikon der Ägyptologie*
MDAIK *Mitteilungen des Deutschen Archäologischen Instituts, Abteilung Kairo*
MFA Museum of Fine Arts, Boston
MMA Metropolitan Museum of Art, New York
OIP Oriental Institute Press, University of Chicago
OMRO Oudheidkundige Mededeelingen uit het Rijksmuseum van Oudheden te Leiden
OUP Oxford University Press
PEQ *Palestine Exploration Quarterly*
PPS *Proceedings of the Prehistoric Society*
PSBA *Proceedings of the Society of Biblical Archaeology, London*
RdE *Revue d'Egyptologie*
RT *Receuil de Travaux Rélatifs à la Philologie et à l'Archéologie Egyptiennes et Assyriennes*
SAE Service des Antiquités de l'Egypte, Cairo
SAK *Studien zur Altägyptischen Kultur, Hamburg*
WA *World Archaeology*
ZÄS *Zeitschrift für Ägyptische Sprache und Altertumskunde, Leipzig and Berlin*

1. Introduction

PAUL T. NICHOLSON AND IAN SHAW

During the last two decades the nature of Egyptology has gradually changed, and new technological and socio-economic questions are now being asked of the archaeological data. With this change has come a renewed interest in many aspects of Egyptian materials and technology. So great has this interest become that it is no longer possible for the traditional Egyptologist alone to tackle such questions as the composition of materials, provenance and the means by which different types of artefacts were produced. Many new analytical techniques have been developed and applied and the results are now available, providing a great deal more precision than was previously imaginable.

These new approaches currently being adopted in Egyptology are reflected in the structure of this book. Each chapter has been written by one or more specialists, drawing not only on conventional Egyptological skills but also on expertise in the natural sciences as applied to archaeological data. All the contributors are either involved in recent field projects in Egypt (not least the important Egypt Exploration Society excavations at Amarna and Memphis), or at the forefront of laboratory-based analysis of archaeological materials.

It will be obvious to many readers that this volume has been inspired by Alfred Lucas's classic work *Ancient Egyptian Materials and Industries*, which has long served Egyptologists as a standard work of reference. First published in 1926, Lucas's book has been revised several times, most recently in 1962, when it was updated, primarily in terms of its bibliographic references, by J.R. Harris (see Lucas 1926, 1934, 1948, 1962). Even the fourth edition still primarily reflects the analytical work of a single individual employing the necessarily limited equipment available in the 1920s (see Brunton 1947 and Gilberg 1997 for assessments of the life and work of Alfred Lucas). Despite the importance of Lucas's work, it has long been recognised that a more modern multi-disciplinary treatment is required, giving not only the result of analyses and technological investigations but also explicitly stating the means by which they were obtained.

While this current volume will not 'replace' Lucas's work, and is not intended as a revised edition of it, it is hoped that it will provide a free-standing source of reference on its subject. Thanks to modern analytical techniques, some chapters will almost entirely supersede those provided by Lucas, while others will provide updated approaches concentrating on new data and new questions. The study of ancient Egyptian material and technology is a vibrant one, with research being conducted by many scholars all over the world (a situation reflected in the diverse list of contributors here). This is quite unlike the situation in the 1920s and 1930s, when most Egyptologists were interested in linguistic and architectural questions, and Lucas was one of a relatively small group of scholars concerned with the analysis of artefacts. As a result of the new vigour of the subject, this volume will perhaps not enjoy the very long currency of Lucas's work but will, we hope, provide a solid basis for future work.

Here we are fundamentally concerned with the study of the procurement and processing of the raw materials employed by the ancient Egyptians. The book is not meant to be an art historical typology of objects produced in any given material, nor a text book on the scientific analysis of such materials. Each chapter is intended to provide an overview of the current state of research on the material in question. In some cases, this is not possible, either because modern research on certain materials (e.g. leather, meat, basketry) has only just begun or because the quantity of data has become so great in recent years that the most meaningful approaches tend to be those that focus on particular problems (as in the case of the chapters on pottery, stone and mummies).

The basic structure and coverage of the book were finalised at a seminar involving most of the contributors in 1994, when it was agreed that chapters on food technology should be included, as these represent a fruitful area of research that has almost entirely emerged in the years since Lucas's time. The contributors have made every effort to provide explicit information on the scientific analyses conducted, since the lack of such detail has been an increasing problem in judging the value of some of Lucas's conclusions. It was also agreed that some indication of the workings and limitations of relevant analytical techniques was necessary so that non-specialists would be better able to judge the results of earlier and current research.

References

Brunton, G. 1947. Alfred Lucas, 1867–1945. *ASAE*, 47: 1–6.

Gilberg, M. 1997. Alfred Lucas: Egypt's Sherlock Holmes. *Journal of the American Institute for Conservation*, 36: 31–48.

Lucas, A. 1926. *Ancient Egyptian Materials and Industries*. 1st edn. London: Longman, Green and Co.

1934. *Ancient Egyptian Materials and Industries*. 2nd edn. London: Edward Arnold.

1948. *Ancient Egyptian Materials and Industries*. 3rd edn. London: Edward Arnold.

1962. *Ancient Egyptian Materials and Industries*. 4th edn., rev. J.R. Harris. London: Edward Arnold.

Part I.
Inorganic materials

2. Stone

BARBARA G. ASTON, JAMES A. HARRELL AND IAN SHAW

Introduction

Although most recent research into Egyptian quarrying has tended to concentrate on the large-scale procurement of limestone, sandstone and granite in the Pharaonic period, the exploitation of stone in the Nile valley can be traced back at least as early as 40,000 BP, when the Middle Palaeolithic inhabitants of Middle Egypt were quarrying and working cobbles of chert along the limestone terraces on either side of the Nile (Vermeersch *et al.* 1990). Most of the earliest sites simply consist of pits and trenches for surface extraction, but Site 4 at Nazlet Khater, dating to the Upper Palaeolithic and radiocarbon-dated to 35,000– 30,000 BP, includes vertical shafts and underground galleries which provide a foretaste of the fully developed quarrying techniques of the Pharaonic period. The early chert quarriers used gazelle and hartebeest horns as picks, and several of these were found in the subterranean galleries at Nazlat Khater 4. The excavations also revealed many large hammerstones, apparently used for rougher quarrying.

The prehistoric quarrying of such materials as chert was essentially a question of small communities procuring locally available materials in order to produce the tools and weapons necessary for their immediate needs. Although there is evidence to show that such *ad hoc*, small-scale quarrying and mining continued to be undertaken to some extent in the Pharaonic period, in the case of certain materials (e.g. alabaster gypsum at Umm el-Sawwan, galena at Gebel Zeit and perhaps also New Kingdom procurement of travertine at Hatnub, see Kemp 1989: 191, 246–8; Castel and Soukiassian 1985, 1989; Shaw 1994: 111–14), such stones as granite, limestone and gneiss began to be exploited on a large scale for building, sculpture and stone-vessel carving. These large-scale expeditions differed in a number of ways from the quarrying undertaken by small groups of individuals: first they were official operations controlled either by the king or a local provincial governor, secondly they were often commemorated by the creation of rock-carvings and hieroglyphic inscriptions at the quarries themselves, and thirdly a new ideological and political element gradually emerged, whereby the king seems to have exercised a virtual monopoly on the quarrying and mining of many raw materials. The king was able to use this monopoly not only as a means of rewarding officials (by granting them blocks of freshly quarried stone to be carved into sarcophagi or false doors, for instance, see Lichtheim 1973: 18–23) but also as a means of gaining favour with the god's. The reliefs and inscriptions in the treasuries of some of the major Greco-Roman temples indicate that the god's shrine was intended to be a microcosm of the universe, including all the essential vegetable and mineral components (see Aufrère 1991: 731–48, 809–20; Shaw 1998: 253–6). There was therefore not only a practical impetus for mining and quarrying in terms of the acquisition of materials necessary for the creation of temples, tombs and funerary equipment, but also an ideological spur, in that the king was obliged to 'recreate' the cosmos by gathering together its fundamental elements and placing them in the temple treasuries (e.g. the use of black basalt to create temple pavements symbolising the fertile silt of the Nile valley).

The first section of this chapter discusses the general evidence for quarrying, primary processing and transportation of different types of stone in the Pharaonic period. In the second section, specific quarries of the Pharaonic, Ptolemaic and Roman periods are described in the form of an alphabetically arranged list of the various stone types. The third section comprises a short summary of research into ancient Egyptian stone-working technology. The fourth section summarises the current state of the subject in terms of techniques of identification and provenancing of stone.

Quarrying, *in situ* processing and transportation

The creation of the first tombs incorporating stone masonry, in the Early Dynastic élite cemeteries at Abydos and Saqqara (*c.* 3000–2649 BC), was the stimulus for a rapid growth in the quarrying of building stone such as limestone and granite. At the same time, the growing need for tombs to be filled with stone vessels symbolising the wealth of the deceased led to the large-scale procurement of such materials as travertine, alabaster gypsum, limestone breccia, basalt, limestone, granite, granodiorite, greywacke, sandstone, siltstone, andesite porphyry, serpentinite, tuff and anorthosite gneiss, which were the preferred materials for funerary vessels in the Early Dynastic period. It is clear from the jewellery found in some of the First-Dynasty tombs (particularly that of King Djer at Abydos) that such gemstones as turquoise and cornelian were also being heavily exploited in the first two Dynasties (and probably considerably earlier, see Beit-Arieh 1980), along with the various precious metals obtained from the Eastern Desert, the Sinai peninsula and Nubia.

During the Old Kingdom (*c.* 2649–2152 BC), the construction of numerous royal pyramid complexes in the Memphite necropolis resulted in an unprecedented demand for stone which probably peaked in the Fourth Dynasty, when the largest pyramids were built. Lehner (1985: 109) calculates that 9 million tons of limestone alone were quarried between the reigns of Sneferu and Menkaura for the pyramid complexes at Dahshur and Giza. It was also at this time that many other stones began to be exploited on a large scale for buildings: granite and granodiorite from Aswan, basalt from the Fayum and travertine from Middle Egypt.

Soft-stone quarrying methods

The vast majority of quarrying during the Pharaonic period was concerned with the procurement of the two principal 'soft stones' used for ceremonial, religious or funerary structures: limestone and sandstone (the quarries for which are discussed below). Limestone, virtually all deposits of which are found at numerous locations between Cairo and Esna, was exploited from the end of the Early Dynastic period until the Eighteenth Dynasty (after which its importance as a building stone went into decline). Sandstone, on the other hand, is found in Upper Egypt, from Esna down to Sudan, and was used in the south from the Eleventh Dynasty onwards. Most of the important surviving temples of the period between the Eighteenth Dynasty and the Roman period were constructed from sandstone.

Outcrops of limestone and sandstone most suitable for quarrying were those having a uniform colouration and fine texture, at least moderate hardness and thick layers with widely spaced vertical fractures. The ancient quarrymen would identify a single rock layer (or series of layers) with the requisite properties and then quarry it at one or more places along the margins of the Nile valley, wherever it was best developed. In many cases it was the quality of the rock rather than its accessibility that dictated where a quarry was located. This is evident from the fact that many ancient quarries are found on the upper slopes of hills and escarpments rather than at their base, where similar but lower quality rock occurs.

Blocks of sandstone and limestone were extracted by the following means, more than one of which might sometimes be combined in one quarry:

(1) large open excavations;
(2) the removal of the vertical faces or horizontal tops of cliffs; and
(3) the excavation of deep adits and galleries (usually in order to reach the best quality rock).

All three of these methods were used for limestone and travertine. However, with the exception of some Middle Kingdom galleries in part of the Gebel el-Silsila sandstone quarry, all sandstone and hardstone quarries were 'open-cut' (i.e. not of the gallery type).

The open-cut process generally comprised a number of stages, beginning with the removal of surface material such as sand or rubble. The next step usually consisted of the marking of the cleaned surface either with painted lines or sequences of chisel-cut indentations in order to indicate where the rows of blocks were to be cut out (each separated from the next by a trench ranging from at least 20 to 60 cm in width, depending on the sizes of the blocks). These trenches were then excavated to a depth which was usually at least 30 cm below the bases of the blocks, thus leaving rows of rock stumps, as in the case of the limestone quarry beside the Fourth-Dynasty pyramid of Khafra at Giza.

In the case of limestone and travertine, the removal of blocks from a vertical cliff face was sometimes the first stage in a process of deeper gallery-style extraction (see Owen and Kemp 1994 for a discussion of the common ground between the excavation of rock-tombs and quarries at Amarna), usually when the better quality stone was covered by an upper layer of poorer quality material. The initial face would be scaled by a series of steps cut into the outer face of the rock. The workers would then carve out a corridor along the ceiling of the gallery, thus allowing them to cut down behind the front row of blocks, detaching rows of blocks from the top downwards, gradually moving backwards deeper into the gallery.

Hard-stone quarrying methods

Of all the hard stones available in Pharaonic Egypt, granite and granodiorite were the only ones that were used for building purposes on anything like the scale of limestone and sandstone. The granite quarries at Aswan, which were exploited from the First Dynasty onwards, are the only hard-stone quarries that have been studied in any detail (e.g. Clarke and Engelbach 1930; Röder 1965; Arnold 1991: 36–40; see Fig. 2.3), although there have been recent detailed studies of both quartzite and gneiss quarrying (see Klemm *et al.* 1984 and Stross *et al.* 1988 for quartzite, and Harrell and Brown 1994 for gneiss). On the basis of surviving buildings and other monuments, Röder (1965) estimates that 45,000 cubic metres of stone were removed from the Aswan quarries in the Old Kingdom, when it seems likely that the loose boulders spread across the surface would have been exploited (Reisner 1931: 71). It was in the New Kingdom, however, that the largest quantities of granite seem to have been quarried, including numerous Eighteenth- and Nineteenth-Dynasty colossal statues and obelisks.

Undoubtedly the most important source of knowledge on granite quarrying is the so-called 'unfinished obelisk', which is located in the northern quarries (a few kilometres to the southeast of the centre of modern Aswan; see Fig. 2.4) and probably dates to the 18th Dynasty (see Engelbach 1922; Habachi 1960; Arnold 1991: 37–9). Work on this obelisk, nearly forty-two metres in length, was abandoned at a relatively late stage in the process of its extraction, when significant cracking became apparent. After removing the weathered upper layers of the granite, a trench was excavated, thus marking out the shape of the obelisk, still attached to the bedrock. The surrounding trench has a width of about 0.75 metres and is divided into a series of 0.6–metre-wide working areas (marked out by vertical red lines down the side of the trench), which would have been able to accommodate as many as fifty workmen around the obelisk at any one time. It is clear from the surviving marks made by the quarry-overseers on quarry-faces at Aswan, that the depth of each trench was regularly assessed by lowering a cubit rod into it and marking the top of the rod with a triangle. Once the trench had reached the necessary depth, the workers would gradually undercut the block, a process which was just beginning in the case of the unfinished obelisk. Finally, in order to move the quarried obelisk from its matrix, one end would have to be quarried out completely, thus allowing the obelisk to be pushed horizontally out (a considerably easier task than attempting to pull it vertically upwards out of the hole).

Quarrying tools

There is some uncertainty as to the kinds of tools used for the quarrying of soft stones during the Pharaonic period (see Arnold 1991: 33). The tool marks preserved on quarry walls suggest that some form of pointed pick or axe was used during the Old and Middle Kingdoms, followed by the use of a mallet-driven pointed chisel from the Eighteenth Dynasty onwards (Klemm 1988). In the case of a small number of blocks, a very large stone chisel seems to have been used, judging from the presence of 2.5 cm-wide grooves (see Arnold 1987: pls. 9d and 33b). R. and D. Klemm argue that the majority of the tool marks were made by soft copper chisels in the Old and Middle Kingdoms and harder copper or bronze chisels from the New Kingdom onwards (with the characteristic patterns possibly allowing specific chronological phases to be identified, e.g. a herringbone sequence of marks in the Eighteenth Dynasty). There appear, however, to be at least two problems with the Klemms' proposed sequence of copper tools: firstly the actual surviving chisels (albeit found at construction sites rather than quarries) tend to have a broad, flat cutting edge rather than a point, and secondly the harder forms of copper alloy were already available in the Old and Middle Kingdoms (see Chapter 6, this volume). Chert was also used for stone-working (for further discussion see section on the uses of chert below).

The question of the types of tools used for the extraction of granite and other hard stones is equally controversial. On the basis of long sequences of rectangular wedge holes at the Aswan quarries (see Fig. 2.5), it was once assumed that the granite was removed by inserting wetted wooden wedges into the holes and levering the blocks away from the bedrock. There are now two fundamental objections to this theory: first, that wooden wedges, even when expanded by soaking them in water, would almost certainly not have been strong enough to fracture the granite (although for an extremely laborious but successful attempt see Zuber 1956: 202), and secondly, that the wedge holes have never been dated any earlier than the Ptolemaic period, by which time iron wedges would have been available (Röder 1965). Judging from various studies of the quarries at Aswan (Arnold 1991: 37–9; Aston 1994: 15–18, fig. 6; Engelbach 1922, 1923; Klemm and Klemm 1993: 305–53; Zuber 1956) and the implications of experimental projects (Stocks 1986a, 1986b; Zuber 1956), the actual process of extraction in the Pharaonic period seems to have involved the excavation of open-cut quarries, using hammerstones (e.g. dolerite) to gradually remove the stone from the surface downwards.

There are at least three other instances of extraction marks left by pounders in Egyptian quarries. In the quartzite quarry at Gebel Gulab (on the west bank at Aswan), a broken obelisk inscribed with the name of the Nineteenth-Dynasty ruler Seti I survives *in situ* near the quarry-face from which it was extracted (see Habachi 1960: 225–32; see also Fig. 2.6). The quarry face shows definite traces of the use of stone pounders. The second instance is to be found at Qau el-Kebir, where Clarke and Engelbach (1930: 18) noted marks left by stone pounders in a limestone quarry characterised by unusually dense, hard rock. The third piece of evidence for extraction with pounders is a set of marks in the greywacke sandstone–siltstone quarry at Wadi Hammamat, which were photographed by Klemm and Klemm (1993: 414) and may well date to the Pharaonic period.

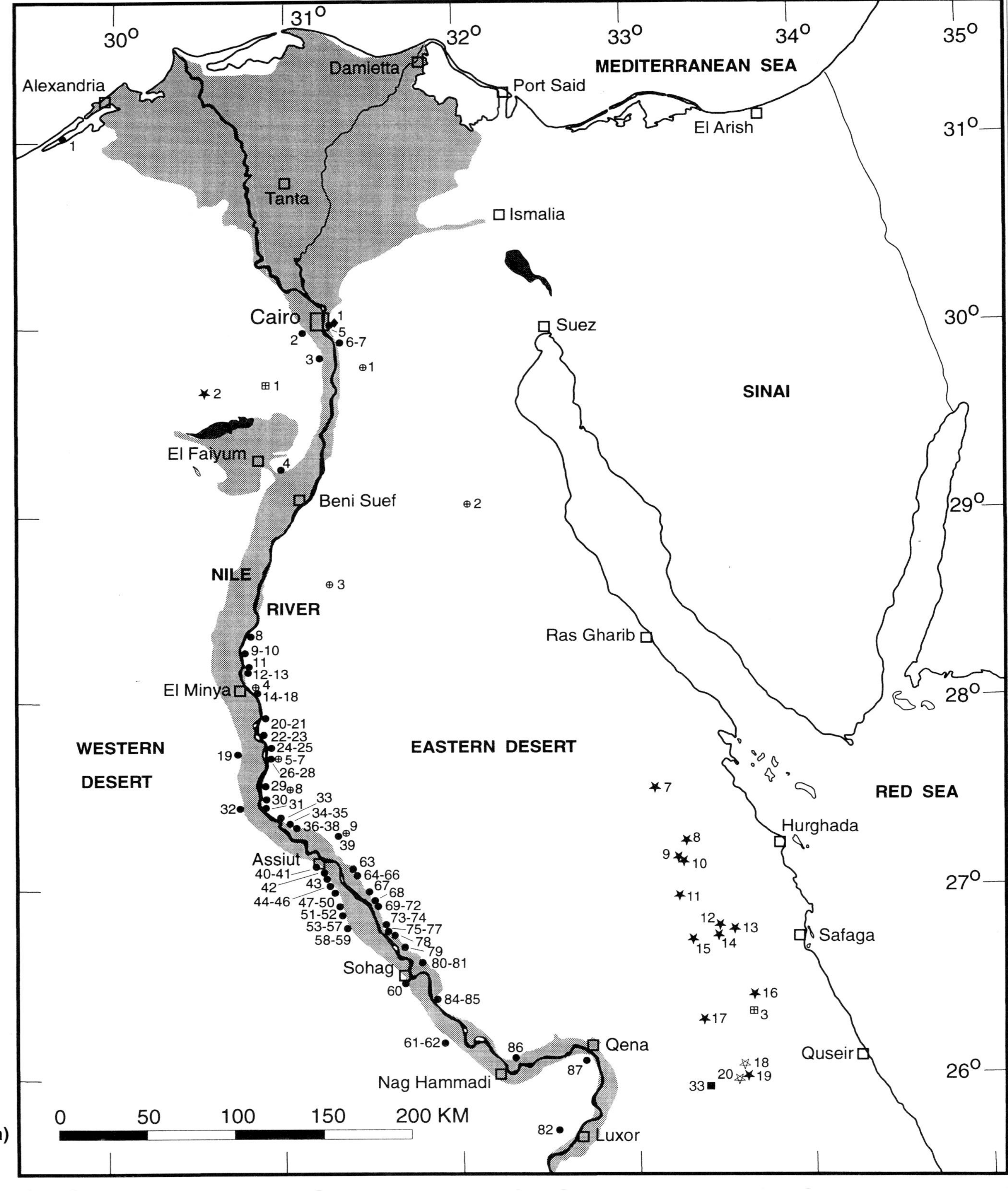

Figure 2.1 Map of Egypt from (a) Luxor to the Mediterranean and (b) Kerma to Luxor, showing locations of the known ancient hard-stone and soft-stone quarries.

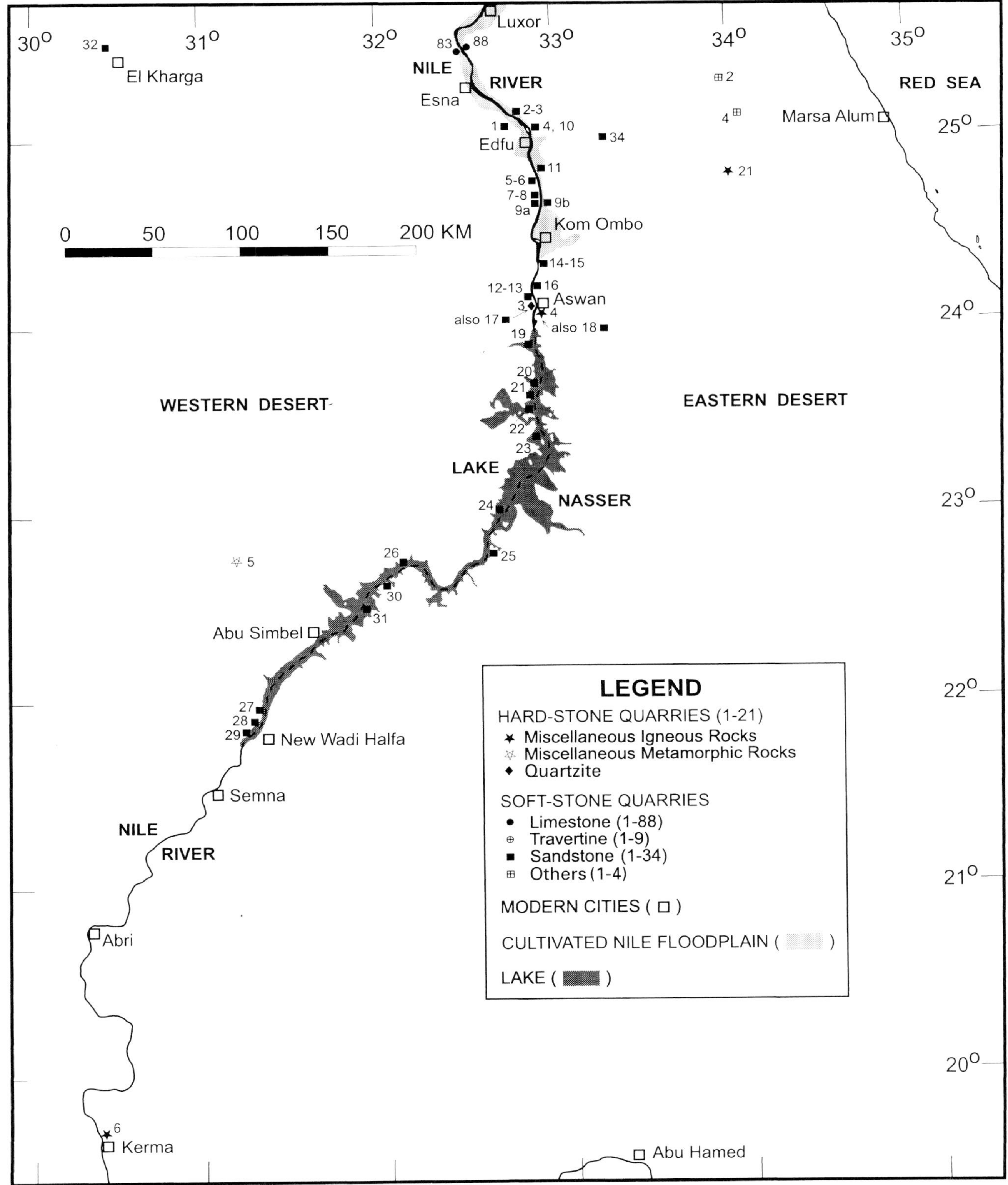

Luxor
NILE
RIVER
Esna
Edfu
Kom Ombo
Aswan
El Kharga
Marsa Alum
RED SEA
WESTERN DESERT
EASTERN DESERT
LAKE
NASSER
Abu Simbel
New Wadi Halfa
Semna
NILE
RIVER
Abri
Kerma
Abu Hamed
0 50 100 150 200 KM
LEGEND
HARD-STONE QUARRIES (1-21)
Miscellaneous Igneous Rocks
Miscellaneous Metamorphic Rocks
Quartzite
SOFT-STONE QUARRIES
Limestone (1-88)
Travertine (1-9)
Sandstone (1-34)
Others (1-4)
MODERN CITIES ( )
CULTIVATED NILE FLOODPLAIN ( )
LAKE ( )

(b)

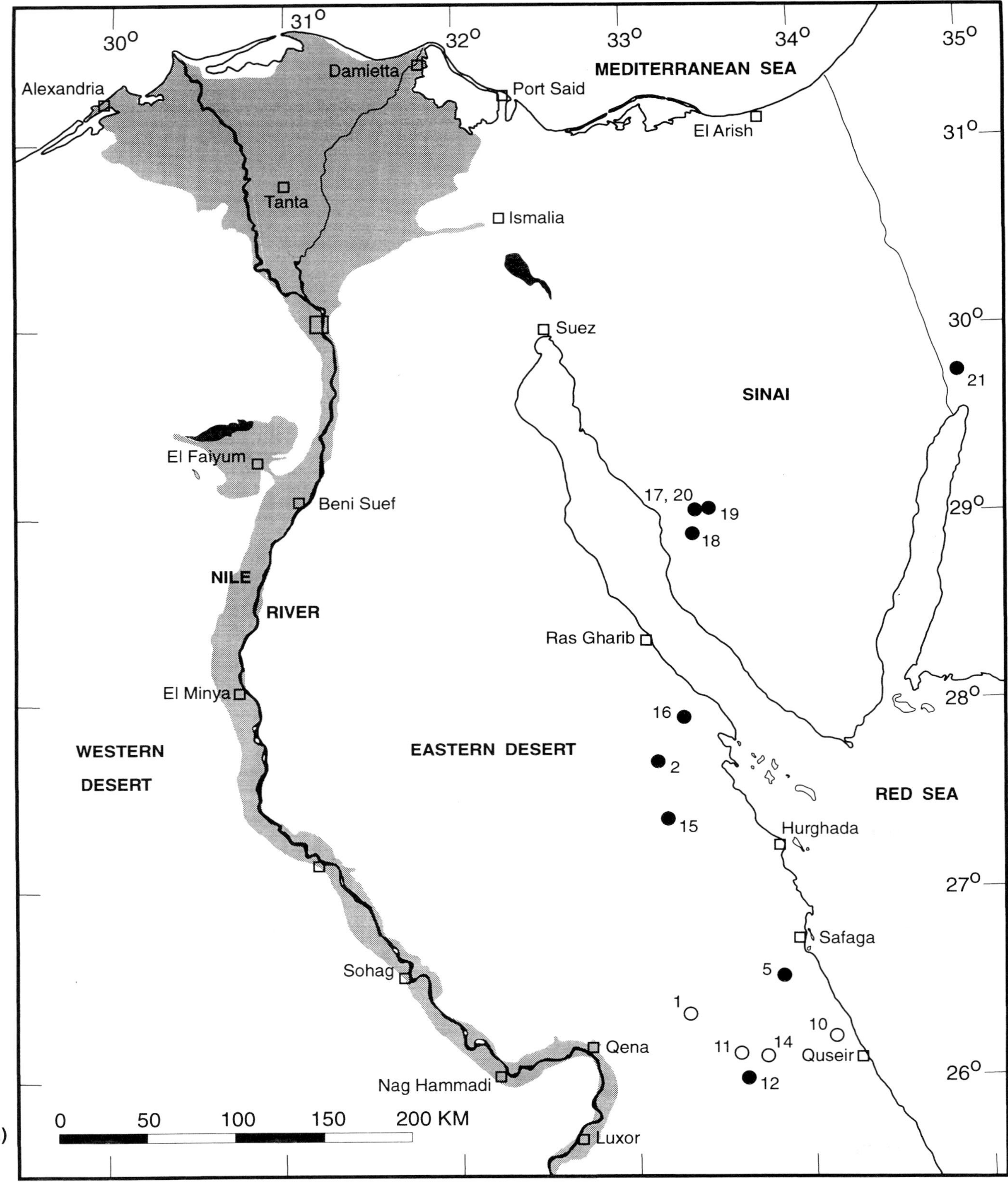

Figure 2.2 Map of Egypt from (a) Luxor to the Mediterranean and (b) Kerma to Luxor, showing locations of quarries and probable ancient sources of gemstones.

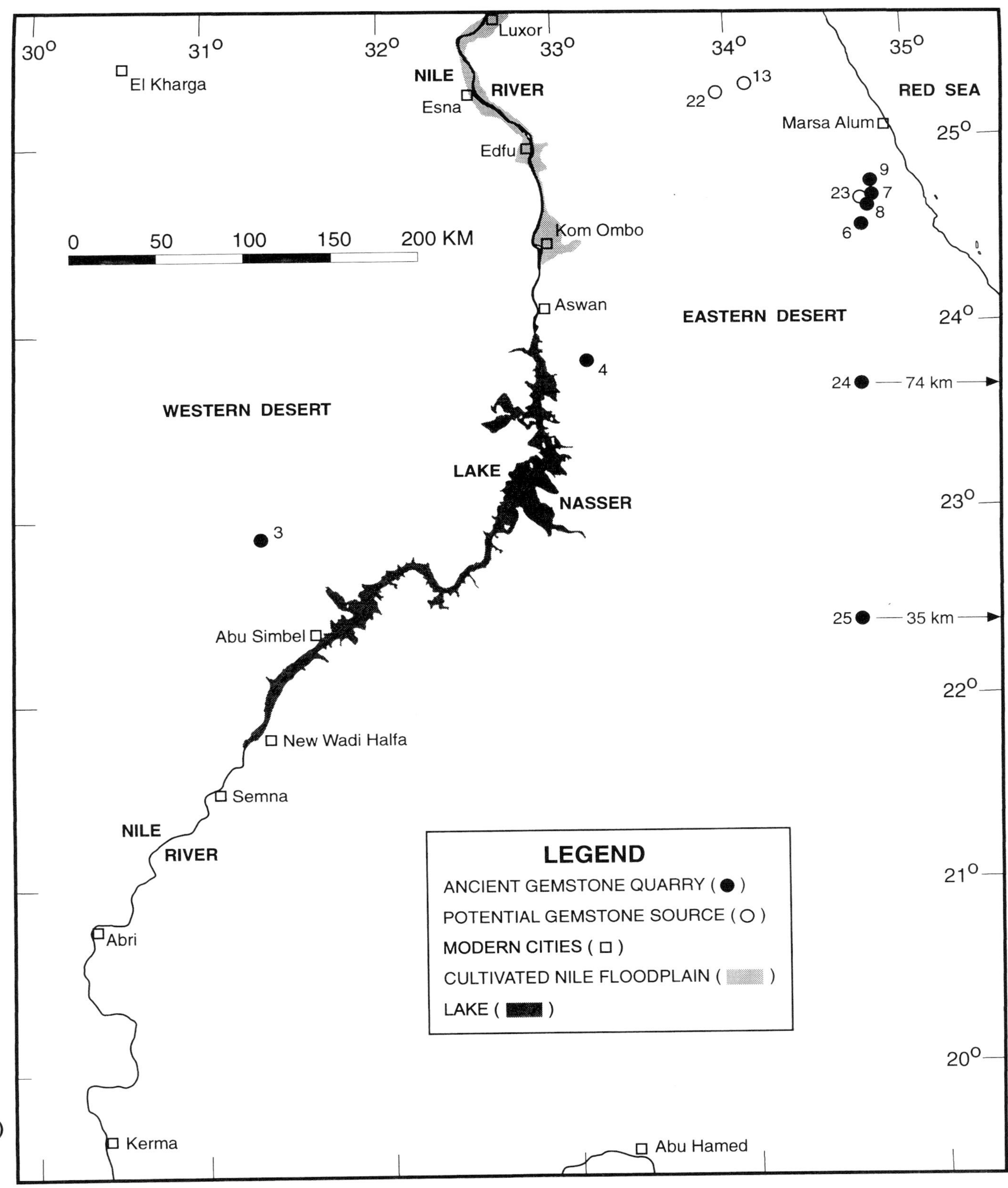
30°
31°
32°
33°
34°
35°
25°
24°
23°
22°
21°
20°
El Kharga
Luxor
NILE
RIVER
Esna
Edfu
Kom Ombo
Aswan
22
13
RED SEA
Marsa Alum
9
23
7
8
6
0
50
100
150
200 KM
EASTERN DESERT
4
24
74 km
WESTERN DESERT
LAKE
NASSER
3
25
35 km
Abu Simbel
New Wadi Halfa
Semna
NILE
RIVER
LEGEND
ANCIENT GEMSTONE QUARRY (●)
POTENTIAL GEMSTONE SOURCE (○)
MODERN CITIES (□)
CULTIVATED NILE FLOODPLAIN ( )
LAKE ( )
Abri
Kerma
Abu Hamed

(b)

Table 2.1. *List of the ancient quarries shown in Figure 2.1*

HARD-STONE QUARRIES

1 QUARTZITE: at Gebel Ahmar, Cairo [30°3.15′N, 31°17.8′E] *(OK-R)*
2 BASALT: at Widan el-Faras on Gebel el-Qatrani, Fayum [29°39.6′N, 30°37.2′E] *(OK)*
3 QUARTZITE: on Gebels Gulab and Tingar near ruins of St. Simon's Monastery [24°6.4′N, 32°52.6′E] *(NK-R)*
4 GRANITE and GRANODIORITE: numerous localities between Aswan and Shellal [24°3.7′N, 32°53.7′E] *(ED-R)*
5 DIORITE-GABBRO and ANORTHOSITE GNEISSES: near Gebel el-Asr, Nubian Desert [22°47.5′N, 31°12.7′E] *(PD-OK, MK:12)*
6 GRANITE and GRANITE GNEISS: near Tumbos at the south end of the Third Cataract, Sudan [19°42.75′N, 30°23.25′E] *(NK?, L:25, NM)*
7 TUFF and TUFFACEOUS LIMESTONE: on Gebel Manzal el-Seyl near Wadi Mellaha [27°32.6′N, 33°7.8′E] *(ED)*
8 ANDESITE-DACITE PORPHYRY and GRANITE: on Gebel Dokhan and in Wadi Abu Maamel (Mons Porphyrites) [27°15.1′N, 33°18.0′E] *(R)*
9 TRACHYANDESITE PORPHYRY: in Wadi Umm Towat near Gebel Dokhan [27°10.2′N, 33°14.4′E] *(R)*
10 QUARTZ DIORITE: in Wadi Umm Balad near Gebel Dokhan [27°9.1′N, 33°16.75′E] *(R)*
11 DIORITE: in Wadi Umm Shegilat near Gebel Abu el-Hasan [26°56.6′N, 33°14.9′E] *(R)*
12 TONALITE GNEISS: between Wadis Abu Marakhat and Umm Diqal near Wadi Fatiri el-Bayda (Mons Claudianus) [26°48.55′N, 33°29.1′E] *(R)*
13 QUARTZ DIORITE: in Wadi Barud near Mons Claudianus [26°43.05′N, 33°34.5′E] *(R)*
14 TONALITE GNEISS: in Wadi Umm Huyut near Mons Claudianus [26°45.08′N, 33°27.95′E] *(R)*
15 QUARTZ DIORITE: in Wadi Fatiri el-Bayda [26°44.0′N, 33°19.3′E] *(R)*
16 GABBRO: in Wadi Umm Wikala near Wadi Semma [26°25.85′N, 33°39.7′E] *(R)*
17 GABBRO: near Wadi Maghrabiya [26°18.65′N, 33°23.7′E] *(R)*
18 SERPENTINITE: near Wadi Umm Esh [26°3.9′N, 33°6.6′E] *(R)*
19 GRANODIORITE: at Bir Umm Fawakhir near wadis Hammamat and el-Sid [26°0.65′N, 33°36.4′E] *(R)*
20 SILTSTONE, GREYWACKE and CONGLOMERATE: in Wadi Hammamat, Eastern Desert [25°59.4′N, 33°34.05′E] *(ED-R)*
21 DOLERITE PORPHYRY: in Rod el-Gamra near Gebel Urf Hamam [24°45.7′N, 33°59.3′E] *(L)*

SOFT-STONE QUARRIES

LIMESTONE

1 Numerous quarries on both sides of Mallahet Mariut marsh near Alexandria: between Abu Sir [30°56.8′N, 29°30.0′E] and Burg el-Arab [30°55.0′N, 29°32.7′E] villages to the SW and Mex village [31°9.25′N, 29°50.6′E] to the NE *Pt-R)*
2 at Giza pyramids [29°58.5′N, 31°7.95′E] *(OK:4)*
3 near Saqqara pyramids: at Djoser pyramid [29°52.15′N, 31°12.9′E] *(OK:3)* and in the desert to the west [29°50.9′N, 31°9.9′E] *(ED-OK?)*
4 near el-Lahun pyramid [29°14.2′N, 30°58.0′E] *(MK:12)*
5 at Zawyet Nasr on Gebel Mokattam near the Citadel [30°1.6′N, 31°16.2′E] *(OK/MK-NK?)*
6 on Gebel Tura near Tura village [29°56.0′N, 31°17.7′E] *(OK-R)*
7 on Gebel Hof near el-Masara village [29°54.9′N, 31°19.2′E] *(MK-R?)*
8 near el-Sawayta village [28°22.5′N, 30°48.0′E] *(NK-L?)*
9 at el-Babein tomb near Beni Khalid village [28°18.1′N, 30°44.9′E] *(NK:19–20)*
10 at and near Deir Gebel el-Tei village [28°16.9′N, 30°45.0′E] *(OK/MK?)*
11 near Tihna el-Gebel village and Akoris ruins [28°11.05′N, 30°46.45′E] *(NK:20, L-R?)*
12 near el-Hawarta village [28°9.95′, 30°46.55′E] *(R?)*
13 near Nazlet Husein Ali village [28°8.4′N, 30°46.6′E] *(R?)*
14 near Sawada village in Zawyet Sultan district [28°4.6′N, 30°48.3′E] *(NK:18)*
15 near Nazlet Sultan Pasha village in Zawyet Sultan district [28°4.1′N, 30°48.9′6E] *(NK-R)*
16 near Zawyet el-Amwat village in Zawyet Sultan district [28°3.2′N, 30°49.8′E] *(NK-R)*
17 in Wadi Sheikh Yasin in Zawyet Sultan district [28°3.1′N, 30°50.7′E] *(NK-R)*
18 near Darb Tila Nufal track in Zawyet Sultan district [28°2.55′N, 30°51.25′E] *(NK-R?)*
19 near Dirwa village and Petosiris tomb [27°44.1′N, 30°41.55′E] *(Pt-R)*
20 near Nazlet el-Diyaba village [27°56.5′N, 30°52.85′E] *(R?)*
21 near Beni Hasan tombs [27°54.9′N, 30°52.2′E] *(OK/MK-R?)*
22 near el-Sheikh Timay village [27°51.7′N, 30°50.7′E] *(OK/MK-Pt?)*
23 near el-Sheikh Ibada village and Antiopolis ruins [27°49.6′N, 30°52.2′E] *(MK-R?)*
24 near Deir Abu Hennis village [27°47.2′N, 30°54.8′E] *(NK?)*
25 in Wadi el-Nakla near Deir el-Bersha village [27°44.9′N, 30°55.4′E] *(NK:18, L:30, Pt)*
26 near el-Bersha village [27°43.2′N, 30°53.7′E] *(age?)*
27 near el-Sheikh Said village [27°42.0′N, 30°53.3′E] *(NK:18)*
28 in Wadi Zebeida near Amarna ruins [27°40.9′N, 30°54.65′E] *(NK:18)*
29 opposite Dairut city on Gebel Abu Foda [27°33.6′N, 30°51.95′E] *(NK?)*
30 near Deir el-Quseir village on Gebel Abu Foda [27°29.6′N, 30°52.2′E] *(age?)*

Table 2.1. (**cont.**)

31 in and near wadis Abu Helwa and Magberi on Gebel Abu Foda [27°25.3′6N, 30°52.7′E] *(OK/MK-NK?)*
32 near Meir village [27°26.0′N, 30°42.2′E?] *(OK/MK?)*
33 at and near Deir el-Amir Tadros monastery on Gebel Abu Foda [27°22.6′N, 30°57.8′E] *(OK/MK?, NK:19)*
34 at and near Deir Abu Mina monastery on Gebel el-Harrana [27°21.3′N, 31°0.9′E] *(age?)*
35 near el-Maabda village on Gebel el-Harrana [27°20.3′N, 31°1.9′E] *(age?)*
36 near Deir el-Gabrawi village on Gebel el-Tawila [27°20.3′N, 31°5.9′E] *(NK:19)*
37 on el-Ketf promontory on Gebel el-Harran [27°19.6′N, 31°2.8′E] *(NK:19)*
38 near Arab el-Atiat el-Bahariya village on Gebel el-Harrana [27°20.0′N, 31°3.9′E] *(Pt-R?)*
39 on Talet el-Hagar promontory near Wadi el-Asyut [27°17.45′N, 31°18.15′E] *(age?)*
40 below el-Izam monastery near Asyut city [27°9.2′N, 31°8.9′E] *(age?)*
41 between Asyut city and Drunka village [27°9.4′N, 31°10.4′E] *(OK/MK?)*
42 at and between el-Aldr Maryam and Sawiris monasteries near Deir Drunka village [27°6.2′N, 31°10.0′E] *(OK/MK?)*
43 near Deir Rifa village [27°4.55′N, 31°10.9′E] *(OK/MK-NK?)*
44 near Sidi Abu el-Haris tomb [27°2.7′N, 31°13.55′E] *(age?)*
45 between Sidi Abu el-Haris tomb and Deir el-Bileida ruins [27°2.3′N, 31°13.65′E] *(age?)*
46 at Deir el-Beleida ruins [27°1.95′N, 31°13.85′E] *(age?)*
47 near el-Balyza village [27°1.25′N, 31°14.2′E] *(age?)*
48 between el-Balyza and el-Abu Khurs village [27°0.4′N, 31°14.55′E] *(age?)*
49 between el-Abu Khurs and el-Zaraby villages [26°59.2′N, 31°14.7′E] *(age?)*
50 near el-Zaraby village [26°58.45′N, 31°15.1′E] *(OK/MK-NK?)*
51 at el-Adra Maryam monastery near Wadi Sarga and Deir el-Ganadla village [26°55.65′N, 31°16.8′E] *(OK/MK?)*
52 near el-Mashaya village [26°54.9′N, 31°17.2′E] *(age?)*
53 near el-Ghanayim Bahari village [26°53.4′N, 31°18.25′E] *(R?)*
54 near Sidi Mansur tomb [26°52.85′N, 31°18.65′E] *(age?)*
55 near el-Ghanayim Qibli village [26°52.15′N, 31°19.15′E] *(age?)*
56 near el-Aghana village [26°51.6′N, 31°14.7′E] *(age?)*
57 near el-Qarya Bil Diweir village [26°50.55′N, 31°19.9′E] *(age?)*
58 near Sid Ab Khiris tomb and Nazlet Imara village [26°47.05′N, 31°21.4′E] *(age?)*
59 near Nag el-Tawalib village [26°46.5′N, 31°22.45′E] *(age?)*
60 near Nag Hamad village and Athribis ruins [26°30.65′N, 31°39.55′E] *(Pt-R?)*
61 near el-Salmuni village and Abydos ruins [26°12.25′N, 31°52.55′E] *(MK-L?)*
62 in Wadi Naqb el-Salmuni near Abydos ruins [26°11.75′N, 31°51.95′E] *(MK-L?)*
63 near Wadi Emu [27°7.15′N, 31°21.35′E] *(age?)*
64 near el-Khawalid village [27°5.6′N, 31°23.2′E] *(age?)*
65 near el-Nazla el-Mustagidda village [27°4.65′6N, 31°23.65′6E] *(age?)*
66 between el-Nazla el-Mustagidda and Deir Tasa villages [27°3.8′N, 31°24.1′E] *(age)*
67 near el-Iqal Bahari village [26°59.55′N, 31°27.4′E] *(age?)*
68 near el-Baiyadiya village [26°57.55′N, 31°27.75′E] *(age?)*
69 near el-Iqal el-Qibi village [26°56.65′N, 31°28.75′E] *(R?)*
70 at el-Hammamiya village [26°56.25′N, 31°29.25′E] *(age?)*
71 between el-Hammamiya village and Antaeopolis ruins [26°55.45′N, 31°29.55′E] *(NK:18)*
72 at and near Qau el-Kebir/Antaeopolis ruins [26°55.5′N, 31°30.05′E] *(OK/MK-NK?, Pt-R)*
73 near el-Nawawra village [26°50.1′N, 31°32.1′E] *(age?)*
74 near el-Khazindariya village on Gebel el-Haridi [26°47.7′N, 31°32.45′E] *(NK:20)*
75 near Nazlet el-Haridi village on Gebel el-Haridi [26°46.35′N, 31°33.25′E] *(age?)*
76 near Abu el-Nasr village on Gebel el-Haridi [26°45.75′N, 31°33.85′E] *(Pt)*
77 between Abu el-Nasr and el-Galawiya villages on Gebel el-Haridi [26°45.75′N, 31°35.6′E] *(OK/MK?)*
78 near el-Galawiya village [26°45.6′N, 31°37.1′] *(age?)*
79 at Istabl Antar between el-Haradna and Urban Beni Wasil villages [26°42.8′N, 31°40.35′E] *(age?)*
80 near Qurnet Salamuni village [26°37.15′N, 31°45.3′E] *(age?)*
81 at el-Salamuni village [26°37.1′N, 31°45.75′E] *(NK?)*
82 near Wadi el-Muluk (Valley of the Kings) [25°44.85′N, 32°37.3′E] *(NK:18, L:26, R)*
83 near el-Ghrera village in Gebelein district (recently destroyed) [25°29.65′N, 32°28.1′E] *(MK – PT?)*
84 near Nag el-Ahaywa village [26°26.0′N, 31°50.3′E] *(age?)*
85 near Sidi Musa tomb on Gebel Tukh [26°24.9′N, 31°50.65′E] *(OK/MK-R?)*

Table 2.1. *(cont.)*

86 near Nag el-Buza village [26°5.75′N, 32°18.1′E] *(age)*
87 on Gebel el-Gir near Tentyris/Dendara ruins [26°6.3′N, 32°41.7′E] *(L:30-R?)*
88 near el-Dibabiya village [25°30.25′N, 32°31.3′E] *(NK:19, 3IP:21, R)*

TRAVERTINE
1 in Wadi Gerrawi near Helwan city [29°48.5′N, 31°27.4′E] *(OK:4)*
2 between Wadi Araba and Wadi Aseikhar [29°4.75′N, 32°3.1′E] *(R)*
3 in Wadi Umm Argub near wadis Muwathil and Sannur [28°39.0′N, 31°15.6′E ?] *(L?)*
4 numerous quarries in el-Qawatir area opposite el-Minya city [28°6.2′N, 30°49.4′E] *(OK/MK-NK?)*
5 in Wadi Barshawi near Amarna ruins [27°42.0′N, 30°56.3′E] *(MK-NK?)*
6 in Wadi el-Zebeida near Amarna ruins [27°41.4′N, 30°54.15′E] *(MK-NK?)*
7 near Wadi el-Zebeida and Amarna ruins [27°40.8′N, 30°55.8′E?] *(NK:19)*
8 at Hatnub near Amarna ruins [27°33.3′N, 31°1.3′E] *OK-4-6, 1IP, MK:12, NK:18)*
9 near Wadi el-Asyut [27°18.75′N, 31°20.7′E] *(NK:18)*

SANDSTONE
1 near Hierakonpolis ruins [25°4.4′N, 32°44.3′E] *(NK:R?)*
2 at el-Mahamid village near Elkab ruins [25°8.25′N, 32°46.8′E] *(NK?, Pt)*
3 at Ramesses II/Ptolemy IX temples near Elkab ruins [25°8.05′N, 32°48.95′E] *(NK:19, Pt)*
4 near el-Keijal village [25°4.3′N, 32°51.65′E] *(age?)*
5 between Nag el-Raqiein and Nag el-Hosch villages [24°44.6′N, 32°55.1′E] *(R?)*
6 at Nag el-Hosch village [24°44.2′N, 32°55.2′E] *(R)*
7 in Wadi el-Shatt el-Rigal [24°41.1′N, 32°55.2′E] *(MK, NK: 18)*
8 near Nag el-Hammam village [24°40.3′N, 32°55.4′E] *(MK-NK?)*
9 at Gebel el-Silsila – West Bank [24°39.1′N, 32°55.6′E *(NK)* and East Bank [24°38.4′N, 32°55.95′E] *(MK?, NK, Pt;R)*
10 near el-Kilh Sharq village [25°3.55′N, 32°52.7′E] *(Pt;R)*
11 at el-Bueib ruins near Wadi el-Sirag [24°48.6′N, 32°54.8′E] *(NK:18)*
12 near Nag el-Fuqani village and opposite el-Kattara village [24°12.4′N, 32°51.4′E] *(Pt)*
13 in Gharb Aswan distrit opposite Geziret Bahrif island [24°9.7′N, 32°52.05′E] *(age?)*
14 from Sidi el-Hasan tomb to Ezbet Ali Amer village in Gharb el-Gaafra district [24°21.4′N, 32°55.7′E] *(Pt-R?)*
15 from el-Hadedoon village to Sidi Abd el-Aziz tomb in Gharb el-Gaafra district [24°18.7′N, 32°54.7′E] *(Pt?)*
16 on Gebel el-Hammam near Khor Abu Subeira (destroyed) [24°13.6′N, 32°52.4′E] *(NK:18)*
17 at Gebel Qubbet el-Hawa opposite Aswan [24°6.05′N, 32°53.15′E] *(OK/MK?)*
18 near Aswan (destroyed) [24°3.7′N, 32°53.7′E] *(age?)*
19 near Dabod temple [23°53.8′N, 32°51.2′E] *(NM/Pt-R)*
20 near Qertassi temple [23°42.0′N, 32°53.1′E] *(Pt-R)*
21 near Tafa temple [23°27.9′N, 32°51.7′E] *(R)*
22 near site of Kalabsha temple [23°33.05′N, 32°51.8′E] *(Pt-R)*
23 between Abu Hor and Merowa villages (may be Sabaya Fm.) [somewhere between 23°29.0′N, 32°53.0′E and 23°26.0′N, 32°54.0′E] *(Pt-R?)*
24 near Qurta temple [23°2.5′N, 32°40.0′E] *(NK:18?, R?)*
25 near Agayba village in the Mitiq district [22°51.0′N, 32°33.5′E] *(age?)*
26 near Tumas village [22°45.1′N, 32°8.8′E] *(NK:18-19)*
27 opposite Gezira Dabarosa village, Sudan [21°57.0′N, 31°18.0′E] *(age?)*
28 near site of Buhen ruins, Sudan [21°53.0′N, 31°15.0′E] *MK:NK?)*
29 at Abd el-Qadir opposite Dorginarti island, Sudan [21°50.5′N, 31°14.0′E] *(NK?)*
30 near Qasr Ibrim ruins [22°38.9′N, 31°59.5′E] *(MK:12?, NK;R?)*
31 at Nag Deira in the Tusha East district [22°30.4′N, 31°53.5′E] *(NK?)*
32 on Gebel el-Teir in Kharga Oasis [25°31.0′N, 30°29.0′E] *(L-R?)*
33 near el-Muweih ruins on Qift-Quseir road [25°56.7′N, 32°33.8′E] *(R)*
34 at Bir el-Kanayis temple in Wadi el-Kanayis on Edfu-Marsa Alum road [25°0.25′N, 33°18.0′E] *(NK:19?, R)*

OTHER STONES
1 GYPSUM: at Umm el-Sawwan, northern Fayum [29°42.5′N, 30°53.0′E] *(ED-OK)*
2 MARBLE: at Gebel Rokham near Wadi Mia, Eastern Desert [25°17.95′N, 33°57.85′E] *(NK-R?)*
3 TALC SCHIST: in Wadi Saqiyah, Eastern Desert [26°19.7′N, 33°39.39′E] *(R)*
4 STEATITE: at Gebel Rod el-Barram, Eastern Desert [25°5.75′N, 34°4.25′E] *(R and earlier?)*

Notes on Locations and Dates: North latitude and east longitude are given in brackets for the centre of the quarry workings at each locality. Quarry dates are given in italics within parentheses. Most dates (those followed by?) are based on the type of tool marks found on the quarry walls (using the tentative chronology of R. and D. Klemm) and/or the age of nearby temples that may have been the destination of the stone. All other ages are based on inscriptions, datable antiquities and/or a definite association with dated ruins. Abbreviations used: PD = Predynastic period, ED = Early Dynastic period, OK = Old Kingdom, 1IP = First Intermediate Period, MK = Middle Kingdom, 2IP = Second Intermediate Period, NK = New Kingdom, 3IP = Third Intermediate Period, L = Late Period, Pt = Ptolemaic Period, NM = Napatan-Meroitic period and R = Roman Period. Numerals preceded by colons refer to dynasties. The "/" in the abbreviation OK/MK means "and/or" and is an undifferentiated date based on tool marks. Hyphenated abbreviations (e.g., "NK-R") indicate that the quarry was worked during and between the periods reported. The dates reported here are based only on the surviving evidence and so it is possible that a given quarry may also have been worked earlier or later than indicated.

Table 2.2. *List of gemstone sources and quarries shown in Figures 2.2*

1. AGATE, CORNELIAN, HAEMATITE and JASPER: at Wadi Abu Gerida [26°21′N, 33°18′E]
2. AMETHYST: at Wadi Abu Had [27°41′N, 33°9′E] (*PD–ED*)
3. AMETHYST and CORNELIAN: near Gebel el-Asr [22°54′N, 31°19′E] (*MK, R*)
4. AMETHYST: at Wadi el-Hudi [23°50′N, 33°10′E] (*MK*)
5. AMETHYST: at Gebel Abu Diyeiba, Safaga region [26°32′N, 33°50′E] (*R*)
6. BERYL and GARNET: at Wadi Gimal [24°31′N, 34°45′E] (*R*)
7. BERYL and GARNET: at Wadi Sikeit [24°40′N, 34°48′E] (*Pt–R*)
8. BERYL: at Wadi Nuqrus [24°37′N, 34°47′E] (*R*)
9. BERYL: at Gebel Zubara [24°45′N, 34°48′E] (*B–Is*)
10. CORNELIAN, HAEMATITE and JASPER: at Wadi Saga [26°13′N 34°08′E]
11. FLUORSPAR: at Umm Esh el-Zarga [26°08′N, 33°35′E]
12. FLUORSPAR: at Umm el-Fawakhir [26°02′N, 33°36′E] (*NK-R?*)
13. FLUORSPAR: at Gebel Ineigi [25°18′N, 34°07′E]
14. GARNET: at Gebel Mitiq [26°07′N, 33°44′E]
15. HAEMATITE: at Gebel Abu Marwat [27°23′N, 33°12′E] (*R*)
16. HAEMATITE: at Wadi Dib [27°55′N, 33°18′E] (*R*)
17. MALACHITE and TURQUOISE: at Bir Nasib [29°02′N, 33°24′E] (*MK–NK*)
18. MALACHITE and TURQUOISE: at Wadi Maghara [28°54′N, 33°22′E] (*ED–NK*)
19. MALACHITE and TURQUOISE: at Serabit el-Khadim [29°02′N, 33°28′E] (*MK–LP*)
20. MALACHITE and TURQUOISE: at Wadi Ba'ba/Wadi Kharig [29°02′N, 33°25′E] (*OK-NK*)
21. MALACHITE: at Timna [29°45′N, 34°56′E] (*NK*)
22. MICROCLINE: at Wadi Higelig/Gebel Migif [25°16′N, 33°56′E]
23. MICROCLINE: at Abu Rushaid [24°38′N, 34°46′E]
24. PERIDOT: at St John's Island (Zabargad) [23°39′N, 36°10′E] (*Pt–R*)
25. SMOKY QUARTZ: at Romit [22°22′N, 35°45′E] (*R*)

Notes on Locations and Dates: North latitude and east latitude are given in brackets for the centre of the quarry workings or source at each locality. Quarry dates are given in italics in parentheses. Most dates are based on the presence of associated datable inscriptions or artefacts. Abbreviations used: PD = Predynastic period, ED = Early Dynastic period, OK = Old Kingdom, MK = Middle Kingdom, NK = New Kingdom, L = Late Period, Pt = Ptolemaic Period, R = Roman Period, B = Byzantine Period, Is = Islamic Period. Hyphenated abbreviations (e.g. NK–R) indicate that the quarry was worked during and between the periods reported. The dates reported here are based only on the surviving evidence and so it is possible that a given quarry may also have been worked earlier or later than indicated. If no date is given, then the site is a potential ancient source but no actual quarry workings have been found.

Processing of stone in situ

As far as stone blocks intended for building were concerned, the amount of processing that took place in the quarries themselves seems to have depended on the type of stone involved. The rough, freshly quarried blocks of soft stone, such as limestone and sandstone, were probably not dressed until they arrived at the storage area beside the construction site of the temple or funerary complex for which they were required. In the case of blocks of hard stone, such as granite or gneiss, however, a certain amount of stone-working may have taken place at the quarries themselves. Arnold (1991: 52) suggests that the skilled workers of hard stones may have been based almost entirely at the quarries themselves rather than the construction sites, leaving only the final polishing to be undertaken at the building itself. Against this view, however, it might be argued that such extensive stone-dressing at the quarries themselves would have resulted in unacceptable damage to the near-finished blocks as they were transported to the building site (and possible confusion on arrival at the latter). The study of mason's marks on stone blocks has, in recent years, begun to yield some important clues in terms of the links between the organisational and bureaucratic links between the quarrying and building processes (see Arnold 1990).

When stone was quarried for items of sculpture, the amount of *in situ* primary processing tended to vary from one quarry to another. One source of evidence for the extent to which items were carved in advance of transportation takes the form of a very small number of surviving depictions of the movement of statues, the best-known being the scene in the tomb of Thuthotep at Deir el-Bersha, showing a colossal statue of the deceased being dragged along by lines of workers pulling on ropes (Newberry 1894). The principal difficulty in interpreting such scenes, however, is the fact that Pharaonic artists often portrayed objects in their finished form even when they were clearly still incomplete – this is particularly evident from the many scenes in which objects are being manufactured in temple workshops. It is therefore uncertain as to whether Thuthotep's statue, for instance, was actually completely carved at the quarries, or simply shown in its finished state as an artistic convention. The archaeological evidence for some *in situ* carving of hard-stone items is fairly convincing, with the survival of near-complete colossal statues in the granite quarries on the east bank at Aswan, a quartzite obelisk of Seti I (to which even the final inscriptions had been added, see Habachi 1960) at Gebel Gulab and the granite gneiss statue of an unknown Twenty-fifth-Dynasty king in the Tumbos quarry (Dunham 1947).

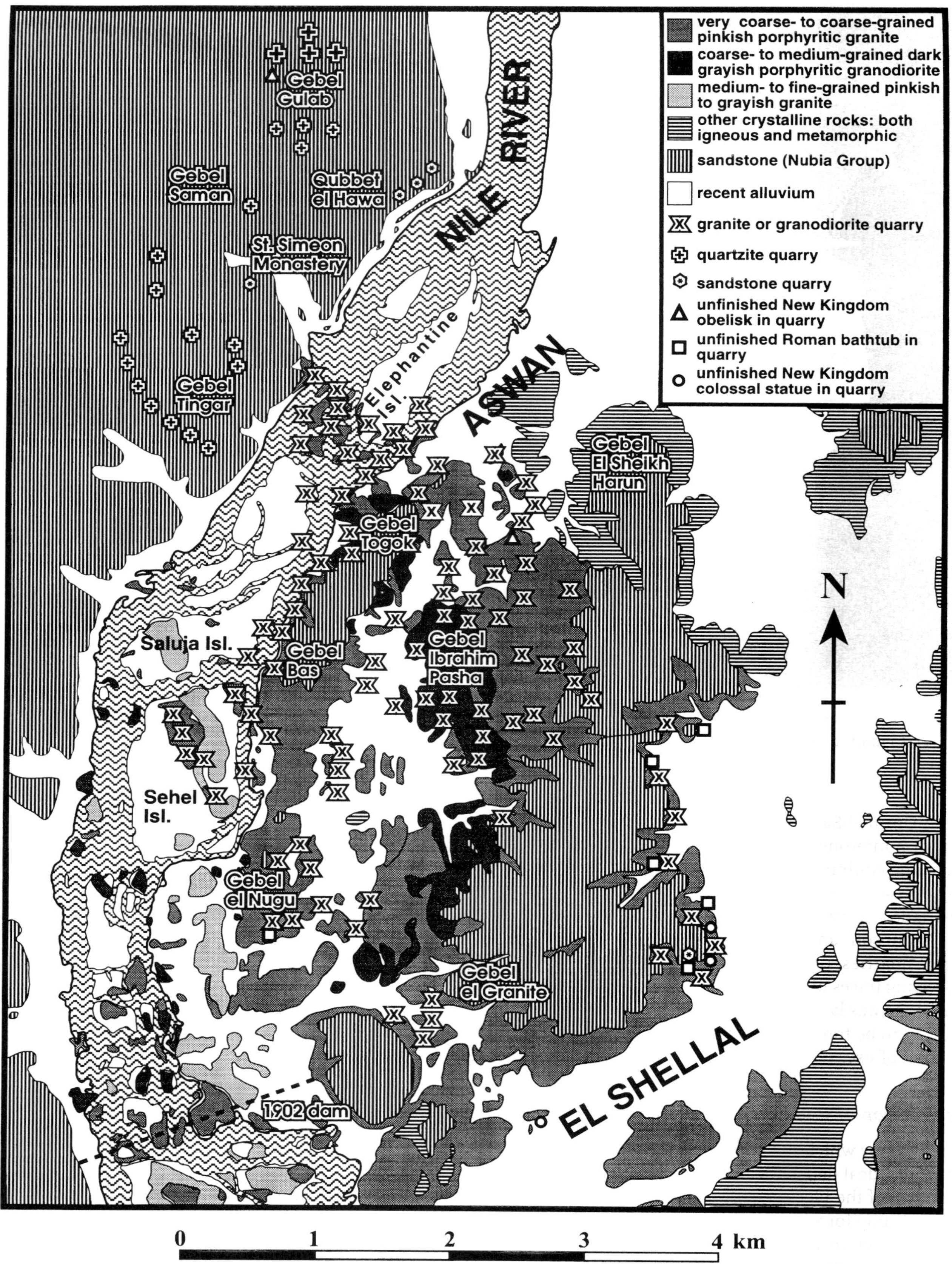

Figure 2.3 Generalised geological map of the Aswan area, showing locations of the granite, quartzite and sandstone quarries.

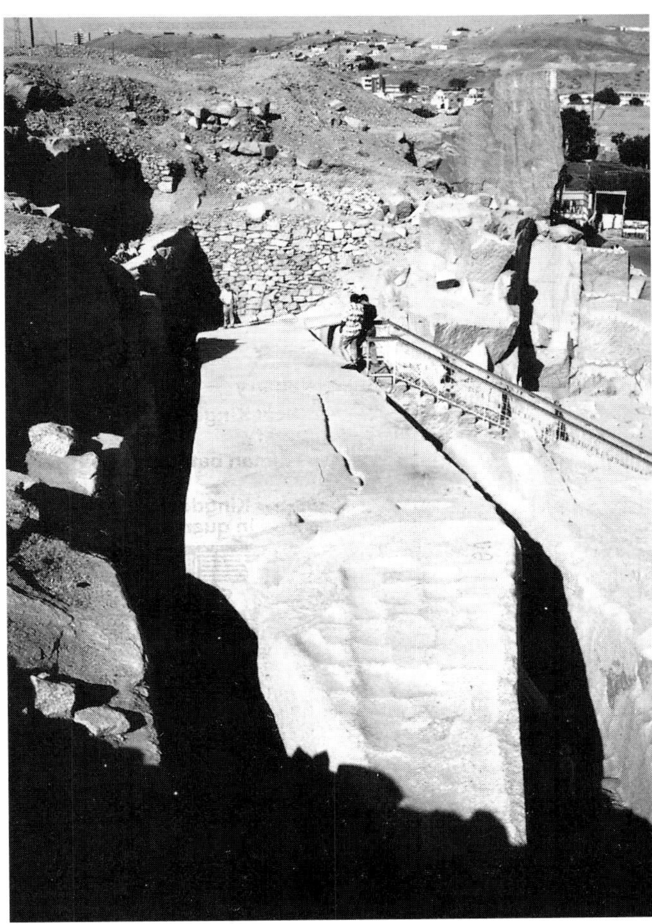

Figure 2.4 The Eighteenth-Dynasty 'unfinished obelisk' in the quarry for coarse pink granite at Aswan.

Figure 2.5 Greco-Roman extraction marks in the quarry for coarse pink granite at Aswan.

Figure 2.6 Quartzite quarry at Gebel Gulab near Aswan, from which the nearby unfinished obelisk of Seti I was extracted.

At the Umm el-Sawwan alabaster gypsum quarries, the survival of numerous unfinished vessels and fragments of chert drilling equipment show that the vast majority of the carving of vessels in this material took place *in situ*, before transportation across to the Memphite necropolis (see Caton-Thompson and Gardner 1934). At the Hatnub travertine quarries, on the other hand, there are relatively few surviving traces of stone-carving at the site, suggesting that the stone was largely carried back in the form of blocks and lumps, to be transformed into vessels and other items at the point of use.

Transportation of stone

The methods by which the quarried stone was transported varied a great deal depending on the locations of the quarries, the size of the blocks and the location of the building site or workshop for which they were intended. In the case of the construction of pyramid complexes and mastaba-tombs in the Memphite necropolis during the Old Kingdom, there were two basic sources of material: the local limestone, which formed the core of the pyramids and the walls of their mortuary and valley temples and the finer stones (e.g. Tura limestone and Aswan granite and granodiorite) which were used for more specialised purposes, such as the smooth outer casing of the pyramids, and usually had to be transported over considerable distances. As with most other raw materials, there were two basic methods of stone transportation in the Pharaonic period: river and land. Arnold (1991: 60) lists the major known examples of heavy monuments transported during the Pharaonic period.

River transport

The importance of water transport in the Egyptian economy as a whole is indicated by the fact that quarrying groups, like many other labour forces (such as the tomb-workers at Deir el-Medina), generally appear to have been organised according to a naval system, being divided in to 'crews' consisting of 'gangs' corresponding to different parts of boats (e.g. starboard and port). In the case of quarrying, this naval organisation must have owed something to the fact that the transportation of the quarried stone would have been as great a task as the procurement itself.

The evidence for the use of boats to transport stone blocks derives primarily from texts and paintings. The causeway in the Fifth-Dynasty royal funerary complex of Unas at Saqqara included depictions of columns (about 10.5 m in height) probably being brought from the Aswan quarries, presumably for Unas's mortuary temple. In addition, it has been suggested that the depictions of emaciated bedouin on Unas's and Sahura's causeways were intended to show the hardships endured in the course of quarrying the stone for the *bnbnt* (or pyramidion) which was placed on the apex of each of the pyramids (Hawass and Verner 1996). The wall-paintings in Old Kingdom private tombs often include depictions of transport-boats conveying a variety of raw materials, but only two tombs include scenes showing the transportation of stone: that of the 5th-Dynasty royal architect and builder Senedjemib Inty (tomb G2370 at Giza; Porter and Moss 1974–81: 85–7) and that of the 6th-Dynasty chief of the estate Ipy (to the west of the pyramid of Pepi I at Saqqara; Porter and Moss 1974–81: 671–2). The captions accompanying the transportation scene in the tomb of Senedjemib Inty indicate that his limestone sarcophagus was brought in a '*satj*-boat' from the Tura quarries, apparently taking about five days to make the journey (see Lepsius 1849–59, II: 76e; Sethe 1903: §66). The Sixth-Dynasty funerary autobiographies of Weni (at Abydos) and Sabni (at Aswan) both describe the building of '*wsḫt*-boats' (as well as '*s3ṯ*-boats' and 'eight-ribbed boats', in the case of Weni) which were specifically commissioned for the transportation of stone (Sethe 1903: §108). Weni also describes the excavation of five canals at Aswan, presumably in order to facilitate the movement of raw materials such as stone through the first cataract. Over 2,000 years later, the Roman historian Pliny described the digging of a canal in order to convey an obelisk to the Nile and then up to Alexandria.

Undoubtedly some of the most impressive instances of the transportation of stone date to the New Kingdom, including the depiction (in the cult temple of Hatshepsut at Deir el-Bahari) of boats carrying two obelisks from Aswan to Thebes. A number of texts from the New Kingdom also concern the movement of cargoes of stone up and down the Nile. Probably the most detailed account is provided by a set of four stone ostraca inscribed with hieratic accounts of the movement of a large number of blocks from the sandstone quarries at Gebel el-Silsila to the Ramesseum at Thebes in the reign of Rameses II (Kitchen 1991). One of these ostraca describes the delivery of sixty-four blocks carried by ten boats, each block weighing between 10,800 and 18,800 kilograms. The resultant calculation that each vessel was carrying about six blocks, weighing a total of some 90,000 kilograms altogether, provides a useful indication of the average load carried by Pharaonic cargo-boats, allowing rough estimates of payloads to be made in the case of other texts, such as the Twentieth-Dynasty Papyrus Amiens (see Gardiner 1941), which simply list the numbers of quarriers and boats despatched on quarrying expeditions. The sizes of the blocks listed in the Ramesseum ostraca correspond quite well to the dimensions of the actual blocks making up the walls of the temple (Kitchen 1991: 86–8).

Land transport: road-building

The commemorative texts carved by the leaders of Egyptian mining and quarrying expeditions frequently mention that routes through the desert were 'opened up' for the workers, and many surviving traces of specially constructed roads have been found in the surrounding areas of mines, quarries and major structures. Indeed, Fischer (1991) has identified various instances of the Old Kingdom titles 'master of the roads' and 'official of the masters of the roads', both in the Memphite necropolis and in the mining areas of the Wadi Hammamat and Wadi Abbad (in the Eastern Desert), suggesting that the coordination and maintenance of land routes was a high priority for the Egyptian administration. In the case of the more extensive rock and mineral sources, which were revisited year after year, considerable time and energy were clearly expended on road construction, the nature of each road being dictated mainly by the bulk and quantities of the materials, the character of the topography and the materials locally available for road-building (see Shaw forthcoming).

The Egyptians' official accounts of quarrying and mining expeditions (usually taking the form of inscriptions or graffiti on the walls of the quarries themselves) routinely emphasise the difficulties and hardships endured by the workmen, perhaps partly in order to increase the prestige of the materials themselves, but, just as the surviving texts largely ignore such practical questions as the process of building pyramids, so they rarely make reference either to the building of roads or to the ways in which cargoes and stone blocks were conveyed along them. Some idea of the construction methods can, however, be deduced on the basis of a number of preserved stretches of ancient roads, causeways and ramps. The occasional survival of such equipment as wooden rollers and sledges also helps to fill in the crucial gaps left by the texts.

The frequent use of wooden sledges to convey large stone blocks or sculptures appears to be confirmed by several funerary reliefs and paintings from different periods, such as those in the tomb of Thuthotep at Deir el-Bersha (*c.* 1900 BC), mentioned above, which show a colossal statue of the deceased being dragged along on a sledge by groups of workmen, their path lubricated by water poured in front of the runners (Newberry 1894: 16–26, pls. XII–XIX; Arnold 1991: 277–8; see also the section on flooring in Chapter 3, this volume). An early Eighteenth-Dynasty relief (*c.* 1500 BC) carved in the limestone quarries at Maʿsara, near Cairo, shows a block carried on a sledge pulled by oxen. There are occasional textual references to the use of donkeys – sometimes numbering several hundred – in the inscriptions describing quarrying expeditions to Sinai, the Tushka region and Wadi el-Hudi (Gardiner and Peet 1952: 11, 114; Simpson 1963: 52–3; Seyfried 1981: 219–20). Harrell and Bown (1995) suggest that, perhaps, blocks of freshly quarried basalt were conveyed on sledges along the paved road leading from the Gebel Qatrani outcrop by the use of a few wooden planks laid across the width of the road; these planks could have been repeatedly removed from the rear of the block and brought round to the front, thus avoiding the need for large quantities of wood.

The longest surviving Egyptian quarry 'road' is the eighty-kilometre route linking the diorite-gabbro and anorthosite gneiss quarries of the Old and Middle Kingdoms (*c.* 2649–1640 BC), near Gebel el-Asr, with the closest Nile embarkation point at modern Tushka. Rex Engelbach undertook two seasons of survey and excavation at the gneiss quarries in 1933 and 1938, including a close examination of the ancient road leading to Tushka (Engelbach 1938: 388–9; Murray 1939a: 108–11). More recently Harrell and Brown (1994) have produced a more detailed map of the area and examined the geological, aesthetic and religious significance of the type of gneiss exploited at the site. The Tushka road was not a paved or drystone structure, as the roads to Hatnub and Gebel Qatrani were; instead it appears to have been simply a cleared track. The road as a whole can be dated at least as early as the Middle Kingdom, on the basis of potsherds described by Engelbach (1938: 388).

Somewhat shorter than the Tushka road, but much better-preserved, is the road stretching for seventeen kilometres between the travertine quarries of Hatnub and the Nile valley at Amarna (Timme 1917; Shaw 1986: 195–8, 1987: 160–2). The course of the main Hatnub road, which incorporates two major causeways across *wadis*, probably dates back to the earliest years of the quarries' use in the middle of the third millennium BC. It is still relatively well-preserved, although there are increasing signs of deterioration through the use of heavy vehicles by modern travertine quarriers. The northwestern end of the road is last clearly visible near the site of Kom el-Nana, an Eighteenth-Dynasty temple complex at Amarna currently under excavation by the Egypt Exploration Society. It must originally have run further to the west, presumably ending in a small harbour, the remains of which would now be buried beneath the cultivated land adjacent to the modern village of Hagg Qandil. Inscriptions at Deir el-Bersha and Hatnub during the Middle Kingdom include references to a hilly region on the east bank of the Nile known as Tjerti, which may well have been the original name of the small settlement at the western terminus of the road (Kessler 1981: 98). In addition to the main Hatnub road there are several others in the surrounding region, leading to smaller travertine quarries in the vicinity. The Old Kingdom travertine quarries at Wadi Gerrawi, although less remote than those at Hatnub, are also said to have been linked with the Nile by a long road, some traces of which still survived in the late nineteenth century (Erman 1885: 623–4; for more recent work at Gerrawi see Dreyer and Jaritz 1983).

The Gebel Qatrani basalt quarries at the northern edge of the Fayum are linked with the Qasr el-Sagha region by a ten-kilometre road (Caton-Thompson and Gardner 1934: 136–7; Harrell and Bown 1995). This road has a nearly uniform width of 2.1 metres and is paved mainly with sandstone slabs and logs of fossil wood. Its characteristics relate to two basic factors: firstly, as with the main Hatnub road, local materials are used (i.e. sandstone slabs, as opposed to the limestone pebbles and boulders at Hatnub); secondly, the need for a built road, as opposed to a simple cleared track, must have been dictated by the bulk and quantity of the basalt blocks being quarried.

Another less substantial road, first documented by Petrie (1888: 33–6, pl. xxvi), stretches southwestwards for about twenty kilometres from the region immediately to the north of Dahshur, beside the Mastabat Faraʿun, probably as far as the northern edge of the Fayum (see also Goedicke 1962; Altenmüller and Moussa 1981; Moussa 1981). Like the 'northern' quarry road at Hatnub and the gneiss-quarriers' road northwest of Tushka, this Dahshur–Fayum route – the so-called 'Dahschurstrasse' – is said to be roughly twenty-three metres wide for most of its length. It is simply a cleared strip of ground rather than a causeway or paved structure. It may have served the Gebel el-Qatrani basalt quarries and/or the Umm el-Sawwan alabaster gypsum quarries during the Old Kingdom, but had begun to be used primarily as a military road by the Late Period (see Shaw forthcoming). Petrie also identified a second road, similar in appearance and dimensions to the 'Dahschurstrasse' and running due westwards from the same origin, apparently crossing 200 kilometres of desert to Bahariya or Siwa oases – presumably this too was a military road.

Local paths and ramps

As well as long-distance quarry roads there were numerous shorter paths and ramps constructed both at the beginning and end of the transportation process. Some have been preserved in the immediate vicinity of the structures for which the raw material was destined. Arnold (1991: 79–101) describes the employment of short drystone, mud-brick and timber roads in the construction of tombs and temples at such funerary sites as Saqqara, Sinki (southeast of Abydos), Dahshur, Meidum, Giza, Lisht and Lahun; he also discusses the evidence for the use of such tools as levers, rockers, sledges and rollers to facilitate the movement of heavy objects. Several of the Lahun Papyri, from the town associated with the pyramid of the Twelfth-Dynasty ruler Senusret II, document the dragging of stone blocks by groups of workers, presumably in the course of the construction of tombs and temples. These papyri include references to *ithw-ı'nru* (stone haulers) as a specialised group within the quarry workforce (Quirke 1990: 171).

Short roads and ramps were often constructed next to the mines and quarries, as at the Wadi el-Hudi amethyst mines, the Serabit el-Khadim turquoise mines, the Qau el-Kebir limestone quarries, the Gebel el-Asr gneiss quarries northwest of Tushka, and the quartzite and granite quarries at Aswan. There are also good surviving ramps in the sandstone quarries at Gebel el-Silsila. At Wadi el-Hudi, immediately to the northwest of the Twelfth-Dynasty amethyst-miners' fortress, there is a small strip of desert cleared of stones and gravel. This may be interpreted either as the southeastern terminus of a major road linking the mining area and the Aswan region (thirty-five kilometres to the northwest) or simply as a formal approach to the fortress (Shaw and Jameson 1993: 92, fig. 3).

The impressive surviving network of roads at Aswan was designed to transport the stone as efficiently as possible to the river-bank, both from the granite quarries on the east bank and the quartzite quarries to the west. On the east bank there was a long north–south road running through a *wadi* parallel to the river, which would have allowed the blocks from the granite quarries to be transported easily to suitable harbours. On the west bank there are numerous short drystone causeways (probably dating to the Greek and Roman periods, judging from the wedge-holes associated with many of the surrounding quarries) by means of which the blocks of quartzite could be dragged through the undulating and boulder-strewn terrain (Klemm and Klemm 1981: Abb. 44). The shorter stretches of road average three to four metres in width and ten to thirty centimetres in height. However, the most substantial surviving stretch of road, leading away southwestwards from the best-preserved ancient quarry-face on the west bank, is about eight metres wide and – at its highest point – about one and a half metres high, making it comparable in dimensions with the causeway near the main quarries at Hatnub.

Types of stone: sources and descriptions

The source identifications and petrological descriptions of building and sculptural stones and gemstones provided in this section are based largely on the field and laboratory work of the present authors. All of the hard-stone and travertine quarries were visited as were also most of those for limestone and sandstone, as well as the principal amethyst, beryl and turquoise mines. Quarry samples and numerous stone artefacts, mainly small vessels, were studied by thin-section petrography, and many of these were further analysed by x-ray fluorescence spectroscopy and other geochemical techniques (see discussion of analytical techniques, pp. 66–9). These petrological analyses are supplemented by those of other investigators for the better-known quarries.

The petrological nomenclature used in this chapter is that widely employed in North America and Europe (see Brown and Harrell 1991, for a review). For example, the mineralogical and textural classification recommended by the International Union of Geological Sciences (IUGS) is used for igneous rocks and igneous precursors of metamorphic rocks (Streckeisen 1973, 1979, see Fig. 2.7). Grain size for igneous and metamorphic rocks is characterised as either aphanitic (grains not distinguishable without magnification) or phaneritic (grains easily visible). The latter tex-

Table 2.3. *The Udden-Wentworth Scale (From Dietrich and Skinner 1979: 181, 189)*

Size (mm)	Fragment	Rock
>256	boulder	boulder conglomerate or breccia
64–256	cobble	cobble conglomerate or breccia
2–64	pebble	pebble conglomerate or breccia
1–2	very coarse sand	
$\frac{1}{2}$–1	coarse sand	
$\frac{1}{4}$–$\frac{1}{2}$	medium sand	sandstone
$\frac{1}{8}$–$\frac{1}{4}$	fine sand	
$\frac{1}{16}$–$\frac{1}{8}$	very fine sand	
$\frac{1}{256}$–$\frac{1}{16}$	silt	siltstone
<1/256	clay	claystone, mudstone or shale

Table 2.4. *Mohs hardness scale (the absolute hardness measures used here are approximately equivalent to those cited in the Rosivale abrasion hardness test).*

Mohs hardness	Comparison mineral	Means of testing	Absolute hardness
1	Talc	Can be easily scratched with fingernail	0.03
2	Gypsum	Can be just scratched with fingernail	1.25
3	Calcite	Can be just scratched with copper coin	4.5
4	Fluorite	Can be easily scratched with steel knife	5.0
5	Apatite	Can be just scratched with steel knife	6.5
6	Orthoclase	Can be scratched with steel file	37.0
7	Quartz	Scratches window glass	120.0
8	Topaz		175.0
9	Corundum		1000.0
10	Diamond		140000.0

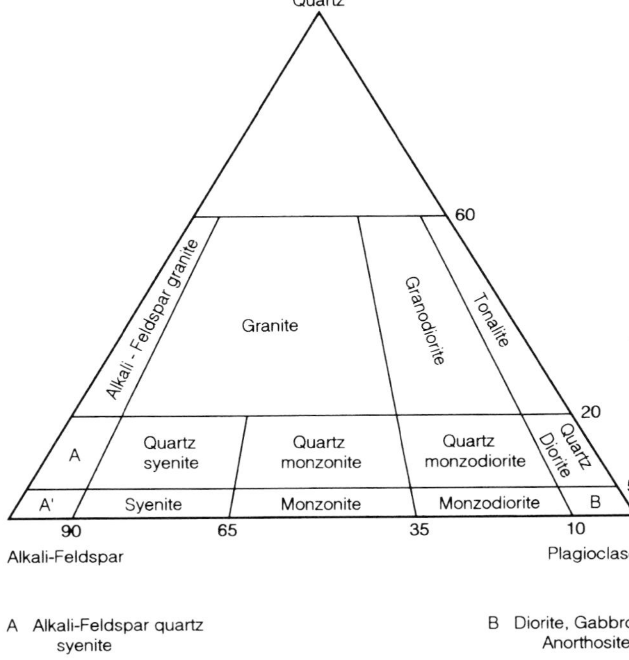

Figure 2.7 Figure showing IUGS classification of plutonic rocks (after Streckeisen 1973).

ture is subdivided into grain-size ranges of fine (less than 1 mm), medium (1–5 mm), coarse (5 mm–3 cm) and very coarse (over 3 cm) grained. Metamorphic rocks are classified on the basis of their structural fabric (foliation) and predominant mineralogy. Although there is no single scheme recommended by an international body as for igneous rocks, there is little disagreement among metamorphic petrologists on nomenclature. A similar situation exists for sedimentary rocks, where relatively few classification schemes are widely used. Accordingly, the limestone nomenclature used here is that of Dunham (1962) and Folk (1962), and the nomenclature for sandstones follows that of Dott (1964) as modified by Pettijohn *et al.* (1972). The standard Udden-Wentworth grain-size scale (see Table 2.3) is used for sandstones and other siliciclastic rocks, whereas for limestones grain size is characterised as fine (less than 2 mm), coarse (2 mm–1 cm) or very coarse (over 1 cm). In Table 2.4, the details of the Mohs hardness scale are given (see Dietrich and Skinner 1979: 21).

The system of nomenclature for different types of quartz material is similar to that used by Sax and Middleton (1992), except that, as well as dividing the main varieties into macrocrystalline (coarse-grained) or microcrystalline (fine-grained), we have subdivided the microcrystalline varieties into the groupings 'chalcedony' and 'chert', the former usually being translucent and the latter opaque (see Table 2.5). Quartz gemstones are thus covered under the headings chert, chalcedony and quartz. Sax and Middleton (1992: 13) point out, with regard to their own system of nomenclature, that 'There are in reality no abrupt transitions or absolute distinctions between the two types or between the varieties of quartz, and the system of nomenclature represents an artificial formalization of the true situation'. The same might be said of the system adopted here.

There has been much confusion over the petrological nomenclature applied to stones used in ancient Egypt. Most of it results from the incorrect use of rock names by archaeologists and other non-geologists who are not well-versed in petrology. The rest of the confusion stems from the correct use of rock names which are derived from competing or obsolete classification schemes. These may include different rock names or give different definitions for the same rock names. For example, the composition of the gneiss from the Roman quarry at Mons Claudianus has been identified as both 'tonalite' (IUGS classification in Brown and Harrell 1995) and 'granodiorite' (Cox classification in Peacock *et al.* 1994). The difference between the IUGS and Cox classifications is substantial because the former is based on quantitative mineralogy from thin-section point counts, whereas the latter uses only major oxide chemistry and does not recognise tonalite as a rock type. It is therefore important that investigators always indicate the classification scheme they are using when assigning rock names. Furthermore, the schemes used should be ones widely accepted by geologists. As in the rest of this book, we have deliberately avoided the discussion of lexicography of ancient stone names, except where it has been absolutely necessary.

Agate *see* chalcedony

Alabaster, satin spar and selenite

Definition

Alabaster is a sedimentary rock formed by chemical precipitation and consisting predominately of the mineral gypsum (hydrated calcium sulphate, $CaSO_4 \cdot 2H_2O$). Note that so-called 'Egyptian alabaster' is actually travertine, a rock

Table 2.5. *System of nomenclature for different varieties of quartz.*

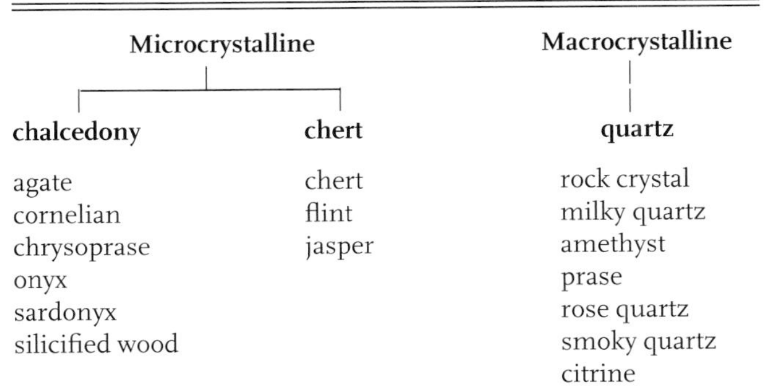

Microcrystalline		Macrocrystalline
chalcedony	**chert**	**quartz**
agate	chert	rock crystal
cornelian	flint	milky quartz
chrysoprase	jasper	amethyst
onyx		prase
sardonyx		rose quartz
silicified wood		smoky quartz
		citrine

composed of the mineral calcite (see TRAVERTINE below). Alabaster is a fine-grained aggregate of gypsum, occurring in massive layers and typically white in colour. Gypsum also occurs as veins of clear, colourless, coarse-grained crystals called selenite and in veins with a fibrous texture, when it is known as satin spar.

Egyptian sources

Workable deposits of alabaster can be found in many areas of the Mediterranean and Red Sea coasts as well as in some of the oases and depressions of the Egyptian Western Desert. Selenite and satin spar occur as thin fracture-filling veins in sedimentary rocks throughout Egypt.

Only one ancient quarry is known; located in the north-east Fayum, it was called 'Umm el-Sawwan' by its discoverer, Gertrude Caton-Thompson. Here the alabaster occurs as vertical seams (approximately 30 cm thick) weathering out of a clay matrix, with thin sheets of selenite running horizontally between the seams. Pebble hand picks were scattered across the alabaster outcrop, and in the cliffs above are three workshop shelters. Mounds of gypsum debris are strewn down the slopes, containing thousands of picks, crescent-shaped flint drill bits and roughed-out alabaster vessels. There are remains of circular stone workmen's huts on top of the cliff, and a wide track, swept free of desert pebbles, leading from the northern Fayum to south Saqqara (see section on transport p. 19). The lack of stratification and the homogeneity of the workshop debris argue against an extended period of exploitation of the site; Caton-Thompson suggested a Third- to Fourth-Dynasty date on the basis of the general shapes of the pottery and stone vessels, although this criterion does not rule out the First and Second Dynasties, when alabaster vessels were, in fact, more common (Aston 1994: 49–50).

There must certainly be other localities that were worked for gypsum (particularly to make plaster) at various times in antiquity, but these have so far gone unrecognised.

Description

The alabaster used for ancient Egyptian vessels is opaque white with occasional yellow patches or reddish brown veins caused by impurities. Its characteristic feature is its extreme softness – it can be scratched with a fingernail. In the past, alabaster has often been confused with travertine although, in fact, it may readily be distinguished from travertine by its softness and lack of effervescence in hydrochloric acid.

Uses

Stone vessels of alabaster were produced in a variety of shapes from the Predynastic period to the end of the Third Dynasty. During the New Kingdom alabaster was used for kohl jars and in the Late Period for alabastra. Lucas (1962: 413) notes that two of the chariot harness saddle knobs from the tomb of Tutankhamun (KV62) are of alabaster, and ashlars of alabaster were employed in a Greco–Roman temple and other buildings at Berenike on the Red Sea coast (Harrell 1996: 107).

From as early as the Predynastic period, gypsum was calcined to make gypsum plaster, a process that requires the heating of gypsum to a modest 100–200 °C. In contrast, burning limestone to produce quicklime requires a temperature of 900 °C, and there is no evidence that lime-burning was carried out in Egypt before the Ptolemaic period. Gypsum plaster was used on walls and ceilings in houses, palaces, tombs and temples, as an adhesive for repairing pottery or stone objects, and as a backing for inlays. Other uses include jar sealings, the modelling on Old Kingdom mummies, and the Amarna portrait masks. Stone masonry was bound with gypsum mortar.

Gesso is, strictly speaking, a term for gypsum plaster, although Egyptologists have commonly used it to refer to whiting plaster which is composed of powdered limestone mixed with glue. Whiting plaster appears as early as the Third Dynasty when it was employed for mounting the blue tiles in the subterranean chambers of Djoser's Step Pyramid and 'southern tomb' at Saqqara (Lucas 1962: 4). It was frequently used in the Eighteenth Dynasty and was later employed as a coating on wooden objects to make a smooth surface for painting or gilding. Whiting plaster was also used extensively for cartonnage mummy masks and coffins.

Examples

1. Cylinder vessel from tomb 2322 at Saqqara, Second Dynasty, *c.* 2770–2649 BC (New York, MMA 12.181.103).
2. Jar from Tomb 1, north necropolis, Abu Rawash, Third Dynasty, *c.* 2649–2575 BC (Cairo JE44351).
3. Gypsum plaster 'mask' of a woman from house P47.2 at el-Amarna, Eighteenth Dynasty, *c.* 1350 BC (height 27 cm; Berlin ÄM 21261; Priese 1991: 124–5).

Bibliography

Caton-Thompson and Gardner (1934: 103–23); Lucas (1962: 74–9); Aston (1994: 47–51).

For photographs of vessels see Aston (1994: pl. 10b) in colour, and el-Khouli (1978: pls. 149: 858, 150: 948) in black-and-white.

Alabaster-calcite *see* travertine

Amazonite *see* microcline

Amethyst *see* quartz

Anhydrite

Definition

Anhydrite is anhydrous calcium sulphate, $CaSO_4$, a mineral with the same composition as alabaster gypsum, but lacking water. It is usually white, but it may be grey or tinted blue. It generally occurs as massive granular aggregates which may be termed 'anhydrock' or 'rock anhydrite', or the rock may simply be called by its mineral name.

Egyptian sources
Ordinary white anhydrite has been quarried in modern times near the Gulf of Suez (Hussein 1990: 559), but the source of the distinctive blue anhydrite used in ancient times has not yet been discovered. White anhydrite was also used in ancient times as a building stone; ashlars of this rock were the main building material for the Serapis temple and a few other buildings at Berenike. Either anhydrite or alabaster gypsum was the stone used to build the Roman fort at Abu Sha'ar and buildings in several other Greco–Roman sites along the Red Sea coast. The quarry for Berenike has not been located but was certainly somewhere on the nearby Ras Banas peninsula, where there are large deposits of both alabaster gypsum and anhydrite.

Description
The ancient Egyptians exploited an attractive blue-tinted variety of anhydrite, which takes a good polish, and plain white anhydrite was also used to a limited extent. A small cosmetic vessel from Elkab (Ashmolean 1896–1908 E.2134) has a body of white anhydrite and a rim of blue anhydrite. White anhydrite has sometimes been confused with travertine or limestone, but it may be easily distinguished from both of these by its greater softness and the fact that it does not effervesce in dilute hydrochloric acid.

Petrie called anhydrite 'blue marble', a misconception which was repeated by subsequent writers until Lucas analysed the rock and published the correct identification in the second edition of *Ancient Egyptian Materials and Industries* (1934). Like limestone and travertine, marble is composed of calcium carbonate and will effervesce briskly in hydrochloric acid whereas anhydrite will not.

Uses
The earliest known instance of the use of anhydrite was for a Predynastic bull's head amulet now in Brussels (Musées Royaux d'Art et d'Histoire E 2335). The next example chronologically is the base of a statuette from an Eleventh-Dynasty Theban tomb (TT 51) at Deir el-Bahari (New York, MMA 26.3.220), but by far the most common use of anhydrite was for small vessels during the Middle Kingdom and Second Intermediate Period. Several categories of finely modelled vessels – including some with monkeys modelled in relief, some in the shape of monkeys holding a cosmetic jar and some in the form of trussed ducks – were produced almost exclusively in anhydrite.

Examples
1. Squat cosmetic jar with two monkeys in relief, blue anhydrite, Twelfth Dynasty (height 4.2 cm; BM EA20759).
2. Squat cosmetic jar with two monkeys in relief, white anhydrite, Twelfth Dynasty, (height 2.2 cm; Cambridge, Fitzwilliam E.266.1939; Bourriau 1988: 142).
3. Trussed duck vessel, Middle Kingdom (height 15 cm; Boston, MFA 65.1749).

Bibliography
Terrace (1966); De Putter and Karlshausen (1992: 49–50); Aston (1994: 51–3).

For colour photographs see De Putter and Karlshausen 1992: pl. 4) and Aston (1994: pl. 11a).

Anorthosite gneiss *see* gneiss: anorthosite, diorite, gabbro, granite and tonalite

Azurite
Definition
This mineral is a deep blue form of copper carbonate ($Cu_3[CO_3]_2[OH]_2$), also called chessylite, which results from the oxidisation of copper sulphide. It occurs in association with copper deposits.

Egyptian sources
Found in the Eastern Desert and at Wadi Maghara and Serabit el-Khadim in the Sinai.

Description
Blue ore of copper not suited to carving.

Uses
The Egyptians may have used azurite as a blue pigment, but the evidence is so far fairly tenuous (see Chapter 4, this volume).

Bibliography
Spurrell (1895); Lucas (1962: 340); Blom-Böer (1994: 61–2).

Basalt
Definitions
'Basalt' is a volcanic igneous rock with an aphanitic groundmass consisting largely of intermediate to calcic plagioclase feldspar (labradorite and bytownite) and various ferromagnesium minerals, especially pyroxene and olivine. 'Dolerite' (or, synonymously, 'diabase') is a rock with the same composition as basalt but with a medium- to mainly fine-grained phaneritic texture. Many objects labelled as dolerite by Egyptologists are actually basalt.

Egyptian sources
Occurrences of basalt are widespread in Egypt. They include a broad, serpentine outcrop starting near Abu Rawash and continuing past Giza and across the northern Fayum; and numerous scattered, small outcrops to the northeast and east of Cairo, on the east bank of the Nile near Gebel el-Teir and on the west bank near el-Bahnasa and Abu Simbel. Despite basalt's availability at numerous localities, only one ancient quarry is known. It is located at Widan el-Faras on Gebel el-Qatrani in the northern Fayum (see Fig. 2.8), and was worked during the Old Kingdom in the Fourth to Sixth Dynasties and perhaps as early as the

Third Dynasty (see Harrell and Bown 1995). It seems likely that basalt outcrops elsewhere would also have been worked, especially after the Old Kingdom.

Description

The basalt from Widan el-Faras consists mainly of labradorite, augite pyroxene and basaltic glass with minor magnetite and rare hornblende amphibole, olivine, quartz and apatite. The rock is slightly porphyritic with moderate grey labradorite and dark green augite phenocrysts up to 7 mm across. The groundmass is mostly aphanitic but grain size occasionally ranges up to 2 mm. The brown discoloration commonly seen on this otherwise dark grey to black rock results from devitrification of glass in the groundmass.

Uses

Buildings

Basalt was widely exploited during the Old Kingdom for pavements in pyramid temples of the Memphite necropolis where it probably symbolised the black, life-giving Nile mud from which ancient Egypt derived its name, Kemet (the 'black land'). Basalt pavements (and occasionally walls) are found in the mortuary temples of the following kings: Djoser (Third Dynasty), Userkaf (Fifth Dynasty) and Pepi I (Sixth Dynasty) at Saqqara; Sahura, Neferirkara and Niuserra (Fifth Dynasty) at Abusir; and Khufu (Fourth Dynasty) at Giza. Also at Giza, extensive use of basalt was made for walls and pavement in Khufu's valley temple and causeway.

Sculpture and vessels

This rock was first used for small vessels in the late Predynastic period and continued to be commonly employed for this purpose until the Sixth Dynasty and rarely thereafter. Determining the other ancient uses of basalt is complicated by the misuse of petrological nomenclature by Egyptologists. For example, many sculptures labelled as basalt are actually siltstone or greywacke from Wadi Hammamat or non-porphyritic granodiorite from Aswan. These rocks were employed for most, if not all, of the so-called basalt sarcophagi and pyramidia of the Old and Middle Kingdoms. It is also occasionally found that basalt objects have been mislabelled as 'black granite'. After giving due allowance to these nomenclatural errors, it appears that basalt was seldom used after the Old Kingdom and then mainly for statuary, especially in the Late Period and Greco-Roman period.

Figure 2.8 Basalt quarry at Widan el-Faras in the northern Fayum.

Examples

1. Libation bowl, Twenty-sixth Dynasty, *c.* 664–525 BC (diameter *c.* 75 cm; BM EA1386).
2. Colossal kneeling naophorous statue of Wahibra, late Twenty-sixth Dynasty, *c.* 530 BC (height 1.8 m; BM EA111).
3. Sarcophagus lid (possibly royal) carved in the high relief form of a male figure, Twenty-seventh Dynasty/ Persian period, *c.* 525–404 BC (BM EA90).

Bibliography

Lucas (1962: 61–62, 410); el-Hinnawi and Maksoud (1968, 1972); Heikal *et al.* (1983); De Putter and Karlshausen (1992: 51–54); Hoffmeier (1993); Klemm and Klemm (1993: 413–22); Aston (1994: 18–21); Harrell and Bown (1995).

Beryl (emerald)

Definitions

Beryl ($Be_3Al_2Si_6O_{18}$) is a beryllium aluminosilicate mineral that forms naturally as hexagonal, prismatic crystals in a variety of colours. Of these well-formed crystals, the green and blue varieties (emerald and aquamarine, respectively) have been of commercial interest for thousands of years, although heliodor, a yellow form of beryl, does not appear to have been exploited in the ancient world. Beryl has a Mohs hardness of 7.5–8; it is harder than quartz and can be scratched by few other materials, so that, although difficult to work, it holds a polish well. Deposits of beryl are associated with granitic veins and high-grade metamorphic rocks. The beryl is of emerald quality only when the veins cut across particular types of ultramafic rocks.

Egyptian sources

The principal Egyptian sources of beryl lie in an area of some 1,000 square kilometres in the southeastern sector of the Eastern Desert, roughly circumscribed by Gebel Zubara in the north, Wadi Nugrus in the west, Wadi Gimal in the south, Umm Kabu in the southeast and Gebel Sikait in the east (see Hume 1934). The Sikait-Zubara mines were the only source of emeralds for Europe, Asia and Africa in the Hellenistic period and they continued to be exploited until at least the Middle Ages, when Arab writers document the appearance of larger, heavier stones from the Indian subcontinent.

There is clear documentary evidence for beryl mining in

the Egyptian southeastern desert in 24 BC (Strabo, *Geography* XVII, I: 45, Jones 1917–32; and see also Pliny, *Natural History* XXXVII: 16–18, Rackham 1968), but the Sikait-Zubara mines had fallen out of use by the seventeenth century AD, and even the location of the mines seems to have been temporarily forgotten by the time James Bruce undertook his expedition through Egypt in 1768 (Bruce 1805). In 1816, the French goldsmith, Frédéric Cailliaud, searching for mines on behalf of Muhammad Ali Pasha, rediscovered the Sikait-Zubara mining region (Cailliaud 1821–62). The principal emerald-mining sites in the region were subsequently visited by Giovanni Belzoni, Sir John Gardner Wilkinson and Nestor l'Hôte in the nineteenth century, and the general geology of the region has been described by Oskar Schneider (Schneider and Azruni 1892) and W.F. Hume (1934). The region was also the subject of three scientific expeditions in the early 1900s (MacAlister 1900; Thomas 1909; Murray 1925).

Preliminary examination of surface pottery at four of the principal mining sites in the Sikait-Zubara region (Shaw *et al.* 1999) confirms that the emerald-mining took place over a long period, extending at the very least from the Ptolemaic period at Gebel Sikait to the sixteenth century AD at Gebel Zubara. The full period of exploitation in the Sikait-Zubara region as a whole must therefore have spanned more than 1,500 years. The changing strategies of mining ranged from adventitious removal of surface rock (in the Greco–Roman period) to the use of complex systems of shafts and adits (in the Byzantine and Ottoman periods). An assessment of the precise order in which different parts of the region were mined will require much more detailed sampling of the ceramics associated with each of the individual mines.

Description

In the Sikait-Zubara region, the combination of micaceous schist (i.e. metamorphosed clay-rich sedimentary rock) and granitic fluids (especially pegmatites) provided the appropriate chemistry for the formation of beryl during metamorphism. The rifting that formed the Red Sea also caused uplift of the igneous-metamorphic basement along the eastern margin of Egypt, thus creating the mountains of the Eastern Desert and exposing the emerald deposits within them. Several geologists and archaeologists have published accounts of their visits to ancient Egyptian emerald mines, particularly during the first three decades of the twentieth century. The most recent study (Grubessi *et al.* 1989, 1990) involved the use of x-ray diffraction and infrared spectroscopy (for the former see section on methods of scientific analysis below) to compare the Sikait-Zubara emeralds with those from mines elsewhere in the world.

The geoarchaeological study of several sites in the Sikait-Zubara region (Shaw *et al.* 1999) has demonstrated a number of the ways in which the conditions for growth of emeralds may arise:

(1) at the boundaries of granite intrusions into schist;
(2) adjacent to quartz veins spawned by a granite;
(3) within granite pegmatites; and
(4) in biotite schist lenses within a metamorphosed granite.

One or more of these modes of emerald formation can be found at each of the four sites.

Uses

The Egyptians used beryl only for jewellery. Lucas (1962: 390) analysed a number of supposed beryls in items of jewellery of the Pharaonic period (such as the Middle Kingdom items from Dahshur) and concluded that in all cases the stones were actually green feldspar or olivine. Although an uncut emerald was supposedly identified in a necklace from the Predynastic site of el-Kubaniya, immediately to the north of Aswan (Junker 1919; Lucas 1962: 390), there have been no modern identifications of beryl in the Pharaonic period or earlier, and the stone does not appear to have been used regularly in Egyptian jewellery until the Ptolemaic period.

Examples

1. Silver crown embossed with busts of an Egyptian god and incorporating large beryls, found beside the body of a woman in room 1 of tomb B.114 at Ballana, dating to the X-Group period, *c.* AD 400–600 (Cairo, Egyptian Museum; Object no. 11; see Emery 1938b: 148, 183, fig. 72, pl. 34a).
2. Necklace consisting of gold and hexagonal beryl beads, Roman period, unprovenanced (Yale University Art Gallery 1941.308), overall length 37 cm.

Bibliography

Cailliaud (1821); Wilkinson (1878); Schneider and Azruni (1892); MacAlister (1900); Thomas (1909); Murray (1925); Hume (1934: 110–25); Lucas (1962: 389–90); Grubessi *et al.* (1989, 1990); Hussein and El-Sharkawi (1990: 537–9); Shaw *et al.* (1999).

Breccia *see* limestone breccia

Calcite *see* travertine

Chalcedony: (agate, cornelian, chrysoprase, citrine, onyx, sardonyx, silicified wood)

Definition

Chalcedony is a translucent microcrystalline form of quartz consisting of thin layers of very small parallel-oriented fibres (from which it derives the toughness which makes it so ideal for carved objects). Its basic chemical composition is silicon dioxide (SiO_2) and it has a Mohs hardness of 6.5–7. The characteristic crusts or cavity fillings of chalcedony result from a process of precipitation from silica-bearing ground water.

The term chalcedony, in its widest sense, also embraces agate, chrysoprase, cornelian, onyx, sardonyx and silicified wood, which are all essentially coloured forms of chalcedony (i.e. fibrous microcrystalline quartz ; see Table 2.5). The colours of these various forms of chalcedony are caused by impurities. Thus the brown colouring of agate and sardonyx as well as the red colouring of cornelian are all produced by the presence of higher proportions of iron oxides, while the green colour of chrysoprase is caused by the presence of nickel oxide. Jack Ogden (pers. comm.) speculates that the Eastern Desert may possibly have contained sources of matauralite (an unusual type of green chrome-bearing chalcedony), which is attested in items of jewellery throughout the Roman empire, the only known modern source being in East Africa.

1. Agate

Definition

A form of chalcedony which occurs as spherical or almond-shaped nodules in mafic volcanic rocks, the characteristic banded or stripey appearance being caused by 'rhythmic crystallisation' (i.e. the build-up of thin layers of quartz fibres). The interiors of agates often contain crystals such as amethyst, calcite and smoky quartz, while the uppermost layers tend to form a white crust as a result of weathering. Many agates are simply grey in appearance but they can acquire bright colours and unusual structures through the natural staining of the porous chalcedony with a variety of metallic salts; fire agate, for instance, derives its iridescent colours from the interference of light passing through thin layers of regularly spaced iron oxide crystals within the chalcedony. There are a number of basic types of agate, such as 'fortification agate' (the patterns in which resemble the bastions of fortresses), 'tubular agate' (which is pierced by tubular canals) and 'ribbon agate' (in which the interior of the nodule consists of planar, parallel bands, usually surrounded by other bands which are concentric to the external surface). Ribbon agate was used for cameos and intaglios in the Greek and Roman periods.

Probably the most important variety, however, is 'banded agate', in which the differently coloured irregular layers are continuous, generally of uniform thickness and colour, and are roughly concentric to the external surface of the nodule. The bands alternate between brown or reddish-brown and white, and vary in translucency.

Egyptian sources

Agate (mostly non-banded) is abundant in Egypt, usually occurring in the form of surface pebbles. There is also at least one instance of the occurrence of agate alongside jasper (see CHERT below) and ordinary chalcedony at Wadi Abu Gerida in the Eastern Desert, about seventy kilometres northwest of Quseir (Barron and Hume 1902: 266; Hume 1937: 862).

Description

The agate found in the Eastern Desert usually has concentric bands of white and brown, and occasionally also blue concentric bands.

Uses

From the Predynastic period onwards, agate was used in jewellery in the form of unworked pebbles, beads and drop pendants. In the Pharaonic period, although agate was sometimes also used for amulets, its use in jewellery was comparatively infrequent. It was employed for small vessels in the 25th and 27th Dynasties as well as in the Roman period.

Examples

1. Vessel found in the Eastern Desert and dating to the Late Period (height 7.7 cm; Cairo JE55034).
2. Vessel found in tomb 4 at el-Kurru and dating to the early seventh century BC (Boston, MFA).
3. Fragment of an Eighteenth-Dynasty gold girdle from the tomb of the three princesses of Thutmose III, comprising a glass or faience *ḥtp* hieroglyph and a gold and agate *nb* sign (length 4 cm; New York, MMA; see Winlock 1959: 135, fig. 73).

Bibliography

Barron and Hume (1902: 266); Engelbach (1931); Lucas (1962: 386–7); Habachi and Biers (1969); Aston (1994: 68–9).

For colour photograph of a Late Period vessel (Cairo JE 55034) see Aston (1994: pl.13c).

2. Chrysoprase

Definition

Yellowish green (i.e. 'apple-green') form of chalcedony, larger broken pieces of which are often fissured with irregular colours. It is found only in serpentinite, and the colour derives from the presence of hydrated nickel silicate impurities. Darker shades of chrysoprase can sometimes be confused with prase (a leek-green massive variety of chert).

Egyptian sources

No specific ancient Egyptian sources of chrysoprase have been located.

Uses

From the Predynastic period to the Roman period chrysoprase was used occasionally for beads, amulets and pendants.

Bibliography

Schäfer (1910: 13, 34–5, 37); Lucas (1962: 392); Ogden (1982: 107–8).

3. Cornelian and sard

Definition

Cornelian (or carnelian) is a red to yellowish- or orange-red translucent form of chalcedony, the colour of which is produced by the presence of tiny amounts of iron oxide. It can sometimes be confused with red jasper, although the latter is opaque rather than translucent. The term sard is used to describe the red to brownish-red form of cornelian although in practice it can be difficult to make a clear distinction between the two stones (with some geologists distinguishing between the two in terms of the intensity of the colour rather than its hue). The red of cornelian is due to minute disseminated particles of haematite. The brown in sard probably derives from particles of goethite, a hydrated iron oxide. Both cornelian and sard can be reddened by heating (Frondel 1962: 207).

Egyptian sources

Numerous small water-worn pebbles of cornelian are found scattered across the surface of the desert between the Nile valley and the Red Sea, but larger stones occur at various specific sites in the Eastern Desert, such as the regions of Wadi Abu Gerida (about seventy kilometres northwest of Quseir, see Barron and Hume 1902: 266) and Wadi Saga (about twenty kilometres northwest of Quseir, see Barron and Hume 1902: 221) as well as at the Gebel el-Asr gneiss quarries in the Western Desert, sixty-five kilometres northwest of Abu Simbel (Engelbach 1933: 69, 1938: 370, 372; Little 1933: 79–80), although it is by no means clear in any of these three instances whether ancient expeditions were sent there specifically in order to obtain cornelian.

Description

The flesh-red and reddish-brown forms of cornelian and sard were used by the Egyptians from the Predynastic period onwards, although a yellowish form was also used in the Middle and New Kingdoms.

Uses

One of the earliest gemstones to be carved into beads, cornelian was used from the Predynastic onwards for both beads and amulets. Some Predynastic cornelian beads appear to have been glazed (e.g. at the Armant cemeteries, see Mond and Myers 1937: I, 72). In the Pharaonic period it was used for inlay on jewellery, furniture and numerous items of funerary equipment (such as coffins), as well as for rings, scarabs, amulets (particularly *wedjat*-eyes) and even small vessels. During the New Kingdom, when most inlay had begun to be made from coloured glass, cornelian was one of the few gemstones still frequently used, although it was sometimes imitated by placing rock crystal or milky quartz on red-painted cement.

Examples

1. Predynastic amulet in the form of a bovine head, of unknown provenance, dating to the fourth millennium BC (height 3.8 cm; Hildesheim, Pelizaeus Museum 5159).
2. Squat-shouldered jar with gold foil cap from the tomb of the Second-Dynasty ruler Khasekhemwy at Abydos, *c.* 2700 BC (height 4.2 cm; Cairo JE34941).
3. Eleventh-Dynasty necklace of cornelian beads capped with gold dating to the Middle Kingdom, *c.* 2140–1991 BC (length 74 cm; BM EA24773).
4. Unfinished open-work plaque comprising a scene of Akhenaten, Nefertiti and their daughters embracing one another, Eighteenth Dynasty, *c.* 1350 BC, provenance unknown but probably Amarna; this is one of the largest known worked gemstones from Egypt, and was perhaps intended to be inset into a gold pectoral, with the appearance of a crack at the base of the object probably being the reason for its abandonment (height 5.7 cm; Cambridge, Fitzwilliam EGA4606.1943; Vassilika 1995: 62–3).

Bibliography

Barron and Hume (1902: 221, 266); Engelbach (1933: 69, 1938: 370, 372); Little (1933: 79–80); Lucas (1962: 391–2); Ogden (1982: 108); Aston (1994: 67–8).

For colour photograph of a cornelian vessel (height: 2.7cm; Cairo CG 18777) see Aston (1994: pl. 15b). For colour photograph of a cornelian necklace (BM EA24773) see Andrews (1990: fig. 74c).

4. Onyx and sardonyx

Definition

The term onyx is used in gemmology to refer sometimes to a black form of chalcedony but more often to the ribbon form of agate, in which the regular bands or layers alternate between contrasting darker and lighter colours (usually black or dark brown alternating with white or light grey). Onyx differs from banded agate in that its bands are straight and parallel. Sardonyx is a variety of onyx consisting of alternating bands of white and brown or reddish-brown.

Egyptian sources

According to Lucas (1962: 387), 'onyx and sardonyx probably . . . occur in Egypt, though no mention of them can be found in the geological reports'.

Uses

Onyx was used for beads from the Predynastic period onwards, but both onyx and sardonyx became very popular after the Twenty-first Dynasty, reaching a peak of use (particularly for cameos, intaglios and ring settings) in the Ptolemaic and Roman periods. During the latter two periods, however, onyx is known to have been imported from India (through Greco–Roman ports such as Berenike on the Red Sea), therefore some of the later uses of onyx may not have employed native stone. On the other hand, the 'nicolo' cut of onyx (i.e. an onyx gem cut in such a way that the uppermost layer is bluish white) was known to the Romans as *aegyptilla*, suggesting either an Egyptian source or trade-routes passing through Egypt.

Example

Sardonyx pendant inlaid with a *wedjat*-eye of gold and fused glass, from the pyramidal tomb of the *kandake* (queen)

Amanishaketo at Meroe, late first century BC (height 1.6 cm; Berlin, ÄM 1650).

Bibliography

Petrie, Wainwright and Mackay (1912: 22); Lucas (1962: 386–7); Ogden (1982: 109).

5. Silicified wood

Definition

Also known as petrified wood, it is a pseudomorph of chalcedony formed when circulating water replaces the organic constituents of wood with quartz, thus preserving the original shape and, often, internal structure of the wood.

Egyptian sources

Silicified wood is extremely abundant in Egypt's Eastern and Western deserts as well as in the Sinai. There is a particularly large 'forest' of silicified wood near Cairo.

Description

A number of botanists (e.g. Seward 1935) have identified the various species of silicified wood found in Egypt.

Uses

Since silicified wood is a very hard material, it is difficult to carve. There are therefore only a few instances of its use in the Pharaonic period (including a scarab), although it was shaped into crude hammerstones in the Neolithic and Badarian periods.

Bibliography

Legrain (1906: 55–6); Keldani (1939); Seward (1935); Ibrahim (1943, 1953); Shukri (1944); Lucas (1962: 455–6).

Chert (chert, flint and jasper)

1. Chert and flint

Definition

Chert is an opaque microcrystalline form of quartz or chalcedony (the latter very rarely making up the majority of the rock). It is a layered siliceous rock with no essential fossil content, which occurs either in the form of beds (created by layers of silica-shelled marine organisms) or as nodules and lenses in limestone.

Most geologists distinguish between chert and flint purely in terms of colour; flint being the darker form of chert. This colour distinction, however, also happens to relate to some extent to the two forms of chert – bedded and nodular – thus, most bedded cherts are light grey (or occasionally light blueish-, yellowish- or brownish-grey), whereas most nodular cherts are dark grey, brownish-black or black. The nodular cherts are therefore often described as flint. In the sections below, chert is used in its wider sense (i.e. including both chert and flint) since Egyptologists have tended to make somewhat arbitrary distinctions between the two.

Egyptian sources

In Egypt, all chert occurs as nodules within limestone. The nodules formed where quartz or chalcedony precipitated from silica-rich groundwater and simultaneously replaced the calcite in the limestone. In the Nile valley, these nodules occur in the Eocene limestones that crop out between Esna and Cairo; most of them are the darker chert that would usually be described as flint. They can also be found in Eocene and Cretaceous limestones cropping out in many parts of the Western and Eastern deserts.

Belgian survey and excavation at the sites of Nazlet Khater, Beit Allam, Taramsa and Nazlet Safaha (all situated between Asyut and Qena) have revealed occupation sites with extensive evidence of the extraction and working of cobbles of chert (Vermeersch, Paulissen and Van Peer 1990). These mines may well be the earliest in the world, dating to *c.* 40,000 BP. In addition, Seton-Karr (1898, 1905) and Baumgartel (1960) describe extensive 'flint' mines of indeterminate date in the Eastern Desert at the site of Wadi el-Sheikh, to the southeast of Beni Suef.

Uses

The Palaeolithic and Neolithic inhabitants of Egypt used chert to manufacture tools and weapons from a very early date (*c.* 500,000 BP), but it is also clear that chert continued to be an important material for numerous artefacts long after the appearance of copper in the Predynastic period. Even when copper and bronze became more readily available in the Pharaonic period, chert was still a very cheap and effective material for many of the basic artefacts used in daily life, as well as being a potent medium for more ritualistic and religious objects, such as the *pšs-kf* implement used for the 'opening of the mouth' ceremony (see Van Walsem 1978–9; Macy Roth 1992) and the curved knives used for such rituals as circumcision and embalming.

In the Predynastic and Early Dynastic periods, chert was used not only for tools and weapons but also occasionally for bangles, pendants and vessels. The evidence from Old Kingdom mortuary complexes such as the Step Pyramid complex of the Third-Dynasty ruler Djoser at Saqqara suggests that chert chisels were used for fine surface working of limestone masonry blocks, although the kinds of chisels suitable for fine stone-carving rarely seem to have survived (see Petrie 1890: pl. 16; Nour *et al.* 1962: pl. 15a). It has been suggested that the many crescent-shaped chert tools found in Djoser's complex were probably used to create the fluting of his columns (see Lauer and Debono 1950). At the Abusir necropolis, Vachala and Sroboda (1989: 178) noted the presence of large numbers of hammerstones and chert tools in the vicinity of Fifth-Dynasty limestone buildings, perhaps having been used to dress the stone.

Figure 2.10 Part of the Gebel el-Asr gneiss quarries: the so-called 'great' or 'chisel' quarry is in the foreground.

Figure 2.11 Old Kingdom bowl carved from the lighter-coloured anorthosite gneiss with streaks and speckles (Ashmolean 1896–1908 E.401), Fourth Dynasty, from Mastaba *A (Kaimenu) at Elkab.*

of greater than 50 per cent anorthite) while the plagioclase in diorite is more sodium-rich.

Various scholars have obtained a range of plagioclase compositions. Klemm and Klemm (1993: 425) analysed a statue of Khafra in the Pelizaeus Museum, Hildesheim and determined that the plagioclase was andesine (An 30–50 per cent). Aston (1994: 62, 183) has analysed two stone vessels from Nag el-Deir and recorded finding labradorite (An 50–70 per cent). Harrell and Brown (1994: 52–4) analysed quarry samples which contained bytownite (An 70–90 per cent), and Little (1933: 78) examined quarry samples with a range of plagioclase compositions from oligoclase to anorthite (An 10–100 per cent). Therefore, until more analyses of ancient Egyptian objects made of gneiss are carried out, it is not certain which variety is predominant.

The dark gneiss is typically banded, although the blackish hornblende is sometimes fairly uniformly disseminated within the lighter feldspar matrix (Aston 1994: pl. 14a). The light-coloured gneiss with black streaks and speckles is unusual in having less than 10 per cent dark-colored minerals – a composition known as anorthosite gneiss.

The Gebel el-Asr banded gneiss has sometimes been called 'diorite' or 'Chephren/Khafra diorite' after the four statues of this stone found in Khafra's valley temple; however, these terms are incorrect and should be avoided. The distinct banding clearly indicates the metamorphic nature of the rock, i.e. it has been transformed by heat and pressure from an igneous diorite or gabbro into a metamorphic gneiss. On visiting the Gebel el-Asr quarry both Engelbach (1938: 389) and Harrell and Brown (1994: 54–5) noted a conspicuous blue glow to the gneiss in the strong sunlight. Harrell and Brown have suggested that this iridescence was the reason this stone was particularly prized, attracting the ancient Egyptians to this remote quarry.

Uses

Stone vessels are the earliest objects of gneiss known (see Fig. 2.11); these date from the late Predynastic period to the Sixth Dynasty, and were particularly common in the Third Dynasty (Aston 1994: 63–4). The Second-Dynasty king Peribsen had a gneiss stele carved for his tomb at Abydos (BM EA35597). Statues of gneiss were produced during the Old Kingdom and Twelfth Dynasty; the few examples of later date were almost certainly recarved from earlier sculptures. There is a notable lack of evidence of any New Kingdom (or later) activity at Gebel el-Asr and exploitation of the gneiss quarry would appear to have ceased at the end of the Twelfth Dynasty.

Examples

1. Seated statue of King Khafra with protective falcon from the king's valley temple at Giza, Fourth Dynasty, *c.* 2520–2494 BC (height 1.68 m; Cairo CG14).
2. Statue of King Sahura with a figure personifying the Koptos nome, Fifth Dynasty, *c.*2458–46 BC (New York, MMA 18.2.4).
3. Torso of a statue of King Senusret I, Twelfth Dynasty, *c.* 1971–26 BC (height 47.5 cm; Berlin, ÄM 1205).
4. Sphinx with the head of King Senusret III, Twelfth Dynasty, *c.*1878–41 BC (length 73 cm; New York, MMA 17.9.2).
5. Block statue of Khai-Hapy from Heliopolis, late Nineteenth Dynasty, *c.*1200 BC (height 49.5 cm; Vienna ÄS64).

Bibliography

Engelbach (1933, 1938); Little (1933); Murray (1939b); De Putter and Karlshausen (1992: 77–80); Klemm and Klemm (1993:

423–6); Aston (1994, 62–4); Harrell and Brown (1994); Shaw and Bloxam (1999).

For photographs of the Sahura and Senusret III statues (MMA 18.2.4 and 17.9.2) see Hayes (1953: 70, 197). For colour photographs see De Putter and Karlshausen (1992: pls. 19, 20: Khai-Hapy statue, statue head and vessel); Aston (1994: pl. 14: two vessels); Klemm and Klemm (1993: pl. 16.6: polished slab).

2. Granite gneiss and granite from Tumbos

In the Tumbos district at the southern entrance to the third Nile cataract in the Sudan, there is a large quarry that dates from the Eighteenth and Twenty-fifth Dynasties and the subsequent Napatan–Meroitic period. Two types of rock were extracted here, granite gneiss from the east bank on the north side of Tumbos village, Dabaki Island and near North Akkad village on the west bank, and granite from the nearby Tumbos Island.

Description

The gneiss is light yellowish to pinkish grey, medium- to coarse-grained and well-foliated with conspicuous banding, and consists of quartz, microcline and oligoclase feldspars, hornblende and biotite. It has the same composition as igneous 'granite' and so should be called 'granite gneiss'. The second rock type, which occurs as thick intrusive veins within the gneiss, is a moderate grey, fine- to medium-grained granite with essentially the same mineralogy as the gneiss.

Uses

Both rock types were used only at sites between the third and fourth cataracts in the Sudan, notably in the Napatan–Meroitic temples at Tabo and Kawa, and the New Kingdom and later temples at Gebel Barkal. They were used only for stelae, statues, offering tables and other sculptures.

Examples (granite gneiss)

1. Stele of Thutmose III from Gebel Barkal, Sudan, 18th Dynasty, *c.*1479–25 BC (height 1.73 m; Boston MFA 23.733).
2. Colossal striding statue of King Anlamani from Gebel Barkal, Sudan, *c.*623–593 BC (height 3.8 m; Boston MFA 23.732).
3. Reposing ram of Amun with King Taharqo standing between the forelegs from Kawa, Sudan, *c.*690–64 BC (height 1.06 m; BM EA1779) (another virtually identical ram is Ashmolean 1931.553).
4. Stele of an unknown Twenty-fifth-Dynasty king from Gebel Barkal, Sudan (height 1.24 m; Cairo JE 48865).
5. Stele of King Tanutamani from Gebel Barkal, Sudan, 664–53 BC (height 1.32 m; Cairo JE 48863).

Examples (granite)

1. Stele of King Tanyidamani from Gebel Barkal, Sudan, 110–90 BC (height 1.58 m; Boston MFA 23.736).
2. Recumbent sphinx with the head of King Taharqo from Kawa, Sudan, Twenty-fifth Dynasty, *c.* 690–64 BC (length 75 cm; BM EA1770).

Bibliography

Dunham (1947); Harrell (forthcoming (b)).

3. Tonalite gneiss from Mons Claudianus

An enormous Roman quarry, known in antiquity as Mons Claudianus (see Fig. 2.12), consists of over 130 excavation sites within and between wadis Abu Marakhat, Umm Hussein and Umm Diqal. The quarry was worked during the first to third centuries AD.

Description

The rock is mottled light grey and greenish black, medium-grained 'tonalite gneiss' with oligoclase plagioclase, biotite mica and hornblende amphibole plus minor microcline feldspar and accessory minerals (apatite, magnetite, sphene and zircon). Foliation is well-developed, with the dark minerals occurring in short, straight, parallel streaks but also in irregular patches. 'Quartz diorite gneiss' is another acceptable name for this rock because in many classification schemes tonalite is considered a quartz-rich subvariety of quartz diorite. The metamorphic rock has previously been misidentified as igneous 'granite', 'granodiorite', 'quartz diorite' and 'diorite'.

Uses

The Mons Claudianus stone was exported throughout the Roman Empire but objects made from it are especially common in Rome and Tivoli, Italy. It was used mainly for large whole columns and basins, and also for smaller objects such as pedestals and pavement tiles. Perhaps the best known examples are the 12.2-metre-long columns (seven of the eight) in the portico of the Pantheon in Rome. No examples of sculptures are known.

Bibliography

Kraus and Röder (1962a, 1962b); Gnoli (1988: 148–50); Peacock (1988, 1992); Marchei *et al.* (1989: 222–3); Galetti *et al.* (1992); Klemm and Klemm (1993: 395–408); Peacock (1992); Peacock *et al.* (1994); Brown and Harrell (1995).

For colour photographs of polished slabs see: Mielsch (1985: pl. 23–796), Lazzarini (1987: fig. 3), Gnoli (1988: fig. 112), Marchei *et al.* (1989: fig. 72a) and Klemm and Klemm (1993: pls. 16.1–16.2).

4. Tonalite gneiss from Wadi Umm Huyut

Located six kilometres southwest of Mons Claudianus, this small quarry near Wadi Umm Huyut was worked during the first and second centuries AD.

Description

The quarry produced tonalite gneiss that is mineralogically and texturally identical to that from Mons Claudianus. The two rocks do differ markedly, however, in their foliation: at

Figure 2.12 Tonalite gneiss quarry at Mons Claudianus, Eastern Desert. The broken column in the foreground is eighteen metres long with a diameter of 2.6 metres.

Wadi Umm Huyut the dark minerals occur mainly in long wavy stringers, whereas at Mons Claudianus they form short, straight streaks.

Uses

It was quarried by the Romans for export from Egypt. Until very recently, the existence of the Wadi Umm Huyut quarry and its stone had gone unrecognised. Where found, the stone has undoubtedly been incorrectly attributed to Mons Claudianus. However, the diminutive size of the workings at Wadi Umm Huyut indicates that, unlike at Mons Claudianus, the rock was used for relatively small objects such as basins, pedestals and pavement tiles. The best of the few known examples of its use is a 2.1–metre-diameter basin from Porto, near Ostia in Italy, now used as a fountain on the Via dei Fori Imperiali beside the Parliament building in Rome.

Bibliography

Brown and Harrell (1995); Harrell *et al.* (forthcoming); Sidebotham (1996).

Granite and granodiorite

Definitions

'Granite' and 'granodiorite' are phaneritic igneous rocks with similar, gradational compositions. Granite consists largely of quartz and alkali feldspar (microcline or orthoclase) whereas granodiorite contains comparable amounts of quartz but less alkali feldspar. Both rock types also include variable amounts of sodic to intermediate plagioclase (oligoclase or andesine), mica (muscovite or biotite) and hornblende amphibole plus small amounts of various accessory minerals.

Egyptian sources

These rocks are widely distributed throughout the Eastern Desert and in the Nile valley where they form the cataracts in the Nile. They were quarried anciently at three localities: in the Nile valley at Aswan and Tumbos (see GNEISS); and in the Eastern Desert at Bir Umm Fawakhir (see map in Fig. 2.1).

1. Granite from Aswan

Description

Extensive outcrops of granite are found east of the Nile between Aswan and the Shellal district as well as on the islands in the river. Ancient quarrying occurred at scores of sites within this region (see Fig. 2.3). Two rock varieties were extracted.

Variety 1

Very coarse- to mainly coarse-grained granite with quartz, microcline, oligoclase and biotite plus minor hornblende and accessory minerals (mostly apatite, sphene, zircon and iron oxides). This is the so-called 'monumental red or pink granite' of Egypt. The rock is commonly porphyritic with microcline phenocrysts up to 4 cm across. When biotite is present in only minor amounts, the rock has a pinkish or occasionally reddish appearance, but when this mica is abundant the rock is much darker with a black and pink mottling. The granite commonly exhibits a pronounced parallel or subparallel arrangement of the feldspar and biotite grains. This is a type of foliation caused by magmatic flowage and such rocks may be described as 'gneissoid granite'. They could also be called 'granite gneiss' but most petrologists prefer to restrict this terminology to rocks with foliation caused by metamorphism.

The granite quarries are located mainly between the city of Aswan and the el-Shellal district to the south. Additional quarrying occurred along the east bank of the Nile between Aswan and Sehel Island, and also on Elephantine, Saluja, Sehel and other islands. Numerous objects were left in the quarries unfinished, including an Eighteenth-Dynasty obelisk (Fig. 2.4), three colossal statues of apparently New Kingdom date, and seven Roman bathtubs (see Fig. 2.3 for locations). These quarries were worked from the Early Dynastic period to the Roman period, but most of the visible remains are Greco-Roman (see Fig. 2.5).

Variety 2

Medium- to mainly fine-grained granite with a mineralogical composition identical to that of the Variety 1 granite. Phenocrysts are absent. This rock occurs as thin veins cutting Variety 1 and the Aswan granodiorite (see below), and occasionally contains fragments (xenoliths) of these rock types. The Variety 2 granite usually exhibits foliation, as evidenced by the parallel alignment of biotite flakes, and so may be described as 'gneissoid granite'. Variations in the amount and coloration of microcline cause the rock to vary from light grey or pinkish to occasionally a reddish colour.

The principal outcrops are on Saluja and Sehel islands, and on the east bank south of the latter island. No ancient quarry workings have been reported. The few that once existed may have been destroyed during construction of the 1902 dam when this rock was extensively quarried and used for fill. This granite variety was rarely used in ancient times, and the few known examples date from the New Kingdom onwards.

Uses

Buildings

The coarse pink granite (Variety 1) was initially used for building purposes in the First Dynasty for a pavement in the tomb of King Den at Abydos. From the Third to the Twelfth Dynasty Variety 1 was widely employed in pyramids for lining burial chambers and passages (for example, those for the Third-Dynasty king Djoser at Saqqara and the Fourth-Dynasty kings Khufu, Khafra and Menkaura at Giza), and also occasionally for exterior facing (as on the Khafra and Menkaura pyramids) and capstones (as on the Middle Kingdom pyramids of kings Amenemhat II and Khendjer at Dahshur and Saqqara, respectively). From the Second Dynasty onwards, Variety 1 was extensively used in temples for door frames, columns and wall linings (for example, door frames in the Second-Dynasty temple of King Khasekhemwy at Hierakonpolis, and interior wall lining and exterior facing in Khafra's valley temple at Giza).

Sculptures

Variety 1 was especially popular from the Early Dynastic period to the Roman period for private, royal and other statuary (from statuettes to colossi), sarcophagi, stelae, naoi, obelisks (New Kingdom only), and small vessels (until the end of the Old Kingdom); it was used for the same building and sculptural applications as the granodiorite from Aswan (see below), with no obvious preferences shown except in the case of the Eighteenth-Dynasty granodiorite statues of the lioness-goddess Sekhmet from the temple of Mut at Karnak, and the New Kingdom and Ptolemaic Apis-bull sarcophagi of granodiorite in the Serapeum at Saqqara. Far more granite was employed overall, however, and this is probably simply a consequence of its much greater abundance at Aswan. The Variety 2 granite was rarely used, undoubtedly because large, fracture-free blocks were difficult to obtain from the veins in which it occurred.

Examples (Variety 1: coarse pink granite)

1. Standing statue of an unknown king from Saqqara, late Fifth or early Sixth Dynasty, *c.* 2400–300 BC (height 74 cm; Cairo JE39103).
2. Colossal standing statue of the Twlefth-Dynasty ruler Senusret I, from Karnak, Thebes, *c.* 1971–26 BC (height 3.1 m; Cairo JE38287).
3. Standing statue of an unknown Eighteenth-Dynasty king, usurped by Rameses II and Merenptah, *c.* 1550–1307 BC (height 2.63 m; BM EA61).
4. Seated statue of King Sobkemsaf I, Seventeenth Dynasty, *c.* 1630 BC (height 1.64 m; BM EA871).
5. Two recumbent lions from Gebel Barkal, Sudan (the so-called 'Prudhoe lions'), but originally from Soleb, Eighteenth Dynasty, *c.* 1391–23 BC (height 1.1–1.2 m; BM EA1 & EA2).
6. Colossal head, possibly of King Amenhotep III, from Karnak, Thebes; Eighteenth Dynasty (height 2.9 m; BM E15).

Examples (variety 2: fine granite)

Very few objects made from Variety 2 are known, but some notable examples are:

1. Head and torso of a colossal statue of Rameses II from the Ramesseum at Thebes, Nineteenth Dynasty, *c.* 1290–24 BC (height 2.67 m; BM EA19) [the head is cut from fine pink granite and the torso from Aswan granodiorite, with a vein of the former cutting through the latter; many of the other examples of the use of this granite are similar in that the objects consist of both the granite and granodiorite].
2. Head and crown of the colossal seated statue of Rameses II at the entrance to the first pylon at Luxor temple. Part of the head and the rest of the body are Aswan granodiorite.
3. Relief in fine pink granite of Ptolemy II from a temple at the Delta-site of Sebennytos, near modern Samannud, *c.* 285–46 BC (height 1.32 m; Cincinnati Art Museum 1952.8).
4. Unprovenanced Greco-Roman funerary shrine (height 1.3 m; Alexandria 25774).
5. Greco-Roman stelae from Akhmim (height 74 cm; Cairo CG22034).

Bibliography

De Morgan *et al.* (1894); Ball (1907); Weigall (1910: 407–10); el-Shazly (1954); Attia (1955); Gindy (1956); Lucas (1962: 57–9, 412–3); Röder (1965); Ragab *et al.* (1978); Meneisy *et al.* (1979); Soliman (1980); De Putter and Karlshausen (1992: 81–6); Klemm and Klemm (1993: 305–53); Aston (1994: 15–18); Brown and Harrell (1998).

For colour photographs of polished slabs see: **Variety 1, coarse granite** Mielsch (1985: pl. 22–749); Lazzarini (1987: figs 1, 2); Gnoli (1988: fig. 111); Marchei *et al.* (1989: figs. 74a–b); De Putter and Karlshausen (1992: pl. 54c–10,11); Dodge and Ward-Perkins (1992: pl. 1d) and Klemm and Klemm (1993: pls. 10.1–10.6); **Variety 2, fine granite** Mielsch (1985: pl. 22–756, 769); Gnoli (1988: figs. 113–14); De Putter and Karlshausen (1992: pl. 54c–12) and Klemm and Klemm (1993: pl. 11.6).

2. Granodiorite from Aswan

Description

This so-called 'monumental black or grey granite' is coarse- to mainly medium-grained granodiorite to occasionally

Figure 2.14 Limestone quarry in Wadi Zebeida near Amarna.

Figure 2.17 Limestone quarry at Beni Hasan.

Figure 2.15 Pillars inside an underground limestone quarry at Qau el-Kebir.

Figure 2.18 Limestone quarry at el-Sawayta.

Figure 2.16 Limestone quarries (open-cut on the left and gallery on the right) at Qau el-Kebir

2. *Serai Formation of the Thebes Group* (early Lower Eocene)
Highly dolomitic, fine-grained, sometimes silty/sandy and clayey, abundantly to mostly sparsely fossiliferous mudstones, wackestones and packstones with mainly globigerinids and nummulitids [fossiliferous microsparites, and sparse to packed biomicrosparites].

3. *Drunka Formation of the Thebes Group* (late Lower Eocene)
Slightly dolomitic, fine-grained mudstones, wackestones, packstones and grainstones with mainly echinoids and non-skeletal carbonate grains, and lesser amounts of pelecypods [fossiliferous microsparites, and sparse to packed bio/oo/pel/intra microsparites and sparites].

4. *Minia Formation* (late Lower Eocene to early Middle Eocene)
Slightly dolomitic to dolomite-free, fine- to coarse-grained packstones and grainstones with mainly echinoids and nummulitids, lesser amounts of pelecypods, and exceptionally with other foraminifera (alveolinids and operculinids) dominating [packed biomicrosparites and biomicrosparudites, and biosparites and biosparudites].

5. *Samalut Formation* (early Middle Eocene)
Slightly dolomitic to dolomite-free, coarse- to mainly very coarse-grained packstones and grainstones with mainly nummulitids, and lesser amounts of echinoids [packed biomicrosparudites and biosparudites].

6. *Mokattam Formation* (late Middle Eocene)
Slightly to moderately dolomitic, fine-grained, silty/sandy, occasionally clayey mudstones, wackestones and packstones with mainly globigerinids, and lesser amounts of nummulitids and echinoids [fossiliferous microsparites, and sparse to packed biomicrosparites].

7. *Alexandria Formation* (Pleistocene)
Dolomite-free, fine-grained, occasionally silty/sandy, friable, highly porous packstones to mainly grainstones (calcarenites) with mostly non-skeletal carbonate grains (especially ooliths and coated grains) [packed oomicrosparites and oosparites].

Uses

Buildings

Limestone was perhaps the first rock used for building purposes in Egypt. The earliest examples are a possibly late Predynastic tomb at Qau el-Kebir, and some First-Dynasty tombs at Abydos and in the Memphite region. At these sites limestone was used for flooring, wall-lining and roofing in burial chambers. By the Second Dynasty it was widely employed for tombs and beginning in the Third Dynasty it was also used in the construction of pyramids and temples. Limestone continued as the principal building stone north of Thebes throughout antiquity. In the Theban region and southward it was replaced by sandstone beginning in the Eighteenth Dynasty. The southernmost limestone structures are the Third-Dynasty el-Kula pyramid near Hierakonpolis, and the Hathor temple at Gebelein dating from the Third Dynasty and later periods.

Sculptures

Although used primarily as a building stone, limestone was also widely employed for reliefs, statuary and a variety of other carved objects. This usage is more a reflection of its easy workability and availability than its aesthetic qualities. Many, if not most, limestone statues were originally painted to conceal the rock's bland appearance. The Mokattam limestone from the Tura and Maʿsara quarries, however, is of exceptional quality and was in demand throughout the Nile valley for sculptures, reliefs and pyramid casings. This rock's uniform pale grey colour and dense, fine-grained texture make it both attractive and durable. A distant second in quality are the limestones of the Serai Formation.

Limestone may have been the first rock used for statuary in Egypt, judging from the fact that various sculptures dating from either the late Predynastic period or the First Dynasty (including two colossal standing statues of the god Min) were found at Koptos, near modern Qift, and a torso deriving from a statue of similar date was found at Hierakonpolis. These sculptures are now in the Petrie Museum, University College London (the two 'Koptos lions') and the Ashmolean Museum, Oxford (the statues of Min: 1894.105c–e, a bird and a lion from Koptos: 1894.105a-b, and the torso from Hierakonpolis: 1896–1908/E.3925).

Examples

1. Stele of Rahotep from his tomb in Meidum, Fourth Dynasty, *c.* 2570 BC (height 79 cm; BM EA1242).
2. Seated figure of a scribe from Saqqara, Fifth Dynasty, *c.* 2465–2323 BC (height 51 cm; Cairo JE30272).
3. False door of Ptahshepses from his tomb at Saqqara, Fifth Dynasty, *c.* 2465–2323 BC (height 2.66 m; BM EA682).
4. Standing statue (painted) of Nenkheftka from his tomb at Deshasha, Fifth Dynasty, *c.* 2465–2323 BC (height 1.34 m; BM EA1239).
5. Colossal bust of Amenhotep III from his funerary temple in Thebes, Eighteenth Dynasty, *c.* 1391–53 BC (height 1.5 m; BM EA3).
6. Seated pair statue of a man and his wife, Eighteenth Dynasty (1.32 m high; BM EA36).

Bibliography

Lucas (1962: 52–5, 414); Meyers and Van Zelst (1977); Boukhary and Malik (1983); Mansour *et al.* (1983); Middleton and Bradley (1989); Hermina *et al.* (1989); Klitzsch (1988); Said (1990: 451–86); De Putter and Karlshausen (1992: 61–9); Harrell (1992); Klemm and Klemm (1993: 29–197); Aston (1994: 35–40).

For colour photographs of cut slabs see: Klemm and Klemm (1993: pls 1.1–5.6).

Limestone breccia

Definition

Limestone breccia is a sedimentary rock containing large, angular fragments of limestone. The term 'breccia' denotes a rock with angular fragments (in contrast to the rounded fragments in a conglomerate), but it is also essential to indicate the composition as well as the texture by prefixing the name with 'limestone'.

Egyptian sources
Limestone breccia occurs sporadically in the Nile valley and on the adjacent desert plateaux between Esna in the south and el-Minya in the north. Traces of ancient stone working have been found at Wadi Abu Gelbana, east of Akhmim (Klemm and Klemm 1993: 189), but no other ancient quarries are known.

Description
The limestone breccia used in ancient times consists of pebble-size (and, less commonly, cobble- to boulder-size) angular fragments of white or grey limestone and occasionally chert. The limestone fragments are commonly surrounded by dark red iron-rich rims, sometimes with a visibly layered structure, and they are set in a matrix of reddish brown to red, fine-grained calcite and iron oxides (haematite and goethite) with some non-carbonate impurities. Contrary to the claims of some geologists, this rock is not restricted to the top of the Issawia Formation of Pliocene age. It occurs in several Eocene limestone formations as a 'collapse breccia' formed from the collapse of the roof of a limestone cave, a feature of karst topography.

Uses
Limestone breccia was used for a wide variety of small objects in the Predynastic period, including animal figurines, maceheads, ornamental combs and gaming pieces (Petrie 1920: pls. 8:26, 26:27 and 60, 30:17, 46:32) as well as for stone vessels. It was among the earliest stones used for vessels, as it is first attested in the Naqada I period, and it occurs frequently in the First to Fourth Dynasties, although it was rarely used thereafter (only a few vessels of Middle Kingdom and New Kingdom date are known). There is one surviving statue of Late Period date (see below in list of examples).

Examples
1. Pear-shaped macehead dating to Naqada III, *c.* 3150–3000 BC (height 6.9 cm; BM EA32089).
2. Bowl of First Dynasty date from Abu Rawash, *c.* 3000–2770 (Cairo JE44332).
3. Small jar from tomb 2190 at Saqqara, dating to the Second Dynasty, *c.* 2770–2649 BC (New York, MMA 12.181.160).
4. Statue of Taweret dating to the Late Period, after 600 BC (BM EA35700; see Fig. 2.19).

Bibliography
Hermina *et al.* (1989: 213); De Putter and Karlshausen (1992: 57–8); Ahmed (1993); Klemm and Klemm (1993: 189–91); Aston (1994: 53–4).

For colour photographs see De Putter and Karlshausen (1992: pls. 8, 54a–3); Klemm and Klemm (1993: pl. 6.2); and Aston 1994: pl. 11b).

Figure 2.19 Limestone breccia statue of the hippopotamus-goddess Taweret, Late Period (BM EA35700).

Malachite

Definition
A vivid green hydrous copper carbonate ($Cu_3[CO_3]_2[OH]_2$) mineral, which occurs in the oxidation zone of copper ore deposits, often interbanded with blue azurite ($Cu_3[CO_3]_2[OH]_2$) and other copper-bearing materials such as green to greenish-blue chrysocolla ($CuSiO_3 \cdot 2H_2O$). It is a relatively soft gemstone, having a Mohs hardness of only 3.5–4, and effervesces in hydrochloric acid.

Egyptian sources
Malachite occurs both in the Eastern Desert and in the Sinai peninsula, with particular indications of ancient workings, alongside the procurement of copper and turquoise, at Wadi Maghara, Serabit el-Khadim, Bir Nasib and Timna, the three former in the Sinai and the latter in the Wadi Arabah, just inside the southern border of mod-

ern Israel, about thirty kilometres north of Eilat. Malachite comprised the majority of the copper ore at Serabit el-Khadim and Wadi Maghara, with azurite and chrysocolla occurring in much smaller quantities at both sites. The principal problem in interpreting the mines in the Sinai is the fact that many of the inscriptions do not make it clear whether turquoise, copper or malachite were primarily being sought by the Egyptians (or perhaps all three), and even when they clearly state the object of the expedition as the procurement of *mfk3t*, the interpretation of this term as turquoise or malachite is still a matter of some debate (see Levene 1998). When H.G. Bachmann describes the Bir Nasib mining and smelting region, he stresses the fact that a number of copper-related materials were being exploited simultaneously: 'Bir Nasib, the largest smelting site in Sinai, is also a place of copper ore and turquoise mining . . . The small adits visible in the sandstone cliffs surrounding the smelting area . . . show green lumps consisting of malachite, paratacamite and quartz' (Bachmann, unpublished comment, quoted in Rothenberg 1987: 7).

Description

In Egyptian artefacts, malachite has occasionally been misidentified as green feldspar (see MICROCLINE) and *vice versa*, although the latter is clearly distinguished by its much higher Mohs hardness (6) and absence of effervescence in hydrochloric acid.

Uses

From the Badarian period onwards, it was primarily mined either as copper ore or in order to be ground up into powder for use as a green eye-paint. Malachite has survived in Predynastic graves not only as a pigment stain on cosmetic palettes and grinding stones but also occasionally in the form of quantities of the raw material held in small linen or leather bags (as well as the kohl itself stored in shells, reeds, leaves or jars), usually preserved among funerary equipment. The green malachite-based form of eye-paint (*wḏw*) seems to have been used only until the middle of the Old Kingdom, when it was replaced by the black galena-based form of kohl (*msdmt*; see Chapter 6, this volume, for discussion of galena mining; and see also Hassan and Hassan 1981 for an early source of galena). These ground pigments appear to have been mixed with water to form a paste and were probably applied with the fingers until the introduction of the 'kohl pencil' in the Middle Kingdom. Malachite was almost certainly also used, from at least the Fourth Dynasty onwards, as one of the essential ingredients in the production of the synthetic pigment 'Egyptian blue' (see Chapter 4, this volume). It was very occasionally used as a green pigment in its own right, although green frit seems usually to have been preferred for this purpose.

There are a number of instances of malachite beads, amulets and inlays in both the Predynastic and Pharaonic periods. There appear to be only two examples of the carving of malachite into vessels, one complete flask of unknown provenance dating to the period between the Naqada III phase and the Early Dynastic (BM EA36356) and the other a fragment from the tomb of the First-Dynasty ruler Djer at Abydos (Oxford, Ashmolean 1896–1908 E.1592). There is some evidence for the trading of malachite with Crete, perhaps from the Middle Kingdom onwards (see Warren 1995: 5–10).

Examples

1. Several large, roughly worked beads from Girga, Predynastic period (Cairo JE 44488).
2. Diadem of gold, turquoise, garnet and malachite beads from the burial of a woman at Abydos, late Predynastic period, *c.* 3250 BC (overall length 31.2 cm; BM EA37532).
3. Small vessel dating between the Naqada III and Early Dynastic periods, *c.* 3150–2649 BC (height: 5.3 cm; BM EA36356).

Bibliography

Lucas (1962: 80–84, 204–5, 400–1); Ogden (1982: 101–2); Hassan and Hassan (1981: 77–82); Rothenberg (1987); Aston (1994: 71–2); Warren (1995: 5–10).

For colour photograph of a malachite vessel (BM 36356) see Aston (1994: pl. 16c).

Marble

Definition

'Marble' is a metamorphic rock consisting predominately of calcite or dolomite with subordinate amounts of any of a wide variety of other minerals. Depending on the mineralogy, the coloration can vary from pure white to any other colour or combination of colours. Textures are usually uniform and contorted internal laminations are common.

Egyptian sources

Large, workable marble deposits are known from only three localities in Egypt, all in the Eastern Desert: in Wadi Dib northwest of Hurghada, at Gebel Rokham near Wadi Mia, and in Wadi Haimur near Wadi Allaqi. In addition to these, small veins of marble occur in association with serpentinite at numerous sites in the Eastern Desert. Gebel Rokham provided the best quality marble and was closest to the Nile valley. Consequently, it alone appears to have been worked in ancient times (see map, Fig. 2.1). The ancient workings at Gebel Rokham have been destroyed by modern quarrying, but the original tailings still exist and have yielded potsherds of the New Kingdom and Roman period (Brown and Harrell 1995).

Description

The rock from Gebel Rokham is fine-grained marble consisting mainly of calcite with subordinate amounts of brucite and dolomite plus rare quartz. Most specimens exhibit distinctive thin, cross-cutting veins of two types: whiter, finer-grained, brucite-free calcite; and dark grey, graphite-bearing calcite. The carbon and oxygen isotopic ratios for the rock are +3.45 (d[13]C) and −11.91 (d[18]O), respectively (see Brown and Harrell 1995). In terms of its isotopic character and brucite content, this marble appears to be compositionally unique among the known white marbles quarried in ancient times in the Mediterranean region.

Uses

The only demonstrated uses of the Gebel Rokham marble are Eighteenth-Dynasty sculptures, including several statues of Thutmose III and a few other objects from the reigns of Akhenaten and Tutankhamun. White marble was used extensively for statuary during the Ptolemaic and Roman periods, and upon examination some of it may be found to come from Gebel Rokham. Most of this stone, however, was probably imported from sources in the eastern Mediterranean. A white marble was occasionally used for small vessels in the Early Dynastic period but its source is unknown.

Examples

1. Kneeling statuette of Thutmose III from Deir el-Medina in Thebes, Eighteenth Dynasty, *c.* 1479–25 BC (26.5 cm high; Cairo Museum, JE 43507A).
2. Bust of Thutmose III from Deir el-Bahari in Thebes, Eighteenth Dynasty, *c.* 1479–25 BC (face [height 18 cm]: Cairo JE90237, rest of statue [height 42.6 cm]: New York, MMA 07.230.3).
3. Marble vessel from the valley temple of Menkaura at Giza, Fourth Dynasty(?) (height 6.2 cm; Boston, MFA 11.1593; Aston 1994: 56).

Bibliography

Alford (1901: 14–15); Lucas (1962: 414–15); Ramez and Marie (1973); Lilyquist (1989); De Putter and Karlshausen (1992: 108–10); Klemm and Klemm (1993: 427–9); Aston (1994: 55–6); Brown and Harrell (1995).

For colour photograph of a polished slab see: Klemm and Klemm (1993: pl. 6.1).

Mica

Definition

The term mica is used to describe a group of potassium aluminosilicate minerals, usually with an admixture of iron and magnesium. The principal types of mica are dark brown or black biotite ($K[Mg,Fe]_3[OH,F]_2AlSi_3O_{10}$), colourless to pale yellow muscovite ($KAl_2[OH,F]_2AlSi_3O_{10}]$), coppery yellow to brown phlogopite ($KMg_3[OH, F]_2AlSi_3O_{10}]$) and pink to pale purple lepidolite ($KLi_2Al[F,OH]_2Si_4O_{10}$). They are all glistening in appearance and have excellent cleavage, usually splitting into very thin translucent sheets. Their Mohs hardness varies between 2 and 3. While biotite and muscovite are rock-forming minerals occurring in a wide variety of igneous and metamorphic rocks, phlogopite occurs mainly in metamorphic rocks, and lepidolite occurs only in igneous pegmatites. It is possible that the only form of mica used in ancient Egypt was muscovite.

Egyptian sources

Deposits of muscovite are recorded at Rod Um el-Farag in the Eastern Desert, although there is no evidence to indicate whether these were exploited in ancient times. Numerous outcrops of mica schist (a rock composed primarily of flaky grains of mica) have been identified in Eastern Desert, particularly in the Gebel Sikait region (see Hume 1934: 109–13 and Aston 1994: 61–2). A deep adit close to the Roman amethyst mines at Wadi el-Hudi, about thirty-five kilometres southeast of Aswan, was identified by Fakhry (1952: 14) as a 'mica mine', but there has not yet been any modern confirmation as to whether this is an ancient working, or even as to whether it is indeed a mica mine (see Shaw and Jameson 1993: 86).

Uses

From the Predynastic period onwards mica was used to a small extent for beads, pendants and mirrors. Most surviving examples of worked mica, however, derive from Upper Nubia during the Classic Kerma period, *c.* 1750–1500 BC, in the form of decorative plaques sewn onto leather caps. Lucas (1962: 263) notes that the collection of the Metropolitan Museum, New York, includes Middle Kingdom mica pendants and a New Kingdom necklace incorporating mica.

As far as mica schist is concerned, Aston (1994: 61) notes three instances of vessels made from this material (BM 58139, Cambridge, Fitzwilliam 94.1954 and New York, MMA 13.2816), all dating to the Predynastic or Early Dynastic periods.

Examples

1. Triangular vessel of mica schist, probably dating to the Predynastic or Early Dynastic periods (length 9 cm; BM EA58139).
2. Mica cap ornament carved in the form of four lion's heads, from Grave 1044, Tumulus KX at Kerma, *c.* 1750–1550 BC (height 5.6 cm; Leipzig, Karl-Marx Universität, Ägyptisches Museum 3792).
3. Mica cap ornaments (displayed on a restored cap) from Kerma, *c.* 1750–1550 BC (height of cap 13.3 cm; Boston MFA 20.1768).

Bibliography

Reisner (1923: 272–80); Fakhry (1952: 14); Hayes (1953: 20; 1959: 193); Lucas (1962: 262–3); Wenig (1978: 150–2); Shaw and Jameson (1993: 86).

For colour photograph of a mica schist vessel (BM 58139), see Aston (1994: pl. 13b).

Microcline (amazonite)

Definition

Feldspar is a mineral group which makes up 60 per cent of the earth's crust. The group consists of calcium, sodium or potassium aluminosilicates, but there are two main types: (1) sodium-potassium alkali (or potash) feldspars, mainly consisting of microcline and orthoclase ($KAlSi_3O_8$), and (2) sodium-calcium plagioclase feldspars. Besides the common pink to light gray alkali feldspars found in granite and other igneous rocks, there are two gemstone varieties: moonstone (an opalescent form of orthoclase which is transparent to translucent and yellowish-brown to bluish-white) and amazonite (or amazonstone, a form of microcline which is opaque and green to bluish green).

Egyptian sources

Amazonite is found mainly in the Eastern Desert in the area of Wadi Higelig and Gebel Migif, about forty kilometres to the west of Gebel Zubara (see Ball 1912: 272). It is also found in the Libyan Mountains north of Tibesti (Dalloni and Monod 1948: 133, 153–4), although there is no proof that the latter source was actually exploited by the ancient Egyptians. Hussein and El-Sharkawi (1990: 563–4) report that it occurs in pegmatite veins intruded into the gneisses of Gebel Migif and Wadi Gimal, and that it also occurs as a constituent of the metasomatically altered gneisses of Abu Rushaid.

Description

Amazonite was one of the Egyptians' six most precious stones, and inscriptions during the Pharaonic period often associate it with turquoise and lapis lazuli. The colour of amazonite derives from the presence of traces of lead and crystalline water. It has frequently been confused with other green stones such as turquoise or beryl.

Uses

It was carved into small beads from the Predynastic period onwards, with a particular peak of popularity in the jewellery of the Middle Kingdom. It was also used for amulets, inlay and small vessels in the New Kingdom.

Examples

1. Early First-Dynasty green amazonite vase, originally gilded on the neck, from Abydos, *c.* 2900 BC (height 7.3 cm; BM EA4711).
2. Small amazonite kohl-pot from the tomb of the 'three wives of Thutmose III' in Wadi Gabbanet el-Qirud, western Thebes, Eighteenth Dynasty, *c.* 1479–25 BC (New York MMA; see Winlock 1948: 51).
3. Unprovenanced amazonite amulet carved in the form of a seated anthropomorphic figure of Amun, dating to the Napatan period, *c.* 785–270 BC (height 8.4 cm; Munich, Staatliche Sammlung Ägyptischer Kunst ÄS6293).

Bibliography

Ball (1912: 272); Dalloni and Monod (1948: 133, 153–4); Lucas (1962: 393–4).

Obsidian

Definition

The term obsidian is used to describe a volcanic glass formed from magma which has cooled too rapidly for minerals to crystallise. It is usually felsic in composition and is commonly black in colour, although it may be brown, red or colour-banded. It has a characteristic conchoidal fracture and a glassy lustre, and while opaque in the mass, it is translucent at the edges. Its Mohs hardness is 5–5.5.

Sources

Lucas (1942, 1947) published the first substantial comparisons between the physical properties of obsidian objects from Egypt and samples from possible source locations. He concluded that the density and refractive index of most Egyptian objects corresponded with sources in Abyssinia (modern Ethiopia and Eritrea), but did not correlate with any of the Mediterranean, Armenian or Arabian sources tested. Since the 1960s, modern analytical methods such as optical emission spectroscopy, neutron activation analysis, x-ray fluorescence and electron microprobe analysis have been employed to characterise obsidian based on its major, minor and trace element content. Distribution patterns for obsidian from the Mediterranean and Near Eastern sources have been outlined (Zarins 1989: 341), but the range of these objects does not appear to extend south of southern Israel or into the Sinai. Obsidian sources in the Arabian peninsula and Eritrea are not so well documented, but Tykot (1996) reports that three New Kingdom objects match the composition of a sample from Arafali on the Buri peninsula in Eritrea. Obsidian from sector TKY–5 in the Dhamar-Reda area in Yemen also has a high barium content, characteristic of the Egyptian samples, but other trace elements present in the Egyptian pieces correspond with the Arafali rather than the Yemeni obsidian.

In an ongoing provenancing study of Egyptian obsidian, Bavay *et al.* (2000) have used laser-ablation inductively coupled plasma mass spectrometry to analyse a vessel fragment from the Early Dynastic royal cemetery at Abydos (Brussels, Musées Royaux d'Art et d'Histoire E4833a), as well as a number of artefacts from Ethiopia and Syria. The results indicate that the northern part of the East African Rift Valley in Ethiopia was the most probable source for the Abydos vessel, given that two trace element ratios (Th/Ta and Th/U) were found to be very similar in the Egyptian and Ethiopian samples, and quite different from those found in the Syrian artefacts. The same team is currently analysing further Predynastic and Early Dynastic objects, as part of a more general study of trade patterns in the Early Bronze Age (see Bavay 1997).

Thus recent analyses tend to corroborate Lucas' contention that most of the obsidian found in Egypt originated in Ethiopia. It is possible, however, that different results might be obtained if samples from Lower Egypt were analysed, since an Upper Egyptian site such as Abydos might have been more likely to obtain obsidian from an African source, whereas a Delta site might have been more accessible to Asiatic sources (Laurent Bavay pers. comm.). Furthermore, obsidian sources throughout the Red Sea region still need further investigation.

Description

Nearly all of the imported obsidian found in Egypt is of a pure jet-black variety. Lucas records one finger amulet of Twenty-sixth-Dynasty date, the dull grey appearance and physical properties of which correspond to obsidian from Melos, and indeed, the presence of some obsidian from Aegean sources would not be remarkable in Egypt during the Late Period.

Uses

Obsidian was imported into Egypt beginning in Naqada I, and occurs in the Predynastic period as flakes and blades (including sickle blades), beads, pendants and as one material of fish-tail knives (Zarins 1989: 361–5). Obsidian vessels of First-Dynasty date have been found in the large *mastaba*-tomb excavated by de Morgan (1897) at Naqada, and in several of the royal tombs at Abydos. A fragmentary obsidian dish in the shape of a hand was discovered in the tomb of Den, recently re-excavated by the German Archaeological Institute, Cairo.

There is a notable lack of evidence for obsidian from the Second to Fourth Dynasties, but it reappears as a material for the pupils of inlaid eyes beginning in the Fifth Dynasty (Saleh and Sourouzian 1987: no. 47). Further examples of obsidian used for the inlaid eyes of statues survive from the Sixth Dynasty, while obsidian eye inlays of Middle Kingdom and New Kingdom date commonly derive from coffins and masks, and this usage continued into the Roman period (Wainwright 1927: 88, 91).

Model vessels in 'opening of the mouth' sets were occasionally made of obsidian during the Sixth Dynasty, and a small number of cosmetic vessels of obsidian survive from the Middle Kingdom, Second Intermediate Period and New Kingdom (Aston 1994: 25, 140). Amulets and scarabs were also made of obsidian, beginning in the Middle Kingdom, and three obsidian sculptures of Middle Kingdom date and four of the New Kingdom are known (Wainwright 1927: 88, 91; Lacovara *et al.* 1996: 174).

Examples

1. Pupils of inlaid eyes in copper statues of Pepi I and his son(?), Sixth Dynasty, *c.* 2289–46 BC (overall height of Pepy I statue 1.77 m; Cairo JE33034; Quibell and Green 1902: pls. 50–4).
2. Obsidian and gold mirror handle of Sithathoriunet from her tomb at Lahun, inlaid with cornelian, faience and electrum, dating to the reigns of Senusret II–Amenemhat III, *c.* 1897–1797 BC (height of whole mirror 28 cm; Cairo CG52663; JE44920; Brunton 1920).
3. Five cosmetic vessels of Merit from her tomb at Dahshur, dating to the reigns of Senusret III–Amenemhat III, *c.* 1878–1797 BC (heights ranging from 45 to 70 cm; Cairo CG18772–6; de Morgan 1895: pls. 25.60–62).
4. Face, ear and fragments of foot and neck(?) of a life-size (presumably composite) statue of Amenhotep III from the Karnak cachette, *c.* 1391–53 BC (face, foot and neck: Cairo CG42101; ear: Boston MFA 04.1941; see Tykot 1996).

Bibliography

Wainwright (1927); Lucas (1942, 1947, 1962: 415–16); Zarins (1989); De Putter and Karlshausen (1992: 111–13); Aston (1994: 23–6); Lacovara *et al.* (1996); Tykot (1996); Bavay *et al.* (2000).

For colour photographs see Saleh and Sourouzian (1987: nos. 5:1, 113) and De Putter and Karlshausen (1992: pl. 40).

Olivine (peridot)

Definition

A silicate mineral, also known as chrysolite, which occurs in two compositional subvarieties: iron-rich fayalite ($FeSiO_4$) and magnesium-rich fosterite (Mg_2SiO_4). It has a Mohs hardness of 6.5–7. The transparent gem variety of olivine is known as peridot (perhaps from the Arabic *faridat*: 'gem'). Peridot (which may be either fayalite or fosterite, but not a combination of both) is coloured yellow-green, olive-green or greenish brown although its typical appearance is a warm yellowish green (caused by a relative dearth of iron). It almost always forms in mafic and ultramafic igneous rocks such as serpentinite.

Egyptian sources

Olivine occurs commonly as minute grains in basalt and as such is found at various locations in the Eastern and Western deserts. However, the only known Egyptian source for the larger crystals of peridot is the island of Zabargad (St John's Island) situated in the Red Sea, about eighty kilometres southeast of the Ptolemaic and Roman port of Berenike (Couyat 1908; Keller 1990: 119–27). The island consists mostly of mafic and ultramafic rocks, and it is in the latter that the peridot occurs. This island appears also to have been the principal source of peridot for the whole ancient Mediterranean region. In the Roman period, Scipio and Strabo knew peridot as 'topaz' (a term now used by geologists to refer to a different mineral).

Uses

From the Predynastic period onwards, olivine was used for jewellery (beads, pendants and amulets), but peridot does not appear to have been used until the Ptolemaic period, when it became a popular material for intaglios and cabochons. An Eighteenth-Dynasty scarab identified by Petrie (1917: 8) as peridot has not yet been subjected to modern analysis. Peridot has often been misidentified as green beryl (emerald).

Examples

1. Late Predynastic (Naqada II) necklace of olivine beads from Mostagedda (BM EA63100).
2. Late Predynastic (Naqada II) olivine pendant, forming part of an anklet from Matmar (BM EA63695).

Bibliography

Couyat (1908); Wainwright (1946); Lucas (1962: 390, 402); Ogden (1982: 102–4); Keller (1990: 119–27).

For colour photograph of fine cut peridot (as well as crystals and rough mass) from St John's Island, see Woodward and Harding (1987: 30).

Onyx *see* chalcedony

Peridot *see* olivine

Porphyry, volcanic: andesite, dacite, trachyandesite and others

Definition

'Porphyry' is a textural term applied to volcanic igneous rocks which consist of phaneritic crystals (phenocrysts) floating in an aphanitic groundmass. Volcanic porphyries occur in a wide variety of rock types. Those used in ancient Egypt are mainly dacite, trachyandesite and especially andesite. When the phenocrysts constitute over 20 volume per cent, the rock is described as a 'porphyry', and if the phenocrysts make up only 10–20 per cent, it is described as being 'porphyritic'. The name of the rock type must be used in conjunction with 'porphyry' or 'porphyritic' to indicate the composition of the rock.

Egyptian sources

Volcanic porphyries are widely distributed in the mountains of the Eastern Desert and are especially abundant in the region northwest of Hurghada. Only two ancient quarries are known and both date from the Roman period: Gebel Dokhan (Mons Porphyrites, see Fig. 2.20), and Wadi Umm Towat (see maps in Figs. 2.1a–b). The sources of other porphyries used for vessels in the Predynastic and Early Dynastic periods (see Fig. 2.21) are unknown.

1. Andesite-dacite porphyry from Gebel Dokhan (Mons Porphyrites)

Description

On the eastern flank of Gebel Dokhan, high on the hillslopes on the west and east sides of Wadi Abu Maamel, are six quarrying areas collectively called Mons Porphyrites by the Romans. From north to south, those on the west side are the northwest, west (or Lycabettus) and southwest (or Rammius) quarries (see Fig. 2.20); and those on the east side are the northeast, east and southeast (or Lepsius) quarries. These were all worked from the middle of the first to the late fourth century AD. The porphyry varies in composition from trachyandesite and trachydacite to mainly andesite and dacite. Three varieties were extracted and these are distinguished by their colour.

Figure 2.20 Gebel Dokhan (Mons Porphyrites), Eastern Desert, with the southwest (left arrow) and west (right arrow) quarries from which the purplish-red 'imperial' andesite-dacite porphyry was extracted. Note the Roman causeway descending on the right from the west quarry.

Variety 1: purplish-red porphyry

This rock has a purplish-red aphanitic groundmass of oligoclase-andesine and hornblende with minor biotite and accessory minerals (mainly magnetite). The phenocrysts are medium-grained oligoclase-andesine (up to 3 mm across) with colours of either pale pink to mainly white (northwest quarry) or all pink (west, southwest and southeast quarries). The groundmass is coloured by haematite

Figure 2.21 Andesite porphyry vessel, late Predynastic or Early Dynastic period (BM EA35304).

(red) and piemontite (pinkish-purple), and the latter mineral is also responsible for the pink colour of the phenocrysts. In part of the west quarry, a brecciated porphyry was extracted. Variety 1 is the so-called 'imperial porphyry' of ancient Rome and most of the rock quarried at Mons Porphyrites is of this variety. The Romans called it *lapis porphyrites* (purple stone) and it is from this term that the modern words 'porphyry' and 'porphyritic' derive.

Variety 2: greenish-black porphyry

This rock, which comes only from the east quarry and one of the excavations in the northwest quarry, has a greenish-black aphanitic groundmass, and pale green and white medium-grained phenocrysts (up to 5 mm across). It has the same mineralogy as Variety 1 except that it lacks haematite and piemontite but contains abundant chlorite and epidote. It is these latter two minerals that give the rock its green coloration.

Variety 3: black porphyry

This variety comes only from the northeast quarry and one of the excavations in the northwest quarry. It has a black aphanitic groundmass, pale green to mainly white medium-grained phenocrysts (up to 5 mm across), and the same mineralogy as Variety 2 except that chlorite and epidote are rare. The Romans apparently called it *lapis porphyrites nero.*

Uses

Buildings

All three varieties were quarried for export from Egypt by the Romans, who used them for pavement and wall tiles as well as, in the case of the imperial porphyry, small whole columns and drums for larger columns.

Sculptures

The Romans made extensive use of the imperial porphyry for sarcophagi, basins and statues, and this same variety was also occasionally used for small vessels during the Early Dynastic period, although no Early Dynastic workings have yet been identified in the Gebel Dokhan area. They may have been destroyed by Roman quarrying, or perhaps the rock was not quarried and the abundant boulders of imperial porphyry found in the nearby *wadis* were used instead. Alternatively, the material for the stone vessels may have been obtained from other localities in the northern part of the Eastern Desert where the same rock type can be found as, for example, in Wadi Umm Esh in the Esh-Mellaha range near Hurghada.

Examples (all Variety 1)

1. Fragmentary bowl with vertical fluting, from tomb Q80 at Ballas, Early Dynastic period (height 16.1 cm, diameter 23.7 cm; Petrie Museum UC5989).
2. Half of a vessel lid from the Step Pyramid at Saqqara, Early Dynastic period (Cairo JE69493).
3. Torso of a draped female figure from Italy, second century AD (BM GR1947.12–29.2).
4. Column fragment from Egypt, Roman period (length *c.* 3 m; BM GR1802.7–10.3).
5. Bust of a Roman emperor (possibly Maximinus) from Benha, *c.* AD 300 AD (height 23 cm; Cairo JE10176).
6. Headless colossal seated statue, possibly of Pantocrate, from Alexandria, Roman period (height 2.82 m; Alexandria 5934).

Bibliography

Hume (1934: 276–84); Andrew (1938); Meredith and Tregenza (1950); Lucas (1962: 417–18); Kraus *et al.* (1967: 157–99); Gnoli (1988: 122–3, 133–5, 138); Klein (1988: 55–88); Marchei *et al.* (1989: 272, 274, 278); De Putter and Karlshausen (1992: 119–21); Klemm and Klemm (1993: 387–95); Harrell (1995); Aston (1994: 21–3); Peacock and Maxfield (1994, 1995, 1996); Brown and Harrell (1995).

For colour photographs of polished slabs see: Variety 1 – Mielsch (1985: pl. 21–698, 702); Gnoli (1988: figs. 90–1); Marchei *et al.* (1989: fig. 116a); De Putter and Karlshausen (1992: pl. 54f–23); Dodge and Ward-Perkins (1992: a in pl. 1) and Klemm and Klemm (1993: pls. 14.1–15.1); Variety 2 – Mielsch (1985: no. 714 in pl. 21), Gnoli (1988: fig. 93); Marchei *et al.* (1989: fig. 120a); Klemm and Klemm (1993: pl. 15.3); and Variety 3 – Mielsch (1985: pl. 21–719); Gnoli (1988: fig. 92) and Marchei *et al.* (1989: fig. 114a).

2. Trachyandesite porphyry from Wadi Umm Towat

Description

In Wadi Umm Towat, on the southwestern flank of Gebel Dokhan, is a small Roman quarry of indeterminate age but probably dating from the first two centuries AD. The rock is a trachyandesite porphyry with moderate grey, medium- to coarse-grained andesine phenocrysts (most less than 1 cm across) and white quartz amygdules (up to 1.5 cm across). The black, aphanitic groundmass consists of andesine plus minor pyroxene and rare magnetite.

Uses

This rock was quarried for export from Egypt by the Romans but was little used. The few known examples include small columns and pavement tiles. No sculptures are known.

Bibliography

Scaife (1935); Gnoli (1988: 139); Marchei *et al.* (1989: 276); Brown and Harrell (1995).

For colour photographs of polished slabs see: Gnoli (1988: fig. 94); Marchei *et al.* (1989: fig. 118a).

3. Andesite porphyries from other sources

Description

A further four varieties of andesite porphyry with generally white phenocrysts and black groundmass appear among the stones used by the ancient Egyptians. The first variety is characterised by very large (up to 3 cm long) rectangular white feldspar phenocrysts, fairly sparsely scattered within the black matrix (Aston 1994: pl. 3a Type A; De Putter and Karlshausen 1992: pl. 46), while the second variety contains more numerous but much smaller (about 1 cm long) phenocrysts (Aston 1994: pl. 3b Type B). The third variety has elongated feldspar phenocrysts (about 1–2 cm long) commonly forming clumps of crystals. Some examples also contain numerous round green amygdules (Aston 1994: pl. 4a Type C; De Putter and Karlshausen 1992: pl. 54g–25). The fourth variety is densely packed with phenocrysts (most 0.5–2 cm long) having a greenish tint (De Putter and Karlshausen 1992: pls. 47, 54g–26). No quarries for the first three varieties have been located, but the rock almost certainly comes from the Eastern Desert, where similar porphyries are common. For example, Aston's Type C andesite porphyry exists on Gebel el-Hammaliya in the Esh-Mellaha range near Hurghada. There is no evidence of quarrying here, but boulders of porphyry are abundant in the ravines draining into Wadi Umm Dirra el-Qibli and these may perhaps have been used for the small number of objects which are known. The quarry for the fourth variety of porphyry has been discovered at Rod el-Gamra, near Gebel Urf Hamam, in the southern Eastern Desert (Harrell and Brown, 1999).

Uses

Aston's Type A porphyry is restricted to the period from Naqada III to the Second Dynasty, and was used for vessels, maceheads, animal figurines and weights. Vessels made from her Type B variety date from the middle of the Predynastic through the Early Dynastic period and possibly into the Old Kingdom. Aston's Type C porphyry is only known from the Predynastic period and the First Dynasty, when it was used for vessels and animal figures, while her Type D variety was used in the Late Period (e.g. two Thirtieth-Dynasty statues in the Louvre, see De Putter and Karlshausen 1992: 124, pl. 47).

Examples

1. Jar from tomb 1257 at Naqada, dating to the Naqada II period, *c.* 3300–3100 BC (height 13 cm; Ashmolean 1895.166), Type B porphyry.
2. Frog statuette dating from the late Predynastic period to the early First Dynasty, *c.* 3100–2900 BC (height 12.3 cm; BM EA66837), Type C porphyry.
3. Large shouldered jar dating to the Early Dynastic period, *c.* 3000–2649 BC (height 29.9 cm; BM EA35698), Type A porphyry.
4. Rectangular dish from the Step Pyramid galleries, Saqqara, dating to the Early Dynastic period, *c.* 3000–2649 BC (Cairo JE88382), Type A porphyry.
5. Dish from the Step Pyramid galleries, Saqqara, dating to the Early Dynastic period, *c.* 3000–2649 BC (Cairo JE88385), Type C porphyry.
6. Head of a man with shaved head, dating to the Thirtieth Dynasty, *c.* 380–43 BC (height 13.5 cm; Louvre E10973), Type D porphyry.

Bibliography

De Putter and Karlshausen (1992: 122–4); Aston (1994: 21–3).

Prase *see* quartz, 4

Quartz (amethyst, milky quartz, prase, rock crystal, citrine, rose quartz, smoky quartz)

Definition

Quartz (silicon dioxide, SiO_2) is one of the commonest minerals in the Earth's crust. It has a Mohs hardness of 7, making it one of the hardest materials worked by the ancient Egyptians. Pure quartz is either white, due to abundant minute water-filled vacuoles (i.e. milky quartz) or, when vacuole free, colourless (i.e. rock crystal and macrocrystalline aggregates lacking crystal form). Chemical impurities have produced a wide range of quartz gemstones, each with distinctive colours, patterns or optical effects, including amethyst, citrine, rose quartz and smoky quartz. The colours of these gems can sometimes fade over time.

'Massive' (i.e. high purity) deposits of quartz occur in the form of two different types of depost: (1) vein quartz, which is formed by the intrusion of a silica magma into a fracture (only in igneous and metamorphic rocks), and (2) cavity-filling quartz, which is formed by the precipitation of quartz inside an open cavity from silica-rich, usually hydrothermally charged, ground water (in any kind of rock). Rock crystal is the colourless form of cavity-filling quartz. Vein quartz is therefore the term used to describe any kind of quartz that occurs in an intrusive igneous vein; it can be colourless, milky white or pink in colour. When it occurs alone as a white rock (i.e. milky quartz), it is commonly described by geologists as 'hydrothermal quartz', which is a reference to the abundant water-filled vacuoles that produce the milky colour. Aston (1994: 65) notes that Egyptian artefacts made from milky quartz have often been identified incompletely as 'crystal' (e.g. Ashmolean 1896–1908 E.1144, 1185, 1245–6, 1311, 1677) or wrongly as 'quartzite' (e.g. BM EA64357; New York, MMA 66.99.2; Cambridge, Fitzwilliam 274.1954).

Bibliography

Frondel (1962).

1. Amethyst

Definition

A translucent violet-coloured, macrocrystalline form of quartz in which the colour is produced by the presence of trace amounts of ferric oxide. 'Amethystine quartz' is a compact formation of amethyst, usually streaked and banded with milky quartz.

Egyptian sources
Amethysts were being used in Egyptian jewellery (and amethystine quartz for small vessels) from the late Predynastic period onwards. The mines in the Stele Ridge area of the Gebel el-Asr gneiss quarries are a possible early source, although all of the known pottery from the quartz-mining part of the site dates to the Middle Kingdom or Roman period (see Engelbach 1933: 69 and Little 1933: 77 for discussion of amethystine quartz at Gebel el-Asr). Another early source, dating to at least the First Dynasty, is suggested by the results of a survey in the Wadi Abu Had, in the northern part of the Eastern Desert (Bomann 1995).

The Wadi el-Hudi region, covering an area of *c.* 300 square kilometres in the Eastern Desert, about thirty-five kilometres southeast of Aswan, was the primary location for amethyst mining in Egypt from the Eleventh Dynasty until the end of the Middle Kingdom, during which time the use of amethysts in jewellery reached a peak of popularity (see Fakhry 1952; Sadek 1980–5; Shaw and Jameson 1993; Shaw in press (a)). It has been exploited for its minerals (including barytes, gold, amethyst and possibly also mica) since at least the early second millennium BC, and modern miners and quarriers are still extracting haematite and building stone from the immediate area. The amethyst occurs in cavities in the granite.

The mines at Wadi el-Hudi were rediscovered by the geologist Labib Nassim in 1923 (Nassim 1925), but the first proper archaeological examination of the site did not take place until 1939, when it was visited by G.W. Murray and Ibrahim Abdel ʿAl of the Egyptian Topographical Survey (see Rowe 1939). Sites 5, 6 and 9, in the western part of the region, constitute an area of intense Middle Kingdom mining activity. Site 5 consists of a hilltop miners' settlement and an adjacent amethyst mine. The L-shaped amethyst mine at site 5 – perhaps better described as an open-cut quarry – is located at the southern end of the hilltop settlement. The deposits of amethyst appear to have been completely worked out in the Pharaonic period. Incorporated into the walls of the adjacent settlement are numerous rock-carvings and inscriptions, five of which are securely dated to the first two years of the reign of Nebtawyra Mentuhotep IV, the last ruler of the Eleventh Dynasty. The pottery, present in large quantities throughout the settlement, also dates mainly to the early Middle Kingdom. Site 9 is a large rectangular stone-built fort, probably dating to the Twelfth Dynasty. To the northeast of the fort are two amethyst mines, while to the northwest there is a short, well-preserved section of ancient road. Roughly midway between sites 5 and 9 is a conical hill, the summit of which is decorated with many inscriptions and rock-carvings, mainly dating to the Middle Kingdom (site 6). There is some evidence for the continued exploitation of amethyst at Wadi el-Hudi after the Middle Kingdom: site 12, for instance, is almost certainly an amethyst mine of the Roman period (Shaw and Jameson 1993: 86; Shaw in press (b)). During the late Middle Kingdom the principal Egyptian amethyst mines may possibly have been located at the northern end of the Gebel el-Asr gneiss quarries (the so-called 'Chephren diorite quarries'), about sixty-five kilometres northwest of Abu Simbel (see Engelbach 1938: 370; Murray 1939a: 105; Lucas 1962: 389; Shaw and Bloxam 1999; Shaw in press (a)).

In the New Kingdom, amethyst was less commonly used for personal adornment, and it is even possible that there was a temporary dearth of known sources. By the Roman period, however, they had apparently regained their popularity (or availability), and, apart from site 12 at Wadi el-Hudi, there are Roman amethyst quarries in the Safaga region near Gebel Abu Diyeiba (midway between the phosphate mines of Wasif and Umm Huetat), where the amethyst has formed in cavities in the red granite following the courses of quartz veins reportedly extending for hundreds of metres (Murray 1914: 179; Lucas 1962: 389). In modern Egypt the natural reserves of amethysts appear to have been virtually exhausted, and they now have to be imported from South America.

Description
It is difficult to determine the precise character of the amethyst mined at Wadi el-Hudi, since the stone is now completely worked out, but judging from the surviving Middle Kingdom jewellery incorporating amethyst beads, it was of a dark violet hue. The amethysts reported by Engelbach at the Gebel el-Asr gneiss quarries appear to be of a much paler colour, and according to Ogden (1982: 107), 'some Egyptian amethysts are so pale they could almost pass for rose quartz'.

Uses
Amethyst was primarily used as a gemstone, and is almost entirely restricted to items of jewellery dating either to the Middle Kingdom or the Roman period, although there are a few instances of its use for beads and small vessels between the late Predynastic period and the end of the Old Kingdom. It was, however, also occasionally used for small vessels (in the Predynastic and Early Dynastic periods) or small amulets (mainly in the Old Kingdom). There is a certain amount of evidence for the trading of amethyst with Crete from at least the Middle Kingdom onwards (perhaps in exchange for such products as animal horns, oils and lichen, see Warren 1995: 5–10).

Examples
1. Vessel from the Step Pyramid at Saqqara, dating to the Naqada III period or Early Dynastic period, *c.* 3150–2649 BC (height 9 cm; Cairo JE65416).
2. Gold, amethyst and turquoise bracelet from the tomb of King Djer at Abydos, First Dynasty, *c.* 3000–2770 BC (length 15 cm; Cairo JE52010).
3. Falcon amulet dating to the Old Kingdom, *c.* 2649–2152 BC (height 1 cm; BM EA57803).

4. Twelfth-Dynasty gold and amethyst girdle from the tomb of Sithathoriunet (in the vicinity of the pyramid of Senusret II at Lahun), dating to the reigns of Senusret II–Amenemhat III, *c.* 1897–1797 BC (length 82 cm; New York, MMA 16.1.16, Brunton 1920).

Bibliography

Murray (1914, 1939a); Nassim (1925); Engelbach (1938); Rowe (1939); Fakhry (1946, 1952); Frondel (1962: 171–81); Lucas (1962: 388–9); Sadek (1980–85); Shaw and Jameson (1993); Aston (1994: 66–7); Bomann (1995); Warren (1995: 5–10); Shaw in press (a), (b).

For colour photograph of the amethyst vessel Cairo JE65416 see Aston (1994: pl. 15).

2. Milky quartz

Definition

Cloudy white form of vein quartz, the milky hue of which is caused by abundant, disseminated, submicroscopic vacuoles or cavities filled with ion-charged water.

Egyptian sources

Milky quartz is abundant virtually everywhere that there are outcrops of igneous and metamorphic basement rocks in Egypt. It is also a common constituent of the modern *wadi* gravels between these outcrops and the Nile valley; the many ancient river deposits in the Nile valley contain large amounts of gravel including many milky quartz clasts. According to Ball (1907: 84–5) there are indications of ancient milky quartz workings to the north of Aswan.

Uses

From the Naqada III period until the end of the Early Dynastic period, milky quartz was frequently carved into pendants and funerary vessels, the latter particularly at Abydos and the Memphite necropolis. It was also used for the model vessels employed in the funerary ceremony of the 'opening of the mouth' in the Fourth to Sixth Dynasties, and became a popular material for inlay and beads in the Middle Kingdom. Many of the red inlays in the jewellery of Tutankhamun have been identified as milky quartz or rock crystal placed over a bed of red cement, probably in imitation of cornelian or red glass.

Examples

1. Late Predynastic or Early Dynastic statuette of a recumbent lion, perhaps from Gebelein; *c.* 3100–2900 BC (length 25 cm; New York, MMA 66.99.2).
2. Miniature vessel from tomb E21 at Abydos; Sixth Dynasty, *c.* 2250 BC (height 8.1 cm; Ashmolean 1910.488a).

Bibliography

Ball (1907: 84–5); Little (1933: 77); Frondel (1962: 189–92); Lucas (1962: 402–3); Aston (1994: 64–5).

For colour photograph of a milky quartz vessel, see Aston (1994: pl. 15a).

3. Rock crystal

Definition

Colourless, transparent form of quartz, which is sometimes described as 'quartz crystal', especially when it occurs in its distinctive six-sided, prismatic crystal form.

Egyptian sources

Rock crystal is reportedly found in the region of the Western Desert between the Fayum and Bahariya Oasis, as well as in the Sinai peninsula.

Uses

Used from the Predynastic period onwards for beads and small vessels. From the Old Kingdom onwards it was regularly used for the corneas of artificial eyes on statuary and coffins, as well as for the miniature vessels serving the 'opening of the mouth' ritual. In the New Kingdom it was frequently used for inlay (sometimes over red cement so as to imitate cornelian) and as a decorative component of prestige goods such as weaponry or funerary equipment. Lucas (1962: 403) argues that Tutankhamun's iron dagger, with its rock crystal pommel, may have been an import. On the other hand, there appears to be some evidence that rock crystal, like malachite and amethyst, was being exported to Crete as a raw material (see Warren 1995: 5–10).

Examples

1. Corneas in the inlaid eyes of a squatting scribe statue, Fourth Dynasty, *c.* 2575–2465 BC (Cairo CG36).
2. Amulet carved into the shape of a baboon, unprovenanced, Twelfth Dynasty, *c.* 1991–1783 BC (Fitzwilliam E.121.1939).

Bibliography

Frondel (1962: 192–4); Lucas (1962: 402–3); Aston (1994: 64–5); Warren (1995: 5–10).

4. Other types of quartz (rose, smoky, citrine, prase)

Definition

The pink (and occasionally slightly violet) colour of rose quartz is caused by the presence of manganese or titanium impurities. Some rose quartz contains many tiny rutile needles which produce a star-like effect, especially when the gem is cut as a cabochon (a round or oval stone with plain, curved surfaces). Smoky quartz is a brown or black form of vein quartz, the colour of which derives from the presence of aluminium impurities, while citrine is a yellow to yellowish-brown form of vein quartz, its colour deriving from iron impurities.

Prase is a leek-green, semi-translucent variety of quartz which derives its colour from the presence of vast numbers of minute fibres of green amphibole minerals such as hornblende or actinolite. Although technically it differs from chrysoprase (an apple-green form of chalcedony), in practice the two are easily confused.

Egyptian sources
No specific ancient source of rose quartz in Egypt has yet been discovered. Traces of smoky quartz have been found in a Roman gold mine at Romit in the Eastern Desert (Ball 1912: 353).

Uses
During the Early Dynastic period and the Old Kingdom, rose quartz was very occasionally used for funerary vessels. Prase was occasionally used for beads during the Pharaonic period.

Examples
1. Rose quartz round-bottomed dish from tomb 1207 at Armant, First Dynasty (SD80), *c.* 3000–2770 BC (Cairo; Mond and Myers 1937: pl. 17).
2. Rose quartz cylinder vessel from the valley temple of Menkaura at Giza, Fourth Dynasty, *c.* 2490–2472 BC (Cairo; Reisner 1931: 188, fig. 60.7).

Bibliography
Ball (1912: 353); Frondel (1962: 181–9, 219); Lucas (1962: 402); Aston (1994: 65–6).

Quartz diorite *see* diorite, quartz diorite and gabbro

Quartzite

Definition
Sedimentary quartzite is a sandstone in which the sand grains are so tightly cemented by quartz that the rock breaks across the grains rather than around them. This is also termed an 'orthoquartzite'. Some geologists prefer to call this rock 'siliceous sandstone' to distinguish it from metamorphic quartzite, although the quartzite used by the ancient Egyptians is entirely of the sedimentary variety. The term 'quartzose sandstone' is ambiguous and should be avoided as the quartzose could refer to either the quartz cement or grains.

Egyptian sources
Hard quartzites are widespread in the Eastern and Western Deserts and are also occasionally encountered in the Nile valley. In these places abundant quartz cementation has developed on exposed outcrops and in the shallow subsurface of otherwise friable sandstones of the Nubia Group and younger formations. There are only two known ancient quarries and these are located where silification has been unusually deep and pervasive: Gebel Ahmar near Cairo, and on and between Gebels Tingar and Gulab near Aswan (see maps in Figs. 2.1a and b). The rock at Gebel Ahmar belongs to the Gebel Ahmar Formation of Oligocene age and was worked from the Old Kingdom onwards. The quartzite near Aswan occurs in the upper part of the Timsah Formation and the lower part of the overlying Umm Barmil Formation (both units belong to the Nubia Group of late Cretaceous age). The quarry workings on Gebel Gulab date from the New Kingdom to the Roman period (see Fig. 2.6). Those on Gebel Tingar and elsewhere in the area may date, in part, from the same time but most of the visible workings are probably associated with the construction of the nearby St Simeon's monastery, dating to the seventh to tenth centuries AD.

Descriptions
The quartzites used in ancient Egypt vary from fine- to very coarse-grained, frequently exhibit cross-bedding, and commonly contain pebble-rich layers. In some cases the pebbles predominate over the sand grains and the rock is more correctly described as a 'siliceous conglomerate'. The predominant colour is brown but other colours are occasionally encountered including light grey to nearly white, and various shades of yellow, orange, red and purple. The different colours are caused by variable amounts of iron oxides (haematite and goethite) in the quartz cement. Manganese oxides are probably responsible for the purplish coloration in some samples.

The quartzites from the two widely separated quarries are usually indistinguishable megascopically but, in thin section, they differ markedly in the roundness of the sand grains. Those from Gebel Ahmar are predominately round to subround whereas those from Aswan are mostly angular to subangular in cross-section. This is the only consistent difference but the type of quartz cement will also be definitive for some samples. Quartz cement normally occurs as optically continuous overgrowths on quartz sand grains. This is the type of cement that occurs at Aswan and predominates at Gebel Ahmar, but at the latter quarry there also occurs a rare form of quartz cement that appears in the form of a finely polycrystalline mosaic resembling chert. It has also been suggested that the two quarries can be distinguished by the presence or absence of detrital anatase sand grains and chert pebbles with the former occurring only at Aswan and the latter occurring only at Gebel Ahmar. These distinctions appear to be valid but the two grain types are not always present. The chert pebbles are significant, however, in that they are the only difference between the quarry stones that can be recognised megascopically. The chert has a microcrystalline texture and greyish colour whereas most of the other pebbles (at both quarries) are coarsely crystalline, milky white quartz. Trace elements have also been proposed as discriminators and they have shown some promise. However, their reliability is questionable for small samples given the inherently variable composition of quartzites.

Uses
Quartzite was employed sparingly as a construction material from the Old Kingdom onwards. Its use was largely limited to doorway thresholds in temples (as in the mortuary temple of the Sixth-Dynasty King Teti at Saqqara) and wall-linings in burial chambers (as in the Twelfth-Dynasty pyramid of King Amenemhat III at Hawara). It was also

used extensively for statuary and sarcophagi from the Old Kingdom onwards. At the Gebel Gulab quarries there is an unfinished obelisk of Seti I still *in situ* (Habachi 1960: 224–31; 1977: 32–3, pl. 6). Quartzite was also the material used for the 'rubbers' with which Egyptian woodworkers finished and smoothed pieces of timber, a process which was depicted in some tomb-paintings and reliefs (e.g. Wild 1966: pl. CLXXIV; see Chapter 15).

Examples

1. Head of an old man, Twenty-fifth Dynasty, after 730 BC (height 23.5 cm; BM EA37883) [white rock].
2. Two colossal heads of Amenhotep III from his funerary temple in Thebes, Eighteenth Dynasty, *c.* 1391–53 BC (height *c.* 1.2 m; BM EA6–7) [pebbly, light grey and brown rock].
3. Standing figure of prince Khaemwaset, son of Rameses II, from Asyut, Nineteenth Dynasty, *c.* 1290–1224 BC (height 1.46 m; BM EA947) [pebbly, light grey and brown rock].
4. Statue of the god Thoth in the form of a baboon; Eighteenth Dynasty, *c.* 1390 BC (height 67 cm; BM EA38) [brown rock].
5. Stelophorous statue of Amenwahsu, Eighteenth or Nineteenth Dynasty, *c.* 1550–1196 BC (height 56 cm; BM EA480) [purplish red rock].

Bibliography

Shukri (1953, 1954); Habachi (1960); Lucas (1962: 62–3, 418–9); Bowman *et al.* (1984); Klemm *et al.* (1984); Niazi and Loukina (1987); Stross *et al.* (1988); De Putter and Karlshausen (1992: 95–9); Klemm and Klemm (1993: 283–303); Aston (1994: 33–5).

For colour photographs of cut slabs see: Klemm and Klemm (1993: pls. 8.1–9.6).

Rock crystal *see* quartz, 3

Sandstone

Definition

Sandstone is a sedimentary rock consisting predominately of sand-size grains (0.063–2 mm) of detrital (transported) rock and mineral fragments that are held together by quartz, calcite, iron oxide, clay or other cements.

Egyptian sources

Outcrops of sandstone are widespread in Egypt. They occur continuously in the Nile valley and on the adjacent desert plateaux from Esna southward into northern Sudan and are interrupted only at the Nile cataracts where more resistant igneous and metamorphic rocks crop out. A total of thirty-four ancient quarries are identified, together with their ages, in Table 2.1 and on the maps in Figures 2.1a–b (see Figs. 2.22–2.24 for photographs of specific quarries). This rock is commonly described as 'Nubian sandstone' because it belongs to the stratigraphic sequence known as the Nubia Group. The quarries may be tentatively assigned to the following geologic formations within this group: Duwi (1–4), Quseir (5–11 and possibly 33–34), Umm Barmil (12–16 and possibly 32), Timsah (17–18), Abu Aggag (19–23) and Sabaya (24–31). Except for the quarry near the Buhen ruins (28) and the workings at the higher elevations near Qertassi (20), all quarries south of Aswan are now under Lake Nasser. As this region received relatively little attention prior to flooding, it is likely that there are more quarries than those shown in Figure 2.1b. The same is true for quarries in the Western and Eastern Deserts. In the Nile valley north of Aswan, however, the list of quarries is probably reasonably complete.

Figure 2.22 Sandstone quarry on the east bank at Gebel el-Silsila.

Figure 2.23 Sandstone quarry at Nag el-Hoch.

Figure 2.24 Sandstone quarry at el-Mahamid.

Identifying the quarry of origin for sandstone objects is not possible at present. However, the formation and hence the general geographic area, can sometimes be established from the grain size and bedding characteristics. This determination can be made megascopically but large blocks are needed to recognise the bedding characteristics. For the quarries investigated north of Aswan, no systematic change in mineralogy has been noted either geographically or stratigraphically. It is possible that trace element analysis may permit more detailed provenance determinations but too little is yet known from quarry samples to evaluate this possibility. It seems unlikely, however, that this would be an effective approach when using small samples because of sandstone's great compositional variability on the scale of individual quarries.

Descriptions

Virtually nothing is known about the character of the sandstone south of Aswan. From Aswan northward, however, quarry samples indicate that the rock almost always contains at least 75 volume per cent quartz grains with most of the remaining percentage consisting of feldspar grains (mainly microcline). The sandstone thus varies from a sub-feldspathic arenite to a quartz arenite, with the former restricted to the finer-grained rocks. The sandstones are highly porous and only loosely cemented with quartz, iron oxides (goethite and minor haematite) and chlorite clay. All three cements are almost always present, and commonly kaolinite clay and rarely calcite also contribute. Because it is incompletely cemented, the sandstone is friable and thus relatively easy to quarry and carve. Its strength and durability is imparted by the sparse but omnipresent quartz cement, and iron oxides give the sandstone its typical brownish colour.

The sandstones encountered in ancient quarries and tombs come from the following six geologic formations (all date from the upper part of the Cretaceous Period; stages and alternative formation names are given in parentheses and brackets, respectively).

1. *Duwi Formation* [or 'phosphate formation'] (Late Campanian to Early Maastrichtian): almost nothing is known about this sandstone; it may be similar to the underlying Quseir Formation.
2. *Quseir Formation* [or 'variegated shale'] (Early to Late Campanian): very fine- to fine-grained, flat-bedded and ripple cross-laminated sandstone.
3. *Umm Barmil Formation* [or 'Taref sandstone'] (Santonian to Early Campanian): coarse-grained to mainly fine- to medium-grained, mostly tabular cross-bedded sandstone.
4. *Timsah Formation* (Coniacian to Santonian): very little is known about this sandstone; it appears to be relatively fine-grained and may be similar to the overlying Umm Barmil Formation.
5. *Abu Aggag Formation* (Turonian): fine- to very coarse-grained but mainly medium- to coarse-grained, mostly trough cross-bedded, kaolinitic sandstone with common, thin granule to pebble conglomerate interbeds.
6. *Sabaya Formation* (Albian to Early Cenomanian): relatively little is known about this sandstone; it may be fine- to coarse-grained and mostly trough cross-bedded with occasional conglomeritic interbeds.

Uses

The earliest known use of sandstone for building purposes was for pavement and wall-lining in the burial chamber of an Early Dynastic tomb at Hierakonpolis. It was not until the Eleventh Dynasty, however, that it was first used on a monumental scale in the mortuary temple of Nebhepetra Mentuhotep II at Deir el-Bahari in Thebes. Here a purplish sandstone was employed along with limestone. The source of this distinctively coloured sandstone, which was apparently not used elsewhere, may be Gebel el-Silsila West or Nag el-Hammam (nos. 8–9 in Table 2.1 and Fig. 2.1b). Sandstone was next used for portions of a few Twelfth-Dynasty temples, including that of Senusret I at Karnak and others nearby at Qift and Nag el-Madamud. It was not, however, until the Eighteenth Dynasty that this rock became the principal building material for temples in Thebes and other sites to the south. It was occasionally imported into the limestone region north of Thebes as, for example, when it was used for portions of the Hathor temple and associated buildings at Dendara, and for the temples of Seti I and Rameses II at Abydos.

The ascendancy of sandstone as the building material of choice coincided with the re-establishment of royal and religious authority at Thebes at the beginning of the New Kingdom, and the concomitant discovery that sandstone was superior to limestone in terms of the size and strength of the blocks that could be extracted from quarries. These attributes facilitated the construction of enormous temples with long architraves in the New Kingdom and later periods.

As a sculptural medium, sandstone was decidedly inferior to limestone, which was more durable and could be more intricately carved. Sandstone was, however, easily worked and readily available and thus widely used for reliefs and statuary outside the limestone region. Objects made from this rock were typically painted.

Examples

1. Osirid statue of King Amenhotep I from Deir el-Bahari, western Thebes, Eighteenth Dynasty, *c.* 1525–1504 BC (height 2.69 m; BM EA683).
2. Painted kneeling statue of the Theban general Intef, from his tomb chapel in the Assasif region of Thebes, Eleventh Dynasty, *c.* 2050 BC (height 58 cm; Cairo JE89858 and 91169).
3. Upper part of a colossal Osirid statue of King Akhenaten, from east Karnak, Eighteenth Dynasty, *c.* 1350 BC (height 1.37 m; Louvre E27112).

Bibliography

De Morgan *et al.* (1894); Weigall (1910); Lucas (1962: 55–7); Van Houten and Bhattacharyya (1979); Ward and McDonald (1979); Klitzsch (1988); Hermina *et al.* (1989); De Putter and Karlshausen (1992: 91–4); Klemm and Klemm (1993: 225–81).

For colour photographs of cut slabs see Klemm and Klemm (1993: pls. 7.1–7.6).

Sardonyx *see* chalcedony

Satin spar *see* alabaster

Schist *see* siltstone, greywacke and conglomerate

Serpentinite (serpentine)

Definition

Serpentine is a hydrated magnesium silicate of the composition $Mg_6Si_4O_{10}[OH]_8$ which is formed by the alteration of magnesium-rich silicates by hot water solutions. The three serpentine minerals – chrysotile, lizardite and antigorite – are differentiated by the degree of substitution of magnesium by iron. 'Serpentinite' rocks contain one or more of these minerals plus minor amounts of brucite, talc, tremolite, magnetite and/or dolomite.

Egyptian sources

Serpentinite is widely distributed in the Eastern Desert. Some of the larger and more accessible outcrops are in Wadi Hammamat and in the tributary wadis of Atalla and Umm Esh to the north. Only one ancient quarry is known and it is Roman in date (Brown and Harrell 1995). It is in an unnamed tributary of Wadi Umm Esh near its confluence with Wadi Atalla. A modern quarry has now destroyed the ancient workings but the remains of stone huts of the Roman period can still be seen. The sources of the two different varieties of serpentinite utilised in the Pharaonic period are not known, although it is possible that one of them (Variety 1 below) may have come from the Wadi Umm Esh area.

Description

Two general varieties of serpentinite were used in the Pharaonic period: Variety 1 is greyish to mostly greenish (often with a mottling of yellowish and darker shades) with black veins or patches; and Variety 2 is mostly black and speckled with grains of grey or brown. Both varieties may be hydrothermally altered peridotites. The blackish serpentinite (Variety 2), for example, has a matrix of antigorite showing mesh structure with granules of iron oxide outlining the boundaries of original olivine grains, and scattered pseudomorphs after pyroxene crystals. Variety 1, from the Wadi Umm Esh quarry, consists mainly of fine-grained antigorite with rare chrysotile and lizardite plus minor dolomite (in veins) and accessory minerals (magnetite, talc and tremolite). The black veins of magnetite are particularly prominent when the surface has been weathered to a greenish-white colour. A translucent subvariety of the greenish serpentinite was called 'green noble serpentine' by Petrie (1937: 2).

Uses

Translucent greenish serpentinite with black patches was used for small vessels and amulets in the Predynastic period and First Dynasty. Blackish serpentinite was a common material for statues and kohl vessels in the Middle Kingdom and Second Intermediate Period though rarely occurs outside this time. Greenish serpentinite with black veins was used for small vessels from the Predynastic period (Naqada II) to the Eighteenth Dynasty. It was also used for small funerary objects, such as heart scarabs and *shabti* figures, in the New Kingdom.

The Wadi Umm Esh serpentinite was quarried for export from Egypt by the Romans who used it for pavement tiles and sculptures – an especially fine example is the figure of a dog in the Palazzo dei Conservatori in Rome. The only known earlier example of its use is a column drum, still *in situ* at Bir Umm Fawakhir, at the eastern end of Wadi Hammamat, which is inscribed with the name of Ptolemy III Euergetes and comes from a temple dedicated to this king that once existed at the same locality.

Examples

1. Bird-shaped vessel from tomb 89 at Naqada, dating to the Naqada II period, *c.* 3500–3100 BC (height 5.5 cm; Oxford, Ashmolean 1895.217) [green with black veins].
2. Kohl jar from the mastaba of Sehetepibraankh at Lisht, Twelfth Dynasty, *c.* 1991–1783 BC (New York, MMA) [green with black veins].
3. Statuette of a girl holding a kohl jar, Twelfth Dynasty (BM EA2572) [granular black].
4. *Shabti* of Amenhotep II, Eighteenth Dynasty, *c.* 1427–1 BC (29 cm; BM EA35365) [green with black veins].

5. *Shabti* of Amenhotep III, Eighteenth Dynasty, *c.* 1391–53 BC (Louvre N 649) [green with black veins].

Bibliography

Akaad and Noweir (1972); Gnoli (1988: 159); Marchei *et al.* (1989: 291); De Putter and Karlshausen (1992: 136–9); Klemm and Klemm (1993: 376–8); Aston (1994: 56–9); Brown and Harrell (1995).

For colour photographs of two varieties of serpentine used in the Pharaonic period see Aston (1994: pl. 12), for the *shabti* (Louvre N 649) and a vessel of green serpentine with black veins see De Putter and Karlshausen (1992: pls. 51–2), and for polished slabs see Mielsch (1985: pl. 20–668), Gnoli (1988: fig. 115), Marchei *et al.* (1989: fig. 129a), De Putter and Karlshausen (1992: pl. 54h–30, 31, 32), and Klemm and Klemm (1993: pls. 13.1–13.2).

Siliceous sandstone *see* quartzite

Siltstone, greywacke and conglomerate

Definition

Siltstone, greywacke and conglomerate are types of sedimentary rock formed from fragments of pre-existing rocks. They are classified by the Udden-Wentworth scale (see Table 2.3) according to the size of their constituent grains. Greywacke is a poorly sorted variety of sandstone which contains a range of grain sizes including at least 10 per cent silt and clay matrix, and is characteristically dark-coloured, hard and dense.

Egyptian sources

The hard green siltstone, greywacke and conglomerate used by the ancient Egyptians belong to the Hammamat Series of late Precambrian age and are widely distributed in the northern and central parts of the Eastern Desert. Only one ancient quarry is known, located in the Wadi Hammamat, which was worked from the Predynastic through the Roman Period (see Fig. 2.25). Over 250 inscriptions and numerous quarry workings occur along a stretch of the wadi just over one kilometre in length, west of the confluence with Wadi Atalla. A Roman ramp runs up the south side of the wadi, while on the floor of the wadi on the north side are the ruins of a chapel of the Thirtieth Dynasty. The green conglomerate workings are in the western part of the quarry, but the most prominent of these, where there are many quarried blocks, dates from the present century. On some surviving blocks (partially broken-up, by twentieth-century quarry-workers), there are New Kingdom inscriptions, including two from the reign of Rameses IV (which is probably significant given that the conglomerate sarcophagus of Rameses VI originally belonged to Rameses IV; Harrell 1992b: 104).

Description

The Hammamat siltstone is composed of fairly well-sorted silt-size grains (primarily measuring 0.01–0.05 mm), while the greywacke consists mainly of fine to very fine sand grains (0.06–0.2 mm) with rare pebbles. The grains are

Figure 2.25 Siltstone-greywacke quarry (arrow) in Wadi Hammamat, Eastern Desert.

mostly quartz with minor oligoclase-andesine plagioclase and felsic to intermediate volcanic rock fragments plus rare muscovite. These are tightly cemented by chlorite and sericite micas plus minor amounts of epidote and calcite. The chlorite-sericite matrix was formed from the original clay-rich matrix by compaction and recrystallization during long, deep burial. Some geologists consider that the heat and pressure which partially recrystallised the original clay to chlorite and epidote are sufficient for these to be called 'slightly metamorphosed'; they would therefore append the prefix 'meta-' to all varieties, i.e. metasiltstone, metagreywacke and metaconglomerate. The colour of the siltstone and greywacke ranges from dark grey to mainly greyish green; the texture is fine, hard and dense. The dark grey variety is restricted to the eastern part of the quarry.

Siltstone and greywacke may be distinguished by the visibly granular nature of the greywacke. In greywacke, the sand-size grains are visible to the naked eye and can be clearly seen with a hand lens, whereas siltstone has a fine uniform appearance, and individual grains are so small they cannot be distinguished without a microscope. The relative quantities of siltstone and greywacke utilised anciently are not yet known, and more accurate identifications are needed. Preliminary indications are that the siltstone comes mainly from the central part of the quarry, especially around the tributary wadi on the north side.

In a study of stone vessels, all five vessels of this stone which were examined in thin-section (from Giza, Saqqara, Tarkhan and Nag el-Deir) were found to be siltstone, as was a statue of Menkaura (Aston 1994: 29, 31, 32). On the other hand, a series of Fifth- and Sixth-Dynasty royal sarcophagi from Saqqara (Unas, Teti, Pepi I, Merenra), hitherto assumed to be of basalt, are actually made of greywacke (Wissa 1994: 387).

Siltstone and greywacke have sometimes been called 'slate', though the pronounced foliation (layering) and conspicuous flaking and splitting which characterise slate are absent from the Wadi Hammamat rocks. The so-called 'slate' palettes of the Predynastic period are actually of siltstone; the rock is identical to that used for stone vessels and statuary in the Pharaonic period (Klemm and Klemm 1993: 369).

'Schist' is another erroneous name which has previously been applied to the Hammamat rocks. Schist is a medium- to coarse-grained metamorphic rock with pronounced layering, completely unlike the fine-grained, homogeneous siltstone and greywacke of Wadi Hammamat. Dark grey siltstone and greywacke are occasionally confused with basalt – a crystalline, igneous rock formed directly from lava. Ironically, the English word 'basalt' actually derives from the ancient Egyptian word for siltstone-greywacke – *bḫn* – through Greek basan and Latin *basanites* (Harrell 1995: 30–3).

The conglomerate quarried in Wadi Hammamat has an overall greenish appearance but contains pebbles of a wide variety of colours, including white, pink, red, yellow, brown, green and grey. The pebbles are well-rounded, range in size up to 25 cm in diameter with most less than 4 cm, and consist mainly of volcanic rock fragments with lesser amounts of granite, chert, vein quartz, quartzite and other rock types. The rock has an unusual 'diamictic' texture where the pebbles are surrounded and supported by a matrix of coarse- to very coarse-grained sand compositionally similar to that in the greywacke. The conglomerate is tightly cemented with chlorite, sericite and epidote plus minor amounts of calcite and iron oxides.

The Romans had a very descriptive name for this conglomerate: *lapis hecatontalithos* ('stone of a hundred stones'). Italian stonemasons, who recycled stone that had been brought to Italy by the Romans, called this rock *breccia verde antico* or *breccia verde d'Egitto*, and this is the origin of the frequently encountered name 'green breccia'. However, in modern terminology, breccia is a rock composed of angular fragments, whereas in conglomerates such as this one the fragments are rounded.

Uses

In the Predynastic period siltstone was used for the so-called 'slate' palettes, and beginning in the Naqada II period also for stone vessels and other small items such as bracelets and spoons. During the Early Dynastic period siltstone was first employed for statuary, and siltstone vessels are particularly numerous. From the Old Kingdom onwards, siltstone and greywacke were employed for large objects such as statuary, stelae, sarcophagi and naoi, and this fine, hard stone was particularly favoured by the Egyptian élite in the Twenty-sixth and Thirtieth Dynasties.

Only a few examples of the use of green conglomerate are known from the Pharaonic period, including the inner sarcophagus of Rameses VI and the sarcophagus of Nectanebo II. The Romans quarried it extensively for export to Italy; it was used for basins, small columns, pavement tiles and rarely for statues.

Examples

1. Palette of the First-Dynasty king Narmer from Hierakonpolis, *c.*3000 BC (height 64 cm; Cairo JE32169) [siltstone].
2. Statue of the Second-Dynasty king Khasekhemwy, from Hierakonpolis, *c.*2700 BC (height 56.5 cm; Cairo JE32161) [siltstone].
3. Statue of Menkaura and Queen Khamerernebty from Menkaura's pyramid complex at Giza, Fourth Dynasty, *c.*2490–72 BC (height 1.4 m; Boston MFA 11.1738) [siltstone].
4. Face from lid of inner sarcophagus of Rameses VI from his tomb in the Valley of Kings (KV9) (height 80 cm; BM EA140) [green conglomerate].
5. Slab inscribed with the Memphite Theology, dating to the reign of the Twenty-fifth-Dynasty king Shabaqo, from Memphis (the so-called 'Shabaka Stone'), *c.* 712–698 BC (length 1.37 m; BM EA498) [conglomerate].
6. Pair of obelisks of Nectanebo II *c.* 360–43 BC (height 2. 59 m and 2.42 m; BM EA523, 524) [siltstone].
7. Sarcophagus of Nectanebo II, *c.* 360–343 BC (length 2.98 m; BM EA10) [green conglomerate].
8. Ptolemaic sarcophagus lid of troop commander Pedimahes, from Tell el-Muqdam (length 2.16 m; Philadelphia PA, University Museum E16134) [greywacke].

Bibliography

Couyat and Montet (1912); Weigall (1913: 37–51); Lucas and Rowe (1938); Andrew (1939); Shiah (1942); Goyon (1957); De Putter and Karlshausen (1992: 59–60, 87–90); Harrell and Brown (1992a, 1992b), Klemm and Klemm (1993: 355–76); Aston (1994: 28–33); Wissa (1994); and Harrell (1995).

For colour photographs of polished slabs see De Putter and Karlshausen (1992: pls. 54d–16, 54e–19 greywacke; 54a–4 green conglomerate) and Klemm and Klemm (1993: pl. 12.1–2 greywacke, 12.3 siltstone, 12.5–6 green conglomerate).

Slate *see* siltstone, greywacke and conglomerate

Sodalite *see* lapis lazuli

Steatite (soapstone)

Definition

Steatite is a rock composed primarily of the mineral talc in which the flakes of talc are oriented randomly, resulting in a massive, homogeneous texture. When the talc flakes are aligned in layers, the rock is called talc schist. Talc is a hydrated magnesium silicate of the composition $Mg_3Si_4O_{10}(OH)_2$ which is characterised by extreme softness (it can be scratched by a fingernail) and a soapy feel (hence 'soapstone', the alternative name for steatite).

Egyptian sources
Steatite occurs widely in the central and southern parts of the Eastern Desert. Some of the largest exposures are immediately to the north and south of Wadi Barramiya, and in the area of Gebel Salatit north of Wadi Barramiya there are large-scale modern quarrying operations. Near here, at Gebel Rod el-Barram, there is a large, recently discovered, steatite quarry that dates from the Roman period (and possibly earlier). The steatite from this quarry is a mottled grey and brown variety identical to that used for ancient vessels. Another newly discovered quarry is in Wadi Saqiyah in the central Eastern Desert , where a greenish talc schist was quarried by the Romans during the first two centuries AD.

Description
Steatite is generally grey, greenish grey or brown in colour, and ancient Egyptian vessels of steatite exhibit a mottled grey and brown appearance. The surface has a dull, waxy lustre, often with many scratches as a consequence of the extreme softness of the stone. A thin section of the Gebel Salatit steatite reveals lenticular masses of fine-grained (0.04–0.08 mm) talc flakes with a few large, patchy grains of magnetite and many fine, scattered shreds of haematite.

Uses
Lucas notes that steatite was used for beads as early as the Badarian period and also commonly for scarabs which were often glazed (1962: 421). Its use for statuary is not clear as it has sometimes been confused with serpentinite, however it was certainly used for cosmetic vessels in both the Middle and the New Kingdoms.

Examples
1. Kohl jar from tomb E3 at Abydos, Twelfth to Thirteenth Dynasties, *c.* 1991–1640 BC (height 2.6 cm; Ashmolean 1896–1908 E.2175).
2. Tubular kohl jar held by a monkey from tomb E10 at Abydos, dating to the Eighteenth Dynasty, *c.* 1550–1307 BC (height 4.7 cm; Ashmolean 1896–1908 E.2339).
3. Head from a statuette of Queen Tiy from the temple of Hathor at Serabit el-Khadim, Eighteenth Dynasty, *c.* 1391–53 BC (height 7.2 cm; Cairo JE38257; Petrie 1906: pl. 133).

Bibliography
Lucas (1962: 155–6, 220–1); De Putter and Karlshausen (1992: 140–3); Klemm and Klemm (1993: 378–9); Aston (1994: 59–60).
For colour photograph of the kohl jar (Ashmolean 1896–1908 E.2175) see Aston (1994: pl. 13a), and of the statuette of Queen Tiy (Cairo JE38257) see Saleh and Sourouzian (1987: no. 144).

Travertine ('Egyptian alabaster')

Definition
Travertine is a sedimentary rock and a variety of limestone consisting largely of calcite (calcium carbonate, $CaCO_3$) or aragonite (another form of calcium carbonate). The travertine used in ancient Egypt is frequently described as 'Egyptian alabaster' or simply 'alabaster'. This terminology, however, is incorrect, since true alabaster, as recognised by geologists, is composed of gypsum (see ALABASTER). As a compromise for those uncomfortable with the name travertine, the terms 'calcite' and 'calcite-alabaster' have been suggested, but they are not recommended here. The former is a mineral name (and hence inappropriate for a rock) and the latter is a hybrid name not recognised by geologists.

Egyptian sources
Small deposits of travertine occur sporadically in the Eocene limestones of the Nile valley and adjacent desert (mainly Eastern) plateaux between Esna and Cairo. A total of nine ancient quarries are known and these are shown, together with their ages, in Table 2.1 and on the map in Figure 2.1a. The most famous Egyptian travertine quarries were located eighteen kilometres to the southeast of Amarna in Middle Egypt. Texts from the Old Kingdom onwards refer to this site as Hatnub ('mansion of gold'). The inscriptions, graffiti and archaeological remains at Hatnub indicate that it was intermittently exploited by the Egyptians for a period of about 3,000 years, from at least as early as the reign of Khufu until the Roman period (see Fig. 2.26). The site of Wadi Gerrawi, near Helwan, was also an important travertine quarry, exploited primarily in the Old Kingdom (see Murray 1945–6; Dreyer and Jaritz 1983; and see Fig. 2.27).

Description
Egyptian travertine is a dense (non-porous) rock consisting entirely of calcite and is a variety known as 'calcareous sinter' (or 'calc-sinter'). A porous, spongy-looking variety called 'calcareous tufa' occurs outside Egypt (e.g. at Tivoli in Italy), and is the one more commonly associated with the name travertine. The Egyptian deposits formed in subsur-

Figure 2.26 The main travertine quarry at Hatnub, Eastern Desert.

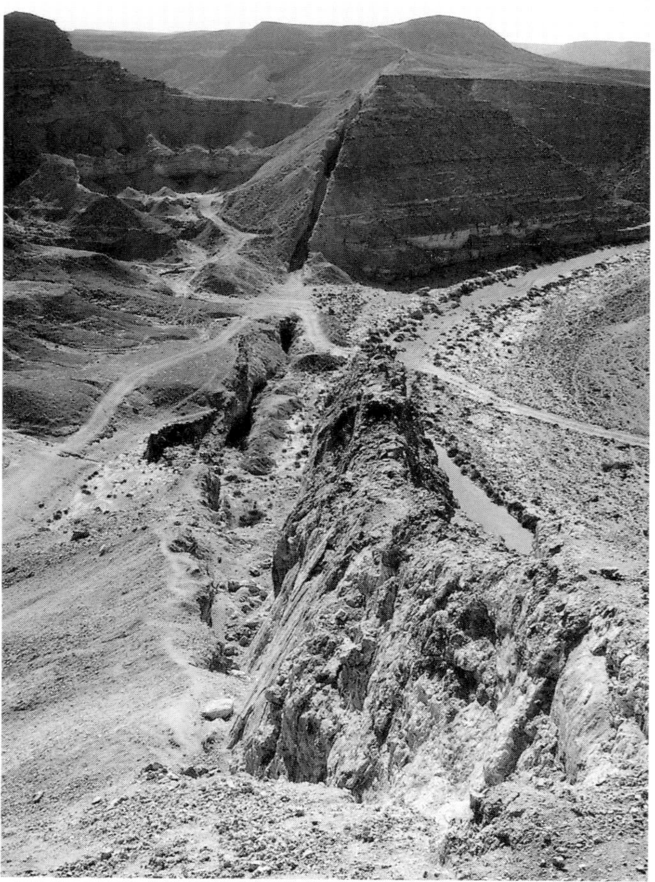

Figure 2.27 Travertine quarry in Wadi Gerrawi, Eastern Desert.

face caverns and fissures in the Eocene limestone bedrock, and consist of the same material from which cave stalagmites, stalactites and other flowstone spelothems are made. There is some evidence suggesting that hot springs may also have played a role in the formation of these deposits. The travertine occurs in three forms:

(1) an opaque, milky white calc-sinter that is fine-grained (crystals <1 mm) with little or no layering;
(2) a translucent calc-sinter that is coarse-grained (crystals 1 mm to several centimetres across), fibrous, coloured in shades of pale brown or yellowish- to orangish-brown with faint to marked layering; and
(3) a strikingly banded calc-sinter that is an interlayering of the first two forms.

Only the last two types were commonly used in ancient Egypt. The brownish colouring fades to white after exposure to the sun, as in the case of the Muhammad Ali Mosque in Cairo's Citadel. This mosque was built between 1830 and 1848, using exterior and interior veneers of Type 3 travertine, and over the last 150 years the exterior has faded badly. This rock is called *alabastrites* by the Greeks and Romans, but the original meaning of the name was forgotten during the Middle Ages, when it was given its modern definition and applied to a variety of gypsum superficially resembling Egyptian travertine.

Uses

Travertine was widely used from Early Dynastic times onwards for pavements and wall-linings in temple passages and rooms. A particularly well-known example of a pavement is in the valley temple of the Fourth-Dynasty king Khafra at Giza. It was also used extensively for small New Kingdom shrines (such as those of Amenhotep I/Thutmose I and Thutmose III in the open-air museum at Karnak), and for small vessels from the late Predynastic to the Roman period. In addition it was commonly employed for other small objects such as canopic jars, statuettes, *shabtis*, offering tables, bowls and dishes. Because large blocks were difficult to obtain from quarries, travertine was only occasionally used for sarcophagi, large statues and *naoi*.

Examples

1. Statue of the Fourth-Dynasty king Khafra from Mitrahina, *c.* 2520–2494 BC (Cairo).
2. Sphinx of the Eighteenth-Dynasty king Amenhotep I, from Karnak, *c.* 1525–1504 BC (44 cm long; Cairo CG 42033).
3. Colossal pair-statue of the crocodile-god Sobek with the Eighteenth-Dynasty king Amenhotep III, from Dahamsha, *c.* 1391–53 BC (2.56 m high; Luxor J 155).
4. Statuette of Akhenaten from house N48.15 at Amarna, Eighteenth Dynasty, *c.* 1353–35 BC (height 12 cm; Berlin ÄM 21835).
5. Sarcophagus of King Seti I from the Valley of Kings (KV17), Nineteenth Dynasty, *c.* 1306–1290 BC (length 2.84 m; London, Sir John Soane's Museum).
6. Statue of King Seti I from the 'Karnak cachette', Thebes (height 2.38 m; Cairo CG 42139).
7. Bust from a statue of King Merenptah, Nineteenth Dynasty, *c.* 1224–14 BC (Louvre E25474).

Bibliography

Petrie (1894); Timme (1917); Lucas (1962: 59–61, 406–7); Akaad and Nagger (1964a, 1964b, 1965); el-Hinnawi and Loukina (1972); Dreyer and Jaritz (1983); Shaw (1986, 1987); Harrell (1990); De Putter and Karlshausen (1992: 43–6); Klemm and Klemm (1993: 199–223); Aston (1994: 42–7).

For colour photographs of polished slabs see: Mielsch (1985, pl. 1–1, 5, 8, 17); Gnoli (1988: figs. 224–5); Marchei *et al.* (1989: figs. 4a–b); De Putter and Karlshausen (1992: pl. 54a–1, 2) and Klemm and Klemm (1993: pls. 6.3–6.6).

Tuff and tuffaceous limestone

Definition

Tuff is a rock consisting of pyroclastic debris (ash and cinders) thrown into the air by a volcanic explosion and accumulating in air-fall or water-laid deposits. Although tuffs are usually considered to be volcanic igneous rocks, they are also equally volcanoclastic sedimentary rocks. A tuffaceous limestone is a sedimentary limestone which contains up to 50 per cent pyroclastic debris.

Egyptian sources

The green tuff and tuffaceous limestone utilised for stone vessels in the Early Dynastic period come from Gebel Manzal el-Seyl, in the upper reaches of Wadi Mellaha near Gebel Mellaha, in the Eastern Desert (see map in Fig. 2.1a and photograph in Fig. 2.28). This quarry site was discovered by an expedition led by Harrell in 1994 (Harrell *et al.*, forthcoming). About 200 small workings are scattered along a three-kilometre-long, ridge-like *gebel*. Within the workings and also in fifteen workshop areas among them are hundreds of roughed-out vessels along with the stone tools used to produce them. The tools are made from locally available dolerite and are mostly hand-held mauls (pounders), but some are notched to take a wooden handle. Alternating layers of tuff and tuffaceous limestone occur in the quarry and workings are present in layers of both rock types.

Description

The tuff at Gebel Manzal el-Seyl is a highly calcareous and chloritic andesite ash tuff. There are two gradational varieties: a dark green vitric tuff and a lighter olive-green vitric-crystal tuff. It is the chlorite that gives the tuffs their green colour, whereas an occasional bluish tint is probably due to the luminescent properties of the calcite. Both varieties consist of andesine plagioclase crystals, andesitic rock fragments (lithics), and rare quartz crystals in a groundmass of microcrystalline quartz and feldspar (originally glass shards, but now devitrified and partially replaced by calcite and chlorite). All of the mafic minerals and some of the plagioclase in the lithic fragments are also replaced by chlorite and calcite. In the dark green vitric tuff, glass shards predominate with fine-grained (less than one millimetre) plagioclase crystals making up less than 33 per cent of the rock. Although the original glass shards have devitrified to microcrystalline quartz and plagioclase, in many cases the outlines of the shards are still visible. Up to a few per cent of lithic fragments and quartz crystals are present. The light green vitric-crystal tuff differs in containing over 33 per cent plagioclase crystals. It has a grainy surface, due to the crystals, whereas the vitric tuff has a smooth surface. Less chlorite makes this rock lighter in colour, and conspicuous dark specks are commonly present. These specks are lithic grains and iron oxide ghosts of mafic minerals. Both tuffs are commonly banded, with laminations varying from less than one millimetre to a few tens of centimetres. However, many vessels were cut from the thicker layers and so show no banding.

Both tuffs are gradational with tuffaceous limestone, which consists predominately of sparry calcite with grains up to one millimetre across. The limestone also has minor amounts of plagioclase crystals and devitrified glass plus occasional quartz grains and andesite lithics. Secondary chlorite gives it a light green colour, which is commonly bluish or, when stained by iron oxides, brownish. The rock surface appears grainy due to the coarseness of the calcite, and it exhibits the same conspicuous dark specks as are seen in the vitric-crystal tuff. The tuffaceous limestone closely resembles the vitric-crystal tuff, and the two rocks are not easily distinguished megascopically. The tuffaceous limestone occurs in thick (up to several tens of centimetres), lamination-free layers and so vessels carved from it rarely show the kind of banding common in the tuff.

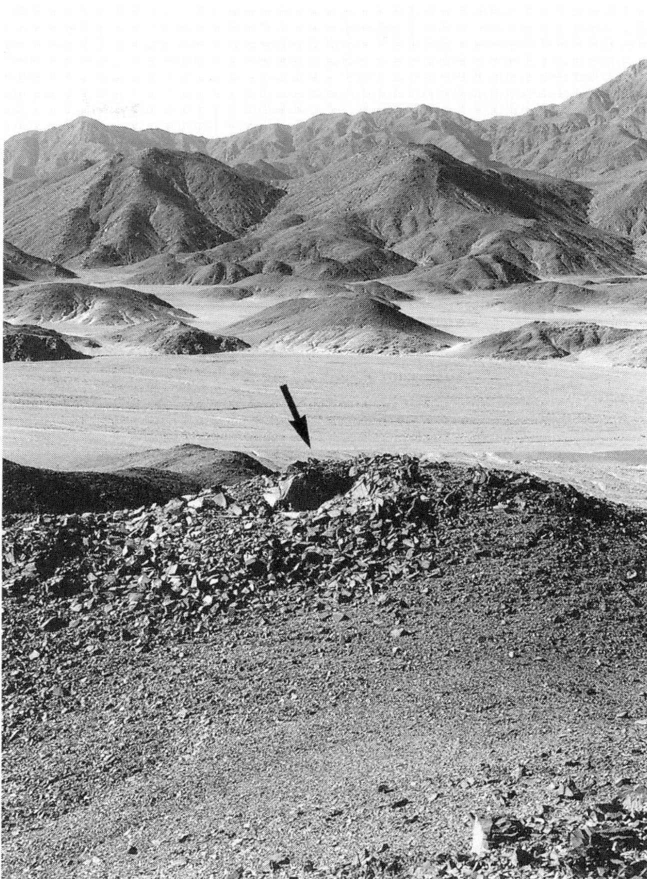

Figure 2.28 One (arrow) of numerous small quarries for calcareous tuff and tuffaceous limestone on Gebel Manzal el-Seyl, Eastern Desert.

Another variety of tuff utilised by the ancient Egyptians is yellowish brown in colour with purple bands. The source of this rock is unknown. In composition it is a lithic andesite tuff with scattered crystals of feldspar and bands rich in iron oxides. Examples of known provenance consist of fragments of three vessels from the First-Dynasty royal tombs at Abydos (Aston 1994: 27, colour photograph pl. 5b).

Tuff and tuffaceous limestone have sometimes been incorrectly called 'volcanic ash' (e.g. Caton-Thompson and Gardner 1934: 87; Petrie 1937: 2). 'Ash' refers to unconsolidated volcanic fragments and when these are compacted and/or cemented into rock the result is a tuff. The dark green tuff may be confused with the Wadi Hammamat siltstone as these rocks closely resemble each other megascopically. However, they are easily distinguished with the aid of dilute hydrochloric acid: only the tuff contains substantial calcite and so effervesces.

Uses

Tuff and tuffaceous limestone was used during the First and Second Dynasties for small vessels, including bowls of various types (Aston 1994: nos. 51, 59) and cylinders. Known examples of vessels come from tombs at Abydos, Nag el-Deir and Saqqara (Petrie 1901b: 43, Aston 1994: 27). The vessels in the Gebel Manzal el-Seyl quarry, though crudely shaped and not hollowed out, have the forms of bowls, dishes and cylinders. These rough pieces would have been carried to the Nile valley for final carving and polishing.

Examples

1. Unprovenanced beaker dating to the Naqada III or Early Dynastic period, *c.* 3150–2649 BC (height 12.6 cm; Cambridge, Fitzwilliam E.110.1994).
2. Dish from tomb 1513 at Nag el-Deir, Second Dynasty, *c.* 2770–2649 BC (Hearst Museum of Anthropology, University of California, Berkeley 6–132).
3. Cylinder vessel from the Step Pyramid at Saqqara, dating to the Early Dynastic period, *c.* 3000–2649 BC (height 16.5 cm; Cairo JE 65422).
4. Purple-striped tuff vessel from the tomb of King Qa'a (tomb Q), Umm el-Qa'ab, Abydos, First Dynasty, *c.* 2770 BC (height 13.6 cm; Ashmolean 1896–1908 E.3235).

Bibliography

Lucas (1962: 419–20); Aston (1994: 26–7); Harrell *et al.* (forthcoming).

For colour photographs of the dish from Nag el-Deir (Berkeley 6–132) and the vessel from Abydos (Ashmolean 18961908 E.3235) see Aston (1994: pls. 5b–c), and for the cylinder vessel (Cairo JE 65422) see Saleh and Sourouzian (1987: no. 20).

Turquoise

Definition

The chemical composition of turquoise is hydrated phosphate of copper and aluminium ($CuAl_6[PO_4]_4[OH]_8 \cdot 4H_2O$). Its colour is opaque blue-green or pale sky blue and its Mohs hardness is 5–6. It forms as veins and nodules usually in trachytic volcanic rocks in arid regions.

Egyptian sources

The two principal ancient Egyptian sources of turquoise are in the Sinai peninsula at Wadi Maghara from the Early Dynastic period to the Middle Kingdom and at Serabit el-Khadim from the Middle Kingdom until at least the Late Period (see also Beit-Arieh 1980 for evidence of prehistoric mining at this site).

The mines at Wadi Maghara, located in the southern Sinai, 225 kilometres southeast of Cairo, were particularly exploited during the Old and Middle Kingdoms. When Petrie examined the site in 1904–5 he found an Old Kingdom hilltop settlement on the opposite side of the wadi from the adits and rock-carvings, as well as two unfortified groups of stone huts on the floor of the wadi, the latter also dating to the Old Kingdom (Petrie and Currelly 1906; Chartier-Raymond 1988).

The mines at Serabit el-Khadim (Barrois 1932; Starr and Butin 1936; Giveon 1978; Bonnet *et al.* 1994; Chartier-Raymond *et al.* 1994; see Fig. 2.29), about eighteen kilometres to the north of Wadi Maghara, were also accompanied by rock-carved stelae, as well as an unusual associated temple complex dating to the Middle and New Kingdoms (*c.* 2040–1070 BC). In the temple precincts and the surrounding area, many rock-cut and free-standing stelae were dedicated by mining expeditions to the goddess Hathor in her aspect of *nbt mfk3t* ('lady of turquoise') and the god Soped 'guardian of the desert ways'. Among the results of Israeli work at Serabit el-Khadim and Wadi Maghara between 1967 and 1982 (Beit-Arieh 1977; Giveon 1972) was the discovery that one of the mines contained equipment concerned with the processing of copper. This find has added to the controversy regarding the ancient Egyptians' precise aims in the Sinai. Many of the inscriptions at Wadi Maghara and Serabit el-Khadim refer to the procurement of a substance called *mfk3t*, which was once translated as malachite and has more recently been taken to mean turquoise. It is possible that the main focus of Egyptian operations at these two sites was the obtaining of copper and malachite, with turquoise perhaps being only a convenient by-product of this mining (see Rothenberg 1987; Levene 1998). It is interesting to note in this context that the surviving examples of turquoise as a gemstone actually form quite a minor component in Egyptian jewellery, compared with the vast quantities implied by the numerous adits, shafts and stelae at Wadi Maghara and Serabit el-Khadim.

Description

Mined by the Egyptians from the late Predynastic period onwards, the greener variety of turquoise appears to have been highly prized by the ancient Egyptians, who preferred it to the more porous blue variety, which tends to fade when exposed to the sun or water.

Uses

Turquoise was used primarily for jewellery from the Predynastic to the Greco-Roman period. There is no evidence that powdered turquoise was used for a pigment (see Chapter 4, this volume), although Jack Ogden (pers. comm.

Figure 2.29 Turquoise mine at Serabit el-Khadim, Sinai, with a rock-cut stele of the Twelfth-Dynasty ruler Amenemhat III just above the entrance.

and Chapter 6, this volume) argues that it may have been used extensively in powdered form in the production of glazes.

Examples

1. Bracelet consisting of thirteen gold and fourteen turquoise *serekh*-plaques, each crowned by a falcon, from the First-Dynasty tomb of King Djer at Umm el-Qa'ab, Abydos, *c.* 3000 BC (overall length 15.6 cm; Cairo CG52010).
2. Gold pectoral of Sithathoriunet, from her tomb at Lahun, incorporating turquoise, lapis lazuli and cornelian inlay, Twelfth Dynasty, *c.* 1830 BC (height 4.5 cm; New York, MMA 16.1.3).
3. Gold arm band of Herihor set with an unusually large nugget of turquoise, Twentieth Dynasty, *c.* 1080 BC (diameter 9 cm; Hildesheim, Pelizaeus Museum, on loan from the Niedersächsische Sparkassenstiftung; Eggebrecht 1996: 76, fig. 71).
4. Gold human-headed *ba*-bird pendant inlaid with turquoise and lapis lazuli, of unknown provenance and dating to the Twenty-sixth Dynasty or later, after *c.* 600 BC (width 5 cm; BM EA3361).

Bibliography

Brugsch (1868); Weill (1908); Petrie and Currelly (1906); Barron (1907: 209–12); Thomas (1912); Barrois (1932); Starr and Butin (1936); Clère (1938); Gardiner and Peet (1952); Cerny (1955); Lucas (1962: 404–5); Rothenberg (1970; 1979: 13780); Giveon (1972, 1974, 1974–5, 1978, 1983); Beit-Arieh (1977, 1980); Chartier-Raymond (1988); Bonnet *et al.* (1994); Chartier-Raymond *et al.* (1994); Levene (1998).

Volcanic ash *see* tuff and tuffaceous limestone

Stone-working technology

A great deal of the impact of Egyptian civilization derives from the products of stone-working technology. On the largest scale there are the techniques of stone-dressing, masonry and civil engineering employed in the construction of such ceremonial buildings as *mastaba*s, pyramids, temples and palaces. In addition, however, a substantial amount of skill and energy was expended on the carving of stone sculpture and such characteristically Egyptian artefacts as offering tables, sarcophagi and stone vessels. Finally there was a highly-developed area of technology devoted to the conversion of gemstones into items of jewellery. The section below provides brief summaries of the technologies associated with each of these types of stone product. Given that this is a wide area, we have concentrated both on the provision of bibliographical information and on the discussion of recent developments.

Masonry

As far as stone masonry is concerned, many volumes have been published describing the surviving remains of pharaonic temples and tombs, whether in the form of travellers' accounts, archaeological reports or architectural histories (Badawy 1954–68 and Smith 1958 being the first attempts to provide comprehensive historical surveys). Although there have been many meticulous studies of specific sites or buildings, only a few – notably Petrie's surveys of the pyramids at Giza and Meidum in 1883 and 1892 – have focused on the technological aspects of the structures. On the other hand, it is remarkable that, despite Petrie's concern with the minutiae of many aspects of craftwork and tools, his general works include no study of the structural engineering of the Pharaonic period.

This gap in the literature began to be filled in the 1920s with Reginald Engelbach's studies of obelisks (Engelbach 1922, 1923), Ludwig Borchardt's many detailed studies of pyramid complexes and sun temples (e.g. Borchardt 1926, 1928) and the first edition of Alfred Lucas' *Ancient Egyptian Materials and Industries* (Lucas 1926), which included a substantial section devoted to the scientific study of stone working. However, the first real turning point arrived in 1930 with the publication of *Ancient Egyptian Masonry*, in which Engelbach collaborated with Somers Clarke to produce a detailed technological study of Egyptian construction methods from quarry to building site (Clarke and Engelbach 1930).

The meticulous excavations of George Reisner at Giza and elsewhere soon afterwards bore fruit in the form of the publication of *The Development of the Egyptian Tomb down to the Accession of Cheops* (Reisner 1936), and Reisner's work at Giza was later supplemented by the architectural reconstruction of the Step Pyramid of Djoser at Saqqara by Jean-Philippe Lauer, whose *Observations sur les pyramides* (Lauer 1960) was also informed by a sense of the fundamental practicalities of ancient stone masonry. Both I.E.S. Edwards (1947, 5th edn. 1993) and Rainer Stadelmann (1985) produced general books on Egyptian pyramids which built on the observations of Borchardt, Reisner, Lauer and others, including substantial discussion of the technological problems encountered by Pharaonic builders. Christopher Eyre (1987) has provided a detailed study of the textual and visual evidence for the organisation of labour in the Old and New Kingdoms, which includes a great deal of data relating to quarrying and building (particularly covering such questions as the composition, management and remuneration of the workforce involved in procuring, transporting and working stone, as well as the timing of quarrying and construction projects).

Most recently, Dieter Arnold's *Building in Egypt: Pharaonic Stone Masonry*, published in 1991, is a wide-ranging study of the data, including meticulous discussion of the surviving evidence for quarrying and stone-working tools, and sophisticated, well-illustrated studies of the grooves and marks on stone blocks which can indicate many of the ways in which they were transported, manoeuvred into position and interlocked with the rest of the masonry. Like Clarke and Engelbach's *Ancient Egyptian Masonry*, it serves as an essential and welcome basis for all future study of Pharaonic stone masonry. Arnold's primary concern is with the technology rather than the materials; for a detailed discussion of the different types of stone utilised by the Egyptians in art and architecture, see De Putter and Karlshausen (1992).

An area of structural stone-working that has still received comparatively little treatment is the study of the procedures and techniques of rock-tomb architecture as opposed to free-standing buildings. The Eighteenth-Dynasty élite rock-cut funerary chapels at Amarna represent a useful opportunity to observe various stages in the process, since they were all abandoned before final use, many of them at a relatively early point in terms of ancient excavation and decoration. Owen and Kemp (1994) have made a preliminary study of the unfinished tombs at Amarna, noting that the characteristic procedure was to cut out the first part of the outer hall of the chapel at ceiling level, and then to cut downwards towards the intended floor-level, usually hollowing out first the transverse area at the front and then the aisle between the colonnades further in. The stone-workers then seem to have gradually hollowed out the rest of the tomb from the ceiling downwards, resulting in a stepped effect when the work was stopped prematurely. The blocked-out outlines of lintels and columns are often visible, the latter being cone-shaped initially in order to accommodate the eventual column-base, as well as leaving plenty of excess rock for the process of decorative cutting. Owen and Kemp (1994: 3) also make the point that all this initial work seems to have been executed with a 'metal bar chisel' (Pendlebury 1951: I, 72, II, pl. LXXIX.3.30), whereas the next stage – the dressing of the surfaces – was accomplished, probably by a different, more skilled set of workmen, using a chisel with a narrower blade, the marks from which are visible in the form of shallow chisel marks cut at a greater variety of angles than the rougher first-stage chiselling.

The related topic of the carving of monolithic columns, which was first scientifically addressed by Engelbach (1928), in the form of an experimental study of the method of production of a Fifth-Dynasty example from the pyramid complex of Sahura at Abusir, has more recently been examined by the Martin Isler (1992), following on from an earlier study of the production of obelisks (Isler 1987) and drawing on his personal experience as a stone sculptor. Like Owen and Kemp, he argues that columns were quarried in such a way that the major part of a column, obelisk or sculpture could be completed by a relatively unskilled stone-cutter, thus minimising the numbers of sculptors who would be required at any one time (Isler 1992: 54).

Vessels

Like the creation of stone masonry, the carving of stone vessels reached a comparatively early peak in ancient Egypt, and became firmly established as one of the most characteristic products of Egyptian craftsmen from the Predynastic period onwards. Indeed, the great antiquity of this area of technology appears to be confirmed by the fact that the Egyptian term for 'craftsman' (*ḥmwty*), written with a determinative sign in the form of a drill, was initially used only to refer to those workers who drilled out stone vessels.

Until the publication of Barbara Aston's *Ancient Egyptian Stone Vessels* in 1994, the only general publications on this topic were the catalogue of stone vessels in the Cairo Museum compiled by Friedrich von Bissing (1907) and a typological study of stone and metal vessels by Flinders Petrie (1937). A few other publications have appeared in recent years, but all these have concentrated on specific periods (e.g. el-Khouli 1978 on Early Dynastic vessels; Reisner 1931, 1932 and Bernard 1966–7 on Old Kingdom vessels; el-Khouli *et al.* 1994 on the vessels from the tomb of Tutankhamun; and Lilyquist 1996 on Second Intermediate Period and New Kingdom vessels). Aston's study of the materials and forms of ancient Egyptian stone vessels combines field survey and petrographic analysis to produce a thorough study of changing materials and forms.

The initial stages of vessel production clearly consisted of a process by which the fragment of stone was roughly shaped and smoothed with stone tools. No monograph has yet tackled the question of the means by which the interiors of stone vessels were hollowed out, although a number of insights have been provided by ethnoarchaeological and experimental studies (Hester and Heizer 1981; Stocks 1986a, 1986b, 1993). In 1972, Thomas Hester and Robert Heizer undertook an ethnographic and technological study of the modern 'alabaster' workshops at the Upper Egyptian village of Sheikh Abd el-Gurna on the west bank opposite Luxor, both in order to record a unique modern cottage industry and in an attempt to gain new insights into ancient techniques of vessel carving and drilling (Hester and Heizer 1981).

Denys Stocks has studied such pictorial evidence as Old and New Kingdom hieroglyphs representing boring tools (Stocks 1993: fig. 3) and depictions of the use of the so-called twist-reverse-twist drill (or TRTD) in various tombs, including that of Mereruka at Saqqara (Sixth-Dynasty; Duell 1938), that of Pepyankh at Meir (Twelfth-Dynasty), and those of Rekhmira at Thebes and Iby at Thebes (Eighteenth-Dynasty and Twenty-sixth-Dynasty; see Stocks 1986b: fig. 1). On the basis of such depictions, Stocks succeeded in creating modern replicas of the figure-of-eight stone borer and the TRTD, thus producing an experimental limestone vessel. With a height of 10.7 cm and a diameter of 10 cm, the vessel took 22 hours, 35 minutes to make (including the exterior shaping, interior tubular drilling and stone boring). Stocks points out that bow-driven tubes produce a tapering drill core, whereas the use of the TRTD results in a parallel-sided core, as in the case of an uncatalogued alabaster gypsum vase in the Petrie Museum. Although bow-driven tubes would have been five times faster than the TRTD, they would have provided insufficient leverage and control, and Stocks' experiments showed that the vessels could actually be broken by the additional mechanical stresses involved in using a bow.

The final stage of the ancient production process consisted of the smoothing and polishing of the vessel both inside and outside, which took place largely with the use of stones and quartz sand. The more delicate parts of the vessels, such as lugs, handles and lips, would have been worked with fine copper chisels.

Gemstones

From as early as the Neolithic period, the Egyptians were using gemstones for jewellery. By the Pharaonic period they were carving and piercing a wide variety of stones, including amethyst, cornelian, chrysoprase, garnet, haematite, milky quartz, sard, jasper, malachite, agate, mica, rock crystal, serpentinite, lapis lazuli, olivine, fluorspar, turquoise, microcline and beryl. The earliest beads were probably created with the use of flint or chert tools, but as early as the Naqada period copper drills were being used to perforate the stone, while copper wires were employed to cut small gems, sometimes leaving serrations that are still visible on the stone. Both the drills and wires achieved their effect by combination with quartz sand and emery abrasives. By the New Kingdom, jewel-makers were employing sophisticated bow-drilling equipment in order to drive the drills.

As with stone vessel production, the study of gemstone working has been significantly advanced by the experimental work of Denys Stocks (1986c, 1989). Six Theban tombs, dating to the Eighteenth and Nineteenth Dynasties, contain scenes showing the drilling of stone beads, including one instance of the drilling of three beads simultaneously (in the tomb of Rekhmira). Although no archaeological examples of such multiple drills have survived, Stocks used the information provided by the six tomb-scenes to construct a replica multiple drill and bow (hypothesising that the bow shaft was probably made from some kind of bamboo-like reed (e.g. *Arundo donax*). He notes not only that the bows depicted in the tomb of Rekhmira were longer than those represented in other tombs (at about 120 cm in length) but also that the operators of the drills had their fingers entwined in the bow-strings at the far end. His experimental work shows that this technique was essential for multiple drilling.

Sculpture

In a culture characterised by the anonymity of the artist and craftworker, it is no doubt significant that those who sculpted statues were not only frequently described by their peronal names in the captions accompanying funerary scenes of sculptors' workshops, but were also sometimes shown in contexts other than the working environment (e.g. eating, carrying offerings, or accompanying the deceased on hunting trips), and were evidently taken on as individual employees, rather than simply being part of the permanent workforce of the deceased. Rosemarie Drenkhahn (1995) therefore argues that sculptors (and also the painters who decorated statues) were higher in status than other craftsmen, and would have been much more closely involved with their employer:

> The carving of a statue created a close and personal relationship between the patron commissioning the work and the sculptor, for the statue was an embodiment of the patron that was placed in his tomb and as such formed an essential precondition for his continued existence in the next world. (Drenkhahn 1995: 339)

Because of Egyptian artistic conventions, ancient depictions of sculptors' workshops (e.g. those in the Eighteenth-Dynasty Theban tomb-chapel of Rekhmira, see Fig. 2.30) tend to show the statues in their finished state, even when they are clearly at comparatively early stages in the process. However, a great deal of information on the various stages of statue-carving has survived in the form of unfinished sculptures of many periods (e.g. the Twenty-sixth-Dynasty semi-worked limestone statue of a standing man in the Institute of Arts, Detroit, and a number of unfinished statues of the Third-Dynasty king Djoser from his Step Pyramid complex at Saqqara, now in the Egyptian Mu-

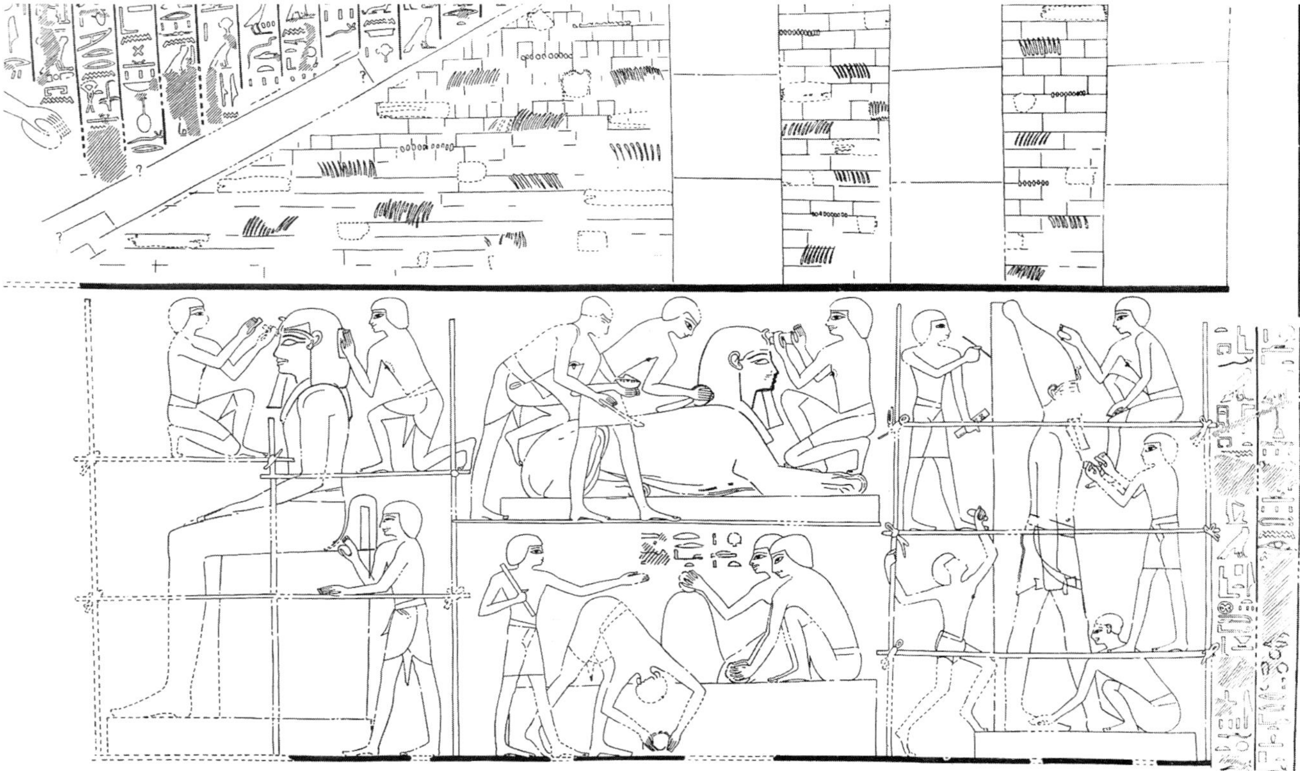

Figure 2.30 Scene from the tomb of Rekhmira at Thebes (TT100), showing sculptors polishing and inscribing colossal statues of Thutmose III.

seum, Cairo), and excavations of settlement sites have revealed the contents of several sculptor's workshops at the Eighteenth-Dynasty city of Amarna. The finds from the studio of Thutmose at Amarna (Roeder 1941; Krauss 1983) show that sculptors may have copied plaster 'masks' and busts in order to standardise the facial portraiture of statues of members of the élite. Such workshops also contain various parts of composite statues, such as separately carved limbs, torsos, heads and headgear, carved from several different types of stone.

These archaeological remains show that the basic sculpting process was to rough out a cube of rock, which then had preliminary drawings executed on all sides, thus providing guidelines for the sculptors (which, in the case of colossal statues, comprised large teams of workers perched on scaffolding) as they worked inwards simultaneously from each side. In the Pharaonic period, they primarily used stone tools for the initial roughing out, but then gradually employed finer copper or bronze tools, until the final minute details were incised with pointed chisels and/or drills. As with the stone vessels, the statues were eventually polished with rubbing stones and quartz sand, although the final production stage was the application of coloured pigments.

Summary of methods of scientific analysis

Introduction

Rock and mineral deposits are usually heterogeneous on the scale of outcrops and quarries, and sometimes can even be quite variable on the scale of individual artefacts. Any petrological analysis of archaeological stone must therefore incorporate a sampling plan that takes this heterogeneity into account. Obtaining a statistically representative sample is easy for outcrops and quarries but not for artefacts which would be damaged by such sampling. Thus samples of artefacts tend to be very few (often only one), very small (less than one gram) and taken from only certain areas (hidden or broken sides), and consequently may not be representative of the object as a whole. Any conclusions based on the analytical results must be qualified accordingly. If, however, a megascopic examination of an artefact reveals it to be compositionally uniform and, in the case of rocks, fine-grained, then a single small sample will probably suffice.

Once a sample of archaeological stone is collected, two questions need to be answered: what is it, and where does it come from? Approaches to answers for these questions are discussed in the next two sections. With the exception of megascopic analyses, the analytical methods described below can be performed by commercial laboratories and, for a fee, by some university laboratories affiliated with geology or chemistry departments.

Identifications

Megascopic analyses

Many rocks and minerals can be identified, at least preliminarily, by a megascopic examination. Good general reference books with excellent colour photographs of typical specimens are Mottana *et al.* (1978), Pellant (1992), and Hall (1994). Less well illustrated but more authoritative reference books are Klein and Hurlbut (1993) for minerals, and Raymond (1995) and Blatt and Tracy (1996) for rocks. Brown and Harrell (1991) provide a good summary of rock classifications suitable for megascopic work.

Equipment and supplies needed include: a hand lens (preferably with 5 × to 10 × magnification and large diameter lens, at least 20 mm, for a wide, bright field of view); a toothbrush with stiff bristles for cleaning surfaces; a small magnet; dilute (5%) hydrochloric acid for testing carbonate content; a small plate of unglazed porcelain for testing streak colour; and, for testing the Mohs scratch hardness, a steel pocket knife or dental pick, a copper or bronze coin, and a small plate of glass. Even better are commercially available sets of metal-tipped scribers representing all the Mohs hardnesses from 2 to 9. Portable hydrometers, used to determine specific gravity (i.e. density) are also commercially available and easy to operate. Minerals can be identified from their unique set of physiochemical properties, including some combination of the following: external crystal form, colour, lustre, streak, cleavage or fracture, scratch hardness, magnetism, specific gravity, reaction to acid, and others. Rocks are classified on the basis of their composition (varieties and relative abundances of minerals present) and texture (grain size, grain articulation – crystalline or clastic, and structures such as foliation for metamorphic rocks).

Thin-section petrography

This is the best method for identifying minerals in rocks, determining their volumetric percentages, and describing their textures. The descriptions of rocks in this chapter are based primarily on thin-section petrography.

A thin-section is a thirty micron-thick slice of rock mounted on a glass slide. These can be prepared from rock chips of any size or shape, but the chip must be at least five millimetres thick to accommodate standard equipment. Thin-sections are examined using a 'polarising transmitted-light (i.e. petrographic) microscope'. Good reference books on thin section petrography are: Ehlers (1987), Nesse (1991), Mackenzie and Guilford (1980) and MacKenzie and Adams (1994) for minerals; Williams *et al.* (1982), MacKenzie *et al.* (1982) and Yardley *et al.* (1990) for igneous and metamorphic rocks; and Scholle (1978, 1979), Adams *et al.* (1984) and Carozzi (1993) for sedimentary rocks.

Analytical methods

There is an enormous variety of analytical methods that can potentially be applied to rocks and minerals. Those described below are only the ones most commonly used in petrological studies. Informative summaries of these methods, with bibliographies, are given in Tucker (1988: 191–354) and Lewis and McConchie (1994: 144–81).

X-ray powder diffraction (XRD)

Sub-gram size, powdered rock or mineral samples are irradiated with x-rays in a 'x-ray powder diffractometer'. Diffraction of x-rays by atoms in the crystal structures of the minerals present permits their identification as well as a semi-quantitative determination of their relative abundances. After thin-section petrography, this is the best method for identifying minerals, except in the case of clay minerals, where XRD is superior to thin-sectioning. Examples of the use of XRD on Egyptian rocks all involve limestone and include Bradley and Middleton (1988), Middleton and Bradley (1989), Campbell and Folk (1991), Harrell and Penrod (1993) and Ingram *et al.* (1993).

X-ray fluorescence spectrometry (XRF)

Five or fewer grams of a powdered rock sample are irradiated with x-rays in an 'x-ray fluorescence spectrometer'. Analysis of wavelengths and intensities of the secondary x-rays emitted by the sample permits identification of the elements present and a fully quantitative determination of their relative amounts. The results are normally presented as weight percents of the oxides for the elements (e.g., calcium and iron would be reported as CaO and FeO, respectively). The method works best for major and minor elements (those present in amounts exceeding 0.001 weight percent or 10 ppm) with atomic numbers larger than about eight. XRF is an essential method for analysing volcanic igneous rocks where the groundmass is usually too fine-grained for thin-section petrography. Thin sections are still needed, however, to identify the phenocrysts and other coarser phases in these rocks. XRF is also a popular method for all other rock types when an inexpensive whole-rock chemical analysis is needed. Examples of the use of XRF include Klemm and Klemm (1981: fig. 9), Harrell (1992) and Harrell and Penrod (1993) for limestone; el-Hinnawi and Loukina (1972) for travertine; Klemm *et al.* (1984) for quartzite; and Klemm and Klemm (1993; partial data only) and Brown and Harrell (1995) for a wide variety of igneous and metamorphic rocks.

Scanning electron microscopy (SEM)

Gold- or carbon-coated pieces of rock or mineral are illuminated with an electron beam in a 'scanning electron microscope' to reveal details of grain morphologies and textures too small to be seen in thin sections. Magnifications of at least 30,000 × are possible and range up to

100,000 × or higher depending on the instrument. These magnifications are not only far higher than those attainable with petrographic microscopes (normally at most 500 × to 750 ×, depending on the lenses used), but, unlike thin sections, SEM provides three-dimensional images of surfaces and these are especially useful for investigating textures and grain morphologies. More useful, however, are the semi-quantitative elemental analyses obtainable from a microscope equipped with an 'energy dispersive x-ray analysis system' (EDS). EDS is very similar to x-ray fluorescence spectrometry but has the advantage of being able to irradiate an area on a sample specimen as small as one micron across. Although the resulting elemental analysis is only semi-quantitative, it can still be useful for identifying the mineralogy of a specific grain. This may be needed, for example, when a rare or unfamiliar mineral cannot be identified in thin section. The thin section itself can then be examined with SEM.

Another instrument sometimes attached to the microscope is the 'wavelength dispersive spectrometer' (WDS). This is essentially an x-ray fluorescence spectrometer but differs from the XRF instrumentation in that excitation of secondary x-rays from elements is caused by an electron beam rather than primary x-rays. Unlike the EDS, WDS provides fully quantitative elemental analyses. Examples of the use of SEM-EDS all involve limestones and include Bradley and Middleton (1988), Middleton and Bradley (1989), Harrell and Penrod (1993), Ingram *et al.* (1993) and Klemm and Klemm (1993: 34–44).

The 'electron microprobe' (or 'probe') is a more specialised and efficient combination of a scanning electron microscope and multiple wavelength dispersive spectrometers. It is the instrument of choice for performing fully quantitative elemental analyses of micron-size areas on rock and mineral specimens. 'Electron microprobe analysis' (EMPA) has been applied to tonalite gneiss by Peacock *et al.* (1994).

Instrumental neutron activation analysis (INAA)

Whereas the scanning electron microscope and electron microprobe provide elemental analyses of parts of a single grain, 'instrumental neutron activation analysis' provides the same information for whole-rock samples. It is especially good for carbonate rocks like marble, limestone and travertine. For these and other rock types, the elements most commonly analysed by this method are those with atomic numbers 57 and above. Depending on the elements sought and the detection limits desired, one to thirty grams of powdered rock are needed. The sample is placed within a nuclear reactor or synchroton and irradiated with neutrons. The resulting radioactivity generated by the sample is analysed by a gamma-ray spectrometer to determine the amounts (in parts per million) and types of elements present. INAA is especially good for trace element analyses but the large sample sizes required often makes it inappropriate for artefacts. Examples of the use of INAA include: Meyers and van Zelst (1977) for limestone; and Heizer *et al.* (1973), Bowman *et al.* (1984) and Stross *et al.* (1988) for quartzite.

Atomic absorption spectrophotometry (AAS)

This method is a popular alternative to INAA for quantitative whole-rock elemental analyses. It has the advantages of providing lower detection limits, requiring only 0.1 gram samples, and detecting more (over fifty) elements. Samples are dissolved in acid and the solution aspirated into a flame in the 'atomic absorption spectrophotometer'. The wavelengths and amounts of incident light absorbed by the heated atoms indicate the concentrations (in parts per million) and types of elements present. A closely related method, 'flame photometry', determines elemental composition from the wavelengths and intensities of light emitted by the heated atoms. This latter method is normally used only to analyse Li, Na, Ca, K, Sr and Rb. Examples of the use of AAS include Oddy *et al.* (1976), and Campbell and Folk (1991) for limestone; Klemm *et al.* (1984) for quartzite; and Klemm and Klemm (1993; partial data only) for virtually all rock types.

Inductively-coupled plasma spectrometry (ICP)

The atomic absorption spectrophotometer is now being replaced by the 'inductively-coupled plasma spectrometer' which can analyse more elements simultaneously, and more rapidly with lower detection limits. AAS, however, is still superior for detection of Na and K. An acidised sample solution is combined with argon gas in radio-frequency coils to form a high-temperature plasma. The atomised and ionised sample is then analysed by either of two procedures. ICP-optical (or atomic) emission spectrometry (ICP-AES or ICP-OES) is similar to flame photometry in that the wavelengths and intensities of light energy emitted by the excited atoms in the plasma are used to identify the elements present. In ICP-mass spectrometry (ICP-MS), in contrast, the elements in the plasma are identified by a mass spectrometer. An example of the use of ICP-AES is Ingram *et al.* (1993) for limestone.

Stable isotope fractionation

Isotopes of oxygen (16 and 18), carbon (12 and 13) and sulphur (32 and 34) are now widely used to characterise carbonate rocks such as limestone, travertine and especially marble. The relative amounts (fractionation) of the isotopic pairs are determined in sub-gram, powdered samples using a 'mass spectrometer'. The analyses are time-consuming and labour-intensive, and so there are relatively few laboratories offering this service. Examples of the use of this method all involve marble and include Brown and Harrell (1995) and Harrell (1996).

Thermogravimetric analysis (TGA)

Limestone and rock gypsum contain minerals that, when

heated, evolve gases such as water vapour, carbon dioxide and sulphur dioxide. This characteristic is useful for distinguishing among varieties of these rocks. In TGA, a subgram, powdered sample is gradually heated within a 'thermogravimeter', which records the progressive reduction in weight due to loss of volatile components with increasing temperature. 'Differential thermal analysis' (DTA) is a closely related method that measures, with increasing temperature, changes in the heat content of a sample due to any of a variety of possible reactions. An example of the use of TGA on limestone is Harrell and Penrod (1993).

Provenance studies

Provenance studies seek to discover the ancient quarry supplying a rock or mineral, or, at the very least, a localised geographic area (or areas) where outcrops of the same material can be found. In order for this to be possible, a comprehensive, detailed geologic database must exist where all rock formations and mineral deposits in an area have been described and mapped, and all ancient quarries have been located and petrologically characterised. In the case of Egypt, such a database is still incomplete. However, good descriptions of the geology of Egypt are given in Said (1990), and an excellent series of geologic maps covering the country have been published by Klitzsch *et al.* (1986–7), with explanations provided by Hermina *et al.* (1989). For maps and reports on specific areas within Egypt, the publications of the Egyptian Geological Survey and Mining Authority should be consulted.

All the major and most of the minor quarries of ancient Egypt have been located (Harrell *et al.* 1996); these are listed in Tables 2.1 and 2.2 and their locations are shown on the maps in Figures 2.1a and b and 2.2. Petrological descriptions of the rocks from these quarries are given in relatively few sources: Akaad and Naggar (1964a, 1964b, 1965); Klemm (1986); Klemm and Klemm (1979, 1981 and 1993); Klemm *et al.* (1984); Harrell (1992, forthcoming (a) and (b)); Brown and Harrell (1995); Harrell and Bown (1995); Harrell and Brown (1994); and Harrell *et al.* (forthcoming).

There have been relatively few attempts at provenancing ancient Egyptian materials based on petrological analyses. Aston (1994) analysed, by thin-section petrography, all the different rock types used for stone vessels from the late Predynastic period through the Old Kingdom. She also collected some quarry samples, and based on these and the geological literature was able to determine the provenance of many of the materials. Meyers and van Zelst (1977) investigated the trace element content (by INAA) of limestone artefacts from numerous sites along the Nile River, but did not sample limestone outcrops or quarries. On the basis of the trace element 'signatures', they were able to distinguish between artefacts coming from the areas near Thebes and north of Thebes. Middleton and Bradley (1989) also analysed limestone artefacts from many sites between Thebes and Giza, and included samples from two ancient quarries. By using a combination of thin-section petrography, SEM-EDS and XRD, they were able to distinguish among limestone objects originating from the Thebes-Abydos, Deir el-Bersha and Cairo areas.

The most contentious investigation of provenance involved analyses of quartzite by Heizer *et al.* (1973), Bowman *et al.* (1984) and Stross *et al.* (1988) using thin-section petrography and INAA, and by Klemm *et al.* (1984) using thin-section petrography, XRF and AAS. Samples from the Colossi of Memnon in western Thebes and other quartzite artefacts were collected by these investigators and compared with samples from the only known ancient quarries for this rock type at Gebel Ahmar near Cairo and the Gebels Tingar-Gulab area near Aswan (see section on quartzite above for additional discussion). McGill and Kowalski (1977) re-analysed the INAA data of Heizer *et al.* (1973) using a variety of multivariate statistical methods.

The study of the provenance of the tonalite gneiss quarried during the Roman period at Mons Claudianus, involving the analysis of numerous samples of similar-looking rocks from sites throughout the Roman empire, was undertaken by David Peacock *et al.* (1994), using megascopic and chemical identification. They employed XRF to compare variations in Y and Zr, and EPMA to compare variations in the Mg and Fe content of the amphiboles, and the Ti and Al content of biotites. They were able to distinguish clearly between three principal ancient sources: (1) Mons Claudianus, (2) the Kozak Dag area of Turkey, and (3) the Cavoli region of Elba, thus demonstrating that the tonalite gneiss (or 'granito del foro') from Mons Claudianus was used in a much smaller number of sites than previously thought (various monuments in Rome, Diocletian's Mausoleum in Split, and possibly Hagia Sophia in Istanbul). Peacock *et al.* (1994: 229) thus conclude that 'the distribution and restricted use contrasts markedly with that of other great decorative stones such as the granite from Aswan . . . all of which suggests that Mons Claudianus may have been a rather special stone, perhaps restricted to the emperor himself'.

There have been few provenance studies of Egyptian gemstones, although some recent analysis has been undertaken on samples of beryl from the Sikait-Zubara region in the Eastern Desert. Grubessi *et al.* (1989, 1990) used XRD and infrared spectroscopy to characterise the emeralds from Gebel Zubara, comparing them with others from mines in Brazil, Austria, Columbia and the Urals.

References

Adams, A.E., MacKenzie, W.S. and Guilford, C. 1984. *Atlas of Sedimentary Rocks under the Microscope*. New York: John Wiley.

Ahmed, S.M. 1993. Collapse and solution red breccia of the Issawia Sharq locality, Nile valley, Upper Egypt. *Egyptian Journal of Geology*, 37/2: 187–202.

Akaad, M.K. and Naggar, M.H. 1964a. Petrography of the Egyptian alabaster of Wadi Al Assyuti. *Bulletin of the Faculty of Science, Alexandria University*, 6: 157–73.

1964b. The deposit of Egyptian alabaster at Wadi El Assyuti. *BSGE*, 36: 29–39.

1965. Geology of the Wadi Sannur alabaster and the general geological history of the Egyptian alabaster deposits. *Bulletin de l'Institut du Desert de l'Egypte*, 13/2: 35–63.

Akaad, M.K. and Noweir, A.M. 1972. Some aspects of the serpentinites and their associated derivatives along Qift-Quseir Road, Eastern Desert. *AGSE*, 2: 251–70.

Alford, C.J. 1901. Gold mining in Egypt. *Transactions of the Institute of Mining and Metallurgy* (London), 10: 2–28.

Altenmüller, H. and Moussa, A.M. 1981. Die Inschriften der Taharkastele von der Dahschurstrasse. *SAK*, 9: 57–84.

Andrew, G. 1938. On imperial porphyry. *BIE*, 20: 63–81.

1939. The greywackes of the Eastern Desert of Egypt, Part I. *BIE*, 21: 153–90.

Andrews, C.A. 1981. *Catalogue of Egyptian Antiquities in the British Museum VI: Jewellery I: From the Earliest Times to the Seventeenth Dynasty*. London: BMP.

1990. *Ancient Egyptian Jewellery*. London: BMP.

Arnold, D. 1987. *Der Pyramidenbezirk des Königs Amenemhet III. in Dahschur* I. Mainz: von Zabern.

1991. *Building in Egypt: Pharaonic Stone Masonry*. New York and Oxford: OUP.

Arnold, F. 1990. *South Cemeteries of Lisht II: The Control Notes and Team Marks*. New York: MMA.

Aston, B.G. 1994, *Ancient Egyptian Stone Vessels: Materials and Forms*. Studien zur Archäologie und Geschichte Altägyptens 5. Heidelberg: Heidelberger Orientverlag.

Attia, M.I. 1955. *Topography, Geology and Iron-ore Deposits of the District East of Aswan*. Cairo: GSE.

Aufrère, S. 1991. *L'univers minéral dans la pensée égyptienne* (2 vols.). Cairo: IFAO.

Badawy, A. 1954–68. *A History of Egyptian Architecture*, 3 vols. Cairo: Urwand (vol. 1); Berkeley and Los Angeles, CA: University of California Press (vols. 2–3).

Ball, J. 1907. *A Description of the First or Aswan Cataract of the Nile*. Cairo: GSE.

1912. *Geography and Geology of South-eastern Egypt*. Cairo: GSE.

Barrois, A. 1932. The Serabit expedition of 1930. *Harvard Theological Review*, 25: 101–21

Barron, T. 1907. *Topography and Geology of the Peninsula of Sinai: Western Portion*. Cairo: GSE.

Barron, T. and Hume, W.F. 1902. *Topography and Geology of the Eastern Desert of Egypt: Central Portion*. Cairo: GSE.

Baumgartel, E.J. 1960. *The Cultures of Prehistoric Egypt* II. London: OUP.

Bavay, L. 1997. Matière première et commerce à longue distance: le lapis-lazuli et l'Egypte prédynastique. *Archéo-Nil*, 7: 65–79.

Bavay, L., De Putter, T., Adams, B., Navez, J. and André, L. 2000. The origin of obsidian in Predynastic and Early Dynastic Upper Egypt. *MDAIK*, 56.

Beit-Arieh, I. 1977. South Sinai: The Early Bronze Age. Doctoral dissertation. Tel Aviv University, Israel.

1980. A Chalcolithic site near Serabit el-Khadim. *Tel Aviv*, 7: 45–64.

Bernard, M. 1966–7. Les Vases en pierre de l'ancien empire (Ve et VIe dynasties). Unpublished dissertation. Université catholique de Louvain, Faculté de philosophie et lettres, Institut supérieur d'archéologie et d'histoire de l'art.

Bissing, F.W. von 1907. *Steingefäße*. CGC 18065–18793. Vienna: Adolf Holzhausen.

Blatt, H. and Tracy, R.J. 1996. *Petrology: Igneous, Sedimentary, and Metamorphic* (2nd edn.). New York: W. H. Freeman.

Blom-Böer, I. 1994. Zusammensetzung altägyptischer Farbpigmente und ihre Herkunftslagerstätten in Zeit und Raum. *OMRO*, 74: 55–107.

Bomann, A. 1995. Eastern Desert [part of 'Digging Diary' section]. *EA*, 6: 30.

Bonnet, C., Le Saout, F. and Valbelle, D. 1994. Le temple de la déesse Hathor, maîtresse de la turquoise, à Sérabit el-Khadim. *CRIPEL*, 16: 15–30.

Borchardt, L. 1926. *Längen und Richtungen der vier Grundkanten der grossen Pyramide bei Gise*. Cairo: Beiträge zur ägyptischen Bauforschung und Altertumskunde.

1928. *Die Entstehung der Pyramide an der Baugeschichte der Pyramide bei Mejdum nachgewiesen*. Berlin: J. Springer.

Boukhary, M.A. and Malik, W.M.A. 1983. Revision of the stratigraphy of the Eocene deposits of Egypt. *Neues Jahrbuch für Geologie und Palaeontologie Monatshefte*, 6: 321–37.

Bourriau, J. 1988. *Pharaohs and Mortals: Egyptian Art in the Middle Kingdom*. Cambridge: CUP.

Bowman, H., Stross, F.H., Asaro, F., Hay, R.L., Heizer, R.F. and Michel, H.V. 1984. The northern colossus of Memnon. *Archaeometry*, 26/2: 218–29.

Bradley, S.M. and Middleton, A.P. 1988. A study of the deterioration of Egyptian limestone sculpture. *Journal of the American Institute for Conservation*, 27: 64–86.

Brown, V.M. and Harrell, J.A. 1991. Megascopic classification of rocks. *Journal of Geological Education*, 39: 379–87.

1995. Topographical and petrological survey of ancient Roman quarries in the Eastern Desert of Egypt. In *The Study of Marble and Other Stones Used in Antiquity – ASMOSIA III, Athens: Transactions of the Third International Symposium of the Association for the Study of Marble and Other Stones in Antiquity* (eds. Y. Maniatis, N. Herz and Y. Bassiakis). London: Archetype, pp. 221–34.

1998. Aswan granite and granodiorite. *GM*, 164: 33–9.

Bruce, J. 1805. *Travels to Discover the Source of the Nile*, 2 vols., 2nd edn. London: G.C.J. and J. Robinson/Constable.

Brugsch, H. 1868. *Wanderung nach den Türkis-Minen und der Sinaï Halbinsel*. Leipzig: J.C. Hinrichs.

Brunton, G. 1920. *Lahun I*. London: Quaritch.

1930. *Qau and Badari III*. London: Quaritch.

1948. *Matmar*. London: BMP.

Cailliaud, F. 1821–62. *Voyage à l'Oasis de Thèbes et dans les déserts situés à l'orient et à l'occident de la Thébaide, fait pendant les années 1815–1818*. 2 vols. Paris: Imprimerie Royale.

Campbell, D.H. and Folk, R.L. 1991. The ancient Egyptian pyramids – concrete or rock? *Concrete International*, 13/8: 28, 30–9.

Carnarvon and Carter, H. 1912. *Five Years' Exploration at Thebes: A Record of Work Done 1907–1911*. London: OUP.

Carozzi, A.V. 1993. *Sedimentary Petrography*. Englewood Cliffs: Prentice Hall.

Castel, G. and Soukiassian, G. 1985. Dépôt de stèles dans le sanctuaire de nouvel empire au Gebel el-Zeit. *BIFAO*, 85: 285–93.

1989. *Gebel el-Zeit I: Les mines de galène (Egypte, IIe Millénaire av. J.C.)*. Cairo: IFAO.

Caton-Thompson, G. and Gardner, E.W. 1934. *The Desert Fayum*, 2 vols. London: Royal Anthropological Institute of Great Britain and Ireland.

Cerny, J. 1955. *Inscriptions of Sinai* II, 2nd edn. London: OUP.

Chartier-Raymond, M. 1988. Notes sur Maghara (Sinaï). *CRIPEL*, 10: 13–22.

Chartier-Raymond, M. Gratien, B., Traunecker, C. and Vinçon, J.-M. 1994. Les sites miniers pharaoniques du Sud-Sinaï: quelques notes et observations de terrain. *CRIPEL*,16: 31–80.

Clarke, S. and Engelbach, R. 1930. *Ancient Egyptian Masonry: The Building Craft*. London: Humphrey Milford and OUP.

Clère, J.J. 1938. Sur un nom du Wadi Maghara (Sinaï). *JEA*, 24: 125–6.

Couyat, J. and Montet, P. 1912. *Les Inscriptions hiéroglyphiques et hiératiques du Ouadi Hammamat*. Cairo: IFAO, pp. 1–141.

Dalloni M. and Monod, T. 1948. *Mission scientifique du Fezzan VI*. Algiers: Institut de Recherches Sahariennes de l'Université d'Alger.

Debono, F. 1971. Ateliers et carrières pharaoniques: (a) ateliers pour la fabrication d'outils de silex pharaoniques. In *Graffiti de la Montagne Thébaine I/2: La Vallée de l'Ouest* (ed. J. Černy). Cairo: Centre de la documentation et d'études sur l'ancienne Egypte, pp. 43–4.

1982. Rapport préliminaire sur les résultats de l'étude des objets de la fouille des installations du Moyen Empire et Hyksos à l'est du la sacré de Karnak. In *Cahiers de Karnak VII (1978–1981)*. Paris: Editions Recherche sur les Civilisations, pp. 377–83.

De Putter, T. and Karlshausen, C. 1992. *Les Pierres utilisées dans la sculpture et l'architecture de l'Egypte pharaonique: guide pratique illustré*. Brussels: Connaissance de l'Egypte Ancienne.

Desroches-Noblecourt, C. and Vercoutter, J. 1981. *Un Siècle de fouilles françaises en Egypte 1880–1980*. Cairo: IFAO and Louvre.

Dietrich, R.V. and Skinner, B.J. 1979. *Rocks and Rock Minerals*. New York: John Wiley and Sons.

Dodge, H. and Ward-Perkins, B. (eds.), 1992. *Marble in Antiquity: Collected Papers of J. B. Ward-Perkins*. Archaeological Monographs of the British School at Rome No. 6. London: British School at Rome.

Dott, R.H. 1964. Wacke, greywacke and matrix: what approach to immature sandstone classification? *Journal of Sedimentary Petrology*, 34: 625–32.

Drenkhahn, R. 1995. Artisans and artists in Pharaonic Egypt. In *Civilizations of the Ancient Near East* I (ed. J. Sasson). New York: Charles Scribner's Sons and Simon and Schuster Macmillan, pp. 331–43.

Dreyer, G. and Jaritz, H. 1983. Die Arbeiterunterkünfte am Sadd el-Kafara. In *Der Sadd el-Kafara: die älteste Talsperre der Welt*. Braunschweig: Leichtweiss-Institut für Wasserbau der Technischen Universität.

Duell, P. 1938. *The Mastaba of Mereruka*. 2 vols. Chicago: OIP.

Dunham, D. 1947. Four Kushite colossi in the Sudan. *JEA*, 33: 63–5.

Dunham, R.J. 1962. Classification of carbonate rocks according to depositional texture. In *Classification of Carbonate Rocks: A Symposium* (ed. W.E. Ham). Tulsa: American Association of Petroleum Geologists, Memoir 1, pp. 108–21.

Edwards, I.E.S. 1993. *The Pyramids of Egypt*. 5th edn. Harmondsworth: Penguin.

Eggebrecht, A. (ed.) 1996. *Pelizaeus Museum Hildesheim: The Egyptian Collection*. Mainz: von Zabern.

Ehlers, E.G. 1987. *Optical Mineralogy* (2 vols.). London: Blackwell Scientific.

Emery, W.B. 1938a. *The Tomb of Hemaka*. Cairo: SAE.

1938b. *The Royal Tombs of Ballana and Qustul*. 2 vols. Cairo: Government Press.

Engelbach, R. 1922. *The Aswan Obelisk*. Cairo: Department of Antiquities.

1923. *The Problem of the Obelisks: from a Study of the Unfinished Obelisk at Aswan*. New York: George H. Doran.

1928. An experiment on the accuracy of shaping a monolithic column of circular cross section of the Vth dynasty from Abusir. *ASAE*, 28: 144–52.

1931. Notes of inspection. *ASAE*, 31: 126–7, 132–7, pl. I.

1933. The quarries of the western Nubian Desert: a preliminary report. *ASAE*, 33: 65–74.

1938. The quarries of the western Nubian Desert and the ancient road to Tushka. *ASAE*, 38: 369–90.

Erman, A. 1885. *Ägypten und Ägyptisches Leben im Altertum*. 2 vols. Tübingen: H. Laupp'schen.

Eyre, C.J. 1987. Work and organization of work in the Old Kingdom and New Kingdom. In *Labor in the Ancient Near East* (ed. M.A. Powell). New Haven: American Oriental Society, pp. 5–48, 167–222.

Fakhry, A. 1946. A report of the inspectorate of Upper Egypt. *ASAE*, 46: 51–4.

1952. *The Inscriptions of the Amethyst Quarries at Wadi el-Hudi*. Cairo: Government Press.

Fischer, H.G. 1991. Sur les routes de l'ancien empire. *CRIPEL*, 13: 59–64.

Folk, R.L. 1962. Spectral subdivision of limestone types. In *Classification of Carbonate Rocks: A Symposium* (ed. W.E. Ham). Tulsa: American Association of Petroleum Geologists, Memoir 1, pp. 62–84.

Frankfort, H. 1939. *Cylinder Seals: A Documentary Essay on the Art and Religion of the Ancient Near East*. London: Macmillan.

French, C.A.I. 1984. Geomorphology and prehistory at Amarna. In *Amarna Reports* I (ed. B.J. Kemp). London: EES, pp. 202–11.

Frondel, C. 1962. *The System of Mineralogy III: Silica Minerals* (7th edn.). New York: John Wiley and Sons.

Galetti, G., L. Lazzarini and Maggetti, M. 1992. A first characterization of the most important granites used in antiquity. In *Ancient Stones: Quarrying, Trade and Provenance* (eds. M.

Waelkens, N. Herz and L. Moens). Leuven: Katholieke Universiteit Leuven, Acta Archaeologica Lovaniensia Monographiae 4, pp. 167–73.

Gardiner, A.H. 1941. Ramesside texts relating to the taxation and transportation of corn. *JEA*, 27: 19–73.

Gardiner, A.H. and Peet, T.E. 1952. *Inscriptions of Sinai* I (2nd edn.). London: OUP.

Garland, H. and Bannister, C.O. 1927. *Ancient Egyptian Metallurgy*. London: Griffin.

Garstang, J. 1907. Excavations at Hierakonpolis, at Esna and in Nubia. *ASAE*, 8: 135.

Gindy, A.R. 1956. The igneous and metamorphic rocks of the Aswan area, Egypt: their description, origin and age relations. *BIE*, 37/2:83–131.

Ginter, B., Kozlowski, J. and Drobniewicz, B. 1979. *Silexindustrien von el Tarif*. Mainz: von Zabern.

Giveon, R. 1972. Le temple d'Hathor à Serabit el-Khadem. *Archéologia*, 44: 64–9.

1974. Investigations in the Egyptian mining centers in Sinai. *Tel Aviv*, 1: 100–8.

1974–5. Egyptian objects from Sinaï in the Australian Museum. *Australian Journal of Biblical Archaeology*, 2/3: 29–47.

1978. *The Stones of Sinaï Speak*. Tokyo: Gakuseisha.

1983. Two officials of the Old Kingdom at Maghara (southern Sinaï). *Tel Aviv*, 10: 49–51.

Gnoli, R. 1988. *Marmora Romana*. Rome: Edizioni dell'Elefante.

Goedicke, H. 1962. Psammetik I. und die Libyer. *MDAIK*, 18: 26–49.

Goyon, G. 1957. *Nouvelles inscriptions rupestres du Wadi Hammamat*. Paris: Librarie d'Amerique et d'Orient Adrien-Maisonneuve.

Griffith, F.Ll. 1896. *Beni Hasan* III. London: ERA.

Griswold, W.A. 1992. Imports and social status: the role of long-distance trade in Predynastic Egypt state formation. Doctoral dissertation. Ann Arbor: UMI.

Grubessi, O., Aurisicchio, C. and Castiglioni, A. 1989. Lo smeraldo delle miniere dei faroni. *La Gemmologia*, 14: 7–21.

1990. The pharaohs' forgotten emerald mines. *Journal of Gemmology*, 22/3: 164–77.

Gundlach, R. 1980. Lapislazuli. *LÄ*, III: 937–8.

Habachi, L. 1960. Notes on the unfinished obelisk of Aswan and another smaller one in Gharb Aswan. In *Drevni i Egipet* (ed. V.V. Struve). Moscow: Institut Vostokovedeni i a, Akademi i a Nauk USSR, pp. 216–35.

1977. *The Obelisks of Egypt*. New York: Charles Scribner.

Habachi, L. and Biers, J. 1969. An agate bowl from Egypt. *Annual of the Museum of Art and Archaeology: University of Missouri, Columbia*, 3: 29–34.

Hall, C. 1994. *Eyewitness Handbook: Gemstones*. London: Dorling Kindersley.

Harden, D.B. 1954. Vasa Murrina again. *Journal of Roman Studies*, 44: 53.

Harrell, J.A. 1990, Misuse of the term 'alabaster' in Egyptology. *GM*, 119: 37–42.

1992. Ancient Egyptian limestone quarries: a petrological survey. *Archaeometry*, 34: 195–212.

1995. Ancient Egyptian origins of some common rock names. *Journal of Geological Education*, 43: 30–4.

1996. Geology. In *BERENIKE 1995: Preliminary Report on the 1995 Excavations at Berenike (Egyptian Red Sea Coast) and the Survey of the Eastern Desert* (eds. S.E. Sidebotham and W.Z. Wendrich). Leiden: Centre for Non-Western Studies, Leiden University, pp. 99–126.

forthcoming (a). Geology. In *The Survey of Gebel el-Haridi I* (ed. C.J. Kirby). London: EES.

forthcoming (b). The Tumbos quarry at the Third Nile Cataract, northern Sudan. *Meroitica*.

Harrell, J.A. and Bown, T.M. 1995. An Old Kingdom basalt quarry at Widan el-Faras and the quarry road to Lake Moeris in the Fayum, Egypt. *JARCE*, 32: 71–91.

Harrell, J.A. and Brown, V.M. 1992a. The world's oldest surviving geological map: the 1150 BC Turin papyrus from Egypt. *Journal of Geology*, 100: 3–18.

1992b. The oldest surviving topographical map from ancient Egypt (Turin Papyri 1879, 1899 and 1969). *JARCE*, 29: 81–105.

1994. Chephren's quarry in the Nubian Desert of Egypt. *Nubica*, 3/1: 43–57.

1999. A Late-Period quarry for naoi in the Eastern Desert. *EA*, 14: 18–20.

Harrell, J.A., Brown, V.M. and Lazzarini, L. in press. Two newly discovered Roman quarries in the Eastern Desert of Egypt. In *Actes D'ASMOSIA IV: Transactions of the Fourth International Symposium of the Association for the Study of Marble and Other Stones in Antiquity*. Bordeaux: Centre de Recherche en Physique Appliqué de l'Archéologie, Université de Bordeaux.

Harrell, J.A., Brown, V.M. and Masoud, M.S. 1996. Survey of ancient Egyptian quarries. *Egyptian Geological Survey and Mining Authority Paper 72*.

forthcoming. Early Dynastic quarry for stone vessels at Gebel Manzal el-Seyl, Eastern Desert. *JEA*.

Harrell, J.A. and Penrod, B.E. 1993. The great pyramid debate: evidence from the Lauer sample. *Journal of Geological Education*, 41: 358–63.

Hassan, A.A. and Hassan, F.A. 1981. Source of galena in predynastic Egypt at Naqada. *Archaeometry* , 23: 77–82.

Hawass, Z. and Verner, M. 1996. Newly discovered blocks from the causeway of Sahure. *MDAIK*, 52: 177–86.

Hayes, W.C. 1953. *The Scepter of Egypt* I. New York: MMA.

1959. *The Scepter of Egypt* II. New York: MMA.

Heikal, M.A., Hassan, M.A. and El-Sheshtawi, Y. 1983. The Cenozoic basalt of Gebel Qatrani, Western Desert, Egypt as an example of continental tholeiitic basalt. *AGSE*, 13: 193–209.

Heizer, R.F., Stross, F., Hester, T.R., Albee, A., Perlman, I., Asaro, F. and Bowman, H. 1973. The colossi of Memnon revisited. *Science*, 182: 1219–25.

Hermina, M., Klitzsch, E. and List, F.K. 1989. *Stratigraphic Lexicon and Explanatory Notes to The Geological Map of Egypt*. Cairo: Cononco Inc. and Egyptian General Petroleum Corp.

Herrmann, G. 1968. Lapis lazuli: the early phases of its trade. *Iraq*, 30: 21–57.

Herrmann, G. and Moorey, P.R.S. 1983. Lapis lazuli. *Reallexikon der Assyriologie und Vorderasiatischen Archäologie*, VI: 488–92.

Hester, T.R. and Heizer, R.F. 1981. *Making Stone Vases: Ethnoarchaeological Studies at an Alabaster Workshop in Upper Egypt*. Monographic Journals of the Near East. Malibu CA: Undena Publications.

el-Hinnawi, E.E. and Maksoud, M.A. 1968. Petrography of Cenozoic volcanic rocks of Egypt. *Geologische Rundschau*, 57: 879–90.

1972. Geochemistry of Egyptian Cenozoic basaltic rocks. *Chemie der Erde*, 31: 93–112.

el-Hinnawi, E.E. and Loukina, S.M. 1972. A contribution to the geochemistry of Egyptian alabaster. *Tschermaks Mineralogische und Petrographische Mitteilungen (Vienna)*, 17: 215–21.

Hoffmeier, J.K. 1993. The use of basalt in floors of Old Kingdom pyramid temples. *JARCE*, 30: 117–23.

Hume, W.F. 1934. *Geology of Egypt II: The Fundamental Precambrian Rocks of Egypt and the Sudan, 1: The Late Plutonic and Minor Intrusive Rocks*. Cairo: GSE.

1937. *Geology of Egypt II: The Fundamental Precambrian Rocks of Egypt and the Sudan, 3: The Minerals of Economic Value*. Cairo: GSE.

Hussein, A.A.A. and El-Sharkawi, M.A. 1990. Mineral deposits. In *The Geology of Egypt* (ed. R. Said). Rotterdam: A.A. Balkema, pp. 511–66.

Ibrahim, M.M. 1943. The petrified forest, part I. *BIE*, 25: 159–82.

1949. Ornamental stones in Egypt. *Transactions of the Mining and Petroleum Association of Egypt*, 4/1: 9–20.

1953. The petrified forest, part II. *BIE*, 34: 317–28.

al-Idrisi, M.M. 1836–40. La *géographie d'Edrisi*, trans. P.-A. Jaubert, Paris: Imprimerie Royale [facsimile edition published in 1975 by Philo Press Amsterdam].

Ingram, K.D., Daugherty, K.E. and Marshall, J.L. 1993. The pyramids – cement or stone? *JAS*, 20: 681–7.

Isler, M. 1987. The curious Luxor obelisks. *JEA*, 73: 137–47.

1992. The technique of monolithic carving. *MDAIK*, 48: 45–55.

Jeffreys, D.G. and Giddy, L. 1993. The people of Memphis. *EA*, 3: 18–20.

Jones, H.L. (ed. and transl.) 1917–32. *The Geography of Strabo*. 8 vols. London: Heinemann.

Junker, H. 1919. *Bericht über die Grabungen . . . auf den Friedhöfen von El-Kubanieh-Sud*. Vienna: Akademie der Wissenschaften in Wien.

Keldani, E.H. 1939. *Bibliography of Geology and Related Sciences Concerning Egypt up to The End of 1939*. Cairo: Survey and Mines Department.

Keller, P.C. 1990. *Gemstones and their Origins*. New York: Van Nostrand-Reinhold.

Kemp, B.J. 1989. *Ancient Egypt: Anatomy of a Civilization*. London: Routledge.

Kessler, D. 1981. *Historische Topographie der Region zwischen Mallawi und Samalut*. Wiesbaden: Dr Ludwig Reichert Verlag.

el-Khouli, A. 1978. *Egyptian Stone Vessels: Predynastic Period to Dynasty III: Typology and Analysis*, 3 vols. Mainz: von Zabern.

el-Khouli, A.A.R., Holthoer, R., Hope, C.A. and Kaper, O.E. 1993. *Stone Vessels, Pottery and Sealings from the Tomb of Tut'ankhamun*. Oxford: Griffith Institute.

Kitchen, K.A. 1991. Building the Ramesseum. *CRIPEL*, 13: 85–93.

Klein, M.J. 1988. *Untersuchungen zu den kaiserlichen steinbrüchen an Mons Porphyrites und Mons Claudianus in der östichen Wüste Ägyptens*. Bonn: Rudolf Habett GMBH no. 26.

Klein, C. and Hurlbut, jr., C.S. 1993. *Manual of Mineralogy*. New York: John Wiley.

Klemm, R. 1986. Steine und steinbrüche der Ägypter. *Geowissenschaften in Unserer Zeit*, 4/1: 11–8.

1988. Vom Steinbruch zum Tempel: Beobachtungen zur Baustruktur einiger Felstempel der 18. und 19. Dynastie im ägyptischen Mütterland. ZÄS, 115: 41–51.

Klemm, R. and Klemm, D.D. 1979. Herkunftsbestimmung altägyptischen Steinmaterials. *SAK*, 7: 103–40.

1981. *Die Steine der Pharaonen*. Munich: Staatliche Sammlung Ägyptischer Kunst.

1993. *Steine und Steinbrüche im Alten-Ägypten*. Berlin: Springer-Verlag.

Klemm, D.D. Klemm, R. and Steclaci, L. 1984. Die pharaonischen Steinbrüche des silifizierten Sandsteins in Ägypten und die Herkunft der Memnon-Kolosse. *MDAIK*, 40: 207–20.

Klitzsch, E., List, F. K. and Pöhlmann (eds.), 1986–7. Geological Map of Egypt (20 sheets, 1: 500,000). Cairo: Conoco Inc. and Egyptian General Petroleum Corp.

Kozloff A. and Bryan, B. 1992 *Egypt's Dazzling Sun: Amenhotep III and his World*, (exhibition catalogue). Bloomington: Cleveland Museum of Art and Indiana University Press.

Kraus, T. and Röder, J. 1962a. Voruntersuchungen am Mons Claudianus im März 1961. *Archäologischer Anzeiger (Berlin)*, 1962: 693–745.

1962b. Mons Claudianus: bericht über eine erste erkundungsfahrt im März 1961. *MDAIK*, 18: 80–120.

Kraus, T., Röder, J. and Müller-Wiener, W. 1967. Mons Claudianus-Mons Porphyrites bericht über zweite forschungsreise 1964. *MDAIK*, 22: 108–205.

Krauss, R. 1983. Der Bildhauer Thutmose in Amarna. *Jahrbuch preussischer Kulturbesitz*, 20: 119–32.

Kulke, H. 1976. Die lapislazuli-lagerstätte Sare Sang (Badakshan): Geologie, Entstehung, Kulturgeschichte und Bergbau. *Afghanistan Journal*, 3/2: 1–16.

Lacovara, P., Reeves, C.N. and Johnson, W.R. 1996. A composite-statue element in the Museum of Fine Arts, Boston. *RdE*, 47: 173–6.

Lauer, J.-P. 1960. *Observations sur les pyramides*. Cairo: IFAO.

Lauer, J.-P. and Debono, F. 1950. Techniques du façonnage des croissants de silex utilisés dans l'enceinte de Zoser à Saqqarah. *ASAE*, 50: 1–18.

Lazzarini, L. 1987. I graniti dei monumenti Italiani ed i loro problemi di deteriomento. *Materiali Lapidei, Bollettino d'Arte* 41: 157–72.

Legrain, G. 1906. *Statues et statuettes des rois et des particuliers* I. Cairo: Egyptian Museum, Catalogue Generale.

Lehner, M. 1985. The development of the Giza necropolis: the Khufu project. *MDAIK*, 41: 109–44.

Lepsius, K.R. 1849–59. *Denkmäler aus Ägypten und Äthiopien*. 6 parts in 12 vols. Leipzig: J.C. Hinrichs.

Levene, D. 1998. Expedition to Atika. In *Proceedings of the First International Conference on Ancient Egyptian Mining and Metallurgy and Conservation of Metallic Artefacts, Cairo, 10–12 April, 1995*. (ed. F. A. Esmael) Cairo: SCA, pp. 365–78.

Lewis, D.W. and McConchie, D. 1994. *Analytical Sedimentology*. New York: Chapman and Hall.

Lichtheim, M. 1973. *Ancient Egyptian Literature I: The Old and Middle Kingdoms*. Berkeley: University of California Press.

Lilyquist, C. 1989. The marble statue of Tuthmosis III from Deir el Bahari. *GM*, 109: 39–40.

1996. *Egyptian Stone Vessels: Khian through Tuthmosis IV*. New York: MMA.

Little, O.H. 1933. Preliminary report on some geological specimens from the Chephren diorite quarries, Western Desert. *ASAE*, 33: 75–80.

Loewental, A.I. and Harden, D.B. 1949. Vasa Murrina. *Journal of Roman Studies*, 39: 31–6.

Lucas, A. 1926. *Ancient Egyptian Materials and Industries.* 1st edn. London: Longman, Green and Co.

1934. *Ancient Egyptian Materials and Industries.* 2nd edn. London: Edward Arnold.

1933. Appendix 2: The chemistry of the tomb. In *The Tomb of Tut-ankh-amen III* (H. Carter). London: Cassell and Co., pp. 170–83.

1942. Obsidian. *ASAE*, 41: 271–5.

1947. Obsidian. *ASAE*, 47: 113–23.

1962. *Ancient Egyptian Materials and Industries.* 4th edn., rev. J.R. Harris. London: Edward Arnold.

Lucas, A. and Rowe, A. 1938. The ancient Egyptian bekhen-stone. *ASAE*, 38: 127–56.

MacAlister, D.A. 1900. The emerald mines of northern Etbai. *Geographical Journal, London*, 16: 537–49.

MacKenzie, W.S. and Adams, A.E. 1994. *A Color Atlas of Rocks and Minerals in Thin Section.* New York: John Wiley.

MacKenzie, W.S., Donaldson, C.H. and Guilford, C. 1982. *Atlas of Igneous Rocks and Their Textures.* New York: John Wiley.

MacKenzie, W.S. and Guilford, C. 1980. *Atlas of Rock-forming Minerals in Thin Section.* New York: John Wiley.

Macy Roth, A. 1992. The *pšs-kf* and the 'opening of the mouth' ceremony: a ritual of birth and rebirth. *JEA*, 78: 113–47.

Majidzadeh, Y. 1982. Lapis lazuli and the Great Khorasan road. *Paléorient*, 8/1: 59–69.

Mansour, H.H., Philobbos, E.R., Khalifa, H. and Galal, S. 1983. Contribution to the stratigraphy and micropaleontology of the Middle and Upper Eocene exposures southeast of Cairo, Egypt. *Bulletin of the Faculty of Science, Assiut University*, 12/2: 153–72.

Marchei, M.C., Sironi, A. and Gnoli, R. 1989. Repertorio. In *Marmi Antichi* (ed. G. Borghini). Rome: Leonardo-De Luca Editori, pp. 131–302.

Matthiae, G.S. 1992. Una testimonianza dei rapporti protohistorici tr Egitto e Asia anteriore da Abusir el-Meleq. *Contributi e materiali di archaeologia orientale*, 4: 1–9.

Maxwell-Hyslop, K.R. 1995. A note on the Anatolian connections of the Tôd Treasure. *Anatolian Studies*, 45: 243–50.

McGill, J.R. and Kowalski, B.R. 1977. Recognizing patterns in trace elements. *Applied Spectroscopy*, 31/2: 87–95.

Meneisy, M.Y., Ragab, A.I. and Taher, R.M. 1979. Contributions to the petrography, petrochemistry and classification of Aswan granitic rocks, Egypt. *Chemie der Erde*, 38/2: 121–35.

Meredith, D. 1952. The Roman remains in the Eastern Desert of Egypt, I. *JEA*, 38: 94–111.

Meredith, D. and Tregenza, L.A. 1949. Notes on Roman roads and stations in the Eastern Desert. *Bulletin of the Faculty of Arts, Fouad I (now Cairo) University*, 11/1: 97–126.

1950. Mons Porphyrites: the north-west village and quarries. *Bulletin of the Faculty of Arts, Fouad I (now Cairo) University*,12/1: 131–47.

Meyer, C. 1992. The Bir Umm Fawakhir project, 1992: a gold mining camp in the Eastern Desert. *Chicago House Bulletin*, 3/2:1–4.

Meyers, P. and van Zelst, L. 1977. Neutron activation analysis of limestone objects in a pilot study. *Radiochimica Acta*, 24: 197–204.

Middleton, A. and Bradley, S.M. 1989. Provenancing of Egyptian limestone sculpture. *Journal of Archeological Science*, 16: 475–88.

Mielsch, H. 1985. *Buntmarmore aus Rom in Antikenmuseum Berlin.* Berlin: Staatliche Museum Preussischer Kulturbesitz.

Miller, R. 1983. Lithic technology in East Karnak, Egypt. *JSSEA*, 13: 228–36.

1987. Flaked stone from the Workmen's Village. In *Amarna Reports* IV (ed. B.J. Kemp). London: EES, pp. 144–53.

Mond, R. and Myers, O. 1937. *Cemeteries of Armant*, 2 vols. London: EEF.

Moorey, P.R.S. 1983. *Ancient Egypt*, 2nd edn. Oxford: Ashmolean Museum Publications.

1994. *Ancient Mesopotamian Materials and Industries.* Oxford: OUP.

Moran, W.L. 1992. *The Amarna letters.* London: Johns Hopkins University Press.

de Morgan, J. 1895. *Fouilles à Dahchour 1894.* Vienna: Adolphe Holzhausen.

1897. *Recherches sur les origines de l'Egypte* II. Paris: Leroux.

de Morgan, J., Bouriant, U., Legrain, G., Jéquier, G. and Barsanti, A., 1894. *Catalogue des monuments et inscriptions de l'Egypte antique, I: De la frontière de Nubie à Kom Ombos.* Vienna: Adolphe Holzhausen.

Mottana, A., Crespi, R. and Liborio, G. 1978. *Simon and Schuster's guide to rocks and minerals.* New York: Simon and Schuster.

Moussa, A.M. 1981. A stela of Taharqa from the desert road at Dahshur. *MDAIK*, 37: 331–17.

Murray, G.W. 1914. Notes on Bir Kareim and amethysts. *CSJ*, 8: 179.

1925. The Roman roads and stations in the eastern desert of Egypt. *JEA*, 11: 138–50.

1939a. The road to Chephren's quarries. *Geographical Journal*, 94, 97–114.

1939b. An Archaic hut in Wadi Umm Sidrah. *JEA*, 25: 38–9.

1945–6. A note on the Sadd el-Kafara: the ancient dam in the Wadi Garawi; and a diorite quarry of the Roman period in Wadi Barud (Eastern Desert). *BIE*, 28: 33–46.

Nassim, L. 1925. Minerals of economic interest in the deserts of Egypt. In *Congrès international de géographie, le Caire, April 1925*, III, p. 167.

Nesse, W.D. 1991. *Introduction to Optical Mineralogy*, 2nd edn. New York: OUP.

Newberry, P.E. 1893. *Beni Hasan* I. London: ERA.

1894. *El-Bersheh I: The Tomb of Tehuti-hetep.* London: ERA.

Niazi, E.A. and Loukina, S. 1987. Effects of Tertiary volcanic activity on some continental sediments in Egypt. In *Current Research in African Earth Sciences* (ed. G. Matheis and H. Schandelmeier). Rotterdam: A.A. Balkema, pp. 329–32.

Nibbi, A. 1976. *Ḥsbḏ* from the Sinai. *GM*, 19: 45–7.

Nour, M.Z., Osman, M.S., Iskander, Z. and Moustafa, A.Y. 1960. *The Cheops Boats* I. Cairo: General Organisation for Government Printing Offices.

Oddy, W.A., Hughes, M.J. and Baker, S. 1976. The washing of limestone sculptures from Egypt and the Middle East. *Lithclastia*, 2: 3–10.

Ogden, J. 1982. *Jewellery of the Ancient World*. London: Trefoil.

Owen, G. and B. Kemp, 1994. Craftsmen's work patterns in unfinished tombs at Amarna. *CAJ*, 4/1: 121–9.

Payne, J.C. 1968. Lapis lazuli in early Egypt. *Iraq*, 30: 58–61.

Peacock, D.S. 1988. The Roman quarries of Mons Claudianus, Egypt: an interim report. In *Classical Marble Geochemistry, Technology, Trade: Proceedings of The NATO Advanced Workshop on Marble in Ancient Greece and Rome* (eds. N. Herz and M. Waelkens). Boston: Kluwer Academic Publishers, pp. 97–101.

1992. *Rome in the Desert: A Symbol of Power*. Inaugural lecture delivered at the University of Southampton, UK, December 3, 1992, Southampton: University Printing Service.

Peacock, D. and Maxfield, V. (eds.), 1994. *The Roman Imperial Porphyry Quarries: Gebel Dokhan, Egypt. Interim Report 1994*. Southampton and Exeter: Universities of Southampton and Exeter.

1995. *The Roman Imperial Porphyry Quarries: Gebel Dokhan, Egypt. Interim Report 1995*. Southampton and Exeter: Universities of Southampton and Exeter.

1996. *The Roman Imperial Porphyry Quarries: Gebel Dokhan, Egypt. Interim Report 1996*. Southampton and Exeter: Universities of Southampton and Exeter.

Peacock, D.S., Williams-Thorpe, O. Thorpe, R.S. and Tindle, A.G. 1994. Mons Claudianus and the problem of the 'granito del foro': a geological and geochemical approach. *Antiquity*, 68: 209–30.

Pellant, C. 1992. *Eyewitness Handbooks: Rocks and Minerals*. London: Dorling Kindersley.

Pendlebury, J.D.S. 1951. *City of Akhenaten* III, 2 vols. London: EES.

Petrie, W.M.F. 1888. *A Season in Egypt*. London: EEF.

1890. *Kahun, Gurob and Hawara*. London: EEF.

1894. *Tell el Amarna*. London: BSAE/Methuen and Co.

1901a. *Diospolis Parva: The Cemeteries of Abadiyeh and Hu, 1898–9*. London: BSAE.

1901b. *The Royal Tombs of the Earliest Dynasties* II. London: EEF.

1917. *Scarabs and Cylinders with Names*. London: Quaritch.

1920. *Prehistoric Egypt*. London: Quaritch.

1937. *The Funeral Furniture of Egypt/Stone and Metal Vases*. London: BSAE and Quaritch.

Petrie, W.M.F. and Currelly, C.T. 1906. *Researches in Sinai*. London: John Murray.

Petrie, W.M.F., Wainwright, G.A. and MacKay, E. 1912. *The Labyrinth, Gerzeh and Mazghuneh*. London: Quaritch.

Pettijohn, F.J. Potter, E. and Siever, R. 1972. *Sand and Sandstone*. New York: Springer-Verlag.

Pliny see Rackham 1968.

Porada, E. 1980. A lapis lazuli figurine from Hierakonpolis. *Iranica Antiqua*: 175–80.

1982. Remarks of the Tôd Treasure in Egypt. In *Societies and Languages of the Ancient Near East: Studies Presented in Honour of I.M. Diakonoff* (eds. M.A. Dandamayef, J.N. Postgate and I.M. Diakonoff). Warminster: Aris and Phillips, pp. 285–303.

Porter, B. and Moss, R. 1974–81. *Topographical Bibliography of Ancient Egyptian Hieroglyphic Texts, Reliefs and Paintings* III, 2nd edn., rev. J. Malek. Oxford:Griffith Institute.

Quibell, J. and Petrie, W.M.F. 1900. *Hierakonpolis* I. London: ERA.

Quibell, J. and Green, F.W. 1902. *Hierakonpolis* II. London: ERA.

Quirke, S. 1990. *The Administration of Egypt in the Late Middle Kingdom: The Hieratic Documents*. New Malden: SIA Publishing.

Rackham, H. (transl. and ed.) 1968. *Pliny (the Elder): Natural History*, 2nd edn. Loeb Classical Library. Cambridge MA: Harvard University Press.

Ragab, A.I., Meneisy, M.Y. and Taher, R.M. 1978. Contributions to the petrogenesis and age of Aswan granite rocks, Egypt. *Neues Jahrbuch für Mineralogie Abhandlungen*, 133/1: 71–87.

Ramez, M.R.H. and Marie, A.A. 1973. The geology and petrography of the basement rocks at Gebel El Rukham area, Eastern Desert. *Journal of Egyptian Geology*, 17/2: 147–62.

Raymond, L.A. 1995. *The Study of Igneous, Metamorphic and Sedimentary Rocks*. Boston: Wm. C. Brown.

Reisner, G.A. 1923. *Excavations at Kerma I–V*, 2 vols. Cambridge MA: Harvard University Press.

1931. *Mycerinus, the Temples of the Third Pyramid at Giza*. Cambridge MA: Harvard University Press.

1932. *A Provincial Cemetery of the Pyramid Age: Naga-ed-Dêr, III*. Oxford: OUP.

1936. *The Development of the Egyptian Tomb down to the Accession of Cheops*. Cambridge MA: Harvard University Press.

Roeder, G. 1941. Lebensgrosse Tonmodelle aus einer altägyptischen Bildhauerwerkstatt. *Jahrbuch der preussischen Kunstsammlungen*, 62: 145–70.

Röder, J. 1965. Zur Steinbrüchgeschichte des Rosengranits von Assuan. *Archäologischer Anzeiger*, 467–552.

Rothenberg, B. 1970. Archaeological survey of south Sinai. *Palestine Exploration Quarterly* 102: 4–29.

(ed.) 1979. *Sinai: Pharaohs, Miners, Pilgrims and Soldiers*. Berne: Kümmerly and Frey.

1987. Pharaonic copper mines in south Sinai. *Newsletter of the Institute of Archaeo-Metallurgical Studies*, 10/11: 3–7.

Rowe, A.E. 1938. Provisional notes on the Old Kingdom inscriptions from the diorite quarries. *ASAE*, 38: 391–6.

1939. Three new stelae from the south-eastern desert. *ASAE*, 39: 187–91.

Sadek, A.I. 1980–85. *The Amethyst Mining Inscriptions of Wadi el-Hudi*, 2 vols. Warminster: Aris and Phillips.

Said, R. (ed.) 1990. *The Geology of Egypt*. Rotterdam: A. A. Balkema Publishers.

Saleh, M. and Sourouzian, H. 1987. *The Egyptian Museum, Cairo: Official Catalogue*. Mainz: von Zabern.

Sax, M. and Middleton, A.P. 1992. A system of nomenclature for quartz and its application to the material of cylinder seals. *Archaeometry*, 34/1: 11–20.

Scaife, C.H.O. 1935. Two inscriptions at Mons Porphyrites (Gebel Dokhan), also a description, with plans, of the stations between Kainopolis and Myos Hormos together with some other ruins in the neighborhood of Gebel Dokhan. *Bulletin of the Faculty of Arts, Fouad I (now Cairo) University*, 3/2: 58–104.

Schäfer, H. 1910. *Königliche Museen zu Berlin I: Ägyptische Goldschmiedearbeiten*. Berlin: Königliche Museen zu Berlin.

Scharff, A. 1926. *Das Vorgeschichtliche Gräberfeld von Abusir el-Meleq*. Leipzig: J.C. Hinrichs.

Schneider, O. and Azruni, A. 1892. Der Ägyptische Smaragd nebst einer vergleichenden mineralogischen Untersuchung der Smaragd von Alexandrien, vom Gebel Sabara und vom Ural. *Zeitschrift für Ethnologie*, 24: 41–100.

Scholle, P.A. 1978. *A Color Illustrated Guide to Carbonate Rock Constituents, Textures, Cements, and Porosities.* Tulsa: American Association of Petroleum Geologists, Memoir 27.

1979. *A Color Illustrated Guide to Constituents, Textures, Cements, and Porosities of Sandstones and Associated Rocks.* Tulsa: American Association of Petroleum Geologists, Memoir 28.

Sethe, K. 1903. *Urkunden des Alten Reichs* I. Leipzig: J.C. Hinrichs.

Seton-Karr, W.H. 1898. Discovery of the lost flint mines of Egypt. *Journal of the Royal Anthropological Institute*, 27: 90–2.

1905. How the tomb galleries at Thebes were cut and the limestone quarried at the prehistoric flint-mines of the Eastern Desert. *ASAE*, 6: 176–87.

Seward, A.C. 1935. *Leaves of dicotyledons from the Nubian sandstone of Egypt.* Cairo: GSE.

Seyfried, K.J. 1981. *Beiträge zu den Expeditionen des Mittleren Reiches in die Ostwüste.* Hildesheim: Hildesheimer ägyptologische Beiträge.

Shaw, I. 1986. A survey at Hatnub. In *Amarna Reports* III (ed. B.J. Kemp). London: EES, pp. 189–212.

1987. The 1986 survey of Hatnub. In *Amarna Reports* IV (ed. B.J. Kemp). London: EES, pp. 160–7.

1994. Pharaonic quarrying and mining: settlement and procurement in Egypt's marginal regions. *Antiquity*, 68: 108–19.

1998. Exploiting the desert frontier: the logistics and politics of ancient Egyptian mining expeditions. In *Social Approaches to an Industrial Past: The Archaeology and Anthropology of Mining* (ed. B. Knapp) London: Routledge.

in press (a). The evidence for amethyst mining in Nubia and Egypt. In *Proceedings of the International Symposium: Recent Research into the Stone Age of Northeastern Africa* (eds. L. Krzyzaniak *et al.*) Poznan.

in press (b). Gold and amethyst mining at the Lower Nubian site of Wadi el-Hudi in the Roman period. In *The Second International Conference on Ancient Mining and Metallurgy and Conservation of Metals* (eds. F.A. Esmael *et al.*). Cairo: SCA.

forthcoming. The roads of Pharaonic Egypt.

Shaw, I. and Bloxam, E. 1999. Survey and excavation at the ancient pharaonic gneiss quarrying site of Gebel el-Asr, Lower Nubia. *Sudan and Nubia: Bulletin of the Sudan Archaeological Research Society*, 3.

Shaw, I. and Jameson, R. 1993. Amethyst mining in the Eastern Desert: a preliminary survey at Wadi el-Hudi. *JEA*, 79: 81–97.

Shaw, I., Jameson R. and Bunbury, J. 1999. Emerald mining in Roman and Byzantine Egypt. *Journal of Roman Archaeology*, 12.

el-Shazly, E.M. 1954. *Rocks of Aswan.* Cairo: GSE.

Shiah, N. 1942. Some remarks on the bekhen stone. *ASAE*, 41: 199–205.

Shukri, N.M. 1944. On the 'living' petrified forest. *BIE*, 26: 71–5.

1953. The geology of the desert east of Cairo. *Bulletin de l'Institut du Desert d'Egypte (Cairo)*, 3/2: 89–105.

1954. On cylindrical structures and coloration of Gebel Ahmar near Cairo, Egypt. *Bulletin of the Faculty of Science, Cairo University*, 32: 1–23.

Sidebotham, S.E. 1996. Newly discovered sites in the Eastern Desert. *JEA* 82: 181–92.

Sidebotham, S.E., Zitterkopf, R.E. and Riley, J.A. 1991. Survey of the Abu Sha'ar–Nile road. *AJA*, 95: 571–622.

Simpson, W.K. 1963. *Heka-nefer and the Dynastic Material from Toshka and Arminna.* New Haven CT and Philadelphia PA: Peabody Museum of Natural History of Yale University and University Museum of the University of Pennsylvania.

Smith, W.C. 1965. The distribution of jade axes in Europe (with a supplement to the catalogue of those of the British Isles). *Proceedings of the Prehistoric Society*, 31: 2533.

Smith, W.S. 1958. *The Art and Architecture of Ancient Egypt.* 1st edn. Harmondsworth: Penguin [2nd edn., rev. W.K. Simpson 1980].

Soliman, M.M. 1980. Geochemistry of some granodiorites, granites, pegmatites and associated gneisses from Aswan, Egypt. *AGSE*, 10: 611–26.

Spurrell, F.C.J. 1891. The stone implements of Kahun. In *Illahun, Kahun and Gurob: 1889–90* (ed. W.M.F. Petrie). London: EES, pp. 51–6.

1894. Flint tools from Tell el Amarna. In *Tell el Amarna* (W.M.F. Petrie). London: EES, pp. 37–8.

1895. Notes on Egyptian colours. *Archaeological Journal*, 52: 222–39.

Stadelmann, R. 1985. *Die ägyptischen Pyramiden.* Mainz am Rhein: von Zabern.

Starr, R.F.S. and Butin, R.F. 1936. Excavations and protosinaitic inscriptions at Serabit el-Khadim. *Studies and Documents*, 6: 15–20.

Stocks, D. 1986a. Experimental archaeology I: sticks and stones of Egyptian technology. *Popular Archaeology*, April 1986: 24–9.

1986b. Egyptian technology II: stone vessel manufacture. *Popular Archaeology*, May 1986: 14–18.

1986c. Egyptian technology III: bead production in ancient Egypt. *Popular Archaeology*, June 1986: 2–7.

1989. Ancient factory mass-production techniques: indications of large-scale stone bead manufacture during the Egyptian New Kingdom period. *Antiquity*, 63: 526–31.

1993. Making stone vessels in ancient Mesopotamia and Egypt. *Antiquity*, 67: 596–603.

Strabo see Jones 1917–32.

Streckeisen, A.L. 1973. Plutonic rocks: classification and nomenclature recommended by the IUGS subcommission on the systematics of igneous rocks. *Geotimes*, 8/10: 26–30.

1979. Classification and nomenclature of volcanic rocks, lamprophyres, carbonatites, and melitic rocks: recommendations and suggestions of the IUGS subcommission on the systematics of igneous rocks. *Geology*, 7: 331–5.

Stross, F.H., Hay, R.L., Asaro, F., Bowman, H.R. and Michel, H.V. 1988. Sources of quartzite in Egyptian sculpture. *Archaeometry*, 30: 109–19.

Terrace, E.L.B. 1966. 'Blue marble' plastic vessels and other figures. *JARCE*, 5: 57–63.

Thomas, E.S. 1909. The mineral industry of Egypt: emeralds. *CSJ*, 3: 267–72.

1912. The mineral industry of Egypt: turquoise. *CSJ*, 6: 56–90.

Timme, P. 1917. *Tell el-Amarna vor der Deutschen ausgrabung in Jahre 1911.* Leipzig: Wissenschaftliche Veröffentlichung der Deutschen Orient-Gesellschaft 31.

Tregenza, L.A. 1950. A Latin inscription from Wadi Semna. *Bulletin of the Faculty of Arts, Fouad I (Cairo) University*, 12/2: 85–9.

1951. The curator inscription and other recently found fragments from Wadi Semna. *Bulletin of the Faculty of Arts, Fouad I (Cairo) University*, 13/2: 39–52.

1955. *The Red Sea Mountains of Egypt*. London: OUP.

1958. *Egyptian Years*. London: OUP.

Tucker, M. (ed.), 1988. *Techniques in Sedimentology*. London: Blackwell Scientific.

Tykot, R.H. 1996. The geological source of an obsidian ear (04.9941) from the Museum of Fine Arts Boston. *RdE*, 47: 177–9.

Vachala, B. and Sroboda, J. 1989. Die Steinmesser aus Abusir. *ZÄS*, 116: 174–81.

Van Houten, F.B. and Bhattacharyya, D. 1979. Late Cretaceous Nubia formation at Aswan, Southeastern Desert, Egypt. *AGSE*, 9: 408–19.

Van Walsem, R. 1978–9. The *pšs-kf*: an investigation of an ancient Egyptian funerary instrument. *OMRO*, 59: 193–249.

Vercoutter, J. 1992. *L'Egypte et la vallée du Nil I: Des origines à la fin de l'Ancien Empire*. Paris: Nouvelle Clio.

Vermeersch, P.M., Paulissen, E., Gijselings, G., Otte, M., Thoma, A., Van Peer, P., Lauwers, R., Drappier, D. and Charlier, C. 1984. 33,000–year-old chert mining site and related Homo in the Egyptian Nile valley. *Nature*, 309: 342–4.

Vermeersch, P.M., Paulissen, E. and Van Peer, P. 1990. Palaeolithic chert exploitation in the limestone stretch of the Egyptian Nile valley. *The African Archaeological Review*, 8: 77–102.

Wainwright, G.A. 1927. Obsidian. *Ancient Egypt*, 13: 77–93.

1946. Zeberged – the shipwrecked sailors island. *JEA*, 32: 31–8.

Ward, W.C. and McDonald, K.C. 1979. Nubia Formation of central Eastern Desert, Egypt : major subdivisions and depositional setting. *American Association of Petroleum Geologists Bulletin*, 63: 975–83.

Warren, P.M. 1995. Minoan Crete and Pharaonic Egypt. In *Egypt, the Aegean and the Levant: Interconnections in the Second Millennium BC* (eds. W.V. Davies and L. Schofield). London: BMP, pp. 1–18.

Weigall, A.E.P. 1910. *A Guide to the Antiquities of Upper Egypt, from Abydos to the Sudan Frontier*. New York: Macmillan.

1913. *Travels in the Upper Egyptian Deserts*. London: W. Blackwood and Sons.

Weill, R. 1908. *La presqu'île du Sinaï*. Paris: H. Champion.

Weisgerber, G. 1982. Altägyptischer Hornsteinbergbau im Wadi el-Sheikh. *Der Anschnitt*, 34: 186–210.

Weisgerber, G., Slotta, R. and Weiner, J. (eds.), 1980. *5000 Jahre Feuersteinbergbau - die Suche nach dem Stahl der Steinzeit*. Bochum: Deutsches Bergbau-Museum.

Wendorf, F. and Schild, R. 1975. The Paleolithic of the lower Nile valley. In *Problems in Prehistory: North Africa and the Levant* (eds. F. Wendorf and A.E. Marks). Dallas: Southern Methodist University Press, pp. 127–69.

Wenig, S. (ed.), 1978. *Africa in Antiquity: The Arts of Ancient Nubia and the Sudan II: The Catalogue*. New York: Brooklyn Museum.

Wild, H. 1966. *Le tombeau de Ti*, fasc. III. Cairo: IFAO.

Wilkinson, J.G. 1878. *The Manners and Customs of the Ancient Egyptians*. vols. I–III (ed. and revised by S. Birch). London: John Murray.

Williams, H., Turner F.J. and Gilbert, C.M. 1982. *Petrography: An Introduction to the Study of Rocks in Thin Sections*. San Francisco CA: W.H. Freeman.

Winlock, H. 1948. *The Treasure of the Three Egyptian Princesses*. New York: MMA.

Wissa, M. 1994. Le sarcophage de Merenrê et l'expedition à Ibhat (I). In *Hommages à Jean Leclant* I (eds. C. Berger, G. Clerc and N. Grimal). Cairo: IFAO, pp. 379–87.

Woodward, C. and Harding, R. 1987. *Gemstones*. London: Natural History Museum Publications.

Wyart, J. *et al.* 1981. Lapis lazuli from Sar-e-Sang, Badakshan, Afghanistan. *Gems and Gemmology*: 184–90.

Yardley, B.W.D., MacKenzie, W.S. and Guilford, C. 1990. *Atlas of Metamorphic Rocks and Their Textures*. New York: John Wiley.

Yoyotte, J. (ed.), 1987. *Tanis, l'or des pharaons*. Paris: Association française d'action artistique.

Zarins, J. 1989. Ancient Egypt and the Red Sea trade: the case for obsidian in the predynastic and archaic periods. In *Essays in Ancient Civilization Presented to Helen J. Kantor* (ed. A. Leonard jr. and B. Beyer). Chicago: OIP, pp. 339–68.

Zuber, A. 1956. Techniques du travail des pierres dures dans l'ancienne Egypte. *Techniques et Civilisations*, 29/5: 161–78; 30/5: 196–215.

3. Soil (including mud-brick architecture)

BARRY KEMP

Introduction

Soil has been one of the most widely used building materials since the Neolithic, particularly in arid and semi-arid parts of the world. Commonly termed adobe, it still has considerable potential. Almost any kind of soil can be used (although some modification is often necessary to add strength), it is relatively easy to work with, and its plasticity and chemical stability give it great versatility. It can be moulded by hand or within rigid moulds into building blocks (bricks), can be rammed between formwork to create walls directly, and is equally suited for plastering to produce smooth or moulded finishes. Its vulnerability to erosion and damage do, however, create a constant need for maintenance in the form of replastering and actual repair.

Architectural applications do not exhaust the industrial uses to which soil was put in ancient Egypt. It was, of course, a prime ingredient of pottery, and in the study of composition and methods of handling there is a degree of overlap with pottery research. It was used in certain small applications which also relate more closely to pottery-making in the degree of manipulation of the clay that was involved. These include the administrative practice of sealing, and the making of small mud objects, such as figurines and beads. This section is, however, limited to soil architecture. Most of the evidence that can be cited in this context is archaeological, but it is important to note that a vocabulary of words exists in Egyptian texts which probably or certainly deal with soil architecture (Badawy 1957; Simpson 1963: 56–8, 72–80; Spencer 1979a: 3–4). Uncertainties in translation, however, make it hard to use these sources constructively.

The mud-brick ruins which have been most accessible to archaeologists have principally been constructions on new sites, frequently in the desert and including the brickwork of tombs. This gives a very distorted frame of reference. Most building in brick at any period was done on sites, often long-occupied, which were situated on the floodplain. Moreover, brick architecture in ancient Egypt included huge palace complexes which are still very poorly documented. Even when fragments are excavated they are normally no more than foundations. We must make allowance for such buildings originally having risen to considerable heights and possessing elaborately constructed interiors which utilised a level of building skills now meagrely represented by what has survived. A modern account of soil architecture in ancient Egypt is almost bound not to do it justice.

History of soil architecture in Egypt

Soil was used for building in Egypt before the making of mud bricks was developed (Lacovara 1984). Although a precursor to brick, these simpler uses are bound to have continued into historic periods. Thus the practice of setting criss-crossed twigs in the tops of walls seen in some New-Kingdom representations of houses is clearly related to wattle-and-daub technique (Davies 1929), which was perhaps the building medium originally in empty foundation trenches of the New Kingdom or later at western Thebes (Hölscher 1939: 71–2). We find its beginnings at a number of Predynastic sites, at its simplest in the lining of fire-pits and in the coating of the basketry and matting that was employed to line grain silos or to cover circular hut-bottoms. Examples are known from settlements where no more substantial use of soil has been detected, suggesting that, locally, this technology might have preceded a full and independent structural use of soil. The sites in question include the middle levels at Merimda and Wadi Hof (el-Omari) (Hayes 1965: 104–15, 117; Debono and Mortensen 1990: 17–20). The remains of clay coating to interwoven branches was reported at Maadi (Rizkana and Seeher 1989: 40; Rizkana 1996: 178), although at the same site mud bricks had also been used (see p. 79).

At Hemmamiya North Spur, nine hut circles and a straight wall 8.2 metres long had been built from a mixture of mud and limestone fragments during a period defined initially by sequence-dates 35–45 and now known to have commenced during the transition from Badarian to Amratian. A radiocarbon date for a layer of fill in one of them (re-examined in 1989) is 3830–3625 BC (Brunton and Caton-Thompson 1928: 82–8; Holmes and Friedman 1994: 118–24, 134–5). The imprint of stalks, pressed vertically against the mud on the outside of the huts whilst still moist, showed that reeds had been used to give added height, whilst wooden posts had been set at thirty-centimetre intervals along one face of the straight wall. The shallowly sunken hut floors had been made of beaten mud. A slightly more advanced technique was employed for similar hut circles at Merimda (Junker 1930: 45–7; 1932: 44–6; Hayes 1965: 105–6; cf. Badawi 1978: 48–9). Whilst some had been built from superimposed rings of Nile mud, others had used rough blocks of the same material containing a binder of chopped straw. Mud had also been used to plaster the interiors and floors of the huts. These huts belong to the latest phase of Merimda (late fifth millennium BC).

Evidence for the moulding of bricks in small numbers for limited use appears quite early on settlement sites in Upper Egypt, sometimes accompanied by evidence that buildings (often rectangular in plan) were still primarily made with reed walls supported by posts and sometimes plastered with mud (wattle-and-daub). Sites 29 and 29A on the desert at Hierakonpolis illustrate this situation well and belong to the Gerzean and possibly Amratian periods (Holmes 1992; Hoffman 1980). Also at Hierakonpolis (site 24) and at several other Gerzean settlements which lack evidence for brick houses, long narrow bar-like bricks were used to support clay vessels built into brick-lined tunnels which were then fired, probably in the process of brewing beer (Peet and Loat 1913: Chapter I, pl. I; Peet 1914: 7–9, pl. I.8; Geller 1992: 21–3). The survival of a wattle-and-daub tradition long after brick-making developed leaves ambiguous the original material of the fired-clay model of a rectangular house found in a tomb at el-Amra of the Gerzean period (Randall-Maciver and Mace 1902: 42, pl. X.1,2; Baumgartel 1960: 132–3, pl. XII.3).

True mud-brick buildings of the Predynastic period still remain few. Petrie excavated the corner of a walled mud-brick settlement in the 'South Town' at Naqada which subsequent fieldwork has indicated belonged most probably to the late Gerzean period (Petrie and Quibell 1896: 54, pl. LXXXV; for dating, see Baumgartel 1970: 6, pl. LXXII; Hassan and Matson 1989: 312). Bricks were also used to line the burial chambers of élite tombs at Naqada (cemetery T) and Hierakonpolis (tomb 100, the Decorated Tomb) at a time which must fall within the Gerzean period (*c.* 3400 BC), and on the Umm el-Qaʿab (cemetery U) at Abydos in the period preceding the First Dynasty (Dreyer *et al.* 1996), but no evidence of superstructure has been found. We can also infer the use of mud brick in the construction of buttressed enclosures depicted in the art of the late Predynastic period (Spencer 1979a: 5).

In northern Egypt the advent of mud-brick architecture is one of the principal signs of major culture change shortly before the First Dynasty. It appears with apparent suddenness in excavated sequences at a number of sites in the Nile Delta, including Buto (von der Way 1992, 1993). Brick fragments from here have been compared with a remarkable use of long mud slabs to revet the wall of an underground chamber at Maadi (Rizkana and Seeher 1989: 54–5, pl. XV.1–2). They measured 50–65 × 9–10 cm along their sides, were probably about 10–15 cm thick, and had been laid in mud mortar. It was not recorded whether straw temper had been used, but this was certainly a feature of a few fragments of bricks found loose in other parts of the settlement. From earlier strata at Buto (Naqada IIb at the latest) come several cylinders or 'nails' of baked clay closely similar to objects which were used as a form of mosaic decoration in brick temple walls in the Uruk culture of Mesopotamia. There is the inevitable suggestion that, in another part of the site, a brick building of Mesopotamian style had been constructed.

In general it would seem that brick came into limited use in the Nile Valley and probably Delta from at least the beginning of the Gerzean period, and probably before, but also that wattle-and-daub remained the preferred medium for most buildings until close to the beginning of the First Dynasty, when all-brick towns began to appear throughout the country.

The hardening of soil through heating must have been a very ancient observation. The use of bricks and clay bars in late Predynastic brewing kilns such as at Abydos, the results of major conflagrations in some of the large First-Dynasty tombs which were subsequently repaired (Emery 1961: 180), and of several major burnings of town walls and houses, visible now on archaeological sites (e.g. Tell Edfu, Elephantine, Abydos and especially Kom Ombo), would have been especially dramatic evidence of the effects of burning on brickwork. The widespread preference for unfired soil architecture was thus through choice rather than ignorance. This is borne out by occasional exceptions, such as the fired clay tiles used in streets in Middle Kingdom fortresses in Nubia (Reisner *et al.* 1967: 118–19, pl. XLIXB; Emery *et al.* 1979: 8, 15–16, 35, fig. 19, pl. 92B). From the New Kingdom onwards these exceptions become a little more frequent: specially shaped bricks for friezes on tomb façades (Borchardt *et al.* 1934; Spencer 1979a: 140–1, pl. 37); the lining of burial chambers at Tell Nabasha (Petrie 1888: 18–19; Spencer 1979a: 44); and on to a little catalogue of examples from the Twenty-first Dynasty to the Hellenistic period (Spencer 1979a: 141; Petrie 1906: 49). One factor inhibiting the use of fired brick has presumably been the added cost of the fuel needed for the firing, as well as the need for a more suitable (and expensive) mortar, which, in the Hellenistic period, was lime.

The composition of mud bricks

Although 'mud-brick' is the term most often used in Egyptology, 'adobe' has a more widespread currency. The ancient Egypt word for mud brick, *djebet*, passed, via the Coptic ⲧⲱⲃⲉ into Arabic as طوب *tub(a)* and thence probably into Spanish to give the word adobe (Wiesmann 1914; Černý 1976: 181; Vycichl 1983: 210–11; Mond and Myers 1934: 48, n. 2; Simpson 1963: 76, n. 16).

The study of adobe architecture has wide geographical range and its literature extends to manuals of use for constructing sophisticated modern buildings in dry environments, especially in the USA (McHenry 1976, 1984). Modern views stress the simplicity of the techniques.

> Adobe building bricks are a very simple material. They are simple to make, and by following a few rules can be laid by anyone with a strong back, using a reasonable amount of care. A great deal of misinformation, myth, and old wives tales has been circulated about this great building material. (McHenry 1976: 50)

Suitable soils are widespread. They should contain four elements:

> coarse sand or aggregate, fine sand, silt, and clay. Any one may be totally absent and the soil may still make satisfactory bricks . . . The aggregate (sand) provides strength, the fine sand is a filler to lock the grains of aggregate, and the silt and clay (generally identified by particle size rather than chemical analysis) acts as a binder and plastic medium to glue the other ingredients together. Soil structures with a high percentage of aggregate (sand) may be strong when dry, but are more vulnerable to erosion from rain. Soil structures high in clay may be much more resistant to water and erosion, but less strong. (McHenry 1984: 48) (Also Brown and Clifton 1978; Hughes 1988.)

This is a valuable perspective from which to view the practice of ancient Egyptian builders, who seem not to have worked to a standard formula. It should be noted, however, that the characteristics of soils differ to the point that expert opinion derived from the study of one region (and much of the technical study of soil architecture has been done in the Americas) is not necessarily transferable to other regions. Local studies are essential, and so far few have been done in Egypt. Moreover, physical composition is not the only variable. 'Soluble salts are a major component of most soils and are as important as clay minerals for cementing the silt- and sand-sized particles' (Hughes, pers. comm.). They, too, vary from one region to another. Many of those who work the land develop an intuitive sense of soil character and whether a particular one is suited to brick-making and, if so, how it might be modified. Anecdotal evidence and personal observation suggest that in modern Egypt the generally preferred material, which produces the hardest bricks, is cultivated topsoil (*khart*) which will have seen a thorough mixing of particle sizes through regular turning by the farmer and will have been enriched with deliberately added organic material. Other soils can, however, also be made usable.

The most significant departures from the norm in ancient Egypt occurred on a minority of sites which were constructed in the desert and where local soils differed markedly from those available in the floodplain. In turning to nearby materials, as they often seem to have done, the ancient builders produced bricks with a different appearance from those normally employed, but it is probably a mistake to consider such bricks as necessarily inferior for the job that they were intended to do. They were simply different.

> Many naturally occurring soils will require some modification, more often to deal with the presence of too much clay, rather than the lack of it. The soil abundant in clay may be modified by the addition of sand, coarser aggregates, or vegetal matter such as straw, hay, or manure. It is perhaps unrealistic to try to establish rigid proportions in view of the nature of the material sources and the lack of difference in the performance of the finished product. (McHenry 1984: 50)

In order to judge the extent to which the soil of ancient Egyptian bricks was modified, particle analysis is required not only of samples of ancient bricks but also of local soils to provide a basis for comparison. A set of analyses by French at East Karnak (1981) and at Amarna (1984) has attempted to do just this (compare a similar study at Lachish in Palestine, Goldberg 1979). The contrasting characteristics of the two sites make these studies particularly valuable: East Karnak is part of a *tell* of long occupation located near the river and sufficiently far from the desert to imply an alluvial origin for the mud of its bricks. Amarna, by contrast, was situated on the desert edge, and the ancient brick-makers had available to them a much wider variety of soils. Figure 3.1 is a summary of the results.

The samples were first crumbled. Once any gravel fraction and other large inclusions had been removed by passing the resulting soil through a two-millimetre mesh sieve they were separated by means of the hydrometer method of particle size analysis into three basic components: fine to very fine sand (2–4 Ø), medium silt (5–7 Ø) and clay. At Amarna, the natural sediments from the river bank displayed a wide variety of mix when taken from different beds: pale brown sand, brown silt and dark brown silty clay loam, the products of a combination of seasonal changes in the amount of sediment carried by the Nile and the changing velocity of river flow. The most appropriate comparison at Karnak was with agricultural soil used for the manufacture of modern local bricks, a brown silt loam, probably alluvial, containing pottery fragments. In three out of these four samples medium silt was the dominant material.

At Karnak, a sample of eight bricks, ranging in date from the early second millennium BC to the late centuries BC/early centuries AD, together with a modern local brick, gave particle-analysis results showing very small to zero amounts of clay, and a silt proportion that varied between 28 per cent and 52 per cent. There is a difference in the silt–sand ratio – a reduction in silt – between the bricks and the single sample of natural alluvium from which they are made. Unless the brick-makers were, on other occasions, choosing soils of 60–70 per cent sandiness, they presum-

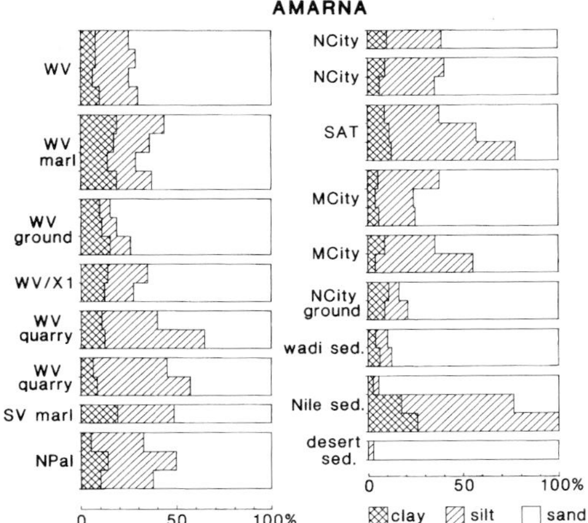

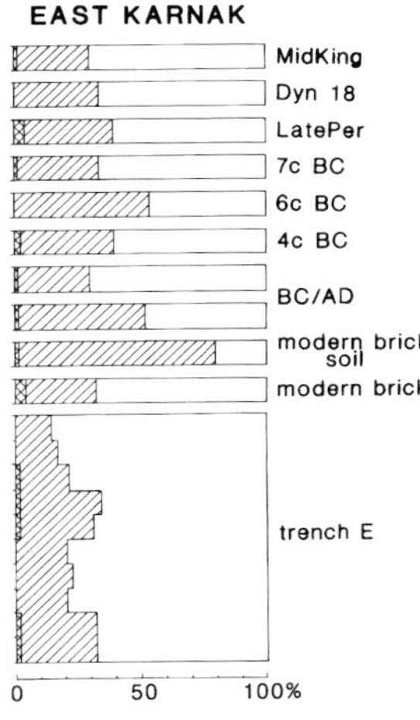

Figure 3.1 The relative proportions of clay, silt, and sand in samples of brick and soil from Amarna and East Karnak (after French 1981, 1984). Each small vertical division represents a single sample. WV = Workmen's Village; SV = Stone Village; NPal = North Palace; NCity = North City; MCity = Main City; SAT = Small Aten Temple. The bottom three sets of samples in the middle column are derived from natural sediments from the floor of a desert wadi*, the river bank, and the desert. The samples from WV ground, NCity ground, and trench E derive from archaeological deposits between or beyond walls.*

ably added sand to the mix (French's own explanation that the silt is puddled out during manufacture is hard to envisage on the scale required). Except for the two latest (which had been partially fired to an orange-brown colour, 7.5 YR 5/4 on the Munsell scale), all of the ancient bricks and the modern brick and sample of alluvium were a similar greyish-brown in colour (10YR 4/2–3 or 5/2–3). A further comparison comes from samples taken at intervals down stratigraphic trenches in the settlement strata (represented by Trench E) which in large part must be derived from the decay of mud brick structures. The generally larger proportions of sand presumably represent the combined effects of the wind in depositing sand and removing the finer silts.

At Amarna all of the bricks sampled were of the same period (*c.* 1350 BC), but came from widely dispersed parts of the site. The most valuable reference set derived from the Workmen's Village, where bricks could be divided into two broad groups on the basis of colour. One, from the village enclosure wall and of the common greyish-brown colour, was deemed to have been made from mud from the alluvial plain; the other group, of varying shades of orange and grey and often quite pebbly, was almost certainly made from marl locally dug from quarries adjacent to the village. Neither group had been given a straw temper. They differ principally from the Karnak bricks in the higher proportion of clay (6–10 per cent) at the expense of silt (17.5–20 per cent), but still were generally sandier than two of the three samples from the local alluvial beds from the banks of the Nile. Again we should accept intervention by the brickmakers. In the case of the marl bricks, comparison with source material can be made more confidently than is usually possible because the quarries which provided it are identifiable. A set of marl bricks, despite their distinctive appearance, broke down into proportions of clay and silt (13.75–18.75 per cent and 15–25 per cent) which were higher than the alluvial bricks but not substantially so. The natural samples from the quarries (6.25–12.5 per cent clay and 28.75–52.5 per cent silt) are again somewhat siltier than the bricks derived from them but the contrast is less marked. At a separate but similarly located site (the Stone Village) the analysis of a single marl brick gave a result closer to that from the Workmen's Village quarries. Samples from an ancient ground surface show, as with its equivalent (Trench E) at Karnak, an increase in sand.

Within the main parts of the city, which were much closer to the course of the river, the composition of bricks varies considerably. From the quantities of grit and pebbles and from the pale greyish colour which can so commonly be seen in the bricks it is likely that local desert materials were a common and deliberately added part of the mud mix (gravel was not present in the samples analysed). The analyses done were confined to fourteen samples of bricks which, from their superficial appearance, seemed to be alluvial. They showed the same persistence of clay (3.75–13.75 per cent) but a general tendency to greater siltiness (18.75–65 per cent) than the alluvial bricks from the Workmen's Village. Quite striking is the variation in the silt/sand ratio of three bricks from different parts of the Small Aten Temple, the third sample being almost identical in composition to one of the natural deposits from the river bank. One ancient ground deposit from the North City showed the increase in sand.

Several lessons can be drawn from these analyses. One is the regular appearance of a mix in which sand was generally in the region of 60–70 per cent implying that the brickmakers had a preferred mix, detectable by the feel of handfuls of the mud, to be achieved either by selection of soils or by the addition of sand. The East Karnak–Amarna comparison also shows that the near absence of clay did not hinder brick-making. A third lesson is that, whilst gross colour differences in bricks (sometimes expressed simply by terms such as 'marl', 'sandy') can be a general guide to the origin of their soils, it actually tells one little about their particle composition, which tends to be the same. Colour differences are more the product of chemical weathering. Thus the distinctive reddish-yellow colour (7.5YR 6/8) of the desert marl at Amarna is due to a high oxidized iron content.

A further lesson is perhaps that particle-size analysis of a few sample bricks on their own is likely to have very limited value. Bricks are the products of geological deposits modified by human intervention. To go beyond repeating what is probably a fairly common basic makeup, brick analyses need to be part of an integrated study of soils within the general locality. If this is the case, analyses which aim to identify sources of raw material can be undertaken which will take one further than the quantification of basic components. The heavy mineral species that are present might indicate, if they can be identified, the source of the sediment, whilst the shape of the quartz particles might distinguish abrasion by fluvial and/or aeolian transportation (French 1981: 277).

The source of the soil used in making bricks is connected to the question of where they were made and who made them. Some soil is invariably required at a building site for mortar and plaster, and one way of proceeding is to make the bricks also at the site, assuming that there is sufficient empty space to create a temporary brickyard. A common occasion for building must have been replacement of houses and other constructions within existing towns. A proportion of whole bricks could have been rescued for re-use from the demolition of the old structures, but the principal demolition product is likely to have been rubble which would then have been available for breaking down into the raw material for new bricks and mortar. The likelihood of recycling is an important factor in any study of the composition of bricks on other than virgin sites.

Soil particle analysis of this kind describes the gross material of the bricks. Extraneous material, added either deliberately or accidentally, can often be observed in ancient bricks, and can include ash, sherds, fragments from stoneworking, and even the occasional bead or other small artefact. Reisner comments from personal observation:

> The only material which is now deliberately added to the mud is dust and broken straw, by preference the sweepings of the threshing-floor; but even street-sweepings, which usually contain a certain amount of wind blown straw, are used by poor people. (Reisner 1931: 72)

The value of added temper is that it redirects the stresses that arise as the bricks shrink as they dry. This reduces shrinkage and provides a reinforcing structure which limits cracking.

Particular interest attaches to the addition of vegetal matter, especially chopped straw and chaff (ancient Egyptian *dḥ3*, Arabic *tibn*). To judge from the impressions of *tibn* left in ancient bricks this was a widespread form of added temper and represents a practice that has survived to modern times. It was evidently a preferred temper. One New-Kingdom model letter contains a complaint about local unavailability of straw for the making of bricks (Caminos 1954: 188; cf. Simpson 1963: 75). The Old-Testament story of the failure of straw deliveries to the Israelite brick-makers whilst resident in Egypt (Exodus 5:1–19; Nims 1950; Kitchen 1966: 156) has given added significance to the practice (although, since other forms of temper can be just as good, the story reflects ancient prejudice). Indeed, despite much expert comment to the contrary, the omission of straw is still sometimes seen as producing bricks of lesser quality, even on desert sites (e.g. Meidum, Borkowski and Majcherek 1991: 27; cf. Nims 1950: 26). A robust comment is provided by McHenry:

> Straw is sometimes suggested as a necessary ingredient. It is not! Most adobes made with reasonable adobe soil don't need it. If the organic content is too high, or the clay content too low, it may be necessary to add straw for strength, and for speed in drying. (McHenry 1976: 51)

This is borne out by Clarke and Engelbach:

> With a good sand and alluvium he [the brick-maker] can make tolerably hard bricks, and dispense with the chaff which, in the southern parts of Egypt, is expensive . . . if there is no *tibn* the bricks are made without it, but sand is often added with good effect. (Clarke and Engelbach 1930: 208, n. 2 and 209)

In modern Egypt *tibn* is widely available only for a time following the harvest. For it to have been available round the year in ancient times it would have been necessary to maintain stocks. The city of Amarna, it should be noted, was largely built of bricks without straw, the normal temper having been coarse sand with some gravel. The possibility of insect infestation of the organic content of bricks has not (to my knowledge) been investigated for Egypt, although on desert sites it can lead to its total loss from termites.

The generally simple approach to the distribution of loads by ancient Egyptian builders meant that compressive strength was the prime physical requirement of mud bricks, which have normally weak tensile strength (large bricks often break in two if carried carelessly). Even so, one set of tests of compressive strength of Fourth-Dynasty mud bricks with chaff temper, and of mud and sand mortar, concluded that the results 'belong to the lowest-known compressive strength values for materials used in architectural monuments' (Borkowski and Majcherek 1991: 29). Making walls thick obviously compensates, but, apart from this, it is also clear from particular examples that walls of, say thirty centimetres in thickness, were capable of reaching heights of between three and four metres and of supporting the added weight of two roofs (Kemp 1995: 147–9). Moreover, modern mud bricks made with similar mixes of materials emerge as perfectly adequate in this respect (Fathy 1969: 241–2, 287–8). It is important to realise that the characteristics of ancient mud bricks are likely to have altered over time, so that one is making judgements which, whilst important in assessing present conservation needs on a mud-brick building, need not have been relevant at the time when the bricks were made and used. Thus a binder of *tibn* (or any organic material) can be lost to insect infestation; on the other hand, long exposure to low levels of humidity, which are likely to be present even on open desert sites, probably leads to the concentration of soluble salts (principally calcium carbonate) in exposed brickwork, especially towards the surface of bricks, and hence to an increase in hardness.

The making of mud bricks

Evidence from ancient Egypt that relates to brick-making, other than the bricks themselves, is not extensive. It is rarely illustrated in tomb scenes. The principal example is in the mid-Eighteenth-Dynasty tomb of Rekhmira (TT100; Davies 1935: pls. XVI, XVII, XXIII; Davies 1943: 54–5, pls. LVIII, LIX, LX; Mekhitarian 1954: 48; Lhote 1954: pls. 97–9, 101; Arnold 1991:97, fig. 3.52). There is also a questionable Twelfth-Dynasty example at Deir el-Bersha (Newberry [1895]: pls. XXIV, XXV; Klebs 1922: 118). The Rekhmira artist changed his colour convention from pinky-grey for bricks as they were being made, to pink and white once they were dry and in the hands of the builder, an attempt to convey the substantial change that does take place during drying. The scene helps to define the meaning of the key word used for making or 'striking' a brick, *sẖt* (Badawy 1957: 63–4; Simpson 1963: 77–8; Spencer 1979a: 3–4). Brick-making was also an occasional subject for the wooden tomb models of the early Middle Kingdom (e.g. Breasted 1948: 52, pl. 46C, from Deir el-Bersha; Garstang 1907: 131, fig. 129, from Beni Hasan; Nims 1950: fig. 2). A small number of actual ancient brick moulds, all made of wood, are known (Petrie 1890: 26, pl. IX.23; 1917: 42 pl. XLVII.55; David 1986: pl. 18; Clarke and Engelbach 1930: fig. 263e), some of them models from temple foundation deposits (Weinstein 1973: 98–9, 232, 296, 419). The remains have also been recorded of at least one place where bricks had been made in ancient times (Vercoutter 1970: 214–16). This very limited documentation shows a way of working that seems to be identical to that of traditional brick-making in modern Egypt which has often been described (e.g. Clarke and Engelbach 1930: 208–9; Reisner 1931: 72–3; Petrie 1938: 4; Nims 1950: 26–7; Spencer 1979a: 3).

One estimate of daily output by a pair of early modern brick-makers and a mud mixer is from 4,000 to 6,000 (Reisner 1931: 72–3; comparable to Nims 1950: 27). Since modern bricks are small this is likely to be a considerable over-estimate if applied to the numbers produced in Pharaonic times; on the other hand, if output is measured in terms of volume, the ancient rate of production is likely to have been higher, since the larger moulds would have meant a more efficient use of the brick-maker's labour.

A question that is bound to arise in the case of a society which, like that of ancient Egypt, was much given to large-scale public works and to the administration of labour and commodities, is the existence of administered brickyards, either permanent or set up for large-scale projects. Estimates of 24.5 million bricks originally in the pyramid of Senusret III at Dahshur and 4.6 million for Buhen fortress give an idea of the size of demand that could arise (de Morgan 1895: 47, n. 3; Emery *et al.* 1979, 40), and a few texts record the exact number of bricks used on a project (e.g. Reisner 1923: 511). The written evidence is, however, ambiguous. A Middle Kingdom administrative papyrus from Kahun concerned with large numbers of bricks could as easily be dealing with brick-laying as brick-making or delivery (Griffith 1898: 59 pl. XXIII.24–40; Simpson 1960). A section of Papyrus Reisner I (of the reign of Senusret I) from Naga el-Deir also covers several operations involving the structural use of soil, including the making of mud bricks, each operation being the subject of precise calculation (Simpson 1963: 56–8, 72–80), but imprecisions in our understanding of the technical vocabulary again hinder understanding.

Being in charge of brick-making did not earn a specific official title. It is possible, particularly in view of the fact that brick-making in traditional societies is a very widespread skill, that it was normally treated as a form of peasant labouring, and the necessary output was obtained through whatever means of coercion was practised at a given time. In the Rekhmira brick-making scene (Davies 1943: 54–5) the labour used is explicitly identified as being foreign captives, their output intended for storerooms for the temple of Amun at Thebes. Given the nature of the administered sector of the ancient Egyptian economy, which was able to transport materials over long distances to meet the needs of individual schemes, the existence of administered brickyards raises the possibility that sometimes bricks or, at least, some of the raw materials, were brought in from a distance, and thus that their composition owes nothing to local sediments.

Perhaps the clearest evidence for administered supervision is the practice of impressing bricks with an official stamp (Fig. 3.4a), which is known from the beginning of the Eighteenth Dynasty to as late as the Thirtieth (Spencer 1979a: 144–6), the Eighteenth Dynasty providing the broadest spread of examples. If at a brickyard the person wielding the stamp from time to time walked down an aisle between fields of recently made bricks and impressed a stamp every few paces, the relatively small number of stamped bricks that would result, and their irregular distribution in loads which might be made up by workmen carrying them away in a different order from that in which they were visited by the stamp-wielder, could well produce the haphazard way in which they appear in constructions. Just as interesting are buildings in which they were not used, the Great Palace, Kom el-Nana, the North Palace and the Great Wall around the North Riverside Palace at Amarna being conspicuous examples. Should we deduce that not all brickyards possessed stamps, and see this as evidence that the sources of supply available to the king did not all have the same status?

A possible precursor to the use of stamps was the tracing of a simple design on to the top of a brick by means of a finger. Examples have been found on the bricks used in Middle Kingdom pyramids (de Morgan 1895: 49, fig. 110; Arnold 1979: 7, pls. 2–3; 1987: 82, Abb. 40). Finger-markings occur on bricks at Amarna, often a single diagonal line (visible in Nicholson 1989: 67, fig. 3.3; 68, fig. 3.4).

Bricks as artefacts

In rare instances individual bricks served a special need. They were used as markers in the course of laying out structures (e.g. parts of the Small Aten Temple at Amarna; the alignment of the boat slipway at Mirgissa, Fig. 3.8a); they had a restricted use in ritual contexts: bricks in early Middle Kingdom temple foundation deposits sometimes contained inscribed plaques (Weinstein 1973: xvii, 'Mud bricks'; Arnold 1979: 50), and in New Kingdom tombs 'magical' bricks were inscribed with short texts of protection which actually specify 'bricks of unbaked clay' (Thomas 1964).

When in their normal use as a building material bricks, as artefacts, are open to systematic recording by the archaeologist. Spencer (1979a: 1) has put forward a set of standard headings under which brick details should be routinely recorded:

1. The composition of the bricks, and whether burnt or unburnt.
2. The dimensions of the bricks.
3. The bonding, preferably described by means of a Corpus of bonds.
4. The distribution of any reed-matting or timber tie-beams in the brickwork.
5. The nature of the mortar.
6. Details of any plaster.
7. Whether stamped bricks occur.
8. Any special usages, or bricks of special form.

We will consider brick sizes first, since measuring ancient bricks is perhaps the most obvious thing to do with them. The first aim of brick measurement is to identify the output of individual factories or brick-making teams, initially for the purpose of internal comparisons. These usually relate to a site's chronology. Although the potential is also perhaps there for a study of how many sources of supply there might have been for a given building project, the variables are probably uncontrollable. Moreover, brick measurement itself is complicated by the nature of the data to be collected.

Even if bricks are formed from a mould that has been made true, the result, from the traditional style of brick-making, is not a simple geometric shape but one with a complex topography that is individual to each and every brick. The reasons for irregularity lie partly in the shrinkage that is bound to have taken place as the bricks dried, particularly since a fairly wet mix is likely to have been used (if one takes modern traditional brick-making as a guide). Moreover, each time that a mix of mud was prepared the proportions of its constituents are likely to have varied slightly, leading to a slightly different degree of shrinkage. A further cause of irregularity is disturbance whilst drying. Modern traditional brick-makers tend to lay out their bricks very close to one another. As the brick-maker lifts the wooden mould free from the most recently made brick, jiggling it to prize it free, it is very easy for him to bump it against the neighbouring brick in the previously made row, distorting it slightly. With the larger-sized bricks favoured at certain periods in the past the jiggling of the mould as it was removed will probably also have distorted each brick as soon as it was made. Furthermore, bricks are normally made on an earth surface which has not been prepared with great thoroughness. The undersides of bricks can therefore be more irregular than the other faces and bear the impressions of loose debris left on the working surface, whilst a slight convexity sometimes develops on the top surface during drying.

Given the imprecisions of manufacture, the proposal to measure ancient bricks to the nearest millimetre (Mond and Myers 1934: 49; Hesse 1970, 1971, endorsed by Spencer 1979a: 147) is not easily met, for brick faces are often not true planes. A dimension exactly recorded, therefore, can itself be a compromise. A high level of precision implies that many measurements will be taken of each individual brick and then be subject to a procedure of statistical reduction. Furthermore, complete bricks, the best basis for measurement, are available only if removed from a wall. If one chooses bricks from the uppermost preserved course, which will at least offer complete top surfaces to measure, one is making the assumption that this arbitrarily chosen layer is representative of the wall as a whole. A random selection of bricks chosen for measurement from the wall is not then possible. If one measures lengths and breadths below the uppermost preserved courses then inevitably these dimensions will not come in true pairs, but each length and breadth will belong to a different brick. Furthermore, weathering or the original smearing of mortar over the wall face often makes it difficult to discern the original edges of the bricks. My own view, formed in the course of trying to measure large numbers of bricks, is that accuracy beyond the nearest half centimetre runs the risk of being illusory (accepted by Hesse 1970: 104, his objection to rounding being the temptation to round to the same value; his histograms have half-centimetre divisions; note his view, however, that the arbitrariness of measurement in millimetres makes it easier to plot individual bricks as a scatter of points since few will be identical and thus occupy the same position on the graph). On the other hand, as outlined below, one of the things that one is looking for is

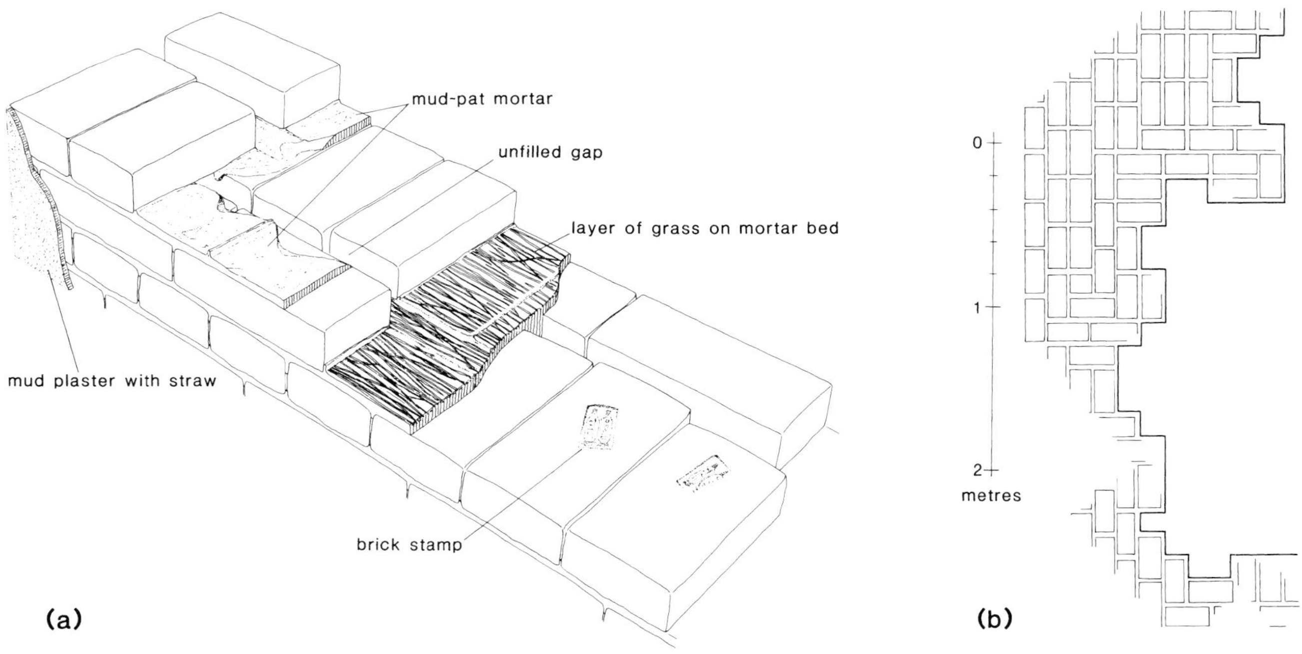

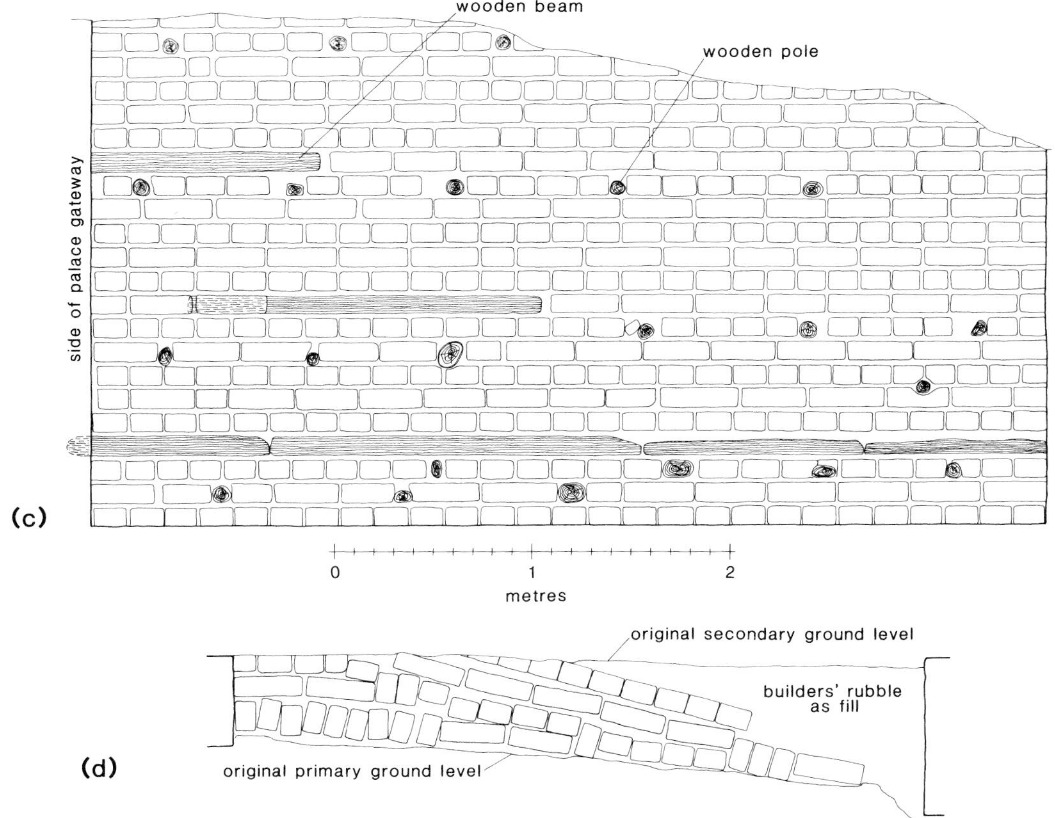

Figure 3.4 The laying of bricks. (a) Features of a mud-brick wall of the New Kingdom; (b) Pattern of bricklaying to achieve the niched façade effect, Early Dynastic Period, Hierakonpolis (after Weeks 1971–2); (c) Part of the enclosure wall of the North Riverside Palace at Amarna (the back wall of the niche north of the Great Gateway), showing the pattern of bricklaying and insertion of timbers; (d) Side wall of a buried portion of a ramp at Amarna (Kom el-Nana), showing how bricks laid on their edge were used to increase the thicknesses of brick courses.

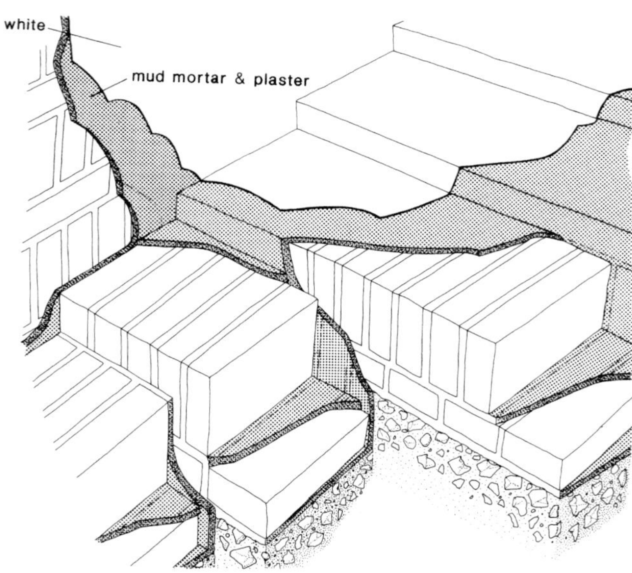

Figure 3.5 A common method of making the steps of a staircase was to use bricks laid on their edge, as here at the Ramesseum (after Thorel 1976: 50). Note the header courses of bricks laid on their edge in the wall beside the steps.

a corpus of bonds (Mond and Myers 1934: 47–52, pls. CXII–CXIV; Spencer 1979a: 7, 136–9, pls. 1–20). It should, however, be normal for the archaeologist to make explicit the pattern or patterns (bonding) used, and most definitely not to draw unmeasured brick shapes on plans simply as a space-filling convention to indicate brickwork. This can easily disguise the fact that, on larger projects, considerable variation in the pattern of laying was tolerated, and even conspicuous departures from the horizontal in courses which had to pass over uneven ground and instead ran parallel to the natural slope (Fig. 3.12 = Mirgissa; Reisner *et al.* 1967: 155–6; Vercoutter 1970: pl. VIII; Serra East: Hughes 1963: pls. XXVIIb, XXIX). Complicated patterns made it even more difficult for the builders to maintain accuracy and regularity. An example is the Early Dynastic palace-façade wall inside the town at Hierakonpolis, where the detailed archaeologist's plan shows numerous anomalies in the bricklaying (Fig. 3.4b; Weeks 1971–2). Another case of intricate patterning in brick is provided by the elaborate sets of archer's loopholes in some of the Middle Kingdom fortresses in Nubia (Fig. 3.11c; Emery *et al.* 1979), but the regularity with which they were laid out raises the possibility that they were formed around wooden shapes. Bricks could also be made to special shapes, some of them curved, but this aspect is reserved for a later section.

Part of the bricklayer's job was to compensate for unevennesses, accidentally developed through variability in brick sizes, uneven foundations, or poor workmanship (Fig. 3.4d); others arose deliberately, when walls were built with inward-sloping (battered) surfaces or the bedding planes were sloping or curved (see pp. 91–2). Mud bricks are easy to break or cut in order to provide pieces to fill small or uneven spaces, but there were a few simple tricks to employ as well. Bricks laid on their long edge added thickness to a course (and were useful in making staircases, Fig. 3.5); wide internal spaces either left open or filled with mortar (Fig. 3.4a) enabled wall thickness to be adjusted and irregular brick lengths in header courses to be lost to sight; bricks laid diagonally were also a means of adjusting thickness (Hölscher 1910: 29, Abb. 23; Thorel 1976: 44). Because vertical joints were often narrow or negligible it was easier to maintain regularity of bonding with bricks which approximated to the 2:1 ratio of length to width (see the discussion above on brick sizes). Nevertheless, actual examples show that it was sometimes necessary to introduce a half brick in a stretcher course to return the courses to their intended pattern of bonding (Fig. 3.4c, courses 3 and 11 from the top). Although walls were normally plastered, many well-preserved examples display considerable care and skill in achieving an even pattern of laying, and the likelihood that the makers of brick moulds sometimes departed from the 2:1 ratio to accommodate an extra header joint adds to the impression that we are often looking at the work of a skilled trade.

One danger which builders strove to avoid was the cracking of walls through uneven distribution of loads. A common measure to prevent this was to insert amongst the courses horizontal timber beams or narrower poles, both laterally and longitudinally, at vertical intervals that could vary from five to fourteen courses (the latter at Elkab; Figs 3.4c, 3.13c). They were particularly needed in very thick masses of bricks where, for the bricks in the interior, careful bonding of courses was normally abandoned, and sometimes even the use of mortar. Since timbers only started at the first interval above ground level, a wall needs to be

Figure 3.6 Section of niched 'palace-façade' brickwork at First-Dynasty tomb 3507 at Saqqara. Note the impressions of cylindrical wooden poles over the tops of the niches.

preserved to a height of a least half a metre for this to be detectable. The practice was often accompanied by spreading a layer of thick grass or reeds over an entire working surface that might or might not coincide with the level at which the timber was being inserted (Figs 3.4a, 3.7; Clarke and Engelbach 1930: 210; Spencer 1979a: 131–2, 135), a practice which is probably illustrated in the brick-making and building scene in the tomb of Rekhmira (TT100), where yellow fronds are shown protruding from a wall (Davies 1943: 55–6, pl. LX). Examples of timber and grass insertions are sufficiently widely spread chronologically to suggest that this was a continuous tradition in larger constructions from the Early Dynastic period onwards. The amount of timber (probably acacia in many instances) required would have been substantial: an estimate of 3,700 logs has been made for Mirgissa fortress, for example (Reisner *et al.* 1967: 157, Uronarti). More rarely, vertical timbers protected corners (Reisner *et al.* 1967: 21). In the brickwork of a Fourth-Dynasty tomb at Meidum (no. 6, Rahotep) logs of trees up to three metres long had been set, nearly upright (Petrie 1892: 16).

From the New Kingdom onwards builders seem to have begun to understand better the forces at work inside very thick masses of brickwork and to have adapted their techniques. The most obvious signs are to be seen in later temple enclosure walls. These were built as a series of blocks of brickwork in which the bricks of each alternate block were laid in beds that were concave along the wall's length, the courses of the other blocks being either all horizonal or all convex (Figs 3.13, 3.15). This alternation was often emphasised, too, by alternating the thicknesses of the blocks. The term 'pan-bedding' has sometimes been applied. Careful preparations were made to ensure that the curve of the bedding-planes was even and regular. At Philae a massive stone bed had been laid out in a curve as a foundation for the pan-bedding of the brick wall above (Petrie 1938: 11, pl. IV.15); at Edfu the pan-bedded sections of brickwork stand on a deep foundation of horizontally-laid bricks (Spencer 1979a: 81); in other cases stonework reinforcing the corners also retains the slope of the curve (Spencer 1979a: 78). Examples occur between the Nineteenth-Dynasty (enclosure wall of the temple of Seti I at Abydos, Frankfort 1933: 13, pl. XIII.1) and Roman times (the wall of this type at the Kom el-Sultan, Abydos – Figure 3.15 – is of the Late Period not the Middle Kingdom, as Petrie 1903: 6, pls. XLVIII.3, XLIX supposed). The style was applied to the building of cellular foundation platforms where the sides were also given concave lines in plan (e.g. Fougerousse 1933; Spencer 1979b), a feature which sometimes appears in the plans of walls, too (Fig. 3.13). It also came to be used for the walls of towns and large houses and other buildings, at least in Greco-Roman times (e.g. at Karanis in the first century AD, Husselman 1979: 33–5, pls. 12–14; Clarke and Engelbach 1930: 211; Spencer 1979a: 117; house models: Davies 1929: 250, fig. 14; Engelbach 1931: pl. III). An alternative, illustrated by the Medinet Habu outer enclosure wall of Rameses III, was to run the concave beds perpendicular to the wall face (Fig. 3.13a; Hölscher 1951: 3, pl. 41). Concave beds did not replace the use of timber inserts; they continued to be laid into the brickwork as an added binder (Fig. 3.13c).

Figure 3.7 *Niched brickwork on the Second-Dynasty 'funerary palace' at Abydos, the Shunet el-Zebib. In the main mass of the brickwork the more pronounced horizontal planes mark layers of grass.*

The design is very well-suited for overcoming structural problems: of uneven settlement of the underlying ground, scaling or spalling of the surface of the brickwork, distortion as the bricks dried leading to cracking, and shear cracking especially in the case of a foundation platform which is going to bear the load of building above (e.g. Clarke and Engelbach 1930: 210–11; Petrie 1938: 10–12). Chevrier (1964) has provided mathematical support and experimental verification, and powerful witnesses are the tall Roman houses at Karanis built in this way, which continued to stand to considerable heights after the town had been abandoned yet remained free from cracking until buried in drift sand (Husselman 1979).

The building of large temple enclosure walls was included amongst the pious acts of kings and formally commemorated as such, at least from the Eighteenth Dynasty onwards (Traunecker 1975). Often made to look like the walls of a fortress (Kemp 1972; Golvin and Hegazy 1993), they were seen symbolically as providing essential protection against the forces of disorder. It is conceivable, therefore, that their design drew upon mythology, although this does not preclude the possibility that symbolic interpretation was secondary to a design which arose from practical utility. One explanation of this kind (Barguet 1962: 31–2; also Spencer 1979a: 114–5) looks to an element of temple mythology, in which each temple was thought to stand upon the primaeval mound of creation, newly emerged from the waters of Nun. The undulations of the wall convey the watery environment. An example at Deir el-Medina preserves battlements and a walkway along the top, and these actually retain the undulations of the bedding-planes of the individual sections of the wall and so emphasise that they were integral to its appearance (Golvin and Hegazy 1993). On the other hand, the employment of concave bedding at Medinet Habu, because it ran at right-angles to the face, was invisible from the outside.

Whatever the original thought behind it was (and I would support those who see it as esentially a technological improvement) we seem to be dealing with an important and distinctive development in architectural aesthetic, the substitution of curving for straight lines. It appears in large buildings where, in contrast to stone-built temples, the outlines were not so strictly dictated by specific design models, and their general visibility would have been a startling contribution to the built environment.

Soil for mortar, plaster, and flooring

Soil provided the mortar used for laying bricks, its compositional relationship to the bricks depending to a large extent on whether the bricks were made on site, and thus from the same earth, or were imported. In the latter case bricks and mortar could be significantly different, as with the whitish mortar of desert clay mixed with straw used with alluvial mud bricks in the Eleventh-Dynasty temple at Deir el-Bahari (Arnold 1979: 6, 16, 25). Coarse filler such as chopped straw was, however, often not used. Cases have been noted where gypsum appears to have been used as mortar when adjacent to stonework (Martin 1989: 9, 12). It is important to be sure that this was a deliberate choice and not the accidental consequence of gypsum used for the bedding of stones spreading into the normally open vertical joints of adjacent brickwork (Mallinson 1995: figs 5.6, 5.9).

Mortar normally formed a bed beneath each new course. It was often (at least in the New Kingdom) laid down as separate little piles which the weight of the new brick would spread out into circular pats (two per brick, Fig. 3.4a). Vertical joints tended to be very close and with little or no mortar within them. Moreover, where brickwork had considerable depth, as in pylons, enclosure walls, and pyramids, the internal brickwork could be laid without mortar at all (e.g. Golvin and Hegazy 1993: 149, pl. IIa; Hölscher 1951: 3). The plastering of wall surfaces above ground, inside and out, made 'pointing' (when the bricklayer smooths and presses mortar into all joints) unnecessary. Nevertheless, the practice was known and occurs on the foundation courses of some good quality buildings (at Amarna, at least), thus below the level of the plastering. Whether or not it was the intention, it would presumably have provided a barrier against the fauna that likes to live in wall cavities.

It is important to distinguish mortar from plaster. They do different things and this is reflected in composition. Plaster not only improves the appearance of a wall and helps to protect it against weathering, it also adds to its mechanical strength (Petrie 1938: 6–7). In composition what normally distinguishes plaster from mortar is the high concentration of straw, the inclusion of which reduces cracking. Subsequent loss of straw from insect attack leaves it very friable and, since it was also the normal medium on which painting was done, wall paintings from domestic or religious buildings of mud brick only survive in exceptional circumstances. An unusual mix of a silt-lime plaster with straw chaff has been identified in the Fourth-Dynasty *mastaba* of Nefermaat and Atet at Meidum (No. 16) (Borkowski and Majcherek 1991: 28–9).

Floors are an aspect of soil architecture which tend to receive less attention than walls, yet are, at the same time, often less straightforward to deal with, the reason being that it is not always clear how deliberate their creation has been. Floors can be deliberate layers of mud plaster over a base of mud bricks, which were sometimes made specifically for flooring and have sets of dimensions of their own, often exactly or approximating a square, of between 30 and 43 cm (Spencer 1979a: 119; see also above for fired brick tiles used to create floors). In the case of compact muddy surfaces over open areas, however, the possibility exists that they came into existence through the combined action of trampling and of wetting the ground, a puddling process in itself. Such by-products of human behaviour can recur over the same area to produce a laminated effect. Deliberately made mud floor plaster probably benefits in the same way that wall plaster does in being given a relatively high organic content, usually derived from chopped straw, and being applied in a fairly plastic state, thus without the addition of too much water. Another form of external mud rendering, midway between the plaster of walls and floors, was the surfacing of sloping revetments, such as the glacis of a fortress (e.g. at Mirgissa: Reisner *et al.* 1967: 151).

The detailed study of the composition of floors leads one into a vital aspect of archaeological interpretation, for floors can contain a record not only of how they were made but also, from material that subsequently becomes incorporated into them, of what activities were carried out on them (a clear example is Hecker 1986). The evidence is often microscopic, but a technique has been developed for taking and studying large thin-sections of archaeological deposits which include floors (Matthews and Postgate 1994). Specialist skill and access to an appropriate laboratory are required, but first results (not from Egyptian sites) are so promising as to imply that the technique could play an important part in interpreting the results of excavation on settlement sites in Egypt, whether in the desert or on the floodplain.

One specialised use of spread soil took advantage of its lubricant property when wet. Used in conjunction with reinforcing timbers to take the weight, a layer of mud was the basis for prepared roads over which heavy loads were dragged. The best-preserved example is a slipway near the Middle-Kingdom fortress of Mirgissa in Nubia which had enabled boats (presumably loaded on sledges) to be hauled past a particularly difficult stretch of the river (Fig. 3.8a; Vercoutter 1970: 204–14). The remains of similar examples have been found at a quarry at Lahun and beside one of the pyramids at Lisht (Arnold 1991: 86–92). These examples need to be interpreted in the light of the well-known scene of the transport of a colossal statue in the tomb of Thuthotep at Deir el-Bersha (Newberry [1895]: 16–26, pls. XII–XIX; Arnold 1991: 277–8) and a similar one in the tomb of Ty at Saqqara. As it is dragged on its sledge a man pours water, presumably to ease the gliding, an effect which modern experiments have replicated (Chevrier 1970: 20–5).

Roofing

An important sub-section of the topic of soil architecture is roofing, which took two forms: flat roofs of mud laid over wooden beams, and vaults and domes of brick. Occasionally actual roofs of ancient buildings have survived but mostly the roofs of above-ground structures will have collapsed. Even then, at least on desert sites, evidence for roofing can still be found amongst the fragments of rubble. In the past this has often been ignored by archaeologists. As a result there is insufficient evidence for judging the relative frequency of the two kinds, both by historical period and by type of building. The plan of a building might sometimes point to the answer; for example, vaults need a certain thickness to accommodate both the springing and, if not balanced by a parallel vault, the lateral force that a vault creates. On the other hand the presence of columns might be thought to indicate a flat roof, although the throne room in the palace at Medinet Habu possessed long vaults above the columns (Hölscher 1941: 38–9, pl. 26; 1951: 29).

Flat roofs require a rigid framework of beams to take weight, and a covering surface laid over them to provide a ceiling or roof. The evidence for ancient practice shows that the covering surface could consist of a layer of bricks (e.g. Emery 1949: 74, fig. 36; 1961: 184–5, fig. 108) or (probably more commonly) of a layer of plant material (thin poles, the central ribs of palm leaves – *gereed* – coarse grass, or woven matting) covered by a thick layer of mud (Fig. 3.8b; Petrie 1890: 23; 1891: 8; Peet and Woolley 1923: 57–8, fig. 6; Frankfort and Pendlebury 1933: 5, 9–11; Lacovara 1990, 8, fig. 2.11; Kemp, 1985: 8–11; Tytus 1903: 13, are variations but are the reconstructions reliable?). The width of spans would depend on the thickness of the timber cross beams which could be given intermediate support from columns. At Amarna flat roofs were usually not more than about 3.5 metres across. For aesthetic reasons the underside, including that of the protruding beams, could also be plastered with straw-rich mud plaster, which could then be painted. When ceilings and roofs of this kind collapse, the mud coverings break into pieces which will continue to retain the impressions of beams and other supporting material (which will normally eventually decay). Such roofing-fragments are important structural evidence and should be looked for and recorded during excavation.

Vaulted roofs are better documented, partly because of their use in tombs where they have had better chances of survival. The earliest examples recorded come from the First-Dynasty necropolis at Saqqara (Fig. 3.9a = Tomb 3500: Emery 1958: 102, pls. 116, 120; 1961: 185, fig. 90); domes have been recorded in Fourth-Dynasty tombs at Giza (Fig. 3.9d; Junker 1941: 25, 30–3, Taf. III; Larsen 1950; Abu-Bakr 1953: 129–43; for later examples see Spencer 1979a: 48, 123–6). Vaults are known to have covered spans of around five metres (Martin 1989: 55–6; Hölscher 1951: 29) and more, one in the mortuary temple of Amenhotep son of Hapu reaching 7.70 metres (Robichon and Varille 1936: pl. XI; Spencer 1979a: 87, following Hölscher, cites a possible case of a span of 8.60 metres at Medinet Habu). In order to create a flat surface above adjacent vaults, either for a roof or for the floor of an upper storey, the intervening spaces had to be filled. Bricks or rubble were used in the only surviving examples (Fig. 3.9b; Emery and Kirwan 1935: 34, 37, fig. 13, pls. 6 and 9; Ghazouli 1964: 145, pl. XVIA; Thorel 1976: 34, 41–2, 47) but by Coptic times smaller relieving vaults were being built into these spaces instead (e.g. at St Simeon's Monastery at Aswan). A further use of vaulting was to create relieving arches to protect doorways or chambers which lay within large masses of masonry (e.g. Minault-Gout and Deleuze 1992: pls. 11–19).

Most ancient vaults seem to have been of the pitched type in which each arc of bricks was laid at a slight angle to the vertical, so that the weight of each new one was borne by those already in place (Fig. 3.9; Van Beek 1987: 81). It has remained a living tradition especially in Nubia (e.g. Mileham 1910: 8–10; also Fathy 1969: 16–18, pls. 7–18). Its attraction is that it enables vaults to be constructed without the use of temporary supports. Although ordinary bricks can serve for this type of vault, special bricks were sometimes made. Normally they have two distinguishing characteristics. They were thinner, resembling tiles (Fig. 3.10), and did not need the standard 1:2 length:width ratio. Specimen dimensions are 41 × 23 × 5 cm (Martin 1989: 55–6); 60 × 22 × 7.5 cm (Ghazouli 1964: 144); 40 × 19 × 37 × 6 cm (Robichon and Varille 1936: 38); 40 × 20 × 40 × 7 cm (Frankfort 1933: 143), the last two with a slightly wedge-shaped design, which in other cases was accompanied by a slight curvature of the edges (Spencer 1979a: 142, fig. 90). The other characteristic was a scoring of one face (to be the underside), or even of both faces, by dragging the fingers down its length during

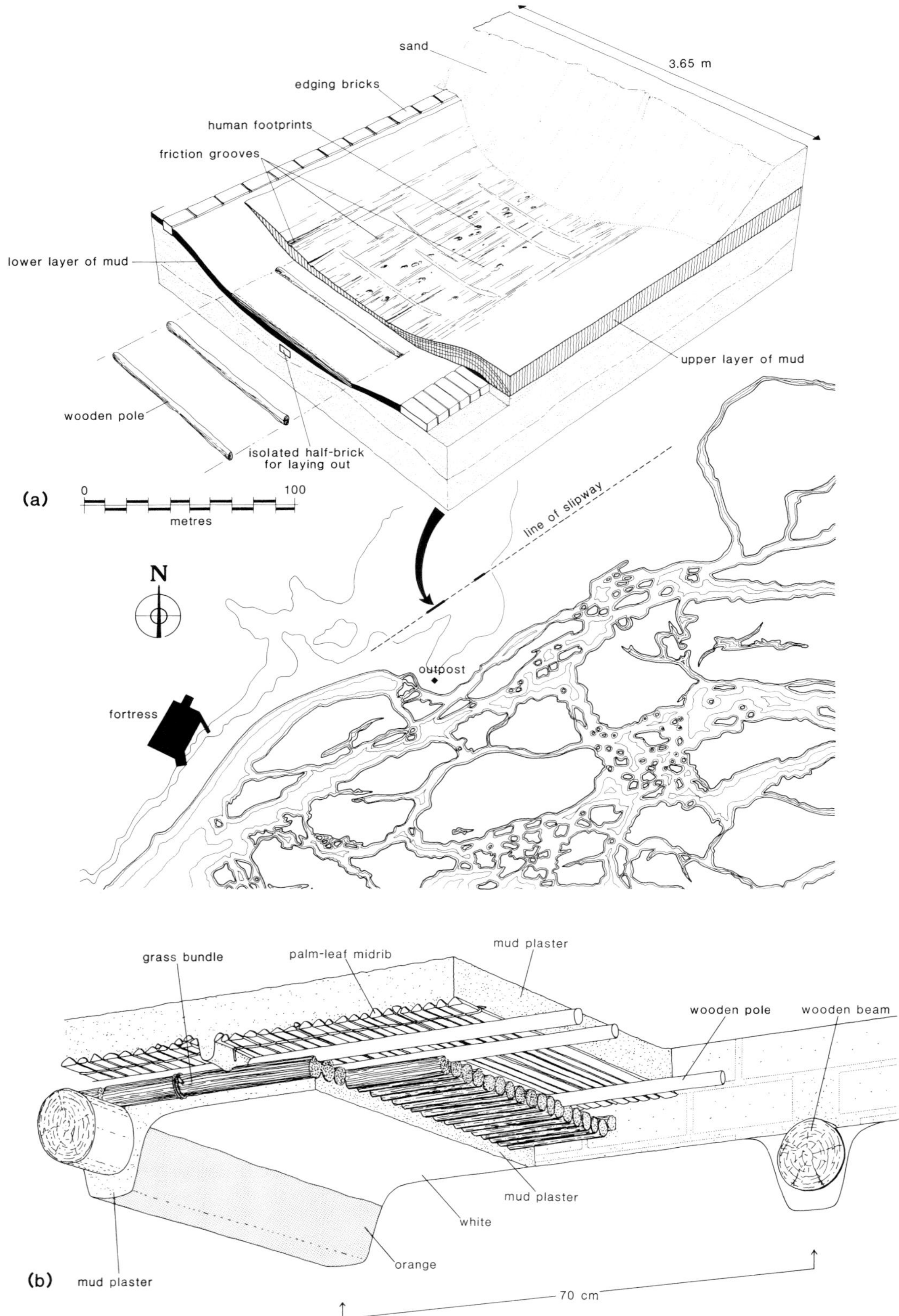

Figure 3.8 Uses of spread mud layers. (a) In a boat slipway at Mirgissa, Nubia (after Vercoutter 1970); (b) As a roof covering in a reconstruction of roof design at Amenhotep III's palace at Malkata, site E, square af21 (1973 excavations of the University Museum of Pennsylvania).

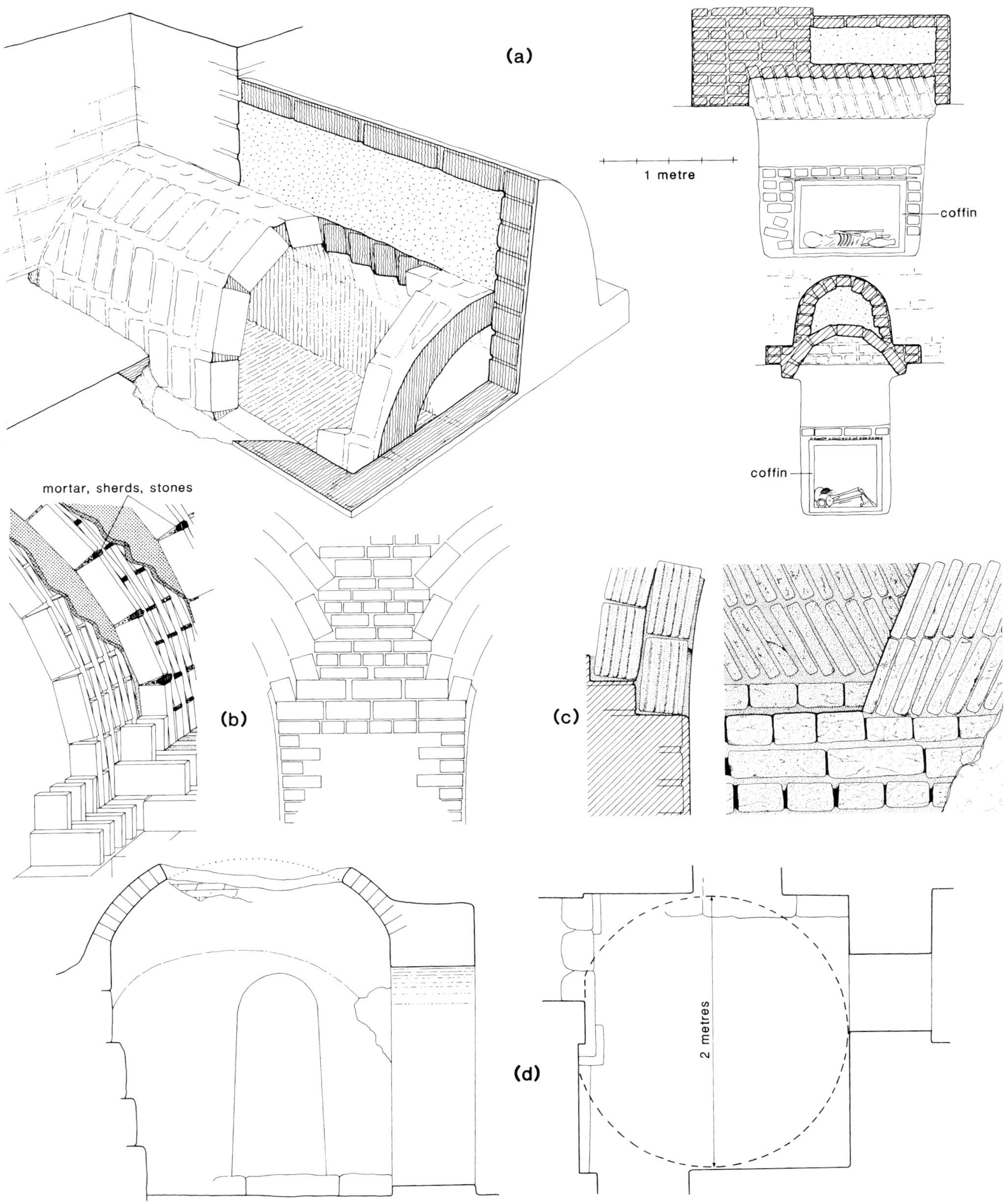

Figure 3.9 *Brick vaults and domes. (a) The earliest example, which covers a subsidiary burial at Saqqara tomb 3500, First Dynasty (after Emery 1958); (b) Brick vaulting at the Ramesseum with alternate pitching for double or multiple vault layers (after Thorel 1976); (c) A detail of the same, showing the grooved surfaces of the vaulting bricks; (d) Domed brick chapel at the Fourth-Dynasty tomb of Seneb at Giza (after Junker 1941).*

(a)

(b)

Figure 3.10 Brick vaulting at the magazines beside the temple of Seti I at Abydos. (a) Junction of pitched vaulting with wall; (b) Vault end, showing the use of roofing-bricks turned at right-angles to fill the space left by the vault pitch.

manufacture to create 'frogging' (Fig. 3.9c). This keyed the dried mortar on to the otherwise smooth surface of the brick and so helped to prevent shear loads from above splitting it away, and also perhaps augmented the suction of the wet mortar by allowing it to act on a greater surface area (Martin 1989: 51). It is important to identify fragments of such roofing tiles if found loose in rubble during excavation.

In some examples of pitched vaults the tiles or bricks were laid in two (and even up to four) layers, often with alternating angles of tilt (Fig. 3.9b, 3.9c; Emery and Kirwan 1935: 37, fig. 13, 43, fig. 22, pls. 6 and 9; Martin 1989: 51, pls. 46 and 157; Ghazouli 1964: pl. XIIB; Frankfort 1933: 14, pl. XI.4; Van Beek 1987: 79, 81). In a well-preserved cellar vault at Amarna pairs of reeds were inserted between the rings of the vault (Frankfort and Pendlebury 1933: 52–3, fig. 6).

To what extent true vaults were built using vertical arcs of brick is not clear. A Sixth-Dynasty chapel at Giza is one example, built with specially shaped bricks with interlocking zig-zag edges (Fig. 3.11a = Fisher 1924: 114–7, pls. 13.2, 17–19). The vertical placing of the arcs was necessary to the creation of an effect of rounded ribs on the underside, which was part of the moulding (see the section on special shapes). True vaults are more likely to require wooden formwork which will temporarily support the arcs. Sets of square holes for the ends of wooden beams in arc-patterns preserved in stone walls at Medinet Habu probably derive from such a building system, but the appearance of the roof and ceiling (was it also ribbed?) is now lost (Hölscher 1941: 38–9, pl. 26, 1951: 29; Spencer 1979a: 87). One should not rule out the possibility that, for large building projects, professional (or at least specialised) vault-builders were employed, who came with their own equipment. Support would also have been needed for arches, commonly built over doorways, but this could have been achieved very simply, through the use of lengths of bent palm-leaf rib or more substantial pieces of curved wood.

Many examples, mainly from tombs, are also known of corbel vaults of brick, in which the space was gradually closed by slightly projecting each course of bricks beyond the one beneath until the bricks of both sides met in the middle (Spencer 1979a: 126–7).

Soil as filling material

Large building (and perhaps demolition) projects in ancient Egypt required the use of extensive ramps for the movement of building materials between different levels. In one method of construction parallel walls or a network of chambers were built of brick and then filled with soil (desert or alluvial) (Badawy 1957: 64–5; Arnold 1991: 86–98; Petrie 1912: 55, pl. XXXII). A comparable practice was also employed for foundation platforms of large buildings (e.g. Janosi 1996) and occasionally for thick walls (e.g. Ziermann 1993). The most notable examples come from the Late Period, when civil and religious buildings were often set upon massive cellular pedestals filled with soil (e.g. Fig. 3.14; Kemp 1977; Petrie 1888: 52–61, pls. XLIII, XLIV; Holladay 1982: 31–1, pl. 40). These examples notwithstanding, Egyptian builders often display a preference for creating required mass (e.g. in thick enclosure walls and temple pylons) through solid brickwork.

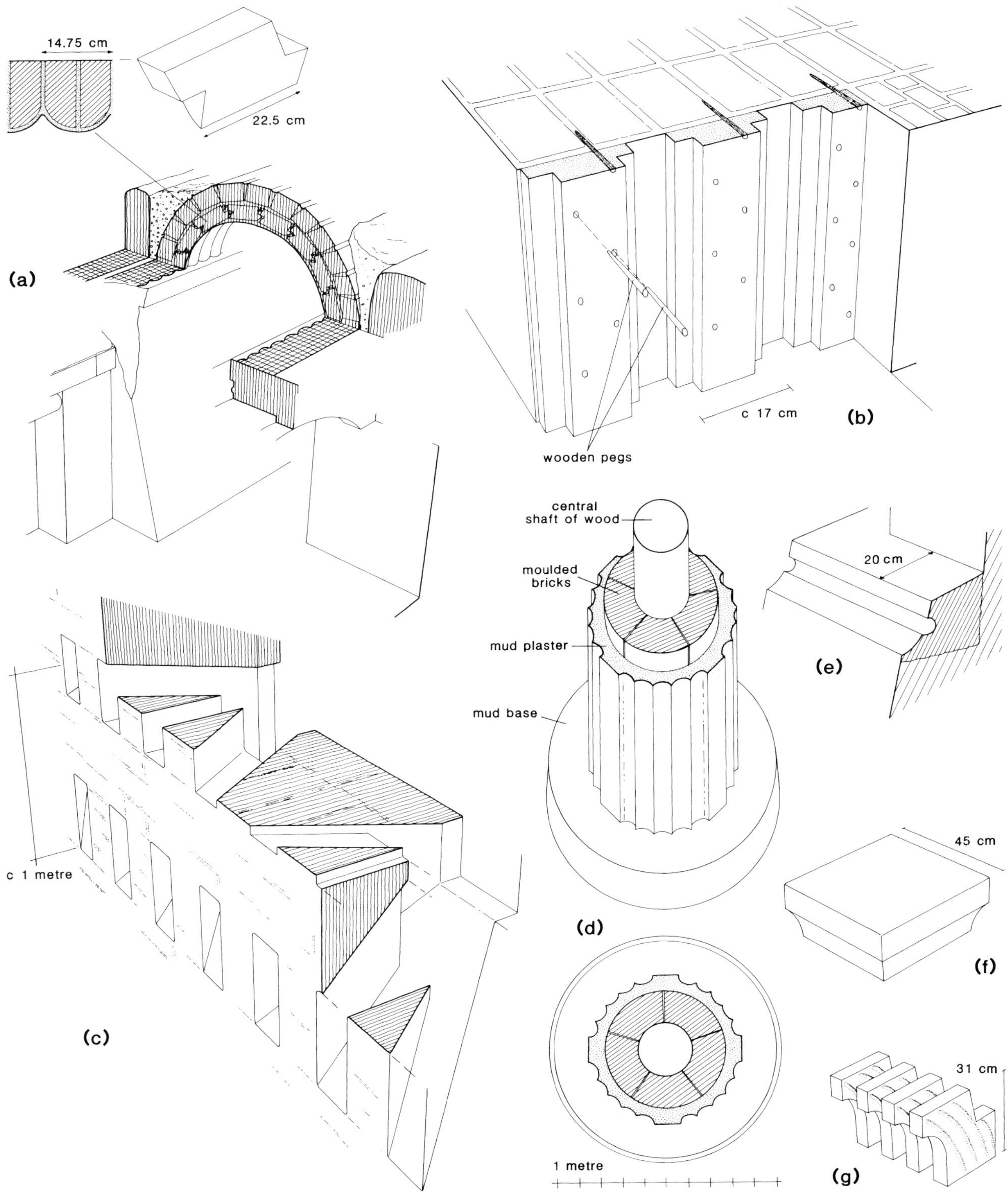

Figure 3.11 *Architectural mouldings in mud. (a) Ribbed vaulted roof in a Fourth-Dynasty chapel at Giza which used specially moulded bricks (after Fisher 1924); (b) Moulded mud panels fixed to a Third-Dynasty tomb façade (no. 3070) at Saqqara by wooden pins (after Emery 1968); (c) Archers' loopholes in the fortress wall at Buhen, Twelfth-Dynasty (after Emery* et al. *1979); (d) composite column from building R41.5 at Amarna; (e) Parapet moulding for an ornamental pool at Maru-Aten, Amarna (after Peet and Woolley 1923: 119, fig. 19, pl. XXXVII); (f) and (g) Cornice mouldings from Deir el-Medina (after Bruyère 1926).*

Some of the evidence for the use of loose soil also comes from building texts, although vocabulary difficulties still hinder translation (Simpson 1963: 73–5, 78). In the best known (P. Anastasi I) the soil is sand, and the interpretation seems to be that the removal of the free-flowing sand allowed a heavy mass, a colossal statue in this case, to be set up vertically on its pedestal (Arnold 1991: 70).

The claim has been made by Badawy (1957: 59–60) that the Egyptians used the rammed-earth method of construction, citing as examples 'platforms replacing pavement in archaic huts, enclosure walls constructed of two facings filled in, constructional ramps consisting of a network of coffers in brick filled in with earth'. If, as I suspect, these examples involved the filling of spaces defined by permanent walls then the term 'rammed earth' is not appropriate. It is better kept for the technique in which earth is rammed by compression between temporary formwork (usually of wood) which, when removed, leaves a solid construction behind. The key to success is to use an almost, but not quite, dry mix of soil in which the action of ramming is not impeded by the need to expel a lot of water. A large amount of strong wooden planking is required and the means of fixing it securely as the mud is compressed. The result can be more solid than that achieved by building in bricks made by the traditional method. I know of no examples of true rammed earth construction in ancient Egypt, but, especially on damp floodplain sites, they might be difficult to identify. A Fourth-Dynasty *mastaba* at Meidum (no. 16, of Nefermaat) had been filled with 'layers of Nile mud, poured in and left to harden before a fresher mass was applied' (Petrie 1892, 1938: 8), but nor is this a true example of the practice; nor the brick quarry ramp at Qau el-Kebir, made from parallel brick walls filled with loose mud (Petrie 1930b: 16, pl. XXII.4; Arnold 1991: 93).

Special shapes and vernacular style

The Egyptian architectural style took its inspiration from wood and plant forms. We are most familiar with the formalised shapes as they were rendered in stone, starting with the Step-Pyramid enclosure. Sporadic examples show, however, that the same or related forms could be reproduced in mud as well, sometimes through the use of specially shaped moulds. Examples are vaults from Old-Kingdom chapels at Giza, sometimes painted red, shaped to represent curved ceilings of reed bundles (Fig. 3.11a = Fisher 1924: 114–7, pls. 13.2, 17–19; Abu Bakr 1953: 129–43; Spencer 1979a: 25, 142; Kuhlmann 1996); *cavetto* cornices and *torus* mouldings at Deir el-Medina and Amarna (Fig. 3.11e, f, g; Spencer 1979a: 142; Frankfort and Pendlebury 1933: 6–7; Pendlebury 1951: 141, fig. 20; Kemp 1985: figs 1.4, 1.5, 2.3); and, again at Amarna, columns of rounded mud bricks built around a central wooden post and faced with fluted mud mouldings (Fig. 3.11d = Pendlebury 1951: 22, 109). Curved bricks made in curved moulds were used at Amarna for column bases (Clarke and Engelbach 1930: 215; Pendlebury 1951: 132) and for circular grain silos (personal observation, house Q44.1). They are also attested in vault construction (Deleuze 1981; Minault-Gout and Deleuze 1992: 72).

The substitution of mud and mud bricks for stone could extend to moulded lotus-clump columns with screen walls (Pendlebury 1951: 139, pl. LV.4) and to statues, although surviving examples are extremely rare: the bulls' heads modelled in clay, into which real horns were inserted, laid out along the base of some First-Dynasty tombs at Saqqara (Emery 1954: 8–9, pl. VII; 1958: 6–8, 75; 1961: 71, pls. 8, 9); statue groups of plastered brick added to some of the corridors of the Ramesseum in the Third Intermediate Period (El-Achirie and Fonquernie 1976: 11–13, pls. XXXIV–XLIa–b; Schumann Antelme 1976: 71–6, 172–4); figures of Bes moulded in high relief in a Ptolemaic shrine at Saqqara (Quibell 1907: 12–14, pls. XXVI–XXIX).

The First Dynasty had also seen, however, the introduction of a style of ornamental brickwork used for palace façades and the tombs of the élite which might well have been independently inspired by the brick architecture of Mesopotamia. Panelling and imitation dooways formed the basis of the lower parts of walls (Figs. 3.6 and 3.7). (In one case the panelled effect itself was achieved by means of pre-cast mud slabs fastened to the façade by long wooden pegs, an early form of architectural cladding, Fig. 3.11b = Emery 1968). The upper parts bore complex patterns which are known mainly from artistic representations, and these, according to one excavator, were sometimes moulded in mud (Emery 1954: 139; 1961: 181, but without illustrations). The same was true of decorative elements in

Figure 3.12 Part of the lower ramparts of the Twelfth-Dynasty fortress at Mirgissa, Nubia. Note the angled bedding-planes to take the brickwork uphill.

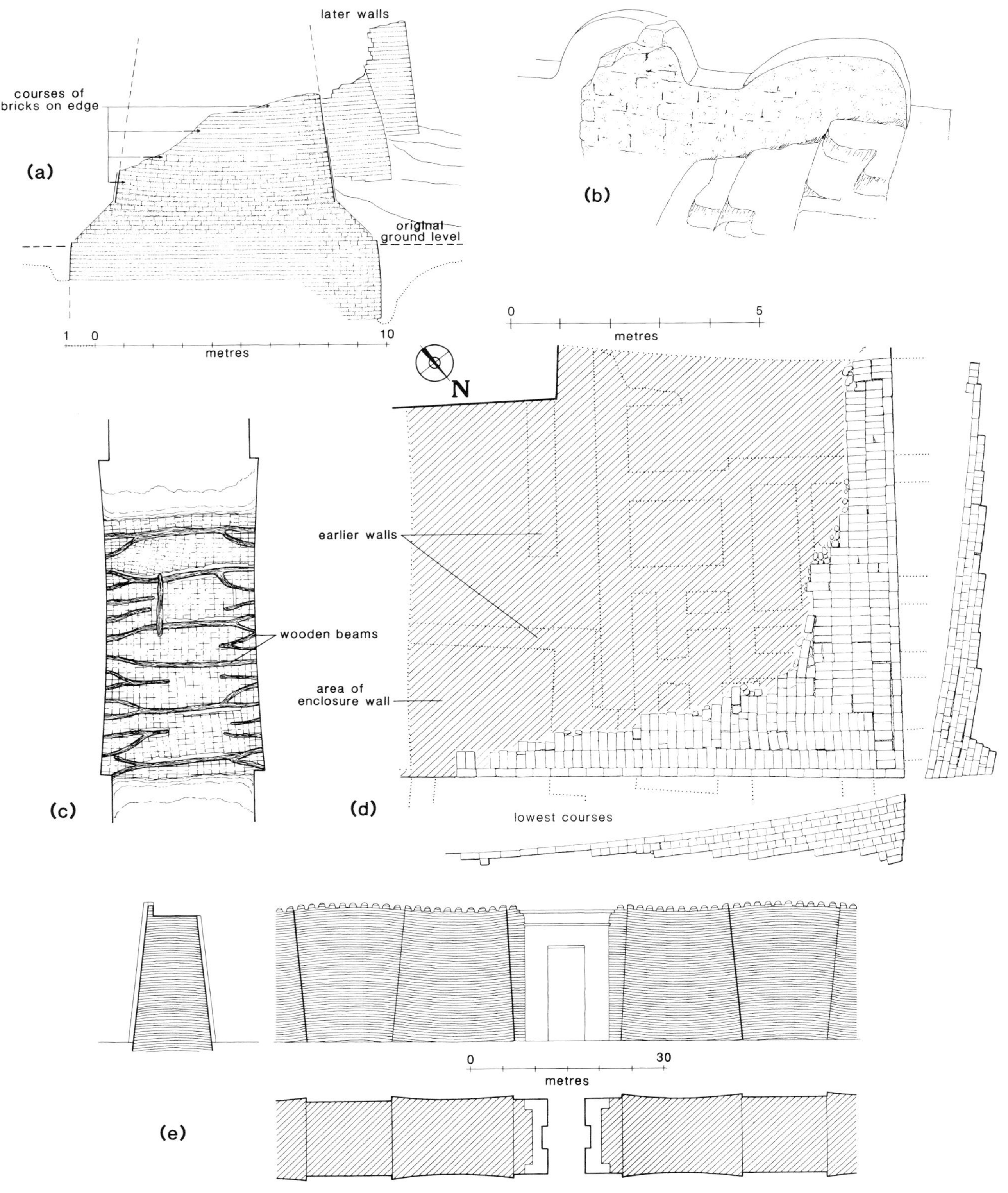

Figure 3.13 New Kingdom and Late Period ramparts. (a) Section through the enclosure wall at Medinet Habu (after Hölscher 1951); (b) Sketch of preserved brick crenellations at the Late-Period fortress on Dorginarti Island, Nubia (after Knudstad 1966: pl. XXIVa); (c) Plan of one course of bricks and timber beams in the enclosure wall of the Montu temple at Karnak (after Christophe 1951: pl. VI); (d) Plan of the foundation brickwork at the north corner of the Monthu temple at Karnak, built over earlier constructions (after Christophe 1951: pls. XVI, XVII); (e) Reconstruction of the centre of the east side of the Thirtieth-Dynasty enclosure wall at the Amun temple at Karnak (after Golvin and Hegazy 1993).

Figure 3.14 Cellular brick foundation platform for the Palace of Apries at Memphis, viewed to the north. The cellular chambers were originally domed.

Amarna houses (Frankfort 1929: 55, 57). Fortifications in mud brick, which used curved walls, elaborate systems of loopholes, and crenellated battlements (Figs 3.11c, 3.12, 3.13b; for two surviving examples see Knudstad 1966: 185, pl. XXIVa; Golvin and Hegazy 1993) provided builders with yet a further set of models.

The lack of tensile strength in mud can make fancy shapes difficult to achieve without reinforcement. Occasional finds of reinforcement in the form of wood or rope which will normally have survived only as impressions in the mud show that simple means to overcome this were understood, as in the case of window grilles, roughly square in section, moulded from mud around wooden cores at Amarna (Frankfort: 1929, 57; Frankfort and Pendlebury 1933: 10; also Fig. 3.11d). Linen can also be useful. It has been noted at Amarna laid over mud columns, to which paint was applied (Pendlebury 1951: 139), and Emery (1954: 139; 1961: 182) cites architectural elements from Early Dynastic tombs at Saqqara which were 'of extraordinary strength and weight, obtained apparently by reinforcing the mud with small strips of flax linen and drying it when under great pressure'. One product was a lintel measuring, in its broken state, 63 × 18 × 10 cm.

Figure 3.15 A section of the Late Period pan-bedded enclosure wall at the Kom el-Sultan, Abydos, built over house walls of the Old Kingdom.

The total evidence for architectural detailing in mud is not great, but, in view of its vulnerability to decay and of the fact that ancient buildings frequently survive only as foundations, this is not really surprising. The evidence certainly points to an awareness by builders of the potential of soil architecture for producing both decorative and utilitarian shapes, but whether they employed it to bring into existence a class of vernacular architecture, primarily domestic, is impossible to tell in the present state of knowledge. Since the forms of brick buildings would have contributed significantly to how ancient Egypt really looked, this is an important field of research.

Acknowledgements

Dr Katherine Spence kindly read a draft-version of this chapter and made many valuable suggestions which I have incorporated into the final text.

References

Abu-Bakr, Abdel-Moneim 1953. *Excavations at Giza 1949–1950*. Cairo: Government Press.

Arnold, D. 1979. *The Temple of Mentuhotep at Deir el-Bahari*. The Metropolitan Museum of Art Egyptian Expedition. New York: MMA.

1987. *Der Pyramidenbezirk des Königs Amenemhet III. in Dahschur*. Band I. Die Pyramide. Deutsches Archäologisches Institut, Abteilung Kairo, Archäologische Veröffentlichungen 53. Mainz am Rhein: von Zabern.

1988. *The Pyramid of Senwosret I*. The South Cemeteries of Lisht I. New York: MMA.

1991. *Building in Egypt; Pharaonic Stone Masonry*. New York and Oxford: OUP.

Ayrton, E.R., Currelly, C.T. and Weigall, A.E.P. 1904. *Abydos Part III*. 1904. London: EEF.

Badawi, F.A. 1978. Die Grabung der ägyptischen Altertümerverwaltung in Merimda-Benisalâme im Oktober/November 1976. *MDAIK* 34: 43–51.

Badawy, A. 1957. Philological evidence about methods of construction in ancient Egypt. ASAE 54: 51–74.

Barguet, P. 1962. *Le Temple d'Amon-rê à Karnak: essai d'exégèse*. Recherches d'Archéologie, de Philologie et d'Histoire 21. Cairo, IFAO.

Baumgartel, E.J. 1960. *The Cultures of Prehistoric Egypt* II. Oxford: Griffith Institute.

1970. *Petrie's Naqada Excavation: A Supplement.* London: Quaritch.

Borchardt, L., Königsberger, O. and Ricke, H. 1934. Friesziegel in Grabbauten. *ZÄS*, 70: 25–35.

Borkowski, J. and Majcherek, G. 1991. Mastaba of Neferma'at and Itet. Report of the Polish–Egyptian restoration mission, 1986–1988. In *Meidum* (eds. A. el-Khouli and G.T. Martin). The Australian Centre for Egyptology, Reports 3. Sydney: The Australian Centre for Egyptology, pp. 22–42.

Breasted, J.H. 1948. *Egyptian Servant Statues.* The Bollingen Series, XIII. Washington: Pantheon.

Brown, P.W. and Clifton, J.R. 1978. Adobe I: the properties of adobe. *Studies in Conservation*, 23: 139–46.

Brunton, G. and Caton-Thompson, G. 1928. *The Badarian Civilisation and Predynastic Remains Near Badari.* London: BSAE and Quaritch.

Bruyére, B. 1926. *Rapport sur les fouilles de Deir el Médineh (1924–1925).* Cairo: IFAO.

Caminos, R.A. 1954. *Late-Egyptian Miscellanies.* London: OUP.

Černý, J. 1976. *Coptic Etymological Dictionary.* Cambridge: CUP.

Chevrier, H. 1964. Technique de la construction dans l'ancienne Egypte. I.– Murs en briques crues. *RdE* 16: 11–17.

1970. Technique de la construction dans l'ancienne Egypte. II. – Problèmes posés par les obélisques. *RdE*, 22: 15–39.

Christophe, L.A. 1951. *Karnak-Nord III (1945–1949).* Fouilles conduites par C. Robichon. Fouilles de l'Institut français d'Archéologie orientale du Caire 23. Cairo: IFAO.

Clarke, S. and Engelbach, R. 1930. *Ancient Egyptian Masonry: The Building Craft.* London: OUP.

David, A.R. 1986. *The Pyramid Builders of Ancient Egypt: A Modern Investigation of Pharaoh's Workforce.* London, Boston and Henley: Routledge and Kegan Paul.

Davies, N. 1929. The town house in ancient Egypt. *Metropolitan Museum Studies*, 1: 233–55.

Davies, N. de G. 1935. *Paintings from the Tomb of Rekh-mi-re' at Thebes.* New York: MMA.

1943. *The Tomb of Rekh-mi-re' at Thebes.* New York: MMA.

Debono, F. and Mortensen, B. 1990. *El Omari. A Neolithic Settlement and Other Sites in the Vicinity of Wadi Hof, Helwan.* Deutsches Archäologisches Institut, Abteilung Kairo, Archäologische Veröffentlichungen 82. Mainz am Rhein: von Zabern.

Deleuze, P. 1981. Note sur une particularité de construction. *BIFAO*, 81, 214.

Dreyer, G., Engel, E.-M., Hartung, U., Hikade, T., Köhler, E.C. and Pumpenmeier, F. 1996. Umm el-Qaab. Nachuntersuchungen im frühzeitlichen Königsfriedhof 7./8. Vorbericht. *MDAIK*, 52: 11–76.

El-Achirie, H. and Fonquernie, B. 1976. Reconnaissance des differentes campagnes de construction pour les annexes nord-ouest (I''') étude detaillée de la salle à colonnes (I''' a–b). In *Le Ramesseum*, X. Collection scientifique, no. 35. Cairo: Centre d'Etudes et de Documentation sur l'Ancienne Egypte, pp. 1–27.

Emery, W.B. 1938. *Excavations at Saqqara: The Tomb of Hemaka.* Cairo: Government Press.

1949. *Excavations at Saqqara: Great Tombs of the First Dynasty,* I. Cairo: Government Press.

1954. *Excavations at Saqqara: Great Tombs of the First Dynasty,* II. London: EES.

1958. *Excavations at Saqqara: Great Tombs of the First Dynasty,* III. London: EES.

1961. *Archaic Egypt.* Harmondsworth: Penguin.

1968. Tomb 3070 at Saqqâra. *JEA*, 54: 11–13.

Emery, W.B. and Kirwan, L.P. 1935. *The Excavations and Survey between Wadi es-Sebua and Adindan 1929–1931.* Cairo: Government Press.

Emery, W.B., Smith, H.S. and Millard, A. 1979. *The Fortress of Buhen: The Archaeological Report.* 49th excavation memoir. London: EES.

Endruweit, A. 1994. *Städtischer Wohnbau in Ägypten: Klimagerechte ehmarchitektur in Amarna.* Berlin: Gebr. Mann.

Engelbach, R. 1931. Recent acquisitions in the Cairo Museum. *ASAE* 31: 126–31.

Fathy, H. 1969. *Gourna, a Tale of Two Villages.* Cairo: Ministry of Culture.

Fisher, C.S. 1924. *The Minor Cemetery At Giza.* The Eckley B. Coxe Jr. Foundation, new series, I. Philadelphia: University Museum.

Fougerousse, J.L. 1933. L'édifice en briques crues. In Montet, P. *Les nouvelles fouilles de Tanis (1929–1932).* Paris: Les Belles Lettres, pp. 76–88.

Frankfort, H. 1933. *The Cenotaph of Seti I at Abydos.* 39th Excavation Memoir. London: EES.

(ed.) 1929. *The Mural Paintings of El 'Amarneh.* London: EES.

Frankfort, H. and Pendlebury, J.D.S. 1933. *The City of Akhenaten* II. London: EES.

French, C.A.I. 1981. An analysis of the sediment at East Karnak. *JSSEA*, 11: 263–78.

1984. A sediments analysis of mud brick and natural features at El-Amarna. In *Amarna Reports* I (ed. B.J. Kemp). London: EES, pp. 189–201.

Garstang, J. 1907. *The Burial Customs of Ancient Egypt, as Illustrated by Tombs of the Middle Kingdom.* London: Constable.

Geller, J. 1992. From prehistory to history: beer in Egypt. In *The Followers of Horus; Studies Dedicated to Michael Allen Hoffman 1944–1990.* (ed. R. Friedman and B. Adams). Oxbow Monograph 20. Oxford: Oxbow Books, pp. 19–26.

Ghazouli, E.B. 1964. The palace and magazines attached to the temple of Sety I at Abydos and the facade of this temple. *ASAE*, 58: 99–186.

Goldberg, P. 1979. Geology of Late Bronze Age mudbrick from Tel Lachish. *Tel Aviv*, 6: 60–7.

Golvin, J.-C. and Hegazy, El-S. 1993. Essai d'explication de la forme et des caractéristiques générales des grandes enceintes de Karnak. *Cahiers de Karnak, IX 1993.* Paris: Editions Recherche sur les Civilisations, pp. 145–60.

Griffith, F. Ll. 1898. *Hieratic Papyri From Kahun and Gurob (Principally of the Middle Kingdom).* London: Quaritch.

Hassan, F.A. and Matson, R.G. 1989. Seriation of predynastic potsherds from the Naqada region (Upper Egypt). In *Late Prehistory of The Nile Basin and The Sahara* (eds. L. Krzyżaniak and M. Kobusiewicz). *Studies in African Archaeology*, 2. Poznań: Muzeum Archeologiczne w Poznaniu, pp. 303–15.

Hayes, W.C. 1965. *Most Ancient Egypt.* Chicago and London: University of Chicago Press; and Toronto: University of Toronto Press.

Hecker, H.M. 1986. Report on the excavation of floor [873] of the outer hall of Chapel 561/450. In *Amarna Reports* III (ed. B.J. Kemp). London: EES, pp. 80–9.

Hesse, A. 1970. Essai techno-chronologique sur la dimension des briques de construction. In *Mirgissa* I (ed. J. Vercoutter). Mission Archéologique au Soudan sous la direction de Jean Vercoutter, I. Paris: CNRS, pp. 102–14.

1971. The measurement of ancient bricks and its archaeological interest. In *Mathematics in the Archaeological and Historical Sciences* (ed. F.R. Hodson, D.G. Kendall and P. Tăutu). Edinburgh: University Press, pp. 432–5.

Hoffman, M.A. 1980. A rectangular Amratian house from Hierakonpolis and its significance for predynastic research. *JNES*, 39: 119–37.

Holladay, J.S. 1982. *Cities of the Delta, III: Tell El-Maskhuta*. ARCE. Malibu: Undena Publications.

Holmes, D.L. 1992. Chipped stone-working craftsmen, Hierakonpolis and the rise of civilization in Egypt. In *The Followers of Horus; Studies Dedicated to Michael Allen Hoffman 1944–1990*. (eds. R. Friedman and B. Adams). Oxbow Monograph 20. Oxford: Oxbow Books, pp. 37–44.

Holmes, D.L. and Friedman, R.F. 1994. Survey and test excavations in the Badari region, Egypt. *Proceedings of the Prehistoric Society* 60: 105–42.

Hölscher, U. 1910. *Das hohe Tor von Medinet Habu; eine Baugeschichtliche Untersuchung*. 12. Wissenschaftliche Veröffentlichung der Deutschen Orient-Gesellschaft. Leipzig: Hinrichs.

1939. *The Temples of The Eighteenth Dynasty*. Oriental Institute Publications 41. Chicago: University of Chicago Press.

1941. *The Mortuary Temple of Ramses III*, part I. Oriental Institute Publications 54. Chicago: University of Chicago Press.

1951. *The Mortuary Temple of Ramses III*, part II. Oriental Institute Publications 55. Chicago: University of Chicago Press.

Hughes, G.R. 1963. Serra East: The University of Chicago excavations, 1961–62: a preliminary report on the first season's work. *Kush*, 11: 121–30.

Hughes, R.E. 1988. The geotechnical study of soils used as structural materials in historic monuments. In *The Engineering Geology of Ancient Works, Monuments and Historical Sites; Preservation and Protection* (eds. P.G. Marinos and G.C. Koukis). Rotterdam and Brookfield: Balkema, pp. 1041–8.

Husselman, E.M. 1979. *Karanis Excavations of The University of Michigan In Egypt 1928–1935. Topography and Architecture*. Kelsey Museum of Archaeology, Studies 5. Ann Arbor: University of Michigan Press.

Jánosi, P. 1996. Die Fundamentplattform eines Palastes (?) der späten Hyksoszeit in 'Ezbet Helmi (Tell el-Dab'a). In *Haus und Palast im Alten Ägypten/House and palace in ancient Egypt* (ed. M. Bietak). Untersuchungen der Zweigstelle Kairo des Österreichischen Archäologischen Institutes, 14. Vienna: Österreichische Akademie der Wissenschaften, pp. 93–8.

Junker, H. 1930. Vorläufiger Bericht über die zweite Grabung der Akademie auf der vorgeschichtlichen Siedlung Merimde-Benisalâme vom 7. Februar bis 8. April 1930. *Anzeiger der Akademie der Wissenschaften in Wien, Philosophische-historiche Klasse* 1930, Nr. V–XIII, 21–83.

1932. Vorbericht über die von der Akademie in Wien in Verbindung mit dem Egyptiska Museet in Stockholm unternommenen Grabungen auf der neolithischen Siedlung von Merimde-Benisalâme vom 6. November 1931 bis 20. Januar 1932. *Anzeiger der Akademie der Wissenschaften in Wien, Philosophische-historiche Klasse* 1932, Nr. I–IV, 36–100.

1941. *Gîza V. Die Mastaba des Snb (Seneb) und die umliegenden Gräber*. Akademie der Wissenschaften in Wien, Philosophisch-historische Klasse, Denkschriften, 71. Band, 2. Abhandlung. Vienna and Leipzig: Hölder-Pichler-Tempsky.

Kemp, B.J. 1972. Fortified towns in Nubia. In *Man, Settlement and Urbanism* (eds. P.J. Ucko, R. Tringham and D.W. Dimbleby). London: Duckworth, pp. 651–6.

1977. The palace of Apries at Memphis. *MDAIK*, 33: 101–8.

1995. Site formation processes and the reconstruction of house P46.33. In *Amarna Reports* VI (ed. B.J. Kemp). London: EES, pp. 146–68.

(ed.) 1985. *Amarna Reports* II. London: EES.

Kitchen, K.A. 1966. *Ancient Orient and Old Testament*. London: The Tyndale Press.

Klebs, L. 1922. *Die Reliefs und Malereien des mittleren Reiches (VII.-XVII. Dynastie ca 2475–1580 v. Chr.)*. Abh. der Heidelberger Akad. der Wissenschaften. Phil.-hist. Klasse 6. Abh.

Knudstad, J. 1966. Serra East and Dorginarti. *Kush*, 14: 165–86.

Kuhlmann, K.P. 1996. Serif-style architecture and the design of the archaic Egyptian palace ('Königszelt'). In *Haus und Palast im Alten Ägypten* (ed. M. Bietak). Untersuchungen der Zweigstelle Kairo des Österreichischen Archäologischen Institutes, 14. Vienna: Verlag der Österreichischen Akademie der Wissenschaften, pp. 117–37.

Lacovara, P. 1984. Archaeology and the decay of mudbrick structures in Egypt I: wattle and daub. *NARCE*, 128: 20–21.

1990. *Deir El-Ballas. Preliminary Report on the Deir el-Ballas Expedition 1980–1986*. ARCE Reports 12. Winona Lake: Eisenbraums.

Larsen, H. 1950. True vaults and domes in Egyptian architecture of the Early Kingdom. *Acta Archaeologica*, 21: 211–34.

Lhote, A. 1954. *Les chefs-d'oeuvre de la peinture égyptienne*. Paris: Hachettte.

McHenry, P.G. 1976. *Adobe; Build It Yourself*. Tucson: University of Arizona Press.

1984. *Adobe and Rammed Earth Buildings; Design and Construction*. New York: John Wiley and Sons.

Mallinson, M. 1995. Excavation and survey in the Central City, 1988–92. In *Amarna Reports* VI (ed. B.J. Kemp). London: EES, pp. 169–215.

Martin, G.T. 1989. *The Memphite Tomb of Horemheb Commander-in-Chief of Tut'ankhamun*. Vol. I. The reliefs, inscriptions, and commentary. 55th Excavation Memoir. London: EES.

Matthews, W. and Postgate, J.N. 1994. The imprint of living in an early Mesopotamian city: questions and answers. In *Whither Environmental Archaeology?* (eds. R. Luff and P. Rowley-Conwy). Oxbow Monograph 38. Oxford: Oxbow Books, pp. 171–212.

Mekhitarian, A. 1954. *Egyptian Painting*. The Great Centuries of Painting. Geneva, Paris, New York: Skira.

Mileham, G.S. 1910. *Churches in Lower Nubia*. Eckley B. Coxe Junior Expedition to Nubia: II. Philadelphia, University Museum.

Minault-Gout, A. and Deleuze, P. 1992. *Balat II. Le mastaba d'Ima-Pépi. Tombeau d'un Gouverneur de l'Oasis à la fin de l'Ancien Empire*. Fouilles de l'Institut français d'Archéologie orientale 33. Cairo: IFAO.

Mond, R. and Myers, O.H. 1934. *The Bucheum*. 41st memoir. London: EES.

1937. *Cemeteries of Armant* I. London: EES.

de Morgan, J. 1895. *Fouilles à Dahchour, mars–juin 1894*. Vienna: Holzhausen.

Newberry, P.E. [1895]. *El Bersheh*, part I (The Tomb of Tehuti-hetep). London: EEF.

Nicholson, P.T. 1989. Report on the 1987 excavations. The pottery kilns in Building Q48.4. In *Amarna Reports* V (ed. B.J. Kemp). London: EES, pp. 64–81.

Nims, C.F. 1950. Bricks without straw. *The Biblical Archaeologist* 13: 22–8.

Peet, T.E. 1914. *The Cemeteries of Abydos, part II. 1911–1912*. London: EEF.

Peet, T.E. and Loat, W.S. 1913. *The Cemeteries of Abydos, III: 1912–1913*. London: EEF.

Peet, T.E. and Woolley, C.L. 1923. *The City of Akhenaten* I. London: EES.

Pendlebury, J.D.S. 1951. *The City of Akhenaten* III. London: EES.

Petrie, W.M.F. 1888. *Nebesheh (Am) and Defenneh (Tahpanhes)*, published with Tanis, part II, 1886. London: EEF and Trübner.

1890. *Kahun, Gurob and Hawara*. London: Kegan Paul, Trench and Trübner.

1891. *Illahun, Kahun and Gurob 1889–90*. London: Nutt.

1892. *Meydum*. London: Nutt.

1903. *Abydos*, part II. London: EEF.

1906. *Hyksos and Israelite Cities*. London, BSAE and Quaritch.

1912. *The Labyrinth Gerzeh and Mazguneh*. London: British School of Archaeology and Quaritch.

1917. *Tools and Weapons*. London: BSAE.

1930a. *Beth-Pelet I (Tell Fara)*. London: BSAE and Quaritch.

1930b. *Antaeopolis; The Tombs of Qau*. London: BSAE and Quaritch.

1938. *Egyptian Architecture*. London: BSAE and Quaritch.

Petrie, W.M.F. and Quibell, J.E. 1896. *Naqada and Ballas 1895*. London: Quaritch.

Petrie, W.M.F., Wainwright, G.A. and Mackay, E. 1912. *The Labyrinth Gerzeh and Mazghuneh*. London: BSAE and Quaritch.

Quibell, J.E. 1907. *Excavations at Saqqara (1905–1906)*. Cairo, IFAO.

Randall-Maciver, D. and Mace, A.C. 1902. *El Amrah and Abydos. 1899–1901*. London: EEF.

Reisner, G.A. 1923. *Excavations at Kerma*, parts IV–V. Harvard African Studies 6. Cambridge, Mass: Peabody Museum.

1931. *Mycerinus: the Temples of the Third Pyramid at Giza*. Cambridge MA: Harvard University Press.

Reisner, G.A., Wheeler, N.F., and Dunham, D. 1967. *Uronarti Shalfak Mirgissa*. Second Cataract Forts, vol. II. Boston: MFA.

Ricke, H. 1939. *Der Totentempel Thutmoses' III. Baugeschichtliche Untersuchung*. Beiträge zur Ägyptischen Bauforschung und Altertumskunde, Heft 3 (1). Cairo: Schweizerisches Institut für Ägyptische Bauforschung und Altertumskunde in Kairo.

Rizkana, I. 1996. The prehistoric house. In *Haus und Palast im Alten Ägypten* (ed. M. Bietak). Untersuchungen der Zweigstelle Kairo des Österreichischen Archäologischen Institutes, 14. Vienna: Verlag der Österreichischen Akademie der Wissenschaften, pp. 175–83.

Rizkana, I. and Seeher, J. 1989. *Maadi III. The Non-Lithic Small Finds and The Structural Remains of The Predynastic Settlement*. Deutsches Archäologisches Institut, Abteilung Kairo, Archäologische Veröffentlichungen 80. Mainz am Rhein: von Zabern.

Robichon, C. and Varille, A. 1936. *Le temple du scribe royal Amenhotep fils de Hapou I*. Fouilles de l'Institut français du Caire 11. Cairo: IFAO.

1939. Médamoud. Fouilles du Musée du Louvre, 1938. *Cd'E* 14, no 27: 83–7.

Schumann Antelme, R. 1976. Description archéologique. In *Le Ramesseum*, X. Collection scientifique, no. 35. Cairo: Centre d'Etudes et de Documentation sur l'Ancienne Egypte, pp. 52–223.

Simpson, W.K. 1960. The nature of the brick-work calculations in *Kah. Pap.* XXIII, 24–40. *JEA*, 46: 106–7.

1963. *Papyrus Reisner I. The Records of A Building Project In The Reign of Sesostris I*. Boston: Museum of Fine Arts.

Spence, K. 1996. Review of A. Endruweit, Städtischer Wohnbau in Ägypten. *JESHO*, 39: 50–2.

Spencer, A.J. 1979a. *Brick Architecture in Ancient Egypt*. Warminster: Aris and Phillips.

1979b. The brick foundations of Late-Period peripteral temples and their mythological origin. In *Orbis Aegyptiorum Speculum: Glimpses of Ancient Egypt; Studies in Honour of H.W. Fairman* (eds. J. Ruffle, G.A. Gaballa, and K.A. Kitchen). Warminster: Aris and Phillips, pp. 132–7.

Thomas, E. 1964. The four niches and amuletic figures in the Theban royal tombs. *JARCE*, 3: 71–8.

Thorel, G. 1976. Les salles voutées du groupe I'. In *Le Ramesseum*, X. Collection scientifique, no. 35. Cairo: Centre d'Etudes et de Documentation sur l'Ancienne Egypte, pp. 28–51.

Traunecker, C. 1975. Une stèle commémorant la construction de l'enceinte d'un temple de Montou. *Karnak V. 1970–1972*. Centre franco–égyptien d'étude des temples de Karnak. Cairo: CNRS and IFAO, pp. 141–58.

Tytus, R. de P. 1903. *A Preliminary Report on the Re-excavation of the Palace of Amenhetep III*. NewYork: Winthrop Press.

Van Beek, G.W. 1987. Arches and vaults in the ancient Near East. *Scientific American*, 257, no. 1: 78–85.

Vercoutter J. 1970. *Mirgissa* I. Mission Archéologique Francaise au Soudan, 1. Paris: CNRS.

Vycichl, W. 1983. *Dictionnaire étymologique de la langue copte*. Leuven: Peeters.

Watanabe, Y. 1986. *The Architecture of 'Kom El Samak' At Malkata-South; A Study of Architectural Restoration*. Studies in Egyptian Culture, no. 5. Tokyo: Waseda University.

von der Way, T. 1992. Indications of architecture with niches at Buto. In *The Followers of Horus; Studies Dedicated to Michael Allen Hoffman 1944–1990*. (eds. R. Friedman, and B. Adams). Oxbow Monographs 20. Oxford: Oxbow Books, pp. 217–26.

1993. *Untersuchungen zur Spätvor- und Frühgeschichte Unterägyptens*. Studien zur Archäologie und Geschichte Altägyptens, 8. Heidelberg: Heidelberger Orientverlag.

Weeks, K.R. 1971–2. Preliminary report on the first two seasons at Hierakonpolis. Part II. The Early Dynastic Palace. *JARCE*, 9: 29–33.

Weinstein, J.M. 1973. *Foundation Deposits In Ancient Egypt*. Ann Arbor, Michigan: University Microfilms, no. 73–24, 237.

Wiesmann, H. 1914. Adobe. *ZÄS*, 52: 130.

Ziermann, M. 1993. *Elephantine XVI. Befestigungsanlagen und Stadtentwicklung in der Frühzeit und im frühen Alten Reich*. Deutsches Archäologisches Institut, Abteilung Kairo, Archäologische Veröffentlichungen 87. Mainz am Rhein: von Zabern.

4. Painting materials

LORNA LEE AND STEPHEN QUIRKE

Introduction

The present colour of an object may be due to intrinsic coloration or to colours applied as paints or dyes, the appearance of which may have altered since application due to degradation. Colour is to be distinguished from pigment, the organic or inorganic colouring substance. A paint on the other hand is defined as a mixture of a pigment and a binding medium, and may be applied directly to the object or onto a painting ground. At present, few analyses of ancient Egyptian binding media have been undertaken, a problem which reflects difficulties of analysis and limited availability of well-provenanced samples. Results of organic analysis can be difficult to interpret because organic materials in a paint sample may be due not only to the binding medium, but also to original coatings such as a varnish applied over paint layers, as well as to more modern additions (binding media are discussed separately with other adhesives in Chapter 19, this volume).

Once sufficient analyses of binding media have become available, it will be necessary to reunite the analyses of both pigment and medium with consideration of the painting ground, which may be expected to affect pigment selection and texture. This chapter primarily addresses the problem of identifying pigments and, to a lesser extent, their provenance, before presenting the more recent findings on methods used in ancient Egypt for preparing ground, and above all the preparation of painted plaster surfaces in the Theban tomb-chapels of the Eighteenth Dynasty.

Egyptian pigments before the Roman period are in most instances inorganic substances, explaining the extraordinarily good preservation of colour on many Egyptian antiquities and monuments. The chemistry of inorganic materials has offered fewer problems for analysts than the identification of organic components of ancient samples, but the researcher needs to be aware of certain complications affecting all methods of scientific research. The ideal sample comes from an undisturbed stratum of a securely dated and provenanced object; the historian is required to help select for analysis the most suitable items, and to identify any problems associated with their archaeological context. Ideally samples should be taken by the analyst, rather than supplied; at the least the analyst should be familiar with the particular sampling method, as well as with conditions of retrieval in the case of field sampling, and of storage in the case of museum sampling. Previous methods of treatment and storage can present a major obstacle to clean sampling, as adequate recording of treatment began only relatively recently; this creates a modern prehistory of the monument or object which is unknown to the analyst before beginning work, but which may affect, and possibly seriously distort results. Selection of a sample thus depends both on a historical sensibility to the relative importance of different items, in the endeavour to cover an informative geographical, historical or socio-economic range, and on appreciation of conditions in the field or at the place of storage. The exact original location of the sample within the painted surface must be recorded, because this is crucial for later interpretation of results; for example, unexpected components may in some cases be explained by the direct intrusion of adjacent pigments, or contamination from the degradation patterns of those pigments, or indeed later restorations. The condition of the sample remains an important consideration throughout laboratory testing, and, in the case of non-destructive testing, in storage after analysis.

If the analyst is insufficiently sensitive to the historical context and questions concerning a sample, or the historian is insufficiently informed on the methods and potential of analysis, they remain unable as a team to extract secure data from their sample. Moreover, both must be aware that their analysis is of the *modern* condition of the object; pigments may degrade over time, producing new colours and losing their original identity, and this possibility must be taken into account. Therefore the scientific monitoring of the presently visible colour ought to follow analysis of the pigment and medium, if any indication of the ancient colour value is to be obtained. Distinction of hues is generally less problematic for polychromatic colouring traditions, as in Dynastic Egyptian art, than for colouristic traditions as in Renaissance and later Western European art.

Nevertheless, linguistic demarcations of the colour spectrum inevitably reflect cultural and individual selection, often subjective and rarely self-conscious; this creates a need for some objective scheme of colour measurement. For instrumental measurement of present colour of ancient Egyptian painted surfaces, see Strudwick (1991); where instrumentation is not available, it is useful to refer to visual aids such as the Munsell code to define fields of colour.

An additional problem for comparison and collation of results by different teams is material nomenclature. In view of the variations in terminology, Table 4.1 lists the chemical formulae of materials as named by us in this article. Without the chemical formula, it is not possible to guarantee the identity of one analysed sample with another; the list is a summary, and does not give details of the possible variations under the names, particularly in the cases of red ochre (containing haematite) and Egyptian blue. It should be remembered that one chemical formula may apply to more than one pigment, and that definitions in chemical terms provide only the first step toward identifying a material by its provenance and manufacture.

The most extensive single project of analysis for ancient Egyptian pigments to date has been that conducted between 1980 and 1991 by the Max-Planck Institut für Kernphysik in Heidelberg, with the Egyptological assistance of the Institute of Egyptology at Heidelberg University (1980–2), the Institute of Ancient History at Konstanz University (1982–4), and the Pelizaeus-Museum, Hildesheim (1989–91; see Blom-Böer 1994). This project involved analysis of 1,380 pigment samples from painting on stone surfaces (tomb-chapels, sarcophagi, temples) and wall-paintings (tomb-chapels, burial chambers), ranging from the Fifth Dynasty to the early Roman period but predominantly of the late Old, early Middle and New Kingdoms, with the weight of the evidence from Thebes. The samples were analysed in reflective light, with scanning electron microscopy (SEM), and electron microprobe techniques (EMPA).

Table 4.1. *List of chemical formulae of compounds cited in the text (in alphabetic order)*

anhydrite	$CaSO_4$
atacamite	$Cu_2Cl(OH)_3$
azurite	$Cu_3(CO_3)_2(OH)_2$
calcite	$CaCO_3$
cassiterite	SnO_2
chrysocolla	$CuSiO_3.2H_2O$
cobalt blue	$CoO.Al_2O_3$
copper wollastonite	$(Ca,Cu)_3(Si_3O_9)$
cuprorivaite	$(Ca,Cu)Si_4O_{10}$
dolomite	$Ca,Mg(CO_3)_2$
Egyptian blue	mainly cuprorivaite $CaCu(Si_4O_{10})$with copper wollastonite $(Ca,Cu)_3(Si_3O_9)$, silica SiO_2 and glass
goethite	the alpha form of FeOOH
gypsum	$CaSO_4.2H_2O$
haematite	Fe_2O_3
huntite	$Mg_3Ca(CO_3)_4$
iron ochre	natural earth pigment consisting of silica (in an Egyptian context this will be quartz) and clay, coloured with iron oxide (see red ochre and yellow ochre)
jarosite	$KFe(SO_4)_2(OH)_6$
kaolinite	$Al_2Si_2O_5(OH)_4$
limonite	general field term for poorly characterised hydrated iron oxides
malachite	$Cu_2(CO_3)(OH)_2$
natron	sodium sesquicarbonate: $Na_2CO_3.NaHCO_3.2H_2O$
orpiment	As_2S_3
pararealgar	the gamma form of AsS
paratacamite	$Cu_2(OH)_3Cl$
pyrite	FeS
pyrolusite	MnO_2
realgar	the low temperature form of AsS
red ochre	type of iron ochre coloured by anhydrous iron oxide (haematite: Fe_2O_3)
silica	SiO_2
titanomagnetite	$Fe_3O_4.Fe_2TiO_4$
vermilion	HgS
yellow ochre	type of iron ochre coloured by various hydrated forms of iron oxide, mainly goethite (FeOOH)

The British Museum project of pigment analysis

Introduction

As part of a conservation project for the treatment of painted papyri, particularly for consolidation prior to facing for removal of acidic backing-paper, samples of nine colours from eight manuscripts dating from the New Kingdom to the Roman period have been analysed since 1991 by the authors. From the collections of the Department of Egyptian Antiquities in the British Museum, six historical phases were identified in the history of colour illustration on papyrus:

1. mid-Eighteenth Dynasty;
2. Nineteenth Dynasty;
3. Twentieth Dynasty;
4. Twenty-first to early Twenty-second Dynasties;
5. Twenty-sixth Dynasty to early Ptolemaic;
6. late Ptolemaic to early Roman.

(These phases may require modification when extended to other collections, e.g. fusion of (3) and (4), division of (5) into earlier and later phases).

Representatives of colour range in each historical phase were selected for sampling and the pigments analysed using x-ray fluorescence (XRF), x-ray diffraction (XRD), and examination under polarised light microscope (PLM) of particles mounted in *Meltmount*. Where further elemental analysis was required, samples were mounted on a carbon block and examined by scanning electron microscope with energy dispersive x-ray analysis (SEM).

Methods of analysis used in the British Museum project

Sampling

In the British Museum conservation project, the sample was limited where possible to the minimal amount (~25 μg); where a lake pigment (an organic dye on an inorganic substrate) was thought to be present, a larger sample (~0.5 mg) was taken in order to allow separation of the organic dye from the inorganic substrate. If the nature of the artefact allowed, two small samples of each colour were taken, the first on a gelatin strip, and the second a powder sample of a few particles only, directly into a small gelatin capsule. Position of the sample on the original object was recorded on a photograph or xerox.

The limitations of small sample size should be borne in mind; if the sample is taken from a less homogeneous pigment, the results may be misleading. It should also be noted that a series of layers may be present, as has been detected with the ochre and orpiment layering of yellow on Theban temples, and sampling should be sensitive to layering as well as ground preparation. In the case of the papyri, there is no ground to be analysed; ground has generally been analysed less often, except in studies of Theban tomb-chapels.

X-ray fluorescence spectroscopy (XRF)

XRF is a non-destructive method of analysis, and is used for identification of the predominant elements in a pigment sample (Goffer 1980); it can be applied directly to pigment mounted on a gelatin strip. Elements within the sample absorb the incident x-rays and re-emit x-rays, the energies of which are characteristic of the elements. XRF analysis gives a spectrum consisting of a series of peaks; the energy at which peaks occur indicate the elements present and the area of the peaks relates to their apparent abundance in the sample.

The limitations of XRF are as follows: elements lighter than magnesium (relative atomic mass = 24), such as sodium, cannot be detected without a vacuum attachment. Other elements, including aluminium, silicon, phosphorus, sulphur and chlorine will only be detected if present in substantial amounts. Nevertheless XRF has the advantage of offering a rapid means of preliminary investigation of a pigment sample.

X-ray powder diffraction (XRD)

This is a means of examining the crystal structures present in the pigment sample (Goffer 1980). As with XRF, XRD is undertaken directly and non-destructively using the sample on the gelatin strip. XRD with a Debye Scherrer camera produces a film containing a series of lines, the positions and relative intensities of which are characteristic of the crystalline material or materials present in the sample. The XRD pattern of the unknown substance can then be compared with lines produced by known materials.

The limitations of XRD are as follows: a large library of XRD data is available for comparison with unknowns, but this library (ICDD) consists primarily of patterns collected from pure substances. Ancient pigment samples are often a mixture of components and may include dirt and dust obscuring the identification process. Pigments applied to a gesso or ground layer cannot always be sampled without inclusion of substrate components, and the latter may then interfere with analysis. If the pigment is microcrystalline or non-crystalline, it will not produce a distinct XRD pattern; ill-defined patterns may also result from pigments which have degraded since application. In certain cases, different compounds produce similar XRD patterns, e.g. the copper chlorides atacamite and paratacamite.

Polarised light microscopy (PLM)

The sample of powder particles collected from the pigment in the gelatin capsule is examined under a microscope; if only a limited sample is available, it is possible to use the material collected on the gelatin strip, but this may be difficult to remove. The sample is mounted on a glass microscope slide using *Meltmount*, a material of known refractive index (1.66), and is then examined in transmitted light using a polarised light microscope, at up to 40 × (objective) magnification. This method allows the researchers to determine the number of components present in a pigment. Several features of each component particle can be assessed; the colour, refractive index (taking into account that of the mounting medium), shape and size of the particles become clear in plane polarised light, and this information can be corroborated and expanded by subsequent observation between crossed polars. Identifications are made by comparison with mounted reference pigments and in conjunction with the results from the previously described instrumental techniques. The limitations of PLM are as follows: certain pigments, such as haematite and vermilion, have similar characteristics, and this could confuse identification if PLM were to be used in isolation without confirmation from other methods of analysis. Unusual materials may lie beyond the reach of the available reference sources. Some pale colours may appear almost colourless when dispersed onto a microscope slide and viewed at high magnification, as occurs for example with small particles of Egyptian blue. Therefore it is useful to view such samples in reflected light before examination with transmitted light; PLM reveals limited information in the case of opaque particles, although the size and shape of the opaque particles and the characteristics of any associated materials can be very informative. Very finely ground pigments can also present problems due to the minute size of the particles. Insufficient data may be gained from some pigments, particularly Egyptian copper pigments. The latter often contain a number of phases within one particle, and the characteristics of the particle will therefore be a combination of those of each phase; this can result in confusing information, as discussed below for Egyptian blue.

Results of the analyses

The results of the analyses of pigments on papyrus combine with those from earlier identifications during the conservation of coffins, tomb-chapel wall-paintings, linen and other objects in the British Museum collections.

Together, the conservation analyses from the British Museum form a substantial database for comparison with the results of the Heidelberg project, as well as those given by Lucas (1962) from earlier studies, and extend the range of study into areas and periods which have received less attention, notably the organic surfaces painted in the First millennium BC. It should be remembered that the range of painting grounds and colours available for analysis varies from one period to another, with the broadest range in the New Kingdom and Ptolemaic to Roman periods. This is particularly important in considering the historical implications of analyses for the New Kingdom and Third Intermediate Period; in these periods, without analyses of pigments from organic surfaces, the analyses of pigments from stone surfaces alone might give the impression that the palette changed at the end of the New Kingdom simply because so few Third Intermediate Period coloured stone surfaces are available for sampling. Similarly, the earliest attested appearances of the less widespread mineral pigments huntite (white), realgar (orange-red) and orpiment (yellow) were from the early New Kingdom in the earlier analyses, predominantly from painted plaster and stone surfaces, but the British Museum analysis of organic surfaces such as wooden coffins has now extended the attested date-range for huntite and orpiment back to the late Middle Kingdom, a period for which few painted stone and plaster objects are available for sampling. Most recently huntite has been reported from late Old Kingdom painted figures (Heywood forthcoming) and more research is clearly needed in this area.

In the context of the present book, material of the Ptolemaic and Roman periods has generally been excluded except when it has been necessary to draw a contrast with usage attested in the various phases of the Dynastic Period. However, it should be noted that the latest Dynastic evidence cited may extend into the Ptolemaic Period owing to the homogeneity of funerary workshop products in the fourth to third centuries BC (Late Period to early Ptolemaic Period); further research is needed to establish secure criteria for distinguishing material from before and after the arrival of Alexander the Great in Egypt in 332 BC.

Pigments of the Predynastic and Early Dynastic periods

Pyrolusite, a natural black ore of manganese obtainable from Sinai, was found at the Lower Egyptian Predynastic site of Maadi (Lucas 1962: 340), and might have been used as a pigment or as eyepaint. For Upper Egypt, the evidence is somewhat less scarce. From Gebelein, Schiaparelli retrieved Predynastic paintings of human figures and boats on linen, now preserved in the Egyptian Museum, Turin (Inv. Suppl. 17138). Petrie reported, but did not identify, plastered and painted cloth, with red, green, black and white pigments, and leather painted in red, green, black (or blue) and yellow, from Predynastic contexts at Naqada (Lucas 1962: 338). These pigments on organic materials would be among the most important surviving evidence for the history either of organic dyes or of inorganic pigments. The most extensive Predynastic painted surface is the burial chamber of a ruler of the late Naqada Period, at Hierakonpolis, excavated by Quibell and Green at the end of the nineteenth century (see Kemp 1973); this was subsequently dismantled, and substantial fragments are displayed in the Egyptian Museum, Cairo. From this monument, Quibell and Green (1902: 21) reported that the black pigments 'do not seem to be pounded charcoal'. They also noted, but did not identify, a white pigment. No modern analyses of Predynastic pigments are available to us, other than studies of the decorated pottery. The characteristic Predynastic purple-decorated buff ware of the Naqada period has been analysed in the post-War period (Hope *et al.* 1981).

There are no recent reports of identifications of Early Dynastic pigments available to us. Lucas (1962: 338) noted painted mud-brick corridors and walls with black, blue, red and yellow motifs among the First-Dynasty *mastaba* tombs at Saqqara, but also commented that the pigments were not identified. In addition, he cites the excavation report on the Third-Dynasty *mastaba* of Hesyra at Saqqara (S2405 [A3]) the mud-brick walls of which bear paintings in red, brown, yellow and, to a lesser extent, black, green and white (Quibell 1913: 5–9, pls. VIII–XIV). Identification of the green pigment would be of considerable importance for our knowledge of the early history of artificial green and blue pigments (see pp. 108–13 under blue and green).

Pigments of the dynastic period (Fourth–Thirtieth Dynasties)

Introduction

The following discussion includes material from the Fourth to the Thirtieth Dynasties, with some comparative material of the Ptolemaic and Roman periods (fourth century BC to fourth century AD). Although it has not proven practicable at this stage of research to avoid the colour-by-colour approach of the Lucas' *Ancient Egyptian Materials and Industries*, the shortcomings should be noted: it creates a foreign and anachronistic focus on English-language colour terms, few if any of which can be said to correspond exactly to the Egyptian perception of colour, and it reinforces the impression of a small range of colours, in marked contrast to the great range of hues present in any Theban tomb-chapel, for example in the ranges of browns, reds and pinks.

At present, the colour-by-colour approach may be justified to some extent at least by the relatively small range of materials used in the paintings of the Dynastic period, as opposed to the great variety in mixtures and techniques of application. It should be emphasised, however, that the object of study is not so much single colours, as the various palettes in use for particular surfaces across the different periods of ancient Egyptian history. When more data become available, it will be convenient to group results of pigment analyses secondarily by colour, and first by workshop along perhaps the following lines: stone sculpture and relief; painting on wood (particularly the funerary workshops); painting on papyrus (again primarily funerary in the surviving record); painting on plaster, subdividing into the domestic and funerary spheres (see pp. 117–19 for a discussion of the types of painting ground).

Within a composition according to the rules of Egyptian canonical art, each pigment is applied evenly across an outlined surface, the artist aiming at polychromatic effect rather than colouristic shading (Brunner-Traut 1977: 121, 127 n. 51). The emphasis of the palette thus falls on the pure and intense colours, with a consequent delimitation of the materials in use. The principal colours may be summarised as three pairs: black and white; red and yellow; and blue and green; variants to this framework include brown, grey, orange, pink and purple. The painting ground plays its part in selection of the range and hue of colour in each composition. While factors such as royal privilege and economy are often important influences on colour choice, the nature of the painting ground itself is also an influential factor. The importance of the ground can be seen in the use of pure orpiment for yellow on New Kingdom royal red quartzite sarcophagi and, on a smaller scale, non-royal funerary manuscripts, as compared with mixed orpiment and ochre on limestone and sandstone temple reliefs of the same period (see pp. 115–16 under yellow). Awareness of background hue and its effect on colour may be seen in the preparation of clean plaster walls of tomb-chapels, and in the apparently deliberately darker walls of sarcophagus chambers in mid-Eighteenth Dynasty royal tombs, evoking the faded brown of an aged papyrus scroll.

Black

In almost every analysis of Egyptian pigments, black has proven to be carbon. Lucas (1962: 339) estimated that the fineness and evenness of particles indicated that it was soot, and suggested that it had been scraped from cooking vessels. One sample of black was found to contain burnt plant material traces characteristic of charcoal (Eton College, Myers Collection, coffin depicting Thutmose III *c.* 960–900 BC).

Lucas (1962: 340) noted the identification of a black pigment in a Twelfth-Dynasty tomb at Beni Hasan as pyrolusite, the manganese ore found at Sinai, but the analysis was undertaken by Spurrell in 1895, and finds no more recent corroboration. Nevertheless, the black on an Eighteenth-Dynasty pottery vessel was more recently identified as oxide of manganese, although here too more information concerning the method of analysis is needed (Lucas 1962: 384). One colour on a Ramesside papyrus (BM EA9949) appeared black, but was found by the present authors to be very dark Egyptian blue, a degradation pattern which may be expected in other instances even if it remains to be explained in detail. In sum, there is almost no evidence for the use of materials other than carbon for obtaining black in painting during the Dynastic period. The exception is the black paint applied to faience objects before firing (cf. Kaczmarczyk and Hedges 1983).

Blue

Egyptian blue

The principal blue pigment was Egyptian blue, discussed here under the headings:

(a) method of analysis;
(b) components and method of production;
(c) texture and hue;
(d) distribution within Egypt;
(e) patterns of degradation; and
(f) attestations outside Egypt.

Other blue pigments identified in analysis are treated at the end of this section.

Method of analysis Egyptian blue is a multi-phase material, and for this reason XRD may be insufficiently sensitive to detect all components. Similarly, PLM cannot be used to identify each of the various phases present. In order to gain more precise information, a sample must be mounted in resin and polished to produce a cross-section; this can then be examined and analysed in a scanning electron microscope with x-ray analysis. However, especially when dealing with pigments taken from objects, the use of this technique is often limited by the required sample size. It is important that sample size be stated in scientific reports, as the quality of the results may depend in part on this.

Egyptian blue was identified in general in the British Museum conservation project using PLM with confirmation from XRD and elemental analysis.

Components and method of production Egyptian blue is a synthetic pigment composed of various phases containing silica, copper and calcium, made by heating together silica, copper alloy filings or a copper ore such as malachite, lime (calcium oxide), and an alkali such as potash or natron (sodium sesquicarbonate $Na_2CO_3.NaHCO_3.2H_2O$, found naturally occurring in Egypt). This may be compared with the description in Vitruvius (*On Architecture* VII: ch. XI, 1), where it is said that *caeruleum* 'blue (pigment)' was manufactured at a factory at Pozzuoli established by Vestorius following procedures found at Alexandria; according to Vitruvius, the Vestorius factory produced its *caeruleum* by fusing together sand, copper filings and *nitrum* 'soda' (Granger 1970, 123–4). Blom-Böer suggests that the three principal ingredients were calcite, malachite and quartz sand, and comments that this substance is fused by heating and ought therefore, strictly speaking, not be termed a frit (Blom-Böer 1994: 62); it has also been suggested that the term 'frit' should be reserved for the initial phase of glass or glaze production (see Chapter 8, this volume). Nevertheless 'blue frit' is widely used in the Egyptological literature as a synonym for 'Egyptian blue'; if frit is defined as a sintered polycrystalline material, use of the term can be justified for Egyptian blue. The melting point was lowered to below 742 °C by the addition of the alkali. Chemically the malachite, silica and calcite turn to cuprorivaite, carbon-dioxide and water vapour:

$$Cu_2CO_3(OH)_2 + 8SiO_2 + 2CaCO_3 \rightarrow 2CaCuSi_4O_{10} + 3CO_2 + H_2$$

This crystalline product consists of rectangular blue crystals, often in many layers. The major component is cuprorivaite, $(Ca,Cu)Si_4O_{10}$, with unreacted quartz, often accompanied by copper-bearing wollastonite, $(Ca,Cu)_3(Si_3O_9)$. There are also varying amounts of alkali-rich glass. By the reign of Thutmose III, copper ore was replaced in at least some cases by bronze filings, as has been deduced from the presence of tin oxide, SnO_2 (Jaksch *et al.* 1983: 533–5). Other minor components noted by the Max-Planck project include pyrite (FeS), titanomagnetite ($Fe_3O_4.Fe_2TiO_4$, thought to be a result of the use of desert sand as a raw ingredient), and cassiterite (SnO_2).

Texture and hue The hardness, texture and resultant colour of Egyptian blue when used as a pigment depend on the initial components, the microstructure of the sintered product, and final particle size after grinding to produce a pigment. Tite, Bimson and Cowell (1987) categorise Egyptian blue as dark blue, light blue or diluted light blue. The dark blue is low in alkali, with a microstructure showing coarse crystals of cuprorivaite. The light blue is also low in alkali, but the cuprorivaite crystals are smaller, and intimately mixed with the other components. The diluted light blue is high in alkali, and as a result contains a large proportion of glass; this results in a paler blue material which is also harder than the low alkali products. The glass-rich materials are often found in the Eighteenth Dynasty and later, and this has been associated with the advanced technology of glass production at this time. Both the light blue and the diluted light blue are thought to have been produced by at least a two-stage process, with regrinding of the material before resintering, to produce the intimate mixture of components revealed in their microstructures. Any of these materials can be ground to form a pigment. Egyptian blue was often thickly applied, with coarse particles up to 50 μm across. In general a higher degree of grinding will produce smaller particles, which appear paler than if they were coarsely ground (see Ullrich 1985). Some paler blue samples were found to contain white, generally calcite or gypsum, although this may be residual $CaCO_3$ in Egyptian blue itself. In some cases the white appeared to be contamination; thus on the Eighteenth-Dynasty shroud of a man named Amenhotep (BM EA73806) calcite was found in the Egyptian blue sample, but the shroud had been folded for many years in storage, possibly already partly in antiquity, and observation suggested that the calcite had offset onto the blue areas due to prolonged contact. This ambiguous result reflects the limitations in removing small samples.

In a report on analyses of blue pigment samples from the Eighteenth-Dynasty Workmen's Village at Amarna, Weatherhead and Buckley (1989: 206–8) have drawn attention to the present visual difference between turquoise-blues and other blues, and they have concluded from their results that a turquoise hue was obtained by adding significantly higher amounts of sodium in the form of impure natron. A similar ratio of copper to calcium was noted as in a green sample, and the future study of intentional variation in hues of artificial pigments needs to demarcate the observed turquoise from the green as much as from the blue. Possible effects of degradation on the present hue must be noted (see 'Patterns of degradation', p. 110).

Distribution within Egypt Spurrell, Laurie and Smith (see Lucas 1962: 342) report Egyptian blue on objects as early as the Fourth Dynasty and the Max-Planck project identified it as the blue pigment in all samples analysed, from the Fifth Dynasty to the Roman period, apart from the grey-blue pigments in the First Intermediate Period tomb-chapels of the local governors Ankhtifi and Setka in el-Moʿalla and Aswan respectively (Blom-Böer 1994: 73). The blue on the famous Eighteenth-Dynasty head of Queen Nefertiti (Berlin, ÄM21300) has also been identified as Egyptian blue (Wiedemann and Bayer 1982). All blue samples in the British Museum conservation project were likewise found to be Egyptian blue, and no tin was detected in these despite their date (New Kingdom to Roman period).

The Theban tomb-chapels of the mid-Eighteenth Dynasty provide variable data concerning blue and green artificial pigment distribution; in general they are sparingly used on these plastered limestone wall surfaces, as in the tomb of Tjanuni (TT74; Brack and Brack 1977: 108), and exceptions may perhaps be explained by the higher importance of the tomb-owner rather than by a chronological difference, as in the extensive use of blue and green in the only slightly later tomb-chapel of Horemheb (TT78; Brack and Brack 1980: 15). In a slightly earlier Theban tomb-chapel from the reign of Amenhotep II (TT104), both blue and green appear in some instances to have been applied thinly and then covered by a layer of a wax-like substance which has now darkened, but this surface has not been analysed or dated (Shedid 1988: 23).

Patterns of degradation One of the most important findings by the Max-Planck project concerned the degradation of artificial blue pigments to superficial green (Schiegl *et al.* 1992). According to these samples from painted stone surfaces, all Old and Middle Kingdom samples of what seemed to be green proved to be originally Egyptian blue; in this, the intense blue cuprorivaite $(Ca,Cu)Si_4O_{10}$ predominates, and the green copper wollastonite $(Ca,Cu)_3(Si_3O_9)$ represents a minor component. From the New Kingdom onwards, the samples which now appear green were shown by analysis to consist of green frit, in which the copper wollastonite predominates over the lesser component of cuprorivaite.

The main conclusion of these analyses was that apparent Old and Middle Kingdom greens were in fact the product of degradation of the multi-phase synthetic pigment Egyptian blue, and that such natural features as plant stems and tree tops were originally painted light blue. Specifically it has been shown that the glass phase in Egyptian blue can devitrify, resulting in the secondary formation of copper chloride and/or malachite. This not only causes colour change, from blue to green, but also renders the pigment spongy and friable. In other cases, loss of the pale blue glass may not result in the formation of chlorides, but the Egyptian blue will become a darker blue. The source of the chlorides for the first of these two degradation patterns has not been identified; if the glass is chloride-rich, some source for this component still needs to be found. It is also not clear at what stage in this decay the degradation products become responsible for the general hue of the pigment. It should be noted too that the small amount of copper wollastonite, present as minute crystals in the interstices of cuprorivaite in Egyptian blue, would also be subject to degradation.

Against the background of these discussions it may be noted that some Old and Middle Kingdom organic surfaces are coloured with apparent emphasis on a strong contrast between green and blue; on the wooden coffin of a lady named Khuit, from Asyut (BM EA46634) the one line of green hieroglyphs runs above a markedly blue *wedjat*-eye pair, and in at least this instance a First Intermediate Period or early Middle Kingdom artist seems to have intended and obtained distinct blue and green pigments on an organic ground. This coffin is unpublished, and has been dated from the offering formula and the style of two statuettes (BM EA45124 and EA45200) which are thought to be from the same tomb; the green pigment was shown in analysis to be malachite (see p. 112 under 'Green').

The selection of pigment and consequently of colour may therefore depend in these cases more on the surface to be painted than the intended colour symbolism or the range of the contemporary palette. In this respect, the identification of binding media as well as the evaluation of texture of pigment may in the future explain the selection of certain pigments and thus the presence of colours on particular types of surface, with possible variations between stone, wood and papyrus. The palettes of the various workshops must therefore be differentiated as carefully as the periods and regional distribution of pigments, the workshops being distinguished provisionally as the following: soft stone, hard stone, painted plaster, and organic (in the surviving record predominantly funerary equipment).

A pale blue glass has also been reported (Schiegl *et al.* 1992); this is produced from similar materials to those used for Egyptian blue, but contains no calcium. It has been suggested that this can degrade to produce copper chloride or malachite, turning green.

Egyptian blue has darkened to appear now as black on one Ramesside papyrus (BM EA9949). The malachite with Egyptian blue that has been detected in samples from the Twentieth-Dynasty Book of the Dead papyrus of the noblewoman Anhay (BM EA10472) appears to be the degradation product of a pigment applied as Egyptian blue. In discussions of degradation it is important to refer back to the object from which a sample has been taken. Degradation of pigments on artefacts in the British Museum has produced a patchy, clearly discoloured appearance, and it seems unlikely that a degradation mechanism in a painted field could result in an evenly coloured alteration product. In future research it may be helpful to define the criteria whereby a colour surface is judged degraded or not.

Attestations outside Egypt Outside Egypt the same compound is found as the material for small artefacts and inlays in Western Asia from the middle of the third millennium BC (Early Dynastic III Period in Mesopotamia). Western Asia is at least as likely as Egypt (and possibly more likely) to be the place of origin for production of the compound as a material for inlays and other plastic forms; we have not found analyses establishing its early use as a pigment in that area (Moorey 1985: 188–93; 1994: 186–9 for material such as inlays, 322–9 for pigments in wall-paintings). It is also attested in the Mediterranean world from at least the end of the Middle Bronze Age or beginning of the Late

Bronze Age. The samples from the Thera frescoes of the sixteenth century BC included tin (Filippakis 1978); this indicates that the introduction of bronze filings to replace copper filings took place either earlier in Egypt than is attested in analysed samples, or outside Egypt with the technology imported back into Egypt from the Mediterranean area in the fifteenth century BC.

It is not certain at what date Egyptian blue began to be produced in Roman Italy. However, the relevant passages in Vitruvius and Pliny (first century AD) seem to imply that manufacture of the material had at that time only recently been established at Pozzuoli (Wallert 1995: 179). Laurie dated the latest examples in Italy to the second to seventh centuries AD, but this range has been extended to the ninth century AD by more recent analyses of pigments in the church of San Clemente, Rome (Lazzarini 1982).

Blue pigments other than Egyptian blue

Cobalt blue is attested in Egypt for the Amarna period on pottery, but not on either the so-called *talatat* blocks (in temples) or the tomb-chapel wall-reliefs of the same period. A source for cobalt has been reported from Kharga Oasis, but a central European provenance is also possible in view of the limited timespan in usage. There seem to have been more intensive Aegean–Egyptian contacts – either direct or via Syria – during the reigns of Amenhotep III and Akhenaten in the late Eighteenth Dynasty, and this might provide the trading network for a short-lived cobalt supply from the far side of the Balkans. Blom-Böer (1994: 62) suggests instead that the limit in time may be linked to a connection between cobalt blue and the sun-cult as interpreted in the reign of Akhenaten. It should also be noted that, apart from the Predynastic period, pottery was commonly painted only in the late Eighteenth to early Nineteenth Dynasties, and that therefore the absence of cobalt as a pigment in other periods might relate more to the choice of surface than to the availability of the mineral within Egypt. Lucas (1962: 344) mentions a report by M. Toch of cobalt blue from the Fifth-Dynasty tomb of Perneb from Saqqara, but he points out that this was later shown to be a misidentification of Egyptian blue (calcium-copper silicate; see Williams 1932: 27, n. 34).

In the First Intermediate Period tomb-chapels of Ankhtifi at el-Moʿalla and Setka at Aswan, the Max-Planck project found blue-grey pigments consisting of a mixture of calcite and carbon black, and of an iron-titanium compound and calcium carbonate (Blom-Böer 1994: 73). These bear greater similarity to the analyses of greys than to those of blues.

Azurite (also designated chessylite), a naturally occurring blue carbonate of copper found in Sinai and the Eastern Desert, was reported by F.C.J. Spurrell (1895) in the following examples: a shell used as a palette in a Fourth-Dynasty context at Meidum, a cloth over the face of a Fifth-Dynasty mummy, also at Meidum, and a number of Eighteenth-Dynasty 'paintings', presumably wall-paintings. There is, however, no more recent corroboration of Spurrell's findings (Lucas 1962: 340). The Max-Planck project (covering the Fifth Dynasty to the Roman period) reported no instances of azurite, and it has been concluded that identifications of blue pigment as natural azurite are not secure; Blom-Böer (1994: 61–2) suggests that the apparent absence of azurite from the Egyptians' palette was perhaps a result of its poor quality and impermanence as a pigment.

It should be noted that there is no evidence that either powdered lapis lazuli or powdered turquoise were used as pigments. According to Lucas (1962: 343–4), the lapis pigment ultramarine is not attested before the eleventh century AD.

Brown

Lucas states that iron oxide or ochre was used for the colour brown, citing analyses of samples dating to the Fourth Dynasty, Amarna period and Late Period (Lucas 1962: 344). He also notes the late nineteenth-century identification by Spurrell of Fourth-Dynasty brown samples as red painted over black. Winlock recorded that the models from the late Eleventh- or early Twelfth-Dynasty tomb of Meketra at Deir el-Bahari included brown pigment obtained by varnishing over a deep yellow ochre. The Max-Planck project identified ochre (generally red, but sometimes brown or yellow) as the material used for brown from the Fifth Dynasty to the Roman period throughout Egypt. Lucas records the Dakhla Oasis as a provenance for good ochre.

The British Museum conservation project found that the brown pigment on one early Eighteenth-Dynasty papyrus (BM EA10477) was a mixture of haematite with orpiment and carbon black. The brown pigment on a Twenty-first- or early Twenty-second-Dynasty papyrus (BM EA10029) was found to contain haematite and carbon black. It should be noted that a green sample containing orpiment yellow and Egyptian blue had turned brown at the edges on one papyrus of the late Ptolemaic or early Roman period (BM EA9916), perhaps from sulphurous emissions in the photochemical degradation of the orpiment component of the green.

A red-brown on a Nineteenth-Dynasty papyrus at the University of Philadelphia Museum was identified by XRF and wet chemical analysis as realgar with iron oxide (Evans *et al.* 1980). The Max-Planck project found that a rare beige hue in samples ranging from the Fifth Dynasty to the Ramesside period, within Upper Egypt, consisted of a mixture of yellow ochre and white pigments; it should be stressed that the hue intended by the artist at application is not always clear from these analyses (Blom-Böer 1994: 73–4).

Green

Although one or two instances of malachite applied as a green pigment are known, the ancient Egyptians generally employed for this colour a synthetic material which is often termed 'green frit' in the literature (for discussion of the use of frit for this product, see p. 109 in the analogous case of Egyptian blue). The major phases of this material are copper wollastonite and a glassy phase rich in copper, sodium and potassium chlorides. It is made in reducing conditions by mixing similar ingredients as for Egyptian blue, but with higher lime, and lower copper content. Two types of green frit have been identified – a glass-rich form, and a wollastonite-rich form; both types may be present in one melt if mixing during manufacture was insufficient. Minor components of green frit may be pyrite (FeS) and covellite (CuS) from a sulphide-rich copper ore.

It has been reported that copper chlorides were used as green pigments from the Fifth Dynasty, and that they were among the first synthetic pigments used. However, the identification of an artificial pigment applied as green before the Eighteenth Dynasty has now been called into question by the results of analyses from stone surfaces by the Max-Planck project. El-Goresy (in Schiegl *et al.* 1992) suggests that copper wollastonite may have been unintentionally produced in highly reducing conditions during sintering of Egyptian blue, but it should be noted that the glassy phase associated with the copper wollastonite would have a much higher calcium content. Basic copper chloride, paratacamite or atacamite, is found in analyses of green pigment samples from surfaces as late as the end of Twelfth Dynasty, but recent investigation by the Max-Planck project led to the conclusion that atacamite may be a degradation product of artificial copper pigments, and that only a few examples of green earlier than the New Kingdom were applied as green, the remainder being applied as light blue. Schiegl specifically disputes that copper chloride pigments were intentionally produced before the New Kingdom, and proposes instead that they are secondary formations due to the degradation of glass-rich phases in sintered materials; weathering of the alkali-rich glass can result in the formation of chlorides and/or malachite, causing the pigment to become paler, spongy and friable (see p. 110, Egyptian blue).

An early Middle Kingdom limestone relief fragment in the Metropolitan Museum of Art, New York, seems to have both water and leaves painted with the same colour, a blue-green. By contrast, the above-cited First Intermediate Period or early Middle Kingdom wooden coffin of Khuit (BM EA44634) has one line of green hieroglyphs and two distinctly blue *wedjat*-eyes; analysis has shown the green of the hieroglyphs to be malachite. This raises the question of whether different painting grounds may have required different media: thus painting on limestone may have excluded green at a time when painting on wood could use both green and blue.

Of three analysed samples of green material identified as pigment from the Eighteenth-Dynasty Workmen's Village at Amarna, two were found to be the green-blue copper ore chrysocolla ($CuSiO_3.2H_2O$), while the third was an artificial material, 'green frit', similar in composition to the turquoise-hue blue pigment samples from the same site (see p. 109 under 'blue'; Weatherhead and Buckley 1989: 208). On papyrus the artificial green pigment or 'green frit' is the pigment of the green colour used in the earliest examples of coloured illustrations, established by analysis of the opening vignette of the mid-Eighteenth-Dynasty Book of the Dead of Nu (BM EA10477). Green frit was probably also the pigment used for the bright green on a Third Intermediate Period papyrus at the British Museum (BM EA9919).

Blom-Böer (1994: 65) reports also a copper-bearing vitreous pigment (*Kupferglas*) from Fifth-Dynasty to Twelfth-Dynasty samples as a possible green pigment, but it ranges in colour from blue to bright green, and its original colour is difficult to assess; samples comprise basic copper chloride and malachite. This may account for the malachite identified as the clearly degraded green on one Thirtieth-Dynasty or early Ptolemaic funerary papyrus (BM EA9944), if not the malachite and calcite mixture on another green from the same papyrus. Malachite was powdered for use as an eye-paint, but no instance of its use as a pigment on stone surfaces was found by the Max-Planck project in samples from the Fifth Dynasty to the Roman period (Blom-Böer 1994: 64, 74–5); it may occur as an ingredient or a 'degradation byproduct' of the 'green frit' discussed above. Malachite has now been found on a First Intermediate Period or early Middle Kingdom coffin at the British Museum (BM EA44634) in a condition which does not suggest degradation from another pigment (see p. 110). However, even if malachite was sometimes applied as a pigment, there was evidently a preference for green frit at most periods.

The Max-Planck project also detected an unexpected possible pre-New Kingdom green in samples of modern red or yellow appearance; these were identified as an iron-bearing vitreous pigment, originally green or brown, which had degraded to the mineral jarosite, with its reddish or yellow hue (Blom-Böer 1994: 63). However, recent analyses by Andrew Middleton and Sylvia Humphrey in the Department of Scientific Research at the British Museum have identified jarosite as a pigment in samples from light yellow colour fields on early Middle Kingdom coffins where there is no sign of degradation on macroscopic observation, and similar results have been reported from the conservation of temple wall paintings at Karnak (see p. 116, under 'Yellow').

The green on a Nineteenth-Dynasty papyrus at the University of Philadelphia Museum was identified by XRF and wet chemical analysis as Egyptian blue mixed with orpiment (Evans *et al.* 1980). This might account for the arsenic sulphide identified from a green pigment from the Royal Tomb at Amarna (Iskander 1987), although the recorded XRD data have been found to be more consistent with a copper compound (Weatherhead 1995: 396). From the late

Ptolemaic or Roman period, the British Museum conservation project found that the green colour on a funerary papyrus (BM EA9916) consisted of Egyptian blue with orpiment. This rare, and presumably more expensive, mixture of blue and yellow to produce a green seems to follow those New Kingdom antecedents, but no parallel can yet be cited from the intervening 1,000 years.

Grey

Lucas reports that a number of Fourth-Dynasty and Fifth-Dynasty samples incorporated a grey obtained by mixing gypsum white with carbon black (Lucas 1962: 346). Reisner had asserted that the grey colour used to paint pottery at the Upper Nubian site of Kerma was obtained from a sandy stone but this is yet to be confirmed (Lucas 1962: 346). Blom-Böer (1994: 74) reports carbon black, or combinations of gypsum with carbon black, from the Fifth to the Twentieth Dynasties, but notes, as with other mixed colours, the difficulty in distiguishing contaminated samples and establishing the original hue intended by the artist at application.

On one of several Ptolemaic and Roman-period papyrus fragments from Elephantine, Ashmunein and the Fayum, a grey pigment was identified by XRD as kaolinite mixed with quartz (Buschle-Diller and Unger 1996: 114).

Orange

Lucas (1962: 346) refers to analyses of orange which identify the colour as red painted over yellow, or else as a mixture of red and yellow, but he does not identify *which* red or yellow pigments, nor does he mention realgar or orpiment in this context. The Max-Planck project found orange in samples from the Sixth Dynasty to the Roman period throughout Egypt to be red ochre, with or without white pigments (Blom-Böer 1994: 5).

In the British Museum conservation project the orange colour used on an early Eighteenth-Dynasty papyrus (BM EA10477) was found to be orpiment or pararealgar with red iron oxide; the orange colours in one Ramesside and one Thirtieth-Dynasty or early Ptolemaic papyrus was identified as pararealgar, and that in a late Ptolemaic papyrus (BM EA9916) was found to be similar to realgar. In at least one Eighteenth-Dynasty funerary papyrus (BM EA9968) realgar has been identified as the substance used for a red-orange ink in a rubric that has now turned into yellow pararealgar (for further discussion of this example, see the section on 'media used on papyrus' in Chapter 9, this volume). On realgar, see p. 114, in the section on 'red'.

Pink

Lucas (1962: 346) refers to the following identifications of pink pigments: Spurrell identified the pink paint used in the Old and New Kingdoms as a mixture of red ochre and gypsum white (see Petrie 1892: 29; Spurrell 1895: 231), while Borchardt (1923: 32) reached the same conclusion concerning the pink paint used on the Nefertiti head from Amarna (Berlin, ÄM). For the Hellenistic and Roman periods, Russell (1893–4: 374–5, 1893–5: 67–71) identified the pink colour in a tomb-painting (presumably on a wall or ceiling) as madder painted over gypsum white. Madder is a dyestuff obtained from the roots of the madder plant, native to Persia and the eastern Mediterranean (Cardon and du Chatelet 1990: 164; and see Chapter 11, this volume). Wagenaar (see Lucas 1962: 346) identified a late pink as finely powdered shell, but this has not been corroborated.

The Max-Planck project found pink on samples from the Fifth to the Twentieth Dynasties to be invariably a red ochre with or without white pigment (Blom-Böer 1994: 75). The unusual bright pink on the Third Intermediate Period papyrus BM EA9919 was found to consist of an organic substance over a gypsum ground, and it is possible that this might be an early example of the use of madder, consistent with the results of Russell (Lucas 1962: 346). The change in palette from the Ptolemaic Period included a greater use of pink, with new inorganic as well as the above-cited organic materials; thus the pink-red on a funerary papyrus of the late Ptolemaic or early Roman period was found to be vermilion (HgS) (BM EA9916).

Purple

True purple seems not to have been used in Egyptian painting, and the colour is not mentioned by Lucas except with reference to Predynastic pottery (Lucas 1962: 384). True purple is not to be confused with the dark red background colour on the inside walls of early Twenty-second-Dynasty anthropoid coffins from Thebes; this appears to be a mixture of yellow and red ochres, judging from the analysis of the paint on two such coffins in the British Museum.

Red

Lucas (1962: 346–8) divided the naturally occurring iron oxides into two groups: red iron oxides (anhydrous oxides of iron) and red ochres (hydrated oxides of iron). The division may be expressed in different terms from the geological standpoint; the ochres are among natural mineral pigments coloured by the presence of iron, either the hydrous iron oxide, 'limonite', or the anhydrous iron oxide, 'haematite' (Thorpe and Whiteley 1954: 631–2). Limonite is a component of yellow ochre, whereas red ochre contains abundant haematite, and the common red pigment is accordingly identified as haematite in analyses; note however that the term haematite tends to be reserved within Egyptology for the mineral in its metallic black appearance, as a material used for carving into beads, kohl-sticks, seals and other small objects (see Chapter 2, this volume).

The Max-Planck project identified most visually red samples as red ochre from the Fifth Dynasty to the Roman period; they noted only a few instances in which haematite appeared to be used (ranging in date from the Sixth Dynasty to the First Intermediate Period and Eighteenth Dynasty) and they defined these simply as particularly rich in iron oxide (Blom-Böer 1994: 75). The analysis of one red pigment from the Eighteenth-Dynasty Workmen's Village at Amarna also indicated the use of haematite (Weatherhead and Buckley 1989: 208–9).

A brighter red colour (closer to orange) can be obtained by using realgar, an arsenic sulphide. It should be noted that, like orpiment, realgar is an extremely light-sensitive pigment; it degrades to pararealgar, which is orange-yellow. The only uses of realgar which Lucas reports are undated references to analyses performed by Spurrell and Barthoux, as well as the mention of a sample of orpiment streaked with realgar which is said to have been found at Tanis (Lucas 1962: 348). As far as non-Egyptian sources of realgar are concerned, Barthoux (1926) mention St John's Island in the Red Sea, while Blom-Böer (1994: 66) cites Asia Minor, a suggestion which may be backed up by the presence of this pigment among the cargo of the shipwreck at Ulu Burun (off the southern Anatolian coast), dating to the late fourteenth century BC (Moorey 1994: 328). The Max-Planck project found two Eighteenth-Dynasty instances of realgar used as orange-red paint at Thebes: the contents of a receptacle found in the tomb-chapel of Kheruef (TT192); and a sample from a wall of the tomb of Thutmose IV in the Valley of the Kings (KV43; Blom-Böer 1994: 73, 75).

Degraded realgar appears to have been found at Amarna, this being the most likely identification of a pigment lump from an unrecorded location at Amarna which is now in the collection of the Bolton Museum (30.24.70); it was streaked with red and identified as arsenic sulphide (Weatherhead 1995: 395). Another probable instance of pararealgar (i.e. degraded realgar) is a quantity of pigment described by the excavators as 'bright orange-red' which was found in a reshaped pottery vessel excavated at Amarna in 1935 (Weatherhead and Buckley 1989: 217–18).

The British Museum conservation project found that examples of red paint were made of haematite/red ochre in most instances, but on one Nineteenth-Dynasty papyrus it consisted of pararealgar with orpiment and a trace of haematite (BM EA9949). It was at one stage reported that realgar could alter to orpiment upon exposure to light, but this is now discounted (Douglass *et al.* 1992). For these reasons realgar is susceptible to misidentification in both laboratory analysis and visual inspection. There remains in addition the problem of identifying pararealgar as a degraded rather than an original pigment (Corbeil and Helwig 1995).

On one late Ptolemaic or early Roman papyrus (BM EA9916) an orange-red pigment was composed of iron oxide, while a pink-red paint consisted of vermilion. The red on a Nineteenth-Dynasty papyrus at the University of Pennsylvania Museum (E2775) was identified by XRF and wet chemical analysis as realgar (Evans *et al.* 1980). Red lead pigments are not attested before the late Ptolemaic or Roman period (Blom-Böer 1994: 66).

White

Lucas (1962: 348–9) reports that the only two white pigments in ancient Egypt were calcium carbonate (whiting, chalk) and calcium sulphate (gypsum). The Max-Planck project recorded both calcium carbonate and calcium sulphate from the Fifth Dynasty to the Roman period, but they found the latter (usually comprising gypsum and anhydrite in varying proportions) to be the more common (Blom-Böer 1994: 66, 75). In addition, their analyses of white pigments from Theban tomb-chapels of the Twelfth Dynasty and Eighteenth to Twentieth Dynasties revealed magnesian calcite, chosen for its intensity as a first layer under main pigment on tomb-chapel walls (Blom-Böer 1994: 67, 75).

Blom-Böer also notes huntite, a magnesium calcium carbonate, as a pigment comparable to orpiment in terms of its quality and brightness (Blom-Böer 1994: 67, 76). Huntite would have been desirable as a painting material not only on account of its colour, but also for its adhesiveness, its small particle size and its very fine grain, which would also have ensured a smooth painted surface. It is attested in the Persian Gulf, and occurs both in land saltlakes and on the margins of magnesium-rich strata, conditions that can also be found in Egypt; the nearest published north African source known to us is far to the west in Tunisia (Perthuisot *et al.* 1990).

The Max-Planck project found huntite to be the material used for white paint in Eighteenth- to Twentieth-Dynasty samples. The suggestion that huntite was used in a Twelfth-Dynasty sample, from the Theban tomb-chapel of Senet (TT60) is considered uncertain because of the method of sampling adopted in that instance (Blom-Böer 1994: 76 n. 157).

Huntite was also identified as a pigment or pigment component in the analyses of samples of pigments from the walls and from the painting equipment of two mid-Eighteenth-Dynasty Theban tomb-chapels (TT80 and TT104). In both of these analyses, which were undertaken by Fuchs and Burmester (see Shedid 1988: 166), huntite was identified in samples either alone or with other pigments, notably with calcite or gypsum in the samples of white.

The British Museum conservation project found huntite used for white colouring on a Twelfth-Dynasty coffin fragment (BM EA46654), an early Eighteenth-Dynasty shroud EA73807), and three papyri, one dating to the early Eighteenth Dynasty (BM EA10477), another to the Nineteenth Dynasty (BM EA9949) and the third to the Twenty-first to Twenty-second Dynasties (BM EA9919). The attested date range of the mineral has thus been extended beyond the New Kingdom, although it should be noted that the absence of later examples among the results of the Max-Planck project is probably to be explained by the fact that the Third Intermediate Period is not well-represented among the surviving coloured stone monuments which form their primary sources. The pigment appears on richly coloured objects, providing a corollary to the selection of orpiment for yellow and realgar for red; in general it occurs on smaller scale surfaces or in lesser quantity than the other white pigments. It would be reasonable to conclude that it belonged to the more restricted and costly palette alongside realgar and orpiment.

Wagenaar (Lucas 1962: 349) identified a white as powdered shell or cuttlefish bone: this has not been corroborated. In this context it should be noted that another papyrus of the Third Intermediate Period (BM EA10029) bore an unidentified white, which contained calcium, phosphorus and low levels of magnesium according to the SEM (EDXA) analysis; this might suggest hydroxylapatite, from bone, but the XRD pattern was not consistent with this, and the material remains enigmatic.

Yellow

This colour is most commonly found to consist of yellow ochre, comprising iron bearing materials, notably goethite (the alpha form of FeOOH) and limonite (the yellow to brown hydrous oxide) together with varying amounts of clay and siliceous matter (see Thorpe and Whiteley 1954: 631). More rarely the arsenic sulphide orpiment has been found. Thus Lucas (1962: 349–50) reports yellow ochre (hydrated iron oxide) and – from the late Eighteenth Dynasty onwards – orpiment, a naturally occurring arsenic sulphide. He also refers to the identification by Reisner (1923: IV–V, 292–3) of the use of ground sandstone for yellow pigment at Kerma, but this requires confirmation. Laurie (1913) identified massicot (a yellow oxide of lead) in a sample of yellow pigment found on a palette dating to *c.* 400 BC, (Lucas 1962: 351) while John had identified vegetal yellow pigments about a century earlier. The yellow in the Theban tomb-chapel of Amenuser, first minister under Hatshepsut in the early Eighteenth Dynasty (TT131), was found by XRD to be yellow ochre (Dziobek 1994: 101).

The Max-Planck project identified as yellow ochre the yellow pigments on samples from Fifth Dynasty to the Roman period, but they found orpiment in pure form only on Eighteenth- and Nineteenth-Dynasty sarcophagi of kings, and on the walls of the tomb of Thutmose IV (KV43). One of the major findings of the project was the mixture of orpiment and yellow ochre applied to New Kingdom temple and tomb walls; Blom-Böer (1994: 63–4, 74) reports layering of first yellow ochre, then orpiment and finally yellow ochre again on the walls of tombs and temples in the New Kingdom, thus giving the ochre the greater intensity of colour characteristic of orpiment. This suggests a differential application of the mineral depending on the surface area and/or status of the monument. With regard to status, however, it should be noted that analyses of samples of yellow pigment from two Eighteenth-Dynasty Theban private tomb-chapels revealed no orpiment, whereas painting materials discovered in the same chapels included pigment blocks identified as orpiment (TT78, tomb-chapel of Horemheb, see Brack and Brack 1980: 100, and TT192, tomb-chapel of Kheruef, see Blom-Böer 1994: 74 n. 149). This suggests that in some instances orpiment, although perhaps present in the tomb-paintings, might simply not have been detected, either because it has faded with exposure to light, and therefore has not seemed to present a coloured surface worth sampling, or because it has been used in a mixture with yellow ochre, and only the ochre stratum of the layered application has been analysed.

With regard to sources for orpiment (arsenic sulphide) outside Egypt, Moorey (1994: 328) cites Julamerk in Kurdistan, Goramis in Iran, as well as Syria and Anatolia, noting that orpiment was part of the cargo on the Ulu Burun shipwreck mentioned above; earlier studies give Kharga Oasis and St John's Island in the Red Sea as possible provenances closer to the Nile Valley.

In the Workmen's Village at Amarna samples of yellow pigment were found on analysis by SEM to consist of (1) quartz grains with a thin iron-rich coating and (2) small inclusions of iron and titanium within the core material. The chemical constituents of these samples therefore appeared to be consistent with the most common yellow pigment of the Dynastic period, goethite or yellow ochre (Weatherhead and Buckley 1989: 209). However, another sample from the 1922 excavation dumps at the Village proved to be orpiment, perhaps deriving from the decoration of the 'South Tombs', the tomb-chapels of members of the royal court which lay a few kilometres to the southeast.

Of even greater importance to the study of Egyptian yellows is a segment of a limestone grinding-bowl on which were found coarse particles of a yellow pigment visually identified as orpiment. This object was found discarded in a well at the industrial area Q48.4 to the south of the central city at Amarna; in her report on the find, Weatherhead (1995: 396–7) suggests that the orpiment may have been ground coarsely because it was intended for application to wood or stone objects, in view of the fact that coarsely applied orpiment was found on a wooden model coffin excavated from the central city. Weatherhead also documents a number of earlier finds at Amarna, including the following: several pieces of yellow pigment excavated in 1921 from a house in the main city (O49.17); fragments found with the painting of the Amarna princesses from the King's House (UC2262, 2289), which originally contained orpiment that is no longer visible (presumably faded on exposure to light); and among the tombs of the nobles (tomb-chapel of Ahmose No. 3), which included at least one instance of orpiment with yellow ochre. She also notes the presence of orpiment on the papyrus fragments from the shrine of the royal statue (BM EA74100), and on the limestone head of Nefertiti from the sculptor's workshop (Berlin ÄM21300). Other instances cited as red-streaked or containing realgar are identified as degradation from realgar, and are thus the degradation product pararealgar rather than orpiment (see section on 'red', p. 114).

The date of the earliest use of orpiment is difficult to determine, although it is certainly earlier than the Eighteenth Dynasty. Analysis of yellow on the late Old Kingdom stele of Sheshi (Louvre E 27.133) revealed a mixture of yellow ochre with an unidentified arsenic compound, and a yellow ochre with traces of sodium chloride and arsenic was identified from the late Old Kingdom tomb-chapel paintings of Metjetji (Louvre E 25.548; Ziegler 1990: 314, 316). These results are strikingly reminiscent of the Max-Planck discovery of layered ochre and orpiment in New Kingdom examples, and may carry the use of orpiment in Egypt back to *c.* 2400 BC.

Unequivocal identifications of yellow as orpiment fix the latest possible date for its introduction as the Twelfth Dynasty, *c.* 1900 BC. In the British Museum conservation project, orpiment was found on a Twelfth-Dynasty coffin in the British Museum (BM EA46644), thus confirming the results of an earlier analysis of pigments on two Twelfth-Dynasty coffins in Boston (Museum of Fine Arts, outer coffin of Thutnakht and fragment 21.816g from the coffin of his wife; Terrace 1968: 167–8). Orpiment was also identified as the yellow pigment on early Eighteenth-Dynasty linen shrouds (BM EA73806–7), papyri of the Nineteenth Dynasty (BM EA9949 and 9968), Twentieth Dynasty (BM EA10472), Third Intermediate Period (BM EA9919 and 10029), Thirtieth Dynasty or early Ptolemaic (BM EA9944) and late Ptolemaic period (BM EA9916). In the case of the Nineteenth-Dynasty papyrus BM EA9949, pararealgar was identified as a minor component alongside orpiment; the two occur naturally together, and this does not affect the identification of the pigment as orpiment. On the early Eighteenth-Dynasty papyrus BM EA10477 the yellow was identified as an arsenic sulphide, the exact structure of which has not been identified. No pigment layers have been detected in the papyri. The darker yellow on the late Ptolemaic example BM EA9916 was found to be pararealgar, a degradation product of orange-red realgar. Orpiment was also the yellow pigment used in a tomb-painting from the Theban tomb-chapel of Nebamun (BM EA37978), of the reign of Thutmose IV in the mid-Eighteenth Dynasty.

Following these analyses of British Museum samples, it has been noted that the buff or dull yellow given by ochre can often be distinguished from bright orpiment by preliminary visual inspection of ancient examples not faded by exposure to light. Orpiment has a laminar structure, creating a scintillating effect quite unlike the matt surface of ochre. However, visual identification should always be confirmed by analysis. The yellow paint on a Nineteenth-Dynasty papyrus at the University of Pennsylvania Museum (E2775) was identified by XRF and wet chemical analysis as orpiment (Evans *et al.* 1980).

Noll originally identified as jarosite the yellow pigment on Eleventh-Dynasty pottery from el-Tarif, and noted it also on the Minoan wall-paintings from Thera. The Max-Planck project encountered additional instances, and Blom-Böer noted Cyprus as a possible provenance for the mineral in the absence of known Egyptian sources. However these additional instances, from tomb-chapel walls (Fifth to Sixth and Eleventh to Twelfth Dynasties, Lower and Middle Egypt), were explained as the result of degradation, and not considered evidence for the use of jarosite as an original ancient Egyptian pigment (Blom-Böer 1994: 63). The analysts suggested that the original material as applied would have been a green or brown vitreous material, perhaps produced in the same manner as – if not identical in composition to – the other vitreous materials used for greens and blues. This hypothesis may now need to be modified in the light of more recent findings such as painting equipment found at Karnak, from which jarosite was identified without reference to degradation, and with note of a possible source for the mineral in the western desert at Aswan (Le Fur 1994: 45 and map p. 32). In addition, Andrew Middleton and Sylvia Humphrey of the Department of Scientific Reseach at the British Museum have identified as jarosite the light yellow pigment on several early Middle Kingdom coffins (unpublished analyses). The question of degradation remains, but needs to be assessed against the original objects as well as the analytical results; there is no obvious reason for the jarosite on the early Middle Kingdom coffins to be considered as the result of degradation. Jarosite, despite being a rare mineral, ought therefore to be considered among the list of known Egyptian pigments.

Gilding

In the context of painting, it may be mentioned that gilding is attested on a small number of illustrated funerary papyri, of New Kingdom and Late Period date, notably the opening vignette of the Book of the Dead of Anhay (BM EA10472), and a large scale vignette in the Book of the Dead of a head-goldsmith named Khar (BM EA9949). Another example earlier in the New Kingdom is found on the Book of the Dead of Tjenena in the Louvre (N3074; de Cenival 1992: 8, 70). Although gold leaf is analagous in these instances to a pigment, it is probably best discussed in the context of metallurgy, see Chapter 6, this volume.

Summary

There appears to be a consistent core palette throughout the Dynastic period, comprising red and yellow ochre, blue and green artificial pigments, carbon black, and calcite or gypsum white. This basic palette is supplemented from at least the late Middle Kingdom onwards by a less commonly attested, perhaps less available (imported ?) set of materials giving more intense colour: orpiment for yellow, realgar for orange-red, and huntite for white. Detailed differences in attestations across time, and reasons for selection of particular materials in particular contexts remain to be studied. Other pigments, such as vermilion, seem to have been introduced only in the late Ptolemaic or Roman period; these, and the implied change in colour appreciation (e.g. the use of pink), may reflect Alexandrian trade and exchange of flora and commodities with the East, notably Persia and India, rather than new exposure to central Mediterranean contacts.

These results concern the basic pigments in the palette, and analysis to identify these inevitably focuses attention on individual samples. Identification of the palette alone can give the impression that the Egyptian artist was constrained by a limited palette for block fields of colour. It leaves to one side the question of different hues of the same colour on one object, where the same broad colour is present in different hues obtained either by different materials or by different application of the same material. There is also the question of shading within one colour field on an object, where the artist applies the material to obtain specific effects of light and shade, volume, or hue. Thick application of pigments on painted plaster gives darker shades, while thin application can help to provide virtually transparent effects, and the addition of white supplies lighter hues; the techniques of painting also provide different results, as when the painter draws a half-dried reed loosely over the surface for thin lines (Shedid 1988: 23–4). These problems fall into the scope of art history, but the identification of pigments provides the basis for an understanding of their application.

The question of the methods used to prepare the raw materials requires further study. At Amarna, the red and yellow pigments appear to have been ground on stone vessels; one pottery vessel with re-shaped hexagonal rim contained a bright orange-red pigment (realgar?), and a pottery vessel base contained an unidentified yellow pigment, but these are presumably painters' pots rather than vessels for grinding (Weatherhead and Buckley 1989: 216–18). The artificial pigments at the same site were found in a small bag shape, indicating the fusion of the raw materials or a second firing of an initially fused pigment, and then shaped either into discs or into round or bowl-shaped cakes of material (Weatherhead and Buckley 1989: 210–16); future research into the industrial areas and analyses of finished and unfinished objects and their moulds may reveal the stage in production at which a distinction was made between, on the one hand, pure painters' materials, and on the other hand, pigments or artificial compositions intended for other purposes (e.g. inlays, jewellery or larger moulded figures such as *shabtis*).

Painting substrates

The various types of surface to which the Egyptians applied pigment may be summarised under the following headings:

Soft stone

Limestone architecture; sarcophagi and statuary; sandstone architecture and statuary (for pottery see Chapter 5, this volume).

These are attested for the whole of the Dynastic period, with peaks of production in the surviving record for the New Kingdom and from the Late Period to the early Ptolemaic period.

Hard stone

The royal quartzite sarcophagi of the New Kingdom were painted in pure orpiment, but for other hard stone architecture and sculpture the presence of ancient pigment is not well-documented. In the case of pink granite relief and architecture, the question is complicated by the nineteenth-century practice of making designs visible with a modern pigment, usually of a distinct red hue, for example a Ptolemaic *naos* in the British Museum (BM EA1134), on which the red pigment is a modern vermilion.

Plaster

The most extensively studied painted surfaces from ancient Egypt are the tomb-chapels on the West Bank at Thebes. In the Theban necropolis the local limestone is rarely fine enough to allow relief carving or other manipulation, therefore the artists generally resorted to preparing a surface of plaster upon which the pigment could be applied in *tempera* rather than in *fresco secco*, in other words they ensured that the pigment adhered to the surface by use of a binding medium without remoistening of the plaster surface. The great majority of these painted plaster surfaces are walls and ceilings of Eighteenth- and Nineteenth-Dynasty tomb-chapels, and sometimes burial chambers. Painted Theban tomb-chapels are less well attested for the Twelfth to Thirteenth and Twentieth to Twenty-fifth Dynasties, and fewer examples of pigment analyses are available from tombs of these periods.

The Theban tomb-chapel of Ineni (TT81) is one of the earliest in the Eighteenth Dynasty for which an accurate description of painting ground and decoration technique is available (Dziobek 1992: 22–6). The highly fragmentary rock surface was smoothed and any unevenness covered by the reinforcing layer of coarse gypsum (five to fifteen centimetres thick); into this mortar some thin limestone flakes were mixed. Over the mortar a layer of probably the same material, only finer, was applied, most carefully on the west wall of the cross-chamber, with 0.1 to 0.3 cm of fine plaster over the mortar; a thicker layer was applied in the statue chamber, before the mortar foundation had dried, causing the cracks in that layer to affect the surface also. Before the plaster was applied, orientation lines were created by flicking a cord over the mortar with a brush giving a line with a thickness of 1 to 2 cm. The pigment chosen for these and other drafting lines was the long-lasting red ochre rather than carbon black, which – although the most durable pigment on surfaces such as papyrus – often seems paler on painted plaster, perhaps because of a difference in binding medium or pigment texture. Over the fine overlay of plaster, red grids of squares were used to guide composition in certain sections only, such as the major scenes on the west wall of the cross-room. Red draft figures followed, and the background colour was then applied; the grids are visible in the tomb of Ineni because the background pigment has fallen away to reveal them. With the drafts still presumably visible through the background colour, the final outlines were drawn with a fine reed, giving contours which were often as thin as 0.05 to 0.1 cm; the method of filling in the colour is not clear in this instance, because all figures are finished.

From the same generation of tomb-chapel decoration, the Theban tomb-chapel of the vizier Useramen (TT61) provides similar evidence (Dziobek 1994: 19–20), with perhaps an additional layer of lime plaster of about 0.5 cm over the coarser mortar containing limestone splinters; the orientation lines, here one to three centimetres thick, may have guided the craftsmen who then applied a layer of fine plaster 0.5 cm thick (0.7–0.8 cm on the south wall of the chamber) upon which any grids were set. The figures were then drafted in red with a 0.2 cm reed, and over these the background colour was painted, followed by the body colouring and, as the final stage, the red outlining of the finished figures.

With regard to Theban tomb-chapels TT80 and TT104, Shedid (1988: 21–3) describes a similar procedure for the next generation of painting on plastered limestone walls, in the reign of Amenhotep II; variations in procedure differ between tomb-chapels and within one tomb-chapel, evidently according to the artists in each team. The variables include (1) presence or absence of grid, presumably depending on the talent of the painter and the complexity of the composition, and (2) presence or absence of draft outlines: these being omitted for example in landscape flora or small details in the long hall of TT80, but included even for figures on a small scale in TT104. No corrections to the red draft figures are attested; instead the figures are coloured directly, the final stages being the outline contours and the black elements of each scene. The final outlines are executed in red-brown, in TT104 and TT80 (cross-room) 0.05 cm for small and 0.15 to 0.2 cm for larger figures, in TT80 (long hall) 0.05 to 0.3 cm for small and 0.2 to 0.4 cm for larger figures. Any amendments to the final outlined figures could be made simply by painting over them in the background colour, at the last stage.

From the brief reign of Thutmose IV come some of the finest surviving examples of tomb-chapel painting, such as the Theban tomb-chapels of Sobekhotep (TT63; Dziobek and Abdel Raziq 1990), Tjanuni (TT74; Brack and Brack 1977) and, extending into the reign of Amenhotep III, Horemheb (TT78; Brack and Brack 1980). The tomb-chapel of Sobekhotep has uneven baserock walls, perhaps resulting from a particularly poor limestone bed, which even an elaborate scheme of mortaring and a final overlay of 0.1–0.5 cm of finer plaster could not remove (Dziobek and Abdel Raziq 1990: 27–8). For the varnishing of specific colours, or entire wall surfaces in the case of Theban tomb-chapel paintings, see Chapter 18, this volume.

Substantial fragments of royal and private palace wall- and floor-paintings survive, although not on the scale available up to eighty years ago; the past 100 years have witnessed the exposure and general destruction of painted walls of late Middle Kingdom townhouses at Lahun, and the painted walls and floors of New Kingdom royal palaces at Deir el-Ballas (Lacovara 1990: 2–3), Malkata (Stevenson Smith 1981: 281–95 with 459–60 nn. 2–34) and Amarna (Weatherhead 1992 and 1994).

Application as *buon fresco* (onto wet plaster) is foreign to Egypt, and is one of the identifying hallmarks of the Aegean painters of the late seventeenth or sixteenth century BC at Tell el-Dabʿa (Bietak 1994: 45), as at Tell Kabri in northern Palestine, although the precise technique of Western Asiatic mural painters has not been identified by analysis (Moorey 1994: 328–9).

Organic surfaces: papyrus, wood, textiles

Papyri are illustrated and painted for apparently non-funerary contexts in the Ramesside period, and for funerary texts from the following periods: Eighteenth–early Twenty-second Dynasty, Twenty-sixth Dynasty, Thirtieth Dynasty to Roman period. Another non-funerary example is provided by the painted fragments from the 'House of the King's Statue' (structure R43.2 in the southeastern central city) at Amarna, dated to the reign of Akhenaten or that of Tutankhamun in the late Eighteenth Dynasty (Schofield and Parkinson 1994). Leather rolls were also sometimes used for illustrated Book of the Dead manuscripts in the Eighteenth Dynasty. Selection of colour in preference to black outline drawings, with some red (the second pigment of the scribal palette) partly reflects cost, but also the factors of ownership and chronologically determined practice in the funerary workshops. Most Eighteenth-Dynasty funerary manuscripts bear coloured vignettes, but the Book of the Dead of Nebseny (BM EA9900) uses only the scribal pigments carbon black and red ochre, apparently because as a copyist, Nebseny himself must have compiled his own funerary papyrus using his personal scribal palette. In other instances, even a limited extension to the scribal palette of black and red is enough to ascribe the manuscript to a funerary workshop specialised in colouring (e.g. the Eighteenth-Dynasty Book of the Dead papyrus of Nebamun: BM EA9964).

The Third Intermediate Period offers a clear instance of change in application of pigments, at least on papyrus (Niwinski 1989). The use of colour seems most extensive in the Twenty-first Dynasty, with richly coloured and illustrated Book of the Dead and Underworld manuscripts, the latter drawing on the Litany of Ra and creation vignettes. In the early Twenty-second Dynasty, the Book of the Dead is generally a hieratic manuscript with only a single vignette at the beginning, showing the deceased offering, and this is often in black and red only, as are the new Underworld manuscripts of the period, drawing on the last four hours of the 'Book of the Secret Chamber which is in the Underworld'. Between the two traditions of colour and scribal palette, the Book of the Dead papyrus of Nestanebtisheru (BM EA10554) bears one of the most extensive series of vignettes, but is executed only in black and red.

It can be seen from this survey that colour use changed sharply between early and mid- Third Intermediate Period funerary papyri; this may serve as a reminder that the artists using colour operated within workshops each with their own tradition, specifically their various histories of access to and use of materials. The rare funerary papyri of the Twenty-sixth Dynasty (Verhoeven 1993: 41–2) include richly coloured Theban and Herakleopolitan manuscripts, but also the Book of the Dead of Psamtek, now in the Vatican Egyptian collections, which is a Memphite papyrus executed only in black and red. The illustrated funerary manuscripts of the Thirtieth Dynasty and Ptolemaic Period have not been dated by groups, but colour seems again to have been an important criterion with probable chronological significance (for a preliminary typology see Mosher 1992).

Surviving painted wooden surfaces are rare before the late Old Kingdom, when non-royal coffins began to be decorated more commonly with painted texts and illustrations. From the Middle Kingdom onwards, wooden canopic chests were also painted, and from the New Kingdom *shabti* boxes. In the first millennium BC, Theban burials included a painted wooden stele set against the coffin within the burial chamber. These categories of object offer a more or less continuous tradition within the funerary workshops of painted organic surfaces from the late Old Kingdom to the Roman period.

Painted textiles do not commonly survive at any period, but include mid-Eighteenth-Dynasty shrouds bearing texts and vignettes from the Book of the Dead. The shroud of Resti, an Eighteenth-Dynasty noblewoman (BM EA73807), revealed the same selection of pigments as that found on contemporary funerary papyri, with huntite for white, orpiment for yellow, Egyptian blue for blue and haematite for red. Surviving textiles suggest that dyeing techniques were introduced into Egypt from Western Asia from the New Kingdom onwards (for colour on textiles, see Germer 1992, and Chapter 11, this volume).

For the application of pigments to basketry (in which patterning of materials of different kind or age, rather than artifical colouring, seems to be the norm) see Chapter 10, this volume; for tattoos, and eye and skin adornment see Chapters 17 and 18; for the dyeing and colouring of leather see Chapter 12; and for the use of varnish see Chapter 17.

References

Barthoux, J. 1926. Les fards, pommades et couleurs dans l'antiquité. *Congrés International de Géographie, Le Caire, April 1925*, IV, pp. 251–67.

Bietak, M. 1994. Die Wandmalereien aus Tell el-Dab^c/Ezbet Helmi. Erste Eindrücke. In *Ägypten und Levante* IV (ed. M. Bietak), pp. 44–58, pls. 14–22.

Blom-Böer, I. 1994. Zusammensetzung altägyptischer Farbpigmente und ihre Herkunftslagerstätten in Zeit und Raum. *OMRO*, 74: 55–107.

Borchardt, L. 1923. *Porträts der Königin Nofret-ete aus de Grabungen 1912/13 in Tell el-Amarna*. Leipzig: Hinrichs.

Brack, A. and Brack, A. 1977. *Das Grab des Tjanuni. Theben Nr. 74* (Deutsches Archäologisches Institut, Abteilung Kairo, Archäologische Veröffentlichungen 19). Mainz am Rhein: von Zabern.

1980. *Das Grab des Haremheb. Theben Nr.78* (Deutsches Archäologisches Institut, Abteilung Kairo, Archäologische Veröffentlichungen 35). Mainz am Rhein: von Zabern.

Brunner-Traut, E. 1977. Farben. *LÄ* II: 117–28.

Buschle-Diller, G., and Unger, A. 1996. Schreib- und Malmaterial auf Papyrus. *Restauro*, 2: 108–14.

Cardon, D. and du Chatelet, G. 1990. *Guide des Teintures Naturelles*. Lausanne: Delachaux et Niestlé.

de Cenival, J.-L. 1992. *Le livre pour sortir le jour, Le Livre des Morts des anciens Égyptiens*. Musée d'Aquitaine et Réunion des Musées Nationaux.

Corbeil, M.-C. and Helwig, K. 1995. An occurrence of pararealgar as an original or altered artists' pigment. *Studies in Conservation*, 40: 133–8.

Douglass, D.L., Shing, C. and Wang, G. 1992. The light induced alteration of realgar to pararealgar. *American Mineralogist*, 77: 1266–74.

Dziobek, E. 1992. *Das Grab des Ineni Theben Nr. 81* (Deutsches Archäologisches Institut, Abteilung Kairo, Archäologische Veröffentlichungen 68). Mainz am Rhein: von Zabern.

1994. *Die Gräber des Vezirs User-Amun Theben Nr. 61 und 131* (Deutsches Archäologisches Institut, Abteilung Kairo, Archäologische Veröffentlichungen 84). Mainz am Rhein: von Zabern.

Dziobek, E. and Abdel Raziq, M. 1990. *Das Grab des Sobekhotep Theben Nr. 63* (Deutsches Archäologisches Institut, Abteilung Kairo, Archäologische Veröffentlichungen 71). Mainz am Rhein: von Zabern.

Evans, D., Hamburg, D. and Mickelson, M. 1980. A papyrus treatment: bringing the Book of the Dead to life. In *Art Conservation Training Programs Conference, April 28–29 1980*.

Newark: University of Delaware, pp. 109–13.

Filippakis, S.E. 1978. Analysis of pigments from Thera. In *Thera and the Aegean World* I (ed. C. Doumas). London: Thera Foundation, pp. 599–604.

Germer, R. 1992. *Die Textilfärberei und die Verwendung gefärbter Textilien im alten Ägypten* (Ägyptologische Abhandlungen 53). Wiesbaden: Otto Harrassowitz.

Goffer, Z. 1980. *Archaeological Chemistry*. New York: Wiley Interscience.

Granger, F. 1970. *Vitruvius, On Architecture*. Edited from the Harleian Manuscript 2767 and translated into English by Frank Granger (Loeb Classical Library). London: William Heinemann; Cambridge MA: Harvard University Press [volume II, Books VI–X].

Heywood, A. forthcoming. Paper presented at *Colour and Painting in Ancient Egypt*. Symposium, July 11–12, 1996, British Museum.

Hope, C.A., Blauer, A.M. and Riederer, J. 1981. Recent analysis of 18th Dynasty pottery. In *Studien zur altägyptischen Keramik* (ed. D. Arnold). Mainz: von Zubern, pp. 139–66.

Iskander, N. 1987. Other analyses. In *Excavations in the Royal Necropolis at El-'Amarna 1984* (eds. A. El-Khouly and G.T. Martin). Supplement to *ASAE* 33: Appendix 4, pp. 35–43.

Jaksch, H., Seipel, W., Weiner, K.L. and El Goresy, A. 1983. Egyptian blue – cuprorivaite: a window to ancient Egyptian technology. *Naturwissenschaften*, 70: 525–35.

Kaczmarczyk, A. and Hedges, R.E.M. 1983. *Ancient Egyptian Faience*. Warminster: Aris and Phillips.

Kemp, B.J. 1973. Photographs of the decorated tomb at Hierakonpolis. *JEA*, 59: 36–43.

Lacovara, P. 1990. *Deir el-Ballas. Preliminary report on the Deir el-Ballas Expedition, 1980–1986* . Winona Lake IN: American Research Center in Egypt.

Laurie, A.P. 1913. Ancient pigments and their identification in works of art. *Archaeologia*, 64: 315–36.

Lazzarini, L. 1982. The discovery of Egyptian blue in a Roman fresco of the mediaeval period (ninth century AD). *Studies in Conservation* , 27: 84–6.

Le Fur, D. 1994. *La Conservation des Peintures Murales des Temples de Karnak*. Paris: Editions Recherche sur les Civilisations.

Lucas, A. 1962. *Ancient Egyptian Materials and Industries*. 4th edn., rev. J.R. Harris. London: Edward Arnold.

Moorey, P.R.S. 1985. *Materials and Manufacture in Ancient Mesopotamia: The Evidence of Archaeology and Art. Metals and Metalwork, Glazed Materials and Glass*. Oxford: BAR-S237.

1994. *Ancient Mesopotamian Materials and Industries: The Archaeological Evidence*. Oxford: Clarendon Press.

Mosher, M. 1992. Theban and Memphite Book of the Dead traditions in the Late Period. *JARCE*, 29: 143–72.

Niwinski, A. 1989. *Studies on the Illustrated Theban Funerary Papyri of the 11th and 10th centuries B.C.* (Orbis Biblicus et Orientalis 86). Freiburg: Universitätsverlag; Göttingen: Vandenhoeck and Ruprecht.

Perthuisot, J.-P., Castanier S. and Maurin, A. 1990. La Huntite ($CaMg_3(CO_3)_4$) de la Sebkha el-Melah (Zarzis, Tunisie): un exemple de microbiodiagenèse carbonatogène. *Bulletin de la Société géologique de France*, 8/VI/no. 4: 657–66.

Petrie, W.M.F. 1892. *Meydum*. London: Nutt.

Quibell, J.E. 1913. *The Tomb of Hesy: Excavations at Saqqara 1911–12*. Cairo: SAE.

Quibell, J.E. and Green, F.W. 1902. *Hierakonpolis Part II*. London: Quaritch.

Reisner, G.A. 1923. *Excavations at Kerma* I–V (2 vols). Cambridge MA: Harvard University Press.

Russell, W.J. 1893–4. Ancient Egyptian pigments. *Nature*, 49: 374–5.

1893–5. Ancient Egyptian pigments. *Proceedings of the Royal Institution*, 14: 67–71.

Schiegl, S., Weiner, K.L. and El Goresy, A. 1992. The diversity of newly discovered deterioration patterns in ancient Egyptian pigments: consequences to entirely new restoration strategies and to the Egyptological colour symbolism. *Proceedings of the Materials Research Society Symposium*, 267: 831–58.

Schofield, L. and Parkinson, R. 1994. Of helmets and heretics: a possible Egyptian representation of Mycenaean warriors on a papyrus from el-Amarna. *Annual of the British School at Athens*, 89: 157–70.

Shedid, A.G. 1988. *Stil der Grabmalereien in der Zeit Amenophis' II. untersucht an den Thebanischen Gräbern Nr. 104 und Nr. 80* (Deutsches Archäologisches Institut, Abteilung Kairo, Archäologische Veröffentlichungen 66). Mainz am Rhein: von Zabern.

Spurrell, F.C.J. 1895. Notes on Egyptian colours. *Archaeological Journal*, 52: 222–39.

Stevenson Smith, W. 1981. *The Art and Architecture of Ancient Egypt* (rev. W.K. Simpson). Harmondsworth: Penguin.

Strudwick, N. 1991. An objective colour-measuring system for the recording of Egyptian tomb paintings. *JEA*, 77: 43–56.

Terrace, E. 1968. *Egyptian Paintings of the Middle Kingdom*. London: George Allen and Unwin.

Thorpe, J.F. and Whiteley, M.A. 1954. *Dictionary of Applied Chemistry* (4th edn.). London: Longmans, Green and Co.

Tite, M, Bimson, M. and Cowell, M. 1987. The technology of Egyptian blue. In *Early Vitreous Materials* (eds. M. Bimson and I. Freestone). London: BMP, pp. 39–46.

Ullrich, D. 1985. Egyptian blue and green frit – characterization, history and occurrence, synthesis. *DACT*, 18.

Verhoeven, U. 1993. *Das Saitische Totenbuch der Iahtesnacht. P.Colon.Aeg. 10207* (Papyrologische Texte und Abhandlungen 41). Bonn: Dr. Rudolf Habelt GMBH.

Wallert, A. 1995. Unusual pigments on a Greek marble basin. *Studies in Conservation*, 40: 177–88.

Weatherhead, F. 1992. Painted pavements in the Great Palace at Amarna. *JEA*, 78: 179–94, pls. 24–5.

1994. Wall-paintings from the North Harim in the Great Palace at Amarna. *JEA*, 80: 198–201.

1995. Two studies on Amarna pigments. In *Amarna Reports* VI (ed. B.J. Kemp). London: EES, pp. 384–98.

Weatherhead, F. and Buckley, A. 1989. Artists' pigments from Amarna. In *Amarna Reports* V (ed. B.J. Kemp). London: EES, pp. 202–40.

Wiedemann, H. and Bayer, G. 1982. The bust of Nefertiti: the analytical approach. *Analytical Chemistry*, 54: 619A–28A.

Williams, C.R. 1932. *The Decoration of the Tomb of Per-neb: the Technique and the Color Conventions*. New York: MMA.

Ziegler, C. 1990. *Catalogue des Stèles, Peintures et Reliefs Egyptiens de l'Ancien Empire*. Paris: Réunion des musées nationaux.

ous inclusions of a particular material, size and shape are found, they are assumed to be filler, whereas inclusions which grade into the silt/clay sized fraction, i.e. the matrix, are thought to be naturally occurring (Kroeper 1992: 30; Riederer 1992). Modal analysis of texture may help here (see Nordström and Bourriau 1993: fig. 2). An important recent study (Redmount and Morgenstein 1996: Table 6, 752–4) of modern Egyptian pottery includes petrographic data for samples made predominantly from Nile silts from Lower Egypt. In this case information about the addition and nature of any filler was available in advance from conversations with the potter. The filler material can be recognised clearly in the thin-section data.

A further role for petrographic analysis lies in suggesting a research design for compositional analysis, such as what elements ought to be included (Hamroush and Zeid 1990: 118–20). Other ways in which petrology has been successful in source studies was in identifying unusual minerals with a narrow geological distribution, or in relating a sample to a control group derived from kiln sites (Williams 1983). Neither of these situations occurs with any frequency in Egypt, though the last will improve as more industrial sites are targetted for excavation.

Level 4: Chemical and mineralogical analyses

The techniques that have been used to determine the composition of Egyptian pottery are those which have become widely used in the examination of archaeological pottery from the rest of the world. Since these are fairly well-known they are given here in summary only, along with key references to the techniques particularly as applied to Egyptian pottery.

- NAA (Neutron Activation Analysis). See Perlman and Asaro 1969; Tobia and Sayre 1974; Brooks *et al.* 1974; Kaplan, Harbottle and Sayre 1982; Riederer 1988; Redmount and Morgenstein 1996; Bourriau 1998.
- INAA (Instrumental Neutron Activation Analysis). See Hancock *et al.* 1986; Hancock *et al.* 1986/7; Allen *et al.* 1989.
- XRF (X-ray Fluorescence). See Ballet and Picon 1990; Redmount and Morgenstein 1996.
- OES (Optical Emission Spectroscopy). See Hennessy and Millet 1963; Payne 1966; Strouhal *et al.* 1988.
- AAS (Atomic Absorption Spectroscopy). See de Paepe 1986; de Paepe *et al.* 1992.
- ICP and ICP-MS (Inductively Coupled Plasma/Mass Spectroscopy). See Redmount and Morgenstein 1996.
- XRD (X-ray Diffraction). See Allen *et al.* 1982; Riederer 1988; Hamroush and Zeid 1990; Hamroush 1992.

OES has been replaced by more accurate techniques such as XRF; NAA, which is extremely costly since it requires access to a nuclear reactor, is being replaced by the cheaper technique of ICP-MS, which has the additional advantage of producing reliable data on a larger number of elements.

The range shows that no one technique suits all situations, and multiple techniques are increasingly being deployed to complement each other. It is important to realise that chemical analysis may not be the best method to differentiate between one fabric and another. Samples may group together on the basis of their chemical composition but show very different mineralogical and textural properties under the microscope.

Any investigation begins with a series of aims and questions:

- Is the aim to characterise a given pottery fabric, to discover the source of its raw material, or both?
- Do the samples adequately (in statistical terms) represent all the material to be analysed?
- If not, is there an existing data set from a previous study that can be utilised? Is it from the same laboratory or from one with whom standards have been exchanged?
- If the source of the raw material is the goal, are there control groups of known origin for comparison?
- What is to be analysed: mineral inclusions, rare earth elements in the matrix, or both?
- In the case of chemical analysis, which elements will be measured and how many?
- Is the technique one which samples the surface of the sherd (XRD) or one which samples the whole thickness, i.e. bulk sampling (NAA). If the former, is contamination from the environment a problem?
- In what form will the analysis appear: as spectra, oxides, compositional percentages or absolute quantities?
- How will the analytical output data be manipulated statistically and by whom?
- Who will interpret the results and in what form will they be published?

A review of published studies of Egyptian pottery, albeit with the benefit of hindsight, shows how rarely such questions have been fully addressed. There seem to be three main reasons for this: the scarcity of samples, which has resulted in the same data being used over and over again (Bourriau 1998); the relatively minor role which archaeologists have played in directing research and analysing the results, with exceptions such as Michael Hoffman at Hierakonpolis; and finally, the failure to exchange standards and to make results truly compatible between laboratories using the same technique. The situation described by Harbottle in 1982 has not significantly changed. A fourth reason may be the reluctance of editors of periodicals to accept reports giving data in full or those presenting negative results.

There has been an evolution from early studies, where testing of the method was of paramount interest (Tobia and

Sayre 1974; Hancock *et al.* 1986), to those where the important questions were archaeological and grew out of a current excavation (Allen, *et al.* 1989; Hamroush and Zeid 1990; Ballet and Picon 1990; de Paepe *et al.* 1992). A similar evolution can be seen from a single method to a multi-method approach and towards more careful sampling and less reliance on inherited data-sets (Redmount and Morgenstein 1996; Bourriau 1998). In forming compositional groups, there is still no consensus as to whether it is better to employ multi-variant analysis which uses all the reliable compositional data, see Fig. 5.8 (Bellido *et al.* forthcoming) or discriminant analysis which selects significant elements or ratios of elements (Hancock *et al.* 1986; Redmount and Morgenstein 1996).

It is essential to understand that the groupings arrived at, if taken from samples of both fired pottery and raw clay, are not directly comparable. The primary and secondary processing which the pottery alone has undergone will have radically changed its elemental and mineralogical composition. A well-known effect is the dilution factor which results from the addition of quantities of sand or limestone to the paste. Sand and limestone contain smaller amounts of trace elements than the clay matrix, and adding them has the effect of lowering the trace element composition overall. If this factor is recognised it can be taken into account at the data analysis stage. This is why compositional analyses need to be used after other methods have been applied to determine what changes the potter has made in his raw material. Some studies, although not of Egyptian clays, have tried to predict them by examining the effect of levigation and firing on raw clays (Allen *et al.* 1982). Some forms of discriminant analysis set out to avoid the problem by utilising elements such as rare earths which are present mainly in the clay matrix of the fabric.

With this *caveat*, how successful have studies been so far in characterising pottery fabrics? Enough compositional data have been published by now for any sherd to be assigned to one of three groups: Nile alluvium; Marl clay; and kaolinite clay (see Figs. 5.8 and 5.9). Using accessible but as yet unpublished data (Bellido *et al.* forthcoming) it is possible to differentiate three sub-groups among the Marl clays corresponding to Marl B, Marl C and Marl D in the Vienna System. It is even easier to distinguish Egyptian from Palestinian pottery by using the large data-sets available. However, it has to be said that an experienced ceramicist using a microscope on a fresh break can do as much (and often very much more). A filler such as fine straw is easy to see, sometimes even by the naked eye, but does not always show up in chemical analysis (by XRF – Ballet and Picon 1990 and NAA – in the study referred to above, Bellido *et al.* forthcoming).

How successful have studies been in identifying the clay sources used by ancient potters? Three studies have succeeded, in relation to Hierakonpolis (Allen *et al.* 1989), el-Omari (Hamroush and Zeid 1990), and ʿAyn Asil (Ballet

Elemental mean concentrations and deviations for Marls and Niles

Element	MARLS		NILES	
	Mean	S.D.	Mean	S.D.
Na	0.830	0.33	1.11	0.36
Al	7.37	1.6	7.42	1.2
Ca	9.54	3.7	3.84	2.3
Sc	16.6	2.5	21.8	2.7
Ti	0.553	0.12	0.873	0.16
V	120	26	149	24
Cr	137	62	156	67
Mn	668	420	1214	660
Fe	4.62	0.62	6.43	0.89
Co	18.7	3.4	29.74	6.2
Rb	42.5	9.9	45.3	14
Cs	2.03	0.75	1.59	0.76
La	33.5	8.0	28.5	9.3
Ce	67.7	11	67.6	18
Sm	6.02	1.3	6.40	1.6
Eu	1.40	0.28	1.82	0.49
Dy	3.93	0.68	4.67	0.88
Lu	0.386	0.072	0.448	0.14
Hf	6.59	1.7	8.18	7.32
Ta	1.36	0.31	1.59	0.38
Th	8.21	1.7	6.94	3.08
U	2.66	0.80	2.18	1.06

Analytical information

Element	Podmore Concentration	Gamma Energy (KeV)	Counting Regime
Al	11.44 %	1779	Short
Ca	1.824 %	3085	Short
Ti	0.6987 %	320	Short
V	152.0 ppm	1434	Short
Mn	404.9 ppm	1811	Short
Dy	6.13 ppm	95	Short
Na	0.0686 %	1368	Inter
Sc	26.0 ppm	889	Long
Cr	121.4 ppm	321	Long
Fe	5.482 %	1099	Long
Co	20.0 ppm	1333	Long
Rb	84.54 ppm	1076	Long
Cs	7.87 ppm	796	Long
La	41.91 ppm	488	Inter
Ce	80.1 ppm	145	Long
Sm	7.35 ppm	103	Long
Eu	1.55 ppm	344	Long
Lu	0.527 ppm	208	Long
Hf	5.484 ppm	482	Long
Ta	1.294 ppm	1221	Long
Th	14.01 ppm	312	Long
U	3.05 ppm	278	Long

Figure 5.8 Compositional data: twenty-two elemental concentrations for 150 samples of Nile silt fabrics and 193 samples of Marl clay fabrics.

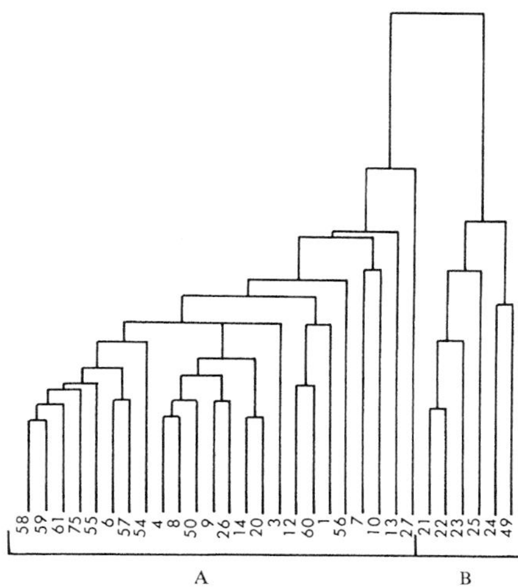

Figure 5.9 Dendrogram showing results of XRF analysis of pottery from ʿAyn Asil. A and B groups were arrived at using seventeen elements. Group A contained samples of a single fabric, in both fine and coarse variants and with/without a filler of plant ash. Group B contained only samples of a different fabric, visually distinguished by the presence of argillaceous inclusions, and used primarily for cooking pots.

and Picon 1990) (see Fig. 5.9), but each study looked at the products of a localised industry and two of the sites (Hierakonpolis and ʿAyn Asil) were production centres, so that the search area was already fairly clearly delineated. Other results have been ambiguous or negative (de Paepe *et al.* 1992) and all have quoted Tobia and Sayre's finding (1974) that chemical analysis alone could not indicate a provenance for pottery made of Nile alluvium, Pliocene clays or mixtures of the two. Tobia and Sayre's ancient pottery sample was too small and unrepresentative to be relied upon (Bourriau 1998); however, their evidence for the homogeneity (in chemical terms) of raw Nile sediments was supported by Hamroush's study (1985) of the distribution of rare earth elements in old and modern Nile sediments, in which he suggested that Nile sediment forming processes had produced an even pattern of distribution for these elements throughout the Nile Valley.

Three subsequent studies, two of modern clays (Hancock *et al.* 1986/1987; Redmount and Morgenstein 1996) and one of ancient pottery (Bourriau 1998) have challenged this view. If further work confirms these three studies, which appear to demonstrate that the differences between samples from different sites are greater than the variation within any single group or the margin allowed for analytical error, then further possibilities for the sourcing of clays are opened up. Even where kilns have not been located, it is usually possible on an archaeological site to identify some Nile silt pottery which must have been locally made, generally because it is too heavy, coarse and fragile to have been worth transporting. Analysis of such pottery groups may eventually allow compositional fingerprints to be established for different regions, periods and classes of pottery.

There have been strenuous appeals for another approach to this same goal, which is to make systematic analyses of all possible sources of raw material (Redmount and Morgenstein 1996: 761; Hamroush 1992: 51). If this is to be done then the initiative must come from archaeologists, since it will not come from scientists in the present research climate. Moreover, in our view, it is only worthwhile if investigations into ancient and modern processing methods are conducted at the same time. In any case, as a first step, efforts should be made towards standardising existing reference sets of data.

The social and economic context of the pottery industry

The place of the pottery industry in the wider social and economic context of ancient Egyptian society is a subject which has received only cursory attention from ceramic specialists (Holthoer 1977: 27–8; Hope 1987a: 7–9), although an increasing interest in the organisation of labour and the economy has touched upon the role of the pottery industry (Eyre 1987a: 27, 30; 1987b: 193; Kemp 1989, 56–63). In this section, the various sources of evidence, literary, artistic and archaeological, are considered in the light of possible modes of production.

Artistic and textual evidence

Scenes of pottery manufacture feature occasionally in tomb representations and models from the Old Kingdom to the New Kingdom (collected by Holthoer, 1977: 5–23; it is not clear that all show pottery manufacture, and the sources cited for the Late Period are not useful in this context). Such scenes have proved invaluable for the understanding of technological developments, but they reveal less about the context in which production took place, in terms either of the organisation of the workshops or their economic circumstances. Such texts as accompany the scenes provide terse and sometimes uninterpretable descriptions of the particular acts depicted, but do not contribute to the wider understanding of the activity. As one would expect from the funerary context in which they occur, they represent assets of the tomb owner, dedicated to his maintenance in the after-life. Consequently, they permit no scope for studying activities which went on outside this framework, such as, for example, any form of centralised or state-controlled industry.

Unambiguous scenes of Old Kingdom pottery manufacture are found in close association with scenes of brewing and baking, and show a very limited repertoire of vessels, usually jars (Holthoer 1977: 6–10, OKA 2, 5 and 9). More doubtful representations, where it is not clear that pottery manufacture is the practice depicted, relate the putative scenes to other industrial processes, such as metal- and leather-working (Holthoer 1977: 6–10, OKA1, 3, 4 and 10). Representations showing the integral association of pottery with the staple provisions, bread and beer, continue to occur into the New Kingdom, but at all periods, baking and brewing scenes are found without accompanying pottery manufacture. This is probably best understood as indicating that pottery production was such an obvious part of the process that it is implicit within the representations of food preparation. After all, the tomb owner required food and drink in the after-life, not the 'empties'.

Models of pottery workshops, from the First Intermediate Period and the Middle Kingdom (Holthoer 1977: 10–11, 15–16, FIB1, 2 and 4; Arnold 1993) are of interest in that they give some indication of where the activity took place. In all cases, potting apparently was carried out outdoors, although sometimes in an enclosed courtyard. The activity is depicted in close proximity to carpentry, metal-working, and in one case stone vase manufacture. In each case only two individuals are at work.

The association of pottery with other craft activities continued into the Middle Kingdom. Only at Deir el-Bersha are potters explicitly associated with bakers and brewers (Newberry 1895: pls. XXIV and XXV). The detailed scenes in three tombs at the nearby site of Beni Hasan place production squarely in an industrial context. The tomb of Amenemhat (BH2) incorporates them amongst depictions of processes such as the manufacture of linen (Newberry 1893a: pl. XI). In the tomb of Bakt III (BH15), the potters are situated below registers showing stock-taking of cattle, and above metal-working (Newberry 1893b: pl. VII). Here, scenes of baking occur at some remove from pottery-making. In the tomb of Khnumhotep III (BH3), the potters are again associated with textile preparation, and also carpentry; bread- and beer-making are pictured several registers below (Newberry 1893a: pl. XXIX). Whether the association with craft activities rather than food production is significant, reflecting different circumstances of production at Beni Hasan (the 'independence' of the pottery-makers suggesting perhaps that pottery is seen here as a commodity in its own right), or merely showing a different lay-out of working space (or indeed a different artistic convention), is impossible to tell, but again it is clear that the manufacturing is part of the activities associated with the tomb owner's maintenance in the after-life, with the same limitations of interpretation.

The tomb of Kenamun (TT93) at Thebes contains the only known New Kingdom scene of pottery manufacture (Davies 1930: pl. LIX). Like many of its precursors, it occurs in association with the preparation of food and drink, but here is an isolated, uninscribed scene, in an obscure position on the rear of a pillar in the outer hall. Its relegation to such an insignificant location prefigures the abandonment of the depiction of potters throughout the rest of the New Kingdom and beyond: although scenes of food production are not uncommon, and other forms of craft activity as part of the work of temple and state institutions are well-attested, the manufacture of ceramic containers is not depicted. The only other representations are informal: a model of the period showing a woman doing something to a pot (UC 15706; Hope 1987a: fig. 2; he suggests she is adding handles, although this is unlikely since handled pots at this period were almost all the result of specialist production, see p. 139–40), and an ostracon from Deir el-Medina which appears to show two children working on a vessel (Hope 1987a: Fig. 1), but Arnold (1993; fig. 15A) identifies the workers as Nubians. Whilst they demonstrate that pottery manufacture was in fact part of daily life, their isolated nature tells us nothing about the framework in which the activity took place.

The representations available suggest that the size of pottery-making workshops was small at all times. The models show only one or two men working in the establishments; the tomb-reliefs are more problematic to interpret, since the actions depicted could be performed at different times by the same or different persons. In most cases the workshops seem to have been situated outside, but close to other industries, and had some recognisable equipment: a turntable or wheel, a kiln or oven. Almost all the representations show the potters to be male, although very limited evidence from the Old Kingdom suggests women may have participated, tending kilns, perhaps as a result of the intimate association at that period with brewing and baking which could also be carried out by women. The New Kingdom depictions of women and, perhaps, children apparently at work on pots also suggest that in fact some modes of production were open to, or made use of, all available labour sources. We can say very little more about the individuals who worked in pottery workshops, but that they had a low social status is clear from texts (for example, P. Sallier II, quoted in Holthoer 1977: 18). To what extent this applied to those working in specialist production centres is unknown. That they did not form part of the recognised social hierarchy is clear from the absence of references to them in the varied inscriptional sources. Holthoer (1977: 17, MKD1) noted only a single stele dedicated by a potter, who had no other titles, at Abydos in the Middle Kingdom.

There is a little further information concerning potters and pottery production, mostly of New Kingdom date, from which one can begin to throw light on the economic context in which some potters worked. By far the most interesting source is the body of texts relating to the supplying of, and the transactions between, members of the community of state-employed craftsmen at Deir el-Medina (Janssen 1975: 485–8). Here, potters were part of the supply staff for the community, although based outside it, and made regular deliveries of vessels. There is little indication of significant ceramic production at the village itself: excavation revealed the remains of a single potter's workshop below house SE1, at the foot of the enclosure wall and outside the village when in use, but no more details are known (Bruyère 1939: 264). It is impossible to say whether the installation belonged to those living in the village, or to their suppliers. Certainly the isolated desert location of Deir el-Medina makes it eminently unsuitable for regular or large-scale production, and there is no other indication of such activity.

The craftsmen also received supplementary goods on top of their basic grain allocation, including vessels of beer, and other commodities which were supplied and/or were measured in *mnt*-jars, including oils and fats, beer, and honey. The *mnt*-jar was a type of pottery vessel particularly associated with wine, and is probably to be understood as a two-handled amphora (Bruyère 1939: 353; for the type and its changes in form over the New Kingdom see Hope 1989: 87–118). The type appears to have been the product of specialist manufacture in a restricted number of centres, and its 'élite' nature, albeit only as a container, is reflected in the nature of goods supplied in it and their expense. However, in general, the many texts which relate the value of commodities arriving at the village fail to attribute values to pottery apart, it seems, from that of the vessel contents, emphasising the cheapness and availability of the product.

The very ubiquity of pottery as an essential means of holding goods probably accounts for the lack of reference to it. One exception is a stele of Rameses II, recounting the commissioning of a group of professional quarrymen to make a statue (Eyre 1987b: 183). On it, the king stipulates that, amongst the abundant supplies he has ordered for them were 'pots made on the wheel, as vessels to cool water for you in the hot(?) season'. These vessels would presumably have been manufactured by potters associated with the great state institutions of the New Kingdom.

Finally, we should give brief consideration to the possibilities that existed for private trade in such commodities as pottery. Small-scale transactions in foodstuffs, as well as in simple manufactured items, are known from the Old Kingdom onwards, and although pottery has not been explicitly recognised as a commodity for exchange, it is likely that it changed hands both as containers and in its own right (Eyre 1987a: 31–2, 1987b: 199–200). Who the sellers were is unclear; as a means of marketing it seems most suitable for small-scale 'domestic' and local production, intended for the local community, rather than state- or estate-based establishments. These would presumably have had the capacity to store excess production until required, especially in view of the apparent lack of value of the product. By the New Kingdom, it is clear that some goods were made for the market; indeed temples employed professional traders on their staff. Considered in the light of the far greater complexity of ceramic production by this time, such traders may well have formed the means by which some types of vessel, not only commodity containers but also vessels clearly not intended for that purpose, spread from their centres of manufacture.

The archaeological evidence

The most commonly recognised features on archaeological sites which reflect the presence of a pottery-making industry are kilns (see Nicholson 1993 and Hope 1993 for a review of the current evidence), which, although it is not always clear whether for pottery or some other industrial process, are often more readily identifiable than other features. The identification of production areas apart from those associated with kilns is rare (although difficult to identify in the archaeological record, Nicholson and Patterson 1985a and 1985b), and the opportunity to examine the installation in a wider context is rarely available.

Taking the evidence of production as manifested by the identification of kilns, pottery manufacture is known from the length and breadth of the Nile valley in Egypt and Nubia, and outside it in the Delta, the western oases and Sinai. Even in the Predynastic period, production at the Upper Egyptian site of Hierakonpolis reached 'staggering proportions' between c. 3800–3500 BC (Hoffman 1982: 142). Here fifteen kiln complexes have so far been identified, and an excavated example is associated with scattered domestic occupation; the potter's house seems to have burnt down on one occasion. The excavated kilns are unsophisticated, but produced at least three different ware types in many different forms, catering for the needs both of the settlement and the nearby cemeteries. It seems that some kilns were used to fire more than one ware, although the coarse ware was intended primarily for the settlement, and the red burnished ware for the cemeteries; one may tentatively suggest that a fully-developed funerary ceramics industry had not developed by this stage. This is borne out at the Delta site of Buto (which, however, fell within a different, lower Egyptian cultural milieu for much of the period), where cemetery and domestic pottery seems to be the same, differing only in quantitative rather than qualitative terms (Köhler 1992: 10).

Examination of the vessels of this period have led to the suggestion that already there was specialised production (i.e. the output of a limited range of wares and forms, often for a specific purpose, and in demand because of it) as far back as Naqada II for certain marl vessels (Mond and Myers 1937: 50; Bourriau 1981a: 44). Painted decoration has also been used as a basis for identifying centres of production and the trade networks emanating therefrom (Aksamit 1992; Finkelstaedt 1980, 1981).

In the late Fifth or early Sixth Dynasty, pottery was manufactured in the mortuary temple of Khentkaus at Abusir (Verner 1992). Here a small workshop was established at a date somewhat after the original foundation, within the funerary temple, apparently in an area of the internal courtyard screened off with matting. The workshop had a preparation and storage area with a wheel and other essentials, and a kiln nearby, also within the temple. The types produced, as deduced from wasters, were beer jugs, bread moulds, stands and miniature vessels, which types were presumably to serve the cult. All of the vessel types were probably of siltware, although this is not explicitly stated; this is the fabric group usually used for these forms. The excavator equated this establishment with a reference in the Abusir papyri (documents from the temple archives of Neferirkara, Posener-Kriéger 1976: 45–6) to a room with potter's wheel. It seems, then, that here the needs of the cult were met from its own resources (although interestingly there is no mention of food production in the same area).

Unfortunately, there is no evidence for similar establishments within other royal funerary complexes, but these may have been served by separate establishments, such as those identified near the north pyramid of Sneferu at Dahshur (Stadelmann 1983), and at Giza near the funerary temple of Menkaura (Saleh 1974, 1996). At Dahshur, firing structures were found in a thin-walled building some distance in front of the pyramid. Nicholson (1993: 112) accepts them as kilns, although the excavator thought they were more likely to be for cooking and the provisioning of the élite personnel associated with the functioning of the complex, since the pottery found therein was said to be of 'household' type, and (apparently) no evidence for pottery manufacture was found. At Giza, part of a large industrial area was excavated which included kilns; the excavator interpreted the whole establishment as dealing with the preparation of food offerings for the cult, which required 'ovens, water jars, bins for grain and ordinary reservoirs of pottery for keeping the goods required'. However, Lehner (1985: 157) has identified what may be installations for levigating clay amongst the structures, suggesting that pottery manufacture was in fact taking place there. Given the intimate association between the preparation of the staples of the diet and pottery-making in the private tombs, it would seem extremely probable that the same association was maintained in state-controlled establishments.

Archaeological examples of pottery production not associated with funerary establishments in the Old Kingdom come from Elephantine (Kaiser *et al.* 1982: 296–9), and Dakhla (Hope 1987b: 33–4). At Elephantine, kilns have been located outside the walled Old Kingdom town, and date from about the mid-Fourth to Fifth Dynasties. They perhaps formed part of a larger industrial area. Although few details are available, it appears that both marl and silt clays were worked there. The Dakhla kilns, which may well have formed part of a potter's workshop, were badly eroded, and little more can be said about this material, apart from the fact that the Old Kingdom pottery from the oasis was closely comparable to the contemporary repertoire in the Nile valley (Hope 1987b: 25).

This homogeneity in form and fabric is a striking feature of the pottery of the period, and extends beyond the Nile valley out to the western oases. The explanation for this is not clear: O'Connor (1974–5: 27) has suggested that the homogeneity of storage jars was due to either restricted production at only a few major centres and/or to a widespread trade in commodities that extended throughout the country. Centralised production could perhaps be cited as a reason for the standardisation of other types. However, what little evidence we have suggests that 'standardised' types were produced in various parts of Egypt (as, for example, at ʿAyn Asil where Old Kingdom forms continued to be made into the First Intermediate Period). Whether there was a high degree of control by the state on potters, who were thereby constrained in what they could manufacture, or whether the homogeneity derived from widespread trade and copying remains to be discovered.

The best example of a town-based workshop complex, of slightly later date, comes from ʿAyn Asil in the Dakhla oasis (Soukiassian *et al.* 1990; see Fig. 5.2). This produced pottery from the end of the Old Kingdom into the First Intermediate Period. Like the workshop at Elephantine, it was situated outside the enclosure wall of the settlement. Whilst of relatively modest size, with a suggested working team of five to ten people, it had the capacity to produce a wide range of forms, and exploit a variety of clays from the area, some of which seem to have been chosen because of their specific properties. The forms included characteristic bread moulds of a type well-known throughout Egypt in the Old Kingdom (Jacquet-Gordon 1981: type A), as well as carinated bowls and cups. The manufacture of bread moulds led the excavators to suggest that there was no 'domestic' production at this time, since, they hypothesised, this would be the type most probably produced by individual households for their own use. These workshops do not seem to have supplied the entire needs of the local population, since there was little evidence in them of the ceramic types found in the town's cemeteries (Soukiassian *et al.* 1990: 164; Minault-Gout and Deleuze 1992: 193–4).

In the Nile valley, the evidence suggests that the apparent centralisation of production or distribution of at least some types of Old Kingdom pottery broke down with the political fragmentation of the First Intermediate Period, and that regional styles developed, which appear to correspond to known political boundaries of the period (Bourriau 1981a: 51; O'Connor 1974–5: 27–8; the evidence he cites for this can be interpreted as showing limited trade across these boundaries). Collapse of state control did not, however, prevent trade outside the frontiers of Egypt; storage jars (presumably commodity containers) continued to arrive in Nubia after Egyptian political control had been lost there (O'Connor 1974–5: 29). Only in the Twelfth Dynasty were the regional styles subsumed back into a more homogenous style which incorporated Egypt and Nubia (except the eastern Delta, where foreign settlements greatly influenced the local repertoire).

Archaeological evidence for pottery production in the Middle Kingdom is slight. Kilns were discovered in the open town at Mirgissa in Nubia, on the periphery of the settlement, but nothing further is known of the workshops (Vercoutter 1970: 79–81 and fig. 23). The open town appears to be the earliest established part of the site, preceding the fort, but it is not clear if this was an Egyptian state-controlled workshop serving state needs, or one serving an 'ordinary' population.

Also in Nubia, an isolated potter's workshop was discovered at Nag el-Baba, in Ashkeit district, dating from the Twelfth Dynasty into the Second Intermediate Period (Site 228: Säve-Söderbergh 1989, 265–7; Holthoer 1977: 16–17). This was a multiple-roomed complex which included clay preparation areas, and had an adjacent kiln of unsophisticated type. Pottery-making tools were identified, including pebbles suggested to be for compacting the surfaces of vessels; the 'palette' from the site, not noted by Holthoer, could well be a rocker stamp for the decoration of vessels, a rare but attested technique in the C Group (for example Wenig 1978: 138, cat. 34). Holthoer also drew attention to a socketed stone set in a low protruding wall in one room, which was coated with an unidentified black substance. This may have been a door pivot, but could also have been for some sort of turntable. No wasters or unfired sherds were mentioned amongst the finds; the fired pottery recovered is a mix of Nubian handmade C-Group, and wheelmade wares, the latter said 'generally' to be imported from Egypt. The question of whether the putative turntable, which does not seem to have been used in the manufacture of C-Group pottery, indicates the manufacture of 'wheelmade' wares here on Egyptian lines (or even by Egyptians) is unanswerable, although the illustrated 'wheelmade' pieces from the site are, unusually, open forms, rather than the usual closed forms required for the import of commodities. There is a certain amount of confusion in that the spouted bowls from the site, illustrated and described under the heading wheelmade, are described in the text as possibly deriving from Old Kingdom Egyptian vessels, which may have 'served as prototypes for contemporary *handmade* pottery, e.g. in the Kerma culture and in C-Group (habitation site no. 228 [i.e.the Nag el-Baba workshop]) and Pangrave context' (my italics, Holthoer 1991: 69). Other finds in the workshop, such as bits of molten copper and mud loom weights suggest that it also manufactured other items.

Specialist funerary production has been posited for some centres in the Middle Kingdom and the Second Intermediate Period, including Beni Hasan and Ballas (Bourriau 1981a: 60; 1986–7). At Beni Hasan, this material is distinguished by its distinctive forms and fabrics, its crude manufacturing technique, and the lack of change in the types used in contrast to the rate of alteration of domestic types. At Ballas, a detailed comparison of the pottery from the settlement and cemeteries identified three ware groups found only in the settlement, and wares common in the cemetery that were under-represented in the settlement (but never exclusively present in the cemetery). Although there is not sufficient evidence to suggest this was the pattern across the whole of Egypt, it seems likely that this was the case.

In the New Kingdom, more evidence is available. At Amarna, several kilns have been identified within the residential areas of the city (Nicholson 1989c), both as part of industrial and private estates. Only one of these, Q48.4, has produced evidence of an associated production area, (Rose 1989). Here the potters worked primarily in siltwares, producing vessels, mainly bowls, of types found in abundance throughout the city. There were, however, also a few unfired marl sherds from closed-form jars. Further evidence for production can be found in surface finds of elements of the bearings of potter's wheels.

Five such bearings have been found (Rose 1989; Powell 1995): one from Q48.4, two from the surface of the South Suburb, a mainly residential area, one of uncertain provenance, and one (Ashmolean 1929.417) from house T36.11 in the North Suburb. In passing, it is worth noting the number of fragments of wheel-bearings identified by Powell in the British Museum and on display in the Cairo museum, most, unfortunately, unprovenanced. It is likely that many others lie, misidentified as door sockets, grinders, or not identified at all, in other museums; a full listing, and their correct identification as surface finds on archaeological sites where their size and weight make them likely to survive well, would probably give a better overview of the widespread nature of pottery making in Egypt than anything else.

More or less contemporary with the Amarna workshop is one found in North Sinai at Haruba, site A-345 (Oren 1987: 97–106). It included preparation areas and kilns, and was situated to east of an area which was apparently not residential, but included magazines used for storing grain. The types produced were mostly made in locally available clay, but the forms were drawn from the Nile valley repertoire, and included 'various types of bowls and kraters; the whole range of drop-shaped vessels', tall 'offering stands', and 'flower pots with heavy, frequently perforated bases bearing deep thumb indentations'. The workshop apparently served as an adjunct of the nearby fortress and produced for the garrisons stationed therein, and perhaps for other fortresses across Sinai, as well as for official convoys passing across the area. The official nature of the establishment is reflected both in its proximity to the fortress and in the occurrence of beer jars stamped with cartouches of Seti I at a nearby site, A-343. The practice of stamping utilitarian vessels, in this case breadcones, has also been noted at Amarna, in the bakeries associated with the temple complex at Kom el-Nana.

Some slight evidence for production comes from the west bank at Thebes. The Deir el-Medina remains have already been mentioned; and kilns seem to have been found behind the mortuary temple of Amenhotep son of Hapu, but no descriptions are available (Varille and Robichon 1935: fig. 1). The latter may have formed part of a

New Kingdom industrial area serving the funerary temples, which ran under the temple.

The evidence from the pottery of the period indicates a greater diversity in production than seen previously, in terms of wares, forms, and surface finishes, and in certain cases specialisation of production can be confidently suggested. The uniformity of fabrics used for wine jars (almost certainly the *mnt*-jars of the Deir el-Medina texts already mentioned, see p. 136) and meat jars, and the standardised features, dimensions and capacities of the vessels, present powerful evidence for specialist manufacture in a very limited number of centres, probably in Lower Egypt because of the clay used. These centres had the capacity to turn out vessels in huge numbers (Hope 1982). Specialist production in centres associated with the major palace complexes has also been suggested for New Kingdom blue-painted pottery, both on stylistic grounds and because of the use of relatively rare pigment in the vessels' decoration (Bachmann *et al.* 1980; Hope 1982), and also for polychrome painted amphorae (Bell 1987) and modelled and sculpted vessels (Bourriau 1982). Certainly in the case of the blue-painted vessels it would seem that they were traded in their own right, since many forms are not suitable as commodity containers, but even so, what is known of their distribution suggests they only reached rural and outlying areas very rarely (for example, very few examples are known from Nubia). This implies that blue-painted vessels imparted a certain status to their owners. At Amarna, where excavations have sampled all classes of dwelling in the city, blue-painted vessels are found everywhere, including the apparently 'poorer' areas; the main differences between areas lies in the quality of the decoration. However, poorly and carelessly decorated specimens still occurred in what would otherwise be thought of as élite areas of the city.

The localisation of certain marl wares into Upper and Lower Egyptian types in the New Kingdom enables the distribution of other vessel types to be examined, and results in the impression that marl pottery was travelling further, and as a commodity in its own right (Nordström and Bourriau 1993: 175–82). An example is the category of 'spinning bowls' at Amarna, a distinctive open vessel with handles affixed to the base or wall on the inside (Nagel 1938: 183–8). The bowls were used in the preparation of flax for plying, and were most commonly made in Upper Egyptian marl (Marl A2). This in itself is unusual; marl clays were usually used for closed forms, to serve as commodity containers, and very rarely for bowls. A property of the clay must have made them particularly desirable for their purpose, perhaps their lack of porosity, since flax fibres are best plied when wet. Siltware examples of the type are rare in comparison with the marl examples. How do the Upper Egyptian vessels come to be at Amarna? Their association with a particular craft may, perhaps, indicate that they were state-supplied, but this seems unlikely, given their widespread distribution over the site; and since weaving was carried on as part of household activities, it seems most logical that the bowls were directly obtained by each household, as required, from traders.

Siltwares are less easy to consider in terms of regional production because of their less distinctive composition, but it may be that examination of prevailing modes of surface treatment by area as applied to similar forms may suggest different areas of production. For example, the commonest type at Amarna, a flat-based bowl with a simple contour and rounded rim, is there invariably red-slipped. At Malkata, an almost contemporary site on the west bank at Thebes, the same form occurs unslipped as well as red-slipped (Hope 1989: 10, fig. 1h). As well as demonstrating more localised production, it also serves to suggest that regional variation is not to be sought only at times of political instability.

A further traceable example of localised production which was traded into the Nile valley is to be found in certain vessels produced in the Dakhla oasis, the fabrics which are distinctive (Aston 1996: 9; Hope 1987b). From the New Kingdom onwards, a limited range of vessel forms from this source were imported into the Nile valley, amphorae and gourds in the New Kingdom, and cigar-shaped vessels thereafter. The vessel shapes indicate clearly that commodities were the items being transferred, but as yet, no synthesis has been undertaken to look at the wares' distribution. However, work on the ceramics of the Third Intermediate Period has identified the pattern familiar from earlier periods of political instability, the development of regional styles (Aston 1996).

Specialist funerary production has been posited for some centres in the New Kingdom, such as Thebes (Rose 1996: 170). Here pots imitating stone and glass were made in a distinctive marl clay that is only used for one other vessel type, the definitively funerary canopic jars. These vessel types do not occur either on non-funerary sites in the region, or in tombs outside the Theban region.

There is less information regarding the pottery industry of the Third Intermediate and Late Periods. A kiln discovered at East Karnak, dated from about the seventh to the late fifth centuries BC, lay in an open space or courtyard in an industrial quarter, not far from a residential area (Redford 1981: 14). No pottery types are mentioned as associated with the use of the kiln. A complex of kilns at Memphis were built over the forecourt of a Ramesside temple adjacent to the enclosure of the main temple, but this had gone out of use and dwellings had been built in the area (Jacquet 1965: 46–50). There were, apparently, some unfired sherds but no information is available on the types.

A final, if uninterpretable, source of evidence which may have some bearing on ceramic production may be found in potters' and painters' marks. The former were made before firing in the leather-hard clay, and may consist of hieroglyphs or simple designs or symbols (marks made after firing may have a separate significance associated with

1982. Keramikbearbeitung in Dahschur 1976–1981. *MDAIK*, 38: 25–65.

1988. Pottery. In *The Pyramid of Senwosret I*. (ed. D. Arnold). New York: Metropolitan Museum of Art, pp. 106–46.

1993. Techniques and traditions of manufacture in the pottery of ancient Egypt. In *An Introduction Ancient Egyptian Pottery*. (eds. D. Arnold and J.D. Bourriau). Mainz: von Zabern, pp. 11–102.

Arnold, D. and Bourriau, J.D. (eds.) 1993. *An Introduction to Ancient Egyptian Pottery. Fascicle I*. Mainz: von Zabern.

Arnold, D.E. 1985. *Ceramic Theory and Cultural Process*. Cambridge: CUP.

Aston, D.A. 1989a. Qantir/Piramesse-Nord – Pottery Report 1988. *Göttinger Miszellen*, 113, 7–24.

1989b. Ancient Egyptian fire dogs – a new interpretation. *MDAIK*, 45: 27–32.

1996. *Egyptian Pottery of the Late New Kingdom and Third Intermediate Period*. Studien zur Archäologie und Geschichte altägyptens 13. Heidelberg: Heidelberger Orientverlag.

Bachmann, H.G., Everts, H. and Hope, C.A. 1980. Cobalt-blue pigment on 18th Dynasty pottery. *MDAIK*, 36: 33–7.

Ballet, P. and Picon, M. 1990. Étude de la céramique. In *Balat III. Les Ateliers de Potiers d'Ayn-Asil* (eds. G. Soukiassian, M. Wuttmann and L. Pantalacci). Cairo: IFAO, pp. 75–165.

Ballet, P. and Vichy, M. 1992. Artisanat de la Céramique dans l'Égypte Hellénistique et Romaine. *CCE*, 3: 109–19.

Bell, M. 1987. Regional variation in polychrome pottery of the 19th Dynasty. *CCE*, 1: 49–76.

Bellido, A., Bourriau, J.D., Bryan, N. and Robinson, V. Forthcoming. Chemical fingerprinting of Egyptian pottery fabrics: a comparison between NAA groupings and the Vienna System.

Bietak, M. 1968. *Studien zur Chronologie der nubischen C-Gruppe: Ein Beitrage zur Frühgeschichte Unternubiens zwischen 2200 und 1500 vor Ch*. Vienna: Böhlaus.

Blackman, W. 1927. *The Fellahin Of Upper Egypt*. London: Harrap.

Bourriau, J.D. 1981a. *Umm el-Ga'ab: Pottery From the Nile Valley Before The Arab Conquest*. Cambridge: CUP.

1981b. Nubians in Egypt during the Second Intermediate Period. An interpretation based on the Egyptian ceramic evidence. In *Studien zur altägyptischen Keramik* (ed. D. Arnold). Mainz: von Zabern, pp. 25–41.

1982. Clay figure vases. In *Egypt's Golden Age: The art of living in the New Kingdom 1558–1085 B.C.* (eds. E. Brovarski, S.K. Doll and R.E. Freed) Boston: Museum of Fine Arts, pp. 101–6.

1985. Technology and typology of Egyptian ceramics. In *Ceramics and Civilization Vol. 1: Ancient Technology to Modern Science* (ed. W.D. Kingery). Columbus, Ohio: The American Ceramic Society, pp. 27–42.

1986/7 Cemetery and settlement pottery of the second intermediate period to early New Kingdom. *BES*, 8: 47–59.

1987. Pottery figure vases of the New Kingdom. *CCE*,1: 81–96.

1996. Observations on the pottery from Serabit el-Khadim. *CRIPEL*, 18: 19–32.

1998 The role of chemical analysis in the study of Egyptian pottery. In *Proceedings of the Seventh International Congress of Egyptologists Cambridge 1995*. (ed. C. Eyre). Leuven: Peeters, pp. 189–99.

Bourriau, J.D. and Nicholson, P.T. 1992. Marl clay pottery fabrics of the New Kingdom from Memphis, Saqqara and Amarna. *JEA*, 78: 29–91.

Bourriau, J.D., Smith, L.M.V. and Nicholson, P.T. in press. *New Kingdom Pottery Fabrics: Nile Clay and Mixed Nile/Marl Clay Fabrics from Memphis and Amarna*. London: EES.

Brissaud, P. 1982. *Les Ateliers de Potiers de la region de Louqsor*. Cairo: IFAO.

Brooks, D., Bieber jr., A.M., Harbottle, G. and Sayre, E.V. 1974. Biblical studies through activation analysis of ancient pottery. In *Archaeological Chemistry* (ed. C.W. Beck). Washington: American Chemical Society, pp. 48–80.

Brunton, G. 1948. *Matmar*. London: Quaritch.

Bruyère, B. 1939. Rapport sur les fouilles à Deir el Médineh (1934–1935). III. Cairo: IFAO.

Butzer, K.W. 1974. Modern Egyptian pottery clay and Predynastic buff ware. *JNES*, 33: 377–82.

Cardew, M. 1952. Nigerian traditional pottery. *Nigeria*, 39: 188–201.

Davies, N. de G. 1908. *The Rock Tombs of El Amarna. Part V – Smaller Tombs and Boundary Stelae*. Archaeological Survey of Egypt. Seventeenth Memoir. London: EEF.

1930. *The Tomb of Ken-amun at Thebes*. The Metropolitan Museum of Art Egyptian Expedition, Vol. V. New York: MMA.

Debono, F. and Mortensen, B. 1990. *El Omari*. MMA.

Eyre, C. 1987a. Work and organisation of work in the Old Kingdom. In *Labor in the Ancient Near East* (ed. M.A. Powell). American Oriental Series 68. New Haven, CT: American Oriental Society, pp. 5–48.

1987b. Work and organisation of work in the New Kingdom. In *Labor in the Ancient Near East* (ed. M.A. Powell). American Oriental Series 68. New Haven, Conneticut: American Oriental Society 68, pp. 167–222.

Fieller, N.R.J. and Nicholson, P.T. 1991. Grain size analysis of archaeological pottery: the use of statistical models. In *Recent Developments in Ceramic Petrology* (eds. A. Middleton and I. Freestone). London: British Museum Research Laboratory, pp. 71–111.

Finkelstaedt E. 1980. Regional painting style in prehistoric Egypt. *ZAS*, 107:116–20.

1981. The location of styles in painting: white cross-lined ware at Nagada. *JARCE*, 18: 7–10.

French, P. 1992. A preliminary study of pottery in Lower Egypt in the Late Dynastic and Ptolemaic periods. *CCE*, 3: 83–93.

Goren, Y., Oren, E. and Feinstein, R. 1995. The archaeological and ethnoarchaeological interpretation of a ceramological enigma: pottery production in Sinai (Egypt) during the New Kingdom period. *KVHAA Konferenser*, 34. Stockholm, 101–20.

Hamroush, H. 1992. Pottery analysis and problems in the indentification of the geological origins of ancient ceramics. *CCE*, 3: 39–51.

Hamroush, H. and Zeid, H.A. 1990. Petrological and chemical analyses of some neolithic ceramics from el Omari, Egypt. In *El Omari* (F. Debono, and B. Mortensen). Mainz: von Zabern, pp. 117–28.

Hancock, R.G., Aufreiter, S. and Elsokkari, I. 1986/87. Nile Alluvium: Soil and Ceramics. *BES*, 8: 61–71.

Hancock, R.G.V., Millet, N.B. and Mills, A.J. 1986. A rapid INAA method to characterize Egyptian ceramics. *JAS*, 13: 107–17.

Harbottle, G. 1982. Provenience studies using Neutron Activation Analysis: the role of standardization. In *Archaeological Ceramics* (eds. J.S. Olin and A.D. Franklin). Washington: Smithsonian Institution, pp. 67–77.

Hennessy, J.B. and Millet, A. 1963. Spectographic analysis of the foreign pottery from the royal tombs of Abydos and Early Bronze Age pottery of Palestine. *Archaeometry*, 6: 10–17.

Hodges, H. 1989. *Artifacts*. London: Duckworth.

Hoffman, M. 1982. *The Predynastic of Hierakonpolis – An Interim Report*. Egyptian Studies Association Publication 1. Cairo and Macomb, Ill.: University Herbarium, Cairo and Department of Sociology and Anthropology, Western Illinois University.

Holmen, K. 1990. Indentification of some plant remains in the el Omari pottery. In *El Omari* (F. Debono and B. Mortensen). Mainz: von Zabern, pp. 129–30.

Holthoer, R. 1977. *New Kingdom Pharaonic Sites: The Pottery*. Scandinavian Joint Expedition to Sudanese Nubia Vol. 5:1. Stockholm: Scandinavian University Books.

1991. The wheelmade pottery in Middle Nubian cortex. In *Middle Nubian Sites* (ed. T. Säve-Söderbergh). The Scandinavian Joint Expedition to Sudanese Nubia publications Vol. 4: 1, 59–74. Partille: Paul Åström Editions.

Hope, C. 1981. Two ancient Egyptian potter's wheels. *JSSEA*, 11: 127–33.

1982. Aspects of ceramic specialisation and standardisation in the New Kingdom. *BL*, VII: 39–41.

1987a. *Egyptian Pottery*. Aylesbury: Shire Egyptology.

1987b. Dakhleh Oasis project – report on the study of the pottery and kilns. In *Ceramics From The Dakhleh Oasis (second season 1979)* (eds. W. Edwards, C. Hope and E. Segnit). Victoria College Archaeology Research Unit Occasional Paper No. 1. Burwood: Victoria College Press, pp. 25–52.

1989. *Pottery of the Egyptian New Kingdom: Three Studies*. Victoria College Archaeology Research Unit, Occasional Paper No. 2. Burwood: Victoria College Press.

1991. Blue-painted and polychrome decorated pottery from Amarna: a preliminary corpus. *CCE*, 2: 17–92.

1993. Pottery kilns from the oasis of el-Dakhla. In *An Introduction To Ancient Egyptian Pottery* (eds. D. Arnold and J. Bourriau). Mainz: von Zabern, pp. 121–7.

Hummel, M and Schubert, S. 1994. Kom el-Ahmar: Ceramic typology. In *The Akhenaten Temple Project 3: The Excavations of Kom el-Ahmar and Environs* (ed. D. Redford). Aegypti Texta Propositaque II. Toronto: Akhenaten Temple Project, pp. 30–82.

Jacquet, J. 1965. The architect's report. In *Mit Rahineh 1956* (ed. R. Anthes). Philadelphia: The University Museum, University of Pennsylvania, pp. 46–59.

Jacquet-Gordon, H. 1981. A tentative typology of Egyptian bread moulds. In *Studien zur altägyptischen Keramik* (ed. D. Arnold). Mainz: von Zabern, pp. 11–24.

Janssen, J.J. 1975. *Commodity Prices From The Ramessid Period*. Leiden: E.J. Brill.

Kaiser, W., Avila, R., Dreyer, G., Jaritz, H., Seidlmayer, F. and S. 1982. Stadt und Tempel von Elephantine. *MDAIK*, 38: 271–345.

Kaplan, M.F., Harbottle, G. and Sayre, E.V. 1982. Multi-disciplinary analysis of Tell el-Yahudiyeh Ware. *Archaeometry*, 24: 127–42.

Kemp, B.J. 1989. *Amarna Reports V*. London: EES.

1995. *Amarna Reports VI*. London: EES.

Kirby, C. 1989. Report on the 1987 excavations: The excavation of Q48.4. In *Amarna Reports V* (ed. B.J. Kemp). London: EES, pp. 15–63.

Köhler, K. 1992. Problems and priorities in the study of Pre- and Early Dynastic pottery. *CCE*, 3: 7–16.

Kroeper, K. (1992) Shape + Matrix = Workshop. Ceramic from Minshat Abu Omar. *CCE*, 3: 23–31.

Leahy, M.A. 1985. The hieratic labels, 1979–82. In *Amarna Reports II* (ed. B.J. Kemp). London: EES, pp. 65–109.

Lehner, M. 1985. Giza. A contextual approach to the Pyramids. *Archiv für Orientforschung*, 32: 136–58.

Makundi, I.N., Waern-Sperber, A. and Ericsson, T. 1989. A Mössbauer study of the black colour in Early Cypriote and Nubian C-group Black Topped pottery. *Archaeometry*, 31: 54–65.

Mesnil du Buisson, Compte du. 1935. *Les noms et signes Égyptiens désignant des vases ou objets similaires*. Thèse complementaire pour le Doctorat des Lettres, Faculté des Lettres de l'Université de Paris.

Minault-Gout, A. and Deleuze, P. 1992. *La mastaba d'Ima-Pépi*. FIFAO XXXIII. Cairo: IFAO.

Mond, R. and Myers, O. 1937. *Cemeteries of Armant I*. London: EES.

Nagel, G. 1938. *La Céramique du Nouvel Empire à Deir el Médineh*. Cairo: IFAO.

Newberry P. 1893a. *Beni Hasan I*. Archaeological Survey of Egypt. First Memoir. London: EEF.

1893b. Beni Hasan II. Archaeological Survey of Egypt. Second Memoir. London: EEF.

1895. *El Bersheh I*. Archaeological Survey of Egypt. Third Memoir. London: EEF.

Nibbi A. 1987. *Ancient Egyptian Pot Bellows and the Oxhide Ingot Shape*. Oxford: DE Publications.

Nicholson, P.T. 1989a. Experimental determination of the purpose of a 'box oven'. In *Amarna Reports V* (ed. B.J. Kemp). London: EES, pp. 241–52.

1989b. *Iron Age Pottery Production in the Hunsrück-Eifel-Kultur of Germany: A World-System Perspective*. Oxford: BAR S-501.

1989c. Report on the 1987 excavations: the pottery kilns in building Q48.4. In *Amarna Reports V* (ed. B.J. Kemp). London: EES, pp. 64–81.

1993. The firing of pottery. In *An Introduction to Ancient Egyptian Pottery* (eds. D. Arnold and J. Bourriau). Mainz: von Zabern, pp. 103–20.

1995a. The potters of Deir Mawas, an ethnoarchaeological study. In *Amarna Reports VI* (ed. B.J. Kemp). London: EES, pp. 279–308.

1995b. Glassmaking and glassworking at Amarna: some new work. *Journal of Glass Studies*, 37: 11–19.

Nicholson, P.T. and Patterson, H.L. 1985a. Pottery making in Upper Egypt: an ethnoarchaeological study. *WA*, 17 (2): 222–39.

1985b. The potters of Deir el-Gharbi. *Popular Archaeology*, February 1985: 5–10.

1989. Ceramic technology in Upper Egypt: a study of pottery firing. *WA*, 21 (1): 71–86.

Nicholson, P. and Rose, P. 1985. Pottery fabrics and ware groups at el-Amarna. In *Amarna Reports II* (ed. B.Kemp). London: EES, pp. 133–74.

Noll, W. 1981a. Bemalte Keramiken Altägyptens: Material, Rohstoffe und Herstellungstechnik. In *Studien zur altägyptischen Keramik* (ed. D. Arnold). Mainz: von Zabern, pp. 103–38.

1981b. Mineralogy and technology of the painted ceramics of Ancient Egypt. In *Scientific Studies in Ancient Ceramics* (ed. M. Hughes). London: BMP, pp. 143–54.

Nordström, H-Å. 1972. *Neolithic and A-group Sites*. Scandinavian Joint Expedition to Sudanese Nubia, Vol. 3:1. Stockholm:

Scandinavian University Books.
Nordström, H-Å. and Bourriau, J. 1993. Ceramic technology: clays and fabrics. In *An Introduction to Ancient Egyptian Pottery* (eds. D. Arnold and J. Bourriau). Mainz: von Zabern, pp. 147–90.
O'Connor, D. 1974–75. Political systems and archaeological data in Egypt: 2600–1780 BC. *WA*, 6: 15–38.
Oren, E.D. 1987. The 'Ways of Horus' in North Sinai. In *Egypt, Israel, Sinai. Archaeological And Historical Relationships In The Biblical Period* (ed. A.F. Rainey). Tel Aviv: Tel Aviv University, pp. 69–120.
Orton, C. 1975. Quantitative pottery studies: some progress, problems and prospects. *Science and Archaeology*, 16: 30–5.
Orton, C., Tyers, P. and Vince, A. 1993. *Pottery in Archaeology*. Cambridge: CUP.
de Paepe, P. 1986. Étude mineralogique et chimique de la céramique néolithic d'el Kadada et ses implications archéologiques. *Archéologie du Nil Moyen* 1: 113–40.
de Paepe, P., Gratien, B. and Privati, B. 1992. Étude Comparative de Céramiques Kerma. *CRIPEL*: 63–81.
Payne, J. 1966. Spectrographic analysis of some Egyptian pottery of the Eighteenth dynasty. *JEA*, 52: 176–8.
Peacock, D.P.S. 1977. Ceramics in Roman and Medieval archaeology. In *Pottery and Early Commerce* (ed. D.P.S.Peacock). London: Academic Press, pp. 21–33.
1982. *Pottery in The Roman World: An Ethnoarchaeological Approach*. London: Longman.
Perlman, I. and Asaro, F. 1969. Pottery analysis by neutron activation. *Archaeometry*, 11: 21–53.
Pollard, A.M. and Heron, C. 1996. *Archaeological Chemistry* . Cambridge: The Royal Society of Chemistry.
Porat, N. and Seeher, J. 1988. Petrographic analyses of pottery and basalt from Predynastic Maadi. *MDAIK*, 44: 215–28.
Posener-Kriéger, P. 1976. *Les archives du temple Funéraire de Néferirkarí Kakaô (Les papyrus d'Abousir)*. Cairo: IFAO.
Powell, C. 1995. The nature and use of ancient Egyptian potter's wheels. In *Amarna Reports VI* (ed. B.J. Kemp). London: EES, pp. 309–35.
Redford, D. 1981. Interim report on the excavations at East Karnak, 1977–78. *JARCE*, 18: 11–41.
Redmount, C.A. and Morgenstein, M.E. 1996. Major and trace element analysis of modern Egyptian pottery. *JAS*, 23: 741–62.
Reisner, G.A. 1923. *Excavations at Kerma*. Cambridge, MA: Peabody Museum of Harvard University.
Rice, P.M. 1987. *Pottery Analysis: A Sourcebook*. Chicago: University of Chicago Press.
Riederer, J. 1974. Recently identified Egyptian pigments. *Archaeometry*, 16: 102–9.
1988. The microscopic analysis of Egyptian pottery from the Old Kingdom. In *Akten des vierten internationalen Ägyptologenkongresses München 1985* (ed. S. Schoske). Beihefte Studien zur altägyptischen Kultur, I. Hamburg: Helmut Buske Verlag. Band I: pp. 221–30.
1992. The microscopic analysis of calcite tempered pottery from Minshat Abu Omar. *CCE*, 3: 33–7.
Rose, P. 1984. The pottery distribution analysis. In *Amarna Reports I* (ed. B.J. Kemp). London: EES, pp. 133–53.
1986. Pottery from the Main Chapel. In *Amarna Reports III* (ed. B.J. Kemp). London: EES, pp. 99–117.
1987. Pottery from Gate Street 8. In *Amarna Reports IV* (ed. B.J. Kemp). London: EES, pp. 132–43.
1989. Report on the 1987 excavations: The evidence for pottery-making at Q48.4. In *Amarna Reports V*, (ed. B.J. Kemp). London: EES, 82–101.
1996. The pottery. In *The Tombs Of Amenhotep, Khnummose and Amenmose at Thebes* (ed. N. Strudwick). Oxford: Griffith Institute, pp. 166–81.
Rye, O.S. 1976. Keeping your temper under control: materials and the manufacture of Papuan pottery. *Archaeology and Physical Anthropology in Oceania*, 11 (2): 106–37.
Saleh, A.A. 1974. Excavations around the Mycerinus pyramid complex. *MDAIK*, 30: 131–54.
1996. Ancient Egyptian house and palace at Giza and Heliopolis. In *House and Palace in Ancient Egypt* (ed. M. Bietak). Vienna: Österreichische Akademie der Wissenschaften, pp. 185–94.
Säve-Söderbergh, T. 1989. *Middle Nubian Sites*. Scandinavian Joint Expedition to Sudanese Nubia, Vols. 4:1 and 4:2. Partille: Paul Åstrom Editions.
Soukiassian, G., Wuttmann M., Pantalacci, L., Ballet, P. and Picon, M. 1990. *Balat III. Les Ateliers de Potiers d'Ayn-Asil*. Cairo: IFAO.
Stadelmann, R. 1983. Die Pyramiden des Snofru in Daschur. Zweiter Bericht über die Ausgrabungen an der nordlichen Steinpyramide. *MDAIK*, 39: 228–30.
Stevenson, R.B.K. 1953. Prehistoric pot-building in Europe. *Man*, 53: 65–8.
Strouhal, E., Urbanec, Z., Čejka, J. and Cejkova, I. 1988. Elemental analysis of pottery from the temple of Queen Khentkaus at Abusir. In *Akten des vierten internationalen Ägyptologenkongresses. München 1985* (ed. S. Schoske). Band I. Beihefte Studien zur altägyptischen Kultur 1. Hamburg: Helmut Buske Verlag, pp. 247–55.
Tobert, N. 1984. Ethno-archaeology of pottery firing in Darfur, Sudan: implications for ceramic technology studies. *Oxford Journal of Archaeology*, 3 (2): 141–56.
Tobia, S.K. and Sayre, E.V. 1974. An analytical comparison of various Egyptian soils, clays, shales and some ancient pottery by neutron activation. In *Recent Advances in Science and Technology of Materials*, Vol. 3 (ed. A. Bishay). New York: Plenum, pp. 99–128.
Varille, A. and Robichon, C. 1935. Quatre nouveaux temples Thebains. *CdE*, 10: 237–42.
Vercoutter, J. 1970. *Mirgissa I*. Paris: CNRS.
Verner, M. 1992. Discovery of a potter's workshop in the pyramid complex of Khentkaus at Abusir. *CCE*, 3: 55–60.
Wenig, S. 1978. *Africa In Antiquity: The Arts Of Ancient Nubia And The Sudan*. 2 vols. New York: Brooklyn Museum.
Whitbread, I. K. 1986. The characterisation of argillaceous inclusions in ceramic thin sections. *Archaeometry*, 28: 79–88.
Wilkinson, T.A.H. 1996. *State Formation in Egypt: Chronology And Society*. Cambridge monographs in African archaeology 40. BAR International Series 651. Oxford: Tempus Reperatum.
Williams, D.F. 1983. Petrology of ceramics. In *The Petrology of Archaeological Artefacts* (eds. D.R.C. Kempe and A.P. Harvey). Oxford: Clarendon Press, pp. 301–29.
Woods, A.J. 1986. Form and function: some observations on the cooking pot in antiquity. In *Ceramics and Civilization*, Vol. 2. (ed. W.D. Kingery). Columbus, Ohio: American Ceramic Society, pp. 157–72.

6. Metals

JACK OGDEN

Introduction

The importance of metallurgy throughout history is underlined by our habit of dividing the past into Bronze and Iron ages, with various subdivisions of these. Such convenient chronological nomenclatures imply a greater segmentation of metal use in the past than is strictly true. The periods of usage of different metals and alloys overlapped and there was often a long delay between the first exploitation of a new technology and its adoption by society at large. Egyptian peasants were still harvesting grain with flint-edged sickles 1,000 years after the pharaoh Pepi I had been immortalised in an over life-size copper statue found at Hierakonpolis (Cairo JE33034).

We know little of the prospecting habits of the Egyptians, but they were thorough and perhaps systematic in their discovery of metalliferous deposits employing a combination of large-scale state expeditions and smaller prospecting/surveying groups. A graffito by Thuthotep, a 'reckoner of gold' around 2000 BC has been found at the remote Abrak well some 240 kilometres southeast of Aswan (de Bruyn 1955). The prospectors might have lacked geochemical knowledge in the modern sense, but they had a practical understanding of nature. No doubt they could recognise the land formations, rock colours and even flora associated with metal deposits. For example, it has been noted that the pine *Pinus halepensis* grows particularly abundantly over the copper gossans on Cyprus (Constantinou 1982), while the presence of acacia trees can reflect the presence of copper and lead ores. Possibly, the association of the goddess Hathor with both mines, as at Timna, and with acacia trees is not coincidental. Acacia wood also served as pit props in some Egyptian gold mines – a function which devotees of Hathor might have found reassuring.

In the ancient Near East, ores were generally treated at or near the mines; it is easier to transport and keep a tally of ingots than bulkier raw materials. Nevertheless, the availability of fuel would dictate the best option for treatment locality. The urban craftsmen were probably far better acquainted with associated craft activities such as faience and glass manufacture than ore recovery and mining processes. However we do not know the economic or other factors that decided which ores should be locally treated near the mines to produce metals or which if any might be transported for use in the pigment and glaze industries.

Our understanding of ancient Egyptian metals comes from the careful study of surviving examples using, increasingly, the analysis and internal study made possible by technological advances. To date, thousands of analyses of Egyptian metals have been published (e.g. Riederer 1978b, 1981, 1982, 1983, 1984, 1988; Lucas 1962; Fleming and Crowfoot-Payne 1979). A good summary of earlier analyses is given by Riederer (1982) and an overall summary of results is provided by Kaczmarczyk and Hedges (1983). There are also numerous other analyses scattered in the conservation and scientific literature, while a huge number undertaken by museums around the world remain unpublished. Most of these analyses have been carried out on supposed Late Period copper alloy objects. Garland noted that

> Amongst archaeologists it is the practice to assign any non-ferrous metal object not found under known and convincing circumstances or not bearing marks by which they may be dated . . . to the Saitic period, generally the 26th Dynasty. (Garland and Bannister 1927: 83)

This tradition is still alive and well. Firm chronological distinction will not be possible until analysis of metal finds becomes as standard a practice in Egyptology as it is in some other archaeological fields. Analysis is now an integral and useful part of archaeology and art history. For example, Riederer, on the basis of his various analyses of over 1,200 Egyptian copper alloy objects, noted that composition sometimes seemed to vary with subject (Riederer 1978b, 1981, 1982, 1983, 1984, 1988). This ties in with Roeder's earlier observation that forms or poses of deity figures tended to differ from place to place within Egypt (Roeder 1956). This is understandable. If the statuettes were usually made at the local temples, their attributes and poses might be expected to replicate those of the cult statues then in use there, while their compositions would reflect the traditions of, and constraints on, the local metalworkers as well as aesthetic and colour considerations.

Our knowledge of ancient sources of ores and other natural products is helped by the published geological studies of Egypt, including much undertaken since the Second World War on metal ore distribution and geochemistry. The reader is thus directed to the specialist geological literature, starting with el-Baz's annotated bibliography (el-Baz 1984). John Harris' 1962 revision of Alfred Lucas' fundamental work *Ancient Egyptian Materials Industries* is, of course, still invaluable and the reader is directed to the older works referenced there, in particular to those relating to excavation reports and ancient documentary sources (Lucas 1962).

Antimony

Antimony is a light, bright, white metal, not unlike silver in appearance, but it is brittle and better suited to casting, not mechanical working. The use of metallic antimony in ancient Egypt has been reported, but such instances were largely discredited by Lucas on the basis of visual study and, where feasible, analysis (Lucas 1962: 195–9). Thus we can now exclude such supposed examples as the 'antimony powder' said to have been found in Tutankhamun's tomb and the 'antimony plating' on an Old Kingdom vessel. Readers are directed to Lucas' comments and can also note that Meyers' more recent re-analysis of the 'antimony plated' vessel confirmed that the surface layer was indeed actually arsenic due, almost certainly, to natural surface enrichment (Lucas 1962: 198; Smith 1970: 102, n. 5).

The only confirmed examples of metallic antimony from ancient Egypt published to date are the small beads, probably of native antimony, of Third Intermediate Period date which were found by Petrie at Lahun and analysed by Gladstone (Lucas 1962; Garland and Bannister 1927: 32). The identification is supported by the existence of occasional excavated (and analysed) finds of metallic antimony outside Egypt – in Western Asia, Transcaucasia and Italy (Caley 1964: 135–6; Moorey 1994: 241–2). The Egyptian beads were probably imports since antimony ores occur as little more than minute traces in Egypt.

Some Iron-Age beads from Tell el-Fara in Israel are described by Dayton (1978: 450) as tin:antimony alloys with about 66 per cent tin and 33 per cent antimony. Although antimony has not yet been found as a principal component in any ancient Egyptian alloys, we might well expect other examples of metallic antimony and antimony-rich alloys to be identified as analysis becomes more routine. As a *caveat*, however, we can note that objects made of antimony alloys occasionally appear in collections that are modern fakes made of easy-to-cast 'type-metal'.

Antimony is common in small amounts in ancient copper alloy objects (usually under about 1 per cent) and as a trace element in lead. It is also found as an ingredient in Egyptian faience from the time of Thutmose III and in glass from about the Amarna period onwards (Kaczmarczyk and Hedges 1983: 98). An antimony compound was also used as an occasional eye-paint in Egypt from the Amarna period onwards, but this was far less common than has generally been supposed – a state of affairs seemingly also true in Mesopotamia (Lucas 1962: 196–9; Moorey 1994: 241). The evidence suggests that antimony, as ore or native metal, was reaching Egypt from the New Kingdom onwards, and was perhaps sometimes confused with tin.

Bronze *see* copper and copper alloys

Electrum *see* gold and electrum

Copper and copper alloys

Copper is a pinkish-yellow metal that occurs native – that is in metallic form – or, far more commonly, as copper-containing ores from which the copper can be extracted by procedures termed smelting. Copper-bearing deposits can contain copper ores of varying complexity and purity and some native copper. Apart from metallurgy, there were a myriad of uses for copper and copper ores in ancient Egypt: in medicines (Weser 1987: 189–94), as pigments (see pp. 153, 154, 156 and Chapter 4, this volume) and as colouring agents in glazes and glass (see p. 156–7 and Chapters 7 and 8, this volume).

Occurrence and retrieval

The main copper-producing regions accessible to the ancient Egyptians were the Eastern Desert and the Sinai, including the Serabit el-Khadim region in the southwest and Timna in the Wadi Arabah, now part of Israel. The epigraphic evidence only refers to the turquoise found at Serabit el-Khadim, but the reported remains of *tuyères*, moulds, crucibles and casting installations suggest local ore treatment (Beit-Arieh 1985: 89–116). Copper slags, ores, crucibles, ingot moulds and other working detritus of Old and Middle Kingdom date have also been found at Wadi Magharah, some twenty kilometres southwest of Serabit el-Khadim. However, it is possible that this was more a treatment centre for ores from the surrounding region than a major mining area (Petrie 1906: 51–2; Lucas 1962: 202–4; Beit-Arieh 1981: 95–127). In view of the turquoise-biased epigraphic material, it is difficult to determine the relative extents to which mining in the Serabit el-Khadim/Magharah area was directed at the turquoise (see Chapter 2, this volume, for discussion of the implications of the term *mfk3t*) or at the copper. However, we can note that the scale of imperial turquoise exploitation in Sinai in the New Kingdom contrasts with the sparse surviving examples of its use in Egyptian jewellery. It is difficult to believe that jewellery was its primary employment. The use of ground turquoise in glaze-making had been suggested by Petrie but rejected by Lucas. Turquoise is an aluminium phosphate. Aluminium is commonly found in glazes due to its presence in sand. However, traces of phosphorus are also found in some Egyptian glazes but have not so far been satisfactorily explained (Lucas 1962: 186–7). Representations of turquoise at the mining sites in the form of cones, apparently of powder, not nuggets or blocks, tend to suggest non-jewellery use.

Our best evidence of ancient copper exploitation in Sinai comes from the Timna mines and smelting sites which have now been excavated and studied in considerable detail. This mining area reveals the recovery and local smelting of copper ores from the fourth millennium BC onwards and the gradual development of the metallurgical processes employed. Traces of manganese in a Predynastic axe and protodynastic copper bands have been taken as evidence that the copper came from Sinai (Lucas 1962: 209). There is little evidence for continued exploitation of the Sinai mines during the First Intermediate Period, but mining was re-started in the Eleventh Dynasty and became extensive in the Twelfth Dynasty, with an increasing documentary record (Mellado 1995). Copper-mining activity at Timna appears to have reached its peak during the Nineteenth and Twentieth Dynasties and represents the largest-scale Egyptian copper-mining enterprise so far discovered (Shaw 1998). The Timna mines were essentially a series of cylindrical shafts which linked underground galleries. According to Craddock:

> The mines were small, shallow and, although linked underground, display little evidence of any overall mining strategy, or of any knowledge of the possibilities of ventilation or drainage. (Craddock 1995: 69)

Timna has been associated with the New Kingdom copper mines at Atika mentioned in Papyrus Harris (Levene 1998). Workings at Timna appear to have ceased abruptly in the time of Rameses V. Strangely, there is no evidence so far for any exploitation of the Timna mines in the Late Period – the period when the production of copper statuettes and the like in Egypt increased exponentially. For a general survey of the Timna mines see Rothenberg (1972).

In Egypt itself, copper ores occur along almost the entire length of the Eastern Desert into Nubia. There is a cluster of copper deposits in the Eastern Desert inland from Safaga, and between Safaga and Quseir there are copper ores with various lead, zinc and nickel associations (Nassim 1949: 143–50). The extent of ancient workings is still largely unknown, but the lead and zinc contents of some of the ores might suggest an origin for the high lead levels in copper glazes from Elkab in the Old and Middle Kingdoms (Kaczmarczyk and Hedges 1983: 235). Copper mines of ancient but uncertain date at el-Atawi/Wadi Sitra (due east of Luxor) might have supplied workshops within the temple complexes at Thebes, where workers carried out such ambitious commissions as the casting of the doors for the temple of Amun at Karnak (as represented in the Eighteenth-Dynasty Theban tomb of Rekhmira, TT100; Davies 1943; see Fig. 6.1). The Ptolemaic bronze foundry recently found at the funerary temple of Seti I at Thebes might well come at the end of a long tradition of temple-based metalworking in the area (Scheel 1989: 41).

The Hammash area, north east of Aswan, has chacopyrite (copper/iron sulphide) ores with some associated gold. The ancient gold and copper workings in this region include some which date back to the Middle Kingdom, if not earlier (Klemm and Klemm 1994).

On the basis of analyses of copper-containing glazes, Kaczmarczyk and Hedges (1983) have recently suggested that the southern Eastern Desert was already being exploited in the Middle Kingdom, and perhaps even as early as the First Dynasty. Simple ores such as malachite, cuprite and atacamite (with the deeper deposits of sulphides with zinc, lead and silver admixtures) also occur at Samiuki in the Eastern Desert, not far from Ras Banas (Anwar 1964: 89–94). Lucas, following Hume, called the mines in this area 'the most important deposits of copper yet discovered in Egypt', and describes the extensive underground workings and the general copper recovery detritus such as ore crushers and slag. According to Lucas (1962: 206–8), the mine at Abu Seyal was 'worked extensively' in ancient

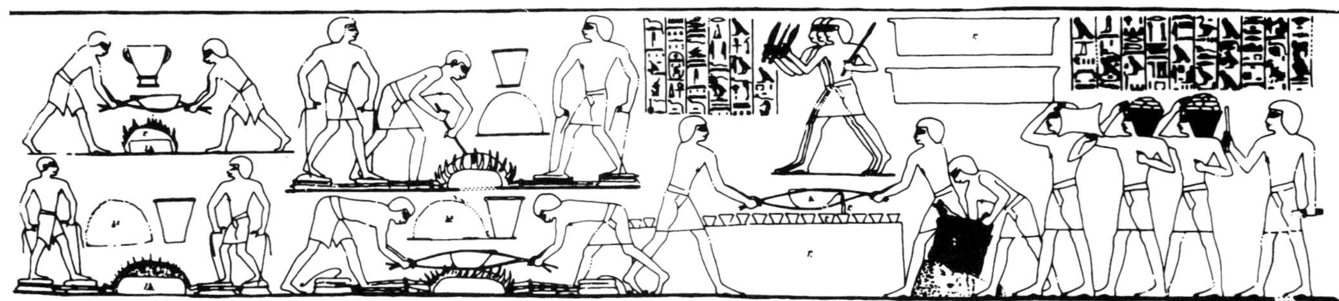

Figure 6.1 Scenes from the Theban tomb of the Eighteenth-Dynasty vizier Rekhmira (TT100), showing metalworking, including the casting of two bronze doors.

times. It has been suggested that at least some of the ore from this area was treated at Quban, where there is abundant slag. A stele from southeast of Aswan refers to the official Hor who had been instructed to collect 'copper from the land of Nubia' during the Twelfth Dynasty (Lucas 1962: 209).

The association of gold and copper ores is not unusual in the Eastern Desert and Nubia. The ore samples found at the Old Kingdom smelting site at Buhen are primarily malachite with a low iron content, but they have been reported to have a remarkably high gold content (el-Gayar and Jones 1989b). The copper derived from these ores is also reported to have included gold particles, but – in view of the ready solubility of gold in copper – these results have been questioned (Craddock and Giumlia-Mair 1993). The Abu Seyal ore, however, appears to be different from that smelted at Buhen and a more southern source for the latter is likely (el-Gayar and Jones 1989a: 31–40).

Literary references to the import of copper into Egypt from the north seem to occur first during the New Kingdom (Lucas 1962: 209), and some of this copper undoubtedly originated in Cyprus. Oxhide ingots – a form characteristic of (but not unique to) Cypriot copper exports – are depicted in the tomb of the Eighteenth-Dynasty vizier Rekhmira at Thebes (TT100). In addition, the famous wreck from Ulu Burun (Turkey) contained copper which is assumed to have been traded from Cyprus to Egypt in the fourteenth century BC (Bass 1986: 269).

Copper and its alloys

Neither native copper nor the copper produced by smelting ores are 100 per cent pure copper. They always contain a variety of other metallic impurities, the nature and amounts of which can reflect the geochemistry of the deposit, the metallurgical processes used in extraction and smelting, and the nature and purity of any intentional alloying metals. The major and minor elemental composition of copper or copper-alloy objects can thus provide potential chronological and geographical information, including evidence for authenticity.

The term 'copper alloy' as used here covers a wide range of alloys in which the predominant metal is copper. In the past the term 'bronze' was often used indiscriminately to cover all copper alloys and even copper alone, but the term 'bronze' is more correctly limited to those alloys which are predominantly copper and tin.

Copper

Some of the earliest examples of copper objects from Egypt – simple, flimsy ornaments and implements from as early as the Badarian period – might possibly have been made from native copper, i.e. copper found in nature in metallic form, not as ores. However the availability of native copper in early Egypt might well have been overstated in the past. For example an Early Dynastic copper chisel found in Nubia has a small silver and gold content which led to its identification as native copper. Lucas, however, felt that it was highly unlikely that such a comparatively large object could be of native copper. He proposed the use of copper ore with a small precious metal association (Lucas 1962: 200–1) – a view now supported by the proved association of copper and gold in some ores as noted above.

The simple 'oxide' copper ore minerals, such as malachite and azurite (both copper carbonates), have bright colours that would attract prospectors and require only fairly elementary smelting procedures. Although even for the simplest ores some pre-treatment, such as hand sorting and crushing 'benefication', would have been important to maximise the yield (Doonan 1994: 84–97). Relatively low temperatures and initially simple crucibles with blowpipes, later small furnaces, would suffice. Experiments have shown that copper can be smelted in clay crucibles with a bank of three or more blowpipes. Up to 90 per cent recovery is possible with simple oxide ores such a malachite and no slag is produced (Craddock 1995: 126–7). The large quantities of crucible fragments, malachite and atacamite and copper prills at Buhen, but no slag, have been taken to indicate crucible smelting of copper here in the Early Dynastic Period (el-Gayar and Jones 1989a, 1989b; Craddock 1995: 130–1).

If we accept that some impurities in the copper, such as arsenic or nickel, are indicative of smelted copper ores, not native copper, the introduction of smelted copper, albeit fairly impure, must have occurred in Egypt by about 4000 BC. In Egypt the low iron levels (average 0.03 per cent) that we see in some of the earlier Predynastic and First Dynasty Egyptian copper alloy objects probably reflect the use of primitive smelting operations using crucible furnaces.

More efficient production, and the ability to exploit more complex and lower grade ores, required higher temperatures and a procedure termed 'fluxing' – the presence or addition of materials to aid the melting and separation of the copper. Iron oxide was the general flux. The smelting of oxide copper ores with iron oxide results in the formation of a mass of mainly iron-minerals, the 'slag', and the reduced copper. This copper is either produced as small prills which are retrieved by crushing the mixed mass of cinders and slag, or, if higher temperatures over longer periods are obtainable, will form a puddle in the base of the furnace which will cool to give a plano-convex or bun ingot. Craddock and Meeks (1987: 187–204) have described the simplest type of early copper-smelting shaft furnace as 'probably the size and shape of a small upturned bucket but lacking its bottom.' We might assume that bag bellows superceded blowpipes for copper-smelting. However, there is little certain evidence for bellows from Egypt until pot bellows appear in the Middle Kingdom (see p. 157). Tylecote calculated that the plano-convex ingots produced at Timna in the more sophisticated shaft furnaces of the New Kingdom weighed between about three or four kilograms a slightly higher estimate than Merkel (1995: 22).

Simple fluxing with slag production was in use at Timna in Sinai by the end of the fourth millennium BC and was soon fairly universal in the Eastern Mediterranean world. Its introduction into Egypt, as evidenced by a sharp rise in iron levels (to an average of about 0.33 per cent) seems to have occurred during the Second Dynasty (Craddock 1985; Craddock and Meeks 1987: 187–204; Cowell 1987; Craddock 1995: 137–40). Recent investigation of slags from Bir Nasib in Sinai show the production of unfluxed copper in Predynastic times and the use of iron ore fluxes by some unspecified time during the Old Kingdom (el-Gayar and Rothenberg 1998; Craddock 1995: 130–1).

The copper produced at the Old Kingdom smelting site at Buhen has an average iron content around 0.5 per cent (el-Gayar and Jones 1989b) and the over-life-size Sixth-Dynasty statue of Pepi I is, according to what is probably the most reliable analysis to date (Desch 1928), almost pure copper with 0.7 per cent iron, enough to indicate a true fluxing process, and 1.1 per cent nickel. Gladstone and Lucas also analysed samples of the Pepi statue and both reported high purity copper and no tin (Lucas 1962: 214).

More efficient copper production was possible when the slag could be run off while molten. 'Tapped-slag' furnaces of this type can probably be dated in the Sinai to the time of the middle to late New Kingdom. It is noteworthy that the average iron levels in Egyptian copper alloy objects drops to around 0.14 per cent by the Late New Kingdom. There are various possible explanations for this. It could reflect the introduction of tapped slag furnaces, the switch to sulphide rather than oxide ores, or, possibly, the employment of manganese rather than iron fluxes utilising the extensive manganese mineral deposits in those areas (Rothenberg 1972: 232; Bachmann 1980: 103–34).

The introduction of more efficient copper-production methods could help explain the exponential increase in cast copper alloy objects during the Third Intermediate Period and Late Period. Sulphide ores were undoubtedly smelted by this time, although the oxide ores, when available, were also still utilised. The smelting of sulphide ores will produce copper with, in theory, lesser amounts of trace elements such as arsenic, antimony and bismuth. For sulphide ores, prior roasting is required and silica, not simply iron oxide, usually has to be present as a flux. The fact that concertina bellows appear to have been introduced in the Near East in the first millennium BC might have aided copper as well as iron production (Craddock 1995: 181–3).

Pure, or near-pure, copper is not easy to cast because it is prone to gas bubbles and tends to shrink, thus producing poor-definition, porous castings. Nevertheless, some surviving Egyptian objects of high purity copper dating right up to the New Kingdom show that the smiths were able to cope with consummate skill.

When first smelted some of the iron from the flux will enter the copper which will thus contain several per cent of iron – as seen in Late Bronze Age copper finds from Timna. Levels of iron up to 1 or 2 per cent are not uncommon in Egyptian copper alloy objects, but higher iron levels – up to 10 per cent or so can enter during smelting – make the copper almost impossible to cast or hammer. The copper has to be refined to remove at least the majority of the iron. It is quite easy to bring the iron contents down to around 0.5 per cent by simply melting the copper and scooping off the oxidised impurities from the surface of the melt. An ingot found in the Wadi Araba, some way from Timna, shows that ingots left the smelting sites in unrefined state.

Copper objects with several per cent iron occur sporadically right through Egyptian history. Examples include a Fifth-Dynasty amulet (Brunton *et al.* 1927: 69) with around 6.5 per cent iron, and a fine, hollow-cast head from a statuette of a Ramesside pharaoh with around 95 per cent copper, 2 per cent lead and 2 per cent iron (Schoske and Wildung 1992: 221–2). We can probably assume such iron contents are fortuitous. A copper cat in Hamburg has been reported to contain almost 12 per cent iron (Riederer 1988: 7). Such an alloy would be extremely difficult to cast and perhaps needs verification – the possibility of contamination of iron from another object or iron wire core supports (see p. 159) should be borne in mind. However, we can note the intentional copper alloys with up to 20 per cent or more iron met with in Iron-Age Italy and elsewhere (Craddock and Meeks 1987: 187–204).

Nickel is a common impurity in ancient copper alloy objects but usually under about 1 per cent. Higher nickel contents are most typically found in zinc-containing copper and thus seldom encountered in Dynastic Egyptian objects. Other trace elements in ancient Egyptian copper and copper alloys include bismuth and cobalt.

Copper–arsenic alloys

Arsenic is present in many ore types and there are at least traces of arsenic in most ancient Egyptian copper and copper alloy objects. Arsenic presence results in the production of wrought copper of far greater hardness – a vital property for implements and weapons – and also greatly facilitates casting by causing the molten metal to flow more easily. The convention is that copper objects with more than about 1 per cent arsenic are regarded as representing the deliberate use of arsenic-rich copper ores or the intentional combining of arsenic and copper ores (Moorey 1994: 242). Almost certainly the higher arsenic levels which appear during the Old Kingdom were not fortuitous (Kaczmarczyk and Hedges 1983: 73). Up to 7 per cent was found in axes in the British Museum (Cowell 1987). Analysis of blue copper-based pigments from more than 110 well-dated Egyptian tombs not only confirms the view that this pigment was made from scrap or by-product copper – as Vitruvius (*De Architectura* VII, Ch. XI, 1; see Morgan 1914) later states – but also provides corroborating chronological information. Arsenic is found first in copper-based pigments in the Fifth Dynasty (el-Goresy *et al.* 1998).

The frequent association of high arsenic with low levels of other impurities is an argument in favour of intentional additions rather than the use of an enriched ore type. We might expect intentional use of arsenic-rich copper ores from an early period followed in time by deliberate additions of arsenic ores to copper or copper ores. However, there is no way to make a definite distinction using current analytical methods.

Analyses have seldom revealed any definite discernible difference between arsenic content and intended use – we would expect low arsenic levels in objects that would benefit from a soft rather than a hard alloy in manufacture. On the other hand, the attractive silver colour of arsenic-rich copper was one motive for its use, regardless of the function or mode of manufacture of the object.

Arsenic is still present in noticeable amounts in a handful of Egyptian copper and copper alloys in the New Kingdom. It is found in copper-based pigments up to the time of Hatshepsut (el-Goresy *et al.* 1998). Arsenic levels in post-New Kingdom copper alloy are typically less than about 1 per cent. When higher levels occur they are presumably, in the main, fortuitous. However, Riederer's analyses (Riederer 1978b, 1981, 1982, 1983, 1984, 1988) show that Late Period cat figurines and cat heads appear to have high arsenic contents more often than might be expected by pure chance. Schorsch (1988) has also referred to a Late Period cat head with a noticeable arsenic content. The two highest arsenic levels recorded by Riederer in post-New Kingdom objects (4.13 per cent and 6.39 per cent) are both in figures of the young god Harpocrates and an intentional colour choice seems possible, given that children were rendered with paler skin than adults in Egyptian art.

It is perhaps relevant that arsenic-based pigment (orpiment – arsenic sulphide) only seems to have come into use in Egypt during the Amarna Period, the very time at which the use of arsenic in copper alloys began to wane. There is no evidence that the ancient Egyptians knew arsenic in metallic form – a state of affairs paralleled in Mesopotamia (Moorey 1994: 240), although supposed examples have been cited from the ancient world.

Antimony is a frequent associate of arsenic and also appears as a trace element in most Egyptian copper alloy objects. Antimony has a similar hardening effect to that of arsenic on copper, but the intentional addition of antimony is unlikely in Egypt until the New Kingdom, after which it might have been used on occasion – perhaps confused with tin. Ancient Egyptian copper or copper alloy objects with over about 1 per cent antimony are unusual, but occasional levels up to almost 4 per cent occur even in the Late Period. Interestingly, Riederer's analyses include only five examples with over 2.5 per cent antimony – two of these are the high-arsenic Harpocrates figures mentioned above.

Copper–tin alloys

When copper is alloyed with tin there is a noticeable increase in the hardness and potential sharpness of copper alloy tools and weapons. The melting temperature drops from 1,083 °C (pure copper) to 1,005 °C for copper with 10 per cent tin. Tin also greatly increases the fluidity of the molten metal, thus facilitating casting. The effects are not dissimilar to those produced by arsenic additions, but are more dramatic and without the very real toxicity hazards. Arsenic additions, intentional or not, permit better casting than pure copper, but the large-scale production of fine-quality castings might have had to await the introduction of copper–tin alloys.

As with arsenic, around 1 per cent tin is usually taken to be the dividing line between accidental and deliberate presence. The deliberate addition of tin (though presumably in the form of an ore, not metallic tin) to copper had occurred in some parts of the Near East by 3000 BC. Tin levels of over 1 per cent have been found in several Early Dynastic objects with the highest reported levels to date being 7 per cent and 9 per cent respectively in a ewer and basin from the tomb of the Second-Dynasty king Khasekhemwy (Cowell 1987; Kaczmarczyk and Hedges 1983: 78). We can also note that Berthelot (1895) found almost 6 per cent tin in a Sixth-Dynasty vessel. Deliberate copper–tin alloys (true 'bronzes') were still the minority in the Middle Kingdom. Examples include the superb Middle Kingdom hollow-cast figure of a man, now in the Louvre (E27153), which contains around 5 per cent tin and about 1 per cent arsenic (Delange 1987). Berthelot noted just over 16 per cent tin in a Twelfth-Dynasty bracelet fragment from the Dahshur treasure (Berthelot 1895).

Copper–tin alloys still had to share the stage with copper and copper–arsenic alloys in the New Kingdom. A Thutmose IV statuette in the British Museum (BM EA64564) is almost pure copper (Craddock 1985), and Lucas remarked that there was still more copper than bronze in the tomb of Tutankhamun (Lucas 1962: 220). We can also note that tin first occurs in copper-based pigments during the reign of Thutmose III (el-Goresy *et al.* 1995: 31). From the Ramesside period onwards, tin is present in the majority of copper alloy objects. Interestingly, the arsenic content of copper alloy objects drops dramatically from the New Kingdom on, and is rare after that time. The way in which tin (and lead – see p. 154) ousts arsenic at this time is matched elsewhere in the Old World and is a strong argument that earlier arsenic additions were intentional. Analyses of Egyptian glazes also show that tin became far more readily available during the New Kingdom. This agrees with the suggestion that the additions to copper alloys were now of metallic tin, not tin ores. This could also explain the appearance of other unusual tin alloys in the New Kingdom (see p. 171 under tin). The source or sources of the tin, however, are still uncertain.

The majority of Egyptian bronzes have up to around 10 per cent tin, as is generally typical in antiquity, but there are occasionally higher levels though very rarely over about 16 per cent. There are some possible chronological variations that deserve further research. For example, there appears to be a dip in average tin content in Third Intermediate Period objects, while Ptolemaic and Roman-period objects more frequently have higher tin levels than hitherto (Kaczmarczyk and Hedges 1983: 90). High tin contents will produce a copper alloy with a silvery colour, indeed a Late Period *menit* in the Fitzwilliam Museum, Cambridge (EGA.54.-1949) is of over 90 per cent copper, while its 'Electrum' inlay is actually composed of a copper–tin alloy with just over 20 per cent tin.

Correlations between object function and composition also deserve further study. It is only to be expected that there should be distinctions between, say, weapons and decorative objects due to working properties of the alloys (i.e. some alloys forming better castings, and some able to be hammered and worked to provide sharper, more durable edges). However, we can also suspect a far wider range of less obvious distinctions, some perhaps based on colour or susceptibility to surface treatments, others due to 'symbolic' reasons. For example, the programme of analyses on tools and weapons in the British Museum revealed that model tools could match the composition of their functional counterparts, although the high purity copper of three models of agricultural tools from Tutankhamun's tomb and of eleven models of tools and weapons from the Fifth Dynasty suggest that this was not always true (Coghlan 1975: 64–7; Maddin *et al.* 1984: 33–41). The potential colour relationships are particularly interesting. For example, among Riederer's recent analysis of some 1,200 Egyptian copper alloy objects, only three statuettes have over 16 per cent tin – all three are figures of the child-god Harpocrates. This suggestion of a link between a pale alloy (see also copper arsenic and antimony alloys p. 152—3) and the rendering of a child-god's skin, raises the question about the factors involved in alloy choice. Sadly, again, far too few excavated copper alloy objects are properly studied, while those currently in collections have often undergone extensive and frequently poorly recorded cleaning and conservation treatments which will have often destroyed much of the evidence for original surface.

In this context we can note recent analyses of New Kingdom stirrup-shaped finger rings, including unpublished analyses by the present writer of examples in the Fitzwilliam Museum, which show that they are typically true bronzes with 8–10 per cent tin (see Giveon 1977: 66–70). It must be assumed that such objects were produced with, or soon obtained in use, polished metal surfaces. The electrum-like colour of the alloy would resemble that of the similarly shaped gold alloy rings. That these rings were intended for use in life is proved by the considerable degree of ancient wear on some examples.

One conundrum is the existence of copper objects containing between 0.1 per cent and 1 per cent tin. Mixed copper–tin ores are rare, and analytical evidence from Timna in Sinai from samples from various stages in the copper recovery process suggest that even such minute amounts might well have been additions. Such low levels would have no noticeable effect on the final hardness or working properties of the metal, but they might have facilitated casting by deoxidising the alloy (Craddock 1980).

Copper alloys with lead

Between 1 and 3 per cent lead in a copper alloy will facilitate casting without detracting from the strength of the alloy. Thus while up to about 2 per cent lead can be fortuitous, lead levels as low as 1 per cent might sometimes be deliberate. This is indicated by an apparent correlation of lead content with copper–tin rather than copper–arsenic alloys prior to the Late New Kingdom (Cowell 1987). Early examples include the Second-Dynasty copper–tin alloy ewer and basin mentioned above which both contain over 1 per cent lead.

Generally speaking, the addition of lead to copper alloys is rare before the Middle Kingdom and lead levels over about 2 per cent are rare prior to the late New Kingdom. The 16 per cent lead recorded long ago by Flight as being present in a Fourth-Dynasty copper alloy statuette is presumably a case of mistaken dating (see Riederer 1982: table 1). However, firstly Phillips did report 8.5 per cent lead in an Eleventh-Dynasty object (see Riederer 1982: table 1), and secondly two Eleventh-Dynasty copper alloy cylinder seals of Mentuhotep, now in the Louvre, have been analysed and shown to have a high lead content (Vandier 1968). It has been stated that an inlaid crocodile statuette in Munich (which originated with the same dealer as the Louvre/Ortiz Middle Kingdom copper alloy statues and is thus assumed to be part of the same Middle Kingdom find) is a leaded alloy (Scheel 1989: 41). However, the contrary view (Delange 1987) has now been shown to be correct (Giumlia-Mair 1996). A leaded alloy figure in the Louvre described as of Second Intermediate Period date (Delange 1987: 176–7) is perhaps, on stylistic criteria, a later archaising work.

The deliberate larger scale addition of lead to copper alloys is generally defined as marking the transition to the Late Bronze Age in archaeological terms. High lead levels – up to 25 per cent or more in some cases – lower the melting point of copper, increase the fluidity of the molten metal and reduce porosity. Around 25 per cent lead can lower the melting temperature of a copper–tin alloy to less than 800 °C. Lead thus facilitated the production of the ubiquitous cast copper alloy objects of the first half of the first millennium BC, but was an unwanted presence in alloys intended for edged tools or weapons.

There are perhaps occasional high-lead objects from the Eighteenth Dynasty, such as a vase with almost 15 per cent lead published by Craddock (1985), assuming that the dating of the object is secure. However, it can generally be assumed that the introduction of lead as a major component of copper took place in the Nineteenth Dynasty. Apparently 25 per cent lead was present in a Nineteenth-Dynasty Osiris figure analysed long ago by Rathgen (see Riederer 1982: table 1) and Craddock (1985) has published a Twentieth-Dynasty *shabti* figure containing about 5 per cent lead. We can note, as a parallel, that the deliberate use of lead compounds in glaze manufacture is a New Kingdom innovation (see Chapter 8, this volume) and, more precisely, lead only became a major component in Egyptian copper-based pigments between the time of Seti II and Tausret in the Nineteenth Dynasty (el-Goresy *et al.* 1998: 31).

In the Third Intermediate Period, copper alloy lead levels are still usually under 5 per cent and the thinner-walled, and more precise hollow castings appear to be tin-bronzes with minimal lead, although copper lead alloys, some with over 20 per cent lead, were becoming more common. However, high lead content is typically a Late Period phenomenon that continued into the Ptolemaic period, when over 20 per cent is not unusual, and over 30 per cent is reported in some instances.

A lead content in copper alloys, even if small, can permit characterisation of the lead isotopes present and thus, potentially, perhaps indicate actual sources of the lead. In recent years there has been much work carried out on lead isotopes in ancient objects in general (see under lead and silver pp. 168, 170), including Egyptian copper alloy objects (Fleming 1982: 65–9), but the validity of the technique is still under review. It should also be noted that lead in a copper alloy can possibly derive from the fluxes used in the smelting process (Rothenberg 1972: 237).

Copper–zinc alloys

Several of the Eastern Desert copper ores contain zinc (sometimes making up a considerable proportion), but these ores would seldom produce an alloy with more than 1 or 2 per cent of zinc. Early use of such mixed ores might explain such objects as a copper pin from a Predynastic grave (no. 218) at Naqada which is stated to contain around 2 per cent zinc and 1 or 2 per cent nickel (Baumgartel 1960: 18).

In Egypt the only pre-Roman use of deliberate copper–zinc alloys – what we term gun metals or brasses – might have been for some late Ptolemaic statuettes and small ornaments. Even some of these, such as some figurines in the so-called 'Alexandrine' idiom, are possibly of early Roman rather than Ptolemaic date. Supposed copper alloy objects or components from Dynastic Egypt with more than 2 or 3 per cent zinc are generally intrusive in the excavation or fake. For an example of the latter see Russmann (1981: 149–56). Here the uraeus was a modern zinc-containing alloy, the statuette itself was a leaded tin-bronze and ancient.

The manufacture of the objects

Copper working 'factories' have now been identified in various parts of Egypt. Here the ingots from the mines, scrap or imported metal were transformed into a plethora of implements, weapons and ornaments for a temple, royal, secular or dead clientele (Scheel 1989).

For example, a major copper-alloy working centre at Qantir, ancient Piramesse, in the Eastern Delta has recently been discovered (Pusch 1990). The excavations have revealed a massive late Eighteenth- to early Nineteenth-Dynasty metal working site covering over 30,000 square metres (see Figs 6.2 and 6.3). Tangible evidence includes crucibles, *tuyères*, moulds, waste, slag and other metal-working tools. This was a centre that included very large-scale copper alloy casting and, perhaps, parallel craft industries. The presence of foreign, including Hittite, armour, weaponry and tools points to foreign craftsmen. The workshop methods revealed can be compared with those depicted in tomb-paintings of the period and with further study of this remarkable site we will undoubtedly gain a far greater understanding of the Egyptian metal-working industry.

There is a wide repertoire of metal-working scenes in tombs (Scheel 1989). For example, the Fifth-Dynasty tomb of Wepemnofret (called Wep) at Giza has scenes showing copper-working (Weinstein 1974: 23–5). These include melting and pouring and, most interestingly, what is probably the earliest reference to annealing with the hieroglyphic caption 'There is no cracking (?) if it is heated excellently'. Annealing is the heating process used to soften, and make more workable, metal that has become hard and brittle due to the build up of stresses during shaping.

Figure 6.2 Scenes from the Theban tomb of Puyemra (TT39), showing metal-working.

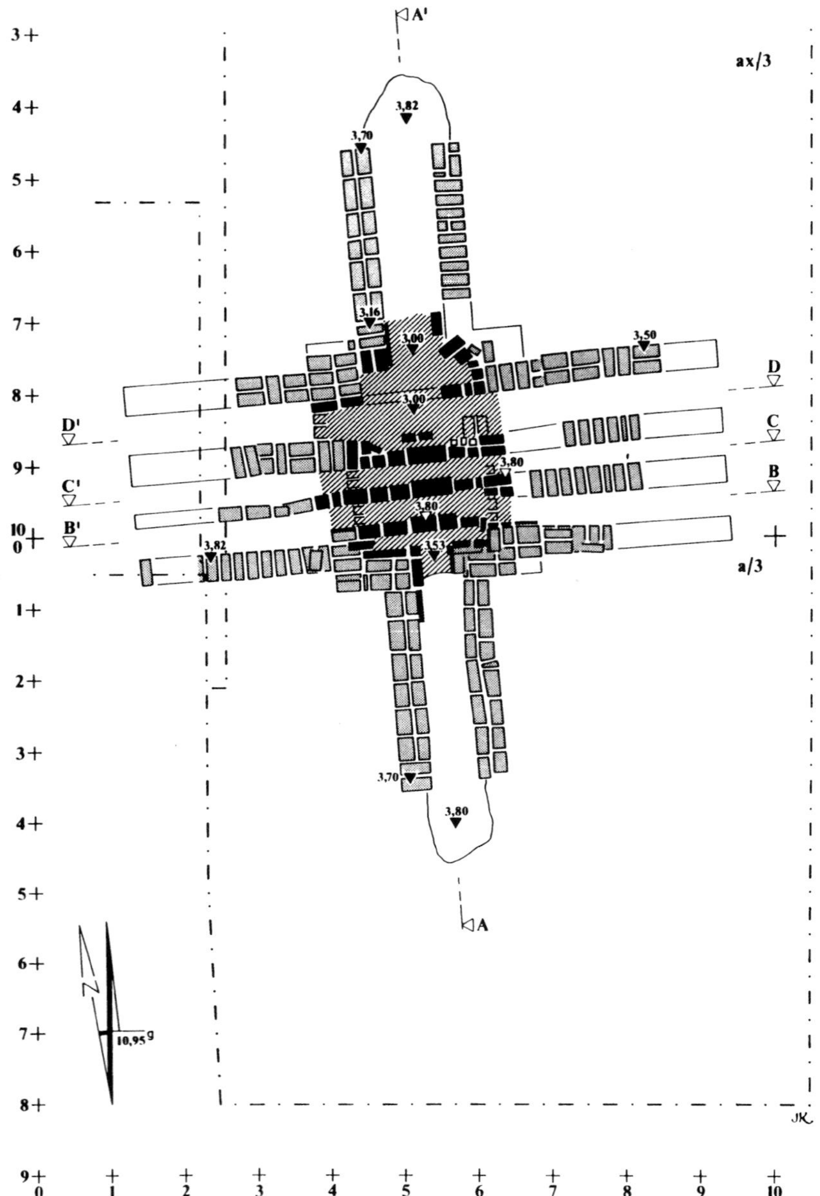

Figure 6.3 Plan of the cross-shaped smelting area at the Delta site of Qantir.

The best-known metal-working scenes are probably those on the wall of Rekhmira's Eighteenth-Dynasty tomb at Thebes (TT100). These show various stages in the large scale production of copper alloy objects – from the arrival of the ingots to the casting of a temple door (Davies 1943; Wainwright 1944: 94–8; see Fig. 6.1).

The ubiquitous copper alloy statuettes representing a near-infinite selection of Egyptian deities are almost invariably from temple not funerary contexts. Enormous quantities of such statuettes have been found: Garland and Bannister (1927: 83), for instance, noted how the draining of the Lake at Karnak 'provided almost a glut of certain varieties', and similar fortuitous finds have sometimes flooded the antiquity market since. A cache of more than 100 copper alloy figurines was excavated at North Saqqara in 1968/9 (Emery 1970). Unfortunately, despite the quantity, quality and almost pristine condition of these pieces (many examples had been wrapped in linen), a proper study of technology, material or surface has never been carried out.

Such caches (paralleled in stone sculpture) do call into question any general policy of recycling 'sacred' copper-alloy objects. This would suggest that temple workshops required a steady source of newly mined raw material. After a review of Egyptian glaze compositions, Kaczmarczyk and

Hedges stated that 'The data . . . lead to one inescapable conclusion: from the sixteenth century BC onwards arsenical copper and tin bronzes were used on a regular basis as a source of copper in the faience industry.' (Kaczmarczyk and Hedges 1983: 90) and 'from the Eighteenth Dynasty on bronze scrap was the primary source of tin in faience' (1983: 239). In consideration of what has just been said, we might suggest that by-products of metallurgy, not recycled objects, might have provided much of the raw material for glaze, glass and pigment manufacture. If so, a close association of metal-working and faience/glass (and perhaps pigment) production must be assumed.

The simplest manufacturing process would be to hammer out small ingots, prills or even bits of native copper into sheets which could then be bent and cut into the required form. The skills needed to raise complex three-dimensional vessels from sheet and to join separate components by rivets and other mechanical methods had been acquired by the First Dynasty. Fine examples include a First-Dynasty find made at north Saqqara some sixty years ago (Emery 1939). Such techniques were usual for metal vessels throughout Dynastic times in Egypt. Vessels were seldom cast, the only common exception being the ubiquitous Late Period situlae with their relief decoration. If the monumental copper figure of Pepi I is of hammered, not cast components, (see p. 158) it would represent the pinnacle of surviving Old Kingdom sheet metal-work.

With the exception of most vessels and containers, and some simple implements, Egyptian copper alloy objects were generally cast to virtually their final form, whereafter only cleaning, and perhaps the addition of details, was needed. Cast weapons and tools however, did require serious mechanical working to harden and toughen the edges enough to be serviceable.

Some sheet-like objects, such as *menits* and mirrors, might have been largely formed by hammering, but the finer, more plastically modelled, openwork *menits* and the comparably worked vase-stands of the Eighteenth Dynasty were probably cast and might indicate the introduction of new casting technology.

The ability to generate the heat to smelt copper meant that the heat necessary to melt and thus cast copper was equally achievable. The main problem lay in generating the concerted heat need to melt and cast reasonable quantities of metal. Blowpipes, sometimes in banks, were used to maximise the heat for melting copper and other metals in the earliest times – they are represented at least as early as the Fifth Dynasty (Lucas 1962: 213, Scheel 1989). Pot bellows, in which a leather top on the flared opening of a pottery nozzle is pumped up and down by hand or foot to force a jet of air out of the narrow end, appear to occur first in the Middle Kingdom (Nibbi 1987; Davey 1979; Tylecote 1981b). However, there is no representational evidence for such bellows prior to the Eighteenth Dynasty. It might be doubted whether larger masses of metal, such as that needed in the initial stages of the manufacture of the Pepi I statue, could be obtained with simple blowpipe technology. However, it has recently been demonstrated that crucible smelting of copper, and thus melting of copper, is quite feasible with a bank of three to six blowpipes (Craddock 1995: 127). There is no evidence that large-scale casting was carried out away from the Nile in the mountainous mining regions where the prevailing winds could have been harnessed.

The simplest form of casting is to pour the molten metal into open moulds carved in stone, shaped in pottery or even formed in sand. More complex, three-dimensional forms required moulds made up of two, three or more sections that could be dismantled to remove the casting. However, at least some of the surviving moulds in terracotta and stone were probably used to make the 'wax' models for use in the lost-wax casting process, not to directly cast the final object.

Objects, such as ingots, flat axes and chisels were being cast by early Predynastic times. Lucas described the earliest Egyptian casting known to him as an axe-head of middle Predynastic date found by Brunton at Matmar which, according to the report by Carpenter, was cast and then hand-worked – either hot-worked or cold-worked plus annealing (Carpenter 1932: 625–6; Lucas 1962: 213). The composition of the axe head was almost pure copper with just minor impurities including 1.28 per cent nickel and 0.15 per cent iron.

In the process of lost wax casting a model of the desired object is modelled or moulded in wax or some other material which is easy to model and has a low melting temperature. The use of beeswax *per se* should not be assumed. In more recent times, a resin/oil mixture or wax/resin has generally been employed and even lead has been used at some periods. Beeswax alone is often too soft particularly for complex or thin articles in warmer climates and today metal-casters can have separate recipes for summer and winter 'waxes'.

The wax model is coated with the 'investment' material, usually clay with an organic binder like dung or chaff, and a hole pierced down from the outer surface to the model. When the clay is fired the wax burns or flows out and molten metal can be poured in. Once cooled and solidified, the mould is broken to extract the casting. The object then typically requires the removal of any surface protrusions or flaws (not the least being the sprue – the attached metal that has solidified in the funnel-shaped pouring hole). The piece is generally given final surface details and polished. A copper alloy statuette of Harpocrates still in its investment has been published (Williams 1919: 3–7).

In practice, certain refinements to the process were required. Air escape holes through the investment would facilitate the complete filling of the mould by metal, as would links between parts of a complex shape. Garland, for example illustrates the 'runners' linking the legs of an unfinished solid cast ibis (Garland and Bannister 1927: 45).

Hollow castings are made by modelling the 'wax' around a central core. Hollow casting would not only save metal but, as Becker *et al.* (1994) have recently pointed out, it would also result in less potential shrinkage and thus less distortion in the mould. The interior core was perhaps most usually made from the same sandy clay/organic material as the investment. Such cores turn black on casting when the organic matter plus any absorbed waxes or resins burn. Blackened cores of this type are typical of Egyptian and other ancient hollow-cast copper alloy objects. There is potential for the dating of such cores by thermoluminescence techniques (Riederer 1978a). Other core materials include gypsum, (presumably plaster suggesting that such a material might also have been used for some investments), calcium carbonate in some form or other (conceivably carved limestone, see Riederer 1982: 30) and even wood (Schorsch 1988). Some cores inside animal figurines were intended to be removed after casting, in order to permit the insertion of a mummified animal (Jett *et al.* 1985).

Lost-wax casting was used for copper objects by the Old Kingdom. The use of casting for large-scale objects, such as the monumental statues of Pepi I and his son, remains unproven. Garland and Bannister (1927) suggested that the fine shaping and detail of Pepi (evident in the best photographs), together with the thickness of the metal, would make hammering a most unlikely option. Assembly of several separate castings would be the only option here, if indeed casting was used. Garland and Bannister did note the visible rivets as evidence for assembly from cast sections, but presumably hammered components would also require rivets.

Early lost-wax castings include the separately made and inserted spouts in some Old Kingdom ewers which date back at least as far as the Fourth Dynasty (Garland and Bannister 1927: 35; Lucas 1962: 215; Schorsch 1992). These, of course, are hollow and thus represent the initial stages towards the production of true hollow-cast objects (Nofal and Waly 1998).

Exceptionally fine figural hollow castings in copper-tin alloys had appeared by the Middle Kingdom – as witness the magnificent Fayum find which included the Louvre statuette mentioned above (p. 153) (Delange 1987: 211–13) and the statuettes now in the Ortiz collection (Ortiz 1994: cat. nos. 33–7). These magnificent hollow-cast statuettes show the ingenious multi-part assembly methods used even as early as the Middle Kingdom. The Louvre standing male figure has slotted-in arms and inserted lower legs and the large Ortiz figure of Amenemhat III (Ortiz 1994: cat. no. 36) has both a separate wig and arms held in place by vertical slotted grooves. This use of fine, thin-walled, hollow casting and mechanically inter-located sections shows a level of fine bronze-working skills hitherto not expected prior to the Ramesside or Third Intermediate Period. Here, as with many of the finer castings, it is difficult to gauge the extent of hand-working. The large female consort from the same group, and also in the Ortiz collection (Ortiz 1994: cat. no. 35), is just as finely hollow-cast with a core still in place (the walls of the arms being only around four millimetres thick).

Most copper alloy statuettes of the Second Intermediate Period and the early New Kingdom appear to be solid cast. Datable examples include one of the Second Intermediate Period, now in Brooklyn, depicting a squatting, nursing mother, her *uraeus* and the inscription identifying the group as a royal princess and her son. This is a consummate one-piece, solid casting, perhaps a copper-tin alloy, with plenty of negative space and with post-casting hand worked detail and inscription (Brooklyn 43.137).

The dearth of early and mid-New Kingdom copper alloy figures, either solid or hollow cast, is quite remarkable (Vassilika 1997). It is noteworthy that the majority of the surviving examples are royal – although, of course, these are the most dateable category and other non-royal examples might well reside in collections with later ascribed dates. The examples include a fine, solid-cast kneeling figure of Thutmose III in black bronze (see p. 160) with gold inlays, which has recently been acquired by the Metropolitan Museum of Art, New York (1995.21; see Hill 1995) and the British Museum statuette of Thutmose IV (BM EA64564) which also appears to be solid-cast. As with the New York piece, the arms are separate and located over square dowels projecting horizontally from the shoulders. There is also careful post-casting hand work.

Fine hollow castings, on the basis of the scanty evidence, appeared again at the end of the Eighteenth Dynasty as witnessed by a black bronze kneeling figure of Tutankhamun now in the museum of the University of Pennsylvania, Philadelphia (Fishman and Fleming 1980). In the Ramesside period, copper alloy sculpture began to become slightly more common. Three fine examples can be seen in the Metropolitan Museum of Art, New York. One is, again, a kneeling figure, perhaps solid-cast, this time of a man wearing characteristic Nineteenth-Dynasty garb (Hayes 1959: 382). The others are a standing figure of a shaven-headed priest and a late New Kingdom, hollow-cast small head with inlaid eyes (Hayes 1959: 381–3) A fragmentary, rather thick-walled, hollow-cast figure illustrated by Garland bears the cartouche of Rameses IV (Garland and Bannister 1927: 47–8).

As noted, complex objects were typically made up from separate components – sometimes part cast, part wrought – and generally joined by mechanical methods. Of these mechanical techniques, the simplest example are rivets as typically used for such purposes as attaching vessel and mirror handles.

The most common ancient joins on figurines are those connecting the arms to the trunk and, as might be expected, the types of join employed tend to mirror those found in woodwork (see Chapter 15, this volume). The simplest are just pegs or dowels, but there are also many variations on the tenon and mortise joint, often with wedge-shaped slots. Just when wedge-shaped rather than straight pegs or tenons were developed remains uncertain. A fine Middle Kingdom male figure in the Louvre has straight tenon shoulder joints (Delange 1987: 211–13), as have the Ortiz kneeling figures of Amenemhat III and his consort (Ortiz 1994: cat. nos. 35 and 37). Once assembled, joint lines could be disguised by hammering or burnishing or concealed by chased details such as arm bands and shoulder straps.

In the Late Period, one-piece castings were more often used, again. In part this was a result of the typically simpler, often cruder, forms, but it was also true that the fluidity of the now popular heavily leaded alloys permitted more complex shapes to be cast in one. When separate components were required – these were most often arms – one or both being made separately and added, depending on size and pose. An over-life-size head of a pharaoh now in Hildesheim was formerly identified as a Ramesside ruler but is in reality almost certainly a Twenty-ninth- or Thirtieth-Dynasty piece and a rare example of near-monumental hollow casting (Eggebrecht 1993: 90–1).

Soldering or braising was very seldom used on copper alloy objects in Egypt during Dynastic times and perhaps never for attaching the various components of statuettes. The use of a silver solder for copper has been reported for joining sheet copper as early as the Fourth Dynasty, when this technique was used for the copper sockets of Hetepheres' canopy supports (Lucas 1962: 216). The seam of a copper (or bronze) trumpet from the tomb of Tutankhamun is similarly assembled (Lucas 1962: 216) and the technique is sporadically reported for other times and places in the ancient world (Ogden 1983a: 67). Both silver and lead were used to plug working defects in an Eighteenth-Dynasty cow vessel – a category of object that represents the rare use of casting for New Kingdom figural objects (Winlock 1936: 147–56). The presence of solder on Egyptian copper-alloy statuettes is usually indicative of recent repair or forgery. Casting-on was sometimes used (see below) and the recent report of the feet of a Third Intermediate Period female statuette being 'welded' on might, rather, be an example of this (Raven 1992).

Roeder noted that the wax models used to cast the ubiquitous Egyptian copper alloy statuettes, both solid and hollow, could be made up from separately formed wax components – torsos, limbs, heads and so on. This would be the natural approach when the figures were being entirely hand-modelled – only the simplest forms could be created from a single initial block of wax. The improvements in precision and the possibilities of mass production permitted by moulding or casting the wax components would be a natural next step and the use of plaster moulds to produce a series of identical components (or occasionally complete figures) is probable. Recent study of copper alloy figurines in Leiden appears to confirm the use of pre-moulded wax parts in just this way (Raven 1992).

The Leiden project has also identified another casting process which is well-substantiated in antiquity in general but seldom reported from Egypt (Garland and Bannister 1927: 69; Raven 1992). This is 'casting on', a process by which a deficient or missing area of a cast is moulded in wax onto the existing metal object and then the whole area coated with the investment and new metal cast in. The apparent presence of the technique on several objects in the Leiden collection suggests that the procedure might have been relatively common. Another Egyptian example is the cast-on base (to a raised vessel) recently described by Schorsch (1992: 145–59). Care must be taken in identification. It can be difficult to differentiate between casting-on and areas where two wax components of the original casting antetype were joined, perhaps with crudely added or smeared-over wax. Metallographic study of a section taken from the area is the best guide, but for obvious reasons seldom resorted to.

Support for the cores during the production of hollow castings also needed consideration. Supports were not required when hollow castings had openings (e.g. on the underside of the bodies or at joins in multi-part objects), because the core would have been in direct contact with, and thus held in place by, the surrounding investment.

Holes cut in the wax would create contact points between core and investment and provide the necessary support. This might explain the mysterious so-called 'dowel holes' both in the Philadelphia figure of Tutankhamun mentioned above (p. 158) (Fishman and Fleming 1980) and in a figure of Min-Amun in the Fitzwilliam Museum, (E49b, 1954 Vassilika 1997), and although this cannot be proved in Egypt, such a technique was later used by Greek metal-casters (Haynes 1992: 70–1). The holes left in the final casting could be plugged or concealed under gesso and gilding.

Late Period copper alloy castings sometimes retain traces of iron wires 'chaplets' used to hold the cores in place (Garland and Bannister 1927: 39–41; Schorsch 1988). Schorsch (1988) has recently pointed out that fakes of Egyptian bronzes often have far more core supports than their ancient counterparts. The recent study of a fine large Third Intermediate Period hollow-cast female figurine in Leiden revealed, rather surprisingly, an internal iron rod support which passed through the trunk and divided down each leg to the heel (Raven 1992). The use of iron wire supports in New Kingdom copper alloy objects is unlikely, but we can note that Renaissance practice as well as recent forgeries of Egyptian copper alloy statuettes demonstrate that relatively pure copper struts can be employed to hold cores in place in leaded copper alloys.

Care had to be taken in all stages of casting and finishing. The fine, thin-walled hollow castings of the Third Intermediate Period and, less so, of the Late Period, were prone to core expansion and cracking at the time of manufacture if the core retained any moisture. As Garland noted, this means that not all cracks and distortion in such objects can be attributed to post-burial corrosion (Garland and Bannister 1927: 43). Hand-finishing of solid castings was quite practical if required. However, the fine, hollow-walled ones, perhaps most typically of Third Intermediate Period date, would be prone to damage by any serious mechanical working and there would have been sense in including as much of the fine detail as possible on the original wax model. The chased detailing of copper objects and the accurate cutting or sharpening up of inlay recesses would be an obvious use of iron tools, but the fine Middle Kingdom copper alloy statuettes show that iron tools were not mandatory.

The quality of workmanship of the Third Intermediate Period figures is, on average, far better than those of the Late Period when, we must assume, the rapid expansion of the industry led to much mass production of poor-quality goods being produced for temple offerings. What this says about changes in Egyptian religious practice at a time of foreign rule is outside the scope of this chapter.

Decorative inlays and overlays on copper alloy objects

The overlaying of all or part of a copper alloy object with gold, electrum or silver sheet is well-known from ancient Egypt. In the simplest technique the precious metal sheet is pressed and shaped over the object and held in place by adhesive, mechanical folds or overlaps. The commonest technique, probably from the late New Kingdom onwards, was to gild with extremely thin gold leaf laid over a thin layer of gesso. To facilitate the adhesion of the gesso to the copper alloy, the object was sometimes roughened by stippling or chiselling (Garland and Bannister 1927: 191; Oddy *et al.* 1988) or by glueing linen to the metal and then applying the gesso over this.

The gold leaf can be extremely thin – down to under 0.005 millimetres (Lucas 1962: 231). The present writer has seen cases where the gold leaf is thin enough to appear greenish by transmitted light. The nature of the adhesives used have not been ascertained but were presumably ordinary animal glues or albumen (see Chapter 19, this volume). In one unpublished Late Period example examined by the writer, minute particles of bird's feather were identified in the glue holding gold leaf to a lead substrate. This might represent the use of feather brushes – a suitable application implement as attested in medieval literature.

It has often been assumed that the even, black colour now seen on some Egyptian copper alloy objects, in particular inlaid examples, was deliberate (Ogden 1983a: caption to fig. 4.1; Craddock and Giumlia-Mair 1993). Recent research has shown that the effect, which is essentially the same as the more recent *shakudo* work from Japan, is due to the addition of a few per cent gold, often containing a little silver, to the alloy. After stringent cleaning and polishing, probably with a vegetable extract or juice as *per* the Japanese technique, the object is treated with an acid solution made from such ingredients as copper sulphate, alum and nitre. This results in a fine, compact and durable bluey-black copper oxide layer. This surface coloration makes an ideal background for inlay work in gold, silver (or electrum) and even copper, and, indeed, this is its most usual function.

The use of this technique in the ancient Old World was first noted on Roman objects. However, observation and analysis soon established its use on earlier Classical pieces – such as for the black inlaid strips decorating the finest Mycenaean dagger blades (Ogden 1993) – and then on Egyptian objects from the Middle Kingdom through to the Late Period (Ogden 1993; Craddock and Giumlia-Mair 1993; Craddock 1994; 1995b; Giumlia-Mair 1996). Middle Kingdom examples of 'black bronze' include the kneeling figure of Amenemhat III in the Ortiz collection (Ogden 1994; Giumlia-Mair 1996), a crocodile from the same group now in Munich (Giumlia-Mair 1996), and also a scimitar blade in Munich (Giumlia-Mair 1996). This latter has a copper alloy blade with a narrow band of black down each side inlaid with inscriptions and designs in gold wire – thus relating it closely to the well-known Mycenaean blades. In the New Kingdom we have the kneeling figures of Thutmose III and Tutankhamum noted above (p. 158). Once into the Third Intermediate Period and Late Period, examples became more plentiful.

Black bronzes tend to have up to about 5 per cent gold and, typically low lead levels, even in the Late Period. Black bronze has been equated with the *ḥsmn-km* (black copper) referred to in Egyptian inscriptions from the early Eighteenth Dynasty onwards (Giumlia-Mair 1996; Craddock 1998). The recent research on what are probably surviving examples of *hsmn-km* vindicates the view of Garland and Bannister three-quarters of a century ago. They noted that the supposed blue colour of some ancient bronzes 'must necessarily have been in great measure due to the composition of the bronze itself, not improbably containing gold' (Garland and Bannister 1927: 82).

Black bronzes are probably just one example of an ancient tradition of deliberately colouring or altering the surface of ancient metals. For example, the New Kingdom cow vessel in the Metropolitan Museum of Art, New York, mentioned above, has a surface which suggests deliberate chemical etching of some type prior to the attachment of the cow figure (Winlock 1936).

As noted below (p. 164), pigment has been observed on some gold and probably silver objects from Egypt and, as seen with copper–tin and copper–arsenic alloys (p. 152–3), some link between alloy and intended colour sometimes seems inescapable. However, the idea that the blackish inlay on the cheek of a Horus falcon deity in the British Museum might be due to deliberate treatment with an arsenic compound (Shearman 1988) has now been rejected (see Craddock and Giumlia-Mair 1993).

A Late Period cast copper alloy situla in the Metropolitan has an unusual surface layer of a high lead copper alloy. This appears to have been applied by dipping the situla into

composite sheet from which objects could be formed (Ogden 1983a: 80–1). This technique was employed for some of the hollow annular 'hair-rings' of the New Kingdom. In one case examined by the writer, the surface layer was electrum with only a marginally higher gold level than the electrum underlying it. It seems economic nonsense to go to so much trouble to plate electrum with electrum, but an explanation might be that the surface layer was just sufficiently higher in gold to permit surface enriching (i.e. to be given a purer gold surface by chemical leaching). This technique, using various mixtures of alum, urine and other substances, has been employed until recent times. The generally accepted rule of thumb is that gold alloys with under about 55 per cent gold cannot be surface 'coloured' in this way.

The plating of silver by dipping into molten electrum, followed by chasing, was possibly used for some small amulet-like statuettes. Oddy *et al.* (1978) described a figure of the god Khons treated in this way, and the same technique appears to have been used on a similar figurine recently examined by the present writer. The use of dip-plating to provide a silver-like lead–copper alloy surface to a copper alloy situla was mentioned above (p. 160). This technique might be most typical of the Late Period, but so far few examples have been discussed.

Gold-working

The methods employed by the ancient Egyptian goldsmiths have been covered in some detail elsewhere (Aldred 1971; Ogden 1983a, 1992a), although there is still a need for a far more comprehensive study. As with copper alloys, all but the most primitive of gold objects would have passed through at least one melting state during their production history. Gold grains, dust or nuggets would be cast together into bars or rings for ease of transport and recording, and every time that gold was alloyed it would be melted with other metals. Early representations, such as that in the tomb of Mereruka at Saqqara (*c.* 2300 BC) show whole banks of workmen with blowpipes melting gold.

Nevertheless, the gold-working tradition of Egypt and the Near East was predominantly one of sheet gold, not casting. Objects were made by hammering out the gold – whether supplied as ingots, fused scrap or, later, coins – into thin sheet, which was then cut and shaped to form the individual components of the jewellery. Even components such as wires and small gold spheres were formed from sheet, the former by various cutting, hammering or twisting operations, the latter by melting small snips of sheet or wire so that surface tension would roll them up into small balls. Even the more massive, solid objects, including some fine, gold amulets were generally made by hand-working gold, not casting.

When casting was employed for gold, it was often in conjunction with hand-wrought work. For example, a gold deity figure might be cast by the lost wax process, but it might also have other components such as a rectangular sheet-gold base, attributes, hammered suspension loop and so on soldered in place. The problem was that casting was potentially wasteful of metal. There was no way to produce a mould or a wax antetype which would employ a pre-determined volume or weight of metal and every cast would have casting fins, sprues and so on which would have to be cut off.

Solid-cast gold objects, like their copper–alloy counterparts, could be made up from several separately cast components. For example the fine Twenty-second-Dynasty gold figure of Amun in the Metropolitan Museum of Art, New York (MMA 26.7.1412) was cast, with fine surface working, but the arms appear to have been made separately (by casting?) and soldered in place. The headdress plumes and base plate are of sheet-gold soldered in place.

In general the use of soldering was common for gold objects, and mechanical joints were more rare, which is exactly the opposite to the situation with copper alloy objects. In general the solders used on gold appear to have been made by adding extra silver, copper or both to some of the gold being worked. For example, one Late Period piece (private collection) was of 92 per cent gold with 7 per cent silver and 1 per cent copper, while the solder used to assemble it was 55 per cent gold, 18 per cent silver and 27 per cent copper.

For finer joints, a soldering process which in essence produced solder within the joint area by reducing a copper compound to copper (colloidal hard soldering or diffusion bonding) was probably used from an early period. A mixture of glue and ground malachite (copper carbonate) as used as a pigment, or verdigris, would have sufficed. The glue held the gold components together until the application of heat burnt the glue to carbon. In the presence of carbon the copper compound was reduced to pure copper which then alloyed with, and diffused into, the adjoining gold, thereby fusing the parts together. This type of technique was probably used for much of the granulation work in ancient times, that is the application of fine lines or patterns in minute gold spheres on a sheet-gold background. However, recent study of an example of Middle Kingdom granulation (Ogden 1992b: 52 UC6482), revealed the apparent use of a silver-based solder alloy, the mode of employment of which is not yet understood.

Granulation first appeared in Egypt during the Middle Kingdom and, particularly in view of some of the earliest examples, was almost certainly an imported idea. It reappeared in the middle to late New Kingdom and was used for some Ramesside jewellery. It is all but unknown among the Third Intermediate Period gold-work from Tanis. Granulation work never seems to have been accepted for use in the more traditional, 'iconographic' Egyptian jewellery forms and was perhaps always at least partly seen as a 'foreign' technique.

In the archetypal, traditional jewellery from Egypt, the forms were high symmetrical, laden with subtle and not-so-subtle imagery and meaning, and inlays of coloured stones were employed more as blocks of pigment than as gems. This means that stones or coloured glass were cut to fit the settings, while the settings were seldom made to employ particularly choice stones. One interesting exception to this rule is a spectacular Twentieth-Dynasty gold bracelet set with a large, irregular piece (perhaps a polished nugget) of turquoise, now in Hildesheim (Pelizaeus Museum, on loan from the Niedersächsische Sparkassenstiftung; Eggebrecht 1996: 76, fig.71).

Even pigment was sometimes applied to gold. In one case examined by the writer, a gold and silver Isis crown from a Third Intermediate or Late Period figure had part of the gold background painted red by the application of red iron oxide pigment over a very thin gesso layer (unpublished, private collection). The use of the red mercury pigment cinnabar has recently been reported on gold-work from the classical world (Williams and Ogden 1994) and in Iberio-Phoenician goldwork of about the fifth century BC (unpublished, private collection).

Enamel is glass which is ground up finely, placed in a hollow, cavity or 'cell' in the metal-work and then heated until it melts and fuses in place. Since the Egyptians were conversant with glass manufacture at least from the early New Kingdom onwards (see Chapter 8, this volume), we might well expect enamel to have been employed in Egyptian gold-work. Use of enamel in various ancient Egyptian objects has been proposed and rejected during the twentieth century (Lucas 1962: 116–17; Aldred 1971: 221 and description to plate 103; Teeter 1981: 319). The only Egyptian gold objects of Dynastic date that are known to the writer and believed likely to be decorated with true enamel are two objects found in the Third Intermediate Period tomb of Wendjebaendjed at Tanis (Ogden 1990/1). The first object is the gold bowl (Montet 1951: 83 and pl. 54; Yoyotte 1987: no. 79). Here the decoration in the centre is an inset rosette motif in the form of a complex rosette (a detail of this is shown in his figure 2). The identification is supported by the similarity in terms of both design and colour palette (white, green and a purplish colour) of a group of six enamelled gold rings found in a Mycenaean tomb at Kouklia (Maryon 1971: 170–1). The other object is one of the pectorals (Montet 1951: 77 and pl. 50; Yoyotte 1987: no. 75). The predominant use of bluish-green in this pectoral is contrary to Egyptian custom, but not surprising with enamel, where red was problematic to produce. Examination of the pectoral strongly suggest that the inlay material is fused in place, certainly it follows very precisely the contours of the cells (particularly the irregularities of the corners), and in places it seems to overlap with the cells.

Even if these two objects are enamelled – and the now-empty wire-bordered tail feathers of Rameses' famous duck bracelets (Cairo CG52575/6) are other possible candidates – enamelling was certainly the exception rather than the rule in ancient Egypt, other than in Meroitic (Ogden 1989) and Ptolemaic contexts. Over the years, various reasons have been put forward (e.g. the absence of lead in Egyptian glass, see Dillon 1907), but a simple explanation might be the close melting ranges of the ancient glasses and the ancient gold alloys used in Egypt. The types of glass used in ancient Egypt had melting temperatures that generally ranged between about 800 and 950 °C, and in practice a temperature around 900–1,000 °C would be necessary for fusing a good enamel. The majority of the gold alloys used by the ancient Egyptians would begin to melt between about 900 and 1,050 °C and some of the solders used would start to melt at well under 900 °C. In practice, Egyptian gold jewellery objects could not be enamelled without the very real risk – in many cases the likelihood – that the gold components would start to distort and even begin to come apart.

The enamelling of copper alloys is also encountered from the Third Intermediate Period onwards, but there has been no systematic study to date.

Iron

There are abundant supplies of iron ore in various parts of Egypt and in the Sinai peninsula (Lucas 1962: 235–6; el-Hinnawi 1965: 1497–509). Iron ores (including magnetite and haematite as well as accessory minerals such as red jasper) are found at Wadi el-Dabba in the Eastern Desert (Akaad and Dardir 1978). Bahariya Oasis in the Western Desert, almost on a latitude with el-Minya, is an important iron-ore source today, supplying haematite, limonite and goethite. El-Baz (1984) provides a good recent bibliography for the iron ores of this region as well as of others such as the iron ores in Aswan sandstone. However, these ore deposits were seemingly seldom if ever exploited in Dynastic times for anything other than pigments (see Chapter 4, this volume) and, we must assume, fluxing agents for copper smelting.

Garland and Bannister refer to old workings at Wadi Abu Gerida in the north Eastern Desert, but these are probably of Roman date (Garland and Bannister 1927: 85). Petrie identified two metal-working sites, possibly for iron smelting, in the Delta – at Naukratis and Tell Defena (Daphnae). He refers to 'the large quantity of iron slag found at Naukratis and occasion [sic] pieces of specular iron ore', dating to the sixth century BC, (Petrie 1886: 39), and he also mentions an 'astonishing' amount of slag – plus a crucible base with slag and charcoal intact – from Defena (Petrie 1888: 79). It is important to remember, however, that copper smelting can also produce a copious amount of iron slag.

Ancient iron can derive from fortuitous examples of meteoric iron (some of which weigh in excess of 30 tonnes), from native iron (telluric iron), or from smelted iron ores. The occasional use of meteoric iron is probably common to most early societies but meteoric iron did not provide a reliable and constant source of supply to early Egypt.

The identification of meteoric iron artefacts in Egypt is

not straightforward. The usually quoted distinction between meteoric and smelted iron is a relatively high nickel content in the former. However, nickel-containing iron can derive from some smelted ores and long buried meteoric iron artefacts can have much, if not most, of the nickel leached from them. Hence Craddock has recently said that

> Some of the well-known small pieces of predynastic and early dynastic corroded iron from Egypt are totally devoid of nickel, but are almost certainly meteoric in origin despite Lucas's statement to the contrary. (Craddock 1995a: 104 and 256; *contra* Lucas 1962: 237–8).

Other examples, such as Predynastic sheet-iron beads (Lucas 1962: 237), are reported to contain 7.3 per cent nickel.

Telluric iron is very rare world-wide and, according to a recent survey by Craddock (1995a), only an occurrence on an island off Greenland was definitely exploited in the past. We must thus assume some confusion of terms in Scheel's suggestion that telluric iron was imported into Egypt from the Peloponnese and from the Near East and that tools of telluric iron appeared during the Saite period (Scheel 1989: 17).

The availability of iron on anything but a fortuitous or sporadic scale had to await the development of iron smelting. The relatively late adoption of this technology owes more to the complexities of the processes than to a lack of supplies, since iron ores are actually abundant world-wide. Iron production requires temperatures of around 1,100–1,150 °C, about the same as for copper smelting.

The initial result of smelting iron ores is a mixed mass of iron, slag and other materials. This has to undergo repeated heating and hammering before relatively high purity and usable *wrought iron* was left. Such iron could be easily hammered into shape (with repeated annealing to keep it workable) and joined by hammer-welding at temperatures around 1,100 °C. Wrought iron of this type could be made into serviceable tools and weapons but had little if any advantage in terms of hardness or ability to take a good edge over copper alloys. About its only noticeable benefit was its tendency to bend not break.

The scattered, supposedly early, ancient Egyptian examples of iron artefacts were possibly metallurgical curiosities as much as evidence of general cultural attainment although they have attracted considerable interest over the last century. Amongst the earliest examples are simple beads made of hammered and bent sheet of Predynastic date found at Girza and examined by Gowland and Desch (see Lucas 1962: 237). The most celebrated instance is the supposed iron sheet found in 1837 near an air passage in the Fourth-Dynasty Great Pyramid at Giza, deep within the masonry and revealed after blasting. The age of this piece has been the subject of much discussion – Lucas, for example, changed his mind about its origin, finally coming down on the side of a non-ancient origin (Lucas 1962: 237).

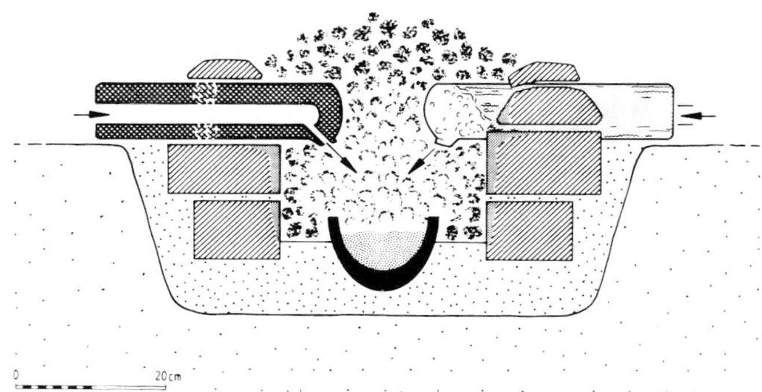

Figure 6.5 Reconstruction of the smelting process used by Ramesside metal-workers at the Delta site of Qantir; the arrows indicate the direction of air forced through the tuyères, while the black semi-circle represents the crucible.

A few years ago this piece was examined metallurgically and an early date again championed (el-Gayar *et al.* 1989c: 75–83). At the same time, Craddock and Lang expressed some doubts and recently published a full reassessment which concluded that the structure and composition of the iron 'strongly suggested that the plate of iron from the Great Pyramid is of no great antiquity' (Craddock and Lang 1989; 1993).

Few would agree with the opinion expressed by Garland and Bannister (1927: 104) that 'iron chisels were in use by the Fourth Dynasty', but it seems likely that a handful of iron objects might have existed from the Old Kingdom onwards. Of the various cited ancient examples, it is difficult to confirm chronology or provenance in most cases. Since small pieces of iron could be by-products of copper smelting using an iron oxide flux, the occasional presence of iron from the early Old Kingdom onwards is only to be expected. Generally speaking, there was some sporadic smelting of iron ores, and production of wrought iron, in the ancient Near East as far back as the third millennium BC, perhaps centred on Eastern Anatolia.

The impetus for iron production might well have derived from copper smelting. It is noted above that iron minerals were added to copper ores as fluxes to aid the smelting process. These could result in copper-iron alloys. However, iron with more than a minute trace of copper becomes unworkable and the true link, if any, between copper and iron production remains in doubt. Another possible link is between the introduction of red iron-based glazes, such as the red faience that appears in New Kingdom Egypt, and the development of iron ore smelting.

By the second half of the second millennium BC, iron was beginning to come into more common use, perhaps mainly deriving from the Hittite world. Documents of the period, such as the Amarna Letters, recount the fine iron objects including daggers received at the Egyptian court from foreign rulers (Lucas 1962: 240). Of the rare surviving New Kingdom Egyptian examples, the most famous is the dagger from the tomb of Tutankhamun (Lucas 1962: 239; Carter No. 256k), with its elaborate gold hilt supporting a finely worked iron blade. Another, less spectacular, example is the miniature headrest amulet also from Tutankhamun's tomb (Lucas 1962: 239).

Steel was being produced in parts of the ancient Near East by the closing centuries of the second millennium BC (Craddock 1995: 258–9). A process termed 'carburisation' adds carbon to the iron which thus provides a 'steel' which can be quench-hardened and tempered to considerable hardness. There are sporadic examples from about the middle of the second millennium BC onwards. Studied examples include a pick from Palestine, identified as carburised, quenched and tempered which has been securely dated to the twelfth century BC (Davis *et al.* 1985: 41–51). The technique of hammering together layers of carburised and uncarburised iron produces a strong tool and examples have now been identified from various parts of the Middle East. Perhaps the earliest Egyptian example is an iron knife in the Petrie collection (Carpenter and Robertson 1930: 428–30). This was initially dated to the late New Kingdom, but a date in the ninth century BC might be more likely (Muhly *et al.* 1977).

By the middle of the first millennium BC the production of iron had increased dramatically, but the exception appears to be Egypt. Indeed the supremacy of iron weapons over the copper-alloy ones has been seen as a major factor in the Persian conquest of Egypt. Moorey has recently noted that iron only became a cheaper metal than copper in Mesopotamia in the Neo-Babylonian Period, that is around 600 BC (Moorey 1994: 263) – the time of the Persian invasion of Egypt. It is perhaps not surprising that the largest group of iron objects from Egypt from this period is a set of almost two dozen iron woodworking tools found in the Delta in association with a Western Asiatic bronze helmet. This group dates to the seventh century BC (Petrie 1897: 18–19, 1909: 106; Williams and Maxwell-Hyslop 1976: 283–305). Four of these tools are steel. Craddock has recently largely dispelled any doubt as to the authenticity of the group (Craddock 1995: 259). It also seems likely that hafted hammers were introduced into Egypt in the Late Period. Hot-working iron with the earlier Egyptian hand-held hammers would have been an unpleasant experience.

With additions of between about 2 and 5 per cent carbon, the melting temperature of iron drops to around 1,200 °C and the result is *cast iron*. Cast iron has little relevance for the ancient Old World and can seemingly be ignored as far as Dynastic Egypt is concerned.

Lead

Native lead is extremely rare, but lead is relatively easy to produce from the main ores galena (lead sulphide) or cerrusite (lead carbonate). Lead can be smelted from galena using a simple charcoal or wood fire. As Moorey (1994: 292) has recently noted, these ores are of readily attractive metallic appearance and would have been easily spotted by early prospectors. Garland and Bannister (1927), as well as Lucas (1962), give the main ancient Egyptian source as Gebel Rosas (Arabic for 'lead mountain') south of Quseir on the Red Sea coast. Galena and cerussite were worked here in the early twentieth century and Garland and Bannister refer to ancient workings in the region (Garland and Bannister 1927: 31). There are, however, numerous other ore localities scattered through Egypt, almost down the entire length of Egypt's Eastern Desert. For example both cerrusite and galena are found at Um Gheig and Samiuki (Bishay *et al.* 1974: 47–53). Hassan and Hassan (1981) have recently published a map of some of the lead ore sources in the Eastern Desert accessible via the Wadi Hammamat, while Stos-Gale and Gale (1981) have provided a list of Eastern Desert galena deposits.

In some parts of the Old World, lead was being extracted from its ores during the sixth and even seventh millennia BC. The smelting of lead thus probably pre-dated the smelting of any other metal, copper included. Perhaps the oldest lead object so far published from Egypt is a hollow figure of a hawk – or perhaps hawk figure casing – found by Petrie in Grave 1257 at Naqada dating to the fourth millennium BC (Ashmolean 1895.137). This has sometimes been described as silver, but recent analysis vindicates Petrie's original view that it is lead, indeed of remarkable purity – 99.99 per cent lead with only minute traces of silver (about 0.025 per cent), antimony, arsenic, gold and copper (Gale and Stos-Gale 1981). The remarkably high purity of the hawk is matched by an unusual lead figure said to have been found at Abydos and obtained by the British Museum (BM EA99.10–11.1188) in 1899 (Krysko 1986). This figure appears to have had its detail, if not its entire form, produced by carving not casting. The surface patina is perhaps evidence of great age, but further study is required to establish its antiquity.

Lead objects seem to have become more common after the beginning of the New Kingdom (Garland and Bannister 1927: 30) for castings, for functional uses such as for filling weight, and as additions to copper alloys (see p. 154–5). This might relate to the increasing import of metallic lead into Egypt from the New Kingdom onwards.

Tin-lead alloys (pewter) are rare anywhere in the ancient world prior to the later part of the Roman Period (see p. 171). One possible New Kingdom example is discussed below under 'tin'.

More research on lead ores within Egypt is clearly needed before galena or lead sources can be clarified. One confusing factor in the past with regard to lead isotope provenance studies has been uncertainty as to whether silver was primarily derived from galena in antiquity (see pp. 170–71). It is not impossible that the galena used in mineral form for eye-paint and the like, was largely derived from Egyptian mines, while metallic lead was more typi-

be placed inside something to protect them from the ash and fuel piled around them. Some kind of lidded vessel would be the most obvious container, and as far as I am aware no such vessel has been found to date, although it may simply have comprised a domestic jar with lid rather than a special type of vessel, and there are numerous fragments of such jars from the site.

One badly damaged mud-brick structure was also unearthed, which may be a kiln. However, this is not yet certain, and it is also possible that it is unconnected with faience manufacture. Until the latter can be more certainly assigned it seems best to assume that firings were of the 'open' type.

Numerous small clay balls (*c.* 0.75 cm in diameter), yet to be analysed, were also discovered. These may be the precursors of those known from Lisht, and perhaps even Amarna. Their function is not clear, although evidence from Lisht and Amarna suggests that they were used as a surface on which beads were fired. A clay disc from Abydos, with finger impressions, each approximately the size of the clay balls, may in some way be connected with these discs.

Nevertheless, it is clear from the 'kilns', as well as from the beads and amulets found showing evidence of manufacturing mistakes, that faience was produced at Abydos, and the results of future excavations may throw much light on manufacturing processes at this time. The question of how the industry was organised, and for whom it was producing must remain open. However, the presence of such an establishment on a site which was already of great religious significance might suggest that it was in some way related to cult activities and may have been connected with a temple.

Middle Kingdom and Second Intermediate Period

This period marks the greatest phase of diversity and experimentation since the Predynastic. The stable conditions following the First Intermediate Period seem to have acted as a stimulus to the accelerated development of the craft. From the site of Lisht comes the first known burial of an overseer of faience workers, which has been dated to the Thirteenth Dynasty (see below).

In addition to modelling, regular use began to be made of the techniques of forming on a core and of shaping over a form or *patrix* (a type of moulding). Shapes approximating to a sphere were sometimes modelled around a ball of straw, a notable example being the popular hedgehog figurines which seem to have had some magico–religious significance. Faience hippopotamus figures were also popular at this time, frequently decorated with scenes of aquatic plants applied in a manganese-based paint.

Vessels of the Middle Kingdom tend to have thick walls, although they were not necessarily clumsily executed, and indeed some, such as the bowls with Nilotic scenes, can be of very fine quality. The use of a fine quartz layer over a coarser body also became widespread, leading to some extemely fine, bright glaze effects. Jars were also made in faience; like bowls, they draw on forms well-represented in pottery. It is characteristic of faience, and later of glass, that the forms used are those first developed in pottery or stone.

Decorative techniques also developed, notably the mixing of two differently coloured body pastes to give a marbled effect, which had been a rare curiosity in the preceding period but now became somewhat more common. The incising and inlaying of faience also became more frequently employed techniques. Carefully executed linear designs in dark paint on a blue background also occurred more often, a critical development in light of its subsequent popularity for scenic compositions on faience vessels of the New Kingdom.

Glazes were frequently applied to objects made up of a fine white layer spread over a coarser body, and the resulting effect can be of the finest quality. The glazes themselves were produced by efflorescence, and by cementation, and it was is in this period that the latter technique is first securely attested. The earliest firm evidence for this process dates to the reign of the Twelfth-Dynasty ruler Senusret I. At Kerma in the Sudan there is evidence for the application of glazes as a slurry (Reisner 1923: 134–75).

Although faience was more widely used and underwent rapid development during this period, it should not be supposed that the use of glazed stone died out. Scarabs became important during the Middle Kingdom, but most were made of stone, perhaps because hieroglyphic inscriptions were clearer in stone than in faience. The development of somewhat harder faience bodies may have partly been an attempt to improve the durability of faience and to make it appear more like stone.

Factory evidence: Lisht

The excavations of the Metropolitan Museum of Art at the Middle Kingdom site of Lisht began in 1907 and continued until 1934, with work in the area around the North Pyramid of Amenemhat I concentrating in the period before 1922. In the 1920–21 season a so-called 'glaze factory' was unearthed in buildings AI.2 and and AI.3. From this area came numerous pieces of faience, mostly beads, and many hundreds of small marl clay balls along with the clay semicircles and possible kiln supports similar to those mentioned above.

Most convincing was the discovery of what may be a kiln. There are photographs of this structure, but it was not particularly well-recorded and there has been some question as to whether or not it could in fact be a grain silo from a later period, cutting into the Middle Kingdom layers. However, recent research by Drs Dieter and Felix Arnold suggests that it may indeed be a kiln. It is a semicircular structure with an external diameter of about 1.5 metres, built into the corner of a room, and apparently filled with an ashy deposit.

The factory was situated immediately south of the probable line of the south wall of the pyramid enclosure. Tomb shaft 879 was located immediately north of the main part of building AI.3, and just a little to the north of the kiln. This shaft is not only the provenance of the famous Lisht Dolphin Jug (Bourriau 1996: 110–11; McGovern *et al.* 1994) but also the findspot of the coffin of Debeni who held the title 'overseer of faience workers' (see p. 178). Along with a mention of such a worker on the faience stele in Edinburgh mentioned earlier, this is a rare reference to such a craftsman. It has been suggested that the tomb is related to the workshop, but chronological considerations are not sufficiently fine to make this a certainty, and the tomb and its contents are currently being studied by J.D. Bourriau and J. Allen. The presence of such an official may be significant in attempting to identify the status of the industry, and might imply that at Lisht production for the royal household was underway, although not necessarily at the site so far identified.

It is clear, then, that faience production was taking place at Lisht in the Middle Kingdom, although the precise technology is not yet known. Examination of the faience by the writer suggests that application glazing was taking place, along with efflorescence. These pieces comprise mostly beads, which possibly derive from flails and amulets. Cementation has not been identified with any certainty.

Factory evidence: Kerma

The site of Kerma in the Sudan is widely regarded as a centre of faience production, although it lacks any *in situ* factory evidence. A series of glazed quartz pebbles are thought to have served as supports for the firing of faience tiles which were apparently produced at the site. Kilns were not certainly identified, the most likely being 'too damaged to be drawn' (Reisner 1923: 135).

The probable 'kiln' structure appears to have been made from a truncated pottery vessel, or perhaps a clay cone fired *in situ*, a practice known from the so-called bread ovens at Amarna and elsewhere. Reisner suggests that the structure was heated from the outside, implying that the clay vessel served as a kind of saggar or separator, preventing the glazes from becoming damaged by ash.

There is evidence for the application of glazes as a slurry (Reisner 1923: 134–75) and Reisner believed that efflorescence glazing was also practiced. The writer has not personally examined any of the faience from the site, but in Reisner's opinion certain of the vessels had been thrown on the wheel, while others were core formed. If correct, Kerma would be the earliest recorded site at which the throwing of faience vessels is attested as a more than occasional practice. Inlaying of one faience paste into another is well-attested here. This faience is the subject of renewed investigations and there is evidence of compositional overlaps between local and imported material (Lacovara 1998).

New Kingdom

This period was the zenith of Egyptian faience-working, with widespread, varied production, masterpiece works, vivid use of polychromy and the dissemination of pieces abroad. It builds on the developments of the previous period, and the better preservation of factory evidence greatly enhances our knowledge.

The open-face mould is developed, and attested by many thousands of finds (see p. 183–4) allowing the production of large numbers of rings, amulets and beads. The making of rings was enhanced by the development of a more robust body which made use of glass in the matrix to fuse it more firmly. This 'glass' probably results from the efflorescence process rather than being a deliberate addition as was once thought (Kuhne 1969: 11–26). At the same time, glass was also used to extend the range of colours that could be produced in faience. Similarly, some of the colorants of glass also became widely used, notably cobalt, antimony and lead (Kaczmarkzyk and Hedges 1983) which occur from the reign of Thutmose III, the pharaoh generally credited with establishing glass production in Egypt. Thus, the establishment of glass-making, with its polychrome characteristics, greatly affected faience production. The harder faience body may have led to the greater use of the material for the production of scarabs, the most magnificent of which were the commemorative scarabs of Amenhotep III.

Faience paste was also used to lute faience elements, such as ring shanks and bezels, together and it is not uncommon to find that the elements of a ring are in different colours, or that the suspension loop of an amulet is of a different colour to the amulet itself. The making of these tiny suspension loops is not fully understood, their extremely small size, commonly less than 2 mm in diameter, often means that there is no trace of the body and all that remains is the glaze. In this respect they are glass objects, albeit with the compostion of faience glaze rather than true glass.

The luting together of faience elements was not confined to small items. The famous *was*-sceptre from Naqada (V&A 437–1895) was made in this way, by joining small sections together. Similarly, the faience lotus chalices, characteristic of the New Kingdom, had a join at the junction of the bowl and stem-foot (Vandiver and Kingery 1987b).

Forming over a *patrix* and around a core continued, as did incising and inlaying. The inlaying technique reached its height at this time, and can be divided into two broad groups. In one the inlay is inserted into a channel cut into relatively dry body-material, and the two shrink away from one another quite markedly, leaving a slight groove around the inlay. Vandiver (Vandiver 1983: A117) notes that at times the body has been allowed to become too dry and the inlay becomes detached. The inlay could also be added more quickly, before the background was so dry, so that shrinkage is much less. This can give the effect of a painted tile, accentuated by the bleeding of copper-based colours into the background colour which is often white. A kind of halo effect is thus produced around areas of the tile, notably foliage. Vandiver (1983: A120) was unable to determine the glazing method for this type of tile, although the shrunken inlay type seems to be produced by efflorescence, and that cannot be ruled out here. Both the polychrome tiles showing prisoners, and the inlays of fish and birds produced at this time are remarkable pieces of craftsmanship. Given our present knowledge of faience-making they would now be extremely difficult to replicate.

The use of faience in architecture should not be underestimated. This was not confined to the use of tiles and hieroglyphic inlays. There were also complicated floral inlays and three-dimensional pieces such as the well-known grape clusters from Amarna. These were mould-made, and could be either flat-backed for attachment to a wall or beam, or fully three-dimensional, made by joining two flat-backed pieces together. It has been suggested that these would have hung from the ceilings of buildings to resemble grapes in a vineyard.

Faience of the New Kingdom was exported around the Mediterranean (Peltenburg 1986) and is well-known from Cyprus and Crete as well as parts of the Greek mainland.

Factory evidence: Malkata

Between 1910 and 1921 the Metropolitan Museum of Art's expedition to Malkata, the palace of Amenhotep III at Thebes, unearthed evidence of faience and glass production. This comprised numerous fired clay moulds, faience objects and lumps of colouring matter. Although chronologically earlier, the Malkata finds are not as well-documented as those discovered by Petrie at Amarna. No faience kilns or furnaces were discovered at either Malkata or Amarna. Subsequent excavations at the site by the University of Pennsylvania and by Waseda University have also uncovered industrial debris, but not in such great quantities. For the moment, the importance of the site lies in the apparent occurrence of faience-making alongside glass production, and in the discovery of several moulds filled with unfired faience paste. These pieces are now in the Metropolitan Museum of Art (MMA 11.215.666–8) (Friedman 1998: 257; Nicholson 1998), and one of them has recently been examined by Wypyski (1998: 265) who believes that the contents may not be faience paste.

Factory evidence: Amarna

The Eighteenth-Dynasty city of Amarna, the Egyptian capital during most of the reign of Akhenaten, has been central to understanding New Kingdom faience, and more especially glass production, ever since Petrie's work in 1891–2. In his publication (Petrie 1894) a thoughtful discussion on faience production is given, although the division between excavated evidence and interpretation is not always clear, and certain details are lacking. For example he mentions finding 'three or four glass factories, and two large glazing works' (Petrie 1894: 25), although precise locations for these are omitted, as is their proximity to one another. It is also unclear whether there were also more minor workshops which are not covered in the account.

The area which is labelled 'moulds' on the map published by Petrie (1894: pl. XXXV) probably represents at least one of these glazing works and refers to the many thousands of fired clay moulds used for forming faience objects, notably amulets and inlays (Petrie 1894: 30). He thought that these would have been pressed against a lump of faience paste material, and the raised image so produced would have been sliced from the lump and put to dry (Petrie 1894: 28). He also believed that they would then have been coated in powdered glass and fired in order to glaze them (i.e. they would have had an applied glaze). Although he found moulds with paste in them, he assumed that this was the remains of fine quartz body material rather than the residue of the paste used in efflorescence, since this method was unknown to him.

As already noted, no kilns were located, although there has been some confusion over this aspect of the work (Vandiver 1983: A30) and, despite discussion of the technological evidence, the remains of actual workshop buildings are not recorded. It is probable that the remains were located in dumps outside the actual working area, or possibly in some part of the courtyard of the workshop. It should be borne in mind that much of the work probably took place out of doors, much as pottery production is undertaken in the simplest Egyptian workshops today (*cf.* Nicholson 1995a).

A recent geophysical survey carried out on the writer's behalf by Mr I. Mathieson succeeded in locating kilns or furnaces just to the south of the modern water tower, believed to cover part or all of Petrie's 'moulds' area. This site, O45.1, is currently under excavation and has yielded what is believed to be a workshop producing glass, faience and pigments (Nicholson 1995b, 1995c). Discriminating between the evidence for these three crafts is not easy, but because the large kilns seem to have been subjected to temperatures higher than those needed for the production of faience they are currently believed to have been used for glass, while a third, less highly vitrified, kiln was probably used for pottery and perhaps faience.

This difficulty in separating crafts, at least in the New Kingdom, may to some extent be an artificial one reflecting our present trend toward distinct, individual crafts. The Egyptians on the other hand, had not long had the use of glass, and they were not only using it as a material in its own right, but according to Kühne (1969: 14) and Vandiver (1983: A108), also adding it to faience body-material in order to strengthen it and extend the range of possible colours (see also Boyce 1989: 161; and discussion p. 182). They might therefore have regarded all these crafts as part of an ancient 'vitreous materials' industry, and while it is important to differentiate the technological processes of each manufacture we should not be surprised to find that different products made in the same workshop were produced using the same kilns/furnaces, possibly by the same group of craftsmen.

The Amarna work has yielded numerous pieces of evidence which are still difficult to interpret. Among these are calcareous plaster trays, usually with their upper surfaces impressed with textile. They may have served as drying trays for faience objects, particularly inlays, which often show textile traces on their underside. Petrie also found this type of tray, of which there are examples in the Petrie Museum (UC40569A, UC40570), although they are not mentioned in any of his publications. There are also small, flattened balls of clay to which adhere tiny faience beads, 2–3 mm in diameter. These are not the calcareous clay balls already known from Lisht, but are of Nile clay. In some cases the beads seem to have been pressed into them to some depth, in others they adhere only at their edges. The exact function of these balls is unknown. The same is true of numerous pieces of coarse yellowish plaster often with layers of crystalline blue pigment adhering to them. This pigment is not yet analysed but may be Egyptian blue.

There are numerous other enigmatic objects from the excavation which will require further study, and further excavation before their function becomes apparent. For the moment all that can be said is that, at least at Amarna, glass- and faience-making seem to be closely linked and that this link probably also extends to other pyrotechnical industries. At present however, there is no evidence of metal-working, which would be a similar technological activity, at O45.1.

Factory evidence: Qantir

In 1928 the Department of Egyptian Antiquities undertook excavations at the late New Kingdom site of Qantir in the Delta (Hamza 1930). These unearthed more than 10,000 fired clay moulds like those known from Petrie's excavations at Amarna, most of which were described as still bearing traces of the coloured faience paste they had contained (Hamza 1930: 42). Numerous faience tiles were also unearthed and cylindrical vessels and 'lumps of the favourite blue colour' (i.e. Egyptian blue pigment) were found.

When Hamza (1930: 42) states that 'the objects discovered make it certain that we are face to face with a faience and glazing factory of great size', he may well be correct, but he goes on to make it clear that these objects were not found in their primary context. He points out that 'the original workrooms had actually vanished, but the debris was full of hundreds of fragments which illustrate the finished objects and furnish us with almost every stage and detail of the mode of manufacture' (Hamza 1930: 45). The recent excavations of the Roemer-Pelizaeus Museum, Hildesheim have found similar remains in such a dump context (*cf.* Rehren and Pusch 1997). Interestingly they have been able to identify many of them with glass production, while some of Hamza's description probably refers to Egyptian blue. This would suggest that this Nineteenth- and Twentieth-Dynasty workshop probably shared close affinities with those at Amarna, and again illustrates the difficulty of separating the various processes. Once again no kilns were located, but a series of cylindrical clay tubes believed to be the nozzles of bellows were discovered. This is quite possible, although again one cannot say to which of several industrial processes they belonged. The text implies that they were found in primary contexts (Hamza 1930: 62) but unfortunately there are no plans or photographs from which to judge.

Hamza (1930: 51) rightly singles out the polychrome tiles as examples of master craftsmanship. These combine numerous colours of paste in a single tile, often depicting their subject in remarkable detail. Of particular quality are the tiles representing bound captives.

Another production centre may have existed at Gurob, but Petrie's descriptions of 'several moulds for rings and amulets and beads stuck together in the baking' are too equivocal to be certain (Petrie 1890: 37; see also Brunton and Engelbach 1927: 3).

From the Third Intermediate Period to the Roman period

By the Third Intermediate Period the technology of faience production had become widespread across the Near East and Mediterranean and it can be difficult to differentiate Egyptian imports from locally made copies.

Antimony and cobalt, introduced in New Kingdom times, almost disappear as constituents of faience in the Third Intermediate Period (Kaczmarczyk and Hedges 1983: 259). Interestingly, this is also a period when there is little evidence of glass production, and although it does not die out (as was once thought), it is certainly true to say that it carried on at a much reduced scale, and that most of the products were of lower quality. Cooney (1981) has suggested that the production of the material known as 'glassy faience' (Fig. 7.4) may account for the decline in glass production. However, this material is not well-defined, falling into a kind of negative category for materials which cannot be safely described as either faience or glass. The material was widely used, particularly for *shabtis*. The brown spots which are found on much faience of this time are believed to have been deliberately produced as decoration on a variety of blue-glazed objects (Bianchi 1996).

The nationalistic revival of the Twenty-fifth and Twenty-sixth Dynasties was evidenced in a renewed attention to traditional arts, including faience. A distinctive apple green colour was introduced, and there was a preference for high quality matt faience rather than the shiny glazes of earlier times. The quality of some of these matt pieces, such as *sistrum* handles is exceptional, with every element of the wigs and jewellery worn by the deities carefully executed.

Application

The final glazing method is that of application, the method formerly assumed to be the only one used for faience glazing (Petrie 1894; Lucas 1962). This was a reasonable view, given knowledge of the glazing processes employed for pottery, and was the method used in glazing stone objects, which predate faience. It is, however, an oversimplified view, which must be borne in mind when consulting early accounts of faience technology.

In this method the glazing materials, comprising silica lime and alkali are ground to a small particle size and mixed with water to form a slurry which is applied to the quartz core. They may be ground together in their raw state, or be partially fritted and then ground, as in the production of a pottery glaze. Fritting allows the materials to react together in the first stages of vitrification, a process which helps the final firing temperature to be lower. The object can be dipped into the slurry, or the slurry can be poured over the object. Brushing is also a possiblility, although Vandiver (1982: 168) found traces of it only on polychrome faience of the New Kingdom. In glazing pottery it is common to fire the body clay and then apply the glaze for a second firing but for faience a primary firing has been found to be unnecessary, and firing temperatures tend to be low so that the glaze does not become too liquid causing excessive flow.

Applied glazes characteristically vary in thickness, and may preserve the traces of kiln supports. The glaze covers all of the object, unless intentionally limited. A tendency to run and drip leads to pooling on the lower surfaces and thicker glaze on bases.

The interface of body and glaze in this method is not well-defined, and since there may be little interstitial glass the body itself may be quite soft (Fig. 7.8). Vandiver (1983: A28) notes that a sharp body–glaze boundary and soft friable body may result from firing below *c.* 900 °C and/or a flux content up to 5 per cent. At higher temperatures or greater flux content the body becomes harder as the glassy phase develops. A thick interaction zone and hard body result from prolonged firing at peak temperature, notably firing above 950 °C and/or flux above 10 per cent.

As with many technological processes, we must remember that faience craftsmen did not necessarily work to rigid formulae, and we should not be surprised to find a combination of techniques used on a single piece. For example, Vandiver and Kingery (1987b) report that a faience chalice of the New Kingdom was formed from a body capable of producing an effloresced glaze. However, when the relief decoration was carved into the surface of the piece it inevitably cut through some of the effloresced salts. This would have left a chalice with only partial glazing, and in order to correct this, the finished piece was dipped in a slurry of the body material. This was actually using the technology of application glazing to an effloresced piece. The new glaze layer was itself efflorescent, and allowed the complete glazing of the object.

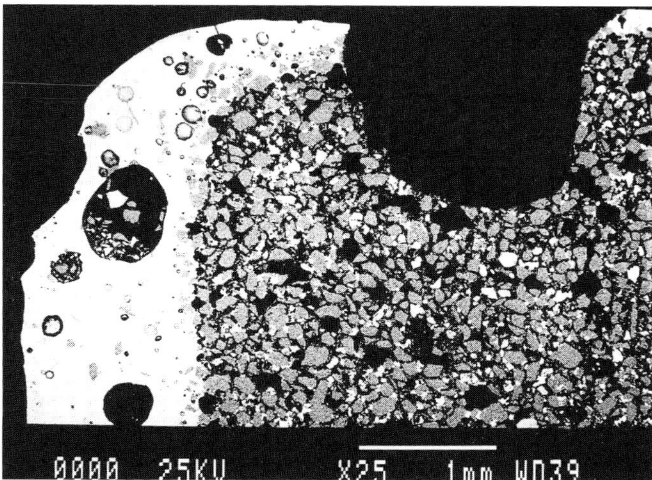

Figure 7.8 Scanning electron microscope photograph of a section through faience glazed by application, from a Late Period shabti *(BM RL16322); the glaze shows as white, the quartz as dark grey, and the voids as black.*

Tite *et al.* (1983: 26) have shown that the glaze composition can be quite variable, and this may be related to changes in the formation of the body, and variations in glazing method, applied regionally and/or chronologically. The forming of the body and glaze varies considerably over time, and according to the status of the workshop. Those workshops enjoying royal patronage presumably had better access to the best raw materials and, more importantly, greater freedom to experiment while smaller local concerns perhaps tended toward conservatism (see Kaczmarczyk and Hedges 1983).

Secondary processing: firing

Through recent experiments that attempt to replicate the ancient production of faience, more is now understood about ancient firing techniques (Vergès 1992; Stocks 1997). Such experimental studies have shown that faience is fired in the range 800–1,000 °C. These studies have been carried out using modern electric kilns and replica faience pastes and, although they are unlikely to be significantly different to the actual firing temperature used, experiment in replica kilns is needed. Such experimentation is required firstly because kiln atmosphere can play an important role in firing, and secondly because it is necessary to ascertain some of the difficulties likely to be experienced in firing this material by traditional means.

The difficulty for modern research is that until recently there were very few kilns known archaeologically. Ironically, the best-known kiln or furnace is the one mentioned by various sources (e.g. Vandiver 1983: A30) as having been found by Petrie at Amarna. This particular Amarna kiln in fact never existed and is a hypothetical reconstruction based on Petrie's finds. Although recent excavations at Abydos and Amarna have supplemented the picture gained from earlier excavations at Lisht, Memphis and Naukratis, the differentiation of glass furnaces from faience kilns/furnaces at Amarna still remains problematic.

Since few kilns have been found, and most of those in old excavations, it follows that the opportunity to examine fuel has been limited. However, charcoal fragments have been found in the recent work at Abydos, and from Amarna, although in this last case the structures with which the fuel is associated are more likely to be for glass production. The Amarna charcoal has been examined by Mary Anne Murray and shown to be of *Ficus sycomorus*. It is not known whether it was deliberately produced, or simply the by-product of incomplete combustion of wood used as fuel, but the fact that some of it takes the form of quite long pieces may suggest that it was the fortuitous product of incomplete combustion (Caroline Vermeeren pers. comm., based on description given by the writer). Further work is needed here.

Petrie (1894: 26) records the discovery at Amarna of what he considered to be a charcoal-burning furnace with large quantities of charcoal inside it. However, whether this was correctly identified, and whether it produced fuel for faience or glass production, or both (or indeed some other purpose) is not known. No analyses were carried out on its contents, and to date it has not proved possible to rediscover the location of this furnace.

Whether or not charcoal was deliberately produced, it is likely that a certain amount of wood and domestic rubbish was burned in the kilns, and animal bone fragments are certainly found among the ash from the kilns at Amarna. This is a likely situation in a country as relatively deficient in timber as Egypt, and one must assume that considerable effort was used in economising on fuel. Petrie (1911: 35) states that the fuel used in the Greco-Roman kilns at Memphis was straw. Although it is possible that straw was among the fuel used, it seems an unlikely choice as the main fuel source, since it burns quickly and huge quantities would be needed for a long firing. Dung might also be a possible source of fuel, perhaps used in combination with wood, but once again experimental work is necessary here.

The objects to be glazed would probably have been protected from the smoke and ash particles of the fire in some way. In efflorescence and application glazing, the pieces probably stood in deep trays or saggars, possibly with lids, to prevent ash from becoming stuck to the glaze. In the case of cementation glazing, they would have been buried in glazing powder, which would itself have been contained in some kind of vessel.

To prevent an all-over glazed object adhering to its saggar or to the kiln, or indeed to neighbouring objects, it would usually be necessary to rest it on some kind of support.

The form of these is not known, but it can be suggested that they were sometimes small cones or bars of clay, possibly rich in alumina which would help to prevent sticking. It is also possible that the numerous small marl clay balls discovered at Lisht may have served this purpose, the bottom of a tray being covered in them, much as modern potters might use alumina powder to prevent pots sticking to kiln shelves in firing. A number of marl clay annuli were also found at Lisht and probably served a similar purpose.

Analytical techniques

The technique by which a multi-part object has been manufactured may be determined by the use of conventional x-ray examination, or more satisfactorily by xero-radiography, as Vandiver and Kingery (1987b) have illustrated, since this clearly shows the joins between components.

The use of the scanning electron microscope (SEM) in determining the method of glazing from an examination of interstitial glass and glaze thickness has already been referred to above. Energy dispersive (ED) and wavelength dispersive (WD) X-ray analyses can be carried out on those instruments equipped for such analyses (see Henderson's contribution to Chapter 8). The SEM is the most satisfactory means for the determination of glazing technique, although examination under the petrological microscope can also be used. In this method a thin section (0.03 millimetres thick) is prepared from the faience and examined under a polarising microscope so that the mineral phases (mostly silica) and glass can be identified. Such sections may need to be consolidated by the addition of a suitable epoxy resin before they are reduced to the correct thickness.

For the most widely used modern study, however, Kaczmarczyk and Hedges (1983) employed x-ray fluorescence (XRF) which examines a small area of the surface of the object (usually 1.5×1.5 millimetres) non-destructively (Tite 1972: 267–72). Primary x-rays are used to bombard the sample which in turn releases energy in the form of fluorescent x-rays whose wavelengths are characteristic of particular elements. A diffraction crystal is used to separate the wavelengths which can then be identified and the concentration of the element measured. The technique is best suited to major elements, but can also detect trace elements.

Kaczmarczyk and Hedges (1983: 10) found that certain elements, notably sodium, magnesium and aluminium were best measured using atomic absorption spectrometry (AAS) (Tite 1972: 264–6), a method which requires the removal of a small sample from the object, twenty milligrammes in the case of their study. This sample is dissolved and the solution atomised in a flame. Focused on the flame is the light from a hollow cathode lamp made from the element to be analysed. The light thus has a wavelength corresponding to that of the element it is sought to examine. Atoms of the element absorb some of the light, and the intensity is measured using a photomultiplier, the quantity of light absorbed indicating the concentration of the element in the sample. The technique is best suited to minor and trace elements, which makes it an ideal complement to XRF.

Other techniques suited to the examination of glass can also be applied to faience and the reader is referred to Chapter 8, this volume, for further details of these.

Acknowledgements (Nicholson)

I would like to thank the Egypt Exploration Society and Mr Barry Kemp for their suppport of my work at site O45.1 at Amarna. I would also like to thank the Wainwright Fund for Near Eastern Archaeology, who funded the work at Amarna, and the Leverhulme Trust (grant F/407/J), who supported the analytical work by myself and Dr Caroline M. Jackson. Mr Ian Mathieson carried out geophysical survey at site O45.1 and I am indebted to him. Ms Susan Cole, Mr Ian Dennis, Dr Jackson, Professor Michael S. Tite and Dr Katharine M. Trott have all worked for the 'Amarna Glass Project' and their hard work is gratefully acknowledged. The work at Amarna would not have been possible without the kind cooperation of the Egyptian Supreme Council for Antiquities to whom I am indebted.

I am also indebted to Dr Dorothea Arnold for giving me the opportunity to examine faience in the Metropolitan Museum of Art, New York, and to Dr Florence Friedman and Dr Matthew Adams for discussions concerning faience and work at Abydos respectively. Dr Adams kindly allowed mention to be made of his unpublished work at Abydos and provided the photographs for Figures 7.2 and 7.3.

Finally, the advice on the production of this chapter given by Professor Edgar Peltenburg is gratefully acknowledged.

References

Allan, J.W. 1973. Abu' L-Qasim's treatise on ceramics. *Iran*, 11: 111–20.

Arnold, Do. 1988. Egyptian art. In *The Metropolitan Museum of Art: Recent Acquisitions: A Selection 1987–1988*. New York: MMA, pp. 6–7.

Aufrère, S. 1991. *L'univers mineral dans la pensée égyptienne*. Cairo: IFAO.

Bellion, M. 1987. *Catalogue des manuscrits hiéroglyphiques et hiératiques et des dessins, sur papyrus, cuir, ou tissu, publiés ou signalés*. Paris: Epsilon Reproductions.

Bianchi, R.S. 1996. Faience and glazes. In *The Macmillan Dictionary of Art Vol. 10*. (ed. J. Turner). London: Macmillan, pp. 46–9.

1998. Symbols and meanings. In *Gifts of the Nile: Ancient Egyptian Faience* (ed. F.D. Friedman). London: Thames and Hudson, pp. 22–31.

Binns, C.F., Klem, M. and Mott, H. 1932. An experiment in Egyptian blue glaze. *Journal of the American Ceramic Society*, 15: 271–2.

Bourriau, J.D. 1996. The Dolphin vase from Lisht. In *Studies in Honor of William Kelly Simpson* I. (ed. P. Der Manuelian). Boston: MFA, pp. 101–16.

Boyce, A. 1989. Notes on the manufacture and use of faience rings at Amarna. In *Amarna Reports* V. (ed. B.J. Kemp). London: EES, pp. 160–8.

Brunton, G. and Engelbach, R. 1927. *Gurob*. London: Egyptian Research Account/British School in Egypt.

Charlesworth, D. 1972. Tell El-Fara'in Egypt: an industrial site in the Nile Delta. *Archaeology*, 25: 44–7.

Cooney, J.D. 1976. *Catalogue of Egyptian Antiquities in the British Museum IV: Glass*. London: BMP.

1981. Notes on Egyptian glass. In *Studies in Ancient Egypt, the Aegean and the Sudan* (eds. W.K. Simpson and W.M. Davis). Boston: MFA, pp. 31–3.

Coulson, W.D.E. and Leonard, A. 1981. *Cities of the Delta I: Naukratis, Preliminary Report on the 1977–1978 and 1980 Seasons*. Malibu: ARCE.

Davies, N. de G. 1902. *The Rock Tombs of Deir el-Gebrawi*. London: EES.

Doran, J.E. and Hodson, F.R. 1975. *Mathematics and Computers in Archaeology*. Edinburgh: Edinburgh University Press.

Drenkahn, R. 1995. Artisans and artists in Pharaonic Egypt. In *Civilisations of the Ancient Near East I* (ed. J.M. Sasson). New York: Charles Scribner's Sons, pp. 331–43.

Friedman, F.D. 1998. (ed.) *Gifts of the Nile: Ancient Egyptian Faience*. London: Thames and Hudson.

Gaballa, G.A. 1979. False-door stelae of some Memphite personnel. *SAK*, 7: 41–52.

Hamza, M. 1930. Excavations of the Department of Antiquities at Qantîr (Faqûs district). *ASAE*, 30: 31–68.

Henein, N.H. and Gout, J.-F. 1974. *Le verre soufflé en Égypte*. Cairo: IFAO.

Kaczmarczyk, A. and Hedges, R.E.M. 1983. *Ancient Egyptian Faience*. Warminster: Aris and Phillips.

Kiefer, C. 1968. Les céramiques bleues pharaoniques et leur procédé révolutionnaire d'émaillage. *Industrie Céramique*, May: 395–402.

Kiefer, C. and Allibert, A. 1971. Pharaonic blue ceramics: the process of self-glazing. *Archaeology*, 24: 107–17.

Kühne, J. 1969 *Zur Kenntnis silikatischer Werkstoffe und der Technologie ihrer Herstellung im 2. Jahrtausend vor unserer Zeitrechnung*. Berlin: Abhandlung der Deutschen Akademie der Wissenschaften zu Berlin

Lacovara, P. 1998. Nubian faience. In *Gifts of the Nile: Ancient Egyptian Faience* (ed. F.D. Friedman). London. Thames and Hudson, pp. 46–7.

Lauer, J.-P. 1938. Fouilles du service des antiquités à Saqqarah. *ASAE*, 38: 551–65.

1976. *Saqqara: The Royal Cemetery of Memphis*. London: Thames and Hudson.

Lilyquist, C. and Brill, R.H. 1993. *Studies in Early Egyptian Glass*. New York: MMA.

Lucas, A. and Harris, J.R. 1962. *Ancient Egyptian Materials and Industries*. 4th edn., rev. J.R. Harris. London: Arnold.

Marucchi, H. 1891. *Monumenta papyrichea Agyptea Biblioteci Vaticani*. Rome: Ex Bibliotheca Vaticana.

McGovern, P.E., Bourriau, J.D., Harbottle, G. and Allen S.J. 1994.

The archaeological origin and significance of the Dolphin Vase as determined by neutron activation analysis. *BASOR*, 296: 31–43.

Moorey, R.S. 1994. *Ancient Mesopotamian Materials and Industries.* Oxford: OUP.

Morgan, M.H. 1914. *Vitruvius: The Ten Books on Architecture*, transl. M.H. Morgan. Cambridge MA: Harvard University Press.

Nenna, M.-D. and Seif el-Din, M. 1993. La vaiselle en faïence du Musée Gréco-Romain d'Alexandrie. *Bulletin de Correspondance Hellénique*, 117: 565–98.

1994. La petite plastique en faïence du Musée Gréco-Romain D'Alexandrie. *Bulletin de Correspondance Hellénique*, 118: 291–320.

Newton, R.G. 1980. Recent views on ancient glasses. *Glass Technology*, 21/4: 173–83.

Newton, R.G. and Renfrew, C. 1976. British faience beads reconsidered. *Antiquity*, 44: 199–206.

Nicholson, P.T. 1993. *Egyptian Faience and Glass.* Aylesbury: Shire Egyptology.

1995a. The potters of Deir Mawas, an ethnoarchaeological study. In *Amarna Reports* VI. (ed. B.J. Kemp). London: EES, pp. 279–308.

1995b. Recent excavations at an ancient Egyptian glassworks: Tell el-Amarna 1993. *Glass Technology*, 36 (4): 125–8.

1995c. Glass making/working at Amarna: some new work. *Journal of Glass Studies*, 37: 11–19.

1998. Materials and technology. In *Gifts of the Nile: Ancient Egyptian Faience* (ed. F.D. Friedman). London: Thames and Hudson, pp. 50–64.

Nicholson, P.T., Jackson, C.M. and Trott, K.M. 1997. The Ulu Burun glass ingots, cylindrical vessels and Egyptian glass. *JEA* 83: 143–53.

Noble, J.V. 1969. The technique of Egyptian faience, *AJA*, 73: 435–9.

Nolte, B. 1968. Die Glassgefäße im alten Ägypten. Munich: *Münchner Ägyptologische Stüden 14*

1977. Fayence. *LÄ* II: 138–42.

Oppenheim, A.L. 1973. Towards a history of glass in the ancient Near East. *JAOS*, 93: 259–66.

Oppenheim, A.L., Brill, R.H., Barag, D. and von Saldern, A. 1970. *Glass and Glassmaking in Ancient Mesopotamia.* New York: Corning Museum of Glass.

Peltenburg, E.J. 1986. Ramesside Egypt and Cyprus. In *Acts of the International Archaeological Symposium 'Cyprus Between the Orient and the Occident'* (ed. V. Karageorghis). Nicosia: Department of Antiquities, pp. 149–79.

1987. Early faience: recent studies, origins and relations with glass. In *Early Vitreous Materials* (eds. M. Bimson and I.C. Freestone), British Museum Occasional Paper 56. London: BMP, pp. 5–29.

Petrie, W.M.F. 1890. *Kahun, Gurob and Hawara 1889–90.* London: Nutt.

1894. *Tell el-Amarna.* London: Methuen.

1909. *Memphis I.* London: Quaritch.

1911. The pottery kilns at Memphis. In *Historical Studies II* (E.B. Knobel, W.W. Midgeley, J.G. Milne, M.A. Murray and W.M.F. Petrie). London: Quaritch, pp. 34–7.

Petrie, W.M.F. and Gardner, E.A. 1886. *Naukratis I.* London: Trübner and Co.

Rehren, T. and Pusch, E. 1997. New Kingdom glass melting crucibles from Qantir-Piramesses. *Journal of Egyptian Archaeology*, 83, 127–41.

Reisner, G.A. 1923. *Excavations at Kerma* IV–V. Harvard African Studies 6. Cambridge MA: Harvard University Press.

Stocks, D. 1997. Derivation of ancient Egyptian faience core and glaze materials. *Antiquity*, 71: 179–82.

Stone, J. and Thomas, C. 1956. The use and distribution of faience in the Ancient East and Prehistoric Europe. *PPS*, 22: 37–84.

Tite, M.S. 1972. *Methods of Physical Examination in Archaeology.* London: Seminar Press.

1986. Egyptian blue, faience and related materials: technological investigations. In *Science In Archaeology* (eds. R.E. Jones and H.W. Catling), Fitch Laboratory Occasional Paper 2. London: British School at Athens, pp. 39–41.

unpublished. Technology of early vitreous materials. *Paper given at Los Angeles Symposium On Archaeometry1992.*

Tite, M.S. and Bimson, M. 1987. Identification of early vitreous materials. In *Recent Advances in the Conservation and Analysis of Artifacts* (ed. J. Black). London: Summer Schools Press, pp. 81–5.

Tite, M.S., Freestone, I.C. and Bimson, M. 1983. Egyptian faience: an investigation of the methods of production. *Archaeometry*, 25/1: 17–27.

Tite, M.S., Shortland, A.J., Nicholson, P.T. and Jackson, C.M. 1998. The use of copper and cobalt colorants in vitreous materials in ancient Egypt. In *La couleur dans la peinture et l'emaillage de l'Egypte ancienne* (ed. M. Menu). Ravello: Centro Universitario Europeo per i Beni Culturali, pp. 111–120.

Vandiver, P. 1982. Technological change in Egyptian faience. In *Archaeological Ceramics.* (eds. J.S. Olin and A.D. Franklin). Washington DC: Smithsonian Institution Press, pp. 167–79.

1983. Appendix A: the manufacture of faience. In *Ancient Egyptian Faience.* (A. Kaczmarczyk and R.E.M. Hedges). Warminster: Aris and Phillips, pp. A1–A137.

Vandiver, P. and Kingery, W.D. 1987a. Egyptian faience: the first high-tech ceramic. In *Ceramics and Civilisation* 3. (ed. W.D. Kingery). Columbus OH: American Ceramic Society, pp. 19–34.

1987b. Manufacture of an eighteenth dynasty Egyptian faience chalice. In *Early Vitreous Material* (eds. M. Bimson and I.C. Freestone). London: BMP, pp. 79–90.

Vergès, F.L. 1992. *Bleus Égyptiens.* Leuven: Peeters.

Verner, M. 1984. Excavations at Abusir: season 1982 preliminary report. *ZAS*, 111: 70–8.

1986. Nouvelles découvertes des égyptologues tchécoslovaques. *Solidarité*, 4: 20–1.

Vitruvius see Morgan 1914.

Weatherhead, F. and Buckley, A. 1989. Artist's pigments from Amarna. In *Amarna Reports* V. (ed. B.J. Kemp). London: EES, pp. 202–40.

Wulff, H.E., Wulff, H.S. and Koch, L. 1968. Egyptian faience: a possible survival in Iran. *Archaeology*, 21: 98–107.

Wypyski, M. 1998. Appendix. In *Gifts of the Nile: Ancient Egyptian Faience* (ed. F.D. Friedman). London: Thames and Hudson, p. 265.

8. Glass

PAUL T. NICHOLSON [TECHNOLOGY] AND JULIAN HENDERSON [ANALYSIS]

[NICHOLSON – TECHNOLOGY]

Introduction and historical summary

Ancient Egyptian glass is among the finest from the ancient world. Despite its great technical competence its origins and technology are still imperfectly understood. Lucas (1962: 179) notes that while glass may have been made sporadically before the 18th Dynasty (*c.* 1550–1070 BC) it was probably a fortuitous product resulting from accidents in faience manufacture, while after that time its production was deliberate. Peltenburg (1987: 16) similarly credits the earliest glass to faience-workers, though he makes the valuable point that these early occurrences form no distinct regional or temporal pattern but are simply sporadic.

Both glass and faience were treated as artificial precious stones, and at least insofar as vessels were concerned neither developed its own distinctive repertoire, rather they copied forms originally made in stone or pottery. The link is further emphasised by the practice of imitating glass vessels in painted wood, in the same way as stone vessels were copied. Examples are known from tombs as rich as that of Yuya and Tuyu (KV46; Davis 1907: 32; Cairo CG3686–9). This also emphasises the high status attached to glass, it was a commodity fit for even the highest individuals, so that while it may have been an artificial precious stone it should not be thought of as a cheap substitute. Indeed Carnarvon considered it to have been sufficiently valuable to have been among the items robbed from the tomb of Tutankhamun (KV62; Reeves 1990: 200).

Beck (1934) and Lucas both summarised known early finds of glass, though by 1962 when Harris's revised edition of Lucas's *Ancient Egyptian Materials and Industries* appeared, many of these had been questioned, and Peltenburg (1987: 17) gives only fifteen occurrences from Egypt. All of these are beads, except for two unprovenanced Twelfth-Dynasty scarabs, (see Martin 1971: nos. 441 and 1198). Lilyquist and Brill (1993: 5–7) also discuss these early occurrences. Most of these 'early' pieces must be treated with extreme caution since many lack secure provenance and/or examination in recent times, and those that have been examined – such as the lion head pendant (BM EA59619) have proved to be of other materials (I. Freestone pers. comm.). Peltenburg (1987: 18) makes a distinction between these occasional pieces, which he calls Stage 1 of glass production and the deliberate products of Stage 2, beginning at around 1500 BC, although the scarabs may be an early outlier of Stage 2 production.

From 1500 BC onwards, glass emerges as a regular, if high-status, product in Egypt. Lucas, like Petrie (1894), took it for granted that glass was *made* in Egypt from its raw materials at least by the time of Amarna, but since his time opinion has shifted toward the view that the earliest glass was imported, or at least that craftsmen were brought in to establish the industry. This view stems from the realisation that the earliest glass is of remarkable technical competence, apparently the product of a fully fledged industry. Petrie himself believed glass to have been introduced into Egypt (Petrie 1926: 229) and then independently manufactured there once it had become established.

Furthermore, the words *ehlipakku* and *mekku*, apparently used by the Egyptians to refer to glass, are of foreign origin and come from Hurrian and Akkadian respectively (Oppenheim 1973, but see also Foster 1979: 21). Oppenheim (1973: 263) argues that the first glass-makers/workers may have been brought to Egypt following the campaigns of Thutmose III (1479–1425 BC) in Mitanni and that Pharaoh requested raw materials, perhaps as cullet or ingots, from which they simply *worked* the glass. The *Annals of Thutmose III* (Breasted, 1906: 204) mention under the tribute of Babylon during the eighth campaign of Thutmose III 'lapis lazuli of Babylon' which Smith (1928: 233) considers to be glass. Glass can also be referred to as 'stones of casting' or 'stone of the kind that flows', *inr n wḏḥ or ʿ3t wḏḥt* (Tatton Brown and Andrews 1991: 26; Nolte 1977a: 614).

Newton (1980:176) states categorically that 'the Egyptians could only melt other people's glass even though they could fabricate the most exquisite items from it . . . glass-melting is a much simpler operation than glass-making . . . [and] the Egyptian court depended for their basic raw material, or for an essential ingredient thereof on imports from Asia'. The question of if and when a truly local production began is currently under investigation (Nicholson 1995 and pp. 200–1, this volume; Nicholson and Jackson, 1998).

Stern and Schlick-Nolte (1994: 25) point out that the largest glass vessel known from Egypt (CG 24804 – not 24808 as stated in their text) which bears a cartouche of Amenhotep II (1427–1401 BC) may be of foreign origin. Whatever the origin of this particular piece, it is clear that glass was of considerable importance, and Nolte (1968: 13) has suggested that glass was a royal monopoly throughout the New Kingdom. Some support for this view is to be found in the mentions of glass in the Amarna Letters (EA14, 25, 148, 235, 314, 323, 327 and 331; for translations see Moran 1992), where glass is clearly said to be imported into Egypt. However, letter EA14 also mentions glass among gifts sent by the Egyptian king to the king of Karaduniyaš (Moran 1992: 27–37).

Whether made, or simply worked, the glass produced was put to a wide range of uses, and subject to various shaping processes. Among the products were beads, amulets, items of sculpture and vessels. It was probably its association with stone which led to glass, as with faience, being used in the making of amulets. Certain types and colours of stone were considered most effective for particular purposes, and glass of the same colour seems to have been credited with the same effects.

Where vessels were produced they too might serve the same function as their stone or pottery counterparts, namely as containers for perfumes, ointments and cosmetics. These tended to be more solid than those favoured in Hellenistic times, and as a result the wide-mouthed forms decline at this later date in favour of a range of miniature 'classical' forms such as *amphoriskoi* and *aryballoi*. Both the container and its contents were costly, and the labour involved in producing both was great. It is not surprising therefore, that in the era before glass blowing (discovered in the first century BC, probably in the Levant) we possess relatively few vessels and that most are of remarkably high quality, the work of the most highly skilled craftsmen.

As well as use for containers of high value substances, and an imitation of precious stones, glass was also valued as a material in its own right. It may have been this which led to its use for sculpture in the round. Such glass sculpture appears to have been an Egyptian invention, and the earliest piece belongs to the reign of Amenhotep II (1427–1401 BC). Until recently the earliest known was a *shabti* figure (Cairo 5319; Cooney 1960: 12). However, since the time of Cooney's article on glass sculpture (1960) this *shabti* has been overshadowed by a head of Amenhotep II himself, in blue glass (Corning 70.1.4) (Goldstein 1979), while the damaged head of a sphinx may also represent this king (BM EA16374). Not only does this point to the acceptance of this novel material for royal portraiture, but further emphasises the status of the medium as a possible royal monopoly. The *shabti*, one of two known, was probably a royal gift. It is notable that both date before the reign of Amenhotep III when large-scale glass production is first suggested by finds from Malkata.

Shabtis require considerably more glass than small vessels, as well as requiring some skill in their finishing, and the same is true of the glass stand of Amenhotep III (1427–1401 BC) (private collection) which may have served as the base for a figurine (Mehlman 1982: 32). Such solid pieces were probably the technological precursors of the headrests described below (p. 202). Pieces such as the Amenhotep II sphinx were probably produced by lost-wax casting, the details probably being refined on removal from the mould. This is contrary to the statement by Stern and Schlick-Nolte (1994: 31) that the technique was unknown during the second millennium BC.

Smaller objects were also produced in glass, though again serving the same purposes as examples in other media. Notable among these is the use of glass as inlay (Bianchi 1983a, 1983b). In these instances the technology as well as the use may have been very much akin to faience production. The changing relationships between these two crafts, and others, through time is a subject requiring further investigation.

At the time of *Ancient Egyptian Materials And Industries*' revision (1962) it was believed that 'from *c.* 1050–400 BC glass is almost unknown in Egypt' (Cooney 1960: 29). However, by the late 1970s evidence for some measure of continuity was beginning to emerge and with evidence such as a glass-inlaid shrine door of Darius (BM WA37496) and a still earlier one of Ahmose II (Emery, 1967: 143). Cooney (1981: 33) revised his opinion in favour of limited continuity. It may be better to think of the period 1050–400 BC as one of 'reduced output' and with a lower standard of craftsmanship yielding vessels such as those from the tomb of Nesikhons, a wife of Pinudjem II, High Priest of Amun, who died during the fifth regnal year of Siamun, a Twenty-first-Dynasty Pharaoh (*c.* 974 BC; see Fossing 1940: 20, fig. 12; Kaczmarczyk and Hedges 1983: 260; Nolte 1968: Taf. XXI and XXVIII). Cooney himself (1960: 33) notes that 'glassy faience', which is known from the Twenty-second Dynasty onwards, may to some extent have taken over from true glass during this period.

From the Late Period (712–332 BC) onwards, Egypt was increasingly drawn into the broader Mediterranean world, and as a result was more open to the influence of the Greeks. Moorey (1994: 199) states that from the Twenty-fourth to Twenty-sixth Dynasties there is no evidence for production of cast or cut vessels in Egypt, and that these are usually assigned to Phoenician workshops, albeit largely on stylistic grounds. From around 550 BC (Tatton-Brown and Andrews 1991: 42) Mediterranean glass workshops flourished and Classical vessel forms were imported into Egypt as well as made there (Nolte 1977b).

The site of Gurob in the Fayum is also likely to have been a production centre, operating from the reign of Amenhotep III (1479–1425 BC) to that of Rameses II (*c.* 1290–1224 BC; Tatton-Brown and Andrews 1991: 31). Petrie recovered a collection of glass vessels from the site (Petrie 1891: 16–18: 1892: 132–3) but these were from domestic contexts, therefore the presence of the workshop itself can only be inferred. It is possible however, that Gurob supplied glass products to Lower Egypt, notably the royal court at Memphis.

As yet the evidence from Qantir (Rehren and Pusch 1997) does not include actual glass workshop remains, only the debris from them. Nevertheless, the detailed work carried out on these finds has reconstructed the specialised process of making red glass (Rehren 1997). Given the nature of the site as the Rammesside capital it is not unlikely that these specialised workshops were also under royal control. As at Amarna, there is ample evidence to suggest that glass production was going on alongside the making of faience objects (see Hamza 1930), again suggesting the possibility of a more generalised vitreous materials industry.

Newberry (1920: 156) records a 'factory site' on the east bank of the Nile, south of el-Mansha (near Akhmim in Middle Egypt). Its status as a factory has been questioned by Keller (1983: 20), who assumes that Newberry had simply been told of the site as a source of artefacts looted elsewhere. However, Newberry in fact seems to have visited the site and found glass manufacturing debris there (1920: 156). Unfortunately it is not possible to speculate further on the nature of this site nor on its connections – if any – with other crafts. Tatton-Brown and Andrews (1991: 33) suggest that this site may have taken over from Malkata as the main supply centre for Thebes.

The work of Keller (1983) at Lisht has already been cited as illustrating clear differences between that site and Amarna, in that the predominant colouring agent for the blue glass seems to be copper. There are numerous reasons why this might be, including preference and chronological differences but it is also possible that it represents a different kind of organisation, perhaps less directly related to royal control. The large block of glass from the site might suggest glass-making, or at least substantial glass-working, but without further excavation it is impossible to tell.

Our evidence suggests that faience, glass and glassy faience may not at all times have been regarded as distinct materials, but rather as part of a generalised vitreous materials industry. In this case the apparent decline in production after the New Kingdom may be apparent to us but not to the Egyptians themselves.

Related materials

In view of the confusion which frequently occurs over faience, Egyptian blue 'frits' and glass, it may be helpful to briefly review these related materials. Recent work (Tite 1986; Tite and Bimson 1987) has resulted in the division of frits into two groups, firstly blue frits, the dominant crystalline phase of which is a calcium-copper tetrasilicate known as 'Egyptian blue' ($CaO.CuO.4SiO_2$) in a very limited matrix of glass, and secondly turquoise-blue frits in which the dominant phase other than quartz is a calcium silicate known as wollastonite ($CaSiO_3$) which is crystallised from the copper rich glass matrix (Fig. 8.5). The frits can each be subdivided into coarse- and fine-textured, the coarse normally representing the first stage of production, after which it would be ground finer and moulded into artefacts or used as a pigment (Weatherhead and Buckley 1989).

Egyptian blue appears to be an Egyptian invention and, although of much greater antiquity, is closely allied to glass. Its texture may be so fine that it is virtually indistinguishable from glass, especially if the latter is weathered. It is known by the Fourth Dynasty (Ullrich 1979) and undergoes gradual refinement, becoming increasingly glass-like, into the early Roman period. It was known to the Greeks as *kyanos* (Cooney 1976: 37), while Vitruvius (VII, 11; see Morgan 1914) refers to it as *caeruleum*, which was believed in his time to have been invented at Alexandria. Egyptian blue, in both coarse and fine form, is a frit. This is the product of a solid state reaction similar to that used in the first stages of Egyptian glass manufacture. Despite the possible confusion with glass, the frits are easily distinguished from faience when a broken section can be viewed, which illustrates the lack of a core; they are homogeneous throughout and have no separate glaze layer.

Egyptian blue may be used both in the manufacture of objects and as a pigment (Chase 1971; Bayer and Wiedmann 1976; see also Chapter 4, this volume).

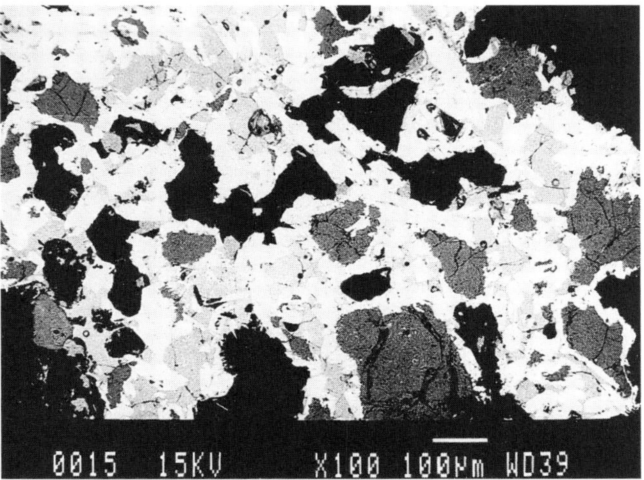

Figure 8.5 Scanning electron microscope photograph of 'Egyptian blue' from a Roman mosaic of the second century AD (BM EB14122). Unreacted quartz appears dark grey, crystals of Egyptian blue as white and the glass matrix as light grey.

[HENDERSON – ANALYSIS]

Chemical analysis of ancient Egyptian glass and its archaeological interpretation

Introduction

Since Lucas (1948) published his account of ancient Egyptian glass, much scientific research has been devoted to its chemical composition. Building on seminal analytical work by Farnsworth and Ritchie (1938) and Turner (1954, 1956a and b), several review papers have been published, discussing the kinds of information that can derive from Egyptian glass analyses. An early paper by Sayre and Smith (1961) provided clear evidence for at least five distinct compositional groupings, of which Egyptian glasses fell into the 'second millennium BC' group (soda-lime-silica, with high magnesia). Despite some criticism of the paper, the groupings have stood the test of time, especially for glasses from reliable archaeological contexts; other compositional types can now be added.

Two early papers by Brill (1963, 1968) provide more clear evidence for distinct compositional groupings of ancient Egyptian glasses, which relate directly to the use of discrete combinations of raw materials in the glass batch. Kaczmarzyck (1986) appeared to show that there was a link between the chemical analyses of cobalt and associated impurities in Egyptian cobalt-blue glasses and faience (Kazmarzyck and Hedges 1983) and the impurities found in Egyptian alum, a source of cobalt. Other review papers which incorporate a discussion of Egyptian glass technology have been published (Henderson 1985, 1989; Freestone 1991). However, of most significance to this work is a recent comprehensive survey of Egyptian glass by Lilyquist and Brill (1993), which includes chemical analyses of glasses dating back to the reigns of Hatshepsut, Thutmose III and Amenhotep II (Lilyquist and Brill 1993: 36, table 2).

The techniques used for the chemical analysis of Egyptian glass

Arc-source emission spectrometry (AES) and its applications

Early techniques used for the analysis of Egyptian glass involved either destruction of the artefact or, at least, the removal of samples. Almost all of these were conventional forms of wet chemical analysis which tended to be time-consuming; wet chemistry involves the dissolution of the material being analysed. They included 'classical' methods such as gravimetric, colorimetric, flame photometric, electrolytic and redox titration determinations.

One of these techniques, the one most frequently used for the chemical analysis of ancient Egyptian glass and other vitreous materials (Hedges and Moorey 1975), from the 1930s until about 1960, was arc-source emission spectrometry (AES). Since spectrometry forms the basis of most analytical techniques to be discussed it should briefly be defined here.

Spectrometry is a form of measurement in which exciting radiation (for example X-rays and gamma-rays) is directed at the glass, and the interaction generates wavelengths of energy which are characteristic of the elements in the glass. If the exciting radiation is of a sufficient energy, such as X-rays, gamma-rays, electrons or protons, ionisations characteristic of the elements in the glass will occur, which, in turn, will yield particles characteristic of the material. In the case of X-ray spectrometry the result of bombarding a soda-lime silica glass is to produce secondary X-rays of sodium, calcium and silicon (among others). X-ray spectrometry therefore involves a primary excitation of the sample and spectrometry of the secondary radiation; the spectrograph records the components in the form of spectra. It is worth noting that the process can be non-destructive.

Arc-source emission spectrometry was being used for archaeological investigations until *c.* 1960, when more accurate, automated and less destructive techniques were introduced for analysing ancient glass. The technique involved a powdered sample. A graphite electrode was positioned so that an arc occurred beween electrode and sample causing the sample to be volatilised and to emit light. The elements present emitted wavelengths which were recorded on a photographic plate. The relative intensities of each line recorded on the photographic plate were measured and could be related to the relative concentrations in the glass; the results were semi-quantitative, not quantitative, but did often provide a basis for chemically classifying the Egyptian glass (Farnsworth and Ritchie 1938).

This analytical technique was time-consuming and destructive. As a result, a relatively small number of analyses were carried out on the materials concerned. For example, many of the analyses cited in *Analyses of Ancient Glasses* (Caley 1962) were carried out using AES.

Using arc-source emission spectrometry, Farnsworth and Ritchie (1938: 159) chemically analysed a series of cobalt-blue Eighteenth-Dynasty glasses, and attributed the colour to the presence of cobalt and copper modified by manganese in the glass; they explicitly stated that they regarded the presence of cobalt as being a deliberate addition (1938: 160). Earlier workers (Neumann, 1929; Neumann and Kotyga 1925) who used wet chemical techniques to analyse Egyptian glasses suggested that copper was responsible for the blue colour and that they were unable to detect cobalt in the glass; the first cobalt being used in fifteenth-century AD Venetian glasses (Neumann and Kotyga 1925: 862). AES was sufficiently precise to be able to show that very low levels of cobalt, later determined as *c.* 0.05 per cent (see Table 8.1b, analyses 6, 8, 15, 20, 23 and 26, p. 215, this volume) were present and produced a deep cobalt-blue colour in Eighteenth-Dynasty glasses. On the basis of their qualitative AES analyses, Farnsworth and Ritchie (1938) went so far as to suggest that Egyptian sources of alum which contain traces of cobalt might have been used as the source of the cobalt-bearing mineral.

Garner (1956a and b) also suggested that a cobalt-bearing ore was used for the coloration of Egyptian glass (Garner 1956a: 148). Farnsworth and Ritchie's work was later expanded upon by Kaczmarczyck and Hedges (1983) and by Kazmarzyck (1986) using X-ray fluorescence analysis (see p. 210). However, Lucas (1934: 218) suggested a Persian source for a cobalt colorant.

Atomic absorption spectroscopy (AAS) and its applications

A more advanced wet chemical analytical technique is AAS (Hughes *et al.* 1976). This technique gradually replaced AES, and in the 1970s AAS was being used to examine archaeological materials on a routine basis.The technique involves very similar principles to those of arc-emission spectroscopy. However the analysis involves the use of a flame to atomise the sample. The sample is dissolved in solution which is then injected into a flame. The basis of the technique is that a hollow cathode light source for a specific element generates light wavelengths characteristic of that element. When passed through the dissolved sample dispersed in the flame, the light is absorbed by the same element if present in the sample. The degree of absorption is a measure of the concentration of the particular element in the sample. AAS is a quantitative technique, and involves the use of standard solutions.

The introduction of computer automation has provided a much faster processing time for AAS. As with all analytical techniques, however, it is not always straightforward. For example, the results can suffer from interference between two or more elements if they occur in the sample together, and solutions have to be made up in order to assess the extent to which the quantitative results are affected (Hughes *et al.* 1976). Analysis of glass by Lambert and McLaughlin (1976) focused principally on Eighteenth-Dynasty glasses, and has shown that they conform basically to a soda-lime-silica composition with low magnesia and potassium oxides.

Robert H. Brill of the Corning Museum of Glass in the USA, one of the most important workers in the field of ancient glass analysis, uses AAS to conduct most of his chemical examinations of ancient glass based on the production of excellent glass standards (Brill 1972). Brill's AAS analyses of a number of Egyptian glass samples, ranging in date between the late sixteenth and fourteenth century BC, provide one of the most comprehensive data sets for the material (Lilyquist and Brill 1993). In *Studies of Early Egyptian Glass,* energy-dispersive X-ray fluorescent analyses (see p. 210) of pre-Malkata glasses by Wypyski have been added to Brill's analyses (Lilyquist and Brill 1993: 47). In Brill's analyses of ancient glasses the level of silica is measured by difference, and the results totalled to 100 per cent (Lilyquist and Brill 1993: 40, n.86). Four groups of glasses were analysed, three of them were from Egyptian sites (pre-Malkata, Malkata and Amarna), and the fourth was from the Mesopotamian site of Nuzi. All three groups of Egyptian glasses were found to be of a similar soda-lime composition, with high magnesia levels. By comparison the potassium oxide levels varied widely: in Egyptian cobalt-blue glasses, in particular, they were found to be lower than in non-cobalt-blue glasses from Egypt and Nuzi (see p. 213 – electron-probe analyses). It is only by analysing this number of securely dated glass samples from a range of periods that such technological information results. It should be noted that there are distinct compositional *similarities* between Egyptian glass and that found at Nuzi. The only difference between the two is the lower soda levels of some of the Nuzi glasses (Lilyquist and Brill 1993: 41), although even this does not separate them compositionally. This example of an analytical project clearly illustrates that, although some pottery fabrics have been chemically fingerprinted using AAS, such results are not obtainable for Egyptian glasses.

X-ray diffraction spectrometry (XRD) and its applications

Another technique which was already available to workers in the 1950s was XRD; it was used specifically to make unambiguous identifications of crystalline material in glasses. Whereas the chemical analysis of Egyptian glass using AAS destroyed the sample and removed its structure, XRD provided a way of identifying the crystals present in glasses. The crystals may be present as undissolved or partially dissolved raw materials such as silica, or as the crystals used to opacify the glasses. The XRD technique involves firing monochromatic radiation at the crystalline material. The diffraction of the radiation with the crystal lattice produces an X-ray pattern characteristic of the structure of the crystal(s). Crystals are composed of lattices built up in a regular pattern; their size and spacing is characteristic of the crystal species. Thus, while it is possible to identify the presence of calcium and antimony oxides by using AAS, elements which make up the commonest opacifying material found in Egyptian glass, calcium antimonate, it is only with X-ray diffraction that it is possible to identify the crystalline species and to distinguish between the two forms $Ca_2Sb_2O_7$ and $Ca_2Sb_2O_6$. Often such crystals are too small to identify with any other method.

Some of the earliest work on the crystalline nature of an Egyptian material was carried out on Egyptian blue using X-ray diffraction analysis (Jope and Huse 1940). Later work by Rooksby and Turner (Rooksby 1962, Turner and Rooksby 1959, 1961, 1963) used XRD to identify definitively a range of opacifying materials for the first time in ancient Egyptian and other ancient glasses. Opacity in Egyptian glass, as in other glasses, is due to the presence of a dispersion of crystals in a translucent glass matrix. All of these opacifiers have been identified by using X-ray diffraction (with supporting imaging using a scanning-electron microscope; see Figs. 8.6 and 8.7). The opaque white, turquoise and yellow Egyptian glasses all contain opacifiers based on antimony (Turner and Rooksby 1959, 1961, 1963; Rooksby 1962; Henderson 1985).

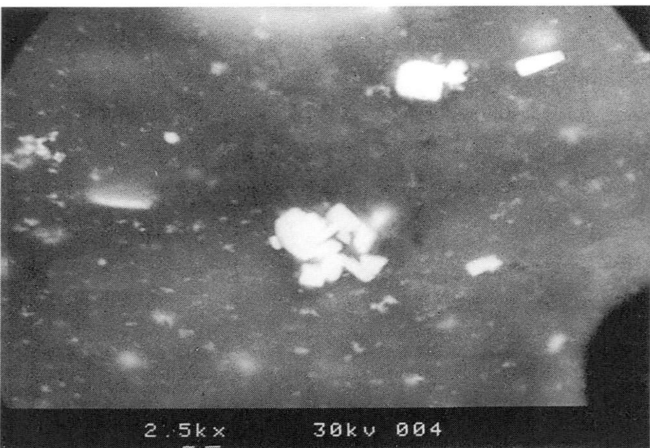

Figure 8.6 Photomicrograph of calcium antimonate crystals in opaque white fourteenth-century BC Egyptian glass (magnification × 2,500).

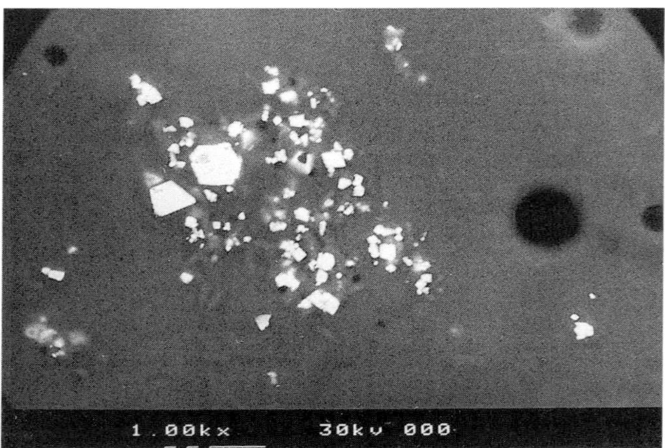

Figure 8.7 Photomicrograph of lead antimonate crystals in opaque yellow fourteenth-century BC Egyptian glass (magnification × 1,000).

The opacifying crystals cause the light to be reflected by the glass and prevent light transmission, thus causing opacity. Calcium antimonate ($Ca_2Sb_2O_7$ or $Ca_2Sb_2O_6$) does not occur naturally as a mineral, therefore antimony needs to be added to the glass where it can react with the calcium to produce calcium antimonate crystals (Turner and Rooksby 1961: 3). In order to produce an opaque turquoise colour in the glass the same procedure is followed as for opaque white glasses, but the antimony is added to a translucent turquoise glass instead of a weakly-tinted glass. The opaque yellow glasses used by the ancient Egyptians are coloured and opacified by the presence of lead antimonate crystals (Rooksby 1962: 23). A lead antimonate occurs naturally as Bindheimite ($Pb_2(Sb,Bi)_2O_6(O,OH)$), so a trace impurity of bismuth in ancient lead antimonate opacified glasses (which would need to be detected using a technique such as electron microprobe or particle-induced X-ray emission) *might* show that this mineral had been used as an opacifier. In the process of heat-treating lead-containing batches, a reaction between lead and antimony would also produce opaque yellow lead pyroantimonate ($Pb_2Sb_2O_7$). No tin-based glass opacifiers were used in ancient glasses until the second century BC (Henderson and Warren 1983, Henderson 1985). Neumann (1929: 835) claimed quite specifically that tin was only found in specimens of three opaque yellow glass specimens used as decoration from Gurob 'Die Trübungsmittel finden sich also nur in den Verzierungsfäden, nicht aber in der Grundmasse' (Neumann 1929: 835). However only compounds of antimony have subsequently been found in opaque Egyptian glasses of the second millennium BC (Brill 1968: 59, table 7; Henderson 1985: 285–6). Figures 8.8–8.10 are energy-dispersive analyses of opaque white, opaque yellow and opaque blue Amarna glasses. It can be seen that for the white and yellow glasses there are significant peaks for antimony (Sb), with no tin oxide detected; in the opaque blue glass a trace of tin (Sn) oxide is visible, but again the dominant peak is antimony. The most likely interpretation, as for the specimens analysed by Neumann (1929: 835) is that the tin was introduced as an impurity in the colorant; all are blue glasses so the impurity would probably have been introduced with the copper present (Sayre and Smith 1967: 297). The only possible yellow opacifier that could have been used for the opaque yellow decoration of the Gurob specimens analysed by Neumann would have been lead antimonate, $Pb_2Sn_2O_7$, (Rooksby 1962), but no lead was detected in the glass compositions published by Neumann (1929: 835) so the results remain anomalous.

The two ionic states of copper produce two correspondingly different colours in Egyptian glasses: a turquoise-blue colour when the cupric (Cu^{2+}) ion is present (Brill 1970: 120) and a dull brown-red colour when the cuprous (Cu^{+}) ion is present (Hughes 1972; Freestone 1987; Guido *et al.* 1984). Again, X-ray diffraction is necessary to unambiguously identify the oxidation state of the copper in opaque reddish-brown glass often used for the decoration of Egyptian glass vessels. The crystals causing the opacity are a form of copper, either copper droplets and/or the reduced form of the oxide, cuprous oxide. All Egyptian opaque red glasses which pre-date the ninth century BC contain lead levels of less than 3 per cent oxide; after this date the lead oxide levels generally rise and a brighter (sealing-wax) red glass colour is produced (Freestone 1987) with the development of different, dendritic, cuprous oxide crystals in the glass. When low levels of lead oxide are present there can be a problem dissolving the copper in the glass. Replication of opaque red glasses has shown that this can be overcome by introducing between 1.37 per cent and 2.29 per cent iron oxide in the glass (Guido *et al.* 1984) – which has been detected in ancient Egyptian glass. This also provides the appropriate (reducing) environment for the precipitation of crystals of cuprous oxide or metallic copper.

proton microprobe), then maps of the distributions of a range of elements in a glass sample can be produced, providing interesting correlations in the occurrence of elements in different glass colours. The technique can be used for the analysis of Egyptian glasses down to parts per million, which is generally a factor of 10 more sensitive than EPMA, but the systems are much more difficult to calibrate than EPMA.

Inductively-coupled plasma-emission spectroscopy (ICPES)
Some fifteen years ago ICPES was added to the range of analytical techniques used by archaeological scientists, but has not yet been used for the analysis of Egyptian glass (see Heyworth *et al.* 1989, Hughes *et al.* 1991; Hatcher *et al.* 1995).

Electron microprobe analysis (EPMA) and its applications
A non-destructive technique which produces high quality results is electron microprobe analysis, also known as electron-probe micro-analysis (EPMA). This followed on from the milliprobe (Hall 1965: 110–11; Hall, Sweitzer and Toller 1973) and its early use for glass analysis (Brill and Moll 1963), becoming commonly used, especially for research in mineral sciences, in the 1970s. Micro-samples as small as 0.5 mm can be mounted and analysed non-destructively, and if necessary repeatedly. The technique involves the use of a micro-beam of electrons which is focused on the sample surface using magnetic lenses. The electrons themselves are generated using an electron gun (see Fig. 8.12). The interaction of the electrons with the sample generates secondary X-rays which are characteristic of the chemical elements in the material. This technique provides an analysis of a shallower layer of glass than with XRF (3–5 microns compared to *c.* 30–50 microns, depending on the conditions employed) and by sampling and preparing the sample carefully, in general, the quality of the results when compared to ED X-ray analysis are far higher, and the technique is considerably less destructive than WD XRF. The samples are normally embedded in epoxy resin and polished flat so that the geometry of the analysis is repeated exactly each time samples are analysed and so as to remove surface roughness. In the process of doing this any weathered material can be removed.

In the case of glass it is essential to defocus the beam in order to minimise or eradicate damage by the electron beam and the volatilisation of the sample surface, causing elements like sodium to be boiled off (Vassamillet and Caldwell 1969; Henderson 1988: 79). In practice during the analysis of glass the beam needs to be deliberately defocused to approximately eighty microns. It is possible to locate the electron beam precisely on the area of the sample to be analysed by moving the sample under a light microscope attached to the system until the beam is located on the desired spot. If compositional heterogeneity is suspected an energy-dispersive detector attached to the system can be used to carry out quick qualitative point analyses before the quantitative WD analyses are performed. It would be possible to quantify the ED results from the system (and defocussing the beam is not necessary) but the levels of precision and detection achieved with the wavelength dispersive probe are of a far higher quality so there is little point (Henderson 1988: 80, table 1; Veritá *et al.* 1994: table 1). This same point can be made for a comparison between the results from an ED spectrometer attached to a scanning-electron microscope and those from a wavelength-dispersive system in an electron microprobe: the levels of detection of the WD system are considerably better. For example, it is often not possible to detect cobalt in a cobalt-blue glass when using the ED system in an SEM , whereas the level of detection for cobalt in a soda-lime glass using WD analysis can be 0.04 per cent cobalt oxide.

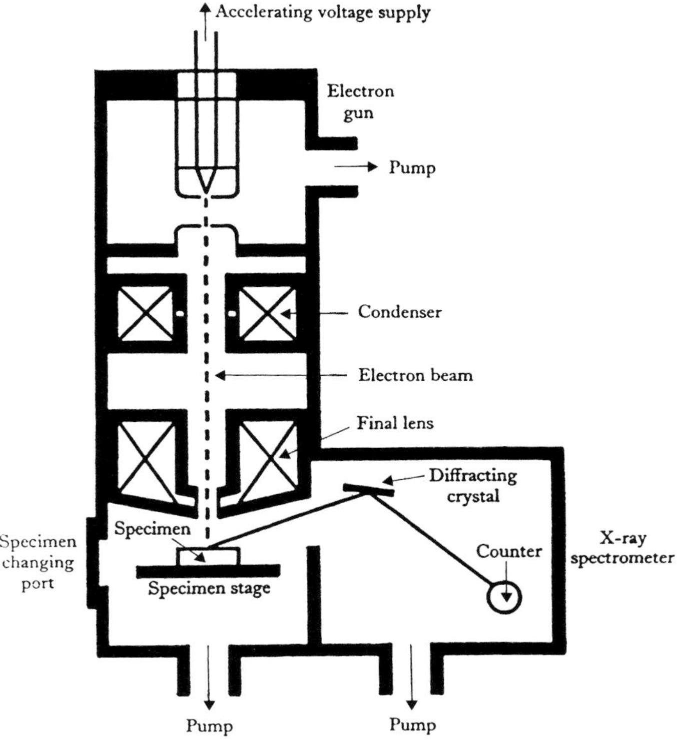

Figure 8.12 Schematic diagram (section) of an electron microprobe. Note the magnetic lenses in the electron gun on the left. The electron beam is focused on the glass samples mounted in a block of epoxy resin. The spectrometer is on the right-hand side of the diagram. It consists of a diffracting crystal and a counter. The system operates under vacuum, hence the presence of three (vacuum) pumps.

Electron microprobe analysis of Eighteenth Dynasty glasses from Amarna

Electron microprobe analysis is a quantitative technique, and given the small beam size it is normal to analyse three to five spots of a homogeneous material, like glass, and average the results. As with any analytical technique, the cross-analysis of a multi-element standard not used in calibrating the system and of proven reliability at the start and end of the analysis will provide two things: the determination of relative analytical accuracy and a means of monitoring any drift in the system. One of the advantages of using EPMA is that the system only provides a total analysis of what it has detected. This means that if the analyst has omitted an important element from the analysis the total will be low. By using analytical techniques which normalise results to 100 per cent there is a danger of distorting the results if one or more element has been omitted from the anlaysis.

Table 8.1b provides electron microprobe analyses of twenty-six samples of Eighteenth-Dynasty Egyptian glasses from Amarna. The range of information that can be derived from these analyses falls into a range of interconnected areas: a definition of the glass compositional type; the identification of the primary components; the identification of the colorants and opacifiers used; the detection of impurities in the glass which help to fingerprint the raw materials used, occasionally allowing the analyst to suggest their sources and an assessment of the compositional variation among the samples. A description of the samples is given in Table 8.1a. It can be seen that glasses of a range of colours have been analysed: translucent turquoise, translucent purple, opaque yellow, opaque white, opaque blue and opaque turquoise. All of these glass samples were taken from vessel fragments which derived from Petrie's excavations and which are now in the Ashmolean Museum, Oxford. All the analyses were carried out using electron-probe microanalysis (for full technical specifications of the wavelength-dispersive electron microprobe used, see Henderson 1988: 78–80).

The basic chemical composition of all the glasses is soda (Na_2O) – 'lime' (CaO) – silica (SiO_2). The only other major component present in some specimens is lead oxide, making lead oxide–soda–lime–silica glasses. Lead oxide is present at levels of up to 9.4 per cent in these glasses (Table 8.1b, analysis 5). X-ray spectra are given in Figures 8.8–8.10 for translucent blue, opaque blue, opaque white and opaque yellow glasses from Amarna; these were obtained using PIXE however.

Table 8.1a. *Description of the Amarna glass samples taken from core-formed vessel fragments*

Sample numbers 1–3
Ashmolean Museum 1924. 118e (55A) Thickened rim fragment with a straight sided neck. Translucent truquoise (1) with combed opaque yellow (2) and opaque white (3) decoration.

Sample number 4–7
Ashmolean Museum 1924. 118b (55A) Thickened rim fragment with a straight sided neck. Translucent turquoise (4) with combed opaque yellow (5), opaque blue (6) and translucent turquoise (7) decoration.

Sample numbers 8–9
Ashmolean Museum 1924. 118a (55A) Opaque pale green vessel wall fragment with combed opaque blue (8) and opaque yelow decoration. Further decorated with an opaque white (9) and blue cable.

Sample numbers 10–11
Ashmolean Museum 1924.416 (55A) An opaque 'apple green' vessel wall fragment (10) with combed opaque white (11) and opaque yellow decoration.

Sample numbers 12–14
Ashmolean Museum 1924. 92 (55A) A translucent purple vessel should fragment (12) with combed opaque yellow (13) and opaque white (14) decoration.

Sample numbers 15–18
Ashmolean Museum 1921.1158 (55A) A deep translucent cobalt blue vessel neck (15) with combed opaque turquoise (16), opaque yellow (17) and opaque white decoration (18).

Sample numbers 19–21
Ashmolean Museum 1936.623 (55A) An opaque yellow vessel wall fragemnt (19) with an inlaid blue band (20) and inlaid stratified eyes of a 'saucer' of blue glass (20) with a superimposed saucer of opaque whtie and a central circular setting of opaque turquoise (21).

Sample numbers 22–24
Ashmolean Museum 1924.117d (55A) An opaque white vessel wall fragment (22) with inlaid stratified eyes with a 'saucer' of opaque blue glass (23) with a dark reddish-brown (24) centres.

Sample numbers 25–26
Ashmolean Museum 1924. 117f (55A) A thick opaque white vessel fragment with inlaid opaque white (25) and opaque blue (26) (bichrome) cables enclosing the possible remnants of an opaque yellow disc inside an opaque turquoise setting.

The alkalies used

It is generally agreed that the principle source of alkali in Egyptian glasses of the second millennium BC was a plant ash of the genus *Salicornia* or *Salsola*, both of which grow in the desert or maritime environments found in Egypt and the Middle East. The compositional characteristics of these halophytic plants (high soda with a relatively high impurity level of magnesia and a low impurity level of potassium oxide) are carried through into the glass made from them, and can be seen in Table 8.1b. Analytical and experimental work by Brill (1970) has shown that samples of *keli*, the ash of the *chinan* plant which grows in the Syrian desert, is characterised by high soda levels (28 per cent), low potassium oxide (5.5 per cent) high calcium oxide (21.1 per cent) and low magnesia (0.5 per cent) (Brill 1970: table 2). Other analyses of soda-rich plant ashes contained considerably higher magnesia levels accompanying the soda. Glasses made in this way are referred to as 'high magnesia

Table 8.1b. *Electron probe analyses of 18th Dynasty coloured glass samples performed by J. Henderson taken from core-formed vessels in the Ashmolean Museum, Oxford, excavated by Petrie from Amarna, Egypt (expressed as the weight percentage of each of the elements in the glasses) For a full description of the vessels sampled see Table 8.1*

Analysis no.	1	2	3	4	5	6	7
Colour	Trans turq	opaque yellow	opaque white	Trans turq	opaque yellow	opaque blue	Trans turq
Na_2O	18.7	15.6	17.8	18.3	12.9	21.6	17.5
MgO	4.8	4.1	4.2	4.2	5.1	3.9	4.0
Al_2O_3	0.5	0.8	0.7	1.2	1.1	5.9	1.2
SiO_2	63.0	61.1	63.0	64.0	56.1	55.9	62.7
P_2O_5	0.1	0.2	ND	0.2	0.2	0.3	0.2
SO_3	0.3	0.5	0.5	0.3	0.4	0.7	0.2
Cl	0.7	0.8	0.7	1.3	0.9	1.8	1.3
K_2O	2.7	3.2	3.0	1.3	3.0	0.9	1.7
CaO	6.4	7.0	6.9	8.6	8.9	5.8	8.8
TiO_2	0.04	0.1	0.06	0.11	0.1	0.1	0.1
Cr_2O_3	0.02	ND	ND	ND	ND	ND	ND
MnO	0.05	0.04	0.03	0.07	0.04	0.3	0.05
Fe_2O_3	0.27	0.5	0.29	0.63	0.8	1.1	0.69
CoO	ND	ND	0.02	0.03	ND	0.21	0.02
NiO	ND	ND	ND	ND	ND	0.08	ND
CuO	1.4	ND	ND	0.7	0.1	0.5	0.86
ZnO	ND	0.17	ND	0.02	0.2	0.31	ND
As_2O_3	0.02	ND	0.12	0.03	ND	0.04	0.02
SnO_2	0.17	0.1	ND	0.06	ND	ND	0.04
Sb_2O_3	0.02	0.39	3.43	0.04	0.9	0.7	ND
BaO	ND	ND	ND	ND	ND	ND	ND
PbO	0.04	6.6	ND	0.06	9.4	0.08	0.06

Analysis No.	8	9	10	11	12	13
Colour	opaque blue	opaque white	opaque green	opaque white	Trans purple	opaque yellow
Na_2O	19.5	18.2	18.7	16.2	16.9	17.0
MgO	3.3	4.2	4.5	4.3	4.0	4.5
Al_2O_3	3.4	0.6	0.6	0.8	1.1	0.6
SiO_2	62.8	61.9	61.6	56.8	65.2	59.7
P_2O_5	0.1	0.2	0.2	0.1	0.1	0.1
SO_3	0.37	0.4	0.5	0.5	0.4	0.4
Cl	1.5	1.1	0.9	0.7	0.9	0.9
K_2O	0.9	3.0	2.6	2.0	1.9	2.5
CaO	5.7	8.0	6.6	11.2	9.0	8.4
TiO_2	0.06	0.04	0.05	0.06	0.06	0.02
Cr_2O_3	0.02	ND	0.02	ND	0.02	ND
MnO	0.31	0.01	0.01	0.01	0.80	0.03
Fe_2O_3	0.57	0.24	0.4	0.37	0.42	0.46
CoO	0.15	0.02	ND	ND	0.02	ND
NiO	0.04	0.04	0.02	0.01	0.02	0.01
CuO	0.83	0.01	1.29	ND	ND	0.08
ZnO	0.11	0.03	ND	0.03	ND	0.25
As_2O_3	0.03	0.12	0.04	0.24	0.06	ND
SnO_2	0.01	ND	ND	0.01	ND	ND
Sb_2O_3	1.21	2.49	0.63	7.56	ND	0.69
BaO	ND	ND	ND	ND	ND	ND
PbO	0.03	ND	1.56	0.01	ND	4.33

Analysis No.	14	15	16	17	18	19
Colour	opaque white	Trans blue	opaque turq	opaque yellow	opaque white	opaque yellow
Na_2O	15.7	18.8	18.4	18.9	13.8	16.5
MgO	4.1	3.6	4.6	4.9	4.7	4.0
Al_2O_3	0.5	3.4	0.7	1.2	2.6	0.8
SiO_2	61.2	62.5	62.3	60.8	63.7	62.7
P_2O_5	0.1	0.1	0.02	0.2	0.2	0.1
SO_3	0.4	0.2	0.21	0.5	0.5	0.2
Cl	0.6	0.6	0.68	1.0	1.1	0.5
K_2O	2.2	0.7	1.6	3.1	3.1	2.7
CaO	12.8	6.8	7.7	8.1	8.9	5.3
TiO_2	0.06	0.06	0.04	0.02	0.06	0.06
Cr_2O_3	ND	0.02	0.02	ND	0.02	ND
MnO	0.03	0.7	0.01	0.04	0.03	0.05
Fe_2O_3	0.27	0.56	0.3	0.35	0.34	0.99
CoO	ND	0.19	0.02	ND	0.02	ND
NiO	ND	0.03	ND	ND	ND	ND
CuO	0.06	0.22	1.51	0.01	ND	0.01
ZnO	0.02	0.14	ND	0.09	ND	0.02
As_2O_3	0.08	ND	0.05	0.05	0.06	ND
SnO_2	ND	0.01	ND	ND	ND	ND
Sb_2O_3	0.91	0.33	1.37	ND	1.92	0.95
BaO	ND	ND	ND	ND	ND	ND
PbO	ND	0.11	ND	1.5	0.1	5.25

Analysis No.	20	21	22	23	24	25	26
Colour	Trans blue	opaque turq	opaque white	Trans blue	opaque red	opaque white	Trans blue
Na_2O	18.6	19.1	20.4	19.1	19.0	19.7	19.9
MgO	3.8	4.5	6.2	5.0	5.2	4.5	4.3
Al_2O_3	0.9	0.9	1.6	2.4	2.7	0.9	3.3
SiO_2	62.4	62.2	62.2	62.9	57.5	63.5	60.3
P_2O_5	0.1	0.1	0.1	ND	ND	0.1	0.1
SO_3	0.2	0.3	0.2	0.2	0.1	0.3	0.5
Cl	0.7	0.6	0.6	0.5	0.4	0.8	0.6
K_2O	3.3	4.0	2.7	2.3	2.9	2.1	1.8
CaO	5.2	5.5	5.2	4.7	5.2	7.4	6.1
TiO_2	0.04	0.04	ND	ND	0.1	ND	0.1
Cr_2O_3	0.02	ND	ND	ND	ND	ND	ND
MnO	0.05	0.04	0.07	0.08	0.16	ND	0.4
Fe_2O_3	0.62	0.54	0.4	0.3	7.6	0.4	0.5
CoO	0.12	0.02	ND	0.08	0.18	ND	0.29
NiO	0.02	0.02	ND	ND	ND	ND	0.06
CuO	0.36	1.27	ND	0.1	1.2	ND	0.06
ZnO	0.02	0.02	ND	ND	ND	ND	0.37
As_2O_3	ND	0.07	0.05	ND	0.4	0.07	0.07
SnO_2	0.08	ND	0.1	ND	ND	ND	ND
Sb_2O_3	0.17	1.0	1.3	0.2	0.3	1.5	1.4
BaO	ND	ND	ND	ND	ND	ND	ND
PbO	1.01	0.04	ND	0.3	0.3	ND	ND

Note: Trans = translucent; turq = turquoise

(soda–lime) glass' (HMG; see Sayre and Smith 1967: 285, 287) to distinguish them from 'low magnesia (soda–lime) glasses', which were later made in Egypt (LMG); the levels of magnesia (MgO) are given in Table 8.1b. The most likely mineral used for the later LMGs was natron (Forbes 1957, 142). Analysis of twelve samples of natron taken from Wadi Natrun and chemically analysed revealed its true crystalline identity to be 'trona', which is a sodium sesquicarbonate, $Na_2CO_3.NaHCO_3.2H_2O$ (Brill pers. comm.). Trona also occurs in the Beheira province of Lower Egypt, a source which was certainly worked in antiquity. During the New Kingdom, however, it has been suggested that ready-made glass was imported from the Middle East (Oppenheim 1973: 260; and see p. 195, this volume). It is worth noting that trona was not only used for glass production but also medically as a detergent and in the process of embalming (see Turner 1956a: 283; see also Chapter 16, this volume). The sodium (kα) X-ray peak is visible at 1.041 KeV in Figures 8.8–8.10. The range of soda (Na_2O) levels detected is given in Table 8.1b.

Silica

Silica in glass-making is provided by sand or quartz pebbles. To locate sand sources obviously does not pose a problem, but to locate sources which have low mineral impurities, such as iron-bearing minerals, is more difficult (Highley 1977). Lucas (1948), among others, has noted the presence of shell fragments in sand which would potentially have provided a major source in the glass batch. Turner (1956b) studied the mineralogical composition of sand from Amarna, from the shore of the river Nile opposite Luxor, and from the Belus river by Haifa in Israel. All the samples contained variable levels of quartz (the silica source), calcite (a calcium source), feldspars, pyroxenes and ilmenite; the sand from Thebes was the only one to contain mud and mica. The sand from Amarna contained between 50 and 55 per cent quartz, 30 and 33 per cent calcite, 5 per cent feldspars, 5 per cent pyroxenes and 1 per cent ilmenite, and can thus be considered a relatively 'clean' sand source.

Lead

Lead (in the form of lead antimonate, $Pb_2Sb_2O_7$) was used from the Eighteenth Dynasty (1550–1307 BC) onwards in Egyptian glasses, specifically for decorative opaque yellow glasses which were normally applied to core-formed vessels. The presence of lead was detected by Turner and Rooksby (1959: 18, table 1B) in glass from Thebes dated to *c.* 1450–1425 BC using X-ray diffraction and confirmed by Sayre (1964). Lead has also been detected in faience (Kaczmarczyk and Hedges 1983). The earliest historical reference to lead can be found in Mesopotamian texts dated to the seventh century BC but thought to have originally derived from a source dating to the twelfth century BC (Brill 1970: 121). *None* of the translucent glasses in Table 8.1b, nor any other translucent glasses dated to periods before the eighth century BC, appears to have been made from lead-rich glasses. Lead is always present in glass as an oxide; although there is no actual archaeological evidence for lead being used as a primary raw material in Egyptian glass production, it must have been added at some point in the production cycle and converted into an oxide.

Crystalline lead antimonate, which can be prepared by heating the oxides of lead and antimony together would have been added directly to the glass as an opacifier (see Fig. 8.7 and p. 208). Work by Brill and co-workers using lead isotope analysis (Brill *et al.* 1993) has shown that characteristic sources of lead (galena) used for Eighteenth-Dynasty glasses (for example) presumably existed somewhere in the Eastern Desert, or possibly along the coast of the Arabian Peninsula (Brill 1993: 59). An X-ray spectrum for an opaque yellow glass from Amarna is given in Figure 8.9. Two lead (Pb) L peaks are visible, as is a series of antimony (Sb) K peaks.

Calcium

Typically, Eighteenth-Dynasty glasses contain calcium oxide levels of between about 6.5 and 9.0 per cent (Table 8.1b), and this indeed is also a common level of calcium oxide found in other soda–lime glasses in the first millennium BC and the first millennium AD (Turner 1956b: 45; Henderson 1985: 277, 1995). Calcium oxide is essential in glass as a network stabiliser; a soda–silica glass would tend to dissolve easily in water.

The surprising feature of Egyptian (and other ancient) soda–lime–silica glasses is that the calcium oxide level is almost invariably between about 6.5 and 9.0 per cent; the analyses in Table 8.1b are no exception. Had the ancient Egyptians used sand sources which were rich in shell fragments, would we expect this repeatable and consistent level of calcium oxide to enter the glass melt? Brill (1970: 109) has suggested that the proportion of shell fragments is always the same in the sand source, resulting in a repeatable glass composition. It is however, much more likely that, as with ancient metallurgy where consistent proportions of mineral-bearing ores would have been purified and melted, the different constituents of the sand were separated so that the shell fragments could be used as a calcium source, but that they would have been added in measured quantities to the glass batch.

Impurities

As to the impurity levels detected in the glasses, the expected high magnesia was detected in all the glasses analysed; however another impurity, potassium oxide, likely to have been introduced with the plant ash used as an alkali, is present at elevated levels in almost all the glasses. Three chemical analyses of blue glasses all contain relatively low potassium oxide levels at levels of 0.9 per cent (analysis 6), 0.9 per cent (analysis 8) and 0.7 per cent (analysis 15); these blue glasses contain the lowest magnesium levels of all the glass samples analysed strongly suggesting that they were fused using a different plant ash source of alkali.

The alumina levels in the glasses are mainly below 1 per cent, except, as expected, in blue glasses (see p. 215). However, three other glasses also contain somewhat higher levels: analysis 18 at 2.6 per cent (opaque white), analysis 22 at 1.6 per cent (opaque white) and analysis 24 of 2.7% (opaque reddish-brown). Again these glasses have evidently been prepared in a slightly different way from the rest and these elevated alumina levels are very unexpected in glasses of this age, especially sample 18, which contains an alumina level more typical of Hellenistic or Roman glass technology. The most likely interpretation of these elevated alumina levels is that they were introduced as an impurity in the sand used as a silica source (Matson 1951: 841); the low alumina levels present in the other glasses is thought to be due to the use of quartz as a silica source. Turner (1954: 441) and Saleh *et al.* (1972) indicate that corrosion of a glass-melting crucible could contribute impurities such as silica, alumina, iron oxide, lime, magnesia and alkalies to the glass melt. However, the generally consistent impurity levels in glass from Tell el-Amarna link to the use of different glass colours suggests that crucible corrosion may only make a minor contribution to the final glass composition: obviously the volume of the melt and consequently the size of the crucible involved will determine whether or not crucible corrosion makes a significant contribution to the chemical composition of the glass.

Glass colour

As noted above the principal colorants detected are as follows: cobalt in both opaque blue (Table 8.1b, analyses 6 and 8) and translucent blue glasses (Table 8.1b, analyses 15, 20, 23 and 26); copper (cupric) in translucent turquoise (Table 8.1b, analyses 1, 4 and 7) and opaque turquoise glasses (16, 21) and manganese in the translucent purple glass analysed (Table 8.1b, analysis 12). The colorants detected in the opaque glasses are calcium antimonate in opaque white glass (Table 8.1b, analyses 3, 9, 11, 14, 18, 22 and 25) and this opacifier combined with other colorants: with cobalt in opaque blue (Table 8.1b analyses 6 and 8), and with copper in opaque turquoise (Table 8.1b analyses 16 and 21). Lead antimonate is the crystalline colorant in opaque yellow glasses (Table 8.1b, analyses 2, 5, 13, 17 and 19). The 'apple' green colour of sample 10 is probably a combination of yellow lead antimonate and a copper (cupric) green glass matrix. The brownish-red sample (24) is coloured and opacified by cuprous oxide; the high level of iron oxide detected (7.6 per cent) will have been added as an internal reducing agent and will also have allowed the copper to dissolve with greater ease (Guido *et al.* 1984: 248). The generation and control of colour in ancient glass is by no means simple. The chemical environment, the redox equlibria in the furnace and subsequent heat treatment of the glass being amongst the determining factors.

Cobalt blue The chemical analyses of Eighteenth-Dynasty glasses presented in Table 8.1b include blue samples with elevated levels of aluminia of *c.* 5.9 per cent; the X-ray spectra for translucent and opaque blue glasses are shown in Figures 8.10–8.11. This is a factor of five or six lower than found in other translucent glass colours. It is also significant that these cobalt-blue glasses, present as Co^{4+} ions (Bamford 1977: 42) are associated with the impurities which Sayre (1964) and Kaczmarczyck and Hedges (1983) have detected in New Kingdom vitreous materials, such as the oxides of manganese, iron, nickel, copper and variable zinc and lead. Peaks for manganese, iron, nickel, copper and antimony are visible in Figure 8.11, in addition to the zinc. In addition to these, zinc and silver are shown to be present in the X-ray spectrum for the opaque blue glass (Fig. 8.10).

Turquoise blue and red-brown opaque glasses The two ionic states of copper produce two correspondingly different colours in Egyptian glasses: a turquoise-blue colour when the cupric (Cu^{2+}) ion is present (Brill 1970: 120) and a dull brown-red colour when the cuprous (Cu^{+}) ion is present (Hughes 1972; Freestone 1987; Guido *et al.* 1984). Weyl (1953: 164–5) notes that the 'green' colour is only produced in the presence of lead oxide in the glass, however several examples of copper-green (translucent turquoise-green) glasses with no detectable lead have been found (Table 8.1b). After brass is introduced, copper and zinc are often found to be associated in ancient turquoise glasses, where scrap brass has been introduced as a colorant.

All Egyptian opaque red glasses which pre-date the ninth century BC contain lead levels of less than 3 per cent oxide; after this date the lead oxide levels generally rise and a brighter (sealing-wax) red glass colour is produced (Freestone 1987) with the development of different, dendritic, cuprous oxide crystals in the glass rather than globular particles.

Iron and manganese Egyptian glasses were coloured 'deliberately' by the probable use of minute quantities of manganese-bearing minerals such as pyrolusite (MnO_2). The chemical compositions of translucent purple Eighteenth-Dynasty glasses (e.g. Table 8.1b, analysis 12) show an elevated manganese oxide level, apparently with few other accompanying impurities, implying that a relatively pure mineral source of colorant, like pyrolusite, was used. The purple colour would be produced by the trivalent Mn^{3+} ion in the glass (Weyl 1937: 118). Manganese, which in later periods is used as a decolorant in glass (Henderson 1985), is present in blue glasses as an impurity and in the purple glass as a colorant, but in the balance of glasses analysed it has either not been detected or only detected at very low levels.

Iron oxide is often present in Egyptian glasses, and may be used to produce a translucent dark brown colour, but generally it occurs only as an impurity which is eclipsed by the addition of colorants like cobalt and copper to the glass melt. The common iron-green glass of later periods is produced by a mixture of ferrous (Fe2+) and ferric (Fe+) ions in the glass melt (Weyl 1953: 91; Bamford 1982: 6; Sellner *et al.* 1979). Newton (1978) was of the opinion that Medieval glassmakers were 'at the mercy of the furnaces they used', so little direct control existed over the available free oxygen. Egyptians, on the other hand, apparently controlled tightly the addition of trace or minor quantities of colorants deliberately.

Other opacifiers The use of opacifiers in Egyptian glass is discussed above (see pp. 207–8). The electron-microprobe analyses in Table 8.1b provide data which conform with the results produced by other workers: opaque yellow glasses were opacified with lead antimonate (analyses 2, 5, 13, 17 and 19), opaque white glasses with calcium antimonate (analyses 3, 9, 11, 14, 18, 22 and 25), opaque blue, green and turquoise with a combination of calcium antimonate crystals and cobalt, copper and iron, and copper respectively. Often the translucent matrices in which the opacifying crystals sit have a colour which may be modified by the presence of other impurities associated with the colorant or other raw materials. Figures 8.8–8.10 are X-ray spectra produced using proton-induced X-ray emission for opaque white, opaque yellow and opaque blue Amarna glasses. It can be seen that there are major peaks for calcium and antimony in all three glasses because calcium antimonate is the opacifier present. Lead is at higher levels in the opaque yellow glass because lead antimonate is present and cobalt is present in the opaque blue glass.

The working properties of Egyptian soda–lime glasses

The chemical compositions of Egyptian glasses determine their working properties (Doremus 1994, 99 figure 1). As we have seen, most Egyptian translucent glasses are soda–lime–silica in composition. The liquidus temperature for a soda–lime–silica glass containing 18.8 per cent soda, 7 per cent calcium oxide and 74.2 per cent silica is 867 °C, which rises to 1,060 °C for a glass containing 17.6 per cent soda, 15 per cent calcium oxide and 64.7 per cent silica (Morey 1964). The former composition is closest to that for second millennium BC Egyptian glasses, however a closer comparison is provided by the work of Brill (1988) where, despite the fact that the glass dates to the fourth century AD, the basic composition is similar to other, earlier, soda–lime glasses (with some important differences in impurity patterns). Brill (1988, 278–81) showed that for a typical soda–lime glass of *c.* 68–73 per cent silica, *c.* 14–17.4 per cent soda and *c.* 7.4–10 per cent calcium oxide ('lime') the liquidus temperarure was *c.* 900 °C, the softening temperature at which the glass could be moulded was *c.* 1,000 °C and the marvering and gathering temperatures were *c.* 1,000–1,100 °C. It is therefore a perfectly valid assumption that the softening and working temperatures for an Egyptian soda–lime–silica glass of the second millennium BC were between *c.* 1,000 and 1,100 °C. The glass would therefore have a relatively short working time, but since the vessels are made with cores, the length of time it took for the wound trails of glass to fuse would not have been a problem. On the other hand a range of (generally opaque) glasses were used in the decoration of the core formed vessels. Some of these had a high lead oxide level (see Table 8.1b) and would therefore have had a much longer working time and a lower softening temperature of *c.* 750 °C, depending on the level of lead oxide involved. The opaque white glasses used for decorative trailing would have been more difficult to work because they contain no detectable lead oxide, or low levels. These glasses would have been applied as opaque rods to the surface of the core-formed vessels (Gudenrath 1991), and would have been continuously re-heated in order to soften them. This, in turn, could have led to distortions of the patterns, but the most difficult part of the operation would have been to avoid distorting the glass vessel while at the same time keeping the rod of decorative glass sufficiently soft to work. The complete decorated core-formed vessels very rarely display any signs that the artisan who made them had problems decorating them.

Chemical analysis and the interpretation of Egyptian glass technology

It is evident from the above discussion of analytical techniques that great strides have been made in the development of both quicker and less destructive techniques. The interpretation of the results has enabled the analyst to contribute to archaeology in a range of new ways. Some of the earliest analytical work, by Farnsworth and Ritchie (1938) showed that even qualitative analyses could enable the investigator to classify the glasses chemically and to suggest a possible source for the cobalt-rich mineral used to colour Eighteenth-Dynasty Egyptian glasses. Even then it was possible to indicate that the glass technology of the Eighteenth Dynasty was well-formed and involved a range of procedures which were standardised by that time.

Any analytical investigation of Egyptian glass before about 1960, and during the time when Lucas was working, tended to be time-consuming and destructive, using techniques such as arc-source emission spectrometry. Consequently, the number of chemical analyses of Egyptian glass was relatively restricted, and the questions asked of the data were connected to the fact that statistical rigour in assembling compositional groupings tended to be lacking. However, some seminal work was carried out by Rooksby and Turner for example (Rooksby 1962; Turner and Rooksby 1959, 1961, 1963) in the investigation of the compounds used to opacify ancient glasses using X-ray diffraction and identified for the first time some compounds only used in ancient glasses. In spite of Neumann's (1929: 835) claim that the opaque colours found in trailed-on decoration was due to tin oxide this is most unlikely in view of the work by Rooksby, Turner and others. Not a single second millennium BC specimen of Egyptian opaque glass has provided further evidence of the use of tin oxide as an opacifier. Nevertheless Neumann (Neumann and Kotyga 1925: 192) did establish the basic chemical characteristics of Egyptian glasses.

Turner (1956c) carried out a further review and substantiated the basic quantitative characteristics of Egyptian glasses and from this he was able to suggest strongly the kinds of primary raw materials that were used for making Egyptian glass (Turner 1956a). He even refers to the chemical analysis of potential sand sources for Egyptian glasses in order to establish some of the potential impurities that could be introduced into the glass (Turner 1956a: 280–1, tables I–III). Turner's investigation of the glass technology at Amarna (Turner 1954) was the first real study of what can be described as an Egyptian glass production site. This involved the relationship of glass chemical composition to working properties and even the ceramic materials used for crucibles. Publication of later Egyptian glass analyses (Turner 1956c: 169, Table III) dating to *c.* 200–100 BC from Elephantine and 'Alexandrian' glasses showed that while the soda–lime–silica glass technology had persisted in use, 'Roman' glass technology had been introduced to Egypt by this time. The main compositional differences from glasses of the second millennium BC was the use of glasses containing markedly lower magnesia and potassium oxide levels due to the probable use of a mineral source of alkali, like natron, instead of a plant ash. The other difference is the occurrence of a generally much higher level of alumina in the later glasses, which is likely to be due to the use of a sand source rich in an alumina-rich mineral impurity such as feldspar or epidote (Matson 1951: 84; Henderson 1985: 271). Although tin oxide is unusual in opaque glasses of the second to first century BC outside Europe, an opaque white glass of this date from Elephantine contained 0.54 per cent tin oxide (and no copper), and therefore may have been opacified by tin oxide (Turner 1956c: table III, 169); only X-ray diffraction analysis of the glass would provide unambiguous evidence for the presence of tin oxide crystals. Bimson and Freestone (1988: 13–15) published the chemical and structural analyses of glass foundation-deposit plaques of Ptolemy III and Queen Berenice dated to between 246 and 221 BC. These analyses also showed that a low magnesia soda–lime glass was in use which was characterised by elevated alumina levels in the 'Roman' tradition.

The use of a far more automated technique, neutron activation analysis (NAA), led Sayre (1964) and Sayre and Smith (1961) to show how soda–lime Egyptian glasses fitted into other ancient glass technologies in a global context. Because the technique allowed Sayre to examine relative levels of glass impurities in detail, he was able to pinpoint Egyptian glass compositions with unusual characteristics (Sayre 1964). Sayre and Smith (1967) also enlarged Turner's (1954) study of raw materials used in Egyptian glasses by examining the impurity levels introduced by different raw materials in detail; he was able to do this because NAA enabled him to carry out a larger number of analyses (although only fifteen glass samples from the second millennium BC were analysed) and thus he was able to establish compositional variability for individual chemical groupings and also to indicate any exceptions from the norm.

The chemical analyses of Egyptian glasses by Fleming and Swan (1986) using a proton probe (PIXE), provided new data which supported the patterns established by Turner (1954) and by Sayre (1964), emphasising, for example, that very small quantities of colorant-bearing materials must have been introduced in the ancient glass melts (Fleming and Swan 1986) in order to bring about a controlled colouring effect in the glass (Henderson 1985: 283). PIXE is an ideal system for this study because it is capable of detecting very low levels of materials.

Electron microprobe analysis, a micro-destructive technique which can produce high quality results, became a relatively widely used analytical technique in the 1970s. The alumina levels detected in the electron probe analyses of Eighteenth-Dynasty opaque glasses published here suggest that the recipe used for making glass at Amarna was not always the same, and indeed the low levels of magnesia in the cobalt-blue glasses detected (Table 8.1b) suggests that a different source of alkali was used in making them (and see Lilyquist and Brill 1993: 41). Other chemical analyses of Amarna glasses have been published by Kühne (1969).

Many of Brill's analyses of Egyptian glasses involved the use of AAS (atomic absorption spectroscopy; see Lilyquist and Brill 1993). Important compositional similarites were noted for glass dating to between the late sixteenth and fourteenth centuries, underlining both that the glass used was the product of a relatively well-established industry, given a relatively low level of compositional variation, and that while the mineralogy of ceramics can sometimes provide a means of 'fingerprinting' them, glass can be far more difficult to characterise as to its regionalised production technology.

Complete chemical analysis of blue and turquoise glass ingots from the fourteenth-century BC Ulu Burun shipwreck, undertaken by Brill, has not yet been published (*cf.* Bass 1986: 282 n. 55; see also section on secondary processing p. 200). In any case it is not yet clear as to whether glass was made from raw materials in Egypt *and* in Mesopotamia in the fourteenth century BC, or imported from Mesopotamia. Although glass was intentionally manufactured in Western Asia from at least as early as *c.* 1500 BC (Moorey 1994: 201) no incontrovertible evidence has been found for the fritting of glass from primary raw materials in either Egypt or Mesopotamia, this being the only certain evidence for primary glass-making at a specific location. Although the earliest glass has been found in Mesopotamia, this does not preclude the possibility that glass was fused from primary raw materials in Egypt later. Further archaeological and scientific investigations need to be carried out in order to investigate this.

If we compare the impurity patterns of magnesia and potassium oxide detected in the Amarna glasses listed here with those from glasses of the late fifteenth to fourteenth centuries BC and thirteenth to twelfth centuries BC from the site of Pella in Jordan (Henderson in preparation) and of fourteenth-century BC date from Tell Brak in Syria (Henderson 1998), as well as Minoan glasses of *c.* fourteenth century BC (Henderson, unpublished analyses), it can be seen that the Amarna glasses form a relatively tight compositional group when compared with the glasses from Tell Brak (see Fig. 8.13). It will be noted that there is also a very interesting compositional distinction between low magnesia thirteenth- and twelfth-century Pella glasses and the earlier high magnesia late fifteenth- and fourteenth-century Pella glasses which, apart from one, fall close to the Amarna glasses. Thus, although from an early period Egyptian glass displays signs of being a conservative technology (Lilyquist and Brill 1993: table 2; see also Table 8.1b and Fig. 8.13 here), and to some extent this is also true of Amarna glass, there is nevertheless some compositional variation, with some relatively high alumina levels occurring in translucent non-cobalt glasses as early as the reign of Thutmose III (Lilyquist and Brill 1993: fig. 57).

The fusion of glass raw materials at high temperatures of up to *c.* 1,400 °C, and the introduction of minute quantities of colorants to the glass in highly controlled ways, are both a testament to the extremely high degree of skill which was involved in glass manufacture in Egypt. Further detailed analytical investigations need to be carried out in order to establish whether glass was made independently from an early period in Egypt; questions still remain as to whether all early Egyptian glass was imported from Mesopotamia and where the glass ingots found on the Ulu Burun shipwreck were originally made, as distinct from being poured into moulds. It is worth noting however, that the moulding of ingots of foreign glass in Egypt, for export to a third country would seem an odd practice unless they were being altered in some way, for example by the addition of a local colorant (see section on secondary processing p. 199). Given the potential variation in the impurity levels of glasses of the second millennium BC in the circum-Mediterranean region (Fig. 8.13), further analytical research is essential.

Acknowledgements [Nicholson]

I would like to thank the Egypt Exploration Society and Mr Barry Kemp for their suppport of my work at site O45.1 at Amarna. The work has been funded by the Wainwright Fund for Near Eastern Archaeology to whom I am indebted, while analytical work by myself and Dr Caroline M. Jackson has been supported by the Leverhulme Trust, grant F/407/J whose support is gratefully acknowledged.

Rene Cappers and Mary Anne Murray kindly provided information on the distribution of glass-making plants and Dr Delwen Samuel gave information on alkali plants. Mr Ian Mathieson carried out geophysical survey at site O45.1 and I am indebted to him. Ms Susan Cole, Mr Ian Dennis, Dr Jackson, Professor Michael S. Tite and Dr Katharine M. Trott have all worked for the 'Amarna Glass Project', and

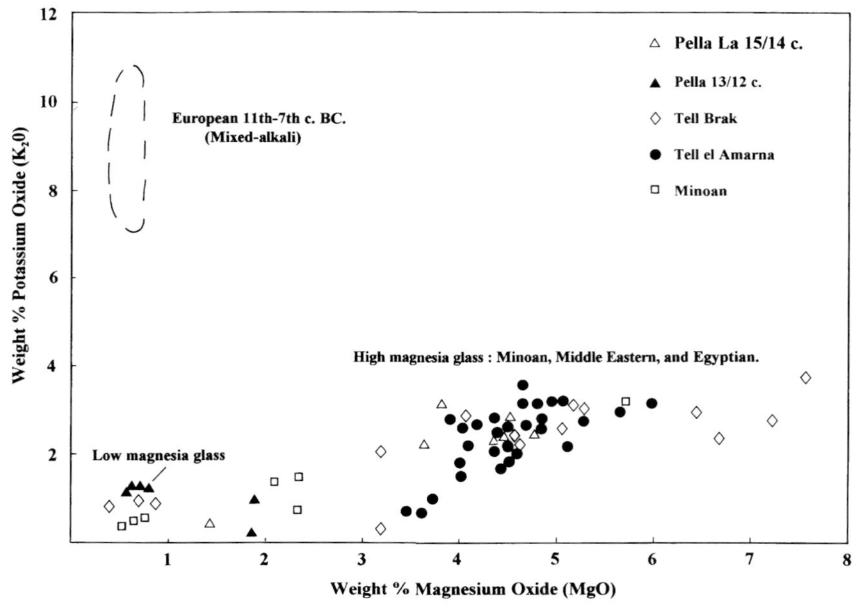

Figure 8.13 A bivariate plot of weight percent of potassium oxide (K_2O) versus weight per cent magnesia (MgO) in glass samples dating to between the fifteenth and twelfth centuries BC from Pella (Jordan); Tell Brak (Syria); Amarna (Egypt); and Minoan samples from Crete. The relative magnesia and potassium oxide levels of some eleventh to seventh century BC glasses from Europe are also plotted to illustrate that an entirely different (mixed-alkali) glass technology also existed slightly later the these soda–lime glasses plotted.

their hard work is gratefully acknowledged. The work at Amarna would not have been possible without the kind cooperation of the Egyptian Supreme Council for Antiquities to whom I am indebted.

Ms Janine Bourriau and Dr Carol Andrews kindly commented on an earlier draft of my section of this chapter and I am indebted to them for their comments.

Acknowledgements [Henderson]

I would like to thank Dr Roger Moorey and Dr Helen Whitehouse of the Ashmolean Museum, Oxford, for permission to sample glass from Tell el-Amarna in order to undertake electron probe microanalyses. I would also like to record my thanks to Dr Ian Freestone and Dr Norman Charnley for discussions over the years on the interpretation of glass analyses, and to both St Cross College, Oxford for a Junior Research Fellowship and the (then) SERC for a Post-doctoral Fellowship at the time when this research was carried out.

References

Bamford, C. R. 1977. *Colour Generation and Control in Glass.* Amsterdam: Elsevier Scientific Publishing.

1982. Optical properties of flat glass. *Journal of Non-Crystalline Solids*, 47 (1): 1–20.

Bass, G. 1986. A Bronze Age shipwreck at Ulu Burun (Kas): 1984 campaign. *AJA*, 90: 269–96.

1987. Oldest known shipwreck reveals splendors of the Bronze Age. *National Geographic*, 172 (6): 692–733.

Bass, G, Pulak, C., Collon, D. and Weinstein, J. 1989. The Bronze Age shipwreck at Ulu Burun: 1986 campaign. *AJA*, 93: 1–29.

Bayer, G. and Wiedmann, H.-G. 1976. Ägyptisch Blau, ein synthetisches Farbpigment des Altertums, wissenschaftlisch betrachtet. *Sandoz-Bulletin* 40, 20–39.

Beadnell, H.J.L. 1901. *Dakhla Oasis: Its Topography and Geology.* Egyptian Geological Survey Report 1899 Pt. 4.1. Cairo: GSE.

1909. *An Egyptian Oasis: An Account of the Oasis of Kharga in the Libyan Desert.* London: John Murray.

Beck, H.C. 1934. Glass before 1500 BC. *Ancient Egypt* (June 1934): 7–21.

Bianchi, R.S. 1983a. Those ubiquitous glass inlays from pharaonic Egypt, part I. *Journal of Glass Studies*, 25, 29–35.

1983b. Those ubiquitous glass inlays, part II. *BES*, 5, 9–29.

Bimson, M. and Freestone, I.C. 1988. Some Egyptian glasses dated by royal inscriptions. *Journal of Glass Studies*, 30: 11–15.

Bimson, M. and Shore, A.F. 1966. An Egyptian model coffin in glass. *BMQ*, 31: 105–9.

Bimson, M. and Werner A.E. 1969a. Two problems in ancient glass: opacifiers and Egyptian core material. In *Annales du 4ª Congrès International d'Etude Historique du Verre* (ed. J. Philippe). Liège: Journales Inernationales du Verre, pp. 262–6.

Bimson, M. and Werner, A.E. 1969b. Problems in Egyptian core glasses. In *Studies in Glass History and Design* (eds. R.J. Charleston, W. Evans and A.E. Werner). Sheffield: Society for Glass Technology, pp. 121–2.

Boyce, A. 1989. Notes on the manufacture and use of faience finger rings at Amarna. In *Amarna Reports* V (ed. B.J. Kemp). London: EES, pp. 160–8.

1995. Collar and necklace designs at Amarna: a preliminary study of faience pendants. In *Amarna Reports* VI (ed. B.J. Kemp). London: EES, pp. 336–71.

Breasted, J.H. 1906. *Ancient Records of Egypt* II. Chicago IL: University of Chicago Press.

Brill, R. H. 1963. Ancient glass. *Scientific American*, 209: 120–31.

1968. The Scientific investigation of ancient glasses. *Proceedings of the VIIIth International Congress on Glass.* Sheffield: The Society of Glass Technology, pp. 47–68.

1970. The chemical interpretation of the texts. In *Glass and Glassmaking in Ancient Mesopotamia* (eds. A.L. Oppenheim, Brill, R. H., Barag, D. and A. Von Saldern). Corning: The Corning Museum of Glass, pp. 105–28.

1972. Chemical-analytical round-robin of four synthetic ancient glasses. *Proceedings of the Ninth International Congress on Glass, Artistic and Historical Communications, Versailles 1971.* Versailles: The International Congress on Glass, pp. 93–100.

1988. Scientific investigations of the Jalame glass and related finds. In *Excavations At Jalame* (ed. G.D. Weinberg) Columbia: University of Missouri Press, pp. 257–94.

Brill, R.J., Barnes, I.L. and Adams, B. 1974. Lead isotopes in some ancient Egyptian objects. In *Recent Advances in Science and Technology of Materials Vol. 3* (ed. A. Bishay). London: Plenum, pp. 9–27.

Brill, R.H. and Moll, S. 1963. The electron-beam probe microanalysis of ancient glass. In *Recent Advances in Conservation* (ed. G. Thompson). Contributions to the International Institute of Conservation Conference, Rome 1961. London: Butterworth, pp. 145–51.

Brill, R.H., Shirahata, H., Lilyquist, C. and Vocke, R.D. Jr. 1993. Lead-isotope analyses of some objects from Egypt and the Near East. In *Studies in Early Egyptian Glass* (C. Lilyquist and R.H. Brill with M. T. Wypyski). New York: MMA, pp. 59–70.

Caley, E.R. 1962. *Analyses of Ancient Glasses 1790–1957.* Corning: Corning Museum of Glass.

Chase, W.T. 1971. Egyptian blue as a pigment and a ceramic material. In *Science And Archaeology* (ed. R.H. Brill). Leiden: Brill, pp. 80–90.

Cooney, J.D. 1960. Glass sculpture in ancient Egypt. *Journal of Glass Studies*, 2: 10–43.

1976. *Catalogue of Egyptian Antiquites in the British Museum IV: Glass.* London: BMP.

1981. Notes on Egyptian glass. In *Studies In Ancient Egypt, The Aegean and the Sudan* (eds. W.K. Simpson and W.M. Davis). Boston: MFA, pp. 31–3.

Daressy, M.G. 1902. *Fouilles de la Vallée des Rois 1898–9.* Cairo: Catalogue géneral des antiquités du musée du Caire.

Davis, T.M. 1907. *Excavations in the Biban el Moluk. The Tomb of Iouiya and Touiyou.* London: Archibold Constable and Co.

Dayton, J.E. 1981. Cobalt, silver and nickel in Late Bronze Age glazes, pigments and bronzes, and the identification of silver sources for the Aegean and Near East. In *Scientific Studies in Ancient Ceramics* (ed. M.J. Hughes). London: BMP, pp. 129–42.

Doremus, R. H. 1994. *Glass Science.* New York: Wiley.

Eisenberg, J. 1996. Archaeological news from San Diego.

Minerva, 7/2, 49.

Emery, W.B. 1967. Preliminary report on the excavations at North Saqqâra. *JEA*, 53: 141–5.

Farnsworth, M. and Ritchie, P.D. 1938. Spectrographic studies on ancient glass. Egyptian glass mainly of the 18th Dynasty, with special reference to its cobalt content. *Technical Studies in the Field of the Fine Arts*, 6/3: 155–73.

Fleming S.J. and Swan C.P. 1986. PIXE spectrometry as an archaeological tool. *Nuclear Instruments and Methods in Physics Research* A242, 626–31.

Forbes, R.J. 1957. *Studies in Ancient Technology* Vol. 5. Leiden: Brill.

Fossing, P. 1940. *Glass Vessels Before Glass Blowing*. Copenhagen: Munksgaard.

Foster, K.P. 1979. *Aegean Faience Of The Bronze Age*. New Haven CT: Yale University Press.

Freestone, I.C. 1987. Composition and microstructure of early opaque red glass. In *Early Vitreous Materials* (eds. M. Bimson and I.C. Freestone). London: British Museum Occasional Paper no. 56, pp. 173–91.

1991. Looking into glass. In *Science and the Past* (ed. S. Bowman). London: BMP, pp. 37–56.

Gadd, C.J. and Thompson, R.C. 1936. A Middle-Babylonian chemical text. *Iraq*, 3: 87–96.

Garner, H. 1956a. The use of imported and native cobalt in Chinese blue and white. *Oriental Art*, 2/3: 48–50.

1956b. An early piece of glass from Eridu. *Iraq* ,18: 147–9.

Geilmann, W. 1955. Beiträge zur Kenntnis alter Gläser III. Die chemische Zusammensetzung einiger alter Gläser, inbesondere deutscher Gläser des 10. bis 18. Jahrhunderts. *Glastechnische Berichte*, 28: 146–56.

Goldstein, S.M. 1979. A unique royal head. *Journal of Glass Studies*, 21, 8–16.

Gudenrath, W. 1991. Techniques of Glassmaking and Decoration. In *Five Thousand Years of Glass* (ed. Hugh Tait). London: BMP, pp. 213–41.

Guido, C.M., Henderson, J. Cable, C., Bayley, J. and Biek, L. 1984. A Bronze Age glass bead from Wilsford, Wiltshire: Barrow G42 in the Lake Group. *PPS*, 50: 245–54.

Hall, E.T. 1965. Recent research at the Research Laboratory for Archaeology and the History of Art, Oxford. *Application of Science in Examination of Works of Art*. Boston: MFA, pp. 105–13.

Hall, E.T., Schweizer, F. and Toller, P.A. 1973. X-ray fluorescence analysis of Museum objects: a new instrument. *Archaeometry*, 15: 53–78.

Hamza, M. 1930. Excavations of the Department of Antiquities at Qantîr (Faqûs district). *ASAE*, 30: 31–68.

Harden, D.B. 1956. Glass and glazes. In *A History of Technology* II (eds. C. Singer, E.J. Holmyard, A.R. Hall and T.I. Williams). Oxford: Clarendon, pp. 311–46.

1968. Ancient glass I: pre-Roman. *The Archaeological Journal*, 125: 46–72.

Harris, J.R. 1961. *Lexicographical Studies in Ancient Egyptian Minerals*. Berlin: Institut für Orientforschung Veröffentlichung 54.1.

Hatcher, H. Tite, M. S. and Walsh, J. N. 1995. A comparison of inductively-coupled plasma emission spectroscopy and atomic absorption spectrometry analysis on standard reference silicate materials and ceramics. *Archaeometry*, 37: 83–94.

Hedges, R. E. M. and Moorey, P. R. S. 1975. Pre-Islamic ceramic glazes at Kish and Nineveh in Iraq. *Archaeometry*, 28/2: 25–43.

Henderson, J. 1985. The raw materials of early glass production. *Oxford Journal of Archaeology*, 4/3, 267–91.

1988. Electron probe microanalyses of mixed-alkali glasses. *Archaeometry*, 30/1, 77–91.

1989. The scientific analysis of ancient glass and its archaeological interpretation. In *Scientific Analysis In Archaeology* (ed. J. Henderson). Oxford: Oxford University Committee for Archaeology, Monograph 19, pp. 30–62.

1995. Ancient vitreous materials. *AJA*, 99: 117–21.

1998. Scientific analysis of glass and glaze from Tell Brak and its archaeological implications. In *Excavations at Tell Brak Vol. I: The Mitanni and Old Babylonian periods*. (D. Oates, J. Oates and H. McDonald). (McDonald Institute Monographs.) Cambridge: The McDonald Institute for Archaeological Research and BSAI, pp. 94–100.

in preparation. Scientific analysis of the glass from Bronze Age Pella.

Henderson, J. and Warren, S.E. 1983. Analysis of prehistoric lead glass. *Proceedings of the 22nd International Symposium on Archaeometry*. Bradford: University of Bradford, pp. 168–80.

Henein, N.H. and Gout, J-F. 1974. *Le verre soufflé en Égypte*. Cairo: IFAO.

Heyworth, M.P., Hunter, J.R., Warren, S.E. and Walsh, N. 1989. The role of inductively coupled plasma spectrometry in glass provenance studies. In *Archaeometry: Proceedings of the 25th International Symposium* (ed. Y. Maniatis). Oxford: Elsevier, pp. 661–70.

Highley, D.E. 1977. *Silica. Mineral Dossier no. 18*. London: HMSO.

Howarth, J.T., Sykes, R.F.and Turner, W.E.S. 1934. A study of the fundamental reactions in the fomration of soda–lime–silica glasses. *Journal of the Society of Glass Technology*, 18, 290–306T.

Hughes, M.J. 1972. A technical study of opaque red glass of the Iron Age in Britain. *PPS*, 38: 98–107.

Hughes, M.J., Cowell, M.R. and Craddock, P.T. 1976. Atomic absorption techniques in archaeology. *Archaeometry*, 18, 19–37.

Hughes, M.J., Cowell, M.R. and Hook, D.R. (eds.) 1991. *Neutron Activation and Plasma Emission Spectrometric Analaysis in Archaeology*. British Museum Occasional Paper no. 82. London: BMP.

Jackson, C.M., Nicholson, P.T. and Gneisinger, W. 1998. Glassmaking at Tell el-Amarna: an integrated approach. *Journal of Glass Studies*, 40: 11–23.

Jenkins, R. 1988. *X-ray Fluorescence Spectrometry*. Chichester: Wiley-Interscience.

Jope, E.M. and Huse, G. 1940. Examination of 'Egyptian blue' by X-ray powder photography. *Nature*, 146: 26.

Kaczmarczyk, A. 1986. The source of cobalt in ancient Egyptian pigments. In *Proceedings of the 24th International Archaeometry Symposium* (eds. J.S. Olin and M.J. Blackman). Washington DC: Smithsonian Institution Press, pp. 369–76.

1991. The identity of *wšbt* alum. *JEA*, 77: 195.

Kaczmarczyk, A. and Hedges, R.E.M. 1983. *Ancient Egyptian Faience*. Warminster: Aris and Phillips.

Keller, C.A. 1983. Problems in dating glass industries of the

Egyptian New Kingdom: examples from Malkata and Lisht. *Journal of Glass Studies*, 25: 19–28.

Kühne, J. 1969 *Zur Kenntnis silikatischer Werkstoffe und der Technologie ihrer Herstellung im 2. Jahrtausend vor unserer Zeitrechnung*. Berlin: Abhandlung der Deutschen Akademie der Wissenschaften zu Berlin.

Labino, D. 1966. The Egyptian sand-core technique: a new interpretation. *Journal of Glass Studies*, 8: 124–7.

Lambert, J. B. and McLaughlin, C. D. 1976. Analysis of early Egyptian glass by atomic absorption and X-Ray photoelectron spectroscopy. In *Archaeological Chemistry* II, (ed. G. F. Carter), Advances in Chemistry Series no. 171. Washington DC: The American Chemical Society, pp. 189–99.

Lilyquist, C. and Brill, R.H. 1993. *Studies in Early Egyptian Glass*. New York: MMA.

Löw, I. 1924–1934. *Die Flora der Juden*. Vienna and Leipzig: R. Lowit, Veroffentlichungen der Alexander Kohut Memorial Foundation 2–4, 6.

Lucas, A. 1933. Appendix 2: The chemistry of the tomb. In *The Tomb of Tut-ankh-amen* III (H. Carter). London: Cassell and Co., pp. 170–83.

1934. *Ancient Egyptian Materials and Industries*, 2nd edn. London: Edward Arnold.

1948. *Ancient Egyptian Materials and Industries*, 3rd edn. London: Edward Arnold.

1962. *Ancient Egyptian Materials and Industries*, 4th edn., rev. J.R. Harris. London: Edward Arnold.

Martin, G.T. 1971. *Egyptian Administrative and Private-name Seals*. Oxford: Griffith Institute.

Matson, F. R. 1951. The composition and working properties of ancient glass. *The Journal of Chemical Education*, 28: 82–7.

Mehlman, F. 1982. *The Phaidon Guide to Glass*. Oxford: Phaidon.

Moorey, P.R.S. 1994. *Ancient Mesopotamian Materials and Industries*. Oxford: Clarendon Press.

Moran, W.L. 1992. *The Amarna Letters*. Baltimore MD: Johns Hopkins University Press.

Morey, G. W. 1964. Phase-equilibrium relations of the common rock-forming oxides except water. *U.S. Geological Survey Professional Paper* no. 440–L, Chapter L.

Morgan, M.H. 1914. Vitruvius: *The Ten Books on Architecture*. Harvard: Harvard University Press.

Neumann, B. 1929. Antike Gläser IV. *Zeitschrift für angewandte Chemie*, 42: 835–8.

Neumann, B. and Kotyga, G. 1925. Antike Gläser, ihre Zusammensetzung und Färbung. *Zeitschrift für angewandte Chemie*, 38, 776–80 and 857–64.

Newberry, P.E. 1920. A glass chalice of Tuthmosis III. *JEA*, 6: 155–60.

Newton, R. G. 1978. Colouring agents used by medieval glassmakers. *Glass Technology*, 21/4: 173–83.

1980. Recent views on ancient glasses. *Glass Technology*, 21 (4): 173–183.

Newton, R.G. and Davison, S. 1989. *Conservation of Glass*. London: Butterworths.

Nicholson, P.T. 1993. *Egyptian Faience and Glass*. Aylesbury: Shire.

1995. Glassmaking and glassworking at Amarna: some new work. *Journal of Glass Studies*, 37: 1–19.

1996. New evidence for glass and glazing at Tell el-Amarna (Egypt). In *Annales of the 13th AIHV Congress*. Netherlands: AIHV, pp. 11–19.

Nicholson, P.T. and Jackson, C.M. 1998. Kind of blue: glass of the Amarna period replicated. In *The Prehistory and History of Glass and Glass Technology* (eds. W.D. Kingery and P. McCray). Columbus, OH: American Ceramic Society, pp. 105–20.

Nicholson, P.T., Jackson, C.M. and Trott, K.M. 1997. The Ulu Burun glass ingots, cylindrical vessels and Egyptian glass. *JEA*, 83, 143–53.

Noll, W. 1981. Mineralogy and technology of the painted ceramics of ancient Egypt. In *Scientific Studies in Ancient Ceramics* (ed. M.J. Hughes). London: BMP, pp. 143–54.

Nolte, B. 1968. *Die Glasgefässe im Alten Agypten*. Munich: Münchner Ägyptologische Studien, 14.

1977a. Glas. *LÄ* II, 614–17.

1977b. An Egyptian glass vessel in the Metropolitan Museum of Art. In *Ancient Egypt in the Metropolitan Museum Journal Vols. 1–11 (1968–1976)*. New York: MMA, pp. 25–9.

Oppenheim, L. 1970. The cuneiform tablets with instructions for glassmakers. In *Glass and Glassmaking in Ancient Mesopotamia* (eds. A.L. Oppenheim, R.H. Brill, D. Barag and A. von Saldern). Corning: Corning Museum of Glass, pp. 22–68.

1973. Towards a history of glass in the ancient Near East. *Journal of the American Oriental Society*, 93: 259–66.

Parodi, H.D. 1908. *La verrerie en Egypte*. Cairo: Khedival Technical School, Bulak. [Thesis at University of Grenoble]

Peltenburg, E.J. 1987. Early faience: recent studies, origins and relations with glass. In *Early Vitreous Materials* (eds. M. Bimson and I.C. Freestone). British Museum Occasional Paper 56. London: BMP, pp. 5–29.

Petrie, W.M.F. 1891. *Illahun, Kahun And Gurob*. London: Nutt.

1892. *Ten Years Digging in Egypt*. London: Religious Tract Society.

1894. *Tell el-Amarna*. London: Methuen & Co.

1909. *Arts and Crafts of Ancient Egypt*. London: Foulis.

1924. *Ancient Egyptians*. H. Spencer's Descriptive Sociology 11.1. London: Williams and Norgate.

1925. Glass found in Egypt. *Transactions of the British Newcomen Society*, 5: 72–6.

1926. Glass in the early ages. *Journal of the Society of Glass Technology*, 10, 229–34.

Pusch, E. 1990. Metallverarbeitende Werkstätten in Qantir/Piramesse-Nord. *Ägypten und Levante*, 1: 75–113.

Reeves, C. N. 1986. Two name-beads of Hatshepsut and Senenmut from the mortuary temple of Queen Hatshepsut at Deir el-Bahri. *Antiquaries Journal*, 66: 387–8.

1990. *The Complete Tutankhamun*. London: Thames and Hudson.

Rehren, T. 1997. Ramesside glass-colouring crucibles. *Archaeometry*, 39/2: 355–68.

Rehren, T. and Pusch, E. 1997. New Kingdom glass melting crucibles from Qantir-Piramesses, Nile Delta. *JEA*, 83.

Riefstahl, E. 1968. *Ancient Egyptian Glass and Glazes in the Brooklyn Museum*. New York: Brooklyn Museum.

Rooksby, H.P. 1962. Opacifiers in opal glasses. *GEC Journal of Science and Technology*, 29/1: 20–6.

Saleh, S.A., George, A.W. and Helmi, F.M. 1972. Study of glass and glass-making at Wadi-el-Natrun. *Studies in Conservation*, 17: 143–72.

Sayre, E.V. 1963. The intentional use of antimony and manganese in ancient glasses. In *Advances in Glass Technology II* (eds. F.R. Matson and G.E. Rindone). New York: Plenum, pp. 263–82.

1964. *Some Ancient Glass Specimens with Compositions of Particular Archaeological Significance.* New York: Brookhaven National Laboratory.

Sayre, E.V. and Smith, R. W. 1961. Compositional categories of ancient glass. *Science,* 133 (June 9): 1824–6.

1967. Some materials of glass manufacturing in antiquity. In *Archaeological Chemistry, a Symposium,* (ed. M. Levey). Philadelphia PA: University of Philadelphia Press, pp. 279–311.

Schuler, F. 1962. Ancient glassmaking techniques. The Egyptian core vessel process. *Archaeology,* 15: 32–7.

1963. Ancient glassmaking: methodology for attacking the Assyrian glassmaking texts. In *Advances in Glass Technology 2* (eds. F.R. Matson and G.E. Rindone). New York: Plenum, pp. 381–3.

Segnit, E.R. 1987. Evaporite minerals from the Dakhleh oasis. In *Ceramics from the Dakhleh Oasis: Preliminary Studies* (W.I. Edwards, C.A. Hope and E.R. Segnit). Melbourne: Victoria College Archaeology Research Unit Occasional Paper 1, pp. 97–102.

Sellner, C., Oel, H.J., and Camera, B. 1979. Untersuchung alter Gläser (Waldglas) auf Zusammenhang von Zisammensetzung, Farbe und Schmelzatmosphare mit der Elektronenspektoskopie und der Elektronenspinresonanz (ESR). *Glastechniche Berichte,* 52: 255–64.

Smith, S. 1928. *Early History of Assyria to 1000 BC.* London: Chatto and Windus.

Stern, E.M. and Schlick-Nolte, B. 1994. *Early Glass of the Ancient World 1600 BC–AD 50.* Ostfildern: Verlag Gerd Hatje.

Täckholm, V. and Drar, M. 1956. *A Student's Flora of Egypt.* Cairo: Anglo-Egyptian Bookshop.

Tatton-Brown, V. and Andrews, C. 1991. Before the invention of glassblowing. In *Five Thousand Years of Glass* (ed. H. Tait). London: BMP, pp. 20–61.

Thompson, R.C. 1925. *On the Chemistry of the Ancient Assyrians.* London: Luzac.

Tite, M.S. 1986. Egyptian blue, faience and related materials: technological investigations. In *Science in Archaeology* (eds. R.E. Jones and H.W. Catling). Fitch Laboratory Occasional Paper 2, London: British School at Athens, pp. 39–41.

Tite, M.S. and Bimson, M. 1987. Identification of early vitreous materials. In *Recent Advances in the Conservation and Analysis of Artifacts* (ed. J. Black). London: Summer Schools Press, pp. 81–5.

Turner, W.E.S. 1954. Studies of ancient glass and glassmaking processes, Part I. Crucibles and melting temperatures employed in ancient Egypt at about 1370 BC. *Journal of the Society of Glass Technology,* 38: 183, 436–44T.

1956a. Studies in ancient glasses and glassmaking processes. Part V. Raw materials and melting processes. *Journal of the Society of Glass Technology,* 40/194: 277–300T.

1956b. Studies of ancient glass and glassmaking processes, Part III: The chronology of glass-making constituents. *Journal of the Society of Glass Technology,* 40: 39–52.

1956c. Studies in ancient glasses and glass-making processes, Part IV: The chemical composition of ancient glasses. *Journal of the Society of Glass Technology,* 40: 162–86.

Turner, W.E.S. and Rooksby, H.P. 1959. A study of opalising agents in ancient opal glasses throughout three thousand four hundred years. *Glastechniche Berichte,* 32K, 8: 17–28.

1961, Further historical studies based on X-ray diffraction methods of the reagents employed in making opal and opaque glasses. *Jahrbuch des Römisch-Germanischen Zentralmuseums,* 8: 1–16.

1963, A study of the opalising agents in ancient glasses throughout 3400 years, part II. *Proceedings of the 6th International Congress on Glass: Advances in Glass Technology* (eds. F.R. Matson and G.E. Rindone). New York: Plenum, pp. 306–7.

Ullrich, D. 1979. Ägyptisch Blau ($CaCuSi_4O_{10}$): Bildungsbedingungen und Rekonstruktionsversuch der antiken Herstellungstechnik. Diploma dissertation. Freie Universität Berlin.

Vandiver, P.B. 1983. The manufacture of faience. In *Ancient Egyptian Faience* (A. Kaczmarkzyk and R.E.M. Hedges). Warminster: Aris and Phillips, pp. A1–A144.

Vandiver, P.B., Swann, C. and Cranmer, D. 1991. A review of mid-second millennium BC Egyptian glass technology at Tell el-Amarna. In *Materials Issues In Art And Archaeology II* (eds. P.B. Vandiver, J. Druzik and G.S. Wheeler). Pittsburgh: Materials Research Society, pp. 609–16.

Vassamillett, L.F. and Caldwell, V.E. 1969. Electron probe microanalysis of alkaline metals in glasses. *Journal of Applied Physics,* 40: 1637.

Veritá, M. Basso, R., Wypyski, M.T. and Koestler, R.J. 1994. X-ray microanalysis of ancient glassy materials: a comparative study of wavelength dispersive and energy dispersive techniques. *Archaeometry,* 36: 241–52.

Weatherhead, F and Buckley, A. 1989. Artists' pigments from Amarna. In *Amarna Reports* V (ed. B.J. Kemp). London: EES, pp. 202–40.

Weyl, W.A. 1937. The chemistry of coloured glass: II. *The Glass Industry* April 1937: 117–20.

1953. *Coloured Glasses.* Corning: The Corning Museum of Glass.

Wosinski, J.F. and Brill, R.H. 1968. A petrographic study of Egyptian and other cored vessels. *Studies in Glass History and Design.* Sheffield, pp. 123–4.

Part II.
Organic materials

9. Papyrus

BRIDGET LEACH AND JOHN TAIT

Introduction

The writing material made from the papyrus plant *Cyperus papyrus* L. was the most important surface for recording written information used by the ancient Egyptians, and they themselves evidently regarded it as the primary writing-ground (general accounts of papyrus in the context of Pharaonic Egypt include Woenig 1886: 74–129; Täckholm and Drar 1950: 99–145; Černý 1952; Lucas 1962: 137–40, 364; Weber 1969: 1–13; Ragab 1980b; Drenkhahn 1982; Germer 1985: 248–50; Manniche 1989: 99–100; Parkinson and Quirke 1995). Various other materials were used for Egyptian scripts written with a pen, such as ostraca (that is, both potsherds and flakes of limestone), animal skins and tablets of wood (or occasionally of stone). The earliest extant papyrus is a blank roll from the Early Dynastic tomb of Hemaka (tomb 3035) at Saqqara, dating to the beginning of the third millennium BC: 'circular wooden box . . . A small flattened roll of uninscribed papyrus was the sole contents' (Emery 1938: 41, pl. 23a). Use of papyrus was continuous throughout Dynastic and Greco-Roman Egypt, into the Byzantine and early Islamic periods. The latest extant papyrus is an Arabic document dated AD 1087 (Pattie and Turner 1974: 7). Texts take the form of whole rolls, or sheets or strips cut from a roll, and, in later periods, codices (that is, books made up of folded sheets, or gatherings of folded sheets, much in the manner of a modern stitched hardback volume). Production of the writing material had declined by the seventh to eighth centures AD, when we see the increased use of animal skins (for example parchment) and of paper made from macerated plant residues.

Taxonomy and distribution of the papyrus plant

The taxonomy of the plant is complex and need not be discussed at length here. The genus name is *Cyperus*, of which there are more than 600 species, one of them being *C. papyrus*. The genus *Cyperus* belongs to the substantial family of *Cyperaceae*, or sedges, which in turn belongs to the larger classification of monocotyledons. These constitute one of the two great divisions of flowering plants: monocotyledons contain one seed leaf, and dicotyledons contain two. *Cyperus papyrus* L. is the botanical name given to the plant. The 'L' stands for Linnaeus, the Latin form of the name of the Swedish botanist Linné, who first classified the plant using the reproductive system in his work *Species Plantarum*, published in 1753 (Linnaeus 1753: I, 47). Various botanists since that time have described it, comparing samples from various geographical areas and naming or re-naming the different sub-species. There are minor botanical differences between these, but the exact sub-species used in antiquity for making the writing material cannot be assessed with any certainty. Ecological shifts over many centuries affecting the content of Nile water and the surrounding soil must have caused changes, small or otherwise, in the plants we are able to examine today. However, certain sub-species of the plant do make better papyrus sheets than others (see p. 228–9).

Today the plant in the wild is widely distributed over large swamplands in Central and East Africa, where it grows profusely (Carter 1953: 3) and also parts of West Africa (Nielsen 1985: 12). In addition it grows in Sicily, and has also been found in Palestine (Täckholm and Drar 1950: 136). It does not grow in the Egyptian Nile Valley today, other than modern horticultural or commercial reintroductions. However, travellers from medieval times until the nineteenth century reported seeing it still growing, particularly in the environs of Damietta and Lake Manzala in Lower Egypt (Täckholm and Drar 1950: 133–4). Because of its disappearance, there has been some debate as to whether papyrus was ever indigenous to Egypt, or might have been imported there as a cultivar (Täckholm and Drar 1950: 139). At the end of the eighteenth century, James Bruce, in his *Travels to Discover the Source of the Nile* (1790) argued against previous writers that neither the main stream of the Nile nor Egypt could have been the proper home of papyrus, remarking that it 'seems to me to have early come down from Ethiopia', that 'its head is too heavy', and that the 'stalk is small and feeble, and withall too tall, the root too short and slender to stay it against the violent pressure of the wind and current, and therefore I do constantly believe it never could be a plant growing in the Nile itself, or in any very deep or rapid river'. (Bruce 1790: V, 1–2; *cf.* Täckholm and Drar 1950: 139–40)

Bruce will have been influenced in his account by his quite incorrect belief that hieroglyphic writing fell into disuse before papyrus began to be employed. However, representational evidence in the numerous depictions of wild papyrus in marshes and hunting scenes, and the major role of the papyrus stem as a symbol, for example in temple architecture, make it implausible to reject the accepted view that the plant was both indigenous and, in the Pharaonic period, widespread in the Egyptian Nile Valley.

The disappearance of the plant from Egypt could perhaps be explained in several ways: ecologically, agriculturally and culturally. Firstly, the silting up and obstruction of the channels and waterways where the papyrus grew must have been a major factor. Täckholm and Drar (1950: 143) draw attention to the fact that certain branches of the Nile in the Delta had completely dried up 'within the Christian and Early Islamic periods', thus inhibiting the flow of fresh water to the papyrus and other plant habitats and depriving the roots of their essential supply of water. The papyrus root-stock is anchored very shallowly in the soil and it would be one of the first plants to disappear if its habitat were altered in such a way. Also, rising salination of the soil, a process which has increased over a long period of time, may have been a factor. As early as 1902, Alfred Lucas (1902: 8) conducted, for agricultural purposes, a survey of the soil and water in the Fayum Province, to determine the presence of injurious salts. Conditions in the Fayum will be different from those in the Nile Valley, but it is remarkable that Lucas found that the salt levels in some soils were indeed high: over ten times the level regarded to be harmful to crops (see p. 242). It is doubtful whether the character of the water of the Nile itself had any bearing on the plant's disappearance. The chemical content of water in the swamp habitats of Uganda, where papyrus still grows wild, is evidently suitable for papyrus growth. In 1953, G.S. Carter carried out an extensive survey of the chemical content of the waters of the papyrus swamps of Uganda (1953: 26). It is comparable to the chemical content of Nile water analysed by Lucas in the early twentieth century, when testing Nile water and soil from various locations in Egypt for the Survey Department in Cairo (Lucas 1908: 30–1). If the two sets of data are reviewed, chlorine content, absorbed oxygen and the presence of nitrogenous matter are comparable, even taking into account fluctuations due to the annual flood (in Egypt) or rains (in Uganda).

Secondly, the Egyptian sources of papyrus might well have simply become depleted, since it was used as a raw material for many items, such as matting, ropes, boats, sandals and numerous kinds of everyday object, quite apart from its decorative uses and its consumption as a food (Dixon 1972; Darby, Ghalioungui, and Grivetti 1977). Täckholm and Drar (1950: 141–2) point out that stocks of any wild plant utilised for centuries would eventually become exhausted, unless carefully cultivated.

Thirdly, as Täckholm and Drar (1950: 141) also note, papyrus habitats were located at the banks of the Nile and its subsidiary channels and waterways; therefore they would naturally be in populated areas. Here, demand for crops and possibly pasturing would eventually have superseded the demand for papyrus, and the land would have been put to other uses.

Aside from these ecological and agricultural reasons, the social and political climate must have played a part in its demise. There is evidence that the Greeks controlled papyrus production (Lewis 1974: 114), to the extent of destroying plants not within their official jurisdiction. This policy was perhaps continued by the Romans and the Arabs. It is difficult to tell if a failure in the supply of papyrus, or a new demand for paper was the more responsible for the fact that the use of paper began increasingly to supplant that of papyrus in the seventh and eighth centuries AD. Paper could be produced from the pulp of several different plants, and therefore its production was not limited to certain locations, as presumably was the case with papyrus. Once the demand for the writing material ceased, the few remaining plantations were perhaps given over to other uses.

The extent to which papyrus was cultivated for making a writing-ground or for other purposes in Pharaonic Egypt, as opposed to growing wild, is not known. Certainly the demand for writing materials in such a bureaucratic state must have been considerable, and it follows that there must have been some control over the way in which it was grown and harvested. Another question that arises is whether the uncultivated variety was suitable for making the writing material. It is possible that only cultivated plants were used for this purpose, while perhaps the wild plants might have been used for other items, such as rope, sandals and boats. The superb appearance of many papyrus rolls surviving from the Dynastic period suggests that great care must have been taken in choosing the correct plant, at the optimum time in its growth. Papyrus of excellent quality is known equally from the Egyptian Old, Middle and New Kingdoms. Although it has often been stated that the overall quality of papyrus worsened during the Greco-Roman and Byzantine periods, such a decline cannot be seen to have begun in Pharaonic Egypt, if attention is confined to the best surviving examples. However, inferior papyrus is also known from all periods. This must raise the question of whether papyrus was sometimes made from wild stock or even from a different sedge plant (see p. 229), thus producing a poorer quality product.

Also, although *Cyperus papyrus* L. is the general name for the plant species, there are many sub-species. They display only minor botanical differences, but these may affect the quality of the finished writing-ground. This was demonstrated in 1968 when a new sub-species of the plant was found growing wild in the Wadi Natrun, West of the Delta. Here, Dr el-Hadidi from the University of Cairo found a small population of *Cyperus papyrus* L., from which he and his colleagues subsequently manufactured some papyrus sheets. Although it was possible to make writing material from these plants, the process was much less successful than that employing plants cultivated from root-stock available in Cairo (Ragab 1980b: 85). It can be only a matter of conjecture whether the ancient Egyptians were aware of the advantages of using a particular sub-species for making the writing-ground, and cultivated it specifically for that purpose.

Papyrus is at present cultivated at several locations in Egypt, to supply the tourist trade in painted papyrus sheets. The first plantation of this type in Egypt was started by Hassan Ragab in 1962, beginning with root-stock from the Zoological Gardens in Cairo (Ragab 1980b: 52), and later with roots of the plant from the Sudan (Ragab 1988: 514–15). How similar this plant is to the ancient variety is difficult to tell, but samples of this material, made in 1975, appear to be of excellent quality: strong, flexible, opaque, of a creamy-white colour and comparable to much ancient papyrus. Unfortunately, mass-production by some manufacturers in recent times has led to the addition of chemicals (caustic soda and bleaches) in the manufacturing process (Ragab 1988: 518), producing poor-quality sheets that are dark, brittle and translucent. Microscopic (SEM) examination of ancient and modern papyrus has shown that it is possible to identify the plant used in some cases (Sturman 1987). It was found that in one modern sheet *Cyperus alopecuroides* Rottb., another sedge plant found plentifully in Egypt, had been used, producing a false papyrus sheet. Interestingly, when a comparison is made between the ancient papyrus samples and modern samples made from *C. papyrus* L., the ancient specimen proves to have a much more ordered and compact cell structure than that of its modern counterpart. In fact the ancient papyrus was as dissimilar from the modern papyrus, as the modern real papyrus was from the false, suggesting that, if these samples were typical, the plant, or the manufacturing process had been significantly different in ancient times.

Description of the plant

Papyrus is a perennial freshwater plant. In Egypt, propagation may be effected by root-stock division in spring or summer (Täckholm and Drar 1950: 100). In modern times, this has been the usual method of establishing new plantations, but plants have also been grown successfully from seed (Ragab 1980b: 55–63). The plant itself is tall, green and leafless. Much of Pliny's description (Nat. Hist. XIII.22 [71]; see Mayhoff 1909; Rackham 1968) is accurate. He says, 'It has a sloping root as thick as a man's arm, and tapers gracefully up with triangular sides to a length of not more than about 15 feet, ending in a head like a thyrsus' (Rackham 1968: 141; see Mayhoff 1909: 442). A thyrsus was 'a rod carried by worshippers of Bacchus [Dionysus] topped by a fir-cone or a cluster of grapes or figs' (Rackham 1968: 140, n. b). The 'head' to which he refers is the umbel, or flower head, and the 'root' is the basal sheath at the bottom of the stem which is about 8 cm thick when fully grown (see Fig. 9.1). Old branches die out continually, leaving a strangled mass of rhizomes. These mount to about 60 cm above soil level, and from them the new shoots grow. For anchorage the plant relies mainly on this heavy basal mass amongst which there is a rapid accumulation of dead plant material and sediment. The roots are soft and able to penetrate only water and water-saturated soil, rich in humus (Bailey 1963: III, 2,472–3). Papyrus, as a sedge, favours marshes and swamps. Shallow water hospitable to the plant occurs chiefly at the edges of quiet bodies of fresh water in sheltered areas, in sluggish rivers, or where the ground is at least waterlogged and free water accumulates on the surface for some period of the year. Hence ideal growing places for papyrus occurred along the banks of the Nile or along one of the numerous river branches and channels in the Delta.

If the stem of the plant, triangular in cross-section, is cut horizontally and the white pith inside exposed, it can be seen that the pith consists of ground-tissue in which fibres are embedded. The ground-tissue is made up of 'parenchyma' cells. In shape these are three-armed cells, and they are stacked in a honeycomb-like network, building up vertical intercellular air spaces called 'aerenchyma', running throughout the length of the stem. In cross-section the parenchyma cells appear to be circularly arranged around the air passages. The parenchyma cells often contain one or more calcium oxalate crystals, but are otherwise empty (Metcalfe 1969: 205–6). Oxalic acid is found in small amounts in nearly all plants, and solid crystals of insoluble calcium oxalate are often found in plant cells (Thatcher 1921: 126). The parenchyma cell walls are mainly cellulose and hemi-cellulose.

Parallel to the air passages run many fibres, or fibro-vascular bundles, embedded in the parenchymous material. These passages serve to carry food and water to the flower head and give the stem its rigidity and support. The fibres are made up of xylem cells which carry water and have lignified walls, and phloem cells which carry food and have cellulose walls (Metcalfe 1969: 205–6; Ragab 1980b: 37–9). It is these fibro-vascular bundles which to the naked eye are such a prominent feature of papyrus sheets, running vertically and horizontally, and it is the parenchymous material that fills and covers this fibre network. Also visible on a finished sheet of papyrus are transversal commissural bundles, also referred to as 'diaphragm cells', which connect the vascular bundles (Metcalfe 1969: 205–6; Ragab 1980b: 39–40). These can be seen very clearly by transmitted light,

(a)

(c)

(d)

(b)

Figure 9.1 *The stems and flowerheads of papyrus plants: (a) the whole plant, (b) the basal sheaths, (c) the stems and (d) the flowerhead or umbel.*

and also with the naked eye, scattered throughout the material.

Manufacture of papyrus as a writing-ground

As can be appreciated from the structure of the plant, it is a very suitable species from which to process this particular kind of writing surface. The vascular bundles serve to give the sheet its strength by forming a structure, in this case a criss-cross network, and the parenchymous material fills and gives body to this framework. The lower portion of the stem is used for papyrus manufacture (see also p. 235). First, it is thicker and has more pith. Secondly, because the fibres run the length of the stem, which tapers at the top, it follows that the fibres are more densely packed at the top, making this part of the stem more fibrous.

The only surviving ancient account of the manufacture of papyrus is given by Pliny (*Nat. Hist.* XIII.23 [74–7]; see Rackham 1968: 142–5; Mayhoff 1909: 442–4). This problematic description has been much discussed (e.g., with bibliographies, Lewis 1974; Bülow-Jacobsen 1976; *cf.* Bülow-Jacobsen 1986). Many modern writers (e.g. Lucas 1962: 138–40; Lewis 1974: 34–69; Nielsen 1985: 58; Menci 1988) consider this account to be correct in basic method, but ambiguous in detail. However, from examination of the ancient examples, and from the experience of various individuals who have made papyrus sheets in more recent years, such as Bruce (1790: v. 5, pp. 9–10), and, in this century, Gunn, Ibscher, Lucas, Baker (Lucas 1962: 138–9), Ragab (1980b: 131–50), Basile (1972; cf. 1977), Leach (1975: 6–14), Owen and Danzing (1993: 36–8), and, most recently, Basile and Di Natale (1996) and De Bignicourt and Flieder (1996: 488–93), the basic method can reasonably be deduced to have been as follows (see Fig. 9.2):

- Cut the stems into manageable lengths and peel away the rind.
- Thinly slice the pith into strips longitudinally, along one of its three flat sides.
- Lay a series of the strips onto a board, side by side, just touching each other, or slightly overlapping, to make the first layer.
- Lay a second similar layer of strips over them at right angles.
- Press or beat the two layers together and allow them to dry.

The basic process seems uncommonly simple. However, questions of craft practice arise, unanswered by Pliny's account, or by the various papyrus-making experiments undertaken in modern times. First, there is still some discussion as to whether the strips were butted up to each other, or overlapped. Examination of ancient material by the authors suggests that both methods could be used, and that in any one papyrus roll the technique employed was fairly consistent. In some badly made ancient papyrus, occasional narrow gaps may be observed in one of the two layers of papyrus, where for a few centimetres the edges of two strips do not quite meet. This may have been due to the use of slightly damaged strips, rather than mere carelessness in laying the strips down.

In modern trials, both methods have been used, with seemingly similar results. In his experiments, Baker favoured butting up, possibly seeking to avoid ridges where the two layers overlapped (Lucas 1962: 139). However, papyrus strips, before pressing or beating, are made up of a considerable amount of air which is expelled during manufacture. The strip is reduced after pressing and drying to less than a quarter of its original thickness (Ragab 1980a: 116). This process allows plenty of scope for unevennesses to be reduced by the time that the papyrus has dried. Therefore the danger of forming ridges is almost negligible. Also, overlapping the strips would naturally reduce the possibility of the gaps that could result if the strips were not butted up to one another sufficiently closely. Baker, however, found that skill in laying down the strips could ensure that no gaps occurred.

Another recently proposed theory as to the manufacture of a papyrus sheet argues that the outer rind was first removed, and then a needle-like implement was used to peel off the pith in an unrolling action, thus obtaining one continuous slice. Two such layers would then be combined to produce a papyrus sheet. Hendriks was the first to investigate this possibility in detail, and it has become known among papyrologists as the 'Hendriks method' or the 'Groningen solution', as samples were used from Botanical Gardens of Groningen State University (Hendriks 1980; 1984; *cf.* comments by Turner 1980; Lewis 1981; Holwerda 1982; Lewis 1989: 16–21). Some experiments have been carried out with fresh papyrus stems using both the slicing and the unrolling methods and comparing them under SEM and a stereo microscope (Wallert 1989). The result was that the 'peeled' papyrus had an uneven surface texture that was identifiable under the microscope.

However, applying the knowledge gained to ancient material has been less successful and ultimately inconclusive. It also appears that it is not easy to peel the pith in this unrolling fashion. Both Wallert (1989: 5) and Owen and Danzing (1993: 37) found it difficult to accomplish without holes, tears and unevenness in the layer. However, it is not impossible that ancient craftsmen might have developed such a skill. Another objection that has been raised is that the stem of the papyrus plant tapers, however slightly, and thus it would be impossible by the Hendriks method to produce a continuous layer in which the fibres continued to run parallel with each other throughout the sheet. If strips are used, the tapering of each individual strip is minimal, and compensation can even be made for this by reversing the direction of alternate strips.

A few instances have been reported of the apparent manufacture of papyrus sheets in three layers. Budge

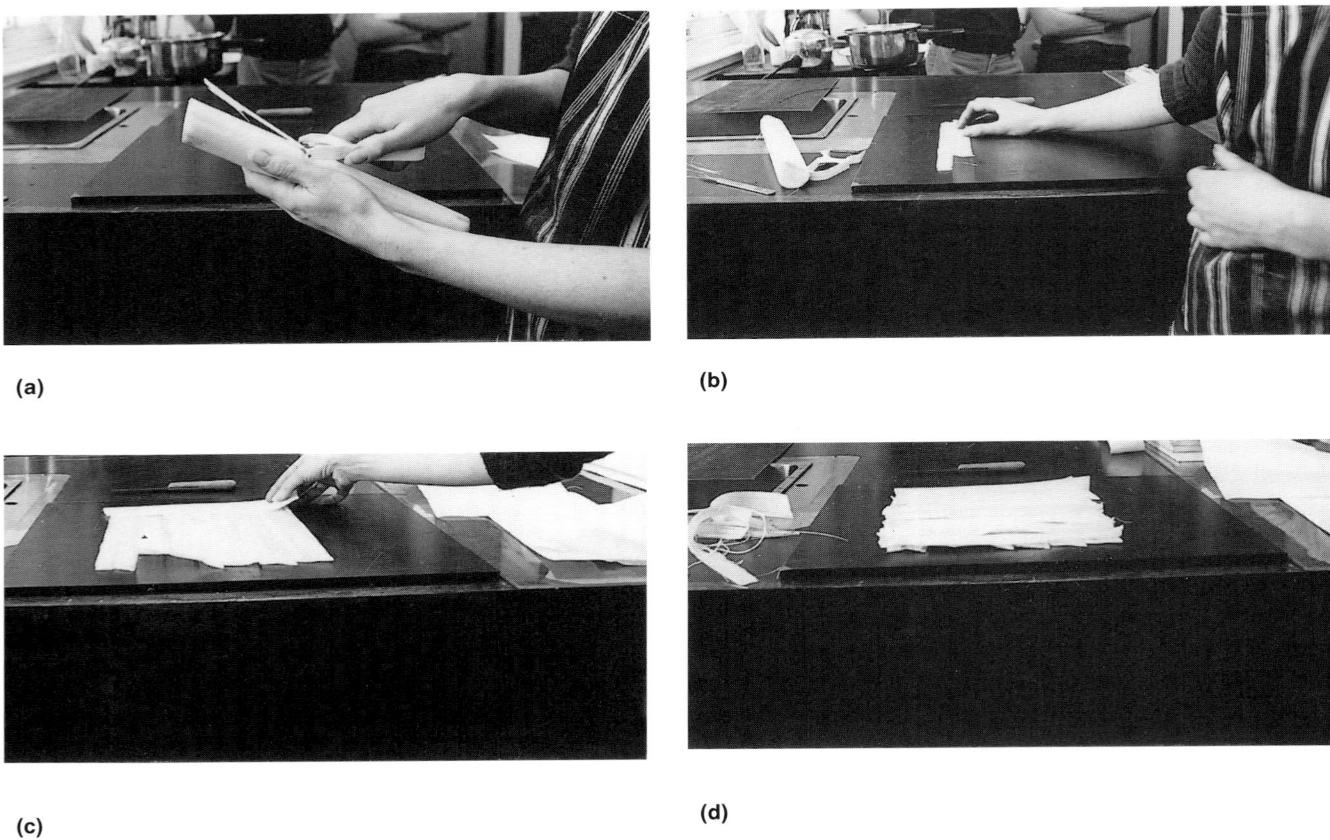

Figure 9.2 Stages of papyrus manufacture: (a) slicing pith into strips, (b) laying down the first layer of strips, (c) laying down the second layer at right angles, (d) two layers ready to be beaten, or pressed together.

claimed that the Greenfield Papyrus in the British Museum (see Fig. 9.3) was written upon papyrus of this kind: 'The material is composed of three layers of papyrus, supplied by plants which measured in the stalks about 4 inches in diameter' (Budge 1912: xxii–xxiii). Unfortunately the papyrus is mounted upon a paper backing, and the structure cannot be assessed from a surface examination. It would be necessary to remove the backing from the papyrus in order to examine it over transmitted light, or to lift up the layers. Neither interference can be justified in the case of a papyrus which is in particularly good condition and needs no conservation treatment. As mentioned by Černý (1952: 31, n. 10), Ebers, in his edition of the medical papyrus that bears his name, quoted Schenk (Professor of Botany at Leipzig) as stating that coarser papyrus was manufactured from three layers (1875: 3). Schenk seems to have examined very few samples, and to have noted three layers in a Book of the Dead in the Leipzig Library. Černý states that he himself had never encountered a three-layered papyrus. Bülow-Jacobsen (1978) describes a Greek literary papyrus, which is probably of the three-layered type.

No example has yet been reported of papyrus originally manufactured in more than three layers. It is necessary to distinguish other reasons that can make papyrus take on a multi-layered appearance. Users of papyri sometimes strengthened and repaired old papyri by pasting on an extra layer of ordinary papyrus. This might vary from a small repair patch to a backing sheet the size of a normal papyrus sheet. Sheet-joins (see pp. 236–7), can occasionally be abnormally wide, especially if they are the amateur work of a user, rather than made by the manufacturer. Although cartonnage (see p. 243) is often readily identifiable, fragments extracted from cartonnage and composed of two or more layers of papyrus still adhering together can give the impression of extremely thick papyrus.

A feature that is quite noticeable is the great thickness of certain papyri of the Late Period or Greco-Roman period. There are certainly only two layers but the strips themselves must have been sliced very thickly. It is widely accepted that the Greek style of reed pen (which in the Ptolemaic period quickly ousted the traditional Egyptian rush pen – even, eventually, for the writing of Demotic) was likely to puncture the thinnest qualities of papyrus, and that this led to a general increase in the thickness of papyrus. However, this characteristic has also been noted in papyri from a rather earlier period. For example, the funerary papyri of Pasheb-

out with the mallet' (Lewis 1974: 41). The phrase 'washed with paste' is a little puzzling. A practical interpretation could be offered: the paste was applied to one sheet along the edge to be overlapped, and the sheet to be attached was laid along the pasted edge, and beaten down. Next, to achieve a smooth join, particularly along the overlapping ridge, extra paste was applied along it before beating down again. However it was done, this task would have to be carried out skilfully in order to beat the four layers of papyrus strips that constitute the overlapping area of the join to a thickness at least comparable with that of the rest of the roll, and to ensure particular smoothness at the overlapping edge, without causing holes or weakening at the underside ridge (see Fig. 9.5). It is noticeable on numerous extant fragmentary papyri that this particular area is very vulnerable, and fractures have often occurred along this edge.

It has been pointed out several times in recent years that some papyri of the Late Period or Greco-Roman period display a refinement in manufacture, presumably designed to provide a smoother finish at the sheet-joins. First, in 1978 Turner reported that John Rea had observed that a then unpublished Oxyrhynchus papyrus of the fourth century AD had only three layers of papyrus for much of the width of the sheet-join (for 2.5 cm of a join 2.75 cm wide). In effect, it seemed likely that a single vertical strip of papyrus had deliberately been omitted at one edge of the sheet (Turner 1978: 20). The papyrus was subsequently published as P.Oxy.li.3624: see the remarks by Rea (1984: 61). Coles described a similar feature in three Rendel Harris papyri (P.Harr. 212, 214, 216) of the fourth century AD, stating that 'at least 3 cm' of vertical fibres are missing (Andorlini *et al.* 1985: especially p. 115). Coles stated that he and Rea had come to see this as a standard feature of papyri of the period. They have found many examples subsequently, and Coles would suggest that appearances hint that it is more likely that a vertical strip was omitted in manufacture than that one was torn away subsequently (R.A. Coles, pers. comm. 1996). One of the authors had independently noticed a slightly different feature in North Saqqara papyri to be dated at least five centuries earlier: frequently the sheets had been 'deliberately made with a short "fringe" of horizontal strips at their left-hand edge, protruding 2–8 mm beyond the last vertical strip' (Tait 1986: 70, with, in n. 56, a reference to Rea's observation). In the Saqqara examples, the only essential difference from the later phenomenon found among the Oxyrhynchus material is that the area of papyrus in the pasted-up roll that consists of only three layers is much narrower. Subsequently Ménei (1993) has independently observed a similar feature in papyri in the Louvre and elsewhere, mentioning a fringe of 1–1.5 cm. One of the authors has examined examples in the British Museum collection and has identified some instances of this type of join. However, without detailed examination, which would involve lifting the layers along the join and would therefore be a rather questionable procedure, it is not easy to say with certainty.

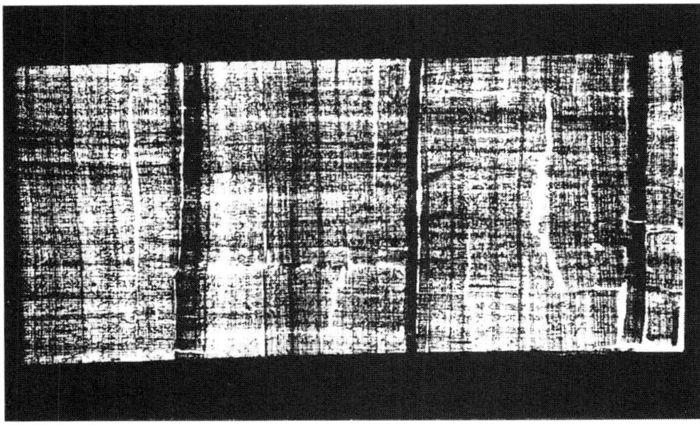

Figure 9.5 The Papyrus of Nesmin (BM EA10188/14, Late Period); the sheet joins are visible when it is seen through transmitted light. The extra thickness of the overlap at the join shows as a dark vertical strip.

One papyrus from the pharaonic period at the British Museum has exceptionally wide sheets, clearly identifiable on the light table. This is a Fifth-Dynasty document from Abusir (BM EA10735/8–9), with sheet widths of 66 cm and 66.5 cm. The well-known 'Hymns to Senusret II' among the Kahun papyri at the Petrie Museum of Egyptian Archaeology, University College London (Kahun, LV.1; UC. 32157) include exceptionally wide sheets measuring 51.5 and 49.5 cm (Griffith, 1898: 1; pls. 1–2). Robinson reports that, in the third century AD, the papyrus rolls used to produce some of the Nag Hammadi codices must have been manufactured with extraordinarily wide sheets, and he surveys the evidence that very wide sheets might have been used for the manufacture of codices at this period (1984: 61–70).

Once the papyrus sheets were pasted together to form a roll, the material was ready for writing. According to Pliny 'rough spots are rubbed smooth with ivory or shell' (Lewis 1974: 39; *cf.* Mayhoff 1909: 445; Rackham 1968: 146–7). However, Pliny then goes on to say that this makes the surface 'shinier and less absorptive'. Hepper and Reynolds (1967), in their account of papyrus-making, suggest that no advantage was to be found in burnishing as it seemed only to loosen the fibres and to make the surface more resistant to ink. However, it has been noticed on many funerary papyri that the inside surface of the roll is smoother than the outside. Indeed, when handling detached fragments from border areas, which bear no text, the inside can be identified by noting the smoother side. On the other hand, in the case of documents typically written on both sides, such as the Late Ramesside Letters, the papyri show no discernible difference between their two surfaces. Those who work with Ptolemaic and Roman papyri are used to seeing a superior finish on the inside surface of rolls.

The application of cedar oil as a preservative (Turner 1968: 3), or a coating of paste (Lewis 1974: 67–8) as a finish has been suggested by several people. It is true that papyrus does have a natural sheen on its surface, and some Demotic papyri in particular appear to have a yellow patina. However, there is no secure evidence for any such application, and on close inspection this can often be seen to be surface dirt or a natural graininess. One of the authors has examined four papyri under the stereoscopic microscope ($\times 30$); a modern example made by Ragab in 1974, an illustrated Book of the Dead from the early Eighteenth Dynasty (BM EA10477/1, *c.* 1450 BC), the Late Period *Lamentations of Isis and Nephthys* (BM EA10188/1, *c.* 300 BC), and a Demotic text (BM EA10710/2, *c.* 550 BC). To the naked eye, the surfaces of all four appeared to have a different appearance. The Ragab example was cream and almost matt, the Book of the Dead darker with a slight sheen and the Late Period and Demotic examples had a yellow to brown, slightly shiny surface. The yellowness of the Demotic example was curious, as it had grains on the surface, particularly along the joins, and it was difficult to know if this was due to over-enthusiastic pasting of the joins, or to dirt, or even to the light paste wash mentioned by Pliny (Lewis 1974: 41). Otherwise, however, under the microscope the surfaces were all comparable, and the sheen appeared to be in the very structure of the material itself, deriving from the glutinous nature of the sap. Even though in his modern practice Ragab washes out the excess starch and gums from his papyrus, the plant still retains much glutinous material, thus imparting the characteristic lustre. The other author has observed a distinctive yellow patina on one surface of many Roman-period papyri from Tebtunis; it would have been the original inside surface of the roll, but was subsequently the outside surface when the roll was reused (see Tait 1977: xi). This surface often shows considerable signs of handling in use; but it is nevertheless possible that the basic overall yellow shade is due to the natural ageing of a layer of paste on the surface.

Media used on papyrus

The Egyptians regularly used black ink for pen-written material. Red ink was freely used alongside black in many kinds of text, for example to distinguish headings (Černý 1952: 24). Many papyri, chiefly religious (for example, the funerary Book of the Dead), are illustrated, and the colours used for this may range from simply black alone to a wide variety of colours. The pigments used for these purposes are covered in Chapter 4 of this volume, and it is necessary here to mention only features of the substances used that are relevant to the study of papyrus.

The black ink employed during the Pharaonic period has to date almost invariably been found to be carbon black (Lucas 1962: 339–40; Green 1995: 90). Carbon ink is made by partially burning organic materials (for example oil or wood; therefore the products obtained are rarely pure carbon, but all contain mineral impurities and hydrocarbons). The carbon derived from it is mixed with a binder, most probably a gum such as gum arabic (Lucas 1962: 6; Green and Leach 1993: 4), to make a solid cake or 'watercolour'. This ink is very stable, as anyone who has worked upon papyri in the many collections around the world can testify.

It is not certain when metallic ink, commonly called 'iron-gall ink', was first used, but Reed (1972: 55) reports that it was in common use by the seventh century AD. Iron-gall ink is made by mixing oak-galls (containing gallotannic acid) with iron sulphate (a liquid, also known as green vitriol or copperas) to produce a writing fluid (ferrous gallotannate) that on exposure to air produces a black colour through oxidation, and becomes ferric gallotannate (Gettens and Stout 1966: 122).

Some interesting analysis has been undertaken quite recently to ascertain the type of ink used on Demotic and Greek texts dating from 252–98 BC in the collection of the Louvre (Delange *et al.* 1990). The PIXE (Proton Induced X-ray Emission) method of analysis was employed, having the advantage of being a non-destructive method. Although the method is not sensitive to carbon, carbon ink could be deduced by its lack of metallic elements compared to iron-gall ink. The results of the analysis were surprising in that it was found that all the Demotic texts were written with carbon ink, and that all the Greek texts, apart from one, were written with metallic ink. One Greek text was dated as early as 252 BC. This is therefore the earliest analysed example of this type of ink on papyrus in Egypt. It was also interesting that the use of metallic ink was directly associated with the writing implement, i.e. a reed pen in the Greek texts, while the demotic texts were always written in carbon ink with a rush pen of traditional Egyptian type, somewhat resembling a brush (see Tait 1988). Also the content of these metallic inks was slightly unexpected, since many different metallic elements were found, suggesting that the ink had been made with a wide variety of components (Ménei 1990: v. 1, p. 64). One significant finding was that, unlike the more modern iron-gall ink which shows a substantial presence of iron and sulphur, these ink samples had a marked lack of sulphur, although it was expected to be found in the same proportion to iron or copper. There was also a predominance of copper as opposed to iron. This in turn led to speculation on the method of ink manufacture, and the effects of ageing, suggesting that perhaps carbonates instead of sulphates were used in manufacture. It has also been proposed that the sulphur may have been incorporated into a gas or liquid compound which could have disappeared over time. Iron-gall ink has, with age, a characteristic brownish appearance, unlike carbon ink, which appears much blacker.

The analysis referred to above found that conclusions drawn from close observation with the naked eye were borne out by scientific analysis. One of the authors has noticed examples of metallic-looking inks on Manichean papyri from the Chester Beatty Collection, dated from the third or fourth centuries AD, and also on BM EA10951, a papyrus dating to the period from the first century BC to the first century AD, in the British Museum collection. However, chemical analysis would be needed to confirm this.

The source of the red ink found on Egyptian papyri is, with rare exceptions, haematite. Haematite, or red iron oxide, Fe_2O_3, is discussed in Chapters 2 and 4, this volume, dealing with the rock and the pigment respectively. A rare exception to this rule is to be found in one example in the British Museum (BM EA9968; Quirke 1993: 29), the Book of the Dead of Ahmose from the early Eighteenth Dynasty. Here the text has the appearance of having been written in black and yellow, which is surprising, as the Egyptian tradition of using red ink was so firmly established. Analysis of the 'yellow' ink was carried out at the British Museum and it was identified as para-realgar (Green 1992), indicating that the original pigment used for the ink was realgar. Realgar, α-AsS, is an orange-red colour of very similar chemical composition to yellow orpiment (arsenic trisulphide, As_2S_3). Exposure to heat (and sometimes light) can bring about changes in this pigment (Green 1995: 88–9), causing it to turn to a yellow colour, 'para-realgar', γ-AsS. The exact chemical reactions, and their causes, are not as yet fully understood, but tests are currently being carried out at the British Museum to try to understand the mechanisms of this change, and the time period involved in it.

Finally it is worth bearing in mind that although vermilion (HgS: red mercuric oxide, from the mineral cinnabar) has not been identified in use as a writing ink, it has certainly been identified as an artist's pigment on a papyrus of the Late Period (BM EA9916/2A; Quirke 1993: 49: Papyrus of Nesmin). When it appeared on the Egyptian palette is not yet known. Gettens and Stout state that it was known in the Classical world (1966: 170–1).

Deterioration of papyrus

Papyrus will deteriorate like any other organic material. Despite this, it has shown remarkable powers of durability. Apart from the purity of the material, this has undoubtedly been aided by the dry climate of Egypt. Finds outside the modern country of Egypt are rare, although well-known discoveries have been made at Derveni, Dura Europus, Herculaneum, Nessana (Anja Hafir, Palestine) and Petra. A survey of these finds, with bibliography, is given by Rupprecht (1994: 7–10; for Petra, see for example Koenen 1996). Deterioration will occur through ageing, and the breakdown of constituents in the material itself, physical damage, insect attack and mould; all these factors are closely associated with the conditions in which the papyri have lain for many years before discovery, and the subsequent treatment they have received. Most forms of deterioration and mould growth take place in the presence of moisture, often with contamination from other organic matter also. Papyrus finds fall very broadly into two categories; those included in tomb assemblages and those excavated from archaeological sites. Tombs can provide relatively dry and stable conditions until discovery, whereas other excavated sites are much less likely to do so. However, because Egypt's water table was relatively low until the present century, and conditions are sometimes favourable, many papyri have also been preserved in non-funerary contexts, and carbonised rolls may survive in relatively damp townsites (see p. 243).

Breakdown of the constituents of papyrus

As we have seen, papyrus is made up of a ground-tissue embedded with fibres. The pith has been analysed by Grant (Wendelbø 1975: 44), and found to be 97 per cent carbohydrates in the form of cellulose, hemi-cellulose and lignin, the remaining 2–3 per cent being made up of proteinaceous material. Further analysis by Weidemann and Bayer (1983) of the cellulose and lignin content of four ancient samples found the cellulose content ranging from 53.29–62.04 per cent, and lignin content from 22.42–32.77 per cent. Recently manufactured samples from Egypt and Sicily showed comparable results, but the Egyptian papyrus sample had 68.96 per cent cellulose content, in contrast to 53.12 per cent in the modern Sicilian papyrus. Examination of the distribution of these constituents showed that the vascular bundles were predominantly lignin and the surrounding material predominently cellulose.

Cellulose is inherently very stable, but it can also break down due to reactions caused by hydrolysis or oxidation. For instance, the degradation of cellulose in modern paper is often caused by acid hydrolysis. Acid hydrolysis involves a chemical reaction catalysed by hydrogen ions. Acidic materials can be present, due to the substances used during paper manufacture, e.g. papermaker's alum, which produces hydrogen ions in the presence of water. Papyrus, being made up of a large proportion of cellulose, will be subject to breakdown, particularly if kept in poor storage conditions, or in contact with acid-producing materials (Thomson 1986: 143–4; 154–6).

The presence of lignin has long been established as one of the factors in the deterioration and discolouration of woodpulp paper (Greathouse and Wessel 1954: 391), particularly when exposed to heat and light. Lignin is a complex aromatic polymeric substance soluble in strong alkalis and converted to soluble form by bleaching agents such as chlorine. Except for mechanically produced woodpulp papers, it is removed, at least partially, from the paper pulp in the paper-making process using various chemical methods to break it down and wash it out. The lignin content of newsprint is 20–30 per cent, and that of chemically treated woodpulp paper commonly 0.5–2 per cent, while good quality paper, made of rag or cotton, contains 0 per cent. Strangely, papyrus contains a proportion of lignin to cellulose similar to that of newsprint, but, unlike newsprint, does not darken when exposed to light, but lightens dramatically. Reflectance measurements with Perkin-Elmer 5515 Ultraviolet-visible (UV-Vis) spectrophotometer taken before and after light ageing (twenty-eight days in Microscal light-fastness tester) of a strip of papyrus showed a 4.1 per cent increase in reflectance (lightening) at 436 nm (Green and Leach 1993: 14).

However, papyrus can discolour or darken with age. Reflectance measurements taken before and after heat ageing (twenty-eight days at 70 °C) showed a 3.6 per cent decrease in reflectance (darkening) at 436 nm. Weidemann and Bayer came to the conclusion that the darkening of papyrus is due to the higher polymerisation of the lignin content, as lignin is a less stable component than cellulose.

Micro-organisms

Being an organic material, papyrus is susceptible to microbiological degradation. Cellulose, lignin, and the sugars in the cell sap of papyrus can be used by micro-organisms for growth. In the early 1970s, Kowalik and Sadurska (1973) of the Institute of Industrial Organic Chemistry in Poland did extensive work on the study of microflora that grow on papyrus, using ancient samples from various museums in Cairo. A very wide range of moulds and fungi were found on the material. They concluded that certain fungi are specific for papyrus and also aspects of Egyptian climatic conditions. Many factors have an influence on fungal growth: moisture, temperature, acidity or alkalinity of the material or its environment, and the presence of nutrients, i.e. nitrogen compounds, from the material itself or from its environment – usually, in the case of papyrus, from the soil. The research carried out by Kowalik and Sadurska found that certain micro-organisms could grow within a wide pH (acid/alkalinity) range: pH 4–10.00 for those growing in the presence of ammonium nitrate and phosphate. The temperatures required for growth were, however, relatively high, 24–6 °C being suitable for many. Fungal growth is extremely destructive to papyrus, as it decomposes it. However, these tests only indicate the possibilities of rapid growth in certain prepared conditions. Although many micro-organisms were isolated from the papyri, spores will always be present on everything in the natural world. It is the actual growth of a fungus that presents a problem, and good environmental conditions will not encourage growth. Also a valid comment on these results was made by Nielsen (1985: 90), that the samples used for the tests had been in museum storage for approximately thirty years, therefore it was not clear whether contamination was due to the nature of the excavation site or museum storage.

Banik and Stachelberger (1987) state that the high salt content of Egyptian soil (see p. 242) has a preservative effect on papyrus, as the salts inhibit microbiological growth. They state that, where sodium chloride is present in a concentration of over 6 per cent, very few micro-organisms can survive. However, although the alkaline soil of Egypt may well have a preservative effect against micro-biological deterioration, mould growth has been found on papyri in various collections (Kowalik and Sadurska 1973; Weidemann and Bayer 1983; Owen and Danzing 1993).

Attack by insects

Papyrus is very vulnerable to insect attack. Most collections have examples of the results of the ravages of insects. The regular patterns of damage are indicative of activity taking place while the papyrus was still rolled. Cockle (1983: 157) states that ancient users of papyrus were aware of this danger and applied *cedrium*, a resinous extract from the juniper, to prevent bookworms from attacking the roll. Many papyri in the British Museum and Petrie Museum collections show evidence of insect attack (see Fig. 9.6); one of the authors, on unrolling a papyrus in 1992, found a dead insect still inside. Fortunately the problem is not a continuing one. Activity dies with the insect, perhaps even before discovery. If papyri are stored in good conditions there is no reason why they should be re-infested.

Deterioration during ancient use

Another factor which will have a bearing on the condition of papyrus rolls is the use to which they were put in ancient times. If the roll was consulted as a reference work, for example the Kahun Medical Papyrus in the Petrie Museum (Kahun, VI.1; UC. 32057; Griffith 1898: 5; pls. 5–6), it will already have been subjected to considerable wear and tear. Sometimes repairs made in ancient times, often with a strip of fresh papyrus, can be observed (see p. 232). A good example of this is the Rhind Mathematical Papyrus in the British Museum (BM EA10057 and BM EA10058; Robins and Shute 1987). Palimpsests are also found, both

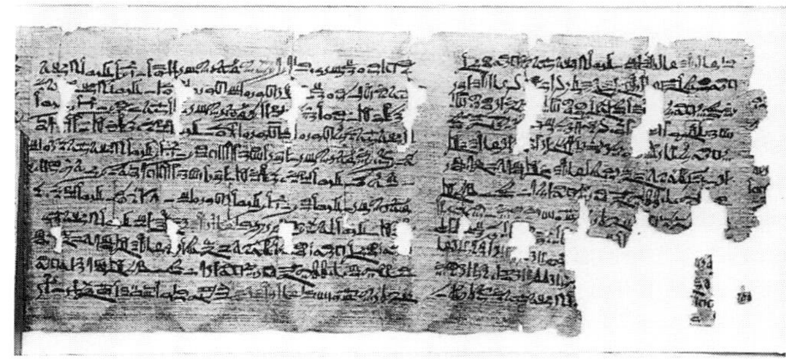

Figure 9.6 A papyrus bearing a liturgy in hieratic (BM EA10819, Eighteenth Dynasty), which has been subjected to insect attack while rolled.

his name and the date on the gelatin film. This type of adhesive with the trade name 'Zapon' was widely used at one time in the restoration of many museum objects (Rathgen 1905: 168–70B). In a solution of amyl acetate, it was used to 'strengthen' archival material. Lucas (1932: 132) refers to the strengthening of papyrus with a 'dilute solution of celluloid', in this case very probably meaning cellulose nitrate adhesive, although he mentions that this was rarely needed. The terms celluloid and cellulose nitrate are often used as if they were synonymous, but we here refer to the film as *celluloid*, and to the adhesive as *cellulose nitrate*. Film made from cellulose nitrate was marketed under the name 'Celluloid' in the USA (Koob 1982: 31). In its early formulation the film was particularly unstable chemically; hence the problem of the possibility of spontaneous combustion. The reactions are complex: in the first stages of degradation, nitrogen dioxide gas is given off, which itself speeds up the degradation. If the gas is able to build up, as in the case of early celluloid film stored in containers intended to be airtight, the reactions are accelerated further, sometimes resulting in combustion (Edge *et al.* 1990). Cellulose nitrate adhesive, being in a less concentrated form, is unlikely to react in this way, although it does become insoluble over time, thus causing other problems.

Of the Ramesseum Papyri treated by Ibscher (and later by his son, as the work went on into the 1920s and 1930s), only two were mounted on celluloid film. Most were attached to gelatin with cellulose nitrate adhesive, or were probably stuck by brushing the gelatin with a little warm water to make it tacky before laying down the papyrus, as no adhesive is visible. One example of the use of cellulose acetate film has been identified (Green 1993), but the rest were attached to waxed glass, or mounted between glass with no support or adhesive.

Salt contamination was observed as a problem from early on, and Rathgen (1905: 155) says that salt crystals were picked off with tweezers. Lucas (1932: 132) states that the only way to deal with salts was to soak the papyrus repeatedly in pure water until the wash water tested free of salt.

For cartonnage, all the early methods used to separate gesso from papyri involved the use of acids, which dissolved the gesso layer more or less completely. Lucas (1932: 134) records that 20 per cent acetic acid solution was employed; at the Sorbonne the use of hydrochloric acid is reported (Wright 1980: 27).

Carbonised papyri presented a particular problem in the past, as they still do. Although one might expect the material to be beyond repair, as indeed some of it is, carbonised papyri have frequently been unrolled, and text revealed. The black ink, in suitable lighting, is still legible against the background of the papyrus, which can take on a grey and 'metallic' colour when it has been subjected to very high temperatures. Many of the Herculaneum papyri were apparently unrolled by means of an elaborate machine, devised by Antonio Piaggio, not long after their discovery in 1752. If we understand correctly, the process involved slowly unrolling the layers onto a sheet of thin animal gut, dilute adhesive being used to relax the roll, and to attach the layers to the sheet (Gilberg 1988). This technique was not universally successful, as might be expected in the case of such fragile material, and sometimes large pieces of the roll broke away. Petrie (1904: 94) gives advice on the handling of finds of carbonised papyri, probably recording his experience at Tanis. He states that 'the objects should be removed from the site by undercutting the earth below and around it'. Later, the individual rolls can be separated using a fine knife and wrapped in soft paper, and 'wrapped thus carefully, a few to a box, they can be transported safely'. Two of the hieroglyphic papyri from Tanis came to the British Museum (Griffith and Petrie 1889), where there are also two small rolls and a box of untreated fragments. The section of the British Library which was formerly the British Museum Department of Manuscripts still has untreated material from Tanis, but the present location of approximately fifty frames of unrolled fragments is unknown. There is some documentation of the treatment received by this material:

> The papyrus fragments have been mounted in frames formed by two sheets of glass, held apart by a thin piece of cardboard round the edges to allow for wrinkles in the papyri; both sides of which can thus be seen. The fragments are kept in place under the glass with shell-lac. The task of mounting the papyri was a simple, although a delicate one. The rolls had been crushed flat, and so consisted of a series of flakes, each the same breadth as the crushed roll. The flakes were removed with a paper-knife from each side of the roll alternately, the order thus obtained being fairly correct. In some cases it was found more convenient to divide the roll in the middle, and, beginning from the centre, to take flakes alternately from each half. (Griffith and Petrie 1889: 2)

Papyrus collections: ongoing deterioration

When papyri have been in museums or private collections for many years their condition will have been affected by the environment in which they have been stored or displayed. All forms of deterioration, whether inherent in the material itself, or due to the nature of the conditions in which they survived before modern discovery, or mechanical handling, or previous treatment, will be accelerated by unstable environmental conditions. One form of deterioration, namely over-exposure to high light-levels, will actually catalyse breakdown of the papyri and some writing or painting media.

We have already seen that exposure to light, particularly ultraviolet light, causes papyri to lighten or 'bleach' (Green and Leach 1993: 11). This is due to photo-oxidation; light as a form of energy will cause chemical breakdown of the cellulose molecule (Thomson 1986: 193–5). Papyri that have been subjected to this type of degradation become irreversibly weak; at worst the fibres and the inter-fibrillar cellulose material readily turns to dust at the slightest movement.

Light can also affect the media used on papyrus. The inks on Egyptian papyri, being carbon black and red iron oxide, remain stable, but iron-gall ink, being an acidic product, ferric gallotannate, is less stable. Most pigments found on Egyptian papyri are mineral pigments and are light-fast, although vermilion and verdigris are known to darken (Thomson 1986: 12). The most light-sensitive pigment is orpiment, arsenic trisulphide, As_2S_3 (see pp. 239, 241). This has long been known, and tests currently being undertaken at the British Museum confirm that orpiment fades extremely quickly, and will eventually lose all colour when exposed to light. The relationship between the amount of light needed to effect the change, and the time factors involved has yet to be established. Orpiment degrades photochemically to arsenic trioxide, As_2O_3, which is almost white in appearance (Green 1995). There are examples of papyri in the British Museum which have lost all the yellow borders commonly drawn above or below the texts of the Books of the Dead. The fact that this is directly caused by exposure to light can be seen when one compares one frame that has been on display with another that has not, from the same papyrus roll: the yellow pigment has invariably faded. Realgar, an orange-red sulphide of arsenic very similar to orpiment, is also subject to photo-degradation (see p. 239).

Relative humidity plays a large part in the efflorescence of salts in those papyri which are contaminated. It manifests itself as small deposits imbedded in the papyrus, or as crystals on the surface, or, when the papyrus is contained in a mount, as a 'bloom' on the glass mount, roughly matching the shape of the mounted fragment (see Fig. 9.9). Analysis of this bloom on the glass has indicated that it consists essentially of sodium chloride (Nielsen 1985: 104–17; V. Daniels, pers. comm., 1996), and other summary examinations known to us have led to the same conclusion.

This 'bloom' forms because of salt migration, as the papyrus takes up moisture from the air. If the papyrus takes in more moisture than it can absorb, it will pass through the material, in its aqueous state, dissolving and carrying salts with it, ultimately to the surface of the papyrus, where it will come into contact with the glass or backing paper. Sometimes it passes through the backing paper to the glass. This is what we see as a 'halo' or 'bloom' on the glass mount.

Thus constant changes in relative humidity (RH) will encourage salt efflorescence. Light and temperature will also play a part in this as they alter the RH (Nielsen 1985: 104–17). Nielsen did tests to establish how far the bloom was caused by these three environmental factors, and found that although a high RH predictably resulted in a bloom on the glass, light exposure also had an effect by causing changes in temperature of up to +11 °C and in turn changes in RH of up to 42 per cent. Bloom resulted on all samples exposed to light even at a low RH setting. Thus papyri displayed for many years at high light levels will be subjected to variations of temperature and RH that can only encourage this type of salt migration. Nielsen's tests involved mounting papyrus fragments between glass and placing them in an environment with the RH at a constant low, constant high, or at a fluctuation, all at 20 °C. She then set the RH at 30, 50 and 80 per cent respectively, and trained direct light on the mounts from lamps switched on and off at six-hourly intervals.

(a)

(b)

Figure 9.9 Papyrus bearing Coffin Texts (BM EA10676/24, Middle Kingdom). Photograph (a) shows it inside a mount, which has developed a bloom on the inside of the glass. Photograph (b) shows the inside of the dismantled mount, with the bloom on the glass corresponding to the outline of the papyrus.

Papyri with salt efflorescence do not always display this 'bloom' on the mount, but salt deposits or crystals are visible under the microscope and sometimes to the naked eye. Aside from the amount of salt in the papyri when they arrive in a museum, the reason for their different behaviour may be due to the rate of drying during a fall in RH. In the case of objects which dry out slowly over a long period of time (i.e. the RH falls slowly and steadily), salts tend to migrate to the edges, or deposit themselves on material in contact – in the case of many papyri, glass. However, if the RH falls rapidly and an object dries quickly, salts are more likely to crystallise centrally, or on the surface of the object (D. Thickett, pers. comm., 1995). Whatever the reasons, some papyri can have a very marked bloom on the glass while the papyrus itself seems to show no salt efflorescence, and *vice versa*. In the latter case the danger is not always immediately visible as the crystals can be very small, but salt crystals repeatedly reforming with changes in RH, and over a number of years, will eventually damage the tissue and shatter the surface irreversibly.

Modern conservation procedures

The approach towards archaeological collections today, has, of course, changed since the time when most objects in our collections were acquired. The tendency is now towards minimum interference, in order to maintain the integrity of the object and of any evidence it can yield. Much repair work continues to be needed, the difference now being that the materials used must conform to conservation standards; this means that they must be chemically stable and have good ageing properties, and that their application should be reversible.

Great emphasis is now placed on 'passive conservation' by endeavouring to achieve satisfactory environmental conditions for storage and display. The recommended environment for pictorial art is 50–60 per cent RH and a temperature of 19 °C (±2 °C) (Bradley 1993: 79). Although 45–55 per cent RH is satisfactory for papyrus, damage can be caused by fluctuating conditions, particularly when those fluctuations are rapid. Light levels also are of crucial importance. Papyrus is subject to photo-degradation when exposed to high light levels, and some pigments used on illustrated papyri are light-sensitive, particularly orpiment. It is recommended that such pigments should not be exposed to light levels above 50 lux, and that the UV content of the light should be less than 75 micro-watts per lumen (Bradley 1993: 79).

The principal reasons for the deterioration of papyri have been outlined in the previous section, but of course all collections are different and will have different problems. Large, well-preserved Books of the Dead need a different approach from that appropriate to badly-preserved and fragmentary excavated material. Early treatments and subsequent museum environments, architecturally and climatically, will vary enormously.

Fungus and insect attack can be a serious problem for conservators and curators alike. Fortunately, this is not often a major problem for collections in temperate climates. However, infestation can occur when new objects are acquired which are already infested, or mould can develop if high RH micro-climates build up in particular areas. Most fungal growth will only occur above an RH of 65 per cent and a temperature of 20 °C (Daniels and Rae 1991: 4), although the spores found on papyri appear to prefer higher temperatures and higher RH (Kowalik and Sadurska 1973: 19), therefore environmental control is very important in order to discourage both insect activity and mould growth.

Many fungicides that have been used in the past are today considered unacceptable for Health and Safety reasons. In the past, after unrolling a papyrus, it was placed between thymol-impregnated blotting paper for several days prior to mounting (Plenderleith and Werner 1971: 46). However, the effectiveness of thymol is questionable (Kowalik and Sadurska 1973: 19), and there is evidence to show that it can yellow both paper and Perspex in the presence of light (Daniels and Boyd 1976). As far as pesticides are concerned, the British Museum, which still acquires much organic material, now uses methyl bromide gas, one of the permitted pesticides, or nitrogen anoxia. Freezing is also a method used for certain artefacts in the British Museum and other museums, although it is not advisable for unstable waxes and glues (Daniels and Rae 1991: 5). Tests prove that papyrus and mounts can be frozen if certain measures are taken (Leach 1995: 158), but as yet this rather drastic action has never been necessary for use on papyrus. More recently, argon gas was used in the Library at Mount Athos (Koestler and Matthews 1994); the gas is used to create a low-oxygen, or anoxic, environment, which kills the insect pests by suffocation. The use of inert gases is not new: nitrogen has been used for many years, most notably in the agricultural industry. Experiments using helium gas are currently planned at the Metropolitan Museum, New York.

The most effective way to guard against both forms of bio-deterioration is basic good housekeeping and staff awareness. Regular inspection of the collections and cleanliness, if done methodically, will ensure minimum risk of infestation or mould growth. Even in difficult climates, and in the case of collections which have no environmental control, much can be achieved by creating airflow. This reduces RH and prevents the formation of micro-climates.

When it comes to dealing with papyri which have evidence of mould growth, the mould deposit should be brushed away (a mask and rubber gloves should be worn for Health and Safety reasons). If the material is very fragile it may be taken away with fine tweezers or a scalpel; the use of magnification (a magnifying lamp, magnifying goggles, or microscope) is always helpful and the conservator can ensure that all the deposits have been removed. This operation should be done in a separate area with dust extraction. As yet, mould has never been encountered on any papyri in the British Museum collections, but unsorted excavation material may have deposits. Evidence has been noted of previous mould growth (or a better term would be microbiological deterioration) on papyri from other collections, where partial dampness at some time in the past has caused a mouldy stain. However, if dried out thoroughly after repair and stored in the correct environmental conditions, the papyrus should not deteriorate further.

Papyri that have been subjected to insect attack are characterised by holes or tunnels where the insect has been, and they may sometimes have very large areas of loss. Occasionally this proves useful for re-orientating fragments of a roll, when the insect has created a regular pattern in the convolutions of the roll while eating its way through the papyrus (Hoffmann 1994). In some instances the insect appears to have confined its movements to a single layer of papyrus (e.g. Tait 1991a: 20).

In the British Museum collection there are still several 'made-up' rolls: that is, papyrus fragments from disparate documents that have been stuck together into a roll shape (see p. 243). They usually present a larger, intact, piece around the outside to cover the scraps inside; other examples are known which are made up of fragments masking a stiff core of some other material. Three of these have been 'unrolled', or separated by the British Museum Department of Conservation in recent years. The method is very simple and involves the introduction of controlled humidity, followed by drying and pressing of the material. The aim is to introduce enough moisture to solubilise the adhesive between the papyrus layers, without harming the inks and pigments, so that the layers can be physically separated. A certain amount of moisture is also needed to 'relax' the papyrus, that is to make it flexible enough to realign and to flatten it out into its original shape. Separation of the layers is accomplished with tweezers or with whatever tool suits the conservator, and the individual pieces can gradually be eased away. It is necessary to re-humidify from time to time as the outer layers are removed. The fragments are then laid between two pieces of blotting paper with an interleaving layer of 'Bondina' or similar material, to act as a support and to stop the papyrus from adhering to them, under a piece of plate glass and weight. The blotting paper can be changed at regular intervals until the papyrus is dry. Much dirt, discolouration and old adhesive can be removed in this way, as it is drawn out of the papyrus into the blotting paper in its aqueous form. Straightforward rolls are approached in very much the same way, which is not unlike the early method of wrapping in damp blotting paper or linen, and leaving perhaps overnight, except that the introduction of moisture is much more controlled.

To achieve controlled humidification of papyrus, two aids have been found particularly useful: the use of an ultrasonic humidifier and the application of a material known by its trade name of 'Gore-Tex'. The ultrasonic humidifier produces water vapour by splitting the water into very fine droplets. The equipment consists of a small water tank with the sonic apparatus below, and a funnel running from it, carrying the water vapour. This produces moisture in a much gentler way than even the finest of sprays. Papyrus can be humidified slowly and gently either by directing the vapour flow directly onto the object, or by creating a humidity chamber and channelling the mist inside. The other method mentioned uses a layer of polytetrafluorethylene membrane (Gore-Tex), which is laminated onto a polyester felt backing. This membrane allows only gases and vapour to pass through it, so that, when it is laid over a damp layer (damp blotting paper or capillary matting), water vapour can pass through to the papyrus, which is laid on top. Again, a humidity chamber can easily be made by placing the layers in a tray and covering with a piece of glass, or by clipping a polythene sheet over it. This is particularly useful for small fragments, as they can be picked out one at a time to be cleaned and repaired. It is also valuable for small rolls or layers of laminated papyrus, as they can be separated in stages and replaced in the tray as more humidification is necessary. For larger papyri that will not fit in a tray, the same layers are used but a piece of glass can be laid on top. The amount of moisture passing through can be controlled by more or less extensive wetting of the damp layer. Distilled water is always used in papyrus conservation, to avoid the various impurities present in tap water.

Papyri that are not too fragile – by which is meant that the material is substantial enough to withstand a minimal amount of handling without disintegration – can be repaired. Small fragments can be picked up with tweezers, but larger pieces are always moved by holding firmly between two sheets of plate glass, with an interleaving layer between the papyrus and the glass as a support. If discoloured, dirty, fractured, misaligned, cockled, creased, or brittle, the papyri can be treated fairly straightforwardly. Humidification to relax the papyri is preceded by testing the inks for fugitivity. The inks are usually stable; only a slight fugitivity is sometimes found, but with proper care in humidification and physical handling this is not a problem. Before humidification, surface dirt can be removed with a soft brush. Once relaxed, if the papyrus is creased, cockled or misaligned it can be gently manipulated into shape. This is often done over a light table, where the fibres of the vertical and horizontal strips can be seen. At this point, any dirt or deposits may be removed. This should not include stains or resinous deposits, e.g. from a burial, which may be regarded as forming part of the object. Lumps of dirt, if necessary, can be picked off with tweezers. Once the papyrus is realigned, it can be repaired. Repairs are made with small pieces, 'tabs', of Japanese paper and wheat-starch paste. Long-fibred, good quality Japanese paper is strong; it can be toned with water colours if desired so that the tabs are not over-noticeable when attached to the papyrus. Gluten-free wheat-starch paste is widely used in conservation and is a good reversible adhesive. Small tabs can be laid over the fractures to rejoin them in the correct position and the papyrus is then pressed until dry. Again, much dirt and discolouration is removed by absorption into the blotting paper during drying. Where dirt or deposits obliterate the text, which is more likely with excavated material, careful use of tweezers and very gentle rolling of damp cotton-wool buds over the area, in the direction of the fibres, can successfully reveal the text. It is always advisable not to over-clean, firstly in order to avoid damage to the ink, and secondly because the absorption of dirt into the blotting paper very often means that on drying-out the text is much clearer than it may have appeared while wet.

Fragments of papyrus often become displaced. This can be due to the condition of the roll itself; if it has been subjected to insect attack it may have fallen into fragments. In addition, separating the layers of a made-up roll only leaves us with a considerable number of fragments which may, or may not, come from the same document. The philologist may be able to judge from the text which fragments may join up, but fortunately it is also possible to match up the horizontal and/or vertical fibres of the papyrus in order to re-orientate the roll or document, even when there has been a certain amount of loss. Because of the way in which papyrus is manufactured, each sheet has a fibre-pattern which can be seen through transmitted light, with or without magnification. Even papyri which are too thick to be viewed through transmitted light can have a visible surface fibre pattern. By lining up matching fibres either horizontally or vertically, it is sometimes possible to get an exact placing of a fragment, although the area immediately around it may be lost. The sheet-joins may also prove helpful. If we know the approximate dimensions of one or two sheets already, we can assume for the purposes of orientation that the remaining sheets will be of approximately the same size (e.g. Tait 1975: 263). Sheet-joins are normally easily recognised, as the horizontal fibre pattern changes, and the join is slightly thicker and darker when viewed by transmitted light because of the overlap. However, sheet-joins can be very difficult to identify in damaged material.

Many papyri in collections have been backed by paper of inferior quality, which has led to cockling, the lifting of small fragments, and fractures. If necessary, and where possible, these backings are removed. In most cases the papyri are very fragile and need to be relined with archival quality materials (Japanese paper and wheat-starch paste), with the advantage, at least, that the fibre pattern can be observed through the new lining. If they are strong enough, the papyri are not re-lined, but may be repaired with tabs only. To effect the safe removal of a backing, the papyrus must be adequately supported during the removal and while applying new repairs. A facing technique has been developed at the British Museum (Walker 1988), which has made it possible to remove backings safely. The technique has also proved satisfactory for illustrated papyri (Leach and Green 1995).

Very friable papyri sometimes need to be consolidated. Often this can be done effectively by humidifying the papyrus slightly, just enough to reactivate the gums, followed by pressing. Another successful method has been to spray on an aqueous solution of funori (0.5 per cent), followed, again, by pressing. Funori is a glutinous extract of three seaweeds, which contains galactose, also found in the natural cell sap of papyrus (Levring *et al.* 1969: 335). Funori has been used in Japan as an adhesive for many centuries, and is widely employed in paper conservation (Winter 1984: 119).

The pigments on an illustrated papyrus may be flaking or crumbling. In this case a suitable consolidant must be applied to reattach the pigment particles to each other and to the papyrus. The consolidants used in conservation such as Klugel G, Paraloid B72, and isinglass have all been tested at the British Museum in recent years: isinglass was found to be the most effective (Leach and Green 1995). It is almost pure collagen, the UK supply being made from the swim bladders of various tropical fish (Foskett 1994: 11). It is a good adhesive, and has a matt appearance which does not alter the colour of the ancient pigments when applied.

When salts are found to be present on papyri, they can, if crystallised on the surface, be removed with fine tweezers, working under magnification. Water-soluble salts may be removed using distilled water, followed by pressing between dry blotting paper to remove the solubulised salt; but this is not necessarily possible if the papyrus is very fragile. Again, not all salts are soluble, and the only safe practice, if the salts cannot be removed or removed completely, is to store or display the papyrus in stable conditions of temperature and RH, with suitable light levels. Salt manifesting itself as a 'bloom' inside a glass mount containing papyrus can be remedied by dismantling the mount, wiping the bloom off the glass, and re-mounting. However, this is not always practicable, or safe for the papyrus. Allowing a little air to circulate inside the mount is helpful in combatting this problem. At the Austrian National Library in Vienna, a small gap is left in the binding tape at the corner of each glass papyrus-mount, and the mount is then placed within a paper folder, as a dust cover. These particular mounts are comparatively small; therefore the method is feasible as well as successful. For collections with much larger papyri, enclosed in correspondingly larger glass mounts, where the papyri are constantly consulted, and the mounts subjected to considerable handling, this method is unfortunately not practicable.

It is widely – although not universally – agreed that papyrus is best stored between two sheets of glass, held together by some form of adhesive tape binding. Glass has several advantages. It has been used for the storage of papyrus for almost two centuries without any apparent harmful effects. It does not normally adhere to the papyrus in any way, and, if necessary, it can easily be cleaned or replaced. It allows the papyrus to be examined and photographed just as it has been stored. Indeed, photographers generally prefer to photograph papyri under glass. The disadvantages of glass should not be disregarded, however. It is heavy, and large collections of papyri when glassed can become very bulky. Sheet glass of three-millimetre thickness is perfectly adequate for small fragments, but the larger the papyrus, the heavier the weight of glass that must be used, and very large papyri require substantial wooden frames, if glass is to be employed with safety. If an accident causes both sheets of a glass mount to break, the papyrus usually remains undamaged, but may be cut, although fortunately the broken edges of the glass usually act in the manner of a guillotine, and sever the papyrus very cleanly. Obviously, care always needs to be taken in the handling of glass and of glass frames.

Papyri stored between sheets of glass should normally be held in place with tabs of Japanese tissue, made to adhere to one side of the glass. If unsupported in this or any other way, small fragments (especially when several pieces of differing thickness are stored in the same frame) can slip or move about. This is, at the least, an annoyance, and greatly increases the risk of damage to the fragments. The effect is exacerbated when the frames are shelved standing vertically, which is the method of storage most commonly adopted. Glass frames cannot be stacked in piles either conveniently or safely, and more elaborate methods of storing papyri horizontally are both expensive and greedy of space.

In modern times, the chief rivals to storage in glass have been various types of transparent plastic folders and Perspex sheets. They have several disadvantages. It is not known whether plastic or Perspex might harm the papyrus as they degrade, plastic folders are not sufficiently rigid to protect papyrus, and Perspex can warp. There is also anecdotal evidence that the static generated by Perspex can tear apart the two layers of a papyrus sheet when the mount is opened; one of the authors has witnessed a papyrus starting to be damaged in this way.

Conclusions

Much experimental and analytical work has been undertaken in recent years to attempt to identify the constituents of papyrus as a writing-ground, and to establish the methods used in the manufacturing process, and the mechanisms of deterioration. Much, however, is still not understood: for example, the type or types of sub-species of papyrus used, and the details of craft practice in the preparation of papyrus sheets (how the strips were cut and pressed together), in joining sheets, and in the finishing processes. In the absence of any Egyptian written sources, these questions may yet be clarified by closer examination and by modern analytical techniques. Much can be deduced from observation, particularly if a substantial corpus of papyri is available for study. However, early methods of mounting papyri, often encountered in long-established papyrus collections, can impede investigation. In the area of conservation, treatments still need to be found for certain problems, such as the insolubility of old cellulose nitrate adhesive used as a repair material at the beginning of this century.

Many papyri in existing collections remain quite unstudied. At the same time, papyri continue to be found in excavations, presenting a wide range of conservation problems. In the last few years, the use of computer scans has rapidly become feasible and almost commonplace, both in the publication of reproductions of papyri, and as a tool in reading them. This topic lies outside the scope of this book, but it is to be expected that computer techniques will play an increasing role in the study and the conservation of papyri: one application already being discussed is the matching of papyrus fibre-patterns, and other new approaches will undoubtedly be developed.

Acknowledgements

We should like to thank Dr V. Daniels, Dr S. Quirke, Mrs G. Roy, Mr T. Springett and Dr M. van der Veen for their help.

References

Andorlini, I., Baccani D., Barbi, R., Baroncelli, V., Bassi, E. and twenty others 1985. *The Rendel Harris Papyri* II. Studia amstelodamensia ad epigraphicam, ius antiquum et papyrologicam pertinentia 26. Zutphen: Terra.

Andrews, C.A.R. 1991. Postscript to PBM 10380A/B. *Enchoria*, 18: 175–6.

Bailey, L.H. 1963. *Standard Cyclopaedia of Horticulture* (3 vols). New York: The Macmillan Company.

Banik, G. 1989. Discoloration of green copper pigments in manuscripts and works of graphic art. *Restaurator*, 10: 61–73.

Banik, G. and Stachelberger, H. 1987. Salt migration in papyrus fragments. In *Recent Advances in the Conservation and Analysis of Artefacts: University of London, Institute of Archaeology Jubilee Conference 1987* (ed. J. Black). London: Summer Schools Press, pp. 199–201.

Barns, J.W.B. 1956. *Five Ramesseum Papyri*. Oxford: Griffith Institute.

Barrandon, J., Irigoin, J. and Schiffmacher, G. 1975. Nouvelles techniques applicables à l'étude du livre de papyrus. In *Proceedings of the XIV International Congress of Papyrologists, Oxford, 23–31 July 1974* (Graeco-Roman Memoirs 61). London: EES, pp. 7–10

Basile, C. 1972. A method of making papyrus and fixing and preserving it by means of a chemical treatment. In *Conservation of Painting and the Graphic Arts*, IIC Lisbon Conference Preprints, pp. 901–5.

1977. Metodo usato dagli antichi Egizi per la fabbricazione e la preservazione della carta-papiro. *Aegyptus*, 57: 190–9.

Basile, C. and Di Natale, A. 1994. *Il Museo del Papiro di Siracusa* (Quaderni dell' Associazione, Instituto Internazionale del Papiro – Siracusa IV). Siracusa: Associazione, Istituto Internazionale del Papiro.

1996. Un contributo alla manifattura dei papiri: esperienze, teorie, nuove ricerche. In *Atti del II Convegno Nazionale di Egittologia e Papirologia, Siracusa, 1–3 Dicembre, 1995* (Quaderni dell'Istituto Internazionale del Papiro – Siracusa VII). Siracusa: Istituto Internazionale del Papiro, pp. 85–135.

Blackman, A.M. 1915a. *The Rock Tombs of Meir II: The Tomb-chapel of Senbi's Son Ukh-hotp (B, No. 2)*. London: EEF.

1915b. *The Rock Tombs of Meir III: The Tomb-chapel of Ukh-hotp Son of Ukh-hotp and Mersi (B, No. 4)*. London: EEF.

Borchardt, L. 1889. Bermerkungen zu den ägyptischen Handschriften des Berliner Museums. *ZÄS*, 27: 118–22.

Bradley, S. (ed.) 1993. *A Guide to the Storage, Exhibition and Handling of Antiquities, Ethnographia and Pictorial Art*. London: BMP.

Bridgeman, C.F. 1973. The radiography of museum objects. *Expedition* (University Museum, University of Pennsylvania), 15 iii: pp. 2–14.

Brissaud, P. 1993. Premières nouvelles de la xle campagne – 1993. *SFFT Newsletter: Bulletin périodique de la Société Française des Fouilles de Tanis* 13: pp. 1–10.

1994. Une campagne intermédiaire. *SFFT Newsletter: Bulletin périodique de la Société Française des Fouilles de Tanis* 14: pp. 1–6.

Bruce, J. 1790. *Travels to Discover the Source of the Nile, in the Years 1768, 1769, 1770, 1771, 1772 and 1773* (5 vols). Edinburgh: Printed by J. Ruthven for G.G.J. and J. Robinson. [Vol. 5 has title: *Appendix: Select Specimens of Natural History, Collected in Travels to Discover the Source of the Nile in Egypt, Arabia, Abyssinia, and Nubia*].

Budge, E.A.W. 1912. *The Greenfield Papyrus in the British Museum: the Funerary Papyrus of Princess Nesitanebtâshru*. London: BMP.

Bülow-Jacobsen, A. 1976. Principatus medio: Pliny, N.H. XIII, 72 sqq. *ZPE*, 20: 113–16.

1978. Papyrus in three layers? P.Haun. 1, inv. no. 5n. *CdE*, 53/105: pp. 158–61.

1986. A short bibliography of papyrus-making. In *Papyrus: Structure and Usage* (ed. M.L. Bierbrier). London: BMP, p. 90.

Caminos, R.A. 1986. Some comments on the reuse of papyrus. In *Papyrus: Structure and Usage* (ed. M.L. Bierbrier). London: BMP, pp. 43–61.

Carter, G.S. 1953. *The Papyrus Swamps of Uganda*. Cambridge: Heffer.

Černý, J. 1952. *Paper and Books in Ancient Egypt*. London: University College (also repr. Chicago: Ares. 1977).

Cockle, W.E.H. 1983. Restoring and conserving papyri. *Bulletin of the Institute of Classical Studies*, 30: 147–65.

Daniels, V. and Boyd, B. 1986. The yellowing of thymol in the display of prints. *Studies in Conservation*, 31: 156–8.

Daniels, V. and Rae, A. 1991. *Guidelines for the Prevention and Control of Bio-Deterioration*. British Museum, London, Conservation Research Section, Internal Report no. 1991/31.

Darby, W.J., Ghalioungui, P., and Grivetti, L. 1977. *Food: the Gift of Osiris* (2 vols). London: Academic Press.

Davies, G. 1922. *The Tomb of Puyemrê at Thebes*. New York: MMA.

De Bignicourt, M.-C. and Flieder, F. 1996. L'Analyse des papyrus. In *Preprints of ICOM Committee for Conservation, 11th Triennial Meeting, Edinburgh, Scotland, 1–6 September 1996*. London: James and James, pp. 488–93.

Delange, E., Grange, M., Kusko, B., and Ménei, E. 1990. Apparition de l'encre métallogallique en Égypte à partir de la Collection de Papyrus du Louvre. *RdE*, 41: 213–17.

Dixon, D.M. 1972. Masticatories in ancient Egypt. *Journal of Human Evolution*, 1: 433–49 (repr. in *Population Biology of the Ancient Egyptians*; ed. D.R.Brothwell and B.A. Chiarelli. London, Academic Press, 1973).

Donnithorne, A. 1986. The conservation of papyrus in the British Museum. In *Papyrus: Structure and Usage* (ed. M.L. Bierbrier). London: BMP, pp. 1–23.

Drenkhahn, R. 1982. Papyrus, -herstellung. *LÄ* 4: 667–70.

Ebers, G. (ed.) 1875. *Papyros Ebers: das hermetische Buch ber die Arzeneimittel der alten Ägypter in hieratische Schrift*. Leipzig: Engelmann.

Edge, M., Allen, N., Hayes, M., Riley, P., Horie, C. and Luc-Gardette, J. 1990. Mechanisms of deterioration in cellulose-nitrate base archival cinematographic film. *European Polymer Journal*, 26 vi: 623–30.

Emery, W.B. 1938. *Excavations at Saqqara: The Tomb of Hemaka*. Cairo: Government Press.

Fackelmann, M. 1985. *Restaurierung von Papyrus und anderen Schriftträgern aus Ägypten*. Studia amstelodamensia ad epigraphicam, ius antiquum et papyrologicam pertinentia 23. Zutphen: Terra.

Foskett, S. 1994. An investigation into the properties of isinglass. *Scottish Society for Conservation and Restoration (Edinburgh) Journal*, 5/iv: 11–14.

Gardiner, A.H. 1955. *The Ramesseum Papyri*. Oxford: Griffith Institute.

Germer, R. 1985. *Flora des pharaonischen Ägypten*. DAIK, Sonderschrift 14. Mainz am Rhein: von Zabern.

Gettens, R.J. and Stout, G.L. 1966. *Painting Materials, a Short Encyclopaedia*. New York: Dover Publications.

Gilberg, M. 1988. Antonio Piaggio and the conservation of the Herculaneum Papyri. In *Early Advances in Conservation* (Occasional Paper 65). London: BMP, pp. 1–6.

Goedicke, H. 1984. *Studies in the Hekanakhte Papers*. Baltimore MD: Halgo.

Greathouse, G.A. and Wessel, C.J. 1954. *Deterioration of Materials*. New York: Reinholt.

Green, L.R. 1992. Analysis of pigments from the Papyrus of Anhay, EA 10472 and yellow used for hieroglyphs on papyrus EA 9968. British Museum, London, Conservation Research Section, Internal Report No. 1992/10.

1993. Analysis of mounting medium of fragments of papyrus, EA 10770/5. British Museum, London, Conservation Research Section, Internal Report no. CA 1993/4.

1995. Recent analysis of pigments from Egyptian artefacts. In *Conservation in Ancient Egyptian Collections: Papers given at the Conference of the United Kingdom Institute for Conservation, Archaeology Section, and International Academic Projects, London, 20–21 July 1995*; eds. C.E. Brown, F. Macalister, and M.M. Wright. London: Archetype Publications, pp. 85–91.

Green, L. and Leach, B. 1993. Investigation of consolidants and facing adhesives for pigments on papyrus. British Museum Conservation Section, Internal Report, 1993/21.

Griffith, F.L. 1898. *Hieratic Papyri from Kahun and Gurob, Principally of the Middle Kingdom* (The Petrie Papyri). London: Quaritch.

Griffith, F.L. and Petrie, W.M.F. 1889. *Two Hieroglyphic Papyri from Tanis* (The EEF, Extra Memoir). London: Trübner and Co.

Griffith, F.L. and Thompson, H. 1904. *The Demotic Magical Papyrus of London and Leiden*. London: Grevel (also issued Oxford: Clarendon Press, 1921).

Harley, R.D. 1970. *Artists' Pigments c. 1600–1835*. London: Butterworths.

Hendriks, I.H.M. 1980. Pliny, *Historia Naturalis* XIII, 74–82 and the manufacture of papyrus. *ZPE*, 37: 121–36.

1984. More about the manufacture of papyrus. In *Atti del XVII Congresso Internazionale di Papirologia*. Napoli: Centro Internazionale per lo Studio dei Papiri Ercolanesi, vol. 1, pp. 31–7.

Hepper, F.N. and Reynolds, T. 1967. Papyrus and the adhesive properties in its cell sap in relation to paper making. *JEA*, 53: 156–7.

Hoffmann, F. 1994. Die Länge des P.Spiegelberg. In *Egitto e Vicino Oriente 17: Acta Demotica: Acts of the Fifth International Conference for Demotists, Pisa, 4th–8th September 1993* (ed. E. Bresciani), Pisa: Giardini, pp. 145–55.

Holwerda, D. 1982. Plinius über die Anfertigung von 'Charta'. *ZPE*, 45: 257–62.

James, T.G.H., 1962. *The Hekanakhte Papers and Other Early Middle Kingdom Documents* (Publications of the Metropolitan Museum of Art Egyptian Expedition 19). New York, MMA.

Koenen, L. 1996. The carbonized archive from Petra. *Journal of Roman Archaeology*, 9: 177–88.

Koestler, R. and Matthews, T. 1994. Application of anoxic treatment for insect control in manuscripts of the Library of Megisti Laura, Mount Athos, Greece. In *Environment et conservation de l'écrit, de l'image, et du son: Proceedings of the ARSAG Conference, Paris, 16–20 May 1994*. Paris: Association pour la Recherche Scientifique sur les Arts Graphiques, pp. 59–62.

Koob, S.P. 1982. The instability of cellulose nitrate adhesives. *The Conservator*, 6: 31–4.

Kowalik, R. and Sadurska, I. 1973. Microflora of papyrus from samples of Cairo Museums. *Studies in Conservation*, 18: 1–24.

Leach, B. 1975. Papyrus. Unpublished student thesis, Camberwell School of Art, London.

1995. Papyrus conservation at the British Museum. In *Il rotolo librario: fabbricazione, restauro, organizzazione interna* (ed. M. Capasso) (Papyrologica lupiensia 3). Lecce: Università degli Studi di Lecce, Dipartimento di Filologia Classica e Mediaevale, Centro di Studi Papirologici, pp. 137–61.

Leach, B. and Green, L. 1995. Removal of unsuitable linings from illustrated papyri: an investigation into suitable consolidants and facings. In *Conservation in Ancient Egyptian Collections: Papers given at the Conference of the United Kingdom Institute for Conservation, Archaeology Section, and International Academic Projects, London, 20–21 July 1995* (eds. C.E. Brown, F. Macalister and M.M. Wright). London: Archetype Publications, pp. 29–35.

Levring, C.T.C., Hoppe, H.A., and Schmid, O.J. 1969. *Marine Algae: A Survey of Research and Utilisation*. Hamburg: Cram DeGruyter.

Lewis, N. 1974. *Papyrus in Classical Antiquity*. Oxford: Clarendon Press.

1981. Open letter to I.H.M. Hendriks. *ZPE*, 42: 293–4.

1989. *Papyrus in Classical Antiquity: a Supplement*. Papyrologica bruxellensia 23. Bruxelles: Fondation Egyptologique Reine Elisabeth.

Linnaeus, C. 1753. *Species plantarum* , 2 vols. Holmiae: Impensis Larentii Salvii.

Lucas, A. 1902. *A Preliminary Investigation of the Soil and Water of the Fayum Province*. Cairo: Public Works Ministry, Survey Department.

1908. *The Chemistry of the River Nile* (Survey Department Paper 7). Cairo: Ministry of Finance.

1932. *Antiquities: their Restoration and Preservation*. London: Edward Arnold.

1962. *Ancient Egyptian Materials and Industries*. 4th edn., rev. J.R. Harris. London: Edward Arnold.

Manniche, L. 1989. *An Ancient Egyptian Herbal*. London: BMP.

Mayhoff, C. (ed.) 1909. *C. Plini Secundi Naturalis historiae libri xxxvii* . . . II. Leipzig: Teubner (repr. Stuttgart, 1967).

Menci, G. 1988. Fabbricazione, uso e restauro antico del papiro: tre note in margine a Plinio, NH XIII 74–82. In *Proceedings of the XVIII International Congress of Papyrology, Athens, 25–31 May 1986*. Athens: Greek Papyrological Society, vol. 2, pp. 497–504.

Ménei, E. 1990. Le Papyrus: conservation, restauration, 2 vols. Unpublished thesis for the Diploma of the Institut Français de Restauration des Oeuvres d'Art, Paris (vol. 2 entitled: 4 Dossiers de restauration).

1993. Remarques sur la fabrication des rouleux de papyrus: precisions sur la formation et l'assemblage des feuillets. *RdE*, 44: 185–8.

1995. Les papyrus carbonisés de Tanis: première étude en vue de la mise au point de méthodes de conservation. *Bulletin de la Société française des Fouilles de Tanis*, 9: 39–50.

Metcalfe, C.R. (ed.) 1971. *Anatomy of the Monocotyledons, V: Cyperacae*. Oxford: Clarendon Press.

Nielsen. I. 1985. Papyrus structure, manufacture and deterioration. Doctoral dissertation. School of Conservation, Copenhagen.

Owen, A. and Danzing, R. 1993. The history and treatment of the papyrus collection at the Brooklyn Museum. *Journal of the American Institute of Conservation, Book and Paper Group*, 1993: 36–43.

Parkinson, R. and Quirke, S. 1995. *Papyrus* (Egyptian Bookshelf series). London: BMP.

Pattie, T.S. and Turner, E.G. 1974. *The Written Word on Papyrus: [Catalogue of] an Exhibition held in the British Museum, 30 July–27 October 1974*. London: BMP.

Petrie, W.M.F. 1885. *Tanis, Part I, 1883–4*. London: EEF.

1904. *Methods and Aims in Archaeology*. London: MacMillan.

Plenderleith, H.J. and Werner, A.E.A. 1971. *The Conservation of Antiquities and Works of Art*, 2nd edn. London: OUP.

Pliny (the elder): see Mayhoff, C. 1909 and Rackham, H. 1968.

Quibell, J.E. 1898. *The Ramesseum*. London: Egyptian Research Account.

Quirke, S.G.J. 1993. *Owners of Funerary Papyri in the British Museum* (Occasional Paper 92). London: BMP.

1995. An early conservation register of work undertaken on Egyptian papyri for the British Museum 1838–1842. In *Il rotolo librario: fabbricazione, restauro, organizzazione interna* (ed. M. Capasso). Lecce: Università degli Studi di Lecce, Dipartimento di Filologia Classica e Mediaevale, Centro di Studi Papirologici, pp. 163–86.

Rackham, H. (transl. and ed.) 1968. *Pliny (the Elder): Natural History*. IV 2nd edn. Loeb Classical Library. Cambridge MA: Harvard University Press.

Ragab, H. 1980a. A new theory brought forward about the adhesion of papyrus strips. *Institute of Paper Historians: Yearbook*, 1980: 113–24.

1980b. *Le Papyrus*. Cairo: Dr Ragab Papyrus Institute.

1988. The quality of recently manufactured papyrus. In *Proceedings of the XVIII International Congress of Papyrology, Athens, 25–31 May 1986*. Athens: Greek Papyrological Society, vol. 2, pp. 513–23.

Rathgen, F. 1905. *The Preservation of Antiquities*. Cambridge: CUP.

Raven, M.J. 1982. *Papyrus, van bies tot boekrol, met een bloemlezing uit de Leidse papyrusverzameling*. Zutphen: Terra.

Rea, J.R. 1984. *The Oxyrhynchus Papyri* LI. Graeco-Roman Memoirs 71. London: EES.

Reed, R. 1972. *Ancient Skins, Parchments, and Leathers*. London and New York: Seminar Press.

Robins, G. and Shute, C. 1987. *The Rhind Mathematical Papyrus: An Ancient Egyptian Text*. London: BMP.

Robinson, J.M. 1984. Introduction. In *The Facsimile Edition of the Nag Hammadi Codices, Introduction*. Leiden: Brill, pp. 1–102.

Roland, J.C. and Mosiniak, M. 1987. Sur l'ultrastructure et la cytochimie des parois cellulaires du papyrus en relation avec la malléabilité, la resistance et l'autoadhésivité des interfaces dans le support d'écriture. *Institute of Paper Historians: Information*, 1987: 133–8.

Rupprecht, H.A. 1994. *Kleine Einführung in die Papyruskunde*. Darmstadt: Wissenschaftliche Buchgesellschaft.

Seider, D. 1976. Pliny on the manufacture of paste for papyrus. *ZPE*, 22: 74.

Shorter, A.W. 1933. Manuscript note entitled: 9912, treatment of in laboratory, to improve legibility. Archives of the Dept. of Scientific Research, BM, London.

Skeat, T.C. 1982. The length of the standard papyrus roll and the cost-advantage of the codex. *ZPE*, 45: 169–75.

Spiegelberg, W. 1917. *Der ägyptische Mythus vom Sonnenauge (der Papyrus der Tierfabeln Ä 'Kufi'), nach dem Leidener Demotischen Papyrus I 384*. Strassburg: Schultz.

Sturman, S. 1987. Investigations into the manufacture and identification of papyrus. In *Recent Advances in the Conservation and Analysis of Artefacts: University of London, Institute of Archaeology Jubilee Conference, 1987*. London: Summer Schools Press, pp. 265–7.

Täckholm, V. and Drar, M. 1950. *Flora of Egypt* II. Bulletin of the Faculty of Science 28. Cairo: Fouad I University Press.

Tait, W.J. 1975. The physical characteristics of the [Saqqara Demotic] papyri. In *Proceedings of the XIV International Congress of Papyrologists, Oxford, 24–31 July 1974* (eds. P.J. Parsons, J.R. Rea, E.G. Turner and R.A. Coles). London: EES, pp. 262–4.

1977. *Papyri from Tebtunis in Egyptian and in Greek*. Texts from Excavations 3. London: EES.

1986. Guidelines and borders in Demotic papyri. In *Papyrus: Structure and Usage* (ed. M.L. Bierbrier). London: BMP, pp. 63–89.

1988. Rush and reed: the pens of Egyptian and Greek scribes. In *Proceedings of the XVIII International Congress of Papyrology, Athens, 25–31 May 1986* (ed. B.G. Mandilaras). Athens: Greek Papyrological Society, vol. 2, pp. 477–81.

1991a. P. Carlsberg 207: Two columns of a Setna-text. In *Demotic Texts from the Collection* (ed. P.J. Frandsen). CNI Publications 15; Carlsberg Papyri 1; Copenhagen: Museum Tusculanum Press, pp. 19–46.

1991b. P. Carlsberg 230: eleven fragments from a demotic herbal. In *Demotic Texts from the Collection* (ed. P.J. Frandsen). CNI Publications 15; Carlsberg Papyri 1; Copenhagen: Museum Tusculanum Press, pp. 47–92.

Thatcher, R.W. 1921. *The Chemistry of Plant Life*. New York: McGraw-Hill.

Thickett, D. 1992. Analysis of adhesive from Papyrus EA 10754/C. British Museum, London, Conservation Research Section, Internal Report No. CA 1992/54.

Thomson, G. 1986. *The Museum Environment*. 2nd edn. London: Butterworths, in association with the International Institute for Conservation of Historic and Artistic Works (also repr. (paperback edn.) Butterworth-Heinemann, 1994).

Turner, E.G. 1968. *Greek Papyri: an Introduction*. Oxford: Clarendon Press.

1978. The terms recto and verso: the anatomy of the papyrus roll. In *Actes du XVe Congrès International de Papyrologie* I. Papyrologica Bruxellensia 16. Brussels: Fondation Egyptologique Reine Elisabeth.

1980. An open letter to Dr I. Hendriks. *ZPE*, 39: 113–4.

Walker, A. 1988. The use of a facing technique in the treatment of fragile papyri. In *Conservation of Ancient Egyptian Materials: Preprints* (eds. S.C. Watkins and C.E. Brown). Bristol: UKIC Archaeology Section, pp. 51–3.

Wallert, A. 1989. The reconstruction of papyrus manufacture: a preliminary investigation. *Studies in Conservation*, 34: 1–8.

Watrous, J. 1967. *The Craft of Old-Master Drawings*. Wisconsin: University of Wisconsin Press.

Weber, M. 1969. Beiträge zur Kenntnis des Schrift- und Buchwesens der alten Ägypten. Inaugural-Dissertation zur Erlangung des Doktorgrades der Philsophischen Fakultät der Universität zu Köln.

Weidemann, H.G. and Bayer, G. 1983. Papyrus, the paper of ancient Egypt. *Analytical Chemistry*, 55 (12): 1220A–1230A.

Wendelbo, Ø. 1975. The freeing of papyri from cartonnage. *Restaurator, International Journal for the Preservation of Library and Archival Material*, 2: 41–52.

Wild, H. 1953. *Le tombeau de Ti, II: La chapelle (première partie)*. Cairo: IFAO.

Winter, J. 1984. Natural adhesives in East Asian paintings. In *Adhesives and Consolidants, IIC, Preprints of the Contributions to the Paris Congress, 2–8 September 1984* (eds. N.S. Bromelle, E.M. Pye, P. Smith and G. Thomson). London: International Institute for Conservation of Historic and Artistic works, pp. 117–20.

Woenig, F. 1886. *Die Pflanzen im Alten Aegypten*. Leipzig: Friedrich.

Wright, M. 1980. The extraction of papyri from cartonnage. Thesis. Institute of Archaeology, University College London.

10. Basketry

WILLEMINA Z. WENDRICH

Introduction

Making baskets has a long tradition throughout the world. In Egypt the traditional technology shows clear parallels with the ancient basketry. Watching a twentieth-century basket-maker helps us to realise that artefacts and assemblages were produced and used by actual people. On the other hand, present-day basketry is not an exact copy of ancient Egyptian basketry. Through the ages basketry techniques have shown a clear development and a definite local variety. A detailed description of techniques employed in making baskets and mats is vital for understanding these developments.

In this chapter the section on materials, tools and techniques gives a general introduction to the materials and technology. Some attention is then given, in the section on representations and imitations, to skeuomorphs of baskets in other materials and the way in which baskets and mats are depicted in tomb paintings. A deeper insight will be given in classification criteria of techniques in the section dealing with classification and terminology and the relations between technique, material, shape and function will be surveyed in the section on function. Some remarks are made on the producers and users of basketry. With the subsequent discard and preservation of basketry objects, the cycle is complete. First of all, however, it is necessary to give a definition of basketry.

Many authors have tried to define what basketry is, only to find that they stumble upon discrepancies between a consistent definition and that which 'common sense' tells them to be basketry (Mason 1904: 193; Lehman 1907: 2; Vogt 1937: 2; Lucas 1962: 128; Leroi-Gourhan 1971: 268, 272; Balfet 1952: 260; Crowfoot 1954: 414; Emery 1980: 210; Forbes 1964: 178; Seiler-Baldinger 1979: 4; Adovasio 1977: 1; Larsen and Freudheim 1986: 38). Basketry and matting are often described as 'textile techniques', but while a cloth and a basket are clearly distinguishable, there is a grey area of objects which can be arbitrarily considered to be made in a textile or a basketry technique. Examples of criteria used in the discussion are the use of tools (looms in various degrees of complexity), the type of raw materials, the shape or the function of the objects. A more extensive discussion of definition, classification and other aspects occurring in this chapter can be found in *The World According to Basketry* (Wendrich, forthcoming).

In this chapter basketry (which includes baskets, bags and mats; sieves, pot stands and nets; brushes and brooms; boxes and coffins; furniture and sandals) is defined as: 'objects made of plant parts of limited length often with a shape specific to that particular plant part'. In other words: what makes basketry techniques fundamentally different from textile techniques is the fact that the basket-maker has to make amends for the often irregular shape of the raw materials and the short strands he or she is working with. Textiles, on the other hand, are made of long yarns, which in theory are uniform in size along the entire length. Mats woven or twined out of string are thus defined as textiles, but nevertheless they will be considered in this chapter. Making a distinction between 'textile' and 'basketry' techniques helps to consider the criteria important for capturing the 'basketness' of objects. Once aware of these criteria, we no longer have to maintain a strict separation. Since string mats are generally considered more 'basket' than 'textile' (here the arbitrariness, not of the definition, but of common sense, becomes clear) they have been included in this chapter.

Basketry materials, techniques, and tools

The term *technology* refers to the knowledge and craftmenship of making basketry, while *basketry technique* is used in a more limited sense to indicate the different interactions of strands making up baskets, mats, bags, nets, brooms or sandals.

Materials

The number of materials from which baskets and mats are made is quite limited, but not quite as limited as the designation 'reed' (which tends to be applied to baskets in publications), might suggest. Very few excavators have made the effort to identify the materials used, but nevertheless have not refrained from publishing ill-founded specifications. In many cases it is impossible to discern the different species macroscopically and a microscopic study of the cross-section or the epiderm patterns to identify plant parts, and the shape and size to identify fibres, is necessary. The work of Greiss (1957) resulted in the most important publications on the subject of plant materials used for basketry. The specification, not only of the plant species, but also of the plant part is of great importance. Thus the term 'palm fibre' which is frequently encountered in the literature, might refer to date-palm leaf, leaf-sheath fibre of the date palm, shredded fruit stem of the date palm, or to dom-palm leaf.

Palm leaf and grass are by far the most important materials for making baskets and mats. The leaves of two palm species are used: the side-leaflets of the large feather-shaped leaves of the date palm (*Phoenix dactylifera*), and strips of the fan-shaped leaves of the dom palm (*Hyphaene thebaica*). A third indigenous palm species, *Medemia argun*, seems not to have been used for basket-making, note also that for Latin names Germer (1985) is followed; alternative names and the extension indicating the botanist who named the plant can also be found in Germer. The long rigid midribs of the date-palm leaves are used for making roofs, doors and screens. At present there is an entire industry making the so-called *gereed* into crates, cages and furniture, but this does not occur until the late Roman period. Similarly, the fibrous leaf-sheaths of the date palm, the most important material for rope-making at present, were not used widely until the Greco-Roman period. In the Predynastic and Pharaonic periods, grass was used instead, being employed widely, not only for making rope, but also for the bundles and strands in twined matting and the bundles in coiled basketry. These tall tough grasses are often referred to as *halfa*, an Arabic term used for both the species *Desmostachya bipinnata* and *Imperata cylindrica*.

Among the less common materials used for making basketry are reeds, sedges and rushes. The culms of reeds are used for matting and making stools, tables and screens. Both the culms of ordinary reed *Phragmites communis* and a tall bamboo-like reed, *Arundo donax* have been identified (Greiss 1957: 148–9), but the former occurs much more often than the latter. *Arundo donax* is nowadays used for making shopping baskets which are light yellow and have a glossy appearance. These baskets, made of the split culms in a stake-and-strand technique, are a relatively recent development. Not only the culms of *Phragmites communis*, the common reed, are used, but also the leaves, identified by Greiss in a matting fragment from el-Omari (Greiss 1957: 107). The leaves of a third type of reed, *Saccharum spontaneum* are used also for making soft mats (*cf.* Greiss 1957: 149, who uses the indication *Saccharum biflorum*) this reed should not be confused with sugar cane, which has been introduced and cultivated in Egypt in modern times.

There is a wide variety of sedges used for making basketry and matting, the best-known being *Cyperus papyrus*, of which the thick triangular culm or just strips of the epiderm are employed in making baskets, boxes, coffins, simple furniture and sandals. Other species, mostly identified in matting, are: *Cyperus alopecuroides*, *C. articulatus*, *C. conglomeratus* and *C. schimperianus*. Sedges have long, leafless stems which are quite spongy inside, thus making them eminently suitable for making mats.

Rushes are less flexible than sedges and were used from the Predynastic period through to the present for making floor mats. The split culms are also used in coiled basketry. In the Roman period a whole new set of techniques were being executed mainly with rushes. The species occurring in Egypt are *Juncus rigidus* and *J. acutus*.

The shrub-like plant *Ceruana pratensis* was used mainly in the Early Dynastic period for making basketry coffins and brushes. Other materials, used especially in the production of mats, furniture webbing and nets, are yarn made of flax (*Linum usitatissimum*) or, from the Greco-Roman period onwards, cotton (*Gossypium species*). For a list of identified applications of each plant species as known at the time of publication see Täckholm *et al.* (1941–69).

The preparation of the raw materials varies from hardly any (*Ceruana pratensis*, leaf-sheath fibres of the date palm, rushes, sedges and grasses), minimal (palm leaf which is cut into strips, soaked and sometimes boiled with dyes) to extensive (flax and cotton).

Techniques

Surveying basket-making in the different periods of Egyptian history involves discerning different techniques, based on basketry found in museum collections, in the literature, and items recorded on site, at excavations of widely varying date. Artefacts in museum collections are often badly provenanced. It is hazardous to draw conclusions from descriptions of the techniques and materials in the literature, because the terminology used is often inconsistent and the identification of the raw materials inaccurate. The terms *plaiting* or *weaving*, for instance, are often used as synonyms for basket-making and may refer to a number of different techniques which bear no relation to plaiting or weaving in the technical sense of the word, e.g. 'straw plaiting' for what seems to be a twined grass mat, 'a small plaited basket' describing twined bags made of grass string, 'woven grass platters or lids' which are in fact made in the coiling technique (respectively: Petrie *et al.* 1913: 13; Bonioanni 1987: 112 and Caton-Thompson and Gardner 1934, caption with pl. xxviii). Other indications such as 'an oval basket of the usual kind' (Peet and Woolley 1923: 74) are not misleading, but just uninformative, although the photographs were clear enough to reveal that the baskets usually found in the Amarna Workmen's Village were coiled baskets. Other authors are much more trustworthy. Carter, for instance, gives quite good, although not very detailed, descriptions of the baskets in the tomb of Tutankhamun (cited by Reeves 1990: 204).

There are nine major basketry techniques in Egypt: coiling, weaving, twining, continuous plaiting, sewn plaits, looping around a core, looping, piercing and binding (see Fig.10.1). Knotted string is often used in making baskets, mats or brooms (for details on rope and knotting see Wendrich 1996). More will be said under **terminology** about the distinction between the different techniques, the classifications and the terminology used, but for the moment a concise description suffices.

Coiling is a technique in which a bundle of material is fixed in a coil, by wrapping the bundle with a strand which holds the bundle in place (Fig. 10.1a). The same technique is used for sandals, but then the term 'coiling' is, strictly speaking, not appropriate. Sandals were not made by laying out one bundle in a coil, but rather by fastening a number of parallel bundles with a wrapping strand.

Weaving is a technique in which a number of strands, usually fixed in a loom, are made into a fabric by interlacing them with crossing strands (Fig. 10.1b).

Twining is a technique in which a number of parallel bundles are held in place by fixing them with two strands which twist around the bundles and around each other (Fig. 10.1c).

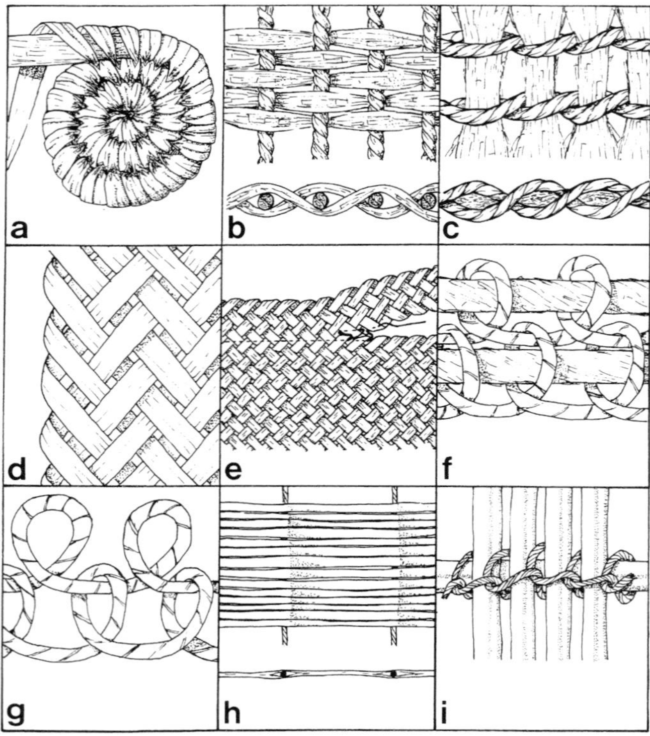

Figure 10.1 Basketry techniques occurring in Egypt: (a) coiling, (b) weaving, (c) twining, (d) plaiting, (e) sewn plaits, (f) looping around a core (g) looping/knotless netting, (h) piercing/sewing, (i) binding.

Plaiting is a technique in which a number of strands, which have not been fixed, are made into a fabric by interlacing them with crossing strands. Usually the strands make a sharp turn at the edge of the fabric and are folded back into the fabric (Fig. 10.1d).

Sewn-plaits technique involves two stages: first long strips are plaited, which are then sewn into a seemingly ongoing fabric (Fig. 10.1e). For rectangular mats a number of strips are fastened parallel to each other, baskets are sewn from one spiralling strip.

Looping (Fig. 10.1g) is a knotless netting technique by linking a row of loops to the previous row. Mats or baskets are made by linking the loops around bundles of grass, which is referred to as looping around a core (Fig. 10.1f).

Piercing involves rigid stems which are connected by yarns or sticks pushed through pierced holes. A similar technique, in which a row of parallel stems or strings are connected, is a form of piercing with needle and thread and therefore perhaps better indicated as 'sewing' (Fig. 10.1h).

Binding involves a number of strands or sticks which are layed out either crosswise or in a coil and fastened with a separate strand (Fig. 10.1i).

Within all these techniques a large number of varieties occur in the pattern or in the spacing. This variation is determined, for instance, by the materials used, by the function of the object, or by local traditions.

Although the continuity in basketry techniques is striking, there are also changes and differences in regional traditions. Although basketry is known from very early periods – and despite the fact that the preservation of organic materials in Egypt, and especially in the desert sites, is unsurpassed – there are no finds pre-dating the Neolithic period. The earliest baskets found are by no means new 'inventions' of mankind. The fine craftmanship shows that the knowledge of basket-making is much older and it is tantalising that we do not know anything about Palaeolithic basketry.

Finds show that by the Neolithic most of the techniques which came to be used throughout the Pharaonic period were already fully developed. In the Fayum A culture (5500 BC) coiling was the most important technique for making containers. Coarse-coiled grain silos (the bundles of grass fastened with winders which, most probably, consisted of palm leaf) were buried in the ground (Caton Thompson and Gardner 1934: pl. xxvii). The winders were lost in most cases, which led Caton Thompson originally to the conclusion that the grain-silos were pits 'lined with coiled wheat straw' (Caton-Thompson 1926: 314). Finely made coiled containers occurred in the settlement (Fig. 10.2). Badarian basketry of roughly the same period, but in the region of Upper Egypt also consisted entirely of coiled containers. The matting was woven, twined and perhaps bound (Brunton and Caton-Thompson 1928: pls. lx, lxi).

The Naqada I period shows a continuity of the basketry techniques. At Merimda (5000–4500 BC) no household

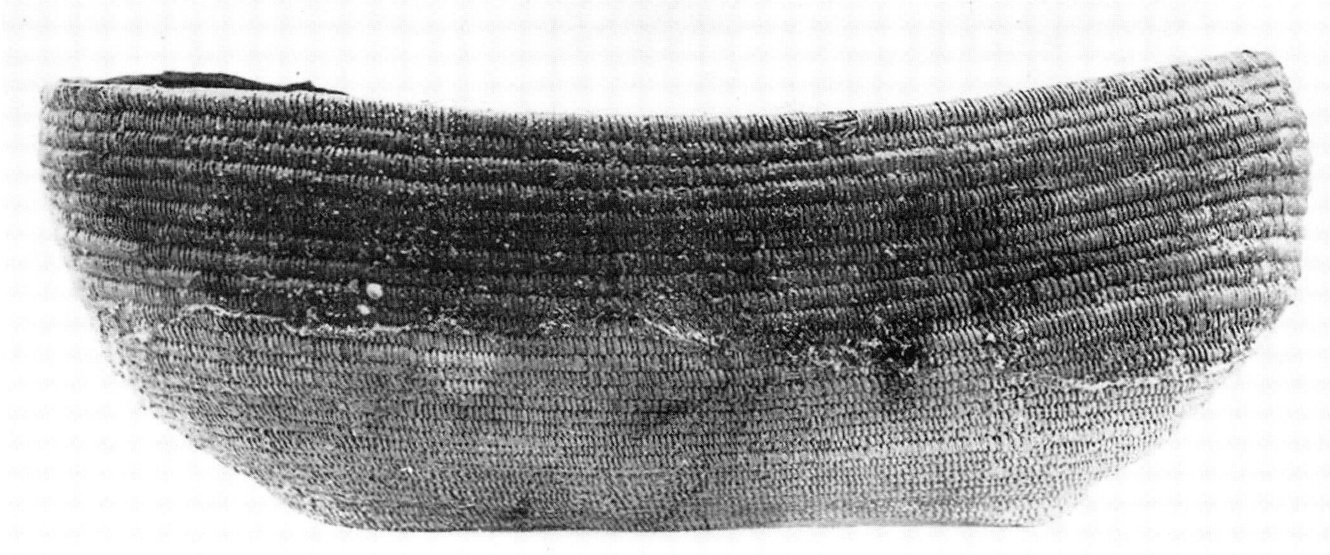

Figure 10.2 Neolithic coiled basket from the Fayum.

basketry was found, but the basketry and matting techniques incorporated in the architecture show the same techniques as the earlier periods. The descriptions and photographs published in Junker's (1929) preliminary reports leave some doubt as to the exact technique and materials, but the large grain silos, buried in the ground were probably made in the coiled technique. The identification of the bundle material as *Arundo donax*, a stiff bamboo-like reed, is puzzling, however, because this species cannot be bent into coils as small as those visible in the photographs (Junker 1929: pl. Vb). Greiss apparently doubted this identification too, because he states that confirmation of the identifiation is required (Greiss 1957: 148–9). Although the text seems to refer to the culms, it is possible that only the leaves of this large reed species were used for making silos. It seems likely that the silos were covered with coiled lids (Junker 1930: 44, pl. IIIa). Housing seems to have been made largely of oval pits built up with matting screens, of which Junker found remains in 1932 (Junker 1932: 52, 53, pl. IIIb). For this type of screen, made in a binding technique, both palm fronds and reeds are eminently suitable. The culms are laid out parallel, or put vertically in the soft mud-plaster and are made into a coherent wall by tying them to two or more levels of horizontal culms, thus forming cross connections in the middle and at the top of the vertical, closely spaced culms (Fig. 10.1i).

Many basketry finds in museum collections, which are supposedly from the Predynastic period, show extremely fine workmanship that is unsurpassed in any later period. A very fine matting fragment, allegedly from the Predynastic period and presently on display in the Egyptian Museum in Cairo (provenance and date are unknown, no registry number is visible, but the fragment is on display in the Predynastic section, room R/U 53, together with the twined fragment JE54546), is made in the pierced technique: culms of rushes have been pierced and a flax yarn has been pulled through the parallel stems (*cf.* Fig. 10.1h). From the same general period dates an extremely finely made twined matting fragment made of grass. The rows of twining, in S-direction, are widely spaced (five centimetres apart). Fragments of coiled basketry from Maadi show an equally fine workmanship (Rizkana and Seeher 1989: pl. VI,1).

Most basketry and matting remains from the Predynastic and Early Dynastic periods are, however, from funerary contexts. In many older publications mat-burials are listed, unfortunately seldom specifying the materials and techniques used (e.g. Petrie and Quibell 1896: 15, 23, 25, 27). In many cases culms of reeds or sedges seem to have been used, which are connected with supple strands by either binding or twining (e.g. Emery 1958: pl. 121b and 122a, Greiss 1957: 107).

The walls of a funerary chapel in the First-Dynasty tomb 3505 at Saqqara (Emery 1958: 10, pl. 26), were not made of reeds, but of much more flexible grass matting, in which bundles of grass were made into a fabric by widely spaced rows of twining. Since S3505 was thought to be an élite tomb, the occurrence of simple twined grass matting as wall cover for the chapel is surprising.

Via the sequence dates of Petrie a number of basketry techniques, also from a funerary context at Tarkhan, occurring in the Early Dynastic period, can be quite closely dated (Petrie *et al.*, 1913: 6, 23–4). Apart from the twined and bound reed mats, two techniques are commonly found among the burials at Tarkhan, which did not occur in the Fayum, Badari and Merimda: bound coffins and woven bed matting. From grave 1004 came a 'basket burial'. It was

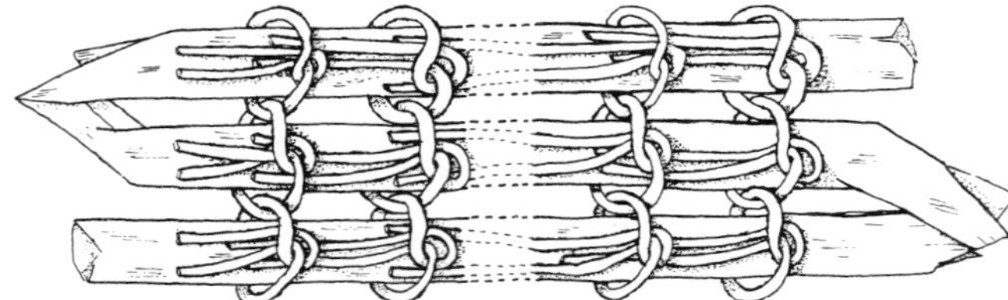

Figure 10.3 Construction drawing of the binding technique of the basketry coffin found at Tarkhan (displayed in room R/U 11 of the Egyptian Museum, Cairo, unnumbered).

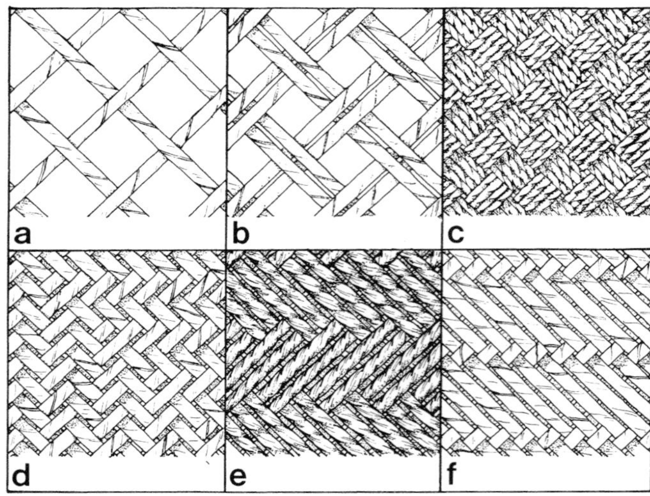

Figure 10.4 Weaving patterns occurring most frequently in ancient Egyptian furniture matting. Tabbies: (a) \1/1\\1 open, S-twisted dom-palm leaf; (b) \2/2\\2 open, S-twisted dom-palm leaf; (c) \4/4\\4 closed, Z-spun flax yarn. Twills: (d) \2/2\\1 closed, S-twisted dom-palm leaf, with pattern shift; (e) \6/6\\2 closed, zS2 grass string, with pattern shift; (f) \1/6\\1 closed, S-twisted dom-palm leaf, with pattern shift.

placed in a recess, bricked across the mouth. (. . .) The basket and body were carried intact to the Cairo Museum' (Petrie *et al.* 1913: 24, pl. xxvi). The oval basketry coffin was made in a binding technique in three parts: base, sides and lid (currently on display in room R/U 11 of the Egyptain Museum, unnumbered). The sides were made by coiling a bundle of papyrus stems (*Cyperus papyrus*) and tying the next row to the lower coil with an irregular, but flexible twig of *Ceruana pratensis*. Each twig was used to tie one half knot of which the ends were held in place by the next knotted twig (Fig. 10.3). The rectangular base and lid of the coffin were made by folding the papyrus bundle sharply at the edge of the rectangle and knotting each bundle to the previous one with the flexible twigs. A First-Dynasty basketry coffin from Helwan was made completely out of bundles of *Ceruana pratensis*, tied with twigs of the same material (Greiss 1957: 108). Coarse First-Dynasty basketry was made by linking loops of, probably, palm leaf around a coiled bundle of grass (Emery 1954: 66, pl. 32).

Wooden bed-frames were woven with matting in a wide variety of weaving patterns. In the First-Dynasty cemetery of Tarkhan, twenty-eight beds were found which were divided into eight different types on the basis of the bed matting and the connection between the matting and the bed (Engelbach in Petrie *et al.* 1913: 23–4). The bed matting was made of twisted rushes, palm leaf or thongs of leather. The weaving patterns of this early bed matting were as varied and intricate as those known from the New Kingdom or later. The photographs in the 1913 publication show two different patterns: a tabby with four parallel strands, made with S-twisted strands ('rushes' according to Engelbach's description but the appearance is more that of palm leaf) and, secondly, a twill pattern woven with two parallel sZ2 strings made of unknown material, probably grass or papyrus rind. The make-up of rope is given in a formula which indicates the direction of spin, ply and cable, as well as the number of strands involved; thus sZ2 string is made of two strands, plied in Z-direction, each of which has been spun in S-direction (see Chapter 11, this volume and Wendrich 1991: 30–2). Figure 10.4 shows a number of tabby- and twill-weaving patterns that occur most frequently in ancient Egypt. Tabbies are patterns in which the shift in the pattern is the same as the number of strands, twills have a shift which is smaller than the number of strands, which gives the pattern an oblique appearance. Both weaving and plaiting patterns can be indicated with a formula: \1/1\\1 is the pattern 'under 1 – over 1 with a shift of one' (a simple tabby). Examples of twill patterns are: \2/2\\1 'under 2 – over 2 with a shift of one', \6/6\\2 'under 6 – over 6 with a shift of two'. An asymmetrical twill pattern is for instance \1/6\\1 'under 1 – over 6 with a shift of one (see Fig. 10.4 and Wendrich 1991: 65–6). Also from a First-Dynasty grave was a mat, probably woven of grass culms and leaves. The excavators published a photograph of the old mat together with 'a modern Egyptian *hasyrah* mat, to show the exact similarity of the work, entirely unchanged in style during 7,000 years' (Petrie *et al.* 1913: 25). The only difference seems to be the material used: rushes rather than grass. Although the appearance of the mats is strikingly similar, a study of technical details, such as the selvedge and finishing off of the bundles could have given valuable information, since it is in such details that the exact production sequence can be inferred and local traditions may become apparent. The photographs and descriptions, unfortunately, do not register such details.

Old Kingdom basketry shows the same general range of techniques as the earlier material: all baskets are made in the coiled technique, mats are woven or twined, furniture matting is woven in the wooden frames of beds, chairs and stools. Twined bags made of string, many examples of which date to the New Kingdom, were also evidently very common during the Old Kingdom, judging from their frequent depiction in tomb paintings (see imitations

p. 263). No actual examples have been published, but just as the coiled baskets were present in large quantities inside every house, these twined bags were used outside and were the Old Kingdom equivalent of our plastic carrier bags. Like these bags, fish traps are depicted in Old Kingdom tomb paintings but these have not been found in any archaeological context.

The binding technique of the Early Dynastic coffins is not found in the Old Kingdom, and nor is the Predynastic pierced matting technique, which seems to be a unique find, not occurring in the Dynastic period or later. Although the sewn plaits technique does not occur until the Greco-Roman period, continous plaiting seems to have developed from weaving during the Old Kingdom, but this technique is not widespread until the Greco-Roman period either. The awnings of Khufu's funerary boat (from his pyramid complex at Giza) are plaited in a twill pattern (\3/3\\1), out of what seem to be four parallel rows of single culms of rushes. Large quantities of this matting were found in the boat pit, and have been stored in a nearby room. The fragment on display in the boat museum at Giza is bordered by two side edges and has a total width of 60 cm. The original length is not known, because the fragment has no top or bottom edges. It is not clear if the width of 60 cm was the standard, so that a number of strips of this width were fastened parallel to each other in order to cover the wooden palisade under which the rowers were seated.

Most surviving Egyptian basketry from archaeological contexts is of New Kingdom date, and especially the late Eighteenth Dynasty onwards, both from tombs and settlements. The coiled technique was used to make all of the household basketry found during excavations in the Workmen's Village at Amarna in 1921–2 and in 1985–6.

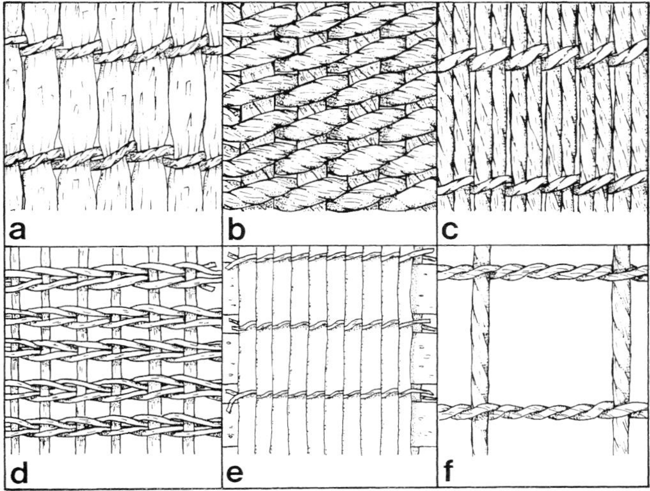

Figure 10.5 Examples of twined basketry: (a) openly twined matting of string around bundles of grass; (b) closely twined matting (made into bags); (c) openly twined seed bag; (d) openly twined sieve grid; (e) twined three-system basket; (f) openly twined carrier net

Peet and Woolley (1923: pl. XXI/4) published one photograph of a basket in sewn plaits technique. This basket was probably a later contamination, its date either contemporary with the late burials, or perhaps even with the excavations, because the workmen used the same type of basketry to move the sand. The fact that the basket seems to have been made of date-palm leaf, while all Eighteenth-Dynasty baskets found at Amarna were made of dom-palm leaf, or in rare cases papyrus, strengthens this suspicion. During the excavations directed by Barry Kemp in the 1980s no plaited basketry was found (*cf.* Wendrich 1989). The mats from Amarna were all made of grass, either woven or twined. These mats were used as floor mats, sleeping mats and awnings, while open twined mats were re-used as roofing material (Fig. 10.5a). Closely twined bags, made of dom palm leaf and grass string possibly served to transport heavy weights on donkey back (Fig. 10.5b), as is still widely done in Egypt at present. These days the closely twined bags are made of the leaf-sheath fibres of the date palm, however. The brushes made of grass or dom-palm leaf were well worn. In general there is a striking absence of date-palm leaf at the Amarna Workmen's Village. Fragments of twined seed bags were found as well as sieves (Figs 10.5c and 10.5d, *cf.* Peet and Woolley 1923: pls. XX/4, XXII/2; note that Fig 10.5d represents a different form of twined grid from that in the sieve depicted in Peet and Woolley 1923).

The basketry of Deir el-Medina has been published by Gourlay (1981); illustrated with clear drawings, a large number of different techniques are presented and classified. Gourlay was handicapped by the low standard of excavation and registration of Bruyère's excavations and has refrained from speculation on the date of the finds. The result is that basketry from the New Kingdom and the Ptolemaic period are presented together and, given the technical innovations in the Greco-Roman period, this limits the usefulness of the publication, as does the fact that no identification of the raw materials is given. Thus it is not known if twined baskets in a three-system technique (Fig. 10.5e) should be dated to the New Kingdom or much later. By far the largest group of baskets used in house-contexts at Deir el-Medina are coiled baskets in a wide range of sizes and shapes. Most frequent are round and oval baskets with conical lids.

There are also many surviving baskets from funerary contexts, for instance from the tombs of Queen Meritamun (DB358), Ramose and Hatnefer, Kha (TT8) and Tutankhamun (KV62). Three very large coiled baskets contained Queen Meritamun's wardrobe. The coiling has a regular appearance because the stitch just picks up the winder covering the previous row, rather than stitching into the previous bundle (*cf.* Fig. 10.6a and b). The baskets are round, about 500 millimetres in diameter and approximately the same in height. Two of them still have their slightly conical lids, which are resting on a supporting ridge formed by an extra coil sewn on the inside of the basket.

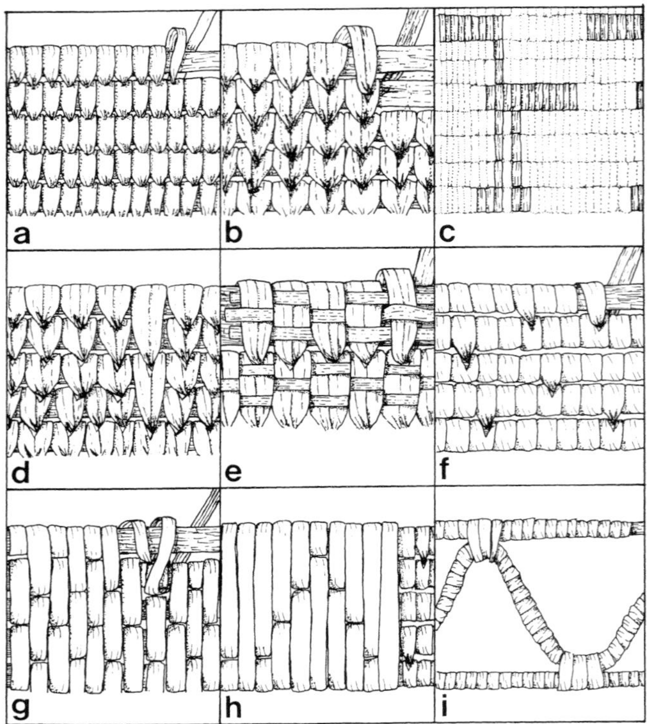

Figure 10.6 Examples of coiled basketry: (a) stitch through the previous winder (smooth appearance); (b) stitch through the previous winder and bundle (stronger than a); (c) coloured winders forming a pattern; (d) vertical rows of stitches over two bundles (for strengthening and decoration); (e) decoration with inlay of horizontal strips; (f) 'lazy basket-maker's stitch' (winding with widely spaced stitches); (g) coiling over alternately one and two bundles; (h) decorative stitches covering the 'lazy basket-maker's stitch'; (i) open coiling, used as decoration of rims and sides.

One basket has two more ridges on the inside, to help maintain the shape and possibly to hold two trays as internal divisions. The bundles, with a diameter of 1.5 cm are made of grass and in one case of the leaves of the ordinary reed. The winders, covering and holding in place the coiled bundles, consist of 1 cm-wide strips of dom-palm leaf. Some of the winding strips are coloured blue and red and thus add a touch of decoration (Cairo JE 55149 A, B and C, presently on display in room R/U 46, case 6186). In a similar fashion, but more lavishly decorated with a pattern of coloured winders which continues on the lid, is a large coiled basket from the early Eighteenth-Dynasty tomb of Ramose and Hatnefer. This basket, 38 centimetres high and about 45 centimetres in diameter, is on display in the Luxor Museum (Journal no. J.18, Cairo JE 66204, for photograph see Anonymous 1978: 80 no. 209 B). The matted furniture and the small basket shown in the same photograph are from Deir el-Medina. The use of coloured winders is sometimes also figurative: three long-necked animal figures, ostriches or giraffes, which stand out in brown winders on a light brown, natural dom-palm leaf coloured background (Fig. 10.6c; currently on display in the Egyptian Museum in Cairo in room R/U 46 in a case with finds from the MMA's excavations from 1929/30 at Deir el-Bahari). Another decorative effect is the regular use of larger stitches, over two bundles rather than one, often arranged in vertical lines over the entire body of the basket (Fig. 10.6d, e.g. Gourlay 1981: pl. XVIII D–F).

Finds from the tomb of Kha, excavated by Schiaparelli in 1906 and now mostly in the Turin Museum, illustrate well the variety of basketry items, the craftmanship of the basketmakers and the importance of this commodity in ancient society. The baskets containing household items, such as food and clothing, were round or oval coiled baskets of several sizes, sometimes decorated with ribs of larger stitches and closed with conical lids (Bonioanni 1987: 115). A large bag of knotless netting filled with dom-nuts was part of his supplies for the after life, as were three small, coiled baskets with condiments. A finely woven sleeping mat decorated with an intricate weaving pattern, chairs and stools with matted seats and a table made of date-palm midribs covered with papyrus culms were among the furniture in the tomb (Bonioanni 1987: 108, 144, 147).

The tomb of Tutankhamun contained 116 baskets, all of them coiled. They range from small containers in which all kinds of foods were stored (see section on function p. 265), to unusual specimens such as decorated bottle-shaped baskets and a round, coiled basket with separate strips interweaving the winders (Fig. 10.6e). In contrast with these finely made objects are the foundation deposits of the Kiosk of Thutmose III in the Asasif. Among these are a number of baskets, crudely made in what could be called the 'lazy basket-maker's stitch': quickly covering the bundle with a wrapping strand, which is stitched into the previous bundle at long intervals (Fig. 10.6f). These items were clearly not made to be used, because this rapid technique results in weak objects and, furthermore, the baskets show no wear marks at all (currently displayed in the Egyptian Museum in Cairo, room R/U 49, unnumbered).

It has been mentioned that in the Greco-Roman period there is a large shift in basketry techniques. Sewn plaits and stake-and-strand baskets were previously unknown, plaiting occurred rarely in Pharaonic Egypt. On the other hand, the traditional Egyptian techniques did not disappear; basketry from Karanis, Qasr Ibrim, Abu Sha'ar and Berenike (Wendrich 1995; Wendrich and Veldmeijer 1996) show a continuity within the long tradition which runs from the Neolithic until at least the New Kingdom. This is reflected in the occurrence of coiled basketry used inside the houses, woven grass mats for sleeping, bound matting for screens, woven bed matting, twined mats as awnings and closely twined bags for outside use. Innovations in coiling techniques are the use of stitches alternating over one and two bundles (10.6g) and the use of decorative wrapped patterns over a roughly coiled foundation made in the 'lazy basket-maker's stitch' (10.6h). The use of widely spaced decorative rims on coiled baskets (10.6i), also a variety of coiling, has not been attested until the third century AD (Qasr Ibrim). Apart from innovations of existing techniques, a number of new techniques were introduced which, by the first century AD had taken over a large part of the 'niche' of the traditional Pharaonic basketry. The most important of these was plaiting. Continuous plaiting, which occurred rarely in the earlier periods, is used widely in the Greco-Roman period, for making small decorative containers, fans and mats (e.g. Petrie 1927: pl. XLI, 162, 163). Coiled sandals were completely replaced by plaited sandals. The sewn-plaits technique, which did not occur at all before the Greco-Roman period, is from then on widely used for making floor mats and flexible baskets (e.g. Petrie 1927: pl. XLI, 167, 168). There are local differences, however. In Middle Egypt the sewn-plaits baskets replaced the twined bags, but the sewn-plaits matting did not replace the woven mats. In Nubia both the baskets and mats are nowadays made in the sewn-plaits technique, the origin of which is at present unknown. Judging from the many texts about Christian monks making this type of basketry (e.g. Wipszycka 1986: 117–44) its spread was fast and wide. Today it is still the most common type of basketry found in the streets of Cairo and rural Egypt alike.

A new type of decorative basket in the Greco-Roman period was the stake-and-strand type. The stake-and-strand baskets, which in ancient Rome were made of quite sturdy and rigid materials, such as willow rods, were in the Egyptian version quite refined because of the thin and relatively flexible rushes used (e.g. Petrie 1927: pl. XLI no. 161, XLII nos. 172–7). Another development of the late Roman period is the occurrence of pierced basketry made of the midribs of the date-palm leaves. This technology gradually replaced the pharaonic production line of furniture and crates made of bound reeds or palm midribs, lined with palm-leaf and flattened papyrus culms (e.g. Petrie 1927: pl. XLI nos. 170–1).

As a general conclusion it can be said that there is a clear continuity between neolithic, Predynastic and Pharaonic cultures, which is in contrast with the basketry revolution taking place in the Greco-Roman period.

Tools

The range of tools necessary to make basketry is limited. Coiled basketry is made with the help of a small needle or awl to make the holes in the bundle through which the wrapping leaf can be pushed. For twined basketry a simple frame is used, the form of which depends on the rigidity of the materials. If reeds are made into a mat, the frame is formed by the reeds themselves and only two fixed points, for instance two pegs in the ground, are needed to fasten the start of the mat. Twining with flexible materials requires a simple loom, consisting of four wooden pegs and two cross-bars holding the warp. The production of twined matting is depicted in tomb reliefs of the Old and Middle Kingdom (DB2; Fig. 10.8e). A slightly less simple loom was used for weaving floor mats with grass or rushes. Although the loom still consists of four pegs in the ground with two cross bars, the warp is run through a heavy beam with holes, which is used to beat the weft. A mat-weaver is depicted in the tomb of Khety in Beni Hasan (BH17; Fig. 10.7). The loom consists of four pegs in the ground to which cross bars have been fastened, holding the tension on the warp, which is running through a heavy beam in front of the mat-maker, who is sitting on top of the finished part of the mat. As Crowfoot (1933) points out, this is a problematic depiction, since the act of sitting on the finished mat would disturb the tension of the warp threads. She is also puzzled by the yellow and green strands in front of the weaver, wondering if an unknown technique of weaving from two sides was depicted. From the study of modern mat-makers it is clear that the weaver is sitting on the finished mat, but supports his weight, by something like a wooden plank on two bricks, running underneath the finished part of the mat in order not to influence the tension of the warp. To have his raw materials close at hand he puts them on the warp threads in front of him, just as is depicted in the tomb of Khety. The yellow and green blocks are the result of weaving with young (green) and slightly older (yellow) rushes in a block pattern. A tool which might be used in weaving mats is a hook with which the rushes are pulled in order to tighten the weft to a greater extent. Weaving on an existing frame (a wooden bed or chair), involves even less tools. The warp is mounted around or through holes in the wooden frame. The weft is beaten with a stick and perhaps some tapering wooden pegs are used for different tasks: as an awl to open up the edges, or to make space for the weaving string in the last phase of the process, when the frame is almost filled.

Figure 10.7 Mat-maker from the tomb of Khety in Beni Hasan (BH17).

For binding and plaiting no tools are necessary, other than a pot with water to soak the palm leaf. For the sewn-plaits technique a large needle is used. A 10 cm-long flat model is known in modern Nubia, and a 30 cm-long round model is attested in modern Middle Egypt. The identification of production areas and tools in excavations is often difficult. Thus a large needle found in a Badarian tomb was suggested to be indicative for mat-making (Brunton and Caton-Thompson 1928: 32). Such large needles are nowadays indeed used for making sewn-plaits mats, but since this technique does not occur until the Greco-Roman period, the large needle found at Badari must have had another function. On the other hand, the awls and needles found, which were thought to have been used for leather working, might have been used for making coiled basketry and pierced matting (Fig. 10.1h).

Representations and imitations

Baskets, chair matting and floor mats are depicted in many tomb paintings, with baskets commonly appearing in the lines of offering bearers and scenes of daily life. The depictions, however, are not always clear, due to the sometimes-stylized ways in which scenes are represented, but it is possible to give a number of indications. Apart from the representations of basketry, there are a number of imitations and decorative patterns derived from basketry.

Representations

In reliefs or painted scenes coiled basketry is represented mostly as half-round or straight-lined forms with horizontal stripes indicating the coiled bundle (Fig. 10.8a), or with horizontal stripes and cross lines indicating the bundle and the winding stitches (Fig. 10.8b). Often the coiled baskets are chequered, with colourful decorations, either representing coloured winders, or as an artistic means of bringing more colour to the walls (Fig. 10.8c). In statues, coiled basketry occurs as round, horizontally ribbed shapes. Statues of beer-brewers, for instance, have a coiled jar stand and a sieve with coiled sides. The grid in the sieves is twined, which is indicated often by a simple cross hatch. Twined bags are depicted most often in relation to agricultural scenes. Sowing is done from the same twined bags in which the harvested wheat and barley is brought in. The writers recording the harvest seem to note the number of bags coming in, which suggests that the twined bags were a measure of contents as well. They are often depicted as a tapering rectangle with cross-hatched lines and two loops at the top, but sometimes the slanting twining pattern is clearly indicated (Fig. 10.8d). In statues and tomb models twined bags are depicted as simply cross-hatched, cushion-like shapes. Model baskets of *shabtis* are also depicted as slightly bulging rectangles, often with cross-hatching, representing the twined seed and harvest bags. From the tomb-paintings one is led to believe that the largest variety of shapes and function is found in twined basketrey. The depictions of carrier bags on donkeys are often twined bags, but also large carrier nets, which are depicted as cross-hatched large ovals (Fig. 10.8i). Although these are flexible

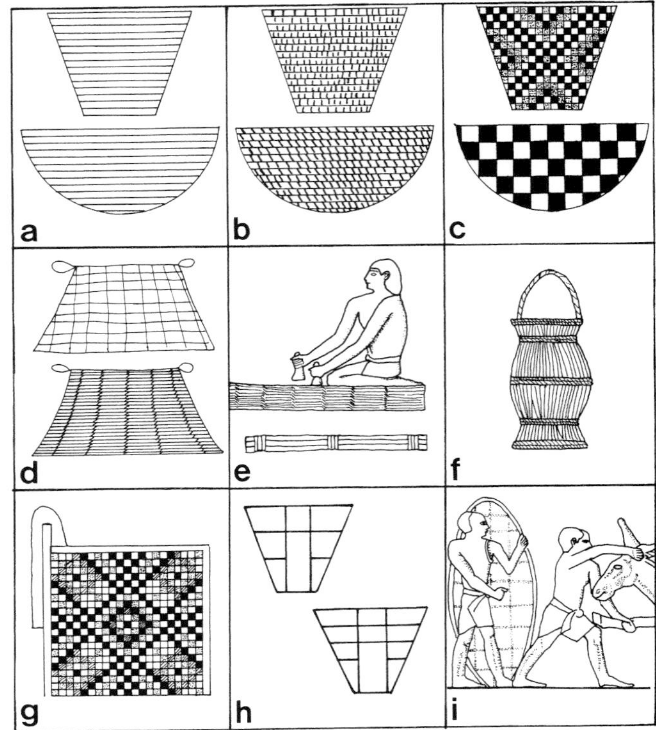

Figure 10.8 Representations of coiled basketry: (a) horizontal stripes representing the coil; (b) horizontal stripes with an indication of the stitches; (c) chequered patterns, in some cases representing coloured stitches, in other cases an artistic liberty. Representations of twined basketry: (d) seed bags are depicted with cross-hatched lines or, more precisely, with rows of oblique stripes; (e) twined mats are stylised as horizontal lines, interrupted by vertical lines. In more precise representations the rows of twining are indicated with oblique stripes; (f) basket with double rows of twining and a rope handle. Representations of other techniques: (g) woven (chair) matting is represented with, sometimes colourful, chequers; (h) rectangular tapering chests, probably made of wood or papyrus; (i) twined or knotted carrier nets are indicated with simple crossing lines.

knotted or twined nets (Fig. 10.5f), they are depicted as being rigid. It is not clear if the fish traps, which are depicted as being made of stakes, fastened by openly spaced rows of twining, were rigid or not, since no archaeological remains have been found (see p. 259).

Quite enigmatic are the square tapering chests often seen with Middle Kingdom offering bearers. They are lidless, usually contain beer jars and seem to have rigid sides. Sometimes a second crate seems to have been put upside down to form a lid. The cross-hatched patterns (mostly black lines on a white background) shows some variation, usually within the same scene (Fig. 10.8h). They might represent boxes, rather than baskets, made of strips of papyrus or palm leaf on a frame of reeds or palm midribs. The square boxes found in archaeological contexts, however, have straight sides rather than the flaring sides of the offering chests. Alternatively they might be plastered wooden boxes.

The chair mat is depicted as a square under the actual line of the seats (Fig. 10.8g), and mostly these matting representations are similar to the chequered coiled baskets. Here we find a clear warning not to try to apply our desire for a consistent iconography to these wall-paintings: the technique indicated is weaving. The weaving patterns on chairs vary from a simple open grid to intricate patterns, but are never coloured. The chequered equivalents on wall-paintings are lavishly coloured and thus do not give a clear image of the actual mats (see Fig. 10.4).

The stylised way of representing mats is as three rectangles with horizontal lines, bordered by three blocks with vertical lines (Fig. 10.8e). This is a depiction of twined matting, the horizontal stripes representing bundles of grass, culms of reeds or sedges and the vertical strokes representing the rows of twining connecting the bundles. Woven mats and (rarely occurring) plaited mats, for instance awnings on ships, are shown as chequered, often colourful rectangles, with the same kind of patterns as the chair matting and some of the coiled baskets (Fig. 10.8g). Terracotta miniature baskets from the Roman period show horizontal lines and sometimes chevron patterns indicating sewn-plaits basketry.

Imitations

Basketry and matting have been used as decorative patterns throughout Egyptian history. The *kheker* motif is thought to represent the top edge of matting, where bundles of reeds are tied together. In the architectural tradition from the Early Dynastic period onwards, mat imitations represent archaic walls. Similarly the zigzag string pattern at the base of walls and along the torus moulding of temple pylons are reminiscent of walls consisting of a frame covered with mats. Although often difficult to discern, because most of the colours on tomb walls have not survived, many walls of niches and false doors in the Old Kingdom *mastabas* are decorated with colourful motifs: chequered and occasionally chevron patterns representing woven matting. Chevron patterns indicate twill-weaving or plait patterns, but their occurrence in decoration is not representative of the number of twill-woven mats occurring. These were very rare, the earliest example being the awnings from the Khufu boat (see p. 259). Sometimes it has proven possible to reconstruct the original patterns from fragments of paint on the wall, for instance in the tomb of Hesyra (Quibell 1913: pl. ix) and tomb S3505 (Emery 1958: pls. 6, 7, 8), both at Saqqara. The drum in the central part of the false door represents a mat, rolled up to give access. The lavishly coloured matting imitations seem to represent an 'ideal' mat, rather than a mat that has been actually present at any time. One of the walls of the funerary chapel of tomb S3505 was, for instance, lined with simple grass matting (see p. 257).

Many of the underground chambers of the Step Pyramid complex of Djoser at Saqqara are lined with matting patterns in faience and plaster. Small faience tiles, measuring about 6 × 4 cm, thick in the middle and sloping down to four sides, are held in on copper wires through a boss on reverse and then plastered. The cushion-like faience tiles represent the bundles of grass or reeds, dented by 'strings' which are twined around the bundles at regular intervals. The strings are imitated in plaster with horizontal lines.

A stone-carved imitation of a twined basket, dated to the Predynastic period, is very detailed and includes the knots which fasten off the twining strands as well as the string tying together the bundles at both ends of the basket (JE 71298, *cf.* Saleh and Sourouzian 1986: no. 13). The importance of placing baskets of stone in a funerary context was probably that these, in contrast with real baskets, represented permanence, and thus outlived eternity for the benefit of the deceased.

From a much later setting, the Nineteenth Dynasty, basket imitations in metal are known. Among the treasures found in 1906 at Tell el-Basta were two jars, one of which had a handle in the form of a gazelle, made of silver. The bodies of both jars are covered with regular rows, of round shapes, and, the second, of heart shapes, imitating the stitches of coiled basketry (Vernier 1927: 415–6, pls. 104 and 105; Saleh and Sourouzian 1986: no. 222).

Classification and terminology

Under 'techniques' (see p. 255) nine basketry techniques were distinguished: coiling, weaving, twining, continuous plaiting, sewn plaits, looping around a core, looping, piercing and binding. It was not specified, however, on what basis this distinction was made, nor was anything said about the terminology.

Classification

The basketry techniques have been classified by discerning the *number of systems* used and the the interaction of these systems. In this context a *system* is a strand, or a number of parallel strands which are made of the same material and have the same orientation and function in building a basketry fabric. An important concept in understanding the interaction of the systems are the terms *active* and *passive*. The active system causes the coherency of the basket, while the passive system forms the base of the structure.

Coiled basketry is made with two systems: a passive bundle, which is fastened in a coil by an active winding strand. Both the active and passive system consist of one *element* (one bundle and one winding strand). The terms active and passive refer not only to the 'task' of the strands in the technique, but also to the production process. The basket-maker concentrates his actions on the active system, while the passive system is usually handled far less. Often the passive system is rigid or completely fixed. An example of the latter is weaving: the passive system, the warp, is fixed in a loom, while the active system, the weft consists of a strand which is woven up and down the warp strands. In the case of weaving, the passive system consists of a number of *elements*, namely the parallel strands making up the warp, while the passive system is one element: the mat-maker weaves the strands one by one.

In coiling the active and passive element are oriented parallel to each other (they both follow a coiling movement from the centre of the base to the rim of the basket). In weaving the active and passive systems are oriented at a right angle.

Twining is very similar to weaving: the passive system is formed by a number of elements, for instance a number of parallel culms of reed, a number of parallel strings or a number of parallel bundles of grass. These are fastened by the active element running at a right angle (Figs 10.1c and 10.5). The active element consists of two *members*, two strings which twist around the bundles and around each other.

Plaiting is a technique in which both systems are active. This is true for continuous plaiting, as well as for the first production stage of the sewn-plaits technique: long strips are plaited out of strands of palm leaf or bundles of grass. In the second stage the plaited strip is the passive system, which is sewn with a string (the active system) into an ongoing fabric (Wendrich 1991: 59–64).

Looping around a core is also a two-system technique: a bundle of, for instance, grass is fixed in a coil by a strand which forms a loop around the bundle and links into the loop of the previous coil. It resembles coiling, in that the two systems follow the same direction, from centre to rim. It is distinguished from coiling because the movement of the active strand is different.

Not all techniques are two-system techniques. Looping (without a core), for instance, is done with one strand only. The coherency of the net is caused by the twist in the palm leaf which results in slightly stiff loops which retain their shape. Apart from one- and two-system techniques, there are also techniques with three or more systems. An example of a three-system twining technique is shown in Fig. 10.5e. Two passive systems are layed out cross-wise, the strands of system one being sandwiched between two layers of strands of system two. They are connected by a third, active, system which twines in between the strands of system one and around the double layer of strands of system two.

Binding occurs as a two- or three-system technique. An example of the former is the Predynastic coffin from Tarkhan, which is made by fixing a bundle of papyrus culms in a coil with knotted twigs (Cairo, Egyptian Museum room R/U11) (Fig. 10.3). A three-system binding technique is found in roof-constructions and wind-screens (Fig. 10.1i). In this case there are two passive systems: a screen of reeds is layed out, and a number of cross-bars are layed on top of this. The two passive systems are connected by a third, active, system: with string or twisted palm leaf the reeds are tied to the cross-bars.

Piercing is a two-system technique in which the passive system is pierced by the active system. The active system can be rigid (such is the case in the *gereed* crates, furniture and bird cages) or flexible, as in the Predynastic matting fragment which consists of parallel stems of rushes, sewn with flax yarn.

Further distinctions can be made for the active and the passive system separately, for instance, by specifying the space between the strands and the rigidity of the strands. Thus all techniques can be classified according to the same criteria, which makes it possible to find out which combinations do and which combinations do *not* occur. Finding explanations for the empty classes is what makes such a classification an important heuristic tool, rather than just a set of pigeon holes (see Wendrich 1991 and forthcoming).

Terminology

'Looped basketry' refers to the looped shape of the active system, while 'coiled basketry' refers to the passive system which is fixed in a coil. 'Stake and strand' basketry describes the flexibility of the two systems (rigid stakes, flexible strands), but in fact comprises a number of techniques: twining, weaving and waling (the latter is a form of twining with three or more elements). Wickerwork, a term used often as an alternative for stake-and-strand basketry, refers to the material used (wicker being an old term for willow rods). It may be clear that the terminology used in this, and many other, publications on basketry is all but consistent. A consistent terminology is based on a consistent classification, but it is debatable whether a consistent terminology is necessary or even preferable. A terminology comprising all aspects which are of importance in discerning one technique from another would result in terms which are multi-composite and, therefore, often unreadable. It is acceptable to use and, if necessary, adapt existing terms, as long as these are clearly defined and, preferably, accompanied by drawings.

Although a generally known basketry term, wickerwork has not been used above. The reason for this is that wickerwork is an English term, referring to a material, willow, which has never been used for making baskets in Egypt and using this term evokes a misleading image of Egyptian baskets. Following this line of reasoning brings to light the most important weakness of both terminology and the underlying classification: it is a construction which not necessarily complies with the world of the Egyptian basket-makers. When working with present-day Egyptian basket-makers it becomes painfully clear that neither a Eurocentric, nor a 'neutral systematic' terminology is in accordance with modern Egyptian basketry classification, let alone with the ancient Egyptian terminology and the classification which silently underlies it.

Function

As this chapter has indicated, basket-makers in ancient Egypt had a number of materials and techniques to choose from, resulting in mats and baskets with different properties. The properties of baskets and mats which are of importance for their functions are size, shape, flexibility and the space between the strands.

Despite the fact that most of the raw materials used were flexible, the baskets themselves were not, due to the technique employed. In particular, coiling results in strong baskets with rigid walls. Rigid materals, such as reeds, papyrus culms and midribs of date-palm leaves, were used for the production of twined or bound screens, (trap)doors, roofs and boxes.

Coiling is not only the most frequently occurring technique, but also the most versatile. Coiled baskets have been found in an enormous variety of sizes and shapes. They were mainly, or perhaps even exclusively, used inside the houses. Personal belongings and jewellery were kept in small decorative baskets, large storage baskets were the ancient Egyptian equivalent of our linen-closet. The contents of the coiled baskets in the tomb of Tutankhamun (KV62) give an impression of what type of goods were stored in baskets. They contained spices, dried fruits, seeds, dom-nuts, wheat and bread. A large coiled dish, with internal divisions, contained dom-nuts, a sealed linen bag, a fragment of bread and a few seeds. The baskets ranged in diameter from about 10 to 50 centimetres. There were thirty-two round baskets, eighty-one oval baskets, often with slightly conical lids, which rested on an extra coil on the inside of the rim and three bottle-shaped baskets, two of which contained dried grapes. Pulses (lentils and chickpeas) were not stored in baskets but in pots (Reeves 1990: 204–7). Of course, the large total of baskets in the tomb, of which there were more than any other kind of artefacts, is unlikely to reflect a normal household situation, but it does show the importance of basketry as storage containers. Pot stands and the rims of sieves were also coiled, while the grids of sieves and strainers were always twined.

The variety in spacing of the active and passive elements mainly reflects the function of twined basketry. For the grid of sieves both the active and passive elements of the twined grid were evenly spaced, the size of the strands and the space between them varying with the function of the sieve. The finest grids were twined out of animal hair. Twined bags were usually made of grass or palm leaf and, when loosely twined, quite flexible. Using the same materials and technique, but pulling the twining strands tightly, resulted in closely twined stiff mats, used, for instance, as saddles. Twined basketry was used mainly outside the house for carrying seeds, grain and other commodities or for moving pots, harvested plants, earth or dung on donkey-back. In the Ptolemaic period, most of the functions of twined basketry were taken over by sewn-plaits basketry, with the exception of the large twined donkey-bags which are still used widely today.

The function of mats is often difficult to determine, because they are used and re-used for a large number of purposes. Twined grass mats were found re-used as roofing material, but they did not end up there until after they had been used extensively as floor mats. Thick, woven mats, which could be easily rolled up, were probably used as sleeping mats, but the context in which they were found at Amarna suggests that they were also used as awnings (Wendrich 1989).

The correlation between function and aspects of size, shape, flexibility and spacing is not a simple linear one. Ethnoarchaeological research shows that the function of baskets is often very specific, and that tradition plays an important role. Furthermore, there is a difference between function and use: a basket might be used for something other than its official function and there are many instances of re-use of baskets and mats, for other purposes than their original function.

Producers and users

Who were the people who made and used the baskets? Both in the Amarna Workmen's Village and the tomb of Tutankhamun (KV62) large quantities were found. The question of who used basketry is therefore easily answered: everybody. Although there were differences between the relatively coarsely coiled and well-worn baskets from the workers and the finely decorated baskets from the tomb.

A tentative identification of the producers is also possible. The production of basketry involves a number of stages. Gathering and preparing the raw materials was probably part of the task of the basket-maker. For some materials, such as grass, or palm leaf, this can be done all year round, whenever the need is felt, but other materials, such as rushes and sedges, have to be gathered at a certain time of year and are dried and stored until needed. The time spent on harvesting and storing requires a certain level of professionalism.

Making coiled basketry does not require a special workshop; it can be made anywhere, the only tools necessary being an awl or needle and perhaps a knife. Although it is a time-consuming process, coiling can be interrupted at any time. Since the baskets seem to have been used only inside the houses it seems likely that they were made by women, perhaps mainly for their own use and whenever their other tasks left them time. Twining and weaving, on the other hand, require the use of looms for which a workspace has to be set apart. This suggests that twined matting, twined bags (which are sewn out of mats) and woven matting were made by part- or full-time professionals. It is a moot point as to whether we should conclude from the male matmaker depicted in the tomb of Khety at Beni Hasan (BH17) (Middle Kingdom), that these mats were generally made by male basket-makers. The producers of sewn-plaits basketry probably were part- or full-time professional males. This is at least true for the early-Christian hermits. Bound matting is mostly used in architectural contexts (screens, doors, walls of huts). The bound matting was probably made on the spot, which would lead to the conclusion that the producers were involved in the building activities. In tomb paintings the builders depicted are always male.

Most probably there was some degree of specialisation, simple coiled basketry being produced by women for their own use, while the other techiques were made by part-time or full-time professionals. This can also be inferred from the fact that the few depictions of basketry producers in tomb paintings are only men, making twined or woven mats. There was also a regional specialisation as is clear from the archaeological material, but also from a painting in the tomb of Rekhmira (TT100; see Fig. 10.9 and 10.10) where part of the tribute from Nubia and the Kharga oasis is a large number of baskets, among which are decorated, finely coiled examples.

From the supposition that there were (semi-)professional basket- and mat-makers follows the possibility that basketry was bought and sold. For the New Kingdom this is confirmed by prices quoted in some of the ostraca found at Deir el-Medina. For some of the prices quoted, it seems likely that they were not sold separately, but that prices included the contents (Janssen 1975: 135). These were probably standard-sized twined bags, containing wheat or barley.

Discard and preservation

Although the basket materials were inexpensive, their production is labour-intensive. Basketry from settlements were found to have been used and re-used extensively. At Qasr Ibrim, for instance, many storage pits were lined with cut-up carrying baskets and mats. Even baskets from funerary contexts often have traces of use, although they are generally in good condition. Baskets found in foundation deposits were produced whimsically and especially for the occasion. Beautifully decorated basketry, on the other hand, survived a number of generations as heirlooms. After a long life of service, the basketry was not thrown away, but many items probably found a final use as fuel for ovens, kilns or fires.

Although the preservation of organic materials is exceptionally good in Egyptian desert sites, the baskets found in excavations, represent only a small portion of the amount that must have been in use. Still, this portion is of vital importance to our understanding of one aspect of Egyptian daily life and serves to correct our view of sites in which the conditions are less favourable.

References

Adovasio, J.M. 1977. *Basketry Technology; a Guide to Identification and Analysis.* Chicago: Aldine.

(a)

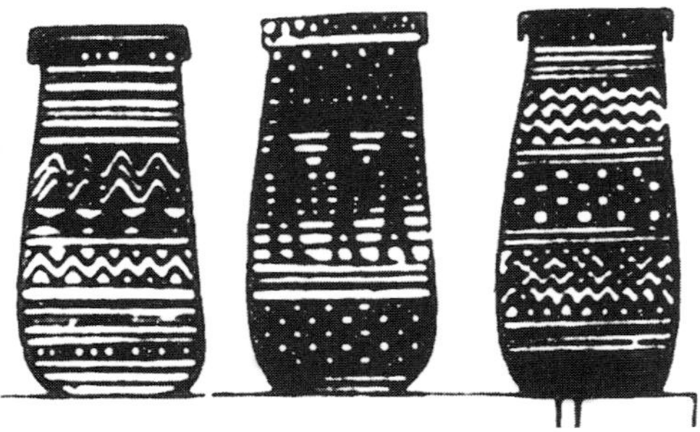

(b)

Figure 10.9 (a) Painting from the Eighteenth-Dynasty Theban tomb-chapel of the vizier Rekhmira (TT100) showing tribute from Nubia, including twined bags and coiled baskets decorated with coloured winders; (b) detail of the coiled baskets with binders.

Anonymous 1978. *Guidebook: The Luxor Museum of Ancient Egyptian Art.* Cairo: EAO.

Balfet, H. 1952. La vannerie; essai de classification. *L'Anthropologie*, 56: 259–80.

Bonioanni, A. 1987. Weaving: mats and baskets. In *Egyptian Civilization: Daily Life* (ed. A.M. Donadoni Roveri). Milan: Egyptian Museum of Turin/Electa, pp. 106–19.

Brunton, G. and Caton-Thompson, G. 1928. *The Badarian Civilisation and Prehistoric Remains near Badari.* London: Quaritch.

Caton-Thompson, G. 1926. The Neolithic industry of the Northern Fayum desert. *Journal of the Royal Anthropological Institute of Great Britain and Ireland*, 56: 309–23.

Caton-Thompson, G. and Gardner, E.W. 1934. *The Desert Fayum.* London: Royal Anthropological Institute of Great Britain and Ireland.

Crowfoot, G.M. 1933. The mat weaver from the tomb of Khety. *Ancient Egypt*: 93–9.

1954. Textiles, basketry, and mats. In *A History of Technology* I (eds. C. Singer, E.J. Holmyard and A.R. Hall). Oxford: Clarendon Press, pp. 413–47.

Emery, I. 1980. *The Primary Structures of Fabrics; an Illustrated Classification.* 2nd edn. Washington DC: The Textile Museum (1st edn. 1966).

Emery, W.B. 1954. *Great Tombs of The First Dynasty* II. London: EES.

1958. *Great Tombs of The First Dynasty* III. London: EES.

Forbes, R.J. 1964 . Sewing, basketry and weaving. In *Ancient Technology* IV. Leiden: Brill, pp. 175–95.

Germer, R. 1985. *Flora des pharaonischen Ägypten.* Mainz: von Zabern.

Gourlay, Y. J.-L. 1981. *Les Sparteries de Deir el-Médineh I, Catalogue des Techniques de Sparterie.* Cairo: IFAO.

Greiss, E.A.M. 1957. Anatomical Identification of Some Ancient Egyptian Plant Materials. Cairo: Imprimerie Costa Tsoumas Mémoires de l'Institut d'Egypte T.55.

Janssen, J.J. 1975. *Commodity Prices from the Ramessid Period.* Leiden: Brill.

Junker, H. 1929. Vorlaufiger Bericht über die Grabung der Akademie der Wissenschaften in Wien auf der neolithischen Siedlung von Merimde-Benisalame (West Delta) vom 1 bis 30. Marz 1929. *Anzeiger der Phil.-hist. Klasse der Akademie der Wissenschaften in Wien*, 66: 156ff.

1930. Voraufiger Bericht über die zweite Grabung der Akademie der Wissenschaften in Wien auf der vorgeschichtlichen Siedlung Merimde-Benisalame vom 7. Februar bis 8. April 1930. *Anzeiger der Phil.-hist. Klasse der Akademie der Wissenschaften in Wien*, 67: 21ff.

1932. Vorbericht über die dritte Grabung der Akademie der Wissenschaften in Wien in Verbindung it dem Egyptiska Museet in Stokholm unernemmene auf der neolithischen Siedelung von Merimde-Benisalame vom 6. November 1931 bis 20. Janner 1932. *Anzeiger der Phil.-hist. Klasse der Akademie der Wissenschaften in Wien*, 69: 36–99.

Larsen, J.L. and Freudenheim, B. 1986. *Interlacing; the Elemental Fabric.* Tokyo: Kodansha International.

Lehmann, J. 1907. *Systematik und geographische Verbreitung der Geflechtsarten. Abhandlungen und Berichte des Königlich Zoologischen und Anthropologisch-Ethnographischen Museums zu Dresden* XI nr.3. Dresden.

Leroi-Gourhan, A. 1971. *L'homme et la matière.* Paris: Editions Albin Michel.

Lucas, A. 1962. *Ancient Egyptian Materials and Industries*, 4th edn., rev. J.R. Harris. London: Edward Arnold.

Mason, O. T. 1904. Aboriginal American basketry: studies in a textile art without machinery. In *Annual Report of the Board of Regents of the Smithsonian Institution, Report of the U.S. National Museum for the Year ending 30 June 1902.* Washington: Government Printing Office, , pp. 171–548, pl. 1/248.

Peet, T.E. and Woolley, C.L. 1923. *The City of Akhenaten* I. London: EES.

Petrie, W.M.F. 1927.*Objects of Daily Use.* London: Quaritch.

Petrie, W.M.F. and Quibell, J.E. 1896. *Nagada and Ballas 1895.* London: Quaritch.

Petrie, W.M.F., Wainwright, G.A. and Gardiner, A.H. 1913. *Tarkhan I and Memphis V.* London: Quaritch.

Quibell, J.E. 1913. *Excavations at Saqqara: the Tomb of Hesy.* Cairo: SAE.

Reeves, N. 1990. *The Complete Tutankhamun.* Cairo: The American University in Cairo Press.

Rizkana, I. and Seeher, J. 1989. *Maadi III. The Non-Lithic Small Finds and The Structural Remains of The Predynastic Settlement.* Deutsches Archäologisches Institut, Abteilung Kairo, Archäologische Veröffentlichungen 80. Mainz am Rhein: von Zabern.

Saleh, M. and Sourouzian, H. 1986. *Die Hauptwerke im Ägyptischen Museum Kairo, offizieler Katalog.* Mainz: von Zabern.

Seiler-Baldinger, A. 1979. *Classification of Textile Techniques.* Ahmedabad, India: Calico Museum of Textiles.

Täckholm, V., Täckholm, A. and Drar, M. 1941–69. *Flora of Egypt*, 4 vols. Cairo: Cairo University Bulletin of the Faculty of Science, 17 (1941), 28 (1950), 30 (1954), 36 (1969).

Vernier, E. 1927. *Bijoux et Orèvreries Catalogue Général des Antiquités Egyptiennes du Musée du Caire no's 52001–53855*, Cairo:IFAO.

Vogt, E. 1937. *Geflechte und Gwerbe der Steinzeit.* Basel: Schweizerische Gesellschaft für Urgeschichte.

Wendrich, W.Z. 1989. Preliminary report on the Amarna basketry and cordage. In *Amarna Reports* V (ed. B.J. Kemp). London: EES, pp. 169–201.

1991. *Who is Afraid of Basketry? A Guide to Recording, Basketry and Cordage for Archaeologists and Ethnographers.* Leiden: CNWS.

1995. Basketry and cordage. In *Berenike 1994, Preliminary Report* (eds S.E. Sidebotham and W.Z. Wendrich). Leiden: CNWS, pp. 69–84.

1996. Ancient Egyptian rope and knots. In *History and Science of Knots* (eds. J.C. Turner and P. van de Griend). Singapore: World Scientific, pp. 43–68.

forthcoming *The World according to Basketry.* Leiden: CNWS.

Wendrich, W.Z. and Veldmeijer, A.J. 1996. Basketry and cordage. In *Berenike 1995, Preliminary Report* (eds. S.E. Sidebotham, W.Z. Wendrich). Leiden: CNWS, pp. 269–96.

Wipszycka, E. 1986. Les aspects economiques de la vie de la communauté des Kellia. In *Le Site Monastique Copte des Kellia; Sources Historiques et Explorations Archáologiques.* Geneva: Mission Suisse d'Archéologie Copte.

11. Textiles

GILLIAN VOGELSANG-EASTWOOD

Introduction

Textiles figured prominently in all aspects of ancient Egyptian life; they were needed from the cradle to the grave. Although many examples derive from Egyptian tombs and represent cloth for the dead, recent excavations of settlement sites have produced a more representative selection of 'daily-life' textiles and these are now available for study. They include the textiles from Kahun and the Workmen's Village at Amarna (Allgrove 1986: 226–52; Eastwood 1985: 191–204), forming an important source of information about the way in which Egyptian textiles were made and used.

It is clear from textiles excavated from both tombs and settlement sites that, as early as the Predynastic period, the Egyptians were proficient spinners and weavers (Caton-Thompson and Gardner 1934: 46, 49, 88, 90). Information about the textile technology of Pharaonic Egypt derives both from the textiles themselves and from representations of the various stages of textile production, from the sowing of the flax-seed in the ground to the weaving of material.

Tomb-paintings and models are a particularly valuable source of information about the production of cloth, in particular spinning techniques and loom forms. The most important paintings are in the Eleventh- and Twelfth-Dynasty tombs at Beni Hasan (BH2, 3, 15 and 17; Newberry 1893: pls. XI, XXIX, 1894: pls. IV, XIII), the Eleventh-Dynasty tomb of Dagi at Thebes (TT 103; Davies 1913: pl. XXXVII), the Twelfth-Dynasty tomb of Thuthotep at Deir el-Bersha (DB2; Newberry n.d.: pl. XXVI.), the Nineteenth-Dynasty tomb of Neferronpet at Thebes (TT 133, reign of Rameses II; Davies 1948: pl. 35) and the Eighteenth-Dynasty tomb of Thutnefer at Thebes (TT 104; Davies 1927b: 233–55). One of the most useful models of a spinning and weaving workshop is from the early Middle Kingdom tomb of Meketra (Cairo JE 46723; Winlock 1955: 29–33; see Fig.11.1). Other models of this type are in the Metropolitan Museum, New York (MMA 32.1.125 and 30.7.3) and the Ny Carlsberg Glyptothek, Copenhagen (A 516).

Figure 11.1 Model of a spinning and weaving workshop from the early Middle Kingdom tomb of Meketra (Cairo, JE 46723).

Fibres

Although ancient Egypt is known for the production of linen cloth, the flax from which it was made was not the only textile fibre in use. Excavated textiles made from sheep's wool, goat hair and palm fibre are also known. Cotton was not in general use in Egypt until the first century AD; the identification of cotton on a mummy has been discounted, as the mummy in question (Philadelphia University Musuem: PUM II) was shipped to America in raw cotton. For the original report about the presence of cotton see Cockburn *et al.* (1983: 52–70). Silk became widely available only after the seventh century AD.

Sheep's wool

The earliest known depictions of sheep in Egypt are the rock drawings of wild barbary sheep in southern Egypt and Lower Nubia, which appear to date from the Neolithic or early Predynastic period. In addition, two species of domestic sheep are depicted in Pharaonic tomb paintings and reliefs. The oldest type of sheep (*Ovis longipes palaeoaegyptiacus*) has long, loosely spiralling horns which come out the side of the skull. It is likely that its wool was coarse. The other form (*Ovis platyura aegyptiaca*) has horns which develop downwards and curl forwards, while keeping close to the head. The wool is shorter than that of *Ovis longipes palaeoaegyptiacus*, with distinct and regular locks and it is likely that it provided reasonably good wool, suitable for weaving.

It has become an established 'fact' that the ancient Egyptians did not use wool. This, however, is a misconception based on several comments by classical authors, notably Herodotus in the fifth century BC and Plutarch in the first century AD (*De Iside et Osiride*: 4). Herodotus states: 'It is, however, contrary to religious usage to be buried in a woollen garment, or to wear wool in a temple' (*Histories* II: 82). The prohibition on wool, if it existed, appears to have applied only to priests since Herodotus also comments that lay-people, especially young men, wore 'linen tunics with a fringe hanging around the legs and called *calasiris*, and a white woollen garment on top of it'.

Wool and woollen textiles were known from the Predynastic onwards, and various excavators record wool from such early contexts. Thus Petrie and Quibell (1895: 44) refer to Predynastic 'brown and white woollen knitted stuff' at Naqada, while Zaki Saad (1951: 44) mentions a woollen cloth wrapped round the skeleton of a man in a First-Dynasty burial at Helwan. A find of wool from Kahun which was originally dated to the Middle Kingdom has recently been radiocarbon-dated to the Roman period (Cooke pers. comm.). From the New Kingdom come several examples of woollen textiles excavated both from the Main City and the Workmen's Village at Amarna. Finally, the unmummified body of an unknown man, was found wrapped in sheepskins in an unmarked coffin within the royal cache of mummies at Deir el-Bahari, Thebes (Andrews 1985: 67, pl. 86).

Goat hair

A small number of goat hair textiles have been found at ancient Egyptian sites. Several of them come from the Workmen's Village, Amarna (Eastwood 1985: 192); one of these was made from dark brown hair, while the others were of cream-coloured fibres. The range of colour suggests that either the goats may have been piebald or perhaps several different coloured goats were being reared. In fact, a wall-painting in the Middle Kingdom tomb of Khnumhotep at Beni Hasan (BH3) depicts goats with fleeces ranging from black to cream (Griffith 1896: pl. III). Piebald goats are also portrayed alongside black- or white-haired goats on a painted papyrus dating to the mid-twelfth century BC (BM EA10016).

Palm fibre

Palm fibre comes from the bast or bark of certain trees, notably the palm tree. It is usually brown in colour, hard to the touch and brittle. It is not commonly found in connection with textiles from the ancient world, but some pieces of cloth from the Workmen's Village at Amarna had a series of possible palm-fibre loops woven into them (Eastwood 1985: 192). It should be noted that some authorities use the term 'coir' to refer to palm fibre, although it strictly refers only to the husk of the coconut, which is not native to Egypt; this term is therefore avoided here.

Grass and reeds

The use of grass and reeds for matting is described in Chapter 10, this volume; it is possible that these fibres were also used for textiles, although this is not certain. Midgley states that some Predynastic fabrics were probably of grass or reed: 'The microscopic structure of the fibre is similar to that used in some Badarian cloths . . . It is apparently some fibrovascular tissue not in any way related to flax' (Mond and Myers 1937: 139–41). He also described some textiles as 'spun from reed fibres', and others as 'made from yarns of grass or reed fibre'. As Lucas (1962: 149) himself noted, much more work is still required on this subject.

Hemp and ramie

True bast fibres identified with ancient Egyptian textiles include hemp (Brunton 1937: 145; Lucas 1962: 149) and ramie (Midgley 1912: 6), but these identifications are not certain and more work needs to be carried out on the textiles in question.

Flax

The majority of ancient Egyptian textiles are of linen which is made from the bast fibre, flax. Flax is a member of the *Linaceae* family, of which there are twelve genera (Catling and Grayson 1982: 13). Although the genus *Linum* has 230 species, only a few are of use for the production of textiles. *Linum* is an annual herb with alternating, lanceolate leaves along the entire length of the stem. The flowers have five petals which can be white, blue or purple. The fruit is a capsule form enclosing ten seeds.

Flax is not a native of Egypt, although its use dates back to the prehistoric period and it is possible that it was imported into Egypt from the Levant (Germer 1985: 101). Two types of flax are believed to have been grown in

Predynastic Egypt: the oldest is *Linum bienne* Mill. (ex *Linum angustifolium*) which grows to one metre high and has small, white flowers. Evidence for the early use of this type of flax has been found in the form of a flax capsule (tomb 3000/object 3) at the Predynastic site of Badari in Middle Egypt (Brunton and Caton-Thompson 1928: 63). The second type of *Linum* known from Predynastic Egypt is *Linum usitatissimum*, which again grows to about one metre high, but it has small, light blue flowers. It is this form of *Linum* which became the main source of flax in ancient times. In some tomb-paintings, the flax flowers are represented by a line of blue paint, which probably indicates that *Linum usitatissimum*, rather than *Linum bienne*, was being depicted.

Turning the flax plant into a piece of cloth is an elaborate process, which took a long time to develop, but it can be shown from excavated textiles from the Fayum region that a variety of types of linen cloth were being produced by the Neolithic period (*c* .5000 BC; see Caton-Thompson and Gardner 1934: 40, 43, 46, 49, 51 and 90).

Sowing and harvesting

The task of sowing flax seeds was carried out in the middle of November following the annual inundation of the Nile Valley. There are numerous representations of sowing scenes in Old and Middle Kingdom tombs, thus allowing the process to be followed and reconstructed. Often the sowing of cereal grain and flax is shown combined, as in the Middle Kingdom tomb of a man called Urarna at Sheikh Saïd in Middle Egypt (tomb 25; see Davies 1901: pl. XVI), where a man is depicted collecting seeds from the storerooms watched over by two officials who note the amount on a writing board (see Fig. 11.2). The seeds are then taken to the fields. In both cases the ground has been prepared by a team of oxen pulling a plough. However, the man sowing cereal grain uses an overarm action, while the man scattering the flax seeds uses an underarm movement which is typical for the sowing of this crop. Finally, flocks of animals, usually sheep, are sent into the fields in order to trample the seeds into the ground.

Flax plants take about three months to mature; once the flowers have died away and the seed heads appear, the plants are almost ready to be harvested. The timing of the harvesting is important, because the age of the plant affects the uses to which the fibres can be put. Thus, if the flax plants are harvested while still young and green then a fine textile can be produced, and if it is harvested when slightly older then the fibres are suitable for a general, good quality cloth. However, if the harvesting takes place when the plants are old, then the resulting flax is usable only for coarse cloth and ropes.

According to various representations of flax harvesting, such as the New Kingdom tomb of Paheri at Elkab (EK3; Tylor and Griffith 1894: pl. III), both men and women were involved in the process. In each case, a bundle of flax stems were grabbed in both hands and then pulled out of the ground. The flax was pulled rather than cut, in order to obtain as long and straight a length of fibre as possible, then the plants were tied into bundles and allowed to dry in the sun. This stage was also portrayed in the tomb of Urarna.

After the flax plants had been thoroughly dried, the seed heads were removed, using several different methods of stripping or 'rippling' the heads. They were often simply removed by hand, but the paintings in the tomb of Paheri show flax stems being pulled between the 'teeth' of a long

Figure 11.2 Scene showing the sowing of flax from the painted decoration of the Middle Kingdom tomb of Urarna at Sheikh Saïd (tomb 25).

board or rippling comb, an example of which was excavated from the Middle Kingdom town-site of Kahun (Manchester Museum Acc. No. 6859). A similar board (this time equipped with a stand) is depicted in the New Kingdom tomb of Menna at Thebes (TT 69; Petrie 1914: 95–6). The seeds of the flax (linseeds) were saved for several reasons: in order to sow the following year, to produce linseed oil, and possibly also as a form of animal-food.

Preparing the flax for spinning

In order to follow the various processes involved in preparing flax for spinning it is first necessary to understand something about the nature of the flax plant and, in particular, of its stem, which is made up of several layers (Catling and Grayson 1982: 13–5, figs. 3–4). Of importance to the production of flax are the fibre bundles (pericyclic fibres), which lie between the phloem and the epidermis and cortex. The bundles contain between twenty and eighty fibre cells (or ultimates) separated by narrow girders of parenchyma cells, and it is these fibres that are used to make the cloth. In order to release the fibre it is necessary to break down and remove the other layers of cells. The preparation of flax for spinning can be divided into two processes: (1) the retting, cleaning or scutching (i.e. the removal of the hard, outer cell layers of the flax stems); and (2) the twisting of the bundles of flax filaments into a rough, preliminary sliver or rove.

With regard to the first stage: once the seed heads have been removed it is necessary to rot or 'ret' the flax stems in order to remove the hard outer bark or cortical tissue of the plant. This is usually achieved by placing the stems in slowly running water; the length of time for which the stems stay in the water depends on the type of flax and the temperature of the water, but ten to fourteen days is normal. After the outer bark of the flax plants has deteriorated, the stems are removed from the water and allowed to dry in the sun.

The second stage in the process of preparing the flax stems for spinning is the beating or bruising of the plants to separate the fibres from the wooden parts of the stem. In the Dynastic period the flax was probably laid on a large stone and beaten with the mallets, but this stage is unfortunately not shown in any of the ancient representations. The excavations of several sites have yielded wooden mallets which may have been used for this task, and such implements were still being used for the same purpose in the Upper Egyptian village of Nahya during the 1930s (Crowfoot 1931: 34).

In order to remove any resistant fibres left over after retting and beating, the lengths of flax were either beaten with a large wooden fan (or 'bat'), to shake out all the loose pieces, or passed between two sticks held in the hand ('scutching'; see Fig. 11.3). The latter technique can be seen in the Middle Kingdom tomb of Dagi (TT 103) and the New Kingdom tomb of Thutnefer (TT 104; Davies 1913: pl. XXXVII; Davies 1927b: fig. 1).

Spinning: producing a linen thread

The ancient Egyptians had two techniques for making a thread: spinning and splicing. Spinning is the twisting together of a fibre or fibres in order to produce a long, cohesive length which is slightly elastic. As the length of individual fibres can vary from about 1 cm (e.g. in cotton), to more than two metres (in jute), different techniques of preparating and spinning have been developed to cope with these variations. It would appear both from actual finds and from representations that the technique of spinning in ancient Egypt was divided into two distinct, but related, processes: firstly the flax fibres were given a loose twist, and secondly they were actually spun in order to produce the thread.

Once the flax fibres had been scutched they were passed on to another inidvidual who transformed them into rough but orderly lengths by rolling the threads either on the

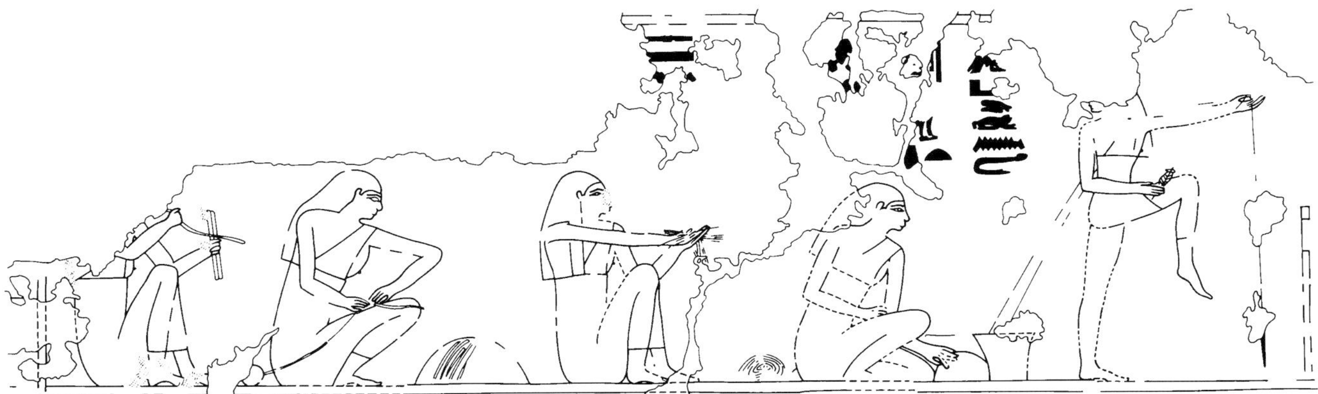

Figure 11.3 Detail of a wall-painting in the tomb-chapel of Dagi at Thebes (TT103), showing the preliminary preparation of flax ; the second woman from the left is probably splicing flax together rather than preparing it for the more conventional spinning of the fibres.

thigh or on a semicircular form placed directly in front of the person. These forms can be seen in various tombs, including that of Thuthotep at Deir el-Bersha (DB2) and those of Dagi and Thutnefer at Thebes (see Fig. 11.3).

The next stage of the process is the winding of roughly spun lengths of flax either into balls, as in the Eleventh-Dynasty tomb of Khety at Beni Hasan (BH 17; Newberry 1894: pl. XIII), or into coils, as in the tomb of Thuthotep at Deir el-Bersha, which seems to show semi-spun lengths being coiled and then passed through an internal loop in a bowl (Newberry n.d.: pl. XXVI). The woman's hands in this scene are held to her mouth, suggesting that she was moistening the fibres. This is of interest because it is normal for flax fibres to be moistened before being spun, in order to produce a coherent thread, usually by wetting the fingers prior to spinning or by moistening the balls or coils of flax with saliva from the mouth. The same method process was still being used by women in certain areas of Upper Egypt and the Sudan until comparatively recently, and two villages – Nahya and Kurdasseh – were famous for the 'women who spin through the mouth' (Crowfoot 1931: 33–5).

Spinning – the technique of twisting together a number of fibres into a strong, continuous thread – is made up of three distinct stages: (a) the drawing-out of the fibres; (b) the twisting of the fibres; and (c) the winding of the thread. Once the spindle is set in motion the spinner pulls or draws out (attenuation, drafting) a few fibres at a time from the mass held in the hand or on a separate holder or distaff. As the spindle turns the fibres, twist or spin is added. When there is sufficient twisted thread, the spindle is stopped and the thread is wound onto the spindle shaft or into a ball. Spun threads may be described as being S-spun (anticlockwise), Z-spun (clockwise), or I-spun (no spin), with the lie of the central bar of each letter indicating the direction of spin. In general, when two or more spun threads are re-spun (plyed) together, it is in the opposite direction to the original spin; thus, for example, an S-plyed yarn may be made up of two or more Z-spun threads.

Numerous forms of hand spinning have been developed throughout the world, employing a range of aids from a stick or stone to more complex forms using bowls, hand-spindles or distaffs. The most common form of spinning equipment used in ancient Egypt is the hand-spindle. A hand-spindle is made up of a stick (the shaft or spindle) and a weight (the whorl), with the latter acting like a fly wheel, keeping up the momentum of the spin. When a sufficient length of thread has been produced, the spindle is stopped and the thread is wrapped around the shaft (Crowfoot 1931; Vogelsang-Eastwood 1992a: 3–17).

A wide variety of materials were used for making whorls in ancient Egypt, including limestone, travertine, clay and wood (examples include Amarna 21/59 in limestone, 21/117 in travertine, 21/447 in clay and TA85.WV. no. 1784 in wood). Most ancient Egyptian whorls are either discoid or dome-shaped. The disc form would appear to be the oldest of the two and has been found at prehistoric sites such as Kom W in the Fayum (Caton-Thompson and Gardner 1934: 33). The dome-shaped whorl appeared at the end of the Middle Kingdom and was in widespread use by the New Kingdom. The shape of the whorl and its precise location on the shaft can vary depending upon local custom: in Egypt, the whorl was usually placed at the top of the shaft. The thread was often secured to the top of the shaft by means of a groove cut into its side around which the thread was secured, probably with a half-hitch knot.

Some whorls have been found to have marks cut into their sides, including three wooden examples from Amarna, one having an elongated V on its side; another with an X and a third bearing a rectangle with two horizontal lines (Vogelsang-Eastwood 1994: 22, fig. 26). A likely explanation for these marks is that they were used to identify the tools as the property of a particular spinner.

Although depictions of men spinning yarn for making nets are known from tombs of the Old Kingdom, it is not until the Middle Kingdom that representations of spinning thread for cloth can be found. There are three basic methods of spinning known from these depictions which and were apparently in use during the Middle and New Kingdom – grasped spindle spinning, support spindle spinning and drop spindle spinning.

Grasped spindle spinning In this method, a prepared rove is passed through a ring or over a support such as a forked stick and then spun on a large spindle grasped in both hands. This technique is shown in the tombs of Bakt III and Khety at Beni Hasan (tombs BH15 and 17) where a forked stick is used (Fig. 11.4a) and in the tomb of Thutnefer at Thebes (TT 104) where a ring is visible (Fig. 11.4b).

Support spindle spinning This technique involves supporting the spindle while it moves. In the tomb of Khety (BH 17) a man is shown sitting back on one heel while drawing a rove from a pot through his left hand and spinning with a spindle held in his right hand (Fig. 11.4c). It is possible that the slightly thicker yarn he was producing was to be used either by a net or mat-maker.

Drop spindle spinning In the third technique, the spindle is rolled on the thigh and is then allowed to drop. This scene is depicted in a number of tombs, notably those of Bakt III and Khety at Beni Hasan. Normally the spinners stand on the ground, but sometimes they are shown standing on blocks in order to achieve a greater height (see Fig. 11.4d). Often the spinners are shown with one or two so-called 'spinning bowls' by their feet (Fig. 11.4b). Spinning bowls have from one to six loops or handles set in the bottom of the vessel (Peet and Woolley 1923: 21, 61, no. 22/591; see also Dothan 1963: 97–112; Vogelsang-Eastwood 1987–88: 78–88). Semi-spun and fully spun threads are passed

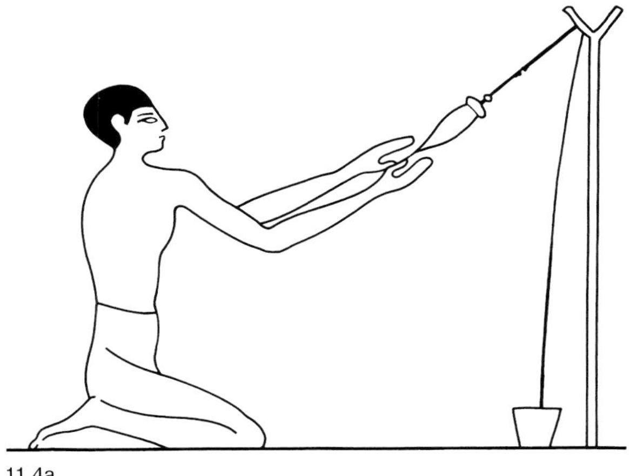
11.4a

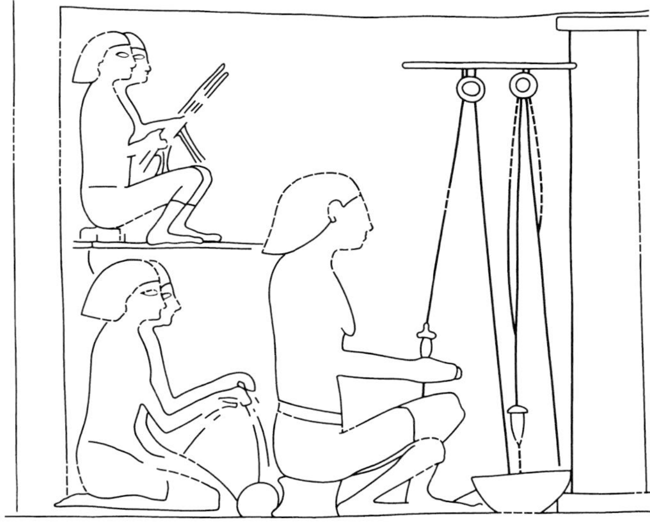
11.4b

11.4c

11.4d

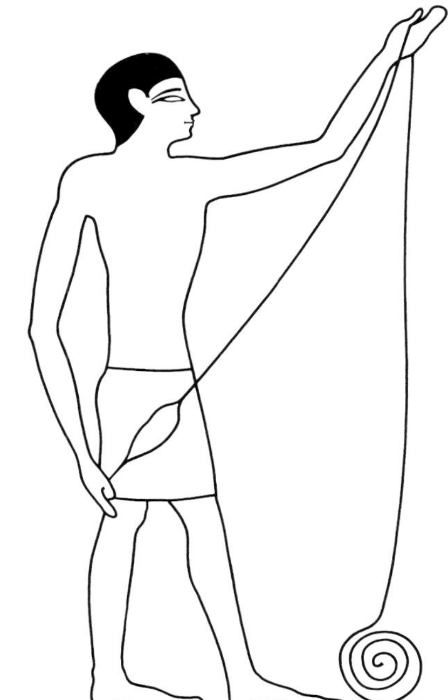
11.4e

Figure 11.4 *Different methods of spinning, as represented in the wall-painting of various Middle Kingdom and New Kingdom tombs. (a) The Middle Kingdom tomb of Khety at Beni Hasan (BH17); (b) The New Kingdom tomb of Thutnefer at Thebes (TT104); (c) The Middle Kingdom tomb of Khety at Beni Hasan (BH17); (d) the Middle Kingdom tomb of Thuthotep at Deir el-Bersha (DB2); (e) the Middle Kingdom tomb of Bakt III at Beni Hasan (BH15).*

through these loops during spinning in order to keep the threads separate and to place a small amount of tension on the thread. The sides of the bowl can vary from a shallow slope to an upright, bucket-like, form. Such bowls are usually made from pottery, but occasional stone examples are known. In the Middle Kingdom tomb of Khnumhotep at Beni Hasan (BH 3), the spinner has two bowls by her feet, one of which is painted red to represent a ceramic vessel, the other is painted red and white, which is probably meant to represent a bowl made from alabaster (Newberry 1893: pl. XXIX).

In recent years, attention has been paid to the ancient processes by which the length of the flax thread was increased. In most cases this was done as part of the attenuation process. In Egypt, however, a second method, splicing, was also developed which gives the effect of two S-spun threads being S-plyed together.

In the case of extremely fine cloth, one to three bundles of between three and twenty ultimates are spun together (Cooke and Brennan 1990: 9). In coarser cloth, however, it would appear that two threads, rather than bundles, were spun together. In both cases it is likely that the fibres were moist when spun and as they dried they set into position, so preventing the threads from unravelling. The length of the splice varies from about 5–20 cm. Splicing seems to have been used occasionally in the Old Kingdom, but by the New Kingdom it was quite common. The use of spliced threads occurs both in extremely fine as well as very coarse cloth. It may be that the technique had to be used to achieve the desired fineness, while in the coarser examples it was a method of using up lengths of thread in the most economical manner possible.

While spinning, it is always a problem to hold enough raw fibres in the hand to continue for as long as possible, before having to stop and collect more fibres in order to continue the process. In the Classical world, the problem was partly solved by using sticks (distaffs), usually of wood, around which the fibres were wrapped, but a slightly different solution was adopted by the ancient Egyptians. They made a small 'yarn carrier' from lengths of wood or palm bound together to form a cage-like structure (Crowfoot 1931: pls. 39–40); the raw flax fibres were then either inserted into the cage or wrapped around it.

Preparing the warp threads

After the flax fibres have been spun into a thread or yarn they are then ready to be woven into cloth. The first task in this process is to remove the thread from the spindle and to warp (warping) the loom. This involves placing the warp threads in position on the loom. Subsequently the threads have to be tensioned. Once this has been done the actual weaving can commence (see below).

Warping involves laying threads of equal length in parallel lines. Three different methods of winding are represented in tomb models and paintings. The first and simplest method, which uses three pegs driven into a wall, is shown in the Eleventh-Dynasty model from the tomb of Meketra at Deir el-Bahari (Cairo JE 46723). The warp thread is either wound off the spindle directly around the pegs or from a previously wound ball; in either case a figure-of-eight shape is created. A second method is illustrated in the tomb of Dagi (TT103), where a woman is shown winding thread around two pairs of uprights which have a cross-beam set about halfway up each of the stands (Davis 1913: pl. XXXVII). The third method of warping is depicted in the Eleventh-Dynasty tomb of Thuthotep I at Deir el-Bersha (Newberry n.d.: pl. XXVI); it involved balls of thread being placed in bowls or containers of some kind, and then groups of perhaps as many as twelve threads either being wound onto a series of pegs driven into a wall (in the manner described above) or being directly wrapped around the warp and cloth-beams of a ground loom.

Weaving

Weaving is the process of interlacing two or more sets of threads according to a pre-defined system to produce all or part of a textile (see Fig. 11.5). The simplest form of weaving is the 'tabby weave' where one weft thread (pick) passes over and under the warp threads (ends). In the next row (throw) the pick passes under one end and over the next, so forming an interlocking structure. All other weaves (e.g. basket weave and tapestry weave) are variations on this idea, although some of the possible variations can be extremely complex.

In tabby weave, the basic binding system or weave is based on a unit of two ends and two picks, in which each end passes over one and under one pick. The binding points are set over one end on successive picks. Various forms of tabby weave have been found in Egyptian contexts. The most common are the simple or balanced tabby weaves whereby there is an equal number of warp to weft threads, and the warp and weft-faced tabby weaves. A faced tabby weave has more threads in one system than the other. Thus a warp-faced tabby has more warp than weft threads per centimetre. Conversely a weft-faced tabby weave has more weft than warp threads.

Basket weave, or extended weave, is a tabby weave in which the warp ends or weft picks move in groups of two or more. Several different forms of basket weaves have been recorded, but most of these are New Kingdom in date. The following forms of basket weave were recorded from the Workmen's Village at Amarna (Eastwood 1985: 195–6): half basket (paired warp threads, single weft-threads); full basket (paired warp and weft threads); warp-faced basket (single warp and paired weft threads); weft-faced half-basket (paired warp threads, single weft threads) and warp-faced half-basket (paired weft threads and single warp threads.

Tapestry weave comprises one warp and a weft. The

latter is composed of threads of different colours which do not pass from selvedge to selvedge but are carried back and forth, interweaving only with the part of the warp that is required for a particular pattern area. Only a few examples of textiles woven in a tapestry weave have so far been found in Egypt and most are associated with royal tombs. Several pieces were recovered by Carter and Newberry from the tomb of Thutmose IV (KV43; Thompson 1904: 143–4). One of the textiles bears the cartouche of Amenhotep II (Cairo JE 46526; dovetail tapestry), while another has a ground decorated with lotus buds and flowers (Cairo JE 46526; Thompson 1904: pl. 1). A further example, worked in slit tapestry weave, derives from an unknown tomb in the Valley of the Kings (Cairo JE 24987; Daressy 1902: 302–3, pl. LVII); it includes a block pattern and a line of hieroglyphs set within a vertical column.

A number of examples of tapestry weave have been identified among the textiles from the tomb of Tutankhamun (KV62). These include several instances of slit tapestry (Carter nos: 367j (JE 62626), 46cc (JE 62674), 367f (JE 62775), 50u (JE 62669), 92g (JE 30/3/34/10) 50t (JE 627082Iff.) and JE 62645), one of dovetailed tapestry (54f (JE 29/3/34/05)), a horse blanket of 'Coptic' or 'bent-weft' tapestry (333 (JE 61992e)) and a form of open-work tapestry (21e (JE 30/3/34/51)).

In addition to the tapestry textiles found in royal tombs, several examples were found in the Eighteenth-Dynasty tomb of the architect Kha (TT8; Schiaparelli 1927), including a piece of material of unknown use which has two large squares of looping set in a tapestry-woven ground (Turin, Mus. Egizio inv. suppl. 8528; Donadoni Roveri 1988: 213, fig. 301). The ground is decorated with a pattern of lotus flowers and buds, and, as in the case of the horse blanket from the tomb of Tutankhamun, the design is worked in a 'bent-weft' system which later became a characteristic feature of Coptic tapestries. These New Kingdom finds indicate that this type of weave has a much longer history than hitherto supposed.

Finally, there is one piece of cloth (Carter no. 21e, JE 30/3/34/51) which has been woven in an unusual variation of tapestry weave. According to Emery's weave classification system it is a form of open-weave tapestry (Emery 1966: 84). So far, however, no near or exact parallels to this type of cloth have been found.

A small number of textiles with warp-patterned type designs have been recorded from various New Kingdom sources. This type of cloth has been variously described as a double weave; compound weave; tablet weave or a warp-pattern weave and it is one of the most complex of the weaves used in the Dynastic period. The weave is a warp-faced form in which the close-pressed warps make the pattern while the weft thread is concealed. Relatively few details are known about the history of this type of weave. In general it is believed to be an imported form because so far it has mainly been found in the tombs of members of the royal family dating to the New Kingdom. There are several surviving textiles in this type of weave. One example, now in the Victoria and Albert Museum, London (VA T251.1921) was found by Carter in an Eighteenth-Dynasty tomb at Thebes (Vogelsang-Eastwood 1994: pl. 38). It is made from coarse flax and has a simple geometric pattern in blue, brown, red and natural, repeating over four throws of the weft. Since there are several, repeating weaving faults, it may be suggested that the cloth was woven using two heddle rods and a shed rod, or possibly three heddle rods (see section on Looms p. 276).

The so-called 'Hood Textile' (VA T21.1940; Crowfoot 1933: 43–5) is possibly from Thebes and probably dates to the New Kingdom; it has a triangular pattern in blue and natural flax. The textile is woven in a warp-faced weave, but

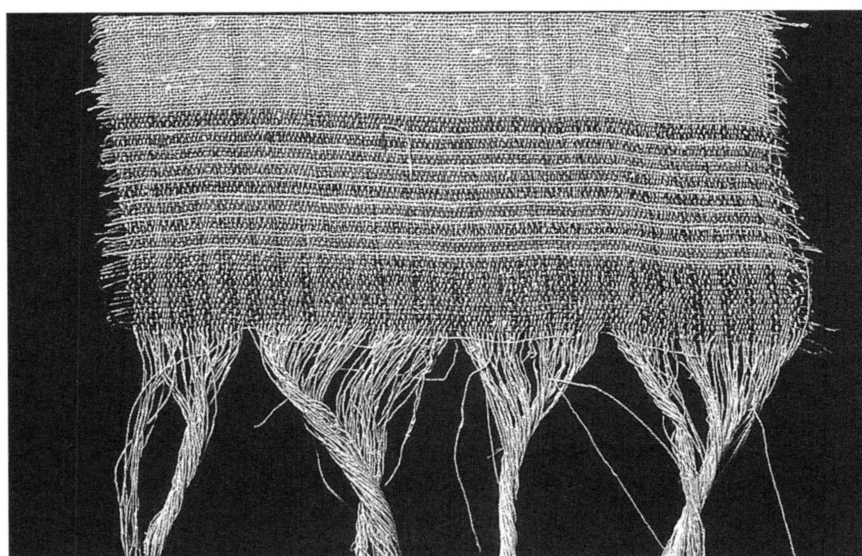

Figure 11.5 Close-up of some fine, warp-faced cloth decorated with a band in red (madder) and blue (indigotin) (Leiden, RMO, no. unknown).

the main pattern is produced by substituting weft for warp threads, which are then used to form a long fringe.

A warp-faced braid, sewn onto a saddlecloth, was found on a mummified horse excavated in front of the Theban tomb of the Eighteenth-Dynasty official Senenmut (TT71; Lansing and Hayes 1937: 10–11, 14, figs. 14–15). Among the textiles in the tomb of Tutankhamun (KV62), such braids were used to decorate the side of one of the king's elaborate bag tunics (Carter no. 367j, JE 62626) as well as a number of the decorated collar-form tunics (Carter nos. 210, JE 62644; 21aa, JE 62643) (Fig. 11.6). One of the largest and most elaborate examples of this type of work is the so-called 'girdle' of Rameses III, which is now in the Liverpool Museum (M 11158; Peet 1933), measures 5.2 metres in length and tapers from 12.7 to 4.8 cm in width, it is decorated with zig-zags, dots and rows of *ankh* signs in blue, red, yellow, green and undyed flax.

Sometimes the ancient weavers also used a combination of various weaving techniques, as in the case of one of the sashes in the tomb of Tutankhamun, the back panel of which was woven in a slit-tapestry technique while the rest was executed in a warp-faced tabby weave (Carter no. 100f; JE no. 62647).

At the beginning of the Middle Kingdom a form of weaving now called weft-looping appeared. This technique involves lifting or looping the weft thread up above the surface of the cloth at regular intervals, producing an effect similar to modern towelling; the Egyptians also created intricate patterns using loops, including chevrons, diamonds and bands. One of the earliest examples of this type of cloth, woven with short loops, comes from the collective burial of sixty soldiers at Deir el-Bahari in western Thebes, dating to the reign of the Eleventh-Dynasty ruler Mentuhotep II (Winlock 1945: 31–2, fig. 3, pl. 30B); similar textiles were found in other Middle Kingdom tombs in the immediate vicinity (Winlock 1945: 32). The use of weft-looping continues well into the New Kingdom and is often found in association with bedding, where looped cloth was used as a mattress (as in the tomb of Kha at Deir el-Medina, see Schiaparelli 1927: pl. 105), although in this later instance the loops are usually long. Cloth with long loops (similar to the symmetrical or ghiorde knot in construction) was also used for matting, such as that found on chariot 120 in the tomb of Tutankhamun. The springiness of the looping would have been used to cushion the movement of the vehicle.

Figure 11.6 Warp-faced braids used on the side edges and lower edge of a tunic from the tomb of Tutankhamun (KV62) (Cairo, JE 62626).

Looms

A variety of written and representational sources suggest that two basic types of looms were in use in Egypt by the Eighteenth Dynasty: the ground (or horizontal) loom and the vertical (or fixed-beam) loom.

The ground (or horizontal) loom

The ground loom has a simple construction, consisting of a horizontal warp stretched in its length between two beams (Roth 1951; Barber 1991: 83–91), the latter being generally kept in place by a pair of pegs driven into the ground (Fig. 11.7). The warp threads are divided into two sets: 1 3 5 7 9 etc, and 2 4 6 8 etc. By lifting up one set of threads using a heddle rod (a stick with a row of long loops attached to it), a shed is created, the first of which is called the natural shed. The countershed is obtained by pulling up a second heddle rod or by individually lifting the warp ends, thus lifting the second set of threads. The weaver starts at one end of the warp and works until the other end is reached, moving the position of the heddle as needed. In order to keep the warps in place, the ground-loom weaver used a 'warp-spacer', consisting of a long rounded bar with slots cut into it at regular intervals (see Petrie 1917: pl. LXVI, nos. 133–6). The length of cloth woven on a ground loom was limited only by the amount of thread spun, as the web or warp thread was simply wrapped around the warp beam and unwound as needed. Thus it was not necessary to have the two sets of pegs set far apart in order to weave long lengths of cloth.

A painting executed on an early Predynastic pottery bowl from a woman's tomb at Badari (Tomb no. 3802; Petrie Museum, UC 9547; see Brunton and Caton-Thompson

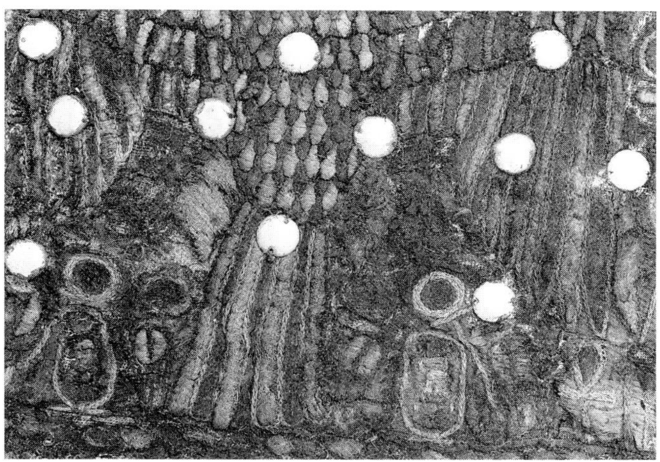

Figure 11.10 Close-up of appliqué and embroidery from a tunic panel (Carter no. 101p; Cairo, JE 62639), tomb of Tutankhamun (KV62).

Various types of braids were in use in ancient Egypt. Sometimes they have small fringes along their longitudinal edges, in which case the braids were placed along the outer edge of a textile. On other occasions, however, there are no fringes and then they are usually found either sewn across the cloth or again down the edges. The size of the braids can vary from about 0.5 to 3 cm. Bands were used in a similar manner to the braids, but they are much wider; one of the best examples of the use of bands can be seen on the embroidered bag-tunic of Tutankhamun mentioned above (Carter no. 367j; Cairo JE 62626). A further example is found on the horse blanket from the tomb of Senenmut (TT71; Lansing and Hayes 1937: 10–11, figs. 14–15). Elaborately decorated bands in red, blue and natural have been sewn down the sides of the garment, both at the front and the back.

Pleating was also used to decorate garments, and the oldest examples seem to be horizontally pleated dresses dating to the Old Kingdom (Riefstahl 1970: 244–9; Hall 1985: 235–45). One of the most elaborate examples (Cairo JE 51513), probably dating to the Middle Kingdom, has three different types of pleating: the first is a simple set of pleats a few centimetres apart; the second is a series of closely set pleats which actually touch each other; and the third is a section of herringbone pleating in which firstly vertical lines were pleated and then secondly, at regular intervals, horizontal lines were pleated to create wide bands with a chevron pattern. Although this example indicates that the Egyptians were capable of complex and decorative forms of pleating, it is still not clear exactly how they achieved this. In some cases, it is likely that the linen was wetted and then pleated by hand so that the pleats set into position as they dried. It is certain, however, that every time a pleated cloth was washed it would have had to be re-pleated, which would have been very time-consuming. Another possibility is that pairs of boards with a series of raised areas, similar to those now used on cigar-making boards, were employed, although it has been suggested that such boards were in fact used for crushing spices (R. Janssen pers. comm.). A third suggestion is that either differences in the spin directions of the weft threads or changes in the weave density have been used to produce the effect of permanent pleating. All of these ideas need to be further explored before any definite answer can be given concerning methods of pleating.

Several surviving linen textiles, dating from the New Kingdom onwards, were painted with designs of varying degrees of complexity. Sometimes these textiles had secular uses, but on other occasions they seem to have been intended for funerary purposes. With regard to secular use, a length of painted cloth was found with a chariot in the tomb of Tutankhamun (Carter 120 [1]; Cairo JE 62746 and 121 [1]; see Littauer and Crouwel 1985: pls. XVIII, XX, XXI); the material has two simple, blue lines painted on it and was placed between the floor of the chariot and the side wall of the frame. In this position the textile would have been subject to hard wear and it is likely that it was necessary to replace it frequently, hence, presumably, the simple method of decoration.

There are numerous examples of textiles which have been elaborately painted in order to represent jewellery (Leiden, RMO AL 48; Raven 1993: 64–5), and such fake jewels were often placed around the wrists of mummies in imitation of bracelets. There are also less elaborately painted examples of cloth bearing the outline of a god, commonly Osiris, which were usually used as shrouds (e.g. the Osiris shroud of Nesitiset, dating to the New Kingdom, see Winlock 1926: 28, fig. 33; Raven 1993: 61). By the Greco-Roman period, more elaborate painted shrouds were in use (Leiden, RMO inv. AMM 8; Vogelsang-Eastwood 1994: 63, fig. 104).

The care of cloth

In ancient times it is likely that textiles and clothes were maintained more carefully than today, holes tended to be mended rather than discarding the garment. Some textiles appear to have been mended three or four times before they were rejected or made into something else. Although there is no direct evidence, it is likely that the care of textiles and clothing was in the hands of women rather than men. It was, for instance, a suitable job for women to carry out while looking after children, as it could be easily interrupted. Sewing, like spinning, is normally a group activity and thus has a social function in bringing people together to make a repetitive task less boring.

One of the few written references to sewing appears in a Nineteenth-Dynasty letter written to Pennesettowy, which was found at the village of Deir el-Medina (O.DM 131; Wente 1990, no. 249). This letter describes the sewing of various garments, including tunics and possibly sleeves, which were then intended to be used to acquire other objects, including some baskets: 'I shall weave two kilts; I shall stitch one tunic; and I shall stitch the pair of sleeves [in exchange for] two baskets and two sieves'.

Sewing equipment

A study of ancient Egyptian sewing shows that a relatively small range of techniques and structural details, such as seams and hems, were used. This situation not only reflects the relatively narrow range of materials then available (a coarse woollen textile requires a different range of seams from a fine silk), but also the ways in which textiles were used in the ancient world. In particular, it illustrates the fact that garments were made in as simple a manner as possible, with drape, rather than tailoring, being emphasised. Before discussing the various types of sewing details it is necessary to look at the range of sewing equipment used in ancient Egypt.

An important point to remember when looking at ancient Egyptian garments is that all sewing tasks were carried out by hand. There were no mechanical devices to help speed up the process or to produce elaborate decorative effects. The basic equipment consisted of a needle, thread and a cutting implement of some kind, although inevitably other items were developed to help with the task at hand.

In addition to fine needles made from pierced fish bones, many bronze, copper and silver needles have been found at sites throughout Egypt; these range in diameter from a few millimetres to a centimetre (e.g. the needles discussed in Petrie 1917: pl. LXV, nos. 65–109; Vogelsang-Eastwood 1994: 35–6). Three different types of metal needles were used in ancient Egypt, each reflecting a different function and quality of stitching when used on cloth. Small, fine, needles pointed at both ends and with one end pierced (New York, MMA 233); needles that were flattened and pierced at one end and sharp at the other end (Leiden, RMO F 1937/1.89) and finally needles that were folded over at one end and sharp at the other (Leiden, RMO F 1937/1.80). In addition to the small needles used for sewing cloth, larger ones were available which were probably used for sewing up the incisions on bodies during the mummification process (e.g. Leiden, RMO AB 145).

Nowadays most people use little finger caps or thimbles while sewing, but the ancient Egyptians used finger guards made out of stone, which were held in place with the other fingers; a Twentieth-Dynasty example is known from Lisht (New York, MMA 11.151.634; Vogelsang-Eastwood 1994: fig. 57).

In order to keep the needles safe, they were often stored in small cases, which have been found at many sites, often still containing needles. They are made from a variety of substances including the hollow leg-bone of a bird, a hollowed-out piece of animal bone or a length of wood. Two such cases – made out of lengths of papyrus rolled up and fastened around the middle with a piece of string – were found in the New Kingdom tomb of the architect Kha and his wife Merit (TT8; Schiaparelli 1927: fig. 62; Donadoni Roveri 1988: fig. 285, Turin inv.suppl. 8379); they contained several copper needles.

Sewing pins were not commonly used, if indeed at all (although cloth is occasionally found with thorns stuck into it). Instead, the cloth was simply held in the hand in order to keep the various elements of a garment together while they were being stitched.

Scissors did not develop until about the first century AD, and there is no evidence to suggest that the ancient Egyptians used them. Similarly, shears did not appear in Egypt until the Ptolemaic period, or possibly even the Roman period (Petrie 1917: 48). Before this date, it is likely that the Egyptians simply tore cloth or used a sharp flint to cut it. Straight cuts were made by simply tearing the cloth, as can be seen in a painting from the Eighteenth-Dynasty tomb of the vizier Rekhmira (TT 100; Davies 1943: pl. LVI). On the other hand, shaped areas, such as neck-lines, were probably cut with a sharp flint, which allows a considerable degree of control to be exerted.

In general, sewing thread was commonly made from two S-spun linen threads which were Z-plyed, although variations such as a three-ply yarn are occasionally found (see van 't Hooft *et al.* 1994: 22–3). The yarn varied in size from fine (0.02–0.3 mm) to coarse (0.6–0.8 mm). Usually the fineness of the sewing thread either matched, or was slightly thicker than, the material being sewed. Although the thread was generally undyed, occasionally a coloured yarn, usually red or blue, can be seen on textiles, especially those dating from the New Kingdom. The blue kerchief found among the textiles in the funerary cache outside the tomb of Tutankhamun was mended with a white thread (New York, Metropolitan 09.184.217–19; Winlock 1916: 238–42 and Winlock 1941).

Sewing techniques

The ancient Egyptians used a narrow range of stitches for functional work such as sewing seams and mending garments. These are the running stitch, overcast stitch, twisted chain stitch and a form of darning similar to that formerly known as 'Swiss darning'. Only a limited range of structural details, such as seams and hems, were used in ancient Egypt. The most common of these were: simple hems, rolled and whipped hems, simple (open) seams, and lap-over seams. Other seams known from the Dynastic period include a form of run-and-fell seam and overcast seams (see Fig. 11.11), but these were rarely used on items of clothing.

When a braid was added to a garment, one of several techniques was used, depending on the nature of the braid and the place where it was to be attached. If it was a fringed braid placed at the lower edge of a garment, it would

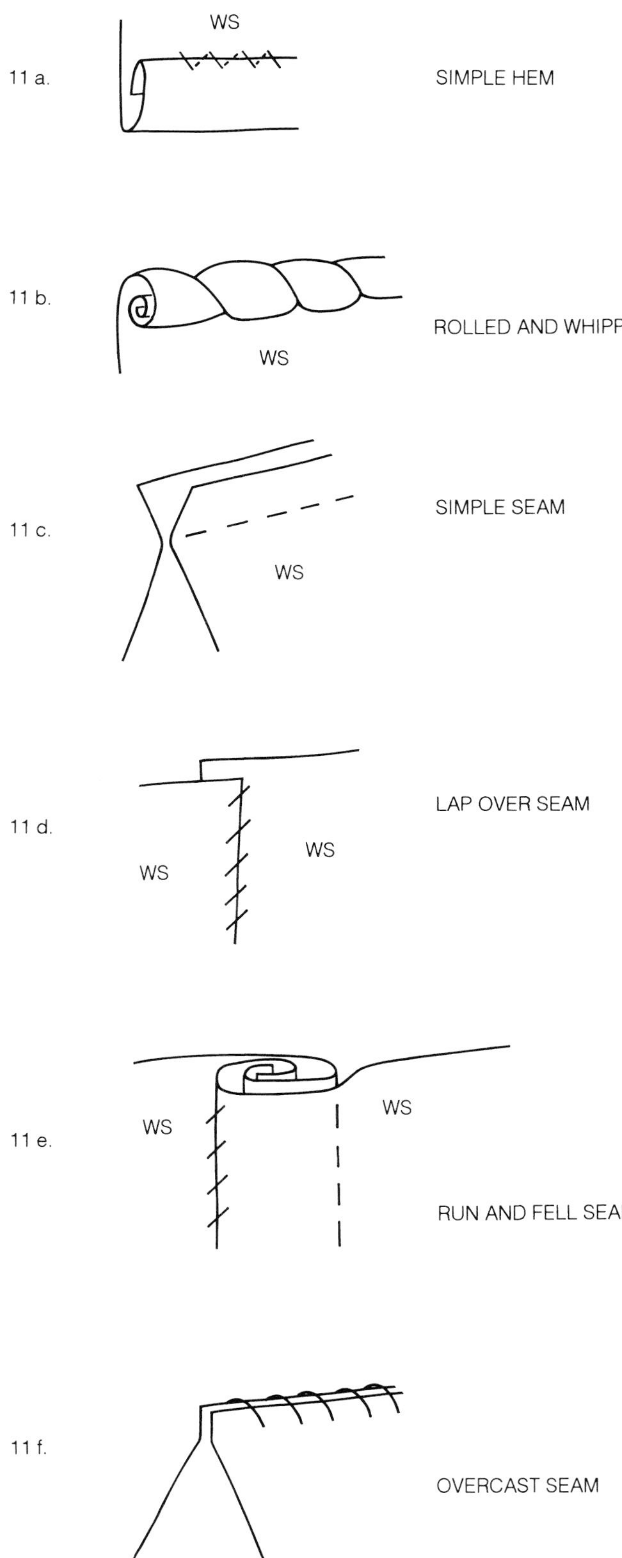

Figure 11.11 Various seams and hems used in Pharaonic Egypt: (a) simple hem; (b) rolled and whipped hem; (c) simple (open) seam; (d) lap-over seam; (e) run and fell seam; (f) over cast seam (WS = wrong side).

normally be secured with one line of overcast stitching (e.g. Carter no. 367i; Cairo JE 62625). On the other hand, two lines of overcast stitching were used to sew on fringeless braids, whether along an edge of a garment or down the middle (e.g. Carter no. 101p; JE 62639).

As today, the quality of sewing in ancient Egypt seems to have depended on the ability of the person actually doing the work. Sometimes, for example, fine cloth was worked with coarse stitching, while a relatively coarse cloth might be neatly sewn. In general, however, the stitching on ancient Egyptian cloth is fine and regular in appearance.

Repairing cloth

There are numerous examples of textiles and garments mended in antiquity. Material has been found which has been stitched on several occasions and it would seem likely that most people took care to keep their clothing in a good state of repair. If, however, an item of clothing became too worn, then it was sometimes made into another, presumably smaller, garment. This process can be seen in a letter written during the reign of Rameses II from the draftsman Pay to his son, Preemheb, who was also a draftsman: 'And you shall be attentive to take this rag of a kilt and this rag of a loincloth in order to re-work the kilt into a red sash and the loincloth into an apron. Don't ignore anything I have told you!' (Černy 1930–5: Nineteenth Dynasty; Wente 1990, no. 218).

As with modern sewing techniques, the repair of ancient textiles can be divided into three basic types, namely, darning, mending and patching. Darning is the method whereby a worn area of cloth is strengthened with lines of stitching before a hole emerges (van 't Hooft *et al.* 1994: 24). The basic darning technique in ancient Egypt consisted of lines of stitching, usually elongated twisted chain stitching being worked over the area. Each line of stitching was isolated, began with a small back stitch and ended with a knot. In most cases it would seem that the area of darning was worked away from the body of the seamstress.

Should a piece of material be torn or a wear hole form, then it is necessary to mend the cloth. Most mending involves holding the two edges of cloth together using one or more lines of stitching. The most common form of ancient mending is that whereby the edges are rolled and then overcast using a whipping stitch. Occasionally more elaborate forms can be found with a double line of stitching, using both a running stitch and a whipped stitch. Another form of 'mending' sometimes encountered amongst ancient cloth is the knotting together of the two edges of the cloth.

Although there are numerous examples of textiles and clothing being either darned or mended, or in some cases both, it is rare to find patched examples. Patching is a method whereby a hole is covered by a second piece of cloth which is then stitched down to the ground material. In most cases, although not all, patched textiles seem to be

Ptolemaic or later in date and this may reflect a Greek or Roman influence.

Many Egyptians were well aware of their appearance and especially the state of their clothes. It is not surprising therefore to find descriptions such as 'this rag of a kilt' or 'shabby loincloth' on Nineteenth-Dynasty ostraca (Černy 1930–35: 19; Wente 1990, no. 218; O.DM 554; Wente 1990, no. 245), or indeed to see the care accorded to many textiles and garments.

The laundry

As an extension to the care taken of textiles and clothing, the laundry played an important role in the life of most Egyptians. Nevertheless, this does not mean that the washerman was held in equal esteem. In the Middle Kingdom text, *The Teaching of Duaf's Son, Khety*, the man who washes the laundry is described as someone to be pitied (although it should be noted that texts of this genre routinely pour scorn on all professions other than that of the scribe):

> And the washerman washes on the shore
> and nearby is the crocodile.
> 'Father, I shall leave the flowing (?) water'
> Says his son and daughter,
> 'for a trade that one can be content in,
> more so than any other trade'
> while his food is mixed with shit.
> There is no part of him clean,
> while he puts himself amongst the skirts of
> a woman who is in her period (?)
> He weeps, spending the day at the washboard
> He is told: 'Dirty Clothes!
> Bring yourself over here', and the (river) edge.
> (Parkinson 1991: 75)

The washerman described in this passage was probably a worker attached to a large estate of some kind. His work was similar to that of the men depicted in several Middle Kingdom reliefs at Beni Hasan (tombs BH2 and 3) and the New Kingdom tomb of Ipuy at Deir el-Medina (TT217; Newberry 1893: pls. XI, XXIX; Davies 1927b: pl. XXVIII; see Fig. 11.12 in this volume). It is likely, however, that the women from smaller establishments also washed the linen of their household.

It is known from a letter dating to the reign of Rameses II that washermen were also assigned to particular households in the Workmen's Village at Deir el-Medina. Various questions are raised in the letter to the scribe Amenemope about the work of one of the village washermen. It would seem that several complaints had been made about the man's inattention to his duties: 'Has the laundryman washed or not? It was only six (?) households that Pharaoh assigned to him. Now see, he has been assigned six households as two days' work, making three households per day' (O.DM 314; Wente 1990: no. 191).

A valuable source of information about the range and amount of work carried out by washermen comes from laundry lists inscribed on ostraca (potsherds or limestone chips). In some cases the lists provide information about the number of garments sent to be washed. In other examples, schematic, but still recognisable garments have been painted onto the sherds (Vogelsang-Eastwood 1992b: 105–11). Various garments can be identified on such sherds, including a loincloth, a tunic and a sash; other items of clothing recorded on the ostraca probably include skirts and kilts.

Judging from the depictions of the washing of cloth on the walls of several tomb-chapels of different dates at Beni Hasan and Deir el-Medina, the basic process appears to have been the same throughout the Middle and New Kingdoms. The first task was to dampen the cloth and then rub it, possibly with a detergent of some kind. During the Dynastic period, the Egyptians were able to use various natural detergents, such as natron (a natural soda), potash and the plant soapwort (*Saponaria officinalis*). The use of natron for washing clothes is incidentally indicated in the letter already quoted above: 'As for Nakhtsobek, I found no natron in his possession although you had given him [some] . . . As soon as you ascertain the [reason for the] delay, they shall procure natron for the (?) cloth' (O.DM 314; Wente 1990: no. 191).

Once the cloth had been rubbed with a detergent it was beaten with sticks or wooden clubs on a stone or a wooden base of some kind. It was then washed in water, rinsed and wrangled. The last task is depicted at Beni Hasan (BH3), where one end of the cloth is shown to have been wrapped around a post while the other was firmly twisted (Newberry 1893, pl. XXIX). The damp cloth was then left to dry in the sun.

The various lengths of cloth were laid flat on the ground and then held in place around the outer edges with stones.

Figure 11.12 A laundry scene depicted in the Middle Kingdom tomb of Khnumhotep at Beni Hasan (BH3).

The drying of cloth is portrayed in a scene in the Twelfth-Dynasty tomb of Sarenput I at Aswan (Müller 1940: Abb.14; Vogelsang-Eastwood 1994: 39, fig. 63). Drying items in this way would also have had the effect of sun-bleaching the various lengths of material. Once the cloth was dry, it could be folded and then stored until needed.

Textile marks

Most Egyptian textiles bear no markings, although a significant number of marked examples have been discovered. The function of such marks is not always clear, and we must look to the size, appearance and positioning of such marks to gain an understanding of their purpose.

Some marks are hieroglyphic or hieratic inscriptions, while others are more abstract in form; almost all were placed in a corner of the material where they would have been unobtrusive but easy to check (e.g. Eastwood 1985: 199, fig. 10.11). It would have been hard to remove such marks without leaving some traces of their original presence. The function of the various marks can be divided into three groups: weaver's/maker's marks; owner's marks and quality marks.

The idea of a maker's mark is quite common and can be found on many ancient objects. In the case of textiles, the mark is woven with an extra, thicker yarn, and is usually made up of a series of lines which travel no more than a few centimetres into the cloth before returning. From a distance of a metre or so the marks cannot normally be seen. The idea that such marks may come from a weaving atelier is perhaps supported by the fact that several pieces of cloth bearing the same mark, but of different qualities, were found at the Workmen's Village at Amarna (Eastwood 1985: 199).

Large quantities of Dynastic-period cloth have been found bearing the mark/name of the owner. Some royal cloth even has the regnal year in which the material was produced. It is likely that this was done not only to keep a check on the amount and quality of cloth within an establishment, but also in order to identify the owner when the cloth was sent to be laundered. Sometimes names were painted in black ink, which did not easily wash out, as in the case of the marks on textiles found in the burial of the so-called slain soldiers of Mentuhotep II at Deir el-Bahari (Winlock 1945: 25–32, pls. XVI–XX). In other cases, the mark was either embroidered or woven into the cloth. For example, a tunic wrapped around the body of Seti II bore the name of Merenptah, a son of Rameses II, embroidered in red and blue thread (Smith 1912: 74–5, diag. 16). Similarly, several of the loincloths from the Eighteenth-Dynasty tomb of Kha at Deir el-Medina (TT8) were embroidered with his name, while other items were inscribed with his name in ink (Schiaparelli 1927: fig. 62). Weavers' marks, inscribed in black ink, were also found on thirty of the seventy-six lengths of cloth recorded from the Eighteenth-Dynasty tomb of Ramose and Hatnefer (the parents of Senenmut) in the Sheikh Abd el-Gurna region of western Thebes (Lansing and Hayes 1937: 26; Porter and Moss 1964: 669); one of these marks was a private name (Boki), while the rest referred to the state or temple stores.

A number of textiles have distinctive patterns woven or embroidered into cloth with a blue or red thread (Leiden, RMO AU 38e; Vogelsang-Eastwood 1994: 41, fig. 66). Although located unobtrusively near the corner of the cloth, the colours of these marks make them considerably more striking than the weavers' marks described above. It is possible that such marks were used on large areas of cloth such as bedding or curtains, rather than on clothing where they would have been more apparent.

The last group of marks to be mentioned are the so-called 'quality marks' which are usually added to the corner of a piece of cloth with black ink (Vogelsang-Eastwood 1994: 41, fig. 67; and see Fig. 11.13). Normally there are two marks, one set above the other. It is likely that the uppermost symbol represents the institute which owned the cloth, perhaps a temple, while the lower mark may indicate the quality of the cloth.

Folding and storage of cloth

The study of how cloth was folded in ancient Egypt is of interest because virtually every country has developed its own method of folding material and clothing. The different styles of folding are related to the range of material used, the types of garments worn, and the methods of textile storage. In countries where large linen cupboards are the main form of storage, cloth is often folded so that there is a neat fold line with all the ends and sides of the material hidden. On the other hand, in places where cloth is stored

Figure 11.13 Various 'quality marks' inscribed on Egyptian textiles of the Dynastic period, all five of which are in the Egyptian Museum, Cairo.

in baskets, it is more appropriate to have a small, flat surface area, in order to store greater quantities.

Several different methods of storing cloth are known to have been used in Pharaonic Egypt. The method used depended not only on the available facilities but also on the size and type of cloth in question. In the wall-paintings of the Eighteenth-Dynasty tomb of Rekhmira (TT100), cloth is depicted in the form of flat lengths of material, long lengths and bundles, as well as having been packed in large sacks and boxes (Davies 1943: pls. XXX, XXXII, LVI, LVII).

Folded cloth was also placed in lidded baskets, as was the case with some of the textiles found in the New Kingdom tomb of Kha and his wife Merit (TT8; Schiaparelli 1927: fig. 80). In more elaborate circumstances, cloth was sometimes stored in boxes. In the Old Kingdom *mastaba* of Mereruka at Saqqara, there are several painted relief scenes showing servants carrying lengths of cloth and chests containing cloth (Duell 1938: pl. 72). Sometimes special linen chests were made, usually having a gabled form with a pair of knobs at one end (Lansing and Hayes 1937: 24, fig. 37). A rope or string could be looped around the knobs in order to fasten the chest securely. Several such linen chests were found in the tomb of Tutankhamun, some of them including lists on the lids which described the contents. According to the inscription on the lid, one chest (Cairo JE61500B) originally contained:

The box of *kdt*-wood . . .
What is in it belonging to the House-of-Repelling-the-Bowman:

Royal linen prepared as *mk*, various *swḥ*-garments 2

Royal linen prepared as *mk*, *ʾıdg3*-garments 10

Royal linen prepared as *mk*, long *sd*-garments 20

Royal linen prepared as *mk*, long shirts 7?

Total of various choice linen 39?

It should also be noted that fold marks in a garment could indicate status; thus, the Thirteenth-Dynasty group statue of Satsobek and her two sons (Leiden, RMO AST 47) includes the depiction of deep fold lines on the kilt of one the sons, while his immaculately pressed attire is used to indicate wealth and status.

The uses of textiles

The uses of cloth in ancient Egypt may be divided as follows: 'clothing'; 'household'; 'outside'; 'economic'; 'ritual' and 'funerary'.

Clothing

The basic form of Egyptian clothing can be divided into two types: wrap-arounds and cut-to-shapes. Wrap-around garments consist of a length of cloth wrapped around the body in various ways; this group includes kilts, skirts, cloaks, shawls and most dresses. Cut-to-shape garments tend to be simple triangles or rectangles, sewn down some or all of the edges and fastened with ties; these garments include loincloths, tunics, and one particular type of dress. There is no evidence to suggest that the garments were normally closely tailored to fit individual figures. Similarly, no garments from the Dynastic period have been recorded with pads, darts or complex shaping, elements which are common to modern clothing.

In ancient Egypt – as in many other cultures – the types of clothes worn by individuals reflect their social status. In general, the more clothes a person wears, the higher is his or her social position. Differences in rank were also indicated more by the quality of the cloth worn than by other factors, such as the way in which a garment was constructed. Loincloths and tunics worn by workmen tended to be made of a strong and solid cloth (Vogelsang-Eastwood 1993: 10–12), while those belonging to a pharaoh such as Tutankhamun were made from a fine, almost silk-like, linen (Carter no. 43g; JE 29/3/34/10a–b; thread count of 112 warps and 32 wefts per centimetre). The basic construction of all of these garments, however, was similar regardless of status. Unlike modern garments, ancient Egyptian clothes were characterised by few variations in the way that they were made, and forms tended to remain the same over long periods. Changes more commonly occurred firstly in the way that garments were draped around the body and secondly in terms of combinations of different garment types.

Loincloths, kilts, skirts, aprons, sashes and 'Archaic wrap-arounds'

Loincloths were worn by most of the population (male and female) for virtually the entire Dynastic period. The loincloth is a simple garment, part of which is wrapped around the waist while the rest is drawn between the legs (Vogelsang-Eastwood 1993: 10–31; see Fig. 11.14); it is, however, a versatile garment which could be worn by itself, either open or closed at the front; tied at the top with a sash or worn under other garments. One of the more unusual garments in the ancient Egyptian's wardrobe was the leather loincloth, which seems be one of the few types of garments which were introduced into Egypt from Nubia, rather than *vice versa*. It was most popular during the New Kingdom and was only worn by men, particularly soldiers, sailors and servants. One surviving example was found in a painted box bearing the name of Maiherpri (Boston, MFA 03.1035; Carter 1903: 46–7; see Fig. 11.15). There were also depictions in the tombs of pharaohs and high court officials, showing loincloths being worn by servants and officials (e.g. Davies 1930: pl. XVI).

One separate item worn by men, either by itself or under another garment such as a kilt (Vogelsang-Eastwood 1993: 32–52), was the apron. It was worn from at least the Old Kingdom onwards, and it consisted of one or more pieces of

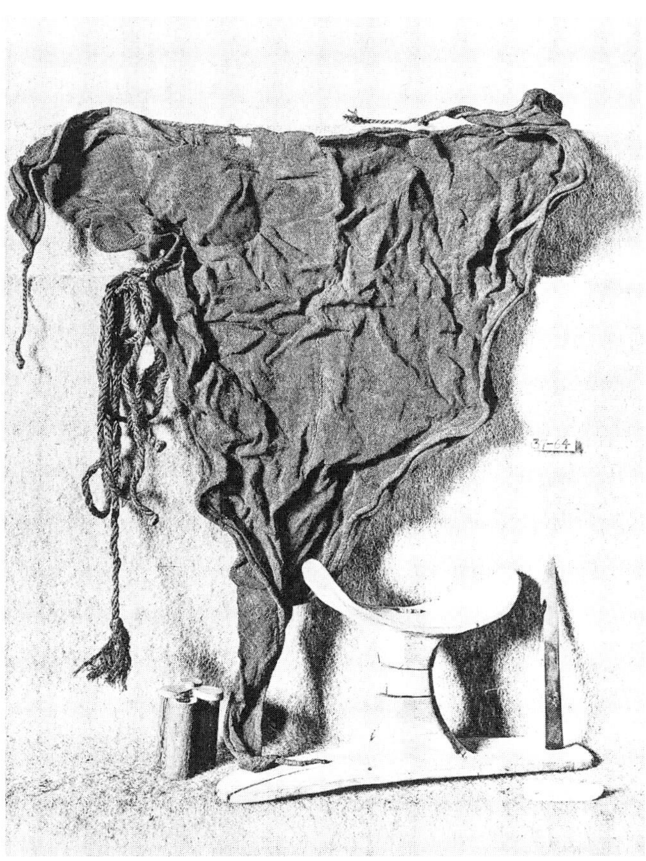

Figure 11.14 A linen loincloth from a 'rectangular gable-topped coffin' at Deir el-Medina.

cloth attached to a belt, sash or band which is fastened around the waist. In general, the apron panel only covers the genital region. Aprons can be simple triangular shapes or elaborately ornate pleated items which extend from the waist to the ankles. Two such are known from the tomb of Tutankhamun, one being made of beadwork (Carter no. 269c (3) [i]) and the other of metal inlaid with glass or gemstones (Carter no. 256j, JE 60685).

Representations of kilts and skirts can be found dating back to prehistoric times. A kilt is a wrap-around garment worn by men, which covers part or all of the lower half of the body (Vogelsang-Eastwood 1993: 53–71). A skirt is a similar garment, but is worn by women. These garments can vary considerably in both size and form. In some cases they are simple items which only covered the hips, but more extreme forms of kilts and skirts could cover all the way from the chest to the ankles. Although the basic construction of kilts and skirts was similar, in general kilts were more elaborate than skirts. Sometimes the men's short kilt was pleated, as portrayed in the painted reliefs of the Fifth-Dynasty *mastaba* of Khafkhufu at Giza (Simpson 1978: fig. 29), and sometimes the pleating extended from half-way around the front to the middle of the back, as depicted in the Sixth-Dynasty *mastaba* of Idut at Saqqara (Macramallah 1935: pl. XX).

In addition to the simple kilts described above there is a second form of kilt known as a sash-kilt, which became fashionable in the New Kingdom. It was worn over other garments, notably the tunic (Vogelsang-Eastwood 1993: 65–71). There were two basic methods of wrapping the sash-kilt: the first method involves a length of cloth which is wrapped around the hips once and then tied with a simple half-knot at the front, as illustrated in the Eighteenth-Dynasty tomb-chapel of Ramose at Thebes (TT55; Davies 1941:

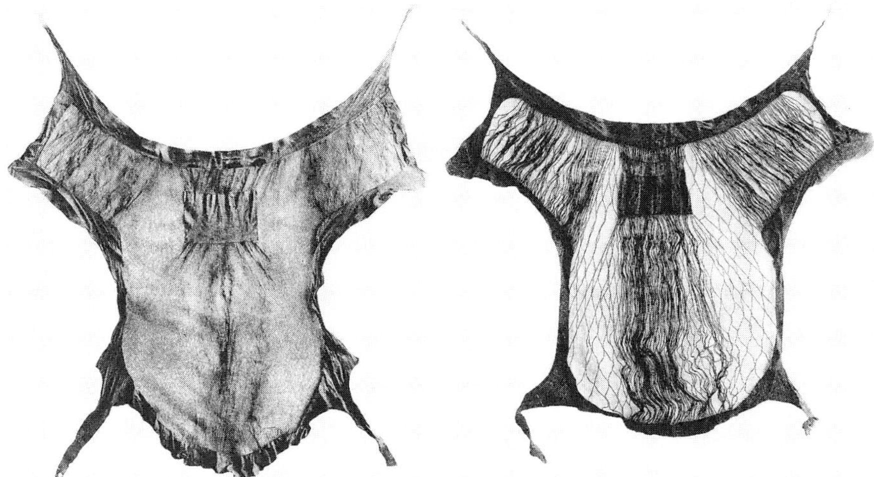

Figure 11.15 Leather loincloths from a New Kingdom box bearing the name of Maiherpri. The cloth on the left is now in the collection of the Museum of Fine Arts, Boston (acc. no. 03.1035), but the present location of the other is unknown.

pl. XXXII); the ends are then allowed to hang decoratively down the front. In the second method, one end of the sash is allowed to hang down from the waist to just above the knees, as in the statuette of Nebnefer (temp. Ramesses II, current location unknown; Wild 1979: pl. 33), while the rest of the cloth is wrapped around the hips (from left to right) and then tucked in at the top.

Sashes are long, narrow lengths of cloth which were worn around the waist. They were often used to secure another garment, such as a kilt or skirt (Vogelsang-Eastwood 1993: 72–87). They can be made of rope (Carnarvon and Carter 1912: pl. LXIX/1), a plain length of cloth (Leiden, RMO Cat. no. 260) or with a fringe for decoration (Carter no. 101m). Sashes decorated with tapestry-weave designs were found in the tomb of Tutankhamun (Carter nos. 21ff, Cairo JE 62645; 21gg, JE 62646). A more elaborately made sash is the so-called 'girdle' of Rameses III (see p. 276). Another form of sash, comprising a back panel with four red streamers, was found in the tomb of Tutankhamun (KV62) (Carter no. 100f, JE 62647).

The 'Archaic wrap-around' is one of the oldest Egyptian clothing types of the Dynastic period. It was worn in a similar manner by both men and women, although in general the female version was much longer than that of men (Vogelsang-Eastwood 1993: 88–94). The effect of an Archaic wrap-around can be recreated using a single rectangle of cloth. The top corner of the material is draped over the left shoulder. The cloth is then passed one or more times around the body and under the arms ending near the left arm-pit. The two top corners are tied together on the left shoulder, giving the impression of a shoulder strap. The garment was then sometimes kept in place with a sash.

Dresses

The dress is a garment specifically worn by women; it generally fits closely to the upper part of the body and has either a flowing or a tightly fitting skirt (Vogelsang-Eastwood 1993: 95–129). It was the most common form of female clothing throughout the Dynastic period and was worn by all women regardless of their social position. There were three basic dress types: wrap-around dresses, V-necked dresses and beaded dresses.

Wrap-around dresses were made out of long lengths of cloth and were wrapped around the body in various ways to produce different effects. They can be divided into two types: simple and complex. The simple wrap-around dress – depicted in Egyptian art from the Old Kingdom onwards – was made out of a length of cloth wrapped between one and three times around the body, depending upon the amount of cloth available. The end of the cloth was tucked in at the top (see depictions in the Eighteenth-Dynasty tomb of Rekhmira at Thebes; Davies 1943: pl. LXIV) and it could be worn either with or without shoulder straps.

Complex wrap-around dresses appeared during the New Kingdom; they could be made out of one or two lengths of cloth, and their principal forms are portrayed on a New Kingdom stele in the British Musem (EA36; Davies 1926: pl. XII, 1941: pl. XI). They were knotted, tucked in or secured in place with a sash, or a with a combination of these fastening methods. On the basis of surviving examples and the study of representations, it would appear that there are two forms of V-necked dress: sleeveless and sleeved.

The sleeveless form has a deep V-neckline and two examples are known. One was found spread over the mummy of a woman (Reisner 1942: 451–2, pl. 42; Roth 1988: 76–7; see Fig. 11.16) and was described by the excavator, George Reisner (1942: 452), as 'a large sheet of linen . . . laid over the body, looking like a tunic with a V-shaped neck, leaving arms and the lower part of the legs exposed'. Unfortunately this example was destroyed during the examination of the mummy, therefore it is not certain how the garment was made. A second example was found more recently at Saqqara (Munro 1983: 102–3) but it was in an extremely poor condition, thus again preventing any analysis of construction methods.

The V-necked dress with sleeves was a cut-to-shape,

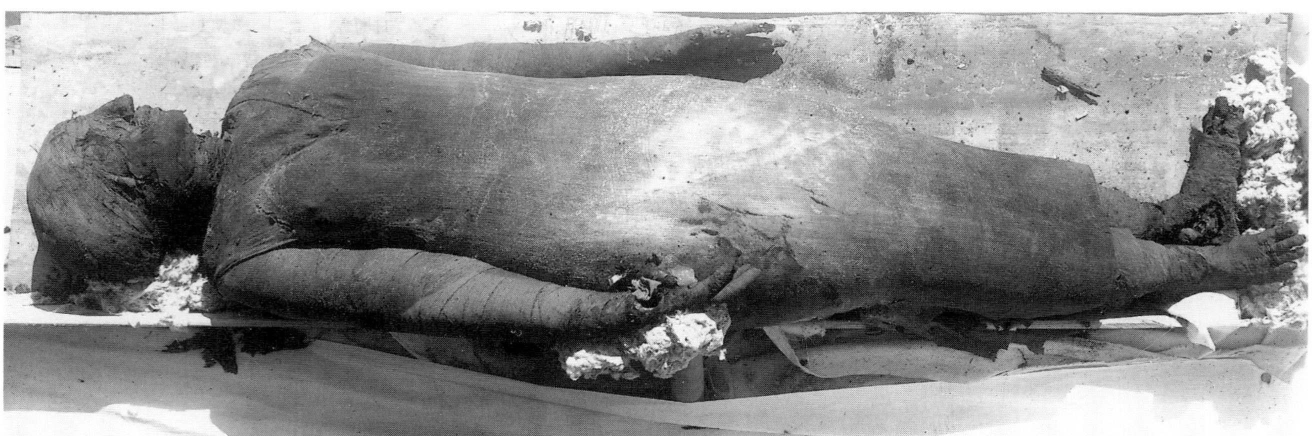

Figure 11.16 Mummy wearing a V-necked dress of the sleeveless type (now destroyed).

usually pleated garment (Riefstahl 1970; Landi and Hall 1979; Hall 1982; Vogelsang-Eastwood 1993: 115–25; see Fig. 11.17). At least fifteen ancient Egyptian examples have been excavated, ranging in date from the Fifth to the Eleventh Dynasty and dying out by *c.* 2000 BC.

Beaded net-dresses were made out of beads strung together in geometric patterns, usually diamonds. So far only two have been identified. The first was found in Mastaba G7440Z at Giza and probably dates to the Fourth Dynasty (Boston MFA 27.1548; Jick 1988) and the second was found in a Fifth-Dynasty tomb at Qau (tomb 978; Petrie Museum UC 17743; Hall 1986: 64–5). The Qau example was made up of a series of beads and the breasts were covered and accentuated by two small caps made out of blue faience with nipples in black (see also Kamal 1901: 34, 38; Brunton 1927: I, 64).

Tunics, shawls and cloaks

The tunic or bag-tunic (*mss*) was made up of a long rectangle of cloth folded in half and sewn up the sides (Janssen 1975: 260; Hall 1981; Vogelsang-Eastwood 1993: 130–54; see Fig. 11.18). There are two forms. The full-length tunic, covering the body from the shoulders to the calves or ankles, was worn by both men and women. The half tunic, stretching from the shoulders to the buttocks (or, less frequently, the knees) was only worn by men. Both the half and full-length tunics were worn by themselves or with other garments.

Occasionally tunics are found with sleeves, which were constructed by two basic methods. In the first method, the sleeve is made out of a single length of cloth which narrows towards the wrist, as in the case of two examples from the Eighteenth-Dynasty Workmen's Village at Amarna (nos. 2674 and 1560 in the unpublished catalogue of textiles from the village; see also Hall 1980: 29). The second form of sleeve is again shaped, but this time there is a flat seam placed at the centre of the back of the sleeve (Vogelsang-Eastwood 1993: 137, fig. 8/4).

Most surviving tunics are plain, but various decorative elements are known to have been used. The basic forms of

Figure 11.17 Old Kingdom V-necked dress with sleeves, from Asyut (Louvre E 12026).

Figure 11.18 Long tunic from the New Kingdom tomb of Kha at Deir el-Medina (TT8; Turin, Museo Egizio, Inv. suppl. 8530).

decoration are: fringing along the bottom edge (Petrie Museum UC 28616Ci and Brussels E.6205), the use of coloured bands woven into the cloth along the selvedges and transverse edges (Leiden, RMO E1), vertical or horizontal bands woven into the garment (Carter no. 261a, Cairo JE 62706; Carter no. 50j, JE 62757), and the use of coloured bands sewn onto the garment along all of the edges of the garment and around the neckline (Carter no. 367i, JE 62626; see also Schiaparelli 1927, fig. 69). In addition, beadwork, sequins of gold and faience, applied pattern bands, and embroidery were sometimes used to decorate tunics (see p. 279ff., decorative techniques).

Shawls and cloaks are outer garments worn by both men and women (Vogelsang-Eastwood 1993: 155–68); they normally consisted of a square or rectangular piece of cloth. Shawls only covered the upper part of the body, while cloaks were much larger and covered most if not all of the body. Shawls were worn over the shoulders and allowed to hang down the back. Two basic types of cloaks are known to have been worn in ancient Egypt. The first was a simple length of cloth wrapped around the body, one example being a protodynastic figurine of a woman (Ashmolean E.326; Quibell 1900: I, pl. IX). The second form was made from a length of cloth with two ties knotted on one shoulder (Davies 1900: I, pl. XVII; Davies 1948: pl. XXVI; see Fig. 11.19).

Leggings
There are three pairs of leggings in the Egyptian Museum, Cairo (nos. 13/1/26/19 and 13/1/26/18). They are made from a long rectangle of cloth folded in half and sewn (overlap seam) down the back, each having a single, very long tie knotted to the front top; this tie was probably wrapped several times around the leg. At the bottom, and set off-centre, there is a V-shaped notch cut out of the material. To date no representations of Egyptians wearing these garments are known. In the late Eighteenth-Dynasty tomb of Ay (KV23), however, there is a depiction of a table bearing various items, including gold collars, gloves and what have been described as 'collars?' (Davies 1908: pls. XXX–XXXI) although they may actually have been leggings.

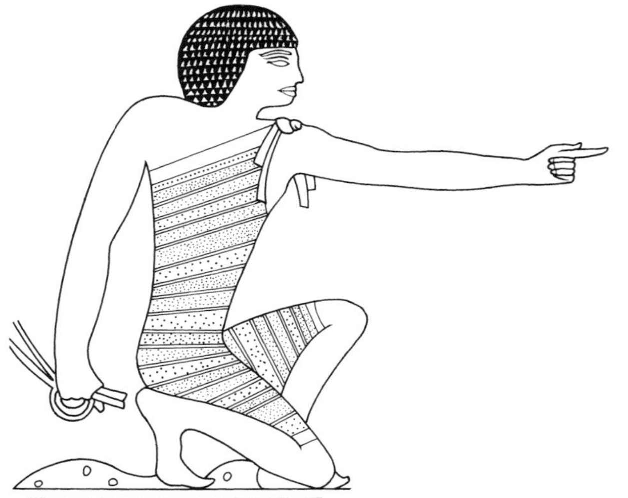

Figure 11.19 Detail from a painted wall-relief in the Old Kingdom mastaba *of Ptahhotep and Akhethotep at Saqqara, showing a hunter wearing a knotted cloak.*

Kerchiefs
A kerchief is a piece of cloth which covers part or all of the head (Vogelsang-Eastwood 1993: 169–78). In general it is made out of a single piece of cloth, usually rectangular, kept in place with a headband of some kind or tied with a piece of string at the back of the nape (e.g. Copenhagen, Ny Carlsberg Glyptotek AE IN 670; Davies 1936: II, pl. XCVII). More elaborate versions, worn by kings and princes (the *khat* headdress), were made out of two semicircular pieces of cloth sewn together (e.g. Winlock 1916; New York, MMA 09–184.217–219; Carter no. 46i, 29/3/34/30a-d). A separate tie or tape was sewn to the centre-top of the semicircle of cloth which was used to fasten the garment to the head. Several examples of these kerchiefs were recorded from the tomb of Tutankhamun (KV62).

Combinations of different garments
The ancient Egyptians used various combinations of the garments described above. The attire of both sexes varies chronologically. Men in the Old Kingdom might wear some combination of loincloths, short wrap-around kilts, long narrow aprons, sashes and long cloaks. In the Middle Kingdom they often wore loincloths, wrap-around kilts of various lengths, long, narrow aprons and triangular aprons, sashes, short shawls and long cloaks might be worn. New Kingdom male attire included loincloths, wrap-around kilts of various lengths (sometimes two worn together), sash-kilts, triangular aprons, tunics, sashes, knotted and wrap-around cloaks of various kinds.

Women in the Old Kingdom wore loincloths, skirts of various lengths, wrap-around dresses (usually simple forms), V-necked dresses, sashes and long cloaks. In the Middle Kingdom they often wore loincloths, skirts of various lengths, wrap-around dresses (usually simple forms), V-necked dresses, sashes and long cloaks. Their New Kingdom wardrobe comprised loincloths, skirts of various lengths, wrap-around dresses (both simple and complex forms), sashes, tunics and long cloaks.

Household uses

Textiles were very widely used in ancient Egypt, and constituted an important part of Egyptian daily life. Perhaps the most obvious and familiar use of cloth was within the household. Although it may be presumed that material was used for curtaining and wall-hangings, it is difficult to find actual evidence. Other household uses ranged from cushions, curtains and bedding to more prosaic items such as spice bags and lamp wicks. Although it is likely that the ancient Egyptians used curtains and wall-coverings, especially on the inside of the buildings, no examples or depictions of such items have yet been found.

Towels

One of the more familiar, modern uses of textiles is that of towels made in order to dry either an object or a person. There are numerous examples of ancient textiles with all-over patterns of looping, similar to modern terry-towelling. Several such cloths were found in the mass-burial of sixty soldiers at Deir el-Bahari (Winlock 1945: 32), and two other textiles of this type were found in an Eleventh-Dynasty tomb at the same site (tomb no. DB813; Winlock 1945: 32; Riefstahl 1944: 16–17, fig. 19). The textiles have a pattern of chevrons, zig-zags and bands of different widths.

Cushions

Ancient Egyptian representations include depictions of a variety of cushions. There were at least four different ways of using them: long, lounging cushions for which a textile now in the Victoria and Albert Museum may have been a cover (VA T251.1921; Davies 1903: I, pl. VII), chair cushions (e.g. the tomb of Huya at Amarna, EA1; Davies 1905: pl. IV), stool/chair cushions (as depicted in the Theban tomb of User, TT260; Greenlees 1923: 131, pl. XXI) and footstool cushions (e.g. the tomb of Huya; Davies 1905: pl. IV). A footstool was found in the Eighteenth-Dynasty tomb of Yuya and Tuyu (KV46; Cairo CG3675); it is made from two roughly rectangular pieces of linen tightly packed with feathers. The size and solidity of this cushion suggests that it was used as a footstool of some kind. A possible long cushion or pillow, made out of red leather and stuffed with bulrush down, was found in the Eighteenth-Dynasty tomb of Ramose and Hatnefer at Thebes (Lansing and Hayes 1937: 16; Porter and Moss 1964: 669).

Beds

Ancient Egyptian beds were made up of rectangular frames mounted on four legs. The base was made from an interlacing structure of rope, sometimes woven into intricate patterns. On top of this matting there was a length of cloth serving as a mattress which had a deep pile made from numerous closely-set loops as in the bed from the tomb of Kha (TT8; Schiaparelli 1927: II, fig. 105; see Fig. 11.20). Over the piled cloth were placed more lengths of material to act as covers or sheets. It is likely that in winter-time additional layers were used, and possibly a woollen blanket. Instead of a pillow a headrest, usually made from wood, was placed at the head of the bed.

More elaborate beds might be surrounded by canopies. A bed canopy was placed inside the tomb of Hetepheres, mother of the Fourth-Dynasty ruler Khufu (Reisner and Smith 1955: 23–7). It measures about 3.20 metres in length, 2.50 metres in width and 2.20 metres in height. It was decorated with gold, and around the inside of the top beams there are small copper hooks which may well have held the drapes covering the top of the canopy and hanging down its sides. Unfortunately, they have not survived, although they may originally have been placed in a long box which was found in the queen's tomb.

Figure 11.20 Bedding from the tomb of Kha (TT8) at Deir el-Medina (Turin, Museo Egizio, Inv. Suppl. 8629–36).

Bags

As with modern bags, the size, range and functions of ancient Egyptian bags were extensive. They were used for carrying spices, as well as small amounts of grain, and were made from lengths of cloth folded in half and sewn down the sides (Leiden, RMO AU 41). Cloth sacks for carrying cumbersome or numerous objects were also in use, judging from depictions in a number of tomb-paintings, such as those in the Eighteenth-Dynasty tomb of Neferhotep (TT 49; Davies 1933: pl. XVIII).

Lamp wicks

The Egyptian hieroglyph for a lamp wick, (Gardiner 1957, sign type V2) clearly shows the basic form of the ancient wick, which was made by twisting a length of cloth or fibres, and then allowing the length to twist back on itself (Eastwood 1985: 202, fig. 10/15). The wick was then allowed to float in the lamp oil.

Seals

The use of cloth as part of a seal has a long tradition in Egypt. Seals were not only used within tombs to fasten and secure doors, but they were also used inside houses, palaces and temples to secure workshops and more particularly storerooms. In addition, they were used on commodities such as jars, with the material placed over the opening of the jar before dropping a plug of clay in place (e.g. Leiden RMO. F.1957/11.4). A second length of cloth was sometimes placed over the clay plug. Occasionally a blob of clay was placed at the ends and then an impression of the owner's mark was made by pressing a seal into the damp clay.

Uses outside the home

The uses of textiles outside the home ranged from items such as the cloths used to cover an object to sacks for the transportation of grain. One of the most widely used methods of extracting oils and juices was to strain the liquid through a piece of cloth. Such strainers would have been strong but flexible, and depictions of the production of wine indicate that two forms of cloth wine strainers were used (see Chapter 23, this volume). One end of the bag could be tied to a fixed support, while the other was fastened to a pole, which was then twisted by several men as depicted in the tomb-chapel of Bakt III at Beni Hasan (BH15; Newberry 1893: pl. VI). In the second method, both ends of the bag were tied to poles and two groups of workmen wrung the bag by turning the poles in opposite directions as in the scene portrayed in the tomb-chapel of Amenemhat at Beni Hasan (BH2; Newberry 1893: pl. XII; see Fig. 11.21).

Another use for cloth strainers was in the production of oils (see Chapter 17, this volume). There are several New Kingdom and later tomb-reliefs which show the production of perfume oils. In most cases the seeds or flowers are placed in a cloth bag. These bags are not as large as those used for wine-making, but they were wrung in the same way as wine bags. A fragment of relief dating to the Ptolemaic period (Turin 1673) depicts the extraction of lily essence by this means.

Textiles were also used in the equipping of animals and the vehicles drawn by them. Donkeys were one of the main pack animals of the ancient world and to protect their backs the animals were covered in a cloth. Back cloths of this type have been depicted in numerous tomb-chapels of the New Kingdom, although no actual examples of this date have been found. A saddle cloth of the first century BC was found at the Red Sea coastal site of Quseir el-Qadim (Vogelsang-Eastwood 1990: 197). It was made from numerous layers of small fragments of cloth sandwiched between two layers of coarse material. Cloths made in an identical manner are in use for donkeys in rural Egypt today and it is probable that the back cloths of the Dynastic period were made in the same way. Occasionally more valuable animals, such as cows and bulls, are shown wearing a cloth covering on their backs as in the Sixth-Dynasty tomb of Isi at Deir el-Gabrawi (Davies 1902: pl. XIX). In such cases it would seem that these blankets were designed to stress the animals' importance, rather than having a more practical function as in the case of the cloths described above. Another form of animal trapping are the blankets worn by horses during the New Kingdom. The remains of such a horse blanket (housing) dating from the New Kingdom were found in association with the mummified horse buried in front of the tomb of Senenmut at Thebes (TT71; Lansing and Hayes 1937: figs. 14–15). A large piece of cloth, with wide bands sewn onto it, was used. Elaborate versions of this type of cloth can be seen in representations of Tutankhamun and Rameses II, riding their chariots into war. Such textiles are also depicted on the hunting chest of Tutankhamun (Carter no. 21; Cairo JE 61467). It is also probable that another textile from the tomb of Tutankhamun (Carter no. 333; JE 61992e) was also part of a horse blanket. There is also a depiction of a horse blanket in the Eighteenth-Dynasty tomb-chapel of Kenamun at Thebes (TT93; Davies 1930: pl. XXII).

Figure 11.21 Detail from a wall-painting in the Middle Kingdom tomb of Amenemhat at Beni Hasan (BH2), showing the use of a cloth grape-juice strainer.

Another use for textiles in relation to chariots is that of coverings for the floor of the vehicle itself, upon which the occupants could stand. Several textiles have been found in the tomb of Tutankhamun (associated with chariots nos. 120 and 122). One cloth is covered with a dense layer of loops, and it is likely that they were used as a springy layer, cushioning some of the bouncing movement of the chariots.

Cloth was also used on ancient Egyptian boats, primarily for sails and awnings but probably also for such purposes as coverings over merchandise, although at present there is little information about the latter more minor uses. Most information about Egyptian sails derives from funerary models and various representations of boats in tomb-paintings. In most cases the sails are shown as large sheets of cloth, one of which was recently found re-used as a set of mummy-wrappings when a mummy was unwrapped in the Musée des Beaux Arts, Lyon (Goyon and Josset 1988: 129–32). The bandages were removed and laid out, and by matching various structural details (seams and hems) it was discovered that the cloth originally came from a shaped sail. The great wooden boat found in a pit near the pyramid of Khufu (see section on boat-building in Chapter 15, this volume) included fourteen poles which were fitted into holes along the sides of the boat forward of the cabin (Landström 1974: 34, Abb.90). These poles were originally used to hold up a large awning, presumably made of cloth, under which the king and his entourage could have sat.

Although there are several references in Egyptian texts and representations to the use of cloth or matting tents, no tents appear to have survived or have been recognised as such. Tents were mainly used by the court or by soldiers while on the move. Military tents (including a possible rolled-up example) are depicted on fragments of relief from the late Eighteenth-Dynasty tomb of Horemheb at Saqqara (Martin 1989: 37–8, 44 and pls. 28, 29 and 35), and they also feature in the depictions of the Battle of Qadesh in several of the temples of Rameses II (Wreszinski 1923–42: II, no. 92a). The use of tents by the New Kingdom court is indicated on one of the boundary stelae (stele F) at Amarna, where there is a reference to a tent made of matting (Davies 1908: 32). In addition, there is a brief literary reference to couriers on the move who used tents: 'be his home of cloth or brick', in the Middle Kingdom work *Satire of the Trades* (see Lichtheim 1973: 188).

Flags played an important part in the decoration of temples and palaces in ancient Egypt. They were used both on the outside of the building and around internal courtyards. For example, in a depiction of one of the palaces at Amarna, flags are shown in such a courtyard (Davies 1903: I, pl. XXXI). Similarly, there are numerous depictions of New Kingdom temples which have two sets of flags set against the outer pylons (Davies 1903: I, pl. XXVII). Rameses II describes the erection of similar flagpoles during the redesigning and extension of the eastern part of the Temple of Amun at Karnak: 'very great flagstaffs, I erected them in the noble courtyard in front of his temple' (Spencer 1984: 10).

The use of decorated cloth for identification purposes by military forces is well-known from various historical sources and is still practised. Each section of the ancient Egyptian army used standards as a means of identification, and they are usually portrayed as plaques with pairs of streamers placed beneath (Davies 1903: I, pl. XV).

'Economic' functions

The ancient Egyptians did not have coinage until the end of the Dynastic period, therefore most transactions were based on a bartering system in which the rough value of most objects was known to both seller and purchaser. Surpluses of any goods were usually bartered in order to make up any deficiencies, and cloth and made-up garments played an important role within this bartering system. All wages in ancient Egypt were paid in kind, frequently in foodstuffs, but also in metalwares, basketry or textiles (although it is not clear whether these goods should be regarded as wages or as rations, see Janssen 1975: 455ff; Kemp 1989: 237). There are various direct references to garments being given as wages. Papyrus Turin 1881 records seventy-eight items of cloth or clothing as the wages of a group of men (see also O.Cairo 25504; Janssen 1975: 492). Cloth and clothing were also among the items sent by Rameses IX to the 'feather-wearing Nubians', according to Papyrus Cairo C-D (Wente 1990: no. 38) in which two garment types are referred to specifically: twenty-five *dw*-clothing (probably kilts) of *sm*-cloth, and twenty-five tunics of 'smooth cloth'.

In addition to being used as wages or rations, textiles were also used in a direct manner to acquire other objects. A Nineteenth-Dynasty letter from the village at Deir el-Medina (O.DM 125; Wente 1990: no. 229) was sent to a woman called Henutudjebu, asking her to acquire a tunic on behalf of the sender 'in exchange for the bracelet and have it furnished to me [in] ten days' (see also O. DM 185; Janssen 1975: 279, 281). Another way in which large households and temples might have acquired textiles was by using the so-called 'traders' (*šwtyw*). These were men who travelled up and down the Nile with surplus goods produced on the estates, trading them for objects that were in short supply within the households or temples.

Income had to be found from various sources in order to support royal expenditure such as the court, temples, building programmes and the army. Part of the income was raised through country-wide tax levies, paid in the form of animals and goods up to a certain value (Kemp 1991: 237). An example of this form of taxation can be seen in the wall-paintings of the Eighteenth-Dynasty tomb of Rekhmira at Thebes (TT100; Davies 1943: pl. XXXI), where the 'recorder' and 'scribe of the recorder' of the town of Wah-set (south of Abydos) are shown delivering linen garments as well as lengths of linen cloth, some carried in a chest.

In addition to using cloth already available in a household, the weaving of lengths of material was sometimes commissioned for specific purposes, including the renting of land. In one of the early Middle Kingdom 'Hekanakhte letters', a farmer writes to his sons telling them to have some cloth woven and to use it, if necessary, to rent some land: 'I said "Weave it", and they shall take it [the cloth] when it has been valued in Nebeseyet and rent land against its value' (P. Hekanakhte no. 1; James 1962: 13).

As well as new cloth, it would appear that there was a thriving trade in second-hand textiles, some of which came from private households, where the selling of excess material in order to purchase other items was not unusual. A New Kingdom story recounts the tale of a woman who sent her servant out to the market in order to sell a length of cloth, perhaps a cloak, but was unable to make the sale because of its poor condition (Janssen 1980). It is also likely that some of the cloth presented for sale at the markets had been robbed from various tombs. This point is reflected in some Twentieth-Dynasty trial records of tomb-robbers. Among the numerous items stolen from various tombs was 'royal linen, *mk* linen, good Upper Egyptian linen, rolled and bound, various garments [total] 63; skeins of thread [total]1' (Peet 1930: 89).

Large quantities of cloth were given by various ancient rulers to each other in order to cement their relationships. When the Mitannian king Tushratta sent his daughter to marry the pharaoh Akhenaten, the dowry included numerous garments and other textiles (Amarna Letters EA14 and 25; see Moran 1992: 32, 80). Similarly, surviving records state that Akhenaten sent the Babylonian king, Burnaburiash II, a total of 1,092 items of 'linen cloth' (textiles and clothes). In addition to cloth being given as part of a dowry or official gift, it is likely that linen was also used to pay obligation gifts. These are gifts which would have arisen out of a duty or obligation to someone else, symbolising the debt owed by one person to another.

Textiles were probably often obtained as booty from

various foreign conquests. In 1457 BC Thutmose III is said to have sacked the city of Megiddo in Palestine, bringing back with him, according to various accounts, quantities of cloth and clothes (Breasted 1906: no. 436), and it is likely that cloth was also brought back to Egypt among the loot and booty of other expeditions. It may even be that in this way both new production techniques and foreign weavers were brought into Egypt during the New Kingdom.

Medical uses

Because of the Egyptians' interest in mummification, the art of bandaging was highly developed at a very early date. Indeed the term *wt* is sometimes used in Egyptian documents to refer to a medical bandager and a bandager of bodies in the course of mummification (Ghalioungui 1983: 6–8). There are various references in the Edwin Smith Surgical Papyrus, to the use of bandages and raw flax for medical and surgical uses (Breasted 1930). There are also references to the use of raw flax being placed on wounds in order to absorb pus or blood and thus serving as a swab (Ghalioungui 1973: 43).

Bandages are described in the surgical thesis of Papyrus Edwin Smith as 'coverings for physician's use' and various different ways of using them are recorded in the case studies, including their employment as covers or splints. Bandages were used both for covering a wound and for keeping medicaments in place. One of the ways in which a flesh wound was treated was by placing a piece of raw meat over it, and keeping it in place with a bandage (P. Edwin Smith, case 32). If the sides of a wound needed to be brought together then paired strips of cloth were used to close the gap (P. Edwin Smith, case 10). It is likely that these banadages were impregnated with wax in order to keep the cloth in place. In addition, various medicaments, such as grease and honey, were soaked into the bandages in order to have healing agents locally applied (P. Edwin Smith, case 14).

The Edwin Smith Papyrus describes three different forms of splint. The first is the mouth splint, whereby pieces of wood bound with cloth were placed in the mouths of patients whose jaws had locked, perhaps because of tetanus, and who could only be fed with liquid food (P. Edwin Smith, case 7). The second form of splint was the so-called soft splint made up of rolled linen used as a plug for a broken nose (P. Edwin Smith, cases 11 and 12); this type of splint was also known as 'posts of linen'. Another form of soft splint was a roll of linen placed behind a wounded ear in order to support it (P. Edwin Smith, case 23). The third type of splint discussed in the papyrus was used for mechanically retaining a major break in position. In such cases wooden splints were padded with linen and then bound around a fracture in the leg or arm. Splints of this type were found around the broken forearm of a Fifth-Dynasty mummy (Smith and Dawson 1924: 161, fig. 69). In the Hearst Papyrus there is a reference to bandages being soaked in some form of starch (Worth Estes 1989: 63); once the starch had dried it took on a hard, stiff form, similar to modern plaster casts.

Religious uses

Mention has been made above of various secular uses of textiles, but cloth also had an important ritual function in temples. One of the rituals which occurred throughout the country on a daily basis was the washing, feeding and clothing of the statues of deities within the various temple sanctuaries. A text in the temple of Seti I at Abydos contains a reference to 'adorning Amun-Ra with red, green and white garments' (Calverley and Broome 1935: pl.12). The exact nature of the 'clothing for the gods' is not clear, but there are two main possibilities: firstly that actual garments were made and either presented to the gods by laying them in front of the image or actually fitted onto the statues; secondly that a length of cloth was wrapped around the statues, perhaps like a cloak, in a manner similar to the ritual figures found in the tomb of Tutankhamun (KV62; Reeves 1990: 130). Of the two possibilities, the second would seem the more likely.

Although the material for clothing the gods was often woven in the temples, textiles were sometimes donated by outsiders. An inventory was made of all the property and goods given by Rameses III to various temples, and among the numerous items are garments and linen which he gave to the gods, including 'wrappings of Horus [total] 2' and 'garments for the august statue of Amon [total] 4' (Breasted 1906: 232). Special garments were made for particular events, such as the Festival of the New Year. As part of the endowment of the temple of Amun at Thebes, Thutmose III ordered that the god should be given new clothing: 'the donning of linen garments and offering of anointing oil in the entire house as is done at the New Year's Day festival . . .' (Cumming 1982: 1255).

In the temple at Medinet Habu, there was a room which is now known as the 'clothing room' (*Medinet Habu* VI/2: pl. 444). One of the wall-reliefs shows the king about to clothe the statue of a god with garments which are depicted as lengths of cloth (rather like an upside-down Y) instead of conventional items of clothing. When it was time to dress the statue again, the old and now 'sanctified' garments were put on one side for other uses, notably as bandages for mummies (Andrews 1984: 25). This detail would suggest that lengths of cloth, rather than actual garments were meant when reference was made to the 'clothing of the gods'.

Funerary uses

One of the most important uses of cloth was related to funerary rites. Tait (Tayt, Tayet), the goddess of weaving, is occasionally associated with funerary practises. Mummy bandages were sometimes known as being or belonging to the 'land of Tait', and one of the earliest references to this goddess appears in Utterance 417 of the Fifth- and Sixth-Dynasty Pyramid Texts, where she is described as clothing (i.e. wrapping with bandages) a dead king: 'While (?) the Great One sleeps upon his mother Nut, your mother Tait clothes you, she lifts you up to the sky in this her name of Kite' (Faulkner 1969: 137).

Most ancient Egyptian burials contained items which were regarded as essential in this life and thus equally important in the next. These objects included pottery, food, jars, cosmetic items, tools and weapons, as well as textiles and clothing. In addition, cloth was placed in the tomb in the form of covers for amulets and statues, and incidentally as cloth being wrapped around cuts of meat and other foodstuffs. The quantity of cloth found in a tomb can be considerable. It has been estimated that Wah, estate manager to the early Middle Kingdom vizier Meketra, had a total of 845 square metres of cloth in his tomb (Winlock 1940: 257), including 375 square metres of linen around the body, the rest being made up of pads and lengths of cloth which ranged in length from 2.56 to 25.6 metres. The tomb of Tutankhamun (KV62) contained at least 400 items of cloth, including clothing, covers for ritual figures, linen arrow quivers, lamp wicks and the trappings for a chariot (Vogelsang-Eastwood and Kemp 1999).

The main element in the furnishing of the tomb was the coffin. This was usually covered with a large length of cloth or pall, the length of which could vary from two or three metres to about twenty, depending on how it was used. In representations of funerals the pall is usually shown as a small piece of cloth, so that the coffin underneath is still visible. The pall was also frequently painted red as this colour was associated with death and regeneration. Tutankhamun was buried inside three coffins, a sarcophagus and four shrines. The second shrine was enclosed by a frame covered with a large sheet of cloth made out of several lengths of material sewn together and decorated with gold rosettes to represent stars (Carter no. 209; Cairo JE 62745a).

A shroud, or cloth cover, was also placed over, and sometimes around, the body. Sometimes only one cloth was placed on the mummy, and in other instances several were used. Most shrouds consisted of a single length of cloth wrapped around the body, sometimes being inscribed in ink with spells, or chapters, from the Book of the Dead, as well as the name of the deceased (see Quirke *et al.* 1995). Occasionally actual garments were used as shrouding; the Eighteenth-Dynasty burial of Ramose and Hatnefer at Thebes, for instance, included at least two tunics covering the outer layer of bandages around the body of Hatnefer (Lansing and Hayes 1937: 19–20; Porter and Moss 1964: 669). A more ornate form of shroud is the so-called Osiris shroud, comprising a linen sheet spread over the bandages and then fastened in place by ties woven for the purpose, an example of which was also found over the mummy of Hatnefer (Cairo JE 66218). This type of shroud is often decorated with a painted life-size figure of Osiris, which may be either a simple outline executed in black ink or a more elaborate painting. Occasionally other gods or human forms are depicted (e.g. Leiden, RMO AMM 8). A more unusual form of shroud, taking the shape of a human being, covered the body of the New Kingdom queen Ahmose Meritamun, who was probably the Great Royal Wife of the early Eighteenth-Dynasty ruler Amenhotep I (Hayes 1990: 54; see Fig. 11.22).

There were various sources of cloth to be used for mummy bandaging, depending on the financial resources to be spent on the funeral (see Benson *et al.* 1979; Wild 1979, and see also Chapter 16, this volume). In most cases the mummifiers used old cloth and clothing which were torn up and wrapped around the body. The Twenty-third-Dynasty mummy of a priestess called Ankhefenkhonsu was wrapped in at least twelve tunics and one or two cloaks (National Museum of Denmark, Copenhagen, Acc. no. 1038). Old cloth and clothes for bandages also formed part of the list of acquisitions prior to military activities, in anticipation of losses. In a Twentieth-Dynasty letter, 'the general of Pharaoh' wrote to the scribe Tjaroy: 'As soon as my letter reaches you, you shall send some old cloths in the form of many strips . . . And don't let them go to waste (?), for they shall be made into bandages with which to wrap up men' (No. 300 Wente 1990: 182).

In more influential households it was possible to obtain what was called 'sanctified mummy wrappings'. These were the old 'clothing of the gods', described above in the section on religious uses (Andrews 1984: 25). In Spell 61 of the Coffin Texts, there is a reference to such garments, which have been used to make bandages for the dead: 'You are dressed in the pure garments of Ptah, in the cast-off garments of Hathor' (De Buck 1935: I, 258).

The amount of cloth used during the mummification process was considerable. It was required to pack the body in order to speed up the dehydration process and to prevent the body from being accidentally crushed (Andrews 1984: 20–6). Linen bags filled with natron were also placed inside the body. After the corpse had been in natron for forty days it was emptied, washed, rinsed and then allowed to dry. Any cavities were again filled with linen and all the facial orifices plugged with cloth. The actual wrapping of the body began about fifteen days later. At this point all the cloth needed was placed into various piles around the room. The piles were for bandages; folded sheets for layering; shaped bundles for wadding; padding, and finally the shrouds. The wrapping of the body began with the fingers and toes and then the arms and legs (Andrews 1984: 26–7; Raven 1993: 21, pl. 21). Gradually the whole body was wrapped in bandages, and pads of cloth were used to fill in certain areas (e.g. under the neck). In addition, if a limb was missing, a substitute was made out of a roll of cloth. Often worn and damaged cloth was used for bandaging the body itself, while the outer bandages were made of material in a better condition.

Figure 11.22 Shroud of Ahmose Meritamun, who was probably the wife of the early Eighteenth-Dynasty ruler Amenhotep I (Cairo, Egyptian Museum).

A wide range of animals, reptiles and birds were also mummified (Andrews 1985: 64–5). In the beginning only certain animals were mummified, notably rams and geese, bulls, cows, crocodiles and falcons, but by the later periods a wide range of animals were mummified including snakes, fish, mice, gazelle, baboons, dogs and cats. The role of cloth during the mummification of animals has yet not been studied in detail.

Conclusions

Until comparatively recently, the study of textiles has lagged behind that of other Egyptian material remains. The study of Egyptian pottery, for example, was initiated over 100 years ago. In contrast, the early reports rarely deal with textiles, providing only occasional references to 'mummy cloth' or simply 'linen'. The situation changed somewhat in the early twentieth century, when various scholars, such as Walter Midgely, Ling Roth, Grace Crowfoot and later Elizabeth Riefstahl each took a specific interest in textiles. After the Second World War, however, there was for some time a general dearth of interest in the subject.

During the last few decades of the twentieth century, there has been a notable change in the attitude of Egyptologists towards the study of ancient textiles. One of the major factors in this change is that the Egyptologists themselves, who once focused primarily on the philological and religious aspects of Egyptian culture, have begun to accept the fact that the material culture of the Pharaonic period is worthy of equal attention.

Changes in the available technology for the analysis of textiles have also played an important role in the study of these objects. Until the development of minimum or non-destructive scientific tests, many museums were reluctant to allow textiles to be used for the analysis of fibres or dyes. The situation is changing, but the growing complexity of analytical techniques has meant that there is an ever-widening gap between the specialist in the field and the person who is analysing the objects; unfortunately it is likely that this gap will widen further in the future.

Despite such problems, the future of the study of ancient Egyptian textiles looks far from gloomy. There is an ever-growing awareness of their intrinsic interest and their value both to scholars and to the general public. More importantly, information about textiles is now more widely available, which means that future generations of students will realise that pieces of linen are much more than simply tatty old rags.

References

Allgrove-McDowell, J. 1986. Kahun: the textile evidence. In *The Pyramid Builders of Ancient Egypt* (ed. A.R. David). London: Routledge and Kegan Paul, pp. 226–52.

Andrews, C. 1984. *Egyptian Mummies*. London: BMP.

Barber, E.J.W. 1991. *Prehistoric Textiles*. Princeton: Princeton University Press.

Benson, G.G., Hemingway, S.R. and Leach, F.N. 1979. The analysis of the wrappings of Mummy 1770. In *The Manchester Museum Mummy Project* (ed. A.R. David) Manchester: Manchester Museum. Manchester: Manchester Museum, pp. 119–32.

Breasted, J.H. 1906. *Ancient Records of Egypt* (5 vols). Chicago: University of Chicago Press.

1930. *The Edwin Smith Surgical Papyrus*. Chicago: University of Chicago Press.

Brunton, G. 1927. *Qau and Badari*. London: BSAE.

1937. *Mostagedda and the Tasian Culture*. London: BMP.

Brunton, G. and Caton-Thompson, C. 1928. *The Badarian Civilization and Predynastic Remains near Badari*. London: BSAE.

Calverley, A.M. and Broome, M.F. 1935. *The Temple of King Sethos I at Abydos* II. London: EES.

Carnarvon, Earl of, and Carter, H. 1912. *Five Years Exploration at Thebes*. Oxford: OUP.

Carter, H. 1903. Report on the general work done on the South Inspectorate. *ASAE*, 4: 43–50.

Cartland, B.M. 1918. Balls of thread wound on pieces of pottery. *JEA*, 5: 139.

Catling, D. and Grayson, J. 1982. *Identification of Vegetable Fibres*. London: Chapman and Hall.

Caton-Thompson, G. and Gardner, E.W. 1934. *The Desert Fayum*. London: Royal Anthropological Institute.

Černý, J. 1930–35. *Ostraca hiératiques* Cairo: Egyptian Museum.

Chassinat, E.G. and Palanque, C. 1911. *Une campagne de fouilles dans la nécropole d'Assiout*. Cairo: IFAO.

Cockburn, A., Barraco, R.A., Peck, W.H. and Reyman, T.A. 1983. A classic mummy; PUM II. In *Mummies, Disease and Ancient Cultures* (eds. A. Cockburn and E. Cockburn). Cambridge: CUP, pp. 52–70.

Cooke, W.D. and Brennan, A. 1990. The spinning of fine royal or byssos linen. *Archaeological Textiles Newsletter*, 10: 9.

Crowfoot, G.M. 1931. *Methods of Hand Spinning in Egypt and the Sudan*. Halifax: Bankfield Museum Notes.

1933. A textile from the Hood Collection of Egyptian antiquities. *Ancient Egypt*: 43–5.

Crowfoot, G.M. and Davies, N. de G. 1941. The tunic of Tutʿankhʿamun. *JEA* 27: 113–30.

Cumming, B. 1982. *Egyptian Historical Records of the Later Eighteeth Dynasty*. Warminster: Aris and Phillips

Daressy, G. 1902. *Fouilles de la Vallée des Rois1898–9*. Cairo: Catalogue Géneral des Antiquités du Musée du Caire.

Davies, N. de G. 1900. *The Mastaba of Ptahhotep and Akhhotep at Saqqara*. London: EES.

1901. *The Rock Tombs of Sheikh Saïd*. London: EEF.

1902. *The Rock Tombs of Deir El-Gebrawi* II. London: EEF.

1903. *The Rock Tombs of El-Amarna* I. London: EEF.

1905. *The Rock Tombs of El-Amarna* III. London: EEF.

1908. *The Rock Tombs of El-Amarna* VI. London: EEF.

1913. *Five Theban Tombs*. London: EES.

1926. *The Tomb of Huy*. New York: MMA.

1927a. The town house in ancient Egypt. *Metropolitan Museum Studies*, 1–2: 233–55.

1927b. *Two Ramesside Tombs at Thebes*. New York: MMA.

1930, *Tomb of Ken-Amun at Thebes*, 2 vols. New York: MMA.

1933. *The Tomb of Nefer-Hotep at Thebes*. 2 vols. New York: MMA.

1936. *Ancient Egyptian Paintings* (2 vols). Chicago: University of Chicago Press.

1941. *The Tomb of the Vizier Ramose*. New York: MMA.

1943. *The Tomb of Rekh-mi-re at Thebes*. New York: MMA.

1948. *Seven Private Tombs at Kurnah*. New York: MMA.

De Buck, A. 1935. *The Egyptian Coffin Texts*. Chicago: University of Chicago Press.

Donadoni Roveri, A.M. 1988. *Egyptian Civilization: Daily Life*. Turin: Museo Egizio di Torino.

Dothan, T. 1963. Spinning bowls. *Israel Exploration Journal*, 13: 97–112.

Duell, P. 1938. *The Mastaba of Mereruka*. Chicago: University of Chicago Press.

Eastwood, G.M. 1985. Preliminary report on the textiles. In *Amarna Reports* II (ed. B.J. Kemp). London: EES, pp. 191–204.

Emery, I. 1966. *The Primary Structures of Fabrics*. Washington: The Textile Museum.

Faulkner, R.O. 1969. The Bremner-Rhind Papyrus I. *JEA*, 22: 121–40.

Gardiner, A.H. 1957. *Egyptian Grammar*. 3rd edn. Oxford: OUP.

Germer, R. 1985. *Flora des pharaonischen Ägypten*. Mainz: von Zabern.

1992. *Die Textilfärberei und die Verwendung gefärbter Textilien im Alten Ägypten*. Wiesbaden: Otto Harrassowitz.

Ghalioungui, P. 1973. *The Physicians of Pharaonic Egypt*. Mainz: von Zabern.

1983. *The House of Life: Magic and Medical Science in Ancient Egypt*. Amsterdam: Hodder and Stoughton.

Goyon, J.C. and Josset, P. 1988. *Un Corps pour l'Eternité, Autopsie d'une Momie*. Paris: Le Léopard d'Or.

Griffith, F.L. 1896. *Beni Hasan* III. London: EEF.

Hald, M. 1946. Ancient textile techniques in Egypt and Scandinavia. *Acta Archaeologica* 17: 49–67.

Hall, R. 1980. A pair of linen sleeves from Gurob. *GM*, 40: 29–40.

1981. The Pharaonic *mss* tunics as a smock?. *GM*, 43: 29–37.

1982. Garments in the Petrie Museum of Egyptian Archaeology. *Textile History*, 13,1: 27–45.

1985. The cast-off garments of yesterday: dresses reversed in life and death. *BIFAO*, 85: 235–45.

1986. *Egyptian Textiles*. Aylesbury: Shire Publications.

Hayes, W.C. 1990. *The Scepter of Egypt*. 2 vols. New York: Harold Abrams.

van't Hooft, P., Raven, M.J., van Rooij, E.H.C. and Vogelsang-Eastwood, G. 1994. *Pharaonic and Early Medieval Egyptian Textiles*. Leiden: Rijksmuseum van Oudheden.

James T.G.H. 1962. *The Hekanakhte Papers and Other Early Middle Kingdom Documents*. New York: MMA.

Janssen, J.J. 1975. *Commodity Prices from the Ramessid Period*. Leiden: Brill.

1980. *De Markt op de Oever*. Leiden: Brill.

Jick, M. 1988. Bead-net dress. In *Mummies and Magic* (eds. S. D'Auria, P. Lacovara and C. Roehrig). Boston: MFA, pp. 78–9.

Kamal, A.B. 1901. *Fouilles à Deir-el-Bersheh*. Cairo: SAE.

Kemp, B.J. 1989. *Ancient Egypt: Anatomy of a Civilization*. London: Routledge.

Landi, S and Hall, R. 1979. The discovery and conservation of an ancient Egyptian linen tunic. *Studies in Conservation*, 24: 141–52.

Lansing, A. and Hayes, W.C. 1937. The Egyptian expedition 1935–1936: The Museum's excavations at Thebes. *BMMA*, 32/2: 4–39.

Landström, B. 1974. *Die Schiffe der Pharaonen*. Munich.

Lichtheim, M. 1973. *Ancient Egyptian Literature* I. Berkeley CA: University of California Press.

Littauer, M.A. and Crouwel, J.H. 1985. *Chariots and Related Equipment from the Tomb of Tutʿankhamun*. Oxford: Griffith Institute.

Loret, V. 1930. Deux racines tinctoriales de l'Égypte ancienne: orcanette et garance. *Kêmi*, 3: 22–32.

Lucas, A. 1962. *Ancient Egyptian Materials and Industries*. 4th edn., rev. J.R. Harris. London: Edward Arnold.

Macramallah, R. 1935. *Le Mastaba d'Idout*. Cairo: Service des Antiquités de l'Egypte.

Martin, G.T. 1989. *The Memphite Tomb of Horemheb*. London: EES.

Medinet Habu, VI/2: The Temple Proper. 1963. Chicago: University of Chicago Press.

Midgley, W.W. 1911. Linen of the IIIrd Dynasty. In *Historical Studies* II (eds. E.B. Knobel, W.W. Midgley, J.G. Milne, M.A. Murray and W.M.F. Petrie). London: Quaritch, pp. 37–9.

1912. Textiles. In *Labyrinth, Gerzeh and Mazguneh* (eds. W.M.F. Petrie, G.A. Wainwright and E. MacKay). London: BSAE, p. 6.

1915. Reports on early linen. In *Heliopolis, Kafr Ammar and Shurafa* (eds. W.M.F. Petrie and E. Mackay). London: BSAE, pp. 48–51.

Mond, R.L. and Myers, O.H. 1937. *The Cemeteries of Armant* I, 2 vols. London: EES.

Moran, W.L. 1992. *The Amarna Letters*. Baltimore: Johns Hopkins University Press.

Müller, H. 1940. *Die Felsgräber der Fürsten von Elephantine*. Ägyptologische Forschungen 9. Glückstadt, Hamburg and New York: J.J. Augustin.

Munro, P. 1983. Der Unas-Friedhof Nord-West 4/5, Vorbericht über die Arbeiten der Gruppe Hannover/Berlin in Saqqara. *GM*, 63: 81–109.

Newberry, P.E. n.d. *El Bersheh I*. London: EEF.

1893. *Beni Hasan* I. London: EEF.

1894. *Beni Hasan* II. London: EEF.

Parkinson, R. 1991. *Voices from Ancient Egypt*. London: BMP.

Peet, T.E., 1930. *The Great Tomb Robberies of the Twentieth Dynasty*. Oxford: Clarendon Press (repr. 1977).

1933. The so-called Ramesses girdle. *JEA*, 19: 143–9.

Peet, T.E. and Woolley, C.L. 1923. *City of Akhenaten* I. London: EES.

Petrie, W.M.F. 1908. *Athribis*. London: BSAE.

1914. The tomb of Menna. *Ancient Egypt*, 1: 95–6.

1917. *Tools and Weapons*. London: BSAE.

Petrie, W.M.F. and Quibell, J.E. 1895. *Naqada and Ballas*. London: BSAE.

Picton, J. and Mack, J. 1979. *African Textiles*. London: BMP.

Porter, B. and Moss, R.L.B. 1964. *Topographical Bibliography of Ancient Egyptian Hieroglyphic Texts, Reliefs and Paintings I: The Theban Necropolis: Part 2: Royal Tombs and Smaller Cemeteries*. 2nd edn. Oxford: Griffith Institute.

Quibell, J.E. 1900. *Hierakonpolis* I. London: BSAE.

Quirke, S., Cruickshank, P. and Morgan, H. 1995. Reawakening Resti: conservation of an eighteenth-dynasty shroud. *Egyptian Archaeology*, 6: 31–3.

Raven, M.J. 1993. *Mummies onder het mes*. Amsterdam: De Tabaafische Leeuw.

Reeves, C.N. 1990. *The Complete Tutankhamun*. London: Thames and Hudson.

Reisner, G.A. 1942. *A History of the Giza Necropolis* I. Cambridge MA: Harvard University Press.

Reisner, G.A. and Smith, W.S. 1955. *A History of the Giza Necropolis* II. Cambridge MA: Harvard University Press.

Riefstahl, E. 1944. *Patterned Textiles in Pharaonic Egypt*. Brooklyn: Brooklyn Museum.

1970. A note on ancient fashions; four early Egyptian dresses in the Museum of Fine Arts, Boston. *BMMA*, 68: 244–9.

Roth, A.M. 1988. Tomb group of a woman. In *Mummies and Magic: The Funerary Arts of Ancient Egypt* (eds. S. D'Auria *et al.*). Boston: MFA, pp. 76–7.

Roth, H.L. 1951. *Ancient Egyptian and Greek Looms*. Halifax: Bankfield Museum Notes.

Saad, Z.Y. 1951. *Royal Excavations at Helwan, 1945–7*. Cairo: Service des Antiquités de l'Égypte.

Schiaparelli, E. 1927. *Relazione sui lavori della Missione Archeologica Italiana in Egitto 1903–1920, II, La tomba intatta dell'architetto Cha nella necropoli di Tebe*. Turin: R. Museo di Antichità.

Simpson, W.K. 1978. *The Mastabas of Kawab, Khafkhufu I and II, G7110–20/30–40/50*. Boston: Museum of Fine Arts.

Smith, G.E. 1912. *The Royal Mummies. Catalogue Général des Antiquités Egyptiennes de la Musée du Caire*, Nos. 61051–61100. Cairo: SAE.

Smith, G.E. and Dawson, W.R. 1924. *Egyptian Mummies*. London: Allen and Unwin [repr. 1991 London: KPI].

Spencer, P. 1984. *The Egyptian Temple: A Lexicographical Study*. London: KPI.

Thompson. W.G. 1904. Tapestry-woven fabrics. In *The Tomb of Thoutmôsis IV* (eds. H. Carter and P.E. Newberry). Cairo: BSAE, p. 143.

Tylor, J.J. and Griffith, F.Ll. 1894. *The Tomb of Paheri at El-Kab*. London: EEF.

Vogelsang-Eastwood, G.M. 1987–88. A note on the so-called 'spinning bowls'. *Ex Oriente Lux*, 30: 78–88.

1990. Textiles from Quseir al-Qadim, Egypt. *OMRO*, 70: 195–200.

1992a. Ancient Egyptian spinning. *Profiel* 4/1: 3–17.

1992b. Deciphering a pictorial clothing list. *GM*, 128: 105–111.

1993. *Pharaonic Egyptian Clothing*. Leiden: Brill.

1994. *De Kleren van de farao*. Amsterdam: De Tabaafische Leeuw.

Vogelsang-Eastwood, G.M. and Kemp, B.J. 1999. The ancient textile industry at Amarna. In *Amarna Excavations II* (ed. B. J. Kemp). London: EES.

Wente, E. 1990. *Letters from Ancient Egypt*. Atlanta: Scholars Press.

Wild, H. 1979. *La Tombeaude Néfer-hotep I et Neb-néfer*. Cairo: IFAO.

Winlock, H.E. 1916. Ancient Egyptian kerchiefs. *BMMA*, 11: 238–42.

1926. The Egyptian expedition, 1924–1925. *BMMA*, 21: 3–28.

1940. The mummy of Wah unwrapped. *BMMA*, 35: 253–259.

1941. *Materials Used at the Embalming of King Tut-Ankh-Amun*. New York: MMA.

1945. *The Slain Soldiers of Neb-hepet-Re-Mentuhotpe*. New York: MMA.

1955. *Models of Daily Life in Ancient Egypt*. New York: MMA.

Worth Estes, J. 1989. *The Medical Skills of Ancient Egypt*. Kanton: Science History Publications.

Wreszinski, W. 1923–42. *Atlas zur altägyptischen Kulturgeschichte* (3 vols). Leipzig: Hinrichs.

12. Leatherwork and skin products

CAROL VAN DRIEL-MURRAY

Introduction

Ever since Lucas emphasised the importance and quality of leather in Pharaonic Egypt, in his ground-breaking *Ancient Egyptian Materials and Industries*, Egypt has tended to be regarded as the origin of all technical expertise in this field. Lively depictions of work scenes in tombs and the preservation of brightly coloured and complex items of leatherwork have contributed to the perception of large-scale and technologically advanced skin-processing skills. As the present study progressed, however, it became clear that Pharaonic skin processing, far from being innovative, remained essentially Neolithic in its technology, and skin products were of marginal importance in comparison to textiles and fibre. Leather-working only came into prominence at times of increased international contact or when pastoralist intruders brought their own traditions with them. Indeed, true leather – in the sense of a water-resistant, impetruscible product tanned with extracts of vegetable origin – was virtually unknown in Egypt until the massive technological changes introduced in the Greco-Roman period.*

The skin products of the Pharaonic period, although here referred to as 'leather', are in fact only lightly cured (so-called 'pseudo-tannages'): the belief in the pre-eminence of Egypt in leather technology, although widespread in the tertiary literature, appears to derive more from the unparalleled conditions of survival than from scientific analysis. These exceptional conditions have, however, resulted in the survival of considerable numbers of artefacts which not only reveal the many purposes to which skin products could be put, but also indicate the variety of processing techniques which were available in antiquity. In contrast to the ancient leather that has survived in the waterlogged conditions of northwestern Europe, Egyptian skin products have often been preserved intact, with the sewing thread still in place, thus permitting a much better appreciation of the production techniques. Other aspects, such as the astounding use of colour and the manner in which highly sophisticated effects can be produced by the simplest methods, need to be more widely recognised and are certainly dirctly relevant to all archaeological research into pre-industrial leather technology. The wealth and variety of the finds from Egypt are a forceful reminder of the limitations which climatic conditions place on our assessment of leather technology at other periods and in other regions where differential preservation may severely distort the material record.

Sources

Much of the surviving artefactual evidence for Egyptian leather-working derives from tombs, the equipment from which cannot simply be regarded as a reflection of daily life in all its aspects, particularly in view of such factors as the ceremonial and symbolic nature of the removal – or retention – of footwear in the presence of deities, kings or superiors. Similarly, the symbolic and cultic significance of tomb and temple depictions means that such scenes need to be interpreted with caution and in a clear historical perspective (see Chapter 22, this volume in particular), but this does not mean that the activities themselves bear no relation to contemporary practice.

Settlement sites such as Middle Kingdom Kahun and New Kingdom Gurob offer a more balanced picture of daily life, but the situation is complicated by the fact that Dynastic-period artefacts from such sites have often become mixed up with Romano-Coptic occupation debris. Unfortunately, it is primarily in the case of the organics – basketry, footwear and textiles – that the dating of individual items is controversial. Thus only one of the sandals from Gurob illustrated by Thomas (1981: pl. 51/470; Petrie Museum UC 28350) dates to the Pharaonic period, while the rest are late Roman. Similarly, an indigo-dyed wool skein from Kahun was recently analysed and shown to be Roman (Germer 1992: 15, 19). The extent of such contamination raises doubts as to the authenticity of the 'Predynastic tannery' at Gebelein, which is discussed below (see p. 305). Because of

---

* Technically, the term 'leather' is restricted to the products of (1) tanning, i.e. the treating of skin with tannin extracts of vegetable origin, and (2) tawing, which refers to treatment with alum. Other processes are described variously as 'curing' or 'pseudo-tannages'.

these problems, the surviving leatherwork from Ludwig Borchardt's controlled excavations at Amarna is particularly important for dating purposes.

By far the richest sources of leatherwork are the Romano-Coptic cemeteries and settlements which, however, fall outside the remit of this contribution. On the whole, the dating of these cemeteries is poorly defined, but items of footwear from recent excavations such as Qasr Ibrim and Mons Claudianus are beginning to provide some refinement within this long period (see Mills 1982; Winterbottom 1990; Petrie 1889: pls. XVIII–XXI; Frauberger 1896). Outside Egypt proper, the Nubian cemeteries reveal a rich and highly skilled leather-working tradition (though still using cured skins and rawhide) from the earliest times. This Nubian leatherwork is unequalled in Egypt, and, especially in the later periods, includes exquisite and spectacularly complex objects of daily use, such as the quivers from Qustul (Williams 1991: figs. 39–47).

In general, a rigorous chronological framework is lacking from many discussions of Egyptian material culture, thus obscuring evidence for technological development or its social and economic background. This shortcoming is particularly apparent in the treatment of Egyptian leatherwork in the secondary literature and popularising studies based on it. Ancient texts are cited without regard for their context or date, and there is little awareness of advances in either philology or interpretation: even Reed (1972: 86–9) includes incorrect translations of Mesopotamian texts, which have subsequently been quoted in numerous publications drawing on this authoritative work. All too often, classical references are inappropriately applied to earlier situations, and modern assumptions as to the advanced nature of Egyptian technology not only colour the translations given but also affect the outcome of specialist research.

Although it may be assumed that the major changes which become visible in Roman times are in fact rooted in earlier traditions, the lack of closely dated comparative material from either the Persian or Ptolemaic periods prevents any insight into the antecedents or indeed, any developments in native technology which may have made craftsmen more responsive to new influences. It is notable that changes in leather technology at this period are echoed in textiles by the major shift from linen to wool and also in basketry techniques (Germer 1992: 18 n. 4; see also Chapters 10 and 11, this volume). Ancient Egyptian leatherwork is in need of a total reassessment, and a research programme undertaking extensive analyses on well-dated samples for both curing and colouring agents is urgently required to establish a framework for future investigation.

Primary processing of animal skin

Butchery

The relative unimportance of leather could be connected to the inefficient and messy manner of butchery, for in hot climates lack of hygiene is one of the chief causes of loss to the leather industry (Aten *et al.* 1978: 28). From Old and Middle Kingdom tombs come particularly detailed scenes depicting the slaughter of cattle and antelope (Eggebrecht 1973), and although all are set in a ritual context, this does not exclude a pragmatic interpretation of the actual sequences (Ikram 1995: 42). Tomb chapels at Meir graphically record the unhygienic conditions of slaughter (Blackman 1914–53: I, pls. X–XI). The vertical throat slit, which was normal in the Old and Middle Kingdom (Eggebrecht 1973: 41), would cause severe spattering of blood, but inadequate bleeding, as carcasses were not hung. Flaying does not seem to have been recognised as a distinct activity, but proceeded piecemeal as the animal was being jointed, thus increasing the likelihood of damage from butchers' knives and contamination with blood and viscera (Eggebrecht 1973: 73–4; Davies 1922: 16, n. 3. pl. LII; Gilbert 1988: 88; see also Chapter 25, this volume). Working from a slit extending from the jaw to the belly (particularly clearly visible in the scene showing the slaughter of cattle and antelope in the Sixth-Dynasty tomb-chapel of Pepyankh at Meir, see Blackman 1914–53: V, pl. XXXV), the butchers first stripped and removed the ritually important right foreleg, leaving folds of skin hanging down from the carcass, which are visible on most depictions (first noted by Davies 1922: 16; see Fig. 12.1a). After removal of the left foreleg and the freeing of the rib-cage, the skin of the back legs was peeled back from vertical cuts, sometimes with the assistance of the butcher's hand or a paddle-like tool (Eggebrecht 1973: 75; Murray 1904: pls. VII, XXI, XIII; Blackman 1914–53: IV, pl. IX; see Fig. 12.1b). Once the beast had been dismembered, the hide was removed using knives and pummelling down with the fists (Fig. 12.1c). All the while, the carcass was rolled about on the dirty floor, with the hide of little more value than a temporary carpet. Indeed, Eggebrecht (1973: 74) suggests that the piecemeal flaying has something to do with keeping the flesh ritually pure, but it is notable that, save for the initial libation, there is no indication of the most obvious form of cleansing: rinsing with water. It is also remarkable that there is apparently no trace of water supply, sluicing or drainage facilities in the surviving remains of an Old Kingdom slaughterhouse at Abusir (Verner 1986). With the skins already heavily contaminated, further processing would be further delayed by the need for transport to a suitable location.

It is perhaps significant that as skin products came to be employed more widely in the New Kingdom, slaughterhouse practices seem to have changed and more attention was paid to the condition of the hides. The deep horizontal throat-cut, which becomes normal in the New Kingdom (Eggebrecht 1973: 49), virtually severing the head (contrast Davies 1930: II, pl. XLII and Fig. 12.1a here), would enable more complete bleeding, while the further separation of the actual slaughteryard from the temple (Haring 1996: 117–18) may have allowed for the provision of hygienic facilities.

though as things stand, and on visual evidence, it is likely that the process was unknown in Egypt until the Greco-Roman period. Vegetable tans are complex polyphenols occurring in two groups, the hydrolysable tannins (pyrogallols) found in such sources as oakwood, galls and sumac leaves, and the condensed tannins (catechols) found in acacia, mimosa and pine. The most common tanning agent in Europe, oak bark, contains both types of polyphenol (Bickley 1991).

Vegetable-tanned leather varies in colour depending on the extracts used, but, in contrast to the white or yellowish products of pseudo-tannages, tends to be darker through the entire thickness of the skin, ranging from ochre to red-brown. The characteristic dark colour of Greco-Roman footwear is caused by iron reactions in the soil, a reaction which also takes place in waterlogged contexts, and which forms the basis of tests for the presence of tannins (Daniels 1993; and see p. 316). Footwear dating to the period *c.* 90 BC–100 AD, from the Roman phase of occupation at the Lower Nubian settlement of Qasr Ibrim, is of tanned leather, while earlier and later native footwear is generally of rawhide (personal examination). By the 'early Christian' levels at Qasr Ibrim, sandals here – as elsewhere in Egypt – are of red-brown or black tanned hide. Bravo (1933: 87, 1948) was clearly puzzled by the total absence of vegetable tannins from his analyses: later compilers – including Lucas (1962: 34, significantly not citing any of his own analyses) – were less cautious and simply ascribed mastery of the techniques to the Egyptians.

The first records of the use of oak galls in tanning appear in Greek sources in the fourth century BC. According to Lau (1967: 56) vegetable tanning is first mentioned in classical literature by Theophrastus (*H. Plant.* III 8.6, 9.1, 14.3, 18.5 and IV 2,8.), although the linguistic differentiation between 'shoemakers' and 'tanners' which appears in the fifth century suggests that in the Greek world the separate processes may have been known earlier. Few of the other sources concerning vegetable tanning (cited by, among others, Forbes 1957; Reed 1972; Thomson 1981) date from before the first century BC.

Contrary to the impression conveyed by the secondary literature, there is no evidence for vegetable tanning in Mesopotamia at an earlier date. The generally quoted texts refer to the Hellenistic period or later, and the translation of *ḫuratu* as 'oak galls' (see *CAD* H; *contra* Sigrist 1981; and much of the tertiary literature) has long been discredited. The Mesopotamian evidence for the terminology of vegetable tanning is discussed by Stol (1983: 534–5) and Van Soldt (1990: 321–57, esp. 347) including the argument that *Puwatu* = *ḫuratu* = madder. Van de Mieroop (1987) proves without doubt that *ḫuratu* (Sumerian *e.rí.na*) is madder (*Rubia tinctorum*), which was grown in Syria and Anatolia on a considerable scale, its shoots and roots being used to colour both textiles and skins. Van Soldt (1990) notes that in the late second millennium BC at Ugarit madder is never

Table 12.1. *The terminological associations between madder and alum in Mesopotamia (after Van der Mieroop 1987: 154).*

First millennium BC	ḫuratû + gabû	madder + alum
Old Babylonian period	ḫuratu + allaḫarum	madder + alum
Isin-Larsa period	ú-háb + allaḫarum	madder + alum

attested without alum (*gabû*) and usually occurs in relation to flax. The references to alum in these texts again point to its use as a mordant. Van de Mieroop (1987: 153–4) extends the link between madder and alum back to the Ur III/Isin period, i.e. *c.* 2000 BC (as far back as the nature of the surviving texts allows), reconstructing the terminological association shown in Table 12.1.

Thus all texts cited in support of tanning with oak galls in fact describe dyeing with madder and its mordant, alum. In northern Europe, tanned leather first seems to appear with the Roman conquest and any prehistoric skin products have survived as a result of exceptional conditions such as frozen deposits, dry salt mines or bogs, where it is subjected to a kind of secondary tannage. In Europe, as in Egypt and Mesopotamia, simple curing methods must have been the norm. In part, the late acceptance of true leather technology has to do with the protracted and complex preliminary working of the hides and skins, the large installations required, the length of time necessary for complete penetration of the liquors (up to two years for ox-hides) and, consequently the high level of skill and investment that was necessary.

A problem in the discussion of the history of true tanning is the status of the so-called 'Predynastic tannery' at Gebelein, where goatskins, supposedly awaiting processing, were found together with large quantities of acacia pods. Although such pods are still used today in local tanning industries, acacia also has many other uses (see Germer 1985), so the presence of pods and leaves alone does not automatically indicate that vegetable tanning was being practised. However, the excavator of the site at Gebelein, Schiaparelli (1921b), seems to have succeeded in convincing Bravo (1933: 86), and through him many others, including Lucas (1962: 34), and thus the 'earliest tannery in the world' has become an established fact, even though, as Bravo himself notes, there was no evidence for vegetable tanning in ancient Egypt, prior to his analyses of material from this site. In fact, the exceedingly summary report of Schiaparelli's excavations makes no mention of any 'tannery', while later accounts stress the long history of occupation of the site, with a major expansion under the Ptolemies when the garrison also housed soldiers of Greek extraction (Schiaparelli 1921b: 126–8; Donadoni Roveri 1989: 134–6). The Greek connection may be the significant factor here: if correct, this could reveal the way in which new technology was introduced. The implication is that analysis of material should take account of both the ethnicity of the settlement from which the finds come as well as the date of the finds in the assessment of results. Under the circumstances, it is perhaps more likely that the Gebelein tannery dates to the later first millennium BC than to the Predynastic period.

Secondary processing: staining and decorative techniques

Colour

The application of colour is inextricably linked to the curing processes. Although it has been suggested that the use of vegetable extracts may have developed from attempts to colour leathers prepared by other methods (Thomson 1981: 143), it is questionable whether there was any awareness that attempts to stain skin with pomegranate or sumac simultaneously enhanced the quality of the leather. The lack of immersion probably prevented the tanning action from penetrating deeply enough to be noticeable, and the same may be true of the alum mordants. The evidence for the sophisticated use of dyes and mordants marshalled by Lucas (1962: 152–4) in fact refers exclusively to the Roman period and later. Even the limited amount of evidence from the Dynastic period is consistent with Germer's finding for textiles (Germer 1992: 137): mineral colours predominate until the Eighteenth Dynasty, when vegetable dyes – madder (red) indigo (blue) and pomegranate (yellow and black) – begin to appear. On leather, colour is generally confined to the grain surface, leaving the lower surface white and indicative of painting or surface staining only. The poor, gelatinous state of much of the decorated work examined makes it difficult to establish the full range of colours, nor is it at present possible to distinguish changes or the emergence of new combinations through time. Red, green, yellow and white seem to be the most popular, but blue was not identified on the material available for study. This is curious, for the blue pigments identified by Kaczmarczyk (1986) could have been applied as a paint like the other mineral colours. Certain shades may, however, be more susceptible to discoloration: circular patches on a pair of green stained shoes in the British Museum (BM EA4408/9), for instance, seem to have been corroded by black metallic pigment decay products. An identical pair from Abydos retain their red stained patches and XRF analysis confirmed that mineral pigments were employed (see Fig.12.15). Red was achieved with iron and perhaps lead compounds, and green was created with copper compounds.

The range of colours appearing on Queen Istemkheb's funerary tent (Cairo) may point to improved knowledge of the properties of mordants and dyestuffs by the Twenty-first Dynasty, although in the absence of modern analyses, further speculation is unfounded. The pink pigment is said to consist of haematite with some lime, the blue is of vegetable origin and the leather is said to be vegetable-tanned (Villiers Stuart 1882). However, the extractive tests for tannins used at that period probably record vegetable dyes rather than tanned skin.

The Mesopotamian craft archive of the Isin period (*c.* 2000 BC.) discussed by Van de Mieroop (1987) illuminates Egyptian practices in the New Kingdom and later. Although he assumes that skins were cured with alum, the listing of the products used in the workshops in fact shows that the skins were oil-cured before being coloured. Four colours were obtained: there is no mention of products for 'white', which must have been regarded as the basic shade. Black was obtained with pomegranate (*nu-úr-ma*) and orpiment (*im-KÙ.GI*: literally 'gold-coloured earth' *cf.* Stol 1983: 35, however, in view of the black deposit caused by the reaction between tannins and iron salts, some other substance may be intended): here, as probably in Egypt, the pomegranate was not used as a tanning agent, but indirectly for the reaction between the tannins and the minerals, giving black. Red leather was already produced with madder and alum, see Table 12.1. From this it is clear that *úháb* is madder and not 'oak galls', since the latter would produce black, leaving the alum superfluous. Finally, copper was used to obtain green: about thirty to thirty-five grams of copper being required for a single skin. For Egypt, a late Nineteenth-Dynasty ostracon from Deir el-Medina (Cairo JE 25596; see Cerny 1935: 33–4) refers to a similar process: oil-cured skins coloured red with *ip* (madder) and *ibnw* (alum).

Decorative techniques

Although Pliny (*Nat. Hist.* XXXV: 42) marvels at the ingenious use made by the Egyptians of the properties of mordants, this expertise must be regarded as a late technological innovation, for New Kingdom leather goods achieve their colourful aspect by intricate and laborious arrangements of separately coloured strips, open-work, appliqué and mosaic patterns. One sandal (BM EA36200; Fig. 12.3) – unfortunately undated and unprovenanced, but, judging from the shape, probably late Eighteenth- or Nineteenth-Dynasty, combines several techniques in a lurid display of colour. Ankle and toe straps are wound round with red stained skin (now faded to pink), the green instep triangle is edged with red, and shapes are scraped away to expose the white surface underneath. Narrow strips of red leather (another dark colour may also be present) are woven through slits in the green-stained insole in a clear imitation of fibre sandals (an interesting and characteristic inversion: in Europe, wooden and fibre shoes imitate leather, whereas in Egypt it is fibre which is the model) and the insole and the thicker rawhide outer sole are attached using a red binding.

Weaving narrow strips of coloured leather through slits

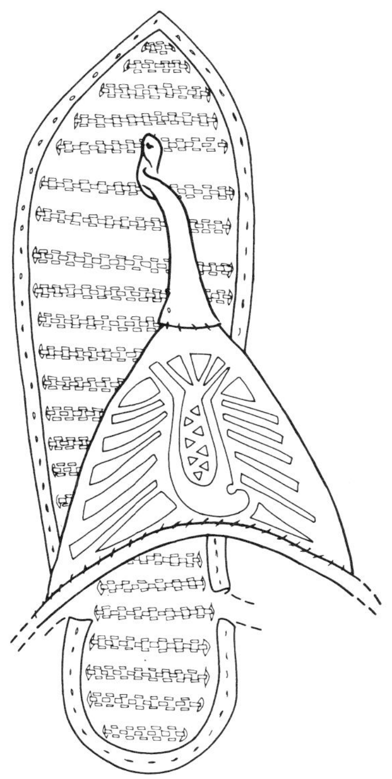

Figure 12.3 Multi-coloured sandal (BM EA36200). Length 268 mm.

is a common decorative technique, also used on quivers and lyres (Ziegler 1978: 113). Similarly laborious is a distinctive technique apparently favoured in the later Eighteenth Dynasty and used on footwear as well as on furnishings and other goods from the city at Amarna. Thin leather strips of slightly different widths are superimposed to give very narrow lines of alternating colours. Sometimes these are made up as separate strips up to three centimetres wide and cut into suitable lengths, but usually they were individually sewn to the backing. Despite being remarkably fiddly to sew, with all these different thicknesses, stitching could be varied to give extra effects, such as the zig-zags and ruffles on certain items from Amarna (Fig. 12.4).

Larger patterns were achieved by appliqués, with open-work revealing differently coloured backgrounds. In view of the knife slips, delicate tools were not employed and the patterns are frequently irregular and coarsely executed. Leather mosaic comes mainly from funerary contexts, and may have been a substitute for other materials, especially jewellery (Schiaparelli 1921a: 14), such as a set of leather plaits with spacers (BM EA23059). Queen Istemkheb's funerary tent with its multicoloured patchwork and elaborate appliqués may also come into this category, for it is surely too hot and airless for actual use in Egypt, although leather tents are well attested in the Roman Period in Europe (van Driel-Murray 1990). On the other hand, the lack of recognisable pieces of coloured mosaic in the extensive collection of leather from Amarna in the Ägyptisches Museum, Berlin could mean that such work only came into fashion after the Eighteenth Dynasty.

Now all too often obscured by dark decay products, these technically simple, but extremely labour-intensive methods must have produced bright and highly effective decoration. Presumably, the explanation for the persistence of such laborious methods is that colours could only be applied to complete skins and that the complex methods of staining and gilding (on the more intractable vegetable tanned leather), common in the Coptic period, were unknown. Instead, patterns were achieved by cutting, arranging and time-consuming stitching or gluing. Appliqué is wasteful of leather since layers are duplicated and snippets from open-work are discarded. The irregular scraps of red goat or gazelle skin used to edge the white rawhide mummy-braces, with their block-stamped presentation scenes, make use of such left-overs. Tooled and stamped designs were used on various items, such as quivers and archers' guards. Lavish use of stamps and tooled lines on sandal insoles is characteristic of the Roman period.

Historical survey

The Predynastic and Early Dynastic periods (c. 5500–2649 BC)

The very survival of anything as fragile as leather from Predynastic graves is quite remarkable: even more remarkable is the care that Flinders Petrie took in the excavation, curation and publication of these fragmentary and unprepossessing organic materials. In the Predynastic period – in contrast to the Dynastic – leather was widely used, and was also handled with considerable skill and confidence, although in the absence of scientific analyses the exact nature of the curing methods is unknown. Brunton and Caton-Thompson (1928: 40) comment on goat and antelope skin garments and wrappings from Predynastic graves at Badari, skin cloaks being worn primarily by men.

Predynastic garments seem to have been simple, some being fastened with toggles made from bone, teeth or tusks (e.g. Petrie and Quibell 1896: pl. LXII, no. 28 with

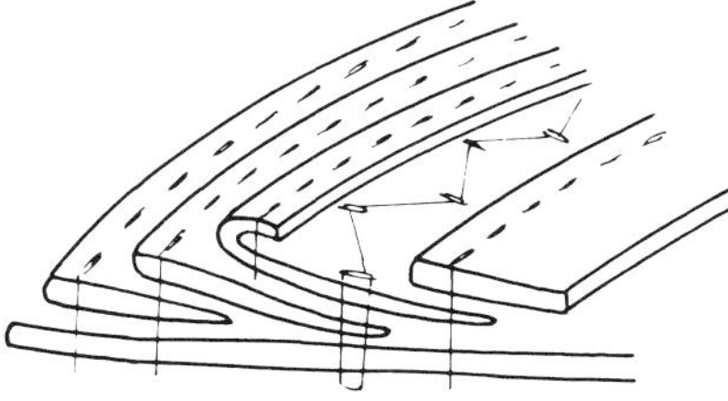

Figure 12.4 Diagrammatic section detail of multi-coloured strips edging an artefact from Amarna (UC 35939). Not to scale (edging c. 30–35 mm wide).

leather thong; Petrie 1920: pl. XXXIII, nos. 28–52) and others knotted on the shoulder (as on a figure of the king on the Early Dynastic Narmer Palette from Hierakonpolis). The tight creases of a large leather knot from grave 1743 at Naqada (Petrie Museum UC 5925) reveals just how supple the leather for such cloaks could be. In addition, a variety of fine stitching and lacing techniques using sinews, twisted thongs and twined thread attest to more complex garments. A small fragment of a bag from grave 1587 at Naqada (Petrie Museum UC 4372) shows the use of a beading strip between seams. Wrappings, covers and pillows were placed in many graves, along with bundles of folded skins, often still covered in hair. Predynastic cowhide, sheep, goat and possibly also gazelle skin can be identified in the collection of the Petrie Museum. Painted fragments of animal skin in some graves are suggestive of decorative leather hangings. Lashings, two-ply thongs and thicker, twisted cables of hide are common in the grave-goods at Naqada and Badari.

Also excavated from a grave at Naqada is a red-painted moulded rawhide container (Petrie Museum UC 36104; see Petrie and Quibell 1896: 29), perhaps confirming the suggestion that some Predynastic vessel shapes are derived from leather vessels. There are also more enigmatic objects such as leather-covered clay cones (e.g. Petrie Museum UC 4372 from tomb 1587 at Naqada, cf. Fig. 12.5a) and a large number of sticks wound about with rawhide thong, which may perhaps be the starting edges of woven leather mats or pot supports; several examples of are in the collection of the Petrie Museum (Fig.12.5). A variety of decorative techniques were employed, including stamping (UC 5053; grave 1592 at Naqada), tooling, in one case resembling basketry (UC 5051; grave 1589 at Naqada) and painting, as in the case of a belt with a pattern of black branches, in imitation of thonged decoration (Petrie and Quibell 1896: 48, no. 103).

Colours on Predynastic leather, presumably mineral-based, include black, red, white and yellow. The frequency of red pigment on objects in graves may well possess a ritual connotation, as in the case of a roughly cut oval of goatskin painted red on both sides from Naqada grave 1611 (Petrie Museum, UC 5924). Petrie suggests that a fragment painted black and yellow was imitating rows of small skins, which, if correct, implies the existence of furry cloaks with free-hanging tails (Petrie and Quibell 1896: 48, pl. LXVII/18). Brunton (1937: 47) also reports 'fur' from burials at Mostagedda. The frequent presence of bone and copper awls is further evidence for the importance of leather as a raw material in these communities (Brunton and Caton Thompson 1928: pl. XX.16). Nibbi (1993) makes a good case for the use of hide-covered boats in the Predynastic and Early Dynastic period: such skins would have had to be oil-cured.

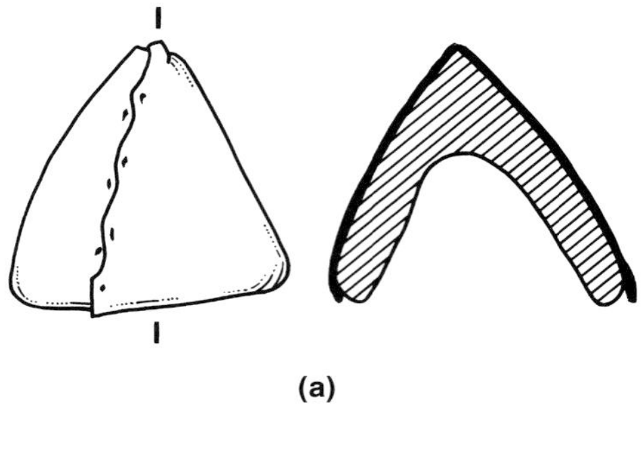

(a)

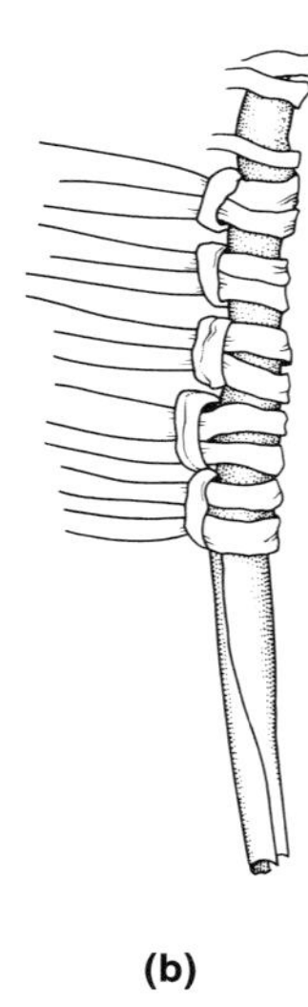

(b)

Figure 12.5 (a) Leather-covered clay cone (Petrie Museum UC 4369; height c. *28 mm) and (b) stick wound round with rawhide (Petrie Museum UC 5058; length* c. *110 mm).*

The Old and Middle Kingdoms (c. 2649–1640 BC)

In complete contrast to the more leather-oriented Predynastic, Nubian and pan-grave societies, Egyptian Old and Middle Kingdoms material culture was much more fibre- and textile-dominated. The decline in leather use seems to be quite abrupt, perhaps in consequence of the increasing use of textile clothing at this period, although metal tools suitable for leather-working do occur in Early Dynastic graves, while Old Kingdom texts and tomb depictions attest to the making of leather sandals and document cases. These two very different leather products could apparently both be made in the same establishment, judging from an inscription on the sarcophagus of Weta, an Old Kingdom official (Junker 1957: 7). However, for Forbes (1957: 27) to state that Weta was 'deeply involved in the leather trade' is a gross exaggeration and a complete misinterpretation of the nature of the text. The general impression from survivals is of a restricted range of leather products and the simplest of manufacturing techniques.

Domestic skin products from the Middle Kingdom town of Kahun seem to be confined to rawhide axe-lashings and moulded rawhide containers such as a rectangular cup containing fat and an oval bird tray, both now in the Petrie Museum (Petrie 1927: pl. 46.37; 47.76; UC 7116, 7128). Remnants of stitched leather were found in a slaughterhouse-cum-workshop at the Middle Kingdom fortress of Mirgissa in Lower Nubia, together with unworked skins in association with tethering stones (incorrectly described as anchors) and wooden pulley wheels (Nibbi 1993: fig. 11, Vila 1970: 189–90). This suggests the processing of the skins by some simple and rapid method (oiling?) directly after slaughter, and then their immediate use. In view of the twenty-two wooden shield grips found in the same room, they were probably used for shield manufacture at Mirgissa. The wooden pulley wheels might even point to the suspension of carcasses to ensure cleaner flaying. The narrow strips of stitched leather are a significant find, given that depictions and models at this time show shields made of differently coloured strips sewn together, as well as of single hides. The Middle Kingdom tombs at Asyut, for instance, include a wooden boss and spine, presumably deriving from a decayed hide shield, and wooden shields and quivers painted to resemble animal skins or coloured strips of hide (Chassinat and Palanque 1911: pls. II/2, XII/3, XIII/1, XIII/3). Winlock (1945: pl. IV) also discusses examples of hide wrist guards.

Cased skins have a very long history of use, and are still widely employed in the Near East as water containers. Small water skins carried on poles are depicted in tombs of the Middle and New Kingdoms (e.g. the Twelfth-Dynasty tomb of Khety at Beni Hasan, BH17; see Newberry and Griffith 1894: pl. XIV) or could be slung over the shoulder on hunting expeditions (as in the Twelfth-Dynasty tomb of Senbi I, no. B1 at Meir, see Blackman 1914–53: I, pl. VII) and a fragment of the tied nozzle of a goatskin bag was preserved at house Q46.2 in the southern part of the Eighteenth-Dynasty city at Amarna (Berlin, ÄM, 1912/13 no. 781). The water bags used by the Roman-period quarriers at Mons Claudianus were larger, employing complex waterproof seams as well as shaped pouring spouts (see Fig. 12.6 and Winterbottom 1990: 78–81). This is just one example of a category of equipment which must have been common on Roman military sites throughout the Empire, but which has only been preserved in Egypt.

Leather balls, made of between four and twelve segments, either in alternating colours or plain white, first appear in Middle Kingdom graves, such as a yellow and red ball from the Twelfth-Dynasty cemetery A at Riqqa (Petrie Museum, UC 31433, see Fig. 12.7). Anthes (1943: 66) mentions a set of six balls, each comprising four segments. Three of the balls are green and red, the others red and white (the latter being described as 'ungefärbt', i.e. the naturally white, cured skin).

The pan-grave culture

In many respects the pan-grave culture of the Second Intermediate Period (*c.* 1640–1532 BC) represents the continuation of Predynastic traditions and skills outside Egypt proper, but with an even stronger pastoral emphasis (e.g. the role of cattle hides and heads in the burial ritual, see Donadoni Roveri 1988: 182–3). Pan-grave leather goods share many traits with contemporary and later Nubian products. The quality of leatherwork in the pan graves excavated at Balabish and Mostagedda is extremely high, exploiting complex decorative techniques – similar to those used in Nubia (see Williams 1983: 65, pl. 106) – to enhance a wide range of items, such as garments, containers, covers and pouches (Wainwright 1920: 28–9, pls. III, IV, XI/2; Brunton 1937: 133). A number of the women's graves included fringed leather cloaks (sometimes stained red), while some of the men's graves included pierced kilts. The careful stitching, sometimes incorporating beads, often adds to the decorative effect, in particular when small pieces of leather have been used in the manner of patchwork (Wainwright 1920: pl. XI/1). Pan-grave footwear is the same as that found in Egyptian burials of the Dynastic period, but the pan-grave examples are usually more neatly finished off (see Fig. 12.8a).

Among the most typical pan-grave leather products are lobate archers' braces, which, although different in overall style compared with those current in the Middle or New Kingdoms, carry purely Egyptian stamped and tooled designs (Brunton 1937: 117, pls. LXXIV/1c, LXXV/49; Wainwright 1920: pl. XII/1–3; Raven 1988: 84–5, found together with a self bow and six arrows). Most drawings ignore the hole at the top of the lobe, through which a cord is looped round the thumb. Similar designs, but in a different medium, appear 2,000 years later in Nubia on the gold and silver braces in Meroitic and X-Group tombs (see Emery 1938: 232–3, fig. 86). The strong, stitched containers found in graves at Mostagedda were interpreted by Brunton (1937: 130) as milk pails (*cf.* BM 63223; and see Fig.12.8b).

The New Kingdom and Third Intermediate Period (c. 1550–712 BC)

Leather was more widely used in the Eighteenth Dynasty, perhaps partly as a result of the introduction of the new weapons technology from the Levant. Colour became increasingly important and elaborate decorative techniques added to the impression of wealth and display, although technologically, the methods of skin processing remained unchanged. Drenkhahn (1976: 130) notes that unlike other processes, the manufacture of chariots combined several skills and materials in integrated workshops which made

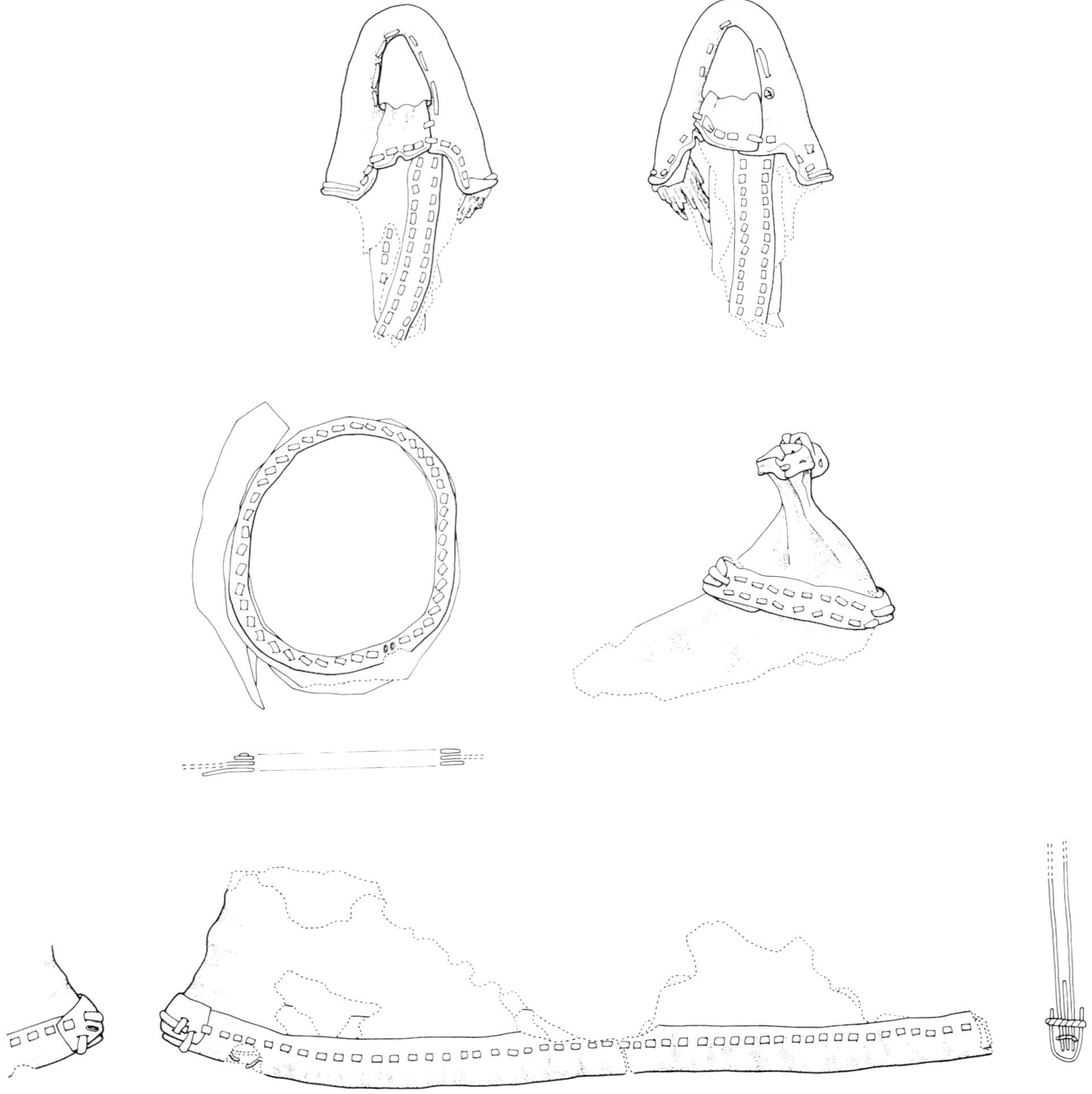

Figure 12.6 Characteristic elements of Roman-period water skins from Mons Claudianus. Scale 1:2.

not only the chariots themselves but also the necessary leather for thongs and harnessing, in addition to the associated equipment such as shields, arm guards and quivers (e.g. those depicted in the Eighteenth-Dynasty tombs of Rekhmira [TT100] and Kenamun [TT93] at Thebes; see Davies 1930: pls. XVI–XX, 1943: pls. LII–LIV). It is not, however, always clear from depictions whether leather, textiles or some other material are intended – the blinkers for Tutankhamun's horses, for instance, are of wood (Littauer and Crouwel 1985: 28).

The manufacture of chariots made sophisticated use of the properties of rawhide, leather and probably also skin-based glues. All surfaces which took stress or abrasion were sheathed in leather, while thick rawhide tyres (shrunk over the composite wheels) stabilised the construction. For display purposes there were even removable red leather tyres (Quibell 1908: 65). Heavy traces, securing the yoke to the central pole served to keep the horses in position (Hansen 1994; Littauer and Crouwel 1985). The introduction of the composite bow stimulated changes in

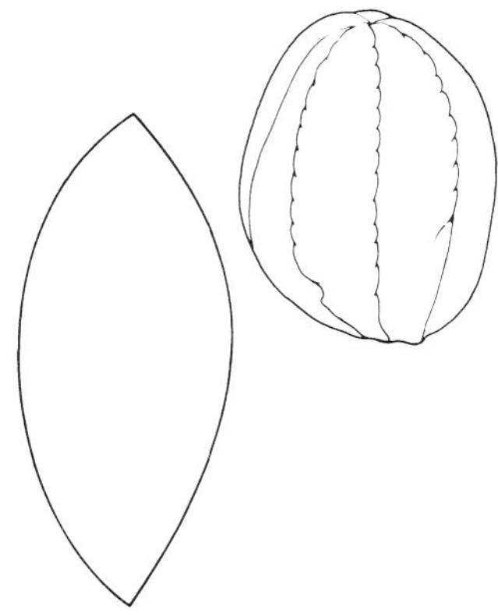

Figure 12.7 *Six-segment red and yellow leather ball from el-Riqqa (Petrie Museum UC 31433) with segment pattern. Scale 1 : 2.*

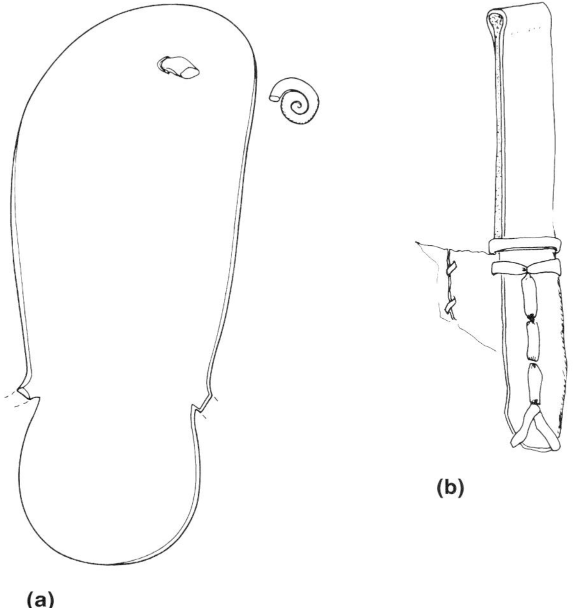

Figure 12.8 *(a) a sandal (BM EA63216; grave 3120; length 234 mm) and (b) reinforced loop from a 'milk pail' (BM EA63223; grave 3133; length c. 186 mm), both from Mostagedda.*

the form of arm guards and quivers. The brightly coloured guards, as depicted in tombs, are tied at wrist and elbow and, in contrast to earlier types, cover much of the lower arm. None seems to have survived and they may have been of padded textile.

The tubular arrow-quivers of the Middle Kingdom were replaced by tapered, round-bottomed types, sometimes using complete animal skins. Though now almost invisible under gelatinous decay, a red quiver in Berlin (ÄM 12476) combines openwork appliqués and couchwork with panels of superimposed coloured strips in red, white, green and black (?), with green, pinked edgings in typically New Kingdom fashion. A quiver from the Eighteenth-Dynasty tomb of Maiherpri in the Valley of the Kings (KV36, dating to the reign of Thutmose III) is unusual not only for its almost perfect preservation, but also for its finely executed, crisp, designs in raised relief (block stamped?), revealing a quality of workmanship which has rarely survived (Daressy 1902: pl. X, nos. 24071–2).

Associated with Nubian mercenaries in the Eighteenth Dynasty, and springing from the pan-grave tradition of pierced leather (see p. 309), are the gazelle-skin net kilts or loincloths (e.g. BM 21999, 2564). The very delicate nets of surviving examples can hardly have served to 'protect' linen loincloths, and they should perhaps be regarded as ethnic markers (Vogelsang-Eastwood 1993: 16–31). Not all such work dates to the Eighteenth Dynasty: a late Roman-period tanned-skin hair-net from Akhmim (Berlin, ÄM 10639) is identical in construction to the 'loincloths' but circular in shape (and a similar Roman netted 'turban' of brown and red wool is described by Winlock 1926: 31–2).

The leatherwork from the Eighteenth-Dynasty city at Armana, much of which is now preserved in the Ägyptisches Museum, Berlin and the Ashmolean Museum, Oxford, is of particular importance in establishing the range of leather goods used in a domestic context in the New Kingdom, especially as finds are in many cases traceable to specific rooms (Borchardt and Ricke 1980). Sandals are common in all houses, as are the rawhide lashings of tool hafting, some of considerable length and intricacy. Larger fragments, suggestive of furnishings or covers, reveal the widespread use of coloured borders and appliqué designs on items of household use. From house N50.1 come at least four sandals, three tool lashings, assorted thongs and straps, odd thongs bound together as handles, several fragments of larger objects edged with coloured strips, a large piece of red rawhide with a green palmette appliqué

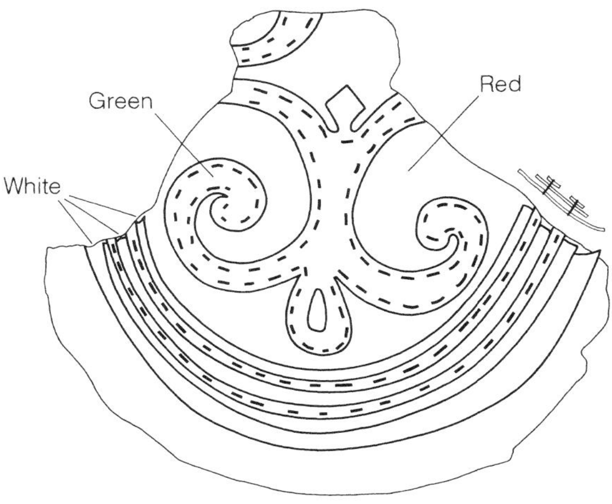

Figure 12.9 *Leather artefact from Amarna (Berlin, ÄM). Scale 1:2.*

(Fig.12.9), and a wide band of composite coloured strips. The excavation of a neighbouring house yielded a small rawhide sheath sewn with red thong or sinew and several rolled up strips that look like buttons. Rawhide belt fragments display an ingenious 'zip fastening', whereby the overlapping ends are interwoven by means of a vertical thong passing through alternating slits.

Offcuts (including both skin edges and the pieces left after cutting out shaped items) are present in the Berlin collection, while Peet and Woolley (1923: 32–3) mention quantities of leather from house P46.14, including unused pieces and numerous trimmings. It is unfortunate that none of the offcuts from P46.14 survives, since this would probably be the earliest attested Egyptian leather-worker's shop.

Many New Kingdom wooden chairs are provided with fibre seats, but folding stools and some Eighteenth-Dynasty 'U-shaped' stools have leather seating-strips. The royal woman named Ahmose, whose tomb in the Valley of the Queens was excavated by Schiaparelli (1921a: 14), was not only buried with leather shoes and substitute jewellery but was also provided with a fine mat, woven of green leather thongs in a large diamond twill pattern.

Skin membranes were also used for lutes, tambourines and lyres (Manniche 1973; Ziegler 1977). Typical for the Twenty-second Dynasty are rawhide mummy-braces: a set of four concave labels (Berlin ÄM 6964/65) still has the red-painted rawhide straps intact.

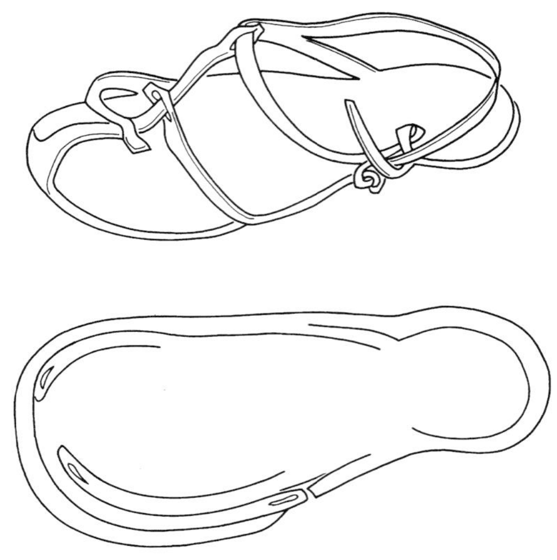

Figure 12.10 Predynastic sandal from Gebelein with reconstructed cutting pattern (Turin, Museo Egizio; dimensions unknown).

Footwear

In most cultures, the most common leather artefact is footwear, although in Pharaonic Egypt fibre was more frequently used for this purpose. On the basis of certain surviving Egyptian magic spells, Bongrani-Fanfoni (1978) proposes that sandals may have fulfilled a protective function in tombs, but the significance of footwear may be more complex than this. Since footwear only appears as an optional extra in tombs already evidencing a moderate degree of wealth, it is possible that sandals may not have been considered appropriate footwear in death, even if, by the New Kingdom, they were widely worn in life (Smith 1992: 219). A statistic according to type (sandals or shoes), materials (fibre, leather or even gold), use (real or models) as well as the sex and occupation of the recipient over a longer period might clarify the role of footwear in tombs. It is, for example, noticeable that Kha, the Eighteenth-Dynasty workman buried in tomb TT8 at Deir el-Medina, had three pairs of sandals, while his wife had none (Schiaparelli 1927: 85), although Mera, a Fifth-Dynasty priestess of Hathor buried at Deshasha possessed two pairs of model sandals, one pair being placed inside her coffin (Petrie 1898: 20). Many of the New Kingdom sandals that the writer was able to examine had indeed been worn: a pair of red-stained sandals from the Eighteenth-Dynasty Tomb N at Gurob (Ashmolean 1889.1086; see Fig 12.11c) are caked with dirt typical of outdoor use with bare feet, as is the colourful example now in the British Museum (BM EA36200; see Fig. 12.3). Although sizes may seem to vary, they still seem to be personal possessions: one of Kha's three pairs of sandals is apparently much larger, but comparison reveals that the largeness lies in the length and width, not in the dimensions of the foot fitting within the straps (Schiaparelli 1927: 85).

No sandals appear to have been found in the Predynastic cemeteries at Badari, Naqada or Mostagedda, but the Egyptian Museum of Turin possesses some Predynastic examples, possibly from Gebelein (Donadoni Roveri 1988: pl. 5). Unlike later Egyptian sandals, these possess interlaced strap-work, formed by partially severing the edges of the sole (Fig. 12.10). Petrie's excavation of a Naqada I-period grave (*c.* 4000–3500 BC) at the cemetery of Diospolis Parva yielded a pair of model sandals painted red, the ragged outline of which resembles the edge-cut strap-work of the Gebelein pair (Petrie 1901: pl. X/U160). Sandals with an apparently similar construction from Nahal Mishmar (a Ghassulian cave-site in Israel; Bar-Adon 1980: 187) may point to a common footwear tradition in the Levant and Egypt for a short time in the Chalcolithic/Early Bronze Age.

In the Old Kingdom, few people other than the king are depicted wearing sandals, although wooden models of sandals begin to appear in tombs, placed in or near the coffin and usually painted white. Although no actual sandals were contained in them, Petrie's so-called 'sandal trays' from graves at Tarkhan may be indicative of the value of footwear in the Early Dynastic period (Petrie 1913: 11, pls. XI/24, XII/10).

There are sandal-making scenes in the tombs of Anta and Shedu at the rather poor Fifth-Dynasty cemetery of

1995 for description of the method). This method is quick and simple, which should make widespread application feasible for the first time. Because it relies on a spot colour change, it is particularly appropriate for use on painted or stained items, since the coloured surfaces can be separated from the body of the leather. Potentially, this is a very powerful tool in the search for the first regular use of tannins in leather processing in Egypt. However, considering the migration of copper salts right through the Ashmolean shoe E2430, revealed by XRF, but invisible to the eye, further research into the depth of penetration of colouring agents is perhaps called for (see Fig. 12.15).

Alum plays a vital role in several, unrelated technological processes: analytical results should not, therefore, be interpreted in isolation. Considering the importance of the substance, a programme of research centred on alum/aluminium itself would be desirable. In particular, the exploitation of Egyptian alum needs to be more closely dated. At present analyses are scarce. Although difficult to detect with x-ray fluorescence spectroscopy, aluminium can be detected with a scanning electron microscope using energy dispersive x-ray analysis (EDXA; V. Daniels pers. comm.). Other techniques sensitive to aluminium could also be applied, but it is important that aluminium is actively sought in all analyses of Egyptian leatherwork otherwise essential information on skin processing methods will be overlooked.

Methods used for the identification of colouring agents on textiles are equally applicable to leather goods as both mineral and vegetable colours could be used (Germer 1992). The XRF scan in Figure 12.15 identifies the mineral-based colours clearly, as well as one of the substances (Ca) used at some stage in processing, but does not reveal details of the curing method or whether alum was used. Furthermore, account needs to be taken of the overlap between mordants and curing agents.

Entrenched assumptions as to the 'antiquity' of many substances and the processes using them have severely hampered scientific investigation. It can only be hoped that a heightened awareness of the importance of undertaking analysis within a clear chronological framework will stimulate research.

A

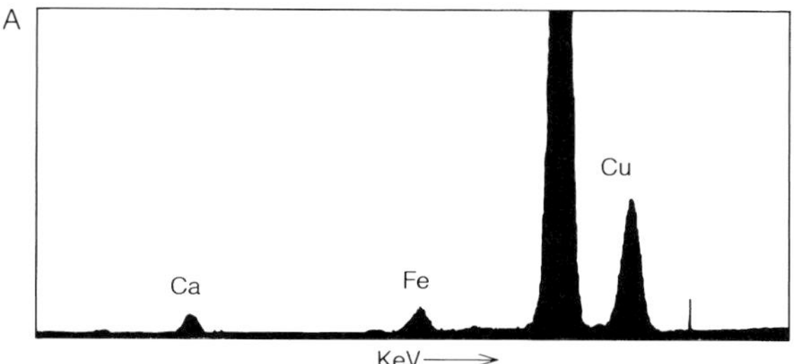

B

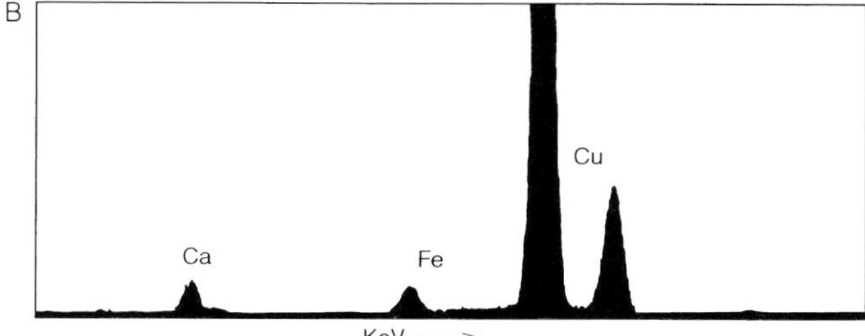

C

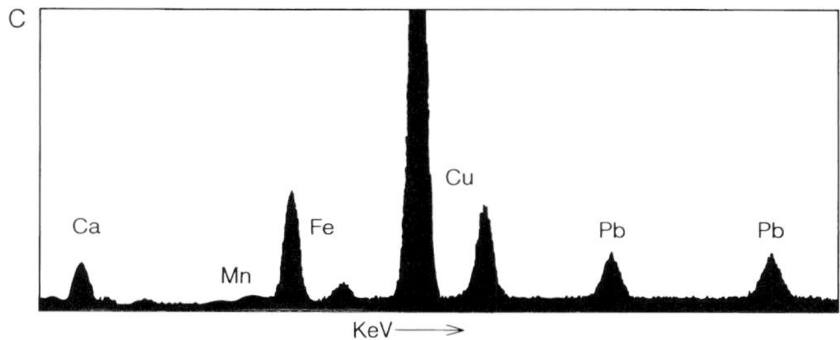

Figure 12.15 XRF scans of three different parts of an ankle-boot: (A) inner surface, (B) top surface and (C) red sole (Ashmolean E2430).

Acknowledgements

This contribution was made possible by a travel grant from the Netherlands Organisation for Pure Research (NWO) which enabled me to examine leather in the collection of several institutions in Britain. I would like to express my thanks to the following for permission to refer to the leather finds in their possession and for valuable and unstinting assistance: Dr H. Whitehouse, Department of Antiquities, Ashmolean Museum, Oxford; Dr J. Spencer and Dr S. Quirke, Department of Egyptian Antiquities, British Museum, London; Dr B. Adams, curator of the Petrie Museum of Egyptian Archaeology, University College, London; Professor Dr G. Wildung and Dr. H. Kischkewitz, Staatliche Museen zu Berlin, Preussischer Kulturbesitz, Ägyptisches Museum und Papyrussammlung. Permission to use objects from their collections for illustrative purposes was generously given by all these institutions. The XRF analysis of Ashmolean E2430, from Abydos tomb W2 was kindly carried out by the Conservation Laboratory staff at the Ashmolean, with the aid of equipment at the Research Laboratory for Archaeology and the History of Art, Oxford, and the results are deposited in the archives of the Department of Antiquities, Ashmolean Museum; I am indebted to Dr Whitehouse for arranging the analyis, and to Dr V. Daniels, British Museum Department of Conservation, for information on analyses and analytical methods as well as permission to refer to unpublished reports. My thanks are also due to Ms B. Wills, Organics Conservation, British Museum for her assistance in locating samples of hippopotamus hide for comparison, and for her advice on this and other matters of identification. I am grateful to Dr C. Cavallo for obtaining copies of the publications by Bravo

(1933, 1948) and for translations of the Italian. With the exception of Figs 12.5, 12.6 and 12.15 the drawings were produced by B. Brouwenstijn and B. Donker (Institute of Pre- and Proto-history, Amsterdam).

References

Alfano, C. 1987. *I Sandali: moda e rituale nell' Antico Egitto*. Città di Castello: Tibergraph.

Anthes, R. 1943. Die Deutschen Grabungen auf der Westseite vom Theben in den Jahren 1911 und 1913. *MDAIK*, 12: 1–68.

Aten, A., Innes, R.F. and Knew, E. 1978. *Flaying and Curing of Hides and Skins as a Rural Industry*. Rome: Food and Agriculture Organization of the United Nations.

Ayrton, E.R., Currely, C.T. and Weigall, A.E.P. 1904. *Abydos* III. London, EES.

Bar-Adon, P. 1980. *The Cave of the Treasure: the Finds from the Caves in Nahal Mishmar*. Jerusalem: Israel Exploration Society.

Bickley, J.C. 1991. Vegetable tannins. In *Leather – its Composition and Changes with Time* (eds. C. Calnan and B.M. Haines). Northampton: Leather Conservation Centre Northampton, pp. 16–23.

Blackman, A.M. 1914–53. *The Rock Tombs of Meir* I–VI. London: EES.

Bongrani-Fanfoni, L. 1978. I sandali e il cammino del' 'Aldila'. *Vincino Oriente*, 1: 1–3.

Borchardt, L. and Ricke, H. 1980. *Die Wohnhäuser in Tell el-Amarna*. Berlin: DOG.

Bravo, G. A. 1933. La lavorazione delle pelli e del cuoio nell'Egitto antico. *Bollettino Ufficiale della R. Stazione Sperimentale per l'industria delle Pelli e delle Materie concianti*, 11: 75–92.

1948. Unpublished typescript in the Egyptian Museum, Turin, dated 15 January, 1948.

Brunton, G. 1937. *Mostagedda and the Tasian Culture: British Museum Expedition to Middle Egypt 1928–29*. London: BMP.

Brunton, G. and Caton-Tompson, G. 1928. *The Badarian Civilization and Predynastic Remains near Badari*. London: BSEA.

Bruyère, B. 1929. *Rapport sur les fouilles de Deir el Medineh (1928)*. Cairo: IFAO.

1937. *Rapport sur les fouilles de Deir el Medineh (1934–5)*. Cairo: IFAO.

CAD 1955 = *Chicago Assyrian Dictionary*. Chicago : Chicago University Press.

Carter, H. and Mace, A.C. 1923. *The Tomb of Tutankhamun I*, 3 vols. London: Cassel.

Carter, H. and Earl of Carnarvon, 1912. *Five Years' Exploration at Thebes*. Oxford: OUP.

Cerny, J. 1935. *Ostraca Hiératiques* I. Catalogue géneral des antiquités égyptiennes du Musée du Caire nos 255501–25832. Cairo: SAE.

Chassinat, É. and Palanque, Ch. 1911. *Une campagne de fouilles dans la nécropole d'Assiout*. Cairo: IFAO.

Cronyn, J.M. 1990. *The Elements of Archaeological Conservation*. London: Routledge.

Daniels, V. 1993. Evaluation of a test for tannin in leather. British Museum Conservation Research Report no. CA1993/1, unpublished manuscript.

Daressy, M.G. 1902. *Fouilles de la Vallée des Rois (1898–1899)*. Cairo: SAE.

Davies, N. de G. 1922. *The Tomb of Puyemre at Thebes*. New York: MMA.

1930. *The Tomb of Ken-Amun at Thebes*. 2 vols. New York: MMA.

1943. *The Tomb of Rekh-mi-Re at Thebes*. New York: MMA.

Donadoni Roveri, A.M. 1988. *Egyptian Civilization: Religious Beliefs*. Milan: Electa.

(ed.) 1989. *Dal museo al museo: passato e futuro del Museo Egizio di Torino*. Turin: Umberto Allemandi and Co.

Drenkhahn, R. 1976. *Die Handwerker und ihre Tätigkeiten im alter Ägypten*. Wiesbaden: Harrassowitz.

Driel-Murray, C. van, 1990. New light on old tents. *Journal of Roman Military Equipment Studies*, 1: 109–37.

Eggebrecht, A. 1973. Schlachtungsbräuche im alten Ägypten und ihre Wiedergabe im Flachbild bis zum ende des mittleren Reiches. Doctoral dissertation. Department of Egyptology, University of Munich.

Emery, W.B. 1938. *The Royal Tombs of Ballana and Qustul*. Cairo: SAE.

Forbes, R.J. 1957. *Studies in Ancient Technology* V Leiden: Brill.

Frauberger, H. 1896. *Antike und Frähmittelalterliche Fussbekleidungen aus Achmin-Panopolis*. Düsseldorf: private publication.

Gall, G. 1961. *Deutsches Ledermuseum*. Offenbach am Main.

Garstang, J. 1907. *Burial customs of ancient Egypt*. London: Constable.

Germer, R. 1985. *Flora des pharaonischen Ägypten*. Deutsches Archäologisches Institut, Abteilung Kairo, Sonderschrift 14. Mainz am Rhein: von Zabern.

1992. *Die Textilfärberei und die Verwendung gefärbter Textilien im Alten Ägypten*. Ägyptologische Abhandlungen 53. Wiesbaden: Harrassowitz.

Gilbert, A.S. 1988. Zooarchaeological observations on the slaughterhouse of Meketre. *JEA*, 74: 69–89.

Haines, B.M. 1991. Mineral, alum, aldehyde and oil tannage. In *Leather – its Composition and Changes with Time* (eds. C. Calnan and B.M. Haines). Northampton: Leather Conservation Centre Northampton, pp. 24–8.

Hansen, K. 1994. The chariot in Egypt's age of chivalry. *KMT*, 5: 50–61.

Haring, B. 1996. Divine households: administrative and economic aspects of the New Kingdom royal memorial temples in Western Thebes. Doctoral dissertation. University of Leiden [publication forthcoming in the Egyptological Series of the Nederlands Instituut voor het Nabije Oosten].

Harris, J.R. 1961. *Lexicographical Studies in Ancient Egyptian Minerals*. Berlin: Akademie-Verlag.

Helck, W. 1975. Alaun. *LÄ*: 130.

Ikram, S. 1995. *Choice Cuts. Meat Production in Ancient Egypt*. Leuven.

Junker, H. 1957. *Weta und das Lederkunsthandwerk in Alten Reich*. Vienna: Sitzungsbericht Österreichische Akademie der Wissenschaften Phil. Hist. Klasse.

Kaczmarczyk, A. 1986. The source of cobalt in ancient Egyptian pigments. In *Proceedings of the 24th International Archaeometry Symposium* (eds. J.S. Olin, and M.J. Blackman). Washington DC: Smithsonian Institution, pp. 369–76.

1991. The identity of *wšbt* alum. *JEA*, 77: 195.

Klebs, L. 1934. *Die Reliefs und Malereien des Neuen Reiches*. Heidelberg: Carl Winters.

Landmann, A. W. 1991. Lubricants. In *Leather – its Composition and Changes with Time* (eds. C. Calnan and B.M. Haines).

Northampton: Leather Conservation Centre Northampton, pp. 22–33.

Lau, O. 1967. Schuster und Schusterhandwerk in der griechisch-römischen Literatur und Kunst. Doctoral dissertation. University of Bonn.

Leach, B. 1995. Tanning tests for two documents written on animal skin. *JEA*, 81: 241–3.

Leemans, C. 1840. *Description Raisonné des Monuments Egyptiens du Musée d'Antiquités des Pays-Bas, à Leide*. Leiden: H.W. Hazenberg.

Littauer, M.A. and Crouwel, J.H. 1985. *Chariots and Related Equipment from the Tomb of Tutankhamun*. Oxford: Griffith Institute.

Lucas, A. 1962. *Ancient Egyptian Materials and Industries*, 4th edn., rev. J.R. Harris. London: Arnold.

Mann, I. 1960. *Rural Tanning Techniques*. Rome: Food and Agriculture Organization of the United Nations.

1962. *Animal By-products: Processing and Utilization*. Rome: Food and Agriculture Organization of the United Nations.

Manniche, L. 1973. Rare fragments of a round tambourine in the Ashmolean Museum, Oxford. *Acta Orientalis*, 35: 29–34.

Martin, G.T. 1987. *Corpus of Reliefs of the New Kingdom from the Memphite Necropolis and Lower Egypt* I. London: KPI.

Mieroop, M. van de, 1987. *Crafts in the Early Isin Period: a Study of the Isin Craft Archive from the Reigns of Išbi-Erra and Šû-Ilišu*. Leuven: Departement Oriëntalistiek.

Mills, A.J. 1982. *The Cemeteries of Qasr Ibrim*. London: EES.

Murray, M.A. 1904. *Saqqara Mastabas* I. London: BSEA.

Newberry, P.E. and Griffith, F.Ll. 1894. *Beni Hassan* II. London: EES.

Nibbi, A. 1993. An early dynastic hide-covered model papyrus boat. *RdE*, 44: 81–101.

Peet, T.E. and Woolley, C.L. 1923. *The City of Akhenaten* I. London: EES.

Perez-Die, M. C. and Vernus, P. 1992. *Excavaciones en Ehnasya el Medineh (Herakleopolis Magna)*. Madrid: Minsterio de Cultura.

Petrie, W.M.F. 1889. *Hawara, Biahmu and Arsinoe*. London: EES.

1890. *Kahun, Gurob and Hawara*. London: EES.

1898. *Deshasheh*. London: EES.

1901. *Diospolis Parva*. London: EES.

1913. *Tarkhan and Memphis V*. London: BSAE.

1920. *Prehistoric Egypt*. London: BSAE.

1927. *Objects of Daily Use*. London: BSAE.

Petrie, W.M.F. and Quibell, J.E. 1896. *Naqada and Ballas*. London: Quaritch.

Quibell, J. E. 1908. *The Tomb of Yuaa and Thuiu*. Cairo: SAE.

Raven, M. J. 1988. The Antef diadem reconsidered. *OMRO*, 68: 84–5.

Reed, R. 1972. *Ancient Skins, Parchments and Leathers*. London: Seminar Press.

Schiaparelli, E. 1921a. *Relazione sui lavori della missione archeologica italiana in Egitto I: Esplorazione della 'Valle delle Regine' nella necropoli di Tebe*. Turin: Museo di Antichita.

1921b. La missione italiana a Ghebelein. *ASAE*, 21: 126–8.

1927. *Relazione sui lavori della missione archeologica italiana in Egitto II: La tomba intatta dell'architetto Cha*. Turin: Museo di Antichita.

Serjeantson, D. 1989. Animal bones and the tanning trade. In *Diet and Crafts in Towns* (eds. D. Serjeantson and T. Waldron). BAR 199. Oxford: BAR, pp. 129–46.

Sigrist, M. 1981. Le travail des cuirs et peaux à Umma sous la Dynastie d'Ur III. *Journal of Cuneiform Studies*, 33: 141–90.

Smith, S.T. 1992. Intact tombs of the seventeenth and eighteenth Dynasties from Thebes and the New Kingdom burial system. *MDAIK*, 48: 193–231.

Soldt, W.H. van, 1990. Fabrics and dyes at Ugarit. *Ugarit Forschungen*, 22: 321–57.

Stol, M. 1983. Leder(industrie). *Reallexikon der Assyriologie und vorderasiatischen Archäologie*. Berlin: Walter de Gruyter, pp. 534–5.

Sykes, R.L. 1991. The principles of tanning. In *Leather – its Composition and Changes with Time* (eds. C. Calnan and B.M. Haines). Northampton: Leather Conservation Centre Northampton, pp. 10–11.

Thomas, A.P. 1981. *Gurob: a New Kingdom Town*. Warminster: Aris and Phillips.

Thomson, R.S. 1981. Tanning – man's first manufacturing process? *Transactions of the Newcomen Society*, 53: 139–56.

Verner, M. 1986. A slaughterhouse from the Old Kindom. *MDAIK*, 42: 181–9.

Vila, A. 1970. L'armement de la forteresse de Mirgissa-Iken. *RdE*, 22: 171–99.

Villiers Stuart, H. 1882. *The Funeral Tent of an Egyptian Queen*. London: John Murray.

Vogelsang-Eastwood, G.M. 1993. *Pharaonic Egyptian Clothing*. Leiden: Brill.

Wainwright, G. 1920. *Balabish*. London: EES.

Williams, B. 1983. *C-Group, Pan Grave and Kerma Remains at Adindan Cemeteries T, K, U and J*. Chicago: OIP.

1991. *Nubadian X-Group Remins from Royal Complexes and from Private Cemeteries at Qustul and Ballana*. Chicago: OIP.

Winlock, H.E. 1926. The Egyptian expedition 1924–25. *BMMA*, Sect. II, March 1926: 5–32.

1945. *The Slain Soldiers of Neb-Hepet-Re Mentuhhotpe*. New York: MMA.

Winterbottom, S. 1990. The leather objects. In J. Bingen, Quatrième Campagne de fouilles au Mons Claudianus. *BIFAO*, 90: 78–81.

Zadok, R. 1985. *Geographical Names According to New and Late Babylonian Texts*. Répertoire Géographique des Textes Cunéiformes 8. Wiesbaden: Reichert.

Ziegler, C. 1977. Tambours conservés au musée du Louvre. *RdE*, 29: 203–14.

1978. *Catalogue des Instruments de Musique Egyptiens*. Paris: Musée du Louvre.

13. Ivory and related materials

OLGA KRZYSZKOWSKA [SCIENTIFIC ANALYSIS] AND ROBERT MORKOT [EGYPTOLOGY]

Introduction

Ivory is a dense and fine-grained material, suitable for carving in the round or in relief, and is ideal for making inlays and veneers, where its natural white colour contrasts well with wood and other materials. Strictly, usage demands that the term 'ivory' be reserved for the dentine of elephant tusks alone; but a somewhat looser definition, encompassing the dentine of other large mammals – hippopotamus, walrus, sperm whale – is gaining acceptance. This allows greater flexibility in discussing and describing the materials and their uses; and moreover, has become essential given recent attention to the role of hippopotamus tusk as a source of ivory in antiquity (e.g. Caubet and Poplin 1987; Krzyszkowska 1988, 1990). Thus whenever possible the terms elephant ivory and hippopotamus ivory should be adopted; but, unqualified, 'ivory' may serve as a useful generic term when distinctions are neither desirable nor practical (e.g. 'ivory workshops').

By Dynastic times, if not earlier, the elephant had become extinct within Egypt proper. Elephant ivory was therefore an import: but several potential sources existed – in Africa itself and also in western Asia. By contrast the hippopotamus was indigenous to the Nile; extinction in the Delta occurring in the seventeenth century AD. It is unlikely that the ivory of other large mammals (e.g. walrus or indeed mammoth) attested in northern Europe, ever reached Egypt. For the use of 'related materials' the evidence – at present – for boar's tusk is scanty; for antler (the boney outgrowths on the skulls of deer) non-existent. But bone itself – readily available as a by-product of hunting and husbandry – is attested in a range of finds, some utilitarian, others decorative. Horn, too, is known from Egyptian contexts: while also an animal product, it is not 'related' to bone and ivory in the physical sense, being a keratinous substance akin to that of hooves.

Until recently, few attempts had been made to identify the types of ivory used in the ancient world, Egypt included. Even today, no systematic study of Egyptian ivories exists; most published objects are described simply as 'ivory' (and behind this label may well lurk objects that are really bone). This lamentable state of affairs seems all the more surprising since the hippopotamus is amply attested in Egyptian art and iconography, and the tusks themselves are easily recognised. However, the poor record of interest and publication inevitably hampers any attempt to discuss the development of ivory-working throughout Egyptian history. Changing sources, patterns of exploitation and use are exceedingly hard to verify. Impressions may indeed be formed from museum catalogues or casual study of displays, but these rarely (if ever) constitute an adequate or representative sample. By stark contrast, ivories from the eastern Mediterranean and the Aegean have been well studied in recent years (e.g. Caubet and Poplin 1987, 1992; Caubet *et al.* 1987; Poursat 1977a, 1977b; Krzyszkowska 1988; 1990). Special attention has been devoted to accurate identification of the types of ivory represented in the archaeological record, to changing patterns of use over time, to regional variations, to manufacture methods, and to workshop material (Krzyszkowska 1992). While full documentation remains a distant (and perhaps unrealistic) goal, significant progress has been made. Certainly, the general trends of ivory use are now fairly clear for the Aegean, Cyprus, the Syro–Palestinian coast, and to a lesser extent Anatolia (Caubet 1991; Bourgeois 1992). Moreover, some general developments seem to be mirrored in Egypt itself, such as a marked increase in elephant ivory in the middle of the second millennium. Egypt, as a major importer, user and 'exporter' of elephant ivory, undoubtedly had some effect on the availability of this material in adjacent areas. Egypt also seems the most probable source of hippopotamus ivory used in Minoan Crete during the third and second millennia BC. Thus a detailed and systematic study of Egyptian ivories would be welcome not only to Egyptologists but also to a wider audience. The present account is meant as broad overview of our current knowledge, often patchy and incomplete; it may perhaps encourage specialist studies in future.

Identification

The accurate identification of ivory and related materials is based on a study of morphology and structure (Krzysz-

constitute unusually rich sources and may therefore skew our picture somewhat, the broad trends seem clear enough.

By the New Kingdom, ivory was used for substantial objects, such as the headrest of Tutankhamun and a variety of cosmetic items. Some were carved from solid pieces of elephant tusk and sizeable ones at that, such as the red-stained ivory 'water dish' from Tutankhamun's scribal equipment (diameter: 16.3 cm; see Reeves 1990: 166). Other large items are composite, but still using sizeable pieces of tusk, such as the ivory headrest representing Shu which is made from two pieces joined with a wooden dowel and four gold nails, the hieroglyphs and details being inlaid with blue pigment (total height: 17.5 cm, length: 29.1, width 9.0; British Museum 1972: no. 37; Reeves 1990: 183). Two game boards from Tutankhamun's tomb (KV62) were also carved from solid blocks of ivory, hollowed and fitted with small drawers to contain the gaming pieces. The dividers for the squares are integral, the squares having been chiselled out (Cairo JE62061, object no. 585; length: 13.5 cm, width: 4.2 cm, height: 2.8 cm; Tait 1982: 17–18, pls. VIII–IX; and Tait 1982: 1–17 pl. VIII object no. 393 this is slightly larger than 585).

There are examples of solid ivory furniture made from small elements, such as the 'folding stool' headrest of four cylindrical ivory duck-headed legs fitted into Bes-head terminals of stained ivory, the flexible neck support being made of three rows of stained ivory pieces (height: 19.2, length: 26, thickness: 10.5; Desroches-Noblecourt 1963: pl. XLIb; Reeves 1990: 183). A small jewel box was made from a solid frame of blocks of ivory with ivory panels for the sides and lid (Desroches-Noblecourt 1963: pl. XXIIIb). More typical is the use of ivory as veneer and inlay in combination with ebony and cedar, as in the case of the portable chest (British Museum 1972: no. 14; Reeves 1990: 189), as well as the chair and footstool (British Museum 1972: no. 16). Thin veneer was glued, while thicker panels were held with ivory pins. The most elaborate use of small pieces of ivory is the veneered box from the tomb of Tutankhamun, with veneers of plain ivory making a frame for a panel of herringbone marquetry of over 45,000 ivory and ebony slivers (Reeves 1990: 191). Examples of small cosmetic objects, many of stained ivory, are closely similar to those described in the Amarna Letters, such as the one in the form of a trussed duck, with a swivel lid from the tomb of Tutankhamun (length: 8.5 cm; Reeves 1990: 158). Goose- or duck-shaped cosmetic boxes can be made in a variety of materials, with parts in ivory, but they also occur in western Asia either as imports or as locally made Egyptianising objects (see Bryan 1996: 50–4). Other similar objects, particularly those in the form of a 'swimming' girl with a duck, made of ivory, wood and ivory and wood alone, have generally been termed 'cosmetic spoons', but are now considered to be ritual implements (see now Kozloff and Bryan 1992: 331–64). Some items of jewellery were also made of ivory, notably bracelets (see, for instance, Reeves 1990: 152).

From Ugarit, a series of bed-panels carved in low relief has been recovered (Caubet and Poplin 1987: 287, figs. 16–17). In the Aegean too, evidence from texts and finds alike point to the use of ivory (often in combination with other materials) to decorate fine furniture (Krzyszkowska 1996: 99–102). There were undoubtedly marked regional differences in the styles of furniture and the way in which it was decorated. For instance, low-relief carving seems to be relatively uncommon in Egypt, a notable exception being a casket from the tomb of Tutankhamun (for body of box see British Museum 1972: no. 21; for lid see Desroches-Noblecourt 1963: pl. V). By complete contrast, in the Aegean, low-relief carving is commonly used to decorate furniture plaques and cosmetic articles alike. In this connection it is worth citing a wooden box lid decorated in low relief from Saqqara, either an Aegean import or carved locally under Aegean influence *c.* 1450 BC or later (Kantor 1947: 85, pl. XXIVA; Hood 1978: 115–16, fig. 101). Certainly in the international climate of the early LBA, the possibility of external influences from the Aegean or eastern Mediterranean on Egyptian traditions must be acknowledged. One type of carving not generally found in Egypt, but common in western Asiatic ivories is open-work in which the design is drilled and fully cut-through (*ajouré*). The only example of this period from Egypt seems to be the arm-band showing Thutmose IV smiting enemies in front of the god Monthu (Berlin ÄM 21685: length: 11.2 cm). The earliest western Asiatic examples appear to be those from Megiddo (discussed by Bryan 1996: 69–72, fig. 14) although most other western Asiatic Egyptianising ivories, like Egyptian ivories, carry incised decorations (Bryan 1996: 60–76, figs. 6–10).

Ivory continued to be depicted in the 'tribute' scenes of the Ninteenth and Twentieth Dynasties, but it has generally been assumed that with the end of the viceregal system in Nubia, ivory along with other exotica ceased to be exported to Egypt or arrived less regularly (*per contra* Morkot 1995: 184–6). There is a scarcity of ivories from the Third Intermediate Period, but aside from a presumed shortage of the raw material, other factors may also be at work, most significantly a change in burial customs. A decline in the craft has also been noted for western Asia during the Early Iron Age (Caubet and Poplin 1992: 94); here, however, the revival began much earlier, with the tenth to eighth centuries BC a veritable heyday (Herrmann 1986: 47–53). It has been generally accepted that the elephant was extinct in western Asia by this time (Barnett 1982: 164–6; Collon 1977). Both documentary and archaeological evidence, although far from unequivocal, points to Africa as the source of the ivory (Morkot 1998). Thus, the impact of 'availability' on the ivory industry of any given area is immensely hard to gauge. Great centres of carving very often arise in areas which lack local supplies; conversely, areas with adequate supplies do not always make use of them. In Egypt, the hippopotamus always provided an alternative – if less versatile – source of ivory, but the extent to which this was exploited during the first millennium BC remains uncertain (see p. 327). The Late Assyrian emperors received ivory and elephant-hides as part of the tribute of the rulers of Phoenicia, and, although the supplies may not have been as regular (or as large) as they were in the New Kingdom (i.e. Late Bronze Age), there is no reason to assume that there was a total cessation of ivory coming from Sudan via Egypt (Morkot 1995: 185–6). There is ample evidence for the continued export of ivory from Sudan during the Egyptian Late Period and Ptolemaic period, but much of this was destined for use in Persia (Morkot 1991: 324–5) or Greece (Gill 1992; Oliver 1992; Burstein 1996; Morkot 1998). Despite the evidence for the export of ivory to the Mediterranean (presumably through Egypt), Barnett (1982: 22, pls. 8b,10f. 11a) drew attention to the relative paucity of Late Period ivory work from Egypt itself: fine items are few and far between. A minor craft, then, not a major art; for originality and inventiveness – hallmarks of Egyptian ivories in the Pharaonic period – were by then increasingly rare.

Hippopotamus ivory: sources and use

Swampy and riverine locations are the natural habitat of the hippopotamus (*Hippopotamus amphibius*). Now confined to sub-Saharan Africa, they survived in the Nile Delta until the seventeenth century AD and were last sighted in Upper Egypt within the past 100 years. Thus, it is reasonable to suppose that they were present throughout much of the Nile Valley, in both Egypt and Nubia, in ancient times (but *cf.* below). This is borne out by numerous representations of the animals from the Predynastic period onwards. Noteworthy are the Egyptian tomb paintings and reliefs depicting the harpooning of the hippopotamus (Säve-Söderbergh 1953; Krzyszkowska 1990: 21, fig. 6). Since hippopotami can cause considerable damage to crops, hunting them was effectively a form of 'pest control'. Obviously this activity yields a useful by-product – ivory. But questions remain. Were tusks always collected after the kill? Were the animals sometimes killed expressly for their tusks? And were tusks ever traded from one part of the Nile Valley to another?

Aside from Egypt, small areas of Syria–Palestine also seem to have supported hippopotamus populations in antiquity. Of these, one was apparently located in the Amuq basin and Orontes Valley, providing a ready source of hippopotamus ivory for Ugarit (Caubet and Poplin 1987: 292–7) and thence to Cyprus. Extinction perhaps occurred early in the first millennium BC. Osteological remains found at Tel Qasile (near modern Tel Aviv) suggest the presence of a second (rather small?) population which evidently survived as late as the fourth century BC (Haas 1953). It is, however, unclear whether Syria–Palestine (and Cyprus) relied solely on local supplies of hippopotamus ivory, or whether they ever had cause to obtain it from the Delta. The Ulu Burun shipwreck of the late fourteenth century BC has yielded a number of hippopotamus tusks (both lower canines and incisors), along with a cut section of elephant tusk (Bass 1986: 282–5, ills. 18–19; Bass and Pulak 1989: 11, fig. 20). The nationality of this ship and its destination are both unknown: but the cargo is very mixed and includes raw materials and products from numerous centres around the eastern Mediterranean and further afield (Bass 1987).

For the export of hippopotamus tusk from Egypt we have some slender evidence, admittedly circumstantial in nature. In Minoan Crete, hippopotamus ivory was used from the pre-palatial period (mid third millennium) onwards; Egypt, rather than Syria–Palestine, seems by far the most likely source for this era (Krzyszkowska 1988: 226–9). The same may well be true for early-mid second millennium, given the strong evidence for Minoan contacts with Egypt during the Middle Kingdom and early Eighteenth Dynasty, e.g. the 'Minoanising' frescoes at Avaris (Bietak 1996: 73–9, pls. III–VIII; and see Warren 1995 for general background on Minoan–Egyptian relations). Although Aegean workshops increasingly depended on elephant ivory during the fourteenth and thirteenth centuries BC (see p. 320), hippopotamus ivory was never wholly abandoned. However, whether the tusks, such as that found in Mycenae, originated in Egypt or Syria–Palestine is quite impossible to say (Krzyszkowska 1984: 124, pl. 13a; *pace* Cline 1995: p. 106 no. 88, pl. 20.6 'probably Syria–Palestine').

In Egypt and Nubia the use of hippopotamus ivory goes back to Predynastic times. The recent Sudan Archaeological Research Society survey in the Dongola Reach recorded one unexcavated tomb of perhaps Neolithic or Kerma date which was covered with hippopotamus teeth. These are also known at Kerma itself. Reisner's excavations yielded the well-known ivory inlays among other items, some of which have recently been identified as hippopotamus (Bonnet 1990: cat. nos. 213–14; 265–6; 276–7. 283, 285, 287–91; see Wenig 1978: cat. nos. 45–51). The Petrie Museum possesses two unworked hippopotamus tusks from the Garstang excavations at Meroe (unpublished).

In Egypt there are ample signs that hippopotamus ivory was used from Predynastic times onwards. Combs, bracelets, pendants, certain vessels and handles are all morphologically feasible in hippopotamus tusk (see Payne 1993 for specific cases). So too are some figurines and other carvings in the round, e.g. gaming pieces (see p. 324). Several bulls' legs (belonging to furniture?) in the British Museum are made from hippopotamus ivory (Spencer 1980: cat. nos. 479–81, ID-OHK 92). This material could also be used for inlays and relief carvings, e.g. a fine ceremonial knife-handle from Hierakonpolis (Petrie Museum UC14864; Adams 1974: cat. no. 324; Drenkhahn 1986 cat. no. 79, Abb. 8). Most of these objects are also feasible in elephant ivory, and smaller ones in bone, therefore it is extremely dangerous (and premature) to generalise about the association of particular end-products with certain raw materials. One must always be alert to cases of 'substitution', whatever the period. Thus Predynastic 'labels' are attested both in hippopotamus ivory (especially incisors) and in bone. Poplin has identified a bull's leg from Abydos as elephant ivory (Louvre E11019A; Desroches-Noblecourt and Vercoutter 1981: 22–3 no. 24). While the wands and clappers of the Middle and New Kingdom were almost always made from lower canines (requiring little modification beyond removal of the enamel), elephant tusk could be used, albeit producing a much straighter shape (Drenkhahn 1986: cat. no. 92). Clearly only systematic study, beginning at site level (e.g. Adams 1974), can reveal local and chronological variations in the selection of raw materials. Of particular concern, too, is the role that hippopotamus tusk came to play in the middle to late second millennium BC, when elephant ivory was acquired in considerable quantitities. Since our documentary evidence suggests the latter may well have been under direct pharaonic control, it is reasonable to ask whether hippopotamus tusk – a locally available material – became the 'poor man's ivory'. Or, did practical concerns alone dictate how and when it was used? Hippopotamus incisors are ideal for making cylindrical mirror-handles, kohl-tubes and the like; to use elephant ivory for these is not only wasteful, but also more labour-intensive. Whether the collapse of long-distance 'trade' in elephant ivory in the Third Intermediate Period (see p. 325) produced a resurgence in the use of hippopotamus ivory is unknown. As indicated above, our information about ivory working during the first millennium BC is generally rather sketchy. One may note, however, that a few figurines of Ptolemaic date have been published as hippopotamus ivory (Randall 1985: 9–10; see also an inscribed inlay of Saite (?) date in the Walters Art Gallery, cat. no. 40). Furthermore it is also worth bearing in mind that we have next to no evidence for the density of hippopotamus populations for any given period or locale. The mere fact that the animal was attested as late as the seventeenth century AD in the Delta tells us nothing about its prevalence during earlier periods. That is, hippopotamus ivory may – at times – have been available only sporadically, as a by-product of occasional hunting. Moreover availability *per se* does not necessarily translate into selection and use. The interplay between the two (availability and use) is complex: even in the Aegean where documentation is fairly good, considerable difficulties have been encountered in providing explanations for the patterns observed (Krzyszkowska 1988: 228–33, esp. 233).

Bone and other materials

As a by-product of hunting and husbandry, bone is one of the most readily-available raw materials known to man. Although the shape and size of bones do place limits on the range of end-products, a surprising variety of objects – both utilitarian and decorative – can be made. Nor should bone necessarily be regarded as inferior to ivory. It is easily worked and can take a fine polish. Unfortunately bone has suffered greatly from prejudices and preconceptions in the archaeological literature. Finely worked and decorative objects are all too often misidentified as 'ivory'; sometimes this even extends to more utilitarian objects, such as a First-Dynasty 'arrowhead' in the British Museum (Spencer 1980: cat. no. 487) which is actually bone (OHK-ID 92). However, on the whole, our documentation for the Predynastic and Early Dynastic periods is reasonable (see pp. 324, 326–7 for ivory; and Adams 1974; Payne 1993); later periods have been less well treated.

It is worth stressing that bone – the raw material – is derived from a variety of anatomical parts. Not all of these were suitable or indeed available for use (Krzyszkowska 1990: 52–8). Only fresh, uncooked, bone can be worked and thus initial selection is determined by dietary needs and further influenced by butchery pratices. Metapodials of the ruminants have little flesh and limited amounts of marrow and are thus natural discards. Moreover, their shafts are straight, thick-walled and immensely strong, thus making them ideal for a wide range of utilitarian and decorative objects. These include tools, pins, inlays, pendants, rings, amulets and small carvings in the round. By contrast, the bones of the upper limbs are covered with more flesh, are less straight, and have thinner walls: altogether less suitable for working. Of the flattened bones, scapulae are probably the most versatile, providing relatively large flat blanks for combs, inlays and plaques; while ribs are more commonly used for tools. Usually the identification of precise bones and species involved will require the attention of a faunal expert, although in the case of heavily worked specimens the designation 'bone' often has to suffice. On a site-level it is also worth attempting to integrate the faunal and archaeological evidence for bone in order to explore the patterns of exploitation and selection.

Horn is attested from Egyptian contexts, although hitherto it has received little systematic study. The material is a keratinous substance akin to that in hooves and forms a sheath over horn-cores, boney outgrowths from the skulls of ruminants, e.g. sheep/goats, cattle and antelope etc. The cores are of no value whatsoever, but sometimes occur archaeologically, with knife marks revealing that the outer sheath had been removed for use. In general, horn survives less well than bone or ivory, yet extremes of dampness and dryness may, in fact, favour its preservation. The most common use of horn seems to have been for vessels (e.g. Ashmolean no. 1895.931; Payne 1993: cat. no. 1214) or handles (Ashmolean no. E.3142; Payne 1993: cat. no. 1234: species identified as oryx). Although presumably most horn used in Egypt was derived from native – or at any rate African – species, circumstantial evidence exists to suggest that the horns of the Cretan wild goat (*agrimi*) might have been imported for making Egyptian composite bows (Warren 1995: 7 with references).

There is no evidence at present for the use of antler or boar's tusk in Egypt. However, a recently re-discovered papyrus from Amarna depicts a battle between Libyans and warriors who *appear* to be wearing Mycenaean boar's tusk helmets (Schofield and Parkinson 1994). A small fragment, said to be from a helmet plaque, has been reported from Qantir in a context dating to the reign of Ramses II (Schofield and Parkinson 1994: 166, n. 64). At best, however, these pieces of evidence point merely to the possibility of ready-made imports, rather than to local manufacture of an imported material.

Manufacture methods

Availability aside, the physical properties of the raw materials have a bearing on their selection and use for particular end-products. Broadly speaking, elephant ivory is the most versatile, placing the fewest constraints on the carver in terms of size and shape of finished product. Hippopotamus lower canines and incisors are considerably smaller and present several obstacles to carving. Bone offers the least amount of solid material. However, in every case, there are benefits to outweigh potential disadvantages. Hippopotamus ivory is denser than that of the elephant and has long been prized by carvers for its gleaming white appearance. Also, for some end-products the actual shape of tusks – large curving lower canines, small straight incisors – have positive advantages. The shapes of bones and their tensile strength make these the 'material of choice' for a wide range of items, especially those subjected to frequent use.

Selection is thus determined by both suitability and by the amount of labour required to transform the raw material into particular end-products. But needless to say, for us to understand the precise mechanisms demands a good grasp of the characteristics of the materials in the unworked state and careful scrutiny of finished products. These observations must go well beyond basic identifications of the materials used. Attention must be given to how items were carved from the tusks or bones. For instance, in the Aegean, circular *pyxides* are almost invariably made from the proximal (root) end of elephant tusks. The natural pulp cavity provides the hollow shape and bases are made separately (the reconstruction in Bass 1987: 726–7 is wrong). In the Aegean, elephant tusks are sectioned longitudinally (never transversely) to produce the flat blanks from which relief plaques and inlays were made; carving ordinarily occurs on the 'inner' face (Poursat 1977b: 253; Krzyszkowska 1992: 26 n. 5). In Syria–Palestine and Cyprus, duck *pyxides* are generally made from lower canines, utilising the angle above the 'commissure' (Caubet and Poplin 1987: 279–81, figs. 8–10; and see below). But exceptions to all these 'rules' do occur: circular *pyxides* with drilled-out centres, and duck *pyxides* cut 'the wrong way' from lower canines or sometimes from elephant ivory. While observations such as these can be made from finished objects alone, many technical aspects can only be understood by studying workshop debris. The Aegean is fortunate in possessing several groups of 'workshop material', notably from Knossos and Mycenae (Krzyszkowska 1992, 1997). However, interpreting material of this kind – offcuts, roughouts, débitage – is no easy matter. And even the most basic step in working an elephant tusk – removal of the natural outer surface, or 'bark' – was evidently effected in several ways, even on the same site (Krzyszkowska 1992: 26). Once again, generalisations are dangerous, and certainly practices attested in the Aegean or eastern Mediterranean are unlikely to be matched precisely in Egypt itself. While much may be learnt by observing how modern 'traditional' craftsmen approach and handle their materials, only systematic study of the archaeological evidence can reveal the specific solutions adopted by Egyptian craftsmen.

In this context it is worth stressing that we have scant evidence for the organisation of ivory workshops and their craftsmen in the ancient world, Egypt included. Ivory-working would have been carried out under centralised control, whether in temple or palace workshops. Although many tomb-paintings, particularly in the Theban region, show artisans at work, only one, the Theban tomb of Menkheperraseneb, appears to depict ivory-working (TT86; Davies and Davies 1933: pl. XI; see Fig. 13.1 here). The scene lacks a caption, but seems to show a tusk being sawn into panels. Many of the tools – saws, chisels, knives, points and drills – employed in ivory-working were those used in woodworking (Barnett 1982: figs. 4b–c; *cf.* Evely

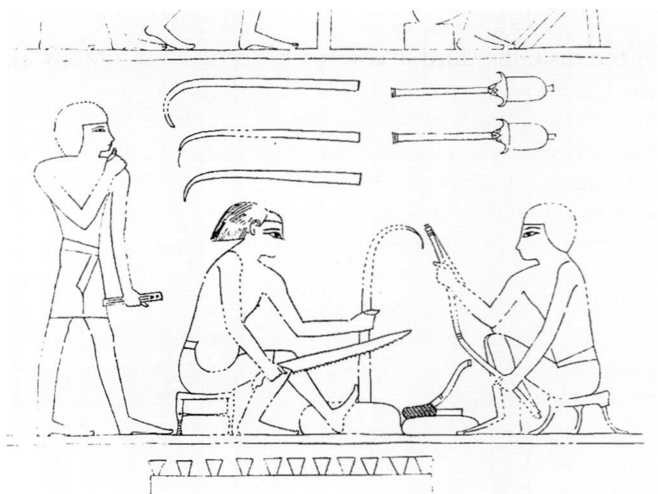

Figure 13.1 Scene possibly depicting an ivory workshop in the Eighteenth-Dynasty Theban tomb-chapel of Menkheperraseneb (TT86).

1992), and the craft may have been practised by the same workers.

Ivory and its relatives are all comparatively soft materials, registering about 2 on the Mohs hardness scale (see Table 2.4). The initial stages of processing could, however, present some obstacles. At the proximal (root) end, an elephant tusk is covered with a somewhat harder (Mohs 4) and slightly ridged outer surface sometimes known as 'bark' or cementum. The distal end or tip lacks any protective outer surface, but the ivory itself is marred with a series of fine black lines or cracks, which may penetrate one to two millimetres within (Krzyszkowska 1990: pl. 1). Thus removal of the 'natural outer surface' is a preliminary step in the carving process, although there are several ways in which this could be effected (Krzyszkowska 1992: 26). Similarly there are various methods for sectioning the tusk and preparing smaller blocks or blanks to form the basis for carving proper: these are closely linked to the end-products intended (see p. 328). A need for economy would persuade carvers to base much of their work on blocks and blanks cut lengthwise from the tusk. There may also have been some practical advantages, i.e. carving 'with the grain', rather than across it, though this suggestion demands further experimental work. In any case, one may observe that even relatively small items, such as Early Dynastic gaming pieces (e.g. Drenkhahn 1986: cat. nos. 67, 70: length: 7 cm) have been cut longitudinally from the tusk. That is, the lamellae indicate that their long axis follows that of the tusk. This approach was essential for larger items, e.g. the ivory 'Shu headrest' from the tomb of Tutankhamun (described on p. 325) and the ivory palette from the same tomb (length: 30.3 cm, width: 4.5 cm, depth: 2.5 cm; Desroches-Noblecourt 1963: pl. IVb).

Compared to elephant tusks, hippopotamus lower canines present the carver with more serious obstacles. In shape they have a marked curve, while in section they are trihedral (Krzyszkowska 1990: 42–7, figs. 17–18, pls. 12–13). Exceptionally hard enamel (Mohs 7) protects two faces of the tusk; the third is covered by 'cementum' (Mohs 4). Cutting through and removing the enamel is thus one of the principal drawbacks of using hippopotamus lower canines. Nonetheless, as Poplin (1974: 85–92, esp. 85–9, figs. 1–6) has demonstrated, the enamel can be cut using string and an abrasive, thus placing this operation within the capability of Predynastic carvers dependent on stone or copper tools. Under natural conditions desiccation causes the enamel to crack and split, and controlled exposure to heat might have been adopted, although proof is lacking (Krzyszkowska 1988: 214). For abrasion there is, however, some evidence, e.g. a segment of lower canine from Knossos, dating to EM IIA, shows clear signs of abrasion across the enamel, though removal by this process alone would have been extremely laborious (Krzyszkowska 1984, pl. XIIIb; Krzyszkowska 1988: 214). A second serious obstacle is the 'commissure', which represents the junction between the surface of the pulp cavity and the newly formed dentine. The slightly 'resinous' appearance of the commisure mars the otherwise dense and gleaming dentine; though it is an immensely useful feature for us in identifying the material (Krzyszkowska 1990: 42–7, figs. 17–19, pls. 14–16). Moreover the commissure represents a line of weakness, along which whole tusks or smaller objects may crack. In the Aegean there is some evidence that carvers sought to avoid 'crossing' the commissure; but if they did impinge on it, the unsightly feature was concealed on the underside of the finished object (Krzyszkowska 1988: 224–6, fig. 5, pl. 30). Finally, tusk size could restrict the range of end-products feasible from lower canines (although of a modern specimen with a length of fifty-eight cm along the outer curve, and a maximum width of 6.5 cm: Krzyszkowska 1990: 38, pl. 12). Yet for all their natural drawbacks, lower canines could yield objects of considerable size and quality: the key lay in skilful sectioning and carving. Regarding incisors, size is the chief obstacle: lengths of about fifty centimetres (of which some forty centimetres is useable) are recorded, but diameters rarely exceed 5.5 cm.

Bone also requires a certain amount of preliminary processing before it can be used. As noted above, only fresh, uncooked, bone can be worked and thus availability is directly linked to diet and butchery techniques. Removal of sinews, marrow and other unwanted elements can be messy but is not especially difficult, and procedure thereafter is dictated by the end-product. Thus in order to manufacture a straight pin or needle from a metapodial, first the epiphyses (joints) would be removed, then the bone would be sectioned lengthwise to provide four blanks of roughly quadrangular section (as demonstrated by unpublished 'workshop debris' from the Aegean). Flat bones, such as ribs and scapulae, are generally split lengthwise, through their cancellous interior, thus providing relatively thin, flat blanks (Krzyszkowska 1990: 53, pl. 20). Unfortunately direct archaeological evidence for bone working – in the form of workshop debris – is even more rare than for ivory-carving. All too often we must fall back on a combination of logic, practical experiment, and ethnographic parallels to reconstruct general approaches.

Finishing techniques

Direct observation of finished objects can yield a limited amount of information on the final stages of ivory (and bone) working. These would involve polishing to remove unsightly tool marks and, in the case of composite items, assembly by means of dowels and mortises (Barnett 1982: 13, fig. 5). Simple inlays or veneers might be provided with a rough scoring on their undersides to assist adhesion. Staining and colouring of ivories is well-attested in the New Kingdom, especially from the tomb of Tutankhamun (e.g. the water-bowl and casket panels). However, the exact substances used and techniques involved require further investigation. Although examples of delicate low-relief carving are known, and one example of open-work, most veneered ivory was left plain or simply incised, sometimes with figures, most frequently with texts. These were often filled with coloured pigment (usually blue).

Conclusions

The wealth of evidence for the use of ivory and related materials in Egypt is great and spans all phases in its history. Systematic study can shed light on a wide range of issues, from sources and procurement of the raw materials to the ways in which they were exploited for particular end-products. There is also huge potential for a detailed investigation into all aspects of working techniques. Last but not least there is undoubtedly scope for further analysis of the changing role that products of ivory and related materials played in Egyptian society and in those of north-east Africa which supplied the raw material. Apart from the economic aspects of ivory, and, from the earliest times, ivory must have been one of the most important items in the Kushite economy, there are also ecological considerations. Both Hellenistic, Roman and early modern sources (such as Petherick 1861) indicate that ivory has often been a by-product of elephants being hunted for food (Morkot 1998: 152). The Assyrian texts refer to elephant-hide, a material which seems not to be noticed yet in Egyptian texts or archaeology. Burstein (1996) has highlighted the effects which over-hunting would have had on elephant populations and migrations; it is also worth considering the relationship with the herders and agriculturalists of the Sudanese savanna. There is still much to be learnt, not only about the details of the ivory trade and ivory-working but also about the wider context, the interaction of people and animals in ancient times. The challenge to future scholars is immense; but the rewards will be felt far beyond the bounds of Egyptology itself.

References

Adams, B. 1974. *Ancient Hierakonpolis.* Warminster: Aris and Phillips.

Barnett, R.D. 1982. *Ancient Ivories in the Middle East.* Jerusalem: Institute of Archaeology, The Hebrew University of Jerusalem.

Bass, G.F. 1986. A Bronze Age shipwreck at Ulu Burun (Kas): 1984 campaign. *American Journal of Archaeology*, 90: 269–96.

1987. Oldest known shipwreck reveals splendors of the Bronze Age. *National Geographic*, 172/6: 693–733.

Bass, G.F. and Pulak, C. 1989. The Bronze Age shipwreck at Ulu Burun: 1986 campaign. *American Journal of Archaeology*, 93: 1–29.

Bénédite, G. 1918. The Carnarvon ivory. *JEA*, 5: 1–15.

Bietak, M. 1996. *Avaris: The Capital of the Hyksos.* London: BMP.

Bonnet, C. (ed.) 1990. *Kerma, royaume de Nubie.* Geneva: Mission archéologique de l'Université de Genève au Soudan.

Bourgeois, B. 1992. An approach to Anatolian techniques of ivory carving during the second millennium BC. In *Ivory in Greece and the Eastern Mediterranean from the Bronze Age to the Hellenistic Period* (ed. J.L. Fitton). BM Occasional Paper 85. London: BMP, pp. 61–6.

British Museum 1972. *Treasures of Tutankhamun.* London: BMP.

Bryan, B.M. 1996. Art, empire, and the end of the Late Bronze Age. In *The Study of the Ancient Near East in the Twenty-First Century* (eds. J.S. Cooper and G.M. Schwartz). Winona Lake IN: Eisenbrauns, pp. 33–79.

Burstein, S.M. 1996. Ivory and Ptolemaic exploration of the Red Sea: the missing factor. ΤΟ ΠΟΙ 6/2: 799–807.

Caubet, A. 1991. Ivoires de Cappadoce. In *Marchands, diplomates et empereurs: études sur la civilisation mésopotamienne offertes à Paul Garelli* (eds. D. Charpin and F. Joannès). Paris: Editions Recherche sur les civilisations, pp. 123–5.

Caubet, A., Courtois, J.-C. and Karageorghis, V. 1987. Enkomi (Fouilles Schaeffer 1934–1966): inventaire complémentaire. *Report of the Department of Antiquities Cyprus*: 23–48.

Caubet, A. and Poplin, F. 1987. Les objects de matière dure animale: étude du matériau. In *Ras Shamra Ougarit III: Le centre de la ville* (ed. M. Yon). Paris: Publications de la Mission archéologique française de Ras Shamra-Ougarit, pp. 273–306.

1992. La place des ivoires d'Ougarit dans la production du proche orient ancien. In *Ivory in Greece and the Eastern Mediterranean from the Bronze Age to the Hellenistic Period* (ed. J.L. Fitton). BM Occasional Paper 85. London: BMP, pp. 91–100.

Cline, E. 1995. Egyptian and Near Eastern imports at Late Bronze Age Mycenae. In *Egypt, the Aegean and the Levant: Interconnections in the Second Millennium BC* (ed. W.V. Davies and L. Schofield). London: BMP, pp. 91–115.

Collon, D. 1977. Ivory. *Iraq*, 39: 219–22.

Davies, N.de G. and Davies, N.M. 1933. *The Tombs of Menkheperrasonb, Amenmose and Another. Nos. 86, 112, 42, 226.* New York: MMA.

Desroches-Noblecourt, C. 1963. *Tutankhamen. Life and Death of a Pharaoh.* London: Michael Joseph.

Desroches-Noblecourt, C. and Vercoutter, J. 1981. *Un siècle de fouilles françaises en Egypte 1880–1980.* Cairo: IFAO and Louvre.

Drenkhahn, R. 1986. *Elfenbein im alten Ägypten: Leihgaben aus dem Petrie Museum London.* Erbach: Deutsches Elfenbeinmuseum Erbach.

Evely, D. 1992. Towards an elucidation of the ivory-worker's tool-kit in neo-palatial Crete. In *Ivory in Greece and the Eastern Mediterranean from the Bronze Age to the Hellenistic Period* (ed. J.L. Fitton). BM Occasional Paper 85. London: BMP, pp. 7–16.

Francis, E.D. and Vickers, M. 1983. 'Ivory tusks' from Al Mina. *Oxford Journal of Archaeology*, 2: 249–51.

Gardiner, A.H. 1947. *Ancient Egyptian Onomastica*, 3 vols. Oxford: OUP.

Gill, D.W.J. 1992. The ivory trade. In *Ivory in Greece and the Eastern Mediterranean from the Bronze Age to the Hellenistic Period* (ed. J.L. Fitton). BM Occasional Paper 85. London: BMP, pp. 233–7.

Groom, N. 1981. *Frankincense and Myrrh: A Study of the Arabian Incense Trade.* London and New York: Longman; Beirut: Librairie du Liban.

Haas, G. 1953. On the occurrence of the hippopotamus in the Iron Age of the coastal area of Israel (Tell Qasîleh). *BASOR*, 132: 30–4.

Hayward, L.G. 1990. The origin of the raw elephant ivory used in Greece and the Aegean during the Late Bronze Age. *Antiquity*, 64: 103–9.

Herrmann, G. 1986. *Ivories from Room SW 37 Fort Shalmaneser (Ivories from Nimrud 1949–1963 Fasc. IV,1).* London: British School of Archaeology in Iraq.

Hood, S. 1978. *The Arts in Prehistoric Greece.* Harmondsworth: Penguin.

Kantor, H.J. 1947. *The Aegean and Orient in the Second Millennium B.C.* Archaeological Institute of America Monograph 1. Bloomington, IN: Indiana University Press.

Kozloff, A. and Bryan, B. 1992. *Egypt's Dazzling Sun: Amenhotep III and his World.* Cleveland OH and Bloomington IN: Cleveland Museum of Art and Indiana University Press.

Krzyszkowska, O. 1984. Ivory from hippopotamus tusk in the Aegean Bronze Age. *Antiquity*, 58: 123–5.

1988. Ivory in the Aegean Bronze Age: elephant tusk or hippopotamus ivory? *Annual of the British School at Athens*, 83: 209–34.

1990. *Ivory and Related Materials: An Illustrated Guide.* Bulletin of the Institute of Classical Studies Supplement 59. London: Institute of Classical Studies.

1992. Aegean ivory carving: towards an evaluation of Late Bronze Age workshop material. In *Ivory in Greece and the Eastern Mediterranean from the Bronze Age to the Hellenistic Period* (ed. J.L. Fitton). BM Occasional Paper 85. London: BMP, pp. 25–35.

1996. Furniture in the Aegean Bronze Age. In *The Furniture of Western Asia: Ancient and Traditional* (ed. G. Herrmann). Mainz am Rhein: von Zabern, 85–103.

1997. Cult and craft: ivories from the Citadel House Area, Mycenae. In *TEXNH: Craftsmen, Craftswomen and Craftsmanship in the Aegean Bronze Age* (eds. R. Laffineur and P. Betancourt). Aegaeum 16. Liège: Université de Liège, pp. 145–50.

van der Merwe, N.J. and Lee-Thorp, J.A. 1990. Source-area determination of elephant ivory by isotopic analysis. *Nature*, 346 (23 August 1990): 744–6.

Miller, R. 1986. Elephants, ivory, and charcoal: an ecological perspective. *BASOR*, 264: 29–43.

Moran, W.L. 1992. *The Amarna Letters.* Baltimore MD: Johns Hopkins University Press.

Morkot, R.G. 1991. Nubia and Achaemenid Persia: sources and problems. In *Achaemenid History VI. Asia Minor and Egypt: Old Cultures in a New Empire.* (eds. H. Sancisi-Weerdenburg and A. Kuhrt). Leiden: Nederlands Instituut voor Het Nabije Oosten, pp. 321–36.

1995. The economy of Nubia in the New Kingdom. *CRIPEL* 17 [Actes de la VIIIe conférence internationale des études ubiennes, Lille 11–17 Septembre 1994. I Communications principales]: 175–89.

1996. The Darb el-Arbain, the Kharga Oasis and its forts, and other desert routes. *Journal of Roman Archaeology* Supplement, 19 [Archaeological research in Roman Egypt]: 82–94.

1998. 'There are no elephants in Dóngola': notes on Nubian ivory. *CRIPEL* 17/3 [Actes de la VIIIe conférence internationale des études nubiennes, Lille 11–17 Septembre 1994, 147–54.]

O'Connor, D. 1986. The locations of Yam and Kush and their historical implications. *JARCE*, 23: 27–50.

Oliver, A. 1992. Ivory temple doors. In *Ivory in Greece and the eastern Mediterranean from the Bronze Age to the Hellenistic Period.* (ed. J.L. Fitton). BM Occasional Paper 85. London: BMP, 227–31.

Payne, J.C. 1993. *Catalogue of the Predynastic Egyptian Collections in the Ashmolean Museum.* Oxford: Ashmolean Museum.

Penniman, T.K. 1952. *Pictures of Ivory and other Animal Teeth, Bone and Antler.* Pitt Rivers Occasional Paper on Technology 5. Oxford: Pitt Rivers Museum.

Petherick, J. 1861. *Egypt, the Soudan and Central Africa with Explorations from Khartoum on the White Nile to the Regions of the Equator being Sketches from Sixteen Years' Travel.* Edinburgh and London: William Blackwood and Sons.

Poplin, F. 1974. Deux cas particuliers de débitage par usure. In *Premier colloque international sur l'industrie de l'os dans la préhistoire* (ed. H. Camps-Fabrer). Aix-en-Provence: Editions de l'Université de Provence, pp. 85–92.

Poursat, J.-C. 1977a. *Catalogue des ivoires mycéniens du Musée Nationale d'Athènes.* Paris: Diffusion de Boccard.

1977b. *Les ivoires mycéniens.* Paris: Diffusion de Boccard.

Randall, R.H. 1985. *Masterpieces of Ivory from the Walters Art Gallery.* New York and Baltimore: Hudson Hills Press.

Reeves, C.N. 1990. *The Complete Tutankhamun.* London: Thames and Hudson.

Säve-Söderbergh, T. 1953. *On Egyptian Representations of Hippopotamus Hunting as a Religious Motive.* Uppsala: Horae Soderblomianae.

Schofield, L. and Parkinson, R. 1994. Of helmets and heretics: a possible Egyptian representation of Mycenaean warriors on a papyrus from el-Amarna. *Annual of the British School at Athens*, 89: 157–70.

Scullard, H.H. 1974. *The Elephant in the Greek and Roman World.* London: Thames and Hudson.

Spencer, A.J. 1980. *Catalogue of Egyptian Antiquities in the British Museum V: Early Dynastic Objects.* London: BMP.

Tadmor, H. 1961. Que and Musri. *IEJ*, 11: 143–50.

Tait, W.J. 1982. *Game-boxes and Accessories from the Tomb of Tutankhamun.* Tutankhamun Tomb Series VII. Oxford: Griffith Institute.

Vogel, J.C., Eglington, B. and Auret, J.M. 1990. Isotope fingerprints in elephant bone and ivory. *Nature*, 346 (23 August 1990): 747–9.

Warren, P. 1995. Minoan Crete and Pharaonic Egypt. In *Egypt, the Aegean and the Levant: Interconnections in the Second Millennium BC* (eds. W.V. Davies and L. Schofield). London: BMP, pp. 1–18.

Wenig, S. 1978. *Africa in Antiquity: The Arts of Ancient Nubia and the Sudan II: The Catalogue.* New York: Brooklyn Museum.

14. Ostrich eggshells

JACKE PHILLIPS

Ostriches inhabit the southern desert areas of Egypt, the Sudan and savanna areas of central Africa south of the Sahara, as well as parts of South Africa. Until World War II, they were also found in the Saudi peninsula. In ancient times they apparently penetrated as far north as southern Europe and also spread into eastern Asia up to Mongolia (Fisher and Peterson n.d.: 148). Little specific study has been made of the ostrich in ancient Egypt (apart from Laufer 1926: 16–20; Darby *et al.* 1977: 315–18; Behrens 1985; Houlihan, 1986: 1–5).

The bird was hunted from earliest times by both Egyptians and Nubians, a practice commemorated on rock-drawings along the Nile cliffs and in the Upper Egyptian/ Lower Nubian desert, for example at Silwa Bahari (Houlihan 1986:3, fig. 2). These drawings date to Badarian or Naqada I times, and there are also a surprising number of reliefs and paintings of the Dynastic period, especially on the walls of tombs dating to the Eleventh Dynasty and later, such as those from the tomb of Bakt III at Beni Hasan (BH15; Newberry 1893: pl. IV) and the Eighteenth-Dynasty tomb of Rekhmira at Thebes (TT100: Davies 1943: pl. XLIV). Perhaps the most famous illustration is the scene depicted on Tutankhamun's ostrich-feather fan, showing the pharaoh hunting the birds for the feathers that decorate the fan itself. Ostriches were most valued for their tail- and wing-feathers and their eggs, the former for decoration and the latter for food and the shell. The popularity of these objects is indicated by the numerous scenes on temple and tomb walls showing 'tribute-bearers' with ostrich feathers and eggs, especially from Nubia but also Libya, Syria and Punt. Recent work at Mersa Matruh adds archaeological evidence for this trade (Conwell 1987: 31).

Eggs can be up to fifteen centimetres in length and thirteen centimetres in diameter, with a shell thickness of up to 3.5 millimetres and a weight of up to 1.5 kilograms. Eggs of many kinds were employed in Egypt both for food and as a medicinal ingredient (Caminos 1975; Darby *et al.* 1977: 315–17, 330–2; Behrens 1985: 75–6); they need to be consumed within days of collection, therefore they could not have been carried very far, especially through the desert areas where they were collected. Scenes depicted on the walls of tombs of the Eleventh Dynasty and later show desert animals coralled for noblemen's 'hunting preserves', and during the New Kingdom there is even a hint at ostrich domestication; eggs for consumption may have been collected from such 'farms'. Ostrich meat is edible, and may have been consumed as a delicacy. The use of albumen (egg-white) as a binding medium for paint also has been suggested, although not yet identified in recent analyses (Lucas 1962: 1–2; Davies forthcoming; see also Chapter 19, this volume).

Ostrich eggshells have been recovered from Egyptian graves of the Badarian and Gerzean periods and from Nubian graves of similar and later date, although they were evidently not regarded as a food suitable for the deceased. A few were decorated, and occasionally clay 'eggs' served as substitutes (Kantor 1948). One at Naqada was apparently intended to act as a substitute for the missing head of the deceased (Petrie and Spurrell 1896: 28). The shells were also worked into jewellery from the Badarian period onwards, taking the form of small disc-beads (shaped, drilled and strung together into simple necklaces), larger perforated discs (possibly for ear, forehead or clothing ornaments), and slightly curving flat pendants in a variety of shapes having a suspension hole at one end. At least some of these items of jewellery were probably amuletic in intent (Nordström 1972: 124–6, pls. 1–5; Needler 1984: 306–7, pl. 52). Eggshell jewellery is common in all periods through to at least the Twenty-second Dynasty, even in the Eighteenth to early nineteenth Dynasty (S. Snape pers. comm. and forthcoming, *contra* Lucas 1962: 38, 44; for Eighteenth-Dynasty jewellery. see Kemp 1980: 8).

Few other objects made from ostrich eggshell have been recovered, and remarkably few ancient Egyptian eggshell vessels are known. These date to the Eighteenth Dynasty, and forms include a simple hole-mouthed container, and a cup with drilled hole at one side (probably for a wooden handle); Hayes 1959: 23; Petrie 1890: 32, possibly the same as Thomas 1981: 87, no. 755; Tylor and Griffith 1894: 18, pl. IV; Helck 1985: 77). Recent detailed analysis of unpublished Abydos tomb 1113 A'09, where a hole-mouthed container with a fitted anhydrite neck and rim attachment was recovered, strongly suggests that the vessel is of New Kingdom date rather than the Eleventh Dynasty or early Twelfth

Dynasty date originally assigned to it (Evans 1928: 222, fig. 127; Helck 1979: 268–70; Snape forthcoming).

Eggs were both exported and worked outside Egypt (presumably with their contents removed) and it is noteworthy that, as with ivory (see Chapter 13, this volume), the majority of research on ostrich eggshell vessels has been conducted outside Egypt. Clearly imported fragments have been recovered on Crete in an Early Minoan IIB or III (*c.* 2550–2100 BC) context at Palaikastro and at Knossos in the Middle Minoan IA (*c.* 2100–1900 BC) palace 'Vat Room Deposit', at a nearby Middle Minoan IIIA (*c.* 1760–1700 BC) tomb and elsewhere. During the earlier Late Minoan Bronze period up to at least Late Helladic IIIA1 (*c.* 1600–1370/60 BC), a considerable number of eggshells were adapted into a particular religious vessel type, the *rhyton*, and lavishly embellished with precious metals and faience fittings; these have been found at major sites on Crete, Thera, Kea and the Greek mainland (Sakellarakis 1990). It is unlikely, however, that the earlier finds could ever have been converted into *rhyta*, as the *rhyton* form did not appear until Middle Minoan IIB (*c.* 1800–1760 BC) on Crete (Koehl 1981: 187, Betancourt 1985: 100; *contra* Sakellarakis 1990: 289). Evans's suggested origin of the Middle Minoan IIB-III 'globular alabastron' form of *rhyton* in an Egyptian eggshell hole-mouthed container is negated by the redating of the only example he could cite, the Abydos vessel mentioned above (Evans 1928: 223–6, fig. 129). While the hole-mouthed container form must have been an inspiration for the *rhyton*, its origin should be sought elsewhere than Egypt. A variety of eggshell vessel types, some possibly but none necessarily the source of the *rhyton* form, have also been recovered in Mesopotamia and Syria–Palestine, as well as painted eggshells in Cyprus, Syria–Palestine and Bahrain, and unpainted shells and fragments there and elsewhere including Nubia and beyond (Reese 1985; Vermeule and Wolska 1990: 253–4, 370–1). The presence of both ostriches and artefacts made of ostrich eggshell in the Bronze Age Levant, Saudi peninsula and Mesopotamia precludes any certainty that the Aegean and Cypriote eggshells came from Egypt. Those recovered at the port of Mersa Matruh provide further evidence to suggest that they were being exported from Egypt.

Acknowledgements

I would like to thank Dr Stephen Snape for permission to cite material from his forthcoming book, and also for drawing my attention to the Eighteenth-Dynasty jewellery at Amarna.

References

Behrens, P. 1985. Strauß, Straußenei, Straußenfeder. *LÄ* VI: 72–82.

Betancourt, P.P. 1985. *The History of Minoan Pottery*. Princeton: Princeton University Press.

Caminos, R. 1975. Ei. *LÄ* I: 1185–88.

Conwell, D. 1987. Of ostrich eggs and Libyans: traces of a Bronze Age people from Bates' Island, Egypt. *Expedition*, 29 (3): 25–34.

Darby, W.J., Ghalioungui, P. and Grivetti, L. 1977. *Food: The Gift of Osiris*. London: Academic Press.

Davies, N. de G. 1943. *The Tomb of Rekh-mi-re' at Thebes* II. New York: MMA.

Davies, W.V. forthcoming. *Colour and Painting in Ancient Egypt*. London: BMP.

Evans, A.J. 1928. *The Palace of Minos* II: London: MacMillan and Co.

Fisher, J. and Peterson, R.T. n.d. [c. 1964] *The World of Birds*. Garden City: Doubleday.

Hayes, W.C. 1959. *The Scepter of Egypt* II. New York: Abrams.

Helck, W. 1979. *Die Beziehungen Ägyptens und Vorderasiens zur Ägäis bis ins 7. Jahrhundert V. Chr.* Darmstadt: Wissenschaftliche Buchgesellschaft.

1985. Straußeneiergefaß. *LÄ* VI: 77.

Houlihan, P. 1986. *The Birds of Ancient Egypt*. Warminster: Aris and Phillips.

Kantor, H.J. 1948. A Predynastic ostrich egg with incised decoration. *JNES*, 7: 46–51.

Kemp, B. J. 1980. Preliminary report on the el-ʿAmarna expedition, 1979. *JEA*, 66: 5–16.

Koehl, R.B. 1981. The functions of the Aegean Bronze Age rhyta. In *Sanctuaries and Cults in the Aegean Bronze Age* (eds. R. Hägg and N. Marinatos). Uppsala: Almqvist and Wiksell, pp. 179–87.

Laufer, B. 1926. *Ostrich Egg-shell Cups of Mesopotamia and the Ostrich in Ancient and Modern Times*. Chicago: Field Museum of Natural History Anthropology Leaflet 23.

Lucas, A. 1962. *Ancient Egyptian Materials and Industries*, 4th edn., rev. J.R. Harris. London: Edward Arnold.

Needler, W. 1984. *Predynastic and Archaic Egypt in the Brooklyn Museum*. Brooklyn: Brooklyn Museum.

Newberry, P. 1893. *Beni Hasan* I. London: EEF.

Nordström, H.-Å. 1972. *Neolithic and A-Group Sites*. Uppsala: Scandinavian Joint Expedition to Sudanese Nubia.

Petrie, W.M.F. 1890. *Kahun, Gurob, and Hawara*. London: Kegan Paul, Trench and Trübner.

Petrie, W.M.F. and Spurrell, F.C.J. 1896. *Naqada and Ballas, 1895*. London: Quaritch.

Reese, D.S. 1985. Shells, ostrich eggshells and other exotic faunal remains from Kition. In *Kition V: The Pre-Phoenician Levels Part II*. (ed. V. Karageroghis). Nicosia: Cyprus Department of Antiquities, pp. 371–82.

Sakellarakis, J.A. 1990. The fashioning of ostrich-egg rhyta in the Creto-Mycenaean Aegean. In *Thera and the Ancient World* III:I (eds. D.A. Hardy, C.G. Doumas, J.A. Sakellarakis and P.M. Warren). London: Thera Foundation, pp. 285–308.

Snape, S. forthcoming. *Ostrich Eggs in the Late Bronze Age*.

Thomas, A.P. 1981. *Gurob: A New Kingdom Town*. Warminster: Aris and Phillips.

Tylor, J.J. and Griffith, F.Ll. 1894. *The Tomb of Paheri at El Kab*. London: EEF.

Vermeule, E. and Wolska, F.Z. 1990. *Toumba tou Skourou, a Bronze Age Potter's Quarter on Morphou Bay in Cyprus*. Cambridge MA: Harvard University Press.

15. Wood

ROWENA GALE, PETER GASSON, NIGEL HEPPER [BOTANY]
AND GEOFFREY KILLEN [TECHNOLOGY]

GALE, GASSON AND HEPPER [BOTANICAL SECTION]

Introduction

Despite the paucity of indigenous trees capable of producing timber or wood of sufficient dimensions, the ancient Egyptians used wood extensively to make a broad range of artefacts. Many examples have been excavated from archaeological sites, preserved by desiccation in the arid climate. In antiquity, Egyptian woodworkers developed specialised techniques to incorporate low grade timbers, frequently of narrow dimensions, as components of large, often decorated items (many wooden artefacts were painted or gilded). Precious exotic woods were imported from around the Mediterranean, Africa, the Near East and possibly India. These included aromatic woods such as *Cedrus* and *Juniperus*, which were particularly valued for making architectural features such as monumental doors and ceremonial or ritual items. Ornamental woods were often used as veneers and inlays, sometimes contrasted with ivory, bone, metals or other materials.

The examination and identification of wood

Ancient wood preserved by desiccation usually retains its original volume and shape while its weight and density may be very much diminished; it is invariably fragile and friable. To prevent further deterioration of the anatomical structure, specimens should be kept dry and maintained in carefully monitored arid conditions.

Temporary microscope slides may be prepared using one of the following methods:

a. Where a small piece of wood can be detached from the artefact this should be immersed in hot water and boiled for a few minutes to soften the tissues and remove air trapped in the cells or, if very degraded, soaked in 70 per cent ethyl alcohol to moisten and strengthen the tissues. The wood surfaces should be trimmed to expose the transverse, tangential longitudinal and radial longitudinal planes. Thin sections (*c*. 20 μm thick) can be cut using a freezing module attached to a sliding microtome, or if the sample is sufficiently large and robust, it may be clamped directly into the stage of the microtome. The sections should be mounted in 70 per cent glycerol on a microscope slide and protected with a cover slip.
b. Sometimes the condition of the artefact is such that fragments of sufficient size cannot be removed without causing damage. Sections must then be taken directly from the artefact using a (flexible) razor blade. The relevant surfaces of the wood should be prepared by applying a drop of 70 per cent ethyl alcohol with a small brush. The sections should be mounted as described above.

The prepared microscope slides can be examined using a light-transmitting microscope fitted with optics suitable for observation at magnifications of up to ×400. The anatomical structure must be seen to match reference slides in every respect before a secure identification can be given. Archaeological wood samples frequently show evidence of degradation which may be difficult to recognise and could be mistaken for diagnostic anatomical features. For example, the breakdown of cell walls may expose microfibrils which sometimes resemble tertiary spiral thickenings. Similarly, in the tracheid pitting in conifers, the breakdown of tissue at the margins of the tori (i.e. the thicker region of the pit membrane, circular as seen in radial section) could be confused with the scalloped tori characteristic of *Cedrus* (see Schweingruber 1990: 110–11).

Most woods can be identified only to generic level, but some species, e.g. *Ficus sycomorus* (sycomore fig), which include particular diagnostic characteristics can be named. Caution, however, should be exercised, since the anatomical structure within a species can vary considerably depending on the climatic, edaphic or biotic conditions in which it has grown. Variations in wood structure can also occur in different parts of the same tree, particularly between juvenile and mature growth. By inference, the geographical region from which the artefact was excavated may suggest the most likely species to have been used but it may not be possible to substantiate one species in favour of another on the basis of the wood structure, and given the portable nature of many artefacts (and timbers), it would be unwise to do so.

Types of wood: sources and descriptions

The following account of woods used in Egypt is arranged in alphabetical order by family, genus and species, grouped into dicotyledons, monocotyledons and gymnosperms. The entries include information on the botanical classification, synonymy and morphology of the tree, native distribution, the physical appearance and properties of the wood, references to anatomical descriptions, general (worldwide) uses of the wood and examples of surviving ancient Egyptian artefacts. To avoid perpetuating doubtful or uncertain identifications we have given priority to artefacts which have been identified either by ourselves in the Jodrell Laboratory at Kew or by established plant anatomists at other institutions, although examples cited by Lucas, as well as his modified textual comments, are retained, except when they apply to post-Ptolemaic periods. Therefore species such as mulberry (*Morus nigra*), that have not been identified from pre-Roman artefacts have been excluded. A further list of identified wooden artefacts in various institutions is given by Davies (1995). Nevertheless, many artefacts still await identification, and it is hoped that this chapter will encourage more work in this field.

Dicotyledons

Broad-leafed flowering plants with two seed leaves (cotyledons), providing hard-wood timbers.

Acacia [*Acacia* species (Leguminosae-Mimosoideae)]
Typically flat-topped trees with finely pinnate leaves (see Fig. 15.1). The flowers are yellow or white, clustered in small round heads or short spikes; and the fruits are flat or twisted pods. The acacia tree is found in hot deserts from Egypt to Jordan and Iraq, and it is widespread in tropical Africa. The desert *A. tortilis* Hayne is a small flat-topped tree usually with several stems. *A. raddiana* Savi, often considered to be a subspecies of *A. tortilis*, is similar but with a more distinct trunk and a less flat-topped appearance. *A. nilotica* (L.) Willd. ex Del. is a rounded tree of river sides. *A. albida* Del. (now transferred to *Faidherbia albida* (Del.) A. Chev.), is a larger tree with irregular branching. A few other species of *Acacia* occur in Egypt, but they were never likely to have been common enough to provide much timber.

Wood type
The acacia heartwood is red, hard and durable. For an anatomical description, see Jagiella and Kürschner (1987: 32–9) and Gale and Cutler (1999).

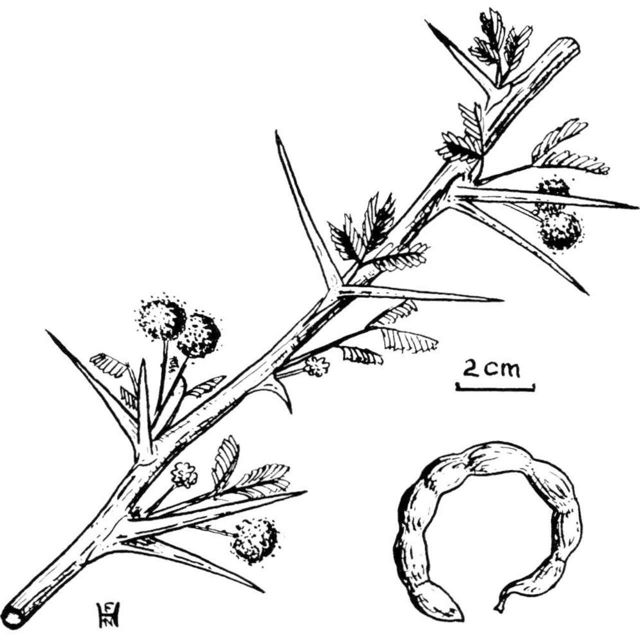

Figure 15.1 Flowering twig of acacia, Acacia tortilis *subspecies* raddiana, *and a pod.*

Uses
The uses of acacia are limited by the small size of timber; in ancient times its charcoal was used for smelting (Scheel 1989: 27). In all periods, acacia wood has been used for boat-building, construction work, furniture, coffins, bows, arrows and dowels (Meiggs 1982; Western and McLeod 1995: 79–80); in addition, acacia blossoms formed part of ancient Egyptian garlands and collars (Beauverie 1935: 138; Germer 1985: 88–92).

When mentioned in ancient Egyptian texts (e.g. the Sixth-Dynasty inscription of Weni from Abydos), it is sometimes said to be obtained from Wawat in Nubia and used for making boats. Herodotus (II: 96; see Godley 1990: 382–5) states that acacia wood was employed by the Egyptians for boat-building, including the masts. Theophrastus (IV: 2, I, 8; see Hort 1916) says that the acacia was an Egyptian tree used for roofing and for the ribs of ships, while Strabo (XVII: I, 35; see Jones 1917–32) simply refers to the 'Thebaic acacia'. Pliny (*Natural History* XIII: 19; see Rackham 1968), apparently quoting Theophrastus, mentions an Egyptian thorn – evidently the acacia from the description – which grew near Thebes and was used for making the sides of ships. Dioscorides (I: 133; see Gunter 1934) says that the acacia grew in Egypt.

Examples
Predynastic: Log (Brunton and Caton-Thompson 1928: 95), roots (Mond and Myers 1937: 7, 138, no. 1408), chisel handle, probably *Acacia* (Ashmolean 1932.911, Payne 1993: 147), and probably a shrine and coffin from Abydos (Fischer forthcoming)

Predynastic–First Dynasty: Coffin from Abydos (Fischer forthcoming), roof beams, arrow fragments (Ashmolean E1381, 1912.559–61; Western and McLeod 1995: 81–3)
First Dynasty: Charcoal (Emery 1939: 70)
First–Third Dynasty: Fragment and charcoal (Mond and Myers 1937: 7, 138, no. 1207)
Third Dynasty: Beam (Ribstein 1925: 194–209)
Third–Fifth Dynasty: Trunks and branches (Lauer *et al.* 1951: 133–4; Ribstein 1925: 194–209)
Sixth–Twelfth Dynasty: Coffin peg (Beauvisage 1896: 85; Ribstein 1925: 194–209; Borchardt 1911: 43), bow fragments (Hearst Museum 6–1588, 6–15346; Western and McLeod 1995: 80), arrow fragment (Hearst Museum 6–1711D, 6–20081, 6–2333X; Western andMcLeod 1995: 83)
Ninth–Tenth Dynasty: Bow (Ashmolean 1921.1301; Meiggs 1982: 404; McLeod 1982: 52; Western and McLeod 1995: 80), headrest (MMA 27.3.160)
Twelfth Dynasty: Sarcophagus dowels, coffin dowels, box dowels, knobs (Osborn 1909: no. 9), stool (MMA 12.182.58)
Second Intermediate Period: Arrow fragment (Manchester University Museum 4223 (a–h); Western and McLeod 1995: 84).
Seventeenth–Eighteenth Dynasty: Table (MMA 14.10.5), arrow fragments (Ashmolean 1892.1464; Western and McLeod 1995: 82, no. 2678)
Eighteenth Dynasty: Part of the body of a chariot (Botti 1951: 192–8), two pegs (Borchardt 1911: 11), dowel (identified at Kew)
New Kingdom(?): Bolt (Borchardt 1911: 56), bow (Ashmolean 1885.375 identified by Western, McLeod 1982: 52; Meiggs 1982: 404; Western and McLeod 1995: 79)
Twenty-sixth Dynasty(?): Arrow fragment (Ashmolean 1886.811b; Western and McLeod 1995: 81, complete arrows (Pitt Rivers Museum 1896–2–1–1, 1896–2–1–3, 1896–2–1–4; Western and McLeod 1995: 85).
First century BC(?): Boning rod (Oakley 1932: 158–9)
Late period: Coffins (Giddy 1992: 36).

Bibliography
Keimer 1984: 19–24; Germer 1985: 89–92; Hepper 1990: 22–3.

Field maple [*Acer campestre* L. (Aceraceae)]
The field maple is a small tree, about fifteen metres high and often shrubby. The leaves are palmate and five-lobed, and the fruits (samara) are winged, with two widely divergent wings. It is found up to an altitude of 2,000 metres above sea-level, throughout Europe and the Balkans, across northern Turkey to the Caucasus and the southern coast of the Caspian Sea. It does not occur in Egypt, but there are several other maples in southwestern Asia (e.g. *A. platanoides* L., *A. cappadocicum* Gled., *A. monspessulanum* L.) which could have yielded usable timber. Another *Acer*, the sycamore tree (*A. pseudoplatanus*), has a wider distribution.

Wood type
The heartwood and sapwood of the field maple are pale or yellowish-brown. The wood is strong and hard with an even grain, and burr wood produces a decorative figuring (i.e. natural patterns on the sawn face of wood, produced by wood cells not growing parallel to the tree's axis, as would usually be the case) on polishing. For an anatomical description of maple wood, see Schweingruber (1990: 176–8) and Gale and Cutler (1999).

Uses
Boxes, culinary utensils, furniture, domestic items, knife handles, musical instruments, boat- and wagon-building, bows, arrows, oxen yokes and charcoal.

Examples
Eighteenth Dynasty: Frame of floor of chariot (Florence 2678; see Botti 1951)

Bibliography
Germer 1985: 106.

Cork wood [*Aeschynomene Elaphroxylon* (Guill. and Perr.) Taub. (Leguminosae-Papilionoideae)]

The cork wood is a soft-stemmed shrub, about two to five metres high. Its leaves have numerous leaflets, and the flowers are large and orange-yellow. It is found on sandbanks in rivers and lakes in tropical Africa.

Wood type
Fibrous, very light-weight and durable. For anatomical description see Metcalfe and Chalk 1950: 526.

Uses
Rafts and floats. This is the only species of *Aeschynomene* that could have provided some sort of timber, but it is fibrous and has a high proportion of thin-walled parenchyma cells, making it very light-weight. It must have been brought into Egypt from further south.

Examples
Third Dynasty: Fragments of furniture (Heidelberg, Ägyptologische Institut 522–4; Ribstein 1925: 206–7).

Bibliography
Germer 1985: 93–4

Silver birch [*Betula pendula* Roth (*B. verrucosa* Ehrh.) (Betulaceae)]
Medium-sized deciduous tree, upright with slender drooping branches and white trunk. The leaves are ovate and acute-toothed, and the flowers are in narrow catkins (see Fig. 15.2). The silver birch is found at an altitude of up to 2,000 metres above sea level, across Europe to northern Greece and the Caucasus, becoming rare in a few scattered places southward, and it does not occur in Egypt.

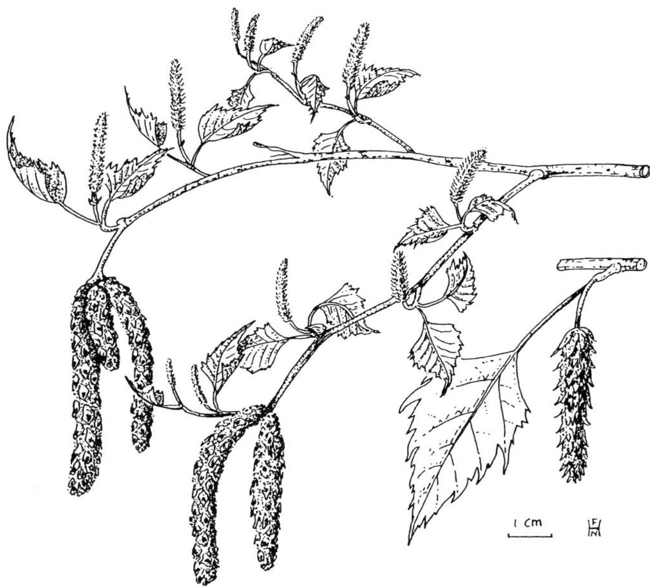

Figure 15.2 Flowering shoot of silver birch, Betula pendula, *with fruiting catkin.*

Wood type
Pale to pinkish-yellow with inconspicuous heartwood, moderately hard and strong but perishable. The bark can be removed in large sheets and has waterproof and insulating properties. For an anatomical description see Brazier and Franklin (1961: 23), Schweingruber (1990: 216–17), Gale and Cutler (1999).

Uses
Boxes, pails, bowls, knife handles, musical instruments, sculpture and boat- and wagon-building.

Examples
The use of this wood is poorly attested in ancient Egypt, only the bark being used to cover items in Tutankhamun's tomb such as bows, a bow box, sticks, a fan-handle, goads and a chariot axle (Hepper 1990: 44). The same parts of the Eighteenth-Dynasty chariot mentioned above (Florence 2678) were also covered with birch bark (see Botti 1951: fig. 2). However, Petrie and Mackay (1911: 10) suggest that certain Old Kingdom staves from Kafr Ammar may be birch.

Bibliography
Germer 1985: 18; Hepper 1990: 45.

Common box [*Buxus sempervirens* L. (Buxaceae)]

A bush or rounded evergreen tree standing up to ten metres high, usually having several slender trunks covered with thin grey bark. The oblong, leathery leaves are about two centimetres long, with a rounded apex (See Fig. 15.3). The flowers are small and yellowish, while the fruits are small and capsular with six beaks. It is found in moist woodland, extending across Europe to the moister areas south of the Black Sea and Caspian Sea, and the hills of western Syria.

Wood type
Golden-yellow with inconspicuous heartwood, strong, hard, heavy and close-grained. For an anatomical description see Schweingruber (1990: 228–9) and Gale and Cutler (in press).

Uses
Sculpture, inlay, knife handles, combs, musical instruments, tool handles, domestic items (bowls, spoons, pins, ladles), gaming pieces and small turned items.

Examples
Seventeenth–Eighteenth Dynasty: Inlay (MMA 14.10.5)
Eighteenth Dynasty: Chair and razor handle (Lansing and Hayes 1937: 13, 28; Hayes 1959: 189), inlay (Hayes 1935: 29)
Twenty-sixth Dynasty: Arrows (Oxford, Pitt Rivers Museum 1896–2–1–2, 1896–2–2–2;Western and McLeod 1995: 85–6).

Since boxwood was used by both the Greeks (Theophrastus V, 3, 7; 7, 7–8) and Romans (Pliny XVI: 28; see Rackham 1968), it is not surprising that a small piece should have been found at the top of a seal dating to the Late Period or Ptolemaic period (see Hayes 1953: 223). Earlier instances of the use of boxwood by Egyptians have, however, also been found, such as the inlay panels dating to the Middle Kingdom (Hayes 1953: 247). Parts of a carved chair, a carved handle for a bronze razor, and applied strips framing inlays of faience on a jewel box, all of Eighteenth-Dynasty date,

Figure 15.3 Leafy shoot of box tree, Buxus sempervirens, *with male and female flowers.*

have been found at Thebes, while several other objects in the Metropolitan Museum of Art, New York (Hayes 1959: 146, 189, 196) and elsewhere (Bothmer 1962: 432) are said to be wholly or partly boxwood. According to the Eighteenth-Dynasty Amarna Letters, the kings of Mitanni and Alashia (Cyprus?) sent boxwood objects and timber to Egypt (letters EA25 and EA40; see Mercer 1939: 145, 147, 205).

Bibliography
Meiggs 1982: 280–2, Germer 1985: 105.

Carob [*Ceratonia siliqua* L. (Leguminosae-Caesalpinioideae)]

Rounded dark evergreen tree, attaining a maximum height of about six metres, with short trunk and spreading branches on which the clusters of pink flowers develop in autumn (see Fig. 15.4). Male and female flowers usually occur on separate trees, and woody pods mature the following year. The carob is found in *maquis* woodland in the Mediterranean region, but in Egypt it is only planted in gardens. The Egyptian name for the carob fruit appears to have been written on a pair of pottery vessels from the First-Dynasty tomb of the official Hemaka at Saqqara (Saad 1938: 51; Keimer 1942: 279–81).

According to Theophrastus (IV: 2, 4) 'some call it the Egyptian fig – erroneously; for it does not occur at all in Egypt, but in Syria and Ionia and also in Cnidos and Rhodes'. Pliny (XIII: 16; Rackham 1968) simply copies Theophrastus, while Strabo (XVII: 2, 2; Jones 1917–32)

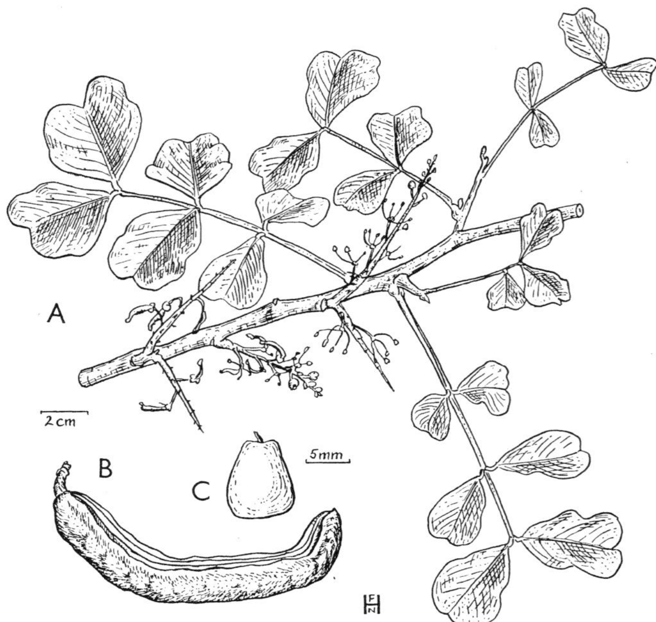

Figure 15.4 Carob, Ceratonia siliqua, *A: leafy, flowering shoot; B: pod; C: seed.*

claims that carob trees are found in abundance in 'Ethiopia'. Breasted (1906) frequently refers to objects of carob wood, but his translations of the term *nḏm* are based on the identification proposed, perhaps incorrectly, by Loret (1893: 111–19), who states that the fruit of the carob tree was known in Egypt from at least the Twelfth Dynasty onwards. Bruyère (1934–5: 108) found it in an Eighteenth-Dynasty context, and Newberry (in Petrie 1890: 47, 48, 50) identified one pod and six seeds of Twelfth-Dynasty date in the town at Kahun, and two pods and a number of seeds in the Greco-Roman cemetery at Hawara.

Wood type
Hard, strong and good quality. For an anatomical description see Fahn, Werker and Baas (1985: 114–15); Schweingruber (1990: 484–5); Gale and Cutler (1999).

Uses
Cabinet-making and furniture.

Examples
Middle Kingdom: Bow (Kew No. 61/1923, 40727)
Roman period: Mummy-labels (BM EA23197, 24497, 24514, identified by Kew).

Bibliography
Keimer 1984: 14–19; Germer 1989: 94–6.

African black or iron wood, Egyptian ebony [*Dalbergia melanoxylon* Guill. and Perr. (Leguminosae-Papilionoideae)

African black/iron wood or ebony (see Fig. 15.5) is found in the dry savanna woodland of tropical Africa (Senegal to Eritrea, northern Ethiopia to Angola, Transvaal) and Western India. Whatever difficulties there may be in the recognition of most of the kinds of wood imported into Egypt, there are none with respect to ebony. The ancient Egyptian name (*hbny*) is well-known and the wood, with its characteristic colour and appearance, is recognised readily without microscopical examination. The ancient Egyptian (Sudan) ebony is not always black, but may be partly or wholly dark brown. Later the truly black wood of species of tropical African *Diospyros*, and especially the south Indian and Sri Lankan *D. ebenum* Koen., acquired the popular name of ebony (Hepper 1977: 109). Records of *Diospyros* in ancient Egypt should be discounted until positively confirmed. However, Western and McLeod (1995: 80, 91–2) discuss the question of Egyptian use of ebony and identify several arrow fragments (Ashmolean E.1371–2) as 'probably *Diospyros* sp.', *D. mespiliformis* being the most likely species.

According to Egyptian textual sources, *hbny* is said to have been imported from a place called Genebteyew(?), as well as from Kush and Punt (Breasted 1906: I, 336, II, 265, 272, 375, 474, 486, 494, 502, 514, 652), but rather than implying that ebony grew in all these areas, these references are simply confirmation that the source(s) lay some-

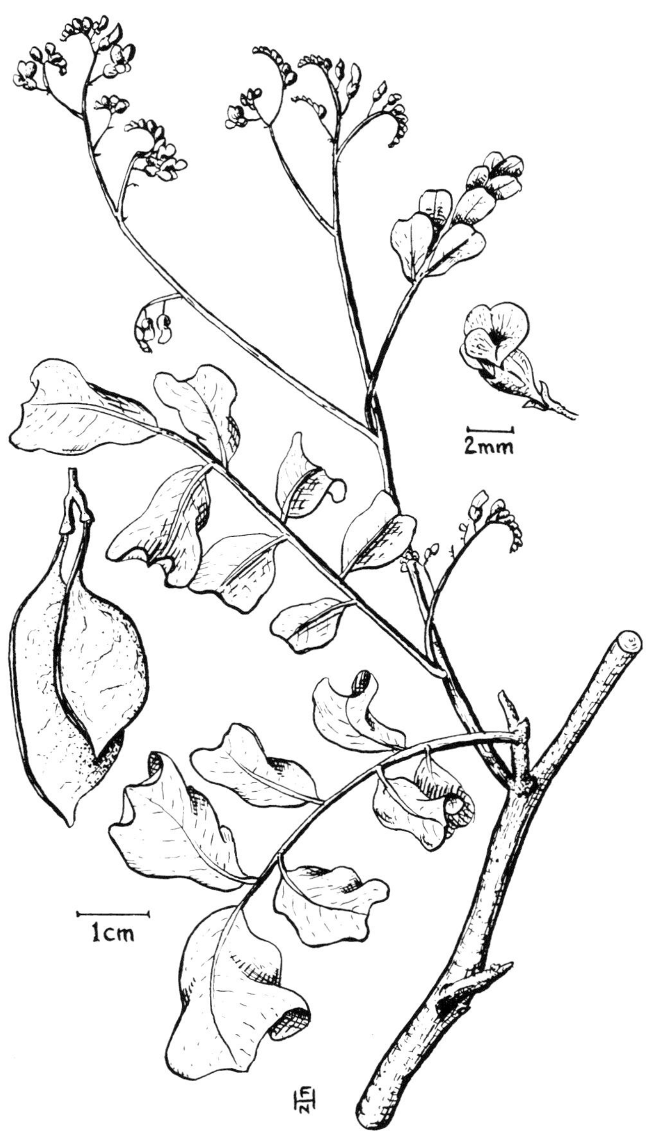

Figure 15.5 Flowering shoot of Egyptian ebony or African black wood, Dalbergia melanoxylon, *with a flower and two pods.*

where to the south of Egypt proper. Burckhardt (1819: 313) reports, as recently as the early nineteenth century AD, that small logs of ebony, about thirty centimetres in length, were being sold at Shendi, just to the north of Khartoum. The scenes depicting the land of Punt, in the cult temple of Hatshepsut at Deir el-Bahari, show Egyptians cutting branches from what are probably ebony trees (Naville 1898: 15). Herodotus (III: 97) describes ebony as an item of tribute from Ethiopia, and it should be noted that Diodorus (I: 3) and Strabo (XVII: 2,2; Jones 1917–32) both claim that ebony trees grew in Ethiopia. Pliny, however, suggests – *contra* Herodotus – that the ebony tree grew neither in Egypt nor in the countries further to the south.

Small ebony objects, such as labels or tablets, have survived from the First Dynasty, and the wood appears to be mentioned by texts as early as the Third Dynasty (Murray 1905: 35). From the Middle Kingdom there are Eleventh-Dynasty ebony arrowheads. Ebony objects of the Eighteenth Dynasty include *shabti* figures of Amenhotep III, various small statuettes (Borchardt 1911: 14) and a panel and door from part of a shrine (Naville 1897: 1; Roeder 1914: 1–11). It should be noted that the well-known Eighteenth-Dynasty head of Queen Tiye in Berlin (ÄM 21834) is not ebony as so frequently stated, but yew: only the inlaid eye-lashes are of ebony (Borchardt 1911: 10). The Eighteenth-Dynasty staff of the princess's butler Thutmose was identified by Richard Moore of Kew as 'a legume, possibly *Dalbergia*, although not dark enough for *D. melanoxylon*, but more likely to be *Pterocarpus*' (Ruffle 1978: 132). This is the only record of *Pterocarpus* in ancient Egypt, but the two genera cannot be reliably separated on the basis of wood anatomy.

Cramps of ebony, thirty to forty centimetres in length, were used to fasten blocks in the Twentieth-Dynasty mortuary temple of Ramses III at Medinet Habu; these have been identified as *Dalbergia melanoxylon*. A specimen of ebony also identified as *Dalbergia melanoxylon* was found at Karanis in the Fayum, dating from the period third to fifth century AD (sent to Lucas by Yeivin).

Some Egyptian texts (Loret 1885: 125–30) indicate that ebony was employed in Egypt for the making of chests, coffins, a harp, shrines, statuettes, staves and whips, although it is not stated whether these items were locally made or imported. Ebony chairs and statues were also obtained as spoils of war. All of these textually attested types of ebony objects (except coffins and harps) have been found among funerary equipment. The ebony objects from the tomb of Tutankhamun, for instance, include a bed, bolts for shrine doors, a complete chair and the legs of a second one, the framework of boxes, a stand for a gaming board, a stool and items with veneer and inlay (Carter 1923, 1927, 1933; Germer 1989: 71; Hepper 1990: 46).

In two of the Amarna letters (EA5 and EA31), Amenhotep III claims to have sent four ebony beds, an ebony headrest, ten ebony footstools and six ebony chairs to the king of Babylonia and thirteen ebony chairs and 100 pieces of ebony to the king of Arzawa (Mercer 1939: 17, 185). One frequent use of ebony in Egypt was as veneer and inlay (generally in conjunction with ivory) for the ornamentation of furniture, boxes and other objects.

Wood type

Heartwood almost black contrasting with the pale sapwood; very hard and heavy, difficult to work but taking a good polish and highly decorative. For anatomical description see Brazier and Franklin (1961: 46); Gale and Cutler (1999).

Uses

Furniture, inlay, veneer, sculpture.

Examples

First Dynasty: Tablets, cylinder seal (Petrie 1901: I: 22, 40; II: 22)
Eleventh Dynasty: Arrowheads (Winlock 1934: 11, 13)
Twelfth Dynasty: Caskets (Mace 1921: 4–6; Winlock 1945: 127)
Eighteenth Dynasty: Staff (Birmingham 474/52; identified by Kew), *shabti* (Borchardt 1911: 14)
Twentieth Dynasty: Cramps (Hölscher 1951: 31).

Bibliography

Germer 1989: 97–8; Hepper 1990: 46–7.

Sycomore fig [*Ficus sycomorus* L. (Moraceae)] (Fig. 15.6)

An erect tree developing massive lateral branches, the leaves being lobed and rough. The fruits (syconium), which develop in clusters on the trunk and branches, are smaller than the common fig and less tasty (Zohary and Hopf 1993: 150–7). It is found in tropical Africa and the Nile valley, extending into lowland Israel and along the eastern coasts of the Red Sea to Yemen and Oman. The spelling 'sycomore fig' is preferable to the often-used 'syc*a*more fig' (see, for instance, Lucas 1962: 440), to prevent confusion with other trees (e.g. *Acer pseudoplatanus* and *Platanus* spp.).

The sycomore fig is represented frequently on tomb walls of the Eighteenth Dynasty at Thebes; it is also commonly mentioned in ancient Egyptian texts. In one Eighteenth-Dynasty document and in another dating to 251 BC (Edgar 1931: no. 59270) sycomore wood is said to have been used for building a boat. Texts dating to the Twentieth Dynasty mention both sycomore-wood statues and sycomore gardens.

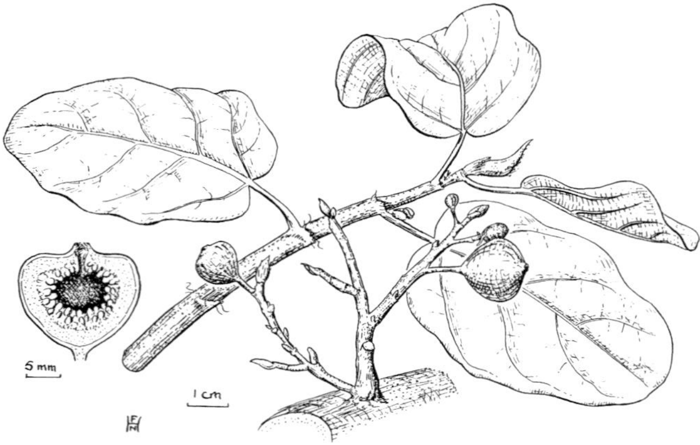

Figure 15.6 Leafy shoot of sycomore, Ficus sycomorus, *with inflorescence on stem, and longitudinal section of a fruit.*

According to Diodorus (I: 3), the sycomore, which he describes as the 'Egyptian fig tree', was grown in ancient Egypt, while Theophrastus (IV: 2, I, 2, quoted by Pliny XIII: 14) provides a description of the sycomore, commenting on the many uses to which it could be put. According to Strabo (XVII: 2, 4; see Jones 1917–32), it grew in Ethiopia.

Petrie and Quibell (1896: 54) note that the sycomore fig has been found among funerary offerings in graves as early as the Predynastic period. There are also attestations of the use of sycomore roots in the Predynastic period, and the sycomore fruit in both the Predynastic period (Brunton 1937: 91) and the First Dynasty (Petrie 1901: 36, 38). There are six clearly identifiable sycomore fig trees in a model garden found by Winlock in an Eleventh-Dynasty Theban tomb, not far from the courtyard of the temple of Nebhepetra Mentuhotep II at Deir el-Bahari, where he also discovered sycomore fig roots (Winlock 1921–2: 26, 2). The Museum of the Royal Botanic Gardens at Kew includes small sycomore branches of Twentieth-Dynasty date (No. 85/1885 26603). The wood was also used for many other artefacts from the Fifth Dynasty to the Roman period and later.

The common fig (*Ficus carica*) was cultivated in Egypt from an early date and is frequently mentioned in offering lists and other texts from the Old Kingdom onwards. However, the only recorded instance of the use of the wood of the common fig is for a mummy portrait of the third century AD in the collection of the Louvre (Coche de la Ferté 1952: 11).

Wood type

Pale, light, fibrous, coarse and of poor quality. For an anatomical description see Fahn, Werker and Baas (1985: 132); Schweingruber (1990: 550–1); Gale and Cutler(1999).

Uses

Roof timbers, coffins, wagons and statues.

Examples

Predynastic: Roots (Mond and Myers 1937: 7)
Fifth Dynasty: Dummy vases (Wittmack 1910: 181–92; Borchardt 1911: 21, 60); Column base (Wittmack 1910: 181–92; Borchardt 1911: 21, 60)
Sixth Dynasty: Coffin of priestess of Hathor (BM EA46634; Davies 1995: 146)
Late Old Kingdom: Coffins (e.g. BM EA46632, 46633, 46637; Davies 1995: 146)
?Sixth Dynasty–First Intermediate Period: Coffin of Nemty-wi (Ashmolean 1911.477)
First Intermediate Period: Coffin fragment and dowels (BM EA46647; Davies 1995: 146)
Middle Kingdom: Numerous coffins (BM EA52950 etc., identified by both Kew and the BM)
Eleventh Dynasty: Roots (Winlock 1922: 26–8)
Late Eleventh–early Twelfth Dynasty: Outer coffin (BM EA41571; Davies 1995: 147)

Early Twelfth Dynasty: Coffins (BM EA29575–6; Davies 1995: 146), coffin fragment (BM EA46642; Davies 1995: 146)
Twelfth Dynasty: Sarcophagi (Osborn 1909, No. 9), coffin and tenons (Osborn 1909,No. 9); coffin (BM EA34259; Davies 1995: 147), box (Osborn 1909, No. 9), coffin (private collection; Oakley 1932: 158–9), statuette (private collection; Oakley 1932: 158–9)
Late Twelfth–early Thirteenth Dynasty: Coffin fragment and dowel (BM EA46654; Davies 1995: 147), coffin (BM EA12270; Davies 1995: 147)
Seventeenth Dynasty: Stele (BM EA55278; Bierbrier 1987, identified by Kew), coffins (BM EA29997, 6652, 6653, 52950, 52951; Davies 1995: 146–7)
Early Eighteenth Dynasty: Coffin (BM EA54350; Davies 1995: 148)
Eighteenth Dynasty: Model building rockers/cradles (private collection; Oakley 1932: 158–9)
New Kingdom (?): Miniature coffins (Borchardt 1911: 102–3)
Third Intermediate Period: Stelae (BM EA22197 etc.; Bierbrier 1987, identified by Kew)
Twentieth–Twenty-sixth Dynasty: Coffin (Chalk 1931–2: 11)
Twenty-fifth Dynasty: Stelae (BM EA8452 etc.; Bierbrier 1987, identified by Kew)
Twenty-sixth Dynasty: Statuette (BM EA11482; James 1982: 156–8)
Saite period: Stelae (BM EA22914 etc.; Bierbrier 1987, identified by Kew)
Late Period(?):Fragment of coffin (Wagenaar 1929: 93–4, 1930: 348–9)
Ptolemaic (?): Wagon (Dittmann 1941: 60–4)
Ptolemaic or Roman: Coffin (Ribstein 1925: 194–209), numerous stelae (BM EA8456 etc.; Bierbrier 1987, identified by Kew).

Bibliography

Germer 1985: 25–7; Baum 1988: 18–28; Hepper 1990: 58–9.

Common ash [*Fraxinus excelsior* L. (Oleaceae)]

Large-sized tree reaching a maximum height of forty-five metres. The deciduous leaves pinnate with nine or eleven leaflets, and the fruits are winged 'keys'. It is distributed throughout Europe to the Caucasus. There are two other species that may have been used instead of the common ash as they are all very similar anatomically: the Syrian ash *F. syriaca* Boiss. (see Fahn *et al.* 1985: 135–6) which has a restricted distribution by streams from the eastern Mediterranean to Iran; and the decorative manna ash *F. ornus* L. (see Schweingruber 1990: 564–5) which occurs as smaller trees on hills in southern Europe and Asia Minor to Lebanon.

The only known specimens of ash from ancient Egypt are (1) the wood of a composite bow from the tomb of Tutankhamun identified by Chalk (Lucas 1962: 429–30) as *F. excelsior*, rather than *F. ornus*, and (2) that used for the axle, the felloes and part of the frame of the floor of the Eighteenth-Dynasty Egyptian chariot in the Museum at Florence.

Wood type

White with inconspicuous heartwood, hard, strong and resilient but perishable. For anatomical description see Schweingruber (1990: 566–7); Gale and Cutler (1999).

Uses

Furniture, tool handles, bowls, boxes, statuary, wheels, paddles, barrels, boat-building, architectural mouldings, shoes, agricultural implements, ladder rungs, arrows and spears.

Examples

Eighteenth Dynasty: Composite bow (*F. excelsior*; Lucas 1941: 144; Germer 1989: 76; Hepper 1990: 47), axle, felloes and frame of floor of chariot (Florence 2678; *F. ornus*; Botti 1951)
Twenty-sixth Dynasty: Arrow (Pitt Rivers 1896-2-2-6; Western and McLeod 1995: 87)

Bibliography

Germer 1985: 152; Hepper 1990: 47.

Storax tree [*Liquidambar orientalis* Miller (Hamamelidaceae)]

A medium to large deciduous tree up to thirty metres high, with palmate (five-lobed) leaves like those of a maple, and globose heads of flowers, which develop into hanging balls of woody seed vessels (see Fig. 15.7). The storax is restricted to the islands of Rhodes and Cos and the adjacent Turkish mainland. It has long been familiar in connection with ancient Egypt because of its use for the production of the

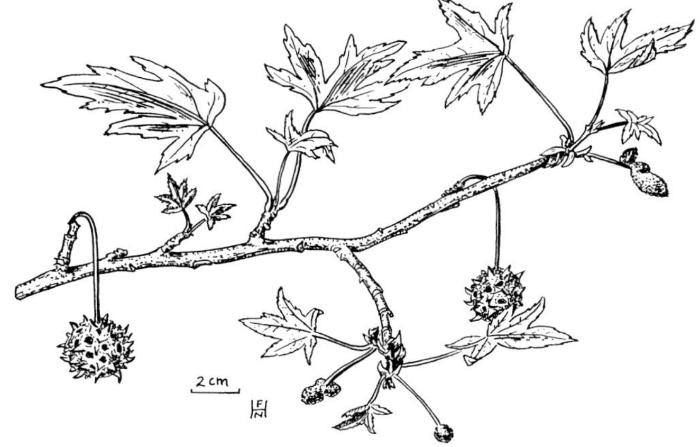

Figure 15.7 Flowering and fruiting shoot of storax tree, Liquidambar orientalis.

storax balsam, which was used in perfumery and in embalming. However, only one surviving specimen of the wood has so far been found, namely a fragment from the Eighteenth-Dynasty tomb of Tutankhamun. This fragment is eighteen centimetres long, with an almost square section measuring 8 × 10 millimetres; one end is shaped like the cutting end of a chisel and the other end is square. Its connections and purpose are unknown, and no reference is made to it in Carter's records, suggesting that it may have been found on the floor of the tomb (KV62).

Wood type

Brown and close-grained. For anatomical description see Gale and Cutler (1999).

Uses

The wood appears to have few recorded uses but since the mature tree attains relatively large dimensions it seems likely that the timber would have been used locally.

Examples

Eighteenth Dynasty: Worked fragment (Lucas 1941: 144, identified by Kew)

Bibliography

Germer 1985: 65, 1989: 77; Hepper 1990: 47–8.

Persea [*Mimusops laurifolia* (Forssk.) Friis (*M. schimperi* Hochst.) (Sapotaceae)]

A medium-sized evergreen tree up to twenty metres in height, with leathery oval leaves clustered towards the end of the twigs, and yellow fruits, the size of pigeon's eggs (see Fig. 15.8), the persea is found in the mountains of Ethiopia and Yemen, and was probably cultivated in ancient Egypt.

Figure 15.8 Flowering and fruiting shoots of persea, Mimusops laurifolia.

It is mentioned in Egyptian texts from the Eighteenth Dynasty onwards (Erman and Grapow 1926–31: IV, 435/10–14; Baum 1988: 87–90) and is discussed by several of the classical writers. Thus Theophrastus (IV: 2, 1, 5, 8) describes it as an Egyptian tree that grew in abundance in the Theban region; he states that it was evergreen (which it is) and that the wood, which was strong and black (said to be whitish by Lucas 1962: 445), like that of the nettle tree (*Celtis australis*), was used for making statues, beds, tables and other objects. Dioscorides (1: 187) notes that the persea was an Egyptian tree, bearing an edible fruit that was good for the stomach, while Pliny (XIII: 17; XV: 13) mentions the tendency, in his day, to confuse the persea with the *persica* (peach).

Twigs and leaves of persea have been found in tombs of various dates from the Twelfth Dynasty (Newberry 1899: 304; Petrie 1890: 49, 1889: 48, 53) to Greco-Roman times. In the Eighteenth-Dynasty tomb of Tutankhamun there were bouquets (several very large) made of twigs with leaves (Carter 1927: 33; Germer 1989: 20; Hepper 1990: 15) together with dried fruit and two glass models of the fruit. Twigs were also found in the Eighteenth-Dynasty Theban tombs of Kha (TT8; Schiaparelli 1927: 166) and Meritamun (DB358; Winlock 1932: 52), although the Meritamun twigs may have been deposited in the Twenty-first Dynasty. Persea fruits have been found in many tombs (see Loret and Poisson 1895: 88–9; Beauverie 1935: 133–4; Schiemann 1941: 128), the earliest specimens being of the Third Dynasty, from the Djoser pyramid complex at Saqqara (Lauer *et al.* 1951: 129–30).

Wood type

Light brown to whitish with yellowish tint (as described by Lucas 1962: 445). There appears to be no published information concerning its anatomical description.

Uses

Joinery, carpentry and construction.

Examples

Middle Kingdom: Corner piece of coffin (BM EA24800, identified by Kew)

New Kingdom: Headrest (Heidelberg University Museum 290; Ribstein 1925:194–209).

Bibliography

Germer 1985: 148–9; Friis, Hepper and Gasson 1986: 201–2; Hepper 1990: 15.

Olive [*Olea europaea* L. (Oleaceae)] (Fig. 15.9).

A small evergreen tree with rounded crown; the trunk of aged trees becoming massive but hollow and with holes marking former branches. Willow-like leaves grey green.

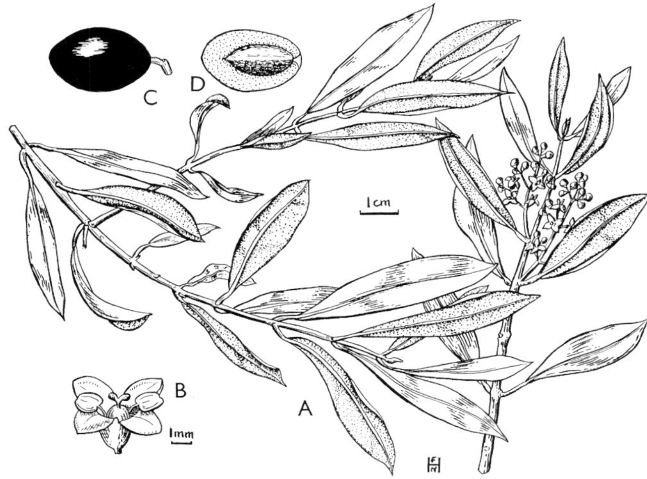

Figure 15.9 A: leafy and flowering shoots of olive, Olea europaea*; B: a flower; C: ripe fruit; D: longitudinal section of fruit showing stone.*

White flowers with four lobes and two stamens. Fruits the well-known black or green olive with a single stone, i.e. seed (Zohary and Hopf 1993: 137–43). The olive tree is essentially found in the 'Mediterranean zone' with cool moist winters and hot dry summers for fruit production, i.e. bordering the Mediterranean Sea.

Although olive trees are cultivated for the sake of their fruits and olive oil is obtained from them (see Chapter 17, this volume), small pieces of olive timber have long been used in Mediterranean lands. In ancient Egypt, however, the only records have been from Late-Period (and possibly Roman-period) wooden stelae.

Wood

Mottled brown, sometimes with a decorative figuring. Hard, heavy, strong and durable. For anatomical description see Fahn, Werker and Baas (1985: 136–7); Schweingruber (1990: 572–3); Gale and Cutler (1999).

Uses

Large timber is difficult to obtain owing to the old trees becoming hollow, so branches of less diameter are used to provide small pieces of wood from trees no longer required for fruit production. Carving, furniture, dowels and small items.

Examples

Late Period: Numerous stelae (e.g. BM EA24526, 26446)

Bibliography

Germer 1985: 150–1; Hepper 1990: 16.

Plum [*Prunus domestica* L. (Rosaceae)]

A deciduous tree, up to six metres high, with elliptical leaves and white flowers. The fruit (drupe) has a glossy skin and succulent flesh around the hard stone. The 'Egyptian plum' mentioned by Theophrastus (IV: 2, 10) is the *myxa* (*Cordia myxa* L.), while the fruit mentioned by Pliny (XIII: 19) is probably another species of *Prunus*. The plum tree originated in cultivation by hybridisation and selection from European species. Although the spokes of an Egyptian chariot at Florence have been identified as plum (*P. domestica*), it is not possible to distinguish the wood with any certainty from almond using anatomical characters, the almond being more likely in Egypt.

Wood type

See Almond.

Uses

See Almond.

Examples

Eighteenth Dynasty: Spokes of chariot (Florence 2678; Botti 1951)

Bibliography

Germer 1985: 61.

Almond [*Prunus dulcis* (Miller) D.A. Webb (Rosaceae)]

A deciduous tree up to eight metres high with erect branches becoming spreading with age, leaves narrow, flowers whitish or pink, fruits (drupe) velvety with a hard stone containing the edible seed (see Fig. 15.10 and Zohary and Hopf 1993: 173–7). The botanical nomenclature of almond has a confusing history. References occur under its synonyms *Amygdalus dulcis* Miller, *A. communis* L. and *Prunus amygdalus* Batsch. It originated in southwestern Asia but is now widely cultivated for its nuts.

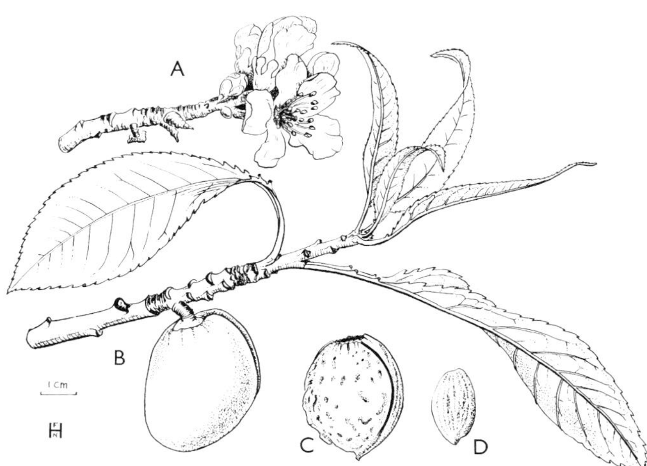

Figure 15.10 Almond, Prunus dulcis*; A: flowering twig; B: leafy and fruiting shoot; C: the stone and D: the seed.*

Wood type
Heartwood reddish-brown, close-grained, strong and hard. For anatomical description see plum (*P. domestica*), and Schweingruber (1990: 628–43); Gale and Cutler (1999).

Uses
Furniture, turnery, carving, bowls, tool handles, arrows and spear shafts.

Examples
Eighteenth Dynasty: Walking stick from Thebes (Kew Museum No. 61/1923 40670); fragment of arrow from the tomb of Tutankhamun (KV62; identified by Boodle at Kew; see Hepper 1990: 44).

Bibliography
Keimer 1984: 25–6; Germer 1985: 59, 60; Hepper 1990: 62.

Turkey oak [*Quercus cerris* L. (Fagaceae)]

A large deciduous tree with a stout trunk, as well as oblong, coarsely toothed or shallowly lobed leaves. The acorn cups have long, narrow downy scales. The Turkey oak is found in southern and central Europe to Asia Minor.

L.A. Boodle identified one of the dowels from the large gilt shrines enclosing the sarcophagus of Tutankhamun as oak (Germer 1989: 74; Hepper 1990: 48). Other specimens of dowels from the shrines were also examined at Kew, and they were all found to be cedar (*Cedrus*) and sidder (*Ziziphus*) apart from one, which was of acacia. Parts of some Middle Kingdom tomb models (e.g. Winlock 1955: 73) and the lid of a coffin of New Kingdom date (Borchardt 1909: 75) are said to be oak, but in neither case can the identification be regarded as certain. The pole, axle and spokes of the Eighteenth-Dynasty chariot now in Florence, initially said to be oak, were later identified as willow, ash and plum respectively (Botti 1951: 192–8). Oak bark was found among the remains of the so-called 'Predynastic tannery' at Gebelein (Bravo 1933: 87; see also Chapter 12, this volume for a discussion of the date of the 'tannery') and a pair of cork soles, stated to be from the cork oak, *Quercus suber*, were found in the Greco-Roman cemetery at Hawara (Newberry and Petrie 1890: 52). Both Theophrastus (IV. 2, 8) and Pliny (XIII: 19) report that the cork oak grew in the vicinity of Thebes. The cork oak occurs in the western Mediterranean region. An arrow made from oak has been recorded from Twenty-sixth-Dynasty Thebes (Western and McLeod 1995: 87).

Wood type
Heartwood, light tan or brown, hard, strong and durable but not such high grade wood as some other species. For anatomical description see Schweingruber (1990: 400–9); Gale and Cutler (1999).

Uses
Oak wood has been used for construction, furniture, joinery, coffins, water pipes, flooring, wagon- and boat-building, ladder rungs, domestic items, tool handles, agricultural equipment, roof shingles, statuary, carving and veneers.

Examples
Eighteenth Dynasty: Dowel (Kew Museum 26754; Carter 1927: 39, 1933: 153)
Twenty-sixth Dynasty: Arrow (Pitt Rivers Museum 1896–2–2–5; Western and McLeod 1995: 87)

Bibliography
Germer 1985: 20–1; Hepper 1990: 48.

Willow [*Salix subserrata* Willd. (*S. safsaf* Delile) (Salicaceae)]

Small tree or branched shrub, with narrowly lanceolate, slightly toothed leaves, and male and female flowers in catkins on separate trees. It is found on the banks and islands of the River Nile (Baum 1988: 196–9). The handle of an Egyptian flint knife of protodynastic date has been identified as probably willow, another example of its early use being for a box of the Third Dynasty. The same or another protodynastic knife handle examined by Ribstein (1925: 194–209) may have been either willow or poplar (*Populus euphratica*) which is rare in Egypt. Poplar leaves have been identified in a garland of uncertain date in the Louvre (Loret and Poisson 1895: 187–8), but no other record of the wood is known. The pole of an Eighteenth-Dynasty chariot in the museum at Florence (No. 2678) was formerly identified as oak (*Quercus* sp.) and later thought to be elm (*Ulmus* sp.), but it is now known to be willow wood (*Salix* sp.; see Western and McLeod 1995: 77).

Leaves of the willow tree were used for making funerary garlands; Eighteenth- and Twenty-first-Dynasty examples of such garlands, some from the tomb of Tutankhamun (Newberry in Petrie 1927: 191–2; Germer 1989: 15; Hepper 1990: 17), are in the Cairo Museum. Other such garlands were also found in the tomb of Queen Meritamun (Winlock 1932: 51). In a papyrus dating from 243 BC there is a request for willow for making tent poles (Edgar 1931: no. 59353).

Wood type
Pinkish-white to reddish-brown in colour, soft, perishable, non-splintering. For an anatomical description see similar species in Schweingruber (1990: 674–9); Fahn, Werker and Baas (1985: 157–9); Gale and Cutler (1999).

Uses
The small stature of the tree limits the usefulness the wood, but willow has been used for bowls, chariots, boats, shields and small domestic items. Willow withies have traditionally been used for basketry.

Examples
Protodynastic: Knife handle (Wittmack 1910: 181–92; Möller and Scharff 1926: 47)

ThirdDynasty: Parts of a box (Heidelberg, Ägyptologische Institut 520–1; Ribstein 1925: 194–209)
Eighteenth Dynasty: Pole of a chariot (Florence 2678; Botti 1951; Western and McLeod 1995: 77)
Late Period: Stelae (BM EA24561, identified by Kew).

Bibliography
Germer 1985: 16–17: Hepper 1990: 17.

Tamarisk [*Tamarix aphylla* (L.) Karsten (*T. articulata* Vahl) (Tamaricaceae)]

A bark-fissured evergreen tree, up to fifteen metres high (but usually much smaller), the leaves of which are reduced to scales along the apparently jointed (articulated) branchlets. The flowers are pinkish-white in short cylindrical heads. The tamarisk is found along water courses and saline places in desert regions in Egypt, Arabia, Iraq, southern Iran and Pakistan (Baum 1988: 200–6). The Nile tamarisk (*T. nilotica* (Ehrenb.) Bunge) does not develop as large a trunk as *T. aphylla*, therefore it is unlikely to yield timber of any size. *T. jordanis* is a small tree growing in rivers such as the Jordan, and others in Syria, but not the Nile.

Semi-carbonised stems and branches of considerable size, supposedly dating to the late Quaternary, have been found in the Wadi Qena by Sandford (see Lucas 1962: 447), and tamarisk wood has been identified from as early as the Neolithic (Caton-Thompson and Gardner 1934: 45–6, 88–9), the Badarian period (Brunton 1937: 33, 59, 67) and other phases of the Predynastic, until as late as Greco-Roman times, when two species (*T. nilotica* and *T. aphylla*) were used at Karanis in the Fayum (Lucas 1962: 447). A flange of Amenhotep III's chariot was identified by Western (1973: 93) as probably *T. jordanis*.

The tamarisk is occasionally mentioned in ancient texts from the Old Kingdom onwards (Keimer 1924: 155–6) and Twentieth-Dynasty inscriptions refer to bundles of tamarisk wood (see Breasted 1906: IV, 241, 379, 392). Herodotus (II. 96) states that certain rafts used in connection with boats were tamarisk. Winlock found evidence to show that a grove of tamarisk trees once existed in front of the Eleventh-Dynasty temple of Nebhepetra Mentuhotep II at Deir el-Bahari (Winlock 1921–2: 26–7).

Wood type
Coarse and dense. For an anatomical description see Fahn, Werker and Baas (1985: 166); Jagiella and Kürschner (1987: 154–5); Gale and Cutler (1999).

Uses
Construction, coffins and fuel.

Examples
Late Quaternary: Stems and branches (Sandford 1929: 503)
Neolithic: Twigs (Greiss 1949: 262–73); worked sticks (Caton-Thompson and Gardner 1934: 45–6)
Badarian: Fragments (Brunton and Caton-Thompson 1928: 38)
Predynastic: Root and twigs (Mond and Myers 1937: 137–8), fragments (Brunton and Caton-Thompson 1928: 62)
First–Third Dynasty: Charcoal (Mond and Myers 1937: 137–8)
Sixth Dynasty: Coffin (BM EA46629; Davies 1995: 146)
?Sixth Dynasty–First Intermediate Period: Coffin pegs (Ashmolean 1911.477)
First Intermediate Period: Bow fragment (Hearst Museum 6–2778; Western and McLeod 1995: 80)
Eleventh Dynasty: Roots (Winlock 1921–2: 26–8)
Middle Kingdom: Walking stick and throw stick (Kew Museum No. 61/1923 26522, 40726; Lucas 1962: 441), coffin (Ashmolean E3907 identified by Western; Meiggs 1982: 404), headrest (Ashmolean 1912.600 identified by Western; Meiggs 1982: 404), coffin dowels (BM EA46646, 47594; Davies 1995:147; EA44631, 47596; identified by Kew and BM)
Early Twelfth Dynasty: Coffin (BM EA46631; Davies 1995: 146)
Seventeenth Dynasty: Coffin dowels (BM EA29997; Davies 1995: 147)
Eighteenth Dynasty: Lid of box (New York, MMA; Hayes 1935: 29), foot of pall support and throw stick (Chalk 1932–3: 12, identified by Kew), flange of chariot-wheel (Ashmolean 1923.663, identified by Western 1973), bed (MMA 20.2.13), chair (MMA 12.182.28)
New Kingdom: Twig (Greiss 1949: 262–73), statuette of Osiris (Ashmolean 1971.74, identified by Western; Meiggs 1982: 404), wooden peg or dowel (Ashmolean 1971.74)
Twentieth–Twenty-sixth Dynasty: Coffin (Chalk 1931–2: 11), coffin pegs (Chalk 1931–2: 11)
Twenty-fifth Dynasty: Stele (BM EA8453, identified by Kew; Bierbrier 1987)
Ptolemaic: Stele of Horus (Ashmolean 1874.279a).

Bibliography
Germer 1985: 124–5; Hepper 1990: 48.

Lime [*Tilia* × vulgaris Hayne (*T. europaea* of authors) (Tiliaceae)]

A large tree up to about forty metres in height, with broadly ovate leaves, and fruits in the form of round nuts with a persistent bracteole forming a rotating wing. The lime is a hybrid, the parents of which are *T. platyphyllos* and *T. cordata*, both being naturally widespread in Europe. *T. x vulgaris* may not only have not been imported into Pharaonic Egypt, but might in fact not have existed at that date. Either one of the parents or the silver lime (*T. tomentosa*) are more likely candidates for wood of this type deriving from ancient Egypt.

Newberry (1890: 46) recorded two flowers of a lime tree (which are fragile and short-lived objects that are most likely to have been imported in the Greco-Roman cemetery at Hawara), but Lucas (1962: 437) suggests that one or more of these specimens may have been cultivated in the Fayum region. There is, however, no modern record of *Tilia* being able to tolerate the Egyptian climate.

Wood type
Pale brown, soft, light and perishable with an even grain. For anatomical description see Schweingruber (1990: 722–3); Gale and Cutler (1999).

Uses
Carving and statuary, inlay, small domestic items (plates, spoons, brush-backs), shields, rakes, measures, boxes, spindles, coffins, toys, plough-parts and deck-planks.

Examples
Late fourth century BC: Coffin (Wittmack 1910: 181–92)

Bibliography
Germer 1985: 119–20.

Elm [*Ulmus minor* Miller (*U. carpinifolia* Suck., *U. campestris* L. or *U. nitens* Moench) (Ulmaceae)]
A medium to large tree, usually twenty metres or more in height, bearing ovate leaves (with toothed margins) and thinly winged fruits with one central seed. It is found in shady, moist places across Europe, the Balkans, the Caucasus, and from Turkey to Iran, but is relatively uncommon in southwestern Asia.

The specimens of elm in Tutankhamun's tomb were two pieces from one of the chariots (one from a wheel and one from the body) and also two other pieces (found on the floor) from another chariot from the same tomb, which were either from the axle or from the pole, probably from the pole. The species of elm could not be positively identified but is probably *U. minor*. Elm is also known from another Eighteenth-Dynasty Egyptian chariot now in the museum at Florence, where it was used for the yoke and its appendages, the curved handrail of the body, the spindles of the wheels and other parts. Fasolo (in Botti 1951) suggested that these parts of the chariot were made from hornbeam (*Carpinus betulus*), but it later proved to be elm wood. Neither the pole nor the axle of this chariot is elm, as has been stated, the one being willow (*Salix*), the other ash (*Fraxinus*). Elm was also noted in a chariot of Amenhotep III. Although chariots in Egypt were probably originally imported from western Asia, they were being made by Egyptian craftsmen from at least the Eighteenth Dynasty onwards, and this industry was depicted on the walls of several tombs of that period (see Wilkinson 1878: 227, 232; Curto 1973; Strouhal 1992: 204–5, fig. 224). During the reign of Solomon (*c.* 970 BC), chariots are said to have been imported into Palestine from Egypt (I Kings 10: 29; 2 Chron. 1: 17).

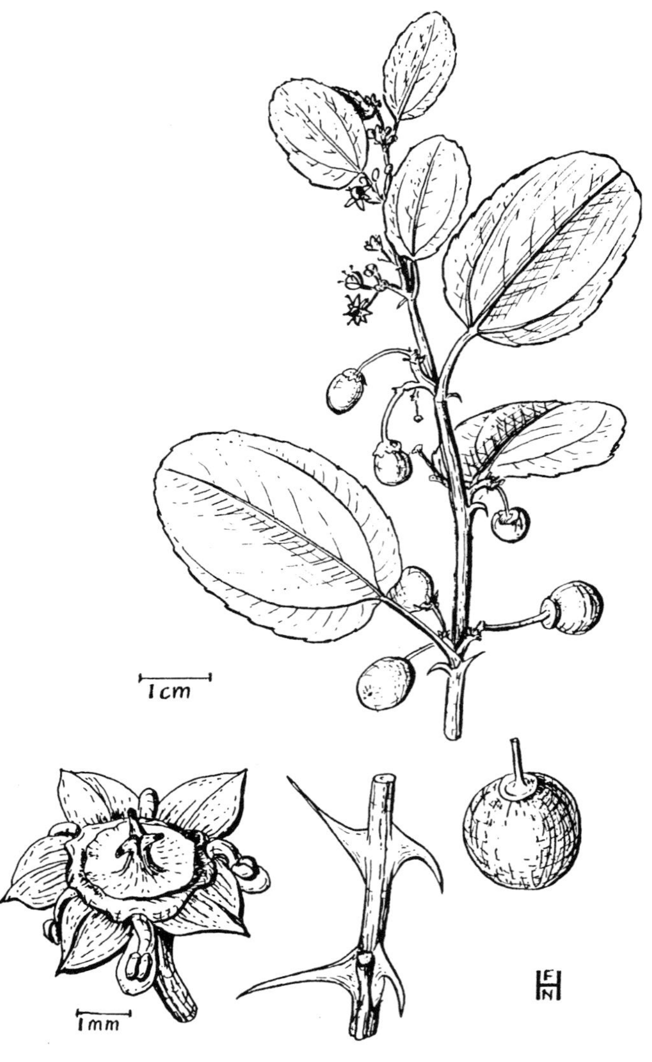

Figure 15.11 Sidder, Ziziphus spina-christi, *with flower and fruit.*

Wood type
Heartwood pale to reddish-brown, tough and durable when permanently wet. For an anatomical description see Schweingruber (1990: 726–7); Gale and Cutler (1999).

Uses
Construction, roof shingles, coffins, wagons and carts, boat-building, water pipes, tool handles, cart wheels, brushes and bows.

Examples
Eighteenth Dynasty: Yoke, handrail and other parts of chariot (Florence 2678; Botti 1951), body and wheel of chariot, pieces of pole or axle of chariot (identified by Chalk: Lucas 1941: 144), nave of chariot (Ashmolean 1923.663, identified by Western 1973).

Bibliography
Germer 1985: 22; Hepper 1990: 49.

Christ's thorn, sidder, nabk [Ziziphus spina-christi *L.* *(Rhamnaceae)*]
Small tree, up to five metres in height, with one or more stems. It has branchlets with paired sharp spines, and leaves with three strong nerves (see Fig. 15.11). The flowers are small and yellowish, and the fruits are ovoid, about three centimetres long, with yellow flesh surrounding a single stone. The Christ's thorn is found in dry country in Palestine, North Africa and drier parts of West Africa.

The dried fruit is known in Egypt from the Predynastic period onwards (Petrie 1921: 44) and it has often been found in tombs (Loret and Poisson 1895: 193–4; Beauverie 1935: 140), for instance in the First-Dynasty tomb of Hemaka at Saqqara (Cairo CG1248–1253; see Saad 1938: 52; Keimer 1943: 279–81), in the Djoser Step Pyramid complex at Saqqara (Lauer *et al.* 1951: 131–2), and in the Eighteenth-Dynasty tomb of Tutankhamun. This tree, although not large enough to have provided the planks that formed the main parts of the shrines mentioned (those of Tutankhamun and Queen Tiye respectively) is sufficiently large to have been used for dowels and, as it grows in the country and is a good hard durable wood, it is not to be wondered at, if the amount of cedar (*Cedrus*) available were not sufficient for all the dowels, that local woods should have been used for most of the remainder. One of the woods used in the construction of a Third-Dynasty plywood coffin from Saqqara was sidder (see Lucas 1936).

Wood type
Hard and durable. For an anatomical description see Fahn, Werker and Baas (1985: 141); Gale and Cutler (1999).

Uses
Boats, coffins, dowels and small items. This is the most likely species to have been used for such purposes as boat-building, since the trunk is well-developed and provides reasonably large pieces of timber. *Z. lotus* (L.) Lam. is a small diffuse bush, while *Z. mucronata* Willd. is a small tree occurring in the savanna well south of Egypt.

Examples
Third Dynasty: Coffin (identified by L. Chalk, see Lucas 1936, 1962: 440–1)
Ninth Dynasty: Fragment from Matmar (Brunton 1948: 53)
First Intermediate Period: Bow fragment (Hearst Museum 6–2757; Western and McLeod 1995: 80)
Middle Kingdom: Coffins (BM EA46630, 47596, 6655, identified by Kew and the BM)
Late Eleventh Dynasty: Coffin (BM EA46630; Davies 1995:146)
Late Twelfth–early Thirteenth Dynasty: Coffin dowels, tenons and pegs (BM EA46654; Davies 1995: 147 (see also sycomore fig above)
Seventeenth–Eighteenth Dynasty: Stool (MMA 14.10.4)
Eighteenth Dynasty: Bow (Lucas 1962: 440), stick (Lucas 1962: 440), dowels (identified by Chalk (1931–2: 11) and Kew)
Meroitic: Kohl tube (Williams 1991: 103, identified by US Forest Products Laboratory, Madison)

Bibliography
Germer 1985: 114–15; Hepper 1990: 68.

Monocotyledons

Flowering plants with one seed-leaf (cotyledon), producing fibrous timber.

Dom/doum palm [*Hyphaene thebaica* (L.) Mart. (Palmae)]
A slender-stemmed palm up to ten metres high, with characteristic forked trunks and large palmate leaves. The fruits are fist-sized, brown and shiny. The dom palm is widespread in the dry savanna of Africa, along the Nile to the region of Abydos (as well as an outlying clump near Eilat, on the Red Sea coast). It is represented in an unmistakable manner in several Eighteenth-Dynasty tombs in the Theban necropolis (Baum 1988: 90–106). Theophrastus (IV: 2, 7) says that the dom palm was an Egyptian tree, commenting upon the characteristic bifurcation of the trunk, which in the palm family is exceptional, and he contrasts it with the undivided trunk of the date palm; he describes the wood as being very compact and hard and, therefore, very different from that of the date palm, and he states that it was employed by the Persians for making the feet of couches.

Wood type
Hard and compact. For an anatomical description see Fahn, Werker and Baas (1985: 179–80); Gale and Cutler (1999).

Uses
Boat-building, carpentry and as a veneer.

Examples
The fruit has been found in graves from the Predynastic period onward, including that of Tutankhamun (Germer 1989: 224; Hepper 1990: 59; Täckholm and Drar 1950: 293: 300; Beauverie 1935: 122–3; Loret and Poisson 1895: 182), but no instance of the use of the wood of this species has been recorded.

Bibliography
Täckholm and Drar 1950: 273–98; Keimer 1984: 64–7; Germer 1985: 2134–5; Hepper 1990: 59–60.

Date palm [*Phoenix dactylifera* L. (Palmae)]

A tall slender palm reaching twenty metres in height, the unbranched trunk of which is covered with old leaf-bases and fibres. The huge leaves are pinnate (like a feather), and there are male and female flowers on separate trees. The fruits (dates) hang in large clusters (see Zohary and Hopf 1993: 157–62); fruit stones of a wild date (*Phoenix sylvestris*) were found in a deposit of late Pleistocene age (early Upper Palaeolithic) in the Kharga Oasis (Caton-Thompson and Gardner 1932: 384).

The date palm originated in Mesopotamia, and was subsequently cultivated in the desert countries to the east and west. It is attested in Egypt from very remote times and is often represented on tomb walls (e.g. in a number of Eighteenth-Dynasty tomb-chapels in the Theban necropolis). Because of its loose fibrous texture, date-palm wood is unsuitable for joiners' work, but the split trunk of the tree was employed in ancient times for roofing (and is occasionally still used for the same purpose today). A Second- or Third-Dynasty tomb at Saqqara was roofed with palm logs, (Quibell 1923: 21) and in a tomb of early date at Qau (Villiers Stuart 1882: 83) near Asyut, in a Fourth-Dynasty tomb adjoining the pyramid of Khafra and in the Fifth-Dynasty tomb of Ptahhotep at Saqqara a roof of this kind has been copied in stone. In the Greco-Roman city of Karanis in the Fayum palm wood was employed in the houses, (Boak and Peterson 1931: 52) in the form of trunks sawn longitudinally into long or short beams (of semicircular cross-section) used mainly for roofing (sent to Lucas by S. Yeivin). The cultivation and use of both date and dom palm in Greco-Roman Egypt have been discussed by Hohlwein (see Lucas 1962: 444), with reference to the classical sources.

Wood type

Soft, fibrous and of poor quality. For an anatomical description see Fahn, Werker and Baas (1985: 180); Schweingruber (1990: 172–3); Gale and Cutler (1999).

Uses

Roof timber, door lintels, statuary and as a decorative veneer.

Examples

First–Third Dynasty. Roof of tomb at Saqqara (Quibell 1927: 21)

New Kingdom. Fragment of box (Schiemann 1941: 128; Anthes 1943: 62).

Bibliography

Täckholm and Drar 1950: 203ff.; Germer 1985: 232–3; Hepper 1990: 62.

Gymnosperms

Coniferous (i.e. cone-bearing) trees (sometimes with berries) providing 'soft-wood' timber.

Cilician fir [*Abies cilicica* (Ant and Kotschy) Carr. (Pinaceae)]

Large tree, up to thirty metres in height, with deeply fissured greyish bark on old trunks. Young branchlets are greyish-brown, with a few stiff bristles, while the evergreen linear leaves are 2–3.5 cm long, *c.* 3 millimetres wide, and pale beneath (see Fig. 15.12). The fir-cones are cylindrical, *c.* 20 cm long and covered with thin stiff scales. Cilician firs are found on mountains between 1,200 and 2,200 metres above sea level in Lebanon, Syria and adjacent parts of Turkey. According to Campbell Edgar (1931: no. 59157), 300 fir trees were planted in Egypt in the middle of the third century BC, but this translation must be regarded as suspect, since fir trees are inhabitants of humid mountains and would not have survived in the Egyptian climate.

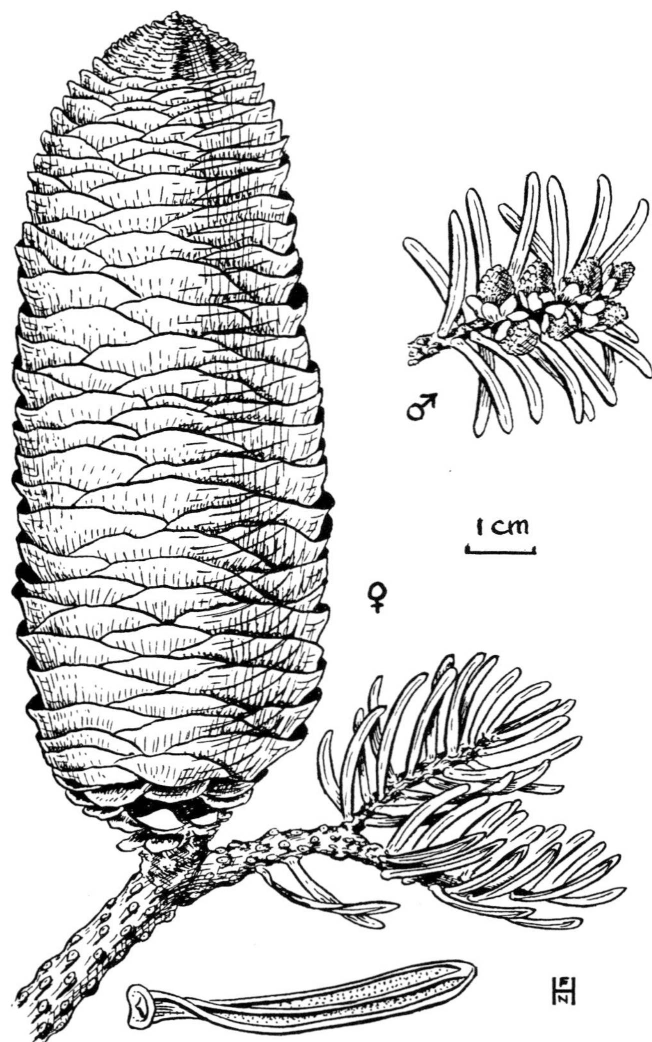

Figure 15.12 Cilician fir, Abies cilicica, *with male and female cones.*

Wood type

Yellowish-white, easily split, flammable and perishable. For an anatomical description see Gale and Cutler (1999). Other species are described in Schweingruber (1990: 108–9).

KILLEN [TECHNOLOGY]

Procurement and primary processing

Felling

Scenes showing woodcutters are occasionally found in tomb-paintings and reliefs throughout the Dynastic period. The tomb of Sekhemkara at Giza, which dates to the reign of the Fourth-Dynasty pharaoh Khafra (LG89; Hassan 1943: 115, fig. 60), contains a depiction of a man felling a tree (see Fig. 15.17); he has chopped a deep notch at the base of the trunk, and the tree is falling away from him. There is also a scene showing two men felling a tree, using the 'double-notch' technique, in the Fifth-Dynasty tomb of Nefer and Kaha at Saqqara (Moussa and Altenmüller 1971: pl. 20).

The scenes on the relief fragments from the tomb of Sekhemkara show the large size of the felled timber (Fig. 15.17). An overseer, who is shown holding a staff, supervises men who are removing the branches from the trunk. Wall-paintings in the Twelfth-Dynasty tomb of the nomarch Khnumhotep III at Beni Hasan, show three woodcutters felling a small tree and feeding its foliage to gazelles (BH3; Newberry 1893: pl. XXIX). In a similar scene in the tomb of Ipuy at Thebes the woodcutter is removing branches from the tree (TT217; Davies 1927: pl. XXX). The care with which timber was felled, so preventing the possibility of 'thunder shakes' being impacted into the grain, is seen in a relief dating to the reign of Seti I on the northern exterior wall of the Great Hypostyle Hall in the Temple of Amun at Karnak. Woodcutters are shown felling what is probably a tall Lebanese cedar. One man is using an axe at the base of the trunk while two others are holding the tree with ropes tied to the upper branches, thus allowing more control over the speed and direction of the tree's fall (Beekman 1949–55: fig. 7.09).

Branches were sometimes used almost unaltered, as in the case of Predynastic bedframes, which were constructed from four branches with natural right-angled 'elbows'. A round hole was bored into the elbow in which was housed the longest straight end of the opposing branch, with the short part of the branch forming the legs (Petrie 1913: pl. VIII/4). The technique of removing branches was also used as a conservation measure, particularly with those exotic trees which would have provided the materials for inlays and veneer. In the cult temple of Hatshepsut at Deir el-Bahari, the depictions of an expedition to the land of Punt include a scene showing Egyptians and Puntites cutting branches from what is thought to be an ebony tree (Naville 1898: pl. LXX). They can also be seen carrying small logs of this timber to ships, for transportation to Egypt, along with complete trees carried in large pots (Naville 1898: pl. LXXIV).

The coniferous wood trade from regions north of Egypt was well-established by the reign of the Fourth-Dynasty ruler Sneferu, when the Palermo Stone records that forty ships sailed to the Lebanese coast where trees such as cedar were felled (Breasted 1906: 146). These were rafted and towed along the Mediterranean coast to be stored in timber yards in the Delta. During the New Kingdom coniferous timbers were being extensively used in shipyards. One of the surviving shipyard accounts comprises details of the procurement of large quantities of timber over a period of seven months in the reign of Thutmose III (BM EA10056; Glanville 1931: 105–21, 1933: 7–41). Planks used for masts could measure up to thirty cubits in length, while some timbers were an impressive four palms (29.6 cm) wide. Most planks, however, ranged between twelve and nineteen cubits (6.2 and 9.9 metres) in length and Glanville estimated that 2,000 feet (607 metres) of planking was used during this relatively short period.

By-products: bark and charcoal

Egyptians used all the products of the tree, employing its leaves for fodder, basketry and matting. Bark was used from as early as the Neolithic period (e.g. Caton-Thompson and Gardner 1932: 88, 122), and in later periods it is clear that objects covered with bark held special significance to Egyptians (e.g. a bow bound with bark, dating to the Second Intermediate Period, New York MMA 28.9.9; see Hayes 1959: 29). During the Eighteenth Dynasty, bark was used as a decorative finish to timber; a number of objects in the tomb of Tutankhamun were covered with bark from the silver birch (*Betula pendula*, see p. 336).

Charcoal, the burnt by-product of timber, has been found in graves dating from the Badarian period (Brunton and Caton-Thompson 1928: 8–9). It was used as a fuel from an early date, and an extensive charcoal-burning industry flourished in the Sinai and the Eastern Desert (Petrie and Currelly 1906: 52), probably contributing signifi-

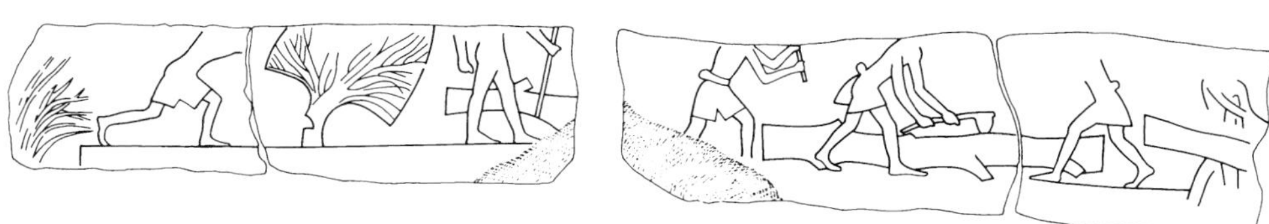

Figure 15.17 Scene of woodcutters from the Fourth-Dynasty tomb of Sekhemkara at Giza, LG 89.

cantly to the loss of Egypt's trees. It was used extensively in the smelting of metal ores, since it enabled high temperatures, sometimes exceeding 1,000 °C, to be reached. In 1985 Rainer Stadelmann took samples of charcoal from a Ptolemaic foundry discovered at the site of the mortuary temple of Seti I in western Thebes; these proved to be composed of *Acacia nilotica* and probably *A. raddiana* (Scheel 1989: 27).

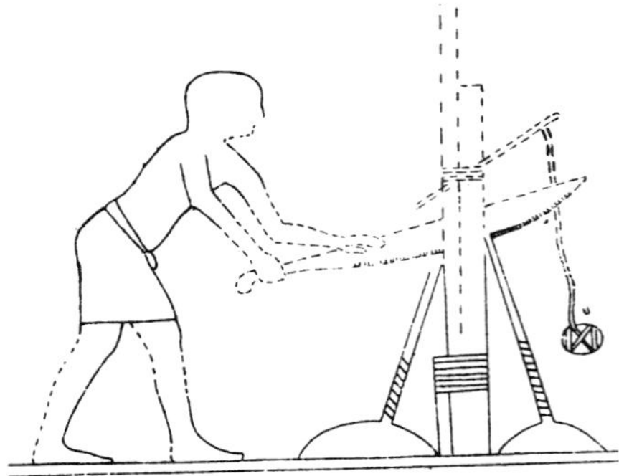

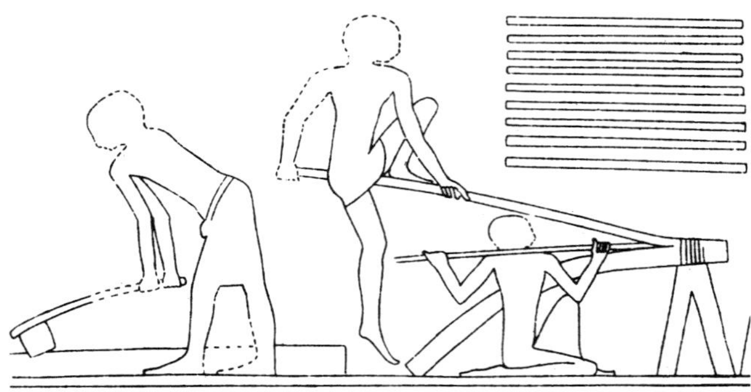

Figure 15.18 Scene in the Sixth-Dynasty tomb of Iteti at Deshasha, showing craftsmen cleaving a tree trunk and other timber conversion processes.

Conversion from timber to wood

After felling, it is essential that the trees are converted into timber promptly in order to prevent the development of defects such as 'shakes' (splits in the timber which open into holes either radially from the centre of the trunk or around its growth rings). The trees would perhaps have had to be sawn horizontally in order to obtain the longest of the planks recorded in the Thutmose III shipyard accounts already mentioned. However, we have no evidence, either from tomb-scenes or texts, to support this process. The technique whereby two men use a double-handled saw over a saw-pit (one man standing below the log in the pit and the other standing above), is considered to be a Roman-period development. In the Dynastic period, it is more likely that long planks were split from the trunk which would have made it all the more vital for woodcutters to select straight-grain timber with few defects.

The technique of cleaving was well-understood and practised from as early as the Predynastic period, as in the case of crudely constructed burial boxes made from irregular shaped planks which are bound together (e.g. from the Predynastic cemetery at Nag el-Deir; Lythgoe 1965: 345, fig. 155a–d). An experienced craftsman could split a trunk of straight-grain growth into thin planks with ease, and we can establish that the trunk has been split by following the lines of cleavage which will tend to follow the grain, usually down the tree's rays, through its weaknesses and irregularities. The process of cleaving timber is depicted in the Sixth-Dynasty tomb of Iteti at Deshasha (Fig. 15.18). Two men are shown splitting a log, which is strapped to a trestle, with the point of a long pole being driven into the split; a third man is preparing a log with an axe, probably defining the edges of the planks to be cleaved (Petrie 1898: pl. XXI). This scene also shows that timber conversion was achieved by a saw, with the log being bound with rope to a vertical sawing post, suggesting that accurately sawn planks would usually not have been greater in length than the height of the sawyer.

Although a scene in the Sixth-Dynasty tomb-chapel of Pepyankh at Meir shows a man sawing a long plank at an angle, with the sloping board tied against a vertical post (Blackman 1953: pl. XVIII), most of the depictions of timber conversion in tomb-chapels indicate that the wood was placed vertically against a post, which was firmly fixed into the ground and occasionally held upright by a pair of taut guide ropes attached to the top of the post and fastened to the workshop floor (Śliwa 1975: 35–7, fig. 13).

The conversion of 'green' timber would have caused the saw to jam, therefore wedges were employed to keep open the kerf (i.e the channel left in the wood by the set of the saw teeth). Occasionally a lever mechanism was passed through the rope bindings in order to increase the tension on the strapping like a tourniquet (see Fig. 15.18; Petrie 1898, pl. XXI). Whether this stone-weighted lever was fixed into the kerf is uncertain, although by the New Kingdom it appears to have been discarded.

The examination of the planks of timber which make up the carcass of Early Dynastic coffins shows that the early sawn conversion of timber was a difficult process to achieve with only the small handsaws which were available, since the saw lines run across the surface of these planks in many directions (Petrie 1913: 26, pl. XXIV). An excellent depiction of the use of this type of saw can be seen in the Fifth-Dynasty tomb of Ty at Saqqara (Wild 1966: pl. CLXXIV). However, the quality of sawn timber improved by the end of the Old Kingdom with the introduction of the large pullsaw, which is represented in the Sixth-Dynasty tomb-chapel of Iteti at Deshasha (Fig. 15.18); it differs from the handsaw in that it was usually manufactured without a wooden handle, since the latter would otherwise have been pulled off during the cutting stroke, given that its teeth point towards the sawyer.

Seasoning

In freshly felled 'green' timber, the moisture (most of which is trapped in the sapwood) has to be reduced by a process of seasoning. The moisture content of planks prepared by 'through and through' cutting varies across their width. Thus, the drying of planks is another important process, for if it is achieved too quickly the planks are likely to warp or 'cup'. Some timber used for statues or panels may have been radially cut ('quarter sawn') or cleaved, i.e. the wooden element may have been cut at right angles to the growth rings; if this method is used, shrinkage on both faces of the board is equal and it is unlikely to warp, although it may shrink or swell.

To season timber, air must be allowed to circulate around the boards. The traditional process of stacking boards horizontally and placing spacers between them is also illustrated in the Sixth-Dynasty tomb-chapel of Iteti (Fig. 15.18). Boards may have also been either rested against the outside walls of a carpenter's workshop or stacked in wigwam fashion. To control the rate of drying, reed mats may also have been placed over the timber. Egyptian carpenters were experienced in estimating the moisture content in timber to a point where timber of between 8 per cent and 12 per cent would have been regarded as suitable for most woodworking processes. Samples of timber taken from the Fourth-Dynasty funerary boat of Khufu at Giza, which had been sealed from atmospheric changes, showed a moisture content of 10 per cent when analysed (Landström 1970: 28).

Woodworking techniques

Tools

During the Predynastic period, native timbers were commonly employed, and there was little demand for imported wood, but this changed by the beginning of the Early Dynastic period, with the introduction of specialised copper woodworking tools. This new technology created opportunities for resistant materials, such as timber, to be worked with a high degree of accuracy. A fine collection of woodworking tools was discovered by Emery (1949: 30–7, 42–8) in the Early Dynastic tomb S3471 at Saqqara.

With the copper saw it became possible not only to convert timber into good quality boards but to cut these to various lengths across the grain and to form sophisticated joints in them. These simple saws were developed from the knife, and were 25 to 40 cm in length. In profile they were similar to the knife, having curved edges with a round blunt nose and a rib along the centre of the blade. Along one edge were closely spaced teeth which were nibbled out and irregular in both shape and pitch. Each tooth was pressed over on the same side, providing an unusual set not like that found on a modern saw, where each tooth is set alternately to the left and right of the blade. The ancient set explains why short saws would bind when carpenters were using them to convert timber, since one side of the blade was always in contact with the wet and possibly resinous kerf. The edges of the blade were beaten to reduce the cutting edge and to increase the blade's hardness. From the rib extended a tang which was covered by a wooden handle (Emery 1949: 30–1, fig. 18).

By the Fifth Dynasty, this type of saw had gradually evolved into one which had a straight back and a wooden handle moulded to fit the carpenter's hand, but it was still being used to convert timber into planks. By the late Old Kingdom carpenters were using only the pullsaw to convert 'green' timber by sawing down the long grain. The pullsaw was longer, with its teeth pointed towards its integral metal handle; it has a straight back with a pointed nose and was used with both hands, the sawyer pulled in down at an angle cutting through the timber (Newberry 1893: pl. XXIX). The shape of the teeth were larger and the pitch greater, which made it an efficient saw to rip down timber.

The adze was used to true and shape timber. The shape of its metal blade developed throughout the Dynastic period (and is best recorded in Petrie 1917: 16–18, pls. XV–XVIII), and it was occasionally ground with a cutting edge on both surfaces but generally only on one like that of the modern plane blade. It was attached to a shaped wooden shaft with leather thongs which would have been soaked in water so that as they dried they tightened and pulled this assembly together. Occasionally cord or linen strapping were used to secure the blade to the handle. These handles needed to be elastic and perhaps would have been made from ash. During the Early Dynastic period, adze shafts were straight (Emery 1949: fig. 19), but by later dynasties adzes with shaped shafts were being used. They were manufactured in a variety of sizes, small ones being used to shape wood and larger ones to remove bark and true timber after it had been converted. A scene in the Fifth-Dynasty tomb of Nefer and Kaha at Saqqara shows two men dressing a log with large adzes (Moussa and Altenmüller 1971: pl. 20).

A number of small copper chisels, probably used to chop holes and grooves in timber (Killen 1980: 16, pl. 10b), have survived from the Predynastic period. These were employed like a modern cold chisel, i.e. the end of the metal chisel was burred over by repeated hitting of the head by a hard implement. By the Early Dynastic period carpenters were using both mortise chisels and firmer chisels which had wooden handles. The mortise chisel had a stout square section blade which was fixed into a large cylindrical, flat-topped handle (Emery 1949: 42–6, fig. 22). The flat top indicates that it was struck with a wooden mallet (see Śliwa 1975: 33–4). The chips of wood could be prised out of the mortise without fear of bending or breaking the blade. Firmer chisels were smaller, with a rectangular section blade and a flared cutting edge, while the top of the wooden handle was rounded, suggesting that it was designed to fit the carpenter's hand being used for handwork and carving (Emery 1949: 42–6, fig. 22).

Also discovered by Emery in tomb S3471 at Saqqara were thin-blade awls (which could be used to bore holes in timber) and small engraving tools (Emery 1949: 47–8, figs. 23–4). All these tools would have needed to be sharpened at regular intervals, therefore the carpenters' workshops were each equipped with a small forge where blades could be reformed and heat-treated. The final sharp edge was then ground on to the blade. This process was achieved by honing the blade at an angle on a slate hone, an example of which is in the British Museum (BM EA36728, dating to the New Kingdom; Killen 1980: 18, pl. 14). This hone has grinding marks along the length of the hone and a few across its width, showing that the carpenter turned the blade over after honing on the sharp edge, in order to wipe away the tissue-thin burr which occurs on metal blades sharpened by this process. To help lubricate the hone, oil from a flask was applied to its surface. One such oil flask (BM EA6037, dating to the New Kingdom; Killen 1980: 18, pl. 15), formed from a horn, has a wooden stopper at one end and a spoon-shaped wooden spout at the other; the spout has some cord tied around it, perhaps indicating that it was hung in the workshop on a peg with the hone, which has a hole bored through it at one end.

In the Eighteenth-Dynasty tomb-chapel of the vizier Rekhmira at Thebes (TT100) are illustrations which show carpenters at work in a joinery workshop (Davies 1943: pl. LV). One carpenter sits on a stone seat and works at a wooden bench which is rebated across the front. This helps him to hold timber firmly and enables him to saw lengths of timber to size. His adze is embedded in the top of the bench, presumably in order to protect his fingers and feet from its sharp edge. This scene shows the ancient carpenter's emphasis on the measuring and setting out of timber; he used a straight edge or cubit rod to test that the timber element was true, and a try square and mitre-cutting aid were also part of his equipment (Śliwa 1975: 39–40). During the Old and Middle Kingdoms these tools would have been kept in a large wooden chest stored in the workshop (Winlock 1955: 35, pls. 28–9), but New Kingdom carpenters seem to have used a basket with handles for this purpose (similar to a modern carpenter's hold-all or bass). An example of such an ancient hold-all is preserved in the Pitt Rivers Museum, Oxford (Location No. I. 49), and a depiction of a pair of carpenters with their tool basket can be seen in the Ramesside tomb of Ipuy at Thebes (TT217; Davies 1927: pl. XXXVII).

The first depiction of the bowdrill appears as part of the painted reliefs in the Fifth-Dynasty tomb of Ty at Saqqara, although this tool must presumably have been used earlier to bore the large holes which pierce the bovine shaped legs of Early Dynastic bed frames. An Early Dynastic *mastaba* tomb at Naqada included a small piece of timber which would have formed the side panel of a tray (de Morgan 1897: 191, figs. 696–7); the slots in the edges of this element were chain-drilled (a series of contiguous holes) and then pared to size with a chisel. In the bottom of each hole can be seen the circular drill marks of the bit. Old Kingdom bowdrills were made from conveniently shaped branches which had a slight elbow; at the short end a cord was fastened to a hole, while at the long end the cord was looped over a lug. The earliest example of this type of bowdrill is a Twelfth-Dynasty one from Kahun, now in the Petrie Museum, London (bow: UC7085, drill: UC7084). New Kingdom bows had holes at each end through which the bowstring was tied (e.g. BM EA6040); they were much longer and therefore turned the drill more efficiently. When finishing and smoothing timber, carpenters used hand-held abrasive blocks of quartzite (siliceous sandstone) which they rubbed along the grain. This process was used throughout the dynastic period and is depicted in the Fifth-Dynasty tomb of Ty at Saqqara (Wild 1966: pl. CLXXIV) and the Ramesside tomb of Ipuy at Thebes (TT217; Davies 1927: pl.XXXVII). The convention of sanding with the grain was understood, since rubbing these blocks across the grain would scuff the timber and damage its appearance.

Laminating

Egyptian carpenters began to laminate thin sheets of timber as early as the Third Dynasty in an attempt to fabricate a large sheet of material which was dimensionally stable and equally strong in all directions. An example of six-ply wood, where the grain of one sheet is at right-angles to the next, was discovered in a sarcophagus within the Third-Dynasty Step Pyramid complex of Djoser at Saqqara. These sheets of 'plywood' formed the sides, ends and base of a coffin. The thickness of each leaf was approximately four millimetres and their widths were found to range from between forty to three hundred millimetres. Being of various lengths, each piece was edge jointed and arranged like a laminated patchwork of various woods, that were held together with small flat pegs (Makkonen 1969: 30–1, Fig. 20). The edges of the centre four leaves were bevelled to provide a shouldered mitred joint which was strengthened in the bottom corners by additional wooden battens (Fig. 15.19). The surface of the coffin had been carved with a corrugated pattern before being covered with gold sheet that was held in position along its edges with small gold nails (Firth *et al.* 1935: 42, pl. 19/1, 2).

Bending and turning

Carpenters were also experienced in artificially bending unseasoned timber. In the tomb of the Fifth-Dynasty vizier Ptahshepses at Abusir men can be seen damping poles, while a scene in the Fifth-Dynasty tomb of Ty at Saqqara shows the actual bending process: set into the ground is a

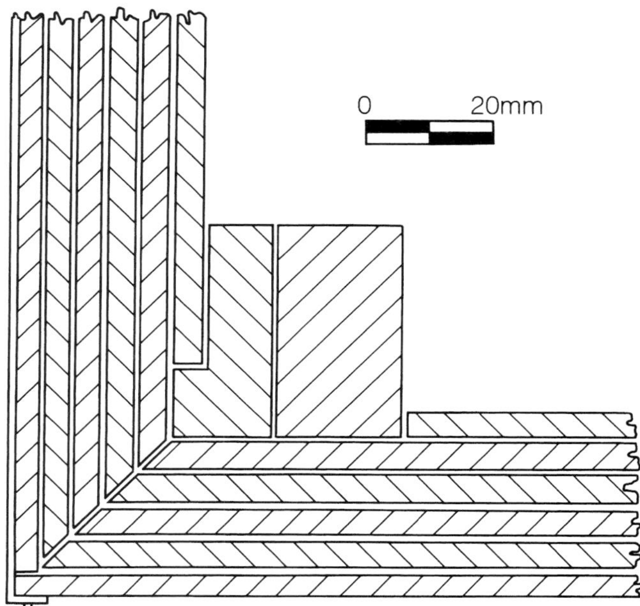

Figure 15.19 Plywood construction on a coffin found in Gallery V under the eastern part of the Third-Dynasty Step Pyramid of Djoser at Saqqara.

Figure 15.20 Scene in the Middle Kingdom tomb of the nomarch Amenemhat at Beni Hasan (BH2), showing craftsmen steam-bending timber bows.

wooden post to which is attached at an angle a forked pole with rope strung across the top of the open fork; beneath this has been placed the damp pole which the craftsman wished to bend. After he had forced the free end of the pole downwards (creating the desired shape by sitting on the end of the pole) he then tied it back to the post. A further strut was next wedged under the bend to maintain the tension until the pole dried and took up its new shape (Wild 1966: pl. CLXXIV).

A wall-painting in the tomb of the Middle Kingdom provincial governor Amenemhat at Beni Hasan (BH2) shows a carpenter steam-bending a length of timber (Fig. 15.20). He holds the stick above a bowl of hot water, softening the wood by allowing the hot vapour to penetrate the timber's already saturated cellular structure. A second man is shown bending these sticks into hoops. To maintain the tension on the hoops, while they dried to shape, their ends were buried in the ground (Newberry 1893: pl. XI). Above the man who is steam-bending can be seen a stack of partly and fully formed bows which this process was well-suited to achieve. Steam-bending would have also been used by wheelwrights in the manufacture of chariot parts. Only strips of unseasoned timber could be bent by this method; seasoned timber of large cross-sectional dimension can only be softened with the use of a steam chest and there is no evidence that this apparatus was used in ancient Egypt.

The art of rotating timber on a fixed centre and scraping the wood away was known to Egyptians, but – despite the fact that the process of turning other materials was practised from the earliest times – the precise date of its introduction is not clear. The first illustration of carpenters working on a lathe (Fig. 15.21) is seen in the Ptolemaic tomb of Petosiris at Tuna el-Gebel (Lefèbvre 1923: pl. X). The wooden bed of this lathe appears to be mounted vertically and is firmly set into the ground. Two adjustable stocks, in which were fixed the dead centres, held the piece of wood to be turned. It is possible that both stocks were fastened to the bed by wedges. This arrangement would allow the wood to be fastened between the centres and that various lengths of timber could be turned on this simple machine.

One man turned the timber with a length of rope which is twisted about the turned element, while the other man scrapes the wood away with a chisel, using the bed of the lathe as a tool rest. The scraping would have been done on both the forward and reverse movements of the work resulting in the chisel producing chatter and score marks on the timber. This type of light lathe would not have been able to produce the heavier, more intricate turned legs of the Roman period, for which horizontally mounted pole lathes would have had to be developed. It is often difficult to

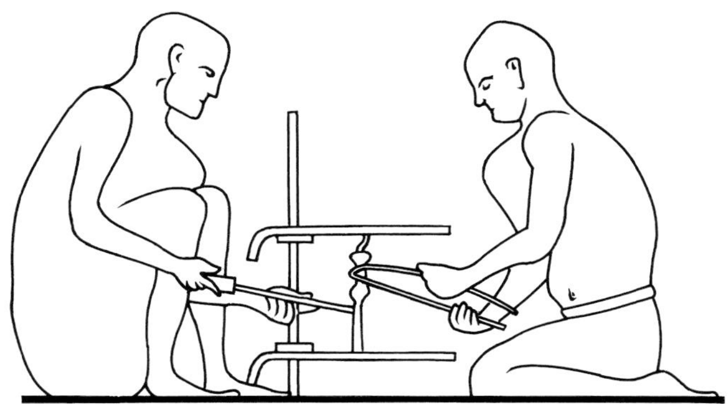

Figure 15.21 Scene showing a carpenter turning wood on a lathe, from the early Ptolemaic tomb of Petosiris at Tuna el-Gebel.

establish from the examination of surviving pieces of 'turned work' whether the piece was turned on a lathe or rotated between centres by hand and the wood ground away with sandstone blocks.

Most round-legged stools of the early New Kingdom were neither turned nor hand-worked between centres. They are irregular in profile and not circular (Killen 1980: 48, pls. 79–81). They show no evidence of being supported between centres and those lines which are incised about them are uneven. The shoulders are not machined square and a spike (not seen on turned legs) extends from the top of the leg to be jointed into a hole on the underside of the seat frame. However, just because this type of stool leg was not turned, we cannot assume that other smaller objects were not. A small Twelfth-Dynasty lid preserved in the Petrie Museum, London (UC7123) has a hole in the centre of the lid; it is uncertain whether this hole was for holding the lid against a centre or whether it was simply the socket in which the lid's handle was fixed. Similar lids are turned on very primitive lathes by workmen at the roadside in Afghanistan. It is not circular as might be expected but symmetrically elliptical, with its major axis aligned along the grain. This distortion can be explained in terms of the timber's shrinkage across the grain which is always more than along the grain which is negligible for most timbers.

Evidence of turning can be found on a pair of early New Kingdom stools in the British Museum; one (BM EA2475) is in a fragmentary state, thus allowing its construction to be examined in detail. The one surviving complete leg (Fig. 15.22) is circular, measuring twenty-eight millimetres in diameter at the foot. Under the foot is a clear pivot hole, while at the other end, above a pair of crossing mortises, the pivot has been removed. From the top of the leg to the stretcher's mortise, this leg has been worked parallel and then smoothed with sandstone. Below the stretcher joint the leg is of a simple spindle shape. Within the deep, parted groove below the stretcher joint are clear chatter marks and long scores which have not been removed by sanding (see Killen 1997: 10–25).

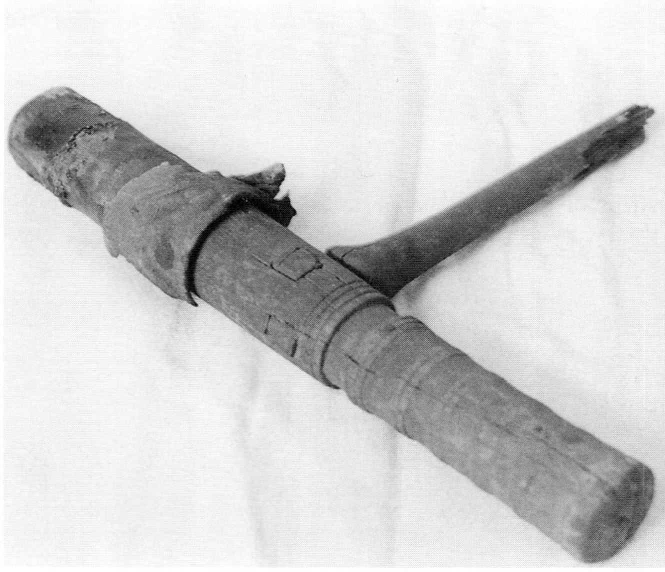

Figure 15.22 Fragment of a turned leg (BM EA2475).

The second of the two stools (BM EA2474) is in almost perfect condition. Its form is similar to the first, and the spindle-work below the stretcher joint is very accurate, the profile being well formed and symmetrical. There are comparable stools from Thebes in the Metropolitan Museum of Art, New York (MMA 14.10.4) and in the Egyptian Museum, Cairo. The tomb of Montuherkhepeshef at Thebes (TT20), which dates to the reign of Thutmose III, yielded a highly polished hardwood stool leg which has a pivot hole under the foot, which Davies (1913: 5, pl. XVII) cites as proof of it being turned. However, this assumption, and that of turning wood in the New Kingdom, is questioned by Peter der Manuelian (1981: 125–8).

Constructional details

From as early as the Predynastic period the Egyptians established the concept of constructing timber in one of three forms: box, frame and stool (or a combination of all three using joints). These systems were found to exploit two of the timber's physical properties: firstly the fact that a timber's strength is along the grain, and not across it, and secondly the fact that shrinkage of timber is negligible along the grain.

During the Predynastic period, burial boxes (i.e. early coffins) were made from a carcass of solid boards. The use of the solid carcass continued until the introduction of the frame with its individual stiles and cross-rails during the Old Kingdom. Although there is some evidence to suggest that Early Dynastic carpenters understood the principles of frame construction (Emery 1954: fig. 50). The strength of the frame is that the long grain of the timber runs along both its width and height. The Early Dynastic bed frames discovered by Petrie in the Early Dynastic cemetery at Tarkhan involve the use of the 'stool', the third constructional form. Each of these traditional constructions was used throughout the Dynastic period. They were enhanced by the introduction of a primitive 'plywood' and by the fact that carpenters understood how to artificially bend timber.

Butt joints

Many Predynastic burials have the body placed on a matting made from plant fibres and twigs supported on a pair of roughly shaped poles (Reisner 1910: 126, fig. 78, pl. 25e). Another burial shows that the body rested on a wooden frame or in a coffin which had butt-jointed corners (see Fig. 15.23 and Reisner 1910: 116, fig. 69, pl. 26a–b). Those

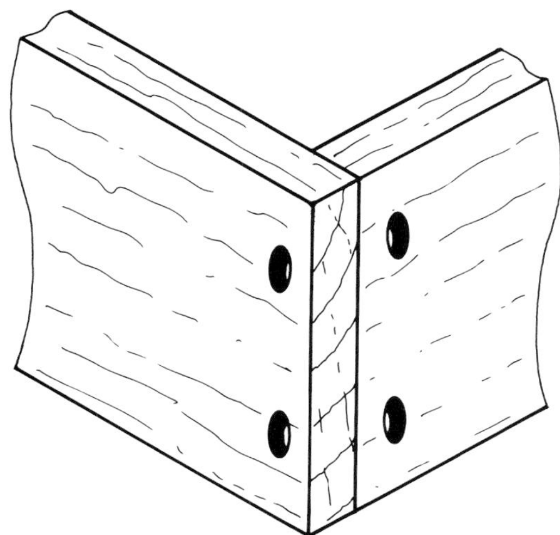
Figure 15.23 Butt joint.

Figure 15.24 Edge joint (tied).

Predynastic burials which were found in coffins gave protection to the body and supported the walls of the grave. A coffin from grave N 7531, in the Predynastic cemetery at Nag el-Deir, was made from planks of cleaved timber butt-jointed together, with the corners tied to upright wooden pillars (Lythgoe 1965: 345, figs. 155 a–d). The simple butt joint is used at all periods and every example is held in place with some type of mechanical fixing. Egyptian carpenters discovered, very early, that glue could not be used on a timber's end grain, as the empty wood cells absorb and transport the glue away from the line of fixture making it difficult to obtain a satisfactory glue line.

Edge joints

Tied joint (Fig. 15.24)

An Early Dynastic *mastaba* at Naqada contained a number of ivory fragments that may have derived from a small box (de Morgan 1897: 191, figs. 693–5). Each piece of ivory had a red-stained band across its face, through which were bored holes exiting either on the back surface or on an adjoining edge. These pieces would have been sewn together with strips of leather. A tray from the Early Dynastic tomb S3504 at Saqqara was constructed by means of a similar technique of binding the sides to the base of this tray (Emery 1954: 43, fig. 27, pls. XVIII and XXXI).

Loose tongue or tenon (Fig. 15.25)

In the same Naqada mastaba mentioned above, de Morgan (1897: 191, figs. 696–7) also found two badly charred box fragments. The end of one piece (Cairo JE31789) shows a pair of diagonal holes indicating that it was butt-jointed at a right angle to another element. More interesting are pairs of slots which have been cut into the edges to accept loose tongues or tenons. Each cavity appears to have been chain-

Figure 15.25 Edge joint (loose tongue or tenon).

drilled and then pared to the required shape. This allowed strips of timber to be inserted into the slots which were then connected to other boards. What is surprising is that no mechanical means was used to secure the loose tongue or tenon in its cavity.

The New Kingdom linen box of Perpawty (Bologna, Museo Civico Archeologico, Inv. No. KS. 1970) incorporates panels made from two irregularly shaped boards which have been matched together and then secured with pairs of loose tongues or tenons. These are held in position by small dowels which pass through the sides of the board and pierce the tongue or tenon above and below the line of fixture (Killen 1994a: 42, fig. 55, pl. 39). Mummy cases were made of a complex patchwork construction of shaped boards which were often edge-jointed using loose tongues or tenons (Leospo 1986: 20–39), we also find the use of edge dowels in this type of construction.

Dowelled edge-joint (Fig. 15.26)
Dowels were also used to edge-joint timber elements together, as in the case of the lid of a Twelfth-Dynasty box discovered by Petrie at Kahun (Oxford, Pitt Rivers Museum, Location No. L. 48), which is made from seven thin slats of matched timber that have holes drilled along their edges in which are placed small dowels. The quality of the drilling is poor, and the sides of many holes have broken through the faces of these strips, thus exposing the dowels (Killen 1994a: 13, figs. 15 and 16, pls. 5, 6, 7 and 8).

One of Tutankhamun's footstools (JE62052) which is of a plain construction, uses edge dowels to connect the side panels to the surface frame (Killen 1994a: 90, fig. 86, pl. 72). What is interesting is that the side supports have been repaired with pieces of timber that have been let in at each end. From this we can see that the quality of such woodwork was variable, and Egyptian cabinet-makers often had to work with offcuts.

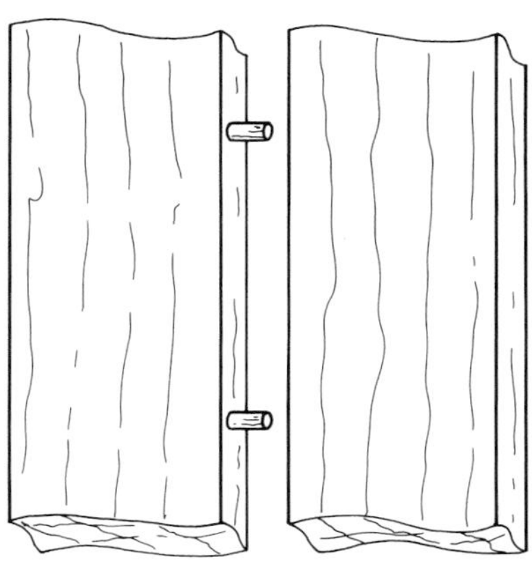

Figure 15.26 Edge joint (dowelled).

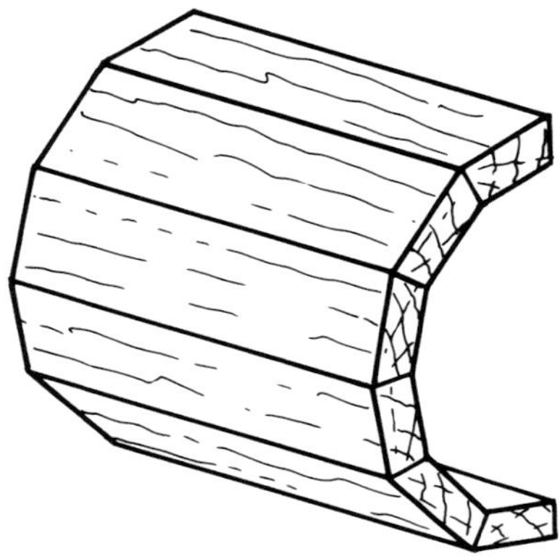

Figure 15.27 Coopered joint.

Coopered joint (Fig. 15.27)
When constructing a carcass with a shaped surface the coopered joint is useful. It is similar to the edge joint but the joining edges are slightly angled to accommodate the planned curvature. This joint was used from as early as the Third Dynasty, in the tomb of Hesyra at Saqqara are wall-paintings which show a number of barrels made from a stave construction. The paintings of these barrels are particularly fine, showing the attractive figure of the grain sweeping around the live knots in the timber planks (Quibell 1913: pl. XIII). Each of the barrels is constructed from vertical boards which are held together with hoops, square in section at the top and bottom and semi-circular around the waist of the barrel. This method of construction is portrayed in the Twelfth-Dynasty tomb of Amenemhat at Beni Hasan (BH2; Newberry 1893: pl. XI).

The coopered joint is also seen on a box with a deep bowed front which was discovered in the tomb of Tutankhamun (Cairo JE61495 ; Killen 1994a: 77, fig.77, pl. 62). The curved front is made from vertical boards which have bevelled edges. To support the assembly, horizontal strips of veneer have been bonded to the curved face of the box with glue. The hulls of ships were constructed from large planks of timber in a similar fashion (Landström 1970: fig. 86).

Half-lap joints

Probably the simplest formed cut joint is the half lap joint (Fig. 15.28: rebated butt). An early example from the Predynastic period was found connecting the corners of a burial box in grave N7454 at Nag el-Deir (Lythgoe 1965: 280, figs. 124d and 124f). The box measured 1,570 millimetres in length by 710 millimetres in width and was excavated from a depth to suggest it was 180 millimetres deep. The tray dating from the Early Dynastic period that was discovered by Emery at Saqqara in tomb S3504 had half-lap jointed corners which would have been sewn together (Emery 1954: 43, fig. 27, pls. XVIII and XXXI).

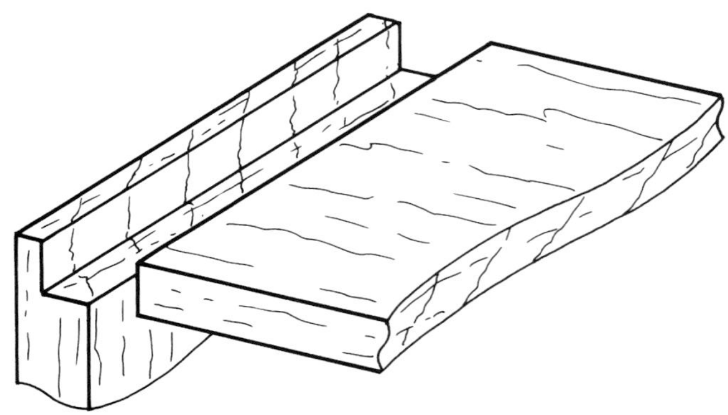

Figure 15.28 Half-lap joint (rebated butt).

Housing joints

The Early Dynastic tray from tomb S3504 at Saqqara (described above in the section on tied and half-lap joints) is also divided into compartments using partitions which are housed into the carcass of the tray. Both the 'through' (Fig. 15.29) and 'stopped' variants of this joint were employed (see Killen 1994a: 2, fig. 3).

Halving joints

This group of joints, where timber is removed from each element, is another way of joining two or three pieces of wood together at an angle. A simple halving joint can be found on the stud work of a cabin end wall on a model ship from the Ninth- or Tenth-Dynasty tomb of Mesehti at Asyut (Cairo JE4918; Reisner 1913: 79, figs. 295–6). A fine example of a triple joint, can be found on a small pot stand, dating to the New Kingdom, which has six legs that are braced by a complex joint (Fig. 15.30: BM EA2471, see Killen 1980: 71, fig. 38, pl. 118).

Bridle joints (Fig. 15.31)

At Saqqara, Emery discovered a large number of timber rail and stile fragments that were dated to the First Dynasty. One fragment had been cut with a bridle joint (Emery 1954: no. 207: 52, fig. 46a). This joint was secured with a single dowel which passes through the face of the joint. The same joint was also used to connect the blade and stock of Egyptian try-squares, such as the Ptolemaic example in the Petrie Museum (UC 6925; see Killen 1980: 12, pl. 3), in which the joint is held by a pair of metal pins and carefully wedged to enclose a perfect right-angle.

Mortise and tenon joints

Those joints which form the mortise and tenon type were extensively used by ancient Egyptian carpenters, joiners, cabinet-makers, builders and sculptors. They discovered that the strongest joint had a tenon one third the thickness of its rail.

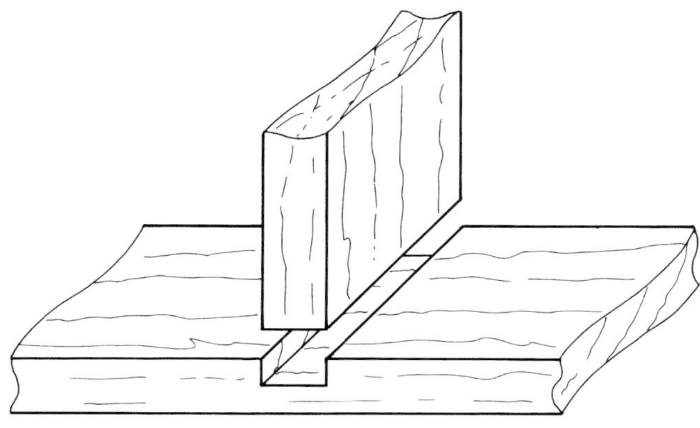

Figure 15.29 Housing joint.

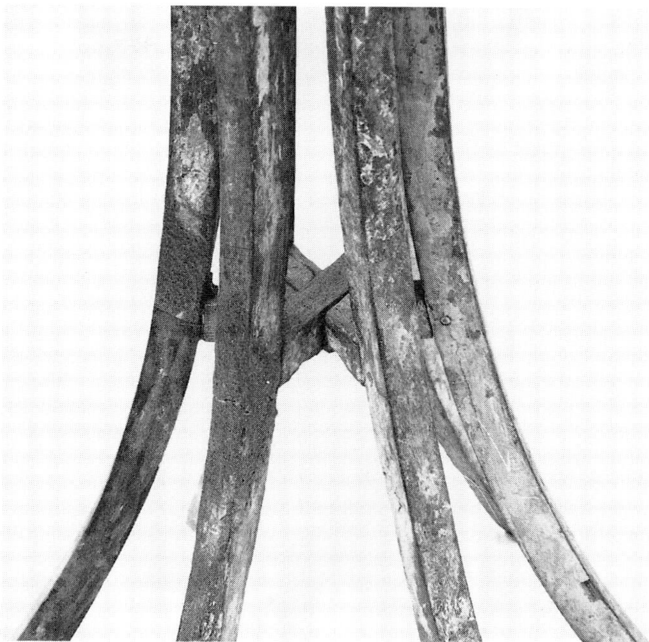

Figure 15.30 Pot stand triple halving joint (BM EA2471).

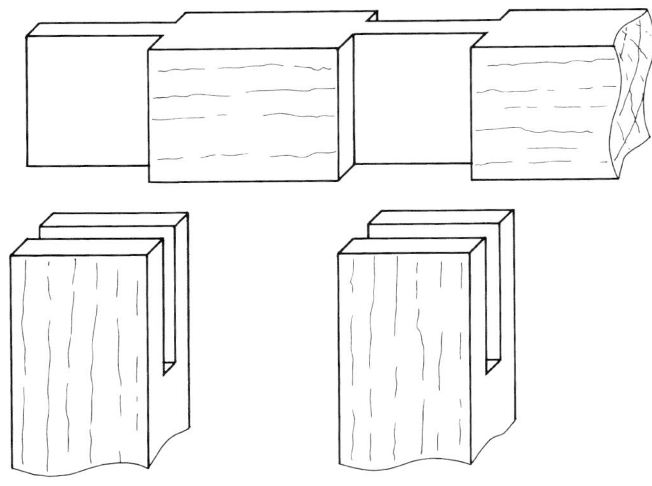

Figure 15.31 Bridle joint.

Common through mortise and tenon with square shoulders

This joint, in which the tenon is taken completely through the opposing rail, was used in the construction of the simple bed frames discovered by Petrie at the Early Dynastic cemetery of Tarkhan (Killen 1980: 24, pls. 27–9), and examples are preserved in the Ashmolean (1912.617, see Fig. 15.32) and Liverpool Museum (55.82.109d–g). The

Figure 15.32 Common through mortise and tenon joint with square shoulders (Ashmolean 1912.617).

Figure 15.33 Common through mortise and tenon joint with scribed shoulders (Manchester 5429).

same type of joint was sometimes used for both stool and chair construction. The seat rails of a Middle Kingdom stool discovered by Garstang in tomb 569 at Beni Hasan (Ashmolean E 4162; see Killen 1980: 39, pls. 51–3) are connected to its legs by common through mortise and tenons, a typical Middle Kingdom design, which prevents the seat rails from lying in the same horizontal plane. These joints would have been secured by driving wedges between the faces of the mortise and the cheeks of the tenon; sculptors commonly employed this method when fastening the arms to statues, such as the life-size figure of the chief lector-priest Kaaper at Saqqara, which has come to be known as the 'Sheikh el-Beled' (Cairo CG34; Saleh and Sourouzian 1987: no. 40).

Common through mortise and tenon with scribed shoulders

This joint was also found at Tarkhan, on bed frames which are supported by bovine shaped legs (Killen 1980: 25–6, fig. 6, pls. 31–4). The curved or scribed shoulders below the tenon, which projects from the top of the leg, mould around and support the side poles of the bed frame (Fig. 15.33). The same technique was used for New Kingdom folding stools, which have the ends of the diagonal spindles formed with goose heads. The tenon takes the form of the goose's protruding tongue and it is mortised into the floor rail, while the beak forms the scribed shoulder of the joint. The stretchers which brace the seats of round legged stools are also attached with a similar joint and on some, ivory ferrules carved in the form of a papyrus flower are scribed and placed around the joint (BM EA2472; Killen 1980: 49, fig. 23, pls. 82–3).

Barefaced tenons

To allow the seat rails to lie in the same plane the technique of halving the tenon and allowing one to pass over the other in the legs mortises is seen on New Kingdom chairs (Fig. 15.34; BM EA2479; Killen 1980: 54, fig. 29, pl. 86). Again the practise of wedging such a joint was preferred to glue.

When the cross-rail was thinner than the stile, Egyptian carpenters also used either a barefaced tenon (without shoulders) or alternatively a barefaced tenon with a single shoulder. This joint was used on the chair described above (BM EA2479), the front and back stretchers of which are jointed to the leg (Fig. 15.35).

Stub tenons

This joint has applications on stool-and-frame constructions where the mortise is 'stopped' (i.e. not chopped completely through the stile). It can be found on the back support-frames of chairs (BM EA2479). The joint cannot be externally wedged, therefore it is held in place with a single dowel passing through the face of the joint and the cheek of

Figure 15.34 Barefaced tenon with single shoulder (BM EA2479).

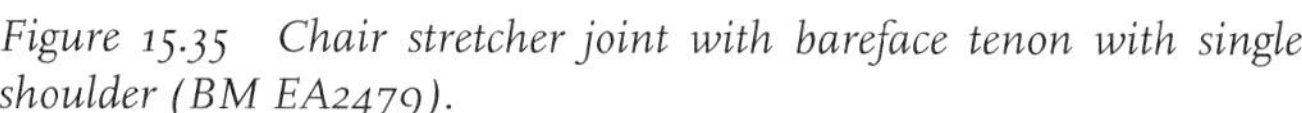

Figure 15.35 Chair stretcher joint with bareface tenon with single shoulder (BM EA2479).

Figure 15.36 Stub tenon joint on chair back rest (BM EA2479).

the tenon (Fig. 15.36). Occasionally it was used on seat-rail joints, but here the ends of the tenons are cut with a mitre so that they meet at a right-angle within the joint. The frames of New Kingdom boxes are predominantly held together with stub tenons, while the boxes from the tomb of Tutankhamun were held with gold pins.

Dovetail-shaped tenons (Fig. 15.37)
This unusual joint is found connecting the corners of a *cavetto* cornice on a Late Period cabinet (Cairo Inv. No. 29.12.25.6); it is prone to failure, due to the stresses applied to the wedge-shaped mortise by the dovetail-shaped tenon. This failure can in fact be seen on the Cairo cabinet, in that a wedge-shaped piece of timber has fallen away from the joint (Killen 1994a: 85, fig. 83).

Dovetail joints (Fig. 15.38)

The technique of cutting tapering tails on one element which would have located in a matching socket has been identified on fragments of ivory discovered in the Early Dynastic royal tombs at Abydos (Petrie 1901: pl. XLIV). The Fourth-Dynasty tomb of Queen Hetepheres I at Giza contained a large collection of furniture, but much of the wood had perished, leaving little more than the gold and copper

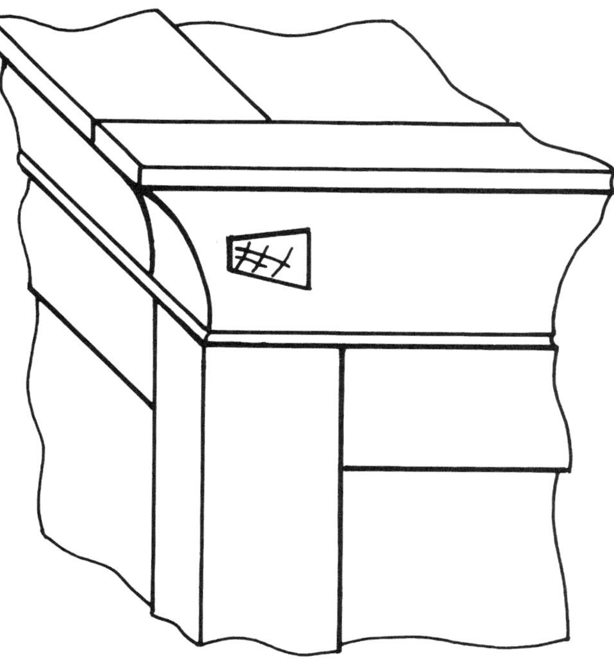

Figure 15.37 Dovetail-shaped tenon joint.

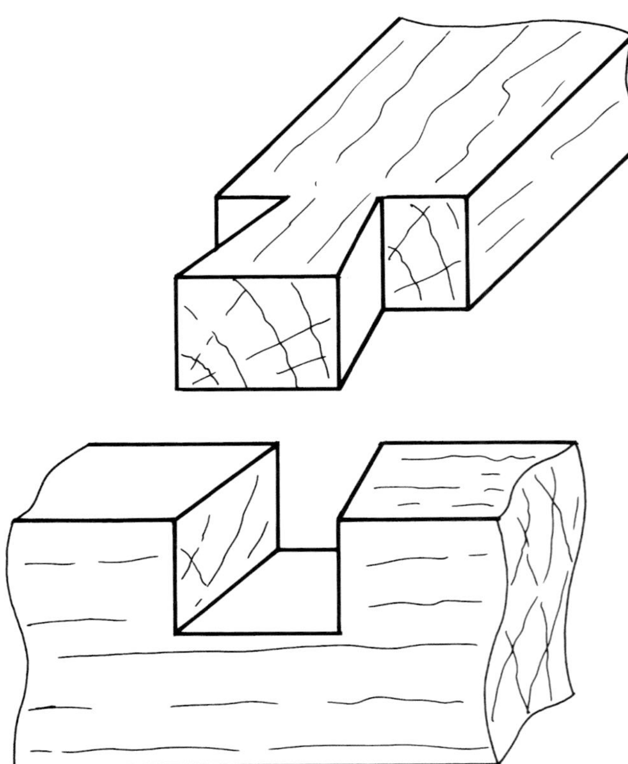

Figure 15.38 Dovetail joint.

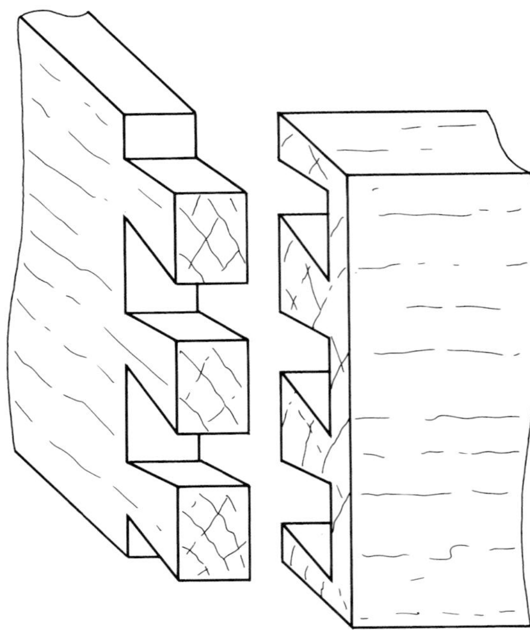

Figure 15.39 Lapped dovetail joint.

sheaths that had been attached to these wooden elements. From the positions of these sheaths, however, it has proved possible to reconstruct much of the furniture, including a bed canopy in which the roof poles are dovetailed into the roof beams, and the vertical back pillars and roof beam are jointed by barefaced dovetails (Reisner and Smith 1955: 23–5, pls. 9e and 10b, figs. 25–6).

On an Eighteenth-Dynasty box in the Louvre (N 2922), it is possible to see a dovetailed shaped tongue extending from under the lid and engaging as a simple lock in a socket in the front of the box (Killen 1994a: 45, fig. 56). A dovetail joint was also used on one of the cross-beams of a small sledge found near the Twelfth-Dynasty pyramid of Senusret III at Dahshur (Cairo JE4928; see Reisner 1913: 88–9, fig. 326).

Lapped dovetail joint (Fig. 15.39)
The main application of this joint is in carcass and drawer construction, as in the case of the drawer in the front of the Twelfth-Dynasty box of Kemni (MMA 26.7.1438; see Killen 1994a: 26–7, fig. 46, pl. 12).

Common through dovetail joint (Fig. 15.40)
Another variation on this joint type, which was used to fasten the corner-boards of boxes, can be observed on a box in the Petrie Museum (UC30704). The sides of rectangular coffins could also be dovetailed, as in the case of an Eighteenth-Dynasty example from the family tomb of Neferkhaut and his family at Asasif in western Thebes, near the causeway of the cult temple of Thutmose III (TT729; Hayes 1935: 19).

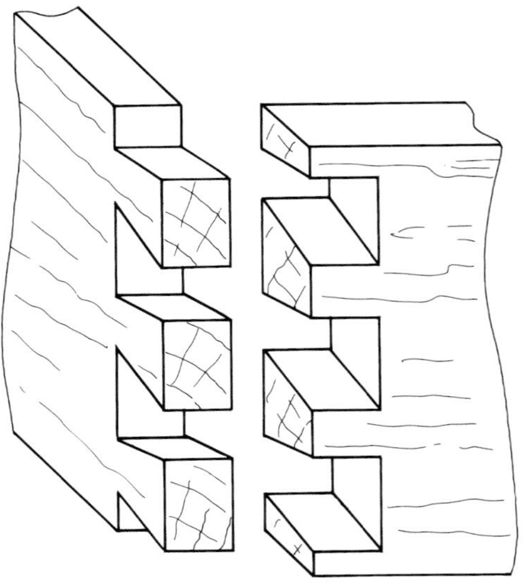

Figure 15.40 Common through dovetail joint.

Mitre joints

Simple plain mitre joint (Fig. 15.41)
One of the earliest examples of the simple, plain mitre joint was found connecting the corner of a burial box, in grave N 7338, in the Predynastic cemetery at Nag el-Deir (Lythgoe 1965: 205, figs. 90a and d). A First-Dynasty ivory frame discovered by Emery in tomb S3507 at Saqqara has

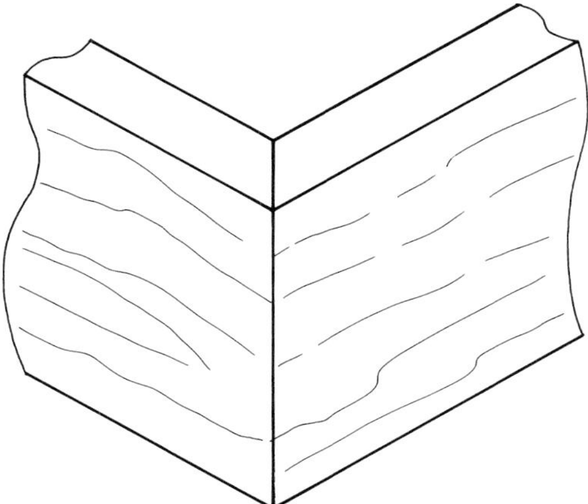

Figure 15.41 *Simple plain mitre joint.*

plain mitred corners (Emery 1958, cat. nos. 75–8: 84, pl. 100 [a]). The back support-frame of an armchair from the tomb of Queen Hetepheres I appears to have been jointed with a mitred halving (Reisner and Smith 1955: 28–29, pls. 15–16, fig. 31). Large coffins were also mitred, as in the case of the Twelfth-Dynasty inner and outer cedar coffins of Amenemhat from Deir el-Bersha, both of which are preserved in the Egyptian Museum, Cairo (CG28091–2). These mitres are held together with copper ties and wooden pegs.

Mitred shoulder joints

The process of jointing the ends of boards to form boxes and coffins could also be achieved with a number of different mitre shoulder joints. The shoulder mitre (Fig. 15.42) and double shoulder mitre (Fig. 15.43), were first identified by Mackay (see Petrie and Mackay 1915: 23–30, pl. XXV). While the butt joint surmounting a long plain mitre (Fig. 15.44) and the half dovetail surmounting a long plain mitre (Fig. 15.45) were confused by Mackay as a mitre housing and a dovetailed mitre housing. The definition of a housing

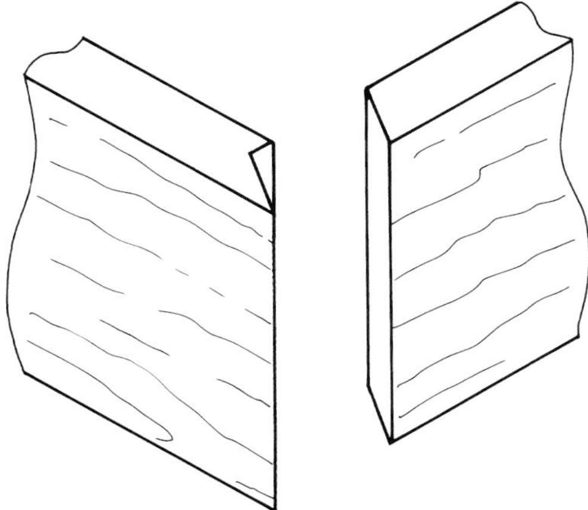

Figure 15.42 *Shoulder mitre joint.*

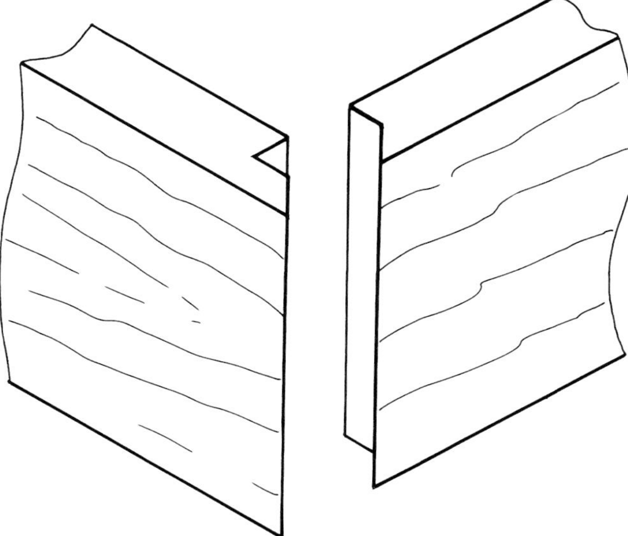

Figure 15.43 *Double shoulder mitre joint.*

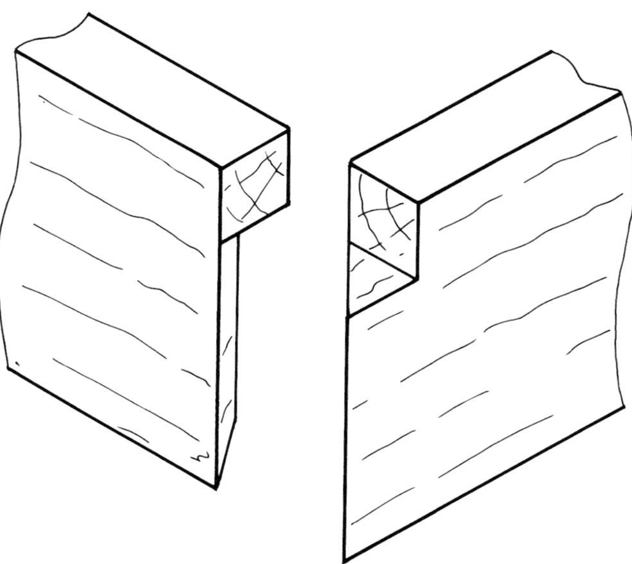

Figure 15.44 *Butt joint surmounting a long plain mitre.*

and a dovetailed mitre housing. The definition of a housing is that it has a wood face on either side of the joint (see Fig. 15.29).

Scarf joints

Common scarf with butterfly cramp locking piece (Fig. 15.46)

Egyptian timbers were often short, and the scarf joint was employed to fasten two lengths of timber together. The faces which come into contact were cut at an angle and a double dovetail socket was cut across the splice. Into this socket was driven a butterfly-shaped wooden cramp that securely locked the battens together.

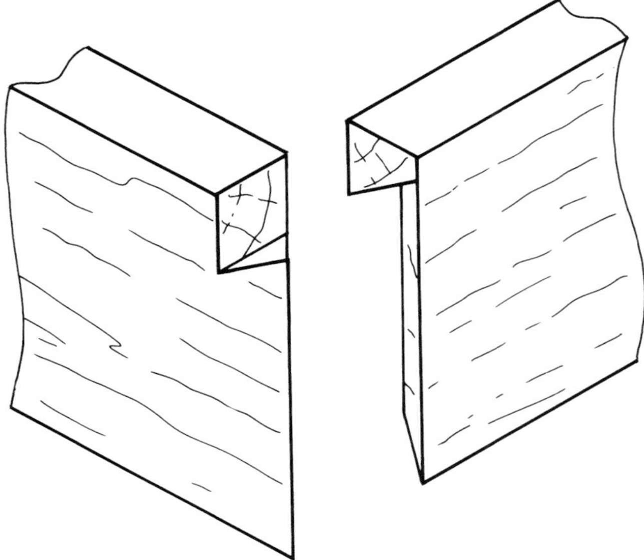

Figure 15.45 Half dovetail surmounting a long plain mitre.

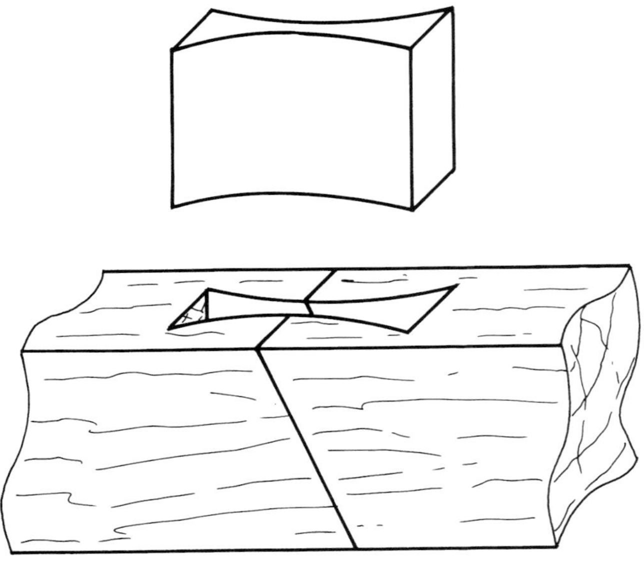

Figure 15.46 Common scarf joint with butterfly cramp locking piece.

Tied hook scarf joint (Fig. 15.47)
Another type of scarf joint was used when constructing the hull of boats. This joint was used when the ends of large timbers were brought together. Holes were cut above and below the line of fixture and ropes were bound through these to fasten the joint. Another variant of this joint, the spliced scarf joint, was also used in boat-building and has flat contact faces (Fig. 15.48).

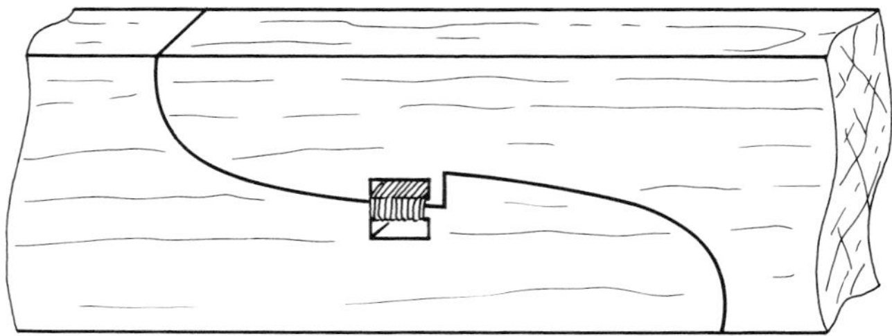

Figure 15.47 Tied hooked scarf joint.

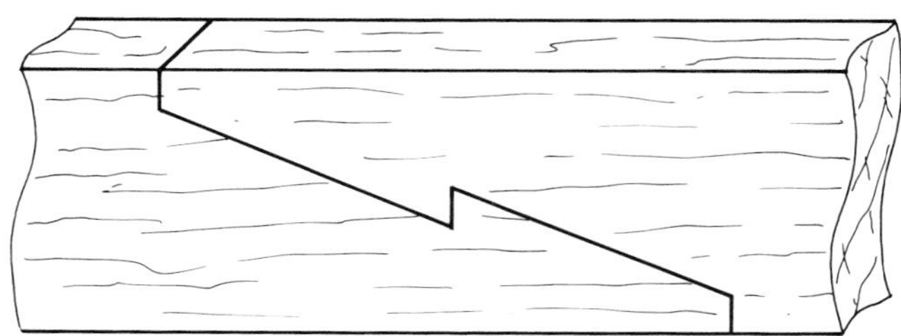

Figure 15.48 Spliced scarf joint.

Veneering and inlay

Veneer was used either constructionally, in the manufacture of plywood for coffins, or as a decorative layer to disguise poor quality timber. Decorative timber veneers were cut with a thin blade saw, unlike the modern process of slicing or rotating the log against a knife. Large amounts of ivory strip that are incised with twisting, crossing, diagonal and zigzag patterns have been discovered at a number of Early Dynastic sites and were dowelled to furniture in early attempts at veneering (Killen 1994a: 6, fig. 6). The Fourth-Dynasty carrying chair of Queen Hetepheres I, from her tomb at Giza, was veneered with ebony strips into which were inlaid gold hieroglyphs (Reisner and Smith 1955: 33–4, fig. 34, pls. 27–9). The Twelfth-Dynasty tomb of Princess Sithathoriunet at Lahun contained ivory veneer panel fragments from a jewellery box. It proved possible to reconstruct the box using both the panel fragments and a number of gold *djed* symbols from the same context (Winlock 1934: 12–17, fig. 3, pl. 1B).

Many of the boxes that were constructed during the New Kingdom had their legs and panels edged with ebony veneer in an attempt to give an impression of a rich frame and panel construction. A small New Kingdom jewellery box in the British Museum (BM EA5897) was decorated in this way (Killen 1994a: 30–4, figs. 49–50, pls. 18–20). The rectangular boxes discovered in the tombs of Yuya and Tuyu (KV46) and Tutankhamun (KV62) were surface-treated in a similar fashion. A scene in the Eighteenth-Dynasty tomb of Rekhmira at Thebes shows a carpenter applying hot glue to a leaf of veneer with a brush (TT100; Davies 1943: pl. LV).

The technique of inlaying (i.e. embedding a variety of materials into wood) was widely practised during the Early Dynastic period. In tomb S3504 at Saqqara, Emery discovered a fragment of timber that had been lightly gessoed and had triangular pieces of faience inlaid into it. These pieces had been fitted into precisely chiselled cavities with a bonding agent (Emery 1954: 38, fig. 16, pl. XXXI [C]). Another First-Dynasty fragment (Ashmolean E1255 and E138), has one surface inlaid with triangular pieces of wood and faience.

A small box from the First-Dynasty tomb of Hemaka (S3035) at Saqqara is inlaid with wood and ivory strips (Emery 1938: 41, fig. 11, cat. no. 433), while another box from the same tomb is inlaid with different coloured woods (Emery 1938: 41, pl. 23a, cat. no. 432). A curtain box discovered in the Fourth-Dynasty tomb of Queen Hetepheres I at Giza is inlaid with faience. The sides and lid of this long box were carved with cavities in the shape of the designs and hieroglyphs to a depth of four millimetres, then gold leaf was burnished around the edge of each cavity prior to the insertion of the inlay along with a binding medium (Reisner and Smith 1955: 25–7, figs. 28a–b, pls. 7b, 12, 13c).

A number of pieces of furniture from Tutankhamun's tomb have been skilfully embellished using the techniques of marquetry and parquetry. For instance, the technique of parquetry (applying geometric shaped pieces of material to timber) was used on two small boxes (Cairo JE61461–2); thousands of tiny slivers of ebony and ivory are placed on the box's panels in herringbone, diamond and crisscross patterns (Killen 1994a: 57 and 64, pls. 51, 53).

Finishing techniques

Gypsum, a hydrated form of calcium sulphate which occurs naturally in Egypt, was made into a thick plaster which could be applied to timber to disguise the grain. If paint was to be applied, then gesso, made from whiting and gum, was used as a foundation. Gesso could also be used to hold inlays in position.

Gilding was another popular means of finishing or decorating timber. One of the earliest examples of this process is seen on a fragment, perhaps part of a furniture rail, which was discovered at Abydos (*c.* 2900 BC; Ashmolean E1255 and E138). The edges of the fragment are carved with a bound rush pattern commonly used at this period. The surface was overlaid with fine linen on to which the gold leaf was applied and burnished into the bound rush pattern (Killen 1994b: 22, fig. 24). Gesso was also used as an adhesive holding the gold leaf to the wooden core. This technique was used throughout the Dynastic period and is seen on much of the royal furniture discovered in the Eighteenth-Dynasty tombs of Yuya and Tuyu and Tutankhamun. The Egyptians also used thicker gold sheet, as well as silver, beaten, pressed and punched into and around wooden cores. These metal sheaths were held in position with small nails, a technique which was used on the legs of a bed frame supposed to have belonged to Queen Hatshepsut of the Eighteenth Dynasty (BM EA21574; Killen 1980: 10, pl. 1).

Boat building

The acacia (*A. nilotica*), sycomore (*Ficus sycomorus*) and tamarisk (*T. nilotica*) grew abundantly in Egypt until the early medieval period, and all of these woods were used in ancient times to build boats. Theophrastus says that acacia could be converted into planks of twelve cubits (6.24 metres) in length (see Boreux 1925: 237), and Janssen (1975: 373–5) has translated documents from the Ramesside period recording that beams of tamarisk could be purchased at lengths of between 4.5 and 8 metres. The timbers identified in the New Kingdom shipyard records preserved in the British Museum (BM EA10056) probably refer to timber such as Cedar of Lebanon (*Cedrus libani*; see Glanville 1931, 1933). The quality of these imported coniferous timbers, which have straight fine grain, allowed good quality planks to be converted to greater lengths.

In the Predynastic period, tree trunks may have been hollowed out to form simple dug-out canoes, although during the Naqada II period some boats began to be made from thick planks of carved timber. The sides of the craft were sewn to the shaped bottom of the boat and were braced with a number of thwarts which prevented the boat collapsing and made the structure rigid. During the Early Dynastic period it became customary to envisage that the deceased would be carried to the netherworld on a boat, therefore models of such boats were sometimes placed in or near the burial (Emery 1961: 54, fig. 17).

Around the Fourth-Dynasty pyramid of Khufu at Giza were buried five boats, three on the eastern side of the pyramid with a further pair, dismantled in pits, on its southern side. One pit on the southern side measured 31.2 metres in length, 2.6 metres wide and 3.5 metres deep and contained 407 assembled wooden parts of a boat which had been stored in thirteen layers. The tomb, unlike that of Queen Hetepheres I which was close by, had remained both water- and airtight and the boat's timbers were found to be in good condition. When all the assembled parts were dismantled for examination and conservation it was found that the boat comprised of 1,224 elements ranging in length from 22.73 metres to just 100 millimetres (Lipke 1984). Those large timbers were found to be cedar while the smaller parts, such as the loose tongues or tenons used to join the hull planks, were either made of sycomore (*Ficus sycomorus*) or sidder (*Ziziphus spina-christi*).

Once fully assembled, the funerary boat of Khufu measured 43.4 metres in length and 5.9 metres across the beam, having a displacement of about 40 tons. The cedar planks which formed the hull were an impressive 130–40 millimetres in thickness. Their edges were bevelled and held together with loose tongues or tenons and transverse lashings of rope which passed through angled channels chiseled in the inner face of the planks. These hull planks were butted together and fastened with hooked scarf joints. The boat's construction shows that it had no keel and the sides were braced with sixteen frames.

At the necropolis site of Dahshur were discovered six Middle Kingdom papyriform craft which may have been the funeral boats of Senusret III. Four were sufficiently well-preserved to show the constructional techniques which were employed in their manufacture. They were smaller than the Khufu boat, the longest being 10.20 metres. Their hull design was very different being constructed around a spine made from three central planks which were butted and tied together and protrude below the hull's curvature. Against these were placed boards, irregular in shape, which construct the curved hull. The hulls of the Dahshur boats were held rigid by through-going beams which were pegged to the uppermost planks of the hull. Across these beams was placed the deck-planking which appears to have been pegged down. On two boats the crossbeams are rebated to accept the ends of the deck-planking.

Excavations at the early Twelfth-Dynasty site of Lisht, which was probably in use about a century before the Dahshur boats, revealed boat timbers buried as foundations for building ramps and causeways connected with the construction of pyramids and *mastabas*. These massive timbers appear to derive from the frame of a freighter, thus offering a good contrast to the ceremonial Giza and Dahshur boats. The planking demonstrates a previously unrecorded manner of construction using intricate fittings with deep mortise and tenons held with plaited lashings. The frame is locked together with a stringer of wood 500 × 500 millimetres in section set deep in the hull to provide a low centre of gravity, which made this boat suitable to carry heavy deck loads (Haldane 1992: 102–12, pls. 115–33).

One further development was the introduction of the hogging truss, which tensioned the stem and stern of the boat and was supported on wooden beams held in vertical forked pillars above the deck. This strengthening system characterised two different types of boat depicted in the temple of Queen Hatshepsut at Deir el-Bahari: sea-going vessels loading materials in the land of Punt (Naville 1898: pl. LXXIII) and an obelisk barge being towed from Aswan to Thebes (Naville 1908: pl. CLIV).

Many scenes of boat-builders practising their trade are portrayed in Old Kingdom funerary reliefs, such as those in the Fifth-Dynasty tomb of Ty at Saqqara, where a large workforce is depicted making a number of boats that are at various stages of construction. Craftsmen are fitting a side hull plank and between the slightly open line of fixture can be seen several edge pegs. In another part of this scene, two men sit on a cross-beam which is supported on trestles. They are mortising rope holes in the edges and adjoining faces of the beam. Other men are seen planing the outer surfaces of the boat with adzes to achieve its correct profile. This could be done without fear of damaging the boat's structural integrity for its joining system was internal (Wild 1953: pl. CXXIX).

Conclusion [Gale, Gasson and Hepper]

In common with other Egyptian antiquities, a large number of wooden artefacts are now dispersed worldwide in private and public collections. Comparatively few have been scientifically examined or the woods identified, although some collections, such as that housed in the British Museum, are currently undergoing comprehensive surveys. Wooden artefacts originating from dynasties preceding the Ptolemaic era span a period of some three millennia or more and represent an as yet mainly untapped and potentially important source of information. The comparative analysis of uses of wood over such a period may indicate preferential or functional selection. In many cultures, both ancient and modern, certain woods (or trees) have been considered apotropaic, symbolic of named deities or credited with peculiar powers (Brown 1935; Grigson 1958; Rock 1974; Cooper 1978; Webster 1986). The same values probably applied in Egypt and venerated woods may have been reserved for ritual purposes. For example, some of the numerous objects associated with mortuary customs (e.g. mummy-labels and stelae) have been identified as *Cedrus*, and it seems that this wood was used even though it was hidden by decoration and painting; the option of using an inferior (and cheaper) wood was apparently not taken. Social rank, contemporary fashions or local availability may have determined the choice, or perhaps, the artisans were merely making the most of a scarce commodity by using offcuts or recycled pieces of wood. There is still much work to be done in identifying the woods used, their sources and functional uses.

Acknowledgements

Geoffrey Killen would like to thank Dr Cheryl Haldane (Institute of Nautical Archaeology) for her advice on the section dealing with boat-building; Dr Stephen Quirke and Mr Vivian Davies of the British Museum for their assistance in studying BM EA10056 and other objects; Lorraine March-Killen for her photographs; Dr Jaromir Malek for his help in consulting the archives of the Griffith Institute; and Dr Dorothea Arnold, the Lila Acheson Wallace Curator of Egyptology at the Metropolitan Museum of Art, for her assistance in studying objects.

References

Anthes, R. 1943. Die Deutschen Grabungen auf der Westseite von theben in den Jahren 1911 und 1913. *MDAIK*, 12: 1–68.

Baum, N. 1988. *Arbres et arbustes de l'Egypte ancienne*. Leuven: Département oriental.

Beauvisage, G. 1896. Recherches sur quelques bois pharaoniques. *RT*, 18: 78–90.

1897. Recherches sur quelques bois pharaoniques. *RT*, 19: 77–9.

Beauverie, M.A. 1935. Description illustrée des végétaux antiques du Musée égyptien du Louvre. *BIFAO*, 35: 115–51.

Beekman, W.B. 1949–55. *Hout in alle tijden*. Deventer: A.E. Kluwer.

Bierbrier, M.L. 1987. *Hieroglyphic Texts from Egyptian Stelae*. London: BMP.

Blackman, A.M. 1953. *The Rock Tombs of Meir* V. London: EES.

Boak, A.E.R. and Peterson, E.E. 1931. *Karanis*. Ann Arbor: Michigan University Press.

Borchardt, L. 1909. *Das Grabdenkmal des Königs Nefer-ir-ka-Re*. Leipzig: Hinrichs.

1910–13. *Das Grabdenkmal des Königs Sahu-Re*. Leipzig: Hinrichs.

1911. *Der Porträtkopf der Königin Teje*. Leipzig: Hinrichs.

Boreux, C. 1925. *Etudes de nautique Égyptienne: l'art de la navigation en égypte jusqu'à la fin de l'ancien empire*. Cairo: IFAO.

Botti, G. 1951. Il carro del sogno (per un grato ricordo personale). *Aegyptus*, 31: 192–8.

Bravo, G. A. 1933. La lavorazione delle pelli e del cuoio nell'Egitto antico. *Bollettino Ufficiale della R. Stazione Sperimentale per l'industria delle Pelli e delle Materie concianti*, 11: 75–92.

Brazier, J.D. and Franklin, G.L. 1961. Identification of hardwoods: a microscope key. *Forest Products Research Bulletin* 46.

Breasted, J.H. 1906. *Ancient Records of Egypt I*. Chicago: Chicago University Press.

Brown, F.B.H. 1935. Flora of south eastern Polynesia III: Dicotyledons. *Bernice P. Bishop Museum Bulletin*, 130.

Brunton, G. 1937. *Mostagedda and the Tasian Culture*. London: Quaritch.

1948. *Matmar*. London: Quaritch.

Brunton, G. and Caton-Thompson, G. 1928. *Badarian Civilisation*. London: BSAE.

Bruyère, B. 1924–53. *Rapports sur les Fouilles de Deir el Médineh*, 17 vols. Cairo: IFAO.

Burckhardt, J.L. 1819. *Travels in Nubia*. London: H. Colburn.

Carter, H. 1923–33. *The Tomb of Tut.Ankh.Amen*, 3 vols. London: Cassell.

Caton-Thompson, G. and Gardner, E.W. 1932. The prehistoric geography of Kharga Oasis. *Geographical Journal*, 80: 371–406.

1934. *Desert Fayum*, 2 vols. London: Royal Anthropological Institute of Great Britain and Ireland.

Chalk, L. (1931–2). *Eighth Annual Report*. Oxford: Imperial Forestry Institute.

(1932–3). *Ninth Annual Report*. Oxford: Imperial Forestry Institute.

Coche de la Ferté, E. 1952. *Les Portraits Romano-Égyptiens du Louvre*. Paris: Louvre.

Cooper, J.C. 1978. *An Illustrated Encyclopedia of Traditional Symbols*. London: Thames and Hudson.

Curto, S. 1973. *L'arte militare presso gli antichi egizi*. Turin: Edizioni d'Arte Fratelli Pozzo.

Davies, N. de G. 1913. *Five Theban Tombs*. London: EES.

1927. *Two Ramesside Tombs at Thebes*. New York: MMA.

1943. *The Tomb of Rekh-mi-re*ʿ *at Thebes*. New York: MMA.

Davies, W.V. 1995. Ancient Egyptian timber imports: an analysis of wooden coffins in the British Museum. In *Egypt, the Aegean and the Levant*. (eds. W.V. Davies and L. Schofield). London: BMP, pp. 146–56.

Description de l'Egypte I: Histoire Naturelle. 1809. Paris: Institut d'Orient.

Diodorus Siculus *see* Oldfather 1935.

Dittmann, K.H. 1941. Der Segelwagen von Medînet Mâdi. *MDAIK*, 10: 60–78.

Ebers, G. 1884. *Der geschnitzte Holzsarg des Hatbastru im aegyptologischen Apparat der Universität zu Leipzig*. Leipzig: S. Hirzel.

Edgar, C.C. 1931. *Zenon Papyri* II. Cairo: IFAO.

Emery, W.B. 1938. *Excavations at Saqqara: The Tomb of Hemaka*. Cairo: Government Press.

1939. *Excavations at Saqqara: Hor-Aha*. Cairo: Government Press.

1949. *Excavations at Saqqara: Great Tombs of the First Dynasty* I. Cairo: Government Press.

1954. *Excavations at Saqqara: Great Tombs of the First Dynasty* II. London: EES.

1958. *Excavations at Saqqara: Great Tombs of the First Dynasty* III. London: EES.

1961. *Archaic Egypt*. Harmondsworth: Penguin.

Engelbach, R. 1931. Ancient Egyptian woods. *ASAE*, 31: 144.

Erman, A. and Grapow, H. 1926–31. *Wörterbuch der ägyptischen Sprache*, 5 vols. Leipzig: J.C. Hinrichs.

Fahn, A., Werker, E. and Baas, P. 1986. *Wood Anatomy and Identification of Trees and Shrubs from Israel and Adjacent Regions*. Jerusalem: Israel Academy of Sciences and Humanities.

Fay, B. 1990. *Egyptian Museum, Berlin*, 4th edn. Berlin and Mainz: von Zabern.

Firth, C.M., Quibell, J.E. and Lauer, J.-P. 1935. *Excavations at Saqqara: The Step Pyramid*, 2 vols. Cairo, IFAO.

Fischer, M. (forthcoming). Umm el-Qaab/Abydos report excavation report. MDAIK.

Friis, I., Hepper, F.N. and Gasson, P. 1986. The botanical identity of the *Mimusops* in ancient Egyptian tombs. *JEA*, 72: 201–4.

Gale, R. and Cutler, D. 1999. *Plant Remains in Archaeology*. London: Westbury and Royal Botanical Gardens, Kew.

Germer, R. 1985. *Flora des pharaonischen Ägypten*. Mainz am Rhein: von Zabern.

1989. *Die Pflanzenmaterialien aus dem Grab des Tutanchamun*. Hildesheim: Gerstenberg.

Giddy, L.L. 1992. *The Anubieion at Saqqâra II: The Cemeteries*. London: EES.

Glanville, S.R.K. 1931. Records of a royal dockyard of the time of Tuthmosis III: P. BM EA10056. *ZÄS*, 66: 105–21.

1933. Records of a royal dockyard of the time of Tuthmosis III: P. BM EA10056 (part II). *ZÄS*, 68: 7–41.

Godley, A.D. 1990. *Herodotus I: Books I–II*. Loeb Classical Library. Cambridge MA and London: Harvard University Press.

Greiss, E.A.M. 1949. Anatomical identification of plant material from ancient Egypt. *BIE*, 31: 249–77.

Grigson, G. 1958. *The Englishman's Flora*. London: Phoenix House Ltd [repr. Frogmore: Paladin, 1975].

Haldane, C. 1992. The Lisht timbers: a preliminary report. In *The Metropolitan Museum of Art Egyptian Expedition XXV: The Southern Cemeteries at Lisht III: The pyramid complex of Senwosret I at Lisht* (ed. D. Arnold). New York, Metropolitan Museum, pp. 102–12, pls. 115–33.

Hamilton, W.R. 1809. *Remarks on Several Parts of Turkey, I: Aegyptiaca*. London.

Hassan, S. 1943. *Excavations at Giza IV: 1932–1933*. Cairo: Fouad I University Press.

Hayes, W.C. 1935. The Egyptian expedition, 1934–1935. *BMMA*, 30 (November 1935): II, 3–36.

1953. *The Scepter of Egypt* I. New York: MMA.

1959. *The Scepter of Egypt* II. New York: MMA.

Hepper, F.N. 1977. On the transference of ancient plant names. *PEQ*, 109: 129–30.

1990. *Pharaoh's Flowers: The Botanical Treasures of Tutankhamun*. London: HMSO.

1992. Timber for the carpenter. In *The Illustrated Encyclopedia of Bible Plants* (ed. F.N. Hepper). Leicester: Inter-Varsity Press, pp. 156–65.

forthcoming. A shabti in juniper wood. *JEA*.

Herodotus *see* Godley 1990.

Hölscher, U. 1951. *The Excavation of Medinet Habu* IV. OIP. Chicago: University of Chicago Press.

Hort, A.F. (transl. and ed.) 1916. *Theophrastus: Enquiry into Plants*, 2 vols. Loeb Classical Library. Cambridge MA and London: Harvard University Press.

Ilic, J. 1991. *CSIRO Atlas of Hardwoods*. Berlin: Springer-Verlag.

Iskander, Z. 1947. Foundation deposits of Thothmes IIIrd (M.A. Mansour). *ASAE*, 47: 157.

Jagiella, C. and Kürschner, H. 1987. *Atlas der Hölzer Saudi Arabiens: Die Holzanatomie der Wichtigsten Bäume und Sträucher Arabiens mit einem holzanatomischen Bestimmungsschlussel*. Wiesbaden: Ludwig Reichert Verlag.

James, T.G.H. 1982. A wooden figure of Wadjet with two painted representations of Amasis. *JEA*, 68: 156–65.

Janssen, J. 1975. *Commodity Prices from the Ramesside Period*. Leiden: Brill.

Jones, H.L. (ed. and transl.) 191732. *The Geography of Strabo*, 8 vols. London: Heinemann.

Keimer, L. 1924. *Die Gartenpflanzen in alten Ägypten* I. Hamburg: Hoffmann und Campe (repr. Hildesheim 1967).

1931. Pendeloques en forme d'insectes faisant partie de colliers égyptiens. *BIFAO*, 31: 145–86.

1943. Note sur le nom égyptien du jujubier d'Egypte (Zizyphus spina Christi, Willd.). *ASAE*, 42: 279–81.

1984. *Die Gartenpflanzen in alten Ägypten* II (ed. R. Germer). Mainz am Rhein: von Zabern.

Killen, G. 1980. *Ancient Egyptian Furniture* I. Warminster: Aris and Phillips.

1994a. *Ancient Egyptian Furniture II: Boxes, Chests and Footstools*. Warminster: Aris and Phillips.

1994b. *Egyptian Woodworking and Furniture*. Aylesbury: Shire Publications.

1997. Wood turning in ancient Egypt. *Journal of the Tools and Trades History Society*, 10: 10–25.

Lansing, A. and Hayes, W.C. 1937. The Egyptian expedition 1935–6: The museum's excavations at Thebes. *BMMA* (Egyptian Supplements January 1937): 4–39.

Landström, B. 1970. *Ships of the Pharaohs: 4000 Years of Egyptian Shipbuilding*. London: Allen and Unwin.

Lauer, J.-P. 1933. Fouilles du Service des Antiquités à Saqqarah (secteur nord) (Novembre 1932–Mai 1933). *ASAE*, 33: 155–66.

Lauer, J.-P., Täckholm, V.L. and Åberg, E. 1951. Les plantes découvertes dans les souterrains de l'enceinte du roi Zoser à Saqqarah (IIIe dynastie). *BIE*, 32: 121–57.

Lefèbvre, G. 1923–4. *Le Tombeau de Petosiris*, 3 vols. Cairo: SAE.

Leospo, E. 1986. *Museo Archeologico di Asti La Collezione Egizia*, Torino: Regione Piemonte, Collana Musei e Gallerie a cure del Servizio Musei, Assessorato alla Cultura.

Lipke, P. 1984. *The Royal Ship of Cheops: A Retrospective Account of the Discovery, Restoration and Reconstruction*. Oxford: BAR.

Littauer, M.A. and Crouwel, J.H. 1982. *Chariots and Related Equipment from the Tomb of Tutankhamun*. Oxford: Clarendon Press.

Loret, V. 1885. L'ébène chez les anciens égyptiens. *RT*, 6: 125–30.

1892. *La Flore Pharaonique*, 2nd edn. Paris: Ernest Leroux.

1893. Recherches sur plusieurs plantes connues des anciens égyptiens. *RT*, 15: 105–30.

Loret, V. and Poisson, J. 1895. Etudes de botanique égyptienne. *RT*, 17: 177–99.

Lucas, A. 1931. 'Cedar'-tree products employed in mummification. *JEA*, 17: 13–21.

1936. The wood of the third Dynasty ply-wood coffin from Saqqara. *ASAE*, 36: 1–4.

1941. Notes on some of the objects from the tomb of Tutankhamun. *ASAE*, 41: 135–47.

1962. *Ancient Egyptian Materials and Industries*, 4th edn., rev. J.R. Harris. London: Edward Arnold.

Lythgoe, A.M. 1965. *The Predynastic cemetery N7000. Naga-ed-Der* IV (ed. D. Dunham). Berkeley CA: University of California Press.

McLeod, W. 1982. *Self Bows and Other Archery Tackle from the Tomb of Tutankhamun*. Oxford: Clarendon Press.

Makkonen, O. 1969. *Ancient Forestry* II. Helsinki: Suomen metsätieteellinen seura, Metsäntutkimuslaitos.

Manuelian, P. der 1981. Notes on the so-called turned stools of the New Kingdom. In *Studies in Ancient Egypt, the Aegean and the Sudan: Essays in Honour of Dows Dunham* (eds. W.K. Simpson and W.M. Davis). Boston: MFA, pp.125–8.

Meiggs, R. 1982. *Trees and Timber in the Ancient Mediterranean World*. Oxford: Clarendon Press.

Mercer, S.A.B. 1939. *The Tell el-Amarna Tablets*. Toronto: Macmillan Co. of Canada.

Metcalfe, C.R. and Chalk, L. 1950. *Anatomy of the Dicotyledons*. Oxford: Clarendon Press.

Miles, A. 1978. *Photomicrographs of World Woods*. London: HMSO.

Möller, G. and Scharff, A. 1926. *Das vorgeschichtliche Gräberfeld von Abusir El-Meleq*. Berlin: DOG.

Mond, R. and Myers, O.H. 1934. *The Bucheum*. London: EES.

1937. *Cemeteries of Armant* I. London: EES.

de Morgan, J. 1897. *Recherches sur les Origines de l'Egypte: Ethnographie Préhistorique: Le Tombeau Royal de Négadah*. Paris: Ernest Leroux.

Moussa, A. and Altenmüller, H. 1971. *The Tomb of Nefer and Ka-hay*. Mainz am Rhein: von Zabern.

Murray, M.A. 1905. *Saqqara Mastabas* I. London: BSAE.

the skin surface with natron and other substances to make it soft and pliable. Embroidered clothes, boots and linen sheets replaced the layers of bandages. The practice of mummification finally ceased with the arrival and spread of Islam following the Arab conquest of Egypt in AD 641.

The application of scientific techniques to the study of mummified remains

Radiology

As a totally non-destructive method, radiography has been used for many years to examine Egyptian mummies. The first radiographs of mummified remains (a child and a cat) were obtained by W. König (1896) in Frankfurt, and in the same year, the English pioneer Thurston Holland (1937: 45, 61) X-rayed a mummified bird. In 1898, Flinders Petrie was the first Egyptologist to use this procedure for human remains (Petrie 1898: pl. XXXVII) and in 1904, G. Elliot Smith and H. Carter X-rayed the mummy of Thutmose IV in Cairo (Smith 1912a: iii–iv). One of the earliest comprehensive surveys – of the Egyptian and Peruvian mummies in the Chicago Field Museum – was undertaken by R.L. Moodie (1931), and since the 1960s, P.H.K. Gray carried out a series of systematic radiological studies in Britain and Europe, documenting some 193 mummies in museums including the major collections in the Rijksmuseum, Leiden, the British Museum and the City of Liverpool Museum (Gray 1973, 1966; Dawson and Gray 1968; Gray and Slow 1968). Also since the late 1960s, J.E. Harris and K.R. Weeks have undertaken a survey of the royal mummies in the Egyptian Museum, Cairo (Harris and Weeks 1973 and Harris and Wente 1980), in order to gain further information about mummification techniques – brain removal, arm position, presence of artefacts – and the age at death of the pharaohs as well as aspects of the genealogy of the royal family.

Figure 16.3 Wooden coffin for a mummified cat (Manchester Museum). Late period, c. 600BC.

However, until the 1970s most mummies had been radiographed on site, with the consequent limitations imposed by the need to use mobile compact equipment capable of being attached to local electricity supplies or associated with suitable isotope sources. Such conditions did not permit accurate comparisons to be made with modern examples.

In the radiological survey undertaken by the Manchester Egyptian Mummy Research Project from 1973 (Isherwood *et al.* 1979, 1984), it was possible to establish standardised conditions by removing the collection of twenty-one human mummies and thirty-four animal mummies from the Manchester University Museum to the Department of Neuroradiology at the Manchester Royal Infirmary and the Department of Diagnostic Radiology at the University's Medical School. Here, under near-ideal conditions, a procedure was established for radiographing the mummies, using orbiting, fluoroscopic and tomographic equipment.

Fluoroscopy (the visualisation of transmitted X-rays on a television screen) was carried out as a first procedure on all the mummies, to evaluate the nature of the contents and their disposition within the wrappings. Each was also subjected to tomography (a method of obtaining X-rays of a section or slice of tissue in a plane). A limited selection of the mummies was investigated further by means of computed tomography (CT). This X-ray transmission technique was developed in Britain by Sir Godfrey Hounsfield in the 1970s; it is designed to obtain transverse body sections 5–13 millimetres in thickness, and provides information which may not be visualised by plain radiography or conventional tomography. The transmission data are processed by computer and made available either as digital information or, by analog conversion, as a pictorial display on a television monitor. The use of such sophisticated equipment under controlled conditions is now standard in most radiological investigations of mummies, and in recent years, there have been several important studies

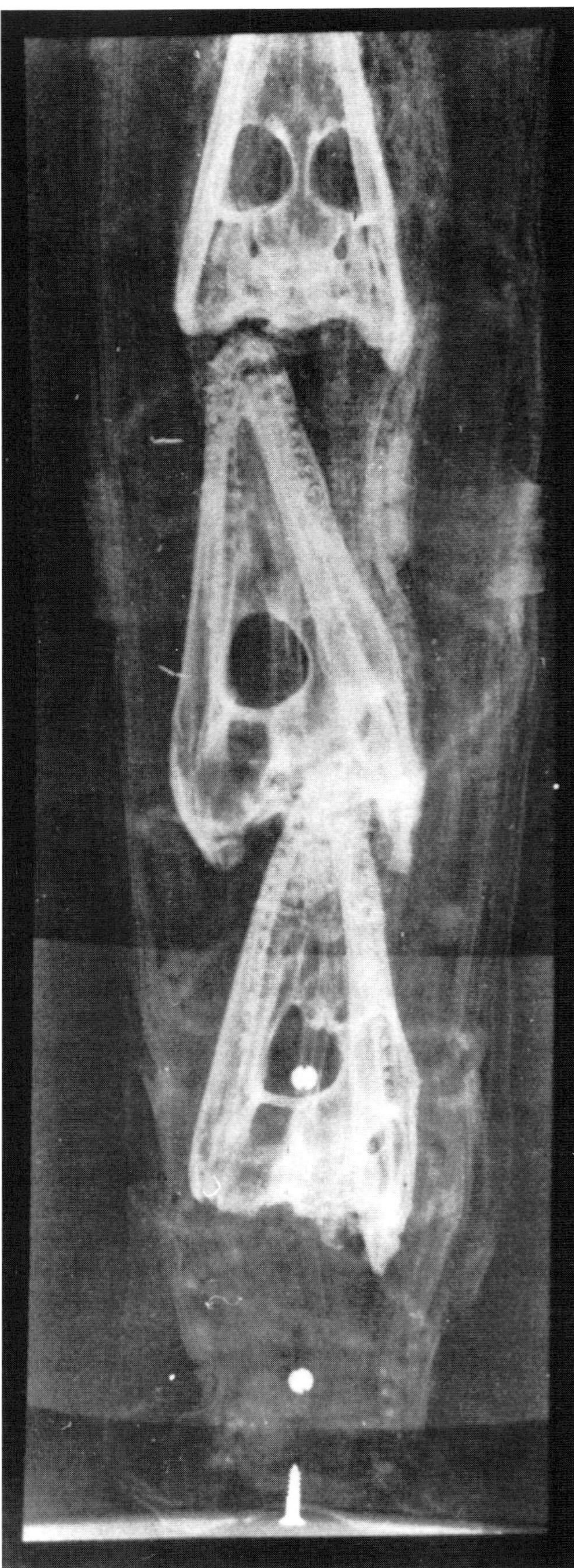

carried out as part of multidisciplinary projects (including Kristen and Reyman 1980; Bard, Fauré and Massare 1985; Raven 1993; Llagostera 1978).

Radiological investigations of mummified remains provide evidence in two main areas. The first concerns the archaeological interest of the mummy and its relationship to its cultural background; the second is the scientific study of disease, injury and causes of death. With regard to the archaeological context, X-ray examination provides a unique opportunity to evaluate skeletal maturity and development. This is based on the ossification of bone in each individual, with particular reference to six sites on the body: the hands, feet, elbows, knees, shoulders and hips. Some problems, however, have resulted from the use of modern European and North American radiological standards to define the bone age of Egyptian mummies. There is a general tendency towards earlier skeletal maturity in the ancient Egyptians and there are significant differences, relating to genetic and nutritional influences, between these ancient and modern populations. Truly accurate radiological studies, it has been argued, should be based on examples from the same ethnic group and from a contemporary population. Generally, however, it is possible to suggest the age at death with reasonable accuracy when the event occurred during the period of active growth (from three months to twenty years), but for adults beyond this range, the presence of other ageing processes such as osteoarthritis or arterial calcification have to be considered.

The X-rays also often provide confirmation of inscriptional evidence (if it is present) or the only evidence (if inscriptions are absent) of the gender of the owner of the body; direct visualisation of the genitalia, or the size and shape of the pelvis, skull and appendicular skeleton from the radiographs can supply this information. In addition, detailed radiological studies have added to our knowledge of mummification techniques and associated funerary customs. The posture of the body within the wrappings and particularly the position of the arms and hands have been examined; Gray (1972), for instance, reviewed and evaluated the position of the arms and hands on one hundred and eleven mummies.

Residual brain tissue has been found in a number of mummies. One CT examination of a shrunken Egyptian brain (Lewin and Harwood Nash 1977) revealed ventricular cavities together with grey and white matter discrimination. Stanworth (1986) was able to examine six detached heads in the Manchester collection on the basis of the evidence provided by X-rays; these showed that fluid levels were present within the skulls, indicating either resin or putrified brain, and material subsequently obtained from

Figure 16.4 When X-rayed, one crocodile-shaped wrapping was found to contain four skulls (three shown here) rather than a complete crocodile.

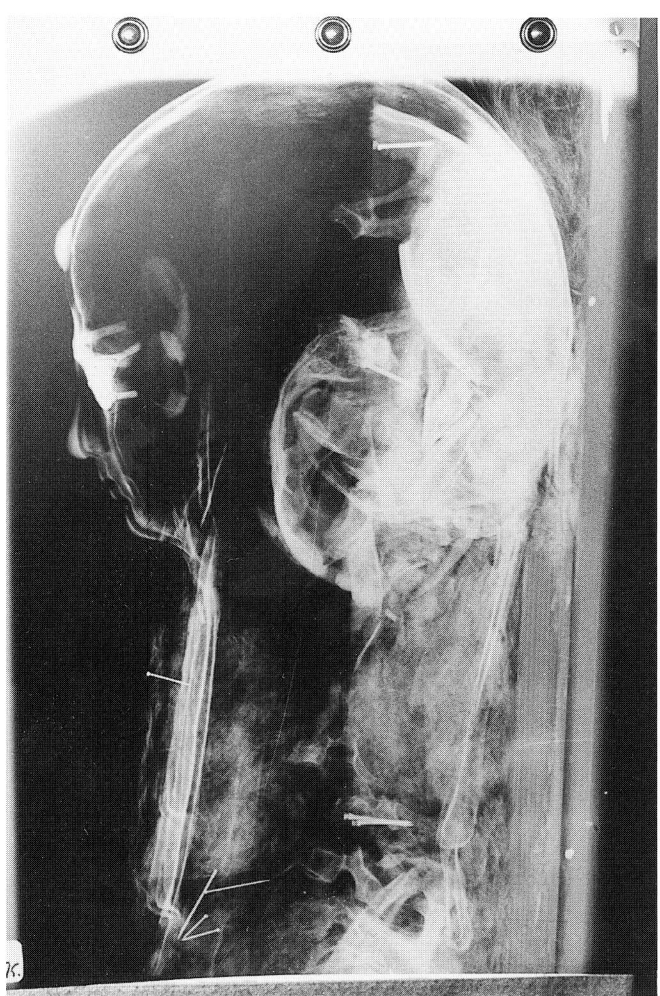

Figure 16.5 Lateral radiograph of the cartonnage face mask and the skull collapsed within, belonging to Mummy 1770 (Manchester Museum).

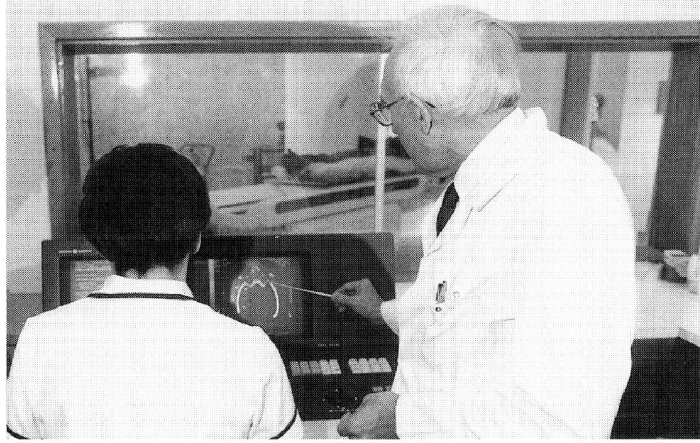

Figure 16.6 A mummy enters the CT Scanner in the Department of Diagnostic Radiology, University of Manchester, and the whole body is subjected to a transaxial sectional survey.

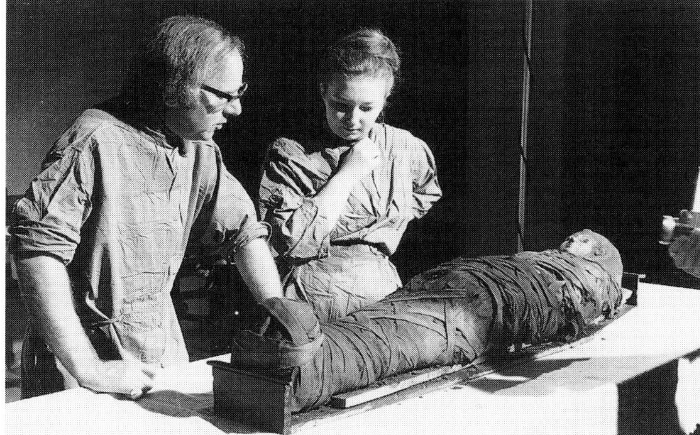

Figure 16.7 Mummy 1770 was unwrapped and autopsied in 1975 by a multidisciplinary team at the University of Manchester.

this source by means of endoscopy was examined further using specialised neuropathological techniques (Thompson *et al.* 1986). It was also possible to determine that the normal routes of entry into these heads to remove the brain tissue, as part of the mummification process, were via the orbits or the nose.

There has been much discussion regarding embalming excerebration (Leek 1969b: 112–16). However, although most scholars claim that this procedure only started in the New Kingdom, indisputable evidence has been presented of four cases of brain removal attributable to the Twelfth Dynasty (1991–1783 BC; see Strouhal 1986). In the Manchester project, evidence for brain removal was also found in seven of the complete mummies; this was demonstrated by means of detailed thin section tomography together with stereoscopy of the thin ethmoidal plates separating the nasal cavity from the anterior cranial fossa. Radiological studies will continue to provide information relating to this particular subject and to the methods of excerebration which were employed.

Radiological studies also supply evidence about other aspects of the mummification process, such as the presence of natron or of layers of resinous material in the abdominal and thoracic cavities. Tomography enables the varying densities of parcels and packing material within the bodily cavities to be identified, thus indicating whether they contain mummified viscera or merely bandages and packing. Such details can assist in identifying the historical period to which the mummy should be attributed.

Ceramic or metal amulets are also readily detected radiologically and their exact position within the layers of bandages can be accurately determined. Embalmers' restorations (such as the insertion of ceramic, mud or linen subcutaneous packing in the face, the restoration of eyes and the use of prosthetic limbs) can also be observed (Smith and Wood Jones 1910: 124; David 1979: 37, 86–9; Gray 1967b; 1971).

Radiological studies can indicate the presence or absence of disease and trauma in the skeleton and any remaining soft tissue. This in turn can lead to conjecture about the possible cause of death. There is generally a notable absence of 'modern' diseases such as cancer, syphilis, tuberculosis and rickets. However, as might be expected, radiology not infrequently provides evidence of pathogenic parasites in the mummies. In the Manchester collection alone (Isherwood *et al.* 1979: 38), linear calcification in residual bladder tissue was observed in two mummies, strongly indicating that they were infected with *Bilharzia haematobium* (*Schistosoma haematobium*); and in a third, a calcified nodule from the anterior abdominal wall was X-rayed and proved to be the remains of a Guinea worm (*Dracunculus medinensis*); infection with this worm is still common in some parts of Africa, the Near East and India.

Recent studies have indicated that the occurrence of alkaptonuria (ochronosis) in mummies is unlikely to be as frequent as originally suggested. In two cases (Simon and Zorab 1961; Wells and Maxwell 1962), it was proposed that the intervertebral disc opacification radiologically observed in these mummies was due to ochronosis, a disease which causes the joints to become arthritic and calcification to occur in the intervertebral disc and articular cartilages. When this problem was addressed by Gray (1967a), he reviewed sixty-four mummies from British museums, with particular reference to the radiological appearances of intervertebral disc spaces, and he observed calcification in eighteen examples. This was an unexpectedly high frequency, and he attributed these appearances to the effect of the embalming procedure rather than to the presence of this otherwise rare metabolic disorder.

When the Manchester mummies were examined radiologically, ten (out of a total of seventeen) showed disc-space opacification. Subsequently, a study of these changes, involving spectroscopy and biochemistry of bone biopsy material, was carried out on one of the mummies, and it was confirmed that these changes could not have occurred during life, and were in fact the result of embalming techniques rather than disease (Isherwood *et al.* 1979: 37–8).

The situation was further elucidated (Wallgren *et al.* 1986) when a new study was made of the evidence obtained from the mummy first examined in 1962. Dissection revealed a black pigment in the intervertebral spaces, and nuclear magnetic resonance (NMR) spectroscopy demonstrated the similarity of this pigment to that of a juniper resin from another Egyptian mummy. Energy dispersive X-ray (EDX) analysis of the radio-opaque crystalline material, which was also found in the intervertebral space, demonstrated that it was natron. It was concluded that both the black pigment and the natron were embalming agents; from these findings, it could be suggested that the intervertebral space had opened up because of extreme dehydration and contraction of the soft tissues during the mummification process, thus allowing some of the liquid resin, poured into the abdomen, to wash residual natron into the space. This conclusion is more acceptable than any attempt to explain why a rare disease in modern times (with an incidence of one in 5 million) should occur in ancient Egypt in one in four examples of the mummies that have been examined.

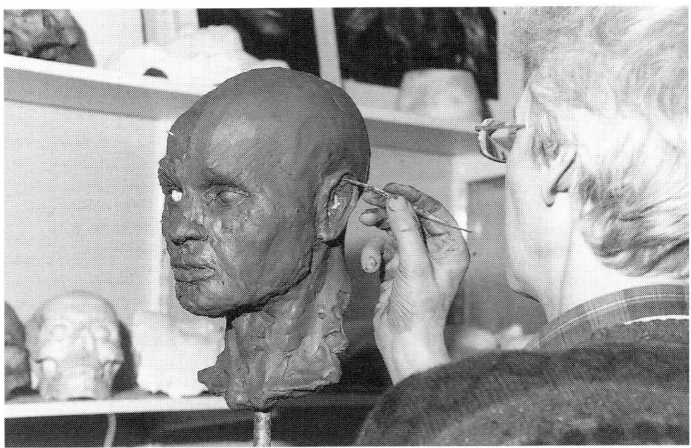

Figure 16.8 Completing the reconstruction of the head of the Leeds Mummy, Natsef-Amun. X-ray computer tomography enabled a polystyrene replica of this skull to be produced.

Radiology is not only a powerful investigative technique in its own right; it also plays an important role in dental studies, endoscopy and scientific facial reconstruction. In the latter field, X-ray computer tomography has been used in the process of reconstructing the heads and faces of mummies (Neave 1992; Drenkhahn and Germer 1991). Previously, direct access to the skull or cast of the skull was required before a face could be reconstructed (Neave 1979) but it is now possible, using X-ray computer tomography, to obtain digital data of the skull of a wrapped mummy. Held on magnetic tape, this record is then transferred to a computer screen so that a three-dimensional image can be displayed. A solid replica of this image can subsequently be produced, using a sophisticated numerically-controlled milling machine which carves the replica from a block of polystyrene. Finally, the appearance of the soft tissue of the face and head can be built up on the replica skull, enabling the appearance of the wrapped mummy to be recreated without unwrapping or damaging the head.

Dental studies

Many multidisciplinary projects have included studies of the dentitions of the ancient Egyptians, and both dry skulls and mummified remains have been available for this purpose. In many instances, not only the teeth – the most indestructible of human remains – but also the supporting soft tissue is preserved, and it has been possible to study dental disease and pathology in large numbers of mummies, thus enabling a good understanding of the general dental health of the ancient Egyptians to be obtained.

There have been several major studies, including the annual University of Michigan expeditions to Egypt since 1965 (Harris 1969; Harris and Ponitz 1980); these teams have examined the mummies of high officals at Giza, dating to the Old Kingdom (*c.* 2800 BC), priests and officials at Luxor dating to the New Kingdom (*c.* 1250 BC), and the royal mummies in the Egyptian Museum, dating from *c.* 1550–1070 BC (Harris and Weeks 1973; Harris and Wente 1980). There has also been an investigation of oral health and diseases in modern Egypt, particularly in Nubia (Harris *et al.* 1970: 578–96), which has assisted in elucidating the ancient evidence. In addition, some studies have concentrated on diet and age determination (for example, Goodman 1986; Stack: 1986; Puech and Leek 1986; Hillson 1986).

The existence of dry skull collections in museums and elsewhere has provided a further basis for the study of ancient Egyptian dentitions, providing researchers with a knowledge of many pathological and non-pathological abnormalities. Such information is invaluable in interpreting the radiographs taken of mummified and wrapped heads, where details can often be obscured by the superimposition of the hard, leather-like tissue of the face, and the various funerary wrappings and artefacts placed over the head by the embalmers.

Despite its limitations, radiology remains the only non-destructive method by which the dental condition of mummified remains can be assessed, and it is sometimes possible to augment the normal projections, in selected cases, by using tomographic techniques to provide records of sections of tissues and, for detached heads, to employ the 'orthopantomograph unit' which will provide a panoramic view of all the teeth and their supporting structures.

Thus, most dental surveys, based on visual and radiological examinations (Leek 1979; Leek 1986), have their limitations. However, the scientific investigation of the mummy of the priest Natsef-Amun enabled a complete picture of his dentition, together with detailed views of the jaw bones, facial skeleton, neck and skull vault, to be obtained. When the mummy was unwrapped in 1828, the mouth was found to be open with the tongue protruding, and in the 1991 investigation, this enabled direct intraoral radiographs to be taken of individual sections of the mouth, as in a living patient (Miller and Asher-McDade 1992).

In general, studies have shown that the dentitions of the early Pharaonic period are notably free of caries, although this condition appears to be more widespread in mummies of the Greek and Roman periods (332 BC–AD 395), perhaps because of dietary changes and the introduction of different eating habits. The most common abnormality seen in the dentitions of the earlier periods is attrition of the cusps of the teeth. It has been demonstrated that the major factor behind this occurrence was the contamination of the bread, which formed the staple element of the Egyptian diet. Examination of samples of bread from tombs has demonstrated that the flour contained many impurities (from the soil, storage and grinding techniques, as well as wind-blown sand) (Leek 1966, 1969a, 1971a, 1972a).

There has also been much discussion concerning the existence of a specialised dental profession in dynastic Egypt. Evidence has been proposed to support the claim that such a profession, capable of undertaking sophisticated dental procedures, did practise in the early dynasties (Harris and Ponitz 1980: 50–1; Harris *et al.* 1975; Ghalioungui and El Dawakhly 1965: 12). However, Leek (1967a, 1967b, 1969a, 1972b) has argued against this theory.

Palaeopathology

Palaeopathology – the study of disease in ancient populations – has been developed since the beginning of this century. The term was first used by M.A. Ruffer who, as Professor of Bacteriology in Cairo, laid the foundations of this science (Ruffer 1921). Palaeopathology, which includes anthropology, archaeology and palaeontology, attempts to trace the appearance, development and disappearance of diseases; it can also indicate the effects of some diseases on ancient societies (Stenn 1981; Brothwell and Sandison 1967).

For most ancient populations, only the evidence of skeletal remains survives and in these situations the skulls and skeletons can provide only limited information, namely about those diseases that leave their traces upon the bone. Nevertheless, in those cultures where preservation of the body tissues had occurred either intentionally or unintentionally, it is possible to trace and identify some of the diseases which have affected these tissues. An important technique, palaeohistology, was originated by Fouquet in 1889 (see Stenn 1981) and subsequently developed by Ruffer, who applied this procedure to the examination of mummies which were then being unwrapped. This was the starting point in applying scientific techniques to the study of preserved human remains. The basic technique includes several stages; these soften (rehydrate), fix and selectively stain sections of mummified tissue which can then be examined histologically. Although studies have been undertaken on tissue taken from preserved bodies from other ancient societies, the best results to date have been gained from Egyptian mummies, and in recent years, there have been considerable advances in methods of obtaining tissue samples, of processing them by means of rehydrating, fixing and staining, and finally, of examining them for evidence of structural components and disease (Tapp 1979b, 1984; Sandison 1955; Reyman and Dowd 1980). These methods – autopsy and endoscopy, histology, light and electron microscopy, and immunohistochemistry – will now be considered.

Autopsy and endoscopy

During the 1970s, a number of autopsies were carried out on mummies, enabling teams of multidisciplinary researchers to gain access to samples for further detailed analyses. An important series of studies were undertaken on mummies in the collections of the Pennsylvania University Museum (PUM I–IV) and the Royal Ontario Museum (ROM I) (Cockburn *et al.* 1980 52–70; Reyman and Peck 1980; Millet *et al.* 1980; Cockburn *et al.* 1975; Hart *et al.* 1977). As part of the Manchester Mummy Project, one mummy in the collection was autopsied and dissected (Tapp 1979a). Preliminary radiographs were taken of the mummies prior to unwrapping and autopsy. However, in the Manchester mummy, in the course of unwrapping, artefacts were found (prosthetic limbs and phallus, nipple amulets, sandals, and toe-nail and finger-nail covers, see Fig. 16.9), as well as evidence of disease (Guinea worm infestation), which provided information not obtainable from the preliminary radiographs.

Although such autopsies stimulated renewed interest in this field and demonstrated the range of scientific possibilities now available to researchers, they are by definition destructive, and during the 1980s, the Manchester team sought to develop virtually non-destructive techniques of investigation, based on the use of endoscopy (Tapp *et al.* 1984: 65–77; Tapp and Wildsmith 1986).

Endoscopy is a medical technique whereby a narrow tube is introduced through one of the natural orifices of the body or through a small incision in the chest or abdominal wall. This allows the doctor to see structures which cannot normally be examined and permits parts of these structures to be removed for subsequent examination under the microscope. The techniques of medical endoscopy are also used extensively in industry to allow examination of otherwise inaccessible areas.

In the investigation of Egyptian mummies, where tissue is hard and unyielding, the rigid endoscopes have proved most successful. Existing orifices in the mummies – often those used by the embalmers, or small holes caused by later damage – can be used as routes of entry. Direct visualisation of the tip of the endoscope on a radiographic screen provides information about the exact position of the instrument within the body. A small retrieval forceps attached to the endoscope and manipulated from outside the mummy is then used to take biopsy samples of the tissue, which is subsequently processed and examined histologically.

In this way, several examples of disease were identified in the Manchester mummies, including a hydatid cyst (caused by the parasitic worm *Echinococcus granulosus*) in lung tissue biopsied from one mummy, and sand pneumoconiosis in lung tissue taken from two mummies (Tapp *et al.* 1984: 70–3). Evidence of a hydatid cyst was also found in one of the detached heads thus examined.

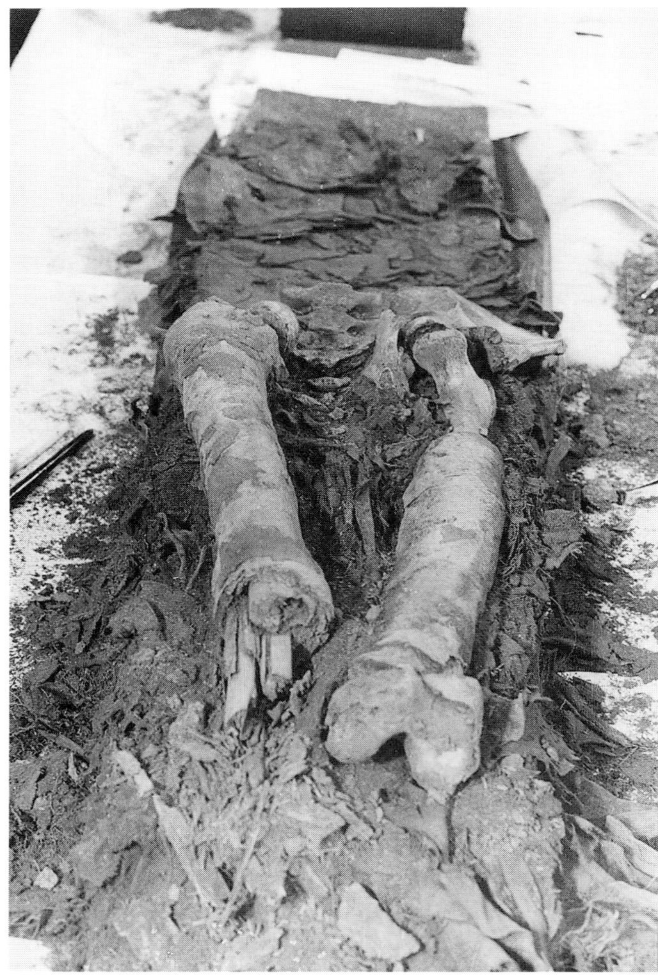

Figure 16.9 Legs of Mummy 1770, revealed during unwrapping, showing amputations and prosthetic limbs inserted alongside the bones.

In addition to enabling researchers to gain access to histological samples, endoscopy can also provide information about embalming techniques. It is possible to visualise the state of preservation of the body and the tissues, the presence or absence of viscera within the thoracic and abdominal cavities, the extent of any insect attack, and the embalming procedures used within the skull. Endoscopy has been of particular value in investigating 'fluid' levels seen radiologically within several skulls, since material could be removed from here and then biopsied, and examined to determine if it were resin or decomposing brain, and also it has assisted researchers in identifying the presence of disease in this area (Tapp *et al.* 1984: 65–77).

In the investigation of the Leeds mummy, which had been initially autopsied in 1828 (George 1828), it proved possible for the 1991 investigation to combine further autopsy techniques with endoscopy. Histological examination of the tissues subsequently allowed reassessment of some of the 1828 findings, and the project provided a significant

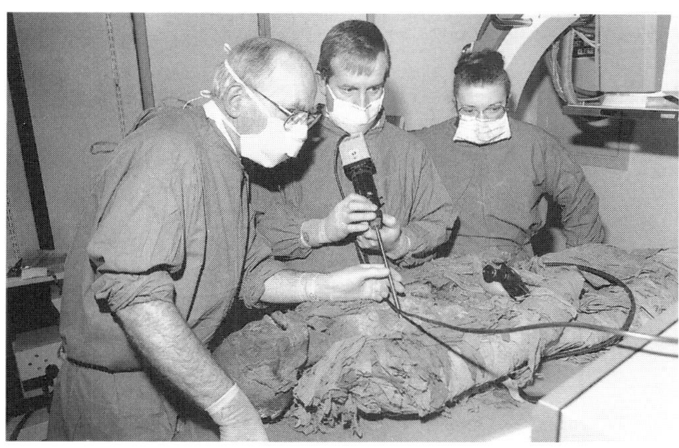

Figure 16.10 An endoscope has been introduced through the chest wall of a mummy to see whether or not the viscera packages are present.

opportunity to compare modern techniques and results with an earlier study (David and Tapp 1992).

Histology and histopathology

Pathology – the scientific study of disease processes – includes several methods of investigation. Microbiology, virology, bacteriology and parasitology can isolate and identify many of the organisms which cause diseases; blood group serology enables a specific blood group to be assigned to a particular individual; and chemical pathology analyses and quantifies the various substances within the blood, urine and other body fluids and, as the normal constituents of these fluids vary in health and in disease, they can provide an indication of the individual's physical condition.

Some research has been carried out to analyse the chemical constituents of mummified tissue and it has been suggested that a correlation can be shown between the degree of preservation of mummified tissue and the level of natron in the tissue and the method of natronisation (Barraco 1978). Large molecular weight substances such as lipoproteins and proteolipids have been isolated and studied (Cockburn *et al.* 1975), and lead and mercury content of bone has been analysed (Cockburn *et al.* 1975; Nielsen *et al.* 1986), although there is much scope for future research in detecting poisons such as arsenic and heavy metals in mummified tissue.

Two branches of pathology which have provided most information about disease in Egyptian mummies are morbid anatomy and histopathology. Morbid anatomy involves naked-eye study of mummies by autopsy and the study of parts of mummies, and was the main method of examination available to such pioneers as Elliot Smith and Margaret Murray (Smith 1912; Smith and Wood Jones 1910; Murray 1910). However, histology (the study of the microscopic structure of the tissues) has since provided one of the most important techniques for studying disease in mummies. Ruffer first combined morbid anatomy with microscopical examination of tissues in 1911 (Ruffer 1911), and between 1910 and 1917 published a series of papers on palaeopathology that were later edited as a book (Moodie 1931). Later work by Sandison (1955, 1969, 1980) laid the foundations for the major advances in the 1970s and 1980s, when histology, immunohistochemistry and electron microscopy added new dimensions to this study (Cockburn *et al.* 1980; Tapp 1979b, 1984, 1986; Krypczyk and Tapp 1986; Reyman 1974; Reyman *et al.* 1976).

The same basic techniques used to process modern tissue can be successfully adapted, with certain modifications, for mummified tissue. Mummification is essentially a process whereby the water is removed from the tissue, thus preventing the tissue enzymes (which are only able to function if water is present) from destroying the tissue. To prepare mummified tissue for histological examination, it is necessary first to replace this water in the tissue and then to fix it to prevent degeneration. Workers in this field have experimented with various methods, including a technique which allows the rehydration and fixation of the tissue to occur simultaneously. Once the tissue has been reconstituted and fixed, it is then processed normally. It is either frozen or surrounded by paraffin wax and cut into thin sections for examination under the microscope. Selective staining is then carried out to allow the structure of the tissue to be seen more clearly: different dyes are used because of their particular ability to pick out various parts of the tissue or cells.

Histology enables the normal structure of mummified tissue and changes produced in the tissue by mummification to be examined, while histopathology is the study of changes in the tissue caused by disease. Some studies have concentrated on particular areas, such as the skin (Verbov 1986; Giacometti and Chiarelli 1968) and the eye (Sandison 1986b; Tapp and Wildsmith 1992: 146–8). Sandison was able to demonstrate that the rehydration of a mummified head could reveal remnants of the globes of the eyes, while Verbov's study showed that the preservation of ancient skin depends more on adequate desiccation and resistance to decay and trauma before completion of the drying process than on its age.

Immunohistochemistry and electron microscopy

In continuing research, immunohistochemistry and electron microscopy have added new dimensions to the study of mummified tissue. Histochemical stains allow a limited number of chemical substances in cells to be identified, but advances in immunohistochemistry have led to a great improvement in the identification of cell constituents. The stains used in this process rely on a specific immunological reaction between a particular protein in the tissue (the antigen) and its specific antibody which is attached to a visible dye in the stain. The use of immunohistochemical stains applied to mummified tissue has produced some interesting and worthwhile results (Thompson *et al.* 1986; Krypczyk and Tapp 1986).

The development of the application of electron microscopy in this field has added further information. A histologist who wishes to examine tissue at magnifications greater than 800 times normal size will use this method since it allows much greater resolution of the detailed structures of the cells in the specimen.

Transmission electron microscopy (TEM), analytical electron microscopy (AEM) and scanning electron microscopy (SEM) have all been used in the examination of Egyptian mummies (Horne and Lewin 1977; Riddle 1980; Leeson 1959; Lewin 1967, 1968; Lewin and Cutz 1976; Macadam and Sandison 1969; Curry 1979; Curry *et al.* 1979; Hufnagel 1974).

The early investigations concentrated on fossilised and ancient bone, but Leeson (1959) published the first study of dried human tissue, rehydrated according to Sandison's procedure (1955), and was able to describe cell membranes, nuclear membranes, and chromatin in the skin of an Amerindian dried body from Columbia. Lewin (1967 and 1968) was the first to use TEM to investigate the ultrastructure of ancient Egyptian mummified material; this was skin and muscle tissue from an Egyptian head, and the published micrographs showed nuclear and cytoplasmic membranes, nuclear pores and tonofilaments.

In the Manchester Project (Curry *et al.* 1979), tissue was taken from canopic jars belonging to the Two Brothers' tomb-group, and in one specimen, the ultrastructure of liver tissue was shown to be well-preserved, and remains of parasites (possibly part of the liver fluke, *Fasciola hepatica*) were identified. Lung tissue from the same source contained numbers of dense, crystalline particles which, when investigated by AEM, were identified as silica particles, indicating the presence of the disease sand pneumoconiosis. In another mummy, intestinal tissue examined by TEM showed worm and cyst remains, possibly of the genus *Strongyloides*.

Histopathological studies have shown a diversity of parasites present in the relatively small number of mummies that have been examined. Examples of these include a round worm (*Ascaris*) found in PUM II (Cockburn *et al.* 1980: 52–70); Bilharzia infestation, a cyst originating from a *Trichinella* infestation, and eggs of the *Taenia* species in ROM I (Millet *et al.* 1980: 71–84); and *Filaria* worms in the Leeds Mummy (David and Tapp 1992: 151–2). Another environmental disease identified in a number of mummies, sand pneumoconiosis, has also been reported in modern desert populations (Tapp *et al.* 1975). In addition to looking for evidence of disease, AEM has also been used to examine mummified tissue for the presence of heavy metals, which accumulate in small quantities in the body (Curry *et al.* 1979; Cockburn *et al.* 1980).

The scanning electron microscope – a machine which examines the surface of solid objects – has been employed to examine the hair of mummies (Curry *et al.* 1979). In other research on ancient hair, the transmission electron microscope has made its contribution to studies of its structure and diseases (Birkett *et al.* 1986, and see also Chapter 20, this volume). However, perhaps the main field for which SEM has been used is in the identification of insects found in the mummies (Curry 1979). Generally, mummies acted as hosts to a variety of insects and evidence of this has

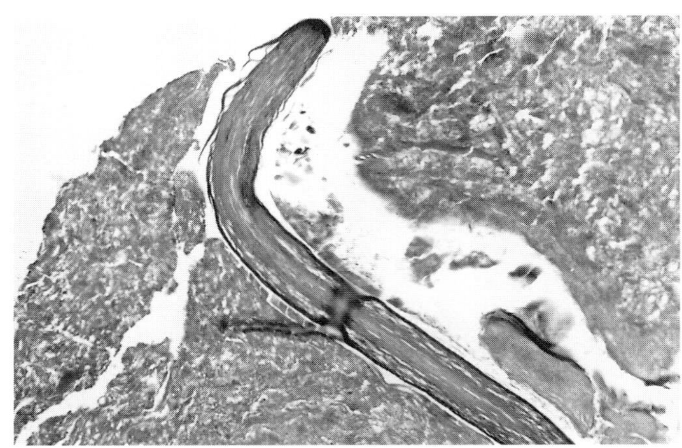

Figure 16.11 A photograph taken through a microscope to show a worm present in tissue taken from the groin of a mummy. The appearance of this worm indicates that it is of the filarial species. These worms block the lymphatic channels, resulting in swelling of the groin and legs.

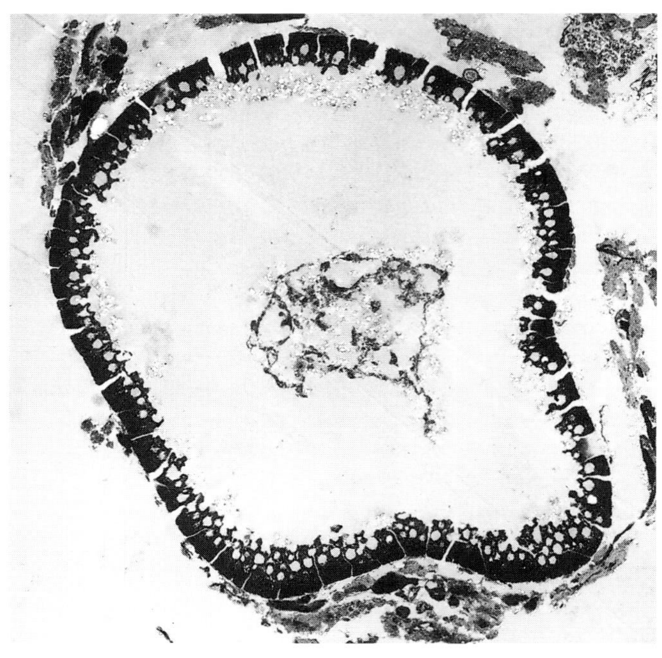

Figure 16.12 Section through the intestinal wall showing the remains of a parasitic worm, magnification: × 3,000. The tissue was taken from a mummy, and examined by transmission electron microscopy; the worm has been tentatively identified as Strongyloides.

been found in a range of contemporary investigations (Stefan 1982; Strong 1981). The effects of insect attack upon mummies will be considered below (see p. 384–5).

Palaeoserology

Since the 1930s, several studies have been carried out on blood-groups in ancient human remains (Boyd and Boyd 1934; Candela 1936; Flaherty and Haigh 1986; Lippold 1971; Henry 1980), and it has been shown that the serologic micromethod (SMM) and the inhibition agglutination test (IAT) are applicable to the study of this material (Hart, Kuas and Soots 1977). As well as offering a potential means of tracing population movements, or identifying the present day descendants of ancient peoples, serology provides a possibility of elucidating familial relationships. One important study attempted to prove kinship between the mummy of Tutankhamun and the body found in Tomb 55 in the Valley of the Kings (presumed to belong to Smenkhkara) (Harrison 1966; Connolly and Harrison 1969; Harrison and Connolly 1969; Harrison and Abdalla 1972).

Since ABO substances exist in tissues other than blood, such as muscle, skin and brain, it is possible for such examinations of ancient tissues to be carried out (Flaherty and Haigh 1984, 1992), but there can be difficulties in interpreting the results. One problem is that the A and B substances are both sugars which may deteriorate with the passage of time, so that only the group A substance may remain detectable. Again, there can be contamination of the samples by associated material such as the various substances and plants which may have been applied during the mummification process, or the micro-organisms present in the tissue itself or in the surrounding soil. It is possible for these contaminants to appear to react as blood-groups and thus give false positive reactions. A survey of the methods that can be employed and of the associated problems is provided by Hart *et al.* (1977).

DNA analysis

Until the middle of the 1970s the study of proteins from ancient mummified remains, especially blood group antigens, provided the only attempts to determine how the genes of ancient organisms exerted their function. Some of the problems associated with these techniques and results have been outlined above. However, since 1985, pioneering work by Pääbo resulted in the development of techniques which enabled DNA to be identified in mummified tissue (Pääbo 1985, 1986). Only a small sample is required for this procedure and it can be taken from any part of the body since almost every cell carries the total genetic information of an individual.

Although the earliest studies involved laborious DNA cloning and sequence reading strategies to analyse specimens, it has been possible to change to more routine techniques of analysis currently used for medical diagnosis (David *et al.* 1993), and to demonstrate that relatively routine molecular techniques can be used with ancient preserved tissues. New molecular genetic techniques have been developed in recent years; one key advance is the polymerase chain reaction (PCR), sometimes referred to as 'gene amplification'.

Such studies open up several major areas for future work, and there are a gradually increasing number of DNA projects being carried out both on newly excavated mummies and on those already held in museum collections (David *et al.* 1993; Griggs *et al.* 1993). Possibilities now exist to study genetic markers in ancient populations for a better understanding of their origins and migrations, and to use a spectrum of highly polymorphic markers to derive a 'genetic fingerprint' of an ancient individual, and thus test hypotheses of individual familial relationships. Also, by studying the evidence of bacterial, fungal, viral and parasite DNA, it should be possible to gain information about infectious disease pathology both in individuals and in populations in antiquity. There can be little doubt that these techniques will make a major contribution to the future study of mummies.

Conservation

In addition to attempting to understand the process of mummification and expanding the study of disease in ancient remains, modern research has also sought to understand the processes of deterioration in mummies and to indicate methods of conserving these remains, which are a finite and vulnerable source, for future investigation.

Deterioration can be the result of the environmental conditions in which the mummy has been kept; physical damage; or damage caused by previous or inept conservation attempts. The wide range of conservation treatments which are available are discussed by David and David (1995). In one instance, the main objective behind the multidisciplinary study of a mummy (that of Rameses II, *c.* 1250 BC) was to develop a programme of conservation for the mummy and its coffin (Balout and Roubet 1985: 264–366).

The mummification procedure

In Lucas's account of mummification, he concentrated on outlining the early historical development of mummification, and discussing the materials and substances which may have been used in the mummification procedure (Lucas 1962: 272–326). Several of the techniques developed to investigate mummified remains in recent years have not only added to knowledge of disease and diet in the Egyptian population, but have also provided new evidence about the mummification method.

One of the problems addressed by Lucas was the manner in which natron was used as a dehydrating agent. Pathological examination of mummies and evidence from experiments on the carcasses of pigeons and chickens led him to conclude that natron had been used in a dry rather than a fluid state. In more recent experiments, Sandison (1963, 1986a) has strongly argued in favour of the use of dry natron, and Garner (1979) undertook a series of experiments on laboratory mice and rats both to investigate the validity of the methods of mummification described in Herodotus (*Histories* II: 86–8; see de Selincourt 1976), and to examine the factors which may have affected them.

Using artificially produced natron samples, he tested the three methods described by Herodotus, studied the effect of high levels of impurities in the samples on the final results, and compared the preservative properties of the dry natron mixtures with those of the natron solutions. The results indicated that several factors could influence the final condition of the body, such as the composition of the natron and the way it was used; fresh natron was more effective in preserving the tissues than reused samples.

Studies on the optimum period of time required for mummification indicated that, although no absolute time (after which decay would be minimal) could be established, the best results were normally achieved within a period of thirty to forty days. Experiments using salt mixtures containing large amounts of sodium chloride or sulphate resulted in poor preservation when compared with those bodies treated with natron. Also, when solutions rather than dry substances were employed, the results were unsuccessful. In general, Garner concluded that mummification could be readily achieved when dry, solid natron was used, but that the thickness of the skin and the relative amounts of muscle and fat affected the results and the speed with which the animal carcasses could be desiccated. Other important factors were the composition of the natron which was used and the relative volume of dry natron to carcass bulk.

Garner (1986) also studied the effect of insect attack on mummified remains. The body was a food source and even mummification could not provide complete protection against destruction. Electron microscopy (Curry 1979) has aided the identification of the parasitic worms and insects found in the mummies. The parasitic worms, which need living hosts, must have been present during the person's lifetime, but the insects found in the wrappings of the mummy, the coffins, or in the mummified body or contents of the canopic jars, infested these areas after death. Beetles, depending on their habits, may have invaded the body at the time of death, during embalming, in the tomb, during transportation, or even in the museum. Flies, however, require a moist food source when they are in their larval stages, therefore they probably infested the bodies prior to, or during, embalming. Insect remains can be examined by viewing under the dissection microscope or by means of SEM, and several studies have been undertaken of remains found during autopsies of mummies (Curry 1979; Cockburn *et al.* 1975; Harrison 1986). The subject has also been addressed by Cloudsley-Thompson (1976) and Lane (1975).

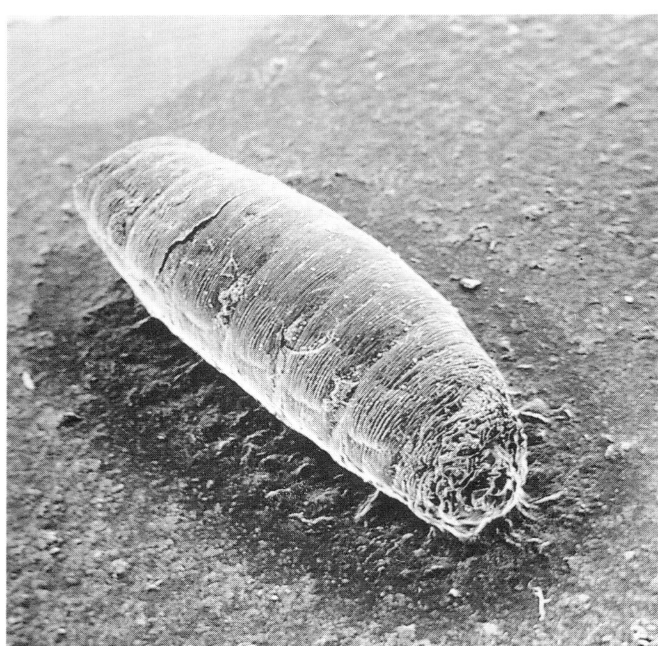

Figure 16.13 Empty puparium of Piophila casei, *magnification: × 29. This was found in Mummy 1770, and infestation by* Piophila *(commonly known as the cheese skipper) probably occurred after death.*

In the study of the mummification process itself, computed tomography can provide information about the methods employed, and can be used, in conjunction with endoscopy, to obtain tissue samples by virtually non-destructive means. Endoscopy can also be used to explore areas where further information may be gained about the embalmers' techniques, such as the removal or otherwise of the viscera, excerebration and the routes of entry into the skull, and the presence and amount of residual brain tissue. It may also be possible to use endoscopy to further explore the theory (Pahl 1986) that the funerary ritual known as 'opening of the mouth' involved actual physical manipulation.

Developments in histology and electron microscopy have enabled major advances to be made in the study of disease, but the use of electron microscopy in particular can demonstrate the remarkable presence of subcellular structures in the tissues and indicate the success or failure of the embalming techniques. In the original investigation of the Leeds Mummy, E.S. George (1828) indicated that the original investigators found that the mummy was greasy to touch and concluded that this phenomenon was produced by the embalming process or by wax being introduced into the tissues during mummification. A.B. Granville (1825) also suggested that wax was employed in the mummification process. However, in the 1991 examination of the

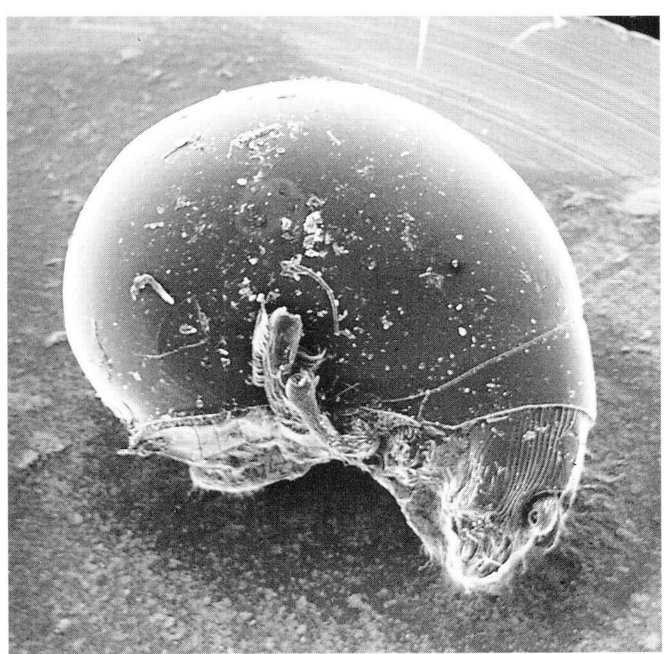

Figure 16.14 An adult hump spider beetle, Gibbium psylloides, *magnification: ×36. Remains of this beetle were found in the mummies and wrappings of the Two Brothers. As a pest of vegetable products, it may have used the bandages as a food source.*

Leeds Mummy, it proved possible to examine the tissues microscopically, and the waxy appearance of the tissues, known as adipocere ('grave wax'), can now be attributed to a natural process (see David and Tapp 1992). Fatty acid crystals (which could be seen microscopically in the mummified tissue) accumulate in the tissues; these crystals originate from the breakdown of neutral fats throughout the body, which is initiated by bacterial and tissue enzymes being released into the tissue after death. M.A. Ruffer (1911) noted small white patches in several internal organs of sand-buried bodies of the Greek and Roman periods, and suggested that these were due to adipocere formation, but the techniques then available did not permit him to confirm this microscopically. Because adipocere formation requires the presence of water and is inhibited by rapid desiccation, it is not often seen in Egyptian mummies, but modern techniques have again been able to resolve this question.

With one of the Manchester mummies, there was the opportunity to describe and identify microscopically and macroscopically the nature of the material of the bandages (Wild 1979). It was also possible to isolate and characterise the materials that may have been applied to the bandages and compare the results with those of previous workers (Benson *et al.* 1979). Thin layer and gas liquid chromatography were used for this, and the results indicated that the bandages had been impregnated with a complex mixture of substances which contained beeswax, bitumen, galbanum and possibly tamarind extract.

The use of plants and plant products in mummification was also discussed at length by Lucas (1962). Recent investigations of mummies have produced new samples of plants, woods and grains; in the examination of Rameses II (Balout and Roubet 1985), the floral ornaments were studied and procedures based on SEM enabled the vegetable micro-remains found in the abdomen, on the mummy and in the sarcophagus to be identified. Testing of the embalming material in the abdomen revealed fragments of *Nicotiana L.sp.* and *Anthemideae*, placed there to kill insects and stop putrefaction. The effect of such procedures in preserving the body is however doubtful (David 1992). In general, botanical studies (Germer 1985) should assist a greater understanding of the use of plants and plant remains in the mummification process.

Animal mummification

Lucas (1962: 302–3) briefly discussed the mummification of animals. Sources such as the inscribed stelae of royal or private persons from the Serapeum (Spencer 1982: 199; Malanine *et al.* 1968) indicate that the process closely followed human mummification. Among recent studies of animals found in ancient Egypt are those by Morrison-Scott (1951–2), Clutton-Brock (1988), Armitage and Clutton-Brock (1981) and David (1979: 13–15). These have mainly concentrated on radiological investigations of wrapped specimens. Continuing projects include radiological studies of the animal mummies from the Sacred Animal Necropolis at Saqqara (Ghaleb-Kirby and Nicholson pers. comm.; Lichtenberg pers. comm.), a catalogue of the human and animal mummies in the Musées Royaux d'Art et d'Histoire, Brussels, Belgium (van Rinsveld 1994), and a study of cats in the British Museum collection (Filer 1994).

References

Armitage, P. L. and Clutton-Brock, J. 1981. A radiological and histological investigation into the mummification of cats from ancient Egypt. *JAS*, 8: 185–96.

Balout, L. and Roubet C. (eds.) 1985. *La Momie de Ramsès II.* Paris: Editions Recherche sur les Civilisations.

Bard, M., Fauré, C. and Massare, C. 1985. Etude radiologique, In *La Momie de Ramsès II* (eds. L. Balout and C. Roubet). Paris: Editions Recherche sur les Civilisations, pp. 68–95.

Barraco, R. A. 1978. Preservation of proteins in mummified tissues. *American Journal of Physical Anthropology* 48: 487–92.

Benson, G.G., Hemingway, S.R. and Leach, F.N. 1979. The analysis of the wrappings of Mummy 1770. In *The Manchester Museum Mummy Project* (ed. A.R. David). Manchester: Manchester Museum, pp. 119–32.

Birkett, D.A., Gummer, C.L. and Dawber, R.P.R. 1986. Preservation of the sub-cellular ultra structure of ancient hair. In *Science in Egyptology* (ed. A.R. David). Manchester: Manchester University Press, pp. 367–9.

Boyd, W. C. and Boyd, L.G. 1934. An attempt to determine the bloodgroup of mummies. *Proceedings of the Society of Experimental Biology and Medicine* 31: 671–2.

Brothwell, D., Sandison, A.T. and Thomas, C.C. (eds.), 1967. *Diseases in Antiquity*. Springfield, IL: Thomas.

Brothwell, D. and Spearman, R. 1970. The hair of earlier peoples. In *Scinece in Archaeology* (eds. D. Brothwell and E.S. Higgs) London: Thames and Hudson.

Candela, P.B. 1936. Blood-group reactions in ancient human skeletons. *American Journal of Physical Anthropology*, 21: 429–32.

Chiarelli, B., Fuhrman, A.C. and Massa, E.R. 1970–1. Nota preliminare sulla ultrastruttura dei capelli di mummia egiziana al microscopio elettronico a scansione. *Rivista di Antropologia*, 57: 275–8.

Cloudsley-Thompson, J. L. 1976. *Insects and History*. London: Weidenfeld and Nicolson.

Clutton-Brock, J., 1988. *The British Museum Book of Cats Ancient and Modern*. London: British Museum Publications and British Museum (Natural History).

Cockburn, A. and Cockburn, E. (eds.) 1980. *Mummies, Disease and Ancient Cultures*. Cambridge: CUP.

Cockburn, A., Barraco, R., Peck, W.H. and Reyman, T.A. 1980. A classic mummy: PUM II. In *Mummies, Disease and Ancient Cultures* (eds. A. and E. Cockburn). Cambridge: CUP, pp. 52–70.

Cockburn, A., Barraco, R., Reyman, T.A. and Peck, W.H. 1975. Autopsy of an Egyptian mummy. *Science*, 187: 1155–60.

Connolly, R.C. and Harrison, R.G. 1969. Kinship of Smenkhkare and Tutankhamen affirmed by serological micromethod. *Nature*, 224: 325–6.

Curry, A. 1979. The insects associated with the Manchester Mummies. In *The Manchester Museum Mummy Project* (ed. A.R. David). Manchester: Manchester Museum, pp. 113–8.

Curry, A., Anfield, C. and Tapp, E. 1979. Electron microscopy of the Manchester mummies. In *The Manchester Museum Mummy Project* (ed. A.R. David). Manchester: Manchester Museum, pp. 103–12.

D'Auria, S., Lacovara, P. and Roehrig, C.H. 1988. *Mummies and Magic*. Boston: MFA.

David, A.R. (ed.) 1979. *The Manchester Museum Mummy Project: Multidisciplinary Research on Ancient Egyptian Mummified Remains*. Manchester: Manchester Museum.

(ed.) 1986. *Science in Egyptology: The Proceedings of the 1979 and 1984 Symposia*. Manchester: Manchester University Press.

1992. Plants and plant products used in mummification. In *Phytochemical Resources for Medicine and Agriculture* (eds. H. N. Nigg and D. Seigler). New York and London: Plenum Press, pp. 15–32.

David, A. R. and David, A.E. 1995. Preservation of human mummified specimens. In *Care and Conservation of Palaeontological Material* (ed. C. Collins). Oxford: Butterworth and Heinemann.

David, R. and Tapp, E. (eds.), 1984. *Evidence Embalmed: Modern Medicine and the Mummies of Ancient Egypt*. Manchester: Manchester University Press.

(eds.) 1992. *The Mummy's Tale: The Scientific and Medical Investigation of Natsef-Amun, Priest in the Temple of Karnak*. London: Michael O'Mara.

David, A.R., Tapp, E., Wildsmith, K., Elles, R., Turnbull, L., Ivinson, A., Dyer, P. and Harris, R. 1993. Medical and scientific examination of the human mummified remains. In *The Tombs of el-Hagarsa* (ed. N. Kanawati). Sydney: Australian Centre for Egyptology, Reports 6, vol. 2, pp. 29–50.

Dawson, W.R. and Gray, P.H.K. 1968. *Catalogue of Egyptian Antiquities in the British Museum (1): Mummies and Human Remains*. Oxford: OUP.

Desarti, V. 1977. The structural reliability of mummy tissue in tracing disease ecology in prehistoric and recent human populations. *American Journal of Physical Anthropology*, 47: 126–7.

Drenkhahn, R. and Germer, R. 1991. *Mumie und Computer: ein multidisziplinäres Forschungsprojekt in Hannover*. Hanover: Kestner-Museums.

Dunand, F. and Lichtenberg, R. 1988. Les momies de la nécropole de Douch en Egypte. *Archeologia* , 240: 30–42.

Filer, J. 1993. Preliminary remarks on the human remains from Soba East. *The Sudan Archaeological Research Society Newsletter*, 4: 16–18.

1994. The SARS Survey from Bagrawiya to Atbara. (b). The contents of five tombs from cemetery 159.2, Wadi Gabati. *The Sudan Archaeological Research Society Newsletter*, 6: 25–7.

Flaherty, T. and Haigh, T.J. 1984. Blood groups in ancient Egypt. In *Evidence Embalmed* (eds. A.R. David and E. Tapp). Manchester: Manchester University Press, pp. 96–103.

1986. Blood groups in mummies. In *Science in Egyptology* (ed. A.R. David). Manchester: Manchester University Press, pp. 379–82.

1992. Blood grouping. In *The Mummy's Tale* (eds. A.R. David and E. Tapp). London: Michael O'Mara, pp. 154–61.

Garner, R. 1979. Experimental mummification. In *The Manchester Museum Mummy Project* (ed. A.R. David). Manchester: Manchester Museum, pp. 19–24.

1986. Insects and mummification. In *Science in Egyptology* (ed. A.R. David). Manchester: Manchester University Press, 97–100.

George, E.S. 1828. *An Account of an Egyptian Mummy*. Leeds: Leeds Philosophical and Literary Society (reprinted Leeds 1928).

Germer, R. 1985. *Flora des pharaonischen Ägypten*. Mainz: Philipp von Zabern.

Ghalioungui, P. and El Dawakhly, Z. 1965. *Health and Healing in Ancient Egypt*. Cairo: Egyptian Organization for Authorship and Translation.

Giacometti, L. and Chiarelli, B. 1968. The skin of Egyptian mummies: a study in survival. *Archives of Dermatology (US)*, 97(6): 712–6.

Goodman, A.H. 1986. Diet and post Mesolithic craniofacial and dental evolution in Sudanese Nubia. In *Science in Egyptology* (ed. A.R. David). Manchester: Manchester University Press, pp. 201–11.

Granville, A.B. 1825. An essay on Egyptian mummies, with observations on the art of embalming amongst the ancient Egyptians. *Philosophical Transactions of the Royal Society*, 269–316.

Gray, P.H.K. 1966. Radiological aspects of the mummies of ancient Egyptians in the Rijksmuseum van Oudheden, Leiden. *Oudheidkundige mededelingen uit het Rijksmuseum van Oudheden, Leiden*, 47: 1–30.

1967a. Calcinosis intervertebralis with special reference to similar changes found in mummies of ancient Egyptians. In *Diseases in Antiquity* (eds. D. Brothwell, A.T. Sandison and

C.C. Thomas), Springfield IL: Thomas, pp. 20–30.
1967b. Embalmers' restorations. *JEA*, 52: 138.
1971. Artificial eyes in mummies. *JEA*, 57: 125–6.
1972. Notes concerning the position of arms and hands of mummies with a view to possible dating of the specimen. *JEA*, 58: 200–4.
1973. The radiography of mummies of ancient Egyptians. *Journal of Human Evolution*, 2: 51–3.
Gray, P.H.K. and Slow, D. 1968. *Egyptian Mummies in the City of Liverpool Museums*. Liverpool: Liverpool Corporation.
Griggs, C.W., Evans, R.P., Kuchar, M.C.J., Rowe, M.J., Woodward, S.R. and Iskander, N. 1993. The genetic and textile analysis of the Hagarsa mummies. In *The Tombs of el-Hagarsa* (ed. N. Kanawati). Sydney: Australian Centre for Egyptology, Reports 6, vol. 2: pp. 51–66.
Harris, J.E. 1969. The University of Michigan's 1969 expedition to Egypt. *Journal of the Michigan Dental Association*, 51: 256–63.
Harris, J.E., Iskander, Z. and Farid, S. 1975. Restorative dentistry in ancient Egypt: an archaeological fact. *Journal of the Michigan Dental Association*, 57: 401–4.
Harris, J.E. and Ponitz, P.V. 1980. Dental health in ancient Egypt. In *Mummies, Disease and Ancient Cultures* (eds. A. and E. Cockburn). Cambridge: CUP, pp. 45–51.
Harris, J.E., Ponitz, P.V. and Loufty, M.S. 1970. Orthodontics' contribution to save the monuments of Nubia: a 1970 field report. *American Journal of Orthodontics*, 58(6): 578–96.
Harris, J.E. and Weeks, K.R. 1973. *X-raying the Pharaohs*. New York: Charles Scribner and Sons.
Harris, J.E. and Wente, E.F. (eds.), 1980. *An X-ray Atlas of the Royal Mummies*. Chicago: University of Chicago Press.
Harrison, I.R. 1986. Arthropod parasites associated with Egyptian mummies with special reference to 1770 (Manchester Museum). In *Science in Egyptology* (ed. A.R. David). Manchester: Manchester University Press, pp. 171–4.
Harrison, R.G. 1966. An anatomical examination of the pharaonic remains purported to be Akhenaten. *JEA*, 52: 95–119.
Harrison, R.G. and Abdalla, A.B. 1972. The remains of Tutankhamun. *Antiquity*, 46: 8–14.
Harrison, R.G. and Connolly, R.C. 1969. Microdetermination of blood group substances in ancient human tissue. *Nature*, 224: 326.
Hart, G.D., Cockburn, A., Millet, N.B. and Scott, J.W. 1977. Autopsy of an Egyptian mummy – ROM I. *Canadian Medical Association Journal*,117: 461–73.
Hart, G.D., Kuas, I. and Soots, M.L. 1977. Blood-group testing (Nakht). *Canadian Medical Association Journal*, 117(5): section 9 in report.
1978. Blood-group testing. *Transfusion*, 18: 474–8.
Henry, R.L., 1980. Paleoserology. In *Mummies, Disease and Ancient Cultures* (eds. A. and E. Cockburn). Cambridge: CUP, pp. 327–34.
Hillson, S.W. 1986. Teeth, age, growth and archaeology. In *Science in Egyptology* (ed. A.R. David). Manchester: Manchester University Press, pp. 475–84.
Holland, T. 1937. X-rays in 1896. *The Liverpool Medico-Chirurgical Journal*, 45: 61.
Horne, P.D. and Lewin, P.K. 1977. Electron microscopy of mummified tissue. *Canadian Medical Association Journal*, 117(5): section 7 of report.
Hufnagel, L.A. 1974. Ultrastructure of tissues from an Egyptian mummy. *American Journal of Physical Anthropology*, 41: 486.
Isherwood, I., Fawcitt, R.A. and Jarvis, H. 1984. X-raying the Manchester mummies. In *Evidence Embalmed* (eds. A.R. David and E. Tapp). Manchester: Manchester University Press, pp. 45–64.
Isherwood, I., Jarvis, H. and Fawcitt, R.A. 1979. Radiology of the Manchester mummies. In *The Manchester Museum Mummy Project* (ed. A.R. David). Manchester: Manchester Museum, pp. 25–64.
Junker, H. 1929–55. *Giza Grabungen auf dem Friedhof des Alten Reiches bei den Pyramiden von Giza*. (12 vols.). Vienna.
Kristen, K.T. and Reyman, T.A. 1980. Radiographic examination of mummies with autopsy correlation. In *Mummies, Disease and Ancient Cultures* (eds. A. and E. Cockburn). Cambridge: CUP, pp. 287–300.
König, W. 1896. 14 photographien mit Röntgen-Strahlen, aufgenommen. *Physikalischen Verein, Frankfurt a M.* Leipzig: J.A. Barth.
Krypczyk, A. and Tapp, E. 1986. Immunohistochemistry and electron microscopy of Egyptian mummies. In *Science in Egyptology* (ed. A.R. David). Manchester: Manchester University Press, pp. 361–6.
Lane, R.P. 1975. An investigation into blowfly succession on corpses. *Journal of Natural History*, 9: 581–8.
Leek, F.F. 1966. Observations on the dental pathology seen in ancient Egyptian skulls. *JEA*, 52: 59–64.
1967a, The practice of dentistry in ancient Egypt. *JEA*, 53: 51–8.
1967b. Reputed early Egyptian dental operation: an appraisal. In *Diseases in Antiquity* (eds. D.R. Brothwell and A.T. Sandison), Springfield, IL: Thomas, pp. 702–5.
1969a. Did a dental profession exist in ancient Egypt? *The Dental Delineator*, 20: 18–21.
1969b. The problem of brain removal during embalming by the ancient Egyptians. JEA, 55: 112–16.
1969c. A technique for the oral examination of a mummy. *X-ray Focus*, 9(3): 5–9.
1971. Bread of the Pharaoh's baker. *NARCE*, 77: 2–4.
1972a. Teeth and bread in ancient Egypt. *JEA*, 58: 126–32.
1972b. Did a dental profession exist in ancient Egypt during the third millennium BC? *Medical History*, 16: 404–6.
1979. The dental history of the Manchester mummies. In *The Manchester Museum Mummy Project* (ed. A.R. David). Manchester: Manchester Museum, pp. 65–77.
1986. Cheops' courtiers: their skeletal remains. In *Science in Egyptology* (ed. A.R. David). Manchester: Manchester University Press, pp. 183–200.
Leeson, J.D. 1959. Electron microscopy of mummified material. *Stain Technology*, 34: 317–20.
Lewin, P.K. 1967. Palaeo-electron microscopy of mummified tissue. *Nature*, 213: 416–7.
1968. The ultrastructure of mummified skin cells. *Canadian Medical Association Journal* , 98: 1011–12.
Lewin, P.K. and Cutz, E. 1976. Electron microscopy of ancient Egyptian skin. *British Journal of Dermatology* , 94: 573–6.
Lewin, P.K. and Harwood Nash, D.C. 1977. X-ray computed axial tomography of an ancient Egyptian brain. *RCS Medical Science: Anatomy, Human Biology, Biomedical Technology, Nervous System*, 5: 78.

Lippold, L.K. 1971. The mixed cell agglutination method for typing mummified human tissue. *American Journal of Physical Anthropology*, 34: 377–83.
Llagostera, E. 1978. *Estudio Radiologico de las Momias Egipcias del Museo Arqueologico Nacional de Madrid*. Madrid: Museo Arqueologico Nacional, Monografias Arqueologicas no.5.
Lucas, A. 1962. *Ancient Egyptian Materials and Industries*. 4th edn., rev. J. R. Harris. London: Edward Arnold.
Macadam, R.F. and Sandison, A.T. 1969. The electron microscope in palaeopathology. *Medical History*, 13: 81–5.
Malanine, M. 1968. *Catalogue des stèles du Serapeum de Memphis*. Paris: Imprimerie Nationale, 5: 1–3.
Maspero, G. 1881. *La Trouvaille de Deir el-Bahari*. Cairo 1889. *Les momies royales de Dier el-Bahari*. Cairo.
Miller, J. and Asher-McDade, C. 1992. The dental examination of Natsef-Amun. In *The Mummy's Tale* (eds. A.R. David and E. Tapp). London: Michael O'Mara, pp. 112–20.
Miller, R.L., Armelagos, G.J., Ikram, S., DeJonge, N., Krijger, F.W. and Deelder, A.M. 1992. Palaeoepidemiology of Schistosoma infection in mummies. *British Medical Journal* 304 (February 29): 555.
Millet, N.B., Hart, G.D, Reyman, T.A., Zimmerman, M.R. and Lewin, P.K. 1980. ROM I: mummification for the common people. In *Mummies, Disease and Ancient Cultures* (eds. A. and E. Cockburn). Cambridge: CUP, pp. 71–84.
Moodie, R.L. 1931. *Roentgenological Studies of Egyptian and Peruvian Mummies*. Chicago: Field Museum of Natural History.
Morrison-Scott, T.C.S. 1951–2. The mummified cats of ancient Egypt. *Proceedings of the Zoological Society of London*, 121: 861–7.
Murray, M.A. 1910. *The Tomb of Two Brothers* (Manchester Museum Handbook). Manchester: Sheratt and Hughes.
Naville, E. and Hall, H.R. 1907–13. *The Eleventh Dynasty Temple of Deir-el-Bahari*. London.
Neave, R.A.H. 1979. The reconstruction of the heads and faces of three ancient Egyptian mummies. In *The Manchester Museum Mummy Project* (ed. A.R. David). Manchester: Manchester Museum, pp. 149–58.
1992. The facial reconstruction of Natsef-Amun. In *The Mummy's Tale* (eds. A.R. David and E. Tapp). London: Michael O'Mara, pp. 162–7.
Nielsen, O.V., Granjean, P. and Shapiro, I.M. 1986. Lead retention in ancient Nubian bones, teeth and mummified remains. In *Science in Egyptology* (ed. A.R. David). Manchester: Manchester University Press, pp. 25–34.
Pääbo, S. 1985. Molecular cloning of ancient Egyptian mummy DNA. *Nature*, 314(6012): 644–5.
1986. DNA is preserved in ancient Egyptian mummies. In *Science in Egyptology* (ed. A.R. David). Manchester: Manchester University Press, pp. 383–8.
Pahl, W. 1986. The ritual of opening the mouth: arguments for an actual-body-ritual from the viewpoint of mummy research. In *Science in Egyptology* (ed. A.R. David). Manchester: Manchester University Press, pp. 211–17.
Petrie, W.M.F. 1892. *Meydum*. London: Nutt.
1898. *Deshasheh 1897*. London: EEF, pl. xxxvii.
Pettit, C. and Fildes, G. 1984. Organising the information: the International Mummy Databank. In *Evidence Embalmed* (eds. A.R. David and E. Tapp). Manchester: Manchester University Press, pp. 150–7.
Puech, P-Fr. and Leek, F.F. 1986. Dental microwear as an indication of plant food in early man. In *Science in Egyptology* (ed. A.R. David). Manchester: Manchester University Press, pp. 239–42.
Quibell, J.E. 1923. *Excavations of Saqqara, 1912–1914*. Cairo: SAE.
Raven, M. 1993. *Mummies onder het mes*. Amsterdam: De Bataafsche Leeuw.
Reisner, G.A. 1913. *Museum of Fine Arts Bulletin*. Boston, Mass: BMFA.
1928 Museum of Fine Arts Bulletin. Boston, Mass.: BMFA
Reyman, T.A. 1974. Histopathology in an Egyptian mummy (*c.* 700 BC). *American Journal of Physical Anthropology*, 41: 500.
Reyman, T.A., Barraco, R.A. and Cockburn, A. 1976. Histopathological examination of an Egyptian mummy. *Bulletin of the New York Academy of Medicine (USA)*, 52(4): 506–16.
Reyman, T.A. and Dowd, A.M. 1980. Processing of mummified tissue for histological examination. In *Mummies, Disease and Ancient Cultures* (eds. A. and E. Cockburn). Cambridge: CUP, pp. 258–73.
Reyman, T.A. and Peck, W.H. 1980. Egyptian mummification with evisceration per ano. In *Mummies, Disease and Ancient Cultures* (eds. A. and E. Cockburn). Cambridge: CUP, pp. 85–100.
Riddle, J.M. 1980. A survey of ancient specimens by electron microscopy. In *Mummies, Disease and Ancient Cultures* (eds. A. and E. Cockburn). Cambridge: CUP, pp. 274–86.
Ruffer, M.A. 1911. Histological studies on Egyptian mummies. *Mémoires de l'Institut de l'Egypte*, 6/3: 1–33.
Ruffer, M.A. and Moodie, R.L. (eds.) 1921. *Studies in the Palaeopathology of Egypt*. Chicago: University of Chicago Press, 49–92.
Sandison, A.T. 1955. The histological examination of mummified material. *Stain Technology*, 30: 277–83.
1963. The use of natron in mummification in ancient Egypt. *JNES*, 22: 259–67.
1969. The study of mummified and dried human tissue. In *Science in Archaeology* (eds. D. Brothwell and E. Higgs). 2nd edn. London: Thames and Hudson, pp. 490–502.
1980. Diseases in ancient Egypt. In *Mummies, Disease and Ancient Cultures* (eds. A. and E. Cockburn). Cambridge: CUP, pp. 29–44.
1986a. Human mummification technique in ancient Egypt. In *Science in Egyptology* (ed. A.R. David). Manchester: Manchester University Press, pp. 1–5.
1986b. The Egyptian mummy eye. In *Science in Egyptology* (ed. A.R. David). Manchester: Manchester University Press, pp. 7–9.
Selincourt, A. de 1976. *Herodotus: the Histories*. Harmondsworth: Penguin.
Simon, G. and Zorab, P.A. 1961. The radiographic changes in Alkaptonuric arthritis: a report on three cases (one an Egyptian mummy). *British Journal of Radiology*, 34: 384–6.
Smith, G.E. 1912a. *The Royal Mummies. Catalogue Général des Antiquités Egyptiennes de la Musée du Caire*, Nos. 61051–61100. Cairo: SAE.
1912b. *Report of the British Association* Dundee.
Smith, G.E. and Dawson, W.R. 1924. *Egyptian Mummies*. London: Allen and Unwin (repr. 1991 London: KPI).

Smith, G.E. and Wood Jones, F. 1910. Report of human remains. *Archaeological Survey of Nubia, Bulletin 2*. Cairo: National Print Department.

Spencer, A.J. 1982. *Death in Ancient Egypt*. Harmondsworth: Penguin.

Stack, M.V. 1986. Trace elements in teeth of Egyptians and Nubians. In *Science in Egyptology* (ed. A.R. David). Manchester: Manchester University Press, pp. 219–22.

Stanworth, P., Wildsmith, K. and Tapp, E. 1986. A neurosurgical look inside the Manchester mummy heads. In *Science in Egyptology* (ed. A.R. David). Manchester: Manchester University Press, pp. 371–4.

Stastny, P. 1974. Antigens in mummified pre-Columbian tissues. *Science (US)*, 183(4127): 864–6.

Stefan, J-R. 1982. L'entomofaune de la momie de Ramses II. *Annales de la Societé entomologique de France*, 18: 531–7.

Stenn, F. 1981. The contribution of paleopathology to modern medicine: an update. *Archives of Pathology and Laboratory Medicine (USA)*, 105(12): 633–7.

Strong, L. 1981. Dermestids – an embalmer's dilemma. *Antenna*, 5(1): 136–9.

Strouhal, E. 1986. Embalming excerebration in the Middle Kingdom. In *Science in Egyptology* (ed. A.R. David). Manchester: Manchester University Press, pp. 141–53.

Tapp, E. 1979a. The unwrapping of a mummy. In *The Manchester Museum Mummy Project* (ed. A.R. David) Manchester: Manchester Museum, pp. 83–94.

1979b. Disease in the Manchester mummies. In *The Manchester Museum Mummy Project* (ed. A.R. David) Manchester: Manchester Museum, pp. 95–102.

1984. Disease and the Manchester mummies – the pathologist's role. In *Evidence Embalmed* (eds. A.R. David and E. Tapp). Manchester: Manchester University Press, pp. 78–95.

1986. Histology and histopathology of the Manchester Mummies. In *Science in Egyptology* (ed. A.R. David). Manchester: Manchester University Press, pp. 347–350.

Tapp, E., Curry, A. and Anfield, C. 1975. Sand pneumoconiosis in an Egyptian mummy. *British Medical Journal* (3 May): 276.

Tapp, E., Stanworth, P. and Wildsmith, K. 1984. The endoscope in mummy research. In *Evidence Embalmed* (eds. A.R. David and E. Tapp). Manchester: Manchester University Press, pp. 65–77.

Tapp, E. and Wildsmith, K. 1986. Endoscopy of Egyptian mummies. In *Science in Egyptology* (ed. A.R. David). Manchester: Manchester University Press, pp. 351–6.

1992. The autopsy and endoscopy of the Leeds muumy. In *The Mummy's Tale* (eds. A.R. David and E. Tapp). London: Michael O'Mara Books, pp. 132–53.

Thompson, P., Lynch, P.G. and Tapp, E. 1986. Neuropathological studies on the Manchester mummies. In *Science in Egyptology* (ed. A.R. David). Manchester: Manchester University Press, pp. 375–8.

Verbov, J. 1986. The skin of Egyptian mummies. In *Science in Egyptology* (ed. A.R. David). Manchester: Manchester University Press, pp. 355–9.

Wallgren, J.E., Caple, R. and Aufderheide, A.C. 1986. Contributions of nuclear magnetic resonance studies to the question of Alkaptonuria (ochronosis) in an Egyptian mummy. In *Science in Egyptology* (ed. A.R. David). Manchester: Manchester University Press, pp. 321–8.

Weeks, K.R. 1980. Ancient Egyptian dentistry. In *An X-ray Atlas of The Royal Mummies* (eds. J.E. Harris and E. Wente). Chicago: University of Chicago Press, pp. 99–119.

Wells, C. and Maxwell, B.M. 1962. Alkaptonuria in an Egyptian mummy. *British Journal of Radiology*, 35: 679–82.

Wild, J.P. 1979. The textiles from Mummy 1770. In *The Manchester Museum Mummy Project* (ed. A.R. David). Manchester: Manchester Museum, pp. 133–6.

Zimmerman, M. R. *et al.* 1981. The paleopathology of an Aleutian mummy. *Archives of Pathology and Laboratory Medicine (USA)*, 105(12): 638–41.

17. Oil, fat and wax

MARGARET SERPICO AND RAYMOND WHITE

Introduction

Whereas today, many of the products used in the home are derived from the petrochemical industry, in the past it was necessary to rely on natural resources. Thus, the ancient Egyptians could have employed vegetable oils and animal fats in cooking, as lubricants, as emollients in themselves, or as a matrix for scented unguents and medicinal preparations. Wax would have been a convenient waterproof sealant or fixative, and all three could have been used as illuminants and in mummification. These substances can also be grouped together by their greasy texture, their hydrophobic tendency, and indeed by a similarity in chemical composition. Production of all three can be divided into two stages: the management of the raw source materials (plants, land and marine animals and bees), and the subsequent industrial processing of them.

Of these natural products, the likely source of ancient wax is perhaps the easiest to delimit. Waxes can be obtained from a number of plants and animals (Mills and White 1994: 49–53), but the source most readily available to the ancient Egyptians was beeswax. Evidence of beekeeping in ancient Egypt is not plentiful, but apiculture is often still practiced as a cottage industry maintaining, as in some parts of the world, close links with traditional methods. Although the collection of honey is often the primary incentive for beekeeping, the production of beeswax could have been an important subsidiary industry.

In fact, most of the sources of oils and fats could have been, and undoubtedly were, used for other purposes. Animals common to both land and marine environments could have been farmed or hunted principally for their meat, and many oil plants could also have been cultivated as food or for other industrial usages. Thus, archaeobotanical and archaeozoological remains, where present, can help establish that a potential source was known, but are not proof in themselves that it was exploited for its oil or fat. More significantly, there have been as yet no securely identified archaeological remains of oil factories or beehives from the Pharaonic period. Furthermore, no tomb scenes show the complete sequence of oil or fat production, and lexicographical difficulties persist.

As all animals possess some body fat, the potential sources are in theory not restricted. The quantity of the deposits (in part related to the size of the animal) and the availability of different species were probably among the prime factors dictating choice. From faunal remains, tombs scenes and textual evidence, the principle domesticated farm animals known to the ancient Egyptians have been identified and information gleaned on hunting and animal husbandry. However, because fat was likely to have been obtained primarily as a by-product of the butchering of animals for meat, there was probably no distinction in the initial farming, hunting, fowling or fishing of the animal depending on usage. Thus, the subject of the production of fat is linked most closely to the killing of the animal and to butchery practices (see Chapter 25, this volume).

In contrast, the identification of sources of vegetable oils has proved more complex. Plants with seeds, kernels, fruits or tubers of a high oil content might seem likely sources, but archaeobotanical evidence of their presence does not always survive, making their history difficult to trace. Moreover, their dates of introduction into Egypt are sometimes still under debate. Rarely can specific plants be named from study of the representations in tomb reliefs. Some botanical identifications have been suggested based on interpretation of texts and in particular, study of the medicinal properties of the plants. While useful, these approaches are seldom conclusive unless the associations are incontrovertible (i.e. toxicity; see Keimer 1924, 1984; Loret 1892; Germer 1979, 1985).

For his list of possible sources of oils, Lucas (1962) drew heavily on later Classical texts. Details of the cultivation of oil crops and oil production are cited in Ptolemaic documents dealing with the newly established oil monopoly, and Classical writers such as Pliny, Theophrastus and Dioscorides provided plant descriptions which enabled modern translators to venture botanical identifications. Based in part on these texts, Lucas proposed balanos, moringa, castor, colocynth, almond, lettuce, linseed, olive, radish, safflower, sesame and malabathrum (cinnamon) as vegetable oil sources. However, lexicographical problems are again inherent (Sandy 1989: 18–24, 30–4; see for example discussions of sesame and radish pp. 397–8, 401–2) and the relevance of these texts is arguably reduced as new plants had been introduced and agricultural practices altered since Pharaonic times (see Chapter 21, this volume). Modern agricultural data can provide some basic information on the plants as long as this is viewed with similar caution. The construction of the Aswan High Dam has altered planting cycles and environmental conditions, such as soil salinity. Crop production has undoubtedly been increased by improved irrigation and better fertilisers and pesticides. Methods of oil and fat extraction have also changed. Today, mechanical presses are used, and chemical solvents added to ensure the maximum oil extraction. Even the chemical composition of the oil plants themselves has sometimes been altered to enhance oil content (Sonntag 1979a: 290).

More recent botanical studies have recognised the oil-producing capabilities of plants such as poppy and tiger nut which were overlooked by Lucas (Germer 1982, 1985: *passim*). Still more sources may have been exploited in antiquity, perhaps discounted today because we perceive them to have an inadequate oil yield, potentially projecting onto an ancient society our own view of cost-effectiveness. Others, currently absent in the archaeobotanical record, may one day be discovered. Therefore, it is important to remember that any list of likely oil sources is formed not by secure evidence, but by extrapolation from the existing available information.

The list which follows revises that produced by Lucas, taking into consideration, where possible, recent botanical theories concerning ancient distribution and some of the new discoveries of archaeobotanical remains in Egypt. Some previous identifications by Keimer (1924, 1984), Loret (1892), Täckholm (1974) and Germer (1985) have been included in this chapter where no further evidence is available. The sources are diverse, and include annual crop plants which would have been cultivated in much the same fashion as cereals (necessitating tilling, sowing, etc. and in some cases, threshing). Thus, consideration of agricultural processes as a whole can help place the agronomy of oil crops into this broader context. Similarly, as oils were produced from fruits and nuts of certain trees, discussions of horticultural practices should also be consulted (on these subjects, see Chapter 21, this volume).

Sources and methods of production of oils, fats and waxes

Vegetable oil sources

Castor (Ricinus communis *L.*)
Family: Euphorbiaceae.
Seeds of castor found in a Predynastic grave at Badari (Brunton and Caton-Thompson 1928: 38) and at Maadi (Keimer 1936: 70) suggest that this plant may have been available to the Egyptians from a very early date. As it is widespread in the ancient Near East (Zohary 1987: 269), its origin is difficult to trace, but it is considered indigenous to eastern Africa and Sudan (Weiss 1971: 3; Zohary 1987: 269) or central Africa (Keimer 1924: 70; Germer 1985: 103). Lucas (1962: 332) believed that it may have been native to Egypt. Found throughout Egypt today, wild castor plants are often seen along the banks of the Nile and irrigation ditches (Weiss 1971: 242). Keimer (1924: 72) noted that it was particularly common in Upper Egypt. In modern times, castor oil production is mainly from wild plants (Weiss 1971: 32), but it may have been cultivated in Ptolemaic times (Sandy 1989: 43–7: Keimer 1924: 72–3).

In Africa, the castor plant is usually fairly tall and multi-branched (see Fig. 17.1), reaching a height of up to twelve

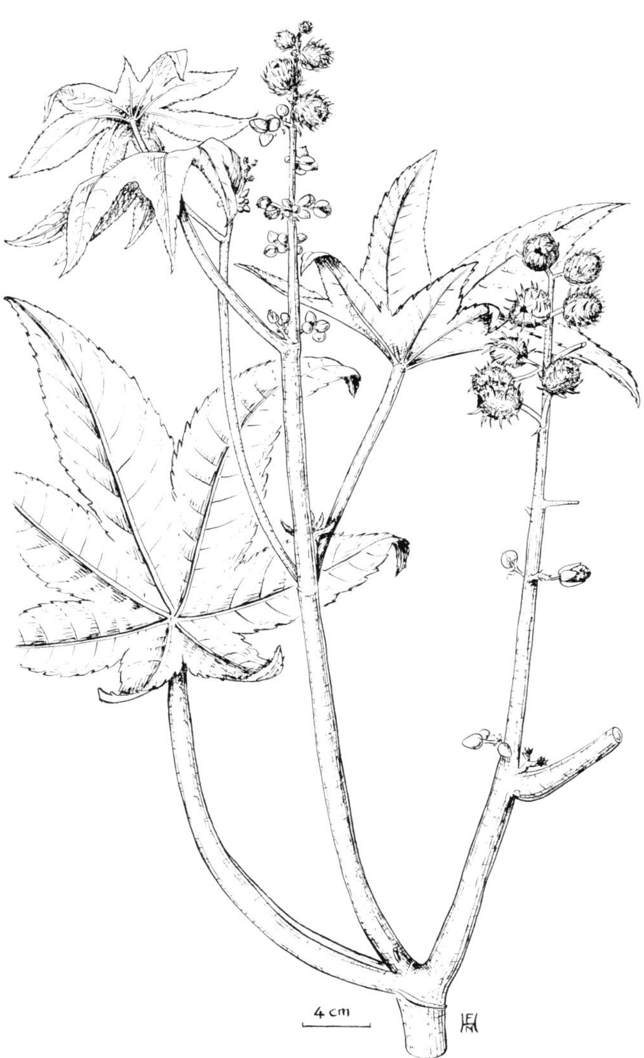

*Figure 17.1 Castor (*Ricinus communis *L.).*

metres (Weiss 1971: 45; Keimer 1924: 70), although three to five metres may be more common (Germer 1985: 103). It is swift-growing and can live for many years (Keimer 1924: 70; Weiss 1971: 45). The plant is characterised by large palmate leaves with serrated edges. The small flowers form on pyramidical racemes at the terminal position on main and lateral branches. Examples in Palestine are said to flower from March to November (Zohary 1987: 269). The lower flowers are yellow and are male, while the upper flowers are red and female (Keimer 1924: 70; Weiss 1971: 46). The fruit formed on the racemes are rounded capsules (about 1 to 3 cm) covered in short firm spines (Weiss 1971: 46; Zohary 1987: 269). The capsules are divided into three chambers, each containing one oval, slightly flattened seed, about one centimetre in size (Weiss 1971: 46; Zohary 1987: 269). The outer surface of the seed is brittle and shiny with mottled colour (Weiss 1971: 46). Examples from Badari were said to be of similar size to wild plants but smaller than cultivated examples (Brunton and Caton-Thompson 1928: 38).

When planted as a crop today, castor is usually sown from seed in November or early December, with the first plants maturing approximately 140 days later (Weiss 1971: 47, 120–1). When ripe, the capsules split open, violently scattering the seeds. Therefore harvesting was probably done by picking the capsule-bearing racemes as they ripened, in order to avoid seed loss due to this dehiscence. The seeds could be released from the capsules in a variety of ways. This could be carried out by hitting the racemes against a tree or rock, having hooved animals tread on the capsules, placing the racemes in a sack and beating them with a stick, or leaving the capsules in a sunny position until they naturally dehisce (Weiss 1971: 201).

Castor was probably seldom interplanted with other edible crops as both the leaves and seeds are toxic. In fact, the seeds contain two toxins, ricin and ricinine. The seeds are a powerful emetic and can be used to induce labour or, when prepared into a paste, as an abortificant and contraceptive (Weiss 1971: 292). Also present is a powerful allergen, known as castor bean allergen (CBA). Today, workers in castor oil factories are carefully screened for respiratory reactions and other allergies (Weiss 1983a: 546–7).

The mildly toxic alkaloid ricinine is not present in cold pressed oil, as it will remain in the pressed seed cake (Salunkhe *et al.* 1992: 514). Conversely, the potency of the extremely poisonous protein, ricin, can be reduced by heating in water, but the allergen would not be destroyed (Weiss 1971: 87, 89; Seegeler 1983: 233). Weiss (1971: 9) noted that the production of castor oil implies a significant knowledge of the plant, as traditional oil extraction by heating and crushing the seeds 'would have produced only a vile tasting, odoriferous poison!'. The cathartic effect and the unpleasant taste of the oil would probably preclude regular culinary use. The oil could also be used in medicinal preparations, as a lubricant, as a skin emolliant and as an illuminant. In Ethiopia, it is reportedly the only oilseed used for lighting (Seegeler 1983: 232). Lucas (1962: 332) mentioned that it is used in modern Nubia for dressing the hair and as a skin emollient.

From Classical texts, it has been suggested that the Greek word κίκι refers to the castor plant, while κροτών refers usually to the seed and oil and more rarely also to the plant (Sandy 1989: 43). If this translation is accurate, Ptolemaic texts indicate that castor was planted either by setting out small plant or shoots or by broadcasting; that it could be planted in February or March, usually on the banks of rivers or lakes; and that it was grown in only eight of the twenty-four nomes in Egypt, for the most part in the Delta, but with a large area devoted to cultivation in Thebes (Sandy 1989: 43–5). Although the spring planting time is unusual, the papyri relate to the Fayum and irrigation practices there may have permitted such a growing season. Its primary use at that time was apparently as an oil for lamps (Sandy 1989: 39–40), notwithstanding its unpleasant odour. Usage in medical preparations is also known (Sandy 1989: 40).

The seed has an oil content of about 47 per cent, while that of the hulled kernel about 66 per cent (Salunkhe *et al.* 1992: 513–14; Seegeler 1983: 234). The oil is pale yellow and transparent, with a viscous consistency, a slight odour and acrid taste. However, it does not easily turn rancid (Weiss 1971: 294).

Balanos (Balanites aegyptiaca (*L.*) Del.)
Family: Balanitaceae or Zygophyllaceae

Although the balanos tree is less familiar to us today, it is believed that the ancient Egyptians used kernels from the fruits of *Balanites aegyptiaca* as a source of oil. Balanos nuts have been found at Predynastic sites in Egypt, such as Hierakonpolis (el-Hadidi 1982: 105) and Naqada (Petrie Museum, UC 36097; see Petrie 1896: 54). A number of later finds have also been noted (Keimer 1984: 2; Lucas 1962: 331).

According to Lucas, the balanos tree was probably more common in ancient times than it is now (Lucas 1962: 331). It is indigenous to east Africa and the Sudan (FAO 1988: 96; Zohary 1987: 258) and may have favoured Upper rather than Lower Egypt (Lucas 1962: 331). Archaeobotanical remains of charcoal from balanos trees dated to 5900–5030 BC have been identified in the central Sudan (Barakat 1995: 104) and the tree remains abundant there today (Axtell and Fairman 1992: 25; Keimer 1984: 3). It is widely distributed in the upper Nile region, particularly in desert *wadis*, oases and along the Red Sea coast (Zahran and Willis 1992: 99, 124, 153, 169).

The tree is said to grow wild in Palestine (Keimer 1984: 3), and Hepper (1992: 55, 150) noted its occurrence in the Engedi oasis and in oases near the Dead Sea. Zohary (1973: 389) stated that the balanos tree 'reaches its northernmost limit (Bet Shean) in the Rift Valley of Palestine'. In addition, a short-leafed variety is found in Syria (Germer 1985: 99). Because of this distribution, it is possible that the oil was imported to Egypt to meet high demand. The oil may also have been used as a base for scented perfumes which were imported.

Balanites aegyptiaca is a small semi-evergreen tree or shrub, generally five to ten metres in height (FAO 1988: 95), but sometimes reaching fifteen metres (Keimer 1984: 3). It is sparsely covered with oval grey-green leathery leaves (see Fig. 17.2). These form on branchlets with long thorns, some as much as 8 to 9 cm in length (FAO 1988: 95). According to Keimer (1984: 3), the thorns are 3 to 6 cm long. Small, green, scented flowers are produced in late May (Bircher 1960: 402–3). The fruits are positioned singly in place of a thorn on some branches (Keimer 1984: 3). In appearance, the oval fruits resemble dates, with a thin skin and very sticky brown flesh. The skin is at first green turning yellow to orange-red in colour, and the flesh is said to have 'a horehound-like flavor' (Osborn 1968: 171). Each fruit contains one oblong, five-angled stone, usually 2–3.5 cm in length (Keimer 1984: 3). The shell of this nut is extremely hard and fibrous, and difficult to crack without crushing the kernel (Hardman and Sofowora 1972: 172). Therefore, it may have required cracking by hand, making the preparation for oil processing quite labour-intensive.

Balanos trees can be grown from seed and do best along river banks and *wadis* (FAO 1988: 98). They can live for more than a century, and can be fruit producing for up to seventy-five years (Axtell and Fairman 1992: 25). The annual crop is approximately 125 kilograms of fruit per tree (Axtell and Fairman 1992: 25).

Many of the archaeological specimens of balanites have a small round hole at one end of the nut, and/or a larger more irregular hole in the central area. These holes were not done to extract oil from the kernel inside, as has been suggested (Täckholm *et al.* 1961: 23). The smaller holes are the result of attack by weevels. Modern studies of balanites confirm that this is the case (FAO 1988: 99; Hussain *et al.* 1949: 730). As this attack is common in windfallen drupes, it is likely that the fruits were picked from the tree by hand as soon as they ripened (Hussain *et al.* 1949: 730). Rodent gnawing clearly caused the larger holes, since the teeth marks are still visible in some of these examples (Delwen Samuel pers. comm.; Germer 1985: 99).

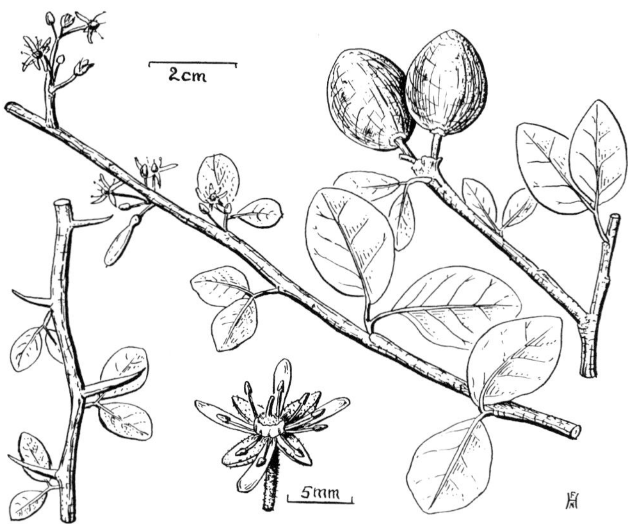

*Figure 17.2 Balanos (*Balanites aegyptiaca *(L.) Del.).*

The kernel within the shell, from which the oil was extracted, is a pale yellow colour and is used for culinary purposes (FAO 1988: 97). If dried, both the fruit and nuts can be stored for a year (FAO 1988: 98) so oil processing need not have taken place immediately. The oil is pale yellow in colour as well as odourless and tasteless, and is particularly suitable for cosmetic preparations (Lucas 1962: 331). It has been noted that the oil content of the kernel is 30–60 per cent (Vaughan 1970: 255; Axtell and Fairman 1992: 25) and that 100 kilograms of fruit will yield about 6.4 kilograms of oil (Schunk de Goldfiem 1942: 237).

The wood of the tree has been used in wood-working (Keimer 1984: 3). A resinous product is also obtained from the flesh of the fruit (Hepper 1992: 141). The bittersweet pulp of the fruit is edible and is today sometimes fermented into an alcoholic drink (FAO 1988: 97; Keimer 1984: 3). The fruits can also be used as livestock fodder (FAO 1988: 97) and this may explain the discovery of balanos nuts in pig pens at Amarna (Samuel, pers. comm.).

*Safflower (*Carthamus tinctorius *L.)*
Family: Compositae

Safflower (Fig. 17.3) could have been used by the Egyptians both as a source of yellow dye and of oil (see Chapter 11, this volume). The origin of the plant has been difficult to establish as it is so widespread, but it probably reached Egypt via western Asia (Zohary and Hopf 1993: 194; Germer 1985: 174). Flower heads and seeds of *Carthamus* sp. have now been identified at Tell Hammam et Turkman in northern Syria, dated to 2500 BC. The seeds show some morphological differences which could indicate 'that the cultivar had not yet developed into the modern one' (van Zeist and Waterbolk-van Rooijen 1992: 158). The presence of flower heads, which by association with the seeds were also identified as *C. tinctorius*, would seem to indicate that the plants were collected for use as dye and 'it remains uncertain whether oil was extracted from the fruits at that time or whether this practice was not developed until later' (van Zeist and Waterbolk-van Rooijen 1992: 158). Seeds dated to 2400–1900 BC again showing this dimorphism were found in northern Syria at Selenkahiye (van Zeist and Bakker-Heeres 1985: 252).

In Egypt, safflower seeds were found at Kahun, but the Middle Kingdom date is dubious (Germer 1989: 38). Claims that safflower dyes were used in the Middle King-

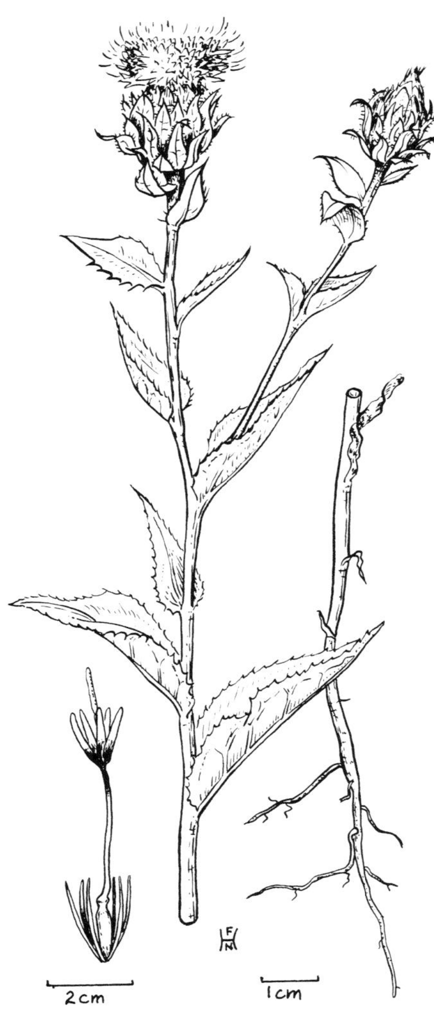

*Figure 17.3 Safflower (*Carthamus tinctorius *L.).*

dom were discounted a few years ago (Germer 1992: 10–15). However, more recently, Germer has published scientific confirmation of safflower dye from Middle Kingdom mummy wrappings (Germer *et al.* 1994: 17–19). Thus, the date still stands, but not on the evidence originally proposed. Flowers of this plant are also known from New Kingdom burials (Keimer 1924: 7). Safflower seeds were found in the tomb of Tutankhamun (KV62; Hepper 1990: 32; Germer 1989: 37–8; de Vartavan 1990: 281, table 12.2) and more recently at Amarna (Samuel 1989: 281, table 12.2). Collectively, such remains have led to the suggestion that safflower was cultivated in Egypt by the New Kingdom (Keimer 1924: 7; Germer 1985: 174) but its use as an oilseed crop is still unconfirmed.

Safflower is grown today as a winter annual in both Upper and Lower Egypt, mainly between Asyut and Aswan (Knowles 1967: 162). It is usually planted as a border crop and will also grow along sandbanks and canals (Weiss 1971: 543; Foaden and Fletcher 1910: 520–1; Knowles 1967: 162). Keimer (1924: 7) noted that in his time, safflower was very widespread, primarily as a secondary crop to Egyptian cereals. It is sown either by drilling or broadcasting in October or November (Foaden and Fletcher 1910: 522; Knowles 1967: 162). Safflower plants normally range in height from 30 to 150 cm (Weiss 1983a: 220). They are highly branched with leaves which, on the lower stem, are large, oblong and deeply serrated, but towards the head are short and ovate or obovate. The plant also becomes increasingly thistle-like towards the head. The inflorescence, forming at the end of each branch, consists of numerous small florets (Weiss 1983a: 223; Salunkhe *et al.* 1992: 329). These flowers, which are the source of the dye, vary in colour from yellow to deep orange. The period of flowering usually begins in mid-March and can continue for several weeks with the seeds first ripening in about mid-April (Wilkinson 1843: 459; Foaden and Fletcher 1910: 523). Harvesting is then carried out until early May (Knowles 1967: 162). Because of the difference in the flowering time and the maturation of the seeds, the plant may have been grown either for dye or oil, but not both.

The harvesting of the seed is comparatively simple. The practice earlier this century was to pull up the entire plant (Foaden and Fletcher 1910: 524). Alternatively, it can also be cut when the seed is ripe (Weiss 1971: 667). As the seeds are indehiscent, threshing can then be carried out by beating with sticks, taking care not to break the stalks, which could then be used as fuel (Foaden and Fletcher 1910: 524). Once the seeds have ripened, the crop can be left standing in the field for up to a month with small loss (Weiss 1971: 667).

The seed, or more properly achene, while resembling a small sunflower seed in shape, is generally cream or white with a fibrous shell covering the dark seed coat (Weiss 1971: 570). The size of the modern cultivated seed is generally between 7–9 mm in length, but the possible examples from Selenkahiye were roughly half that size (van Zeist and Bakker-Heeres 1985: 252). In modern Egypt and the Sudan, the oil content of the seed is about 28–29 per cent (Weiss 1971: 608). Safflower oil is normally pale yellow, but has a slightly unpleasant odour, making it perhaps less suitable as an edible oil (Weiss 1971: 726, 730).

It has been proposed that the Greek κνῆκος refers to safflower oil (Sandy 1989: 85). Based on references in Ptolemaic texts, it would seem that safflower was one of the less common oil sources of that time (Sandy 1989: 87). Whether this was also true of the Pharaonic period remains uncertain.

*Moringa (*Moringa peregrina *(Forssk.) Fiori =* M. aptera *Gaertn.)*
Family: Moringaceae
Although moringa nuts are often mentioned as a source of oil, the earliest secure archaeobotanical remains are from

Hawara and date to the Greco–Roman period (Keimer 1984: 27). Examples were found by Schiaparelli in a Theban grave, but as the burial was disturbed, the date is uncertain (Keimer 1984: 27 gave a date of Twentieth to Twenty-sixth Dynasty or later). While absence of evidence is not evidence of absence, it is interesting that there are no earlier botanical remains of moringa, given that it is often cited as an oil source available from very early times. This is based in part on the translation of the Egyptian word *b3ḳ* as moringa, an interpretation which is still unconfirmed (see olive, p. 399). However, the tree is native to the Sudan (Zohary 1966: 340) and possibly also to Egypt (Lucas 1962: 331). As yet, there is no evidence that another species indigenous to Sudan, *Moringa oleifera* (= *M. pterygosperma*), with characteristic winged nuts, was known to the Egyptians (Hepper 1990: 25. Note that Keimer (1984: 27) stated that *M. oleifera* grows only in India).

Trees of *M. peregrina* are now quite rare, but are known in Lower Egypt. According to Keimer (1984: 27), it is doubtful that moringa ever grew in the Delta, as Loret suggested (Loret 1892: 86). Drar, in his expedition to Gebel Elba, noted that the tree was common in *wadis* between Hurghada and Quseir, with only one or two 'stunted specimens' found at Elba (Drar 1936: 84). Keimer (1984: 27; also Zahran and Willis 1992: 173, 175, 177) noted that it occurs frequently in the eastern desert foothills and *wadis* of Upper Egypt around Akhmim. It also grows in the Sinai peninsula (Zahran and Willis 1992: 291, 293).

Like balanos trees, moringa grows in Palestine, although there is little evidence that it was of economic importance in antiquity (Zohary 1962: 146; 1966: 340). Moringa trees have been found in the Lower Jordan Valley, the Dead Sea area, the Judean Desert, the southern Negev, the Aravah Valley and in Edom (Zohary 1966: 340). It is therefore possible that some oil was imported to Egypt if necessary and moringa oil could have formed the base of perfumes which were sent to Egypt.

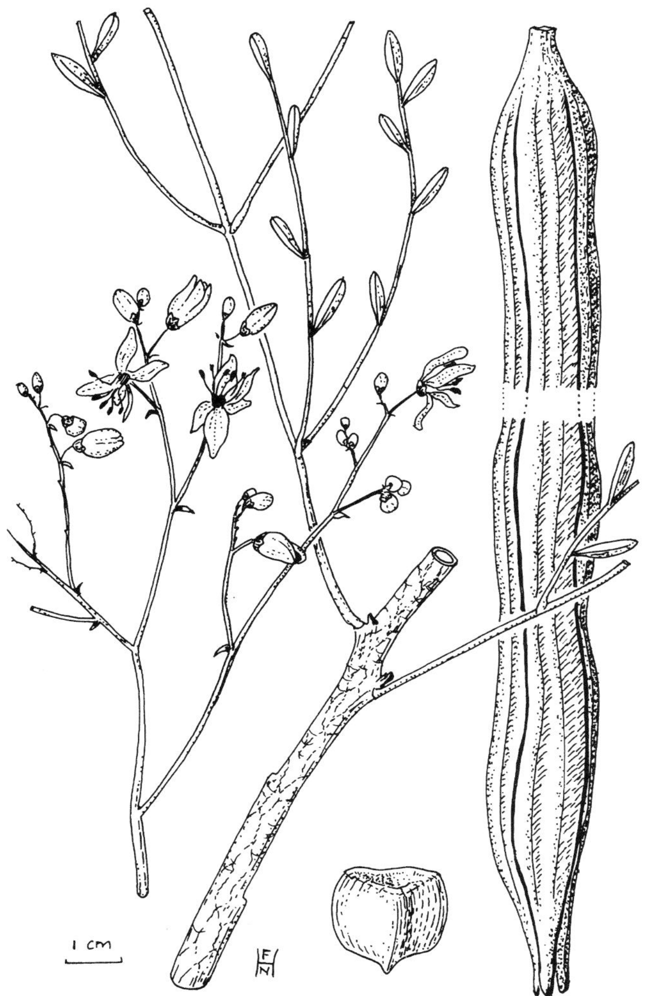

*Figure 17.4 Moringa (*Moringa peregrina *(Forssk.) Fiori).*

This deciduous tree generally is only about six to ten metres high, with a broad crown (Keimer 1984: 27). It is most often described as having 'whip-like branches, with small leaflets' (Lucas 1962: 331; Hepper 1990: 25; Drar 1936: 84; see Fig. 17.4). The pale pink flowers, formed in panicles of up to 30 cm, occur in May (Täckholm 1974: 211; Hepper 1992: 150: Zohary 1966: 340). Long, narrow, brown pods, generally about 20 cm in length with longitudinal grooves or furrows, ripen in October (Täckholm 1974: 211; Zahran and Willis 1992: 172–3; Zohary 1966: 340). The three valves of the pod split to release the nuts, which are at first pale green and then become brown as they ripen. The small nuts (up to 1 cm) are rounded with three sides (Zohary 1966: 340). Each nut contains one white, fleshy rounded kernel, from which the oil is extracted. However, as these pods can remain hanging on the tree for much of the year, 'long after the leaves and flowers have disappeared' (Miller and Stuart-Smith 1988: 210), they may have been picked by hand when needed and then split to release the nuts.

Some data on the harvesting of moringa nuts are available from studies in the eastern desert. There, the trees are restricted to the lower regions of mountains higher than 1500 metres (Hobbs 1990: 40). According to Osborn (1968: 173), collection of the pods is undertaken in August, but Hobbs observed the process in late autumn (Hobbs 1990: 40). Harvesting is carried out by two to five men picking the pods from the tree and 'throwing rocks to dislodge others' (Hobbs 1990: 40). At the end of the day, they remove the seeds from the pods and bag them in burlap sacks (Hobbs 1990: 40). Some of the nuts are used by them to make an oil for culinary purposes, the rest are sold commercially, to be pressed on a large scale (Osborn 1968: 173).

The nuts themselves could have been cracked by hand, as the shell is quite thin. In addition to oil manufacture, the kernels may also have been eaten whole. The oil has a slight yellow colour and although odourless, has a sweet taste (Lucas 1962: 331). The flavour of the root has given rise to the modern name for the tree, the horseradish tree (Hepper 1992: 55).

*Linseed (*Linum usitatissimum *L.)*
Family: Linaceae
It is believed that linseed, cultivated from *Linum bienne* Mill., was introduced into Egypt from the Near East between 6000 and 5000 BC (Zohary and Hopf 1993: 123). Predynastic remains have been identified at Maadi (Kroll 1989: 132; van Zeist and de Roller 1993: 3), el-Omari (Barakat 1990: 112), Merimda (Zohary and Hopf 1993: 123), and the Fayum (Caton-Thompson and Gardner 1934: 46, note 2; 49). Early Dynastic seeds have been found at Buto (Thanheiser 1991: 40–1), Tell Ibrahim Awad in the eastern Delta (de Roller 1992: 112–3), and in the contents of funerary jars at Minshat Abu Omar (Thanheiser 1992: 167). The plant may, of course, also have been grown for flax cloth, which was produced from its fibrous stems (see Chapter 11, this volume). Linen has been identified at several Predynastic sites (see Chapter 11, this volume; Brunton and Caton-Thompson 1928: 65–6; Caton-Thompson and Gardner 1934: 46).

Linseed is an annual plant, grown in both Upper and Lower Egypt. It can be sown by broadcast in late October to mid-November with the seed ripening in March or April (Wilkinson 1843: 459; Hepper 1992: 166; Foaden and Fletcher 1910: 424–5). The plant can reach about one metre in height with a slender erect stem, long, narrow leaves and pale blue flowers (Godin and Spensley 1971: 68; see Fig. 17.5). The seeds form in firm rounded capsules, 7 to 9 mm in size, with five chambers, each holding two seeds. Ancient capsules from Predynastic el-Omari were slightly smaller (Barakat 1990: 112) as were specimens found at Badari, which were also more deeply ridged than modern examples, and therefore described only as a species of flax (Brunton and Caton-Thompson 1928: 63). Modern seeds have an oil content of 35–44 per cent (Vaughan 1970: 141; Salunkhe *et al.* 1992: 506). Measuring about 4 to 6 mm in length, the seeds have a flattened, oval shape, pointed at the lower end, with a smooth, glossy brown fibrous testa.

When grown for oil, the seeds should be sown more thinly than for flax fibre, allowing the plant to become fully branched (Foaden and Fletcher 1910: 425; Hepper 1990: 34). In modern Egypt, linseed is frequently planted for both oil seed and fibre (Foaden and Fletcher 1910: 425–6). However, if the seeds are allowed to ripen completely, the stem can become woody, reducing its range of usage (Foaden and Fletcher 1910: 424; see also Chapter 11, this volume). Tomb-scenes providing agricultural information on oil plants are extremely rare, but linseed crops are shown in some, where the density and upright nature of the plants suggest that they were grown either for fibre or for both

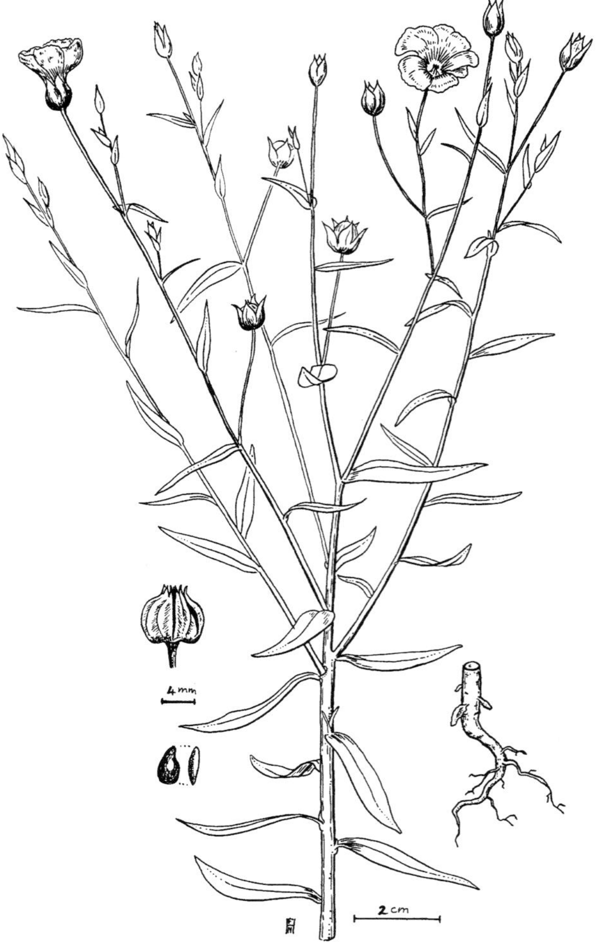

*Figure 17.5 Linseed (*Linum usitatissimum *L.).*

seed and fibre (see Chapter 11, this volume). To obtain the two, the plants are uprooted just as the seed begins to ripen (Foaden and Fletcher 1910: 425–6), a method confirmed by New Kingdom harvesting scenes (e.g. Tylor and Griffith 1894: pl. III). The plants are then bundled, dried and the seed heads stripped from the stems by hand or by dragging the the stems through a comb, a technique known as rippling (see Chapter 11, this volume). The separated indehiscent capsules can then be threshed to extract the seeds (Eckey 1954: 534; Renfrew 1973: 121).

It has been proposed that linseed oil was first used in the Near East and Mesopotamia, where it was of primary culinary importance until the later introduction of sesame (Helbaek 1966: 618). However, this theory has met mixed reception based on lexicographical difficulties with the relevant texts and on the unpleasant taste of the oil (Waetzoldt 1985: 86–7; Bedigian 1985: 164–70). It is certainly true that linseed turns rancid quite quickly, although it has been argued that it is palatable when fresh. Cold pressed linseed oil is still used for cooking and frying in India and eastern

Europe, for example (Salunkhe *et al.* 1992: 509; Eckey 1954: 546), and in the traditional Egyptian bean dish, *ful medammes* (Manniche 1989: 116). The seeds can also be eaten. However, some care is necessary in the preparation of food mixtures containing large quantities. The seeds should be heated in hot water prior to eating as they contain a glycoside which, if soaked in unheated water, can produce poisonous prussic acid (Renfrew 1973: 124; Gallant 1985: 155). Because of its tendency towards rancidity, the oil was probably also seldom used for cosmetic preparations, particularly for those which were imported to Egypt and would have taken some time in transit. In antiquity, it may have been less frequently used for culinary purposes when other sources were available.

λίνον, believed to be the linseed plant, was mentioned numerous times by Classical writers. However, the only reference to linseed oil in Egypt during Ptolemaic times comes from the Revenue Laws, giving rise to the conclusion that production of linseed oil had become uncommon by that time (Sandy 1989: 4–5; Gallant 1985: 155).

*Sesame (*Sesamum indicum *L.)*
Family: Pedaliaceae

The date for the introduction of sesame into Egypt has been controversial. Greek papyri mention the cultivation of *σήσαμον*, translated as sesame, in Egypt, particularly in the Fayum, during the Ptolemaic period (Sandy 1989: 62–7) and it has been proposed that sesame was not grown in Egypt until that time (Loret 1892: 57; Sandy 1977: 29; 1989: 62). Keimer, however, believed that sesame was introduced in the New Kingdom, equating sesame oil to the word *nḥḥ* which first appears at that time (Keimer 1924: 19). The botanical identity of *nḥḥ* is still under debate (Koura 1995; Sandy 1989: 30–1), and yet the New Kingdom date for the introduction of sesame into Egypt is entering into the published literature as secure, based on the tenuous link between *nḥḥ* and sesame (Nayer and Mehra 1970: 27).

Attempts to determine the date of its cultivation in Egypt are hindered by the lack of secure information on the earliest introduction of the plant into the Near East. There has been much discussion of this subject and the debate can only be summarised here. Two locations for the origin for cultivated sesame have been proposed: one in southeast Asia, around India, and one in eastern Africa, perhaps Ethiopia (Nayar and Mehra 1970: 26; Bedigian and Harlan 1986).

For the former, it would seem that sesame subsequently spread west to Mesopotamia, then the Near East and finally to Egypt (Zohary and Hopf 1993: 133). Dates for this dispersion have been difficult to establish. Based on Sumerian texts, some would place sesame's cultivation in Iraq in the middle of the third millennium BC (Bedigian 1985: 142–6, 164), and it has been suggested that it then replaced linseed as the primary oil crop in Mesopotamia (Helbaek 1966: 618, see discussion of linseed, p. 396). The lack of botanical finds dating to this period and, just as for *nḥḥ*, the lexicographical difficulties of the word used in these texts have made this association impossible to establish conclusively. However, seeds of *Sesamum indicum*, dated to the middle of the third millennium BC, have now been identified by M.P. Charles at Abu Salabikh in Mesopotamia (Matthews *et al.* 1994: 183). Further finds from archaeological sites in Iraq may indeed help place this important discovery in the context of the history of sesame cultivation.

Prior to the Abu Salabikh seeds, the earliest botanical remains of sesame were those at Harrapa in the Indus valley (dated 3035–3500 BC), and then a long chronological gap ensues until the Iron Age (900–600 BC), when sesame was found at Karmir Blur in Urartu, north of Mesopotamia (see Bedigian and Harlan 1986: 140, 146 for a summary). At the latter site, evidence of oil manufacture was also found. More recently, nearly 200 seeds were found at Deir Alla in Jordan, dated to Iron Age IIB (*c.* 800 BC) (van Zeist and Neef 1989: 34, 36; van der Kooij and Ibrahim 1989: 82). According to van Zeist and Neef (1989: 36), the Deir Alla material should not be interpreted as evidence of the large-scale cultivation necessary for oil production, which they believe did not occur until the Greek period, but of a limited use of the seeds for culinary purposes. In addition, seed impressions in pots from southern Arabia at Hajar Bin Humeid dated to around the fifth century BC were identified as sesame (Soderstrom 1969: 402; Bedigian and Harlan 1986: 147–8). Clearly, further botanical identifications of sesame in sites in the Near East might alter the existing perspective, but the present evidence would appear to suggest that sesame did not reach Syria–Palestine until at least the Iron Age.

The second possibility, that sesame was introduced to Egypt from eastern Africa, is still more difficult to support. Pollen identified as either *Sesamum indicum* or *S. alatum* (syn. *S. capense*, see Nayar and Mehra 1970: 28), a wild species found in savannas of Africa, has now been reported at Predynastic Naqada (Emery-Barbier 1990: 324). On this species, see Bruce (1953: 17). Similarly, seeds from Predynastic graves excavated by Petrie at Naqada were identified by Thiselton Dyer at Kew as *Sesamum indicum* (Petrie 1896: 54), but no mention was made in Petrie's publication about the state of preservation of the seeds and unfortunately their present whereabouts are unknown. This evidence would be of much earlier date than expected, but as Petrie failed to record from which grave(s) the seeds were taken, it is impossible to rule out later contamination.

Other botanical remains of sesame seeds from Egypt are extremely rare and have not helped resolve questions concerning cultivation. Empty capsules of sesame were found in a grave at Dra Abu el-Naga which had been used as a granary at a later undetermined date, probably in the Greco–Roman period (Keimer 1924: 19). Seeds were found inside storage jars at Deir el-Medina (Bruyère 1937: 109), but the dating again is unclear (Germer 1985: 172). Particularly problematic was the identification of sesame seeds in the tomb of Tutankhamun, examined originally by Boodle at Kew (Germer 1989: 41; Hepper 1990: 27; de Vartavan 1990: 476, table 1; 478, table 2; 486, table 5). Germer mentioned that the samples were described as having no preserved internal structure, but an external form similar to *Sesamum* (Germer 1989: 41). Part of a seed capsule of sesame was found in a Ptolemaic deposit at el-Hiba (Wetterstrom 1984: 57). A single sesame seed was found at Elephantine, dated only to the first millennium BC (Willerding and Wolf 1990: 266). Sesame seeds found at Qasr Ibrim in Nubia are later still, dated to AD 300–500 (Rowley-Conwy 1989: 135). Even if these identifications are accepted as correct, this in itself would not establish that the plant was cultivated in Egypt at that time. Thus, existing archaeobotanical remains from Egypt again seem to point to later cultivation there.

In the Near East and Egypt today, sesame is a summer crop, commonly sown by broadcast in June to mid-July in irrigated areas (Foaden and Fletcher 1910: 496). Such a planting schedule would have been difficult in the Nile valley during Pharaonic times due to the seasonal flooding. Taking *σήσαμον* as sesame, Sandy suggested that, in Ptolemaic times, this may pertain in particular to the Fayum area, where separate spring and fall plantings could be undertaken because 'parts of the Fayum were not subject to the annual flood and . . . perennial irrigation was possible' (Sandy 1989: 64). However, during that period, 'sesame cultivation was principally carried out in the Delta' (Sandy 1989: 65). It has also been noted that sesame oil had become comparatively uncommon in the Roman period (Gallant 1985: 153–4). With so little archaeobotanical evidence for sesame in ancient Egypt, secure agricultural details are difficult to establish.

The sesame plant is an annual of about one and a half metres in height. Fine hairs cover much of the plant and give the stem and leaves a furry appearance. The stem is erect, with multiple branches and the flowers form individually at the axils, the join between the stem and the branches (see Fig. 17.6). The flowers are tubular (2–3.5 cm long) in shape, also furry, and are white or pink in colour. Fifty to one hundred seeds are contained in the subsequently formed capsule which is rectangular with a pointed tip (Salunkhe *et al.* 1992: 372). Harvesting by cutting the plant occurs in October or early November when the leaves have dropped off, but before the capsules split and release the seeds. In modern Sudan, either the entire plant is cut at the base below the branches or each branch is cut to a uniform length (Bedigian and Harlan 1983: 388). The stalks are bundled and left to dry, and then shaken or lightly beaten.

The seeds are well-known for their culinary usages as well as for their oil. They are flattened and oval in shape, but somewhat thinner at the hilum. They are 2.5–3 mm in length and about 1.5 mm wide. The oil content ranges from 37 to 63 per cent (Salunkhe *et al.* 1992: 373; Eckey 1954: 754–6). Colour can also vary from pale cream to dark brown or red, but the oil content appears to be higher for the lighter coloured seeds (Salunkhe *et al.* 1992: 373).

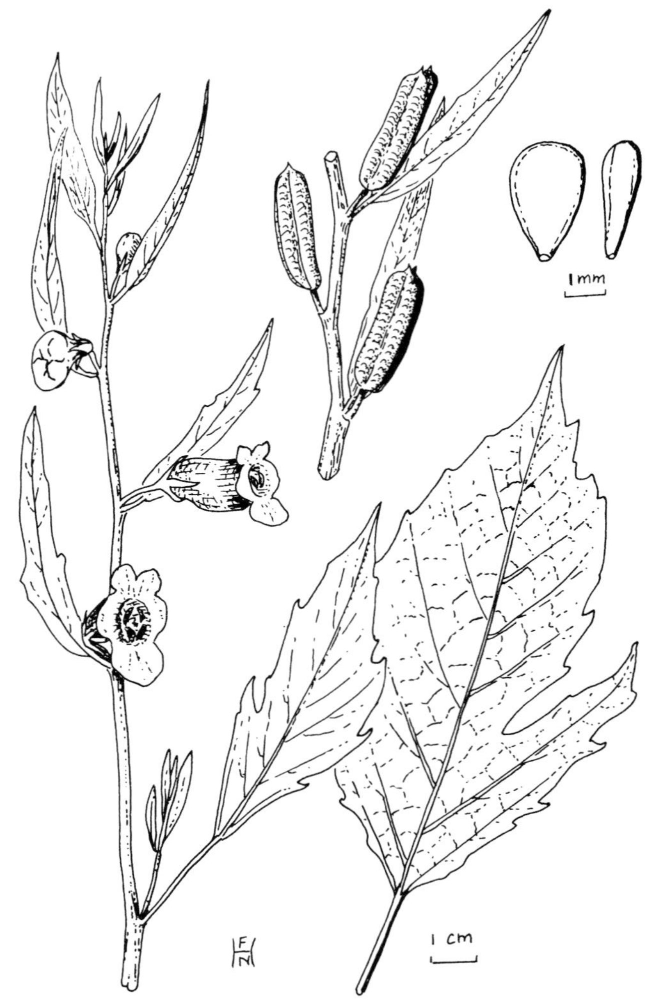

*Figure 17.6 Sesame (*Sesamum indicum *L.).*

*Olive (*Olea europaea *L.)*
Family: Oleaceae

Much has been written on the exploitation of olives in antiquity, particularly regarding their cultivation, distribution and importance as an oil source. In modern Egypt, olive trees will grow under irrigation and they are still the most important crop in the Siwa Oasis (Sears 1994: 4–5; Hepper 1990: 16). However, environmental conditions in Egypt are not conducive to olive production. As a result, the date for the inception of oleoculture in Egypt is unclear. A New Kingdom introduction has been proposed (Meeks 1993: 4–5; Keimer 1924: 29–30) and certainly remains of olive stones become more common on archaeological sites in Egypt from that time, including recent finds at Amarna

(Renfrew 1985: 188). The use of olive leaves in the floral garlands placed on Tutankhamun's coffins led Hepper (1991: 16) to speculate that they 'must have been cultivated locally.' Notably, stones of Middle Kingdom date have been identified at Memphis by Mary-Anne Murray (see Chapter 24, this volume; Giddy and Jeffreys 1991: 5), but whether these were the result of local cultivation is unknown. Transport of raw products certainly took place in antiquity, as the discovery of olives and olive stones among the archaeobotanical remains on the Late Bronze Age shipwreck at Ulu Burun off the coast of southern Turkey attest (Haldane 1993: 352).

To a large extent, the suggested New Kingdom date for cultivation continues to be based on linguistic evidence which is still open to debate (Meeks 1993: 5–6, 8). Some would argue that the product *b3ḳ*, found in texts from Middle Kingdom times, was olive oil; others that it was moringa oil (Loret 1886: 101–6; Keimer 1984: 27; Stager 1985: 174–5; Koura 1995: 82; Baum 1988: 129–30). However, at this point, it is still difficult to accept one translation over the other unreservedly. Yet both identifications have been accepted into the literature (Zohary and Hopf 1994: 142; Manniche 1989: 122; Hepper 1992: 150; Germer 1985: 58; Faulkner 1962: 78).

Although the impetus for the cultivation of olive may have derived from its use as a food stuff (see Chapter 24, this volume), the extraction of oil would also have been of importance. Given the probable late date of introduction of olive into Egypt, it has been assumed that olive oil was one of Egypt's earliest imports. This implies production in excess of local demands and a good comprehension of its horticulture (Gophna and Liphschitz 1996: 147–51). However, it is worth remembering that oil could be extracted from both feral and cultivated varieties and oil production may have originated with wild olives. It is also possible that the olives used for oil were of different varieties from those which were eaten (Zohary and Hopf 1994: 137). Hundreds of varieties of olives are found throughout the Mediterranean (Zohary and Hopf 1993: 137). Wild *oleaster* forms, known as *Olea europaea* L. ssp. *oleaster* (Hoffm. and Link) Hegi or *Olea europaea* var. *sylvestris* (Mill.) Lehr = var. *oleaster* (Hoffm. and Link) DC, often have smaller fruits and more spinescent young branches than cultivated varieties (var. *europaea*) (Zohary and Hopf 1993: 138). In modern Palestine, the wild olive prefers maquis environments and is distributed in Upper Galilee, Golan, Gilead and Ammon (Feinbrun-Dothan 1978: 15). According to Hepper (1992: 104), the hilly region of Samaria and the Shephelah 'is excellent for olives, but Judaea around Hebron rises too high for successful cultivation.' In general, they prefer altitudes of 300–1200 metres and often occur near the shores of the Mediterranean (Godin and Spensley 1971: 98; Cherfas 1994: 29).

Finds of wild olive wood in the Near East date back to Palaeolithic times with remains of olive stones becoming more prevalent from the Chalcolithic period (Liphschitz *et al.* 1991: table 2; Liphschitz *et al.* 1996: 141). However, as the stones of the wild forms can be of similar size to the cultivars, it can be impossible to distinguish between the two, particularly for early archaeological remains (Zohary and Hopf 1993: 138, 141; Feinbrun-Dothan 1978: 15; Liphschitz *et al.* 1991: 444). Nonetheless, finds of ancient olive stones and wood at Chalcolithic (3700–3500 BC) Teleilat Ghassul north of the Dead Sea, have been interpreted as confirmation of its cultivation, as this location is believed to be 'far outside the natural range of olives' (Zohary and Hopf 1993: 141; for other early remains, see also Stager 1985: 188, table I; Liphschitz 1996: 11–14 and Liphschitz *et al.* 1991: table 2). Although this view was further supported by the discovery of olive wood and stones in the upper Jordan Valley (Neef 1990: 300–1), it has been proposed that these could represent wild olives which had been transported to the site (Liphschitz *et al.* 1991: 444, 446). An alternative date for the introduction of oleoculture, based on combined study of wood remains, pollen and olive stones, has been placed in the Early Bronze Age I period (Liphschitz *et al.* 1991: 450–1).

It should be noted as well that olive stones have been found from Neolithic times in Greece and the Early Minoan period on Crete (Runnels and Hanson 1986: 301–2; J. Renfrew 1972: 316–7; Blitzer 1993: 163–5) and the possibility of Aegean sources for olive oil imports to Egypt also deserves consideration. Cultivation may have begun there in the Early Bronze Age (C. Renfrew 1972: 285; Blitzer 1993: 172), but to some extent it is reasonable to question this assumption (Runnels and Hansen 1986: 306). In part, it was based on scientific analysis of jar contents undertaken in the early part of this century and their accuracy can now be challenged (see discussion of chemistry, p. 415). In addition, wild and cultivated olives have been identified in deposits as early as the Neolithic and Chalcolithic periods on Cyprus, but their history there is not clear (Meikle 1985: 1095–6; Zohary and Hopf 1993: 141; for a summary, see Hadjisavvas 1992: 3).

The horticulture of olives is quite complex (see Chapter 24, this volume). Under cultivation, propagation is often by planting the knobs formed at the base of the trunk which root easily when removed and planted (Zohary and Hopf 1993: 138). Other means include cuttings and grafting, although the latter practice appears not to have been developed until Classical times at the earliest (Zohary and Hopf 1993: 135, 138). If grown from seed, it is usually planted in August or September, but the seeds have low germination and are prone to slow growth (Brousse 1989: 467). According to Brousse (1989: 467) 'At least two additional years will be required to develop a tree from seed as compared to cuttings.' There is some indication that propagation by seed is unreliable as the seed often reverts to the wild oleaster type which is less fleshy and has a lower oil content (Zohary and Hopf 1993: 138). However, spontaneous growth of seed from cultivated trees 'doubtless accompanied olive growing from its very start' (Zohary and Hopf 1993: 138).

Olive trees can reach heights of fifteen to twenty metres, but are usually pruned to only four to five metres (Godin and Spensley 1971: 97). The evergreen, oval leaves are leathery with a silvery underside and fine hairs on the upper surface (Meikle 1977: 1095; Greiss 1957: 102). The wood is hard and close-grained, and is not only suitable for woodworking but is termite resistant (Miller 1988: 216; see also Chapter 15, this volume). Fragrant white flowers appear in May and June and form in short panicles at the axil of the leaves on the previous year's shoots (Cherfas 1994: 29; Miller 1988: 216; Brousse 1989: 465–6). A warm, dry climate with an average temperature of 18 °C is necessary during flowering, although trees can tolerate temperatures reaching 40 °C (Godin and Spensley 1971: 97). Godin and Spensley (1971: 97) reported that to successfully produce fruit, the trees must spend about two months at temperatures of around 10 °C, but Cherfas (1994: 29) noted that in order to flower, they must be chilled for some time below about 7 °C. Temperatures below 2 °C will damage the fruit and below −9 °C will damage the tree (Charles 1985: 50).

The ovoid fruit, or drupe, is fleshy, with a hard woody stone encasing a single seed. Immature fruit is dark green in colour, turning yellow, then dark purple and finally black when fully ripe in late summer/autumn (Cherfas 1994: 29; Charles 1985: 46). Olives used for culinary purposes are usually harvested in late September, while those intended for oil are apparently not collected until February of the following year 'when oil content is maximum' (Brousse 1989: 466). Harvesting is by hand-picking or shaking (Hepper 1992: 107). The use of wooden poles to beat the trees is discouraged as this can harm the fruit (Hepper 1992: 107).

Notably, the trees are quite slow-growing and take some time to begin to fruit. According to Zohary and Hopf (1993: 137), production generally starts five to six years after planting, but Sandy (1989: 73) noted that the trees take ten years to fruit, and Godin and Spensley (1971: 99; also Sandy 1989: 73) stated that some trees may take as long as fifteen to twenty years. However, once established, they can bear fruit for decades or even hundreds of years (Zohary 1995: 379). Unlike the other common oil sources, olive oil is obtained by pressing the fruit flesh and not the seed or kernels. It has been reported that the fruit has an oil content of 15–35 per cent (Brousse 1989: 473), but that of the wild oleaster olive is generally lower (Zohary 1995: 380). Fortunately, the bitter component oleuropein, found in the flesh, is not present in the oil (Cherfas 1994: 27).

In the Near East, evidence for olive oil production begins at an early date. Possible remains of crushing basins, dated to the Chalcolithic period, have been found in the Golan Heights in Israel (Epstein 1993: 135–8). At Chalcolithic Tell Abu Hamid and Tell esh-Shuna in the Jordan Valley, quantities of crushed stones (*jift*) have been found, possibly the result of olive oil manufacture (Neef 1990: 298). Large vats and mortars believed to be evidence of olive oil pressing installations have been identified at a number of Early Bronze Age sites (see Stager 1985: 176–7 and Eitam 1993b: 99 for summaries). At EBA Beth Yerah (Khirbet Kerak), the presence of combed decoration on the vats and on associated storage jars led to speculation that contemporary imported combed vessels found in Egypt also contained olive oil (Esse 1991: 33, 123–4; Stager 1985: 176–7) but this has yet to be confirmed by scientific analysis (Serpico and White 1996: 135).

The method of pressing in the Chalcolithic period appears to have been quite simple. The olives were first crushed in a stone basin (usually basalt) with an upcurving rim. The mash was then deposited into a basket and transferred to a large vat with a flat surface and a deep central depression. A heavy stone weight could be placed on the basket, forcing the oil out through the weave and down into the collecting hollow (Epstein 1993: 137; Eitam 1993a: 77; Frankel 1994: 28–31). This method of extraction evidently continued in Palestine until the introduction of the lever or beam press, which came into use during the Iron Age, perhaps as early as the tenth to ninth centuries BC (Stager and Wolff 1981: 96; Eitam 1979: 153; Frankel 1994: 35–40). However, there is some evidence to suggest that a form of this new press was used during the Late Bronze Age at Ugarit in Syria (Callot 1987: 204–8, 1994: 191–6). With this method, additional pressure was brought to bear by a heavy wooden beam. The basket of pulp was placed onto a basin with a circular depression as described above, and a flat stone was then positioned on top of the basket. One end of a long wooden beam was inserted into a niche 'chiselled out of the vertical rockface' positioned horizontally just above the basket (Eitam 1979: 148–9). Stone weights were hung from the beam forcing it down onto the basket with increased pressure like a lever. The oil would collect in the basin, with the sediment trapped in the depression below. Alternatively, the oil could be channelled off into a lower-level collecting basin. The quantities of oil produced by beam press could be quite high and it has been estimated that the oil installations at the site of Ekron in Israel, dating to the seventh century BC, could produce at least 230 tons annually, sufficient to make it a significant exporter of oil (Eitam 1993b: 96; 1996:183; Gitin 1990: 40).

After the Iron Age, further advances in technology followed. In Palestine during the Hellenistic period, a new system of crushing olives evolved which was a precursor of the later *trapetum* and *mola olearia* (Kloner and Sagiv 1993: 121–5; Frankel 1993b: 477–80). Similarly, the more efficient screw weight was developed (Frankel 1993a: 115–16). Mattingly (1988: 37) calculated production in Roman Libya based on a sixty- to ninety-day pressing season. He estimated that the average productive tree would bear an annual yield of 20–100 kilograms of olives per productive tree and, given an oil content of 15–25 per cent, an oil yield of between three and twenty-five kilograms per tree, or 3.36–28 litres.

Although lexicographical problems exist, Classical texts do mention olive cultivation and oil production in Egypt, albeit on a more limited scale than elsewhere in the Mediterranean (Sandy 1989: 19–24). Much of this information follows current practice, indicating an extensive knowledge of the horticulture of olives. Numerous varieties were recognised at the time, and there is some evidence that they were propagated from shoots, planted in January/February and harvested in early October. It was also observed that the fruits would form only on the previous year's growth (Sandy 1989: 76; 80). The Fayum and Memphis were evidently the favoured areas for cultivation, yet the trees were said to grow in other districts, notably Thebes (Sandy 1989: 76–7, 80). In Roman times, the use of olive oil was very common, but apparently less so in the Ptolemaic period and Sandy (1989: 82) commented that 'No Demotic evidence exists for olive oil'.

*Almond (*Prunus dulcis *(Miller) D.A. Webb* = P. amygdalus *Batsch* = Amygdalus communis *L.)*
Family: Rosaceae
Thus far, the earliest finds of almond in Egypt come from the Workmen's Village at Amarna (Renfrew 1985: 189) and from the tomb of Tutankhamun (KV62). A small piece of wood identified by Boodle at Kew as almond was used for an arrow in the tomb (Hepper 1991: 44), as well as around thirty stones and a few entire fruits found in pottery jars (Hepper 1991: 62; Germer 1989: 38). Although often cultivated in Palestine, its indigeneity there is still uncertain (Zohary 1987: 21; Hopf 1983: 589). It grows wild in the Mediterranean (Hepper 1992: 120) and Keimer (1984: 25) proposed that almond could have been introduced into Palestine from Greece. Today in Palestine, the tree flourishes in *maquis* areas, particularly in upper and lower Galilee, Mount Carmel and the Judaean Mountains (Zohary 1987: 21). Archaeobotanical evidence suggests that it was present in Syria and Palestine by Neolithic times (Hopf 1983: 589; Willcox 1996: 149; van Zeist and Bakker-Heeres 1982: *passim*; 1984: 155–7). It was probably cultivated by the Early Bronze Age, but it can be difficult to distinguish between the wild and cultivated forms, and oil could certainly have been manufactured from both (Zohary and Hopf 1993: 176).

The almond may have subsequently reached Egypt from Palestine but, according to Hepper (1991: 62), it was unlikely to have been extensively cultivated in Egypt. In modern times, it grows with difficulty and only in gardens in northern Egypt (Keimer 1984: 25: Lucas 1962: 329). However, a useful reminder of the fact that botanical remains may have been transported over considerable distances is offered by the discovery of almond kernels on the Late Bronze Age shipwreck at Ulu Burun off the southwest coast of Turkey (Haldane 1993: 352).

The almond tree was probably grown from seed in Pharaonic times (Zohary and Hopf 1993: 174). When mature, it is multibranched and tends to spread sideways reaching a height of three to eight metres (Hepper 1987: 55; Zohary 1987: 21). Clusters of large white or pale pink flowers (see Fig.15.10, this volume) appear early in the year (February/March) before the appearance of the leaves (Hepper 1991: 62; 1987: 55; Zohary 1987: 21). The fruit resembles a small peach and is covered with fine hairs (Hepper 1992: 121; Zohary 1987: 21). According to Eckey (1954: 456), the fruit is not edible, but Hepper (1991: 62) stated that, although it can be eaten, it is usually allowed to mature so that the kernels, which are also edible, can fully ripen. The hard, yellowish, pitted stone (approximately 2 × 1.5 cm) contains a single flattened brown kernel (Zohary 1987: 21). Harvesting of the fruits could be carried out by hand-picking or by knocking them down from the tree (Eckey 1954: 456). The stones within the fruits split when dry, making the kernels fairly easy to obtain (Zohary 1987: 21).

Almonds can be grouped roughly into two types, bitter and sweet, based on the respective presence or absence of the glucoside amygdalin in the kernel. The bitterness is due to the hydrocyanic acid produced through the hydrolysis of the amygdalin (Salunkhe *et al.* 1992: 492) by crushing, chewing 'or any other injury' (Zohary and Hopf 1993: 174). Ingestion of 'a few dozen bitter seeds' can be fatal (Zohary and Hopf 1993: 174–5). Oil can be obtained from either sweet or bitter types, but the product known today as 'bitter almond oil' is obtained by distillation (Salunkhe *et al.* 1992: 492), a practice probably not known in Egypt until Classical times (see Chapter 18, this volume). It has been suggested that, because kernels of sweet almonds may have been prized as a food source, the oil may have been extracted from bitter almonds (Salunkhe *et al.* 1992: 492; Hepper 1987: 55; Eckey 1954: 456). As some 75 per cent or more of the seeds from the sweet fruit will produce trees bearing sweet almonds, it is possible that cultivation centred on those trees, with bitter-kerneled fruit trees 'rogued out, a practice still current in some environments' (Spiegel-Roy 1986: 206; Zohary and Hopf 1993: 174). Kernels from sweet almonds have a higher oil content (50–60 per cent) than those from bitter almonds (40–55 per cent, but sometimes as low as 20 per cent) (Eckey 1954: 457). The extracted oil is colourless to pale yellow (Salunkhe *et al.* 1992: 492).

*Radish (*Raphanus sativus *L.)*
Family: Cruciferae
Lucas (1962: 335–6) cited radish as an oil source based on comments by Pliny (XV: 7; XIX: 26; see Rackham 1968) regarding the crop *ῥαφανος*. However, while this was considered one of the most common oil crops in Roman Egypt,

references to the oil in Ptolemaic texts are virtually absent (Sandy 1989: 6, nn. 22, 24; 53). There has also been a suggestion that radish seed has a low oil content and was therefore unlikely to have been a common source of vegetable oil (Keimer 1984: 29). Following on from this, it was proposed that Pliny must have confused another cruciferous oil crop with radish, possibly turnip (*Brassica rapa* L. = *B. campestris* L.) or mustard (*Sinapis alba* L., *Brassica nigra* (L.) Koch, and *B. juncea* (L.) Czern.) (Keimer 1984: 29; Zohary and Hopf 1993: 132).

All of these plants, including radish, have wild progenitors found across western Asia and Europe which may have been exploited for oil, and cultivated forms of both are well-known for their oilseed (Zohary and Hopf 1993: 132; Charles 1985: 61, table 5). In addition, the root vegetable swede or rutabaga (*Brassica napus* L.) is also grown today for its oily seeds. Rape (*B. napus* ssp. *oleifera*) is the oilseed crop related to swede, and turnip rape is a form of turnip, specifically *B. rapa* spp. *oleifera* (Salunkhe *et al.* 1992: 61; McNaughton 1995a: 68, 1995b: 63).

The similar appearance and small size of the seeds of these oil plants (only about 0.1 cm) can make it difficult to distinguish between them, particularly in archaeological samples (Zohary and Hopf 1993: 132; Charles 1985: 47; van Zeist 1985: 37). Perhaps as a result of this, there is a dearth of archaeological evidence for the presence of any of these plants in Pharaonic Egypt, with the exception of radish of uncertain date and a root of *B. rapa* dated to the Roman period (Germer 1985: 50–1, 55–6; van Zeist 1985: 37; see also Chapter 24, this volume). Seeds described as *Brassica* spp. were found in the tomb of Tutankhamun, but more specific identification was not possible (de Vartavan 1990: 478, table 2). Although charred seeds identified as *Brassica* sp. or *Sinapis* sp. were found at Khafājeh in Mesopotamia (*c.* 3000 BC) and it was speculated that they could have produced an oil used in lamps (Delougaz 1940: 154; Bedigian and Harlan 1986: 139–40), there are many species in these genera and this usage cannot be confirmed. Thus, the theory that they were cultivated in the eastern Mediterranean prior to the Greco–Roman period has been founded primarily on ambiguous linguistic grounds (Zohary and Hopf 1993: 132).

Modern corroborative evidence for the exploitation of these plants for oil production in Egypt is sparse. Manniche (1989: 141) stated specifically that radish oil is used by the Copts in Egypt today both in cooking and anointing. However, this does not seem to be supported by Foaden and Fletcher (1910: 538, 540), who make no mention of the cultivation of radish or turnip as oil crops in Egypt.

When grown as vegetables, the seeds of radish and turnip are sown or broadcast from September to late December (see Chapter 24, this volume). Two types of turnip grow in Egypt today, and these are ready for harvest two to two and a half months after planting. The common red radish ripens in about one month, while the *baladi* white radish can take two months to mature (Foaden and Fletcher 1910: 538, 540). Both white and black mustard occur in Egypt today, as winter weeds in fields (Boulos and El-Hadidi 1994: 100; Täckholm 1974: 192).

Confusion of oleiferous species in antiquity still deserves consideration, but the oil content of radish (30–50 per cent) is certainly comparable to many other oilseeds (Eckey 1954: 446). That of rapeseed falls into the same range (33.2–47.6 per cent) (Salunkhe *et al.* 1992: 61). All of these plants furnish edible oils when cold pressed. Less palatable are the hot pressed oils (Eckey 1954: 433).

Tiger nut or chufa (Cyperus esculentus *L.*)
Family: Cyperaceae

Another possibly early source of oil is the tuber from the sedge plant, *Cyperus esculentus*. Rhizomes of this plant were clearly used as food since Predynastic times, although their oleagenous property has also been noted (Germer 1985: 245; for a list of finds and details of dietary importance, see Chapter 24, this volume).

The plant itself is an upright perennial, ranging in height from ten to forty centimetres, with a grass-like appearance. The leaves which form at the base are long, narrow and shiny, and the flowers, which are rare in cultivated plants, are yellow or yellow-brown spikelets, usually about 1 to 1.5 cm long, (FAO 1988: 239; Täckholm and Drar 1950: 61; Negbi 1992: 69). The small yellow or light brown tubers formed on the roots have characteristic transverse rings and are generally 1.5 to 2.5 cm in length (Zohary and Hopf 1993: 186; Täckholm and Drar 1950: 61, 65; see also Fig. 24.9, this volume).

Although this plant has been cultivated in the Delta in modern times (Täckholm and Drar 1950: 67), it occurs in a wild state at various locations in Egypt, often along river banks (FAO 1988: 241; Keimer 1984: 69). It is part of the Mediterranean flora and is also found throughout tropical Africa to the Zambezi (Keimer 1984: 69; Täckholm and Drar 1950: 61). However, Zohary and Hopf (1993: 186) noted that the nuts seem to have been used exclusively in Egypt as there is a lack of 'contemporary records of this tuber-bearing sedge from other parts of the Old World.' In the Delta, it is cultivated by planting the tubers from March to mid-May (Täckholm and Drar 1950: 68). The resulting crop is then harvested four to five months later, when the plants are dug up by spades and beaten by sticks to separate the small yellow-brown tubers (Täckholm and Drar 1950: 68). Most of these lie in the top 15 cm of the soil, rarely at depths below 23 cm (FAO 1988: 242).

The oil content of the tubers is about 20–36 per cent of their dry weight and the tubers can keep for a long time if properly dried (FAO 1988: 240; Eckey 1954: 298). According to Täckholm and Drar (1950: 68), the oil produced from the rhizomes is similar to olive, and has been used in soap manufacture and as a lubricant for watches 'and other fine apparatus'. Like olive, it is not prone to rancidity and has been used to retard the oxidation of other oils (Täckholm and Drar 1950: 68; Eckey 1954: 298). In addition to their uses as food and as an oil source, the tubers may have been utilised in perfume manufacture (Negbi 1992: 67; see also Chapter 18, this volume).

*Colocynth (*Citrullus colocynthus *(L.) Schrad.)*
Family: Cucurbitaceae
Colocynth, which grows wild in the desert of Egypt (Lucas 1962: 332), may have been the progenitor of the watermelon, *Citrullus lanatus* (Zohary and Hopf 1993: 182; Hepper 1991: 56; see also Chapter 24, this volume). Few finds of colocynth have been attested in ancient Egypt, but these include seeds found at Neolithic Armant (Lityńska 1993: 353) and at the Predynastic sites of Naqada (Wetterstrom 1996: 68; Zohary and Hopf 1993: 182) and el-Omari (Barakat 1990: 113). The colocynth also grows wild in Palestine (Feinbrun-Dothan 1978: 275) but evidence for its early exploitation there is scant. Zohary and Hopf (1993: 182) referred to seeds found in the Pre-Pottery Neolithic cave at Nahal Hemar in Israel, but these are in fact from a mixed deposit of later date (Kislev 1988: 76).

Colocynth is a creeping perennial herb, with trailing branches (Täckholm 1974: 374). The lobed leaves are rigid, triangular-ovate in shape, with a pale green colour above, and grey undersides which are covered with hairs (Feinbrun-Dothan 1978: 275; see also Fig. 17.7). They range in size from 1.5 to 11 cm in length and from 1.4 to 6.5 cm in width (Jeffrey 1977: 676). Single, pale yellow flowers form from May to August (Chakravarty and Jeffrey 1980: 194; Jeffrey 1977: 676; Feinbrun-Dothan 1978: 275). The extremely bitter fruits or gourds measure 5 to 8 cm in diameter, with a spongy white pulp (Zohary and Hopf 1993: 182; Feinbrun-Dothan 1978: 275). They are dark green, sometimes mottled or striped, and turn yellow as they ripen

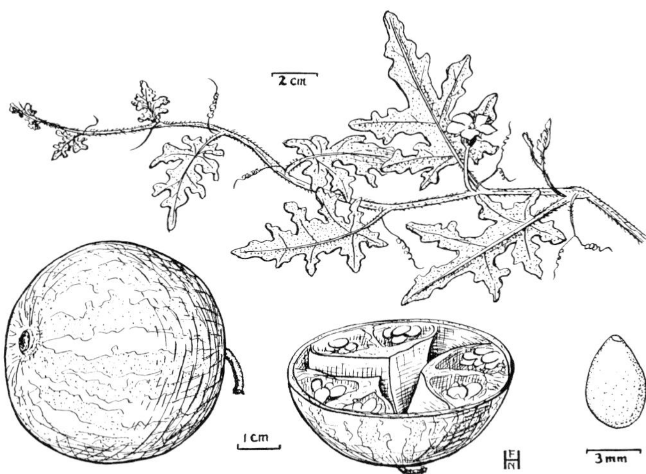

*Figure 17.7 Colocynth (*Citrullus colocynthus *(L.) Schrad.).*

(Täckholm 1974: 374; Hepper 1991: 56; Feinbrun-Dothan 1978: 275). When mature, the gourd becomes partially hollow, thus loosening the seeds (Chakravarty and Jeffrey 1980: 194). Both the seeds and the pulp are violent purgatives (Chakravarty and Jeffrey 1980: 196; Feinbrun-Dothan 1978: 275; Zohary and Hopf 1993: 182), but the seeds can be eaten after soaking in water or boiling (Osborn 1968: 167).

The glossy brown seeds are obovate, about 6.5–10 mm long, 3.5–5 mm wide and 1.5–2.5 mm thick (Jeffrey 1977: 677; Chakravarty and Jeffrey 1980: 194). Measured ancient examples from the site of el-Omari were somewhat smaller (Barakat 1990: 113). Modern seeds have an oil content of 13–20 per cent (Eckey 1954: 766; Vaughan 1970: 63), but the golden yellow oil is rarely in use (Lucas 1962: 332; Vaughan 1970: 63). Chakravarty and Jeffrey (1980: 196) stated that in modern times the seeds are of no commercial value. Osborn (1968: 167), who discussed the uses of colocynth in Egypt, mentioned the use of a tar extracted from the seeds as a treatment for mange and for tanning skins, but made no reference to its use as an oil source.

According to documentary sources, the plant *κολόκυντος* was grown in Egypt in Ptolemaic times as a source of oil, and this may be a reference to colocynth, although potential confusion with other gourds cannot be eliminated (Sandy 1989: 4, n. 14). Agricultural information on its cultivation is absent, and this oil is not otherwise mentioned in any other sources (Sandy 1989: 4–5).

*Lettuce (*Lactuca sativa *L. and* Lactuca serriola *L.)*
Family: Compositae
Finds of lettuce seeds have been extremely rare and of questionable date (see Chapter 24, this volume), but it has been maintained – on the basis of tomb reliefs – that this plant was grown in Egypt at least since Old Kingdom times. In addition to the traditional use of cos lettuce (*Lactuca sativa*) as an edible vegetable, the seeds from this and another species, *Lactuca serriola* could have been exploited as a source of oil (Boulos and el-Hadidi (1994: 72).

The relationship between *L. sativa* and *L. serriola* has been the subject of some debate. According to Zohary and Hopf (1993: 186), *L. serriola*, which occurs throughout the Mediterranean, is the 'closest wild relative' of *L. sativa*. However, Ryder and Whitaker (1995: 54) reviewed the evidence and concluded that 'the origin of cultivated lettuce is uncertain, and critical tests to resolve the problem have not been devised'. While it may be tempting to consider *L. serriola* simply as the wild form of the cultivated lettuce, *L. sativa*, the taxonomy of the two remains somewhat abstruse and it is evident that there are gradations in the extent to which they have been brought into cultivation. For example, in modern Egypt, *L. serriola* is found growing freely along roadsides and waste ground (Boulos and el-Hadidi 1994: 72), although Knowles (1967: 162) observed that it was deliberately planted in Upper Egypt 'in much the same manner as safflower', with its oil used for culinary purposes. Foaden and Fletcher (1910: 562), noted that in addition to *Lactuca sativa*, a prickly lettuce (*Lactuca scariola* var. *sativa*) was grown in Egypt, and another form of this, *Lactuca scariola oleifera*, was cultivated in Upper Egypt for its oleagenous seeds. As *L. scariola* L. can be considered synomymous with *L. serriola* L. (Feinbrun-Dothan 1978: 436; Boulos and el-Hadidi 1994: 72), these may be grouped with the latter. Alternatively, Lindqvist (1960: 338) suggested that *L. scariola* f. *oleifera* Lam., found in Upper Egypt and the Sudan, could be one of the semi-wild forms of *L. sativa*, which were 'encouraged, rather than cultivated, for the purpose of extracting oil from the seeds or as fodder for animals'.

Along these lines, el-Hadidi (1992: 323–4) made a distinction between *Lactuca serriola*, a summer weed in Egypt, and a species he named *Lactuca sativa* L. subsp. *minii* Hadidi, subsp. *nov* which occurs as a winter weed in the Sohag and Qena provinces. The latter has smaller, thicker, dark green leaves and larger achenes than the usual cultivated lettuce. Seed morphology also differs. The leaves of the wild species were said to have been collected locally and eaten as a salad, while the mature seeds are harvested as a source of oil 'reputed to promote high fertility in men' (el-Hadidi 1992: 324). He also drew attention to the similarities in appearance between this lettuce and the examples illustrated in connection with the god Min.

Clearly further research is necessary to clarify the taxonomy of the genus and to identify the source(s) of the oil, but the oleiferous forms do seem to belong to the *L. sativa/serriola* complex. In modern Egypt, cultivated *L. sativa* lettuce is sown by broadcast continually from mid September to November, and also again in late February (Foaden and Fletcher 1910: 562). It is grown first in a nursery bed and then transplanted thirty to thirty-five days later with the plants spaced 20 to 30 cm apart. Harvesting usually takes place forty-five to sixty days after transplanting (Foaden and Fletcher 1910: 563; for further information, see Chapter 24, this volume). In contrast, *Lactuca serriola* is an annual or biennial plant, generally reaching a height of between 30 and 80 cm, with a leafy stem. Leaf shapes vary and can be prickly, but are usually oblong, positioned vertically in the sunlight (Feinbrun-Dothan 1978: 437). Pale yellow flowers form in heads, alone or in clusters (Feinbrun-Dothan 1978: 437). The seeds are grey-brown ribbed achenes, about three millimetres in length with an elliptical shape and nearly white pappus (Feinbrun-Dothan 1978: 437; Boulos and El-Hadidi 1994: 72). *Lactuca scariola* can be planted much like *L. sativa*, but takes longer to mature and is not harvested until two and a half to three months after transplanting (Foaden and Fletcher 1910: 563). The oil content of *Lactuca scariola oleifera* seeds was reportedly 35–8 per cent (Eckey 1954: 785; Foaden and Fletcher 1910: 562).

*Poppy (*Papaver somniferum *L.)*
Family: Papaveraceae

This species is better known as the opium poppy, but in addition to the narcotic, the plant is also cultivated for its seeds. These are used for culinary purposes and as a source of oil. Zohary and Hopf (1993: 128) distinguished two cultivars, subsp. *somniferum* Corb., the source of the opium, and subsp. *hortensis* (Hussenot) Corb., that of the oil. The wild progenitor of *Papaver somniferum* is *P. setigiterum* DC, which has a distribution in the western Mediterranean, only as far east as Italy (van Zeist 1985: 37; Zohary and Hopf 1993: 129, map 14). Cultivated plants have larger capsules and are non-dehiscent (Zohary and Hopf 1993: 128). As an annual, the opium poppy grows quite quickly and can reach heights of about one metre, with an erect stem and serrated leaves (Hepper 1992: 152, Wilkinson 1843: 461). Also related is *Papaver rhoeas* L., the corn or field poppy, whose seeds were used for medicinal purposes but do not appear to have been pressed for oil (Renfrew 1973: 177–8). Corn poppy seeds can be distinguished from those of the opium poppy as they are smaller than the latter (Renfrew 1973: 177). Flower colour also differs. Those of the corn poppy are often red or crimson but those of the opium poppy range from pinkish white to mauve, sometimes with darker patches at the base of the petals (Hepper 1992: 152).

Germer (1985: 44) reported identification of a corn poppy seed at Meidum dated to the Fourth Dynasty. Conversely, while finds of opium poppy seeds are common in Europe from Neolithic times and occur in Greece during the Bronze Age (Zohary and Hopf 1993: 130; Merlin 1984: 110–46), a date for its introduction to the Near East is uncertain and archaeobotanical remains have not yet been identified there (van Zeist 1985: 37). Evidence from Egypt is also controversial. A capsule of *Papaver somniferum* was found in a storage jar at Deir el-Medina (Bruyère 1937: 109). Although this might suggest a New Kingdom introduction, the date and identification of the find have been disputed (Germer 1982a: 190; Merlin 1984: 278, 280). Earlier claims of the presence of opium in a jar from the Eighteenth-Dynasty tomb of Kha at Deir el-Medina have also been shown to be unsubstantiated (TT8; Bisset *et al.* 1996b: 201). Some have argued for the use of opium by the New Kingdom on textual evidence but this is still under debate (Merlin 1984: 272–80).

Merrillees (1962: 289) proposed that trade in opium had reached Egypt by the Eighteenth Dynasty. He based his theory on the distinctive shape of Cypriot base ring ware pottery juglets introduced into Egypt at that time, which he believed resembled the head of a poppy. Studying artistic designs said to represent this poppy, and the diminishing occurrence of base ring ware juglets after the Amarna period, he made the controversial suggestion that the cultivation of *P. somniferum* in Egypt had begun by the reign of Amenhotep III, resulting in a reduction in the demand of the imported product (Merrillees 1962: 291; for a discussion, see Merlin 1984: 260–72, 278). These views have met with mixed acceptance (e.g. Germer 1981: 125–9; Hepper 1992: 152; Merlin 1984: 251–9) and scientific support has been limited (Bisset *et al.* 1996b). It has been reported that chemical analysis of two sherds from unprovenanced juglets of this type found traces of alkaloids characteristic of opium and also evidence of a vegetable oil (Evans 1989: 153–4). Unfortunately, the results were not discussed in detail. More recently, opium has again been identified in a vessel of this type using TLC, GC/MS and radioimmunoassay (Koschel 1996; Bisset *et al.* 1996a). These finds begin to raise hope that it may be possible to confirm a connection between the jars and their contents. However, Bisset *et al.* (1996a: 203–4) cautioned that the possibility of re-use cannot be excluded and that these few, unprovenanced jars do not establish that opium was used during the Eighteenth Dynasty in Egypt, nor could they as yet be 'looked upon in any way as a vindication of Merrillees' hypothesis concerning the origin and purpose of these juglets'.

Egypt was once apparently 'an important country in the world opium trade' (Veselovskaya 1976: 16), although it has clearly now lost its economic standing in this respect. The drug is obtained by slitting the outer surface of the unripe rounded capsules. The numerous seeds found inside the capsule can be white to yellow, grey, brown-red, blue or black, measure about one millimetre in size and contain about 40–55 per cent oil (Salunkhe *et al.* 1992: 455). The cold pressed oil is yellow, with a pleasant smell and taste and is good for culinary purposes. On the other hand, the hot extracted oil is dark yellow with an unpleasant odour and is more suited for industrial use (Veselovskaya 1976: 2). There is apparently no mention of the cultivation of poppy for oil in Ptolemaic times (Sandy 1989: 6).

*Malabathrum or cinnamon oil (*Cinnamomum verum *J. Presl*=Cinnamomum zeylanicum *Nees)*
Family: Lauraceae
Lucas (1962: 333) noted the possible importation of cinnamon leaves (*malabathrum*) from India in the Roman period for production into oil in Egypt. There is also an indication that in Classical times, there was confusion between cinnamon and cassia (*Cinnamomum cassia* Blume), which has a similar spicy fragrance and is indigenous to China (Hepper 1992: 138; Lucas 1962: 308). However, there is no secure evidence as yet for the large-scale importation of cinnamon-scented leaves from either India or China during the Pharaonic period (Hepper 1992: 138–9; Germer 1985: 14; see also Chapter 24, this volume). Instead, cinnamon-based products available to the ancient Egyptians may have derived from the East African camphor tree (*Ocotea usamarensis* Engl.; Lüchtrath 1988: 44–8; on this species, see Verdcourt 1996: 10–1). In any case, it is more plausible that the product obtained from the leaves was a volatile oil, manufactured by means of distillation and of a different chemical composition to the oils discussed here (see Chapter 18, this volume). Such a volatile oil is still produced today for use in perfumery (Arctander 1960: 167–8).

Discussion

From the overview above, it is clear that oil-producing sources of tubers, seeds and fruit would be available at different times of the year. Some were labour-intensive cultivated crops, grown annually and for the most part maturing in spring. Others may have required less dedicated attention. Nuts from trees such as balanos and moringa need not have been cultivated, while both cultivated and wild olives or almonds could have been collected for oil. Castor bushes can live for a number of years, making annual planting unnecessary, or wild castor may have been harvested for its seeds on an *ad hoc* basis. In addition, special care would have been required for the handling and storage of castor seeds because of their toxicity and allergic properties. With the exception of the olive, with its more delicate fruit, seed crops and tubers could have been stored for months without appreciable loss in oil content, if kept cool, dry and pest-free. Moringa and balanos fruits could have been stripped of their fruit, and the uncracked nuts set aside until required. The only restriction to bulk storage of raw materials may have been size, as the need for considerable space may have dictated priority in processing in some cases. These variables suggest that oil production could have taken place primarily twice a year as sources became available in spring and fall or could have been spread over much of the year. Unfortunately, our understanding of the seasonality of the oil industry remains restricted by the lack of secure information regarding the sources in use.

Oil extraction

Little is known concerning methods of oil manufacture in ancient Egypt. However, taking modern techniques of extraction as a guideline, it is clear that before pressing, some additional processing was necessary. Four preliminary stages (cleaning, dehulling, grinding and heating) are used today (Carr 1989: 231–4) and these were probably also employed anciently (Charles 1985: 51–2). Some of the stages discussed here (grinding, boiling, pressing) were also used in antiquity for the formulation of scented ointments using an oleagenous base. This overlap is apparent in the existing ancient Egyptian textual and artistic evidence, where it is often difficult to determine whether the information relates to oil or perfume processing (see Chapter 18, this volume). The steps outlined below follow the basic modern stages of oil production.

Cleaning
Foreign material and botanical débris which might cause contamination, such as twigs, leaves, other seeds, sand and dirt should be removed from the oilseeds, tubers or fruits.

This could have been done by hand-picking, sieving and/or winnowing (Head *et al.* 1995: 21).

Dehulling (decortication)

Many oilseeds, such as sesame, have an outer shell or thin seed coat which could have been removed by soaking in hot water, drying and then rubbing. Removal of these coats would facilitate pressing. This process is also mentioned in Classical texts (Gallant 1985: 154). In modern Egypt, the hulls of safflower seeds are removed by cracking the seed with stone rollers (Knowles 1967: 162).

Grinding or mashing

In ancient Egypt this was probably done with a mortar and pestle. Quantities of oilseeds, tubers or fruit would be crushed to produce a softer pulp, thereby releasing the oil and increasing the yield. In modern Sudan, sesame seeds are ground in a mortar and pestle, then placed on a stone, clay or gourd slab and kneaded by hand into a paste before extraction (Bedigian and Harlan 1983: 393).

Cooking or 'conditioning'

The mashed oleagenous pulp could then be mixed with water and cooked. Today, temperatures for this stage range from 80–105 °C (Carr 1989: 235). The length of time depends on factors such as the hardness of the seeds. In the absence of some type of press, cooking alone may have been used to extract oil. In this process, also known as the *hot water flotation method*, the ground seed is placed in water and boiled for at least thirty minutes, until the oil floats to the surface. The oil is then collected from the top with a shallow dish and heated to remove the excess water (Head *et al.* 1995: 22–3). This process was used in Syria as recently as the last century and also in 'the rural areas of many developing countries' (Head *et al.* 1995: 22; Amouretti 1986: 158). Moringa oil is extracted by bedouin in Egypt using this means (Osborn 1968: 173). In Ethiopia, castor oil prepared for medicinal purposes is heated in water to temperatures of 32–8 °C (Seegeler 1983: 232) and this flotation method is also still used in Uganda and Sudan for the extraction of sesame seed oil (Head *et al.* 1995: 56). Through laboratory experimentation, it was established that from half a kilogram of sesame seed, 108 ml of oil can be produced, giving an extraction efficiency of 41 per cent (Head *et al.* 1995: 56–7). However, the procedure is quite lengthy and the oil yield tends to be lower than by pressed methods (Head *et al.* 1995: 23). As a slight variation, Bedigian and Harlan (1983: 393) reported that, in the Nuba culture in Sudan, boiling water is simply poured over ground sesame paste and the oil skimmed off as it rises to the surface.

Cooking times may have been dictated by the availability of fuel sources. In some instances, and most economically, plant remains themselves (such as the stalks of sesame or castor plants once the seeds had been removed) could have been burned. Alternatively, cooking could have been eliminated altogether, with the mash then 'cold pressed'. Lucas (1962: 332) cited Classical texts which suggested that castor seed was prepared in this manner.

Little is known of the ancient Egyptian oil industry, but titles translated as 'the oil boiler' do occur (*ps sgnn*, *nwdw*). The presence of the hieroglyph for fire in some writings indicates that the process is associated with heating, but words for oil such as *sgnn*, *nwd* and even *mrḥt* can refer both to oils and to scented oil-based mixtures. Thus, these titles are ambiguous (see Chapter 18, this volume). It is also unclear whether and in which circumstances these terms extended to animal fats.

Pressing

Representations specifically showing the method of extracting oil in ancient Egypt are absent, but judging from scenes of perfume manufacture (see Chapter 18, this volume), it is known that the bag press was available and may well have been used for processing both oils and scented ointments.

In its simplest form, a cloth sack could be filled with ground seed, tuber or fruit pulp and hung so that the oil, termed free run oil, would flow out through the weave (Carr 1989: 229). More efficiently, as representations of perfume manufacture show, wooden poles could be inserted through loops at either ends of the bag and twisted by hand in opposite directions to increase the oil flow (see Chapter 18, this volume). A large pottery vessel could be placed beneath the bag to catch the oil as it was wrung out from the sack. This type of press might seem quite crude, but ethnographic studies and past commentaries by travellers in Italy and Turkey show that the exact same method, including the use of wooden poles, was still in use in those countries until the early twentieth century to extract olive oil (Amouretti 1986: 159; see Fig. 17.8). The first press was 'cold' using just the mashed fruit. After that, the paste was soaked or boiled in hot water and then wrung again. Notably, this method continued in use even after the introduction of more 'sophisticated' stone presses.

Figure 17.8 Nineteenth-century print showing oil being extracted by the process of wringing it out of a bag into a pottery vessel.

The sack press remained in use during the Pharaonic period but some variations did occur over time. Again based on scenes of perfume manufacture, it is known that by the Middle Kingdom, the ancient Egyptians had developed a more elaborate form of torsion press, set in a wooden framework (see Chapter 18, this volume). Further slight modifications in the attachment of the press to the framework appear to have taken place in the New Kingdom. It seems reasonable to assume that the use of these various presses extended to the processing of oils, although this cannot as yet be confirmed.

It is interesting that there is as yet no evidence that the methods of pressing in the Near East, namely by means of stone weights or the more advanced beam press, reached Egypt in Pharaonic times (see discussions of the olive, p. 400). It could be argued that the methods used in the eastern Mediterranean had evolved specifically around oleoculture and, as olives were probably not grown in Egypt until the New Kingdom, there was no incentive to transfer the technology. However, as it would seem equally feasible to process any mashed oilseeds or tubers by this method, this does not seem to be an entirely satisfactory explanation. Similarly, if the bag press had been recognised as superior, it is difficult to understand why that method was not adopted in the Near East.

Clarification of oil (filtering or refining)

Pressed oils will usually contain some solid debris which can be removed by settling or boiling. In the former, the fresh oil is left to stand for several days until the solids, termed the 'foots', settle to the bottom. The clear oil can then be poured or siphoned off (Head *et al.* 1995: 38). In the boiling method, the fresh oil is strongly heated in water in a proportion of 10 per cent by weight to the oil. As the water evaporates, the oil can be poured off, leaving the settlings at the bottom (Head *et al.* 1995: 38). In both methods, the 'foots' can be dredged off, placed in cloth and pressed to remove any residual oil or can be re-heated and then filtered through cloth (Carr 1989: 237; Head *et al.* 1995: 38). However, clarification is not always considered necessary as in some areas still using traditional oil extraction methods the flavour of the unrefined oils is preferred (Axtell and Fairman 1992: 6–7).

It would seem then, that the principal means of oil extraction available to the ancient Egyptians were boiling and/or pressing. Given the simplicity of these techniques, it is likely that production was undertaken both on a large industrial scale and on a smaller domestic level. More specific information on the degree of specialisation is unclear. Some processors may have focussed on one or two particular oils, some may have processed whatever sources were available. A number of factors also require consideration. Extraction of castor oil would have necessitated careful cleaning of equipment or a separate set of paraphenalia to avoid contamination with its potent toxin and allergen. Because olives bruise easily, their pressing season was probably restricted to a few weeks and it certainly would have been easier to import olive oil than to transport the olives themselves for pressing in Egypt. Access to fuel supplies may also have affected production.

Archaeological evidence for Pharaonic oil workshops has been lacking, perhaps partly because of the fact that much of the equipment used for oil processing is not exclusive to that process. The significance of pieces of cloth or bags and wooden poles might easily be missed, botanical remains may not be preserved, and some pressed cakes may have been used as animal feed. Large pottery vessels are unlikely to have survived intact. Mortars and pestles deserve closer scrutiny, but in the past, have most often been interpreted as evidence of bakeries. It should be remembered too, that it is only fairly recently that the remains of pressing installations and the existence of the lever press have been recognised in Palestine. These discoveries could provide useful comparative information. It is to be hoped that, in the future, sufficient evidence may be found to identify sites of ancient oil production in Egypt.

Sources of animal fats

All animals have internal fat deposits to a greater or lesser degree. While any animal source could therefore supply fat, the most substantial amounts were likely to have been obtained primarily through the butchery of wild and domesticated animals for meat or hides (see Chapters 25, this volume; Chapter 12, this volume). Collectively, the various sources available were numerous, but some of the preeminent ones can be summarised here. These include the principal domesticates of cattle (*Bos taurus*), sheep (*Ovis aries*), goat (*Capra hircus*), pig (*Sus domesticus*) and donkey (*Equus asinus*) all of which would have been available from predynastic times onward (Houlihan 1996: 11–13; Zeuner 1963: *passim*; Epstein 1971: *passim*; Epstein and Mason 1984: 8–12). Among the later introductions was a fat-tailed woolly sheep, which may have first reached Egypt via Western Asia in the Middle Kingdom but, by the New Kingdom, it had become the dominant type (Zeuner 1963: 183; Ryder 1983: 109). The tails of this sheep can weigh as much as twenty pounds and are 'one of the most important sources of edible fat' in Iran today (Ryder 1983: 716). Another possible introduction was the zebu (*Bos indicus*), a type of cattle with a distinctive hump of fat behind the neck. It has been suggested that this might have been brought to Egypt early in the New Kingdom, although this is based on pictorial evidence still in dispute (Houlihan 1996: 11; Epstein and Mason 1984: 12; Ikram 1995: 13). It would be expected that the importance of cows and donkeys as draft animals or beasts of burden, or providers of dairy products may well have increased their economic value beyond that of simple food and fat sources.

An assortment of wild land animals could also have been hunted or kept in captivity to provide meat and perhaps fat. To list a few, these species include aurochs (*Bos primigenius*), boar (*Sus scrofa*), oryx (*Oryx gazella dammah)* and *Oryx leucoryx*), addax (*Addax nasomaculatus*), hartebeest (*Alcelaphus buselaphus buselaphus*), gazelle (including *Gazella dorcas* and *Gazella soemmeringii*), ibex (*Capra ibex nubiana*), hare (*Lepus capensis*), and even hyena (*Hyaena hyaena*) (Boessneck 1988: 36, table 7; Houlihan 1996: 41–73); Ikram 1995: 20–1). Of these, aurochs seems to have become extinct in Egypt at some point after the reign of Amenhotep III (Ikram 1995: 13). Deer (Cervidae) have been identified in tomb reliefs, but their presence in Egypt is controversial as their indigenisation on the African continent is still questioned (Houlihan 1987: 243).

Waterfowl such as geese (*Anser* spp. and *Branta* spp.) and ducks (*Anas* spp.) would have been excellent sources of fat. Other possible sources may have been cranes (*Grus grus* and *Anthropoides virgo*), herons (*Ardea* spp.), and doves (*Streptopelia turtur*). Game birds such as partridges (*Alectorius barbara and Ammoperdix heiji*) and quail (*Coturnix coturnix*) were also available (Ikram 1995: 26–7). More exotic migratory birds as well as perhaps the ostrich (*Struthio camelus*), may also have been exploited on occasion (Houlihan 1986: *passim*).

A wide range of fish thrived in the Nile (Brewer and Friedman 1989). Unfortunately, little is known of the oil reserves of ancient Egyptian species. The best modern commercial sources of fish oil (herring, mackerel, cod, etc.) are not among those present in Egypt. Some species of carp and eel do have moderate amounts of fat, but others, notably tilapia, are considered to have a low fat content (Pigott 1996: 241, table 6.7; Ackman 1995: 131).

Big game animals, such as lions and hippopotami were certainly hunted, and although medical texts suggest that fat obtained from them could be included as an ingredient in prescriptions, their usage must have been rare (Lucas and Harris 1962: 330–1; Chassinat 1922: 451–2; Helck 1977: 205). The lexicography is sometimes still problematic, but medical texts also seem to suggest that fat from a variety of unexpected sources could have been exploited, including snake, crocodile and mouse (Chassinat 1922: 451–2; Helck 1977: 205).

Fat rendering

In land animals, there are three primary sites for fat deposits (Bender 1992: 20). The largest quantities are obtained from storage deposits under the skin and around the organs. Much smaller amounts are derived from the intermuscular fat visible between the muscle fibres, often known as 'marbling'. Finally, a low percentage of intramuscular fat deposits are found within the muscle structure. As a guideline, in modern times, fats can amount to 18–30 per cent of the carcass weight of market steers (Dugan 1987: 103).

Modern terminology distinguishes between cow/sheep fat and pig fat. Although these two fats are of similar composition, that from cattle or sheep is known as tallow, while that obtained from pig is called lard. Traditionally, lard was obtained only from the fat deposits surrounding the kidneys and bowels of pigs, but the term is now used for any pig fat (Bolton and Pelly 1924: 99). Similarly, the internal fat of cattle, in particular kidney fat, is familiar to us as suet (Elsdon 1926: 355). Today, fat deposits around the kidney, heart, intestines etc. are termed 'killing fats' as they are obtained when the animal is slaughtered (Love 1996: 3). 'Cutting fats' are those removed from the animal when it is cut apart (Love 1996: 3; see also Chapter 25, this volume). In general, killing fats are harder and 'have better flavour stability' than cutting fats (Love 1996: 3). Tallow from sheep is usually harder than beef tallow, is more prone towards rancidity and has a more unpleasant taste (Bolton and Pelly 1924: 99).

Within the household, small quantities of fat derived from inter- and intramuscular sources may have been produced incidentally through the cooking of meat for food. However, animal fats produced on an industrial scale were probably rendered primarily from the 'killing' or storage deposits. Rendering can be defined as the process by which fat is separated from other substances (protein, water, carbohydrates and mineral components) found in fatty animal tissue (Dugan 1987: 103). The extraction is usually carried out by heating which releases the fat by rupturing the cells containing fat (Weiss 1983b: 68; Love 1996: 6). Edible animal fats and marine oils are usually rendered within a few hours of killing (Norris 1979: 480–1).

Specific details of the rendering techniques used by the ancient Egyptians are not known, but were probably based on methods of 'dry' and 'wet' rendering. Dry rendering could have been carried out by the traditional 'open kettle' procedure, in which fatty tissue is cooked to dryness at temperatures ranging from 230–40 °F in an open vessel (Weiss 1983b: 68; Sonntag 1979a: 332). Alternatively, the fat could simply be melted over a low heat. This is the method recommended for preparing suet in modern cookery books, although the use of hardened animal fats in ancient Egyptian cookery is unconfirmed. According to one recipe (Bishop 1861: 30), the membrane and veins in the kidney fat are first removed; then the fat is placed in a pan 'some distance from the fire' and allowed to melt gradually. Once liquified, it is poured into a pan of cold water, and when hard, wiped, folded into white paper and placed in a linen bag. If kept in a dry, cool place, it can be kept for up to a year. In a similar 'wet' process, the tissue could have been steamed in a small amount of water in a closed container at lower temperatures (Sonntag 1979a: 332). The rendered fats could then be 'drawn off after standing for a sufficient length of time to form a separate layer' (Weiss 1983b: 68). Again, as for vegetable oils, any contact with copper or copper alloys would have caused rapid rancidity of the fats (Weiss 1983b: 65).

In addition to tallow and lard, other fats may also have been produced. These include neat's-foot oil and sheep's-foot oil. Both are extracted in a similar fashion. Neat's-foot oil is obtained by boiling the feet of cattle in water after the hair, skin and hooves have been removed (Elsdon 1926: 372; see also Chapter 12, this volume). The oil then rises to the surface and can be skimmed off as in the hot water flotation method used to process oilseeds. Bone fat from the shin bones of cattle can also be extracted by this method.

Scenes of fat-rendering are rare in ancient Egyptian tombs. Ikram (1995: 177) mentioned two possible New Kingdom scenes from the temple of Seti I at Abydos, both in Room 17 off the butcher's yard, and one from tomb KV11 at Thebes. In one of the Abydos scenes (Ikram 1995: 178, fig. 55), the fat is being chopped up by two men, then heated over a fire in a large vessel and finally wrung out with a bag press over a large vat. Such a procedure would be identical to that for extracting vegetable oils (see pp. 405–7). Ikram (1995: 177) rightly questioned the necessity of the press for the processing of fat, particularly in the second less well-preserved example from the temple. This may be an instance where a method known to have been used for oil extraction was extended without basis to the rendering of fat by an unwitting artist, but the closeness of the processing of oils and fats is evident from New Kingdom jar labels at Amarna where both are produced by the *ps sgnn*, or oil boiler (Pendlebury 1951: p. xxiv, no. 258).

The scene in KV11 was described as badly damaged, but seems similar to the Seti I examples, showing the chopping up of the fat, the heating of the vessel and the press (Ikram 1995: 177). Again, the identification is somewhat speculative.

Ikram (1995: 179) also raised the interesting possibility that some of the Middle Kingdom wooden models, particularly from the tomb of Meketra at Thebes, may represent fat-rendering. Some show a pot on a three-legged stand positioned over a fire. The contents of the pot are painted red and white, which could exemplify either the boiling of the fat or the making of blood pudding. Although the interpretation is uncertain, Ikram (1995: 179) noted that the idea that the models show the processing of fat should not be discounted.

Dairy products (milk, butter, cheese)

Milk could have been obtained from cows, goats and sheep. Milk-based processed products like butter and cheese may also have been available. Lucas (1962: 330) further distinguished between butter and butter fat. The former he described as 'material produced by churning milk or cream until the individual globules of fat previously in suspension coalesce'. Butter fat was defined as a product 'made by melting butter by heat and allowing it to stand until the water and casein settle out, when the fat is poured off'. This is the modern Egyptian *samn* or *ghee*, which is used for culinary purposes.

Cheese can be manufactured by adding an acidic component to milk, causing it to ferment. There are several possible sources for this component. In a warm climate such as that of Egypt, bacterial growth in stored milk can produce sufficient acid to induce this conversion (Fox 1993: 1). Alternatively, acidic rennet derived from the enzymes in animal stomachs can be added to milk, and it may have been recognised in ancient times that milk stored in skins made from animal stomachs turned to cheese (Fox 1993: 2). Today, calf rennet is most common, but pig, hare, kid and lamb rennets are also used (Scott 1986: 3, 170). Exudates of some plants, notably the latex of the fig tree (*Ficus carica*), can also cause milk to coagulate (Scott 1986: 179).

Any movement of the storage vessel containing this acidified mixture would cause it to separate into curds and whey (Fox 1993: 2). The whey could be drained through a cloth or strainer, leaving the solid curds. In modern Egypt, the curds are placed in reed mats, left to drain and then squeezed (Dagher 1991: 66). Both curds and whey are edible and whey can be consumed as a 'pleasant, refreshing drink' (Fox 1993: 2). If dehydrated and salted, the curds could then be stored for future use. Dehydration could be carried out by cooking, stirring, pressing and salting the curds (Fox 1993: 9). Varieties of cheese can be attributed, for example, to differences in local milk supply, the growth of mould, or the presence of other micro-organisms (Fox 1993: 4). The stages outlined here (acidification, coagulation, dehydration, pressing and salting) are still the basis of cheese manufacture today (Fox 1993: 9; Dagher 1991: 62–6).

Beeswax

Both honey and beeswax are produced by honeybees, including *Apis mellifera*. Within this species, there are a number of geographical variants 'characterised by their adaptation to the environment in which they live' (Dietz 1992: 36). For example, the Egyptian honeybee is *Apis mellifera lamarckii*, while south of Egypt and in other parts of the Mediterranean, a number of other variants are indigenous (Dietz 1992: 37–8). The Egyptian honeybee builds smaller colonies than the European types and is considered an 'aggressive' bee (Crane 1983: 39). The warm climate of Egypt is well-suited for beekeeping, but bees also need water (Crane 1980: 6), a resource of more limited supply in Egypt. Because of this, the Delta region would have been particularly favourable for apiculture, and bees could also live in the oases and along the Nile Valley.

Within a honeybee colony, beeswax is used for the construction of the combs, each consisting of hundreds of hexagonal cells. These are used for the storage of pollen, nectar, honey, water, and as a nursery for raising young. Beeswax is produced by the female worker honeybee. The liquid wax is secreted from glands under the abdomen and hardens into plates (Crane 1980: 3). These in turn are removed by the hind legs of the bee, transferred to the fore legs and then placed in the mouth, chewed, and finally applied to the combs (Schmidt and Buchmann 1992: 961).

After a few days of wax production, the worker bee flies out of the hive to forage for pollen, nectar, water and propolis (Crane 1980: 4, 11). Pollen and nectar are foodstuffs; and propolis, a brown or greenish-coloured resinous secretion or exudation of plants. The latter is used on its own or mixed with wax to repair and make waterproof the hive or nest cavity, to varnish the comb cells, and occasionally to reduce the size of the entrance hole (Crane 1980: 5).

The purest and whitest beeswax is obtained from newly built honeycombs, which have always been valued for their honey. Wax from the broodcombs (i.e. the part of the hive where the young are reared) is darker in colour. In traditional hives, the yield of beeswax may be about 8 per cent of the honey yield (Crane 1980: 3). As the collection of honey is undertaken by removing the wax combs, both of these products can be gathered concommitantly. The process can be divided into three stages: the harvesting of the combs, the extraction of the honey and the rendering of the wax.

At what date the shift from collecting wild honey to harvesting man-made hives occurred is not known (Crane 1980: 109). The earliest evidence of beekeeping comes from Egypt. A relief in the Fifth-Dynasty sun temple of Niuserra at Abu Gurob shows beehives and honey harvesting (Crane and Graham 1985: 2, 3, fig.1). Three other later scenes are known: one in the Eighteenth-Dynasty tomb of Rekhmira (TT100; see Fig. 17.9), one in tomb TT73 at Thebes (*c.* 1450 BC) and one in tomb TT279 at Thebes (dated 660–625 BC). These representations indicate that the hives were all used horizontally, were roughly cylindrical, and were stacked one on top of the other. The shapes of the individual hives differ slightly; the examples from Rekhmira (Fig. 17.9) having a larger, more rectangular shape than the ones shown in tomb TT279. In the Rekhmira and tomb TT279 reliefs, the hives are a blueish-grey colour, suggesting that they were made of unbaked clay (Crane and Graham 1985: 4–5).

No actual hives from ancient Egypt have been identified, but the stacking construction shown in the ancient reliefs continues to the present day. Cylindrical or 'pipe' clay hives, longer and narrower than those shown in the reliefs, are stacked eight to ten high, 300–500 together (Crane 1983: 40). Traditional hives now used are constructed of sun-dried mud made with the aid of matting or a piece of miniature paling (Crane pers. comm.). Details of construction were given by Mellor (1928: 19–21).

Once formed, the ends of the cylinders were sealed with a disc made of mud and straw (Mellor 1928: 19). The simplest type of man-made hive had a small opening at the front through which the bees entered. To extract the honeycombs, the beekeeper would remove the disc covering the back. A better hive had a removeable disc at both front and back. Smoke could be blown into the back opening, driving the bees towards or out of the entrance without killing them. The honeycombs could then be removed at the back of the hive (Crane and Graham 1985: 5). This is the procedure in use in Egypt during this century (Mellor 1928: 19). The most unequivocal evidence of the beekeeper opening the hive from the back is in the scene in tomb TT279, where the bees appear to be flying out of the entrance with the harvesting taking place at the back (Crane and Graham 1985: 5).

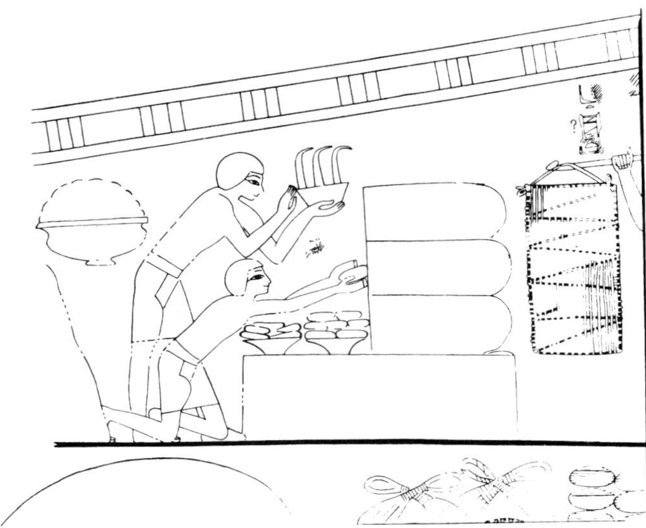

Figure 17.9 Scene from the tomb of Rekhmira (TT 100) showing removal of honeycombs from the hive.

The depiction of rounded combs in the Rekhmira relief is particularly interesting. Davies (1943: 45) commented that although this is the usual shape, 'how the bees were induced to give it this shape is not clear'. However, Kuény noted that when the hives are constructed, the beekeeper can place a used, round comb near the entrance which, combined with the shape of the hive, will result in the formation of round combs (Kuény 1950: 90–1).

Earlier this century, the harvesting of beeswax and honey from traditional hives was generally undertaken twice a year in Egypt with the first collection in April/May and the second, the principal harvest, carried out in November (Kuény 1950: 90; Mellor 1928: 26). However, in the provinces of Girga, Qena and Aswan, only one collection was undertaken, in September (Mellor 1928: 26). Mellor gave an excellent account of the harvesting process, based on ethnographic evidence from the Delta and the Memphite region, which can be summarised here (Mellor 1928: 28–9). A hive was opened at the back and the combs removed as described above. They were then thrown into a cow or water buffalo skin with two openings, one large and one small, the latter having been tied shut. When the skin was full, the combs were stamped on to break them and release the honey.

The next stage is the extraction of the honey. According to Mellor's account (1928: 30–1), a more thorough trampling of the bag holding the combs was undertaken and the smaller opening at the base was untied. The first honey that ran out of the bag was decanted directly into jars. The remaining contents (combs, honey, debris) were then emptied into a large copper pan and washed by hand with water at a ratio of about 10 parts honey to 1–1.5 parts water. This was subsequently poured into a large pottery jar known as a *zir*, with a small hole in its blunt-ended base. A sieve of two crossed sticks and halfa grass was placed inside the jar over the hole. This would trap the dirt and wax, but allow any honey to flow into a container below.

Rendering of wax

Although tomb scenes sometimes depict honey being poured from one vessel to another, none shows the process of rendering the beeswax. The simplest method would be to melt the drained combs until fluid (the melting point of wax is 62–65 °C) and then to remove the dirt and debris by either straining the liquid wax or allowing it to cool and solidify, and finally scraping the debris from the bottom of the wax cake where it would tend to collect (Crane: in press). However, because of its inflammable nature, wax is more safely heated in water. This is the most basic method for rendering beeswax, known as the 'hot water technique' (Tew 1992: 686). Mellor (1928: 30–1) noted that such a procedure was in use in Lower Egypt earlier this century and it is also very similar to a description provided by Columella (XI.16.1; see Crane in press). According to Mellor (1928: 30–1), the combs from the traditional hives were placed in a large copper vessel, which was about quarter-full of water. This mixture was then brought to a boil. Next, straw was added and the liquid again allowed to boil. In Columella's account, the combs were washed before boiling and there was no mention of the addition of straw, although the wax was strained through straw or rushes between boilings.

Mellor recounted that, after boiling, the beeswax was poured into sacks and either squeezed in the manner of the bag pressing technique used for oil (see pp. 406–7) or placed in a wax press. The latter was similar to the contemporary screw press used for olives, which would not have been available in Pharaonic times (see discussions of olives and pressing, p. 400). Using this procedure, Mellor calculated the average yield of one cylinder hive at 0.957 kg of honey and 0.062 kg of wax (Mellor 1928: 33). In present-day Tanzania, the same bag press method is used but, after straining, the wax is placed in a second bath of cold water and the wax skimmed off as it hardens and rises to the surface (Ntenga and Mugongo 1991: App. II, 1). As in the dry technique, any debris can be slaked off the bottom of the cake.

Archaeological remains of some wax objects suggest that the Egyptians did use relatively pure beeswax, but whether wax contaminated by pollen, propolis or other detritus was also utilised is not known. Some ancient wax objects are darkly coloured and until further scientific research is carried out, it is unclear whether this is natural or the result of some added components. Figures of the Four Sons of Horus made from red wax certainly appear to have been deliberately coloured. Raven (1983: 29) noted that some ancient Egyptian wax samples have a higher melting point than might be expected, and he attributed this to added propolis, but this theory has yet to be supported by scientific evidence (see p. 422). Pure beeswax often has a yellow tinge. In addition, Mellor's account noted that the wax was heated in a copper vessel, and there is some evidence that this can turn the wax green (Grout 1946: 546). The wax can be bleached (whitened) by rolling softened wax into thin sheets or shreds and leaving them in the sun for a few weeks (Root 1978: 661; Grout 1946: 547–8).

Although a Ptolemaic papyrus in the Zenon archive included a request for donkeys to move hives away from irrigation flooding, there is no evidence that migratory beekeeping was practised in ancient Egypt (Crane 1983: 42). However, in recent centuries, hives have been transported on boats from Upper Egypt to Lower Egypt, starting in late October to follow the flowering season down the Nile. These would stop repeatedly along the way to allow the bees to forage.

Summary of the uses of oil, fat and wax

As noted above, these products were used for a variety of purposes (see pp. 419–20 for further discussion). In daily life, oils and fats were undoubtedly employed in cookery and as a preservative for meat (see Chapter 25, this volume). Industrially, oils and fats could have been applied, for example, as lubricants for chariot-wheels and potters' wheels (Lucas 1962: 328; Powell 1995: 318; 327–33) and as a means of curing hides (see Chapter 12, this volume). Texts confirm their importance in illumination and they were used, apparently more so than wax, to coat linen wicks (Chapter 11, this volume; Černý 1973: 43–6). In addition, beeswax could have served as an adhesive, as a sealant, as a paint binder and for making models for metal casting (Lucas 1962: 2–3; see Chapter 19, this volume). There is also some evidence that beeswax was used to coat paintings in New Kingdom tombs (Mackay 1920).

All oil, fat and wax could also have played an important role in the personal toilet. Pure oils and fats could have been used as emollients for moisturising the skin. In the absence of soap, mixtures with alkali substances such as lime or natron could have been used to cleanse the body (Lucas 1962: 85). They could also be used with make-up or applied to the hair (Lucas 1962: 84–5). Notably, these natural products could have been mixed with other components, such as flowers, resins, herb, spices and aromatic woods to form scented ointments (see Chapter 18, this volume). These could have been used in daily life, in religious ceremonies and in funerary preparations, including those used in mummification. They also could have been used in medicinal preparations (Germer 1979 passim; Chassinat 1922).

Archaeological remains and textual evidence suggest that the ancient Egyptians believed beeswax to have special magical powers, perhaps due to its inflammable nature (Raven 1983: 24–32). The ability to model softened beeswax made it suitable for use in the manufacture of detailed animal, human and divine figures (Raven 1983: 9–22).

Chemical composition of oils, fats and waxes and their detection in ancient samples

Oils and fats

Many of us are now familiar with certain terms associated with oils and fats, such as *triglycerides, saturated* and *polyunsaturated fats, fatty acids* and *cholesterol*, because of their dietary importance and potential effect on our health. However, the relationship of these products to the chemical composition of oils and fats is rarely explained.

Oils and fats are very similar in composition and are collectively known as lipids (see Gunstone *et al.* 1994 for a summary of lipid chemistry). In fact, oils differ from fats in that they are normally fluid at room temperature. Major sources of lipids include plants, land mammals, marine animals and dairy products. The lipids from all of these sources contain mixtures of different glycerides and in particular, triglycerides (also known as triacylglycerols). These are compounds consisting of a glycerol molecule to which three fatty acids are bonded (Fig. 17.10). Most triglycerides will be composed of two or three different fatty acids. It is rare for triglycerides to consist of the same three fatty acids. The range of principal fatty acids found in the likely ancient lipid sources is actually quite small, but many different combinations of triglycerides can be formed from them. For example, fifty-five different triglycerides can be made using the five fatty acids found in linseed oil (Mills and White 1994: 33). Because of this complexity, and the resulting high molecular weight of the triglycerides, lipids are usually discussed not by their triglyceride composition, but by the relative abundance of the different fatty acids found in them.

These fatty acids are in themselves also very similar in composition (see Fig. 17.11). The distinctions are based on the number of carbon atoms present (usually in even numbers and most commonly in chains of sixteen or eighteen carbons in vegetable oils and animal fats) and the number, position and geometry of double bonds. Fatty acids with no double bonds are termed *saturated* while those with double bonds are known as *unsaturated*. Fatty acids with one double bond are sometimes referred to more specifically as *mono-unsaturated* and those with two or more double bonds as *poly-unsaturated*. As unsaturation increases, the melting point of the lipid decreases. Unsaturated fatty acids are more common in vegetable oils and this is the reason that they are more likely to be fluid at room temperature than animal fats. At body temperature, both fats and oils are liquid.

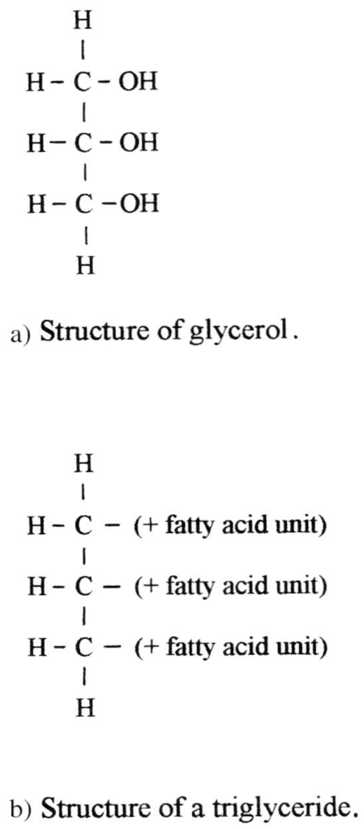

```
        H
        |
    H - C - OH
        |
    H - C - OH
        |
    H - C - OH
        |
        H
```

a) Structure of glycerol.

```
        H
        |
    H - C - (+ fatty acid unit)
        |
    H - C - (+ fatty acid unit)
        |
    H - C - (+ fatty acid unit)
        |
        H
```

b) Structure of a triglyceride.

Figure 17.10 Molecular structure of a glycerol molecule (a) and a triglyceride (b). H = hydrogen, C = carbon, O = oxygen.

The principal fatty acids found in oils and fats include palmitic acid with sixteen carbon atoms and no double bonds (commonly expressed as 16:0), stearic acid (18:0), oleic acid (18:1), linoleic acid (18:2) and linolenic acid (18:3). As well as these common names, fatty acids have systematic names which provide information on their structure. For example, the systematic name of palmitic acid is hexadecanoic acid. For the sake of simplicity, the common names are used here (see Mills and White 1994: 33, table 3.1 for a concordance). Animal fats and dairy products can also contain other saturated fats including lauric acid (12:0) and myristic acid (14:0). The fatty acid composition of some of the likely sources known to the ancient Egyptians is shown in Tables 17.1 and 2. For some, the compositional data is

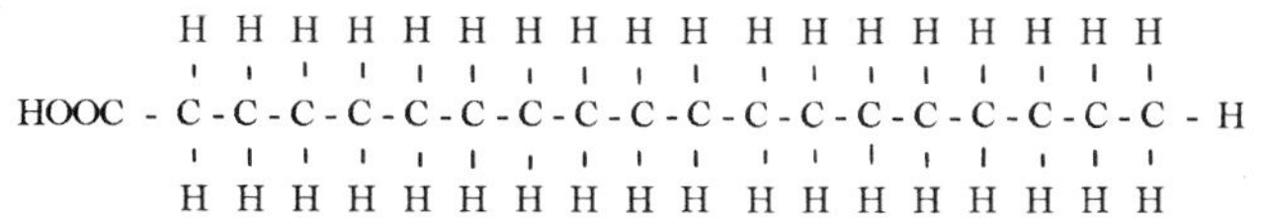

```
        H H H H H H H H H H H H H H H H H H
        | | | | | | | | | | | | | | | | | |
HOOC -  C-C-C-C-C-C-C-C-C-C-C-C-C-C-C-C-C-C - H
        | | | | | | | | | | | | | | | | | |
        H H H H H H H H H H H H H H H H H H
```

a) Structure of stearic acid (no double bonds).

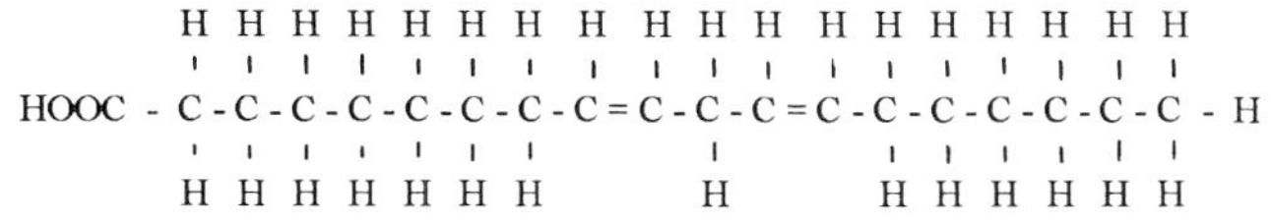

```
        H H H H H H H H H H H H H H H H H H
        | | | | | | | | | | | | | | | | | |
HOOC -  C-C-C-C-C-C-C-C=C-C-C=C-C-C-C-C-C-C - H
        | | | | | | |     |       | | | | | |
        H H H H H H H     H       H H H H H H
```

b) Structure of linoleic acid (double bonds at C_9 and C_{12}).

Figure 17.11 Structures of stearic and linoleic fatty acids. C = carbon, H = hydrogen, O = oxygen. Note the presence of double bonds at the C_9 and C_{12} position of the chain in linoleic acid.

limited and in need of further study. Despite the appearance of specific amounts for some sources in the table, the percentage of any one fatty acid is never fixed. This variation can be due to numerous factors. Climatic conditions, soil type, seasonal alterations, geography and health of the plant can affect the fatty acids found in vegetable oils (Sonntag 1979c: 4). Similarly, animal fat composition is influenced by factors such as the location of the fat within the body and the diet of the animal. The latter is also true for milk fats (Sonntag 1979a: 311). Marine lipids can differ according to the temperature of the water and whether the source was an oceanic or freshwater species (Sonntag 1979c: 4).

Most importantly for ancient samples, lipid composition will change over time due to environmental factors, such as exposure to light, air or moisture. These degradation and oxidative changes begin, for example, as soon as the seed has ripened or the animal killed. Such alterations have been studied because of their importance to the modern commercial lipid industry. For example, as the polyunsaturated fatty acids break down, some of the triglycerides will crosslink to form larger molecules. This polymerisation can cause the oil to become sticky, semi-solid and eventually dry, a crucial property today for oils used in paints. Based on the list of probable oil sources presented above, the only drying oil available to the ancient Egyptians would have been the highly unsaturated linseed oil. Because of this tendency, it would be less likely that linseed was used in preparations which might be stored for long periods of time, such as cosmetics. In contrast, non-drying oils would have been especially suitable for this purpose. Using this property as a guideline, the oil sources used by the ancient Egyptians can be divided into three groups: non-drying oils, semi-drying oils and drying oils (Table 17.3). Thus, the choice of oil for a particular usage might have been linked in part to its susceptibility to solidify.

Another change brought about by degradation and oxidation is the breaking of the bonds between the fatty acids and the glycerol molecule, thus 'freeing' the fatty acids. In the oil industry today, oils are graded according to the amounts of free fatty acids present. As the percentage of these increases, the quality of the oil is diminished. For example, for olive oil to be described as 'extra virgin,' it must contain less than 1 per cent of these acids (Cherfas 1994: 29).

In ancient lipids, the amounts will increase further and the alteration become more extensive, although some triglycerides may remain. In this regard, the presence of double bonds in fatty acids is important, since these are most susceptible to cleavage as degradation/oxidation progresses, forming smaller carbon chain molecules. Hence, in ancient samples, saturated fats such as stearic and palmitic acid may remain present in some quantity, but unsaturated fats may, in part, have broken down into similar molecules of shorter carbon chains (seven, eight or nine carbons; Mills and White 1994: 39–40; Evershed *et al.* 1992b: 199). From this, it is clear that, once degraded, it would become still more difficult to distinguish between the different aged oils and fats based on their composition.

Changes in consistency can also occur in ancient samples. Aged lipid matter can sometimes have a fairly dry, solid texture. Other examples are soft, sticky or rubbery. Lucas (1962: 328) suggested that those with an elastic consistency were probably unsaturated oils which had polymerised. In fact, this elasticity is the result of cleavage of those unsaturated fatty acids characteristic of oils which then form crossed-linked and scission products. When in a massive state as opposed to a thin film, these swell the matrix and make it rubbery. While this undoubtedly provides a highly useful means for distinguishing between oils and fats in ancient samples, it should be remembered that the presence of added components could alter the pliable texture. Therefore, this distinctive feature is best taken into consideration in conjunction with scientific analysis where the presence of a lipid has been established.

Another property which might have affected choice is the taste of the lipid. Fresh oils and fats are often bland or pleasant to taste, but can alter over time. This is also linked to degradation, as short carbon chain compounds particularly ketones, aldehydes and lower acids (e.g. caproic (C_6), caprylic (C_8) and capric (C_{10})) form from the fatty acids by oxidative scission at points of unsaturation (Sonntag 1979b: 140). These can produce a rancid taste in oils, and their abundance will increase as degradation progresses. Because unsaturated fatty acids are more susceptible to the formation of these products, there is, in a broad sense, a correlation between the tendency to dry and rancidity. Thus, for culinary purposes, non-drying oils or certain semi-drying oils might be preferable (Table 17.3). This is

Table 17.1. *Proportions of principal fatty acids found in some oils*

	Palmitic (16:0)	Stearic (18:0)	Oleic (18:1)	Linoleic (18:2)	Linolenic (18:3)	Other fatty acids	Ref.
Olive	8–18%	2–5%	56–82%	4–19%	0.3–1%		1
Linseed	6–7%	3–6%	14–24%	14–19%	48–60%		1
Safflower	6–7%	2–3%	12–14%	76–78%	tr.		2,5
Castor	1–2%	1–2%	3–6%	4–7%	–	(+83–89% ricinoleic acid)	1
Sesame	7–12%	3–6%	35–50%	35–50%	–		3,5,12
Balanos	12–17%	8–12%	23–34%	37–44%	–		3,4,9
Moringa	3–9.3%	3.5–12%	72–78%	1–8.6%	0.6–1.6%	(+4% higher fatty acids)	4,11
Poppy	9–10%	1.5–2.5%	10–30%	62–72	0–5%		1,6
Almond	5.5–7.5%	1.2–3%	66.4–77%	17–23.5%	–		6,7
Colocynth	8.9%	5.6%	17.2%	65%	–		8
Lettuce*	1.9–4.3%	1.3–4.1%	37.6–40.2%	51.1–56.9%	–		8
Radish	6.3	1.8%	21.7%	11%	9%	(+35.1% erucic acid (22:1) and 10% arachidic (20:0))	14
Rape**	3.2–3.8%	–	11.2–26.6%	13.7–17.5%	8.1–8.8%	(+31–52.3% (22:1)	10
Tiger nut	12	3	77	6–15%	–	and 9.6–11.8 (20:0))	8,13

* *Lactuca scariola* ** includes *Brassica napus* and *B. campestris*

References: **(1)** Mills and White 1994: 33, table 3.2, 2; **(2)** Weiss 1971: 725; **(3)** Hilditch and Williams 1964: 234, 269, 315; **(4)** Busson 1965: 206, 326; **(5)** Sonntag 1979a: 399; **(6)** Salunkhe *et al.* 1992: 455, 492; **(7)** Axtell and Fairman 1992: 143; **(8)** Eckey 1954: 298, 446, 766, 785; **(9)** Hussain *et al.* 1949: table IV; **(10)** Downey and Röbbelen 1989: 356; **(11)** Somali *et al.* 1984: table II; **(12)** Deshpande *et al.* 1996: 468; **(13)** Oderinde and Tairu 1992: 280, Table 2; **(14)** O'Donoghue *et al.* 1996: 544, Table 1

Table 17.2. *Proportions of principal fatty acids found in some animal fats*

	Caprylic (8:0)	Capric (10:0)	Lauric (12:0)	Myristic (14:0)	Palmitic (16:0)	Stearic (18:0)	Oleic (18:1)	Linoleic (18:2)	Linolenic (18:3)	Ref.
Pig fat				1–2%	20–28%	13–16%	42–45%	8–10%	0.5–2%	1
Beet tallow				2–3%	23–30%	14–29%	40–50%	1–3%	0–1%	1
Mutton tallow				6%	26%	30%	30%	1.5%	0.2%	1
Duck fat				0.2–1.4%	22–25%	6–11%	46.5–53%	10.5–13%	0.1–1.8%	3
Goose fat				0.8%	25%	9.5%	51%	9.1%	0.3%	3
Cow's milk	1–2.5%	2–3%	2–3%	9–11%	22–30%	11–15%	25–31%	1–2.5%	1–2.5%	1
Goat's milk	2.8%	10%	6%	12.3%	27.9%	6%	21.1%	3.6%	–	2
Sheep's milk	2.2	4.8%	3.9%	9.7%	23.9%	12.6%	26.3%	5.2%	–	2
Hen's eggs				tr.	27%	9%	44%	13.5%	0.5%	1

References: **(1)** Mills and White 1994: 33, table 3.2; **(2)** Sonntag 1979a: 310; **(3)** Foures 1996: 262, table 15.

Table 17.3. *Classification of oils according to their drying properties.*

Drying oils	Linseed
Semi-drying oils	Safflower Colocynth Lettuce Poppy Sesame Balanos Almond
Non-drying oils	Olive Moringa Tiger nut Castor Rape Radish

not a hard and fast rule, as castor, to take an example, has a disagreeable flavour and a laxative effect. Also, some of the oils contain compounds known as anti-oxidants which can retard spoilage. Sesame, for example, is classed as a semi-drying oil but contains powerful anti-oxidants to hinder its rancidity (Sonntag 1979c: 75). Conversely, it is important to remember that taste can be subjective and oils which we feel have an unpleasant taste today might not have been shunned by the ancient Egyptians. Of the oils, linseed turns rancid quite quickly and yet is still used today for food preparation in some parts of the world (see p. 396–7). Similarly, availability or cost may have dictated choice more than taste.

In addition to compounds associated with rancidity, others can produce characteristic changes in flavour or odour over long periods of time. Lucas and others noted a distinctive odour of coconuts in recently excavated fatty matter (Lucas 1962: 329; Petrie 1896: 39; Chapman and Plenderleith 1926: 2615). This is most likely due to formation of long and short-chain ketones as degradation occurs. One short-chain ketone which contributes to the odour and flavour of coconuts, methyl nonyl ketone (Sonntag 1979c: 77), is probably responsible for the presence of that scent in the ancient examples.

As the short-chain ketones are easily volatilised, the coconut odour does not persist. Once dissipated, the waxy scent of the long-chain ketones can become more readily apparent. Thus, very rarely will the contents of jars stored in museums still retain a faint coconut smell unless they are covered. A waxy scent is more common, notably in deposits from uncovered jars. Most frequently, no odour will remain because of prolonged exposure to light and air without protection.

From a review of earlier analyses of ancient samples from Lucas's time, it is noticeable that many times lipids were identified as an animal fat based on the detection of saturated palmitic and stearic acids (Lucas 1962: 328; Merrillees and Winter 1972: 128–30). While these acids may well have been present, it is also possible that in some cases the analyst was unaware of the preferential survival of saturated fats over unsaturated fats in aged samples. For the most part, the tests they were using, such as determination of melting point, solubility, saponification and iodine values, could do little to identify molecular structures and for the most part, provided information on the physical properties of the organic components (Evershed 1993: 75). Because of this, some might easily have been led to the conclusion that the source was an animal fat, as these contain a higher proportion of saturated fats than vegetable oils. It is clear that the techniques widely used by Lucas and his contemporaries were unable to provide sufficient detail on molecular structure.

Today, more modern techniques of analysis, such as infrared spectroscopy (IR), Fourier transform infrared spectroscopy (FT-IR), thin layer chromatography (TLC), nuclear magnetic resonance (NMR), high performance or high pressure liquid chromatography (HPLC), gas chromatography (GC) and gas chromatography/mass spectrometry (GC/MS) have increasingly been applied (for further information on these methods, see Mills and White 1994: 15–22). All of these techniques are based on comparison of ancient samples to known modern ones.

Fourier transform infrared spectroscopy (FT-IR) and IR analyses are based on the ability of different chemical bonds between atoms to absorb infrared radiation at specific wavelengths thus enabling them to be distinguished. Each bond type will have its own natural vibration. Radiation at this frequency will be absorbed by the bond and cause it to vibrate. The energy input causing this vibration will be observed in the resulting spectrum as a reciprocal drop in intensity (i.e. an absorption peak) at a frequncy corresponding to that of energy input. The spectrum of peaks in a sample enables the analyst to identify certain combinations of atoms within a molecule, but does not give detailed information about the complete molecular structure of components. Moreover, since in archaeological material, a complex mixture of original components, oxidation products and random polymeric species can be present, the number of different groups of atoms (and their corresponding bonds) grows, and with them the number of absorption bands. This proceeds to such an extent, even after a few decades of ageing, that the bands begin to overlap and become much broader, making identification less secure. As a result, IR and FT-IR can sometimes provide a general indication that a lipid is present but, it is rarely possible to make more precise identifications, and mixtures containing lipids are notably difficult to characterise (Fig. 17.12; Mills and White 1994: 21; Serpico and White 1998: 1038–9; White 1992: 6; Pilc and White 1995: 73–84; Heron *et al.* 1991a: 642; Heron *et al.* 1991b: 338; Evershed *et al.* 1992a: 16). Nonetheless, FT-IR and IR can often distinguish between broad classes of natural products such as glycerides, resins, beeswax and amber, and this in itself can be valuable. These techniques can also be useful when applied to large numbers of samples, making it possible to subdivide bulk samples into groups of similar spectra.

NMR uses very high frequency radio waves to interact with atomic nuclei. NMR can help determine the presence of hydrogen and carbon atoms, provide information on the bonds present and identify and locate the position of oxygen-based (functional) groups along the hydrocarbon chain (Pollard 1986: 406). However, mixtures are difficult to characterise and minor but potentially important compounds can be missed (Mills and White 1994: 23–4; Evershed *et al.* 1992a: 16).

In addition to these techniques, there are a number that rely on chromatographic analysis. These are based on the concept that compounds within a sample can be separated by their differing rate of transport across a stationary adsorbent. In TLC, the adsorbant (or stationary phase) coats a thin glass plate. A sample is applied as a small spot near one end of the plate. This end is then dipped into solvent which will draw the components of the sample up the plate at different rates by capillary action. Thus, the components are separated into a series of spots along the plate. The position and intensity of the resulting sequence of spots can then be matched to similar patterns found in modern reference materials. However, this technique cannot identify the molecular composition of the compounds and the results can be ambiguous. Often chemical compounds can only be separated into chemical classes rather than individual components. Degradation of ancient samples 'can produce complex patterns that may differ significantly from the pattern given by the original material' (Heron *et al.* 1991b: 334; also Mills and White 1994: 15; Evershed *et al.* 1992a: 15).

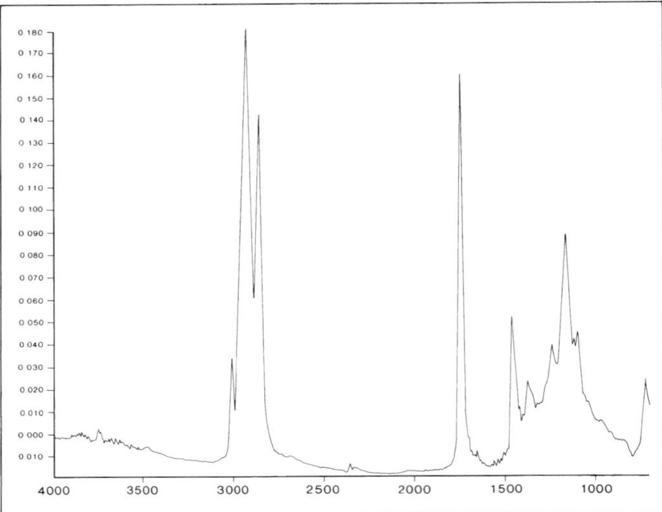

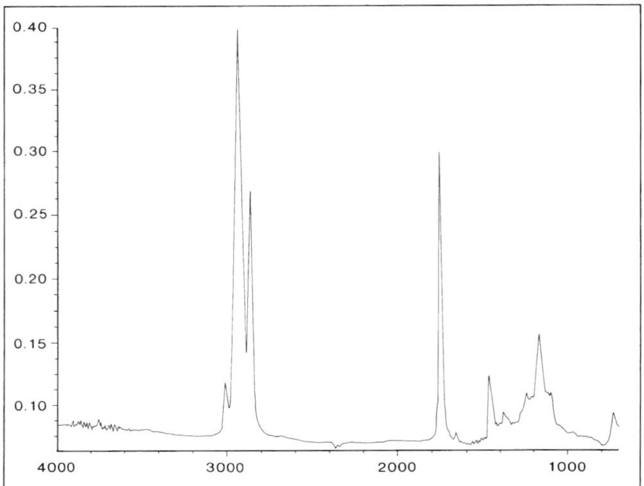

Figure 17.12 Infrared spectra of modern oils, demonstrating their similarity. Top: olive oil (transmittance spectrum, infrared microscope). Bottom: sesame seed oil (transmittance spectrum, infrared microscope).

Gas chromatography (GC) and GC/MS are based on the similar method of column chromatography. In the latter technique, the sample is dissolved in solvent(s) and applied to the top of a (glass) column packed with an absorbent material instead of the glass plate. Solvents of varying composition are applied to the top of the column and slowly percolate down under the action of gravity. Depending on their composition, the various components within the mixture of solvents and sample will 'stick' or be adsorbed to the stationary phase packing material in much the same fashion as in thin layer chromatography. However, in GC, the sample is carried by gas through the column. Movement of the different components will be impeded by the stationary phase causing them to elute from the outlet at the base of the column at different rates corresponding to their length of time (retention time) within the column. When they exit the column, the compounds are detected (for example by a flame ionisation detector) in relation to their retention time as a series of peaks, the area under each reflecting the amount of the compound present. This sequence of peaks can then be matched to a known reference sample. Thus, different fatty acids will elute at different times and, in fresh samples, the size of the peaks will emulate their abundance in an oil or fat. Unfortunately, in ancient samples, this pattern of intensity is not as reliable and many of the original components may have altered. Moreover, some complex molecules will stick to the column and not pass through. One means of overcoming this is through pyrolysis (Py-GC), whereby the sample is rapidly heated to break it into smaller fragments.

In GC/MS, the compounds enter a mass spectrometer as they leave the column and are bombarded with high energy electrons which cause the compounds to break into fragmental patterns determined by their molecular structure. Different compounds will have preferred fragmentation patterns which can be diagnostic. With GC/MS the components can not only be separated, but their molecular structure and weight can be elucidated, making it possible to identify the specific fatty acids and smaller chain molecules produced through degradation (Fig. 17.13).

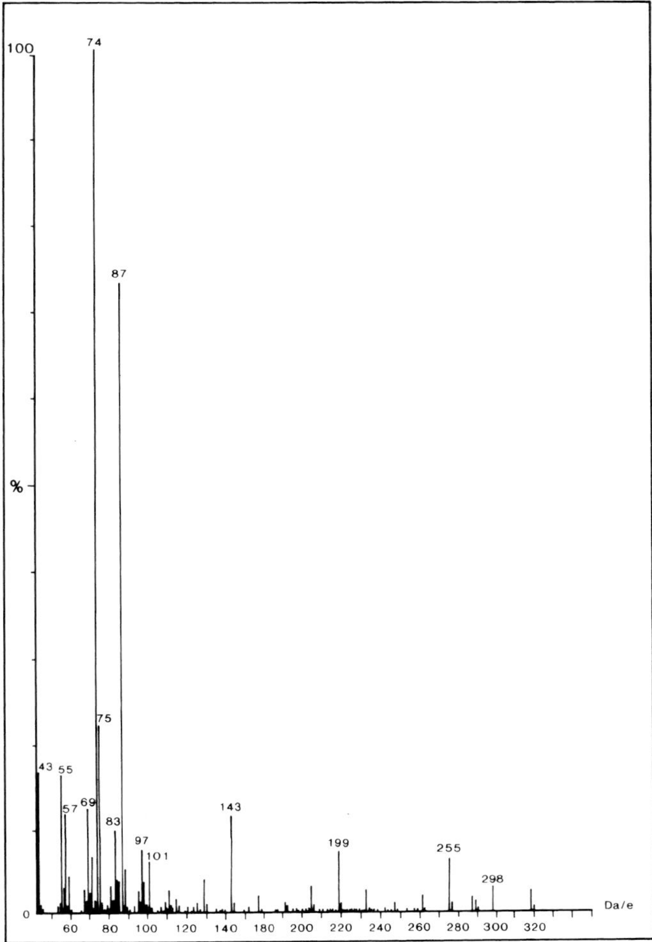

Figure 17.13 Mass spectrum (electron impact mode 70 ev) of a component from a trans/thermolytically methylated sample taken from the contents of a New Kingdom one-handled pottery jar with painted decoration (BM EA4902). The component is identified as the methyl ester of stearic acid.

High pressure liquid chromatography (HPLC) is another variation, in which the sample is carried through the column not by gas but by a liquid medium. With the use of shorter stainless steel columns and high pressure injectors, this technique has great potential, but has not had the application it deserved due to limitations imposed by the range of available detectors. Interface with mass spectrometers, which could provide crucial information on molecular structure, has been difficult and problematic. With the introduction of more reliable and cheaper mass-produced interfaces, such as thermospray, electrospray and atmospheric pressure ionisation techniques, coupled with the use of mini-bore, microbore and capillary HPLC columns, this situation is likely to improve significantly. While this technique holds much promise, for the moment, GC/MS is the most widely used and successful method for analysing ancient lipids and waxes.

Fortunately, with GC and GC/MS the components are not only able to be separated, but their molecular structure can be elucidated, making it possible to identify the specific fatty acids and smaller chain molecules produced through degradation (Fig. 17.14). Thus, GC/MS is undoubtedly the best procedure for the identification of ancient organic material, such as lipids. Even with GC/MS, distinction between ancient animal fats and vegetable oils is problematic. Although it is possible to identify the specific fatty acids present, this in itself will not lead to a secure genus identification as their remaining detectable proportions may bear little relationship to their original amounts (White 1992: 5).

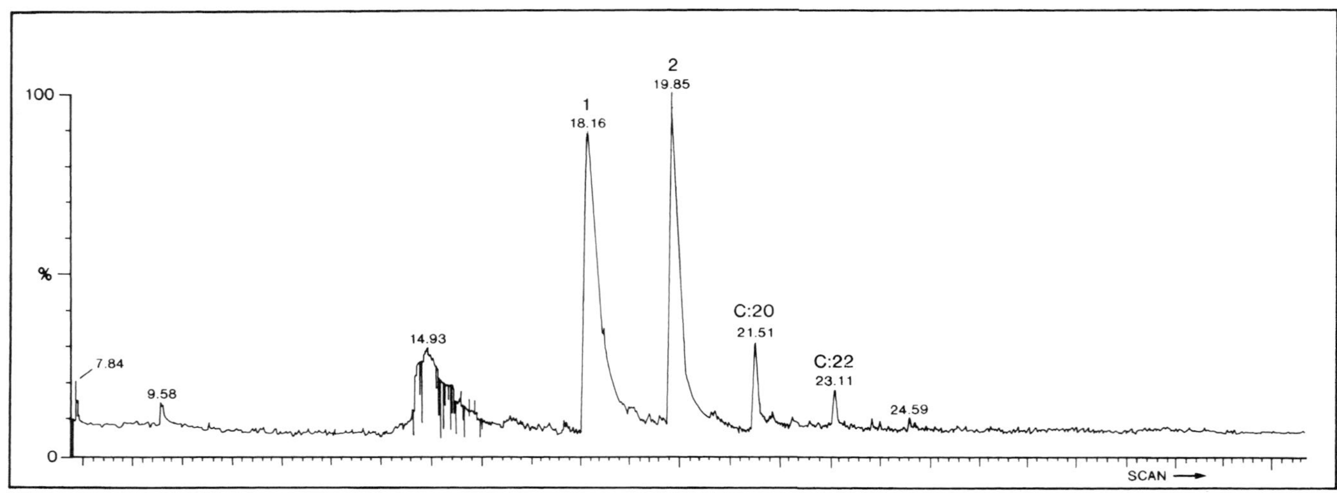

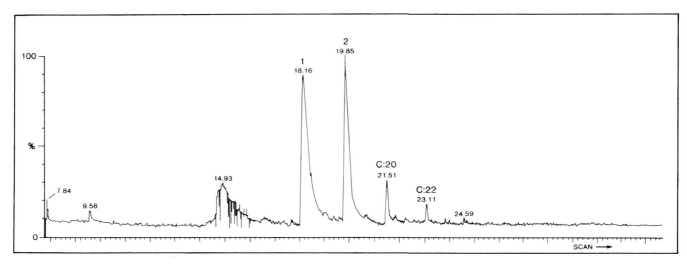

Figure 17.14 Total ion chromatogram of a trans/thermolytically methylated sample taken from the contents of a New Kingdom one-handled pottery jar with painted decoration (BM EA4902). Peak 1 is identified as the methyl ester of palmitic acid. Peak 2 is identified as the methyl ester of stearic acid. The raised area to the left of these is indicative of oxidation/degradation products.

There are some possible exceptions to this. Castor oil contains a high proportion of the comparatively stable compound ricinoleic acid, not found in the other possible lipid sources. Detection of even small quantities of this acid would allow for an identification of castor oil (Mills and White 1994: 32, 33, table 3.2; Serpico and White 1996: 133). Second, given the abundance of mono-unsaturated erucic acid (22:1) in *Brassica* spp. and *Sinapis* spp. oils, sufficient amounts may remain detectable in ancient samples to indicate a cruciferous oil. In addition, oils derived from marine sources often comprise fatty acids with longer polyunsaturated carbon chains than those found in land animals and vegetable sources (Sonntag 1979c: 36–7; Deal 1990: 7; Patrick *et al.* 1985: 233). Again, the presence of these would be fairly conclusive. As yet, no samples from ancient Egypt have been shown to be castor, cruciferous or marine oils, but this may change with time.

Milk fats can sometimes be distinguished because they contain lower saturated fatty acids (C_4 to C_{10}) than other lipid sources (Mills and White 1994: 33; Evershed *et al.* 1992b: 203; Evershed 1993: 85). In milk fats, myristic acid would be present at a level representing about 40 per cent of the palmitic acid, with the lauric acid amounts at about 10–20 per cent. Some years ago, the contents of a First-Dynasty pottery jar from Saqqara were identified as cheese (Zaky and Iskander 1942). Although the techniques used were less advanced than those today, it was possible to establish that lipids were present, as well as calcium, phosphates and nitrogen as part of protein. This combination is indeed compatible with an identification of cheese, or possibly whole milk. Notably, nitrogen would remain in these dairy products, and is also found in eggs (White 1984: 5). However, eggs would not contain the lower fatty acids found in milk at a significant level. In addition, nitrogen is absent in butter. GC/MS can provide relevant data on the composition of these components (White 1984: 10–11), but for the quantification of the amino acids found in proteins, HPLC would be more instructive. Another means of distinguishing between proteinaceous materials would be through fluorescent antibody techniques (on these methods, see Chapter 19, this volume).

Although oil and fat source identifications are clearly problematic, some information can be obtained from study of the preserved saturated fatty acids. As palmitic and stearic acids are more stable than the unsaturated fatty acids, it is possible that the relative proportions of these may be useful. It has been noted that in fresh oils, the ratio of palmitic to stearic acid is generally closer to 2:1, while in animal fats, it is closer to 1:1 (Mills and White 1994: 171–2; Patrick *et al.* 1985: 233; Charters *et al.* 1995: 121). Notably, the palmitate/stearate ratio in poppy seed oil is significantly higher (4:1) than the other likely ancient sources and this has enabled its identification in modern paint media (Mills and White 1994: 171). At the moment it would seem that tiger nuts would have a high palmitate to stearate ratio, but more research would be necessary to confirm this. Moreover, because composition can vary even in fresh oils, caution is necessary and it is less clear whether this ratio on its own could be reliable.

Another possible means of distinguishing between animal fats and vegetable oils is through the quantification of the shorter-carbon-chain products formed when the fatty acids degrade. As vegetable oils, particularly oils such as linseed, contain high quantities of unsaturated acids, it would be reasonable to expect a higher proportion of short-chain products in these degraded oils than in animal fats (Serpico and White 1996: 130, 132). Further research is now being undertaken to assess this, and if confirmed, would provide a useful means of differentiation.

At present, distinction between vegetable oils and animal fats is usually made not by fatty acid composition or identification of their degradation products, but by the presence of compounds known as sterols (see Fig. 17.15). Best known of these is cholesterol, found in animal fats. Vegetable oils contain phytosterols, such as sitosterol. The sterol content in fats and oils is very low (less than 1 per cent) (Sonntag 1979c: 54), and they have rarely remained in detectable levels in ancient samples. Like fatty acids, oxidation will alter their composition (White 1992: 6). If the oxidation products of these components are preserved, then their isolation can allow differentiation between animal fats and vegetable oils (Mills and White 1994: 41; Serpico and White 1996: 132; Heron *et al.* 1991b: 332; Evershed *et al.* 1992b: 199; Evershed 1993: 80–1). More recently, selected ion monitoring (SIM)-GC/MS has been shown to be particular effective in detection of sterols. It is worth noting, however, that with such sensitive techniques as GC/MS, cholesterol and also certain lipids can be present as a contaminant if the sample has been handled by humans (Evershed 1993: 88, 90).

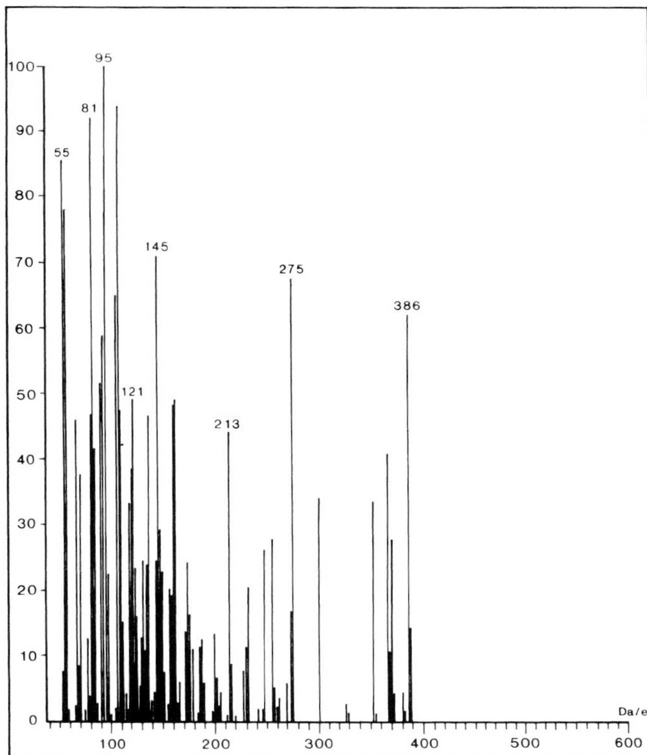

Figure 17.15 Mass spectrum (electron impact mode 70 ev) of one of the components found in a sample of the contents of a late Eighteenth-Dynasty one-handled calcite cosmetic jar (BM EA24708[11]; part of the toilet box of Tutu). The component is identified as cholesterol.

Very little scientific research has been carried out on lipids specifically from ancient Egypt in the past few years. Analysis of a group of jars from the First-Dynasty tomb of Djer at Abydos suggested that both plant and animal sources may have been in use by that time. This was determined by a combination of factors including the palmitate/stearate ratio, the relative abundance of dicarboxylic degradation products, and the presence of sterols. It was also possible to demonstrate differences in the contents found in vessels of similar shape, establishing that commodities were not correlated to specific jar types (Serpico and White 1996: 138–9). Most of the vessels were of Palestinian origin, but as the contents sometimes showed signs of re-use, the lipids need not have been imported. One residue showed traces of a coniferous resin mixed with the fat or oil. This may indicate the presence of a deliberately scented ointment (see Chapter 18, this volume).

Lipids found in cosmetic jars might of course have been used on their own as emollients, but it is also possible that added volatile components had disappeared over time (see Chapter 18, this volume). This may be the case with the contents of a distinctive one-handled jar with painted decoration in the style of New Kingdom 'dummy' vases. Vessels of this shape have been linked to the 'Seven Sacred Oils' and in particular to *nẖnm* ointment. However, GC/MS analysis of the contents revealed only the presence of lipid matter (Fig. 17.14). No sterols could be detected and the amount of shorter-chain dicarboxylic acids was small. These factors, along with the dry friable consistency of the residue would seem to favour identification of an animal fat, but this cannot be confirmed unreservedly.

As well as high amounts of palmitate and stearate, cholesterol was isolated by GC/MS in a residue found in another small cosmetic jar in the British Museum (BM EA24708.11). This was a late Eighteenth-Dynasty one-handled jar found in a toilet box belonging to an individual named Tutu in Thebes (Fig. 17.15). The sample was taken from beneath the surface of the deposit, reducing the likelihood that this component was present as a result of contamination. This indicates that the jar contains an animal fat. Again, no volatile compounds could be detected.

Published literature includes the report of a lipid mixture in a jar dated to the Twenty-sixth Dynasty (Seher *et al.* 1980: 397–9). Based on the amounts of saturated fatty acids present, the lipid was identified as most closely matching beef tallow. However, cholesterol was not noted to add support to this. Traces of volatile essential oils, particularly those associated with coniferous products were found, but no indication of conifer resin (see Chapter 18, this volume).

In addition, oil was reportedly amongst the components found on the outer layer of wrappings and the body of mummy in Munich analysed by IR, X-ray fluorescence, ion chromatography and mass spectrometry (Storch and Schäfer 1985: 331, table I; see Chapter 18, this volume).

Lipids have been found in other products associated with funerary practices. A fatty substance was the primary component identified in a sample of black 'anointing fluid' poured over a polychrome painted and varnished Third Intermediate Period cartonnage now in the Museum of Fine Arts, Boston (72.4823a). This was based on analysis, using microscopic techniques, FT-IR, GC/MS and HPLC (Newman unpublished). The cause of the blackened colour was not evident, and is certainly not apparent in other aged lipid samples. Similar 'anointing' residues have been noted on a number of other contemporary cartonnages and coffins, but had previously been believed to be a resin (Niwiński 1992).

Lipid matter was also identified as a minor component in some resin varnishes applied to New Kingdom funerary equipment (Serpico and White in press; these varnishes are discussed in greater detail in Chapter 18, this volume). In one instance, traces were found in the yellow resin varnish coating the Nineteenth to Twentieth Dynasties outer anthropoid coffin of Henutmehyt in the British Museum (BM EA48001A). In another instance, traces were also found in a black resin varnish covering a *shabti* of the Nineteenth-Dynasty Queen Nefertari (Boston, MFA 04.1767).

In contrast to the dearth of analyses of ancient Egyptian material, there has been a burgeoning wealth of research into lipids from other archaeological sites in both the Old and New Worlds. Although this material may differ in many respects from ancient Egyptian samples (in terms of environmental conditions, age, etc.), it is easy to see its potential relevance. These advances extend not only to research into visible residues (e.g. those adhering to pottery and stone jars) but also to analysis of lipids invisible to the eye, which had become absorbed into pottery vessels but could be extracted using solvents. The theory behind this process is simple. Since pottery fabrics are, to a greater or lesser degree, porous, any products – especially liquids – could be expected to migrate into the walls of a pot. Experiments conducted over the past few years have confirmed this migration in ancient Roman amphorae (Condamin *et al.* 1976). While the burnishing of vessels or the application of a slip could reduce the degree of migration, these treatments are only common on the interior of open vessels in Pharaonic times. GC/MS is again the best technique for this procedure. FT-IR and IR are much less suitable for absorbed residues.

Potential surface contamination or exchange with organic components in the soil, while occurring, does not appear to restrict the identification of absorbed contents. Condamin *et al.* (1976) were able to establish that, in fact, the reverse was possible, namely that the soil could pick up traces of the contents. Although extensive studies have not been carried out, absorption of lipid matter into the ceramic matrix of a jar seems to reduce microbial activity, which can occasionally result in better preservation than for some visible residues (Heron *et al.* 1991a: 655–7; Evans 1991: 290; Evershed 1993: 77). However, degradation is not eliminated by this entrapment, and alterations due, for example, to prolonged vessel use or burial in damp conditions can occur (Evershed *et al.* 1995: 91). Determination of re-use of jars may still be problematic for solvent-extracted residues (Charters *et al.* 1995: 124; Deal 1990: 6).

Research also suggests that heating need not destroy evidence of ancient oils and fats. Lipid matter can even be detected in strongly heated samples from both visible and adsorbed residues (Evershed 1993: 77; Charters *et al.* 1995: 125: Evans 1991: 290), although sterols may be less well-preserved, making it difficult to distinguish between plant and animal sources (Serpico and White 1996: 134).

There are several potential areas of study which might provide further information on lipid residues. One new line of research is based on the detection of the preserved triglycerides and diglycerides. In the past, archaeological samples were often saponified, a procedure which breaks down any remaining triglycerides etc. into their fatty acid components. This procedure can be useful for establishment of the palmitate/stearate ratio, for example. However, by using high-temperature GC and GC/MS, intact di- and triglycerides can be detected (Evershed *et al.* 1990: 1340). This can provide additional information on the degree of preservation of the sample and, in studies of large numbers of samples, help target the best candidates for more complete study.

Recently, analysis of radish seeds of the sixth century AD from Qasr Ibrim involved the use of gas chromatography combustion/isotope ratio-mass spectrometry (GCC/IRMS) to determine the $d^{13}C$ values of the fatty acids and thus secure the botanical identity of the seeds (O'Donoghue *et al.* 1996: 554–5). Further research is necessary, but if applied to ancient lipids, this technique could potentially help distinguish oils derived from plants in sufficiently disparate groupings on the genetic evolutionary tree, or help separate vegetable oils from individual animal fats (Woodbury *et al.* 1995: 2688–9; Deal 1990: 9–10).

Beeswax

As in oils and fats, the composition of beeswax is dominated by long straight chain compounds. However, these include an array of different components, such as fatty acid esters, free fatty acids and hydrocarbons (molecules consisting of only hydrogen and carbon) (Tulloch 1980). Palmitic and stearic acids are again present, but in reduced quantities to lipids. The ratio of these acids is much higher (4 or 5:1) than for fats or oils (1 or 2:1) and this will remain true in aged beeswax. Furthermore, whereas in oils and fats, compounds of more than twenty carbon atoms were rare, in beeswax these are most common. Particularly characteristic are saturated hydrocarbons of odd-number carbon atoms, usually C_{25} to C_{35}, with C_{27} most frequent. The principal wax esters comprise even-carbon-number saturated alcohols and fatty acids. The total carbon number ranges from around C_{38} to C_{52}. The total fatty acid fraction ranges from C_{16} to C_{36}, but the C_{24} ester is especially abundant, even in aged samples (Mills and White 1994: 50; White 1978: 58).

As a result of these saturated components, the composition of beeswax is comparatively more stable than the majority of other natural products. Thus, many of the earlier analyses of Lucas's time would still be valid today (e.g. Lucas 1962: 2–3, 303, 336–7). Moreover, in unmixed beeswax samples of sufficient size, FT-IR and IR analyses, known to be of limited value for the identification of oils and fats, can be reliable (Fig. 17.16) (Mills and White 1994: 50; Shearer 1987: 254; Kühn 1960). GC, GC/MS and pyrolysis-mass spectrometry (Py-MS) have also been used effectively, and are more dependable than IR methods for smaller samples or where mixtures are present (Mills and White 1994: 54; White 1978: 62). The use of beeswax in mummy wrappings and cartonnages dating from the Late Period to the Roman period has been established by GC and Py-MS (Wright and Wheals 1987: 205–6; see also White 1978: 67–8; see also Chapter 19, this volume).

Mixtures of beeswax with products such as resins, lipids and bitumen can also be distinguished with GC/MS (see Chapter 18, this volume). In composites of beeswax and lipid, for example, the ratio of palmitic and stearic acids may be raised higher than in pure lipid matter and the range of fatty acid esters would be more extensive (White, unpublished results; Charters *et al.* 1995). In addition, beeswax has been isolated in a number of samples taken from mummies which often contained complex admixtures (see Chapter 18, this volume for a more detailed discussion of substances used in mummification). These include GC and GC/MS analyses of deposits taken from the wrappings of a mummy dated to *c.* 600–500 BC, and from the interior of the abdomen of a Roman mummy (Connan and Dessort 1991: 1448–9, Fig. 1, nos. 182 and 237), as well as residues from the visceral packing, interior of the skull and the linen between the knees of a Ptolemaic mummy now in Lyon (Connan and Dessort 1989) and TLC and MS analysis of residues on the bandages of a Roman mummy in Manchester (Benson *et al.* 1979; 124–8). GC/MS analysis also identified beeswax in residues taken from the foot of a mummy (*c.* 300 BC) and in two canopic jars (*c.* 600 BC) now in Berlin (Connan 1991: 35). IR, X-ray fluorescence, ion chromatography and mass spectrometry were used to identify beeswax in deposits from the head, thorax, and also on the bandages of a mummy in Munich (Storch and Schäfer 1985: 330–31).

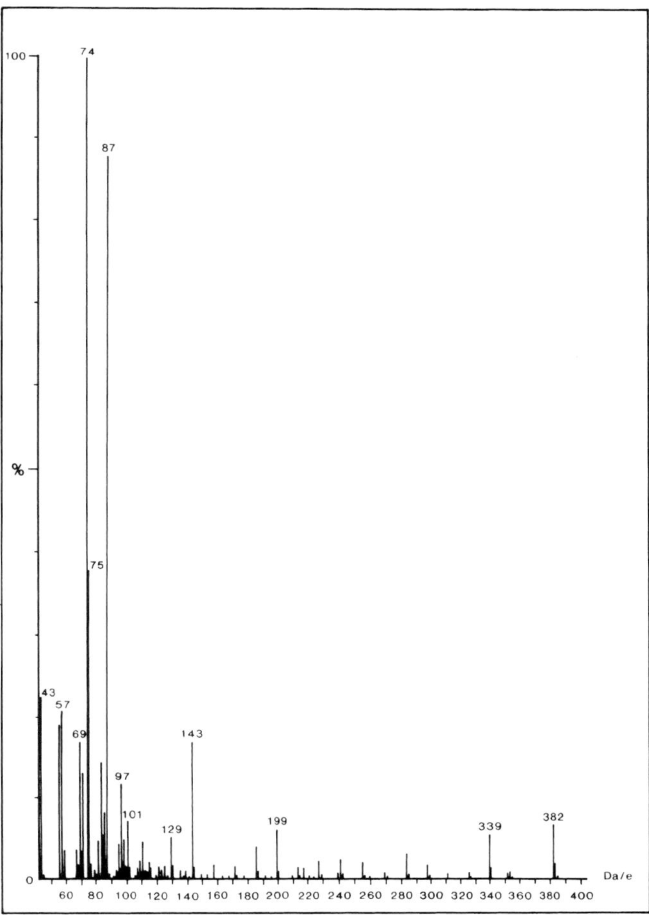

Figure 17.17 Mass spectrum (electron impact mode 70 ev) of one of the components from a trans/thermolytically methylated sample taken from the black varnish coating of a shabti *of Rameses IX (BM EA8571). The component is identified as methyl tetracosanoate (C_{24}), indicative of beeswax.*

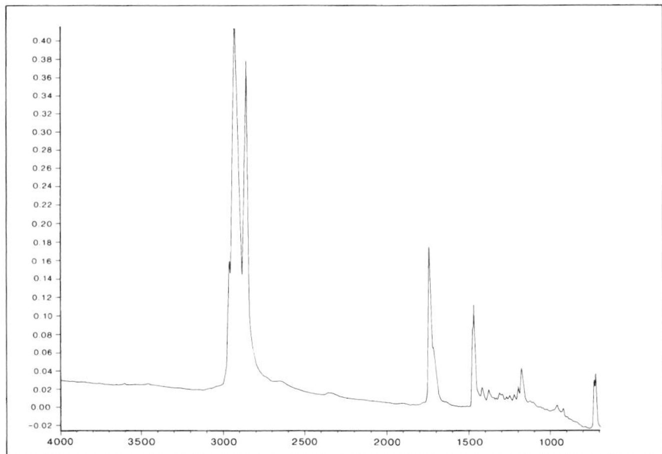

Figure 17.16 Infrared spectrum of a fragment of modern beeswax fragment (transmittance spectrum, infrared microscope).

These analyses reflect the variety of applications of beeswax in the mummification process. In addition, its use as a binder for inorganic pigments has been posited, based on MS and X-ray analyses of a sample from the famous bust of Nefertiti in Berlin (Wiedermann and Bayer 1982: 622A, 624A; see Chapter 19, this volume).

The ability to distinguish mixtures of beeswax and resin is relevant to the proposal by Lucas (1962: 3) and Raven (1983: 29) that ancient beeswax may have contained resinous propolis. This was offered as an explanation for the higher melting point of some ancient beeswax samples, in particular those from wigs (Raven 1983: 29). In fact, scientific research indicates that the higher terpenoids characteristic of resin are not present in propolis, making it possible to differentiate any mixes of wax and propolis from those of wax and resin (Walker and Crane 1987: 328–31; see Chapter 18, this volume). This has been demonstrated by some of the mummy samples and also recently in a study of a deposit from a New Kingdom wig, which was shown to consist, not of beeswax and propolis, but of beeswax and resin (Cox 1977: 69; see also Chapter 20, this volume). This might well explain the higher melting point noted in the past. Unfortunately, no information was given on the technique used or details of the analysis. Nonetheless, it is evident that beeswax and mixtures with beeswax can be identified relatively easily using modern analytical techniques.

Conclusions

From this overview of oil, fat and wax, a number of the potentials and problems of chemical analysis are apparent. While identification of beeswax may be relatively straightforward, it is clear that determination of the sources of oils and fats would rarely be possible. Because of this, some of the most fundamental questions, such as which oils or fats were in use and for what purposes, or how frequently these sources were used in comparison with each other, cannot easily be answered. Distinction between imported sources of oil and those which were locally available is also unlikely at this time.

Although this might seem disappointing at first, it is still possible to gain valuable archaeological information by forming new strategies for research. Most promising would be studies of groups of material which could be used to address specific archaeological questions, rather than 'one-off' analysis of a single sample. For example, it might be possible to associate certain vessel types with lipid storage or usage. In this context, GC/MS examination of Saxon lamps in northern England provided evidence of degradation which could be attributed to heating of an animal fat consistent with its use as lamp fuel (Heron *et al.* 1991b: 335). Detection of sterols in a number of similar lamps could indicate whether animal fats or vegetable oils were more commonly used for this purpose. Analysis of lamps from different periods or sites could establish changes or variations in the types of fuel in use.

Gas chromatography/mass spectrometry (GC/MS) analysis of residues from cooking pots at the same site, concommitant with study of the distribution of the organic matter in the vessels, suggested the use of lipid matter in food preparation (Charters *et al.* 1993). For such studies, it is important to consider possible re-use of jars and any chemical alterations caused by prolonged or intense heating or post-depositional factors. Further investigations into questions concerning re-use would certainly be of value to archaeologists.

However, the appropriate selection of technique is only one aspect of the analysis. A number of other criteria are also relevant, including:

1) the utilisation of a careful and definite sampling methodology;
2) the comprehensive study of modern reference samples for chemotaxonomic comparison;
3) the choice of sample preparation procedure by the analyst;
4) the specific analytical protocol used;
5) the recognition of any possible evidence of contamination, re-use etc.; and
6) the integration of relevant archaeological data.

These factors need to be assessed, and their effect taken into consideration, in any evaluation of scientific results.

Acknowledgements

We would like to thank Mr F.N. Hepper for permission to use the botanical drawings included in this chapter. For reading an earlier draft of portions of this chapter and for his very useful comments, we thank Dr Carl Heron, Department of Archaeological Sciences, University of Bradford. Similarly, we also thank Dr Eva Crane, Honorary Life President and Scientific Consultant to the International Bee Research Association, for comments and advice on the historical aspects of beekeeping and wax-rendering. For suggestions regarding sesame, we consulted Dr Delwen Samuel (McDonald Institute for Archaeological Research, Cambridge) and Mr Mark Nesbitt (Institute of Archaeology, London). Ms Mary-Anne Murray also assisted with some botanical aspects. Any errors, of course, remain our responsibility. We also acknowledge the kind permission of museum curators to analyse the samples we mention here from our own research. These include Mrs Barbara Adams, Petrie Museum of Egyptian Archaeology, University College London, and Mr W.V. Davies (Keeper), Mr T.G.H. James (former Keeper) and Dr A.J. Spencer of the Department of Egyptian Antiquities, British Museum, London. We also thank Dr Richard Newman, Department of Objects Conservation, Museum of Fine Arts, Boston, for bringing his unpublished results to our attention.

References

Ackman, R.G. 1995. Composition and nutritive value of fish and shellfish lipids. In *Fish and Fishery Products: Composition, Nutritive Properties and Stability* (ed. A. Ruiter). Wallingford, Oxon: CAB International, pp. 117–56.

Amouretti, M.-C. 1986. *Le pain et l'huile dans la Grèce antique*. Paris: Annales Littéraires de l'Université de Besançon.

Arctander, S. 1960. *Perfume and Flavor Materials of Natural Origin*. Elizabeth, NJ.

Axtell, B.L. and Fairman, R.M. 1992. *Minor Oil Crops: I, Edible Oils; II, Non-edible Oils; III, Essential Oils*, Rome: FAO Agricultural Services Bulletin 94.

Barakat, H. 1990. Plant remains from el Omari. In *El Omari – A Neolithic Settlement and Other Sites in the Vicinity of Wadi Hof, Helwan* (eds. F. Debono and B. Mortensen), DAIK. Mainz: von Zabern, pp. 109–14.

Barakat, H.N. 1995. Middle Holocene vegetation and human impact in central Sudan: charcoal from the Neolithic site at Kadero. *Vegetation History and Archaeobotany*, 4: 101–8.

Baum, N. 1988. *Arbres et arbustes de l'Egypte Ancienne: la liste de la tombe Thébaine d'Ineni (no. 81)*. Orientalia Lovaniensia Analecta 31. Leuven: Dept. Oriëntalistiek.

Bedigian, D. 1985. Is *se-gis-i* sesame or flax? *BSA*, 2: 159–78.

Bedigian, D. and Harlan, J.R. 1983. Nuba agriculture and ethnobotany, with particular reference to sesame and sorghum. *Economic Botany*, 37(4): 384–95.

1986. Evidence for cultivation of sesame in the ancient world. *Economic Botany*, 40/2: 137–54.

Bender, A. 1992. *Meat and Meat Products in Human Nutrition in Developing Countries*. Rome: FAO Food and Nutrition Paper 53.

Benson, G.G., Hemingway, S.R., and Leach, F.N. 1979. The analysis of the wrappings of Mummy 1770. In *The Manchester Museum Mummy Project* (ed. A.R. David). Manchester: Manchester Museum, pp. 119–31.

Bircher, W.H. 1960. *Gardens of the Hesperides*. Cairo: The Anglo-Egyptian Bookshop.

Bishop, F. 1861. *Wife's Own Book of Cookery*. London: Ward and Lock.

Bisset, N.G., Bruhn, J.G. and Zenk, M.H. 1996a. The presence of opium in a 3500 year old Cypriote base-ring juglet. In *Ägypten und Levante* VI (ed. M. Bietak). Vienna: Verlag der Österreichischen Akademie der Wissenschaften, pp. 203–4.

Bisset, N.G., Bruhn, J.G., Curto, S., Holmstedt, B., Nyman, U. and Zenk, M.H. 1996b. Was opium known in 18th Dynasty ancient Egypt? An examination of materials from the tomb of the chief royal architect Kha. In *Ägypten und Levante* VI (ed. M. Bietak). Vienna: Verlag der Österreichischen Akademie der Wissenschaften, pp. 199–201.

Blitzer, H. 1993. Olive cultivation and oil production in Minoan Crete. In *Oil and Wine Production in the Mediterranean Area* (ed. M.-C. Amouretti and J.-P. Brun). Athens: Ecole français d'Athènes, pp. 163–75.

Boessneck, J. 1988. *Die Tieswelt des Alten Ägypten untersucht anhand Kulturgeschichtlichen und zoologischen Quellen*. Munich: C.H. Beck.

Bolton, E. R. and Pelly, R.G. 1924. *The Resources of the Empire: Oils, Fats, Waxes, and Resins*. London: Ernest Benn.

Boulos, L. and el-Hadidi, M.N. 1994. *The Weed Flora of Egypt*. 2nd edn. Cairo: American University in Cairo Press.

Brewer, D.J. and Friedman, R.F. 1989. *Fish and Fishing in Ancient Egypt*. Warminster: Aris and Phillips.

Brousse, G. 1989. Olive. In *Oil Crops of the World: their Breeding and Utilization* (eds. G. Röbbelen, R.K. Downey and A. Ashri). New York: McGraw-Hill Publishing, pp. 462–74.

Bruce, E.A. 1953. Pedaliaceae. In *Flora of Tropical East Africa* (eds. W.B. Turrill and E. Milne). London: Crown Agent for the Colonies, pp. 1–23.

Brunton, G. and Caton-Thompson, G. 1928. *The Badarian Civilization and Predynastic Remains near Badari*. London: BSAE.

Bruyère, B. 1937. *Rapport sur les fouilles de Deir el Médinah (1934–1935). Deuxième partie: La nécropole de l'est*. Cairo: IFAO.

Busson, F. 1965. *Plantes alimentaires de 'ouest african*. Marseilles: L'Imprimerie Leconte.

Callot, O. 1987. Les huileries du Bronze Récent a Ougarit: premiers éléments pour une étude. In *Le Centre de la Ville. Ras Shamra-Ougarit* III (ed. M. Yon). Paris: Editions Recherche sur les Civilisations, pp. 197–212.

1994. *Le tranchée 'Ville Sud': Etude d'architecture domestique. Ras Shamra-Ougarit* X. Paris: Editions Recherche sur les Civilisations.

Carr, R. 1989. Processing of oilseed crops. In *Oil Crops of the World: Their Breeding and Utilization* (eds. G. Röbbelen, R.K. Downey and A. Ashri). New York: McGraw-Hill Publishing, pp. 226–59.

Caton-Thompson, G. and Gardner, E.W. 1934. *The Desert Fayum*. London: Royal Anthropological Institute of Great Britain and Ireland.

Černý, J. 1973. *The Valley of the Kings*. Cairo: IFAO.

Chakravarty, H.L. and Jeffrey, C. 1980. Cucurbitaceae. In *Flora of Iraq* IV. (eds. C.C. Townsend and E. Guest). Baghdad: Ministry of Agriculture and Agrarian Reform, pp. 191–209.

Chapman, A. C. and Plenderleith, H.J. 1926. Examination of an ancient Egyptian (Tut-ankh-Amen) cosmetic. *Journal of the Chemical Society*, 1926/II: 2614–19.

Charles, M.P. 1985. An introduction to the legumes and oil plants of Mesopotamia. *BSA*, 2: 39–61.

Charters, S., Evershed, R.P., Blinkhorn, P.W. and Denham, V. 1995. Evidence for the mixing of fats and waxes in archaeological ceramics. *Archaeometry*, 37/1: 113–27.

Charters, S., Evershed, R.P., Goad, L.J., Leyden, A., Blinkhorn, P.W. and Denham, V. 1993. Quantification and distribution of lipid in archaeological ceramics: implications for sampling potsherds for organic residue analysis and the classification of vessel use. *Archaeometry*, 35/2: 211–23.

Chassinat, E. 1922. Le mot dans les textes médicaux. In *Recueil d'études égyptologiques dédiées à la mémoire de Jean-François Champollion* (Bibliothèque de l'école des hautes études). Paris: Librairie ancienne Honoré Champion, pp. 447–65.

Cherfas, J. 1994. Gift of the gods. *Kew*, Spring 1994: 27–9.

Condamin, J., Formenti, F., Metais, O., Michel, M. and Blond, P. 1976. The application of gas chromatography to the tracing of oil in ancient amphorae. *Archaeometry*, 18(2): 195–201.

Connan, J. 1991. Chemische Untersuchung altägypticher Mumien-Salböle. In *Mumie und Computer* (eds. R. Drenkhahn and R. Germer). Hanover: Kestner-Museum.

Connan, J. and Dessort, D. 1989. Du bitume de la Mer Morte dans les baumes d'une momie égyptienne: identification par critères moléculaires. *Comptes Rendus de l'Académie des Sciences*, série II, 309/17: 1665–72.

1991. Du bitume dans des baumes de momies égyptiennes (1295 av. J.-C.–300 ap. J.-C.): détermination de son origine et évaluation de sa quantité. *Comptes Rendus de l'Académie des Sciences*, série II, 312/12: 1445–52.

Cox, J.S. 1977. The construction of an ancient Egyptian wig (*c.* 1400 B.C.) in the British Museum. *JEA*, 63: 67–70.

Crane, E. 1983. *The Archaeology of Beekeeping*. London: Duckworth.

1980. *A Book of Honey*. Oxford: OUP.

in press. *History of Beekeeping and Honey Hunting: Bees as a World Resource*. London: Duckworth.

Crane, E. and Graham, A.J. 1985. Bee hives of the ancient world. *Bee World*, 66: 25–41, 148–70.

Dagher, S.M. 1991. *Traditional Foods in the Near East*. Rome: FAO Food and Nutrition paper no. 50.

Davies, N. de G. 1943. *The Tomb of Rekh-mi-re' at Thebes*, 2 vols. New York, MMA.

Deal, M. 1990. Exploratory analyses of food residues from prehistoric pottery and other artifacts from Eastern Canada. *Society for Archaeological Sciences*, 13/1: 6–12.

Delougaz, P. 1940. *The Temple Oval at Khafājah*. Chicago: University of Chicago Press.

Deshpande, S.S., Deshpande, U.S. and Salunkhe, D.K. 1996. Sesame oil. In *Bailey's Industrial Oil and Fat Products*, Vol. 2, 5th edn. (ed. Y.H. Hui). New York: John Wiley and Sons, Inc., pp. 457–96.

Dietz, A. 1992. Honey bees of the world. In *The Hive and the Honey Bee*, 2nd edn. (ed. J.M. Graham). Hamilton, Illinois: Dadant and Sons, pp. 23–71.

Downey, R.K. and Röbbelen, G. 1989. *Brassica* species. In *Oil Crops of the World: Their Breeding and Utilization* (eds. G. Röbbelen, R.K. Downey and A. Ashri). London: McGraw Hill, pp. 339–62.

Drar, M. 1936. *Enumeration of the Plants collected at Gebel Elba during Two Expeditions*, Technical and Scientific Service Bulletin No. 149, Ministry of Agriculture. Cairo: Government Press.

Dugan, L.R., Jr. 1987. Fats. In *The Science of Meat and Meat Products*, 3rd edn. (ed. J.F. Price and B.S. Schweigert). Westport, CT:Food and Nutrition Press, pp. 103–14.

Eckey, E.W. 1954. *Vegetable Fats and Oils*. New York: Reinhold Publishing Corp.

Eitam, D. 1979. Olive presses of the Israelite period. *Tel Aviv*, 6: 146–55.

1993a. 'Between the [olive] rows, oil will be produced, presses will be trod . . .' (Job 24,11). In *Oil and Wine Production in the Mediterranean Area* (eds. M.-C. Amouretti and J.-P. Brun). Athens: Ecole Français d'Athènes, pp. 65–90.

1993b. Selected oil and wine installations in ancient Israel. In *Oil and Wine Production in the Mediterranean Area* (eds. M.-C. Amouretti and J.-P. Brun). Athens: Ecole Français d'Athènes pp. 91–106.

1996. The olive oil industry at Tell Miqne-Ekron in the Late Iron Age. In *Olive Oil in Antiquity* (eds. D. Eitam and M. Heltzer). Padua: Sargon srl., pp. 16–96.

Elsdon, G.D. 1926. *The Chemistry and Examination of Edible Oils and Fats, their substitutes and adulterants*. London: Ernest Benn.

Emery-Barbier, A. 1990. L'homme et l'environnement en Egypte durant la période prédynastique. In *Man's Role in the Shaping of the Eastern Mediterranean Landscape* (eds. S. Bottema, G. Entjes-Nieborg and W. van Zeist). Rotterdam: A.A. Balkema, pp. 319–26.

Epstein, C. 1993. Oil production in the Golan Heights during the Chalcolithic period. *Tel Aviv*, 20: 133–46.

Epstein, H. 1971. *The Origin of the Domesticated Animals of Africa*, 2 vols, rev. in collaboration with I.L. Mason. London: Africana Publishing Co.

Epstein, H. and Mason, I.L. 1984. Cattle. In *Evolution of Domesticated Animals* (ed. I.L. Mason). London: Longman, pp. 6–27.

Esse, D.L. 1991. *Subsistence, Trade and Social Change in Early Bronze Age Palestine*. OIP. Chicago: University of Chicago Press.

Evans, J. 1989. Report. In Merrillees, R.S.: Highs and lows in the Holy Land: opium in Biblical times. *Eretz-Israel*, 20: 148–54.

1991. Organic traces and their contribution to the understanding of trade. In *Bronze Age Trade in the Mediterranean* (ed. N.H. Gale). Studies in Mediterranean Archaeology XC, Jonsered: Paul Åströms Förlag, pp. 289–94.

Evershed, R.P. 1993. Biomolecular archaeology and lipids. *WA*, 25/1: 74–93.

Evershed, R.P., Charters, S. and Quye, A. 1995. Interpreting lipid residues in archaeological ceramics: preliminary results from laboratory simulations of vessel use and burial. *Material Research Society Symposium Proceedings* 352: pp. 85–95.

Evershed, R.P., Heron, C. and Goad, J. 1990. Analysis of organic residues of archaeological origin by high-temperature gas chromatography and gas chromatography-mass spectrometry. *Analyst*, 115: 1339–42.

Evershed, R.P., Heron, C., Charters, S. and Goad, J. 1992a. Chemical analysis of organic residues in ancient pottery: methodological guidelines and applications. In *Organic Residues in Archaeology: their Identification and Analysis* (eds. R. White and H. Page). London: United Kingdom Institute for Conservation, Archaeology Section, pp. 11–25.

1992b. The survival of food residues: new methods of analysis: interpretation and application. In *New Developments in Archaeological Science: A Joint Symposium of the Royal Society and the British Academy, Feb. 1991* (ed. A.M. Pollard). London and Oxford: British Academy and OUP, pp. 187–208.

Faulkner, R.O. 1962. *A Concise Dictionary of Middle Egyptian*, Oxford: Griffith Institute.

FAO, 1988. *Traditional Food Plants: A Resource Book for Promoting the Exploitation and Consumption of Food Plants in Arid, Semi-arid and Sub-humid Lands of Eastern Africa*. Rome: FAO Food and Nutrition Paper 42.

Feinbrun-Dothan, N. 1978. *Flora Palaestina, Part Three: Text*. Jerusalem: Israel Academy of Sciences and Humanities.

Foaden, G.P. and Fletcher, F. 1910. *Textbook of Egyptian Agriculture* II. Cairo: Department of Agriculture and Technical Education, National Printing Department.

Foures, C. 1996. Fats from land animals. In *Oils and Fats Manual* I (eds. A. Karleskind and J.-P. Wolff). Paris: Lavoisier Publishing, pp. 247–66.

Fox, P.F. 1993. Cheese: an overview. In *Cheese: Chemistry, Physics and Microbiology* I, 2nd edn. (ed. P.F. Fox). London: Chapman and Hall, pp. 1–36.

Frankel, R. 1993a. Screw weights from Israel. In *Oil and Wine Production in the Mediterranean Area* (eds. M.-C. Amouretti and J.-P. Brun). Athens: Ecole Français d'Athènes, pp. 107–18.

1993b. The *trapetum* and the *mola olearia*. In *Oil and Wine Production in the Mediterranean Area* (eds. M.-C. Amouretti and J.-P. Brun). Athens: Ecole Français d'Athènes, pp. 477–81.

1994. Ancient oil mills and presses in the land of Israel. In *History and Technology of Olive Oil in the Holy Land* (ed. E. Ayalon). Arlington, VA: Oléarius Editions, pp. 19–89.

Gallant, T.W. 1985. The agronomy, production and utilization of sesame and linseed in the Graeco-Roman world. *BSA*, 2: 153–8.

Germer, R. 1979. *Untersuchung über Arzneimittelpflanzen im Alten Ägypten*. Hamburg: Universitat Hamburg.

1981. Einige Bemerkungen zum Angeblichen Opiumexport von Zypern nach Ägypten. *SAK*, 9: 125–9.

1982a. Mohn. *LÄ*, 4: 190.

1982b. Öle. *LÄ*, 4: 552–5.

1985. *Flora des pharaonischen Ägypten*, DAIK Sonderschrift 14. Mainz am Rhein: von Zabern.

1989. *Die Pflanzenmaterialien aus dem Grab des Tutanchamun*. Hildesheim: Gerstenberg.

Germer, R., Kischkewitz, H. and Luning, M. 1994. Neueste Forschungen in der Mumiensammlung des Ägyptischen Museums Berlin: Die Mumie des In-em-achet. *Jahrbuch der Berliner Museen*, New Series, 36: 7–21.

Giddy, L.L. and Jeffreys, D.G. 1991. Memphis 1990. *JEA*, 77: 1–6.

Gitin, S. 1990. Ekron of the Philistines, part II: olive-oil suppliers to the world. *Biblical Archaeology Review*, March/April: 33–42, 59.

Godin, V.J. and Spensely, P.C. 1971. *Oils and Oilseeds*, TPI Crop and Product Digests #1, Tropical Products Institute, England.

Gophna, R. and Liphschitz, N. 1996. The Ashkelon trough settlements in the Early Bronze Age I: new evidence of maritime trade. *Tel Aviv*, 23: 143–53.

Greiss, E.A.M. 1957. *Anatomical Identification of Some Ancient Egyptian Plant Materials*. Mémoires de l'Institut d'Egypte 55. Cairo: Costa Tsoumas and Co.

Grout, R.A. 1946. Production and uses of beeswax. In *The Hive and the Honeybee* (ed. R.A. Grout). Hamilton, IL: Dadant and Sons, pp. 536–54.

Gunstone, F.D., Harwood, J.L. and Padley, F.B. 1994. *The Lipid Handbook*, 2nd edn. London: Chapman and Hall.

el-Hadidi, M.N. 1982. The Predynastic Flora of the Hierakonpolis Region. In *The Predynastic of Hierakonpolis – An Interim Report* (M.A. Hoffman). Egyptian Stuides Assoc., Pub. No. 1 Giza: Cairo University Herbarium and Dept of Sociology and Anthropology, Western Illinois University, pp. 102–15.

1992. Notes on Egyptian weeds of antiquity: 1. Min's lettuce and the Naqada plant. In *The Followers of Horus, Studies Dedicated to Michael Allen Hoffman 1944–1990* (eds. R. Friedman and B. Adams). Oxford: Oxbow, pp. 323–6.

Hadjisavvas, S. 1992. *Olive oil processing in Cyprus from the Bronze Age to the Byzantine period*. Studies in Mediterranean Archaeology XCIX. Nicosia: Paul Åströms Förlag.

Haldane, C. 1993. Direct evidence for organic cargoes in the Late Bronze Age. *WA*, 24/3: 348–60.

Hardman, R. and Sofowora, E.A. 1972. A reinvestigation of *Balanites aegyptiaca* as a source of steroidal sapogenins. *Economic Botany*, 26: 169–73.

Head, S.W., Swetman, A.A., Hammonds, T.W., Gordon, A., Southwell, K.H. and Harris, R.V. 1995. *Small Scale Vegetable Oil Extraction*. Chatham Maritime, Kent: Natural Resources Institute.

Helbaek, H. 1966. The plant remains from Nimrud. In *Nimrud and its Remains* II (ed. M. Mallowan). London: Collins, pp. 613–19.

Helck, W. 1977. Fett. *LÄ* 2: 204–5.

Hepper, F.N. 1987. *Planting a Bible Garden*. London: HMSO.

1990. *Pharaoh's Flowers: The Botanical Treasures of Tutankhamun*. Royal Botanic Gardens, Kew. London: HMSO.

1992. *Illustrated Encyclopedia of Biblical Plants: Flowers and Trees, Fruits and Vegetables, Ecology*, Leicester: Inter Varsity Press.

Heron, C., Evershed, R.P. and Goad, L.J. 1991a. Effects of migration of soil lipids on organic residues associated with buried potsherds. *JAS*, 18: 641–59.

Heron, C., Evershed, R.P., Goad, L.J. and Denham, V. 1991b. New approaches to the analysis of organic residues from archaeological remains. In *Archaeological Sciences 1989: Proceedings of a Conference on the application of scientific techniques to archaeology, Bradford, Sept. 1989* (eds. P. Budd, B. Chapman, C. Jackson, R. Janaway and B. Ottaway), Oxbow Monograph 9. Oxford: Oxbow, pp. 332–9.

Hilditch T.P and Williams, P.N. 1964. *Chemical Constitution of Natural Fats*. London: Chapman and Hall.

Hobbs, J.J. 1990. *Bedouin Life in the Egyptian Wilderness* (reprinted 1989 University of Texas Press edition). Cairo: American University in Cairo Press.

Hopf, M. 1983. Appendix B: Jericho plant remains. In *Excavations at Jericho* V (eds. K.M. Kenyon and T.A. Holland). London: British School of Archaeology in Jerusalem, pp. 576–621.

Houlihan, P.F. 1986. *The Birds of Ancient Egypt*. Warminster: Aris and Phillips.

1987. Some remarks on deer (Cervidae) in ancient Egypt. *JEA*, 73: 238–43.

1996. *The Animal World of the Pharaohs*. London: Thames and Hudson.

Hussain, S.A., Dollear, F.G. and O'Connor, R.T. 1949. Oil from the kernels of lalob fruit, *Balanites aegyptiaca*. *Journal of the American Oil Chemists' Society*, December: 730–2.

Ikram, Selina. 1995. *Choice Cuts: Meat Production in Ancient Egypt*. Leuven: Peeters.

Jeffrey, C. 1977. Cucurbitaceae. In *Flora of Cyprus*, Vol. I (ed. R.D. Meikle). Kew: Royal Botanic Gardens, pp. 675–9.

Keimer, L. 1924. *Die Gartenpflanzen im Alten Ägypten* I. Hamburg-Berlin: Hoffmann und Campe Verlag.

1936. Bericht über in Maadi 1931 und 1932 gefundene Samen. In *The Excavations of the Egyptian University at the Neolithic Site at Maadi: Second Preliminary Report, Season 1932* (eds. O.

Menghin and M. Amer) Cairo: Government Press, pp. 69–71.

1984. *Die Gartenpflanzen im alten Ägypten* II (ed. R. Germer). DAIK. Mainz am Rhein: Philipp von Zabern.

Kislev, M. 1988. Nahal Hemar Cave: dessicated plant remains: an interim report. *ʿAtiqot*, 18: 76–81.

Kloner, A. and Sagiv, N. 1993. The olive presses of Hellenistic Maresha, Israel. In *Oil and Wine Production in the Mediterranean Area* (eds. M.-C. Amouretti and J.-P. Brun). Athens: École français d'Athènes, pp. 119–36.

Knowles, P.F. 1967. Processing seeds for oil in towns of Turkey, India and Egypt. *Economic Botany*, 21: 156–62.

van der Kooij, G. and Ibrahim, M.M. 1989. Reconstruction: the history of Tell Deir Alla. In *Picking up the Threads . . . A Continuing Review of Excavations at Deir Alla, Jordan* (eds. G. van der Kooij and M.M. Ibrahim). Leiden: University of Leiden Archaeological Center, pp. 74–90.

Koschel, K. 1996. Opium alkaloids in a Cypriote base ring I vessel (Bilbil) of the Middle Bronze Age from Egypt. In *Ägypten und Levante* VI (ed. M. Bietak). Vienna: Verlag der Österreichischen Akademie der Wissenschaften, pp. 159–66.

Koura, B. 1995. Ist *b3q* Moringaöl oder Olivenöl? *GM*, 145: 79–82.

Kroll, H. 1989. Die Pflanzenfunde von Maadi. In *Maadi III: The Non-Lithic Small Finds and the Structural Remains of the Predynastic Settlement* (eds. I. Rizkana and J. Seeher), DAIK, Mainz am Rhein: Philipp von Zabern, pp. 129–36.

Kuény, G. 1950. Scènes apicoles dans l'ancienne Egypte. *JNES*, 9: 84–93.

Kühn, H. 1960. Detection and identification of waxes, including Punic wax, by infra-red spectrography. *Studies in Conservation*, 5(2): 71–9.

Lindqvist, K. 1960. On the origin of cultivated lettuce. *Hereditas*, 46: 319–50.

Liphschitz, N. 1996. Olives in ancient Israel in view of *Dendroarchaeological* Investigations. In *Olive Oil in Antiquity* (eds. D. Eitam and M. Heltzer). Padua: Sargon srl., p. 7–13

Liphschitz, N., Gophna, R., Hartman, M. and Biger, G. 1991. The beginning of olive (*Olea europaea*) cultivation in the Old World: a reassessment. *JAS*, 18: 441–53.

Liphschitz, N., Gophna, R., Bonani, G. and Feldstein, A. 1996. Wild olive (*Olea europaea*) stones from a Chalcolithic cave at Shoham, Israel and their implications. *Tel Aviv*, 23: 135–42.

Lityńska, M. 1993. Plant remains from the Neolithic site at Armant: preliminary report. In *Environmental Change and Human Culture in the Nile Basin and Northern Africa until the Second Millennium B.C.* (eds. L. Krzyzaniak, M. Kobusiewicz and J. Alexander). Posnan: Posnan Archaeological Museum, pp. 351–4.

Loret, V. 1886. Recherches sur plusieurs plantes connues des anciens égyptiens. *RT*, 7: 101–14.

1892. *La Flore Pharaonique*. Paris: Ernest Leroux.

Love, J.A. 1996. Animal fats. In *Bailey's Industrial Oil and Fat Products* I, 5th edn. (ed. Y.H. Hui), New York: John Wiley and Sons, pp. 1–18.

Lucas, A. 1962. *Ancient Egyptian Materials and Industries*. 4th edn., rev. J.R. Harris. London: Edward Arnold.

Lüchtrath, A. 1988. Tj-šps, der Kampferbaum Ostafrikas. *GM*, 101: 43–8.

Mackay, E. 1920. On the use of beeswax and resin as varnishes in Theban tombs. *Ancient Egypt*, 5: 35–8.

McNaughton, I.H. 1995a. Swedes and rapes. In *Evolution of Crop Plants* (eds. J. Smartt and N.W. Simmonds). Harlow, Essex: Longman Scientific and Technical, 2nd edn, pp. 68–75.

1995b. Turnips and relatives. In *Evolution of Crop Plants* (eds. J. Smartt and N.W. Simmonds). Harlow, Essex: Longman Scientific and Technical, 2nd edn, pp. 62–7.

Manniche, L. 1989. *An Ancient Egyptian Herbal*, London: BMP.

Matthews, W. and Postgate, J.N. with Payne, S., Charles, M.P and Dobney, K. 1994. The imprint of Living in an Early Mesopotamian City: Questions and Answers. In *Whither Environmental Archaeology* (eds. R. Luff and P. Rowley-Conwy). Oxford: Oxbow Books, Oxbow Monograph 38, pp. 171–212.

Mattingly, D.J. 1988. The Olive Boom. Oil Surpluses, Wealth and Power in Roman Tripolitania. *Libyan Studies* 19: 21–41.

Meeks, D. 1993. Oléiculture et viticulture dans l'Égypte pharaonique. In *Oil and Wine Production in the Mediterranean Area* (eds. M.-C. Amouretti and J.-P. Brun). Athens: École français d'Athènes, pp. 3–38.

Meikle, R.D. 1977. *Flora of Cyprus* I. Kew: Royal Botanic Gardens.

1985. *Flora of Cyprus* II. Kew: Royal Botanic Gardens.

Mellor, J.E.M. 1928. Beekeeping in Egypt: Part I. An account of the Beladi Craft, that is to say the Craft native to the Country; with observations made upon it from September 1926 to January 1928. *Bulletin de la Société Royale Entomologique d'Égypt*, XII.

Merlin, M.D. 1984. *On the Trail of the Ancient Opium Poppy*. London: Associated University Press.

Merrillees, R.S. 1962. Opium trade in the Bronze Age Levant. *Antiquity*, 36: 287692.

Merrillees R.S. and Winter, J. 1972. Bronze Age Trade between the Aegean and Egypt. Minoan and Mycenaean Pottery from Egypt in the Brooklyn Museum. In *Miscellania Wilbouriana* I. New York: Brooklyn Museum, pp. 101–33.

Miller, A.G. and Stuart-Smith, S. 1988. *Plants of Dhofar, The Southern Region of Oman: Traditional, Economic and Medicinal Uses*, Office of the Adviser for Conservation of the Environment. Sultanate of Oman: Diwan of Royal Court.

Mills, J.S. and White, R. 1994. *The Organic Chemistry of Museum Objects*. Oxford: Butterworth-Heinemann Ltd. Second Edition.

Nayar, N.M. and Mehra, K.L. 1970. Sesame: Its Uses, Botany, Cytogenetics, and Origin. *Economic Botany*, 24: 20–31.

Neef, R. 1990. Introduction, development and environmental implications of olive culture: The evidence from Jordan. In *Man's Role in the Shaping of the Eastern Mediterranean Landscape* (eds. S. Bottema, G. Entjes-Nieborg and W. van Zeist). Rotterdam: Balkema, pp. 295–306.

Negbi, M. 1992. A sweetmeat plant, a perfume plant and their weedy relatives: a chapter in the history of *Cyperus esculentus* L. and *C. rotundus* L. *Economic Botany*, 46(1): 64–71.

Newman, R. unpublished. Examination report on the analysis of a Third Intermediate Period inner coffin (72.4821b and c) and cartonnage (72.4821a) of Bes. Boston: MFA.

Niwiński, A. 1992. Ritual protection of the dead, or symbolic reflection of his special status in society? The problem of the black-coated cartonnages and coffins of the Third Intermediate Period. *Studia Aegyptiaca*, 14: 457–71.

Norris, F.A. 1979. Handling, storage, and grading of oils and oil-bearing materials. In *Bailey's Industrial Oil and Fat Products* I (ed. D. Swern). New York: John Wiley and Sons, 4th edn., pp. 479–510.

Ntenga, G.M. and Mugongo, B.T. 1991. *Honey hunters and beekeepers: A study of traditional beekeeping in Babati District, Tanzania.* Uppsala: Swedish University of Agricultural Sciences, International Rural Development Centre Working Paper 161.

O'Donoghue, K., Clapham, A., Evershed, R., and Brown, T. A. 1996. Remarkable preservation of biomolecules in ancient radish seeds. *Proceedings of the Royal Society, London B*, 263, 1996: 541–7.

Oderinde, R.A. and Tairu, A.O. 1992. Determination of the triglyceride, phospholipid and unsaponifiable fractions of yellow nutsedge tuber oil. *Food Chemistry*, 45: 279–82.

Osborn, D.J. 1968. Notes on medicinal and other uses of plants in Egypt. *Economic Botany*, 22(2): 165–77.

Patrick, M., de Koning, A.J. and Smith, A.B. 1985. Gas liquid chromatographic analysis of fatty acids in food residues from ceramics found in the Southwestern Cape, South Africa. *Archaeometry*, 27(2): 231–6.

Pendlebury, J.D.S. 1951. *The City of Akhenaten III.* 2 vols. London: EES.

Petrie, W.M.F., and Quibell, J.E. 1896. *Naqada and Ballas*, London: Bernard Quaritch.

Pigott, G.M. 1996. Marine oils. In *Bailey's Industrial Oil and Fat Products* I, 5th edn. (ed. Y.H. Hui). New York: John Wiley and Sons.

Pilc, J. and White, R. 1995. Application of FT-IR to the analysis of paint binders in easel painting. *National Gallery Technical Bulletin*, 16: 73–84.

Pliny *see* Rackham 1968

Pollard. M. 1986. Nuclear magnetic resonance spectroscopy (high resolution). In *Analysis of Oils and Fats* (eds. R.J. Hamilton and J.B. Rossell). London: Elsevier Applied Science Publications, pp. 401–34.

Powell, C. 1995. The nature and use of Ancient Egyptian potter's wheels. In *Amarna Reports* VI (B.J. Kemp). London: EES, pp. 309–35.

Rackham, H. (transl. and ed.) 1968. *Pliny the elder: Natural History.* Loeb Classical Library. London: Heinemann.

Raven, M.J. 1983. Wax in Egyptian magic and symbolism. *OMRO*, 64: 7–47.

Renfrew, C. 1972. *The Emergence of Civilization: The Cyclades and the Aegean in the Third Millennium BC.* London: Methuen.

Renfrew, J.M. 1972. The plant remains. In *Myrtos: An Early Bronze Age Settlement in Crete* (P. Warren), British School of Archaeology at Athens, London: Thames and Hudson, pp. 315–17.

1973. *Palaeoethnobotany: The Prehistoric Food Plants of the Near East and Europe.* London: Methuen.

1985. Preliminary report on the botanical remains. In *Amarna Reports* II (B.J. Kemp). London: EES, pp. 175–90.

de Roller, G-J. 1992. Archaeobotanical remains from Tell Ibrahim Awad, seasons 1988 and 1989. In *The Nile Delta in Transition; 4th–3rd Millennium B.C.* (ed. E.C.M. van den Brink). Tel Aviv: E.C.M. van den Brink, pp. 111–15.

Root, H.H. 1978. Wax. In *The ABC and XYZ of Bee Culture*, 2nd ed. (ed. A.I. Root, rev. E.R. Root, H.H. Root, J.A. Root and L.R. Goltz). Medina, OH: The A.I. Root Company, pp. 651–67.

Rowley-Conwy, P. 1989. Nubia AD 0–500 and the 'Islamic' Agricultural Revolution: preliminary botanical evidence from Qasr Ibrim, Egyptian Nubia. *Archéologie du Nil Moyen*, 3: 131–8.

Runnels, C.N. and Hansen, J. 1986. The olive in the prehistoric Aegean: the evidence for domestication in the Early Bronze Age. *Oxford Journal of Archaeology*, 5(3): 299–308.

Ryder, M.L. 1983. *Sheep and Man.* London: Duckworth.

Ryder, E.J. and Whitaker, T.W. 1995. Lettuce. In *Evolution of Crop Plants* (eds. J. Smartt and N.W. Simmonds). Harlow, Essex: Longman Scientific and Technical, pp. 53–6.

Salunkhe, D.K., Chavan, J.K., Adsule, R.N. and Kadam, S.S. 1992. *World Oilseeds: Chemistry, Technology and Utilization*, New York: Van Nostrand Reinhold.

Samuel, D. 1989. Their staff of life: initial investigations on ancient Egyptian bread baking. In *Amarna Reports* V (ed. Barry J. Kemp). London: EES, pp. 253–90.

Sandy, D.B. 1977. *Oils in Ptolemaic Egypt.* Ann Arbor, MI: University Microfilms International.

1989. *The Production and Use of Vegetable Oils in Ptolemaic Egypt.* Atlanta, Georgia: Bulletin of the American Society of Papyrologists Supplement 6, Scholars Press.

Schmidt, J.O. and Buchmann, S.L. 1992. Other products of the hive. In *The Hive and the Honey Bee* (ed. J.M. Graham). Hamilton, Illinois: Dadant and Sons, rev. edn., pp. 927–88.

Schunck de Goldfiem, J. 1942. Étude chimique de *Balanites aegyptiaca* (Del.). *Bulletin de la société botanique de France*, 89: 236–7.

Scott, R. 1986. *Cheesemaking Practice*, 2nd edn. London: Elsevier Applied Science.

Sears, C.S. 1994. The Oasis of Siwa: visited and revisited, comprising an updated ethnography and photo-essay covering the changes and acculturation of the past fifty years. *NARCE*, 165: 1–10.

Seegeler, C.J.P. 1983. *Oil Plants in Ethiopia, their taxonomy and agricultural significance.* Wageningen: Centre for Agricultural Publishing and Documentation.

Seher, A., Schiller, H., Krohn, M. and Werner, G. 1980. Untersuchungen von 'Ölproben' aus archäologischen Funden. *Fette, Seifen, Anstrichmittel*, 10: 395–9.

Serpico, M. and White, R. 1996. A report on the analysis of the contents of a cache of jars from the tomb of Djer. In *Aspects of Early Egypt* (ed. J. Spencer). London: BMP, pp. 128–39.

1998. Chemical analysis of coniferous resins from ancient Egypt using gas chromatography/mass spectrometry (GC/MS). In *Proceedings of the Seventh International Congress of Egyptologists* (ed. C. Eyre). Leuven: Peeters, pp. 1037–48.

in press. The identification and use of varnishes on New Kingdom funerary equipment. In *Colour and Painting in Ancient Egypt* (ed. W.V. Davies). London: BMP.

Shearer, G. 1987. Use of Diffuse Reflectance Fourier Transform Infrared Spectroscopy in art and archaeological conservation. In *Recent Advances in the Conservation and Analysis of Artifacts* (ed. J. Black). London: Summer Schools Press, pp. 253–6.

Soderstrom, T.R. 1969. Appendix III: impressions of cereals and other plants in the pottery of Hajar Bin Humeid. In *Hajar Bin Humeid: Investigations at a Pre-Islamic Site in South Arabia* (ed. G.W. Van Beek). Baltimore: Johns Hopkins Press, pp. 399–407.

Somali, M.A., Bajneid, M.A. and Al-Fhaimani, S.S. 1984. Chemical composition and characteristics of *Moringa peregrina* seeds and seed oil. *Journal of the American Oil Chemists' Society*, 61(1): 85–6.

Sonntag, N.O.V. 1979a. Composition and characteristics of individual fats and oils. In *Bailey's Industrial Oil and Fat Products I* (ed. D. Swern). New York: John Wiley and Sons, Fourth Edition, pp. 289–477.

1979b. Reactions of fats and fatty acids. In *Bailey's Industrial Oil and Fat Products I* (ed. D. Swern). New York: John Wiley and Sons, 4th edn., pp. 99–175.

1979c. Structure and composition of fats and oils. In *Bailey's Industrial Oil and Fat Products I* (ed. D. Swern). New York: John Wiley and Sons, 4th edn., pp.1–98.

Spiegel-Roy, P. 1986. Domestication of fruit trees. In *The Origin and Domestication of Cultivated Plants* (ed. C. Barigozzi). Oxford: Elsevier, pp. 201–11.

Stager, L.E. 1985. The firstfruits of civilization. In *Palestine in the Bronze and Iron Ages: Studies in Honour of Olga Tufnell* (ed. J.N. Tubb). London: Institute of Archaeology, 172–88.

Stager, L.E. and Wolff, S.R. 1981. Production and commerce in temple courtyards: an olive press in the sacred precinct at Tel Dan. *BASOR*, 243: 95–102.

Storch, W. and Schäfer, H. 1985. Chemische Untersuchungen an der Müncher Mumie ÄS 73B: Ein Beitrag zür Aufklärung des Mumifizierungsverfahrens. *SAK Beihefte*, 1: 328–38.

Täckholm, V. 1974. *Students' Flora of Egypt*, 2nd edn. Cairo: Cairo University.

Täckholm, V. and Drar, M. 1950. *Flora of Egypt* II. Cairo: Fouad I University Press.

Täckholm, V., El-Duweini, A.K., Greiss, E.A.M. and Iskander, Z. 1961. Botanical identification of the plants found at the Monastery of Phoebammon. In *Le Monastère de Phoebammon dans la Thébaïde* III. Cairo: Société d'archéologie copte, pp. 3–37.

Tew, J.E. 1992. Honey and wax - a consideration of production, processing and packaging techniques. In *The Hive and the Honey Bee*, 2nd edn. (ed. J.M. Graham). Hamilton, IL: Dadant and Sons, pp. 657–704.

Thanheiser, U. 1991. Untersuchungen zur Landwirtschaft der vor- und frühdynastischen Zeit in Tell-el-Fara^cin-Buto. In *Ägypten und Levante*, II (ed. M. Bietak), Vienna: Verlag der Österreichischen Akademie der Wissenschaften, pp. 39–45

1992. Plant remains from Minshat Abu Omar: first impressions. In *The Nile Delta in Transition; 4th–3rd Millennium B.C.* (ed. E.C.M. van der Brink). Tel Aviv: E.C.M. van den Brink, pp. 167–70.

Tulloch, A.P. 1980. Beeswax - composition and analysis. *Bee World*, 61(2): 47–62.

Tylor, J.J. and Griffith, F. LL. 1894. *The Tomb of Paheri*. London: EES.

de Vartavan, C. 1990. Contaminated plant-foods from the tomb of Tutankhamun: a new interpretative system. *Journal of Archaeological Science*, 17: 473–94.

Vaughan, J.G. 1970. *The Structure and Utilization of Oil Seeds*. London: Chapman and Hall.

Veselovskaya, M.A. 1976. *The Poppy: Its Classification and Importance as an Oleiferous Crop*. Translated from a Russian edition dated 1933. New Delhi: Amerind Publishing Co.

Verdcourt, B. 1996. Lauraceae. In *Flora of Tropical East Africa* (ed. R.M. Polhill). Rotterdam: A.A. Balkema.

Waetzold, H. 1985. Ölpflanzen und Pflanzenöle im 3. Jahrtausend. *BSA*, 2: 77–87.

Walker, P. and Crane, E. 1987. Constituents of Propolis. *Apidologie*, 18(4): 327–34.

Weiss, E.A. 1971. *Castor, Sesame and Safflower*. New York: Barnes and Noble, Inc.

1983a. *Oilseed Crops*. London: Longman.

Weiss, T.J. 1983b. *Food Oils and their Uses*. Chichester: Ellis Horwood.

Wetterstrom, W. 1984. The plant remains. In *Archaeological Investigations at el-Hibeh 1980: Preliminary Report* (ed. R.J. Wenke). ARCE Reports. Malibu: Undena, pp. 50–77.

1996. L'apparition de l'agriculture en Égypte. *Archéo-Nil*, 6: 51–75.

White, R. 1978. The application of gas chromatography to the identification of waxes. *Studies in Conservation*, 23: 57–68.

1984. The characterization of proteinaceous binders in art objects. *National Gallery Technical Bulletin*, 8: 5–14.

1992. A brief introduction to the chemistry of natural products in archaeology. In *Organic Residues in Archaeology: their Identification and Analysis* (eds. R. White and H. Page). London: United Kingdom Institute for Conservation, Archaeology Section, pp. 5–10.

Wiedermann, H.G. and Bayer, G. 1982. The bust of Nefertiti. *Analytical Chemistry*, 54(4): 619A–628A.

Wilkinson, G. 1843. *Modern Egypt and Thebes: being a Description of Egypt* I. London: John Murray.

Willcox, G. 1996. Evidence for plant exploitation and vegetation history from three Early Neolithic pre-pottery sites on the Euphrates (Syria). *Vegetation History and Archaeobotany*, 5: 143–52.

Willerding, U. and Wolf, G. 1990. Paläo-ethnobotanische Untersuchungen von Pflanzenresten aus dem 1. Jahrtausend v. Chr. von Elephantine. *MDAIK*, 46: 263–7.

Woodbury, S.E., Evershed, R.P., Rossell, J.B., Griffith, R.E. and Farnell, P. 1995. Detection of vegetable oil adulteration using gas chromatography combustion/isotope ratio mass spectrometry. *Analytical Chemistry*, 67(15): 2685–90.

Wright, M.M. and Wheals, B.B. 1987. Pyrolysis-mass spectrometry of natural gums, resins, and waxes and its use for detecting such materials in ancient Egyptian mummy cases (cartonnages). *Journal of Analytical and Applied Pyrolysis*, 11: 195–211.

Zaky, A. and Iskander, Z. 1942. Ancient Egyptian cheese. *ASAE*, 41: 295–313.

Zahran, M.A. and Willis, A.J. 1992. *The Vegetation of Egypt*. London: Chapman and Hall.

van Zeist, W. 1985. Pulses and oil crop plants. *BSA*, 2: 33–8.

van Zeist, W. and Bakker-Heeres, J.A.H. 1982. Archaeobotanical studies in the Levant 1. Neolithic sites in the Damascus Basin: Aswad, Ghoraifé, Ramad. *Palaeohistoria*, 24: 165–256.

1984. Archaeobotanical studies in the Levant 2. Neolithic and Halaf levels at Ras Shamra. *Palaeohistoria*, 26: 151–70.

1985. Archaeobotanical studies in the Levant 4. Bronze Age sites on the North Syrian Euphrates. *Palaeohistoria*, 27: 247–316.

van Zeist, W. and Neef, R. 1989. Plants. In *Picking up the Threads: a Continuing Review of Excavations at Deir Alla, Jordan* (eds. G. van der Kooij and M.M. Ibrahim). Leiden: University of Leiden Archaeological Center, pp. 30–6.

van Zeist, W. and de Roller, G.J. 1993. Plant remains from Maadi, a Predynastic site in Lower Egypt. *Vegetation History and Archaeobotany*, 2: 1–14.

van Zeist, W. and Waterbolk-van Rooijen, W. 1992. Two interesting floral finds from third millennium B.C. Tell Hammam et Turkman, northern Syria. *Vegetation History and Archaeobotany*, 1: 157–61.

Zeuner, F.E. 1963. *A History of Domesticated Animals*. London: Hutchinson and Co.

Zohary, D. 1995. Olive. In *Evolution of Crop Plants* (ed. J. Smartt and N.W. Simmonds). Harlow, Essex: Longman Scientific and Technical, pp. 379–82.

Zohary, D. and Hopf, M. 1993. *Domestication of Plants in the Old World*. Oxford: Clarendon Press.

Zohary, M. 1962. *Plant Life of Palestine*. New York: The Ronald Press Co.

1966. *Flora Palaestina. Part One, Text*. Jerusalem: Israel Academy of Sciences and Humanities.

1973. *Geobotanical Foundations of the Middle East* II. Stuttgart: Gustav Fischer.

1987. *Flora Palaestina. Part Two, Text*. Jerusalem: Israel Academy of Sciences and Humanities.

18. Resins, amber and bitumen

MARGARET SERPICO WITH A CONTRIBUTION BY RAYMOND WHITE

Introduction

In the past, the similar, glossy appearance of resin, amber and bitumen has often resulted in confusion between them in ancient samples. Objects with resinous features, notably a red-brown or reddish-orange colour and a lustrous surface, have varyingly been described as resin or amber, and dark, shiny deposits have been called bitumen or a heated resin pitch. That these three natural products have attracted speculation is not entirely surprising. Given the dearth of supplies within Egypt, they provide important evidence of trade. No deposits of amber within Egypt are known, and while limited quantities of resin and bitumen do exist, there is as yet no evidence that they were exploited by the ancient Egyptians. Both resin and bitumen reached Egypt in Predynastic times, although their usages at that time can be unclear (Prag 1986: 71–2, 73; Raven 1990: 10–13; Connan *et al.* 1992). Amber may also have been imported then (Doran 1937: 96–100), but this has yet to be corroborated by more recent scientific analysis. The most common employment of amber would have been in the manufacture of small items, such as amulets, beads, or other types of jewellery. These may have been carved in Egypt from the raw material or imported as a completed object. Resin could have been shaped or moulded for a similar purpose, again leading to potential confusion in the identification of the source (Raven 1990: 11–14).

Other possible usages of resins and bitumen are quite diverse. The pleasing odour of many resins undoubtedly made them valued as incense, and they could also have been ingredients (perhaps along with aromatic woods, herbs, spices and flowers) in scented ointments. These were of importance not only in the everyday toilet but also in religious ceremonies and funerary rituals. Both resins and bitumen may have been applied to the body of the deceased as part of the mummification process and their possible usage as a varnish on funerary furniture during the New Kingdom may be a further reflection of their religious importance. On a more pragmatic level, resins, and perhaps bitumen, could have been employed as adhesives and possibly as mortar (Lucas 1962: 7–8, 75; see Chapter 19, this volume).

Resins

Botanical sources

Most resins are obtained by making incisions into the bark of a tree or shrub and collecting the exudate either in a fluid state or after it had hardened. Some slight variations in procedure may have occurred from place to place, for example, with regard to the types of instruments used, the length of time for harvesting, or the nature and frequency of the incisions. In a few instances, the root, or the swollen galls which result from insect attack are tapped. Modern references to resin tapping can provide useful parallels, but accounts often only given the common name of the source. Some of these words for resins, such as *mastic* and *galbanum*, can be applied not only to different species within a genus but to different genera altogether (see p. 434, 442). It has also been argued that certain species are only resin-producing in certain areas or have ceased to produce resin since antiquity (discussed below). For some species, this question cannot be adequately resolved due to the lack of reliable information on resin production.

There is little evidence that the Egyptians themselves were involved in the tapping of resins in foreign locations. Reliefs such as one which depicts the cutting of coniferous trees in Western Asia during the reign of Seti I (Naville 1912: pl. XXI), suggest that the Egyptians may occasionally have visited areas where resins were produced. In Hatshepsut's Punt reliefs, the lumps of gum-resin are shown, as are the trees (Naville 1898: pls. LXIX, LXXIX), but not the tapping. Thus, it is likely that resins were obtained primarily through middle-men at major trading centres.

A number of botanical studies in the past have considered the possible sources (Lucas 1962: 90–7, 316–26; Germer 1985: 5–12, 65, 106–11; Hepper 1987b: 107–114; and Täckholm *et al.* 1941: 45–79). The distribution of the different resins can be divided by their geographical locations: east Africa/Arabia, the Mediterranean, and central Asia. Within these groups, some can be considered 'primary' sources, namely those which Egypt could, in theory, have obtained through direct contact with the areas. 'Secondary' sources most likely reached Egypt indirectly. The latter category would include some of the resins found in Iraq and Iran, which could require long distance land routes to reach Egypt. Other resins indigenous to western Africa, such as sandarac (*Tetraclinis articulata* (Vahl) Mast.) found in Algeria and Morocco, are unlikely to have played a significant role in resin trade and are mentioned only in passing. Similarly, a few sources have only limited resin production. These include broom, box, euphorbia, tamarisk, elderberry and oleander (Hepper 1987b: 114).

Mediterranean coniferous resins

Perhaps best-known of the Mediterranean resins are the conifers. The relevant genera can be found in two families: Pinaceae, which includes pine, cedar, fir and spruce, and Cupressaceae, which includes juniper and cypress. Although spruce (*Picea orientalis* (L.) Link) was mentioned as a source by Lucas (1962: 319), it has been established that this tree is indigenous only to the eastern Black Sea area (Kayacik 1955: 482), and is therefore not likely to have been widely available. Moreover, only one example of spruce wood has been identified from Egypt (Meiggs 1982: 404). As this is an unprovenanced handle for a tool of uncertain date and purpose (Ashmolean Museum, Oxford, 1927.3046, published by Clark *et al.* 1974: 371), its antiquity is not certain and few conclusions can be drawn (Dr Helen Whitehouse, Ashmolean Museum: pers. comm.). Another species, *Picea abies* (L.) Karsten, is apparently restricted to northern Greece (Jalas and Suominen 1973: 14–15).

In general, coniferous resins are pale yellow in colour and translucent, but it is the turpentine obtained from the distillation of the wood or resin for which many of these trees, notably the pines, are best known today (Mills and White 1994: 95–7; Howes 1949: 104). In addition, softwood pines are excellent sources of pitch and tar, produced by strong heating of the resin (see p. 450). Although most of these coniferous resins are obtained by slashing the bark, the resin of the fir collects in ducts or 'blisters' on the trunk which can then be punctured (Howes 1949: 154).

*Cedar (*Cedrus libani *A. Richard)*
Family: Pinaceae
Perhaps the most controversial of the resin-producing conifers is the cedar (see Fig. 15.13). For many years, this was linked to the Egyptian word *ˁš*. However, earlier this century Loret proposed instead that *ˁš* was probably fir, *Abies cilicica*, or more generally any conifer, especially pine (Loret 1916: 50–1). He argued that ancient Egyptian representations of *ˁš* wood are not red, as would be expected of cedar, but yellow; that texts imply that *ˁš* was a straight, tall tree, while cedar was squat and often had a twisted trunk; and that other conifers were at least as common in Lebanon as cedar (Loret 1916: 45–8).

The problems presented by the colour of *ˁš* persist but there is some indication that in dense forests *Cedrus libani* could have a tall, upright habit (Meiggs 1982: 407). Moreover, as various wood artefacts ranging in date from Predynastic through to Greco-Roman times have been identified as cedar, the tree was clearly not unknown to the Egyptians (Chapter 15, this volume; Meiggs 1982: 409; Davies 1995: 150, table I). In addition, many botanists now accept that, since antiquity, there has been significant deforestation of cedar (Beals 1965: 679–94; Mikesell 1969: 10; Zohary 1973: 345; Meiggs 1982: 48–64; 405–9). Meiggs (1982: 377) suggested that this diminution probably occurred between the sixth and seventeenth to eighteenth centuries AD.

Zohary noted that, in Lebanon, 'where the cedar forests are affected by men, the removed cedar trees are largely replaced by the rather weedy *Juniperus excelsa* which, both in the Lebanon and in some places of the Taurus, has won areas formerly in possession of the cedar' (Zohary 1973: 346). Thus, while deforestation has reduced the prevalence of some trees, others may have had a more restricted distribution in antiquity than they do today.

In the mountains of Lebanon, *Cedrus libani* grows at altitudes between 1,400–1,950 metres above sea level (a.s.l.), favouring humid regions with rain and snow. It is often found in mixed woods with oaks, junipers and, in the north, fir (Browicz and Zieliński 1982: 15). Cedar also occurs in Syria, Turkey, and, as *C. libani* subsp. *brevifolia*, on Cyprus (see Table 18.1). Lucas (1962: 432) acknowledged that while *C. atlantica* grows, for example, in Morocco, it is unlikely to have been exploited in Pharaonic times. Dallimore and Jackson (1931: 175) dated the introduction of this cedar to northern Africa to the last century.

*Fir (*Abies cilicica *Ant. et Ky.)*
Family: Pinaceae
Abies cilicica (Fig. 15.12) is generally divided into two subspecies, ssp. *cilicica* and ssp. *isaurica*. In Syria-Palestine, *Abies cilicica* ssp. *cilicica* is distributed over much the same area as the cedar and the two are often associated (Table 18.1). In Syria, these trees grow on the humid northwest and western slopes at altitudes between 1,200 and 1,500 metres a.s.l., mixed with oaks, junipers and other trees, while in Lebanon, as the dominant species, it can reach altitudes of 2,000 metres a.s.l. (Browicz and Zieliński 1982: 13). Both *A. cilicica* ssp. *cilicica* and *A. cilicica* ssp. *isaurica* are found in Turkey and another species, *Abies nordmanniana* (Stev.) Spach, also grows there, but only along the northern coast (Coode and Cullen 1965b: 69, map 5).

Notably, the fir does not extend as far south into Lebanon as *Cedrus libani*. Meiggs (1982: 56) suggested that this may be the result of overcutting or, more likely, because the higher temperatures and low rainfall of this area preclude the growth of fir in that region. When considered in combination with the known deforestation of cedar,

Table 18.1. *Mediterranean distribution of the principal resin-producing coniferous trees and shrubs.*

	S. Med. Coast			E. Med. Coast				N. Med. Coast and Aegean					
	Eg	Si	NA	Is	Jo	Le	Sy	ET	WT	Cy	Cr	AI	Gr	References
Pinus halepensis Mill.			X	X	X	X	X	X		O			O	6,7,9–15,17,19.
Pinus pinea L.				O		X		?	?	O	O	X	X	2,10,12,13,17,19.
Pinus brutia Ten.						X	X	X	X	X	X	X	X	2,4,6,7,9,10,12–16,18,19.
Pinus nigra Arn.							?	X	X	X	O	X	X	1,2,6,10,12,15–19.
Cedrus libani A. richard						X	X	X	X	X				3,6,8,10,12,13,19.
Abies cilicica Ant. et Ky.						X	X	X	X					3,6,12,13,19.
Juniperus oxycedrus L.				X		X	X	X	X	X	X	X	X	1,3–5,10,13,15–19.
Juniperus communis L.								X	X				X	1,3,5,15,17.
Juniperus drupacea Labill.						X	X	X	X				X	1,3,5,13,15,17.
Juniperus phoenicia L.		X	X		X				X	X	X	X	X	1,3–5,10,15,17–19.
Juniperus foetidissima Willd.						X		X	X	X		X	X	1,3–5,10,13,15,17.
Juniperus excelsa Bieb.						X	X	X	X	X		X	X	1,3–5,10,13,15,17,19.
Cupressus sempervirens L.			X		X	X	X	X	X	X	X	X		3–5,10,12,13,15–19.

Abbreviations: Eg = Egypt, Si = Sinai, NA = North Africa, Is = Israel, Jo = Jordan, Le = Lebanon, Sy = Syria, ET = south Eastern Turkey (east of 32°), WT = south Western Turkey (west of 32°), Cy = Cyprus, Cr = Crete, AI = Aegean Islands, Gr = Greece.
Concordance: X = present, O = distribution in dispute, ? = possibly indigenous.

References: (1) Boratyński *et al.* 1992: 130–7, 174; (2) Browicz 1994: 16–8; (3) Browicz and Zieliński 1982: 7–11, 13–5; (4) Carlström 1987: 46; (5) Coode and Cullen 1965a: 76, 78–84; (6) Coode and Cullen 1965b; 68, 71, 74–5; (7) Critchfield and Little 1966: 12–3; (8) Dallimore and Jackson 1931: 175; (9) Jalas and Suominen 1973: 22–3; (10) Meikle 1977: 22, 24–32; (11) Mirov 1967: 253; (12) Mouterde 1966: 15–9; (13) Post and Dinsmore 1933: 797–802; (14) Rackham 1983: 306; (15) Rechinger 1943: 82–3, 85–6; (16) Turland *et al.* 1993: 34; (17) Tutin *et al.* 1993: 42–3, 45, 47–8; (18) Zaffran 1990: 69–71; (19) Zohary 1973: 341–9, 351.

Table 18.2. *Mediterranean distribution of some non-coniferous resin-producing plants.*

	S. Med. Coast			E. Med. Coast				N. Med. Coast and Aegean					
	Eg	Si	NA	Is	Jo	Le	Sy	ET	WT	Cy	Cr	AI	Gr	References
Pistacia atlantica Desf.		X	X	X	X	X	X	X	X	O		O	X	2,11,14,19,22–4.
Pistacia terebinthus L.				X	X	X	X	X	X	X	X	X	X	1,3,5,11,12,14,15,17,19,20,22–4.
Pistacia khiniuk Stocks	X	X			X		X	X						2,12,16,19,21,22–4.
Pistacia lentiscus L.			X	X	X	X	X	X	X	X	X	X	X	1,3,11,12,14,15,17,19,23–4.
Pistacia eurycarpa Yalt.							X	X						2,19,24.
Cistus creticus L.				X	X	X	X	X	X	X	X	X	X	1,2,5,7,11,12,14,15,17,18,20,23.
Cistus laurifolius L.			X					X	X				X	1,4,7,9,10.
Liquidambar orientalis Mill.									X			X		1,5,13,15.
Opopanax chironium(L.) W. Koch									X				X	6,8,18.
Opopanax hispidium Griseb.							X	X		X	X	X	X	6,8,11,12,15,17.
Opopanax syriacum Boiss.						X	X							12.

Abbreviations: Eg = Egypt, Si = Sinai, NA = North Africa, Is = Israel, Jo = Jordan, Le = Lebanon, Sy = Syria, ET = south Eastern Turkey (east of 32°), WT = south Western Turkey (west of 32°), Cy = Cyprus, Cr = Crete, AI = Aegean Islands, Gr = Greece.

Concordance: X = present, O = distribution in dispute, ? = possibly indigenous.

References: (1) Boratyński *et al.* 1992: 58–9, 145, 178–9; (2) Browicz 1988: 5–7, 18–9; (3) Browicz 1984: 6–7; (4) Browicz 1983: 6–8; (5) Carlström 1987: 54, 67,82; (6) Chamberlain 1972: 472; (7) Coode 1965: 507–9; (8) Hartvig 1986: 714; (9) Hepper 1987a: 31, 46; (10) Hepper 1987b: 110, 142; (11) Meikle 1977: 182–3, 366, 368–9, 758; (12) Mouterde 1970: 471–2, 550, 615–6,646; (13) Peşman 1972b: 264; (14) Post and Dinsmore 1932: 142, 286–7; (15) Rechinger 1943: 109, 247, 285, 412; (16) Täckholm 1974: 339; (17) Turland *et al.* 1993: 36, 55–6, 151–2; (18) Tutin *et al.* 1968: 183, 283, 360; (19) Yaltirik 1967: 544–6, 548; (20) Zaffran 1990: 198, 209; (21) Zahran and Willis 1992: 177, 293; (22) Zohary 1973: 368–9; (23) Zohary 1972: 297–300, 336–7; (24) Zohary 1952: 200–1, 204–12.

these factors support the need for a re-evaluation of the view that cedar was less abundant in antiquity than fir. Although perhaps due to chance preservation, there have also been fewer identifications of fir wood than of cedar (see Chapter 15, this volume; Davies 1995: 150, table I).

*Pine (*Pinus *spp.)*
Family: Pinaceae
Four species of pine are relevant: *Pinus halepensis* Mill., *P. pinea* L., *P. brutia* Ten., and *P. nigra* Arn. Of these, both *P. halepensis* and *P. brutia* are highly invasive and *P. pinea* has been widely cultivated for its edible nuts (Zohary 1973: 343–4; Mouterde 1966: 16). Notably, in the nineteenth century, forests of *P. pinea* were planted in the area between Beirut and Sidon, where cedar had formerly grown (Meiggs 1982: 397; Zohary 1973: fig. 134).

Of these pines (and also of Pinaceae in general), only *Pinus halepensis* (Fig. 15.16) extends as far south as Israel and Jordan (Table 18.1). In Lebanon and Syria, it is found in the lower mountain ranges commonly at altitudes ranging from 0–1000 metres a.s.l. (Zohary 1973: 341). Recently, it has been suggested that *P. halepensis* rarely grew in Israel in antiquity. The increase in the distribution of the species was dated to the twentieth century (Liphschitz 1992: 33–46; Liphschitz *et al.* 1988–1990: 141–50) but further research is needed to clarify this point. Specimens on Cyprus are said to have been introduced, although the date of this was not given (Meikle 1977: 26).

In the near eastern Mediterranean, *Pinus brutia* replaces *P. halepensis* and the two can sometimes hybridise where they overlap (Rechinger 1943: 86; Browicz 1994: 16–17). This tree is found along the coast at altitudes from sea level to 1,500 (–1,700) metres a.s.l. in Lebanon and Syria (Zohary 1973: 343; Table 18.1).

In contrast, the distribution of *Pinus pinea* is more scattered and sparse (see Table 18.1). It is indigenous to Lebanon and according to Zohary (1973: 345), prefers altitudes of up to 500 metres a.s.l. However, Browicz (1994: 18) wrote that it reaches 'its highest elevation of 1200 m' there. Zohary (1973: 345) mentioned the possibility that this pine formerly grew along the coast of Israel, despite any evidence of this today. Germer (1985: 9) stated that *Pinus pinea* occurs in Syria, but this is not confirmed by other published flora, some of which state specifically that examples in Syria were planted (Mouterde 1966: 16; Browicz 1994: 18). Its indigeneity on Cyprus and Crete is also doubtful (see Meikle 1977: 27; Gaussen *et al.* 1993: 43; Zohary 1973: 342, 344–5) and in the recent edition of *Flora Europaea*, *P. pinea* was considered only 'possibly native' to Greece and Turkey (Gaussen *et al.* 1993: 43).

The final pine for consideration, *Pinus nigra* may occur in western Syria although some flora have omitted it (Zohary 1973: 344, map 137; Mouterde 1966: 15–17) (see Table 18.1). Its ancient status on Crete is, like *Pinus pinea*, again dubious (Turland *et al.* 1993: 34; Zaffran 1990: 69; Gaussen *et al.* 1993: 42). This pine not usually mentioned as a source of pine wood or resin in ancient Egypt, but one of the beams used in the doorway into the burial chamber of Tutankhamun was reported to be either *Pinus halepensis* or *Pinus laricio* (Germer 1989: 72), the latter now considered synonymous with *P. nigra* Arnold (Coode and Cullen 1965b: 74). As was the case for fir, evidence for pine in ancient Egypt is scarce until the Greco-Roman period (Chapter 15; Davies 1995: 150, table I).

*Juniper (*Juniperus *spp.)*
Family: Cupressaceae
Like some pines, certain junipers, which are commonly shrubs or small trees, are also invasive. Several species are known in the eastern Mediterranean, including *Juniperus oxycedrus* L., *J. communis* L., *J. drupacea* Labill, *J. phoenicia* L., *J. foetidissma* Willd. and *J. excelsa* Bieb. Another species, *J. sabina* L., was mentioned by Germer (1985: 12) but occurs only in eastern Turkey, inland Greece and Iran (Coode and Cullen 1965a: 82; Boratyński *et al.* 1992: 137).

The Mediterranean distribution of these species is somewhat diverse (see Table 18.1). The shrub-like *J. communis* is found only in northern and western Turkey and Greece (Browicz and Zieliński 1982: 8–9). Three species are of more substantial size. In Lebanon, *J. excelsa* (Fig. 15.15), can reach some twenty metres in height, and is common at altitudes of 300–1,720 metres a.s.l. along with cedar, fir or pine forests (Browicz and Zieliński 1982: 9). Another tree, *J. foetidissma* often grows in both broad-leaved and coniferous forests at altitudes of 500–1,700 metres a.s.l. (Zohary 1973: 349). *J. drupacea*, a slightly smaller tree than the previous two, is also found in coniferous forests, preferring altitudes of about 1,000–1,500 metres a.s.l. (Browicz and Zieliński 1982: 9).

Within this genus, only two, more shrub-like, small trees (less than ten metres in height) reach further south. These are *J. oxycedrus*, which occurs in Israel, and *J. phoenicia* which occurs not only in western Jordan, but also in northern Africa and northern Sinai. Generally a maquis component, *J. phoenicia* grows in Jordan at 1,500 metres a.s.l. (Boratyński *et al.* 1992: 136). In southwest Jordan, this species has been found mixed with other species including *Pistacia terebinthus* ssp. *palaestina* (Browicz and Zieliński 1982: 11). Zohary (1973: 349) noted that *J. oxycedrus* has a wide ecological range and is usually found at altitudes ranging from sea level to 1,900 metres a.s.l. 'in slopes facing the Mediterranean Sea'. This species is also highly invasive and may have spread since antiquity (Zohary 1973: 349).

Juniper berries have been found in a number of Egyptian burials, from Predynastic to Greco-Roman times. Most of these were attributed by Täckholm *et al.* to the species *J. oxycedrus*, although a few may be *J. drupacea* (Chapter 15, this volume; Täckholm *et al.* 1941: 75–9). Identifications of juniper wood are comparatively rare (Chapter 15; Davies 1995: 150, table I), perhaps because a number of the more

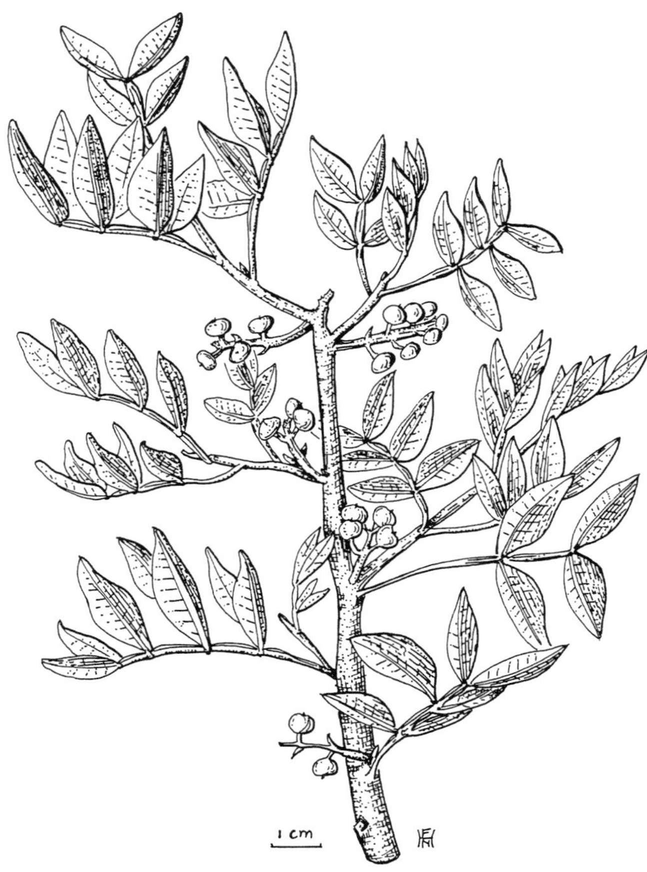

Figure 18.1 Pistacia lentiscus *L.*

shrub-like species discussed here are not suitable for use as timber.

*Cypress (*Cupressus sempervirens *L.)*
Family: Cupressaceae
The final conifer for consideration is the cypress, *Cupressus sempervirens* L (Fig. 15.14). This tree is found in Syria, Lebanon and Jordan (see Table 18.1). In Edom, south of the Dead Sea, a small population is found at an altitude of about 1,500 metres a.s.l. (Browicz and Zieliński 1982: 7). In Lebanon, it can be found in pure stands or mixed with *P. brutia*, at elevations from sea level to 1,000 metres a.s.l. According to Zohary (1973: 347–8), remnants of cypress forests in Palestine suggest that it may have been more common there in antiquity.

Although some examples of cypress wood have been identified from ancient Egypt (Chapter 15; Davies 1995: 150, table I), the resin-producing capability of this species was questioned by Lucas. He also dismissed juniper and cedar as non-resinous (Lucas 1962: 319), but offered no evidence for this conclusion. Although these conifers may not be copious resin-producers, some resin can be obtained from certain species (Mills and White 1977: 18; 1994: 103–4).

Mediterranean non-coniferous resins

In addition to the conifers found throughout the Mediterranean, a range of other, perhaps less well-known resins, could also have been obtained. For some, their use in Egypt cannot yet be confirmed. If they did reach Egypt, whether these were supplied in conjunction with the trade in coniferous products, or separately, remains unclear.

*Pistacia (*Pistacia *spp.)*
Family: Anacardiaceae
Like the coniferous sources, several species within the genus *Pistacia* produce resin and are found throughout the Mediterranean. Loret (1949) considered this genus the most likely source of the resin known as *snṯr* which was used as incense (see p. 456–9). Among the relevant species is the shrub, *Pistacia lentiscus* L. (Fig. 18.1), which exudes the pale yellow 'tears' known as mastic. Although this term, *mastic*, is often applied to resin from *P. lentiscus*, there is some need for caution as it has all too frequently been applied to resins from any species of pistacia or even to describe certain bituminous products (see p. 456). To avoid confusion, it is used here strictly for the resin produced from *P. lentiscus*. This species is quite widespread in the Mediterranean (see Table 18.2). Zohary (1972: 299) noted that, in Palestine, it favours *maquis* environments along the coast and lower hills up to elevations of 300(–500) metres a.s.l..

Today, mastic is only produced on a commercial scale on the island of Chios, off the west coast of Turkey. The resin is used for chewing gum, as picture varnish and to make a flavoured spirit, *mastica*.

Notably, its resin-producing capability in other Mediterranean locations is quite controversial. Some have argued that it is only the cultivated *P. lentiscus* var. *chia* (Desf.) Poir found on Chios, which yields resin (Browicz 1987: 189–95; Hepper 1990: 26; 1992a: 195). Meikle, however, cited some evidence that, at least in the past, specimens of *P. lentiscus* on Cyprus could yield resin although possibly of a lesser quality than that found on Chios (Meikle 1977: 366). Further research is necessary, but if it is only produced by Chian trees, then one could question its accessibility in Pharaonic times.

Because it has remained in large-scale production on Chios, the process of tapping (by incision into the bark) has been documented (Davidson 1948: 189). The first tappings begin when the tree is six years old, but only a small amount (fifteen grams) of resin is produced. After ten years, this may increase to about thirty grams. Mature trees of fifty to sixty years have an average yield of 157–88 grams, but in a particularly good year some trees may yield as much as 1,250 grams. The average total annual production in 1948 was about 318,250 kilograms. (Davidson 1948: 190).

Figure 18.2 Pistacia terebinthus *L.*

As well as mastic, certain species of pistacia produce a resin generally known as *terebinth*. Loret (1949) proposed that the small tree, *Pistacia terebinthus* L. (Fig. 18.2) was the prime source of this resin in ancient times. (Here, following Yaltirik (1967: 546–8), *P. terebinthus* includes ssp. *terebinthus* and ssp. *palaestina* (Boiss.) Engler in DC, although some prefer to keep them as separate species). Stands of this tree grow in Syria, Lebanon, Israel and Jordan (see Table 18.2). Browicz (1984: 7) noted its occurrence both in coastal and inland sites, along river valleys and elevated areas, including mountain foothills, usually at elevations between 600 and 800 metres a.s.l. Like *P. lentiscus*, this pistacia is found in many Mediterranean locations (see Table 18.2), but may have been yet more common in antiquity. It has been noted that many stands of *P. terebinthus* have been destroyed in modern times, leaving only remnants (Currid 1984: 5–6; Zohary 1973: 369).

Loret's comments on two other species, *P. atlantica* Desf. and *P. mutica* F. and M. require some revision. He acknowledged that the tree, *P. atlantica* Desf., which he considered a strictly African species, could produce substantial quantities of resin (Loret 1949: 54). Conversely, he dismissed *P. mutica* F. and M. as a possible source perhaps because of Post and Dinsmore's suggestion that *P. mutica* F. and M. had been introduced to Palestine from Asia Minor (Loret 1949: 53; Post and Dinsmore 1932: 286). However, *P. mutica* F. and M. is now considered synonymous with *P. atlantica* and is acknowledged as indigenous to the eastern Mediterranean (Zohary 1952: 205; Yaltirik 1967: 545; Browicz 1988: 5–6). Thus, *P. atlantica* Desf. can be accepted as a common eastern Mediterranean tree and an excellent source of resin.

Zohary (1940: 161) noted the promising use of *P. atlantica* as a timber tree and described it as 'one of the most beautiful and long-lived trees of our region'. Although sometimes rare, *P. atlantica* is very widely distributed in the Mediterranean region (see Table 18.2). According to Browicz (1988: 6), it is frequently found at altitudes between 800 and 2,400 metres a.s.l., and in the Negev desert at 600–1,000 metres a.s.l. It now seems probable that, like *P. terebinthus*, it suffered from deforestation in Syria–Palestine caused by a number of factors, especially spreading agriculture (Kislev 1985: 133–8; Hepper 1992b: 33; Hepper and Gibson 1994: 95; Browicz 1988: 6; Zohary 1940: 160). Its status on Rhodes and Cyprus has also not been sufficiently explained (Browicz 1988: 6; also Meikle 1977: 368).

It is likely that there has been considerable confusion between the trees of *P. atlantica* and *P. terebinthus* through the years (Mills and White 1989: 38). Thus, terebinth resin could be derived from either *P. atlantica* or *P. terebinthus* and it could be misleading to call the resin terebinth without secure botanical identification. Meikle, discussing the occurrence of *P. atlantica* Desf. on Cyprus, noted that it 'was frequently misnamed *P. terebinthus* by older authors, and it will often be found that references to mastic-producing trees . . . relate, not to *P. terebinthus* as stated, but to *P. atlantica*' (Meikle 1977: 368; note here also the confusing use of the word 'mastic' to describe resin from these species). It has recently been suggested that *P. terebinthus* in fact yields little resin (Mills and White 1989: 38). This, taken in conjunction with the earlier suggestion that it may be only the *P. lentiscus* var. *chia* (Desf.) Poir found on the island of Chios which yields resin, would greatly reduce the possible sources of Mediterranean pistacia resin.

Of particular note is *Pistacia khinjuk* Stocks which, exceptionally, is found within Egypt itself (see Table 18.2). Rare examples are known from the eastern desert of Middle Egypt, at Wadi Galala and Wadi Rigbeh, and from Gebel Elba on the southeast border between Egypt and the Sudan, while larger stands have also been found in southern Sinai, and along the northwest coast of Arabia. Along the eastern Mediterranean coast, *P. khinjuk* is found in Jordan and Syria. There, it is said to grow with other trees and shrubs in dry steppe-forest or steppe areas, on rocky sections of mountains or gorges, or on limestone hills often in association with *Pistacia atlantica* (Browicz 1988: 7). It also occurs further inland in eastern Turkey, as well as in Iraq, Iran and Afghanistan (Yaltirik 1967: 546). Unlike other pistacia species, the resin of *P. khinjuk* is obtained from large galls which form on the leaves of the shrub as a result of damage, primarily from insects (Whitehouse 1957: 318).

Mention should also be made of *P. aethiopica* Kokwaro (syn. *P. lentiscus* L. var. *emarginata* Engl.) found in Ethiopia, Somalia, and perhaps in Eritrea, although now apparently extinct (Gilbert 1989: 530, 532). It has been noted that this species is particularly abundant in southern Ethiopia and is often tapped for its high quality resin (Gilbert 1989: 532). Another possibly relevant species, *Pistacia chinensis* Bge. var. *falcata* (Beccari) Zoh. (syn. *P. falcata* Mart.) occurs in Somalia, Sudan, Ethiopia and Arabia (Gilbert 1989: 532; Zohary 1952: 217). Loret drew attention to New Kingdom texts which list both *snṯr* and *ʿntyw* from Punt, and cited this species as a possible source of African *sn<u>t</u>r*. Loret (1949: 590) called it *P. falcata* Martelli. Another species, *P. eurycarpa* Yalt. was formerly considered a variety of *P. atlantica*, namely *P. atlantica* var. *kurdica*. This species is found in eastern Turkey, as well as in Armenia, Afghanistan, Iraq and northeastern Syria (see Table 18.2) and is, therefore, less likely as the most common source of the resin for the ancient Egyptians.

In summary, four species of pistacia can be considered as primary sources of resin from the Mediterranean. These are *Pistacia atlantica*, *P. terebinthus*, *P. khinjuk* and *P. lentiscus*. Two species, *P. aethiopica* and *P. chinensis* var. *falcata*, may have been exploited in Africa. While it is now clear that *P. atlantica* would have been an exceptionally good source of resin, more research is necessary to clarify the resin-producing capabilities of *P. terebinthus* and *P. lentiscus*. *P. khinjuk* is significant as it is the only source to occur in Egypt.

Archaeobotanical evidence which could confirm that the ancient Egyptians were familiar with pistacia trees is scant. During recent excavations at the site of Kom Rabiʿa at Memphis, a few charred fruits of pistacia were found in Middle Kingdom levels. The archaeobotanist for the expedition, Mary Anne Murray, has identified these as a species of *Pistacia* (Chapter 24, this volume). The fruits of some of these species are very similar in appearance, making a more precise identification unlikely. However, it is interesting that the fruits were clearly not of *P. khinjuk* and therefore must have been imported. This resemblance in the appearance of nuts of *Pistacia atlantica* and *P. terebinthus* has hindered assessment of archaeobotanical remains across the Mediterranean.

Kislev discussed the possibility of distinguishing between the two by slight morphological differences, concluding that examples found at the New Kingdom mining site of Timna were *Pistacia atlantica* (Kislev 1988: 238–9). He also provided a useful summary of earlier archaeobotanical identifications of pistacia in the Mediterranean and western Asia. Based on this, he concluded that 'almost all' of these were of *Pistacia atlantica* (Kislev 1988: 239). In fact, few of these identifications were linked to a specific species, doubtless due to the morphological problems. Among the early finds, Renfrew (1973: 24–6) claimed to have found examples of *P. atlantica* at two prehistoric sites in Greece, while van Zeist (1972: 14) made a similar identification for fruits from Çayönü in south west Turkey dated to 7500–6500 BC. Broken endocarps also said to belong to *P. atlantica* were found at Chalcolithic Nahal Mishmar in Israel (Zaitschek 1980: 223). Helbaek identified remains from various sites, including Early Bronze Age Lachish, Pre-Pottery Neolithic Beidha in Jordan, and Çatal Hüyük in southern Turkey, and Late Bronze Age Kalopsidha in Cyprus as *P. atlantica* (Helbaek 1958: 311; 1966a: 62–3; 1964: 123; 1966b: 117). However, his grounds for these identifications are not always clear and further research into the morphological differences cited by Kislev could prove useful.

Undoubtedly the most significant find of pistacia resin in modern times is the discovery of several dozen amphorae containing this commodity on the Late Bronze Age shipwreck at Ulu Burun off the south coast of Turkey (Bass 1987). This clearly has implications for Loret's theory that *sn<u>t</u>r* was pistacia resin and these will be discussed in greater detail in conjunction with the scientific analyses undertaken on the resin (see p. 456–9).

Industrially, the fruits of the *Pistacia* species have a number of uses. They have been used in soap-making and tanning, and the resin has been used in medicines (Jeffrey 1980: 494). In Egypt, the exudate of *P. khinjuk* is used as chewing gum and in perfume manufacture (Jeffrey 1980: 496). The fruits of some species, such as *P. atlantica* and *P. terebinthus*, are edible, while the fruit kernels of *P. khinjuk*, are more commonly eaten (Zohary 1972: 298; Whitehouse 1957: 318; Jeffrey 1980: 496). Undoubtedly best known of these are the pistacio nuts obtained from *P. vera* L., which grows in more eastern locations.

*Labdanum or ladanum (*Cistus *spp.)*
Family: Cistaceae

In the past, it was suggested that the evergreen rock rose shrubs of the genus *Cistus*, grew in Egypt, although this was subsequently discounted (Lucas 1962: 94, *contra* Newberry 1929: 94). Of the number of species within this genus known throughout the Mediterranean, three are generally presumed the most likely sources of the resin ladanum (or labdanum) in antiquity. These are *Cistus creticus* L., *C. laurifolius* L. and *C. ladanifer* L.

Cistus creticus (syn. *C. incanus* L., *C. villosus* L., and *C. tauricus* (Presl) Gross. See Coode 1965: 507; Meikle 1977: 182) is the most widespread of the resinous species (see Table 18.2) but its exploitation has seldom been discussed (Hepper 1987b: 110; Meikle 1977: 182–4). Distributed throughout Syria/Palestine, it favours the northern forests of Lebanon where cedar (Bsharri, Ehden) and fir (Ehden) are also found. Although it will occasionally grow in the pine and oak forests of Israel, it more commonly occurs in areas of devastated *maquis* and forest edges at altitudes up to 800–900 metres a.s.l. (Browicz 1988: 18–9; Zohary 1972: 336).

In contrast, *Cistus laurifolius* (Fig.18.3), which is said to be very resinous (Hepper 1987b: 110) is found only in Turkey and in the northeastern corner of Greece along the Turkish coast (see Table 18.2), although Warburg (1968: 284) gave Italy as its most eastern location. Boratyński *et al.* (1992: 59) noted that examples also occur in the Atlas Mountains of Morocco. Another source of ladanum, *C. ladanifer*, is common to Spain but is again said to occur in northwest Africa (Hepper 1987b: 110). In addition, some easterly spread is known, for example, in Cyprus, probably as an introduction (Meikle 1977: 187).

Figure 18.3 Cistus laurifolius *L.*

Given its distribution, it is possible that *C. creticus* could have been known as the Levantine myrrh (*ʿntyw*) of ancient times (Hepper 1987b: 110). However, unlike myrrh and other plants which exude resin from incisions into the bark, ladanum is obtained from the leaves. On the methods of collection on Cyprus, an account dated to 1886 (Dyer 1886: 386) recorded three different methods in use: 1) with a stick drawn over the ground, 2) from the bells of goats, and 3) combed from the beards and other long hair from the goat's body. The collection was carried out from May to August. In Crete, a whip-like tool with leather thongs was used (Dyer 1885: 301–2; Newberry 1929: 94). The straps were dragged over the leaves and the collected resin scraped off with a knife and then made into cakes. The rate of collection was estimated at about three pounds per day. Dyer (1885: 301) noted that, at that time, 6,000 pounds were exported annually from Crete and 2,500–2,800 pounds from Cyprus.

*Liquidambar (*Liquidambar orientalis *Mill.)*
Family: Hamamelidaceae

A confusion of species has been suggested for storax resin. The small tree or shrub *Styrax officinalis* L., common in the eastern Mediterranean, has been named as the source, although it has been commented that today this tree does not produce resin. Hanbury, in 1857, believed that *Styrax officinalis*, while recognised as the source of storax in classical times, had since ceased to produce resin, as references to the resin come to an end after 1769 (Hanbury 1857: 465). This point was recently reiterated by Meikle (1985: 1089). Thus, it has been proposed that the resin from *Liquidambar orientalis* L. was the product known as storax more recently and *stacte* in classical times (Hepper 1987a: 49). The identity of the latter substance has long been disputed. Steuer (1933: 31–48) argued that it was a name given to the essential oil which was obtained from myrrh by pressing (on essential oils see discussion of lower terpenoids, pp. 446–8). Lucas, however, demonstrated that it would be impossible to separate the volatile component through pressing (Lucas 1937: 31–2).

The tree *Liquidambar orientalis* Mill. (Fig. 15.7) is found only in Western Turkey and Rhodes (see Table 18.2). According to Howes (1949: 162), the yellow-brown resin is obtained by beating the bark in the spring and collecting the resin in the autumn (see also Hanbury 1857: 463). Identifications of liquidambar in archaeological contexts have been rare and thus far only one piece of worked wood, from Tutankhamun's tomb, has been identified as *Liquidambar* sp. probably *L. orientalis* (see Chapter 15, this volume).

*Opopanax (*Opopanax *spp.)*
Family: Umbelliferae

The most likely source of opopanax, often thought to have an unpleasant odour, is *Opopanax chironium* (L.) W. Koch (Cooke 1874: 62). This species, which resembles the parsnip, is found in northwest Turkey and possibly Greece (see Table 18.2). It is a two-metre-high perennial with yellow flowers. The gum-resin, opopanax, is obtained by breaking up the root, which produces a milky juice which dries to yellowish lumps or, more rarely, opaque reddish lumps or tears (Cooke 1874: 62–3). Again, one must be aware of a possible confusion of terms. It has been noted that 'the name opopanax is derived from that of its original source *Opopanax chironium*, but production today is entirely from *Commiphora* spp.' (Coppen 1995: 84. See p. 440).

Alternatively, two other species *O. hispidum* Griseb. and *O. syriacum* Boiss. have been proposed as possible sources. The former is found in Syria, Iran, Iraq (Rechinger 1987: 438–9) as well as Cyprus, Turkey, Greece, Crete and islands in the Aegean (see Table 18.2). In contrast, *O. syriacum* Boiss. is found in Syria and Lebanon (Mouterde 1970: 615–6 as *Smyrniopsis syriaca*; Stol 1979: 63–4. Mouterde noted that this plant is endemic in Lebanon and

Syria and grows in rocky, preferably wooded locations. In Lebanon, it is found at altitudes between 1,400 and 2,000 metres a.s.l., in some instances, at locations where cedar (Hadeth, Ehden) or fir (Ehden) also grow. Mouterde also mentioned that the plant occasionally produced 'un peu de resine'. The resin producing capabilities of both of these sources have yet to be confirmed, however.

East African and Arabian sources

The resinous products which immediately come to mind in this category are frankincense and myrrh. Over the years, the extent to which the Egyptians knew and used both frankincense (*Boswellia* spp.) and myrrh (*Commiphora* spp.) has been the subject of considerable debate. The topic cannot be covered in depth here, but a few relevant points can be summarised. Notably, reliefs such as those at Hatshepsut's temple at Deir el-Bahari (Naville 1898: pls. LXIX–LXXVI) imply that the Egyptians did travel south to areas which may have been able to supply frankincense and myrrh. Through study of the flora and fauna shown in these reliefs, it has been suggested that the location, known to the Egyptians as Punt, was positioned somewhere in the region of Sudan/Somalia/Ethiopia. Kitchen (1993: 603) suggested that it may be located in eastern Sudan, along the northern and northwestern sides of the Ethiopian highlands but not into Somalia. However, definitive establishment of the location has been elusive (to mention only a few discussions: Groom 1981; Bradbury 1996: 39; Fattovich 1990; Herzog 1968; Kitchen 1971).

The primary resinous import of this region was called *ʿntyw* which some have translated as frankincense, others as myrrh. Hepper, who studied the *ʿntyw* trees shown in the Hatshepsut reliefs admitted that they are very stylistic, but believed they more closely resembled *Boswellia* rather than *Commiphora* (Hepper 1992b: 136). He also commented that there are some observable variations in the appearance of the two genera, particularly when leaves, fruit or flowers are present (Hepper 1992b: 137–8). However, the possibility of confusion between frankincense and myrrh trees in antiquity cannot be conclusively eliminated.

For those who would take *ʿntyw* as myrrh, *sntr*, another Puntite product, might be interpreted as frankincense (e.g. Germer 1985: 110). This would seem to imply that both products were accessible from the area known as Punt, lending particular importance to the geographical distribution of frankincense and myrrh. Although of secondary importance to *ʿntyw* in the Punt reliefs, *sntr*, and to some extent *ʿntyw*, are also cited as imports from Syria-Palestine, especially in the New Kingdom. This has led to the suggestion that gum-resins from Arabia were reaching Egypt via Western Asia at that time (Saleh 1972; 1973). Alternatively, Loret (1949) proposed that *sntr* might be *Pistacia* resin, as species of that genus occur in both locations (see pp. 456–9).

Clearly, the botanical identities of these products remain to be resolved. Scientific analysis of ancient resin samples is now contributing to this discussion and these results are summarised below. Botanical data is also of potential significance.

*Frankincense (*Boswellia *spp.)*
Family: Burseraceae
Frankincense, obtained from African and Arabian species of *Boswellia*, is still well-known today. There are over two dozen species within the genus but the taxonomy of the most likely sources of the gum-resin has been in some dispute. A summary of taxonomic changes was provided by Groom (1981: 101–9), incorporating the earlier work by Hepper (1969: 72). Five species were discussed by Hepper at that time. These included the Arabian source, *Boswellia sacra* Flueck., and the African sources, *B. carteri* Birdwood, *B. frereana* Birdwood, *B. papyrifera* (Del.) Hochst., and *B. bhau-dajiana* Birdwood. However, regarding the latter, he stated that, although resinous, it 'remains inadequately known and it may not be a really distinct species' (Hepper 1969: 69). More recently, Hepper has classed *B. frereana* and *B. carteri* also as *B. sacra* (Hepper 1992b: 136). Baum, on the other hand, following Thulin and Warfa (1987),

*Figure 18.4 Frankincense (*Boswellia sacra *Flueck.)*

considered *B. carteri* and *B. bhau-dajiana* as synonymous with *B. sacra* leaving *B. frereana* and *B. papyrifera* as separate species (Baum 1994: 25). Despite these differences, it is clear that the main sources of frankincense were in Arabia and areas of Africa south of Egypt.

According to Thulin and Warfa, *Boswellia sacra* (Fig. 18.4) grows in both Somalia and southern Arabia, while *B. frereana* is restricted to Somalia, for the most part in the same areas there as *B. sacra* (Thulin and Warfa 1987: 490, map 1; 498, map 2). In contrast, *B. papyrifera* is found further to the northwest and west of those species, and its distribution includes Sudan, Ethiopia, and other east African locations (Hepper 1969: 68; Vollesen 1989: 443; Groom 1981: 99; Gillett 1991: 5).

All of these species are small trees up to eight to ten metres high, with peeling papery bark, compound oblong leaves and small five-petalled flowers clustered at the ends of the shoots (Hepper 1992b: 136; Gillett 1991: 5). The colour of the inflorescence ranges from white (*B. sacra*), to pinkish-white (*B. papyrifera*) to reddish or greenish red (*B. frereana*) (Thulin and Warfa 1987: 490, 495; Gillett 1991: 5). The trees prefer dry, rocky locations such as stony hillsides (Gillett 1991: 5).

The procedure of tapping *Boswellia* trees was discussed by Hepper (1969: 71). He noted that, using herbarium samples, the best quality frankincense was obtained from *B. frereana*, while that of *B. carteri* was inferior (Hepper 1969: 68). More recently, Vollesen commented that the resin of *B. papyrifera* is widely collected in northern Ethiopia, but is considered of a lesser quality than *B. sacra* (Vollesen 1989: 443). According to Thulin and Warfa (1987: 489, 495), both *B. sacra* and *B. frereana* are copious resin producers. The tear-shaped resin globules are milky white in colour at first but then dry either to a pale yellow (*B. frereana*) or a yellowish-brown (*B. sacra*). Commercially, frankincense is sometimes also called olibanum.

Although seldom noted, it has been observed that trees of *B. rivae* Engl. are tapped for gum-resin in Ethiopia and Somalia, which is used locally as incense or to freshen the breath (Bekele-Tesemma 1993: 116; Goettsch 1991: 116). Moreover, this gum-resin is in greater demand in southern Ethiopia than that obtained from the other most common species, *B. papyrifera* (Goettsch 1991: 116). *B. rivae* is a shrub or small tree, reaching six or seven metres in height, with pink flowers and peeling bark (Vollesen 1989: 443; Gillett 1991: 5, 7). It prefers wooded grassland or bushland on limestone hills (Vollesen 1989: 443; Gillett 1991: 7).

*Myrrh (*Commiphora *spp.)*
Family: Burseraceae
The taxonomy of *Commiphora*, with some 190 or more species spreading from Africa to India, is very complex (Groom 1981: 100; Gillett 1991: 9). However, it is generally accepted that myrrh is obtained from *Commiphora myrrha* (Nees) Engl. (syn. *C. molmol* (Engl.) Engl. See Gillett 1991: 30; Vollesen 1989: 452). This species (Fig. 18.5) shows much variation in form, but is usually a thorny, multi-stemmed shrub or small tree (up to four metres high), with small white four-petalled flowers, ovoid drupes, and grey-green oval leaves which are present for only a small part of the year (Hepper 1992b: 137; Gillett 1991: 29). It favours rocky slopes and semi-desert conditions, and its distribution includes southwest Arabia, eastern Ethiopia, and northern, central and southern Somalia (see Table 18.3) (Gillett 1991: 29–30; Groom 1981: 116, 119; Hepper 1992b: 137; Vollesen 1989: 452). The gum-resin is a translucent yellow colour when it exudes and is said, in fact, to have little scent (Gillett 1991: 29; Groom 1981: 122).

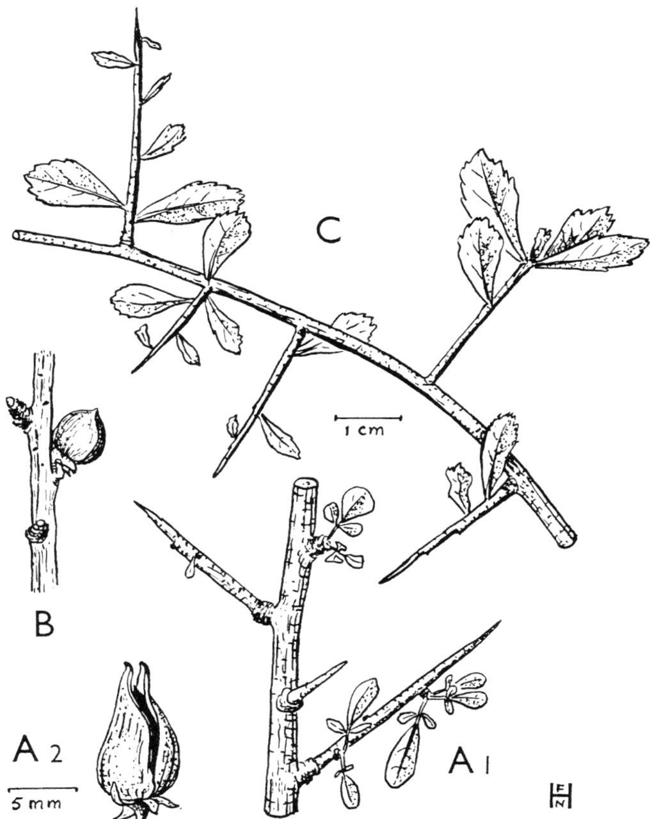

*Figure 18.5 Myrrh (*Commiphora myrrha *(Nees) Engl.).*

It is perhaps less appreciated that many other species of *Commiphora* are also resinous. These have a number of physical features in common with *C. myrrha*. They are generally spiny shrubs or small trees, often with a peeling bark, and, while producing a gum-resin, the exudate may differ in colour, consistency and odour (Gillett 1991: 8–9; Groom 1981: 125). Table 18.4 enumerates the members of this genus which have been cited as sources of gum-resin. However, it is readily apparent from this list that there is no general consensus regarding the identification of the sources, and that information on the appearance and consist-

Table 18.3. *Distribution of species of* Commiphora *said to produce gum-resin*

Species	Sudan	Somalia	Ethiopia	Arabia	Palestine	Egypt
C. myrrha (Nees) Engl. (syn. *C. molmol* (Engl.) Engl.)		N, C, S	NE, SE	SW		
C. habessinica (Berg.) Engl. (syn. *C. abyssinica*)	?	NW	All	SW		
C. schimperi (O. Berg) Engl.	?	N, S	N, W, S, C	SW		
C. kataf (Forssk.) Engl.						
ssp. *turkanensis Gillett*		C	X	–		
ssp. *kataf*		N	E	S		
C. erythraea (Ehremb.) Engl.	NE	X	E, SC	X		
C. africana (A. Rich) Engl.	C	N	N, C, S, SE, W	X		
C. hildebrandtii (Engl.) Engl.		X	SE			
C. ogadensis Chiov.		X	SE			
C. mukul Engl.				?		
C. pedunculata (Kotschy & Peyr) Engl.	C, S	?	?			
C. boranensis Vollesen		S	SE			
C. corrugata Gillett & Vollesen		C, S	SE			
C. playfairii (Oliv.) Engl.		NE				
C. samharensis Schweinf.						
ssp. *samharensis*	X	X	E			
ssp. *terebinthina* (Vollesen) Gillett		X	S, SC			
C. quadricincta Schweinf.	NE	N	NE	X		
C. hodai Sprague		X	E			
C. kua (R. Br. ex Royle) Vollesen		N, C, S	E	X		
C. gileadensis (L.) C. Chr. (syn. *C. opobalsamum* (L.) Engl.)	NE	X	E	X	X	X
C. truncata Engl.		X	E			
C. foliacea Sprague				X		
C. campestris Engl.						
ssp. *campestris*			S			
ssp. *glabrata* (Engl.) Gillett		S				

Key: X = present; ? = uncertain; N = north; S = south; E = east; W = west; C = central; NE = northwest; SE = southeast; SW = southwest; SC = south-central.

References: Primarily Gillett 1991 and Vollesen 1989, supplemented by Andrews 1952: 323–5; Groom 1981; Miller *et al.* 1996: 20–1; Rees 1995.

ency of the exudates is scant. Thus, it is impossible to determine which, if any, species may have been exploited in antiquity and if so, what distinctions may have been made between them. In modern Somalia, for example, a range of exudates from different *Commiphora* trees and shrubs is available, each with its own local name, and it has been noted that the sources of these gum-resins 'have never been fully described or correlated with the trees' (Groom 1981: 117. Also Rees 1995: 58). Moreover, further data on the resin-producing capabilities of these species are necessary. To take one example, *C. africana* (A. Rich.) Engl. was named as a source by Rees (1995: 58) and Howes (1949: 153), but Hepper (1992b: 145, n. 2) called it 'one of the least resinous species of the genus'. These factors make it unlikely that any such list of sources would remain unaltered over time.

As Table 18.4 indicates, these different *Commiphora* species are said to be the source of various gum-resins, such as bdellium, opopanax, or opobalsam (Hepper 1992b: 145, n. 2). The grounds for distinguishing these exudates from myrrh or from each other is not entirely clear. Groom (1981: 123) suggested that bdellium was a name given in classical times to gum-resins of *Commiphora* more strongly scented than myrrh.

Details on the distribution of the different species are given in Table 18.3. Again, there is a lack of consensus for much of this data. In some cases, earlier identifications of species in different regions have come into dispute; in others, taxonomic problems have led to confusion. Gillett (1991: 81, 83) suggested that another source mentioned by some modern authors, *C. erythraea* (Ehrenberg.) Engl., is in fact 'no more than a variety' of *C. kataf* subsp. *kataf*

Table 18.4. *Details on the exudates produced by certain species of* Commiphora

Species	Citations as resinous	Description of exudate
C. myrrha (Nees) Engl.	All	A hardly scented, viscid exudate resulting in a hard translucent yellowish gum-resin.
C. habessinica (Berg.) Engl.	2, 3, 6, 7	Faintly scented gum-resin.
C. schimperi (O. Berg) Engl.	2, 3, 5, 7	Called a bdellium. Exudate usually sparse. A hard, yellowish gum-resin.
C. kataf (Forssk.) Engl.	3, 5, 7	Faintly apple-scented gum-resin, called opopanax.
C. erythraea (Ehrenb.) Engl.	2, 3, 5	Gum-resin also called bisabol myrrh, sweet myrrh, opopanax, and perfumed bdellium.
C. africana (A. Rich) Engl.	2, 4, 5, 6, 7	A hard, slightly scented gum-resin. Exudate sparse, called bdellium.
C. hildebrandtii (Engl.) Engl.	3, 5, 7	Called a bdellium. A brittle, white gum-resin.
C. ogadesnsis Chiov	1, 7	White exudate.
C. mukul Engl.	3, 5	Source of bdellium.
C. pedunculata (Kotschy & Peyr) Engl.	5, 7	Opaque exudate called bdellium.
C. boranensis Vollesen	1, 7	Colourless, very aromatic exudate.
C. corrugata Gillett & Vollesen	1, 7	Colourless in twigs; milky and very resinous in trunk.
C. playfairii (Oliv.) Engl.	3, 4	Called a bdellium. White to reddish brown in colour.
C. terebinthina Vollesen	1, 7	Clear exudate with a terebinthine odour.
C. quadricincta Schweinf.	2, 6	
C. hodai Sprague	2, 6	
C. kua (R. Br. ex Royle) Vollesen	2, 6	Creamy, barely scented exudate forming a hard, yellowish gum-resin.
C. gileadensis (L.) C. Chr.	1, 2, 3, 5, 6	Called an opobalsam.
C. truncata Engl.	2, 6	
C. foliacea Sprague	3	
C. campestris Engl.	6, 7	Exudate not copious. Described varyingly as having a strong turpentine or pear-scented odour.

Citations as resinous based on (1) Baum 1994; (2) Goettsch 1991; (3) Groom 1981; (4) Howes 1949; (5) Rees 1995; (6) Vollesen 1989; (7) Gillett 1991.
Descriptions of the gum-resins compiled largely from Gillet (1991), Rees (1995) and Groom (1981).

(Gillett 1991: 83). In modern times, the exudate of *C. kataf* has been called *opopanax* (Rees 1995: 58; Howes 1949: 153), a clear instance where a general term has been confusingly applied to different genera (see discussions of opopanax above). Groom (1981: 27, 123) not only kept *C. erythraea* and *C. kataf* separate but also suggested that *C. erythraea* was the ancient source of the product known by the Egyptians as *ʿntyw*.

With regard to discussions concerning *snṯr* and *ʿntyw*, two further species are especially relevant. *C. samharensis* Schweinf. ssp. *terebinthina* (Vollesen) Gillett, is said to have a clear exudate with a terebinthine, or pistacia-like odour, possibly causing the gum-resin of this species and the resin of *Pistacia* spp. to be used interchangeably in antiquity (Baum 1994: 31). Moreover, *Commiphora gileadensis* (L.) Chr. may have been the source of an aromatic variously known as the Biblical Balm of Gilead, Mecca balsam or opobalsam (Hepper 1987b: 110–1; Rees 1995: 58). This species is found in Somalia, eastern Sudan, eastern Ethiopia, and Arabia (Vollesen 1989: 477), but it 'seems to have been cultivated in the tropical conditions of Jericho and Engedi . . . based on Josephus' comments about the precious balm' (Hepper 1992b: 140–1). According to Hepper (1992b: 148), if the species did occur in Palestine, it is still not clear whether it was indigenous or had been introduced in antiquity from Arabia. He also argued against *Balanites aegyptiaca* as the source of this balm, as some have suggested (Moldenke and Moldenke 1952: 55; see Chapter 17, this volume).

If indigenous, it is possible that *C. gileadensis* was the source of the Levantine *ʿntyw* or *snṯr* mentioned in ancient Egyptian texts, for example in the *Annals of Thutmose III* (Baum 1994: 34, 38–9). Notably, Zahran and Willis cited the occurrence of *Commiphora opobalsamum* (= *C. gileadensis*) in the Gebel Elba region in Egypt (Zahran and Willis 1992: 177–8; also Baum 1994: 33–4). Vollesen (1989: 477) stated that it may have been 'possibly originally introduced' to that part of Egypt, but it is clear that the flora of the Gebel Elba district is in many ways distinct from the rest of Egypt.

Germer noted that seeds of *C. gileadensis* were found in a Theban grave of unknown date (Germer 1985: 108; 1988: 30–1; the species given by Germer is *C. opobalsamum* Engl. which is synonymous with *C. gileadensis* (L.) Chr.). Like African species of *Boswellia* and *Commiphora*, the resin of *C. gileadensis* is obtained by incisions in the bark. The method was summarised by Hepper (1987b: 109). The resin collection begins in December, but is most profuse between March and May. In general, resins obtained from *Boswellia* and *Commiphora* can differ in appearance. Dried frankincense is usually pale yellow or white in colour, while dried myrrh often has a darker yellow-brown appearance (Hepper 1987b: 109).

Through scientific analysis (see p. 458–9), a convincing argument is emerging for the identification of *snṯr* obtained from Syria-Palestine as *Pistacia* spp. If so, the identity of *ʿntyw* is still very much open, particularly given the number of species within the genera of *Boswellia* and *Commiphora*. It is also feasible that some confusion between frankincense and myrrh did occur or, though perhaps less likely, that the botanical source of *snṯr* in Syria–Palestine differed from that of *snṯr* from Punt.

Asiatic sources

*Galbanum and asafoetida (*Ferula *spp.)*
Family: Umbelliferae

The modern distribution of the sources of galbanum and asafoetida would suggest that they were not readily available and their usage in antiquity is unclear. The most likely source of the gum-resin galbanum, the tall perennial plant *Ferula gumosa* Boiss. grows only in Iran today (Chamberlain and Rechinger 1987: 410. Hepper (1987a: 31; 1987b: 142), calling it *Ferula galbaniflua* Boiss. and Buhse (Fig. 18.6), discussed its possible ancient usage. Lucas (1962:

*Figure 18.6 Galbanum (*Ferula galbaniflua *Boiss. and Buhse).*

94) and Manniche (1989: 132) both listed *Peucedanum galbaniflora* as a source of galbanum. This species can perhaps be equated to *Peucedanum galbanifluum* (Boiss. and Buhse) Baill. which, like *F. galbaniflua* Boiss. and Buhse, is synonymous with *F. gumosa* (Chamberlain and Rechinger 1987: 410). In addition, Manniche (1989: 132) suggested *Peucedanum officinale* (without attribution) as a source of galbanum but the taxonomy of this species is confusing and further information is needed.

The greenish-coloured, translucent, irregular tears of *F. gumosa* can be obtained from incisions in the stem near the root (Cooke 1874: 60). Fragments of the fruit of this plant, now in Berlin, were found at Antinoë and dated to AD 300 (Germer 1988: 31).

A number of sources have been suggested for the resin asafoetida. These include *Ferula foetida* (Bunge) Regel, *F. assa-foetida* L. and *F. narthex* Boiss., which are found mainly in Iran and Afghanistan (Chamberlain and Rechinger 1987: 393–4, 396–7, 409–10; Hepper 1992b: 142). Chamberlain (1977: 229–33) clarified the earlier confusion of *F. foetida* and *F. narthex* with *F. assa-foetida*. Again, the resin is obtained from the root (Cooke 1874: 50–3). Alternatively, the species *F. persica* Willd. var. *latisecta* Chamberlain and *F. Gabrielii* Rech. have been suggested as sources (Chamberlain and Rechinger 1987: 398, 401).

The existence of closer sources in antiquity is again not clear. As the name implies, however, the resin is today considered to have an unpleasant odour (Howes 1949: 161; Cooke 1874: 50; Chamberlain 1977: 229), but whether it was thought so in antiquity is not known. Moreover, while its odour may suggest that the gum-resin was not used in perfumery, it may, for example, have been used more extensively in medical preparations.

Summary of the botanical survey

Based on the botanical survey, it is clear that a wide variety of resins were available both directly and indirectly. Although the Levantine coast is generally accepted as the most likely centre of access for the resins used in ancient Egypt, this overview indicates that many of the resin-producing species could have been acquired from a variety of locations. While it may remain true that Levantine sources were more accessible, the wide distribution of some of these species suggests that the overall patterns for Mediterranean trade in resins could be quite complex.

However, it is evident that the precise ancient distribution of certain species, such as pine and pistacia, is often difficult to determine with certainty and may have altered over time. Factors such as fires and animal browsing, as well as human activities, such as deforestation and war, have undoubtedly changed parts of the ancient landscape significantly. Conversely, in addition to cultivation, the invasive tendencies of some species, such as pine and juniper, may have also affected ancient distribution. At first, these problems may seem insurmountable, but it is encouraging that careful botanical study of relict forests, like those of cedar and pistacia, has helped determine the ancient distribution more accurately. In view of Loret's comments on the identity of ʿš, the distribution of cedar is particularly significant. Similarly, the more restricted distribution of *Abies cilicica* may lead to a modification of Loret's theory that ʿš was more commonly fir.

Regrettably, the actual process of resin collection leaves little evidence which could be traced by archaeologists. Moreover, the lack of accurate modern field notes on resin production has undoubtedly made it difficult to determine the sources most likely to have been exploited in antiquity. The complexity of the taxonomy and the confusion of species has often rendered the few existing accounts unreliable. Hopefully, now that the extent of these problems has been highlighted, botanists will intervene to set the records straight. Clearly, further research into the resin-producing capabilities of species such as pistacia, juniper, cypress and styrax is necessary and may well have a profound effect on current theories of resin trade. These complications have a serious cumulative effect on the scientific analysis of ancient samples. Because the techniques used for identification of these rely on comparative modern reference samples, botanical identifications have to be secure or the analytical results could be useless. In particular, many modern resins are sold only with their common name. To cite one example, resin called opopanax could in fact be either *Opopanax* spp. or *Commiphora* spp. This indicates a need for more precise botanical labelling of reference material.

The chemistry of resins

The application of scientific analysis to the study of ancient natural products, such as resins, amber and bitumen, has expanded considerably over the past few years. This will undoubtedly continue in the future. However, integration of this data into the archaeological or historical framework of ancient Egypt is often more difficult to achieve. This reflects a growing need for a better understanding of the capabilities of scientific analyses. Certain fundamental questions need to be addressed. What can one realistically expect of such analyses? Do diagnostic compounds exist which will allow these products to be distinguished? Will the age of the sample affect the results? Can the components in mixtures be separated and identified? etc. The overview presented here can in no way be considered a comprehensive study of the chemistry of these products, but is more specifically intended to provide some of the basic background information which can help answer some of these questions.

Most simply, fresh resinous exudates can be divided into true resins (pistacia, cedar, pine, fir, spruce, ladanum, liquidambar, juniper and cypress), which contain only a resin component, and gum-resins (frankincense and myrrh), which are a combination of components found in a true resin and polysaccharidic gum. This distinction can be established by the solubility of the fresh exudate in alcohol and water. True resin components would be soluble in alcohol, but unaffected by water. However, as gum will either dissolve or swell in water, but remain unaffected by alcohol, gum-resins would be partly soluble in alcohol and either partly dissolve or swell in water. While this is a reliable test for distinguishing between fresh samples of resin and gum-resin, it is unclear whether these distinctions would remain true for aged samples. In addition, these tests cannot determine a specific genus for the resin and species identification is impossible and clearly guesswork. Moreover, this test would be inherently less reliable for any mixtures of resins, gum-resins, and gums.

Lucas and his contemporaries relied to a large extent on solubility tests for resin identifications (Lucas 1962: 316–24). In addition, a number of 'spot' tests were also often undertaken, such as the Liebermann-Storch test (Lucas 1911: 22, 24, 26). These tests are based on colour matches produced when certain reagents are applied to fresh resins and ancient samples (Griffiths 1937: 703–7), but they have now been largely abandoned due to their inconsistency. Lucas seems to have been well aware of the limitations of such analyses and was not generally inclined to give firm genus identifications. However, he did occasionally indulge in a certain amount of speculation, and sometimes concluded that a sample was 'probably' a resin of a certain genus (Lucas 1962: 320). Therefore, results can sometimes appear more conclusive than can be supported by the scientific analysis.

Fortunately, as resin chemistry has progressed over the years, more diagnostic chemical components have been identified. Through the identification of these components, using primarily GC (gas chromatography) and GC/MS (gas chromotography/mass spectrometry), it has become possible not only to determine if a sample is resinous but also, in many instances, to establish the botanical source for a resin much more specifically (Mills and White 1994: 109; on these techniques see Chapter 17, this volume). These analyses are largely based on the isolation and identification of components called *terpenes* and *terpenoids*. These compounds, found in most resins, are based on complex six carbon ring systems with attached hydrogen atoms. These rings are shown as hexagonal configurations, for example, in Fig. 18.7 (one ring) and Fig. 18.8 (three rings). When only carbon and hydrogen are in the structure, the compound is known as a terpene. However, when oxygen is also bonded to the carbon rings, the compounds are called terpenoids. Collectively, the term *terpenoid chemistry* is given to the study of these compounds.

Based on the number of carbon atoms and rings, the terpenes and terpenoids can broadly be placed into two groups: lower terpenoids and higher terpenoids. Resins commonly contain varying amounts of both. Each of these terpenoid groups can be further subdivided as follows:

Lower terpenoids

Monoterpenoids	Compounds with ten carbon atoms.
Sesquiterpenoids	Compounds with fifteen carbon atoms.

Higher terpenoids.

Diterpenoids	Compounds with twenty carbon atoms.
Triterpenoids	Compounds with thirty carbon atoms.

As the number of carbon atoms increases, so does the number of rings, reaching a maximum of five rings. Similarly, generally speaking, as the number of these carbon rings increases, so does the mass of the compound and its stability (as the factors which can affect this are numerous and complex, they will not be discussed in detail here; for further details, see Mills and White 1994: 3–4, 8). Thus, it is more likely that the complex higher terpenoids, rather than lower terpenoids, would be preserved in ancient samples. However, other factors can affect the stability of the compound. For example, the presence of double bonds between the carbons in a terpenoid can make the compound more prone to alteration over time. Conversely, some compounds contain a carbon ring with three conjugated double bonds (a benzene ring), which is comparatively stable (see Fig. 18.8 bottom row). Fresh resins con-

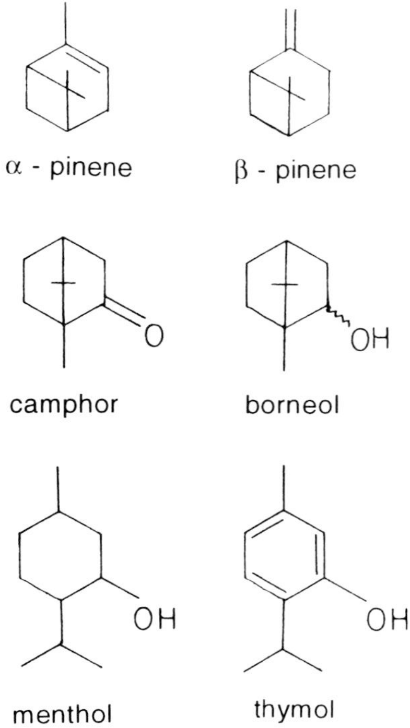

Figure 18.7 Molecular structures of some monoterpenes and monoterpenoids.

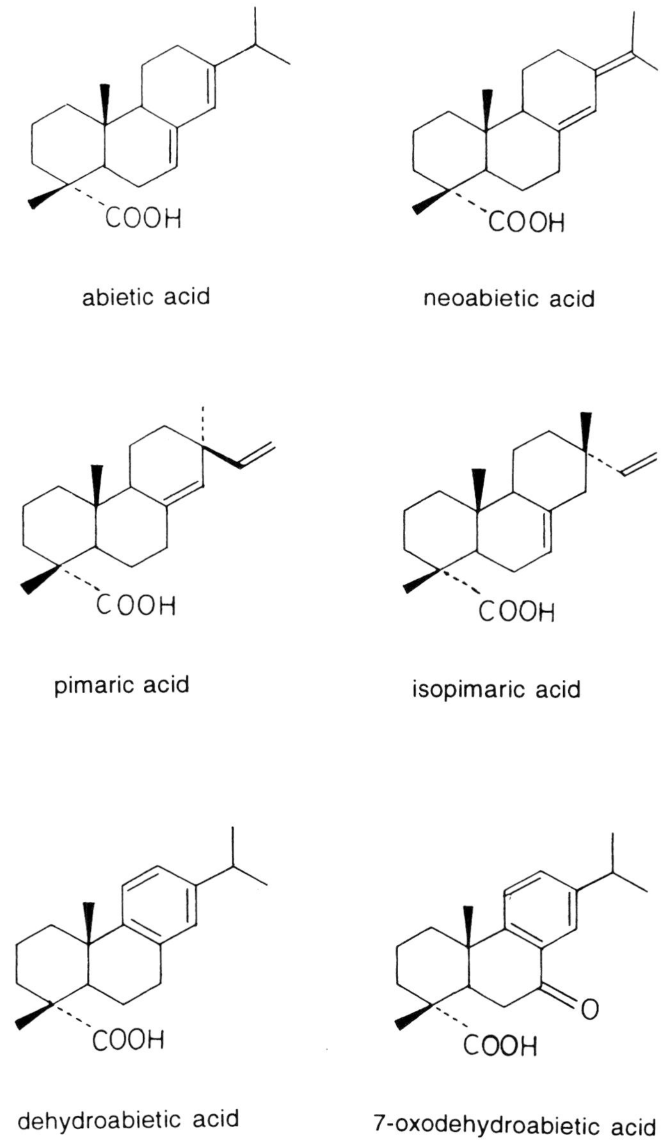

COOH COOH

abietic acid neoabietic acid

COOH COOH

pimaric acid isopimaric acid

COOH O COOH

dehydroabietic acid 7-oxodehydroabietic acid

Figure 18.8 Molecular structures of some of the abietane and pimarane diterpenoids found in conifer resins. Note dehydroabietic and 7–oxodehydroabietic acids found in some ancient samples.

taining such rings are often called *balsams* or *aromatic* compounds, the latter term unrelated to the odour of the component (Mills and White 1994: 5–6, 109).

Therefore, although compounds in each of the terpenoid groups can have a similar or identical ring structure (skeleton), other factors, such as the placement and number of double bonds, can cause them to behave differently from each other. For example, while sesquiterpenoids are composed of fifteen carbon atoms (arranged with one or two carbon rings), there are several hundred known sesquiterpenoids.

As the higher terpenoids are generally more stable, and therefore, more likely to remain detectable over time, they are the first indicator to the identity of a resin. Moreover, nature has provided one important distinction: natural resins containing higher terpenoids will contain either diterpenoids or triterpenoids, but not both. The exceptions to this are the exudates of the Umbelliferae family which are discussed below (see p. 448).

Identification of diterpenoid resins

Of the diterpenoid resins, coniferous resins are particularly relevant to this study. The major Mediterranean resin-producing genera within this group are from the families Pinaceae (pine, cedar and fir) and Cupressaceae (juniper and cypress). Fortunately, the diterpenoids found in the resins of these two families are distinct and, therefore, it should be relatively easy to distinguish between Pinaceae and Cupressaceae resins in fresh samples.

In ancient samples, however, it is rare that these diterpenoids would remain unchanged. Certain compounds characteristic of the Pinaceae family will change over time to form dehydroabietic acid (Fig. 18.8). This compound can be further oxidised, as ageing progresses, to form 7–oxodehydroabietic acid (Fig. 18.8). These two acids are therefore the compounds most likely to be found in ancient samples of the family Pinaceae. However, the diterpenoid pimaradiene compounds found in fresh samples of Pinaceae resins often do not seem to survive as well as dehydroabietic and 7–oxodehydroabietic acid and are therefore comparatively rarer, although not unknown, in ancient samples (Mills and White 1977: 15). Some of the diterpenoids of the Cupressaceae resins can survive. However, communic acids (Fig. 18.9) are readily converted to polycommunic acid and this compound would therefore be more commonly present in aged Cupressaceae samples (Mills and White 1994: 102–3). Because such changes are known, it is clear that ageing will not generally affect the ability to distinguish between Pinaceae and Cupressaceae resins.

Within these families, a more precise identification to a specific genus is more difficult to establish in older samples. In the Pinaceae family, which includes pine, cedar and fir, it is only possible to identify aged fir (*Abies* spp.) resin with some certainty, as it can contain large quantities of the oxidation products of the neutral compound cis-abienol (Fig. 18.10) (Mills and White 1977: 17; 1994: 102). Unfortunately, no diagnostic diterpenoids have been found which could distinguish between aged cedar (*Cedrus* spp.) and pine (*Pinus* spp.), although recent research has explored the possibility that variations in the proportions of diterpenoids might provide a means of distinguishing between members of the Pinaceae family (Hafizoğlu and Holmbom 1987: 142; Hafizoğlu 1987: 34–5). Similarly, within the family Cupressaceae, there are no diagnostic diterpenoids found only in juniper (*Juniperus* spp.) or cypress (*Cupressus* spp.), and therefore, identifica-

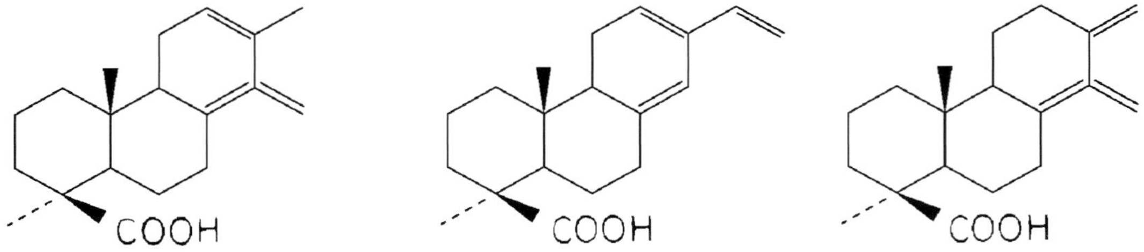

COOH COOH COOH

cis-communic acid trans-communic acid iso-communic acid

Figure 18.9 *Molecular structures of some labdane diterpenoids found as polymer in Cupressaceae resins.*

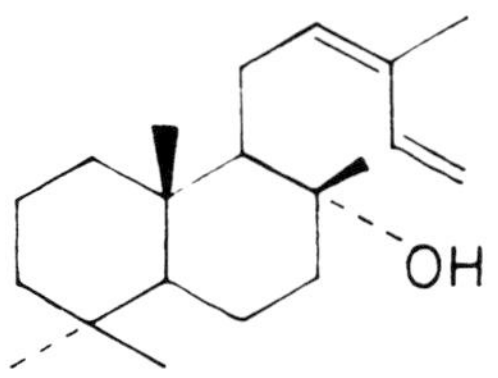

OH

cis-abienol

Figure 18.10 *Molecular structure of cis-abienol.*

tion of either genus cannot be determined by the diterpenoids present. In order to distinguish between cedar and pine, and between juniper and cypress, it would be necessary to detect diagnostic lower terpenoids.

Before turning to these, it should be noted that the ancient Egyptians may have had access to ladanum, the resin obtained from *Cistus* spp. Like resins of the family Cupressaceae, cistus resins contain labdane compounds. Some of these, such as laurifolic acid, labdanolic acid, cistenolic acid, are characteristic of fresh ladanum (Pascual-Teresa *et al.* 1986: 1185; Pascual-Teresa *et al.* 1982: 899–901). Thus, it is unlikely that there would be confusion between ladanum and the Pinaceae and Cupressaceae resins. However, as yet, little work has been done on ancient samples of ladanum, making it difficult to determine the likely products of long-term degradation.

Identification of lower terpenoids

These mono- and sesquiterpenoids (Fig. 18.7) are the components which give the resins their distinctive odours. For example, myrrh contains up to 10 per cent of these compounds (Brieskorn and Noble 1982: 221). The initial, more fluid state in which resins are found is due to their presence, as they are liquid at normal temperatures. Thus, when an abundance of lower terpenoids is present, the fresh resin is often called an *oleoresin* and may have a softer consistency (Howes 1949: 89).

Lower terpenoids can be found in many different parts of a plant, such as the leaf (bay), the flower bud (rose), the seed (cardamom), the rhizome (ginger) or the bark (cinnamon). In fact, these mono- and sesquiterpenoids are perhaps better known as the essential or volatile oils which help give resins, herbs, spices, and flowers their characteristic scents or tastes. However, the description of these components as essential or volatile 'oils' can be misleading as these substances are not true oils, such as olive oil, containing fatty acids, but terpenoids which are for the most part immiscible in water. Recent research has indicated that these lower terpenoids can survive in ancient plant remains. Samples of *Origanum* spp. fragments taken from Greco–Roman funerary wreaths found by Petrie at Hawara were analysed by GC/MS and shown to contain characteristic lower terpenoid compounds of the genus (Edmondson and Bienkowski 1993: 173). This study is encouraging and suggests that volatile components can survive in ancient material.

The isolation of these lower terpenoid components is the basis of much of the perfume industry. While, as in modern times, these essential oils could be obtained by distillation, they could also be obtained by the processes of *enfleurage* or *maceration*, by steeping the resins or plants in a lipid base. Thus, in ancient times, a cedar-scented cosmetic could be manufactured either by dissolving a cedar resin in a lipid base, or by steeping plant parts, such as needles or branches of cedar, into the lipid. If a resin had been used, both diterpenoids and lower terpenoids would be likely to be present, as, in general, resins – if fluid – can be dissolved into a lipid base. However, if maceration or enfleurage of botanical remains other than resin were used, lower terpenoids would dominate.

While detection of diagnostic lower terpenoids in resins could in theory help determine the botanical source of the resin, such analyses are not without difficulties. Even in fresh resin or plant samples, the number of lower terpenoids present and the amount of each specific lower terpenoid can vary according to the species of the plant and its environment. Thus, identification of a botanical source based on the quantities of lower terpenoids present would be prone to inaccuracy.

Furthermore, over time, the amounts of lower terpenoids present can decrease significantly due to their volatility. Unfortunately, this volatility also means that these terpenoids are much more difficult to detect over time, and will often have disappeared altogether in ancient samples. For this reason, it is not always possible to identify the specific genus of an ancient coniferous resin. Nevertheless, in some instances, the lower terpenoids could remain detectable. To some extent, this depends on the size of the sample, its degree of preservation and, particularly for ancient samples, the possible presence of other compounds such as fats, waxes, etc., mixed with the resin. As resins are comparatively complex compounds, small quantities of essential oils do sometimes remain trapped in the sample. Ground or powdered resins, however, would be less likely to have detectable lower terpenoids, because of the increased total surface exposure to air, light, etc.

Unfortunately, little work has been done to date on the identity and stability of the lower terpenoids found in juniper and cypress resins, and thus it remains difficult to distinguish between these two sources. Some analyses of the lower terpenoids found in pine and cedar resins have been undertaken and it is now clear that lower terpenoids can provide a means of distinguishing between these two resins. While the lower terpenoids found in pine resins are predominately monoterpenoids, such as α- and β-pinenes (Fig. 18.7), those in cedar are largely sesquiterpenoids, particularly within the groups known as azulenes and atlantones (Mills and White 1994: 97, table 8.1; de Mayo 1959: 182, 184; Simonsen and Barton 1952: 198–202; Bryant 1969: 291; Pfau and Plattner 1934: 129–57; and Hafizoğlu 1987: 28). Sesquiterpenes are rare in pines, but caryophyllene and longifolene, do occur (Hendrickson 1959: 86). However, longifolene is also found in species of juniper (Akiyoshi *et al.* 1960: 237–9) and fir (Fady *et al.* 1992: 165). Thus, while problematic, detection of the type of lower terpenoid compounds can allow for a genus identification. If both the diterpenoid and lower terpenoid components can be detected in a resin sample, it may be possible to distinguish between pine, cedar and fir. Although Pinaceae sources can also be readily distinguished from juniper and cypress by their diterpenoid content, it is as yet unclear whether it would be possible to isolate juniper from cypress through their lower terpenoids.

For some genera, notably cedar and fir, where the botanical information suggests that only one species is a likely resin source, the resin could therefore be linked to a specific species, such as *Cedrus libani* A. Richard or *Abies cilicica* Ant. et Ky. by process of elimination. However, in general, identification of a resin to a particular species is less secure. Many of the differences between species are probably based on fine distinctions in the percentages of the lower terpenoids, and as noted above, these can vary greatly. One possible exception, however, is *Pinus halepensis*, which can sometimes be distinguished not only from cedar and fir, but also from the other types of pine probably available to the ancient Egyptians. Its identification is based not on the isolation of certain lower terpenoids, but on the ratio of the diterpenoids present, notably 'the preponderance of sandaracopimaric over pimaric acid' (White 1990: 81, 88). Although pimaric acids are rarely preserved in ancient samples, they were identified in a sample taken from the hull of a ship of the first century AD found in Israel at Lake Kinneret. From this ratio, the sample was identified as *Pinus halepensis* (White 1990: 81, 88). This, however, represents a rare example of possible species identification.

Identification of triterpenoid resins

In contrast to the coniferous resins, the triterpenoid resins which could have been available to the ancient Egyptians, such as pistacia, storax, frankincense and myrrh, are somewhat easier to identify as they each contain certain characteristic triterpenoids. The triterpenoids found in *Pistacia* spp. resins have been studied in some detail by Mills and White (1989: 37–44). As well as β-amyrin, tirucallol, and oleanonic acid, which are found in other resins, *Pistacia* spp. resins contain moronic, masticadienonic and isomasticadienonic acids (Fig. 18.11), which, of the possible resin sources, are characteristic of pistacia resins. These components were identified, for example, in samples taken from the Late Bronze Age amphorae from the shipwreck off the coast of Turkey at Ulu Burun (Mills and White 1989: 37–44; Bass 1987: 726–7). Hairfield and Hairfield (1990: 43A–45A) attempted a species identification of the pistacia resin from the shipwreck using thin-layer chromotography (TLC). However, this technique is not as accurate as GC/MS for ancient samples, and can be problematic (Mills and White 1994: 15; see also discussion of TLC in Chapter 17, this volume).

In contrast, comparatively little is known about the chemical composition of aged examples of the gum-resins frankincense and myrrh. However, some of the triterpenoid components of the fresh gum-resins are diagnostic and should remain so over time. For samples of frankincense, *Boswellia* spp., the triterpenoids include not only non-diagnostic compounds and derivatives of α- and β-amyrin and elemadienonic acid, but also characteristic compounds such as β-boswellic acid and its derivative, 11–keto-β-boswellic acid (Fig. 18.13; Snatzke and Vértesy 1967: 121–32. See also Tucker 1986: 425–33). For myrrh, *Commiphora* spp., again α- and β-amyrin would be present, but the detection of commic acids would be diagnostic (Figs 18.12 and 18.13; see Thomas and Willhalm 1964: 3177–83). It should be mentioned that, to date, any attempts to distinguish chemically between modern African and Arabian sources of *Boswellia* spp. or *Commiphora* spp. would not necessarily be relevant for ancient samples (for a summary, see Tucker 1986: 427–8, 430–1). Similarly, it appears that distinction between gum-resins of *Boswellia* spp. and *Commiphora* spp. based on their gum components is unlikely,

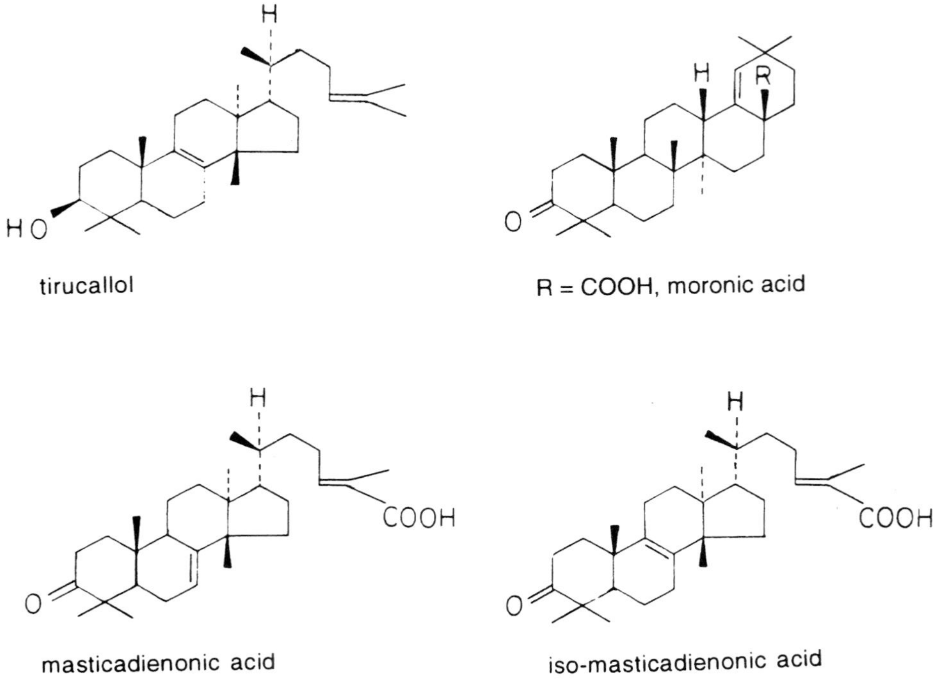

tirucallol

R = COOH, moronic acid

masticadienonic acid

iso-masticadienonic acid

Figure 18.11 Molecular structures of triterpenoid components found in pistacia resin.

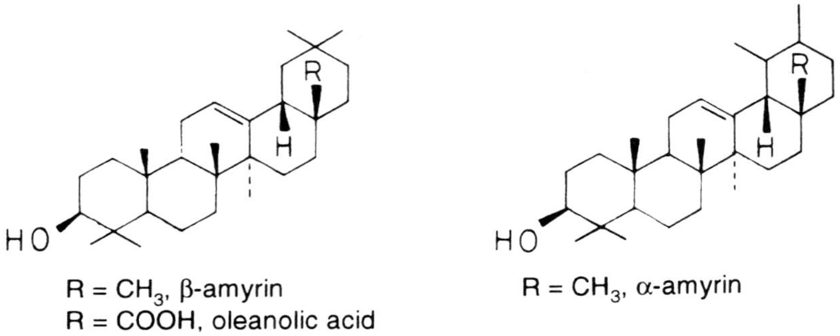

R = CH_3, β-amyrin
R = COOH, oleanolic acid

R = CH_3, α-amyrin

Figure 18.12 Molecular structures of some triterpenoid components.

as they both contain similar saccharides (Mills and White 1994: 77, table 6.1).

Like pistacia resin, oleanonic acid is also present in *Liquidambar orientalis* Miller. But storax also contains the characteristic compounds α- and β-storesin (Hunek 1963: 479). In addition, compounds with a benzene ring, found in 'aromatic' resins, such as cinnamic acid, may also be present (Mills and White 1994: 109). Because no ancient samples of this resin have yet been confirmed, the structure of the degradation products is unknown, although they are probably storesin-based and thus may be recognisable.

Identification of non-terpenoid-based resinous substances

The principal components of the resin-like exudates of *Ferula* spp. and *Opopanax* spp., including galbanum, asafoetida, and opopanax, differ from the terpenoids dis-

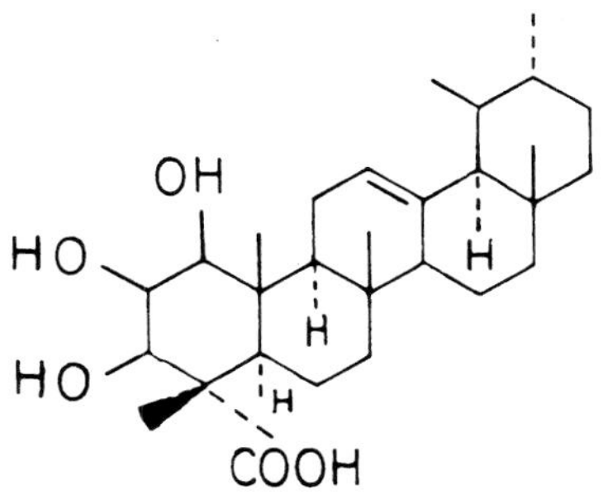

OH
HO
HO
H
H
H
COOH

commic acid E

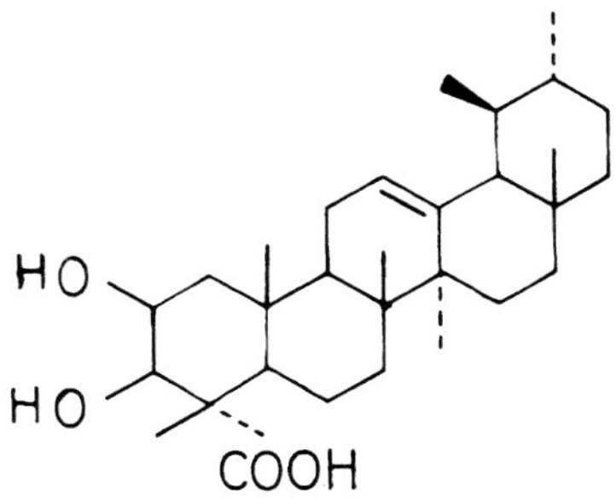

HO
HO
COOH

commic acid D

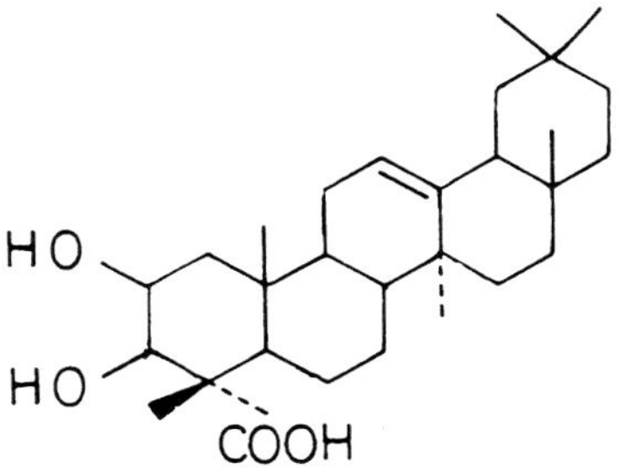

HO
HO
COOH

commic acid C

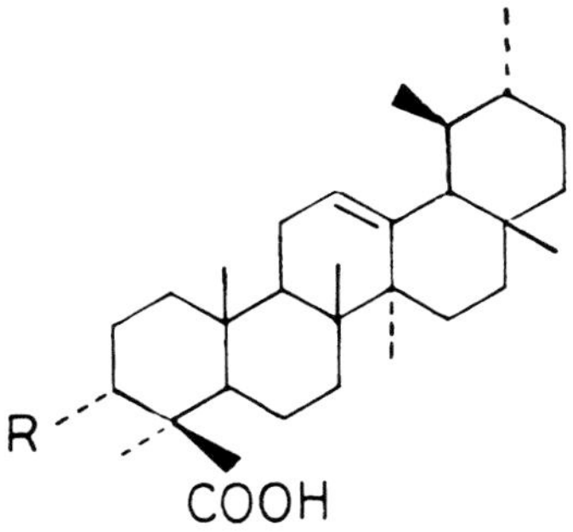

R
COOH

R = OH,
β-boswellic acid
R = AcO,
acetyl-β-boswellic acid

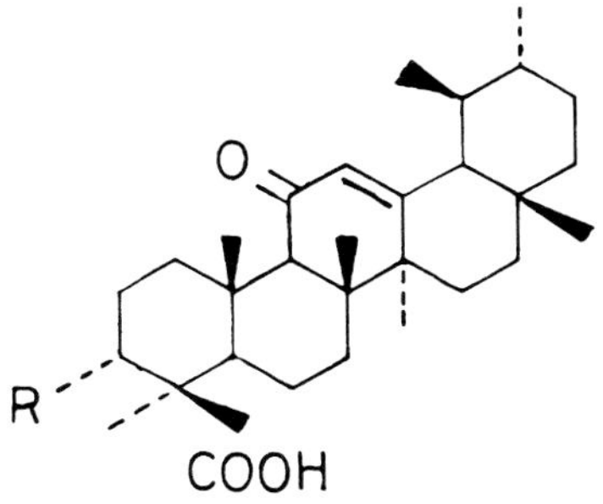

O
R
COOH

R = OH,
11-keto-β-boswellic acid
R = AcO,
acetyl-11-keto-β-boswellic acid

Figure 18.13 Molecular structures of some triterpenoids found in myrrh (commic acids) and frankincense (boswellic acid derivatives).

cussed above. Both belong to the family Umbelliferae, and it is therefore unsurprising that the two contain similar chemical components. A primary constituent is ferulic acid, a comparatively unstable compound, as well as polysaccharide gums and phenolic compounds (on the latter, see Mills and White 1994: 11). These components are prone to cross-linkage over time, making it difficult to identify characteristic components from the resultant polymers.

While the detection of a prevalence of these polymers through GC/MS might suggest the presence of a resin of this type, it would not be sufficient to confirm the identity. The abundance of non-characterisable polymers would make any such samples distinct from the other terpenoid-based resins discussed here.

Identification of pitch and tar

By taking into consideration both the lower and higher terpenoid composition of the various resins, it is often possible to distinguish between different genera in ancient samples. However, the Egyptians could have heated resin to increase the fluid consistency, or they could have obtained products, such as pitch and tar, by heating or distilling resins or resinous woods. Would such treatment affect the identifiable components of the resins?

The words for heated resin products, such as *rosin, turpentine, tar, pitch* and even the word *resin* itself have often been used interchangeably, which has led to much confusion. Such confusion is not new, however, and it has been noted in the past that classical authors also transferred the terms without much regard to their accuracy (Lucas 1931: 16–9; Heron and Pollard 1988: 433–4). The problems caused by this confusion, however, become particularly significant when considering the chemistry of resins. It is therefore necessary to define these terms more accurately.

While today, distillation of aromatic resins or other substances such as leaves, bark, etc., produces essential or volatile oils used in perfumery, the volatiles produced by the distillation of softwood resins, such as pine, are commonly called *turpentine.* Like essential oils, turpentine consists of the lower terpenoids condensed after heating. The remaining product, which contains the higher terpenoids, is known as rosin. It is generally believed that the ancient Egyptians did not capture volatile components, such as turpentine, until Greco-Roman times (see p. 461), but if they did gently heat resin, driving off those volatile components, the residue left, namely rosin, would have been preserved. Significantly, because lower terpenoids are often not preserved in ancient resin samples, rosin bears some resemblance to archaeological samples. Both consist mainly of higher terpenoids of similar composition, and both can have similar degradation products, namely dehydroabietic and 7-oxodehydroabietic acids.

In contrast, tar and pitch are produced through destructive distillation, or pyrolysis. Lucas (1931: 18, n. 1) defined destructive distillation as 'the process of heating, out of contact with the air, a solid material in such a manner that its original composition is destroyed and new bodies are formed, some of which are volatile and are conducted away, the more liquefiable portions being condensed by cooling. This is the opposite of the more usual method of distillation, in which care is taken to avoid decomposition and only the separation of pre-existing bodies occurs.' Tar is usually produced by strongly heating softwood or resin at a temperature of 350 °C (Heron and Pollard 1988: 433). Further heating or distillation of the tar produces a thicker pitch (Robinson *et al.* 1987: 642; Heron and Pollard 1988: 433; Lucas 1962: 325). These compounds, which are black and viscous in consistency, are particularly suited for caulking or waterproofing. Tar is the initial pyrolysate formed from the heating of softwood or resin. Because the tars and pitches obtained from coniferous wood are largely formed from the resin trapped in the wood, the chemical composition of these products bears some similarity to pyrolysed resin (Mills and White 1994: 59, 65).

Generally, the diterpenoid components found in fresh resins, such as abietic acid, and pimaric acid are not preserved in pyrolysed tars, although dehydroabietic acid is present in both Pinaceae softwood and resin tar. In contrast, the oxidation product, 7-oxodehydroabietic acid is usually absent in strongly heated products (Mills and White 1977: 24), although Heron and Pollard (1988: 440) commented that its absence may be due to environmental factors. Both softwood and resin tars will also contain certain characteristic *aromatic* compounds (p. 445), such as norabietatrienes, 1,2,3,4-tetrahydroretene, and retene itself (Fig. 18.14). As a result, isolation of these last three components provides a means of distinguishing between resin and tar. The proportion of retene is further increased during the formation of pitch (Robinson *et al.* 1987: 642).

However, as strong heating to produce a tar or pitch would tend to drive off the lower terpenoids (Evershed *et al.* 1985: 529), it is generally not possible to distinguish between different coniferous sources for the tar based on these components. Nonetheless, it has been shown that there are demonstrable differences between the infrared (IR) and

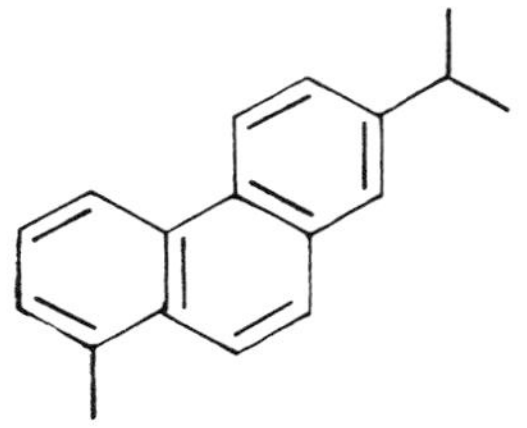

retene

Figure 18.14 Molecular structure of retene, found in some strongly heated ancient coniferous resins.

nuclear magnetic resonance (NMR) spectra of pine and spruce tars which may allow for a genus identification (Robinson *et al.* 1987: 643; Evershed *et al.* 1985: 528–30).

It is apparent that the ancient Egyptians were familiar with the pyrolysis of wood, as it is through this process charcoal is formed. However, the charcoal found in Egypt was probably formed from indigenous, non-resin producing trees and not from the pyrolysis of coniferous resins. Lucas (1962: 326) suggested that any tar or pitch was probably imported and not produced internally as it would seem unlikely that the ancient Egyptians would import large quantities of wood simply to reduce the bulk to tar.

Summary

From this overview, it is clear that it should be possible to distinguish between a number of different types of resins, notably between coniferous resins, Burseraceous resins, labdanum, storax and pistacia resin. At times, it may also be possible to identify the coniferous and Burseraceous resins more specifically, at least to genus. It should be feasible to determine whether the resins had been strongly heated or to distinguish between a resin, an asphalt and a gum.

While identification of a sample to genus or species would of course be preferred, valuable information still can be obtained from less specific identifications. In particular, determination of a link between certain types of resin, for example, coniferous or Burseraceous resins, and specific usages for those resins, such as in mummification or as incense, might prove useful (see discussion of usages pp. 456–68).

Amber

Sources of amber

In addition to the wide array of fresh resins and gum-resins available to the ancient Egyptians, it has been suggested that they occasionally may have had access to imported amber. Although often described as a fossilised resin or gemstone, amber is not a mineral but a wholly organic substance (Grimaldi 1996: 12). It is derived from resin-bearing trees, once clustered in dense now-extinct forests. Millions of years ago (mostly during the Middle Cretaceous to Tertiary periods), fallen trees from these forests, and their resins, were carried via riverine routes to deltas or coastal regions, where they were eventually buried by sediments (Grimaldi 1996: 12–13, 20). The known accumulations of amber, therefore, are secondary redepositions resulting from geologic activity rather than the primary deposits (Beck and Shennan 1991: 16–17; a useful summary of some of the geological events contributing to this is also discussed). These occur throughout both the Old and New Worlds and many varieties are recognised. Due to their prehistoric derivation, these ambers have been given the collective geological name of *resinite* (Anderson and Winans 1991: 2901; on problems of nomenclature see Anderson and Crelling 1995: xi).

Best known is Baltic amber, given the geological name of *succinite*, and found in substantial quantities on the coast of the Baltic Sea. It has been estimated that up to a million pounds of amber a year was dug from the *blue earth* layer of the Samland peninsula in the eastern Baltic earlier this century (Beck and Shennan 1991: 16–17). Natural deposits of succinite are widely dispersed and specimens have been found in locations from Russia to England (Mills and White 1994: 110).

Originally translucent or opaque in appearance with a pale yellow to brown colour, succinite, in common with ambers in general, will darken to a red or brownish-red hue, often after only a few years' exposure (Strong 1966: 14). Numerous cracks in the surface will develop as well. Because fresh resins will undergo similar visual alterations upon exposure to light and air, it is often extremely difficult to distinguish by eye ancient amber artifacts from those made of resin. Over time, other physical properties and chemical components also become altered. Amber, for example, is much harder in consistency than fresh resin and has a much higher melting point (Strong 1966: 1). In contrast to most fresh resins, amber is only incompletely soluble in organic solvents (Mills and White 1994: 110).

It has long been recognised that Baltic amber is not unique and other ambers from this area are also known, such as the friable *gedanite*, the dark, opaque *beckerite*, and the soft, yellow *glessite* (Grimaldi 1996: 53). Elsewhere, varieties of resinite include *simitite*, found in Sicily, *rumanite* found in Romania, and *schraufite*, which occurs in Romania, Poland and Austria. The designation *schraufite* has also been given to resinite of similar composition found in Lebanon, especially between Beirut and Damascus and in the area around Jezzine (Grimaldi 1996: 35). Further deposits occur in Israel and Jordan.

Although these different types of amber have been known in some cases for centuries, there was a common tendency in the past to assume that any resinite used in ancient times was of Baltic derivation, partly because of its sheer plenitude and partly because Classical texts suggested its exploitation at that time (Grimaldi 1996: 149–57; for a summary of Classical references, see Beck *et al.* 1966: 219–220; Hughes-Brock 1993). The recognised use of amber in Crete and Greece from the Middle Bronze Age onwards (summarised in Beck: 1966; see also Hughes-Brock 1993) lent credibility to the theory that resinite may have at least occasionally reached Egypt as a result of trade (Hood 1993: 233).

Suggestions that a range of ancient Egyptian amulets, beads and other items of jewellery, dating as early as the Predynastic period, were made from amber have been published in the past (summarised by Lucas 1962: 387). The possibility that some of the resinous beads in the tomb of Tutankhamun (KV62) were of amber was considered, but subsequently rejected, by Lucas (1962: 388). Notably, Lucas remained sceptical of its abundance in Egypt stating: 'that amber may have been used by the ancient Egyptians especially at a late date, is not denied, but that all the objects termed amber are indeed amber has not been proved, and some at least are almost certainly other kinds of resin' (Lucas 1962: 387–8).

Lucas's comments remain difficult to dismiss, as little scientific analysis has been carried out on proposed resinite objects thus far. More recently, Raven (1990: 8–10, 16–17) echoed Lucas's sentiments concerning the scarcity of amber in Egypt. Conversely, Hood, in a review of the material from Tutankhamun's burial, suggested that some of these items, and a few other New Kingdom pieces, may be of amber based on stylistic grounds (especially parallels to Aegean material), the implied importance of the objects, and their placement in the tomb (Hood 1993: 231–2).

In addition, it should be noted that there is no single, uniform chronological stage at which a resin becomes amber (Langenheim 1969: 1158). Any alteration in the structure or composition of resinites is related not only to composition of the original parent resin and the age of the sample, but also to its post-depositional environment. Therefore, 'sub-fossil' buried resins, which are thousands rather than millions of years old are also known as resinites. This group comprises resins called *elemis* and *copals*. Like amber, these occur throughout the world, including parts of eastern Africa. For these resinites, the botanical sources have been easier to identify, as in some instances, the modern trees are still extant. East African copal from *Hymenaea verrucosa* Gaertn. (syn. *Trachylobium verrucosum* Gaertn.), for example, can be dug up beneath modern specimens of the same trees, also tapped today for their fresh resin (Burkill 1995: 132; Brenan 1967: 134; Howes 1949: 96–7). In general, it would seem unlikely that resinite from this tree, which is found in Kenya and Tanzania, was known to the Egyptians (Burkill 1995: 132; Brenan 1967: 134). The nearest source of copal would probably have been from *Daniellia oliveri* (Rolfe) Hutch and Dalz. which extends as far north as Sudan (Brenan 1967: 132; Burkill 1995: 94–6; Howes 1949: 98). Similarly, the nearest source of fresh and sub-fossilised elemi resin would be *Canarium schweinfurthii* Engl., which occurs in southern Sudan and possibly southwest Ethiopia (Gillett 1991: 2,4; Vollesen 1989: 442; Howes 1949: 143–4). This tree, reaching up to forty metres in height and bearing edible fruits and seeds, is in the Burseraceae family, along with the genera yielding frankincense and myrrh. Again, its possible use in ancient Egypt remains entirely speculative.

Chemistry of amber

For centuries, the chemical composition of amber has attracted much attention and research. In particular, attempts to characterise the varieties of ambers from different geographical sources have met with some, albeit limited, success. One component most often used as an indicator of certain varieties of amber is succinic acid. As Beck *et al.* (1965: 96) commented, 'It had been known since the middle of the 16th century that Baltic amber contains a small amount of a characteristic organic acid which sublimes when the resin is subjected to destructive distillation'. Further research in the last century illustrated that non-Baltic ambers, for example, rumanite and simitite also contained succinic acid in quantities sometimes similar to succinite (up to about 8.0 per cent). Thus, different varieties of amber were broadly classified into two groups: those which contained succinic acid, termed *succinites*, and those which did not, called *retinites* (Langenheim 1969: 1158; Strong 1966: 1–2).

Through isolation and quantification of succinic acid, some of the earliest scientific research attempted to provenance amber artifacts excavated from Minoan and Mycenaean tombs. These were consistently identified as of Baltic origin. However, in an exemplary critical re-assessment, Beck not only pointed out the shortcomings of the earlier methods of scientific analysis, but also demonstrated an inherent bias towards a Baltic origin for them (Beck 1966: 191–211).

More recently, Beck undertook re-examination of a number of these samples using infrared spectroscopy (IR). Although generally of limited value in the characterization of organic compounds (see Chapter 17, this volume), IR can distinguish samples of amber from other organics, such as oils and fats, beeswax, and bitumen (Mills and White 1994: 112; Langenheim 1969: 1160). Moreover, detailed study of IR spectra has indicated that of the European resinites, Baltic amber and only Baltic amber will show a broad, horizontal shoulder between 1250 and 1175 cm^{-1} on its IR spectrum due to the esters of succinic acid (Beck *et al.* 1965: 103). Thus, with IR, samples can be subdivided into Baltic and non-Baltic sources. With this technique, Beck was able to confirm that most of the Mycenaean/Minoan samples were Baltic amber, but there is some evidence that other non-Baltic sources were occasionally used (Beck 1966: 208; 1970: 10).

The recognition that the majority of amber from Bronze Age mainland Greece and Crete are of Baltic amber clearly has implications for possible European trade routes (Hughes-Brock 1993). Similarly, the application of IR to several dozen samples found in Palestine, ranging in date from the Chalcolithic to Arab periods (although none yet from the Early Bronze Age) has also been useful (Todd 1993). The conclusion that some 80 per cent of these samples were of Baltic amber (Todd 1993: 236) again has important ramifications for discussions of trade. Amber in Palestine is not plentiful, and many of these objects were probably or certainly of Mycenaean manufacture, or were from sites which had received Mycenaean products (e.g. Tell Abu Hawam and Akhziv in Israel; see Todd 1985: 295–7; 1993: 239–42).

The results of this study are perhaps somewhat surprising, since Lebanese schraufite along with similar deposits in Israel and Jordan would have been far nearer sources of amber. More detailed characterization of the non-Baltic ambers may shed light on this discrepancy. It may be that these resources were not known or exploited in antiquity, or perhaps the physical characteristics of this amber were also a factor. In particular, the use of this amber for the manufacture of objects may have been limited (for example, to small beads) because of its tendency to fracture (Strong 1966: 2; Grimaldi 1996: 35).

Interestingly, a pendant from a burial outside the Northern Palace at Tell Asmar in Mesopotamia, possibly dating to the second half of the third millennium BC, was subjected to IR analysis by Beck and identified as an east African copal (Meyer *et al.* 1991). A conclusive genus identification was not possible, although Beck pointed out that east African *Trachylobium* spp. copal (now *Hymenaea* spp., see p. 452) would be a likely source (Meyer *et al.* 1991: 297–8). Sudanese *Daniellia olivera* (see p. 452) was not specifically considered. Lucas (1962: 88) noted only one analysis of an ancient Egyptian deposit where copal might be present. This was Kopp's (1934: 75) examination of the resinous contents of an obsidian jar, possibly one of the 'Seven Sacred Oils', found during Winlock's excavations at Middle Kingdom Lahun. Whether analysis with modern techniques would support this conclusion remains speculation. Certainly, the possibility that east African copals were reaching Mesopotamia at that time raises many issues regarding ancient trade, and indicates that continued study of natural products such as resins, amber and bitumen may yet shed light on this subject.

Further subdivisions of resinite varieties using IR have been difficult to establish. It has been noted that some of the non-Baltic sources from different geographical areas 'yield indistinguishable spectra, probably because they share a common botanical origin' (Lambert *et al.* 1988: 249). Moreover, weathering and oxidation processes have adversely affected some ancient samples, causing a diminution in definition in the crucial area of the IR spectrum (Beck *et al.* 1965: 104–7). In recent times, some progress has been made. In 1991, Beck and Shennan (1991: 29) commented that 'we canot say that a spectrum is of Sicilian amber rather than of Romanian amber – we can only say that it is, or is not, of Baltic amber'. Just two years later, Beck and Hartnett (1993: 40–2) published a paper demonstrating the ability to distinguish reference samples of simitite from succinite using IR. Determination of the composition of simitite has been particularly problematic because, in the last century, Baltic amber was imported to Sicily for carving, due to a shortage of simitite (Beck and Hartnett 1993: 36–7).

Infrared spectroscopy (IR) has perhaps been most successfully used to differentiate between varieties of amber when taken in conjunction with other, more informative techniques, such as ^{13}C-NMR, GC/MS and pyrolysis methods (for example, Lambert *et al.* 1988; Boon *et al.* 1993; Stout *et al.* 1995; Galletti and Mazzeo 1993; Poinar and Haverkamp 1985; Anderson and Botto 1993: 1032–8). Of these procedures, the particular advantage of Py-MS and Py-GC/MS, is that they allow examination of the high molecular weight components and polymers found in resinites which are not normally soluble in organic solvents, as well as lower terpenoids trapped in the cross-linkages. Through utilisation of all of these techniques, both the problems of differentiating between various types of amber, and the question of the botanical sources of the ambers, have been addressed.

With regard to the latter issue, it has been recognised for some time that many of the components (e.g. higher and lower terpenoids, etc.), found in resinites are similar to, or derived, from those found in modern resins. This has enabled comparisons to be made. In resinites, these compounds may have become cross-linked and polymerised (Mills and White 1994: 110). For example, succinic acid related compounds are present in amber, but absent in fresh resins. The physical changes in hardness, melting point and solubility in ambers, noted above, can also be attributed to this.

Examination of the solvent-soluble fractions of ambers, particularly by GC/MS, has revealed an array of terpenoids similar to those found in fresh resins (Mills and White 1994: 110–1). Facilitating this research has been the occasional discovery of traces of the botanical remains of the parent trees in some amber samples (Langenheim 1969: 1159). Based on this data, it was suggested that the plant source of Baltic succinite was an extinct coniferous tree, given the name *Pinites succinifer*. This was subsequently changed to *Pinus succinifera* Conw. and the assumption made that the source was a type of pine. However, claims that the amber was based on a polymer of diterpenoid abietic acid, found in pine (Rottländer 1970: 35–52), have been treated with some scepticism. Instead, it has been demonstrated that Baltic amber contains a high proportion of communic acid and communol, along with agathic acid and pimaradiene and abietadiene acids (Gough and Mills 1972: 527–8; Mills *et al.* 1984/5: 35).

These compounds have an affinity with modern species of *Agathis* in the family Araucariaceae rather than pine, although botanical remains found in the amber are closer to other conifers, notably pine (Mills *et al.* 1984/5: 36; Langenheim 1969: 1163). One explanation for this would be that both *Agathis* and pinaceous trees derive from a common ancestor (for a summary of these issues, see Langenheim 1995: 21–4). To reduce confusion, a reversion to the earlier name of *Pinites succinifer* has been advocated (Mills *et al.* 1984/5: 36).

Scientific research has also been applied to studies of the east African copals, *Hymenaea verrucosa* and *Daniellia oliveri*. GC/MS analysis of samples of these resinites has indicated differences from the diterpenoid European ambers. Labdane diterpenoids are again present in *Hymenaea* spp., but high proportions (45–85 per cent) of ozic acid are also found, and abietane or pimarane compounds are absent (Mills and White 1994: 104; Mills and White 1977: 19). *Daniellia oliveri*, in contrast, contains large amounts of the labdane daniellic acid (illurinic acid) (Mills and White 1994: 104). Thus, within the broad grouping of resinites, amber can be distinguished from copals.

Recent research using ^{13}C-NMR has revealed other compositional distinctions in varieties of amber. Lambert *et al.* (1988) established that another type of Baltic amber, gedanite, was similar to succinite and probably related to it. Previously, it had been suggested that it may have been derived from a different species in the same genus as succinite, given the name *Pinites stroboides* (Lambert *et al.* 1988: 253). Also proposed was a division of European ambers into two groups. The northerly one, including succinite, retains the exomethylene group and was linked to *Pinites succinifera* (probably intended as synonymous with *Pinites succinifer*). The more southerly group, including rumanite, lacks the exomethylene group, but contains a tricyclic abietane-like structure which would appear to suggest an angiosperm or coniferous source (Lambert *et al.* 1988: 261).

Some discretion is necessary, however, as it was also shown that, in heated succinite, the exocyclic methylene group is absent (Lambert *et al.* 1988: 252; Mills and White 1994: 113). In fact, the presence or absence of the exomethylene group may be related not just to different palaeobotanical sources but also to the 'maturity' (e.g. both the age and thermal history) of the samples, becoming progressively diminished as the maturity of the resinite increases (Anderson *et al.* 1992: 834; Lambert *et al.* 1988: 255–6).

In another study, using GC/MS, it was shown that the diterpenoid composition of the varieties succinite and gedano-succinite were similar, and that differences in the amounts of the succinic acid based compounds were probably due to 'the diagenetic alteration of a single resin' (Stout *et al.* 1995: 146). A more detailed understanding of how these processes (geologic, environmental, diagenetic, etc.) effect resinites will undoubtedly emerge in the future. Studies such as these clearly indicate that the divisions of amber into different varieties have been subjective, often based purely on geographic location or appearance rather than scientific grounds. It would be more satisfactory to group resinites based on their botanical source and on compositional similarities.

Using Py-GC/MS and ^{13}C-NMR and taking into consideration other published data, Anderson *et al.* (1992: 830, table I) have attempted to synthesise all available information and to formulate just such a classification system. Nearly all of the resinites possibly accessible to the ancient Egyptians (succinite, simitite, schraufite, etc.) are grouped in Class I. These are based on polymers of (primarily) labdatriene carboxylic acids. These were then further divided into three sub-classes. Class Ia consists of resinites, such as succinite, dominated by polymers of communic acid, partially copolymerised with communol, together with succinic acid (Anderson *et al.* 1992: 830, table I). Class Ib resinites are again dominated by polymers of communic acid, with varying degrees of copolymerisation with communol, but lacking succinic acid. Class Ic consists of copals and Leguminosae resins which contain predominantly polymers of ozic acid and/or zanzibaric acid.

Brief mention can be made of German siegburgite, placed in Class III and characterised by natural polystyrenes similar to those found in modern Hamamelidaceae resins, notably liquidambar (Anderson *et al.* 1992: 830, table I, 837–8). The authors caution that 'given the frequency of occurrence of synthetic polystyrene samples in the environment, care is necessary to ensure the authenticity of individual samples' (Anderson *et al.* 1992: 837). The issue of forged amber is clearly important. Other imitations have been manufactured from Bakelite, epoxy resins and various polyesters, some even containing insects and botanical debris much as might be found in true resinites (Shedrinsky and Baer 1995: 141–2; Grimaldi 1996: 133, 137, 140–1). Similarly, it has been noted that 'many amber artifacts in museums . . . have been treated with paraffin, beeswax, or synthetic polymer solutions in order to consolidate them and to improve their superficial appearance' (Beck *et al.* 1965: 108).

In addition, problems of sample size are particularly relevant for resinites. For example, it has been pointed out that solid state NMR techniques often require large samples (50–100 mg) which may not be suitable for museum material (Boon *et al.* 1993: 9). As many alleged amber objects in museum collections are small, often intact artefacts, such as beads, the potential importance of a secure identification must be weighed against the amount of sample needed for analysis.

Bitumen

Sources of bitumen

Bitumen (asphalt) could have been available to the Egyptians from a number of sources (see Fig. 18.15), and there is evidence that these deposits were known and exploited from very early periods in the Near East (Forbes 1964). Like amber, the origins of bitumen stretch back into geologic time. As sediments of organic matter from land and marine-based plants accumulated, the resulting anaerobic conditions and increased temperatures brought about changes in chemical composition, and initiated the formation of petroleum (Mills and White 1994: 57). Bitumen, a further altered petroleum product occurs in different forms, ranging from fluid deposits to solid blocks. In modern Israel, these blocks, some weighing as much as 100 tons but usually less, occasionally rise to the surface of the Dead

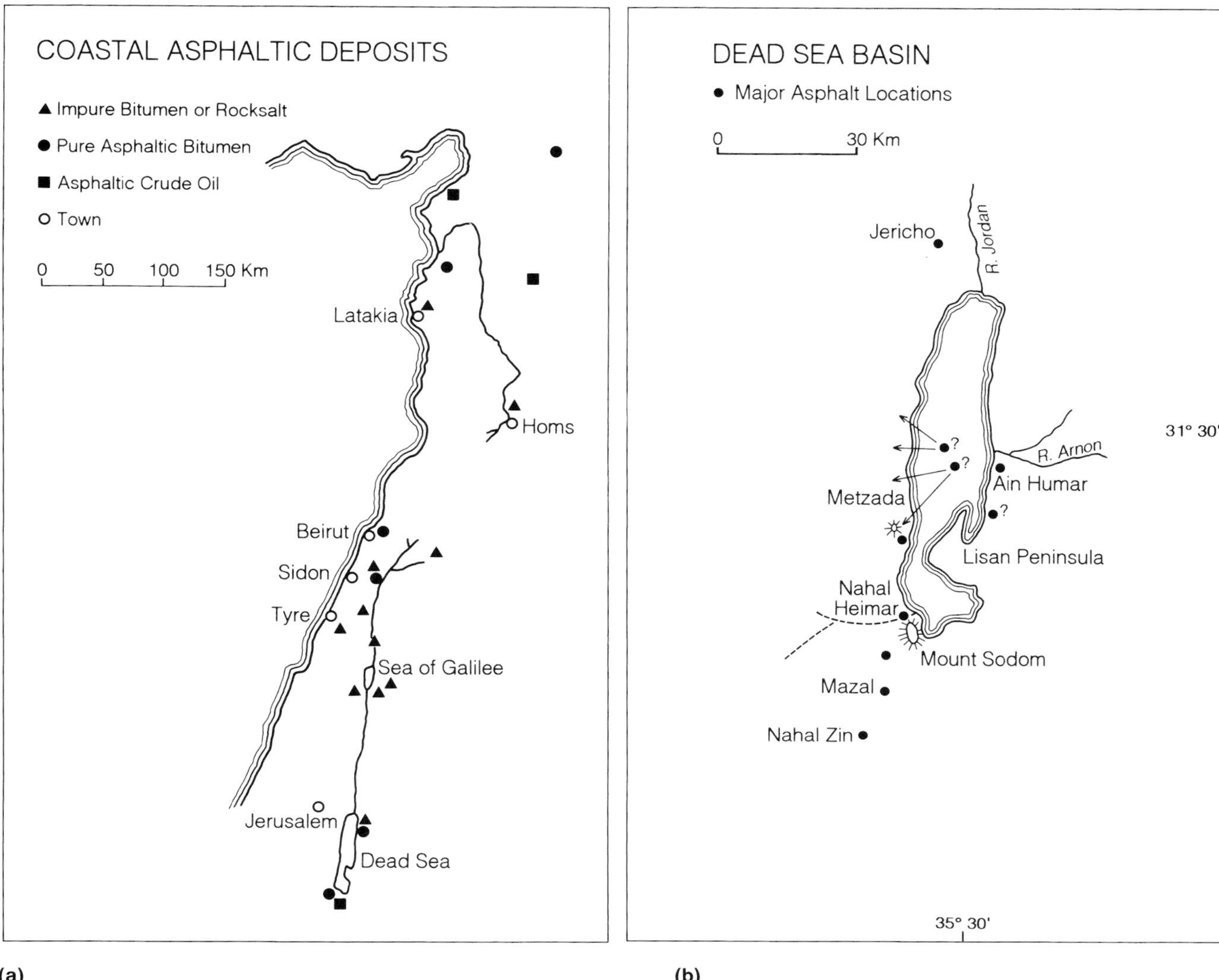

Figure 18.15 Distribution of bituminous deposits in Syria-Palestine.

Sea as a result of tectonic activity (Nissenbaum 1978: 838). Semi-viscous asphalts can be seen dripping from crevices in the sandstone or limestone, particularly in the central areas on both the east and west sides of the lake (Nissenbaum 1978: 838).

Bitumen is also found in areas of Iraq, and in the Luristan and Khuzistan regions of Iran (Marschner and Wright 1978; Connan and Deschesne 1996: 70, 115; Connan 1988). Small deposits of bitumen within Egypt do occur, for example, at the Gebel Zeit area (*Mons Petrolius*) along the Red Sea coast and at Helwan (Aufrère 1991: 640; Forbes 1964: 25–6; Abraham 1960: 214). However, there is as yet no evidence for their use in earlier Pharaonic times. Similarly, although the Near Eastern sources are best known, some asphalt may have been obtained from Ethiopia (Forbes 1964: 26–7). Therefore, it is likely that any bitumen used by the ancient Egyptians was imported, probably from one of the regions mentioned above.

Chemistry of bitumen

Although distinct from fresh resin, bitumen does contain hydrocarbon triterpenes and triterpenoids with skeletons which are similar to resin. Other distinctions have been proposed based on the amounts of associated mineral matter. 'Pure' asphalt normally contains less than 10 per cent mineral matter, while 'rockasphalt' can contain up to 90 per cent mineral matter, often limestone or sandstone (Abraham 1960: 60, 139; Forbes 1964: 5).

For many years, detection of the proportion of sulphur and of the elements nickel, vanadium and molybdenum has been taken as an indication that the substance in question was indeed asphalt (Spielmann 1932: 177–80; Marschner *et al.* 1978: 107; Forbes 1964: table IV; Griffiths 1937: 707; Lucas 1962: 305–6). However, with the increased application of GC/MS to the study of asphalts, more conclusive indicators of asphalt have been found. The chemistry of these compounds is very complex, more so than for resins, and only a very general overview can be presented.

In most recent analyses, the identifications of asphalt are more specifically based on the isolation of solvent-soluble components, including long chain acyclic hydrocarbons, notably pristane (C_{19}) and phytane (C_{20}) (Fig. 18.16), and cyclic compounds, such as hopanes, moretanes, steranes and phytosterols (Fig. 18.16). Identification of aromatics, such as naphthalene, has also been undertaken.

Using these bio-markers, many pieces of bitumen from archaeological sites in Syria-Palestine have been identified. The use of bitumen as an adhesive in ancient Israel has now been established through chemical analysis of a variety of objects ranging in date from the Chalcolithic period through much of the Bronze Age (Nissenbaum *et al.* 1984: 158; Connan *et al.* 1992: 2743–59). Samples of bitumen used as an adhesive were also identified at Ras Shamra in Syria (dated 1600–1200 BC) (Connan *et al.* 1991: 101–3; also earlier work by Venkatesan *et al.* 1982: 517–9).

Bitumen artefacts have been found in both Iraq and Iran (Marschner and Wright 1978; Marschner *et al.* 1978). Recently, an impressive archaeological and scientific study of ancient remains from Susa in Mesopotamia has been published (Connan and Deschesne 1996). There, bitumen was not only used as an adhesive but as building mortar, and as a means of waterproofing. Interestingly, a large number of objects including beads, plaques, sculptured figures, cylinder seals and a wide variety of vessels were manufactured from this material. These range in date from the fourth to first millennium BC. Some were made of asphaltite, an especially pure form of bitumen resembling obsidian (Connan and Deschesne 1996: 43). Others were identified chemically as a type of bitumen mastic (note the potentially confusing use of the word *mastic*, also applied to resin from *Pistacia lentiscus* – see p. 434). While recognizing that *bitumen mastic* often refers to mixtures of bitumen with mineral elements (e.g. sand, crushed pottery debris, etc) and organic components (e.g. straw, reeds, etc.), Connan and Deschesne also applied the term to heat altered bitumen from the Luristan region in northern Mesopotamia (Connan and Deschesne 1996: 110–1). It is this 'annealed bitumen' which was widely used for carving at Susa.

For some of these samples, it was possible to identify the specific source of the asphalt, due to compositional differences. For example, in a large study conducted by Connan (1988: 788), it was possible to conclude, by comparison of samples from ancient Mesopotamia with modern samples from the site of Hit in Iraq, that the samples from Babylon, and only those samples, matched the natural asphalt of Hit. Similarly, from the the analysis of samples from Ras Shamra, the likely source of the asphalt was identified as the area around Kfarie, some twenty kilometres to the northeast of Ras Shamra (Connan *et al.* 1991: 108), and in the study of material from Israel, the samples were shown to match the floating blocks of asphalt found on the Dead Sea (Nissenbaum *et al.* 1984: 160–1).

Of particular importance is a large study of samples from Israel (Connan *et al.* 1992: 2743–59), which included samples from a deposit of black material, originally believed to have been asphalt, found at the Egyptian Predynastic site of Maadi (Gangl 1936: 63). Lucas (1962: 307–8), who subsequently reanalysed the sample, concluded that it 'could not possibly be mineral bitumen (asphalt)' and was most likely a resin. However, in a most recent study, the sample was shown to have been asphalt, and also to have some similarities with the Dead Sea floating blocks. The intended use of the asphalt at Maadi is not clear.

Not only do the results offer some confirmation of the reciprocal contact of Egypt and Palestine in this early period, but they also demonstrate the need to re-evaluate earlier analyses. In addition, the results create a large gap between the occurrence of asphalt at Maadi and the presumed use of asphalt in mummification during the Persian period. Some work has been undertaken to bridge this gap, and these studies will be discussed in greater detail in the context of the Mediterranean resins used in mummification.

The uses of resins, amber and bitumen

A number of usages of resin, amber and bitumen have been postulated and these were summarised above. While further research is necessary to explore the identity and extent to which these products were used as adhesives, sealants, mortar and in jewelry manufacture, an overview of some of the more prevalent applications can be presented here.

Incense

The pleasant aromatic scent of many resins certainly would have made them desirable as incense. Fragrant flowers, leaves, bark and roots, either individually or in mixtures with resin(s), could also have been thrown onto burning charcoal to diffuse their aroma through smoke, thus functioning as a type of incense. However, resins, which would burn more slowly, would have been particularly well suited for this. Certain terms, particularly *snṯr* and *ʿntyw*, are mentioned in numerous texts from Old Kingdom times onward and these are believed to refer to resins or resinous products (see discussions on frankincense, myrrh and pistacia above). Attempts to determine the botanical identity of

phytane

pristane

Ⓢ

Ⓢ = branched sidechains from C_2 to C_{11}

cholestane

H H H H

H H

hopane

H H H H

H H

hopane II

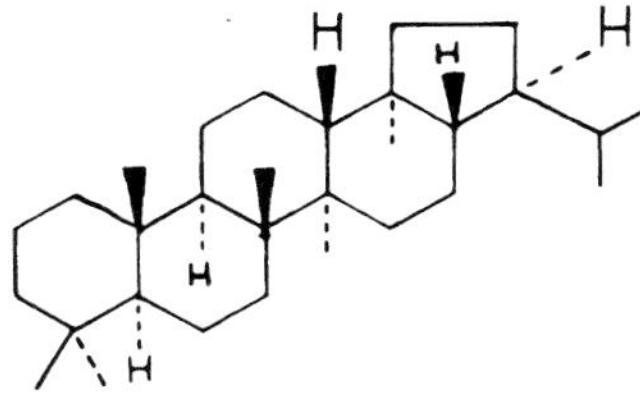

moretane

Figure 18.16 Molecular structures of some components found in bitumen.

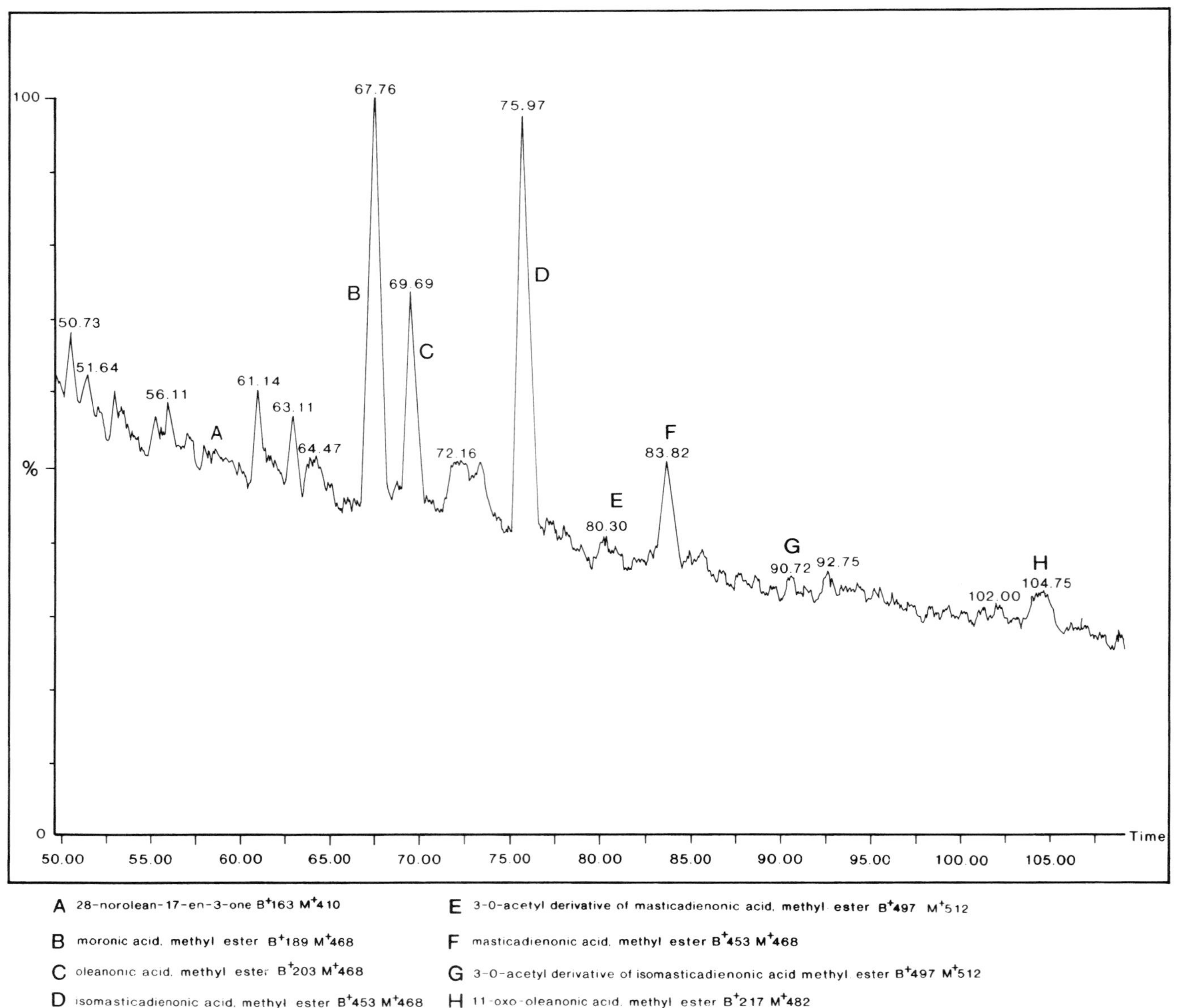

Figure 18.17 Total ion chromatogram of a trans/thermolytically methylated sample taken from the contents of an imported Canaanite amphora from Tell el-Amarna. The principle components, identified by their electron impact mass spectra, indicate the material to be a pistacia resin. The low level of pyrolysis/thermal degradation products, particularly 28-norolean-17-en-3-one, suggests that the resin has not undergone any heating of significance. This conclusion is supported by the strong presence of the masticadienonic acids.

these sources have continued for a number of years and progress has been limited.

The discovery of pistacia resin in amphorae on the Late Bronze Age shipwreck off the south coast of Turkey at Ulu Burun, mentioned previously (Mills and White 1989), recalls Loret's theory that *snṯr*, most often translated as incense, could be linked botanically to pistacia resin. More recently, the same characteristic triterpenoids of pistacia resin have been found (through analysis with GC/MS, see Fig. 18.17) in over two dozen similar imported 'Canaanite' amphorae at the Eighteenth-Dynasty site of Tell el-Amarna in Egypt (Serpico and White; 1998: 1038; in press; Serpico 1996). This confirms that substantial quantities of this resin were reaching Egypt from Mediterranean sources.

Significantly, GC/MS analysis also indicated that pistacia resin coated a number of bowls at Amarna and the contents had clearly been burned as incense (Serpico 1996). This, coupled with the discovery of pistacia resin in some Canaanite amphorae labelled for *snṯr*, the most common ancient Egyptian word for incense, leads to the conclusion that, during the New Kingdom the product *snṯr* consisted predominantly of pistacia resin and was widely used by the Egyptians as incense (Serpico 1996). The identification by IR and chromatography of lumps of resin found at the Karnak temple as *Pistacia lentiscus* suggests that these could be the remnants of loose pieces of incense (Le Fur 1994: 60). Similar amorphous lumps were also found in temple settings at Amarna (Serpico 1996).

A number of possible botanical sources of pistacia resin were mentioned above, but more precise species identifications (e.g. *P. lentiscus*) cannot be established with existing techniques, making it difficult to determine the geographical location of the source(s). However, the consistent occurrence of pistacia resin in amphorae which are believed to have been manufactured in western Asia would suggest that Mediterranean sources are most likely. Further research into the subject of resin trade and the transport of commodities in these amphorae is currently in progress.

As yet, there is little evidence to help establish a botanical identification for the product known as *ʿntyw*. Burseraceous resins (frankincense and myrrh) have rarely been identified thus far in ancient samples (Evershed *et al.* 1997: 667) although myrrh was reportedly found in a jar dated to the Middle Kingdom (see p. 463).

Varnish

Two types of varnish were applied to funerary equipment in the New Kingdom. One was a translucent yellow coating and the other was a dark, more opaque varnish. Lucas discussed the subject at some length, observing that the application of the varnishes ranged in date from the late Eighteenth to the Twenty-sixth Dynasty (Lucas 1962: 357). He believed the yellow varnish to be a resin, originally clear, but darkened over time. After testing a number of samples, he concluded that the black varnish was neither a pitch nor bitumen, but also some type of dark black resin (Lucas 1962: 359). Both coatings were applied to a range of objects, including coffins, *shabtis* and *shabti* boxes, stelae, canopic chests, human and animal figures, statue bases, painted vases and, in the case of the yellow varnish, even coating tomb walls. Many objects in the tomb of Tutankhamun (KV62) were so coated.

More recent visual re-examination of these varnishes has slightly revised Lucas's date range and has shown that both black and yellow types were in use by the time of Hatshepsut/Thutmose III (Serpico and White: in press). Moreover, from our GC/MS study of a number of both yellow and black varnishes on New Kingdom funerary equipment, it is clear that the main component in the yellow varnish was again pistacia resin. The same characteristic triterpenoids found in the contents of the Canaanite jars mentioned above were present in these samples (Figs. 18.18 and 18.19). Some admixtures with lipids and coniferous resin did occur, but only to a very limited degree (Serpico and White in press; Serpico 1996. For an earlier identification of pistacia resin as such a coating on a Twenty-first-Dynasty coffin, see Masschelein-Kleiner *et al.* 1968: 115). Textual evidence establishes that *snṯr* was used as varnish at that time, confirming that these coatings were of religious significance. (Serpico and White in press b). Originally, the resin would have been a pale yellow, almost clear colour. Although still translucent, the varnish had darkened noticeably over time. In addition, some of the samples showed evidence of heating, which was determined by the abundant presence of compounds such as 28-norolean-17-en-3-one (Fig. 18.20). As this heating may well have darkened the resin, it seems likely that both clear and yellowed varnishes were applied to these objects.

In comparison, the black coatings show more variation. GC/MS analysis has indicated that a more strongly heated pistacia pitch was used in some, while mixtures of pistacia pitch, coniferous (Pinaceae) pitch and lipid matter com-

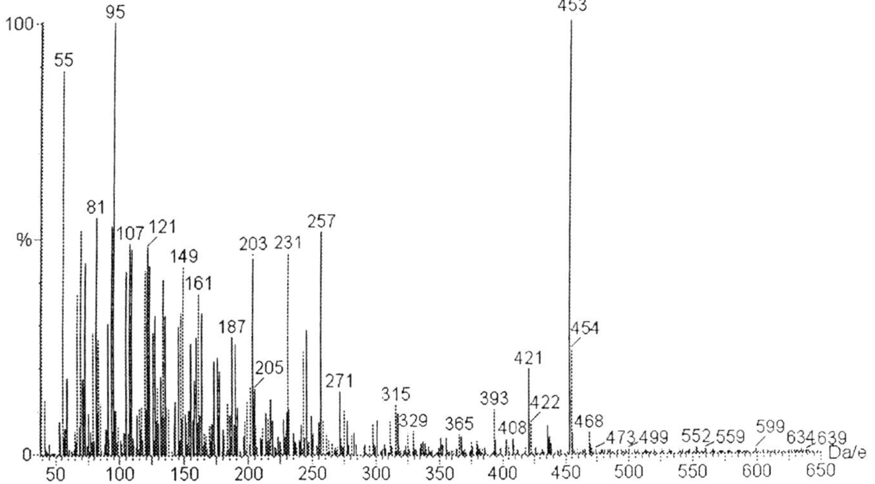

Figure 18.18 Mass spectrum (electron impact mode 70 eV) of one of the components found in a trans/thermolytically methylated sample of yellow varnish on a Nineteenth-Dynasty polychrome shabti *box* (BM EA25711). *The component, identified as methyl isomasticadienonate, occurs in pistacia resin.*

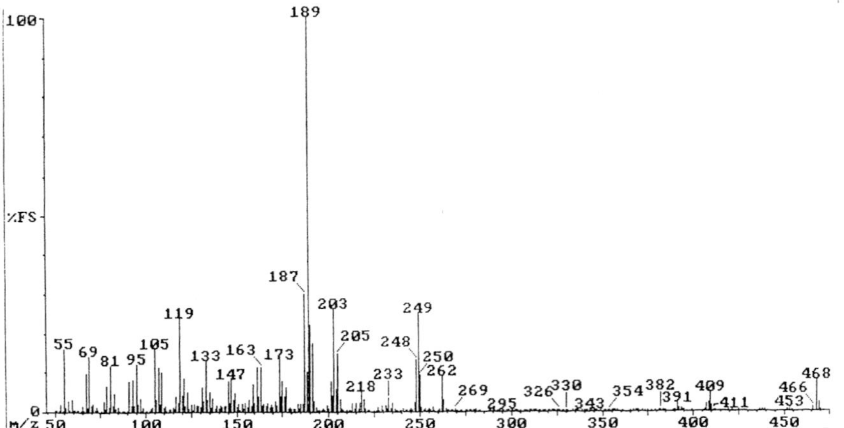

Figure 18.19 Mass spectrum (electron impact mode 70 eV) of one of the components found in a trans/thermolytically methylated sample of yellow varnish taken from a New Kingdom polychrome painted 'dummy' pottery jar (Ashmolean 1955.462). This component is identified as methyl moronate, the methyl ester of moronic acid, which is found in pistacia resin.

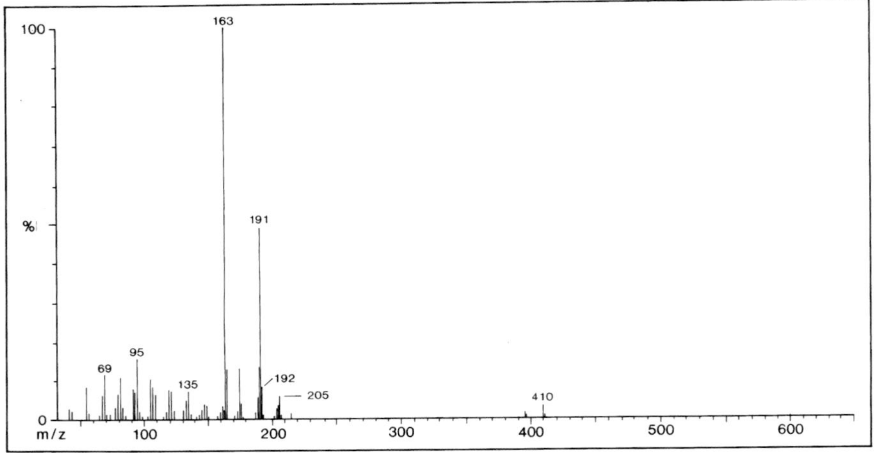

Figure 18.20 Mass spectrum (electron impact mode 70 eV) of one of the components found in a trans/thermolytically methylated sample of yellow varnish from an Eighteenth Dynasty coffin (BM EA 29580). The component, identified as 28-norolean-17-en-3-one and is characteristic of a heated pistacia resin.

prised others (Serpico and White: in press). These results correlate with New Kingdom and later texts mentioning a black substance *ʿ3t nṯrt*, which contained a number of components and was known to have been applied in Ptolemaic times, for example, to religious statues (Serpico and White in press; Chassinat 1990: 214; Aufrère 1991: 329–32, 334, 347).

Notably, two of the Eighteenth-Dynasty samples analysed by GC/MS, one from a coffin (BM EA6661) and one from a canopic chest (BM EA 35808), contained hopanes which established that the black varnish was derived from bitumen (Fig. 18.21; Serpico and White in press. This provides evidence for an association between bitumen and funerary practices as early as the first half of the Eighteenth Dynasty.

The conclusion has therefore been reached that, while these coatings may have been intended to enhance the appearance of the funerary objects, their religious importance was the primary reason for their usage.

Manufacture of scented ointments

It should be noted that the term *perfume* strictly speaking refers to the volatile components distilled from various scented parts of plants (flowers, leaves, bark, etc.). As evidence to contradict Lucas's observation (1962: 85–6) that distillation was practiced only from Greco-Roman times is

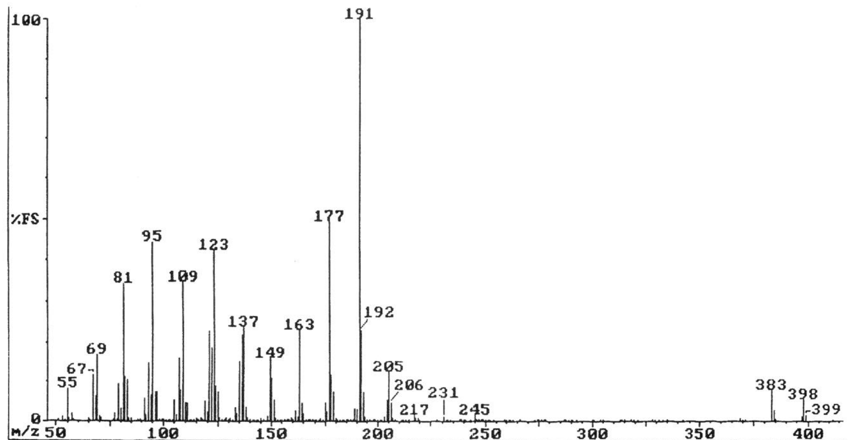

*Figure 18.21 Mass spectrum (electron impact mode 70 eV) of one of the components found in a trans/thermolytically methylated sample of black varnish on an Eighteenth-Dynasty 'black style' private anthropoid coffin (*BM EA6661*). This component, nor-hopane, occurs in bitumen.*

still speculative (see p. 450), it would seem that no true perfumes could have been produced until then. Scented products would have been manufactured using an oil and fat base are therefore best described as cosmetics, unguents or ointments. These composites could have been made in Egypt from imported resins, or imported as a finished product. Although it has been assumed that cosmetic products were widely manufactured in Egypt, perfume industries were also active in Mesopotamia, Crete and mainland Greece and certainly imported pottery vessels did reach Egypt from the Aegean.

While the inclusion of bitumen in ointments manufactured for everyday use might seem impractical, it may well have been a component of religious or funerary preparations, as the analyses of varnishes has shown. Although lexicographical difficulties surrounding the ancient Egyptian words for resins and bitumen persist, the product *mnnn*, translated by some as bitumen, was an ingredient in the Seven Sacred Oils during Ptolemaic times (Chassinat 1955: 66; 1922: 463–4; 1990: 209–10; Loret 1894: 157–62; Aufrère 1991: 640; Dümichen 1879: 97–128). These ointments were used from Old Kingdom times onward not only in mummification but in daily temple ritual and in the Opening of the Mouth ceremony.

Production of scented unguents could have been carried out in a number of ways. Two traditional means, *enfleurage* and *maceration* were noted by classical writers. The technique of cold steeping, known as *enfleurage*, would have been suitable for cosmetics scented with aromatic flowers. Using this method, a layer of animal fat was smeared on a wooden board and then petals were strewn across it. Another board was placed on top and the combination left to steep. The next day, the petals were removed and replaced with fresh ones. This process could be repeated for several weeks until the scent had fully transferred (Dayagi-Mendels 1989: 97; Lucas 1962: 86).

In the hot steeping method, known as *maceration*, the aromatic components were steeped in oil or fat, which was heated above a vessel of boiling water, effectively similar to a modern double boiler. Once heated, the mixture could be left to stand for several days and stirred occasionally (Dayagi-Mendels 1989: 100; Lucas 1962: 86). This type of procedure seems to be recorded in the texts from the laboratories at the Ptolemaic temples of Dendara and Edfu (Dümichen 1879). However, whether the variety of ingredients was as extensive and the procedures as complicated in pharaonic times is open to debate. Some evidence for the use of heating in the manufacture of fragrant unguents is furnished by a relief in Theban Tomb 175, dated to the Eighteenth Dynasty (Wreszinski 1915: pl. 356; Manniche 1989: 56–7). Here, several stages of processing appear to be represented, including straining of raw materials, melting of the lipid matrix, grinding of the aromatics and boiling the mixture in a large vat prior to decanting (Manniche 1989: 57).

As an adjunct to boiling or as another means of producing scented ointments, techniques of torsion pressing might also have been used (Lucas 1962: 86; see Chapter 17, this volume). The earliest representation of a press may date back to the First Dynasty (James 1995: 200), but the scene appears more frequently in the Fourth Dynasty. Depictions continue throughout the Old Kingdom, becoming decreasingly common after that time (for a detailed discussion on the evolution of the press, see Chapter 23, this volume). Most representations pertain to wine-making, but some evidence suggests that the method was the same for both wine and oil. In fact, in tomb depictions showing only the pressing itself with no accompanying text or related scenes, it may be impossible to determine whether oil or wine pressing is represented (Lepsius 1849–59: II, Bl. 13). Texts dating as far back as the Old Kingdom mention the god Shesmu, who was sacred to both the oil and wine press supporting this parallelism, and in the Fifth-Dynasty tomb of Iymery at Giza (G6020), both oil and wine pressing scenes are illustrated and are very similar in appearance (Lepsius 1849–59: II, Bl. 49, 53). The oil pressing scene

(Lepsius 1849–59: II, Bl. 49) is accompanied by a depiction of a row of jars, each inscribed with the name of one of the so-called 'Seven Sacred Oils' (Fig. 18.22). Interestingly, the term 'Seven Sacred Oils' is a modern one; in the ancient scenes, they are known only as *mrḥt*, which is both a general word for oil and a term applied to scented mixtures. Using this process of cosmetic manufacture, the scented components could be placed in a cloth bag, soaked in heated oil as a type of infusion and then wrung out as in the reliefs. There is some evidence that this simple bag press method continued to be used in perfume manufacture in the Late Period (Fischer 1988: 3–2; Lucas 1962: 86).

Another relief which may show oil pressing prior to the Late Period is in the Eleventh-Dynasty tomb of Bakt III at Beni Hasan (BH15), which shows a more advanced press with a wooden framework (Newberry 1894a: pl. VI; Fig. 18.23). An inscription above the press mentions that this is a workshop of *nwd*. Given the context in which the word occurs in other texts, it would seem that *nwd* could refer to a scented cosmetic mixture. Two accompanying vignettes illustrate stages prior to pressing. These represent the grinding or mashing of the raw material and the placement of the mash into the bag.

More recently, Tallet has argued that this scene represents not a cosmetic process, but the preparation of a cooked wine, known as *šdḥ* (Tallet 1995: 487–9). In his interpretation, *nwd* refers to the press itself, a term which became related to scented cosmetics (Tallet 1995: 488). Without doubt, the scenes do appear ambiguous and Tallet's arguments are persuasive.

Certainly, *nwd* does come to be associated with the manufacture of cosmetics (see Chapter 17, this volume). *Nwd* can refer both to the unguent and to the individual involved in the processing (Erman and Grapow 1928: 226). In the New Kingdom, some spellings of *nwdw*, referring to unguents, show a type of press. Two examples of this writing occur in the account of Hatshepsut's expedition to Punt (Sethe 1906: 347/20, 352/13). Another title, *ps sgnn* has often been translated as 'the oil boiler' and some writings clearly suggest that heating (or boiling) was involved (Peet 1930: 91, pl. XI, Rt. 5,8, 106, pl. XVII, Rt. 3, 7–9). Thus, it would appear that both boiling and pressing were used in this industry, either separately or sequentially. At this time, it remains difficult to determine which method(s) for the manufacture of scented ointments were in use at a given time or in a given area.

One more aspect of cosmetic processing should be mentioned. The odour of oils with a strong scent of their own, for example olive, could have been neutralised prior to steeping by adding certain substances such as cyperus or coriander. These would be soaked in water or wine, added to the oil, and then strained off prior to adding the final scent. This preparatory technique was known in classical times as *stypsis* (Shelmerdine 1984: 82–3; Negbi 1992: 66–8; on this and other uses of *Cyperus* see chapters 17 and 24, this volume). There is some evidence that a similar practice was in use in Greece during the Late Bronze Age, roughly contemporary with New Kingdom (Shelmerdine 1985: 38–9). Mycenaean texts also seem to suggest that perfumes in the Aegean were manufactured from a single fragrance rather than complex mixtures (Shelmerdine 1985: 15). This would appear to be in contrast to Egyptian ointments at least from Ptolemaic times, as the recipes given for the 'Seven Sacred Oils' and for the famous *kyphi* of classical times contain a wide array of components (Lucas 1962: 89; Manniche 1989: 57–8; Dümichen 1879). Again, these recipes are of post-pharaonic date and the botanical identifications of the ingredients are sometimes in doubt.

Figure 18.22 Scene of pressing unguents in the Fifth-Dynasty tomb of Iymery at Giza (G6020). Note the jars labelled for the 'Seven Sacred Oils' to the right and the inscription mentioning the pressing of mrḥt.

Figure 18.23 Scene of pressing from the Eleventh-Dynasty tomb of Bakt III at Beni Hasan (BH15).

Scientific analysis of jar contents does seem to confirm that mixtures of oils or fats and resins were utilised. However, even where resins can be shown to have been mixed with lipids in a pottery or stone jar, it may be difficult to determine the intended use of the preparation. Scented oils in costly stone jars placed in a tomb may have been intended for funerary purposes, including as incense, and may never have been applied as cosmetics used in daily life. Some jars, particularly amphorae, may have been used for the bulk transport of resins, as evidence from the Ulu Burun shipwreck in Turkey and our own research into Canaanite amphorae at Amarna has shown (Bass 1987; Serpico and White, 1998: 1038; in press). Thus, it is clear that interpretation of samples from funerary pottery and stone storage jars, particularly unprovenanced examples must be undertaken with caution.

Among the earliest evidence for the possible use of resins in ancient Egypt is the contents of an imported Palestinian 'Abydos ware' jug in the First-Dynasty tomb of Djer at Abydos (Ashmolean E3160). GC/MS analysis of the jar indicated that it contained a mixture of a lipid and resin (Serpico and White 1996: 136–8). Dehydroabietic and 7–oxodehydroabietic acids were found, confirming that the source of the resin was in the family Pinaceae (pine, cedar or fir), but more specific genus identification was not possible. Also present were components indicative of heating, notably retene. However, as the tomb was burned in antiquity, it may well be the case that the contents were originally an unheated resin and not a pitch. It was also clear that the jar had been re-used and that the resin mix was an earlier deposit than that in the base, which did not contain resin. Thus, it is possible that the jar did not reach Egypt until the second deposit had been placed inside.

Dehydroabietic and 7–oxodehydroabietic acids were also found through GC/MS analysis of a small Middle Kingdom calcite cylinder jar at Kahun (Petrie Museum UC7318) (Serpico and White 1998: 1041). As in the Djer jar, retene was present, but the jar shows no sign of external heating and it would seem therefore that the contents consisted, at least in part, of a heated pitch. Fortunately, diagnostic sesquiterpenes characteristic of cedar were also isolated confirming that the Egyptians did import and use cedar products (see Figs. 18.24 and 18.25).

Two Middle Kingdom jars, probably from de Morgan's excavations at Dahshur were analysed by HPLC and diode array detection (Vieillescazes and Coen 1993). In one, masticadienonic and isomasticadienonic acids were found indicating that pistacia resin was present. The authors suggested *P. lentiscus* as the source, but as yet there are insufficient grounds for distinguishing chemically between pistacia species (see pp. 447–8). The contents of the second jar were identified as myrrh (Vieillescazes and Coen 1993: 257–9).

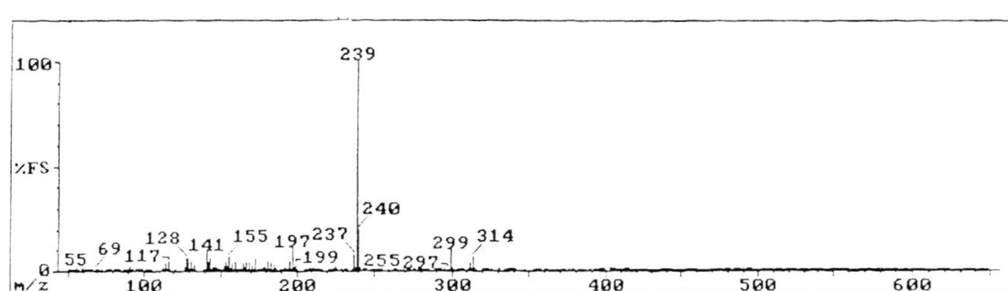

Figure 18.24 Mass spectrum (electron impact mode 70 eV) of one of the components found in a trans/thermolytically methylated sample taken from the contents of a small Middle Kingdom calcite jar from Kahun (Petrie Museum UC7318). This component, methyl dehydroabietate the methyl ester of dehydroabietic acid, is found in coniferous resins of the family Pinaceae.

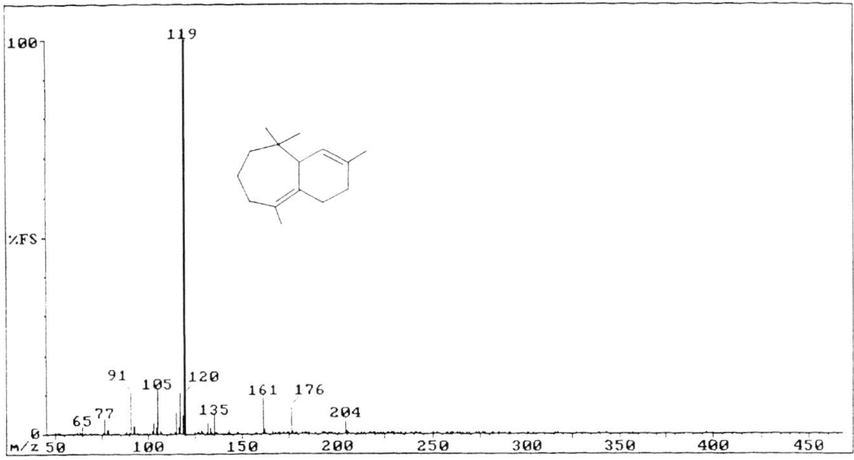

Figure 18.25 Mass spectrum (electron impact mode 70 eV) of another of the components found in the sample from the Middle Kingdom Kahun jar (Petrie Museum UC7318). This compound, identified as tetramethyl-hexahydro-benzocyloheptane, occurs in cedar resin.

The contents of a small unprovenanced amphora of Nile silt clay with two horizontal handles, typical of the late Eighteenth and Nineteenth Dynasties (BM EA58278) have also been examined by GC/MS (Serpico and White 1998: 1043). The residue consisted primarily of a vegetable oil base, but traces of the sesquiterpenoids diagnostic to cedar were again identified. Notably, the higher diterpenoids found in resins were absent. Thus, the cedar component appears to derive not from resin, but possibly from steeping cedar wood, bark, and/or needles into the lipid base to impart the scent (see methods of perfume manufacture p. 461–2). No botanical remains were visible in the residue, perhaps indicating that the cedar products had been removed prior to decanting the mixture. As it was not possible to empty the jar to examine the contents, some botanical debris may be present within the residue below the visible surface. The contents of this jar are particularly important given the proposed link between *ꜥš*, possibly cedar resin, and a related product, *sfṯ*, believed to be either a coniferous pitch or a conifer-scented oil derived from *ꜥš*. While these results cannot establish conclusively that *sfṯ* was a cedar-scented oil, they do confirm that such mixtures were known to the ancient Egyptians.

A similar mixture was reported from a Twenty-sixth-Dynasty jar in the tomb of Padihorresnet at Thebes (TT196; Seher *et al.* 1980: 398–9). The lipid component was said to be consistent with a beef tallow (see Chapter 17, this volume) and a range of lower terpenoids was also present. These suggested the presence of a coniferous essential oil, perhaps cedar as well as other scented components.

Another possible use of resin is as a flavouring for wine or as a coating for wine jars. Lucas found no evidence for the use of resin as a wine additive and concluded furthermore, that jar linings were not applied to the interior of vessels until the Greco–Roman period (Lucas 1962: 20). Evidence for resinated wine from a First-Dynasty tomb at Abydos has been published recently, based on analysis by FT-IR (McGovern *et al.* 1997: 10–11). The authors drew parallels between the spectra of the First Dynasty jar and a Neolithic vessel from Hajji Firuz Tepe in Iran, also analysed by HPLC. Both jars were said to contain a mixture of wine and pistacia resin, most likely from *Pistacia atlantica* (McGovern *et al.* 1996: 480; McGovern *et al.* 1997: 10–1, 20). While the results are potentially of interest, the use of FT-IR, UV-spectral analysis and HPLC as means of distinguishing calcium tartrate, believed to be indicative of wine, have been shown to be problematic at times (Chapter 23, this volume). It is also worth mentioning that, just as for oils and fats, the application of IR and FT-IR for the identification of resins to a specific genus, such as *Pistacia* spp., is rarely reliable and in aged mixtures would be still more difficult (for a discussion of the limitations of IR and FT-IR, see Chapter 17, this volume). Certainly, the abundant use of pistacia resin as incense and varnish during the New Kingdom makes it likely that it was popular in earlier periods, but as yet, there is no secure scientific means of distinguishing *Pistacia atlantica* from other resinous pistacia species.

Pending further investigation into the possible use of resin in wine, it nonetheless remains clear that resins were used in scented unguents. However, the extent of the use of resin in these lipid-based mixtures is difficult to quantify and many more samples would need to be tested. The contents of a number of jars, which were examined but not discussed here (White, unpublished results), had only a lipid component remaining today (see Chapter 17, this volume). This could be due either to the use of pure lipid matter without added fragrance, or the result of the chance preservation of volatile ingredients. This, in turn, raises the possibility that resins were not as widely used for this purpose as previously believed.

Amulets

As yet, little research has been undertaken into the identification of natural products used for the manufacture of jewellery or amulets. One unprovenanced scarab, dated stylistically to the Third Intermediate Period and now in the British Museum (unnumbered) has been analysed by GC/MS. The results suggest that the object is amber. Dehydroabietic and 7–oxodehydroabietic acids were detected, along with labdane components and abietadienes and abietatrienes, consistent with an amber with *Agathis*-like affinities. The fragment appeared to contain heavily cross-linked polymer and only small amounts of ether-soluble terpenoid material were extracted, apart from the large amounts of phthalate plasticiser. From a complex of peaks, methyl Δ8-isopimarate was identified and its spectrum is reproduced in Fig. 18.26. A small amount of methyl 5–β-dehydroabietate was also found, whilst only traces of methyl pimarate and Δ8–pimarate were detectable. Small amounts of dimethyl agathate and, possibly, dimethyl Δ13–isoagathate (from its base peak of $m/z = 189$ and weak molecular ion at $m/z = 362$).

Mummification

Because of their appearance, the blackened deposits found on mummies were often initially described as bitumen (Budge 1893: 173–5). As early as the beginning of the twentieth century, attempts were made to identify these residues more precisely. Notably, Lucas's monograph, *Preservative Materials used by the Ancient Egyptians in Embalming*, published in 1911, pioneered work in this area and remains a standard scientific study on the products used in mummification. For its time, this work contained a fairly comprehensive evaluation centred primarily on unwrapped royal mummies. Based on his research, Lucas concluded that, although often described as bitumen, there was no evi-

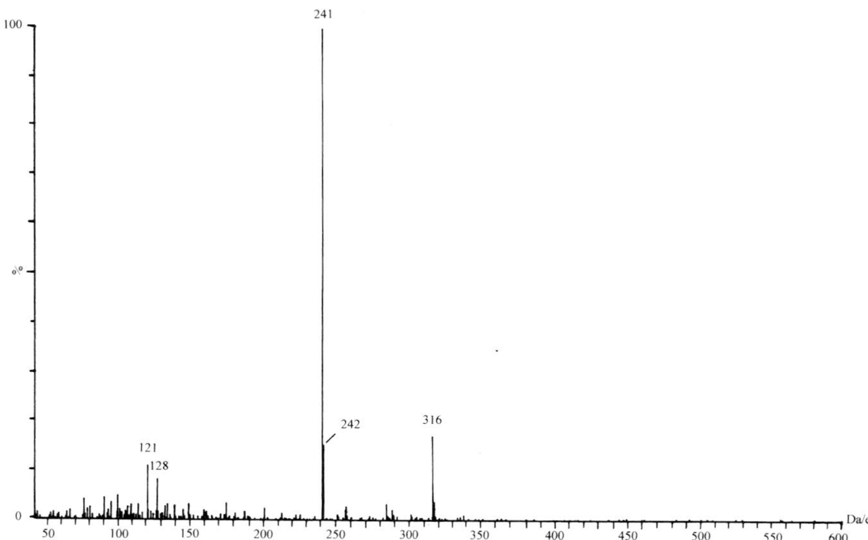

Figure 18.26 Mass spectrum (electron impact mode 70 eV) of one of the components found in a trans/thermolytically methylated sample taken from an unprovenanced Late Period scarab in the British Museum (unregistered). This component is indicative of amber.

dence that this product had been used in mummification until Ptolemaic times. He used tests with a variety of solvents, and for the fluorescence of these solutions, as evidence that a these samples were not bituminous (Lucas 1911: 44–5). He did discuss the possibility that ageing had affected the solubility, but concluded that the samples were unlikely to have changed so dramatically. Thus, he felt that the samples were probably types of resin. This observation was subsequently modified by Harris (Lucas 1962: 306–7), who cited the work by Zaki and Iskander, as evidence that the practice of using bitumen in mummification began as early as the Persian period (Zaki and Iskander 1943: 239–42).

With regard to the blackened skin of mummies, particularly New Kingdom examples, this may have been the result of the treatment of the body with resin or pitch, or possibly some type of scented oil. Lucas offered several other explanations for the blackened skin colour, including fungal growth from damp conditions (Lucas 1962: 297). His suggestion that the colour is due to the 'slow spontaneous combustion' of the body over time is unlikely (Lucas 1962: 297). Of the mummy of Seti I, Smith noted that 'all the exposed areas of the skin, including the face, are quite black, but . . . when the head was first exposed in 1886 the skin was distinctly brown and not black' (Smith 1912: 57). More recently, it was noted that a mummy of Ptolemaic date unwrapped at Pennsylvania, known as PUM II, was initially a light brown colour, but 'within a day of exposure to air it had darkened appreciably. Today the remains are almost black' (Fleming *et al.* 1980: 88). In addition, Lucas noted that the reddish brown colour of desiccated mummy tissue can often resemble resin which could also cause confusion (Lucas 1911: 50–1). As a result of this, it may be difficult to rely on early descriptions of the distribution of resinous material on the body for a reconstruction of the use of resins in mummification. If the face of a mummy is described as 'blackened with resin,' one can question whether a deposit of resin was visible on the face, or whether the blackened skin was merely assumed to have been due to an application of resin.

With this *caveat* in mind, published reports suggest that both reddish-coloured and blackened glossy deposits were clearly employed in a number of different stages of the mummification process. Deposits described as resins have been observed on mummies dating back at least to the Old Kingdom, when they were found with linen as packing for the body cavity or wrapping the body (Smith and Dawson 1924: 74–5; Andrews 1984: 9). Significantly, in a recent publication, Pinaceae pitch was identified on the clavicle of a Sixth-Dynasty mummy using GC/MS (Koller *et al.* 1997: 343–4). Resins apparently continued to be used in the packing of the torso during the Middle Kingdom (Smith 1916: 119), although linen alone has also been noted (Smith and Dawson 1924: 80–1). In some instances, the face, including the eyes, of mummies of this date had been smeared with a resinous substance (Smith and Dawson 1924: 80–1). Other uses of resin dating to this time include the plugging of the embalming wound with linen-soaked resin and the use of resin to coat the bandages wrapping the mummy (Smith 1916: 119; Strouhal 1986: 144). Occasionally, resin was poured over the wrapped mummy or over the coffin (Lucas 1962: 312–3; Mace and Winlock 1916: 17, 18).

Therefore, most of the mummification practices involving resin, with the possible exceptions of resin placed in the cranial cavity or inserted as subcutaneous packing, began at least as early as the Middle Kingdom. The earliest examples of resin packing in the cranium appear to date from the beginning of the Eighteenth-Dynasty, detected primarily through X-ray analysis (Smith and Dawson 1924: 89; Harrison and Abdalla 1972; Strouhal and Vyhnánek 1974: 126; Notman 1986: 256, but see also Strouhal 1986: 141 for more cautious observations). More recently, CT scans have also suggested that there were resinous deposits in crania (Strouhal *et al.* 1986). In the New Kingdom, resinous substances were also smeared on the face and facial apertures, inserted as packing material both internally and subcutaneously, poured over the body and incision wound prior to wrapping, layered with the bandages, and coating the completed mummy (Smith 1912; Smith and Dawson 1924).

Most recently published scientific analyses of residues associated with mummies have focussed on those dating to the Greco-Roman period. While it could be argued that this information is not necessarily relevant for a study of earlier material, a review of this research does provide insight into the products in use. From these, a trend appears to be emerging for the use of coniferous products of the family Pinaceae (pine, cedar or fir), beeswax, and bitumen in both treatment of the body and of the wrappings. Not all of these products are present in every mummy and samples taken from the different areas of a single body or from its wrappings may also vary in composition or in the ratio of the components. In some cases, it has been possible to distinguish different geographical sources for the bitumen. Notably, bitumen from the Dead Sea was used in some, and in others, the source seems to have been Hit-Abu Jir in Iraq (see below).

In one study using GC/MS, bitumen was identified in three mummies, two dated to the early second century AD and one dated to about 200 BC (Rullkötter and Nissenbaum 1988: 619–20). This was found to resemble the solid floating blocks found in the Dead Sea. No reference was made to the presence of beeswax or any coniferous products. Also, no location of the samples on the body was given, making it more difficult to interpret the results. A fourth sample, taken from a coffin dated to *c.* 900 BC, was identified as bitumen, but from a different, unknown source.

Analysis of a sample taken from the foot of a mummy of a small child, dated between AD 100 and 200 AD, has also been published (Proefke *et al.* 1992: 105A–10A). The sample was analysed by GC/MS and FABMS (fast atom bombardment tandem MS). The detection of hopanes confirmed the presence of asphalt in the sample. In addition, dehydroabietic, 7–oxodehydroabietic and 15–hydroxy–7–oxodehydroabietic acids were detected indicating that a Pinaceae resin had been applied.

Connan and Dessort have conducted studies on a number of human remains. Using GC/MS, four samples taken from the Lyon Mummy, dated from 150 BC to AD 90, were examined (Connan and Dessort 1989: 1667–72; Goyon and Josset 1988: 103–7). Two samples were from linen cloth between the knees, one from the visceral packing, and one from the cranial cavity. All contained bitumen, but the results suggested that two different sources of Dead Sea asphalt had been used, one for the viscera, and a second for the knees and cranial cavity (Connan and Dessort 1989: 1669, 1671). Samples taken from the linen in the knee area and from the visceral packing had evidence of beeswax (Connan and Dessort 1989: 1668). Dehydroabietic acid and retene were also present on the cloth between the knees (Connan and Dessort 1989: 1670, fig. 4a), which suggests a resin, possibly a pitch, in the Pinaceae family. Overall, the amounts of bitumen in the samples were relatively small compared to the resin and beeswax.

Also examined by GC/MS were samples taken from the foot of a mummy dated *c.* 300 BC and the contents of two canopic jars dated to 600 BC (Connan 1991: 34). Bitumen was found in all three samples. Those from the canopic jars were shown to match bitumen from the floating blocks of the Dead Sea, while that from the mummy was similar to deposits from Hit-Abu Jir in Iraq (Connan 1991: 35). In addition, the lower terpenoid, longifolene, was also identified, indicating the presence of a coniferous product (Connan 1991: 35). This appeared to be the major component in the deposits, but beeswax was also found.

Samples from four other mummies dating to the Greco–Roman period were examined by Connan and Dessort (1991: 1448) and the results indicated that one or more of these products (bitumen, beeswax, coniferous matter) were still present, although proportions did continue to vary.

In addition, one sample, said to come from a mummy of Nineteenth-Dynasty date in the Cairo Museum, was also analysed. Unfortunately, no further details (object registration number, provenance, etc.) were provided. Nonetheless, the results were interesting. The detection of characteristic steranes and hopanes indicated that the sample contained bitumen, most closely matching samples from the floating blocks in the Dead Sea (Connan and Dessort 1991: 1449, Fig. 1; 1450, pl. II; 1451, tab. II). The sample also had traces of the lower terpenoid, longifolene, which was interpreted as characteristic of certain species of pine (Connan and Dessort 1991: 1447–9, pl. I, fig. 1), although other genera do contain it (see p. 446–7). It would be unwise to attempt to reconstruct a general overview of the the products used in mummification in the New Kingdom from this one sample. However, taken in conjunction with the evidence for the use of bitumen as a varnish on funerary objects from the Eighteenth Dynasty (p. 460), the results from this mummy would appear to confirm an earlier use of bitumen than had been proposed by Lucas.

In a report by Kaup *et al.* (1994: 493), both mono- and sesquiterpenoids were found in a sample taken from a Ptolemaic mummy. These, however, were much smaller in quantity than the main component of the sample. This was shown to be pistacia resin, through comparison to modern specimens of *Pistacia lentiscus* (Kaup *et al.* 1994:

493–5. Note that species identification is in fact highly unlikely). The monoterpenoids were consistent with a *Pinus* spp. product and aromatic alcohols were detected, probably 'originating from smouldering processes'. Sesquiterpenoids found in the sample showed some affinity to those occurring in cedar. It was noted, however, that none of the more stable diterpenoids or retene compounds were identified, nor was there any mention of a lipid component. Like the examples above, where longifolene was present, these results raise an important question. How did these lower terpenoids come to be present in these samples, as they do not seem to be part of a resin or a scented unguent? They could derive from botanical remains within the body (sawdust, leaves, etc.), but there was no mention of this in the reports. Another possibility is that they are somehow the result of a crude distillation process involving the heating of wood chips (Kaup *et al.* 1994: 498). Such a scenario is intriguing, given Lucas's proposed date for the introduction of distillation at around the fourth century BC (Lucas 1962: 85–6).

In addition to these examples, research is currently being undertaken on an unwrapped body of Third Intermediate Period date in the British Museum (BM EA74303) (Serpico and White 1998: 1044). Based on examination of the skull (the pelvic area was damaged), the body is perhaps more likely to be that of a female (Ms Joyce Filer, Special Assistant in Mummified Remains for the Egyptian Dept. of the British Museum, pers. comm.). A sample from the chest cavity was shown by GC/MS to contain dehydroabietic and 7-oxodehydroabietic acids (see Fig. 18.27), indicative of pine, cedar or fir product. Retene was also identified, suggesting that this was in fact a pitch. Beeswax was also present. A second sample taken from the back of the skull again contained substantial amounts of this pitch and possible traces of beeswax. Also included were small amounts of moronic and oleanonic acids, establishing the presence of pistacia resin. These results indicate that the blackened deposits found on the mummy were derived from at least two different resin sources. They also emphasise the need for detailed recording of the specific provenance of the samples.

Most of the analyses discussed above used GC or GC/MS, which are amongst the most reliable means of identifying ancient resins. A few other analyses have been undertaken using a variety of methods. Lower terpenoids were reported in the PUM II in Philadelphia by analysis using X-ray diffraction and thin layer chromatography (TLC) (Coughlin 1977: 7). Again, no evidence of higher terpenoids indicative of a resin was noted. In this study, essential oils from *Juniperus* spp. and *Cinnamomum camphora* (Nees and Eberm.) were said to have been present, in addition to myrrh. However, apart from camphor, the specific lower terpenoids found which led to these identifications were not given. As noted in the botanical discussion in Chapter 17, this volume, *Cinnamomum camphora* is indigenous to the Far East, and a much more likely source might be *Ocotea usamarensis* Engl. Other botanical sources of camphor, such as rosemary, might also need to be considered. Moreover, TLC is often a problematic method of analysis for aged mixtures, such as these (see discussion of TLC in Chapter 17, this volume).

Several samples were taken from various parts of the wrappings, body surfaces and internal areas of a mummy in Munich (Storch and Schäfer 1985: 327–38. Mummy ÄS 73B). These were tested by IR, X-ray fluorescence, ion chromatography and mass spectrometry. The samples from the outer layer of wrapping and the surface of the mummy were identified as mixtures of beeswax and oil, while the wrappings were coated with a mixture of beeswax, oil, resin, gum, soda, and bitumen (Storch and Schäfer 1985: 331, table I). The samples taken from inside the head, thorax and organs were said to have been composed of beeswax, oil, bitumen, gum, soda and fossilised resin (Storch and Schäfer 1985: 331, table I). The identification of

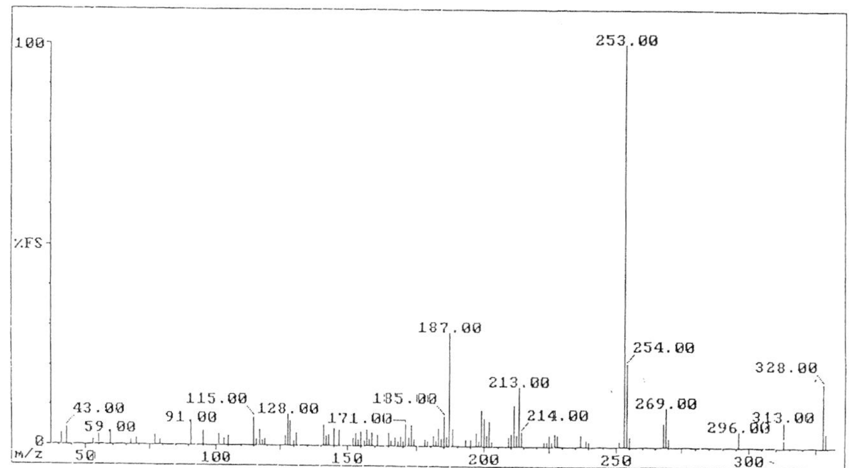

Figure 18.27 Mass spectrum (electron impact mode 70 eV) of one of the components found in a trans/thermolytically methylated sample taken from the chest cavity of a Third Intermediate Period mummy (BM EA74303). This component, 7-oxodehydroabietate, the methyl ester of 7-oxodehydroabietic acid, is characteristic of coniferous resins of the family Pinaceae.

a fossilised resin is especially unusual and would be worthy of more detailed examination to determine its identity more precisely.

Finally, bandages from a mummy examined by the Manchester Museum, dated to *c.* AD 380, were tested with a variety of techniques (Benson *et al.* 1979: 119–30). Stylistically, this mummy of a young girl aged about thirteen or fourteen possibly from Hawara, appears to be Greco–Roman in date (on the problems with the dating, see Hodge and Newton 1979: 137, 146). A Lassaigne test established the presence of sulphur, normally associated with asphalt, on the bandages. Molybdenum and vanadium were detected using atomic absorption spectroscopy and neutron activation analysis. However, GLC (gas-liquid chromatography) analysis of samples of Dead Sea asphalt produced no chromatograms which could be used for comparison (Benson *et al.* 1979: 127, table 8, asterisked footnote). Based on the results, it was concluded that bitumen was present on the inner bandages, but not on the outer ones (Benson *et al.* 1979: 131). Once again beeswax was identified. No coniferous resins were found on the bandages of the mummy examined by the Manchester group, but the results of thin layer chromotography (TLC) analysis led to the conclusion that galbanum was present (Benson *et al.* 1979: 123, 128, fig. 5). This result deserves further research because, as discussed above, galbanum is not easy to trace in aged samples, TLC is less reliable in complex mixtures, such as are present here (see discussion in Chapter 17, this volume) and as yet there has been no conclusive evidence of its presence in ancient material through GC/MS work.

With few exceptions, the results of all analyses using GC/MS do seem similar and suggest that imported coniferous products, sometimes resin, as well as beeswax and asphalt were used specifically in mummification. Where calculated, the amount of asphalt in the samples ranged from 3 to 81 per cent, but most seemed to contain between 10–30 per cent (Connan and Dessort 1991: 1451, Tab. II). It is true that the majority of samples date to the Greco–Roman period, but the presence of bitumen in a sample dated to the Nineteenth Dynasty may indicate that the use of this product in classical times was a continuation of an earlier practice. The indication that bitumen was used as a varnish on funerary equipment as early as the first half of the Eighteenth Dynasty increases the likelihood that bitumen will also be found in mummies of this date, if not earlier.

Of interest in this regard is a black resinous deposit in the one remaining canopic jar of Thutnakht, buried at Deir el-Bersha (Newberry 1894b) in the Middle Kingdom (Museum of Fine Arts, Boston, MFA 21.424.). The cartonnage jar was of human shape and the inscription indicated that it represented Qebehsenuef, guardian of the intestines. Remains of the canopic box, said to have been made of cedar, were also found in the burial (D'Auria *et al.* 1988: 111; the coffin was also cedar). A sample from the jar was shown by GC/MS to contain dehydroabietic and 7–oxodehydroabietic acids, indicating the presence of a resin of the family Pinaceae. In the absence of degradation products of the compound cis-abienol, it would seem that pine or cedar were the most likely sources. Notably, no evidence of asphalt was detected in the sample (Serpico and White 1998: 1041).

Conclusions

Although, in many respects, current study of the use of resins, amber and bitumen in ancient Egypt is a continuation of the work started by Lucas and his contemporaries, the application of new scientific and botanical approaches to this subject is rapidly extending our knowledge. These two disciplines, taken in conjunction with Egyptology, can only benefit from one another. Successful chemical analysis of resins requires well-documented botanical information, while the results of such analyses will shed light on the botanical sources in use.

In this regard, scientists would undoubtedly prefer to acquire modern samples of resin from species growing in the relevant region. For example, although differences in composition may seem minor, it would always be better to obtain authentic modern samples from a species of pine found in the Mediterranean, rather than one indigenous to North America. Conversely, in order to determine which species should be chosen, chemists need secure botanical information. The fact, noted above, that some modern resins are sold only under their common names (opopanax, olibanum, etc.) also emphasises the need for a consensus of nomenclature.

From the results of scientific analysis available, certain trends have already begun to emerge, particularly regarding the identification and use of resins. There does appear to be a relationship between *Pistacia* spp. resin and its use as incense and varnish during the New Kingdom. Combined with the evidence from the Ulu Burun shipwreck, this points to a much more extensive industry for this product than had hitherto been considered. Research is continuing into this subject and will, hopefully, provide new insight into Mediterranean trade. It is also interesting that the apparent abundance of this resin seems to support the increasing evidence that deforestation of *Pistacia* trees has occurred since antiquity, illustrating again the co-dependence of scientific and botanical research.

Another demonstrable connection between product and usage is the recurring choice of coniferous products, beeswax and bitumen in mummification. Further analyses will help to establish whether this correlation extends earlier than the Late Period, as the single analysis of a New Kingdom sample appears to indicate. The discovery of bitumen used as black varnish in the early New Kingdom suggests that this may be the case.

Such relationships are important to note because they can help us to formulate strategies for further research. The benefit of multiple, rather than one-off analyses is also evident. However, it is unlikely that the lines can be so rigidly drawn. What will probably emerge is a simple *predilection* for a particular choice, dependant on a range of factors such as availability, current fashion, cost, and the suitability of the product for that purpose. These connections will be much looser than a strict adherence of a specific substance for a specific usage, but will provide a better understanding of the products as commodities.

Also noticeable at this point is the near absence of scientific identifications for some resinous exudates, such as frankincense, myrrh, juniper and cypress. Too much should not be read into this, as the numbers of samples analysed are still relatively small. Moreover, not all usages have been fully explored, nor for all periods. This is, as yet, an observation which remains to be explored.

With regard to the application of scientific analysis to the study of amber and bitumen in ancient Egypt, the position is more one of demonstrable potential as few analyses have been carried out. However, extensive investigations into these products are underway and, as more ancient Egyptian samples become available, they will be able to conjoin a substantial body of research. The ability to determine the provenance of these products will undoubtedly also supply new insights into ancient trade.

Acknowledgements

We would like to thank Mr F.N. Hepper for permission to include his botanical drawings in this chapter. Thanks are due to Dr Carl Heron, Department of Archaeological Sciences, University of Bradford for reading an earlier draft of portions of this chapter. Also, Dr Helen Whitehouse, Curator, Department of Antiquities, Ashmolean Museum, Oxford; the Egypt Exploration Society, London; Mr Barry Kemp, Director of the Egypt Exploration Society expedition to Amarna; Mrs Barbara Adams, Curator, Petrie Museum of Egyptian Archaeology, University College London; Mr W.V. Davies (Keeper), Mr T.G.H. James (former Keeper), Ms Joyce Filer (Special Assistant for Human Remains), and Drs Stephen Quirke and John Taylor (Assistant Keepers), Department of Egyptian Antiquities, British Museum, London, for assistance with museum material and permission to sample and analyse objects mentioned in this chapter as part of our research.

References

Abraham, H. 1960. *Asphalt and Allied Substances I: Historical Review and Natural Raw Materials.* Princeton, NJ: D. Van Nostrand Company, Inc.

Akiyoshi, S., Erdtman, H. and Kubota, T. 1960. Chemistry of the natural order Cupressales – XXVI: The identity of Junipene, Kuromatsuene, and Longifolene, and of Juniperol, Kuromatsuol, Macrocarpol and Longiborneol. *Tetrahedron,* 9: 237–9.

Anderson, K.B. and Botto, R.E. 1993. The nature and fate of natural resins in the geosphere – III. Re-evaluation of the structure and composition of *Highgate Copalite* and *Glessite. Organic Geochemistry,* 20/7: 1027–38.

Anderson, K.B. and Crelling, J.C. 1995. Introduction. In *Amber, Resinite, and Fossil Resins* (eds. K.B. Anderson and J.C. Crelling). Washington, DC: American Chemical Society, pp. xi–xvii.

Anderson, K.B. and Winans, R.E. 1991. Nature and fate of natural resins in the geosphere 1: Evaluation of pyrolysis-gas chromatography/mass spectrometry for the analysis of natural resins and resinites. *Analytical Chemistry,* 63: 2901–8.

Anderson, K.B., Winans, R.E. and Botto, R.E. 1992. The nature and fate of natural resins in the geosphere – II. Identification, classification and nomenclature of resinites. *Organic Geochemistry,* 18/6: 829–41.

Andrews, C. 1984. *Egyptian Mummies.* London: BMP.

Andrews, F.W. 1952. *Flowering Plants of Sudan* vol. II. Khartoum: Sudan Government Press.

Aufrère, S. 1991. *L'univers minéral dans la pensée égyptienne,* 2 vols. Cairo: IFAO.

Bass, G.F. 1987. Oldest known shipwreck reveals splendors of the Bronze Age. *National Geographic,* 172: 692–733.

Baum, N. 1994. *Sntr*: une révision. *RdE,* 45: 17–39.

Beals, E.W. 1965. Remnant cedar forests of Lebanon. *Journal of Ecology,* 53: 679–94.

Beck, C.W. 1966. Analysis and provenience of Minoan and Mycenaean amber, I. *Greek, Roman and Byzantine Studies,* 7: 191–211.

1970. Amber in archaeology. *Archaeology,* 23/1: 7–11.

Beck, C.W. and Hartnett, H.E. 1993. Sicilian amber. In *Amber in Archaeology: Proceedings of the Second International Conference on Amber in Archaeology, Liblice 1990* (eds. C.W. Beck and J. Bouzek in collaboration with D. Dreslerovà). Prague: Institute of Archaeology, Czech Academy of Sciences, pp. 36–47.

Beck, C. and Shennan, S. 1991. *Amber in Prehistoric Britain.* Oxbow Monograph 8. Oxford: Oxbow Books.

Beck, C.W., Gerving, M. and Wilbur, E. 1966. The provenience of archaeological amber artifacts. Part I: 8th century BC to 1899. *Art and Archaeology Technical Abstracts,* 6(2): 215–302.

Beck, C., Wilbur, E., Meret, S., Kossove, D. and Kermani, K. 1965. The infrared spectra of amber and the identification of Baltic amber. *Archaeometry,* 8: 96–109.

Bekele-Tesemma, A. (with Birnie, A. and Tangnäs, B.) 1993. *Useful Trees and Shrubs for Ethiopia. Identification, Propagation and Management for Agricultural and Pastoral Communities.* Regional Soil Conservation Unit, Swedish International Development Authority.

Benson, G.G., Hemingway, S.R. and Leach, F.N. 1979. The analysis of the wrappings of mummy 1770. In *The Manchester Museum Mummy Project* (ed. A.R. David). Manchester: Manchester Museum, pp. 119–31.

Boon, J.J., Tom, A. and Pureveen, J. 1993. Microgram scale pyrolysis mass spectrometric and pyrolysis gas chromatographic characterisation of geological and archaeological amber and resin samples. In *Amber in Archaeology: Proceedings of the Second International Conference on Amber in Archaeology, Liblice, 1990* (eds. C.W. Beck and J. Bouzek). Prague: Institute of Archaeology, pp. 9–27.

Boratyński, A., Browicz, K. and Zieliński, J. 1992. *Chorology of*

Trees and Shrubs in Greece, Institute of Dendrology. Kórnik: Polish Academy of Sciences.

Bradbury, L. 1996. *Kpn*-boats, Punt Trade, and a Lost Emporium. *JARCE*, 33: 37–60.

Brenan, J.P.M. 1967. Leguminosae, subfamily Caesalpinioideae. In *Flora of Tropical East Africa* (eds. E. Milne-Redhead and R.M. Polhill). Published under Authority of the Ministry for Overseas Development by the Crown Agents for Overseas Government and Administrations.

Brieskorn, C.H., and Noble, P. 1982. The terpenes of the essential oil of myrrh. In *Aromatic Plants: Basic and Applied Aspects* (eds. N. Margaris, A. Koedam and D. Vokou). World Crops: Production, Utilisation, and Description, Vol. 7. The Hague: Martinus Nijhoff, pp. 221–6.

Browicz, K. 1983. *Chorology of Trees and Shrubs in South-West Asia and Adjacent Regions* II. Warsaw: Polish Scientific Publishers.

1984. *Chorology of Trees and Shrubs in South-West Asia and Adjacent Regions* III. Warsaw: Polish Scientific Publishers.

1987. Pistacia lentiscus cv. Chia (Anacardiaceae) on Chios island. *Plant Systematics and Evolution*, 155: 189–95.

1988. *Chorology of Trees and Shrubs in South-West Asia and Adjacent Regions* VI. Warsaw: Polish Scientific Publishers.

1994. *Chorology of Trees and Shrubs in South-West Asia and Adjacent Regions* X. Warsaw: Polish Scientific Publishers.

Browicz, K. and Zieliński, J. 1982. *Chorology of Trees and Shrubs in South-West Asia and Adjacent Regions* I. Warsaw: Polish Scientific Publishers.

Bryant, R. 1969. The Sesquiterpenoids. In *Rodd's Chemistry of Carbon Compounds*, Vol. II, Part C, 'Polycarbocyclic compounds excluding steriods,' (ed. S. Coffey). London: Elsevier Publishing Co.

Budge, E.A.W. 1893. *The Mummy: Chapters on Egyptian Funereal Archaeology*. Cambridge: CUP.

Burkill, H.M. 1995. *The Useful Plants of West Tropical Africa 3*, 2nd edn. Kew: Royal Botanic Gardens.

Carlström, A. 1987. *A Survey of the Flora and Phytogeography of Rodhos, Simi, Tilos and the Marmaris Peninsula (SE Greece, SW Turkey)*. Lund: Univ. of Lund.

Chamberlain, D.F. 1972. *Opopanax* W. Koch. In *Flora of Turkey and the East Aegean Islands* 4 (ed. P.H. Davis). Edinburgh: University Press, pp. 471–3.

1977. The identity of *Ferula assa-foetida* L. *Notes from the Royal Botanic Garden, Edinburgh*, 35/2: 229–33.

Chamberlain, D.F. and Rechinger, K.H. 1987. *Ferula* L. In *Umbelliferae* (ed. I.C. Hedge, J.M. Lamond and K.H. Rechinger). In *Flora Iranica* series (ed. K.H. Rechinger). Graz: Akademische Druck – u. verlagsanstalt, pp. 387–426.

Chassinat, É. 1922. Le mot [hieroglyphs] dans les textes médicaux. In *Recueil d'études égyptologiques dédiées à la mémoire de Jean-Francois Champollion* (Bibliotheque de l'École des hautes Études). Paris: Librairie ancienne Honoré Champion, pp. 447–65.

1955. *Le manuscript magique copte: no. 42573 du Musée égyptien du Caire*. Cairo: IFAO.

1990. *Le temple d'Edfou* II, 2nd edn., rev. S. Cauville and D. Devauchelle. Cairo: IFAO.

Clark, J.D. 1974. Interpretations of prehistoric technology from ancient Egyptian and other sources. *Paléorient*, 2: 323–88.

Connan, J. 1988. Quelques secrets des bitumes archéologiques de Mésopotamie révélés par les analyses de géochimie organique pétrolière. *Bulletin des centres de recherches exploration-production elf-Aquitaine*, 12(2): 759–87.

1991. Chemische Untersuchung altägyptischer Mumien-Salböle. In *Mumie und Computer* (eds R. Drenkhahn and R. Germer). Hannover: Kestner Museums, pp. 34–6.

Connan, J. and Deschesne, O. 1996. *Le Bitume à Suse: Collection du Musée du Louvre*. Paris: Réunion des Musées Nationaux and Fondation Elf.

Connan, J. and Dessort, D. 1989. Du bitume de la Mer Morte dans les baumes d'une momie égyptienne: identification par critères moléculaires. *Comptes rendus de l'académie des sciences*, Série II, 309(17): 1665–72.

1991. Du bitume dans des baumes de momies égyptiennes (1295 av. J.-C. – 300 ap. J.-C.): détermination de son origine et évaluation de sa quantité. *Comptes rendus de l'académie des sciences*, Série II, 312/12: 1445–52.

Connan, J., Deschesne, O. and Dessort, D. 1991. L'origine des bitumes archéologiques de Ras Shamra. In *Ras Shamra-Ougarit VI: Arts et industries de la pierre* (ed. M. Yon). Paris: ADPF, pp. 101–25.

Connan, J., Nissenbaum, A. and Dessort, D. 1992. Molecular archaeology: export of Dead Sea asphalt to Canaan and Egypt in the Chalcolithic-Early Bronze Age (4th–3rd millennium BC). *Geochimica et Cosmochimica Acta*, 56: 2743–59.

Coode, M.J.E. 1965. *Cistus* L. In *Flora of Turkey and the East Aegean Islands* 1 (ed. P.H. Davis). Edinburgh: Edinburgh University Press, pp. 506–8.

Coode, M.J.E. and Cullen, J. 1965a. Cupressaceae. In *Flora of Turkey and the East Aegean Islands* I (ed. P.H. Davis). Edinburgh: Edinburgh University Press, pp. 76–84.

1965b. Pinaceae. In *Flora of Turkey and the East Aegean Islands* I (ed. P.H. Davis). Edinburgh: University Press, pp. 67–75.

Cooke, M.C. 1874. *Gums, Resins, Oleo-Resins, and Resinous Products in the India Museum, or Produced in India*. London: India Museum.

Coppen, J.J.W. 1995. *Flavours and Fragrances of Plant Origin*. Rome: Food and Agricultural Organization of the United Nations.

Coughlin, E.A. 1977. Analysis of PUM-II mummy fluid. *Paleopathology Newsletter*, 17 (March): 7–8.

Critchfield, W.B. and Little, E.L. Jr. 1966. *Geographic Distribution of the Pines of the World*. Washington, DC: US Department of Agriculture Forest Service, Miscellaneous Publication 991, February.

Currid, J.D. 1984. The deforestation of the foothills of Palestine. *PEQ*, 116: 1–11.

D'Auria, S., Lacovara, P. and Roehrig, C.H. 1988. *Mummies and Magic: The Funerary Arts of Ancient Egypt*. Boston: MFA.

Dallimore, W. and Jackson, A.B. 1931. *A Handbook of Coniferae (including Ginkgoaceae)*. London: Edward Arnold.

Davidson, D.F.D. 1948. Report on the gum mastic industry on Chios. *Bulletin of the Imperial Institute*, 46: 184–91.

Davies, W.V. 1995. Ancient Egyptian timber imports: an analysis of wooden coffins in the British Museum. In *Egypt, the Aegean and the Levant: Interconnections in the Second Millenium BC* (eds. W.V. Davies and L. Schofield). London: BMP, pp. 146–56.

Dayagi-Mendels, M. 1989: *Perfumes and Cosmetics in the Ancient World*. Jerusalem: The Israel Museum.

Doran, W. 1937. On Predynastic beads from AR 1370, 1403 and

1424a. In *Cemeteries of Armant I: Text* (by R. Mond and O.H. Myers). London: EES, pp. 96–100.
Dümichen, J. 1879. Ein Salbölrecept aus dem Laboratorium des Edfutempels. *ZÄS*, 17: 97–128.
Dyer, W.T.T. 1885. The collection of gum labdanum in Crete. *The Pharmaceutical Journal and Transactions 1884–1885*, 3rd Series, XV: 301–2.
1886. Notes on Cyprian Drugs. *The Pharmaceutical Journal and Transactions 1885–1886*, 3rd Series, XVI: 385–6.
Edmondson, J. and Bienkowski, P. 1993. Analysis of essential oils in funerary wreaths from Hawara. In Biological Anthropology and the Study of Ancient Egypt (eds. W. V. Davies and R. Walker). London: BMP, pp.1716.
Erman, A. and Grapow, H. 1928. *Wörterbuch der Ägyptischen Sprache* II. Leipzig: J.C. Hinrichs.
Evershed, R.P., van Bergen, P.F., Peakman, T.M. and Leigh-Firbank, E.C. 1997. Archaeological frankincense. *Nature* 390: 18/25 December, pp. 667–8.
Evershed, R.P., Jerman, K. and Eglinton, G. 1985. Pine wood origin for pitch from the *Mary Rose*. *Nature*, 314: 528–30.
Fady, B., Arbez, M. and Marpeau, A. 1992. Geographical variability of terpene composition in *Abies cephalonica* Loudon and *Abies* species around the Aegean: hypotheses for their possible phylogeny from the Miocene. *Trees*, 6: 162–71.
Fattovich, R. 1990. The problem of Punt in the light of recent field work in the Eastern Sudan. *SAK Beihefte*, 4: 257–72.
Fischer, H.G. 1988. The early publication of a relief in Turin. *GM*, 101: 31–2.
Fleming, S., Fishman, B., O'Connor, D. and Silverman, D. 1980. *The Egyptian Mummy: Secrets and Science*. Philadelphia PA: University Museum, University of Pennsylvania.
Forbes, R.J., 1964. *Studies in Ancient Technology* I. Leiden: E.J. Brill.
Galletti, G.C. and Mazzeo, R. 1993. Pyrolysis/gas chromatography/mass spectrometry and Fourier-transform infrared spectroscopy of amber. *Rapid Communications in Mass Spectrometry*, 7: 646–50.
Gangl, J. 1936. Appendix III: Report giving the results of the examination of various materials from Maadi. In *The Excavations of the Egyptian University in the Neolithic Site at Maadi: Second Preliminary Report, Season 1932* (by O. Menghin and M. Amer). Cairo: Egyptian University, Government Press, pp. 63–5.
Gaussen, H., Heywood, V.H. and Chater, A.O. 1993. *Pinus* L. In *Flora Europaea I: Pinaceae*, 2nd edn. (ed. D.M. Moore) (Series eds. T.G. Tutin, N.A. Burges, A.O. Chater, J.R. Edmonson, V.H. Heywood, D.M. Moore, D.H. Valentine, S.M. Walters and D.A. Webb). Cambridge: CUP, pp. 40–4.
Germer, R. 1985. *Flora des Pharaonischen Ägypten*, DAIK, Mainz: von Zabern.
1988. *Katalog der Altägyptischen Pflanzenreste der Berliner Museen*. Wiesbaden: Otto Harrassowitz.
1989. *Die Pflanzenmaterialien aus dem Grab des Tutanchamun*. Hildesheim: Gerstenberg Verlag.
Gilbert, M.G. 1989. Anacardiaceae. In *Flora of Ethiopia* III (eds. I. Hedberg and S. Edwards). Addis Ababa, Asmara and Uppsala: Ethiopian Flora Project, pp. 513–32.
Gillett, J.B. 1991. Burseraceae. In *Flora of Tropical East Africa* (ed. R.M. Polhill). Rotterdam: A.A. Balkema and the East African Governments.
Goettsch, E. 1991. Traditional aromatic and perfume plants in central Ethiopia (a botanical and ethno-historical survey). In *Plant Genetic Resources of Ethiopia* (eds. J.M.M. Engels, J.G. Hawkes and M. Worede). Cambridge: CUP, pp. 114–22.
Gough, L.J. and Mills, J.S. 1972. The composition of succinite (Baltic amber). *Nature*, 239: 527–8.
Goyon, J.-C. and Josset, P. 1988. *Un corps pour l'éternité: autopsie d'une momie*. Paris: Le léopard d'or.
Grimaldi, D.A. 1996. *Amber: Window to the Past*. New York: Harry N. Abrams, Inc. and the American Museum of Natural History.
Griffiths, J.G.A. 1937. Resins and pitch from ancient Egyptian tombs. *Analyst*, 62: 703–9.
Groom N. 1981. *Frankincense and Myrrh: A Study of the Arabian Incense Trade*. London: Longman.
Hafizoğlu, H. 1987. Studies in the chemistry of *Cedrus libani* A. Rich.: I. Wood extractives of *Cedrus libani*. *Holzforschung*, 41/1: 27–38.
Hafizoğlu, H. and Holmbom, B. 1987. Studies in the chemistry of *Cedrus libani* A. Rich.: III. Oleoresin composition of cones and bark from *Cedrus libani*. *Holzforschung*, 41/3: 141–5.
Hairfield, H.H. and Hairfield, E.M. 1990. Identification of a Late Bronze Age resin. *Analytical Chemistry*, 62/1: 41–5.
Hanbury, D. 1857. On Storax. *The Pharmaceutical Journal and Transactions, 1856–1857*, XVI: 417–23; 461–5.
Harrison, R.G. and Abdalla, A.B. 1972. The Remains of Tutankhamen. *Antiquity*, 46: 8–18.
Hartvig, P. 1986. *Opopanax* Koch. In *Mountain Flora of Greece* I (ed. A. Strid). London: CUP, p. 714.
Helbaek, H. 1958. Plant economy in ancient Lachish. In *Lachish* IV (O. Tufnell). London: OUP, pp. 309–17.
1966a. Pre-pottery Neolithic farming at Beidha: a preliminary report. *PEQ*, 98: 61–6.
1966b. What farming produced at Cypriote Kalopsidha. In *Excavations at Kalopsidha and Ayios Iakovos in Cyprus* (ed. P. Åström), Studies in Mediterranean Archaeology 2. Lund: P. Åströms Forlag, pp. 115–26.
1964. First impressions of the Çatal Hüyük plant husbandry. *Anatolian Studies*, 14: 121–3.
Hendrickson, J.B. 1959. Stereochemical implications in sesquiterpene biogenesis. *Tetrahedron*, 7: 82–9.
Hepper, F.N. 1969. Arabian and African frankincense trees. *JEA*, 55: 66–72.
1987a. *Planting a Bible Garden*. London: HMSO.
1987b. Trees and shrubs yielding gums and resins in the ancient Near East. *BSA*, 3: 107–14.
1990. *Pharaoh's Flowers: The Botanical Treasures of Tutankhamun*. Kew: Royal Botanic Garden.
1992a. A corrective note on Pistacia trees and resin. *BSA*, 6: 195–6.
1992b. *The Illustrated Encyclopedia of Bible Plants*. Leicester: Inter Varsity Press.
Hepper, F.N. and Gibson, S. 1994. Abraham's oak of Mamre: the story of a venerable tree. *PEQ*, 126: 94–105.
Heron, C. and Pollard, A.M. 1988. Analysis of natural resinous materials from Roman amphoras. In *Science and Archaeology: Glasgow, 1987* (eds. E.A. Slater and J.O. Tate). Oxford: BAR, 196 (ii), pp. 429–47.
Herzog, R. 1968. *Punt*. Abhandlungen des DAIK, Ägyptologische Reihe, Band 6. Glückstadt: J.J. Augustin.

Hodge, K.C. and Newton, G.W.A. 1979. Radiocarbon dating. In *The Manchester Museum Mummy Project: Multidisciplinary Research on Ancient Egyptian Mummified Remains* (ed. A.R. David). Manchester: Manchester Museum, pp. 137–47.

Hood, S. 1993. Amber in Egypt. In *Amber in Archaeology. Proceedings of the Second International Conference on Amber in Archaeology, Liblice, 1990* (eds. C.W. Beck and J. Bouzek in collaboration with D. Dreslerovà). Prague: Institute of Archaeology, pp. 230–5.

Howes, F.N. 1949. *Vegetable Gums and Resins.* Waltham MA: Chronica Botanica Co.

Hughes-Brock, H. 1993. Amber in the Aegean in the Late Bronze Age: some problems and perspectives. In *Amber in Archaeology: Proceedings of the Second International Conference on Amber in Archaeology, Liblice 1990* (eds. C.W. Beck and J. Bouzek in collaboration with D. Dreslerovà). Prague: Institute of Archaeology, pp. 219–29.

Huneck, S. 1963. Die Triterpensäuren des Balsams von Liquidambar orientalis Miller. *Tetrahedron,* 19/1: 479–82.

Jalas J. and Suominen, J. 1973. *Atlas Florae Europaeae: distribution of vascular plants in Europe,* Part 2. Helsinki: The Committee for Mapping the Flora of Europe and Societas Biologica Fennica Vanamo.

James, T.G.H. 1995. The earliest history of wine and its importance in ancient Egypt. In *Origins and Ancient History of Wine* (eds. P. McGovern, S. Fleming and S. Katz). Luxembourg: Gordon and Breach Publishers, pp. 197–213.

Jeffrey, C. 1980. Anacardiaceae. In *Flora of Iraq* IV (eds. C.C. Townsend and E. Guest). Baghdad: Ministry of Agriculture, pp. 486–99.

Kaup, Y., Baumer, U., Koller, J., Hedges, R.E.M., Werner, H., Hartmann, H.-J., Etspüler, H. and Weser, U. 1994. Zn_2Mg alkaline phosphatase in an early Ptolemaic mummy. *Zeitschrift für Naturforschung C: A Journal of Biosciences,* 49/7 and 8: 489–500.

Kayacik, H. 1955. The distribution of *Picea Orientalis* (L.) Carr. *Kew Bulletin,* 3: 481–90.

Kislev, M.E. 1985. Reference to the Pistachio tree in Near East geographical names. *PEQ,* 117: 133–8.

1988. Fruit remains. In *The Egyptian Mining Temple at Timna* (B. Rothenberg). London: Institute for Archaeo-Metallurgical Studies, Institute of Archaeology, University College London, pp. 236–41.

Kitchen, K.A. 1971. Punt and how to get there. *Orientalia,* 40: 184–207.

1993. The land of Punt. In *The Archaeology of Africa: Food, metals and towns* (eds T. Shaw, P. Sinclair, B. Andah and A. Okpoko), London: Routledge, pp. 587–608.

Koller, J., Baumer, U., Kaup, Y., Etspüler, H. and Weser, V. 1998. Embalming was used in Old Kingdom. *Nature* 391: 22 January, pp. 343–4.

Kopp, A.H. 1934. Appendix. In *The Treasure of El Lahun* (H.E. Winlock). New York: MMA, pp. 74–5.

Lambert, J.B., Beck, C.W. and Frye, J.S. 1988. Analysis of European amber by carbon–13 nuclear magnetic resonance spectroscopy. *Archaeometry,* 30: 248–63.

Langenheim, J.H. 1969. Amber: a botanical inquiry. *Science,* 163: 1157–69.

1995. Biology of amber-producing trees: focus on case studies of *Hymenaea* and *Agathis.* In *Amber, Resinite, and Fossil Resins* (eds. K.B. Anderson and J.C. Crelling). Washington DC: American Chemical Society, pp. 1–31.

Le Fur, D. 1994. *La conservation des peintures murales des temples de Karnak.* Paris: Éditions recherche sur les civilisations.

Lepsius, K.R. 1849–59. *Denkmäler aus Ägypten und Äthiopien.* 6 pts in 12 vols. Leipzig: J.C. Hinrichs.

Liphschitz, N. 1992. Levant trees and tree products. *BSA,* 6: 33–46.

Liphschitz, N., Biger, G., and Mendel, Z. 1988–1990. Did Aleppo pine (*Pinus halepensis*) cover the mountains of Eretz-Israel during antiquity? *Israel – People and Land,* 5–6: 141–50 (in Hebrew with English summary, p. 18).

Loret, V. 1894. Étude de drogueriè égyptienne. *RT,* 16: 134–62.

1916. Quelques notes sur l'arbre *âch. ASAE,* 16: 33–51.

1949. *La résine de térébinthe (sonter) chez les anciens égyptiens.* Cairo: Recherches d'archéologie et philologie et d'histoire XIX.

Lucas, A. 1911. *Preservative Materials used by the Ancient Egyptians in Embalming.* Cairo: Ministry of Finance, National Printing Dept.

1931. 'Cedar'-tree products employed in mummification. *JEA,* 17: 13–20.

1937. Notes on myrrh and stacte. *JEA,* 23: 27–33.

1962. *Ancient Egyptian Materials and Industries,* 4th ed., rev. J.R. Harris. London: Edward Arnold.

Mace, A.C. and Winlock, H.E. 1916. *The Tomb of Senebtisi at Lisht.* New York: MMA.

Manniche, L. 1989. *An Ancient Egyptian Herbal.* London: BMP.

Marschner, R.F. and Wright, H.T. 1978. Asphalts from Middle Eastern archaeological sites. In *Archaeological Chemistry* II (ed. G.F. Carter). Washington DC: American Chemical Society, pp. 150–71.

Marschner, R.F., Duffy, L.J. and Wright, H. 1978. Asphalts from ancient town sites in Southwestern Iran. *Paléorient,* 4: 97–112.

Masschelein-Kleiner, L., Heylen, J. and Tricot-Marckx, F. 1968. Contribution à l'analyse des liants, adhésifs et vernis anciens. *Studies in Conservation,* 13: 105–21.

de Mayo, P. 1959. *Mono- and sesquiterpenoids.* New York: Interscience Publications, Inc.

McGovern, P.E., Glusker, D.L., Exner, L.J. and Voigt, M.M. 1996. Neolithic resinated wine. *Nature,* 381: 480–1.

McGovern, P.E., Hartung, U., Badler, V.R. Glusker, D.L. and Exner, L.J. 1997. The beginnings of winemaking and viniculture in the ancient Near East and Egypt. *Expedition,* 39/1: 3–21.

Meiggs, R. 1982. *Trees and Timber in the Ancient Mediterranean World.* Oxford: Clarendon Press.

Meikle, R.D. 1977. *Flora of Cyprus,* I. Kew: Royal Botanic Garden.

1985. *Flora of Cyprus,* II. Kew: Royal Botanic Garden.

Meyer, C., Todd, J.M. and Beck, C.W. 1991. From Zanzibar to Zagros: a copal pendant from Eshnunna. *JNES,* 50/4: 289–98.

Mikesell, M.W. 1969. The deforestation of Mount Lebanon. *The Geographical Review,* 59/1: 1–28.

Miller, A.G., Cope, T.A. and Nyberg, J.A. 1996. *Flora of the Arabian Peninsula and Socotra* I. Edinburgh University Press, Royal Botanic Garden Edinburgh and Royal Botanic Gardens, Kew. Edinburgh: Edinburgh University Press.

Mills, J.S. and White, R. 1977. Natural resins of art and archaeology: their sources, chemistry and identification. *Studies in Conservation*, 22: 12–31.

1989. The identity of the resins from the Late Bronze Age shipwreck at Ulu Burun (Kaş). *Archaeometry*, 31/1: 37–44.

1994. *The Organic Chemistry of Museum Objects*. London: Butterworth.

Mills, J.S., White, R. and Gough, L.J. 1984/5. The chemical composition of Baltic amber. *Chemical Geology* 47: 15–39.

Mirov, N.T. 1967. *The Genus Pinus*. New York: Ronald Press.

Moldenke, H.N. and Moldenke, A.L. 1952. *Plants of the Bible*. Waltham MA: Chronica Botanica Co. (repr. Dover Publications, Mineola NY, 1986).

Mouterde, P. 1966. *Nouvelle flore du Liban et de la Syrie* I, Texte. Beirut: Éditions de l'imprimerie catholique.

1970. *Nouvelle flore du Liban et de la Syrie* II, Texte. Beirut: Dar el-Machreq Editeurs.

Naville, E. 1898. *The Temple of Deir el Bahari* III. London: EES.

1912. Hebraeo-Aegyptiaca I: The Shittim wood. *PSBA*, 34: 180–90.

Negbi, M. 1992. A sweetmeat plant, a perfume plant and their weedy relatives: a chapter in the history of *Cyperus esculentus* L. and *C. rotundus* L. *Economic Botany*, 46/1: 64–71.

Newberry, P.E. 1893. *Beni Hassan* I. London: EES.

1894a. *Beni Hassan* II. London: EES.

1894b. *El-Bersheh I: The Tomb of Tehuti-hetep*. London: EES.

1929. The shepherd's crook and the so-called 'flail' or 'scourge of Osiris'. *JEA*, 15: 84–94.

Nissenbaum, A. 1978. Dead Sea asphalts – historical aspects. *The American Association of Petroleum Geologists Bulletin*, 62/5: 837–44.

1992. Molecular archaeology: organic geochemistry of Egyptian mummies. *JAS*, 19: 1–6.

Nissenbaum, A., Serban, A., Amiran, R. and Ilan, O. 1984. Dead Sea asphalt from the excavations in Tel Arad and Small Tel Malhata. *Paléorient*, 10/1: 157–61.

Notman, D.N.H. 1986. Ancient Scannings: Computed tomography of Egyptian mummies. In *Science in Egyptology* (ed. A.R. David). Manchester: Manchester University Press, pp. 251–320.

de Pascual-Teresa, J., Bellido, I.S., Basabe, P., Marcos, I.S., Ruano, L.F. and Urones, J.G. 1982. Labdane diterpenoids from *Cistus Ladiferus*. *Phytochemistry*, 21/4: 899–901.

de Pascual-Teresa, J., Urones, J., Marcos, I.S., Barcala, P.B. and Garrido, N.M. 1986. Diterpenoid and other components of *Cistus laurifolius*. *Phytochemistry*, 25/5: 1185–7.

Peet, T.E. 1930. *The Great Tomb-Robberies of the Twentieth Egyptian Dynasty*. Oxford: Clarendon Press.

Peşman, H. 1972a. *Ferulago* W. Koch. In *Flora of Turkey and the East Aegean Islands*, vol. IV (ed. P.H. Davis), Edinburgh: Edinburgh University Press, pp. 453–71.

1972b. *Liquidambar* L. In *Flora of Turkey and the East Aegean Islands* 4 (ed. P.H. Davis). Edinburgh: Edinburgh University Press, pp. 264–5.

Pfau, A.S. and Plattner, P. 1934. Zür Kenntnis der fluchtigen Pflanzenstoffe I: über Atlanton, den Riechstoff der echten Cedernholzöle. *Helvetica Chimica Acta*, 17: 129–57.

Poinar, G.O. and Haverkamp, J. 1985. Use of pyrolysis mass spectrometry in the identification of amber samples. *Journal of Baltic Studies*, 16/3: 210–21.

Post, G.E. and Dinsmore, J.E. 1932. *Flora of Syria, Palestine and Sinai* I. Beirut: American Press.

1933. *Flora of Syria, Palestine and Sinai* II. Beirut: American Press.

Prag. K. 1986. Byblos and Egypt in the fourth millennium BC. *Levant*, 18: 59–74.

Proefke, M.L., Rinehart, K.L., Raheel, M., Ambrose, S.H. and Wisseman, S.U. 1992. Probing the mysteries of ancient Egypt: chemical analysis of a Roman Period Egyptian mummy. *Analytical Chemistry*, 64/2: 105A–11A.

Rackham, O. 1983. Observations on the historical ecology of Boeotia. *The Annual of the British School at Athens*, 78: 291–351.

Raven, M.J. 1990. Resin in Egyptian magic and symbolism. *OMRO* 70: 7–22.

Rechinger, K.H. 1943. *Flora Aegaea: Flora der Inseln und Halbinseln des Ägaischen Meeres*. Vienna: Springer.

1987. *Opopanax*. In *Umbelliferae* (eds. I.C. Hedge, J.M. Lamond and K.H. Rechinger). In *Flora Iranica* (ed. K.H. Rechinger). Graz: Akademische Druck – u. verlagsanstalt, pp. 438–9.

Rees, A. 1995. Frankincense and myrrh. *The New Plantsman*, 2: 55–9.

Renfrew, J.M. 1973. *Palaeoethnobotany: the prehistoric food plants of the Near East and Europe*. London: Methuen.

Robinson, N., Evershed, R.P., Higgs, W.J., Jerman, K., and Eglinton, G. 1987. Proof of a pine wood origin for pitch from Tudor (Mary Rose) and Etruscan shipwrecks: application of analytical organic chemistry in archaeology. *Analyst*, 112: 637–44.

Rottländer, R.C.A. 1970. On the formation of amber from *Pinus* resin. *Archaeometry*, 12: 35–52.

Rullkötter, J. and Nissenbaum, A. 1988. Dead Sea asphalt in Egyptian mummies: molecular evidence. *Naturwissenschaften*, 75: 618–21.

Saleh, A.A. 1972. The *Gnbtyw* of Thutmosis III's Annals and the South Arabian *Geb(b)anitae* of the classical writers. *BIFAO*, 72: 245–62.

1973. An open question on intermediaries in the incense trade during Pharaonic times. *Orientalia*, 42: 370–82.

Seher, A., Schiller, H., Krohn, M. and Werner, G. 1980. Untersuchungen von 'Ölproben' aus archäologischen Funden. *Fette, Seifen, Anstrichmittel*, 82/10: 395–9.

Serpico, M. 1996. Mediterranean resins in New Kingdom Egypt: a multidisciplinary approach to trade and usage. Unpublished PhD thesis, University College London.

Serpico, M. and White, R. 1996. Report on the analysis of the contents of a cache of jars from the tomb of Djer. In *Aspects of Early Egypt* (ed. J. Spencer). London: BMP, pp. 128–139.

1998. Chemical analysis of coniferous resins from ancient Egypt using gas chromatography/mass spectrometry (GC/MS). In *Proceedings of the Seventh International Congress of Egyptologists* (ed. C. Eyre). Leuven: Peeters, pp. 1037–48.

in press. The identification and use of varnishes on New Kingdom funerary equipment. In *Colour and Painting in Ancient Egypt* (ed. W.V. Davies), London: BMP.

Sethe, K. 1906. *Urkunden der 18. Dynastie*, II. Leipzig: J.C. Hinrichs.

Shedrinsky, A.M. and Baer, N.S. 1995. The application of analytical pyrolysis to the study of cultural material. In *Applied Pyrolysis Handbook* (ed. T.P. Wampler). New York: Marcel Dekker, pp. 125–55.

Shelmerdine, C.W. 1984. The perfumed oil industry at Pylos. In *Pylos Comes Alive: Industry and Administration in a Mycenaean Palace* (eds. C.W. Shelmerdine and T.G. Palaima). New York: New York Society of the Archaeological Institute of America and Fordham University, pp. 81–95.

1985. *The Perfume Industry of Mycenaean Pylos*. Gothenburg: Paul Åström.

Simonsen, J. and Barton, D.H.R. 1952. *The Terpenes III: The Sesquiterpenes, Diterpenes and their Derivatives*. Cambridge: CUP.

Smith, G.E. 1912. *The Royal Mummies. Catalogue général des antiquités égyptienne du Musée du Caire, Nos. 61051–61100*. Cairo: IFAO.

1916. Notes on the mummy. In *The Tomb of Senebtisi at Lisht* (A.C. Mace and H.E. Winlock). New York: MMA, pp. 119–20.

Smith, G.E. and Dawson, W.R. 1924. *Egyptian Mummies*. London: Allen and Unwin.

Snatzke, G. and Vértesy, L. 1967. Über die neutralen Sesqui- und Triterpene des Weihrauchs. *Monatshefte für Chemie*, 98(1): 121–32.

Spielmann, P.E. 1932. To what extent did the ancient Egyptians employ bitumen for embalming? *JEA*, 18: 177–80.

Steuer, R.O. 1933. *Myrrhe und Stakte*. Vienna: Arbeitsgemeinschaft der Ägyptologen und Afrikanisten in Wien.

Stol, M. 1979. *On Trees, Mountains and Millstones in the Ancient Near East*. Leiden: Ex Oriente Lux.

Storch, W. and Schäfer, H. 1985. Chemische Untersuchungen an der Münchner Mumie ÄS 73B: Ein Beitrag zur Aufklarung des Mumifizierungsverfahrens. *SAK* Beihefte I: 328–38.

Stout, E.C., Beck, C.W. and Kosmowska-Ceranowicz, B. 1995. Gedanite and gedano-succinite. In *Amber, Resinite, and Fossil Resins* (eds. K.B. Anderson and J.C. Crelling). Washington, DC: American Chemical Society, pp. 130–48.

Strong, D.E. 1966. *Catalogue of the Carved Amber in the Department of Greek and Roman Antiquities*. London: BMP.

Strouhal, E. 1986. Embalming excerebration in the Middle Kingdom. In *Science in Egyptology* (ed. A.R. David). Manchester: Manchester University Press.

Strouhal, E. and Vyhnánek, L. 1974. Radiographic examination of the mummy of Qenamūn the seal-bearer. *ZÄS*, 100: 125–9.

Strouhal, E., Kvicala, V., and Vyhnánek, L. 1986. Computed tomography of a series of Egyptian mummified heads. In *Science in Egyptology* (ed. A.R. David). Manchester: Manchester University Press, pp. 124–39.

Täckholm, V. 1974. *Students' Flora of Egypt*, 2nd edn. Cairo: Cairo University.

Täckholm, V. and Täckholm, G. in collaboration with Drar, M. 1941. *Flora of Egypt* I. Bulletin of the Faculty of Science, No. 17. Cairo: Fouad I University.

Tallet, P. 1995. Le shedeh: étude d'un procédé de vinification en Égypte ancienne. *BIFAO*, 95: 459–92.

Thomas, A.F., and Willhalm, B. 1964. The Triterpenes of *Commiphora*, IV. *Tetrahedron Letters*, 43: 3177–83.

Thulin, M. and Warfa, A.M. 1987. The frankincense trees (*Boswellia* spp., Burseraceae) of northern Somalia and southern Arabia. *Kew Bulletin*, 42(3): 487–500.

Todd. J.M. 1985. Baltic amber in the ancient Near East: a preliminary investigation. *Journal of Baltic Studies*, 16/3: 292–301.

1993. The continuity of amber artifacts in ancient Palestine: from the Bronze Age to the Byzantine. In *Amber in Archaeology: Proceedings of the Second International Conference on Amber in Archaeology, Liblice 1990* (eds. C.W. Beck and J. Bouzek in collaboration with D. Dreslerovà). Prague: Institute of Archaeology, pp. 236–48.

Tucker, A.O. 1986. Frankincense and myrrh. *Economic Botany*, 40/4: 425–33.

Turland, N.J., Chilton, L. and Press, J.R. 1993. *Flora of the Cretan Area*, The Natural History Museum. London: HMSO.

Tutin, T.G., Heywood, V.H., Burges, N.A., Moore, D.M., Valentine, D.H., Walters, S.M. and Webb, D.A. (eds.) 1968. *Flora Europeae II: Cistaceae* 1st edn. Cambridge: CUP.

Tutin, T.G., Burges, N.A., Chater, A.O., Edmonson, J.R., Heywood, V.H., Moore, D.M., Valentine, D.H., Walters, S.M. and Webb, D.A. (eds.) 1993. *Flora Europaea I: Pinoceae* 2nd edn. Cambridge: CUP.

Venkatesan, M.I., Linick, T.W., Suess, H.E., and Buccellati, G. 1982. Asphalt in carbon–14–dated archaeological samples from Terqa, Syria. *Nature*: 295, 11 February: 517–19.

Vieillescazes, C. and Coen, S. 1993. Caractérisation de quelques résines utilisées en Egypte ancienne, *Studies in Conservation*, 38: 255–64.

Vollesen, K. 1989. Burseraceae. In *Flora of Ethiopia* III (eds. I. Hedberg and S. Edwards). Addis Ababa, Asmara and Uppsala: Ethiopian Flora Project, pp. 442–78.

Warburg, E.F., 1968. *Cistus* L. In *Flora Europaea II: Cistaceae*. 1st edn (ed. V.H. Heywood; series eds T.G. Tutin, V.H. Heywood, N.A., Burges, D.M., Moore, D.H., Valentine, S.M. Walters and D.A. Webb). Cambridge: CUP, pp. 282–4.

White, R. 1990. Analysis of resinous materials. In *The Excavations of an Ancient Boat in the Sea of Galilee (Lake Kinneret)* (by S. Wachsmann). *'Atiqot* (English series), 19: 81–8.

Whitehouse, W.E. 1957. The pistachio nut – a new crop for the Western United States. *Economic Botany*, 11: 281–321.

Wreszinski, W. 1915. *Atlas zür Altaegyptischen Kulturgeschichte* I/2. Leipzig: J.C. Hinrichs.

Yaltirik, F. 1967. *Pistacia* L. In *Flora of Turkey* II (ed. P.H. Davis). Edinburgh: Edinburgh University Press, pp. 544–8.

Zaffran, J. 1990. *Contributions à la flore et à la vegetation de la Crete*. Aix en Provence: Publications de l' Université de Provence.

Zahran, M.A. and Willis, A.J. 1992. *The Vegetation of Egypt*. London: Chapman and Hall.

Zaitschek, D.V. 1980. Appendix A: plant remains from the Cave of the Treasure. In *The Cave of the Treasure: The Finds from the Caves in Nahal Mishmar* (P. Bar-Adon). Jerusalem: Israel Exploration Society, pp. 223–7.

Zaki, A. and Iskander, Z. 1943. Materials and methods used for mummifying the body of Amentefnekht, Saqqara 1941. *ASAE* 42: 223–55.

van Zeist, W. 1972. Palaeobotanical results of the 1970 season at Cayönü, Turkey. *Helinium*, 12: 3–19.

Zohary, M. 1940. Forests and forest remnants of *Pistacia atlantica* Desf. in Palestine and Syria. *Palestine Journal of Botany*, R Series, 3: 156–61.

1952. A monographical study of the genus *Pistacia*. *Palestine Journal of Botany*, J Series, 5: 187–228.

1972. *Flora Palaestina II: Text*. Jerusalem: The Israel Academy of Sciences and Humanities.

1973. *Geobotanical Foundations of the Middle East*, 2 vols. Stuttgart: Gustav Fischer.

19. Adhesives and binders

RICHARD NEWMAN AND MARGARET SERPICO

Introduction

A number of natural products found in the ancient world have adhesive properties and could have been used as such by the ancient Egyptians. Lucas (1962: 1–9) listed albumen (egg white), beeswax, glue, gum and resin as the most likely organic adhesives. Analyses since that time have indicated that oils and fats, honey, possibly plant nectars, and bitumen should be added to this list. Inorganic adhesives noted by Lucas, such as clay, gypsum, natron, solder and salt, are discussed elsewhere in this volume where more relevant. Some of the organic products covered here, such as beeswax, resin, oils and fats and bitumen, were used for other purposes and are considered in greater detail in Chapters 17 and 18 in this volume.

Materials and sources

Glue

Glue is an adhesive made from the protein collagen. Collagen, the primary structural protein of animals, is a major component of connective tissues (tendons, cartilage etc.), the principal protein found in skins and hides, and makes up nearly all of the organic part of bones (von Endt and Baker 1991: 157–9; MacGregor 1985: 2–4). The preferred sources of glue in ancient Egypt are not known, but obviously could have included various animals and fishes. Horse is a well-recognised modern source, but it is only after the Hyksos period that their numbers in Egypt increased, and certainly not to the extent that they were commonly available. Today, cow is frequently used, and rabbit-skin glue is also common (Hubbard 1962: 114). In ancient times, the raw materials may well have been obtained as part of the butchery process of domesticated or wild animals slaughtered for food (see Chapters 12 and 25, this volume). It should be noted that hooves and horns consist mainly of another protein, keratin, that is insoluble and cannot be utilised as an adhesive (MacGregor 1985: 20ff.). However, horn tissue grows over a bony core, thus it is possible that collagen could be derived from horn, although this source is considerably less suitable than the widely available more collagen-rich animal materials noted above.

Collagen also occurs in the skins, bones and some other tissues of fish. That made exclusively from the bladders is known today as isinglass, but that made from skins is clearest and of the finest grade (Gettens and Stout 1966: 23). For the best results, the fish should be of a non-oily variety and of a reasonable size, as production requires a ton of fish skins to yield some fifty gallons of liquid glue (Walsh 1962: 126). In current practice, dried and salted fish skins are stored until ready for processing, and the salt then removed (Walsh 1962: 126).

Preparation of glue solutions is simple, and ancient Egyptian methods probably were little different from those used later. To make these glues, the bones, hides, etc. should be cleaned of any extraneous matter and then boiled in water. The mixture should then be strained and cooled to a jellied consistency, and finally, dried to form an odourless, brittle mass, varying in colour from light to dark brown. This can be ground to a powder and mixed with warm water to form the adhesive. The solution must be used warm, since it will gel below about 30 °C. Dried animal glue may be kept indefinitely without any loss of adhesive capability (Hubbard 1962: 116). Fish glues are used while still in a liquid state. Any type of glue solution is prone to spoilage (Gettens and Stout 1966: 45; Walsh 1962: 127). While having poorer adhesive properties and an unpleasant odour, such a partially decomposed solution can still be suitable. One advantage of such partially decomposed glue is that it remains in solution at room temperature.

Animal glues can be mixed with fish glues (Hubbard 1962: 116; Walsh 1962: 127). Neither animal nor fish glue is soluble in oils or waxes, but glue can be combined with these other materials to form an emulsion.

Egg white and yolk

Eggs from wild birds, such as geese or ducks, were readily available in ancient Egypt but domestic chickens (*Gallus*

gallus) were not common until classical times (Lucas 1962: 2; see also Chapter 25, this volume). Egg white, yolk, or a mixture of both can be used as an adhesive or binder. The white is almost entirely made up of proteins. At one time, it was thought that egg white consisted exclusively of the protein albumen, which was used as synonymous with egg white by Lucas (1962: 1). It is now known that this protein (now called ovalbumin) makes up about two-thirds of the protein in egg white (Taborsky 1974: 34). Egg yolk is more complex in composition: about a third of the solids of egg yolk are made up of various proteins, the remainder mostly consisting of lipids, which include oil.

Egg white is a naturally stringy material, unsuitable for use as an adhesive since it cannot be spread easily with a brush. However, whipping of the white breaks up the stringy network of proteins. The liquid beneath the froth that is generated by whipping contains enough protein in solution to make a useful adhesive. Dried egg white can be put into solution, but it is likely that white would have been prepared fresh when needed. Egg yolk, taken out of the sac that contains it in the fresh egg, can be used directly as an adhesive, although it was probably normally diluted with water. Because of its oily component, egg yolk is insoluble after drying and thus should be prepared fresh when needed. Egg white and yolk can be mixed together and diluted with water for use as an adhesive.

Plant gums

Like resins and gum-resins, gums are exudates produced by a variety of trees and shrubs found throughout the world. Although gums, resins, and gum-resins differ in chemical composition, these terms are often used very loosely to describe any plant exudate, resulting in some confusion. For example, the term *aromatic gum* is often applied to scented resins or gum-resins, but in fact, as gums are usually both unscented and tasteless, they would not have been added to perfumes in order to impart a scent. However, as they can be viscous, they could have been used as a thickening agent in perfume or medicinal preparations. Similarly, because they are edible, gums would also be suitable for medicinal purposes. Above all, their sticky consistency would have made them ideal for use as adhesives.

Two genera produce the gums which were probably most widely available to the ancient Egyptians. These are *Acacia* spp. and *Astragalus* spp. Three other sources, locust bean gum, tamarind gum and cherry gum have also been mentioned in the published literature.

Plant gums can be divided into two broad groups: those that are soluble in water, and those that are insoluble. Gums in the latter category were at one time referred to as *bassorin* or *erasin* (Smith and Montgomery 1959: 9). Related to the gums in general composition are plant mucilages, which derive from seeds, flowers, stems, leaves or shoots of various plants.

Acacia gum
Acacia *spp.*
Family: Fabaceae
Acacias are generally small, fast-growing trees or shrubs with a spreading, flat-topped habit and very thorny branches. The leaves are small and the flowers clustered, commonly in racemes. The seed-bearing pods, which are often bean-like in appearance, can in certain species, twist and loop before ripening (Hepper 1992: 63). In some cases, (e.g. *Acacia senegal*), these pods can remain on the tree for several months (Howes 1949: 19; Thulin 1989: 78). Acacias usually favour *wadi* beds and gravelly soils (Hepper 1987: 78; Barakat 1995a: 164). Propagation can be carried out by seed, although Hepper noted these 'are often riddled with insects' (Hepper 1987: 78).

Some 130 species occur as part of the desert flora of Africa (Thulin 1989: 75) and, in one of the most comprehensive studies to date, Anderson (1978) listed some eighty-nine species of Acacia found throughout the world which produce gum. It is also clear that members of this genus have other valuable economic usages. Given the dearth of trees in Egypt, wood from species of acacia would have been of particular value for timber and for use as charcoal (Barakat 1995a: 164–5; van Zeist and de Roller 1993: 13; see also Chapter 15, this volume). It is no doubt also a reflection of their importance that archaeobotanical remains of acacias have been found in Egypt from Predynastic times onward (see Chapter 15, this volume).

The gum obtained from acacia species is soluble in water, forming for the most part, a transparent, viscous solution which can subsequently dry to hard tears (Mantell 1949: 12; Howes 1949: 5). The trees are tapped by incisions in the bark, with long strips of the bark then torn away. The gum collects in places along these wounds. In favourable conditions, the dried tears may be collected after about three weeks, but in poor weather it may take as long as two months for collection to be worthwhile (Howes 1949: 21). Subsequent collections from the same tree usually then take place at ten-day intervals. Tapping must be undertaken during the dry period (in Sudan from October to May or June of the following year), since the gum would dissolve in rain (Howes 1949: 21).

The best acacia gum is obtained from *Acacia senegal* Willd., which is widely distributed in eastern Africa as far north as Sudan (Howes 1949: 17; Thulin 1989: 78; Thulin *et al.* 1993: 370, 372; Brenan 1959: 92–3; Barakat 1995b: 105). The gum from this species is more commonly called *gum arabic*, as historically, major distribution was from Arabian ports (Howes 1949: 16). This shrub or small tree, reaching ten to fifteen metres in height, has white or cream flowers, and linear, dehiscent, yellow-brown or brown pods (Thulin 1989: 78). Its lifespan is only twenty-five to thirty years and apparently in the latter stages it is often subject to insect attack (Howes 1949: 19). Fortunately, the trees are not daunted by difficult environments and, despite their shrubby appearance, 'the largest quantities (of gum) are produced by plants growing under the most adverse conditions' (Twilley 1984: 360; also Glickman 1969: 97). The gum usually exudes in tears or ribbons, although the trees will not produce gum during cold weather (Twilley 1984: 360). According to modern sources (Gettens and Stout 1966: 28), gum arabic is manufactured by grinding the dried exudate to a powder and then slowly stirring it into boiling water at a ratio of one measure of gum to two of water. This mixture is then left to stand for at least a day and can subsequently be decanted for use.

While some two dozen or more species of acacia are indigenous to Sudan, this is the species tapped almost exclusively for commercial purposes today (Howes 1949: 17). Whether gum arabic, and/or any of the other Sudanese acacia gums were imported by the Egyptians is unknown, but contact between Egypt and Nubia is well documented. A number of species of acacia also grow in Egypt itself. Several of these have been mentioned as potential sources of gum (Fig. 19.1; Anderson 1978: 531; Twilley 1984: 382–5; Howes 1949: 20). However, details concerning the quantities produced are often lacking and it is clear that the quality of the gum may also vary. These factors make it likely that any list of sources would be subject to revision as further information becomes available. Nonetheless, a few of these relevant Egyptian acacias can be mentioned.

Notably, the tree *Acacia seyal* Del. is found in Egypt and is widely recognised as a productive source of gum, albeit of a lesser quality to *A. senegal*. Reaching a height of up to nine to ten metres, this tree has a flattened crown, bright yellow flowers, and curved, dehiscent pods somewhat constricted between the seeds (Thulin 1989: 85–6; Brenan 1959: 103; Germer 1985: 92). It has been suggested that the gum collected from this species is only from natural exudations and that tapping does not increase yield (Howes 1949: 20).

Gum could also have been obtained from *Acacia nilotica* (L.) Willd. ex Del. (see Hepper 1990: 22; Gettens and Stout 1966: 27–8), perhaps the best-known of all the Egyptian acacias. Finds of this acacia have been documented for much of Egyptian history (Keimer 1984: 19; Germer 1985: 90). For example, archaeobotanical remains (charcoal, pods), probably of this acacia, have been identified at Predynastic Maʾadi (Kroll 1989: 133; van Zeist and de Roller 1993: 3, 13). Sometimes represented in Egyptian reliefs (Germer 1985: 91), this tree is generally two and a half to fourteen metres high, with bright yellow flowers. The straight or slightly curved indehiscent pods are distinctively contricted between the seeds (Thulin 1989: 86–7).

The Egyptian *Acacia arabica* (Lam.) Willd. is distinguished by its yellow flowers and grey pods (Germer 1985: 92). Twilley (1984: 382) considered *A. arabica* to be synonymous with *A. nilotica* and Täckholm (1974: 290) noted that this species is also sometimes known as *A. nilotica* spp. *tomentosa* (Benth.). Brenan (1959: 111) considered *A. arabica* as synonymous with *A. nilotica* ssp. *leiocarpa* Brenan. Another subspecies, *A. arabica* var. *adansoniana* Dubard, also occurs in Egypt (Täckholm 1974: 290).

Howes (1949: 20) and Zohary (1972: 27) noted that some gum can be obtained from *Acacia albida* Del. (now also called *Faidherbia albida* (Del.) A.Chev., see Thulin 1989: 84; and Chapter 15, this volume), a tree reaching up to thirty metres in height, with white- or cream-coloured flowers, and curved, indehiscent pods of a bright orange or purplish-brown colour (Thulin 1989: 84; Brenan 1959: 78–9; Hepper 1992: 64; Germer 1985: 89). This species was not mentioned in Anderson's comprehensive list of gum sources (Anderson 1978: 531), but was included in Twilley's compendium of gum-yielding genera (Twilley 1984: 382).

Acacia tortilis (Forssk.) Hayne, a tree of some twelve to fourteen metres in height, has white- or cream-coloured flowers and twisted, yellow-brown pods which are indehiscent or gradually dehiscent (Thulin 1989: 87; Täckholm 1974: 290; Brenan 1959: 117–18; Germer 1985: 89). One subspecies, *A. tortillis* subsp. *raddiana* (Savi) Brennan (see Thulin *et al.* 1993: 380; Brenan 1959: 117), was listed as a separate species (= *A. raddiana* Savi) by Zohary (1972: 28) and Täckholm (1974: 290; see Fig. 15.1).

These sources are perhaps the most familiar acacias in Egypt today, but a number of other species are also known to provide acacia gum. Table 19.1 lists the acacias that commonly occur in Egypt and provides some information on their distribution. Brief mention should also be made of *Acacia farnesiana* Willd., discussed by Loret (1887: 39) but now considered to have been introduced to the Sudan (Keimer 1984: 22–3; Twilley 1984: 383; Germer 1985: 92). Thulin (1989: 86) stated that it was probably native to tropical America.

It should also be noted that many of the acacias found in Egypt, and other gum-producing members of this genus as well, occur elsewhere in the supposed sphere of Egyptian contact. As mentioned above, numerous species grow in Sudan, but a variety are also found in Somalia, Ethiopia, and Arabia (Thulin 1989: 78–0; Thulin *et al.* 1993: 370–82; Megahid 1978: 299–300; Brenan 1959: 78–129; Miller *et al.* 1996: 18–21). Moreover, certain acacias in Syria-Palestine also yield gum (Zohary 1972: 27–9; Mouterde 1970: 221). While it is unlikely that these foreign sources were the impetus for Egyptian trade with the outside world, some gums from these areas may have reached Egypt as supplementary items of commerce.

Gum tragacanth
*(*Astragalus *spp.)*
Family: Leguminosae

In contrast to acacia, tragacanth gum has no sources in Egypt and must have been obtained from certain wild species of the genus *Astragalus*, which are found in the dry, exposed slopes of Turkey, Syria–Palestine, Iraq and Iran, at altitudes between 1,200–2,100 m a.s.l. (Howes 1949: 39;

Table 19.1. *A list of acacias found in Egypt, with information on their distribution.*

Acacia species	***Modern distribution in Egypt***
A. seyal Del.	Rare. Nile Valley south of Qena.
A. nilotica (L.) Willd.	Common. Nile Valley; Western Desert including oases. Also found in Sinai.
A. arabica (Lam.) Willd. (syn. *A. nilotica* ssp. *tomentosa* (Benth.))	Rare. Nile Valley, south of Aswan.
A. albida Del (syn. *Faidherbia albida* (Del. A. Chev.))	Rare. Nile Valley including Delta and Faiyum; Eastern Desert.
A. tortilis (Forssk.) Hayne	Rare. Eastern Desert; Red Sea coast; Gebel Elba. Also found in Sinai.
A. raddiana Savi (syn. *A. tortilis* ssp. *raddiana* (Savi) Brenan)	Common. Nile Valley including Delta and Faiyum; all desert areas and oases; Gebel Elba; Red Sea coast; Sinai.
A. mellifera (Vahl) Benth.	Very rare. Eastern Desert; Red Sea coast, Gebel Elba.
A. laeta R. Br. ex Benth.	Rare. Nile Valley including Delta and Faiyum; oases in the Western Desert; Gebel Elba.
A. nubica Benth. (syn. *A. oerfota* (Forssk.) Schweinf.)	Very rare. Gebel Elba.
A. gerrardii Benth.	Very rare. North of Wadi Tumilat; Sinai.
A. erhenbergiana Hayne	Common. Nile Valley including Delta and Faiyum; all desert regios including oases. Sinai.
A. etbaica Schweinf.	Ver rare. Eastern desert; Red Sea coast; Gebel Elba.
A. asak (Forssk.) Wild (syn. *A. glaucophylla* Steud ex A. Rich.)	Very rare. Gebel Elba.

References: Täckholm 1974: 289–91; Boulos 1995: 74–5.

Hepper 1992: 148). In general, these are small, spiny shrubs about thirty to sixty centimetres tall (Gentry *et al.* 1992: 29). They feature clusters of small flowers, one-seeded pods, and sharp-tipped stalks which remain after the leaves have fallen (Gentry *et al.* 1992: 29; Hepper 1992: 148).

There are over 1,500 species of *Astragalus*, but of these, only about two dozen produce gum in Iran, and fewer still in Turkey (Dogan *et al.* 1985: 330). The taxonomy is often problematic and it has recently been noted that 'A new systematic revision . . . is badly needed' (Gentry *et al.* 1992: 29). Traditionally, the best gum-producing species was thought to be *Astragalus gummifer* Labill., found in forests, steppe and hill slopes in Turkey, Syria and Lebanon (Chamberlain and Matthews 1970: 121; Mouterde 1970: 349). However, it has been suggested that the primary sources are in fact *A. microcephalus* Willd., *A. gossypinus* Fischer and *A. echidnaeformis* Sirjaev (Dogan *et al.* 1985: 330; Gentry *et al.* 1992: 29). *A. gummifer* was considered a minor producer of a much poorer grade of gum (Dogan *et al.* 1985: 330; Gentry *et al.* 1992: 29).

From the distribution of these three other sources, only one species, *A. gossypinus*, would seem relevant. The nearest Mediterranean distribution of the cushion-shaped shrub *A. microcephalus* is in Turkey, but it only grows in the interior regions (Chamberlain and Matthews 1970: 132). Similarly, although *A. echidnaeformis* was noted by Gentry *et al.* (1992: 29), this species is not recorded in Turkey, Syria or Palestine. However, it is a significant source of gum in parts of Iran (Gentry 1957: 47). In constrast, *A. gossypinus* (syn. *A. gossipinoides* Hand.-Mazz), a dwarf shrub which is only about 10 to 15 cm in height, not only occurs in southern and eastern Turkey, northern Iran and Iraq, but also in Syria (Chamberlain and Matthews 1970: 142; Mouterde 1970: 351; Post and Dinsmore 1932: 394). In some areas of Iran, it is one of the most important commercial species (Gentry 1957: 49).

A few sources found closer to Egypt may also have been exploited. It has been noted, for example, that some gum can be obtained from *A. bethlehemicus* (Hepper 1992: 148; Zohary 1972: 78). This dwarf shrub grows in semi-steppe environments in Syria, Lebanon, Israel and Jordan (Mouterde 1970: 353; Zohary 1972: 77; Post and Dinsmore 1932: 397). Zohary noted that this species and another similarly small shrub, *A. cruentiflorus* Boiss., are tapped for gum in Palestine (Zohary 1972: 78; also Post and Dinsmore 1932: 396).

Several other gum-producing species with Mediterranean distributions have been noted as well (Gentry 1957: 50). *A. kurdicus* Boiss., for example, also furnishes a gum (Twilley 1984: 386; Howes 1949: 39; Gentry 1957: 50). This dwarf shrub, usually only 10 to 20 cm high, grows in Turkey (Chamberlain and Matthews 1970: 148), and Syria (Post and Dinsmore 1932: 397). *A. parnassi* Boiss. subsp. *cylleneus* (Boiss. and Heldr.) Hayek (syn. *A. cylleneus* Boiss. and Heldr.), is another dwarf shrub found in both Turkey and Greece, and the small shrub, *A. creticus* Lam., occurs in southern Turkey, Crete, and the Greek island of Samos (Chamberlain and Matthews 1970: 122, 166).

Although tragacanth gum can be obtained from spontaneous natural exudates or wounding of the trunk, the finest quality is furnished by tapping the roots. The best plants are smaller, cushion-like shrubs, ordinarily less than 30 cm in height (Gentry 1957: 41). The first tapping usually takes place after the plants are two years old, and they are generally productive for only about seven years (Howes 1949: 41). The season begins in June and can continue for several months, until the onset of the rainy season (Gentry 1957: 58; Hepper 1992: 148). To obtain the gum, the top 5 to 20 cm of earth are removed from the base of the plant stem, one or two longitudinal or cross-angled incisions are then made into the root, and a piece of wood positioned in the cut to keep it open (Mantell 1949: 16; Gentry 1957: 56; Howes 1949: 40; Hepper 1992: 148). Ribbons of gum will exude from the central gum cylinder in the root at a rate of about two and a half centimetres each half hour and, to preserve their purity and pale colour, are best collected fairly soon after tapping, perhaps only two days later (Howes 1949: 40; Gentry 1957: 43; Hepper 1992: 148). The highest quality of gum is produced from the first three collections undertaken within ten days of the initial cutting (Gentry 1957: 56). Alternatively, the roots can be repeatedly punctured to produce long thin pieces known commercially as 'vermicelli', doubtless because of their characteristic shape (Howes 1949: 41). Because of these more lengthy procedures, gum tragacanth has traditionally been more expensive and less widely used than gum arabic (Mills and White 1994: 77). Hepper noted that collection can also be difficult 'as the plants are scattered over the hillsides, and several species may occur, each with its own characteristic gum, which should not be mixed with another' (Hepper 1992: 148; see also Gentry 1957: 56). It is estimated that, on average, one plant can produce about 16.12 grams of gum per season, although local inhabitants in Iran claim this can reach as much as 30 gm (Gentry 1957: 62).

In contrast to the water-soluble acacia gum, tragacanth gum will generally absorb water and swell to form a viscous, thick, mucilaginous jelly but will not dissolve (Howes 1949: 5, 10). Because of this, only a small quantity of ground tragacanth mixed with water is necessary to produce the adhesive (Gettens and Stout 1966: 28). In modern technology, this gel must be strained through a cloth, and an homogenous consistency is not easily achieved (Gettens and Stout 1966: 28; Glickman 1969: 21). After standing for one or two days, the mixture will separate (Glickman 1969: 21; Howes 1949: 10). Research has indicated that the gum actually consists of two distinct water-soluble fractions and an insoluble one (Aspinall and Baillie 1963: 1708–14). At one time, the term *bassorin* was used to describe the major component of the insoluble fraction (Meer *et al.* 1973: 289).

Locust bean gum
Ceratonia siliqua *L.*
Family: Fabaceae
Both Glickman (1969: 131) and Mills and White (1994: 77) mentioned the use of this gum as a binder for mummy wrappings, but without citing a specific reference. It can also be used as a thickening agent in cosmetic and medicinal preparations (Germer 1985: 94). The gum is obtained from the brown seeds, similar in size and shape to those of watermelon, of the cultivated tree *Ceratonia siliqua* L., better known as the carob (Glickman 1969: 133). This evergreen tree (see Fig. 15.4) is indigenous to the eastern Mediterranean, although some archaeobotanical remains have been found in Egypt and it is cultivated there today (see Chapters 15 and 24, this volume). The oval, flattened seeds (about 8–9 mm long) are encased in brown pods which have been widely used as a food source (Howes 1949: 46). Within the seeds, the sticky component is found in the layer of white, semi-transparent endosperm between the central embryo and the dark seed coat (Glickman 1969: 133). For maximum viscosity, this hard layer must be separated and heated in water. However, not only is this separation difficult to achieve, but the necessary layer will also contains small amounts of insoluble matter and impurities (Howes 1949: 46; Glickman 1969: 135). Thus, it is only with 'the development of ingenious mechanical processes' that this has been accomplished to the extent that locust bean gum has become commercially viable (Howes 1949: 46).

Given these difficulties and the comparative ease of procuring gum from acacia and even tragacanth, it is highly unlikely that locust bean gum was widely used by the Egyptians. Further scientific research will be necessary to establish the extent of its use.

Tamarind gum
Tamarindus indica *L.*
Family: Fabaceae
Like locust bean gum, this product is obtained from the seeds located inside the large, indehiscent pods of the tree *Tamarindus indica* L. (Mills and White 1994: 77). The tamarind, an evergreen tree (three to twenty-four metres high), featuring oblong leaves and yellow flowers, is found in India and southeast Asia (Mills and White 1994: 77; Twilley 1984: 392). However, its indigeneity there has been questioned and the tree is now believed to be native to tropical Africa (Thulin 1989: 66; Thulin *et al.* 1993: 358). It occurs today in Somalia and Ethiopia and is frequently cultivated (Thulin 1989: 66; Thulin *et al.* 1993: 358). Although chemical analysis of some ancient Egyptian samples has indicated the possible presence of tamarind gum, (see p. 488), the results were not exclusive of other sources and thus, the possibility that this product was used in Pharaonic times remains speculative.

Cherry gum
Prunus *spp.*
Family: Rosaceae
Chemical analysis has led to the possibility that this gum may have been used by the ancient Egyptians. However, the suggestion that the source may have been *Prunus serrulata* (Masschelein-Kleiner *et al.* 1968: 110, see discussion p. 488) would seem unlikely as this tree, more commonly

known as the Japanese cherry, would not have been available in the Pharaonic period. Wild cherries (*P. fruticosa* Pallas) do occur in Europe and northern Turkey, but it is doubtful that these were cultivated until the Classical period (Zohary and Hopf 1993: 171–2).

Interestingly, despite their botanical differences, gums obtained from a variety of fruit trees have also been called cherry gum or *Bassora* gum (Howes 1949: 78; Twilley 1984: 366). These include almond (*P. dulcis* (Miller) D.A. Webb), apricot (*P. armeniaca* L. syn. *Armeniaca vulgaris* Lam.), plum (*P. domestica* L.) and peach (*Persica vulgaris* Miller, syn. *Prunus persica* (L.) Batch). However, like cherry, it is unlikely that plum, apricot or peach were cultivated prior to classical times (Zohary and Hopf 1993: 169–72; Howes 1949: 78; Twilley 1984: 390–1), although there is some evidence that almond was available during the Late Bronze Age (see Chapter 17, this volume). In general, these gums are darker in colour, less soluble, and 'inferior in adhesive properties' to acacia gum (Howes 1949: 78).

Other plant gums or mucilages

Masschelein-Kleiner *et al.* (1968: 110) suggested plantain as a possible source of sugars found in an adhesive. Seeds of various members of the plantain family (*Plantago* spp.) supply mucilages (Smith and Montgomery 1959), but nothing is known otherwise of their use for this purpose in ancient Egypt.

Honey and plant sugars

These materials are mentioned here since a few identifications of their uses as adhesives or binders have been made in literature since the fourth edition of Lucas (see discussion p. 488). Lucas (1962: 25–6) considered honey to have been the only source of sugar in ancient Egypt, and its use there has long been documented (Chapter 24, this volume). Other sweeteners mentioned by Lucas (1962: 27) are grape and date juices. Juices from other fruits, of course, are also sweet and contain natural sugars.

Starch

Starch occurs as small granules in roots, bulbs, tubers and seeds of plants. It has been used as an adhesive by other cultures, but there are no indications that it served this purpose in ancient Egypt.

Beeswax

Beeswax was utilised for a number of purposes in ancient Egypt (see Chapter 17 in this volume for a more thorough discussion). For example, it was often used to model figures and was also employed in the mummification process. Lucas cited a few examples of Middle Kingdom and New Kingdom date where wax had been used as an adhesive (Lucas 1962: 2–3). Details on the composition and production of beeswax are given in Chapter 17 in this volume.

Oils and fats

These substances were well-known in ancient Egypt as components in the formulation of scented cosmetics and were also used as the fuel for lamps. Some of the oils known to the ancient Egyptians, such as linseed and poppyseed, are capable of drying to form solid films and could have been used as adhesives or binders. Both of these oils were widely used as paint media in modern times (Mills and White 1994: 171–2).

Because animal fat is solid at room temperature but can be liquified with mild heating, a warmed animal solution could have been used as an adhesive. However, there is virtually no evidence for the use of either oils or fat as an adhesive in Pharaonic Egypt. The compositions and sources of oils and fats are discussed in Chapter 17 of this volume.

Natural resins and bitumen

Resins from northeastern Africa and the Mediterranean were widely used by the Egyptians as incense and in the manufacture of scented cosmetics (see Chapter 18, this volume). In addition, there is some evidence that they were also applied as adhesives, perhaps as early as the First Dynasty (Lucas 1962: 7–8). Bitumen was imported to Egypt from Western Asia during the Pharaonic period and, by the Early Bronze Age, was often used in Syria–Palestine and Iraq as an adhesive and fixative (see Chapter 18, this volume). This increases the possibility that bitumen may have been employed for similar purposes in Egypt, although evidence for this is still lacking. The compositions and sources of these materials are discussed in Chapter 18 of this volume.

Evidence from ancient Egypt

Representations showing the application of adhesives are rare. One scene which has been interpreted as such comes from the Eighteenth Dynasty tomb of Rekhmira at Thebes (TT100). Davies interpreted the scene as the spreading of glue onto the surface of a box prior to gilding (Davies 1943: 51, pl. LV). The adhesive seems to be prepared first by grinding it into a powder and then heating it over a fire. From this, it would seem that the adhesive was more likely to have been an animal glue heated in water than an acacia gum. The latter would also have been heated in water, but usually then left to stand. In this scene, the glue is applied with a brush. Today, in some instances hairs can still be seen in remains of adhesive on some Egyptian objects, notably between lids and cases of New Kingdom and Third Intermediate period coffins.

Davies (1943: 51) suggested that the glue in the Rekhmira scene was ground with a red (sandstone?) rubber. While the material used for the rubber is uncertain, it can be observed that some residues of ancient Egyptian adhesives in museum collections have a noticeably pink colour. These are generally powdery in consistency and may be the remains of a gesso, perhaps intentionally tinted, although more research is necessary to determine the precise composition.

Composition and analysis of organic adhesives and their detection in ancient Egyptian materials

Glue

Composition and analysis

Like all proteins, collagen is a natural polymer formed from amino acids. A single molecule of a particular protein can be made up of several hundred to thousands of individual amino acid molecules. There are nearly two dozen common naturally-occurring amino acids, some of which are shown in Figure 19.1. Individual proteins can be distinguished from each other in several ways: by their molecular weights, by their physical structures, and by the types and relative amounts of different amino acids contained in them (Table 19.2). Collagens from different animal and fish sources can vary to some extent in molecular weight as well as in their quantitative amino acid compositions (Kulonen and Pikkarainen 1970: 82ff.). Preparation methods can also affect molecular weights, since more extensive boiling can cause breakdown in the collagen strands; as already mentioned, bio-deterioration, to which collagen solutions are quite susceptible, also reduces strand lengths.

(+)-Aspartic acid	Asp D	$HOOCCH_2CHOO^-$ $^{+}NH_3$
(+)-Glutamic acid	Glu E	$HOOCCH_2CH_2CHOO^-$ $^{+}NH_3$
(-)-Hydroxyproline	Hyp	HO, 4, COO-, N, H, H (ring structure)
(-)-Serine	Ser S	$HOCH_2CHOO^-$ $^{+}NH_3$
Glycine	Gly G	CH_2COO $^{+}NH_3$
(+)-Alanine	Ala A	CH_3CHCOO^- $^{+}NH_3$
(-)-Proline	Pro P	4, COO-, N, H, H (ring structure)
(-)-Leucine	Leu L	$(CH_3)_2CHCH_2CHCOO^-$ $^{+}NH_3$
(-)-Phenylalanine	Phe F	CH_2CHCOO^- (on benzene ring) $^{+}NH_3$

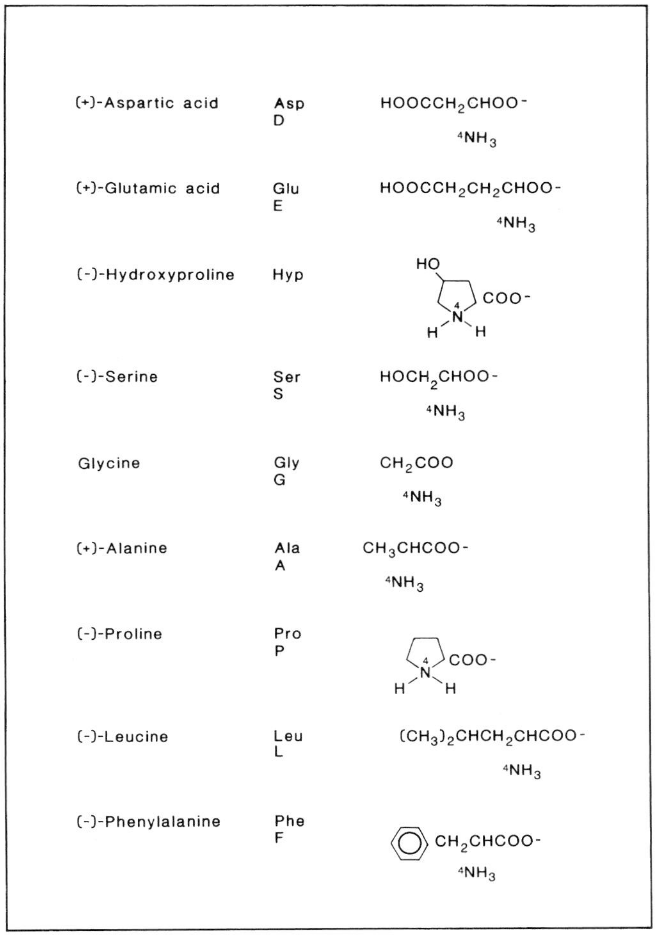

Figure 19.1 Structures of some amino acids.

Identification of collagen in samples from archaeological artefacts can be carried out in several ways. FT-IR spectrometry (discussed in Chapter 18, this volume) can detect protein, but cannot distinguish between different proteins; a further limitation of this technique is that inorganic materials (pigments etc.) often complicate interpretation of the sample spectrum, and may even completely mask contribution from the organic component(s) of a sample.

In studies of archaeological and art objects, one major approach to specific protein identification involves amino acid analysis. Collagen, like other proteins, can be chemically broken down by heating in weak acid solution or exposing to acid vapours (procedures known as hydrolysis) into amino acids. The amino acids liberated by this treatment can then be separated and the relative amounts of each in a particular sample determined by chromatography.

In thin layer chromatography (TLC), small spots of the amino acid solution are positioned near the bottom of a specially-coated inert plate (glass or plastic). The plate then is placed in a solvent chamber, with a small amount of solvent (or a solvent mixture) in the bottom. The solvent is wicked up the plate, dissolving and carrying the amino acids in the sample spot along with it. The different amino acids travel up the plate at varying rates. After drying, the plate is sprayed with a reagent that produces coloured spots on the plate, or spots that are visible under ultraviolet light. Amino acids that are most abundant produce stronger, or more dense, spots on the chromatography plate; the colours produced by different acids can also vary. Specific amino acids and reference proteins are run simultaneously with samples and the patterns compared for identification of the unknown (Striegel and Hill 1996: 39–45). Related to TLC is paper chromatography, in which separation is carried out on a strip of paper; this technique is not often utilised today.

Gas chromatography, a technique described in Chapter 17 of this volume with respect to analysis of oils and fats, can also be applied to analysis of amino acids (Schilling *et al.* 1996; Schilling and Khanjian 1996). Sample preparation is more complex than with TLC, since the amino acids liberated by hydrolysis must be reacted with certain chemicals to produce new compounds (derivatives) that are

Table 19.2. *Amino acid compositions of some proteins and other materials used in adhesives.*

Amino acid	Collagen (glue)*	Egg white*	Egg yolk*	Casein*	Rice starch†	Gum arabic†	Gum tragacanth†
Glycine	24.7	3.6	3.5	1.7	12.7	7.7	5.8
Alanine	10.1	6.3	5.6	2.7	10.5	4.7	5.7
Valine	2.2	8.3	6.4	7.2	5.6	2.9	8.3
Leucine	3.7	10.3	9.2	9.0	6.9	5.2	4.9
Isoleucine	1.2	6.2	5.1	6.0	5.3	1.0	3.2
Proline	13.0	4.5	4.5	13.2	7.4	9.0	9.0
Phenylalanine	1.6	5.2	3.9	5.1	3.0	1.1	3.5
Tyrosine	0.0	1.4	2.8	5.5			
Serine	4.0	5.8	9.1	4.0	8.3	16.5	11.6
Threonine	2.2	3.7	5.6	2.7	6.0	7.3	4.4
1/2 cystine	0.0	1.9	1.9	0.0			
Methionine	1.4	1.2	2.3	2.3	1.7	0.0	0.0
Arginine	8.2	6.8	5.5	4.0			
Histidine	1.5	2.4	2.4	3.6			
Lysine	4.1	8.0	5.7	6.7	2.1	3.1	5.6
Aspartic acid	5.0	10.5	11.5	6.1	14.5	7.6	8.3
Glutamic acid	9.7	13.9	15.0	20.2	16.1	4.6	5.8
Hydroxyproline	7.4	0.0	0.0	0.0	0.0	29.2	24.0

Data souces: *J. Mills and R. White 1994: 86 and references therein. †M. Schilling *et al.* 1996: 51.
Amino acid amounts are given as weight percentages, calculated so that all of the analysed amino acids give a total of 100%. Note that the analyses of starch and the gums did not include all of the amino acids analysed for the four proteins; blanks are left for amino acids not analysed.

amenable to GC analysis. Determination of the relative amounts of different amino acids in a given sample, of which there may up to nearly twenty different types, can be more accurately carried out by this instrumental technique than by TLC, which generally cannot fully resolve the entire range of amino acids present in protein-containing binders or adhesives.

Currently, the most common instrumental technique for amino acid analysis is high performance liquid chromatography (HPLC). In this technique, the mixture of amino acids is carried in solution through a stainless steel column, usually 15–30 cm long, that is packed with small spherical particles of a solid resin (of which there are various types). As with GC, amino acids usually need to be derivatised before they can be analysed by HPLC. The derivatives of different amino acids travel at various rates through the column, thus reaching the instrument's detector at different times after sample injection. There are several available HPLC amino acid analysis procedures. Analysis of paint samples that contain various inorganic materials (pigments) can produce somewhat anomalous results, but separation of pigments from organic binder is not feasible with very small samples, such as can typically be taken from artefacts. Thus, interpretation of results needs to take maximum account of the influences of specific inorganic materials on the observed amino acid profile. Identification of glue in an ancient adhesive sample involves matching the amino acid profile of the sample with modern collagen. Based on analysis of some ancient Egyptian samples, collagen seems to survive in virtually unaltered state, so the effects of ageing, at least in the case of this material in typical Egyptian burial environments, seem unimportant with respect to identification. HPLC can produce excellent quantitative results (Halpine 1992; Halpine 1995). However, since the amino acid compositions of collagens from different sources are fairly similar, it has yet to be proven that specific sources of a collagen sample from an archaeological object can be positively determined by amino acid analysis alone. A specialised form of liquid chromatography, a dedicated *amino acid analyser*, has also been utilised in some studies. More recently, amino acid analyses have typically been carried out with HPLC systems that have been configured to separate and detect these compounds.

Two other modern analytical approaches have been taken, with regard to the analysis of glue in ancient artefacts, and these approaches are also applicable to all other organic adhesives. Both involve pyrolysis, which is rapid controlled heating of a solid samples to a high temperature at which the organic molecules of the binder chemically break down into smaller fragments (Wampler 1995). Under carefully controlled pyrolysis conditions, the fragmen-

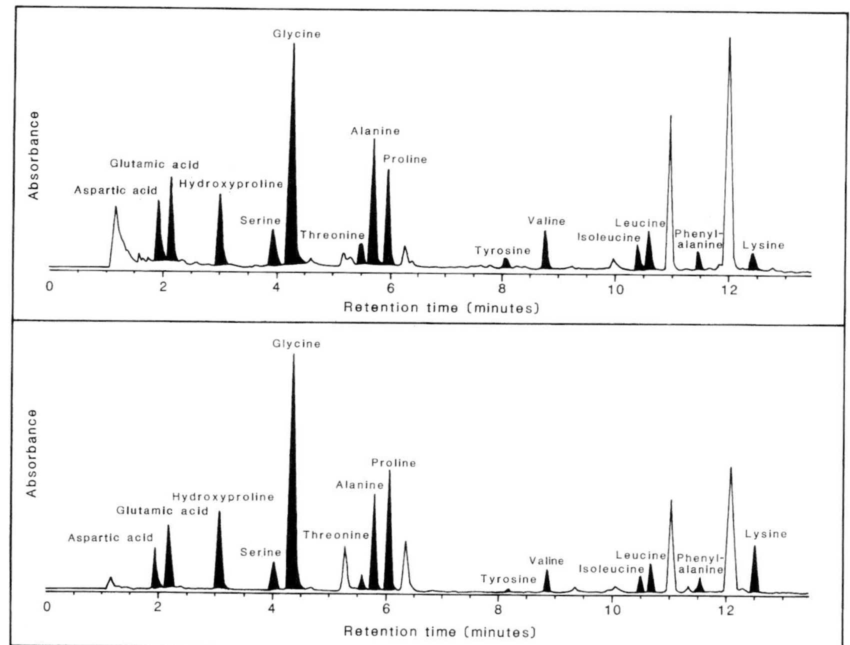

Figure 19.2 Chromatograms from amino acid analysis of reference collagen (top) and a sample of paint from a wooden sculpture (bottom) from Deir el-Bersha (Table 19.4, no. 12). Analysis carried out by high performance liquid chromatography (phenylthiocarbonyl derivatives).

tation procedure is reproducible, and interference from pigments can be minimised. The fragments produced by pyrolysis can then be analysed by two different techniques. In one technique, the pyrolysis device is connected to a gas chromatograph, and the fragments are separated in the GC (pyrolysis-GC or Py-GC). The resulting chromatogram can contain dozens (even hundreds) of different peaks; identification of an unknown sample is based on the comparison of its chromatogram with chromatograms of pyrolysed standard reference binders or adhesives. In the second case, the pyrolysis device is connected to a mass spectrometer, which separates the fragments by mass (Py-MS). The result is compared to mass spectra generated by analysis of reference binders under the same conditions. Pyrolysis can be carried out rapidly, or it can be carried out more slowly, the pyrolysis temperature being ramped from a relatively low beginning point to a high final temperature. In the latter case, mass spectra from different stages of pyrolysis (that is, pyrolysis fragments generated at different temperatures) can be acquired, providing some separation of data, which can make interpretation of results more straightforward, particularly in the case of complex samples that may contain more than one adhesive and pigments. Both Py-GC and Py-MS can be used to identify proteins, but only applications of Py-GC to ancient Egyptian samples have been published to date. Both pyrolysis procedures seem to be capable of distinguishing different proteins from one another. Once again, while collagen can be specifically identified, the source of the collagen cannot be determined.

Detection in ancient Egyptian samples

Only a few identifications of glue in ancient Egyptian artefacts have been published since the fourth edition of Lucas. Paint from the Old Kingdom tomb of Nefer at Saqqara was said to be bound with glue (LeFur 1994: 59); identification technique(s) were not noted (the reported analysis is from an unpublished thesis). The white ground on a wooden Romano–Egyptian sarcophagus was identified by pyrolysis GC as glue (Shedrinsky 1989: 402–3); paint from the same sarcophagus was identified by TLC and GC as bound with glue (Striegel and Hill 1996: 43–4). An adhesive on a very late (third to fourth century AD) fabric painting was identified by amino acid analysis in an automatic amino acid analyser (Sack *et al.* 1981: 20–2). Glue was also identified as an adhesive used to hold the outer linen fabric wrappings of a Roman period mummy together using paper chromatography and automatic amino acid analysis (Benson *et al.* 1979: 124). Glue has also been identified as the medium of a Fayum-region mummy portrait from the second quarter of the third century AD (Alexopoulou-Agoranon *et al.* 1997: 90). Identification was based on solubility tests (it was noted that the paint was insoluble in chloroform, which would dissolve wax, but swelled in water); a sample was also tested with a biological stain that reacts with proteins.

Glue was tentatively identified in the light blue fill in cloissons on the gold collar of a Nubian stone alabastron dating to the seventh century BC (Newman 1994: 35–6). Identification was by HPLC amino acid analysis. However, the amino acid profile was not a very good match for collagen, suggesting that another amino acid-containing material could also be present. The material was tinted with

Table 19.3. *Monosaccharide and uronic acid compositions of some gums and mucilages.*

	Arabinose	Rhamnose	Galactose	Glucose	Mannose	Xylose	Fucose	Glucuronic acid	Galacturonic acid
Acacia senegal[**]	++	+	++					+	
Acacia seyal[*]	++	+	++					+	
Acacia nilotica[*]	++	++					+		
Acacia arabica[*]	++		++				+		
Gum tragacanth[†]	+		+			+	+		+
Apricot gum[‡]	++		++		+			+	
Cherry gum[**]	++		+		+	+		+	
Tamarind seed gum[††]	+		+			+		+	+
Locust beam[**]			+		++				

'++' indicates a major component; '+' indicates a minor component.
Sources of data: [*]Anderson and Karamalia 1966: 763. [†]Aspinall and Baillie 1963: 1702–14. [‡]Twilley 1984: 381. [**]Mills and White 1994: 77. [††]Whistler and BeMiller 1973: 398. Note that some of the above analyses are of heterogeneous materials; some gums contain seveal polysaccharides that have quite distinct compositions.

calcite and Egyptian blue. This latter analysis serves as an example of how caution is necessary in interpreting results, even those in which quantitative amino acid analysis is carried out. Most organic materials contain at least small amounts of amino acids. The burial environment, handling or treatment of the object from which a sample was taken can contribute amino acids, as can other organic materials that may have part of the original sample. Thus, interpretation of a result may not be straightforward.

Glue has been identified in paint and ground samples from a number of painted wood artefacts from the Museum of Fine Arts, Boston (Table 19.4; Newman and Halpine in press). All of these analyses have been carried out by HPLC, specifically using the *PicoTag* procedure, developed and marketed by Waters Chromatography (Milford, Massachusetts, USA). A typical chromatogram is shown in Figure 19.2, along with a chromatogram of modern reference collagen. In a number of samples, the amino acid patterns were very close to those of modern collagen. In others, collagen appeared to be present, but apparently with some other source or sources of amino acids. In still other instances, the amino acid profile could not be correlated with any reference binder.

While the number of analyses carried out since the fourth edition of Lucas are comparatively few, it is clear that glue was a major adhesive that served many purposes in ancient Egypt. However, caution should be exercised in interpretation of identifications of glue, perhaps more than in the case of the other ancient adhesives discussed in this chapter. Glue or gelatin (essentially identical in composition to glue, but a purer material since it is manufactured under more stringent processing conditions and control than glues) are still commonly used as adhesives in conservation procedures, including setting down of flaking paint or consolidation of powdery paint. There is no common analytical method by which modern glue or gelatin can be distinguished from ancient glue (ancient glues often contain a small amount of lipid, which would not be present in modern glue or gelatin, but since lipids are present in other materials, detection of lipid in a glue sample cannot be taken as proof that the glue is ancient). An originally glue-bound paint sample consolidated with glue during a conservation procedure would obviously show the amino acid profile of collagen, but it could not be concluded from the analysis that glue was the original binder in the sample.

Egg white and yolk

Composition and analysis

All of the techniques applicable to the analysis of the protein collagen, discussed above, can also be applied to the analysis of egg. Amino acid analysis can reliably point to the use of egg, but since the amino acid profiles of egg white and yolk proteins are similar to one another, yolk and white cannot be distinguished with great confidence by amino acid analysis alone. The major protein of egg white, ovalbumin, is present in hen's eggs and wild bird eggs. While ovalbumin from these different sources varies somewhat in amino acid composition and probably structure (Taborsky 1974: 36), it does not appear that amino acid analysis can reliably distinguish between egg white from different bird sources, nor likely could yolk from different bird's eggs be distinguished. As already mentioned, about two-thirds of egg yolk solids consist of lipids. About two-thirds of these lipids are triglycerides, the same kinds of molecules that occur in vegetable oils and animal fats. Analysis of this portion of the yolk can be carried out by the same methods used to analyse oil and fats, as discussed in Chapter 17 in this volume.

In the case of egg proteins, some techniques not applicable to collagen can potentially be used for specific identification. Fluorescent antibodies can in principal specifically identify ovalbumin (for example, see Kockaert *et al.* 1989: 183–8). Aged samples can present difficulties; it is not clear whether this procedure could produce a useful result for samples of ancient Egyptian age. A novel staining procedure based on detection of a very minor component of egg white, avidin, has been published (Wolbers 1988: 249–50), but once again it is not certain that this procedure could be successfully applied to quite old samples.

Detection in ancient Egyptian samples

In recent research on paintings from the tomb of Nefertari (QV66), it was observed that coatings (or varnishes) had been applied selectively to the surfaces, particularly on red and yellow colours. In some samples of these coatings, synthetic resin (clearly from a restoration campaign) was found, in others natural resin. Egg white was identified in one sample (Stulik *et al.* 1993: 63). Identification of egg white was by a microchemical test, which presumably established the presence of protein, followed by HPLC amino acid analysis. Analysis of the paint from this tomb showed that the binder was gum. It is not certain whether the egg white was a restoration material. If the egg white *varnish* is original, the selective use of the material could have been to produce different degrees of glossiness in various passages of the painting. Apparently a natural resin was also used for the same purpose on some areas of the paintings (see Chapter 18, this volume).

The only other reasonably reliable identification of an egg binder in ancient Egypt is from a mummy portrait of the fourth-century AD in the collection of the Petrie Museum (UC14768). Egg yolk was identified as the binder by GC analysis of the lipid (oil) fraction (Ramer 1979: 6–7), which showed a pattern characteristic of the non-drying oil in egg yolk.

Plant gums and mucilages, honey and plant nectars or juices

Composition and analysis

Plant gums and mucilages are polysaccharides, or large, complex molecules formed by bonding together simple sugars (monosaccharides) and, in many cases, sugar acids. Hundreds or even thousands of simple sugar molecules may be bonded together to form a single gum molecule. Typically plant gums that contain sugar acids exist as salts of those acids (usually calcium or magnesium salts). The molecules in gums from different plants vary in terms of

(1) their size,
(2) the identity and relative amounts of the monosaccharides and sugar acids found in them, and
(3) the manner in which these small molecules are bonded together to form the polysaccharide molecule.

Chemical breakdown of gums by heating in acid solution (hydrolysis) yields monosaccharides (simple sugars) and, when present, sugar acids (uronic acids). There are only about six common monosaccharides found in plant gums; a typical gum may contain from two to four or five different monosaccharides. In addition, although there are two common types of sugar acids found in gums, the two almost never occur together in a single gum. Figure 19.3 shows the structures of the monosaccharides and sugar acids. Table 19.3 lists the monosaccharides and sugar acids that have been identified in various polysaccharides.

Analysis of gums can be carried out by several methods. Earlier identifications were often based exclusively on microchemical reactions (e.g. Feigl 1960: 425–6; Stulik and Florsheim 1992: 278–9). While simple to carry out and reasonably sensitive, these tests could *point to the presence* of plant gum, but they cannot positively *prove* it. FT-IR spectrometry, in circumstances where there is no significant interference from inorganic materials (such as pigments), can indicate the presence of plant gum. While there are some differences in the spectra of different gums, in general this technique is restricted to simply

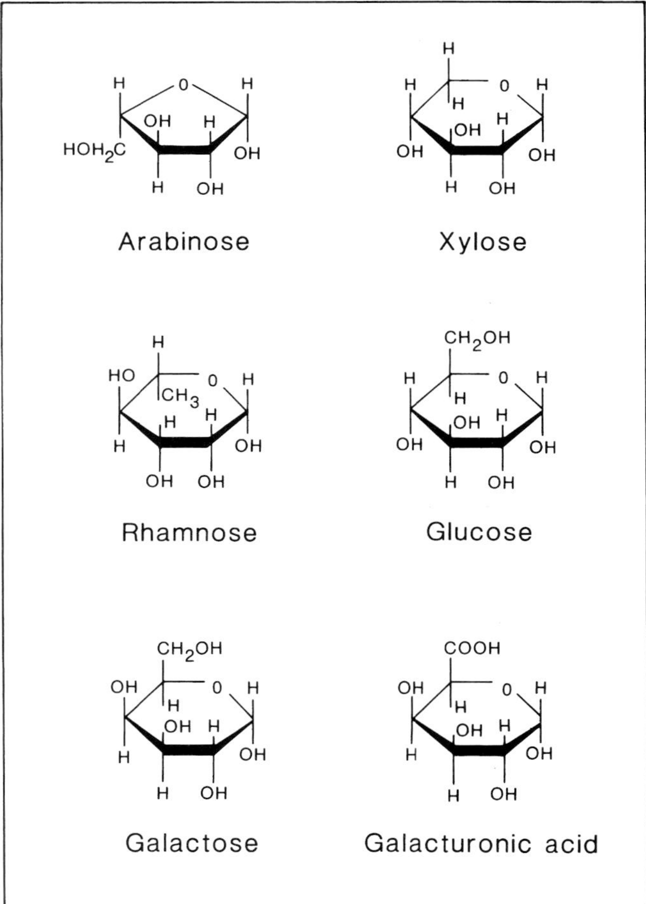

Figure 19.3 Structure of some monosaccharides and uronic acid.

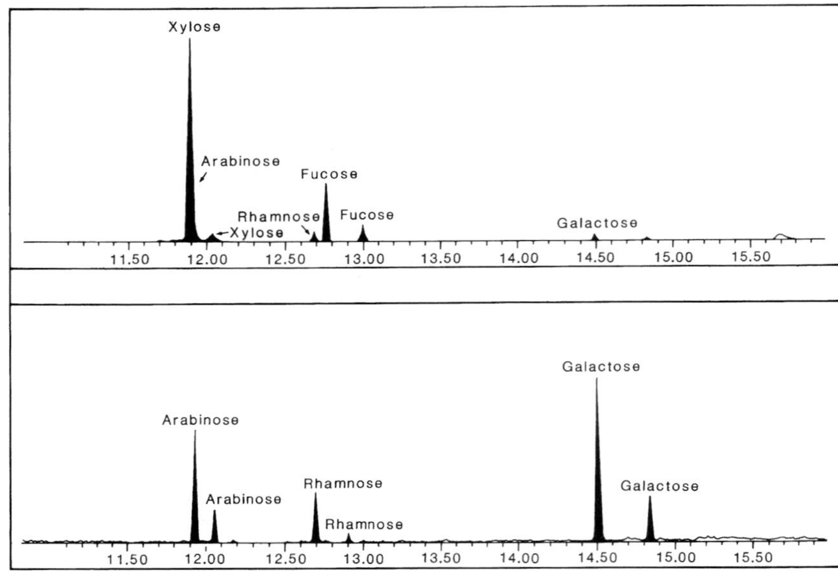
Xylose
Arabinose
Fucose
Rhamnose
Fucose
Xylose
Galactose
11.50 12.00 12.50 13.00 13.50 14.00 14.50 15.00 15.50
Galactose
Arabinose
Rhamnose
Galactose
Arabinose
Rhamnose
11.50 12.00 12.50 13.00 13.50 14.00 14.50 15.00 15.50

(a)

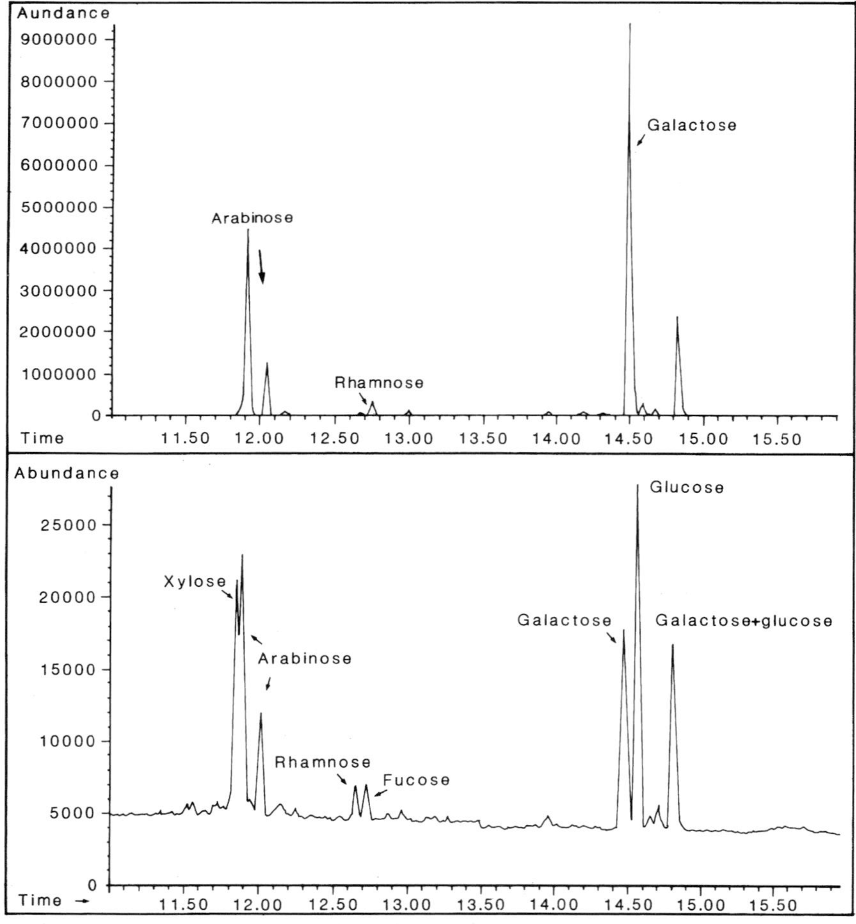
Adhesive from linen wrapping on goose mummy.
Aundance
9000000
8000000
7000000
6000000
5000000
4000000
3000000
2000000
1000000
0
Galactose
Arabinose
Rhamnose
Time
11.50 12.00 12.50 13.00 13.50 14.00 14.50 15.00 15.50
Abundance
25000
20000
15000
10000
5000
0
Glucose
Xylose
Galactose
Galactose+glucose
Arabinose
Rhamnose
Fucose
Time
11.50 12.00 12.50 13.00 13.50 14.00 14.50 15.00 15.50

(b)

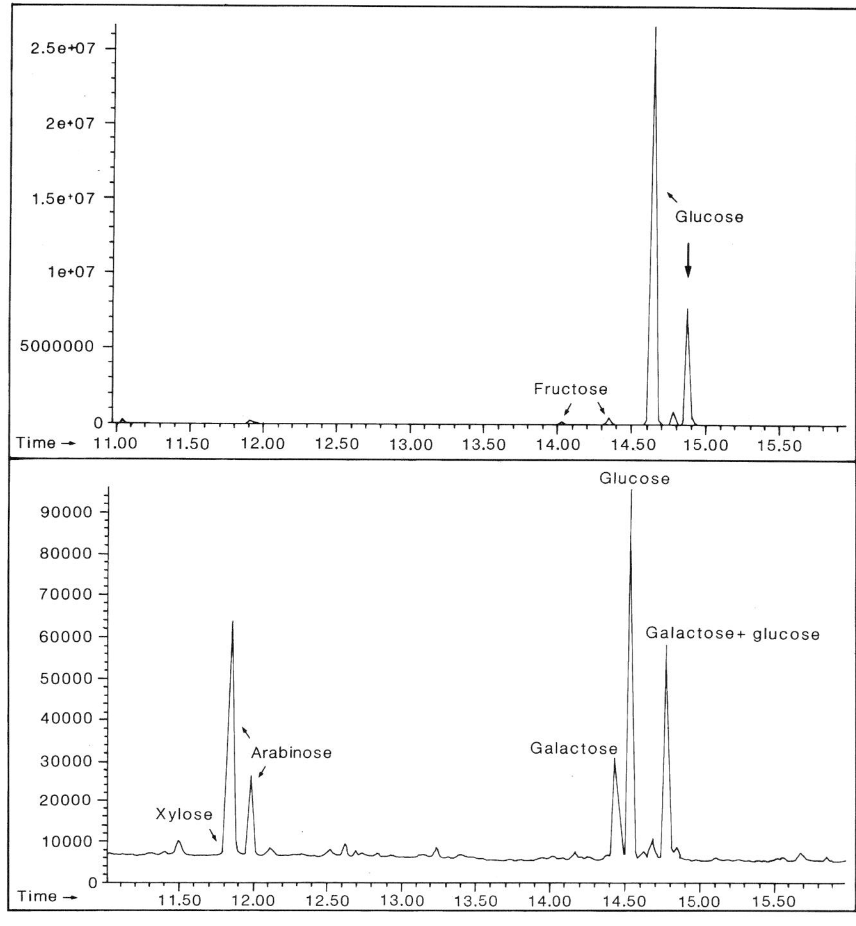

Figure 19.4 Chromatograms from monosaccharide analysis of two reference gums and some samples from ancient Egyptian objects. Analysis by GC/MS (oxiome/ trimethylsilyl derivatives) (a) Top: gum arabic (Acacia senegal); *bottom: gum tragacanth (botanical source uncertain); (b) Top: Blue paint from falcon (Table 19.4, no. 22); bottom: Red paint from painted wood fragment (Table 19.4, no. 32); (c) Top: Adhesive from wrappings on goose mummy (Table 19.4, no. 18); bottom: Yellow paint from canopic chest (Table 19.4, no. 28).*

indicating that a gum is present. Examples of the detection of gum by FT-IR spectrometry in ancient Egypt paints include LeFur (1994) and Newman (1993: 63).

The same instrumental analysis techniques that currently are applied to the identification of proteins can be applied to plant gums. Hydrolysis of a gum into its constituent monosaccharides and sugar acids can be followed by TLC, GC or HPLC analysis. Of these three procedures, HPLC has been very rarely utilised to date, perhaps primarily because the sample sizes for most of the standard sugar analysis procedures are relatively large. TLC can separate some of the monosaccharides as well as the common sugar acids (for example, Striegel and Hill 1996: 47–51). GC can be used for monosaccharide analysis (Erhardt *et al.* 1988: 74, 82), although it is possible to detect sugar acids with some sample preparation procedures (e.g. Bleton *et al.* 1996: 95–108).

Although only a handful of specific simple sugars go into the makeup of plant gums, the specific combinations of sugars and variations in their relative amounts are often distinctly different in gums from separate genera, for example between acacias and gum tragacanth. However, in some cases gums from different genera could have quite similar compositions.

Different species within a specific genus may also have rather similar compositions, as with the acacias. Because of overlaps in compositions, specific gum identifications are much more difficult to carry out than specific protein identifications. A further limitation comes from the fact that relatively few gums have been analysed; for example, the compositions of considerably less than half of the acacia species from which gums in ancient Egypt could have derived have been published.

Pyrolysis techniques can also be utilised to analyse plant gums. At least some distinctions between different specific gums can be made by pyrolysis GC (Derrick and Stulik 1990). Pyrolysis-mass spectrometry (Py-MS) has been applied as a means of distinguishing between the presence of gums, waxes, resin and some other materials in cartonnage samples (Wright and Wheals 1987); the possibility of distinguishing between different gums was not explored.

Another possible source, honey, is a dissaccharide: each molecule in honey is made up of two different simple sugar molecules bonded together. Neither monosaccharide found in honey (fructose and glucose) is more than a very minor component of plant gums. For this reason, the simultaneous presence of these two sugars in a sample has been used as an indication of the presence of honey. By GC analysis, honey was identified as the binder in a paint sample from a Twenty-first-Dynasty sarcophagus in the collection at Antwerp (Masschelein-Kleiner 1968: 107–10); the presence of fructose and glucose was taken as an indication that honey was one component of an adhesive sample from the same object. Cane sugar is made up of the same disaccharide as honey, although this type of sugar was not available until a much later period in Egypt.

Grape and date juices, and other fruit juices, also contain sucrose, but may contain the monosaccharides fructose or glucose in varying amounts.

Detection in ancient Egyptian materials

Paint from stone columns and blocks in the temple at Karnak dating from a wide range of periods (Eighteenth Dynasty, Nineteenth Dynasty, Ptolemaic and Coptic) were bound with plant gum. An initial publication stated that this was probably an acacia gum (Vieillescazes and Lefur 1991: 97–8), while a later publication, apparently reporting the same data, specifically identified the gum as *Acacia nilotica* (Lefur 1994). Identification was by IR spectrometry and TLC. Realistically, the analyses that were carried out cannot point specifically to this particular species of gum, although they would be able to indicate that it was a possibility.

Wall paintings from the Nineteenth-Dynasty tomb of Nefertari (QV66) in Thebes were found to be bound with a gum, by means of analysis utilising TLC and HPLC (Stulik *et al.* 1993: 63–5). The gum was identified as an *Acacia*, specifically a species that contained only arabinose and galactose; it was noted that a local acacia gum currently sold in the markets at Luxor was virtually identical in composition to that found in the paint samples.

A red wash on an Eighteenth-Dynasty siliceous sandstone sarcophagus was found by GC analysis to contain a number of monosaccharides (Boston, MFA, 04.278; Newman 1993a: 62–5, 1993b: 152–3). In general, the types and relative amounts of monosaccharides detected resembled the overall pattern given by gum tragacanth. This paint also contained glucose, however, implying the presence, perhaps, of plant nectar or juice.

Gum tragacanth has been identified – utilising TLC and GC – in a white filling material from a Twenty-first-Dynasty sarcophagus in Antwerp (Masschelin-Kleiner *et al.* 1968: 107–10). Another filling material from this sarcophagus was concluded to have been bound by an unknown gum mixed with honey. Because a large amount of xylose was detected in this sample, it was speculated that tamarind gum, plantain or a variety of *Prunus* was present. These materials were simply mentioned as possibilities because they are known to contain large amounts of xylose, but there is little evidence of their use in this manner in ancient Egypt. Finally, a paint sample from the same object was apparently bound with honey alone.

In a Py-MS study of organic adhesives from cartonnages, plant gums were identified as binders in several gesso (calcite-containing ground) layers (Wright and Wheals 1987: 208). Gum has been identified as the binder in one Fayum-region mummy portrait (Munich inv. no. 3; Kühn 1960: 73). Identification was by detection of sugars in a water extract using a microchemical procedure.

Analyses of paint samples from a number of painted wooden objects and some stone objects in the Museum of Fine Arts, Boston, have found gums, sometimes mixed with a glucose-containing material, to have been a common

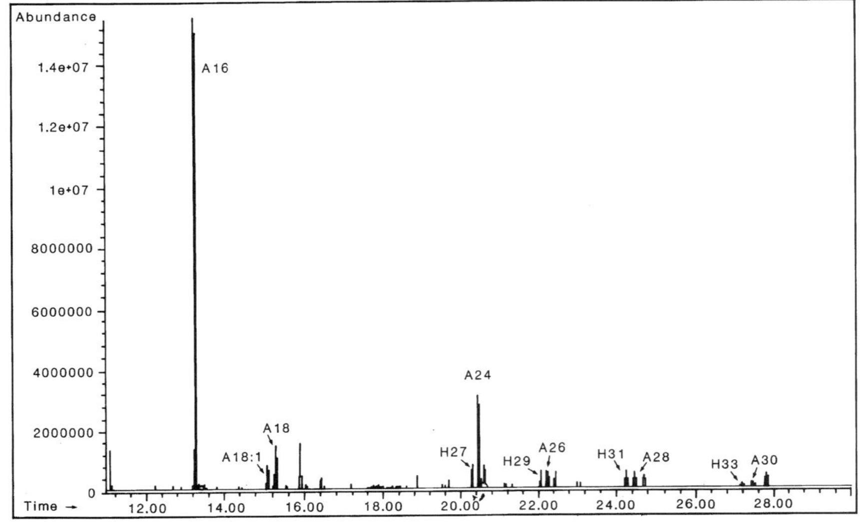

Figure 19.5 Chromatogram from analysis of binding medium of a Fayum mummy portrait, c. AD 150–200 (Boston, MFA, 1974.552). Analysis by GC/MS (saponified, methylated sample). 'A' indicates fatty acid (followed by numbers of carbon atoms and number of double bonds, if any are present). 'H' indicates a straight-chain saturated hydrocarbon (followed by number of carbon atoms).

binder (Table 19.4; Newman and Halpine in press). All of these analyses were carried out by a GC procedure that does not detect uronic acids and cannot fully resolve some of the monosaccharides. Despite these limitations, the variations in types and amounts of different monosaccharides indicate that more than one type of gum was utilised (Fig. 19.4). Many samples contained only galactose and arabinose, the two major sugars in many varieties of acacia. Although quantitative analyses were not carried, the chromatograms indicated that the relative amounts of the two sugars varied considerably, implying that more than one type of acacia served as a source of gum. Rhamnose was almost never detected in this group of samples, thus eliminating certain acacias as possible sources (for example, a major variety of acacia growing in the Sudan, and the principal source of acacia gums today, is *Acacia senegal*, which contains a substantial amount of rhamnose).

Some of the samples from the Museum of Fine Arts at Boston contained a combination of monosaccharides that could indicate the presence of gum tragacanth. The pattern of sugars resembles that of the bulk composition of the mixed polysaccharides in *Astragalus gummifer* (as noted above, it is now thought that most of the gum tragacanth in the market could come from three different species of *Astragalus*, and that *A. gummifer* may not be an important supplier; it is not clear whether earlier published analyses of reference samples of this specific gum were carried out on samples that had been misclassified).

In the analyses of objects from Boston, glucose was frequently detected. There is some ambiguity in interpreting the significance of this. Very small amounts of glucose in a paint sample from a wooden object could conceivably be due to contamination from deterioration of the wood: the major component of wood is cellulose, which yields glucose when hydrolyzed. But in cases where a substantial amount of glucose was detected, this seems less likely. While the source for this sugar is not certain, it must have come from a material added to the plant gum, perhaps for the purposes of making the final paint less brittle, a practice that was common in medieval European manuscript illumination. For the moment, failure to detect fructose in nearly all of the samples in which glucose was detected is curious, since honey and plant nectars contain sucrose, which can be hydrolysed to equal amounts of glucose and fructose. One sample, from a fragment of a painting on a wooden panel, contained both glucose and fructose, indicating honey or plant nectar. No other monosaccharides were detected in this sample, so clearly gum was not the medium.

The tentative identification of tamarind in the linen wrappings from a Roman-period mummy (Manchester Museum 1770; see Benson *et al.* 1979: 128–31) was based on multiple TLC analyses of water and methanol extracts, which were found to give results similar to those given by extracts from tamarind seed pods analysed simultaneously on the same plates. These analyses specifically focused on organic acids found in the pods. In modern commerce, tamarind gum is made from the dried and ground kernels of the seeds. This material contains a polysaccharide (gum) as well as other components, including proteins and lipids. Because of the complexity of its composition, it would seem prudent to base an identification on analysis of several classes of materials (proteins, polysaccharides etc.) rather than to rely on one class.

Beeswax

Composition and analysis

Beeswax is a complex mixture of hydrocarbons, esters of long-chain alcohols and fatty acids, along with some free fatty acids. A more detailed discussion of its composition and the methods by which it can be analysed is presented in Chapter 17, this volume.

Detection in ancient Egyptian materials

Mackay (1920: 35–8) noted, on the basis of the determination of its melting point, that beeswax had been used as 'a fixative or as a varnish' on tombs at Thebes dating to a period in the early Eighteenth Dynasty, between the reigns of Amenhotep I and Amenhotep II, but apparently not earlier or later. There was evidence in some instances that wax had served as a surface coating, applied specifically to coloured areas, sometimes rather carelessly. In some instances, wax was detected within the paint layer itself, implying its use as a binder, although it was noted that application with heat could have driven the wax down into the substrate, so its presence below the surface was not positive indication that it served as the paint binder. More recently, wax was identified in a paint sample from the Eighteenth-Dynasty tomb of Tutankhamun (KV62; LeFur 1994: 59). Again, it is not clear whether this is a coating or the paint binder. More extensive analyses of other samples will be necessary to resolve this question.

The earliest certain use of wax as a binder occurs in the mummy portraits, most originating from the Fayum region, all of which date from about the first to the fourth century AD. Beeswax has been positively identified in some of these portraits by GC analysis (White 1978: 67–8; Alexopoulou-Agoranu *et al.* 1997: 91; Fig. 19.5). What is not entirely clear for the moment is how the wax was prepared and applied. The surfaces of the paintings indicate that paint was both brushed on and applied, or at least moved around, with heated metal implements. No solvent for beeswax appears to have been available at that time, so the wax, if pure, must have been applied melted. Evidence that the wax may have been processed in some way initially came from melting point studies, which showed that the melting point of wax samples from mummy portraits does not match that of pure wax (for example, Dow 1936: 3–17). Various authors have speculated that the medium was beeswax that had been processed by a method described by

Table 19.4. *Binders identified in some objects from the Museum of Fine Arts, Boston.*

No.[1]	Accession no.	Description	Period	Sample colour and type[2]	Binder[3]
Stone substrates					
1	38-4-10	Head	Old Kingdom	Yellow	Gum+sugar
2	38-4-11	Fragment	Old Kingdom		Sugar?
3	35-11-24	Jar	Old Kingdom	Black	?
4	35-11-25	Fragment	Old Kingdom	Red	Gum+sugar
5	none	Hand	Old Kingdom		
6	24.593	False door	First Interm. Period	Red	?
7	29.1.159	Fragment	Middle Kingdom	Red	
8	07.534	Relief fragment	New Kingdom	1. Blue	?
				2. Yellow+gd	?
9	72.653	Head	New Kingdom		
10	04.278	Sarcophagus	New Kingdom		
11	none*	Jar		1. Red	Gum (*Acacia*)
				2. Yellow	Gum (*Acacia*)
Wood substrates					
12	II-A-7	Figure	Middle Kingdom	1. White+gd	Glue+gum
				2. Black	Glue
13	III-A-6	Fragment	Middle Kingdom		
14	none	Coffin board		Blue	Glue+?
15	II-B-3	Figure	Middle Kingdom	Black+gd	Glue
16	21.816 1	Fragment	Middle Kingdom	1. White	Gum?
				2. blue+gd	Gum
				3. Red+gd	Gum
17	01.7431	Mummy mask	New Kingdom	1. Black+gd	Gum
				2. Brown	Gum+sugar
				3. White	Gum
18	37.553a-c	Goose mummy	Dynasty 18	1. Adhesive 1	Sugar+gum
				2. Adhesive 2	Gum (*Acacia*)
19	72.4113	*Shabti*	Dynasty 19	Black coating	Resin (*Pistacia*)+nondrying oil or fat[4]
20	Wray 564	Hand	Dynasty 21	Gd+blue	Gum?
21	72.4732	Mummy mask	Third Interm. Period	Blue+gd	Gum+sugar
22	none	Model falcon	Third Interm. Period	Blue	Gum+sugar
23	72.4836	Outer mummy case	Third Interm. Period	1. Gd	Glue+gum
				2. Blue	Glue
				3. Black coating	Gum+sugar
24	05.96	Baboon mummy coffin	Late Period	1. Gd	Glue
				2. Black+gd	Sugar+gum?
25	72.4074a-c	Ptah-Sokar-Osiris	Late Period	1. Blue	Glue+gum (*Acacia*)
				2. Light green	?
				3. Gd	?
26	03.1625	Ptah-Sokar-Osiris	Ptolemaic	Black+gd	?
27	72.4178	*Ba*-Bird	332-330 BC	Blue+gd	Glue+?
28	98.1127	Canopic chest	Greco-Roman	1. Yellow+gd	Gum+sugar
				2. Red+gd	Gum
29	none*	Servant statue		Gd+yellow	Glue+gum (*Acacia*)
30	72.4796	Braided beard		Black	Gum (*Acacia*)+another gum?
31	1588H	Fragment		Red	?
32	37.537b	Painted fragment		Red+gd	Sugar (possibly honey)
33	13.4360	Painted fragment		Gd	Sugar?
34	none	Scribal palette		1. Red (ink)	Gum (*Acacia*)
				2. Black (ink)	Gum (*Acacia*)

Notes: 1. For the sake of brevity, specific objects are referred to in the text by these numbers.
2. All samples are paint unless otherwise indicated 'gd' indicates a ground layer (usually white, pigmented with calcium carbonate).
3. Identifications by high performance liquid chromatography analysis of amino acids, or gas chromatography/mass spectrometry analysis of monosaccharides. 'Gum (*Acacia*)' indicates that monosaccharide analysis showed arabinose and galactose, suggesting that a tree belonging to the *Acacia* genus could have been the source. 'Sugar' indicates that substantial glucose was detected. Identifications followed by '?' are tentative due to low levels of the characteristic compounds. '?' without an identification indicates that only traces of amino acids or monosaccharides were found, at levels too low to permit a suggestion of the binder to be made.
4. Identification by gas chromatography/mass spectrometry. *Pistacia* resin suggested by presence of some compounds characteristic of resins from this genus. Nondrying oil or fat suggested by presence of palmitic and stearic acids, with only a very small amount of azelaic acid.
*These two items are parts of the same object.

Pliny. Because the method involved treatment with seawater and alkali, this material, known as *Punic wax*, probably contained some breakdown products, in particular salts of fatty acids. The presence of these compounds could account for the melting point deviations. One study by GC has found evidence of such a partial breakdown of the esters in beeswax from one mummy portrait (Petrie Museum UC19612); the same study found no evidence of such breakdown in another portrait (Petrie Museum unnumbered; White 1978: 67–8). Wax processed by such a method can be used as an emulsion in water, and could have been mixed with other materials, such as egg, oil, or gum. To date, however, analyses that have clearly shown the presence of beeswax have not detected any other material admixed with the wax. The use of emulsified wax, alone or mixed with other ingredients, would clearly have practical advantages over ones that require melting, particularly for large-scale projects such as tomb paintings. It is to be hoped that future research will provide more information on the use of wax in wall paintings in ancient Egypt.

Wax has occasionally been identified as an adhesive material. Black pigment in the eye of a bust of the Eighteenth-Dynasty queen, Nefertiti (Berlin ÄM21300) was bound with beeswax, identified by GC and MS (Wiedermann and Bayer 1982: 622A, 624A). A paper on adhesives in cartonnages identified wax in a few ground samples by Py-MS (Wright and Wheals 1987: 205–6, 208).

Natural resins and bitumen

Composition and analysis

Most natural plant resins consist of terpenoid compounds, specifically diterpenoids or triterpenoids. Bitumen contains triterpenes, along with lesser amounts of other types of compounds. The chemistry and analysis of these materials are discussed in Chapter 18 of this volume.

Detection in ancient Egyptian materials

There is little evidence for the use of natural resins as a binder or adhesive. The use of resins in varnishes for paintings, including the 'black varnishes,' is discussed in Chapter 18 of this volume. A study of some Eighteenth-Dynasty tomb paintings has identified resin, specifically *Pistacia lentiscus*, as a paint binder (LeFur 1994: 59). The techniques of identification are not noted, but species identifications of resins are rarely possible (see Chapter 18, this volume). A Py-MS analysis of cartonnage samples identified natural resin as the binder in ground or gesso samples from some objects (Wright and Wheals 1987: 208). However, these results were not confirmed by other techniques, and should probably be regarded as problematic. Amino acid analysis of paint samples from a range of objects ranging in date from the Old Kingdom through to the Greco–Roman period suggested that the binder used most closely matched sandarac resin from *Tetraclinis articulata* (Vahl) Masters (Halpine 1995: 250). This tree, in the coniferous family of Cupressaceae, is found in Morocco and Algeria (Hepper 1992: 160) and was not considered to be a probable source of resin by Lucas (1962: 321). While the identification of sandarac is therefore certainly interesting, it would be desirable to have the results of such a novel approach compared with more traditional methods of resin analysis, such as GC/MS.

The use of bitumen in ancient Egypt dates back at least to the Eighteenth Dynasty (see Chapter 18, this volume). Some identifications of bitumen in the context of mummies and in some Eighteenth-Dynasty varnishes are discussed elsewhere (Chapter 18, this volume). Given the widespread use of bitumen as an adhesive in certain periods and areas in the ancient Near East (also discussed in Chapter 18 of this volume), there is a *possibility* – still unsubstantiated – that it may have been used for similar purposes in ancient Egypt.

Oils and fats

Composition and analysis

Oils and fats are mainly made up of triglycerides, which are esters of glycerol and various fatty acids. The composition and analysis of these materials are discussed in Chapter 17 of this volume.

Detection in ancient Egyptian materials

Oils and fats have not been identified as binding media in ancient Egyptian paints. However, one possible use of such

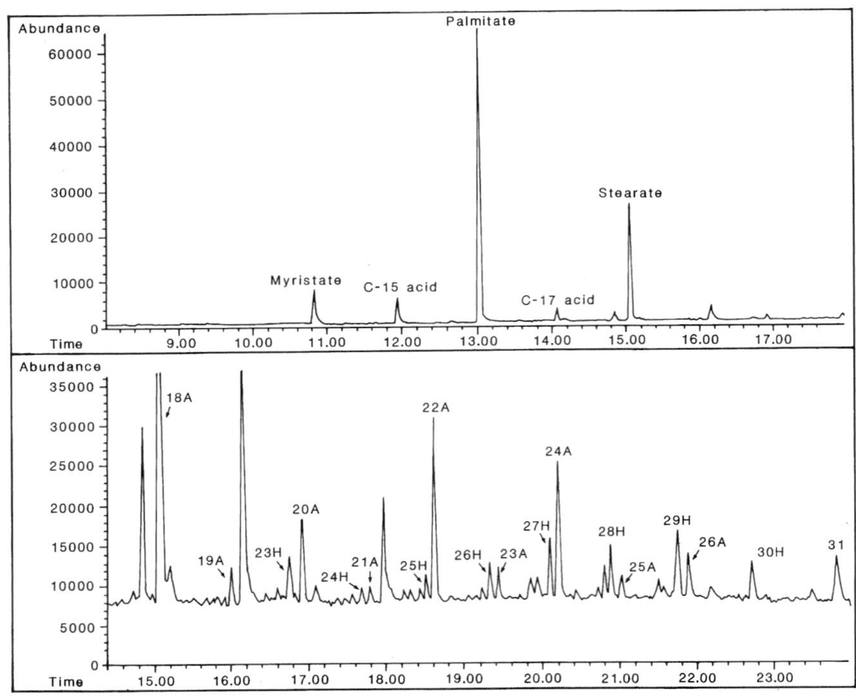

Figure 19.6 Chromatogram from analysis of a fill material on a stone sarcophagus, 1570–1293 BC. Top: detail showing major components. Detail of later part of chromatogram, with expanded vertical scale to show some minor components. Analysis by GC/MS (methylated methylene chloride extract of sample). In bottom detail, 'A' indicates a fatty acid (preceded by number of carbon atoms). 'H' indicates a straight-chain saturated hydrocarbon (preceded by number of carbon atoms).

a material as an adhesive has been found in a brown-coloured mixture used to fill hieroglyphs on a carved stone sarcophagus that was altered some years after it had been originally carved (Boston MFA 04.278; Newman 1993a: 62–5, 1993b: 154–5). The fill material was found by GC analysis (Fig. 19.6) to contain both a fatty substance, perhaps animal fat, and natural resin (*Pistacia* sp.). FT-IR analysis also indicated the presence of a protein. GC analysis did not detect plant gum.

Summary

Attention to the identification of binders and adhesives is clearly increasing, despite the difficulties in differentiating between ancient material and modern conservation applications. There is much scope for further research, including the assessment of any changes in the use of these materials over time. In particular, any distinctions in the binders used for different pigments and in different chronological periods should be considered. It is to be hoped that, as research continues, more distinctive patterns in the use of adhesives and binders will emerge.

References

Alexopoulou-Agoranou, A., Kalliga, A.-E., Kanakari, U. and Pashalis, V. 1997. Pigment analysis and documentation of two funerary portraits which belong to the collection of the Benaki Museum. In *Portraits and Masks: Burial Customs in Roman Egypt* (ed. M. Bierbrier). London: BMP, pp. 88–5.

Anderson, D.M.W. 1978. Chemotaxonomic aspects of the chemistry of *Acacia* gum exudates. *Kew Bulletin*, 32: 529–36.

Aspinall, G. and Baillie, J. 1963. Gum Tragacanth. Part 1. *Journal of the Chemical Society*, 1963/II 1708–14.

Barakat, H.N. 1995a. Charcoals from the Neolithic site at Nabta Playa (E-75–6), Egypt. *Acta Palaeobotanica*, 35(1): 163–6.

1995b. Middle Holocene vegetation and human impact in central Sudan: charcoal from the neolithic site at Kadero. *Vegetation History and Archaeobotany*, 4: 101–8.

Benson, G.G., Hemingway, S.R. and Leach, F.N. 1979. The analysis of the wrappings of Mummy 1770. In *The Manchester Museum Mummy Project* (ed. A.R. David). Manchester: The Manchester Museum, pp. 119–31.

Bleton, J., Coupry, C. and Sansoulet, J. 1996. Approche d'étude des encres anciennes. *Studies in Conservation*, 41: 95–108.

Boulos, L. 1995. *Flora of Egypt Checklist*. Cairo: Al Hadara Publishing.

Brenan, J.P.M. 1959. Leguminosae, subfamily Mimosoideae. In *Flora of Tropical East Africa* (eds. C.E. Hubbard and E. Milne-Redhead). London: Crown Agents for Oversea Governments and Administrations.

Chamberlain, D.F. and Matthews, V.A. 1970. *Astragalus* L. In *Flora of Turkey* III (ed. P.H. Davis). Edinburgh: Edinburgh University Press, pp. 49–254.

Davies, N. de G. 1943. *The Tomb of Rekh-mi-ré at Thebes*, 2 vols. New York: MMA.

Derrick, M. and Stulik, D. 1990. Identifcation of natural gums in works of art using pyrolysis-gas chromatography. In *ICOM Committee for Conservation Preprints, 9th Triennial Meeting, Dresden*. Paris: ICOM Committee for Conservation, pp. 9–14.

Dogan, M., Ekim, T. and Anderson, D.M.W. 1985. The production of gum tragacanth from *Astragalus microcephalus* in Turkey –

a contribution towards a balanced environment. *Biological Agriculture and Horticulture*, 2(4): 329–34.

Dow, E. 1936. The medium of encaustic painting. *Technical Studies in the Field of the Fine Arts*, 5: 3–17.

Endt, D. von and Baker, M. 1991. The chemistry of filled animal glue systems. In *Gilded Wood: Conservation and History* (general eds. D. Bigelow, E. Cornu, G. Landrey and C. van Horne). Madison CT: Sound View Press, pp. 155–62.

Erhardt, D., Hopwood, W., Baker, M. and von Endt, D. 1988. A systematic approach to the instrumental analysis of natural finishes and binding media. In *American Institute for Conservation Preprints of papers presented at the sixteenth annual meeting, New Orleans, Louisiana, June 1–5, 1988*. Washington DC: American Institute for Conservation, pp. 67–84.

Feigl, F. 1960. *Spot Tests in Organic Analysis*, (trans. R. Oesper). Amsterdam: Elsevier.

Gentry, H.S. 1957. Gum tragacanth in Iran. *Economic Botany*, 11(1): 40–63.

Gentry, H.S., Mittleman, M. and McCrohan, P.R. 1992. Introduction of chia and gum tragacanth, new crops for the United States. *Diversity*, 8(1): 28–.

Germer, R. 1985. *Flora des Pharaonischen Ägypten*. DAIK. Mainz: von Zabern.

Gettens, R. and Stout, G. 1966. *Painting Materials. A Short Encyclopaedia*. New York: Dover [reprint of original 1942 edition].

Glickman, M. 1969. *Gum Technology in the Food Industry*. London: Academic Press.

Halpine, S. 1992. Amino acid analysis of proteinaceous media from Cosimo Tura's The Annunciation with Saint Francis and Saint Louis of Toulouse. *Studies in Conservation*, 37: 22–38.

1995. An investigation of artists' materials using amino acid analysis: introduction to the one-hour extraction method. *Conservation Research 1995, Studies in the History of Art 51, Monograph Series 2*. Washington DC: National Gallery of Art, pp. 29–70.

Hepper, F.N. 1987. *Planting a Bible Garden*. London: HMSO.

1990. *Pharaoh's Flowers: The Botanical Treasures of Tutankhamun*. London: Royal Botanic Garden, Kew.

1992. *The Illustrated Encyclopedia of Bible Plants*. Leicester: Inter Varsity Press.

Howes, F.N. 1949. *Vegetable Gums and Resins*. Waltham, MA: Chronica Botanica Co.

Hubbard, J.R. 1962. Animal glues. In *Handbook of Adhesives* (ed. I. Skeist). London: Chapman and Hall, Ltd., pp. 114–25.

Keimer, L. 1984. *Die Gartenpflanzen im Alten Ägypten* I. Hamburg-Berlin: Hoffmann and Campe Verlag.

Kockaert, L., Gausset, P. and Dubi-Rucquoy, M. 1989. Detection of ovalbumin in paint media by immunofluorescence. *Studies in Conservation*, 34: 183–8.

Kroll, H. 1989. Die Pflanzenfunde von Maadi. In *Maadi III: The Non-Lithic Small Finds and the Structural Remains of the Predynastic Settlement* (eds. I. Rizkana and J. Seeher). Cairo: DAIK, pp. 129–36.

Kühn, H. 1960. Detection and identification of waxes, including Punic wax, by infra-red spectrography. *Studies in Conservation*, 5: 71–81.

Kulonen, E. and Pikkarainen, J. 1970. Comparative studies on the chemistry and chain structure of collagen. In *Chemistry and Molecular Biology of the Intercellular Matrix*, 1 (ed. E. Balazs). London: Academic Press, pp. 81–7.

LeFur, D. 1994. *La conservation des peintures murales des temples de Karnak*. Paris: Éditions Recherche sur les Civilisations.

Loret, V. 1887. *La flore pharaonique d'après les documents hiéroglyphiques*. Paris: Librairie J.-B. Baillière & Fils.

Lucas, A. 1962. *Ancient Egyptian Materials and Industries*, 4th edn., rev. J.R. Harris London: Edward Arnold.

MacGregor, A. 1985. *Bone, Antler, Ivory and Horn*. London: Croom Helm.

Mackay, E. 1920. On the use of beeswax and resin as varnishes in Theban tombs. *Ancient Egypt*, 5: 35–8.

Mantell, C.L. 1949. The water-soluble gums - their botany, sources and utilization. *Economic Botany*, 3/1: 3–31.

Masschelein-Kleiner, L., Heylen, J. and Tricot-Marckx, F. 1968. Contribution à l'analyse des liants, adhésifs et vernis anciens. *Studies in Conservation*, 13: 105–21.

Megahid, A.M. 1978. *Flora of Saudi Arabia, Vol. I: Dicotyledons*, 2nd edn. Riyadh: Riyadh University Publications.

Meer, G., Meer, W. and Gerard, T. 1973. Gum tragacanth. In *Industrial Gums* (eds. R. Whistler and J. BeMiller), 2nd edn. New York: Academic Press, p. 289.

Miller, A.G., Cope, T.A. and Nyberg, J.A. 1996. *Flora of the Arabian Peninsula and Socotra* I. Edinburgh: Edinburgh University Press.

Mills, J. and White, R. 1994. *The Organic Chemistry of Museum Objects*, 2nd edn. Oxford: Butterworth-Heinemann.

Mouterde, P. 1970. *Nouvelle flore du Liban et de la Syrie* Tome 2, Texte. Beirut: Dar el-Machreq éditeurs (Imprimerie Catholique).

Newman, R. 1993a. Analysis of red paint and filling material from the sarcophagus of Queen Hatshepsut and King Thutmose I. *Journal of the Museum of Fine Arts, Boston*, 5: 62–5.

1993b. Appendix: analysis of red paint and filling material [appended to P. Der Manuelian and C. Loeben's article: 'New light on the recarved sarcophagus of Hatshepsut and Thutmose I in the Museum of Fine Arts, Boston']. *JEA*, 79: 152–5.

1994. Appendix: technical examination of Aspelta's alabastron. *Journal of the Museum of Fine Arts, Boston*, 6: 33–6.

Newman, R. and Halpine, S. in press. The binding media of ancient Egyptian painting. *Colour and Painting in Ancient Egypt*. (ed. W.V. Davies). London: BMP.

Post, G.E. and Dinsmore, J.E. 1932. *Flora of Syria, Palestine and Sinai*, I, 2nd edn. Beirut: American Press.

Ramer, B. 1979. The technology, examination and conservation of the Fayum Portraits in the Petrie Museum. *Studies in Conservation*, 24: 1–13.

Sack, S., Tahk, F. and Peters, T. 1981. A technical examination of an ancient Egyptian painting on canvas. *Studies in Conservation*, 26: 15–23.

Schedrinsky, A., Wampler, T., Indictor, N. and Baer, N. 1989. Application of analytical pyrolysis to problems in art and archaeology: a review. *Journal of Analytical and Applied Pyrolysis*, 15: 393–412.

Schilling, M. and Khanjian, H. 1996. Gas chromatographic analysis of amino acids as ethyl chloroformate derivatives. Part 2, effects of pigments and accelerated aging on the identification of proteinaceous binding media. *Journal of the American Institute for Conservation*, 35: 123–44.

Schilling, M., Khanjian, H. and Souza, L. 1996. Gas chromatographic analysis of amino acids as ethyl chloroformate derivatives. Part 1, composition of proteins associated with art objects and monuments. *Journal of the American Institute for Conservation*, 35: 45–60.

Smith, F. and Montgomery, R. 1959. *The Chemistry of Plant Gums and Mucilages and Some Related Polysaccharides*. New York: Reinhold, American Chemical Society Monograph Series No. 141.

Striegel, M. and Hill, J. 1996. *Thin-Layer Chromatography for Binding Media Analysis*. Los Angeles: The Getty Conservation Institute.

Stulik, D. and Florsheim, H. 1992. Binding media identification in painted ethnographic objects. *Journal of the American Institute for Conservation*, 31: 275–88.

Stulik, S., Porta, E. and Palet, A. 1993. Analyses of pigments, binding media, and varnishes. In *Art and Eternity. The Nefertari Wall Paintings Conservation Project 1986–1992* (eds. M.A. Corzo and M. Afshar). Marina del Rey, CA: The Getty Conservation Institute, pp. 55–65.

Taborsky, G. 1974. Phosphoproteins. *Advances in Protein Chemistry*, 28: 1–210.

Täckholm, V. 1974. *Student's Flora of Egypt*, 2nd edn. Cairo: Cairo University.

Thulin, M. 1989. Fabaceae (Leguminosae). In *Flora of Ethiopia* 3 (eds. I. Hedberg and S. Edwards). Addis Ababa and Asmara, Ethiopia and Uppsala, Sweden: Ethiopian Flora Project, pp. 49–251.

Thulin, M., Hassan, A.S. and Styles, B.T. 1993. Fabaceae (Leguminosae). In *Flora of Somalia* 1 (ed. M. Thulin). London: Royal Botanic Garden, Kew, pp. 341–465.

Twilley, J.W. 1984. The analysis of exudate plant gums in their artistic applications: an interim report. In *Archaeological Chemistry III* (ed. J.B. Lambert). Washington DC: American Chemical Society, pp. 357–94.

Vieillescazes, C. and Lefur, D. 1991. Identification du liant dans la peinture murale égyptienne (Temple de Karnak). *Bulletin de la Société d' Égyptologie de Genève*, 15: 97–8.

van Zeist, W. and de Roller, G.J. 1993. Plant remains from Maadi, a Predynastic site in Lower Egypt. *Vegetation History and Archaeobotany*, 2: 1–14.

Walsh, H.C. 1962. Fish glue. In *Handbook of Adhesives* (ed. I. Skeist). London: Chapman and Hall, Ltd., pp. 126–8.

Wampler, T. 1995. Analytical pyrolysis: an overview. In *Applied Pyrolysis Handbook* (ed. T. Wampler). New York: Marcel Dekker, pp. 1–29.

White, R. 1978. The application of gas-chromatography to the identification of waxes. *Studies in Conservation*, 23: 57–68.

Wiedermann, H. and Bayer, G. 1982. The bust of Nefertiti. *Analytical Chemistry*, 54: 619A–28A.

Wolbers, R. 1988. Aspects of the examination and cleaning of two portraits by Richard and William Jennys. In *American Institute for Conservation Preprints of papers presented at the sixteenth annual meeting, New Orleans, Louisiana, June 1–5, 1988*. Washington DC: American Institute for Conservation, pp. 245–60.

Wright, M. and Wheals, B. 1987. Pyrolysis-mass spectrometry of natural gums, resins, and waxes and its use for detecting such materials in ancient Egyptian mummy cases (cartonnages). *Journal of Analytical and Applied Pyrolysis*, 11: 195–211.

Zohary, M. 1972. *Flora Palaestina* II, Text. Jerusalem: Israel Academy of Science and Humanities.

Zohary, D. and Hopf, M. 1993. *Domestication of Plants in the Old World*. Oxford: Clarendon Press.

20. Hair

JOANN FLETCHER

Introduction

Quantities of human hair dating from the Predynastic to the Roman period have frequently been found within a funerary context despite their frequent omission from excavation reports. Balls of human hair have been found at the Predynastic cemeteries of Mostagedda (Brunton 1937: 90; Lucas 1962, 31) and Nag el-Deir (Lythgoe 1965: 78, 228, 309–10, 392), and a single example was discovered with the mummy of the Eighteenth-Dynasty Queen Meritamun (from DB358; Winlock 1932: 34; Fletcher and Montserrat 1998: 406). Two such samples wrapped in linen were discovered in a small calcite chest in the tomb of Tutankhamun (Cairo JE61762; Carter and Mace 1923: 200, pl. 66.a; Edwards 1972: No.5; Fletcher and Montserrat 1998: 402, 405–6, fig. 1) and small amounts of hair sealed inside balls of mud have been found in the Eighteenth-Dynasty city at Amarna (BM EA55138; Peet and Woolley 1923: 66) and at the Twelfth-Dynasty town of Kahun (Manchester 6729–30; Crompton 1916: 128, pl. 16).

Individual locks of hair were also deposited in burials as early as the Predynastic period (Amélineau 1904: pl. 1; Lythgoe 1965: 309–10; Brunton 1948: 8), although the most celebrated example of such a practice is the section of plaited hair found inside a miniature coffin (inscribed with the name of Queen Tiye) among the tomb equipment of Tutankhamun (Carter No.320.e; see Carter 1933: 86–8, pl. 25; Lucas 1962: 31; Fletcher and Montserrat 1998: 404–5). Such locks of hair have even been discovered inside mummy wrappings, including those of Rameses V (Cairo CG61085; Smith 1912: 90).

Similar examples could also have served a practical purpose, and it has been suggested that portions of human hair might have been used to apply the various powdered cosmetics with which they were found (Brunton 1927: 36, 55; Brunton 1937: 114; Brunton 1948: 57–8). Hair was also sometimes attached to the heads of female figurines, presumably in an attempt to give a more life-like appearence, and rag dolls of Roman date exhibit fashionable styles made up of human hair (Petrie Museum UC28024; Petrie 1889: 12, pl. 20/22; Petrie 1927: 62, pl. 55/570; Janssen 1996: 231–2; Berlin, ÄM 17954, in Posener 1962: 107; Fletcher 1995: fig. 698), a practice further supported by the discovery of 'a large store of dolls' hair' in a house at Kahun (Petrie 1890: 30).

Hair was also used for threading beads to make necklaces and bracelets in the Predynastic and Early Dynastic periods (Brunton 1937: 85; Brunton 1948: 26; Petrie 1901: 18–19; Lucas 1962: 31), and bracelets made entirely of hair or a hair and fibre mixture have been found in Old Kingdom burials and pan graves (Brunton 1937: 110, 130; Lucas 1962: 31). Although 'the nature of the hair in these cases has not been determined' (Lucas 1962: 31), it would seem quite possible that animal hair was used. Shell beads of the Badarian period are described as strung on animal hair (Brunton and Caton Thompson 1928: 57; Lucas 1962: 31) and a First-Dynasty bracelet was partly made up of 'thick hair, probably from tails of oxen' (Petrie 1901: 18; Lucas 1962: 31). The fly-whisks of Tutankhamun are described as 'probably either horse-hair or donkey hair' (Lucas 1962: 31; Carter 1927: 224, pl. 43), while Middle Kingdom examples from Kerma are composed of 'giraffe-tail hair, possibly mixed with a little goat hair' (Lucas 1930: 31; Reisner 1923: 313–15), and a net-bag from Balabish was made of 'giraffe-tail or elephant-tail hair' (Wainwright 1920: 12, 32, 46).

Wig-making

Hair was predominantly used to construct the wigs and false braids which served as items of daily and funerary attire throughout the Pharaonic period (Fletcher 1995). The hair employed for this purpose was specifically human hair, and in almost every case can be identified as cynotrichous (Caucasian) rather than heliotrichous (Negroid) (Hrdy 1978: 281; Titlbachova and Titlbach 1977: 84–5; Brunton 1937: 45; el-Batrawi 1935: 174–5,194).

Although the precise circumstances regarding the supply of hair as a raw material for wig-making are not known, it seems to have been a valuable commodity, and is listed alongside incense and gold in the 'accounts list' from the town of Kahun (Griffith 1898: 39, 48–50, pls. XIX–XX).

It must have been bought or traded in the Dynastic period, as it later was in Roman times, or alternatively individuals may have utilised their own hair. No trace of animal hair has been found in any of the wigs analysed (Lucas 1930: 192–4; Lucas 1962: 30; Eisa 1948: 9–19; Schoske 1990: 112; Fletcher 1995: 443), although a small amount of unidentified animal fur was discovered in a cache of wig-making equipment at Deir el-Bahari (Laskowska-Kusztal 1978: 87, 89–90, 112, 120).

Before processing began, the hair would have been sorted into lengths, and any tangles or lice eggs removed with a fine-toothed comb. It also seems likely that the hair would have been washed, and samples of a solid soda 'soap' with detergent properties have been found among the aforementioned wig-maker's equipment (Laskowska-Kusztal 1978: 96, 104–5, 119–20, figs. 47, 54). The prepared lengths of hair would then be worked into an assortment of plaits, braids and curls, depending upon the style required, and each piece lightly coated in warmed beeswax, resin, or a beeswax and resin mixture. This acted as a fixative which would harden when cooled, thus setting the shape, and since the melting point of beeswax has been determined at between 60 and 63 °C, this method of anchoring the hair would have proved quite satisfactory (Lucas 1930: 191–2, 1962: 30–1; Cox 1977: 69–70; Schoske 1990: 112; Janssen 1996: 231).

The individual locks could then be fastened either directly on to the natural hair, or on to a foundation net in order to create an actual wig. The foundation net would be made on a head-shaped wooden mount (Laskowska-Kusztal 1978: 106–9, 113, figs. 57–61), and although linen string (Scott 1980: fig. 28; Laskowska-Kusztal, 1978: 87, 110, fig. 10) or leather strips (Laskowska-Kusztal 1978: 92, 111, fig. 19) were occasionally employed in its construction, fine lengths of plaited or woven hair were the preferred material (Cox 1977: 69, fig. 1.3; Schoske 1990: 112; Gauthier-Laurent 1938: 691; Laskowska-Kusztal 1978: 110–11). The separate locks could be attached by weaving them directly into wefts of hair which in turn formed part of the net base, or alternatively they could be knotted into position. A further method was to attach each lock by looping its root end around a part of the net, then press it back on itself; this loop could then be secured by winding a smaller substrand of hair around it, and applying a further coating of the beeswax mixture (Cox 1977: 69–70, figs. 2–3, pl. X.2). The durability of such techniques and the great skill of the wig-makers produced wigs of a standard often equivalent to modern examples, and despite claims that their weight might have been sufficient to cause parietal thinning of the skull (Smith 1912: 36; Ruffer 1914: 244), their lightweight construction would have made them equally easy to wear (Fletcher 1995: 37).

Historical survey of wigs

The practice of attaching false braids directly on to the natural hair dates back to Predynastic times, the earliest examples discovered at Hierakonpolis cemetery HK.43 and dated to *c.* 3500 BC (Fletcher 1998; forthcoming (a)). Further sections of worked hair have been dated to the very beginning of the Dynastic Period, and were found in relatively large numbers in the Early Dynastic Umm el-Qa'ab necropolis at Abydos. Despite their fragmentary nature it is possible to observe complex construction techniques involved in creating the lengths of hair weft, to which a wide variety of curls, ringlets and plaits were attached (e.g. Oxford, Pitt-Rivers Museum No. 1901.40.56; Petrie 1902: 5, pl. IV.7; Cox 1989: fig. 468: and Berlin, ÄM, Inv. No. 18051–2; Amélineau 1904: pl. III; Scharff 1929: 12, pls. 3–4).

Although there is little evidence for the use of false hair in the Old Kingdom, the Eleventh-Dynasty necropolis at Deir el-Bahari has produced a number of interesting examples. One of the men from the mass grave of soldiers of Mentuhotep II was found to have supplemented his locks with tightly wound spirals of false hair, and since his burial had been hastily carried out following battle it cannot be explained as a post-mortem addition and must have been worn in life (Winlock 1945: 9). The oldest wigs found intact also date from this period, the earliest of which would appear to be that found in the tomb of Amunet (at Deir el-Bahari probably pit 25 in the north court of Menthutop's temple) a priestess of Hathor and 'sole royal ornament' of Mentuhotep II. (Cairo, TR 5: 11: 27: 2; Lucas 1930: 196).

Wigs were also discovered within their original storage boxes in a number of Twelfth-Dynasty tombs around the cemetery site of Lisht (Lansing 1933: 26, fig. 39; Gautier and Jéquier 1902: 49–50; Mace and Winlock 1916: 10, 105, pl. 9.A). Although in a poor state of preservation, they all appear to have been made of human hair, with the best preserved example made up of long braids coated in a 'resinous substance' (Lansing 1933: 26).

The range of wigs and false braids which have survived from the New Kingdom reflect the large number of styles fashionable at the time for both men and women. A fine example of the 'double' or 'duplex' style much favoured by officials and noblemen of the period was found in its reed box in a tomb 'behind the small temple of Isis, Thebes' (BM EA2560; Cox 1977: 67–70, fig. 1, pl. X.1; Brovarski *et al.* 1982: 197, fig. 50; Fletcher 1994a: 32–3). It is composed entirely of human hair set in two distinct sections, an upper part of light brown, open-centre curls set over an under-panel of several hundred long thin plaits, originally measuring up to thirty-eight centimetres in length (see Fig. 20.1). Both curls and plaits are attached to a reticulated foundation base of finely plaited hair, and secured with a coating of beeswax and resin. An unprovenanced wig of New Kingdom date (Berlin, ÄM 6911) again features this arrangement of curls and plaits set on a net base, although the curled section is very much more compact and the 46-cm-long plaits are fewer in number (Schoske 1990: 112; Fletcher 1994a: 32).

Figure 20.1 Man's 'double-style' wig from Thebes, New Kingdom (BM EA2560)

A further fragmentary example of the double style would appear to be the portions of Yuya's wig (Cairo CG51185), which were found in his tomb in the Valley of the Kings (KV46; Quibell 1908: 65; Lucas 1930: 195, 1962: 30), while an intriguing sample of 'artificially curled ringlets' suggestive of a similar wig (Fletcher 1995: 387; Fletcher and Montserrat 1998: 206–7; Fletcher forthcoming (b)) was discovered in a small calcite chest (Cairo JE61762) among the funerary equipment of Tutankhamun (see Carter's notes, Griffith Institute; Carter and Mace 1923: 200, pl. 66/a; Edwards 1972: no. 5).

In contrast to such highly artificial examples, the Nubian fan-bearer Maiherpri had been buried (KV36) with a unique coiffure of short tight spirals of heliotrichous hair set over his shaven head, giving the impression of a totally natural style (Cairo CG24100; Daressy 1902: 60, pl.16–17, 1903: 74–5).

It is also quite apparent that women's wigs were considerably less elaborate than those worn by men, and so consequently they appear more naturalistic. The best preserved example of the long full style typical of the New Kingdom was found inside the tall wooden wig box of Merit in the tomb she shared with her husband Kha at Deir el-Medina (TT8; Turin No.S.8499; Schiaparelli 1927: 101; Chiotasso *et al.* 1992: 99–105; Carpignano and Rabino Massa 1981: 229–30, pl. 25; Garetto 1955: 66). It is made up of numerous wavy braids of dark brown hair approximately fifty-four centimetres long, which are set by means of complex knot work around a narrow plait which forms a central parting (see Fig. 20.2). A similar wig composed of long plaits was found on the head of the mummy of Ahmose-Hentempet (from tomb DB320; Cairo CG61062; Smith 1912: 20, pl. 16), who had also been provided with a second wig made up of artificially curled locks, complete with a fringe of small ringlets (Smith 1912: 20–1, pls. 16–17; Lucas 1930: 195, 1962: 30; identified by Fletcher 1995, 387 as Cairo JE46913). In its current flattened state this wig measures thirty centimetres across and twenty-four centimetres from front to back, creating a rather short style when worn.

Figure 20.2 Long wig of Merit, wife of Kha, from tomb TT8 at Deir el-Medina, Eighteenth-Dynasty (Turin, Museo Egizio, Inv. no. S.8499).

In addition to complete wigs, individual braids were also employed to create the longer, wider styles in fashion at this time. The wavy brown hair of Queen Meritamun, probably the wife of Amenhotep II (from DB358), had been filled out around the crown and temples using numerous tapered braids, a duplicate set of which was also provided (MMA 30.3.15.c; Winlock 1930: 15, fig. 14, 1932: 9, 34, 47, 75–6, pl. 13, 32–3; Riefstahl 1952: 15, fig. 4; Lucas 1962: 31; Hayes 1959: 188). Similar sets of false braids were buried with the female relatives(?) of the Eighteenth-Dynasty official Senenmut (eg. MMA 36.3.191–4; Lansing and Hayes 1937: 8, fig. 12; Hayes 1959: 188, 196, fig. 111; Lucas 1962: 31), including a large number of tapered plaits of dark brown human hair which had been attached to the partially grey curls of his mother Hatnefer (Qasr el-Einy Faculty of Medicine Bioanthropological Collection No.1002; Lansing and Hayes 1937: 20, fig. 31; Fletcher forthcoming a). These had been arranged in two thick masses at each side of her head and the ends set in two rounded sections to create the so-called 'Hathor-style' featured in artistic representations (Fletcher 1995: 384). The hair of a man buried at Mostagedda had also been 'artificially lengthened by the addition of human hair fastened on with thread' (Brunton 1937: 123).

Figure 20.3 Short, curled wig of Istemkheb, wife of the high priest Menkheperra, from DB320 at Deir el-Bahari, Twenty-first Dynasty (Cairo JE26252).

False braids were sometimes employed to disguise areas of baldness, most often caused by old age (*alopecia senilis*). The mummy identified as Queen Tetisheri has natural sparse white locks interplaited with rather more substantial plaits of brown hair (Cairo, CG 61056; Smith 1912: 14–15, fig. 2, pls. 9–10), and a similar technique was employed by the hairdressers of Queen Ahmose Nefertari (Cairo, CG 61055; Smith 1912: 13–4, pl. 7; Riefstahl 1952: 15) and Ahmose Hettimehu (Cairo, CG 61061; Smith 1912: 19, pl. 14).

Wigs remained fashionable during the Third Intermediate Period, with the double style well represented by the seven large Twenty-first-Dynasty wigs (Cairo JE26252a–g; Lucas 1930: 190–2; Lucas 1962: 30; Laskowska-Kusztal 1978: 111–12) which were found among the cache of mummies discovered in a shaft-tomb at Deir el-Bahari (DB320) in 1881. They all exhibit the same two part construction of curls and plaits of human hair, although small bundles of date palm fibre were used as an internal padding in order to create their impressive dimensions while economising on hair.

Another wig from the same cache (Cairo JE26270) was found inside a papyrus box bearing the seals of the High Priest Menkheperra; although too fragile to be removed, it was examined *in situ* and found to be 'made up into small curls and plaits and there is no evidence of any foreign fibre in the form of stuffing . . . the material is seen to consist entirely of human hair' (Lucas 1930: 192–3), correcting the earlier description of 'une perruque de grande taille en poil de mouton noir et en cheveux mêlés' (Cairo Museum Guide, 1892: 309, quoted in Lucas 1930: 192–3).

However, the assumption that this large, double-style wig must have belonged to his wife ('the wig of Queen Isemkhebe', according to Lucas 1962: 30) rather than to Menkheperra himself seems equally erroneous (see Fletcher 1994a: 33; Fletcher 1995: 404). The wig to be identified as that of his wife Istemkheb [Isemkhebe] is in fact much smaller and is simply dressed with curls of human hair and typical of the short, feminine style of the time (Cairo JE26252.h; James and Thorpe 1994: 269; Fletcher 1995: 404, figs. 793 and 801; Lucas 1930: 192; Brugsch and Maspero 1881: pl. 28; see Fig. 20.3 here).

The wig of Nany, Chantress of Amun-Ra (MMA 30.3.35), also reflects the fashion for shorter hair, with its sturdy, layered form made up of thick plaits of human hair, ranging from fifteen to twenty-five centimetres in length (Winlock 1930: 19, figs. 22–3, 1932: 55, 81–2; Scott 1980: fig. 28); in contrast to most previous examples however, the plaits of this wig are now set on a foundation of linen string, and the wig of Nany's sister Queen Duathathor-Henuttawy is composed entirely of 'black string' set in narrow spirals thirty-five centimetres long (Cairo, CG61090; Smith 1912: 103, pls. 75–6). The dark brown plaits of the wig belonging to the Twentieth-Dynasty Queen Nodjmet are also described as being 'tied to strings' to form the foundation base, and in addition to her artificial coiffure she had also been provided with false eyebrows made up of fine lengths of hair (Cairo, CG61087; Smith 1912: 96, pls. 69–71).

Despite losing popularity during the Late Period, the fashion for wigs was revived during Roman times. Although the most elaborate examples are made entirely of date-palm fibre (e.g. Cairo TR 18: 1: 26: 26; Lucas 1930: 195, 1962: 30) or grass (Cairo JE33434; Lucas 1930: 194, 1962: 30), hair was still used in the production of wigs (Dunand *et al.* 1992: 51–2, 142, pls. 24, 33) and smaller hairpieces. A section of plaited hair, set in a rigid crescent shape by means of sixty-two bronze pins, was found at Gurob (UC 7833; see Fig. 20.4); known as an 'orbis', it represents 'probably the only example surviving of a well-known hairdressing of the period of Trajan' (Petrie 1927: 5, pl. 4; Fletcher 1994b: 134, fig. 223).

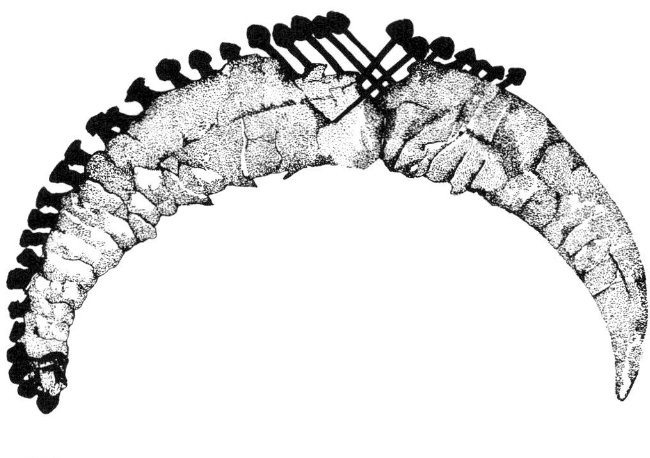

(a)

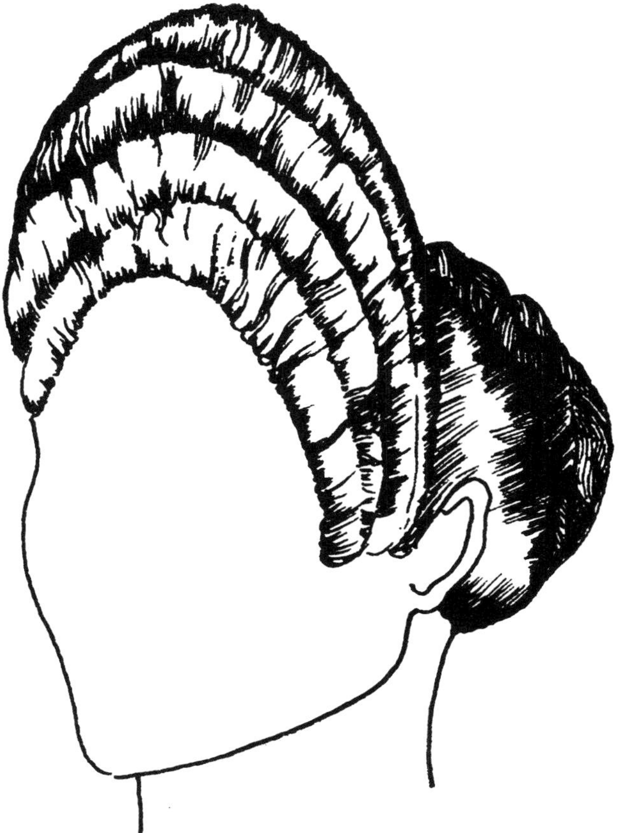

(b)

Figure 20.4 (a) False front of hair ('orbis') from Gurob, dating to the Roman period (Petrie Museum UC7833); and (b) reconstruction showing how the orbis would have been worn.

Analytical techniques

In order to identify and distinguish between both animal hair of different species and human hair of varying ethnic types and to examine its general condition, the scanning electron microscope (SEM) can be used to examine the surface structure (Rabino Massa and Conti Fuhrman 1980: 133–7; Schoske 1990: 112; Paris 1985: 224–30, 240–1; Curry *et al.* 1979: 109–10; Barth 1991: 603; Appleyard 1978). The hair of particular individuals can also be investigated by similar techniques. Thus, the mummy of the 'Elder Lady' found in the tomb of Amenhotep II was identified as Queen Tiye after scanning electron microprobe analysis and ion etching were used to compare a sample of the mummy's hair with the lock of the queen's hair found in Tutankhamun's tomb (KV62; Harris *et al.* 1978: 1149–51). However, this identification is not conclusive, and the results have been criticised due to the lack of comparative data (Germer 1984: 88–9, 1986: 524).

Hair can also be subjected to neutron activation analysis (NAA) to provide information regarding dietary intake and levels of environmental pollution (Paris 1985: 244–53, 255–7; Chatt and Katz 1988: 85–87; Gössler *et al.* 1995: 269–273; Lenihan 1977: 192–4). Microscopic analysis of the hair surface can help to identify a number of diseases (Birkett *et al.* 1986: 367–9; Rook and Dawber 1991: 200–255), and SEM has been used extensively in the study of head lice (*Pediculus humanus capitis*) which can transmit typhus and relapsing fever (Fletcher 1994a: 31–3, 1995: 41–3; Maunder 1983: 21). These parasites have been found in a number of human hair samples (Fletcher 1995: 38–43; Fletcher 1994a: 31–3; Fletcher 1994b: 130, fig. 214), including one Early Dynastic example which was heavily infested with both eggs and adult lice (Manchester No.1198). The discovery of the latter confirms the identification of the hair as natural rather than a wig (as previously assumed), because lice need regular access to the scalp's blood supply in order to feed, and since they can only survive in the natural hair, a wig which could be removed at any time would prove a totally unsuitable habitat (Fletcher 1994a: 32, 1995: 41, 363).

In addition to providing information regarding infestation and disease, hair samples can also be studied microscopically for evidence of styling techniques. SEM examination of the hair ends can help to ascertain the kind of cutting equipment used, with samples dating from the Early Dynastic period exhibiting a relatively smooth unstepped surface indicative of a sharp blade having been used to cut the hair before it had become desiccated and brittle (Fletcher 1995: 363, 442, fig. 733).

The melanin granules in the hair can be examined in order to establish the original colour of the hair (Brothwell and Spearman 1963: 433), which on the surface may have faded over time, or been changed by environmental conditions or the process of mummification (Brothwell and Spearman 1963: 432–3; Hrdy 1978: 281; Titlbachova and Titlbach 1977: 83–4). Vegetable dyes have been found in samples dating back to *c.* 3500 BC and these have been extracted and identified by absorption spectrophotometry and thin layer chromatography (Paris 1985: 221–2, 254, 385–6; Fletcher forthcoming, a; 1998; 1995: 481–2; Penelope Walton Rogers, Textile Research Associates York, pers.comm.17-5-1997 and 3-9-1998).

References

Amélineau, E. 1904. *Les Nouvelles Fouilles d'Abydos, 1897–1904*. Paris: Leroux.

Appleyard, H.M. 1978. *Guide to the Identification of Animal Fibres*. Leeds: Wool Industries Research Asociation.

Barth, J. 1991. Investigation of hair, hair growth and the hair follicle. In *Diseases of the Hair and Scalp*, (eds. A.J. Rook and R.P.R. Dawber). Oxford: Blackwell, pp. 588–606.

el-Batrawi, A.M. 1935. *Report on the Human Remains. Mission Archéologique de Nubie 1929–34*. Cairo: Government Press.

Birkett, D.A., Gummer, C.L. and Dawber, R.P.R. 1986. Preservation of the sub-cellular ultra structure of ancient hair. In *Science in Egyptology*, (ed. A.R. David) Manchester: Manchester University Press, pp. 367–9.

Brovarski, E., Doll, S.K. and Freed, R.E. (eds.) 1982. *Egypt's Golden Age: The Art of Living in the New Kingdom 1558–1085 BC*, Boston: MFA.

Brothwell, D. and Spearman, R. 1963. The hair of earlier peoples. In *Science in Archaeology*, (eds. D. Brothwell, D. and E.S. Higgs). London: Thames and Hudson, pp. 427–36.

Brugsch, E. and Maspero, G. 1881. *La Trouvaille de Deir el-Bahari*. Cairo: Mourés et Cie [transl. as Ragget, V. 1990. *The Royal Mummies of Deir el-Bahri* (ed. C.N. Reeves). London: KPI.

Brunton, G. 1927. *Qau and Badari* I. London: BSAE and Quaritch.

1937. *Mostagedda and the Tasian Culture*. London: Quaritch.

1948. *Matmar*. London: Quaritch.

Brunton, G. and Caton Thompson, G. 1928. *The Badarian Civilisation and Predynastic Remains Near Badari*. London: BSAE.

Carpignano, G. and Rabino Massa, E. 1981. Analisi di un campione di capelli della parrucca appartenente alla moglie dell'architetto Kha. *Oriens Antiquus*, 20: 229–30.

Carter, H. 1927. *The Tomb of Tut.ankh.amen* II. London: Cassell.

1933. *The Tomb of Tut.ankh.amen* III, London: Cassell.

Carter, H. and Mace, A. 1923. *The Tomb of Tut.ankh.amen* I, London: Cassell.

Chatt, A. and Katz, S. 1988. *Hair Analysis: Applications in the Biomedical and Environmental Sciences*. Weinheim: VCH Publishers Inc.

Chiotasso, L., Chiotasso, P., Pedrini, L., Rigoni, G. and Sarnelli, C. 1992. La parrucca di Merit. In *Sesto Congresso Internazionale di Egitto, Atti*, I, Turin, pp. 99–105.

Cox, J.S. 1977. The construction of an ancient Egyptian wig (*c.* 1400 BC) in the British Museum. *JEA*, 63: 67–70.

1989. *An Illustrated Dictionary of Hairdressing and Wigmaking*. London: Batsford.

Crompton, W.M. 1916. Two clay balls in the Manchester Museum. *JEA*, 3: 128.

Curry, A., Anfield, C. and Tapp, E. 1979. Electron microscopy of the Manchester mummies. In *The Manchester Museum Mummy Project*, (ed. A.R. David). Manchester: Manchester Museum, pp. 103–11.

Daressy, G. 1902. *Fouilles de la Vallée des Rois 1898–99*. Cairo: IFAO.

1903. Observations prises sur la momie de Maherpra. *ASAE*, 4: 74–5.

Dunand, F., Heim, J., Henein, N. and Lichtenberg, R. 1992. *La Nécropole de Douch (Oasis de Kharga)*, Cairo: IFAO.

Edwards, I.E.S. 1972. *Treasures of Tutankhamun* . London: BMP.

Eisa, E.A. 1948. A study on the ancient Egyptian wigs. *ASAE*, 48: 9–19.

Fletcher, A.J. 1994a. A tale of hair, wigs and lice. *Egyptian Archaeology*, 5: 31–3.

1994b. Wigs and hair decoration. In *De Kleren van de farao* (ed. G. Vogelsang-Eastwood). Amsterdam: De Tabaafische Leeuw, pp.127–38.

1995. Ancient Egyptian hair: a study in style, form and function. Unpublished doctoral thesis, Manchester University Th.194SS.

1998. Preliminary report on hair samples from Hierakonpolis HK.43 (unpublished excavation report).

forthcoming (a). *Ancient Egyptian Hairstyles and Wigs*. Austin TX: University of Texas Press.

forthcoming (b). The wig and wig box. In *The Clothing of Tutankhamun* (ed. G. Vogelsang-Eastwood). Oxford: Griffith Institute.

Fletcher, A.J. and Montserrat, D. 1998. The human hair in the tomb of Tutankhamun: a re-evaluation. In *Proceedings from the Seventh International Congress of Egyptologists* (ed. C.J. Eyre), Leuven: Peeters, pp. 401–7.

Garetto, E. 1955. L'acconciatura e la cosmesi della donna egizia nel Nuovo Impero, I. *Aegyptus*, 35: 3–85.

Gauthier-Laurent, M. 1935–8. Les scènes de coiffure féminine dans l'ancienne Égypte. In *Mélanges Maspero* I/2. Cairo, pp. 673–96.

Gautier, J.E. and Jéquier, G. 1902. *Mémoire sur les fouilles de Licht*. Cairo: IFAO.

Germer, R. 1984. Die angebliche mumie der Teje, probleme interdisziplinärer arbeiten. *SAK*, 11: 85–90.

1986. Problems of science in Egyptology. In *Science in Egyptology*, (ed. A.R. David). Manchester: Manchester University Press, pp. 521–5.

Gössler,W., Schlagenhaufen, C., Irgolic, K.J., Teschler-Nicola, M., Wilfing, H. and Seidler, H. 1995. Priest, hunter, alpine shepherd, or smelter worker? In *Der Mann im Eis: Neue Funde und Ergebnisse*, (eds. K.Spindler, E. Rastbichler-Zissernig, H. Wilfing, D. zur Nedden and H. Northdurfter) Vienna and New York: Springer Verlag, pp. 269–73.

Griffith, F.Ll. 1898. *Hieratic Papyri from Kahun and Gurob*. London: EEF.

Harris, J.E., Wente, E., Cox, C., Nawaway, I., Kowalski, C., Storey, A., Russell, W., Ponitz, P. and Walker, G. 1978. Mummy of the 'Elder Lady' in the tomb of Amenhotep II: Egyptian Museum Catalog Number 61070. *Science*, 200: 1149–51.

Hayes, W.C. 1959. *The Scepter of Egypt* II. New York: Harold Abrams.

Hrdy, D.B. 1978. Analysis of hair samples of mummies from Semna South (Sudanese Nubia). *American Journal of Physical Anthropology*, 49: 277–82.

James, P. and Thorpe, N. 1994. *Ancient Inventions*. New York: Ballantine.

Janssen, R. 1996, Soft toys from Egypt. In *Archaeological Research in Roman Egypt* (ed. D.M. Bailey). London: Journal of Roman Archaeology Supplement No.19: 231–9.

Lansing, A. 1933. The Egyptian expedition 1932–3: The excavations at Lisht. *BMMA* (Egyptian Supplements November 1933): 4–38.

Lansing, A. and Hayes, W.C. 1937. The Egyptian expedition 1935–6: The museum's excavations at Thebes. *BMMA* (Egyptian Supplements January 1937): 4–39.

Laskowska-Kusztal, E. 1978. Un atelier de perruquier à Deir el-Bahari. *ET*, 10: 84–120.

Lenihan, J.M.A. 1977. Hair and history. *Medical History*, 21: 192–4.

Lucas, A. 1930. Ancient Egyptian wigs. *ASAE* 30: 190–6.

1962. *Ancient Egyptian Materials and Industries*, 4th edn., rev. J.R. Harris. London: Edward Arnold.

Lythgoe, A.M. 1965. *The Predynastic Cemetery N7000. Naga-ed-Der* IV (ed. D. Dunham). Berkeley CA: University of California Press.

Mace, A.C. and Winlock, H.E. 1916. *The Tomb of Senebtisi at Lisht*. New York: MMA.

Maunder, J.W. 1983. The appreciation of lice. *Proceedings of the Royal Institute of Great Britain*, 55: 1–31.

Paris, Musée de l'Homme, 1985. *La Momie de Ramsès II*. Paris: Éditions Recherche sur les Civilisations.

Peet, T.E. and Woolley, C.L. 1923. *The City of Akhenaten* I. London: EES.

Petrie, W.M.F. 1889. *Hawara, Biahmu and Arsinoe*. London: EES.

1890. *Kahun, Gurob and Hawara*. London: EES.

1901. *The Royal Tombs of the Earliest Dynasties* II. London: EES.

1902. *Abydos* I. London: EES.

1927. *Objects of Daily Use*. London: BSAE.

Posener, G. 1962. *A Dictionary of Egyptian Civilization*. London: Methuen.

Quibell, J.E. 1908. *The Tomb of Yuaa and Thuiu*. Cairo: SAE.

Rabino Massa, E. and Conti Fuhrman, A.M. 1980. Early Egyptian mummy hairs: tensile strength tests, optical and scanning electron microscope observation. a paleobiological research. *Journal of Human Evolution*, 9: 133–7.

Reisner, G.A. 1923. *Excavations at Kerma* IV–V. Harvard: Harvard University Press.

Riefstahl, E. 1952. An ancient Egyptian hairdresser. *Bulletin of the Brooklyn Museum*, 13 (4): 7–16.

Rook, A.J. and Dawber, R.P.R. 1991. Defects of the hair shaft. In *Diseases of the Hair and Scalp* (eds. A.J. Rook and R.P.R. Dawber) Oxford: Blackwell, pp. 200–55.

Ruffer, M.A. 1914. Pathological notes on the royal mummies of the Cairo Museum. *Mitteilungen zur geschichte der Medizin und der Naturwissenschaften und der Technik*, 13: 239–48.

Scharff, A. 1929. *Die Altertümer der Vor- und frühzeit Ägyptens*. Berlin.

Schiaparelli, E. 1927. *Relazione sui lavori della Missione Archeologica Italiana in Egitto 1903–1920, II, La tomba intatta dell'architetto Cha nella necropoli di Tebe*. Turin: R. Museo di Antichità.

Schoske, S. (with Grimm, A. and Kriebl, B.) 1990. *Schönheit Abglanz der Göttlichkeit: Kosmetik im Alten Ägypten*. Munich: Ägyptischerkunst.

Scott, N. 1980. *The Daily Life of the Ancient Egyptians*. New York: MMA.

Smith, G.E. 1912. *The Royal Mummies. Catalogue Général des Antiquités Egyptiennes de la Musée du Caire*, Nos. 61051–61100. Cairo: SAE.

Titlbachova, S. and Titlbach, Z. 1977. Hair of Egyptian mummies. *ZÄS*, 104: 79–85.

Wainwright, G.A. 1920. *Balabish*. London: EES.

Winlock, H.E. 1930. The Egyptian expedition 1929–30: The museum's excavations at Thebes. *BMMA* (Egyptian Supplements December 1930): 3–28.

1932. *The Tomb of Queen Meryet-Amun at Thebes*. New York: MMA.

1945. *The Slain Soldiers of Neb-hepet-Re' Mentu-hotep*. New York: MMA.

Part III.
Food Technology

21. Cereal production and processing

MARY ANNE MURRAY

Introduction

The power and prosperity of ancient Egypt has long been regarded as a product of one of the most successful and stable agricultural economies of the ancient world (e.g. Erman 1894: 425; Hassan 1993: 551; Harlan 1995: 113). An array of tools from Predynastic times, including sickle blades, grinding stones and granaries may provide an early testimony to one of the most continuous and defining features of Egyptian culture – the successful production of emmer wheat and barley (Fig. 21.1). At present, it is generally agreed that Egyptian agriculture was probably established some time during the sixth millennium BC with a range of domesticated crops introduced from the Levant (Trigger 1983: 17; Wetterstrom 1993: 201; Zohary and Hopf 1993: 209). Emmer and barley were the staple cereals of this adopted agricultural complex which, along with the herding of domesticated animals, would have originally supplemented, rather than wholly replaced, well-established hunting and gathering practices (Hassan 1984a: 57; Wetterstrom 1993: 167). For the beginnings of

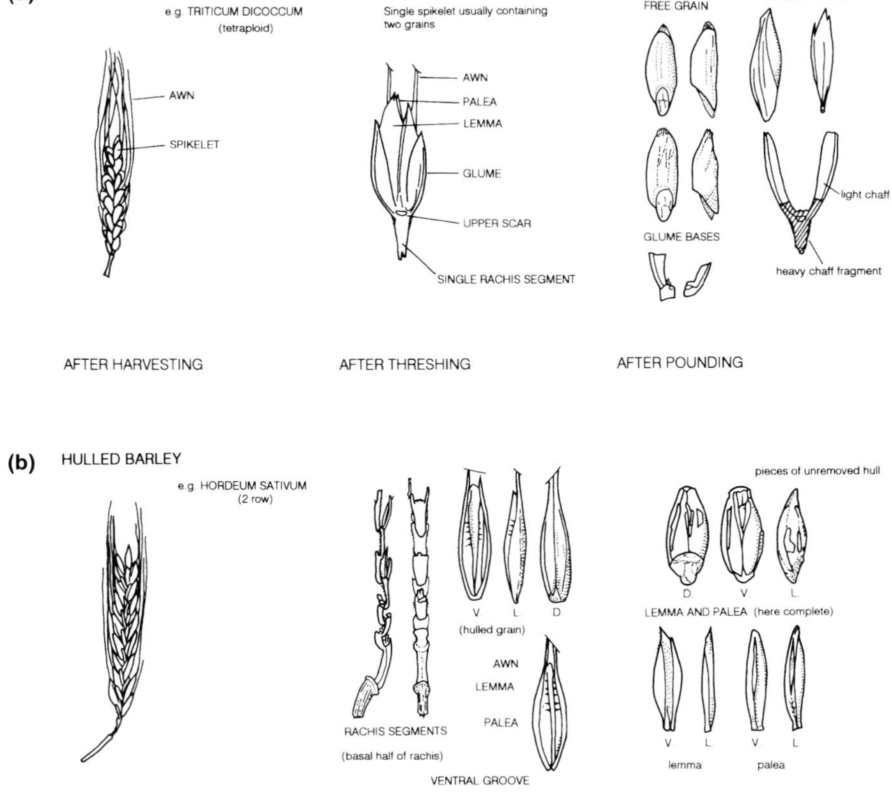

Figure 21.1 Diagrams of (a) glume wheat and (b) hulled barley.

Egyptian agriculture, see Wetterstrom 1993; Butzer 1976; Hassan 1984a, 1986, 1988). Thus far the earliest finds of emmer and barley in Egypt date to 5300–4000 BC from the Fayum oasis and Merimda Beni Salama in the Delta (Caton-Thompson and Gardiner 1934: 46–9; Hassan 1988: 141; Wetterstrom 1993: 201; Zohary and Hopf 1993: 209), thereby marking the beginnings of one of the most accomplished examples of plant–people interaction in history.

This chapter will discuss cereal production and processing during the Pharaonic period; from the initial land preparation prior to sowing, to the storage of the cereals in granaries (Fig. 21.2). The post-storage stages of bread- and beer-making are investigated by Samuel in the following chapter. There has always been an assumption of continuity with regard to both the technology and methods of ancient Egyptian agriculture and many authors have commented on the similarities between ancient and modern practice (e.g. Wilkinson 1878; Erman 1894; Foaden and Fletcher 1908; Blackman 1927; Hurst 1952; Ayrout 1963; Beshai 1993). The exceptional fertility of the annually deposited Nile silts together with the seasonal toil and organisation of the Egyptian farmer combined to create a unique agricultural system which focused on the production and processing of emmer and barley. These staple commodities not only served as vital food and drink to the Egyptians of the Pharaonic period but were also used as an important measure of wealth. Emmer and barley formed an integral part of a complex administrative system of wages and taxation which played a critically important role in the development and relative stability of the economically successful Egyptian state throughout this time (e.g. Gardiner 1941; Cerný 1954; James 1962; Kemp 1972, 1986, 1989, 1994; Janssen 1975, 1986). The complexities of life in Pharaonic Egypt, however, such as an increase in social and economic stratification, 'urbanisation' and cultural influences from outside Egypt, would have introduced any number of variables that might have governed the status of agriculture. A range of natural events, too, such as climatic changes and the annual uncertainties of the Nile flood, held the potential for the catastrophic failure of the annual cereal crop (Butzer 1984: 103; Baer 1960; Bell 1970, 1971, 1975; Parks 1992; Harlan 1995: 115; Hassan 1997). Despite the conservatism of the Egyptian farmer (e.g. Beshai 1993: 265), cultural and environmental factors would have no doubt encouraged the adaptation of long- and short-term adjustments to the agricultural system on the local, regional and national level (Butzer 1976, 1984; O'Shea and Halstead 1989; Parks 1992; Allen 1997; Hassan 1997). Therefore, while examples of agricultural continuity can be found, such as the annual cycle of cereal production and perhaps the basic tools used for it, this important aspect of Egyptian economic history clearly requires a detailed analysis of the available evidence.

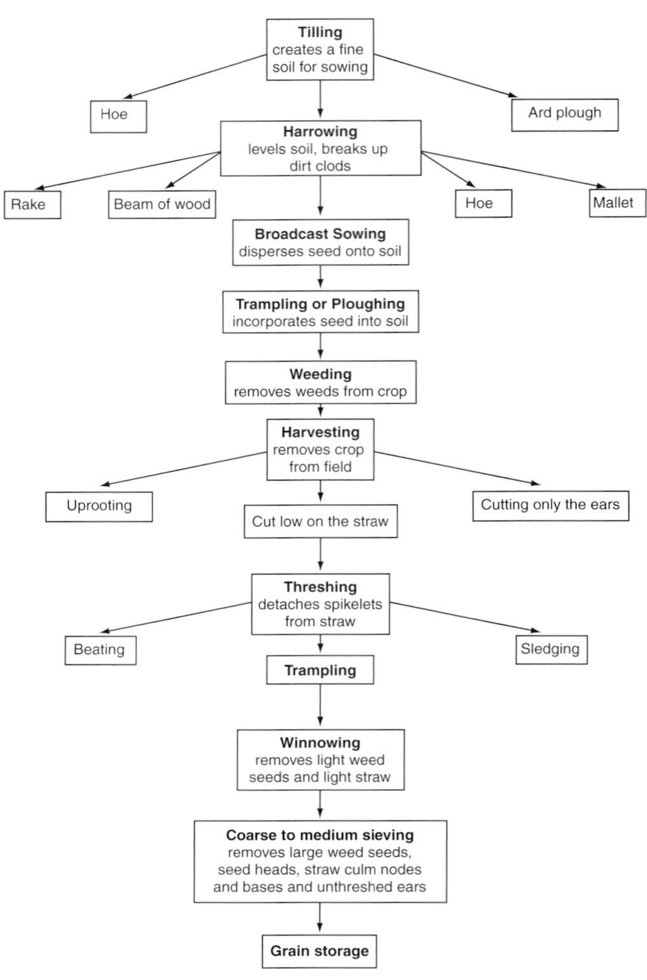

Figure 21.2 Flow chart of pre-storage cereal production and processing stages.

Considering the importance of cereal production during Pharaonic times, a perusal of the literature makes it clear that there is often a rather simplistic view of these agricultural practices, including a misunderstanding of both the order and purpose of its many stages. The preservation of Egypt's uniquely rich artistic and textual records has undoubtedly created a sense that these provide us with all the information we need about agrarian practices, yet due to the many limitations of these data, important questions on the subject remain unanswered. Evidence for the technology of ancient Egyptian cereal production and processing can be derived from a wide and varied array of sources which include:

1) artistic representations in the form of tomb scenes and tomb models;
2) textual and lexicographic data;
3) historical observations;

Table 21.1. *Types of evidence for ancient Egyptian cereal production and processing.*

	Artistic	Textual	Historical	Archaeological*	Archaeobotanical	Ethnographic	Ecological♯	Experimental
Cereal species	N	Y	Y	N	Y	Y	Y	Y
Irrigation	Y	Y	Y	Y	Y	Y	Y	Y
Fallowing	O	Y	O	N	N	Y	O	O
Fertilising	O	Y	Y	N	O	Y	O	O
Tilling	Y	Y	Y	Y	Y	Y	Y	Y
Levelling	O	O	O	O	O	Y	O	O
Sowing	Y	Y	Y	O	Y	Y	Y	Y
Trampling	Y	Y	Y	N	N	Y	N	O
Weeding	O	O	O	N	Y	Y	Y	Y
Harvesting by uprooting	Y	O	O	N	Y	Y	Y	Y
Harvesting low on straw	Y	O	O	O	Y	Y	Y	Y
Harvesting high on straw	Y	O	O	O	Y	Y	Y	Y
Threshing	Y	Y	Y	O	Y	Y	O	Y
Winnowing	Y	Y	Y	Y	Y	Y	Y	Y
Coarse sieving	Y	O	O	Y	Y	Y	Y	Y
Grain storage	Y	Y	Y	Y	Y	Y	Y	Y

Y – Source can provide evidence for or against.
O – Source can potentially provide evidence for or against.
N – Source cannot provide evidence for or against.
* – Archaeological evidence in this context relates to artefactual, architectural and stratigraphic data.
♯ – Ecological evidence includes studies of weed flora, pollen, phytoliths, palaeoentomology, zooarchaeology and geomorphology.

4) archaeological evidence;
5) archaeobotanical finds from tombs and particularly from settlement sites;
6) ethnographic models;
7) ecological evidence; and
8) experimental evidence.

A brief examination of the contribution of each source to the subject must be made at the outset.

Evidence for agrarian practices
Artistic evidence

The paintings and reliefs found in many private tomb chapels have been used extensively, and indeed almost exclusively, as a guide to describe ancient farming in the Nile Valley (e.g. Erman 1894; Montet 1958; Vandier 1978; James 1984; Sist 1987). There is a diverse array of agricultural scenes preserved from the Old and New Kingdoms, whereas much of the relevant Middle Kingdom evidence comes in the form of wooden models depicting everyday activities which were often placed in tombs (Winlock 1955; Vandier 1978). Many of the Old Kingdom tombs are found in the Memphite region, while Middle and New Kingdom tombs are frequently located in the area of Thebes, with a scattering of provincial tombs from all periods. Most farming sequences depicted in tomb-scenes appear to follow the logical order of cereal processing known from traditional Egyptian, Near Eastern and Mediterranean agriculture (e.g. Foaden and Fletcher 1908, 1910; Sigaut 1978, 1988; Hillman 1981, 1984a, 1984b; Jones 1983, 1984; Charles 1990; Peña–Chocarro 1996). Major processing activities, such as ploughing, sowing, the trampling in of seed, harvesting, threshing and winnowing are seemingly well-illustrated, whilst other, less systematic farming practices, such as weeding, are not clearly depicted although this may not necessarily preclude their practice. Many agricultural scenes are accompanied by captions describing the activities portrayed.

With regard to the making of bread and beer in Pharaonic Egypt, Samuel (1989, 1993, 1994a, 1994b and Chapter 22, this volume) has shown that there are certain discrepancies between common interpretations of the artistic record and the evidence drawn from the archaeological and ethnographic records. Indeed, several critical factors highlight the risks of using the artistic record alone to interpret agrarian practices. First, representations in Egyptian tombs are thought not to have been 'art for art's sake' and although the activities portrayed may seem accurately depicted, they were originally designed to create an appropriate environment for the occupier of the tomb in the after-life. These scenes, therefore, are considered to be a representation of an ideal, dictated by strict conventions of iconography and the requirements of a funerary cult, rather than a realistic depiction of each process (Baines and Málek 1984; Harpur 1987; Robins 1994). It is also clear that many scenes were copied repeatedly, that standardised patterns were used in their creation (e.g. Robins 1994), and that while the purpose of each sequence may be clear, often its detail is not (e.g. James 1995: 205). In addition, tomb-paintings and reliefs were created for an élite class and the information they contain may not be representative of Egyptian society as a whole (Crawford 1979: 137–8; Janssen 1979: 505; Samuel 1993: 276). Alternative, small scale-practices of harvesting or threshing, for example, may have been used although these may not be depicted in this rather simplified and selective view of farming activity. Tomb-paintings and reliefs offer a rich source of information and not to examine them for what they contain, however cautiously, would be imprudent, yet it is quite clear that this record alone cannot provide the details required for a thorough investigation of the subject.

Textual and lexicographic evidence

Textual and lexicographic sources, such as literary and administrative texts, private letters and household accounts, offer some insight into the workings of Egyptian cereal production during the Pharaonic period. They are of particular value for data on the use of cereals as wages, grain prices, taxation of harvests, land tenure, measurement systems used for both cereals and land, cereal trade, and data on crop yields (e.g. Cerný 1933, 1939, 1954, 1973; Gardiner 1941, 1947, 1948; Caminos 1954; Nims 1958, Helck 1987; Baer 1962, 1963; James 1962; Janssen 1975, 1979, 1986; Valbelle 1985; Kemp 1986, 1989; Spalinger 1987; Katary 1989; Castle 1992; Eyre 1995). These sources, primarily from the New and Middle Kingdoms, include the Wilbour Papyrus (Gardiner 1948; O'Connor 1972; Adams 1997), the Hekanakhte Letters (James 1962; Baer 1963), and texts from Deir el-Medina (Cerny 1954; Janssen 1975; Valbelle 1985), and are important 'accumulations of small details' (Kemp 1986: 134) which offer glimpses of specific aspects of agriculture but provide an inadequate picture of agrarian practices overall. As with the artistic evidence, there are important limitations, as textual evidence is most likely to document those matters most pertinent to the 'official' class of Egyptian society (Kemp 1977: 199, 1994: 134; O'Connor 1993: 585; Eyre 1995: 186–7). Moreover, certain lexicographic details relating to relevant technical terms and to the cereals themselves have yet to be fully understood, for example, the uncertainty of the possible cereal types *mimi* and *swt* (e.g. Gardiner 1948; Nims 1958; Janssen 1975; Kemp 1994; Eyre 1994; Miller and Wetterstrom 1996; Germer forthcoming). It is also unclear whether the terminology related to cereals remained constant throughout the Pharaonic period (Germer forthcoming). As with the artistic record, the interpretation of texts often suffers from preconceived ideas of the information offered (e.g. Janssen 1975) and would no doubt benefit from evidence provided by the range of specialist studies on agricultural matters.

Historical observations

Other potentially useful sources are the writings of Classical authors, many of whom, such as Herodotus and Pliny, commented on the agricultural practices of their day. Major changes were taking place in Egyptian agriculture during the Greco–Roman period, most notably the introduction of new cereal types and improved irrigation techniques (e.g. Crawford 1971, 1979; Bowman 1990). Although travellers' accounts should be used cautiously, they often provide insight into relevant agrarian matters. While modern, mechanised Egyptian agriculture differs greatly from its ancient counterpart (Hopkins 1987; Ruf 1993: 188), a number of traditional agrarian practices observed in Egypt in earlier periods were still in use by the Egyptian *fellahin* in recent years (e.g. Lane 1860; Willcocks 1904; Foaden and Fletcher 1908, 1910; Willcocks and Craig 1913; Blackman 1927; Ammar 1954; Ayrout 1963; Nessim 1988; Beshai 1993; Hivernel 1996; see also Coult 1958).

Archaeological evidence

The diverse artefactual, architectural and stratigraphic evidence recovered from settlements is essential to our understanding of Egyptian agrarian communities, yet the excavation of settlement sites in Egypt has often been overshadowed by the architecture and objects of temples and tombs (e.g. O'Connor 1972; Butzer 1976; Kemp 1977; Bietak 1979; Smith 1972, 1985; Adams 1992, 1997). Several major Pharaonic settlements have been excavated, including Tell el-Dab'a (e.g. Bietak 1986, 1996), Amarna (Kemp 1984–96, 1989, 1994), Deir el-Medina (e.g. Bruyère 1939), Memphis (Jeffreys *et al.* 1983–96), Abydos (Adams 1992) and Elephantine (e.g. Seidlmayer 1996: Pilgrim 1997). Due to Egypt's arid climate, many tools of otherwise perishable materials associated with the various stages of cereal production and processing have survived, such as hoes, ploughs, rakes, forks, shovels, sieves and winnowing fans, as have sickle blades, mortars, pestles and querns (e.g. Petrie 1891, 1917). Archaeological features, including facilities for the preparation and storage of food stuffs are also vitally important, as are the data on their relative association and distribution (e.g. Kemp 1986, 1994; Samuel 1989, 1993, 1994a, 1994b; this volume, Bietak 1996; Jeffreys forthcoming). Evidence of this kind can be used to monitor changes in technology through time and by region and is also able to reveal important influences from outside Egypt (e.g. Davies and Schofield 1995; Bietak 1996; Bourriau 1981, 1997). At the workmen's villages at Amarna and Deir el-Medina, however, attempts to correlate artefactual remains with the various occupations represented there, including farming, have shown that evidence beyond the archaeological record is clearly necessary to complete the picture (McDowell 1992; Shaw 1992).

Archaeobotanical evidence

Botanical remains have been recovered from Egyptian sites since at least the nineteenth century and hundreds of reports have been written on these finds (see de Vartavan and Asensi Amorós 1997). Most plant assemblages have consisted of offerings recovered from tombs and these have made an important contribution to Egypt's ancient botanical record (e.g. Schweinfurth 1883, 1884; Loret 1892; Täckholm *et al.* 1941; Lauer *et al.* 1950; Germer 1985, 1988, 1989; de Vartavan 1990, 1993; Hepper 1981, 1990; Barakat and Baum 1992). Germer (forthcoming) has noted, however, that these plants were carefully selected assemblages based on religious prescriptions and were not necessarily wholly representative of Egyptian agricultural history or even of those items common to the Egyptian diet. Although such samples are less likely to include the essential clues of agrarian practices that the remains of cereal processing wastes provide (i.e. chaff and weed seeds), a recent detailed analysis of the offerings from Tutankhamun's tomb has indicated that these assemblages are capable of producing useful data on cereal production (de Vartavan 1990, 1993). Tomb offerings have also provided important information on the presence of fruit and vegetable species during the Pharaonic period (see Chapter 24, this volume).

The richest botanical remains, in terms of the agricultural information they provide, have been retrieved from the excavation of ancient settlements. These plant remains are often complex mixtures of cereals, chaff, straw, weed seeds, pulses, fruits, nuts, leaves, stems, roots and tubers, dung, and wood charcoal and can be found on every settlement site. Ancient plants are commonly preserved by charring, which usually occurs during their disposal or use as fuel (Hillman 1981: 155). Archaeobotanists usually recover these remains by a method known as flotation (Fig. 21.3) which, by the use of water, easily separates organic material from deposits selected during excavation. In contrast to desiccated or dried remains (see below) charring acts as a filter which favours those plants most likely to be exposed to fire (e.g. as fuel or household debris) and also those items robust enough to survive the charring process (e.g. Boardman and Jones 1990). It has been noted, however, that in some cases certain items, such as pulses and some types of cereal chaff, are better represented in charred material (van der Veen *et al.* 1996: 239–41). Charred remains are often clearly the result of a specific episode of burning, such as the use of a particular cereal-processing residue as fuel, for example, and this is a most useful characteristic when analysing the various stages of cereal processing.

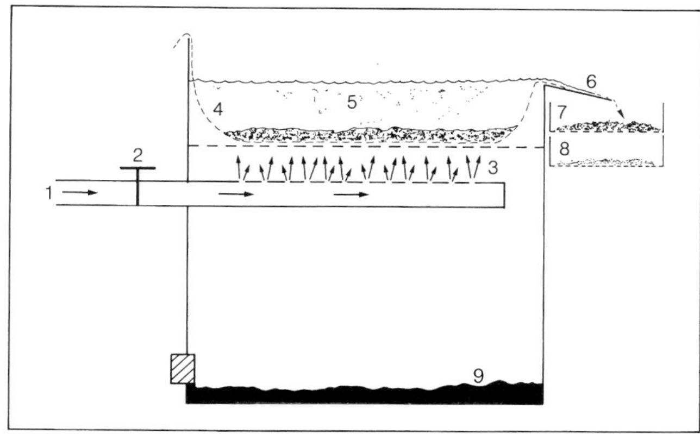

Figure 21.3 Diagram of flotation machine: (1) water in flow pipe, (2) shut off valve, (3) water flowing upwards through holes in pipe, (4) soil deposit taken from excavation, (5) floating plant remains, (6) plant remains flowing over spout into sieves, (7) plant remains retained in 1 mm mesh sieve, (8) plant remains retained in 250–300 μm sieve (9) fine silts as bottom of tank.

Due to Egypt's arid climate, some plants also survive as desiccated (or dried) remains and these assemblages are frequently collected by dry sieving or hand selection, although in many cases, flotation can also safely be used for their recovery. To date, most Egyptian desiccated plant assemblages have been found primarily in dry tombs or desert settlements dating from the Greco–Roman period or later although several Pharaonic sites have also produced these remains, including New Kingdom Amarna and Middle Kingdom Kahun (Renfrew 1985; Samuel 1989; Newberry 1890; Germer forthcoming). Desiccated plant remains often represent a wider array of species and preserved plant parts than are usually present in charred remains (e.g. Rowley-Conwy 1994). Charred and dessicated assemblages from the same site, therefore, may have a very different, although complementary, composition (e.g. van der Veen *et al.* 1996: 239–40; Smith 1997). (For examples of flotation recovery in Egypt, see el-Hadidi 1982; Wetterstrom 1986, 1992; Moens and Wetterstrom 1988; Thanheiser 1987, 1991, 1992a, 1992b, in prep; de Roller 1992; van Zeist and de Roller 1993; Murray 1993, 1994; van der Veen 1996; de Vartavan 1996; Smith 1997; for dry sieving or hand selection, see Hepper 1981;Wetterstrom 1982, 1984; Renfrew 1985; Samuel 1989; Hillman *et al.* 1989; Rowley-Conwy 1989, 1991, 1994; Barakat 1990; Willerding and Wolf 1991; Litýnska 1994; Wasylikowa *et al.* 1995; Cappers 1996; el-Hadidi and Amer 1996).

The identification of cereal grains and chaff is sometimes difficult due to overlapping morphological characteristics and the charring process also can often obscure important identification criteria (e.g. Jacomet 1987; Boardman and Jones 1990; T. Miller 1992; van Zeist and de Roller 1993; Hillman *et al.* 1996). The use of chemical criteria and DNA studies, to aid in the accurate identification of cereal specimens is still in its infancy but has a great potential to establish the identity of problematic cereal grains (e.g. Hillman *et al.* 1993; Brown *et al.* 1993, 1994; Evershed 1993; Dahlberg *et al.* 1995; McLaren 1996). For the Pharaonic period, this is particularly relevant to finds of 'controversial' cereals, such as einkorn wheat (*Triticum monococcum*) and the free-threshing wheats (*T. durum*, *T. aestivum* and *T. compactum*).

Most plant remains arrive on a settlement as the result of human activities, such as when plants are gathered for use as food, medicines, dyes, and building materials. Weed species which often infest cereal fields, for example, are frequently harvested along with the cereal crop. These and other items, including the cereal chaff and straw, must then be gradually removed through various processing operations, such as winnowing and sieving, in order to obtain a clean grain product. In traditional agrarian communities, residues from these processing stages are often disposed of by burning them as fuel in domestic hearths or ovens (e.g. Hillman 1981, 1984a and 1984b). Crop-processing residues preserved in this way are a common component of charred archaeobotanical samples from Egyptian settlements. Detailed ethnographic analysis has shown that not only does each cereal-processing stage create a characteristic product and by-product, but that these assemblages can also be distinguished in the composition of ancient plant remains. Moreover, it is primarily the discarded weeds in these assemblages which provide the most revealing details of the various aspects of cereal husbandry, such as sowing and reaping times, field conditions and tilling and harvesting methods (Hillman 1973, 1981, 1985, 1987a, 1987b; Jones 1983, 1984, 1987). Recognising the products and by-products of cereal processing in archaeobotanical samples is an important first step prior to the investigation of the broader aspects of crop husbandry and site economy (e.g. Jones 1987: 321).

Seeds and other plant parts may have also arrived on an Egyptian settlement in animal dung. Textual and archaeobotanical evidence both show that dung from livestock was often used as fuel in ancient Egypt, particularly where fuel wood may have been scarce (e.g. Caminos 1954; Cerny 1955; Renfrew 1985; Moens and Wetterstrom 1988; Wetterstrom 1982, 1986, 1994; Thanheiser 1992b; Murray 1993, 1994, forthcoming; Litýnska 1994). It has been shown that undigested seeds and other plant parts can pass through the gut of an animal and when the animal dung is burned as fuel, any remaining plant material may then become incorporated into the archaeobotanical record (Anderson and Ertug-Yaras 1997; Miller 1984; Miller and Smart 1984; Bottema 1984; Charles 1997). Plants preserved in this manner are also important indicators of agrarian practices, such as the use of cereals and processing residues for animal fodder, as has been demonstrated at the Old Kingdom settlement of Kom el-Hisn (Moens and Wetterstrom 1988).

The systematic sampling, recovery, analysis and interpretation of ancient plants from the many diverse context types present on ancient Egyptian settlements, including hearths, pits, floors, middens, ovens and storage areas, is able to provide the basis for a detailed and well-informed theory of agrarian practices for any given community (Fig. 21.4).

Ethnographic models

Extensive research into how traditional agriculturalists cultivate and process wheat and barley has produced detailed ethnographic models of how ancient Near Eastern agrarian societies might have operated (Hillman 1973, 1981, 1984a, 1984b, 1985; Jones 1983, 1984). As noted earlier, the products and by-products of the various cereal-processing stages are sufficiently distinguishable by their composition of cereals, chaff and weed seeds that these models can be extrapolated to the archaeobotanical record. The relevance of ethnographic models for recognising cereal-processing activities in ancient assemblages has also been clearly demon-

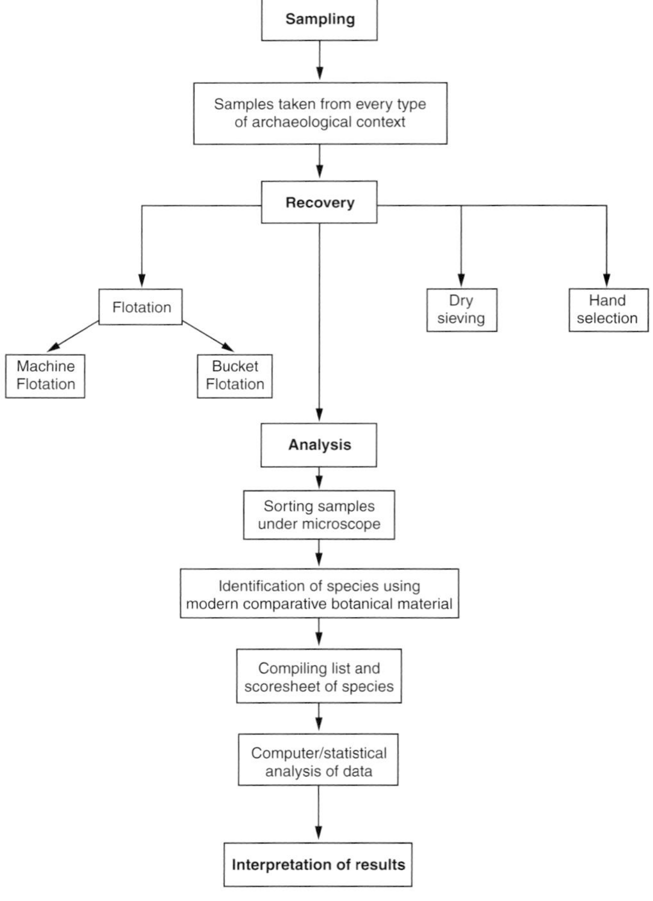

Figure 21.4 Flow chart of basic archaeobotanical process.

strated using multivariate analysis (Jones 1983, 1984, 1987, 1991; van der Veen 1992; Colledge 1994; Smith 1997). The success of these models is largely due to the limited number of ways available to process cereals since in most areas, including Egypt, prior to the introduction of mechanised farming this century, the basic methods and tools for tilling, harvesting, threshing and winnowing remained largely unchanged (Hillman 1981, 1984b, 1991; Jones 1983, 1984). Moreover, many aspects of traditional Egyptian agriculture are typical of the classic Mediterranean and Near Eastern system of cereal production and processing (e.g. Hillman 1981, 1984b, 1991; Jones 1983, 1984; Sigaut 1978, 1988; Charles 1990; Peña-Chocarro 1996). Clearly, ethnographic models should not be used uncritically (Halstead 1987; van der Veen 1992) and are best integrated with other interpretative evidence, particularly the archaeobotanical, archaeological, artistic and experimental records.

Ecological evidence

Ecological evidence is another essential element for the interpretation of archaeobotanical data. Close examination of the various characteristics of the weed seeds present in archaeobotanical samples provides a reliable method of identifying cereal production and processing activities (e.g. Hillman 1981, 1984a, 1984b; Jones 1983, 1984, 1987, 1991, 1992; Kuster 1991; Jones and Halstead 1995; Jones *et al.* 1995; Charles *et al.* 1997), therefore, studies of the Egyptian arable weed flora and other botanical communities offer a vital contribution to the understanding of the weed flora of ancient crops (e.g. Täckholm *et al.* 1941–1969; Kassas 1952; el-Hadidi and Kosinova 1971; Kosinova 1974, 1975; Täckholm 1974; el-Hadidi 1982; 1993; Sa'ad 1980; Boulos and el-Hadidi 1984; Dargie and el-Demerdash 1991; Shaltout and el-Fahar 1991; Cope and Hosni 1991; Zahran and Willis 1992; Fahmy 1995; Boulos 1995). The use of multivariate analyses can also be a useful tool in helping to differentiate the ecological characteristics of archaeobotanical remains (Jones 1983, 1984, 1987, 1991; van der Veen 1992, 1996; Colledge 1994).

Other ecological studies can also contribute to the study of agrarian practices, for example, the analysis of plant phytoliths (silica skeletons) has been used to address questions relevant to the study, including analysing the many uses of cereal straw as roofing, matting and other building material, for example (e.g. Kaplan *et al.* 1992; Rosen 1992, 1996; Pearsall and Piperno 1993; Matthews and Postgate 1994). The integration of animal husbandry into the Egyptian agrarian system was a critical factor in its success and this important evidence must also be considered (e.g. Moens and Wetterstrom 1988; Zeder 1991; Redding 1992). Pollen analysis, too, is able to contribute useful agricultural data (e.g. Ayyad *et al.* 1991, 1992, 1995), including the pollen found in dung remains (e.g. Vermeeren and Kuijper 1993), as is the study of insects as pests of cereal storage (e.g. Kislev 1991; Panagiotakopulu *et al.* 1995; Panagiotakopulu and van der Veen 1997). Soil micromorphology can offer valuable interpretations of ancient occupation levels with regard to activity areas related to cereal processing and preparation (e.g. Matthews and Postgate 1994), while geomorphology and hydrology have provided valuable data on the history of the Nile flood regime (Butzer 1976, 1984).

Experimental evidence

Experimental archaeology, especially using authentic materials to replicate ancient practices, offers a critical means of testing hypotheses concerning ancient cereal husbandry and provides data for the integration of archaeological and ethnographic evidence (Samuel 1989, 1993: 280; Anderson 1992: 182; Kemp 1994: 146; Viklund 1998). Cereal-based experiments have provided important data concerning the growing, harvesting, threshing, winnowing, sieving, grinding and cooking of emmer and barley (e.g. Reynolds 1981; Anderson 1992; Willcox 1992; Samuel 1989, 1993, 1994a and b, Chapter 22, this volume; Meurers-Balke and Lüning 1992; Viklund 1998). Other useful projects, such as the experimental charring of cereals, have demonstrated how the differential preservation of grain and chaff can affect the overall composition of archaeobotanical assemblages (Boardman and Jones 1990), as have investigations into the use of animal dung as fuel (Miller 1984; Miller and Smart 1984; Bottema 1984; Anderson and Ertug-Yaras 1997). The examination and replication of ancient tools, coupled with ethnographic models for their use, have also added to our understanding of the development and function of many tool types (e.g. Rees 1981; Reynolds 1981; Samuel 1989, 1993; Anderson 1992).

It is obvious that a well-integrated, multi-disciplinary approach, using all available data will provide us with the clearest picture of Egyptian cereal production and processing than any single source of evidence alone (Table 21.1). The picture offered by the artistic and textual records is too general for dealing with a specific settlement; while the direct agricultural evidence from archaeobotanical remains, coupled with other lines of investigation, offers a more finely tuned picture of the practices of an individual farming community. Until further comparative data are available from a wider array of Egyptian settlements, however, important questions dealing with temporal and spatial differences, as well as those of the continuity and scale of cereal production and processing practices will remain unanswered.

The Egyptian cereals: emmer wheat and hulled barley

The archaeobotanical record shows that emmer wheat and hulled barley have been cultivated in Egypt since at least the sixth millennium BC (Caton-Thompson and Gardiner

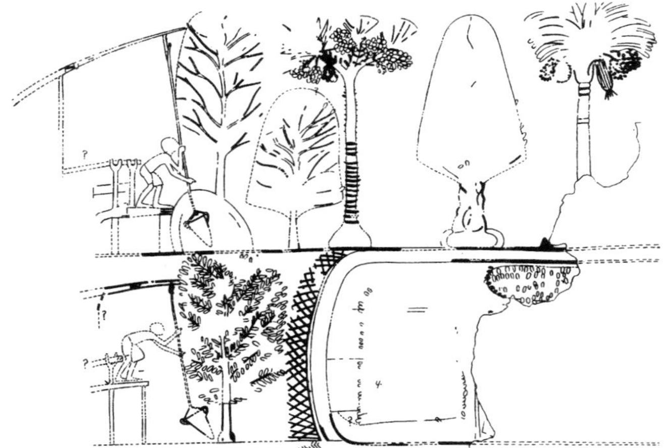

Figure 21.5 Shaduf *scene from the tomb of Neferhotep at Thebes (TT49).*

1934: 46–9; Wetterstrom 1993: 201; Zohary and Hopf 1993: 209) and that they continued to be the two most important cereals produced until Greco–Roman times. Two vital products of emmer and barley – bread and beer – were the main staples in the Pharaonic Egyptian diet. Emmer was primarily used to make bread but also was used for beer-making while barley was most suitable for beer-making (Chapter 22 this volume). Emmer (*Triticum dicoccum* (Schrank) Schübl.) is a hulled wheat, which means that after the threshing process breaks up the cereal ear into spikelets, the spikelets then need to be processed further to rid them of their chaff in order to obtain a clean grain product (Fig. 21.1). Like emmer, hulled barley must undergo a similar process to separate the chaff which is strongly fused to the grain. The archaeobotanical record shows that two-row barley (*Hordeum vulgare* subsp. *distichum* (= *H. sativum* var. *distichum*)) and six-row barley (*Hordeum vulgare* subsp. *vulgare* (= *H. sativum* var. *hexastichum*)) were grown in Egypt, although relatively few finds of the more primitive two-row form have been reported (de Vartaran and Asensi Amorós 1997: 127–8). It is now suggested that four-row barley (*H. tetrastichum*), commonly reported from Egypt, is simply a lax-eared form of six-row barley and that separating these two closely related types in archaeobotanical material is unjustified (Charles 1984: 31; Buurman 1987: 22; Zohary and Hopf 1994: 58) (For detailed descriptions of the grains and chaff of emmer and barley, see Täckholm *et al.* 1941; Charles 1984; Jacomet 1987; Samuel 1989; Zohary and Hopf 1994; Nesbitt and Samuel 1996; Hillman *et al.* 1996). Several finds of naked barley (*H. vulgare* var. *nudum*) have also been recorded although claims for this species in ancient Egypt have been disputed (e.g. Helbaek 1959). While barley thrives on good soils, it also grows well on relatively poor quality land and can endure arid and saline conditions (Zohary and Hopf 1994: 55) and in Egypt, it is often grown after the reclamation of salt land (Foaden and Fletcher 1910: 438; Täckholm *et al.* 1941: 283). Archaeobotanical evidence also shows that barley was an important animal fodder in the past (Wetterstrom 1982, 1994; Moens and Wetterstrom 1988; Murray 1993, 1994, forthcoming) as it is today (Täckholm *et al.* 1941: 284; Ayrout 1963: 51; Barakat 1990: 11).

Determining the predominance of emmer or barley as human food in an ancient Egyptian settlement, and indeed in Egypt as a whole during the Pharaonic period, is not a simple matter. The artistic record offers no distinction between cereals (Erman 1894: 434; Kemp 1994: 145), while the lexicographic data shows that many types of emmer and barley were recognised by the ancient Egyptians who evidently distinguished cereals by colour, by region (i.e. Upper or Lower Egypt) and perhaps for religious reasons (Gardiner 1941, 1947; Dixon 1969; Germer 1985, forthcoming; de Vartavan 1987). These numerous ancient distinctions, however, do not directly correspond to modern botanical taxonomic classification (Gardiner 1947: 222; de Vartavan 1987: 12). While emmer and barley are clearly distinct taxa, it has been suggested that differences in the varieties of ancient cereals were probably more complex than those in modern comparative material, and that these differences may be difficult to determine in the archaeobotanical material (Hillman *et al.* 1996: 197; Willcox 1992: 162; Buurman 1987: 20–1; also Nevo 1995). Distinguishing cereals on the basis of colour and region continued as a practice common to Egyptian farmers this century (Foaden and Fletcher 1910: 430–1; Täckholm *et al.* 1941: 232; 250). Textual sources sometimes also distinguish between cereal types, for example, in administrative documents, letters and even in literature, references to emmer and barley were often written in separate colours, with red for emmer and black for barley (Gardiner 1941, 1947, 1948; Caminos 1954; James 1962; Janssen 1975). This and other linguistic evidence imply that barley was the predominant cereal during the Old and Middle Kingdoms, whereas by the New Kingdom, and certainly from the Twenty-fifth Dynasty until the Ptolemaic period, emmer appears to have become the most important cereal of the two (Gardiner 1941: 27; Kees 1961: 74; Dixon 1969: 138; Janssen 1975: 460; Lloyd 1983: 327). Most textual evidence survives from the New Kingdom and suggests, for example, that emmer was the primary cereal used for the payment of wages and taxes at that time (Gardiner 1941: 27; Kees 1961: 74; Dixon 1969: 138; Janssen 1975: 460).

The apparent shift in the importance of emmer over barley has been attributed to the initial success of the more resilient barley crop under basin irrigation, followed by the more widespread use of emmer after improvements in irrigation during the New Kingdom (Hassan 1984b: 223). Textual sources have also suggested that barley was the primary cereal of Upper Egypt, whereas emmer was the main cereal of Lower Egypt (Täckholm *et al.* 1941: 284;

(Murray forthcoming). Similarly; it has been noted that a decline in the number of wet-loving species in Egyptian samples may be an indication of the successful levelling and drainage of arable fields (Wetterstrom 1986: 9).

Tilling

There is much confusion concerning the order of agrarian operations with regard to tilling; sowing and the trampling in of seed by animals. This is due to variations in the artistic representations of these practices found in tomb-paintings and reliefs. In reality the order of these operations would have undoubtedly varied depending on the type of land under cultivation and its condition; i.e. whether it was freshly inundated or not; how long it had been under water; how long it had been left after drainage; whether it was previously fallowed land; virgin land; horticultural land; etc. Indeed, the evidence seems to suggest that very little tillage, if any, was necessary on land well-inundated by traditional basin irrigation.

Ideally, the practice of tilling creates a loose, friable soil which improves cereal yield by providing an adequate seed cover for germination, aerating the soil and encouraging strong root development (Foaden and Fletcher 1908: 87; Arnon 1972: 430). When necessary, the tilling of soil in ancient Egypt was done primarily using either a hoe or a shallow ploughing ard (Fig. 21.2). An early example of the hoe, used for canal digging, is clearly depicted on the Predynastic Scorpion Macehead (*c.* 3200; Emery 1961: 237). The hoe could be as simple as a modified forked branch, though the most common type consisted of a blade of sharpened wood, either broad and flat or thick and narrow, fastened to a wooden handle at an acute angle and often strengthened by a cord (Fig. 21.6). Like the modern Egyptian *turiah* or fass, the ancient hoe was a versatile tool which could be used for a variety of tasks, such as land preparation prior to sowing, covering sown seed, breaking up dirt clods after ploughing or sowing, weeding, and any number of jobs dealing with the earthworks necessary for irrigation. A study earlier this century found that hoeing was considered the most important tilling operation of Egyptian farming (Foaden and Fletcher 1908: 98).

A natural progression from the simple hoe was the ard-type plough, also commonly depicted in the artistic record. The use of the plough would have significantly increased the agricultural potential of lands previously thought not to be worth the time and effort to prepare. It has been estimated, for example, that using an ox-drawn ard plough is between two and fifteen times faster than cultivating manually (Halstead 1995: 13). The wooden ard would have been attached to draught animals, usually cattle, and scenes from the tomb of Paheri at Elkab, for example, suggest that men, too, may have occasionally pulled the plough (Fig. 21.7). Initially, draught animals were harnessed by a yoke attached to the animals' horns whereas later, a more efficient shoulder yoke was used (David 1986: 147). Based on Old Kingdom tomb scenes, Harpur suggests that the plough may have been more important than the hoe for tillage, the latter perhaps only being used if the ground were very hard (Harpur 1987: 159). Egyptian soils are best ploughed when they are neither too wet nor too dry (Foaden and Fletcher 1908: 91; Arnon 1972: 430); although some tomb-scenes appear to indicate that ploughing may have sometimes commenced amidst pools of standing water (Montet 1958: 108). The optimal time to plough these soils is when the surface has dried out enough to form fine cracks and when the plough can keep fairly clean of soil (Foaden and Fletcher 1908: 91). The artistic record suggests that tilling was done primarily by men.

Tomb-paintings and reliefs depict a variety of tillage practices using both the hoe and plough, throughout the Pharaonic period which variously show:

1) tilling, sowing and then the occasional trampling in of seed by animals;
2) sowing, tilling, (trampling occasionally); and
3) sowing and trampling only.

In the first example, ploughing or hoeing prior to sowing, although commonly depicted, was perhaps most import-

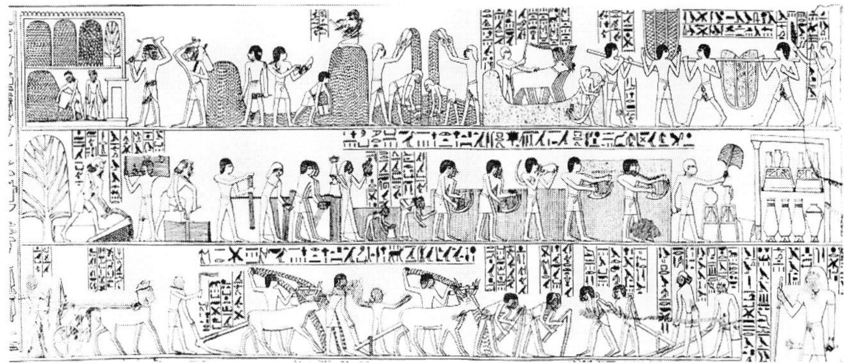

Figure 21.7 Scene showing an ancient Egyptian plough in use, from the tomb of Paheri at Elkab (EK3).

ant for fields left too long after flooding, newly claimed lands, or those fields left fallow or unflooded during the previous year(s). It has been suggested that ploughing prior to sowing, on newly laid Nile silts, would have encouraged moisture loss and therefore would have been disadvantageous in some cases (Foaden and Fletcher 1908: 91; Arnon 1972: 423). In the second sequence, an initial ploughing was deemed unnecessary and tilling was used to incorporate the sown seed into the fresh silt; scenes of this type are found in chapels at Meidum, for example, and associated captions indicate that ploughing was used to cover the sown seeds although no sowers are actually depicted (Harpur 1987: 161). Since sowing was commonly performed simultaneously with ploughing, the Egyptian word *sk3* can mean plough, till or cultivate (Caminos 1954: 13; James 1962: 18; Simpson 1972: 94). The third example, of sowing and trampling, is discussed in the section on Trampling (p. 519).

The nature of the weed flora in archaeobotanical assemblages can provide an indication of the depth of tillage since the ard plough scratches a shallow furrow in the soil without turning it over as heavily as the later mould-board ploughs, and therefore each have a distinct impact on the weed flora. Most notable is that hardy perennial and biennial weeds can survive even after cross-ploughing with an ard (Hillman 1991: 29–30) and this survival is most useful to archaeobotanists when the type of plough being used is in question. It has been widely observed in ethnographic studies of traditional agriculture that ards, hoes and other tools used for levelling or breaking new agricultural ground can differ from those tools later used to cultivate the same land. Similarly, differences may be expected between the tools used for garden crops and those used for cereal husbandry (Reynolds 1981: 104; Hillman 1984b: 116).

A wide variety of ancient agricultural tools have been recovered from Egyptian excavations and demonstrate that, although an array of hoes and ards were available for tilling operations (e.g. Petrie 1917), the basic design of these tools remained largely unchanged throughout the Pharaonic period (Wilkinson 1878; Butzer 1976). It would seem that the general conservatism of farmers world-wide with regard to a useful and effective tool applied to the Egyptian example: if it works, why change it? (e.g. Rees 1981: 72). Indeed, the efficiency of the simple hoe and ard plough on Egyptian soils have ensured their continued importance throughout the twentieth century (Lane 1860; Foaden and Fletcher 1908; Blackman 1927; Tantawi 1941; Ayrout 1963; Nessim 1988; Hivernel 1996).

Raking, harrowing and levelling

The practice of raking or harrowing, either before or after sowing, serves to break up clods of earth, level the soil and ensure a greater cover for sown seed (Fig. 21.2; e.g. Arnon 1972: 423). Soil levelling is a critical part of irrigation agriculture since uneven land requires more water and may also result in differential productivity from unequal water distribution (Foaden and Fletcher 1908: 98; Arnon 1972: 429). The range of tools used for this practice might have included rakes, boards, logs and large bundles of brush, either hand-held or drawn behind animals (Hillman 1984b: 116). The ancient Egyptians may have had no specialised tool for this operation, if indeed it was practised at all, since the inundation may have sufficiently levelled the land for most purposes. No artistic representations of harrowing have been recognised, although Petrie (1917: 54) uncovered rakes from the Twelfth-Dynasty settlement of Kahun which he suggested may have been used for harrowing or covering seed. In addition to the hoe, mallets were also evidently used for breaking up clods of dirt (Erman 1894: 428–9; Tantawi 1941: 238). The practice is clearly depicted in tomb-scenes (e.g. Harpur 1987: 159) and excavated examples of mallets from Kahun might have been well-suited for this task (David 1986: 147; e.g. Petrie 1917: pls. XLV, XLVI). During this century the *zahaffa*, a beam of wood or a palm tree pulled lengthways behind a team of oxen, was commonly used to break up dirt clods and level the soil after ploughing (Foaden and Fletcher 1908: 128; Ayrout 1963: 38). It has been observed that, today, harrowing and levelling are more commonly practised in the Delta (Hopkins 1987: 119) but it would be difficult to determine if the same were true in antiquity.

Sowing

The timing of cereal sowing would have varied somewhat by region and by year since, as noted above, flood waters would have ordinarily receded by early October in the south and four to six weeks later in the northern parts of Egypt (Butzer 1976: 17). Archaeobotanical assemblages from Pharaonic settlements clearly show the pattern of winter sowing and spring reaping for the cereals, on the basis that many of the weed species present in charred remains are those which were in seed in the spring when the cereals were being harvested. Among the most common spring-seeding weeds found in Egyptian archaeobotanical samples, for example, are species of rye grass (*Lolium sp.*) and canary grass (*Phalaris sp.*) (e.g. Renfrew 1985; Wetterstrom 1986, 1992, 1994; Thanheiser 1987, in prep; Samuel 1989; Kroll 1989; Barakat 1990; de Roller 1992; van Zeist and de Roller 1993; Murray 1993, 1994, forthcoming). Studies show that weeds can be reduced significantly by sowing cereals early and in dense stands (Willcox 1992: 168; Foaden and Fletcher 1908: 19).

The cereal grains used for sowing are often known as seed corn, and the issuing of seed corn prior to sowing is sometimes the first activity shown in tomb scenes (Harpur 1987: 159). In traditional Mediterranean and Near Eastern agriculture, cereals are most likely to be sown in spikelet form rather than as clean grain (e.g. Hillman 1984b: 116;

Willcox 1992: 163; Peña-Chocarro 1996: 134) since pounding the grain to rid it of its chaff can damage its usefulness as seed corn. For this reason sowing in the spikelet is likely to have been the case in ancient Egypt as well. The artistic record suggests that cereals were scattered by hand from bags hung around the shoulder or held in the hand. This method of broadcast sowing is common in the Near East and experiments have shown it to be an easier and more time-efficient method than sowing seeds in rows (e.g. Willcox 1992: 164). While tomb representations suggests that twined bags were used for sowing seed (see Chapter 12, this volume), these artefacts may be difficult to positively identify archaeologically since they may also have been used for a variety of other purposes (McDowell 1992: 203). The sower is usually shown standing in front of a plough or a flock of sheep which would later be used to cover the sown seed.

In traditional agriculture, a mixture of two or more cereal or pulse species are sometimes sown together for a variety of reasons (e.g. as a way of reducing the risk of failure of any single species), and these crops are known as maslins. Archaeobotanical samples from Egypt and elsewhere in the Near East often contain a mixture of wheat and barley and based on ethnographic observation, it has been suggested that, in some cases, this mixing of cereals may have occurred at the sowing stage rather than as a later accident of storage or through the subsequent mixing of debris during disposal (Jones and Halstead 1995: 103). Their research has shown that the mixing of species is often the result of the contamination of seed corn by other seeds of similar size, habitat and harvest date. These contaminants can be difficult to separate from the clean grain and are therefore sown together as the seed corn the following year (Jones and Halstead 1995: 112). The highly mixed nature of wheat and barley seed corn in Egypt earlier this century was attributed to this phenomenon (Foaden and Fletcher 1910: 326, 431). Identifying the seed corn as perhaps the primary source of crop contamination may be an important first step in determining the antiquity of growing maslins in Egypt (Jones and Halstead 1995: 112; van der Veen 1995). Due to the potential variation in harvesting dates, between emmer and barley, and the larger-sized emmer spikelets that would theoretically make them easier to separate, the intentional sowing of emmer/barley maslins may not have been a common Egyptian practice (see Harvesting, p. 520). It has been suggested, however, that the use of multivariate statistics is the most likely means for identifying the associated cereal, pulse and weed assemblages of maslin crops in the archaeobotanical record (van der Veen 1995). Further research is required in order to determine if this practice can be detected in the Egyptian archaeobotanical record.

Trampling

As with ploughing, the trampling in of the grain by animals would have protected the seeds from birds and other pests and would have facilitated their germination. This method would have been most effective on the soft earth of newly lain silt and somewhat less effective on land left too long after the flood had receded. Tomb-representations, as well as literary texts, indicate that flocks of sheep and occasionally donkeys were used to trample in seed (Vandier 1978; Harpur 1987) although in the New Kingdom and later periods, artistic and historical sources show that pigs were sometimes used for the job (Herodotus II.14; Wilkinson 1878: 394; Montet 1958: 111; Wreszinski 1915: pl. 97b). Cattle probably would have been too heavy for this task since seed sown too deeply in wet soils can fail from water-logging and lack of air (Foaden and Fletcher 1908: 107). It has been noted that the softer water-logged soils of the Delta were most conducive to the large-scale use of trampling (Lloyd 1976: 77) and indeed Harpur (1987: 163) queries whether the sparse artistic evidence for trampling in Upper Egypt should be regarded as an accident of preservation or an indication that the plough was more commonly used than the trampling method in that region. Tomb-scenes show the chaos of the practice, with stray sheep in disarray before a man holding a stick instils order and encourages them to move in the right direction (Erman 1894: 429; Harpur 1987: 162). The practice of seed trampling was reported by Herodotus (II.14) in the fifth century BC, who rather optimistically noted the relative ease of the method and of Egyptian cereal production in general: '[The Egyptians] do not have to plough the furrow or dig the soil, they can dispense with the tiresome labour in the field that other people must endure. As soon as the river has risen of its own accord, watered the arable land and receded again, each of them sows his own plot and drives pigs onto it to tread the seeds in. Then he awaits the harvest!'.

Between sowing and harvest

There are few tomb-scenes depicting cereal husbandry practices between the sowing of grain and the harvest (Harpur 1987: 164) although ethnographic evidence allows us to speculate on several processes that may have taken place. Additional watering of cereal fields would have been done manually during this time, if required at all. Those cereals to be used as animal fodder may have been cut or uprooted at this stage while the plants were still green (Hillman 1984b: 117; Charles 1990: 62; Peña-Chocarro 1996: 134). Guarding the cereals from pests, especially birds, prior to harvest also would have been an important duty. Bird-infested cereal fields are sometimes illustrated, as are figures using clappers to scare birds away (Harpur 1987: 168). Other pests, such as insects, crop disease and bad weather also held the potential threat of a blighted harvest. Prior to the harvest, cereal fields were also surveyed using pre-measured cords to determine the amount of tax to be paid on the estimated yield, later to be compared to the actual yield after threshing. Textual sources indicate that this task was conducted by a governing body known to have existed since at least the Second Dynasty, yet Berger (1934: 52) notes that its presence does not appear in the artistic record until the Eighteenth Dynasty at Thebes. Ethnographic observation indicates that the early harvest of part of the cereal crop, in order to avoid tax, is not unknown (Hillman pers. comm.).

Weeding

Did Egyptian farmers weed their cereal crops? Weeds directly compete with cereals for light, air, water and nutrients and are most detrimental to young plants, and in the arid Egyptian climate, it is the competition for moisture which can be most damaging (Foaden and Fletcher 1908: 104; Arnon 1972: 479). Once cereals are established, however, they can outgrow weeds, and weeding beyond a certain stage may be disadvantageous due to unnecessary root disturbance (Reynolds 1981: 115; Hillman 1981: 148). Despite having a potentially negative effect on crop yields (Hillman 1984b: 117), ethnographic evidence from traditional agriculture in Egypt and elsewhere shows that cereal crops often contain more weeds than cereal plants (e.g. Foaden and Fletcher 1910: 325; Reynolds 1981: 115; Charles 1990: 54; Peña-Chocarro 1996: 134) and consequently, the seed corn used for sowing the following year is frequently contaminated with field weeds from the previous year's harvest (Foaden and Fletcher 1910: 325; Charles 1990: 54). An analysis of botanical offerings from the tomb of Tutankhamun (KV62; *c.* 1325 BC), for example, has provided a rare opportunity to study the origins of crop contamination. The results from fourteen samples showed that 51 per cent of the contaminant species probably arrived with the harvested crop, while the remainder could be traced to contamination in storage or by other means (de Vartavan 1990: 491). It would seem likely, then, that Egyptian seed corn may have been perpetually contaminated with field weeds from previous years.

Many weeds have beneficial qualities, by providing food for both humans and animals, medicines, dyes and fuel. Weeds can provide grazing, conserve soil moisture, protect against soil erosion and may have been tolerated or even encouraged in some cases (Arnon 1972: 479; Hillman 1984b: 117; Willcox 1992: 168). Exceptions probably included the removal of large and prickly weeds which could hinder harvesting (Hillman 1991: 30; Willcox 1992: 167; Charles 1990: 54). It has been noted that, in some areas, Egyptian farmers today do not generally weed their cereal crops (Hopkins 1987: 119) and observations earlier this century in Egypt, prior to the introduction of weedkillers, show that the weeding of cereals was a rare practice (Foaden and Fletcher 1910: 433). The archaeobotanical evidence from many sites attests the profusion of weeds in ancient Egyptian cereal fields (e.g. Wetterstrom 1986; de Vartavan 1990; Murray forthcoming; Chapter 22, this volume, also see section on Sowing, p. 518), and indeed the artistic record does not clearly depict the practice of weeding. To date, therefore, there is little evidence to confirm anything but the casual weeding of cereals in ancient Egypt.

Cereal processing

Harvesting

Emmer and barley usually ripen about six months after sowing and, depending on the region, sowing times, species sown, water availability, type of land, crop density and harvesting method, the harvest could have been as early as February or as late as May (Foaden and Fletcher 1910: 434; Willcocks and Craig 1913: 768; Hopkins 1987: 118; Willcox 1992: 163; Charles 1990: 55). The barley crop, for example, is likely to have ripened and been harvested a few weeks before the emmer crop (e.g. Pliny N.H. XVIII 7 in Wilkinson 1878: 398; Foaden and Fletcher 1910: 438; Willcocks and Craig 1913: 768). Cereal crops sown in the early winter months would be expected to produce higher yields than those sown later due to late flooding or problems of drainage (Hillman 1981: 146–7; Willcox 1992: 162; Charles 1990: 51). Farming experiments have demonstrated that cereal fields which are densely sown are not only easier to harvest but also tend to ripen more uniformly (Willcox 1992: 163). Observations in Egypt show that cereals are allowed to become 'dead ripe' before harvesting in order to facilitate threshing (Foaden and Fletcher 1910: 434), yet allowing the crop to become over-ripe would result in grain loss, therefore the timing of the harvest would have been a critical decision (Russell 1988: 43). Cereals in Egypt are often harvested in the evening or early morning while they are still moist with dew, in order to minimise grain loss (Foaden and Fletcher 1910: 434; Täckholm *et al.* 1941: 238) and this sensible practice may have taken place in ancient times as well (e.g. Caminos 1954: 307).

The primary tool used for harvesting emmer and barley was the sickle. Originally, sickle blades were made of chipped stone, and were either hand-held or set into a groove within a straight or curved wooden handle. They were sometimes also set into the lower jawbone of an animal (Fig. 21.8). Sickle blades were later made of copper and then bronze, although chipped stone blades continued to be used throughout the Pharaonic period (e.g. Petrie 1891; Bruyère 1939; Miller 1983; Jeffreys forthcoming). An analysis of chipped-stone sickle blades has demonstrated that the microscopic striations which form on these tools during harvesting can vary greatly depending on the number of stems reaped at one time, the degree of humidity, hardness and silica content of the stems, and the ability of the har-

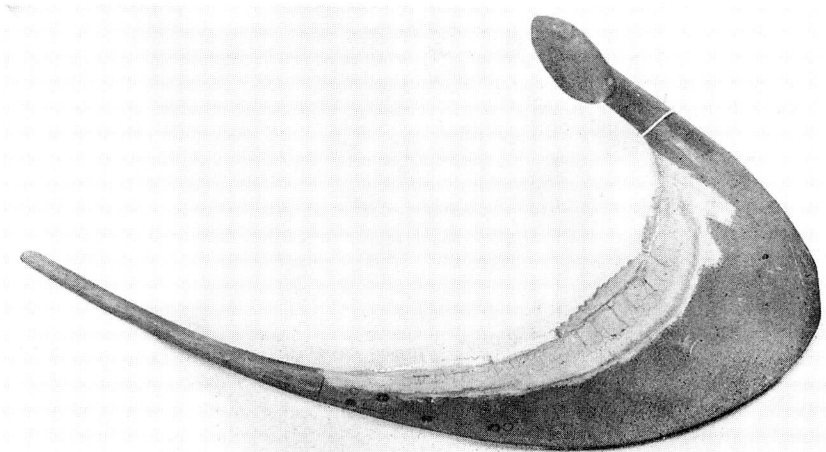

Figure 21.8 Ancient Egyptian sickle.

vester, i.e. the contact with the soil and the motion of harvesting itself (Anderson 1992: 194). An important conclusion of Anderson's research is that, while the presence of sickle blades on a site may represent a harvesting activity, the frequency of the use of the tool and indeed the product being harvested cannot be determined from the microscopic wear patterns; nor do the number of sickles found on a settlement reflect the amount of cereal harvested (Anderson 1992: 205). It had been suggested that wear patterns on harvesting blades could also help determine whether the land had been tilled or not, a question relevant to Egyptian agriculture, but recent experiments show that wear patterns only determine whether a tool was used near to the ground (i.e. 20–30 centimetres from the soil) and do not indicate whether the ground was tilled (Anderson 1992: 194). Striations rarely occur if wheat and barley are harvested high on the straw (Anderson 1992: 196). Sickle blades also may have been used for harvesting other materials, such as reeds and sedges for fuel or building material, or roots and tubers (Anderson 1992: 206).

How were ancient Egyptian cereals harvested? Harvesting could have been done in three ways: 1) by uprooting; 2) by cutting the cereal low in the straw; or 3) by harvesting only the cereal ears, either with a sickle or by hand (see Fig. 21.2; and see Hillman 1981, 1984a, 1984b; Willcox 1992; Anderson 1992). More than one form of reaping may have taken place and in some cases, wheat and barley may have been harvested differently depending on crop density, the scale of operations or the ultimate use of the cereal and its straw.

Harvesting by uprooting the entire cereal plant would have been done either by hand or perhaps by using a blunt sickle blade. Traditionally, uprooting is usually done by grabbing the cereal low on the straw and knocking the roots out of the ground to dislodge as much soil as possible since this may later contaminate the threshing yard and the final grain product (Hillman 1981: 150, 1984b: 118). Although the uprooting of flax is frequently depicted in tomb-scenes, the uprooting of cereals does not appear to be shown.

In traditional Mediterranean and Near Eastern agriculture, harvesting is often done by cutting the cereals relatively low on the straw. Ethnographic and experimental research have found that little effort is made to avoid most weeds using this harvesting method (Hillman 1981: 150; Willcox 1992: 167; Charles 1990: 54) although the distance of the cut from the ground may depend on the height of the prickly weeds to be avoided (Anderson 1992: 189). Cutting cereals low on the straw has the added advantage of leaving cereal stubble in the fields for livestock to graze. Cereals harvested in this way have a relatively long length of straw attached and therefore can be bundled into sheaves (Hillman 1984b: 118). This harvesting method appears to be represented in the artistic record, especially in tomb scenes from the Old Kingdom, such as those of Ty and Mereruka at Saqqara (Épron *et al.* 1939; Duell 1938).

Reaping high on the straw is done when the harvester wants to cut only the ears of the cereal and as little straw as possible. With this method, a handful of cereal stalks are cut simultaneously with a sickle at the base of the lowest ear in the bunch. For both emmer and barley, the height of the ears can vary greatly; as much as a metre from the shortest to the tallest ear within a given field, especially if the crop is sown late (Reynolds 1981: 113; Hillman 1981: 151, 1984b: 119; Anderson 1992: 190). Harvesting in this way means that the cut ears have varying lengths of short straw attached and therefore no cereal sheaves are produced, as there would be with uprooting or cutting low on the straw (Hillman 1984b: 119). If the straw is to be used as fuel, stored fodder, or building material later on, then after the harvesting of the ears, the straw must be cut in a separate operation. An advantage of harvesting only the cereal ears is that there is less straw to thresh and winnow and few, if any weeds to remove. In addition to cutting the ears with a sickle, they can also be harvested by hand. Harvesting experiments have indicated that reaping the cereal ears by hand can be a more efficient method than using chipped stone sickle blades, due in part to the variable heights of cereals in a given field (Knörzer 1971: 103; Reynolds 1981: 113). The slight, natural droop of the cereal ear is an advantage for hand-harvesting, as this feature exposes a section of the stalk to the elements, thus making it more brittle and easier to break off. The ideal time for harvesting in this way would have been just prior to the natural breakage of the ear at this exposed point (Reynolds 1981: 113). The artistic record of harvesting invariably shows the use of sickles rather than harvesting by hand but the possibility of hand-harvesting in certain circumstances certainly should not be excluded.

The artistic portrayal of cereal production in the after-life offers an uncomplicated and idealised view of the harvest where, in the Elysian Fields of the Book of the Dead, emmer is perennially and unifomly three cubits high (*c.* 157.7 cm) (Budge 1898: 171). (Modern emmer from Turkey, for example, can vary in height from 60–*c.* 150 cm (Hillman 1984a: 26) although these soils may be less fertile than those of the Nile valley, and it is also likely that ancient cereals were much taller than present-day varieties (Hillman pers. comm.; D. Zohary pers. comm.). Harvesters in tomb-scenes, are usually shown working in a line across the field, each grasping a handful of consistently high cereal stems and cutting the straw below their hands. The height of the cut is highly variable, as is the height of the straw left standing in the fields, indeed two different heights of cut straw are often indicated (Fig. 21.7). Perhaps the most useful information from this evidence concerns not the actual reaping but rather the harvested cereals themselves. In Old Kingdom scenes, harvested cereals are shown bound into sheaves, indicating that a relatively long straw remained attached to the cereals, as illustrated in the Fifth-Dynasty tomb of Mereruka at Saqqara, for example (Fig. 21.9; see Duell 1938: pl. 169). Sheaving would not have been likely if only the ears, with their varying lengths of short straw, were harvested. Uprooting would have also produced sheaves and although this practice is clearly depicted for the harvesting of flax, it is not shown for cereals. In general, the artistic record from the Old Kingdom suggests that cereals were not harvested by hand-picking, nor by the exclusive cutting of the cereal ears, but rather that they may have been cut relatively low on the straw, as implied by the sheaved cereals. In contrast, New Kingdom tomb-scenes often show that the harvested cereals were not bound into sheaves but rather that the harvested ears were collected in baskets or woven carriers prior to their transport to the threshing floor. Likewise, threshing scenes clearly show animals trampling the harvested cereal ears, as in the Eighteenth-Dynasty tombs of Menna (TT69; Fig. 21.10; Davies 1936: pl. LI) and Paheri (EK3; Fig. 21.7; see Tylor and Griffith 1894: pl. III). In theory, the practice of harvesting by reaping the ears separately from the straw is more indicative of small-scale operations (Hillman 1984b: 119). Nonetheless, the artistic record from the New Kingdom suggests the use of this method.

Several authors have commented on this possible change in harvesting practice as suggested by the artistic record (e.g. Wilkinson 1878; Erman 1894; Vandier 1978; Sist 1987; Casey 1995), although it is clear that this source alone does not provide the detailed evidence required to address this important question in full. Archaeobotanical analysis provides the best means of investigating the issue, since the amount and type of weeds gathered during the harvest vary according to the method of harvest used. For example, a high number of weed seeds present in samples provide some evidence against the harvesting of the cereals by exclusively cutting the ears, which would produce few, if any, weed seeds. If the weed species present are relatively low-growing and arrived on the settlement with the cereal, as is likely, then harvesting was probably carried out by cutting the cereal low enough on the straw to include these weeds in the harvest. Uprooted cereals would tend to have a higher proportion of inseparable twining and climbing species and a relatively high number of straw culm bases (Hillman 1981: 149–51). Specific archaeobotanical research of this type is needed on a site by site basis to determine if there is reliable evidence for a change in harvesting practice through time or by region or if the differences in tomb scenes simply reflect a change in the artistic conventions of the genre.

Harvesting methods may well have varied due a number of factors. Ethnographic examples from Egypt and the Near East show that uprooting occurs most often with the relatively low-growing barley crop or for wheat growing sparsely (Wilkinson 1878: 422–3; Dalman 1933, III: 34–7; Täckholm *et al.* 1941: 283; Hillman 1984b: 118; Halstead and Jones 1989: 43). Experimental harvesting also confirms that cereals are most likely to be uprooted when sparse growing (Anderson 1992: 189) and that, because uprooting tends to contaminate the grain with soil, it is perhaps most suitable for barley to be used as animal fodder (Willcox 1992: 167). The scale of operations may have also dictated harvesting styles, as seen by the gleaners who are often depicted in tomb-scenes collecting cereals into baskets by hand (e.g. Davies 1936). Traditionally, gleaners are the poorer members of the community who are allowed to gather grain that has been missed or left during the harvest (Dalman 1933, III: 60–1; Hillman 1984b: 120) and indeed, in Egypt today, fields of harvested free-threshing wheats are sometimes left open to the gleaners (Hopkins 1987: 119). Petrie (1917) suggested that only the ears were harvested in ancient Egypt and that the straw was later uprooted because it was too valuable to be damaged during threshing. Cereal straw was most likely a valuable product in its own right and was no doubt occasionally in short supply, particularly after a poor harvest or during the summer months and the period of

Figure 21.9 Harvesting sequence from the Old Kingdom tomb of Mereruka at Saqqara.

Figure 21.10 Harvesting sequence from the New Kingdom tomb of Menna at Thebes (TT69).

inundation (Wilkinson 1878: 424–5; Wetterstrom 1994: 6). In some cases, the condition of the straw may not have mattered; i.e. as fuel, fodder, or temper in mud-brick, plaster and pottery; whereas for roofing or trade this may have been more of a consideration. If a change in harvesting did indeed take place in the New Kingdom; then perhaps an increase in the importance of cereal straw may have been a contributing factor. Pliny (*Natural History* XVIII; XLV 161; 162 in Darby *et al.* 1977: 488) observed that in Egypt 'wheat was cut twice; and then a third extravagantly wasted; left for the cattle to eat' and this has been interpreted as three separate harvests of wheat (Darby *et al.* 1977: 488). It has also been suggested that this may indicate that the first cutting of wheat was for the ears; the second for the cereal straw and the third left behind for the cattle was the cereal stubble remaining in the field for grazing (e.g. Casey 1995).

Ethnographic observations from Egypt and elsewhere indicate that harvested cereals are often left to dry in the fields before being taken to the threshing floor (Foaden and Fletcher 1910: 434; Hillman 1984b: 120; Halstead and Jones 1989: 44; Charles 1990: 55; Peña-Chocarro 1996: 138) and that the eventual transport of the cereals is sometimes done at night or in the early morning, when the sheaves are damp enough to prevent grain loss (Hillman 1984b: 121; Peña-Chocarro 1996: 138) although it is not clear whether this was also an ancient Egyptian practice. The artistic record shows harvested cereals being carried by hand or transported by donkey to the threshing floor in a variety of containers, including frames, nets, sacks and baskets. If the straw was harvested separately, it may have been taken to storage at this stage or, as has been ethnographically observed elsewhere, it may have remained stored in the field until required (Hillman 1984b: 126; Charles 1990: 55; Peña-Chocarro 1996: 140).

Threshing

The threshing stage is undertaken in order to separate the emmer spikelets and hulled barley grains from the cereal straw and is achieved by spreading the loosened sheaves or cereal ears onto a threshing floor and subjecting the crop to one of these three most likely methods: 1) beating with a stick; 2) trampling by animals; or 3) threshing by sledge (Fig. 21.2) (e.g. Hillman 1984b). Threshing often takes place during the hottest part of the day when the cereals are at their driest and the grains are most likely to break away from the straw (e.g. Halstead and Jones 1989: 44). The bulk of the artistic and textual evidence indicates that trampling by animals was the primary method used to thresh cereals, although other small-scale methods also may have been used, particularly threshing by beating.

Threshing by beating with a stick or other wooden implement produces spikelets and largely intact straw. A similar method, known as lashing, involves beating the crop against the floor, wall, object, or lashing frame (Hillman 1984b: 121–2; Anderson 1992: 193; Peña-Chocarro 1996: 138). In traditional agricultural communities, including Egypt, threshing by beating is usually done when small quantities are processed, especially by poorer families who have no access to cattle or a threshing yard (e.g. Ayrout 1963: 51). Hillman (1984b: 121) points out just such a case for the threshing of gleanings in *Ruth* 2,17: 'so she (Ruth) gleaned in the field until evening, and beat out that which she had gleaned'. Earlier this century, Blackman (1927: 180) noted that the small-scale threshing of cereals received as wages in kind for helping with the harvest was more 'primitive' than the trampling method, and was done at the household level by beating the crop with a stick. Threshing by beating or lashing also may have been done if the cereal straw needed to be in relatively good condition for thatching or for basketry (e.g. Peña-Chocarro 1996: 138). There appear to be few, if any, Pharaonic tomb scenes which depict threshing by beating, although a painted relief from the early Ptolemaic tomb of Petosiris clearly depicts the practice (Bowman 1990: 102).

Threshing by trampling is done by hoofed animals, usually cattle, which are driven over the harvested cereal crop (thickly laid to prevent the crushing of the cereals). The trampled cereals are repeatedly turned with a fork and new sheaves are added until the crop is fully threshed. This method produces spikelets and trodden straw. As well as being the primary method of threshing depicted in the artistic record (e.g. Figs. 21.7 and 21.10), trampling is also mentioned in texts and the method was still used in Egypt this century (Budge 1898: 171; Tantawi 1941: 239; Harpur 1987: 167). Tomb-scenes show the importance of keeping the animals moving during the threshing process to prevent them from eating the crop underfoot, and captions highlight what a potentially chaotic job threshing by trampling could be (Erman 1894: 432; Harpur 1987: 167).

Threshing by sledge is done using a wooden frame or tribulum fitted with stone or metal teeth, wheels or rollers. The sledge is drawn by an animal in a circular movement over the heaped cereals, producing spikelets and chopped straw. A threshing sledge, known as a *norag*, was commonly used in Egypt this century (Wilkinson 1878; Foaden and Fletcher 1908, 1910; Blackman 1927; Ammar 1954; Ayrout 1963; Beshai 1993). The antiquity of the threshing sledge in the Near East, however, is not yet known (see Ataman 1992), and to date there is no evidence for its use during the Pharaonic period.

Additional tools used for threshing would have included a variety of forks and rakes. If the cereals had been harvested by uprooting or by cutting low on the straw, there would have been large quantities of straw to handle. Threshing scenes often show men using two- and three-pronged forks, presumably to turn the straw over and to place it into the path of the animal, as the pile tends to move outwards due to the circular movement of the animals during the threshing process (Hillman 1984b: 122; see

Petrie 1917: pl. LXVII for examples of each). Forks and rakes also would have been used to separate the coarsest straw from the spikelets, to bring unthreshed spikelets and straw to the surface of the pile, and to allow threshed spikelets to move downwards (Hillman 1984b: 122). Raking is not clearly shown in tomb scenes though wooden rakes have been excavated which may have been used for the purpose (e.g. Petrie 1917). If the crop was threshed by beating or lashing, then raking would have been unnecessary since the straw remains more or less intact and can be stored directly; in contrast, the trampling and sledging methods crush and chop the straw which would then need further separation from the cereal spikelets (Hillman 1984b: 123). At this stage, the separated straw may have been transported for use as fuel, fodder, temper or building material, as was observed by Lane (1860) and Blackman (1927: 173).

Artistic representations from throughout the Pharaonic period show the threshing floor as a circular area delineated by a low wall or platform (Harpur 1987: 167; Davies 1927: 56) and a threshing platform is referred to in texts (e.g. Caminos 1954: 360, 357). Evidence from later periods show that wealthier families had their own threshing floors (Bowman 1990: 104), while most people may have used communal threshing areas. Others, very poor gleaners, for example, might have threshed their own cereals by beating. There is also some textual evidence for the hiring of oxen for the purposes of ploughing and threshing (Gardiner 1941; Caminos 1954; Kees 1961). It is not surprising that there is relatively little archaeological evidence for threshing floors in Pharaonic Egypt as the practice probably would have been conducted away from the domestic area of the settlement, especially if the primary method used was trampling by animals (Hillman 1984b: 125). Threshing waste would appear in the archaeobotanical record as a mixture of spikelets, weed seeds and large numbers of cereal straw nodes (and straw bases if the crop was uprooted) and although threshing waste can be identified archaeobotanically, it is difficult to determine precisely the method used to do the threshing (Hillman 1981: 153). Ethnographic parallels show that threshing floors would have needed to be cleaned and probably resurfaced between threshing sessions (Dalman 1933 III: 67–74; Hillman 1984b: 121) and textual sources also allude to their upkeep (e.g. Caminos 1954: 307).

Winnowing

Primary winnowing is done to separate the threshed cereal spikelets from the remaining straw and other light debris (Fig. 21.2). Evidence from traditional Near Eastern agriculture, as well as ancient Egyptian tomb scenes and texts, indicates that winnowing usually takes place on or near the threshing floor (Davies 1927: 56; Caminos 1954: 357; Hillman 1984b: 125; Harpur 1987: 158). Winnowing is best done in a steady, light, gust-free breeze. The threshed cereals are tossed into the air using forks, shovels or winnowing fans, and the wind carries away the lightest material, including light straw fragments and light weed seeds whereas the spikelets and other relatively heavy material, such as straw nodes and large seed heads, fall to the ground. Depending on the amount to be winnowed and the quality of the wind, winnowing can take a few hours or several days to complete (e.g. Halstead and Jones 1989: 44). Winnowing is the first cereal processing stage in which the composition of the material is altered by the removal of items (Hillman 1981: 155; Jones 1984: 45). Straw and chaff separated through winnowing can be collected and used as temper in mud bricks, dung-cakes and plaster or as fuel or animal fodder throughout the winter and spring seasons (e.g. Hillman 1984b: 124; Charles 1990: 55). Secondary winnowing occurs during post-storage processing, when the emmer spikelets and hulled barley have been processed to a semi-clean grain stage (see Chapter 22, this volume).

The main tools used for winnowing are winnowing fans, forks, brooms, shallow baskets or sieves. Several observers have noted the similarities between the ancient Egyptian tools used for threshing and winnowing and those used this century (Wilkinson 1878; Foaden and Fletcher 1908; Blackman 1927; Tantawi 1941). Ethnographic observation indicates that winnowing forks may be used initially but then, after the bulk of straw has been removed, winnowing shovels are more efficient for tossing the grain into the air (Hillman 1984b: 124; Peña-Chocarro 1996: 139). The artistic record shows that spikelets were continually swept and fanned together, no doubt, in part, to remove the straw fragments which invariably accumulate on the surface of the heaps (see Figs. 21.7 and 2.10; Hillman 1984b: 124). Winnowing fans are like small wooden scoops or shovels designed to fit in each hand (see Figs. 21.7 and 21.10; and for archaeological examples see Petrie 1917: pl. LXVIII) and these and shallow baskets or sieves were then used to winnow the lighter material from the spikelets. If winnowing took place on a small scale, for example, in a backyard or on a roof, then winnowing tools more suited to small-scale processing may have been used (Hillman 1984a: 11, 1984b: 119; Blackman 1927: 180; Samuel 1994b). The heaps of winnowed spikelets were sometimes decorated, possibly with offerings (Wreszinski 1915; Harpur 1987: 158) and a similar practice was observed earlier this century in Egypt (Blackman 1927: 173). The artistic record sometimes shows women carrying out the winnowing process (Harpur 1987: 168).

By definition, the bulk of the light, small weed seeds, light straw and chaff which characterise winnowing in archaeobotanical samples are most frequently swept away with the wind and normally accumulate into two distinct heaps nearby, with the lightest material falling furthest away (Hillman 1984b: 124). These residues may be collected for various uses, although they may be less likely to survive the charring process if used as fuel (Hillman 1981: 155). After this process, the winnower is left with the heavier items of the assemblage, including heaps of cereal spikelets, heavy straw fragments, weed seeds and stones (see Fig. 21.2; Hillman 1984b: 124). Awn fragments and light weed seeds are a common component in archaeobotanical samples, but these items may have also come from the sieving stages which follow winnowing. Both threshing and winnowing would have been repeated as required to break up any ears still attached to the straw and to remove additional weed seeds, barley awns or light straw (Hillman 1984b: 125; Jones 1984: 45; Halstead and Jones 1989: 45).

Coarse to medium sieving

After winnowing, the emmer spikelets and hulled barley must be cleaned further by several sieving operations, although winnowing is often cited in the literature as the final stage of processing before the grain is recorded and stored. Both tomb-scenes (e.g. the tomb of Ty at Saqqara) and ethnographic observations in Egypt illustrate that, like winnowing, the sieving operations also took place in the threshing area (Harpur 1987: 508, 512; Foaden and Fletcher 1910: 435). An initial sieving is conducted using a coarse mesh which allows the cereal spikelets to pass through the sieve while retaining the largest components of the waste, such as straw fragments, unthreshed ears and large seed heads. A second sieving stage is then necessary to remove most of the smaller elements still present with the grain. This is done using sieves with a medium-sized mesh which retain the spikelets and small seed heads while allowing even smaller items, such as loose weed seeds, to pass through the sieve (Fig. 21.2) (Hillman 1984b: 125–6). Winnowing scenes from several tombs clearly show that grain was both retained and passed through sieves (e.g. Harpur 1987: 508, 512). Sieves with different sized mesh would need to be used for emmer and barley since the emmer spikelets are much larger than the hulled barley grains. As with other cereal processing by-products, the residues from coarse to medium sieving would have been useful as animal fodder, fuel or temper. Ethnographic observation shows that processing by-products are often amalgamated, usually with other by-products of similar composition, i.e. residues from winnowing and coarse sieving (Jones 1984: 48).

Some of the cereal grain found on archaeological settlements are tail grains, e.g. terminal spikelets, which are smaller than most grains. These pass through the seives and are therefore lost for use as food, trade or for the following year's seed. Theoretically, by measuring and plotting the dimensions of this grain, an estimate can be made as to the diameter of the mesh size used to sieve the grain (see Hillman 1984a: 23; Jones 1996). The final sieving, using fine-meshed sieves, occurs after the post-storage processing stages of pounding and additional winnowing and will be discussed by Samuel in Chapter 22 of this volume. Archaeobotanical samples from Egypt may often represent the by-products from the later stages of cereal processing, particularly the coarse and fine sieving stages (e.g. Wetterstrom 1992, 1994; Murray 1993, 1994, forthcoming).

Procedures prior to the storage of grain and straw

Artistic and textual evidence show that, after the winnowing and sieving operations, grain was measured using containers of known quantity and the amounts were then recorded by scribes prior to grain storage (Wilkinson 1878: 420; Griffith 1926: 215; Harpur 1987: 169; see Fig. 21.10). Scenes in New Kingdom tombs tend to emphasise the assessment of cereals for taxation purposes, and the final measuring and recording of the grain often appear, not at the end of the usual agricultural cycle but rather in conjunction with offering scenes or those showing the tomb owner's occupation (Manniche 1988: 39). Cereals were measured in *hekat*, *khar* (sacks) and *oipe* at various times during the Pharaonic period (see Gardiner 1941, 1948; Baer 1962; James 1962; Janssen 1975; see Spalinger 1987 for further information). Tomb-scenes commonly show cereals being transported to granaries by donkey and sometimes along the Nile by barge (e.g. Tylor and Griffith 1894, pl. III; Davies 1927: 57; Gardiner 1941). Various studies have demonstrated the pitfalls of attempting to estimate ancient crop yields (e.g. Sigaut 1992) and it will not be attempted here.

As well as cereal grain, the straw and chaff of emmer and barley were no doubt valuable commodities in ancient Egypt. As noted above, they would have been used as roofing, bedding, basketry, fuel, animal fodder, building material, or as temper in pottery, plaster, mud bricks and dung-cakes used for fuel (e.g. Caminos 1954: 65). Van der Veen (1996) has shown at the Roman quarrying site of Mons Claudianus that the presence of chaff and straw from the early stages of cereal processing does not necessarily mean that cereals were cultivated locally since these items may also have been imported for use as temper, fuel, etc. Textual evidence from post-Pharaonic periods also allude to straw and chaff as important commodities (e.g. Bagnell 1993: 156, 224). Even today, cereal residues have a market value in Egypt and due to price controls on wheat in recent years, cereal straw can fetch a higher price than the cereal grain (Hopkins 1987: 118, Ruf 1993: 198). One source notes that, in parts of Egypt today, if cereals are harvested manually they are either cut at the base of the plant with a sickle blade or are uprooted, and that modern harvesting machines are often not used because they do not cut the plant low enough to preserve the valuable straw (Hopkins 1987: 119). For a description of the various types of straw fractions obtained during cereal processing, see Hillman (1984b: 127).

Figure 21.11 Storage facility.

Grain storage

Various sources of evidence suggest that cereal grain was deposited in granaries at this point in the cereal processing sequence, meaning that cereals may have been stored in spikelet form and not as clean grain. Further processing would have been necessary at this stage to obtain a clean grain product; primarily pounding in order to free the grain from the tough glumes that bind emmer and the fused hull that binds barley. Further winnowing and sieving, then would have been necessary to remove the chaff (for these later processing stages see Chapter 22, this volume). It has been suggested that, in areas with dry summers, such as Egypt, it is more typical that cereals would have been threshed and winnowed communally, then processed beyond the spikelet stage to the level of semi-clean grain and then stored in bulk, while in areas with wet summers, grain would have been stored in spikelet form to keep the grain dry which could then be processed further in a piecemeal fashion as required (Hillman 1981: 131 and 138, 1984a: 8, 1984b: 126). The dry climate of Egypt would have indeed allowed farmers to process cereals communally to the clean grain stage prior to storage, but the relatively scant direct evidence on the subject to date does not suggest that they did.

Artistic evidence from Pharaonic tombs, for example, indicates that, after winnowing and sieving, the cereals were recorded by scribes and put directly into storage, evidently still in spikelet form since no further processing, such as the pounding stage, is associated with this sequence (Harpur 1987: 158; and see also Fig. 21.7). Several grain storage facilities have been excavated from the Pharaonic period though, as yet, the evidence needed to clarify this important issue of storage practice has not come to light. Some evidence for the bulk storage of grain in spikelet form has come from model granaries which were often placed in tombs in the Middle and New Kingdoms; presumably to provide a perennial grain store in the after-life (e.g. Winlock 1955). These models frequently contained emmer spikelets and hulled barley, along with weed seeds, chaff and other debris that one would expect with grain stored at this stage of processing. The most notable example is from the tomb of Tutankhamun (KV62; Hepper 1990: 53–4). Several baskets containing emmer spikelets were also found in this tomb and may be taken as further evidence of spikelet storage (Nesbitt and Samuel 1996: 51), although this grain may just as well have represented seed corn for future harvests in the after-life, and not stored grain. Although tomb finds may provide some confirmation for the storage of spikelets, particularly from model granaries, this evidence may not be representative of every-day storage practices.

Further evidence comes from the Eighteenth-Dynasty Workman's Village at Amarna (*c.* 1350 BC). The desiccated remains of broken emmer chaff were found around a mortar emplacement, indicating how emmer spikelets were processed further on a domestic level to obtain clean grain. Many small stone mortars used for dehusking grain were also found, suggesting that each household processed its own spikelets when required (Samuel 1989, 1993). There is also ample archaeobotanical evidence from other Nile Valley settlements in the form of large amounts of chaff, suggesting that cereals were likely to have been dehusked at the domestic level (Wetterstrom 1984; Thanheiser 1987, forthcoming; Moens and Wetterstrom 1988; Murray 1993, 1994, forthcoming). Although much of the available evidence points to the bulk storage of emmer spikelets and hulled barley, important questions remain. Was the bulk storage of spikelets a common practice throughout the entire Dynastic period, in all areas of Egypt and by all sectors of Egyptian society? Were emmer and barley treated similarly in this respect? Archaeobotanical analysis must address these questions directly, taking into account the scale of storage, i.e. small-scale domestic storage or large-scale 'official' storage, and must also consider that finds of spikelets may represent stored animal fodder or seed corn for the following year. As with other aspects of archaeobotanical research, it cannot be assumed that the results from a single site can be extrapolated to include an entire period or region as a whole, however, with further data from additional sites, patterns of cereal storage should eventually become clear.

Storage is the intermediate stage between cereal production and processing and its distribution and consumption (Forbes and Foxhall 1995: 70). The archaeological and artistic records show a wide spectrum of storage facilities for cereals, ranging from the large-scale state- and temple-controlled granaries of the Ramesseum and Medinet Habu, for example, to small-scale domestic arrangements (e.g. Petrie 1891; Hölscher 1941; Badawy 1954, 1966, 1968; Winlock 1955; Kemp 1986, 1989, 1994; Hepper 1990;

Lehner 1994). Most of the harvested grain belonged to the state and not to the individual farmers who had to relinquish much of their yield to the granary system. From this surplus, all manner of Egyptian workers were paid with cereals (e.g. Cerny 1954; Janssen 1975: 460–6). Texts from Deir el-Medina, for example, show that the workmen on the necropolis were given 4 *khar* of emmer (310 litres) and 1.5 *khar* of barley (115 litres) per month (Cerny 1954; Janssen 1975: 460, 1979: 512; Kemp 1994: 134). The storage of the grain within the spikelet would have offered significant protection from insects, fungi and other pests and diseases (Farag *et al.* 1986; Jones *et al.* 1986; Sigaut 1988), especially if cereals were a mobile commodity to be traded and doled out as wages in this manner (Kemp 1994: 151). Grain was evidently issued to workers in sacks and indeed, may have remained stored in this way (Kemp 1994: 151) although small-scale domestic storage might have also included the use of jars, pits, silos, bins or baskets (Ayrout 1963: 51; Darby *et al.* 1977: 462–3; Hillman 1984b: 132; Sigaut 1988; Forbes and Foxhall 1995; and see also Wendrich in Chapter 10, this volume). Observations earlier this century in Egypt indicate that clay or basket-work granaries were often located on the roofs of houses (e.g. Blackman 1927: 173) and the practice can still be seen today. If this method of grain storage was also an ancient practice, it may help to explain the dearth of evidence for small-scale storage facilities at the household level since the eventual collapse of a mud-brick structure might be likely to obscure this evidence (Murray forthcoming).

Archaeological evidence indicates that large storage facilities were attached to temples and palaces. Excavations at Kahun, for example, also show that grain was stored in several locations within the town, rather than a single, central granary (Petrie 1891; Kemp 1986: 134). The excavation of ancient settlements has also revealed that high officials would have had their own storage facilities, such as at Armana (Kemp 1994: 151) and at Memphis, where a residence, most likely belonging to a priest of the nearby Ptah temple, appears to have controlled access to a large, circular silo (Jeffreys forthcoming). It is possible that personal granaries, such as these, were for grain harvested from the officials' own fields (Kemp 1994: 151). A common type of silo was one in which grain was added through a door in the top and removed through a door near the bottom (Fig. 21.11; see Badawy 1954: 53–4). The analysis of Tutankhamun's tomb offerings by de Vartavan (1990, 1993) showed that 31 per cent of the intrusive species present in the offerings sampled could be traced to contamination while the main crop was in storage, most probably due to insufficient cleaning of this common type of storage facility (de Vartavan 1990: 492). The presence of certain species, such as coriander (*Coriandrum sativum*), black cumin (*Nigella sativa*) and fenugreek (*Trigonella foenum-graecum*) from Tutankhamun's tomb could also be interpreted as the deliberate use of these species as insecticides against pests of storage (Panagiotakopulu *et al.* 1995: 708).

Just as modifications to the basin irrigation system helped to deal with the uncertainties of the Nile floods, the storage of surplus grain provided a buffer against variations in cereal productivity. Using documentary evidence from the New Kingdom village of Deir el-Medina, for example, Janssen (1975: 126–7) found no apparent correlation between fluctuations in the price of cereals and the annual agricultural cycle, inferring that grain storage was sufficient to provide a cushion for supply and demand throughout the year. Although possible episodes of famine in ancient Egypt have been documented (e.g. Vandier 1936; James 1962; Baer 1963; Bell 1971; Schenkel 1978), other sources also indicate that, for the most part, the state and temple system of grain storage was sufficient to feed the population during lean years (e.g. Hölscher 1941; Janssen 1975: 126–7; Kemp 1989: 195–6). It has been noted that, although large-scale state-controlled systems of storage can provide an effective buffer against variations in grain supply, they can also be its Achilles heel, due to the centralised nature of a complex system (O'Shea and Halstead 1989: 126). In ancient Egypt, however, the hierarchy of cereal storage suggests that the system was well-organised on the national, regional, local and household levels. A Nineteenth-Dynasty letter states: 'Don't let the granary be lacking in barley or emmer for it is upon its granary that a house stands firm' (Wente 1990: 126) and indeed it seems clear that the ancient Egyptian hierarchy of grain storage was one of the many secrets of its success as a cereal producer.

Conclusions

With attention primarily focused on the spectacular monuments and treasures from the temples and tombs of ancient Egypt, the minutiae of daily life, particularly the details of a unique agricultural tradition, have been often overlooked. The excavation of Egyptian settlement sites and the recovery, analysis and interpretation of botanical remains are an important source for testing a range of specific queries concerning the production and processing of Egyptian cereals. For example, can the alleged shift in the predominance of emmer and barley and the reasons behind it be more clearly defined? Can changes in cereal production or processing be detected through time, particularly during periods of social turmoil, weak government or outside influence (e.g. the First Intermediate Period and the Second Intermediate Period), or during periods of ecological crisis as shown in the records of the Nile floods? There is also a clear need for a regional approach, for example, can differences in land use be detected, such as the supposition that barley was primarily a cereal of Upper Egypt and emmer of Lower Egypt? Could this Upper/Lower Egypt distinction have something to do the variable harvesting times of these two cereals and their early or late availability in these areas? Is there evidence for specialisation or differences in technical knowledge as reflected in tool types through time or by area? Were there regional or temporal differences in harvesting techniques or grain storage, for example? Archaeobotanical evidence is also able to address larger questions of site economy, such as the important distinctions between small and large-scale cereal producer and consumer communities (van der Veen 1991, 1992; Hillman 1984; Miller 1990) and also the internal trade of cereals, straw and chaff between these settlement types, as has been demonstrated for the post-Pharaonic sites of Quseir al-Qadim and Mons Claudianus in the Eastern Desert, for example, where cereals could not be grown locally and had to be imported (Wetterstrom 1982: 374; van der Veen 1996: 137). The processing and use of wild cereals in ancient Egypt also must be considered further, such as the recent evidence for the early use of wild sorghum (Wasylikowa and Kubiak-Martens 1995; Wasylikowa *et al.* 1995; Dahlberg *et al.* 1995). No doubt a continuation of the relatively recent 'Flotation Revolution' in Egypt will recover archaeobotanical data from a wider range of sites to gradually illuminate the many unresolved issues of ancient Egyptian cereal husbandry.

Additional data are needed before a fully integrated study of the ancient Egyptian cereal economy as a whole can be achieved, although this is a necessary aim if we are to test the many common assumptions of agricultural continuity throughout the Pharaonic period. With time, a multidisciplinary approach to the subject will lend new meaning to the agrarian details already found in the artistic, textual and archaeological records and will highlight what were among the most important aspects of daily life for many ancient Egyptians, namely the routine agricultural tasks of sowing, harvesting and processing emmer and barley which, village by village, formed the strong backbone of the ancient Egyptian state throughout the Pharaonic period.

Acknowledgements

The author would like to thank several colleagues for their valuable comments and discussion of earlier drafts or portions of this work, including Drs Hala Barakat, Mike Charles, Sue Colledge, Dominique de Moulins, Jon Hather, Frances McLaren, Mark Nesbitt, Delwen Samuel, Wendy Smith, Marijke van der Veen and Wilma Wetterstrom. Special thanks to Gordon Hillman. Thanks also to Dr Lisa Giddy, David Jeffreys and Ian Casey for Egyptological comments and advice.

References

Adams, M.D. 1992. The Abydos excavation. Final report presented to the American Research Center in Egypt. Unpublished manuscript.

1997. A textual window on the settlement system in ancient Egypt. In *Anthropology and Egyptology: A Developing Dialogue* (ed. J. Lustig). Monographs in Mediterranean Archaeology 8. Sheffield: Sheffield Academic Press, pp. 90–105.

Allen, R. 1997. Agriculture and the origins of the State in ancient Egypt. *Explorations in Economic History*, 34: 135–54.

Ammar, H. 1954. *Growing up in an Egyptian Village: Silwa Province of Aswan*. London: Routledge and Kegan Paul.

Anderson, P. 1992. Experimental cultivation, harvest and threshing of wild cereals and their relevance for interpreting the use of Epipalaeolithic and Neolithic artefacts. In *Préhistoire de L'Agriculture: Nouvelles Approches Expérimentales et Ethnographiques* (ed. P. Anderson). Monographie du Centre de Recherches Archéologiques 6. Paris: Éditions du CNRS, pp. 179–209.

Anderson S. and Ertug-Yaras, F. 1997. Fuel, fodder and faeces: an ethnographic and botanical study of dung fuel use in Central Anatolia. *Environmental Archaeology*, 1: 99–109.

Arnon, I. 1972. *Crop Production in Dry Regions I: Background and Principles*. London: Leonard Hill.

Ataman, K. 1992. Threshing sledge and archaeology. In *Préhistoire de l'Agriculture: Nouvelles Approches Expérimentales et Ethnographiques* (ed. P. Anderson). Monographie du Centre de Recherches Archéologiques 6. Paris: Éditions du CNRS, pp. 305–19.

Atzler, M. 1995. Some remarks on interrelating environmental changes and ecological socio-economic problems in the gradual development of the early Egyptian inundation culture. *Archéo-Nil*, 5: 7–65.

Ayrout, H. 1963. *The Egyptian Peasant*. Boston: Beacon Press.

Ayyad, S., Krzywinski, K. and Pierce, R. 1991. Mud brick as a bearer of agricultural information: an archaeopalynological study. *Norwegian Archaeological Review*, 24/2: 77–91.

Ayyad, S., and Moore, P. 1995. Morphological studies of the pollen grains of the semi-arid region of Egypt. *Flora*, 190: 115–33.

Ayyad, S., Moore, P. and Zahran, M.A.1992. Modern pollen rain studies of the Nile Delta, Egypt. *New Phytologist*, 121: 663–75.

Badawy, A.A. 1954. *History of Egyptian Architecture I: From the Earliest Times to the End of the Old Kingdom*. Cairo: Urwand.

1966. *History of Egyptian Architecture II: The First Intermediate Period, the Middle Kingdom and the Second Intermediate Period*. Berkeley and Los Angeles CA: University of California Press.

1968. *History of Egyptian Architecture III: The Empire (The New Kingdom). From the Eighteenth Dynasty to the End of the Twentieth Dynasty. 1580–1085 BC*. Berkeley and Los Angeles: University of California Press.

Baer, K. 1960. *Rank and Title in the Old Kingdom: The Structure of the Egyptian Administration in the 5th and 6th Dynasties*. Chicago IL: University of Chicago Press.

1962. The low price of land in ancient Egypt. *JARCE*, 1: 25–45.

1963. An 11th Dynasty farmer's letters to his family. *JAOS*, 83: 1–19.

Bagnell, R. 1993. *Egypt in Late Antiquity*. Princeton: Princeton University Press.

Baines, J and Málek, J. 1984. *Atlas of Ancient Egypt*. Oxford: Equinox.

Barakat, H. 1990. Plant remains from El Omari. In *El Omari: A Neolithic Settlement and Other Sites in the Vicinity of Wadi Hof, Helwan*. Appendix IV. (eds. F. Debono and B. Mortensen). Mainz: DAIK, pp. 109–13.

Barakat, H.N. and Baum, N. 1992. *La Végétation Antique de Douch (Oasis de Kharga): Une Approche Macrobotanique*. Cairo: IFAO.

Bell, B. 1970. The oldest records of the Nile floods. *Geographical Journal*, 136: 569–73.

1971. The Dark Ages in ancient history: I. The first Dark Age in Egypt. *AJA*, 75: 1–26.

1975. Climate and the history of Egypt: the Middle Kingdom. *AJA*, 79: 223–69.

Berger, S. 1934. A note on some scenes of land measurement. *JEA*, 20: 54–6.

Beshai, A.A. 1993. Systems of agricultural production in Middle and Upper Egypt. In *The Agriculture of Egypt*. (ed. G.M. Craig). Oxford: OUP, pp. 265–77.

Bietak, M. 1979. Urban archaeology and the 'town problem' in ancient Egypt. In *Egyptology and the Social Sciences*. (ed. Kent Weeks). Cairo: American University in Cairo Press, pp. 97–144.

1986. *Avaris and Piramesse: Archaeological Exploration in the Eastern Nile Delta*. Mortimer Wheeler Archaeological Lecture 1979. 2nd edn. Oxford: OUP.

1996. *Avaris: The Capital of the Hyksos. Recent Excavations at Tell el-Dab'a*. London: BMP.

Blackman, W.S. 1927. *The Fellahin of Upper Egypt*. London: G. Harrap and Company.

Boardman, S. and Jones, G.E.M. 1990. Experiments on the effects of charring on cereal plant components. *JAS*, 17: 1–11.

Bottema, S. 1984. The composition of some charred seed assemblages. In *Plants and Ancient Man: Studies in Palaeoethnobotany*. (eds. W. van Zeist and W.A. Casparie). Rotterdam: A.A. Balkema, pp. 207–12.

Boulos, L. 1995. *Flora of Egypt Checklist*. Cairo: Al Hadara Publishing.

Boulos, L. and el-Hadidi N. M. 1984. *The Weed Flora of Egypt*. Cairo: American University in Cairo Press.

Bourke, S. and Descoeudres, J. (eds.) 1995. *Trade, Contact and the Movement of People in the Eastern Mediterranean: Studies in Honour of J. Basil Hennessey*. Sydney: Meditarch.

Bourriau, J. 1981. *Umm el-Ga'ab: Pottery from the Nile Valley before the Arab Conquest*. Cambridge: CUP/Fitzwilliam Museum.

1997. Before Avaris: the Second Intermediate Period in Egypt outside the eastern Delta. In *The Hyksos: New Historical and Archaeological Perspectives*. (ed. E.D. Oren). University Museum Symposium Series. Philadelphia PA: University Museum Press, pp. 159–82.

Bowman, A.K. 1990. *Egypt after the Pharaohs*. Oxford: OUP.

Brown, T.A., Allaby, R.G., Brown, K.A. 1994. DNA in wheat seeds from European archaeological sites. In *Conservation of Plant Genes II: Utilization of Ancient and Modern DNA*. (eds. R.P. Adams, J.S. Miller, E.M. Golenberg and J.E. Adams). Monographs in Systematic Botany 48. St. Louis: Missouri Botanical Garden.

Brown, T.A., Allaby, R.G., Brown, K.A. and Jones, M.K. 1993. Biomolecular archaeology of wheat: past, present and future. *WA*, 25: 64–73.

Bruyère, B. 1939. *Rapport sur les Fouilles de Deir el-Médineh*. (1934–1935). 3ieme Partie: Le Village, Les Décharges Publiques, La Station de Repos du Col, de la Valée des Rois. Cairo: IFAO.

Budge, W. 1898. *The Book of the Dead*. London: Kegan Paul, Trench, Trübner and Company.

Butzer, K. 1976. *Early Hydraulic Civilisation in Egypt: A Study in Cultural Ecology*. Chicago IL: University of Chicago Press.

1984. Long term Nile flood variation and political discontinuities in Pharaonic Egypt. In *From Hunters to Farmers: The Causes and Consequences of Food Production in Africa*. (eds. J.D. Clark and S. Brandt). Berkeley and Los Angeles CA: University of California Press, pp. 102–12.

Buurman, J. 1987. A Middle Bronze Age corn stack at Twisk, province of north Holland. *Berichten van de Rijksdienst voor het Ondheid kundig Bodemonderzoek*, 37: 7–37.

Caminos, R. 1954. *Late Egyptian Miscellanies*. Brown Egyptological Studies 1. Oxford: OUP.

Cappers, R.T.J. 1996. Archaeobotanical remains. In *Berenike 1995: Preliminary Report of the 1995 Excavations at Berenike (Egyptian Red Sea Coast) and the Survey of the Eastern Desert*. (eds. S. Sidebotham and W. Wendrich). Leiden: Research School CNWS, pp. 319–36.

Casey, I. 1995. A study of ancient Egyptian agriculture and crop processing. BA dissertation. Institute of Archaeology, University College London, England.

Castle, E. 1992. Shipping and trade in Ramesside Egypt. *JESHO*, 35: 239–77.

Caton-Thompson, G. and Gardiner, E.W. 1934. *The Desert Fayum*. London: Royal Anthropological Institute of Great Britain and Ireland.

Černý, J. 1933. Fluctuations in grain prices during the Twentieth Egyptian Dynasty. *Archiv Orientální*, 6: 173–8.

1939. Late Ramesside letters. *Bibliotheca Aegyptiaca*, 9: 1–20.

1954. Prices and wages in Egypt in the Ramesside period. *Journal of World History*, 1: 903–21.

1955. Some Coptic Etymologies. In *Ägyptologische Studien: Hermann Grapow zum 70. Geburtstag gewidmet*. (ed. O. Firchow). Berlin: Akademie-Verlag.

1973. *A Community of Workmen at Thebes in the Ramesside Period*. Cairo: Cairo: IFAO.

Charles, M. 1984. Introductory remarks on the cereals. *BSA*, 1: 17–31.

1989. Agriculture in Lowland Mesopotamia in the Late 4th and Early 3rd Millennia BC. Ph.D. thesis. Institute of Archaeology, University College London, England.

1990. Crop husbandry in southern Iraq: 1900–1960 AD. *BSA*, 7: 47–64.

1997. Fodder from dung: the recognition and interpretation of dung derived plant material from archaeological sites. *Environmental Archaeology*, 1: 111–22.

Charles, M., Jones, G.E.M. and Hodson, J.G. 1997. FIBS in archaeobotany: functional interpretation of weed floras in relation to husbandry practices. *JAS* 24/12: 1151–61.

Colledge, S. 1994. Plant exploitation on Epipalaeolithic and Early Neolithic sites in the Levant. Ph.D. thesis. University of Sheffield, England.

Cope, T. and Hosni, H. 1991. *A key to Egyptian Grasses*. Kew and Cairo: Royal Botanical Gardens and Cairo University.

Coult, L. 1958. *An annotated research bibliography of studies in Arabic, English and French of the* fellah *of the Egyptian Nile (1798–1955)*. Coral Gables: University of Miami Press.

Crawford, D.J. 1971. *Kerkeosiris: An Egyptian village in the Ptolemaic period*. Cambridge: CUP.

1979. Food: tradition and change in Hellenistic Egypt. *WA*, 11(2): 136–46.

ancient Egyptian bread baking. In *Amarna Reports* V (ed. B.J. Kemp). Occasional Publications 6. London: EES, pp. 253–90.
1993. Ancient Egyptian cereal processing: beyond the artistic record. *CAJ*, 3 (2): 276–83.
1994a. Cereal food processing in ancient Egypt: a case study of integration. In *Whither Environmental Archaeology?* (eds R. Luff and P. Rowley-Conwy). Oxbow Monograph 38. Oxford: Oxbow Books, pp. 153–8.
1994b. An archaeological study of baking and bread in New Kingdom Egypt. Ph.D. thesis. University of Cambridge, UK.
Schenkel, W. 1978. *Die Bewässerungsrevolution im Alten Ägypten.* Mainz: von Zabern.
Schweinfurth, G. 1883. *Neuw Beiträge zur Flora des alten Agypten.* Berichte der Deutschen Botanischen Gesellschaft, bd I. Berlin: Gebrüder Borntraeger, pp. 544–6.
1884. *Über Pflanzenreste aus altägyptischen Grabern.* Berichte der Deutschen Botanischen Gesellschaft, bd II. Berlin: Gebrüder Borntraeger, pp. 351–71.
Seidlmayer, S. 1996. Town and state in the early New Kingdom: a view from Elephantine. In *Aspects of Early Egypt* (ed. J. Spencer). London: BMP.
Shaltout, K.H. and el-Fahar, R.A. 1991. Diversity and phenology of weed communities in the Nile Delta region. *Journal of Vegetation Science*, 2: 385–390.
Shaw, I.M.E. 1992. Ideal homes in ancient Egypt: the archaeology of social aspiration. *CAJ*, 2(2): 147–66.
Sigaut, F. 1978. Identification des techniques de recolte des grains alimentaires. *Journal d'Agriculture Traditionelle et de Botanique Appliquée*, 24: 140–70.
1988. A method for identifying grain storage techniques and its application for European agricultural history. *Tools and Tillage*, 6: 3–32.
1992. Rendements, semis et fertilité: signification analytique des rendements. In *Préhistoire de L'Agriculture: Nouvelles Approches Expérimentales et Ethnographiques.* (ed. P. Anderson). Monographie du Centre de Recherches Archéologiques 6. Paris: Éditions du CNRS, pp. 395–403.
Simpson, W.K. 1972. *The Literature of Ancient Egypt: An Anthology of Stories, Instructions and Poems.* New Haven: Yale University Press.
Sist, L. 1987. Food production. In *Egyptian Civilization: Daily Life.* (ed. A.M. Donadoni Roveri). Milan: Electa, pp. 46–75.
Smith, H. 1972. Society and settlement in ancient Egypt. *Man, Settlement and Urbanism.* (eds. P. Ucko, R. Tringham and G. Dimbleby). London: Duckworth.
1985. Settlements in the Nile Valley. *Mélanges Gamal Eddin Mokhtar.* Vol. II, Cairo: IFAO, pp. 287–91.
Smith, W. 1997. The agricultural economy and practice of an Egyptian Late Antique monastery: an archaeobotanical case study. Ph.D. thesis. University of Leicester, England.
Spalinger, A. 1987. The grain system of Dynasty 18. *SAK*, 14: 284–311.
Täckholm, V. 1974. *Student's Flora of Egypt.* 2nd edn. Cairo University Press.
Täckholm, V. and Drar, M. 1941–1969. *Flora of Egypt*, 4 vols. Cairo: Cairo University Press. [vol. 1 with G. Täckholm].
Tantawi, A.R.M. 1941. Comparison with the methods used in ancient Egypt. In *Flora of Egypt* I (eds. Täckholm, V., Täckholm, G. and Drar, M. 1941). Cairo: Fouad I University Press, pp. 238–9.
Thanheiser, U. 1987. Untersuchungen zur ägyptischen Landwirtschaft in dynastischer Zeit an Hand von Pflanzenresten aus Tell el-Daba. Unpublished dissertation. University of Vienna, Austria.
1991. Untersuchungen zur Landwirtschaft der vor- und frühdynastischen Zeit in Tell-el-Fara'in-Buto. *Ägypten und Levante* II: pp. 39–45.
1992a. Plant food at Tell Ibrahim Awad: preliminary report. In *The Nile Delta in Transition: 4th–3rd Millennium BC* (ed. E. van der Brink). Tel Aviv: Edwin van der Brink, pp. 117–22.
1992b. Plant remains from Minshat Abu Omar: first impressions. In *Nile Delta in Transition: 4th–3rd Millennium BC* (ed. E. van der Brink). Tel Aviv: E. van der Brink, pp. 167–70.
forthcoming Über den Ackerbau in dynastischer Zeit. Ergebnisse der Untersuchungen von Pflanzenresten aus Tell el-Dab'a. *Tell el-Dab'a VIII: Interdisziplinaere Studien* (eds. M. Bietak, J. Dorner, J. Boessneck and A. van den Driesch, H. Egger, U. Thanheiser). Vienna: Austrian Academy of Sciences.
Trigger, B. 1983. The rise of Egyptian civilization. In *Ancient Egypt: A Social History* (eds. B. Trigger, B. Kemp, D. O'Connor, and A. Lloyd). Cambridge: CUP, pp. 1–69.
Tylor, J. and Griffith, F. 1894. *The Tomb of Paheri at El Kab.* London: EEF.
Valbelle, D. 1985. *Les Ouvriers de la Tombe: Deir el-Medineh à l'époque Ramesside.* Bibliotheque d'Etude 96. Cairo: IFAO.
van der Veen, M. 1991. Consumption or production? Agriculture in the Cambridgeshire Fens? In *New Light on Early Farming: Recent Developments in Palaeoethnobotany* (ed. J. Renfrew). Edinburgh: Edinburgh University Press, pp. 349–61.
1992. *Crop Husbandry Regimes: An Archaeobotanical Study of Farming in Northern England, 1000 BC–AD 500.* Sheffield Archaeological Monographs 3. Sheffield: J.R. Collis.
1995. The identification of maslin crops. In *Res archaeobotanicae.* 9th Symposium IWGP. (eds. H. Kroll and R. Pasternak). Kiel: Institut für Ur-und Frühgeschichte der Christian-Albrecht-Universität, pp. 335–43.
1996. The plant remains from Mons Claudianus, a Roman quarry settlement in the Eastern Desert of Egypt – an interim report. *Vegetation History and Archaeobotany*, 5 (1–2): 137–41.
van der Veen, M., Grant, A. and Barker, G. 1996. Romano-Libyan agriculture: crops and animals. In *Farming the Desert: The UNESCO Libyan Valleys Archaeological Survey I: Synthesis* (ed. G. Barker). London: UNESCO Publishing, Department of Antiquities (Tripoli), Society for Libyan Studies, pp. 227–63.
Vandier, J. 1936. La Famine dans l'Egypte Ancienne. Cairo: IFAO.
1978. *Manuel d'Archéologie égyptienne VI: Scènes de la vie agricole.* Paris: A. and J. Picard.
van Lepp, J. 1995. Evidence for artificial irrigation in Amratian art. *JARCE*, 32: 197–209.
van Zeist, W. and de Roller, G. 1993. Plant remains from Maadi, a Predynastic site in Lower Egypt. *Vegetation History and Archaeobotany*, 2: 1–14
Vartavan, de C.T. 1987. Egyptian barley: a reassessment. *Wepwawet: Discussions in Egyptology*, 2: 11–14.
1990. Contaminated plant foods from the tomb of Tutankhamun: a new interpretative system. *JAS*, 17: 473–94.
1993. 'Combined-systems' analysis for the interpretation of plant remains from the tomb of Tutankhamun. Ph.D. thesis. University College London, England.

1996. Introduction. *Archéo-Nil*, 6: 5–8.

de Vartavan, C.T. and Asensi Amorós, V. 1997. *Codex of Ancient Egyptian Plant Remains*. London: Triade Exploration Ltd.

Venit, M.S. 1989. The painted tomb from Wardian and the antiquity of the *saqiya* in Egypt. *JARCE* 26: 219–22.

Vermeeren, C. and Kuijper, W. 1993. Pollen from coprolites and recent droppings: useful for reconstructing vegetations and determining the season of consumption? *Analecta Praehistorica Leidensia*, 26: 213–20.

Viklund, K. 1998. *Cereals, weeds and crop processing in Iron Age Sweden: methodological and interpretive aspects of archaeobotanical evidence*. Umeå: University of Umeå Press.

Vleeming, S.P. 1993. *Papyrus Reinhardt: An Egyptian Land List from the 10th Century B.C.* Berlin.

Wasylikowa, K and Kubiak-Martens, L. 1995. Wild sorghum from the Early Neolithic site at Napta Playa, South Egypt. In *Res archaeobotanicae*. 9th Symposium IWGP. (eds. H. Kroll and R. Pasternak). Kiel: Institut für Ur-und Frühgeschichte der Christian-Albrecht-Universität. pp 345–58.

Wasylikowa, K., Schild, R., Wendorf, F., Królik, H., Kubiak-Martens, L. and Harlan, J. 1995. Archaeobotany of the early Neolithic site E–75–6 at Nabta Playa, Western Desert, south Egypt. *Acta Palaeobotanica*, 35(1): 133–55.

Wente, E. (ed.) 1990. *Letters from Ancient Egypt* (ed. E. Melter). Atlanta: Scholars Press.

Wetterstrom, W. 1982. Plant remains. In *Quseir al Qadim 1980: Preliminary Report*. (ed. D. Whitcomb and J. Johnson). Malibu: Undena Publications, pp. 355–77.

1984. The plant remains. In *Archaeological Investigations at El-Hibeh 1980: Preliminary report* (ed. Robert Wenke). Malibu: Undena Publications, pp. 50–77.

1986. *Ecology and agricultural intensification in Predynastic Egypt*. Unpublished final report to National Science Foundation. Washington DC.

1992. *Plant remains from the Giza bakery/brewery*. Unpublished paper delivered to the Society for American Archaeology Annual Meeting.

1993. Foraging and farming in Egypt: the transition from hunting and gathering to horticulture in the Nile valley. In *The Archaeology of Africa: Food, Metals and Towns*. (eds. T. Shaw, P. Sinclair, B. Andah, and A. Okpoko). One World Archaeology. London: Routledge, pp. 165–226.

1994. *Ecology and agriculture in ancient Egypt*. Unpublished manuscript.

Wilkinson, J.G. 1878. *The Manners and Customs of the Ancient Egyptians*, 3 vols. (ed. and rev. S. Birch). London: John Murray.

Willcocks, W. 1904. *The Nile in 1904*. London: E. and F.N. Spon.

Willcocks, W. and Craig, J. 1913. *Egyptian Irrigation*, 2 vols. London: E. and F.N. Spon.

Willcox, G. 1992. Archaeobotanical significance of growing Near Eastern progenitors of domestic plants at Jales (France). In *Préhistoire de L'Agriculture: Nouvelles Approches Expérimentales et Ethnographiques* (ed. P. Anderson). Monographie du Centre de Recherches Archéologiques 6. Paris: Éditions du CNRS, pp. 159–77.

Willerding, U. and Wolf, G. 1991. Paläeo-ethnobotanische Untersuchungen von Pflanzenresten aus dem 1. Jahr-tausend v. Chr. von Elephantine. *MDAIK*, 46: 263–7.

Winlock, H.E. 1955. *Models of Daily Life in Ancient Egypt from the Tomb of Meketre at Thebes*. Cambridge MA and New York: Harvard University Press and MMA.

Wreszinski, W. 1915. *Atlas zur Altaegyptischen Kulturgeschichte*. I. Leipzig: Hinrichs.

Zahran, M.A. and Willis, A.J. 1992. *The Vegetation of Egypt*. London: Chapman and Hall.

Zeder, M. 1991. *Feeding Cities: Specialized Animal Economy in the Ancient Near East*. Washington DC: Smithsonian Institute Press.

Zohary, M. 1973. *Geobotanical Foundations of the Middle East*. Stuttgart: Gustav Fischer.

Zohary, D. and Hopf, M. 1993. *Domestication of Plants in the Old World: The Origin and Spread of Cultivated Plants in West Asia, Europe and the Nile Valley*, 2nd edn. Oxford: Clarendon Press.

22. Brewing and baking

DELWEN SAMUEL

The nature of bread and beer

For most ancient Egyptians, the seasonal routine revolved around the husbandry of the cereal crops. For many, the daily routine was centred on the transformation of these cereals into staple foods. The importance of both bread and beer is widely attested in many documentary sources, including offering lists, proverbs, scribal exercises and administrative records (Breasted 1907: 103; Drenkhahn 1975; Helck 1971). The frequency with which well-furnished tombs were provided with bread loaves and jars of beer, and the many artistic scenes of baking and brewing in tombs, demonstrate how the ancient Egyptians aimed for an equally abundant supply in the after-life. No meal was complete without bread and beer, and everyone in ancient Egyptian society partook of them, from Pharaoh to the labouring peasant. Bread and beer played a number of key roles in ancient Egyptian society. At the most fundamental level, they made a major contribution to nutrition. Together with raw cereals, they were an important part of internal trade, commerce and rations (Kemp 1989: 126). Ritual practice made use of both foods (Darby *et al.* 1977: 503; Helck 1971: 82–94).

Beer and bread are also modern staples and therefore are familiar foods in many societies today. It is thus easy to make assumptions about what these foodstuffs are and how they were made. The variety of beers and breads produced in the present day, though, demonstrates that there is no simple definition for either of them, and that they can vary considerably in almost every aspect of production, from raw ingredients and processing methods to final product. Given this great modern diversity, there is no reason why ancient bread and beer should necessarily resemble any particular present-day type. The very familiarity of these foods makes the study of their ancient counterparts a challenge, because ingrained assumptions must constantly be made explicit and reassessed.

Attempts to define beer and bread are unlikely to be wholly comprehensive, but some definitions are needed, in order to establish a base line for discussion. Beer can be considered to be a liquid made from starchy ingredients, usually cereal grain, which has been fermented into a beverage with at least some alcohol content. Bread may be thought of as a product cooked by direct exposure to dry heat – baked – and normally made wholly or in part from a starchy ingredient, usually cereal grain. Both beer and bread may be made from ingredients other than cereal, or have other ingredients added. Both foodstuffs share many characteristics, most obviously cereal as the usual major ingredient, and may have some preparation steps in common.

Sources of evidence and methods of analysis

Traditional sources

The investigation of ancient Egyptian baking and brewing techniques has relied heavily on the artistic record, which includes wall-reliefs and paintings, statuettes and models. A few examples are given here for each period. Wall decorations and statuettes of baking and brewing figures are most abundant in the Old Kingdom. A group of Old Kingdom statuettes is on display at the Cairo Museum, including a female brewer from the *mastaba* of Meresankh at Giza (JE66624) and a man working with a pottery vessel from the *mastaba* of Ptahshepses at Saqqara (Cairo CG112; Saleh and Sourouzian 1987: nos. 52 and 53 respectively). Perhaps the best-known depiction of baking and brewing is the relief in the tomb of Ty on the west wall of Room II (the 'provisions room'; see Épron and Daumas 1939: pls. 66–7, 70–1; Montet 1925: 230–56; Wild 1966), while the reliefs from the Saqqara *mastabas* of Hetepherakhti now at Leiden (Mohr 1943; Wild 1966: pl. 10) and Kaemrehu now at Cairo (CG 1534; Saleh and Sourouzian 1987: no. 59) are also quite widely cited.

Several Middle Kingdom wall-paintings show baking and brewing. Some of the most notable are at Beni Hasan in the tombs of Amenemhat (BH2; Newberry 1893a: 30–1, pl. 12), Khnumhotep (BH3; Newberry 1893a: 68, pl. 29), Bakht III (BH15; Newberry 1893b: 48, pl. 6) and Khety (BH17; Newberry 1893b: 55–6, pl. 12), as well as the Twelfth-Dynasty Theban tomb of Intefiqer (TT60; Davies and Gardiner 1920: 11–12, 14–16, pls. 8–9A, 11–12A). Models are the most common method of depicting these processes at this period, for example that from the tomb of Wadjethotep (no. 2106) at Sedment, dating to about the Ninth Dynasty, now at the Ny Carlsberg Glyptotek in Copenhagen (Mogensen 1930: 66, pl. 63, AE.I.N. 1571; Petrie and Brunton 1924: 7, pl. 20 no. 3). In the New Kingdom, apart from a few statuettes of millers, certainly votive or ritual (for examples see Breasted 1948: 22–4, pls. 22–4; Gardiner 1906), there are a few wall-paintings. A detailed but damaged scene from the demolished ninth pylon at Karnak, now at the Luxor Museum, depicts bakers and brewers at work in temple workshops at Thebes (Lauffray 1979: pl. 16; 1980: 178–9, fig. 191). One of the latest known depictions is an elaborate but fairly poorly preserved scene in the tomb of Rameses III at Thebes (KV11; Darby *et al.* 1977: 523, fig. 12.14; Wreszinski 1923: pl. 374).

Publications which include funerary representations of brewing and baking occasionally contain a discussion as well as a description of the processes. Examples of these are Borchardt (1897) for various Old Kingdom statuettes in the Cairo Museum; Davies (1902: 26, pl. 20) for reliefs in the late Old Kingdom tomb of Rahenem (no. 72) at Deir el-Gabrawi; Moussa *et al.* (1977: 66–72, pls. 23, 26; 101–4, fig. 13, pls. 34–5) for reliefs in the Fifth-Dynasty tomb of Niankhkhnum and Khnumhotep at Saqqara; and Winlock (1955: 27–9, pls. 22–3, 64–5) for a model from the Eleventh-Dynasty Theban tomb of Meketra. In addition, a number of syntheses have been written, including those by Faltings (1991 – Old Kingdom only); Klebs (1915: 67, 90–94, 1922: 94, 119–21, 1934: 171–9); Sist (1987: 55–6); Vandier (1964: 272–318) and Wreszinski (1926).

A variety of texts deal with bread and beer production. Many of these are scribal exercises, concerned with converting quantities of grain into loaves and beer of specific strength or quantity. Examples of these exercises can be found in the Rhind Mathematical Papyrus (Peet 1923: 112–22). Other documents record deliveries of grain to temple or palace kitchens and the quantities of bread and beer produced (see for example Helck 1961: 437–45, 1971: 33; Spalinger 1986). Deir el-Medina ostraca record that beer was brewed by villagers (Janssen 1980: 146–7). One of the most frequently cited Egyptian texts dealing with beer-making is not Pharaonic at all, but dates to the end of the third or beginning of the fourth century AD, written by the Egyptian Zozimus of Panopolis (Akhmim, see for instance Borchardt 1897: 130; Darby *et al.* 1977: 538; Helck 1971: 40; Lutz 1922: 78). Among the other Classical authors who mentioned or described Egyptian brewing and baking are Herodotus (mid fifth century BC), Pliny (first century AD), Strabo (64 BC–AD 22) and Athenaeus (third century AD; see Darby *et al.* 1977: e.g. 537; Lucas 1962: 13). Helck (1971: 41) and Lutz (1922: 81–2) describe an unlikely sounding Talmudic recipe for ancient Egyptian beer using safflower and salt.

Despite the same fairly limited pool of data (Währen 1961: 1) however, there has been a general lack of consensus about ancient Egyptian baking and brewing methods. Few accounts tally, in major or in minor details (Samuel 1993: 277–8). This does not make the artistic and written records invalid or unusable. On the contrary, they are a rich source of valuable data. There are nevertheless a number of critical problems with these sources which have rarely been addressed. The modern observer, with a set of contemporary experiences and expectations, will view the artistic depictions differently from the Egyptians who made them and who experienced the actual processes. Also, it cannot be established with artistic and documentary evidence alone how widely the practices of the élite, who generated that evidence, can be applied to the technology of the majority of the ancient Egyptian population.

An area of confusion is the extent to which baking and brewing practices changed over time. General accounts often treat the whole span of Pharaonic cereal food production as unchanging. Others have acknowledged that changes did occur, but mechanisms and causes have rarely been investigated. Use of Classical texts to investigate practices during Pharaonic times is likely to be particularly misleading. At least two major changes in cereal processing technology took place in Egypt during Greco-Roman times: emmer, the sole wheat of the ancient Egyptians (see Chapter 21, this volume), was replaced by free-threshing wheat (Crawford 1979: 140; Nesbitt and Samuel 1996: 77; Täckholm *et al.* 1941: 240–1), and the technology of milling switched from saddle to rotary querns (Forbes 1954: 274).

As this brief survey suggests, a great deal has been written about ancient Egyptian bread and beer. This chapter, however, is written on the premise that much of their production has been misunderstood. Discussion has often been heavily based on various assumptions: that ancient Egyptian bread and beer ingredients were similar in character and physico-chemical behaviour to ingredients commonly used today in the Western world; that ancient Egyptian food making technology was fairly crude; and that the limited evidence of artistic depictions provides most of the information needed to understand production methods. As the evidence presented in this chapter makes clear, such assumptions are wrong.

There is actually little consensus for the precise sequence of activities involved in flour production, as Figure 22.1b suggests. Nearly all accounts assume that the cereal which was processed was clean grain with no attached husk. Since this was not the case, as explained later in the chapter, the technology of flour production in particular has been misinterpreted.

Broadly speaking, the most common interpretation of ancient brewing is based on the use of bread (Fig. 22.1a). It has been thought that dough rich in yeast was prepared and lightly baked so that the yeast would not be killed by heat.

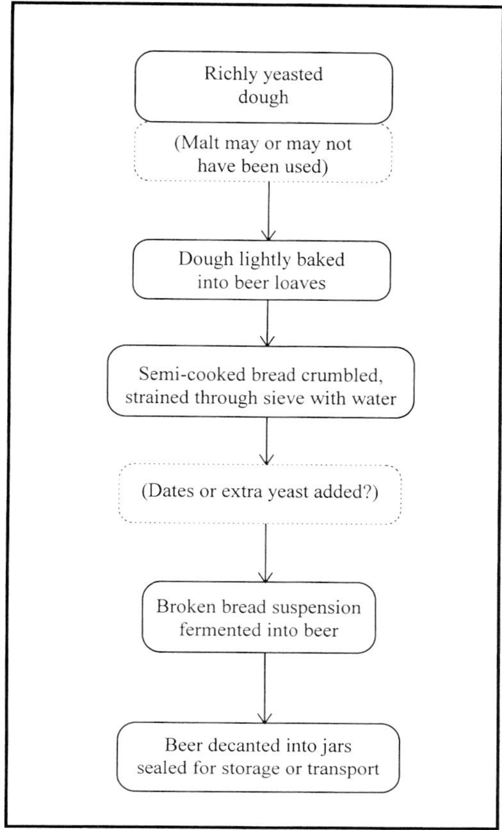

Figure 22.1a Generalised summary of interpretation of ancient Egyptian brewing, based on and adapted from several different sources (see for example references in text). Steps in brackets and broken lines indicate activities which are not widely included in modern accounts of ancient brewing practice, but which are sometimes mentioned.

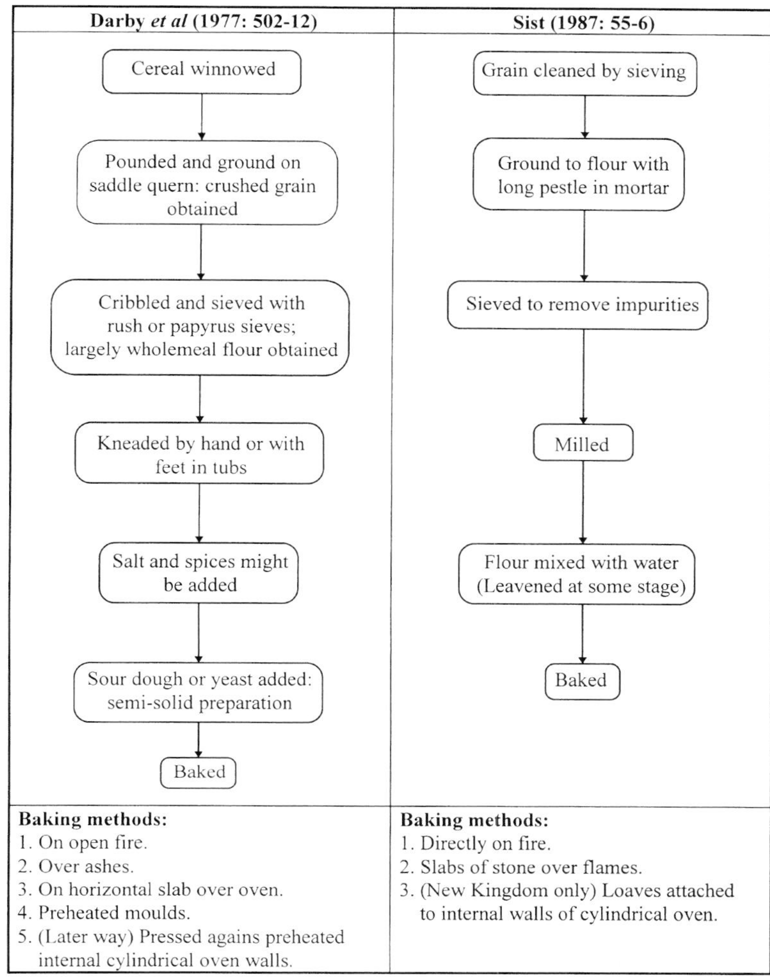

Figure 22.1b Two general accounts of ancient Egyptian baking methods, which are representative of common interpretations of the process.

These loaves were then crumbled and rinsed through sieves with water into vats. In them, fermentation occurred due to the action of yeast from the bread.

In order to take a fresh approach to the subject, the artistic and philological records have been referred to, but have been set aside as primary data sources for the purposes of this chapter. Both have a great deal to offer and their integration with archaeological, ethnographic and experimental evidence will add valuable and unique perspectives. There may now be enough data available from a range of sources to re-evaluate the historical development of ancient Egyptian baking and brewing. Such a study, though, has not yet been undertaken. The evidence for baking and brewing in the New Kingdom is currently the most extensively studied using scientific methods, and is therefore the main focus of this chapter. Figures 22.2 and 22.3 summarise the interpretations presented here, which are based on the sources of evidence set out below.

Archaeological evidence

Sites, tools and installations

The archaeological record has the potential to provide comparable information for all periods, and can give the most direct evidence for ancient Egyptian baking and brewing technology. In the arid Egyptian climate, organic remains are especially well preserved. Archaeologists are beginning to recognise the potential for a much more detailed understanding of cereal processing and food preparation in general (Samuel 1996a). As a result, the deliberate targeting and recording of food-related evidence should become more detailed and precise. At present, there are relatively few excavations which have been published or investigated in sufficient detail to draw accurate conclusions about the technology of cereal food preparation. The following are some of the main available sources.

Glimpses into the roots of Pharaonic brewing have been obtained from two Predynastic sites, those of Abydos and

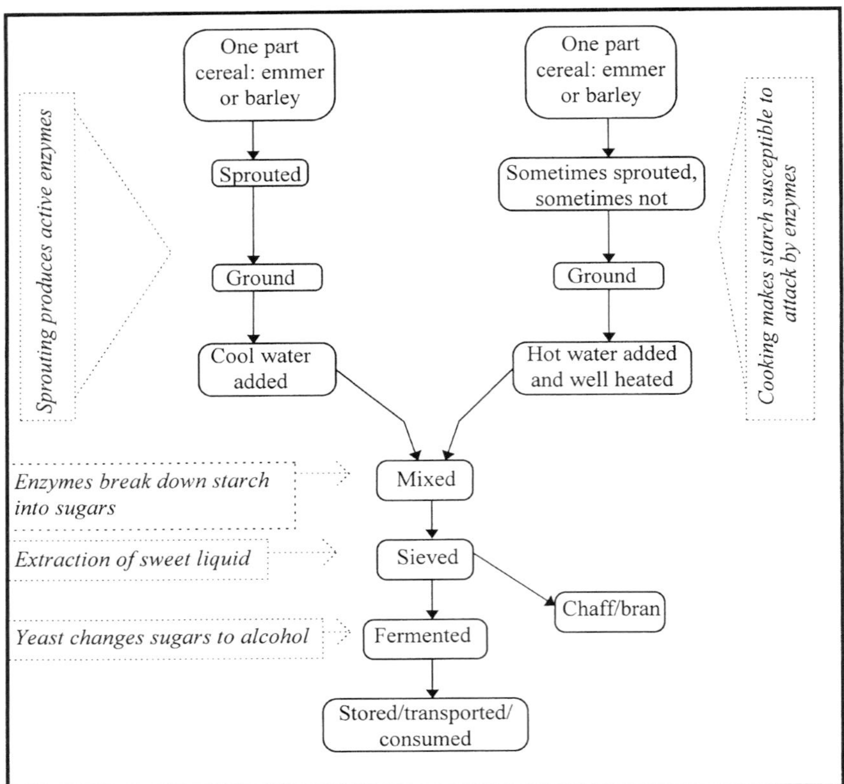

Figure 22.2 The suggested method of ancient Egyptian brewing presented in this chapter, based on microscopy of desiccated brewing residues. Text in boxes with solid lines and rounded corners indicates ancient brewing steps; text in dotted line boxes indicates biochemical changes which occur at each step.

Hierakonpolis. Excavations at both have uncovered installations which may well be connected with brewing (Geller 1992a: 21–4, 1992b: 104–12; Peet 1914: 7–9, pl. I no. 6, 8; Peet and Loat 1913: 1–7, pls. I, XIV/no. 3). They consist of double rows of large vats, supported by distinctive fire-bricks (see p. 79) and surrounded by an elaborate mud-brick shell. Such fire-bricks unassociated with installations have been found at a number of other Predynastic sites. The large quantities of ash and charcoal surrounding the vats, as well as the reddening of the ceramic, attest to the application of fire and the function of these structures as heating installations of some sort. In some cases residues of the vat contents have been preserved. Peet (1914: 9) submitted samples for chemical analysis which determined they were carbon-rich and therefore organic; further study indicated the grain embedded in residues was wheat (Peet and Loat 1913: 7). Residue from the Hierakonpolis vats was also submitted for archaeobotanical analysis, which indicated the major components were emmer chaff and grain (Geller 1989: 47, 1992b: 110).

Although Peet and Loat (1913) suggest these installations were kilns for parching grain, this interpretation is unlikely (for parching see p. 562). Geller (1989: 47–52, 1992a: 21, 1992b: 139, 142–3) has interpreted these structures as brewing installations, probably for mashing – that is, heating the beer ingredients at a moderate temperature for some time. This is based on chemical analytical data, not fully published, purporting to show that the residues are rich in sugars (Geller 1989: 47–8). Geller (1992b: 111, 183, table 8) reports and Maksoud *et al.* (1994) assert that fermentation products can be detected in these residues. The analytical chemical work published to date is unconvincing because the effects of degradation of ancient organic molecules (and therefore the possible presence of molecules that were not part of the original contents) has not been considered. Also, the possibility that micro-organisms contaminated the organic remains after abandonment has not been eliminated.

Nevertheless, the interpretation of these installations as kilns used at some stage in the brewing process is likely for the following reasons.

1) The Abydos residues contain wheat – almost certainly emmer rather than 'common wheat' (*Triticum vulgare*), as stated in the publication (Peet and Loat 1913: 7) – while the residues found adhering to the interior of the Hierakonpolis vats are rich in cereal grain and chaff. Emmer spikelets are clearly discernible in a photograph of residue published by Geller (1992b: 196, pl. 7). The abundant chaff indicates the food being prepared was not related to bread, porridge or other human food (for chaff in food see p. 545), while the roughly broken nature of the chaff indicates it was coarsely processed.

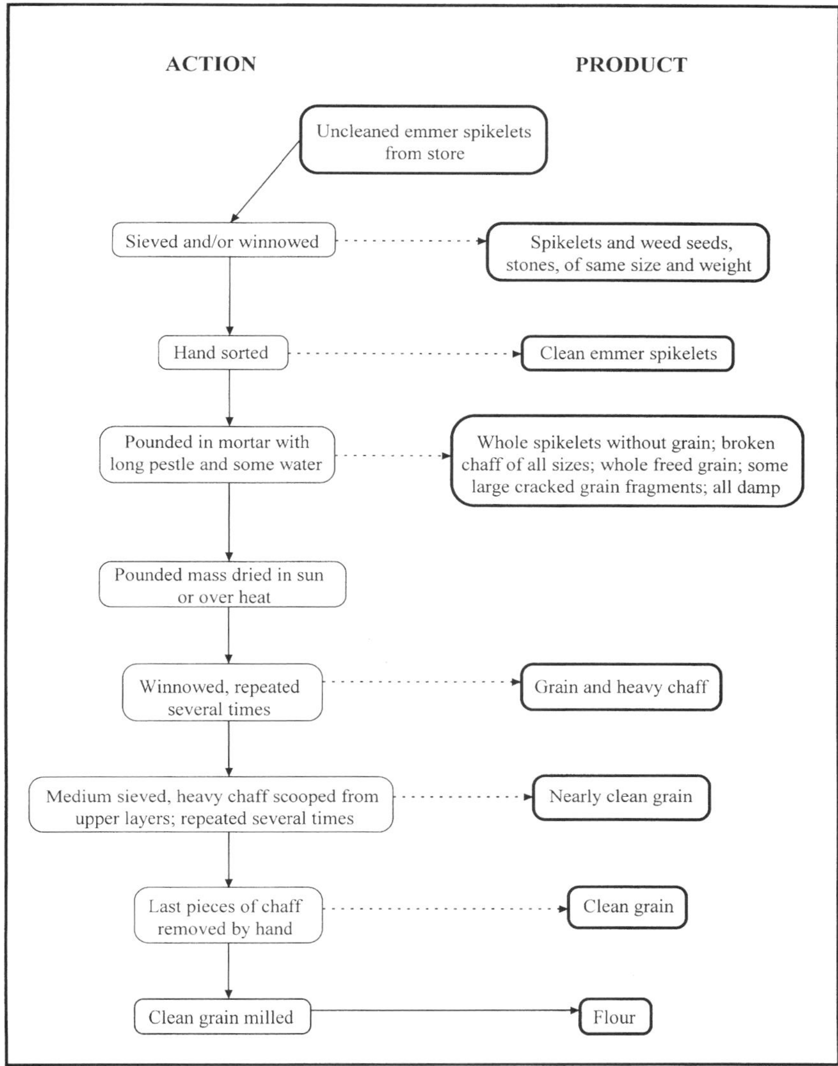

Figure 22.3 A model for ancient Egyptian emmer wheat processing, from removal of the semi-cleaned spikelets from store to flour milling. The reconstruction is based on archaeology (including archaeobotany), ethnography and experimental replication. Each stage of processing is shown on the right, accompanied by the intermediate products associated with that activity on the left.

2) Geller describes the remaining contents as 'a vitreous black residue' (1989: 45), 'in which emmer wheat and possibly barley was embedded' (1992a: 21), but states that this residue was not charred: 'numerous uncarbonised grains, spikelets, and rachillas of emmer wheat [were identified] in [the] sediment from . . . the vat features' (1992b: 110). The thick fused masses caked onto the inside surfaces of the vats are clearly visible in photographs published by Geller (1989: pls. 4, 5). This description indicates that reasonable amounts of water must have been part of the mixture in the vats, because the uncharred residue has fused into a solid mass, something that could not occur by heating dry or damp grain alone (see p. 550).
3) The abundant ash and charcoal surrounding the vats at both Abydos and Hierakonpolis, together with the slight but not extensive reddening of the ceramic, clearly indicate that gentle heat was produced in the structures and applied to the mixture of coarsely broken spikelets and water inside.
4) The Early Dynastic written records indicate that beer was very important at that period, and therefore it must have been well-established in ancient Egyptian culture by that point. It is highly likely, therefore, that Egyptian brewing had its antecedents in Predynastic times.

Recent excavations at Giza, directed by Mark Lehner, have uncovered an Old Kingdom bakery (Lehner 1992: 3–6, 1993: 62–6). This provides valuable insights into baking practices associated with a royal project of some kind. The Giza data currently available throw light on the end process of Old Kingdom bread production, the baking stage.

Excavations at Middle Kingdom Abu Ghalib uncovered ovens, elongated conical moulds and platters in close association (Larsen 1936a, 1936b: 48, 73–6, figs. 2, 4, 10 nos.

1933.499, 1934.51, 1933.498, 1933.500, 14, pls 13b, 19a, 20). Larsen (1936a) discusses the possible baking methods used at this installation, proposing that only bread in moulds was intended for beer and thus was only partially baked, while the platters were lids for covering the oven. Jacquet-Gordon (1981: 16) records Middle Kingdom sites from which similar elongated conical bread moulds have been recovered.

Two sites, both dating to the New Kingdom, and both of comparable structure, have provided particularly rich evidence for the full sequence of baking and brewing methods. These are Deir el-Medina (Bruyère 1939) and the Workmen's Village at Amarna (Kemp 1984, 1985, 1986, 1987a, 1987b; Peet 1921; Peet and Woolley 1923; Woolley 1922). This chapter draws heavily on archaeological finds from these villages and therefore focuses primarily on New Kingdom practice. The data available includes cereal-processing tools such as saddle querns for milling and mortars for pounding, as well as installations such as quern and mortar emplacements and ovens.

Residues and loaves

Amongst the most informative archaeological remains are desiccated loaves of bread and residues of beer. The complete loss of water has prevented most decay processes taking place, but the biomolecules making up the foodstuffs have broken down through ageing. The microstructure is very well preserved and has provided vital evidence for ancient processing methods. For example, starch granules and yeast cells can clearly be distinguished by microscopy.

Several descriptions and studies of surviving ancient Egyptian bread have been made (e.g. Borchardt 1932; Bruyère 1937: 106–7; Darby *et al.* 1977: 517–22; Glabau and Goldman 1938; Grüss 1932; Leek 1972, 1973; Täckholm *et al.* 1941: 248; Währen 1960: 94, 1961: 15, 1963: 24–7; Wittmack 1896, Wittmack 1905: 6–7), but it is not generally recognised that several hundred such loaves survive from ancient times (Fig. 22.4). They are now scattered in museums throughout the world. The loaves vary greatly in size, shape and texture. They have thin crusts which are darker on the upper side and paler on the base, showing that they were definitely baked.

Virtually all surviving bread has been recovered from élite tombs. This means that it relates only to the wealthier members of ancient Egyptian society, and that it is only representative of funerary practice. Without specimens from settlement contexts, it is impossible to know if surviving loaves are the same as bread consumed in daily life, if they were similar to bread baked for religious or ceremonial occasions, or if they were types which were only produced for funerary offerings. Beer residues, in contrast, have been recovered both from tombs and from settlement sites, representing both funerary and daily practice, for the élite and for the humbler members of society.

Figure 22.4 A loaf of bread, roughly made in the shape of a Horus figure (University Museum, University of Pennsylvania, acc. no. 29-87-635). The beak and elongated, flattened falcon-like head can be seen on the left, while the flattened, broader shoulders are human in outline. The loaf was cut while fresh, making a clean, flat surface to the right. On the top of the loaf, just above the cut surface, two faint lines of black ink are visible. The total length is 130 mm and the greatest breadth (across the shoulders) is 75 mm. The body of the loaf is 30 mm high, while the thickest part, at the beak, is 40 mm. This bread loaf is very dense, made of very finely ground flour with a slightly oily texture. The cereal from which this bread loaf is made has not yet been identified. Original provenance: Dra Abu el-Naga, Shaft number 6, New Kingdom.

Beer residues are less clearly identifiable, because unlike bread, they do not have an obvious appearance (Fig. 22.5). Nevertheless, they have been recognised as contents within whole pots (Bruyère 1937: 110; Grüss 1929a, 1929b, 1929c; Petrie 1907: 23; Winlock 1932: 32), within brewing installations (Geller 1989: 45, 47, 49, 1992a: 21; 1992b: 108), and as thin crusts clinging to pottery sherds (Samuel 1994b, 1996b: 5, 1996c: 488, fig. 1; Samuel and Bolt 1995: 29). Other residues which have been called remains of beer are less convincing, if only because they have not been described in enough detail in publications, do not have known parallels or have not been extensively analysed (Firth 1915: 17; Mond and Myers 1937: 60–1; Petrie 1901: 32; 1920: 43). No residues have so far been found in labelled beer vessels. Residues most likely to have been beer or precursors have some or all of the following characteristics. They contain fragments of grain, cereal chaff or bran tissue, are rich in modified starch, have large colonies of yeast cells and perhaps lactic acid bacteria, and are found in small shallow cups likely to have served as drinking vessels, in closed vessels suitable for fermenting or storing beer or, in the case of Predynastic installations, in large open vats used for heating large quantities of processed cereal. The assumption that residues with most of these features are indeed associated with beer, rather than some other cereal food, is based on the fact that beer was a staple food for the ancient Egyptians. The interpretation of many cereal-based resi-

Figure 22.5a A rim sherd with a thin coating of beer residue (dark patches), from the Workmen's Village, Amarna. The sherd comes from a long-necked amphora (Group 21, see Rose 1984: 135, 137), showing that beer containers could be those more conventionally thought to be for commodities such as wine or oil. This view shows the outer surface of the rim, with some fragments of chaff embedded in the residue. The typical cracked surface of such thin coatings can be seen in some areas. Sample TAVR92–58; scale bar is 1 cm.

Figure 22.5b Large irregular lumps of beer residue, now at the British Museum. They are composed mainly of coarsely shredded barley chaff, firmly stuck together with a dark orangey-brown matrix.

dues as beer-related is thus very likely but not absolutely proven.

No adequate survey of surviving residues has ever been carried out, but there may be hundreds in unwashed Egyptian pottery collections obtained from arid locations. Residues may derive from the finished product or the intermediate stages of brewing. Residues of finished beer are thin coatings with a few small fragments of cereal chaff or bran embedded in an orangey-brown matte, or slightly shiny, crust of material, which is usually cracked over the surface (Fig. 22.5a). Intermediate products may look similar to the finished beer, or may be large masses of coarsely shredded chaff, sometimes with coarse pieces of grain, stuck together by thick or thin layers of matte or slightly shiny, orangey-brown matrix (Fig. 22.5b). In some cases, only the friable chaff is left, with very little or no obvious matrix binding it together.

Residues and loaves have been examined by a number of methods. Simple careful observation provides data on colour, texture and quantities of inclusions. For bread, information on shape, size, decoration and method of forming the loaf can be obtained. Ingredients can be identified based on the morphology of features on grain, seeds, chaff fragments and other plant parts and their comparison to modern known plants. Often, though, fragments are so small or abraded that there are not enough features with which to make identifications. In these cases, the anatomical pattern of cells making up the tissues may be useful. Shreds of tissue are carefully removed from the specimen, gently cleaned with alcohol and a fine brush, and the cells may be usefully highlighted with appropriate general stains such as safranin and fast green (Gurr 1953: 205; Jensen 1962). They are then identified by reference to modern tissue mounts from known plants and plant parts (for similar identification techniques see for example Dickson 1987; Hansson 1996; Hansson and Isaksson 1994; Hjelmqvist 1984; 1990; Holden 1986; Körber-Grohne and Piening 1980).

The light microscope allows observation of components such as starch granules, yeast cells and plant tissue (Grüss 1928, 1929a–c). Several crumbs of specimen (from 0.5 to 1 millimetres or more in diameter) are crushed on a glass slide, mounted in a drop of water, covered with a cover slip and observed at magnifications of 100 up to 400 times. Polarised light helps to determine whether the ancient starch has been affected by heat, through the presence or absence of birefringence (French 1973: 1054–5; Goering *et al.* 1974). Appropriate stains can enhance the features viewed with the microscope.

Specimen crumbs can also be embedded in plastic resin and sliced into sections 1–7 μm thick. These are placed onto slides and stained with a variety of stains which can target starch, protein, lipid and other biomolecular components. The structures of starch granules and tissues, and their relationships to each other, can thus be accurately observed.

A highly informative technique to investigate the microstructure of beer residues and bread has been scanning electron microscopy (SEM) (Samuel 1994b, 1996b, 1996c; Samuel and Bolt 1995). Several tiny crumbs from each specimen (from 0.1 to 1 millimetres or more in diameter) are removed and mounted on stubs with double-sided sticky tape. Each stub is then coated with about 20–30 nanometres of gold or gold palladium, to permit conductivity of electrons in the microscope. No further preparation is required, because the material is already completely desiccated. Apart from coating the ancient material with a thin metal layer, SEM is non-destructive. With careful storage, the mounted samples can be archived and re-examined as often as required.

Archaeobotanical recovery and analysis

As Murray (Chapter 21, this volume) has stressed, archaeobotanical recovery and analysis is essential for the accurate understanding of plant resources. At sites where remains are preserved by desiccation, the rare opportunity exists to investigate primary deposition (the places where plant remains were dropped as they were being used) and therefore to locate specific activity areas within constructed spaces. By itself, the function of, for example, an isolated oven or milling stone is difficult to interpret. Set in the surroundings in which it was used, and in relation to other equipment, detailed information can be gathered about cereal-processing methods. The plant remains associated with cereal-processing areas are also invaluable evidence for the reconstruction process. For example, the full assemblage of shredded chaff and whole spikelets lying on the floor of an ancient village house, adjacent to a mortar, has not only allowed the archaeological link to be made between mortars and pounding whole spikelets, but has also provided clues about how the spikelets were pounded, based on the appearance of the shredded chaff (Samuel 1989: 280, 1994a: 117–18).

Some microscopy (e.g. Hallam 1973: 140–1; Palmer 1995; Whymper 1913a) and chemical studies (Barton-Wright *et al.* 1944; Shewry *et al.* 1982; Whymper 1913b) have been made of desiccated Egyptian cereal grain. This work has shown that although raw grain microstructure is remarkably well-preserved, profound biochemical changes have occurred over time. Because DNA and proteins have been badly damaged over the passage of time, it is impossible for desiccated ancient Egyptian grain to germinate now, despite its excellent outward appearance.

In damp areas, in the river flood plain, only charred plant material will survive. Most of this will not be deposited in the area where charred remains were first generated, but was moved in ancient times to rubbish deposits, scattered on floors or other secondary areas. Careful recovery of charred material nevertheless can provide valuable information about ancient foodstuffs, such as the raw ingredients and their distributions.

Ethnographic analogy

Murray (Chapter 21, this volume) has emphasised the importance of ethnographic information about the traditional use of plants. This extends to the study of food processing, although less ethnoarchaeological work on food preparation has been done compared to post-harvest cereal processing up until storage. Preservation, recovery and recording of archaeological and bioarchaeological remains may be excellent, but the interpretation of food processing may be inaccurate if the sequence of activities linking ingredients and tools unfamiliar to the archaeologist is not understood. Traditional methods of preparing foods can only be observed amongst people who still use tools and materials similar to those found archaeologically.

Geographical proximity of ancient and modern cultures is not necessarily an appropriate criterion. In Egypt, for example, the type of oven used today (Rizqallah and Rizqallah 1978) is of very different construction to the cylindrical form used by the New Kingdom Egyptians (Währen 1960: 92). The sole use of geographical proximity as a measure of similarity ignores potential cultural changes that can occur, either as a result of indigenous development, or through new cultures introducing new techniques.

Appropriate ethnographic analogy for ancient cereal food processing involves the same or similar tools and raw materials. This can only be established by careful reference to both archaeological and ethnographic evidence. It requires an understanding of the biology and physical structure of the raw ingredients as well as the end results of specific processing methods. The ethnographic analogies used here are those which involve the same type of tools and installations as those found in the ancient Egyptian archaeological record, or which relate to cereals of the same species or structure as the hulled cereals of ancient Egypt.

Experimental reconstruction

Experimentation is valuable to test hypotheses about ancient processes which have been developed from detailed archaeological analysis and carefully selected ethnographic analogies. It can indicate gaps, demonstrate what is impractical, and provide greater insights into specific processing technologies. Experiments must be designed and carried out with great care in order to be valid, making use of all available archaeological, ethnographic and archaeobotanical data. Methods and equipment must be justifiable on the basis of both archaeobotanical and ethnographic evidence. It is best to use authentic ancient or modern materials if possible. With care, experimentation can be an excellent direct method of assessing and experiencing the results of specific processing activities with the tools and ingredients used in ancient times.

For ancient Egyptian baking and brewing, detailed experiments have been undertaken for producing flour from cereals taken from storage (Samuel 1989: 264–70, 1993, 1994a: 143–66). Some work has been done on baking, but authentic experimental brewing has yet to be carried out. Wherever possible, ancient tools have been used. If these were not sufficiently robust, replicas were constructed with direct reference to the ancient originals, as were installations such as ovens. For steps with no clear indication of the relevant ancient tools, models were taken from appropriate ethnographic analogies. All bread-making experiments were carried out with modern emmer wheat, the cereal which has been found in much of the ancient Egyptians' surviving bread.

Raw materials

Bread requires two essential ingredients: flour, usually from some type of cereal or other starchy food, and water. Leaven is frequently assumed to have been used for baking in ancient Egyptian times, but is an optional bread ingredient. Beer is made from cereal grain, fermenting micro-organisms and water. Extra flavourings can be used for both bread and beer. In the following section, only cereals and leavening will be discussed. Additives will be dealt with separately in the sections on beer and bread. The supply of water is a separate technology which cannot be dealt with here.

Cereals

Murray (Chapter 21, and Fig. 21.1, this volume) describes emmer wheat and barley, the two cereals cultivated by the ancient Egyptians, and their hulled nature which requires extensive processing to obtain clean grain. As Murray explains, there is good evidence to show that emmer and barley grain were stored still hulled, that is, still packaged in a tight envelope of chaff (the 'spikelet' of emmer wheat). Both barley and wheat chaff must be removed during human food processing otherwise the huge amount of coarse roughage introduced into the digestive tract prevents absorption of nutrients (Miles *et al.* 1988; Schweizer and Würsch 1991: 184–5). The extra processing needed to remove chaff is an important distinguishing characteristic of hulled cereals. The wheat used for most bread and pasta today easily breaks up into naked grain and loose chaff when threshed, and only requires the type of sieving and winnowing described by Murray to separate the two fractions.

Cereals are staples for agricultural societies in temperate zones throughout the world (Zohary and Hopf 1993: 15). Their primary contribution to diet is food energy, although they are also important for vitamins and minerals as well as protein (Ranhotra 1991). Cereals, like all other plant foods, lack some essential components for human health, and cannot on their own provide a balanced protein intake. Food energy is supplied by starch, which makes up 69–79 per cent of the cereal grain (Ranhotra 1991: 850).

Starch is composed of two long molecules, the building block of which is the simple sugar glucose. These long molecules must be broken into much shorter chains in order for cereal products to be digested or fermented. Whole starch is stored within the grain in the form of lens-shaped or spherical granules, embedded in a protein matrix (Fig. 22.8a). The outer part of the grain is composed of several layers of tissue, collectively known as the bran, in which much of the vitamin and mineral content is concentrated (Fig. 22.6). At one end of the grain is the embryo which, when exposed to adequate conditions of warmth and moisture, will germinate and develop into a new plant. Concentrated in the embryo and the tissues surrounding it are vitamins, minerals, and much of the fat content of the cereal grain (Angold 1983; Barnes 1989: 374–9; Bradbury *et al.* 1956: 334, 336; Mattern 1991: 15–19; Winton and Winton 1932: 190–201).

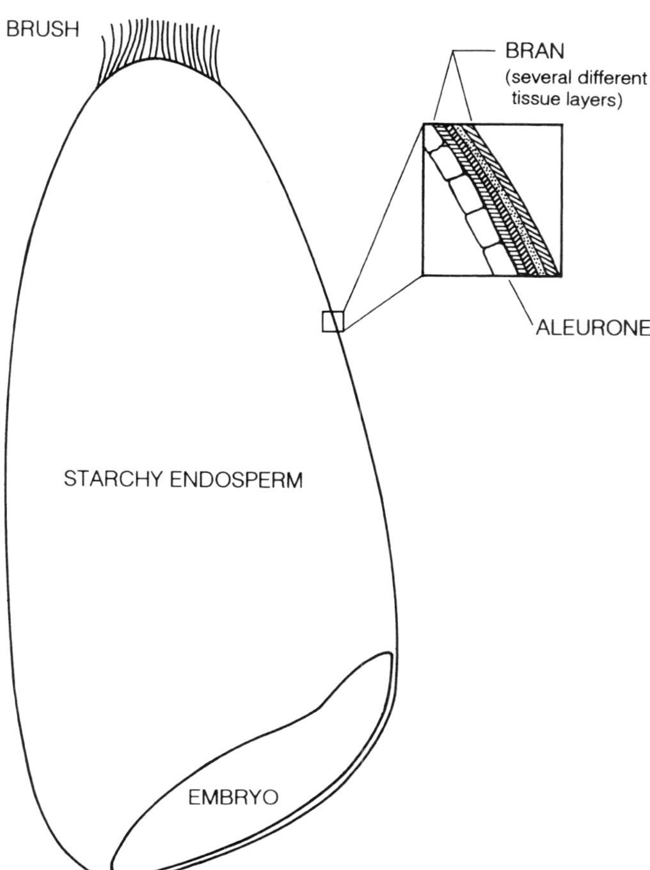

Figure 22.6 Schematic diagram of a cereal grain. At one end of the wheat grain is a distinctive brush of hairs; this feature does not appear on barley grain. The outer surface is the bran, made up of several different cell layers. Beneath the bran is a thicker tissue, called the aleurone layer. During germination, cells of the aleurone produce enzymes which act upon the starchy endosperm. The bulk of the grain is composed of starchy endosperm, cells packed with starch granules embedded in a protein matrix (see Fig. 22.8a). At one end of the grain is the embryo, the structure which eventually grows into a new plant.

Fermentation agents

What is fermentation?

All cells need to generate energy for activity and growth. Many cells, be they unicellular organisms or part of a complex creature such as a wheat plant or a human being, do this by a complex biochemical pathway which requires oxygen. Fermentation, also known as anaerobic respiration (Raven *et al.* 1981: 94), is the chemical pathway by which some cells are able to provide themselves with energy in the absence of oxygen. Without oxygen, the cellular production of energy is much less efficient. The precise chemical pathways of fermentation vary according to cell type, and alcohol is not always an end-product. As with respiration in the presence of oxygen, a major product is carbon dioxide (Raven *et al.* 1981: 94). This gas produces the effervescent or spongy quality of fermented foods.

Alcoholic or ethanol fermentation is the anaerobic respiration process used by the yeasts (Berry 1982: 10–11). In this system, one of the main products is ethanol. The effects of alcohol on human beings are well-known: in moderate quantities alcohol produces a pleasant sensation, in larger amounts it has adverse effects on the body and over the long term, large intake is fatal (Duffy 1992; Hurley and Horowitz 1990). For food preparation, alcohol can be advantageous for preservation and storage by improving keeping qualities. Alcohol is a poisonous substance, at greater or lesser concentrations, for all living things. As yeast cells produce alcohol, to which they have a degree of tolerance, they create an environment toxic to many other bacteria and fungi, preventing food-spoilage organisms from flourishing (Wood and Hodge 1985: 265).

A group of food micro-organisms associated with many cereal products is lactic acid bacteria, of which there are many species. One of their main fermentation by-products is lactic acid (Prìhoda *et al.* 1993: 31; Steinkraus 1983: 337–8). The sour taste can be very pleasant and refreshing if carefully controlled, as in sour dough bread. The build-up of lactic acid creates an acidic environment, which many food spoilage micro-organisms cannot tolerate. Thus, lactic acid fermentation also helps to preserve foods (Cooke *et al.* 1987; Holzapfel *et al.* 1995; Steinkraus 1983: 338).

Both yeast and lactic acid bacteria use simple sugars for their nutrition. Yeast prefers glucose but can use a range of sugars (Brown 1993: 67; van Dam 1986: 122), while many lactic acid bacteria grow on maltose and other complex sugars (Ponte and Reed 1982: 284). Both may also require a range of other nutrients such as certain vitamins and minerals (Berry 1982: 10). When long chains of starch are broken down in the cereal grain during growth or food processing, large quantities of sugars such as glucose and maltose are released (French 1973: 1056; Palmer 1989: 179). These are suitable for both yeast and lactic acid bacteria growth. In many modern commercial baking and brewing systems, manufacturers try to keep very pure yeast cultures and avoid lactic acid bacteria. There are exceptions, such as San Francisco sour dough bread (Sugihara 1985: 251–4) and Belgian lambic beers (De Keersmaecker 1996). Prior to the introduction of large-scale controlled conditions in industrialised times, however, yeasts and lactic acid bacteria were both present in baking and brewing substrates in varying proportions (Sugihara 1985: 249; Wood and Hodge 1985: 280).

Yeast

Morphological characteristics do not give enough information to identify the species of micro-organisms which were used by the ancient Egyptians for baking and brewing. Grüss (1929a) named the yeast he detected in New Kingdom beer residues as a new species, *Saccharomyces winlockii*, in honour of Herbert Winlock, who excavated the vessel in which the cells were found (Winlock 1932: 32). Unfortunately, the contention that the ancient yeast truly is a species new to science cannot be sustained from the only available evidence, the appearance of the yeast.

The identification of yeasts is based on three major approaches (Deák 1991: 180–3). One is morphology, which includes shape, size, method of budding and other characteristics. Since many yeast species look very similar or exactly the same, the second approach (i.e. the differences in physiology and biochemistry) is essential for identification. Physiological studies involve establishing which particular nutrients must be available for survival, compared to nutrients which need not be present for the yeast species to thrive. This information cannot be obtained for the ancient yeast cells, which are dead, and therefore their precise identity cannot be established this way. Biochemical analysis is highly problematic for ancient, degraded biomolecules.

The third approach – the use of genetic analysis through the examination of DNA and RNA – is now very important in the field of yeast taxonomy. In the future it may be possible to obtain more information about ancient yeast species through DNA studies as well. Three major requirements must first be met, however. Most importantly, since modern yeast cells are ubiquitous in the air and on all surfaces, the most stringent conditions of cleanliness and sterility must be maintained. Otherwise it will be modern micro-organism DNA which is isolated and analysed. In order to be able to interpret any results from ancient DNA analysis, the genetic code of modern yeast species must be known. Work is actively proceeding on yeast genetics (Deák 1991: 181) but much remains to be done. Finally, sufficient amounts of ancient yeast DNA, preserved in lengths which encode useable information, must be recoverable from the ancient residues.

Some authors have suggested that the ancient Egyptians scooped off the yeasty froth from the surface of actively fermenting beer, and used this to leaven their bread (Kemp 1989: 120; Wilson 1989: 97). This is possible, but was not necessarily the case. The same species of yeast will change its metabolic activity depending on its environment, but does not adjust quickly. In high sugar concentrations, such as in fermenting beer, yeast behaves anaerobically even if oxygen is present. In low sugar conditions, as in bread made from ordinary cereal flour, yeast switches to aerobic metabolism (Berry 1982: 11; Hough 1991: 115–18). Brown (1982: 58) comments that it was not until after about AD 1700 in Europe that yeast from beer was used to leaven bread, but the technique was not reliable and often made the bread bitter.

Lactic acid bacteria
Only in a few samples of ancient beer have colonies of bacteria been observed. Each bacteria cell is about one micron (one thousandth of a millimetre) in length and usually rod-shaped. When present, they tend to occur in enormous numbers. Sometimes, however, only a few individual cells can be seen, usually in close association with yeast cells. Lactic acid bacteria are commonly associated with yeasts and are often part of fermented cereal foods (Nout and Rombouts 1992: 136S, 141S; Wood and Hodge 1985). Thus, the close association of these ancient bacteria with yeast in a cereal food, their abundance, their shape, their close association with the sample matrix and the usual lack of other types of micro-organisms, all suggest that the small rod shapes are lactic acid bacteria.

No micro-organisms which match lactic acid bacteria in appearance have been observed in ancient bread loaves. Techniques appropriate for the identification of low quantities of minute cells must be developed and applied to samples of ancient desiccated bread before it can be established whether lactic acid bacteria were present in ancient Egyptian loaves as part of their preparation.

Beer brewing
Ingredients

Desiccated residues of ancient beer provide the most direct evidence for ingredients used in ancient Egyptian brewing. The following discussion of ingredients is largely based on analysis of residues, mostly dating to the New Kingdom.

Cereals
Most residues so far studied come from the two workmen's villages of Amarna and Deir el-Medina. They therefore reflect brewing practice of one particular stratum of society. From the evidence of these residues, in New Kingdom times barley appears to be most frequently used for village brewing, while emmer was sometimes used. Occasionally, both cereals were mixed in more or less equal proportions. Thus, both cultivated cereals were used for brewing but barley may have been more common for beer. These residues are too limited to conclude that the pattern holds for New Kingdom artisan-class domestic brewing in general, and cannot yet be extrapolated to New Kingdom society as a whole. Further work on residues from other archaeological sites should help to clarify the question.

Grüss (1929a, 1929b, 1929c) identified only emmer from a range of New Kingdom beer residues. His published drawings, although definitely of cereal tissue, are unfortunately undiagnostic and cannot be assigned either to emmer or to barley.

The use of the two cereals and the proportions in which they were mixed may have been one characteristic whereby the ancient Egyptians distinguished and named different types of beers. The flavour and character of modern wheat beers, primarily produced in southern Germany, but in other northern European regions as well (Jackson 1993: 49), are distinct from barley-based beers. According to Jackson (1993: 48), modern wheat beers tend to be more thirst-quenching and tart in flavour.

Fermentation micro-organisms
Yeast was certainly a key fermentation agent in ancient Egyptian beer. Many thin-crust residues, deriving from the finished beer product, contain large colonies of yeast cells. Cells have sometimes been preserved in the act of budding, showing that these colonies were in an active state of growth at the time they were desiccated. Individual ancient yeast cells are recognisable by distinctive bud scars (Fig. 22.7).

A number of features indicate that yeast cells in the ancient residues are original ingredients of beer and not chance contamination. The cells are of generally uniform appearance, both within individual residues and amongst all residues so far examined. Residues which contain yeast usually have many cells embedded in the residue matrix, not individual cells deposited loosely on the surface. Finally, budding cells, and therefore active growth, show there were abundant nutrients and sufficient moisture to support yeast metabolism for a fairly extensive period of time, up until the residues dried out completely. This would not have happened if, when discarded, the thin deposits on broken potsherds did not already contain yeast. They would have dried out too rapidly to allow large colonies of active cells to be established from chance contamination.

Bacteria, possibly lactic acid bacteria, have been detected with SEM in some beer residues. Lactic acid fermentation can impart a refreshing acidic flavour to beer. In a hot climate, such a thirst-quenching flavour would be highly desirable. If lactic fermentation was indeed a feature of ancient Egyptian beer, it may have had some of the character and flavour of modern-day African beers, in which lactic fermentation plays an important role (Dirar 1993: 80–2; Odunfa 1985: 167; Platt 1964: 70–1). The extent to which lactic acid fermentation occurred in ancient Egyptian brewing is currently uncertain, however, because the very small size of the bacteria makes their consistent detection uncertain. Even when abundant, they can be difficult to observe.

If lactic acid bacteria are uncontrolled in food systems, there may be over-production of acids and other metabolites, which can cause overwhelming and distasteful flavours (Stear 1990: 505). It is thus possible that lactic acid bacteria were important for brewing but that most brews

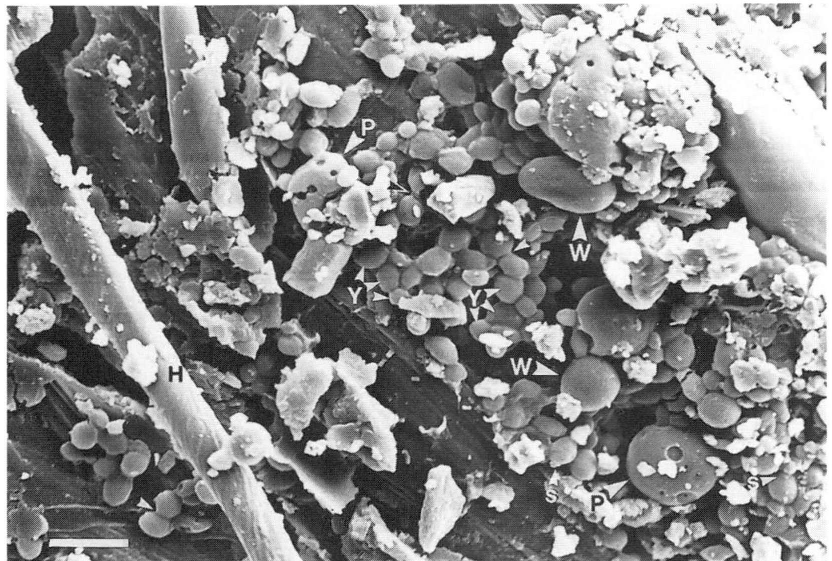

Figure 22.7 Scanning electron micrograph of a desiccated ancient Egyptian beer residue from the Workmen's Village, Amarna (sample TAVR92–72). The residue is a thin coating, similar to that shown in Fig. 22.5a. In this view, whole starch granules (W), pitted starch granules (P), yeast cells (Y) and a brush hair (H) can be seen. The pitted starch indicates that malted (sprouted) grain was an ingredient of the beer. The yeast cells can be identified by their distinctive bud scars (s). Many were desiccated in the process of budding apart (some examples are marked by unlabelled arrows), showing that the yeast was alive and active up until the time the residue dried out. Scale bar is 10 microns.

did not contain huge amounts. If this was the case, the small size of the bacteria together with their relatively low density would make them difficult to locate in the ancient residues. The close association of lactic acid bacteria with yeast in traditional and spontaneously fermented cereal foods today does suggest that ancient Egyptian beers (and bread) were also fermented by yeast-lactic acid bacteria systems. Another possibility which cannot be ruled out is that residues with notably large colonies of bacteria are the remains of beer which were contaminated with undesirable micro-organisms, and therefore discarded.

Other ingredients

Apart from cereals, fermentation micro-organisms and water, there is at present little direct evidence for other ingredients in ancient Egyptian beer. No New Kingdom residues contain obvious large non-cereal plant fragments and most show no microscopic traces of non-cereal tissues. If plant flavourings were standard additions, it would be reasonable to expect that some fragments of tissue from such ingredients would be consistently present and detectable. If extracts and liquids or syrups were added, methods other than microscopy would be needed to identify them. Very little chemical analysis has been applied to ancient Egyptian food remains. Some beers may well have been flavoured with various additives, but the dearth of non-cereal fragments and tissues suggests that, at the New Kingdom workmen's villages, beer was not normally flavoured with extra ingredients.

Unlike most modern European-style beers, the ancient Egyptians did not use hops. The wild hop plant has a northern temperate distribution, growing in latitudes of about 35°–70°N (Neve 1991: 1). (The Egyptian Mediterranean coast is roughly 31°30′N.) Although the modern character of European beers is strongly influenced by hops, in many regions this flavouring was not widespread for brewing until the nineteenth century AD (Neve 1991: 26–7). Other beers, such as traditional African brews (see, for example, Dirar 1993: 224–304; Odunfa 1985: 170–7; Platt 1964: 70–1; Rooney *et al.* 1986: 335–7), do not incorporate any flavourings, and there is no reason to suppose that additives must have been an integral part of ancient Egyptian beer.

A few residues do contain microscopic fragments of plant tissue which are not derived from cereals. Grüss (1929a: 278) located tissue fragments which he identified as *Citrus aurantium* L., sour orange. The identification is unlikely, however. Like other citrus fruit trees, the sour orange probably originates in south east Asia (Zeven and de Wet 1982: 62; Zohary and Hopf 1993: 173). It does not seem to have been generally known to the Mediterranean world until after the medieval period (Zohary and Hopf 1993: 173). No other reliable archaeobotanical identifications of sour orange in Pharaonic Egypt have been substantiated (Germer 1985: 105; De Vartavan and Asensi Amorós 1997: 79). The anatomical structure of this particular tissue has been published by Grüss, and should be reassessed.

A few plant tissue fragments have been found in residues from the Workmen's Village at Amarna and from Deir el-Medina. Their small size and rarity make identification difficult. Microscopy of a range of known modern and ancient plant tissues which may have been beer ingredients do not match anatomically most of the tissue fragments found in these residues. These comparative plants include date fruit (*Phoenix dactylifera* L.), dom fruit (*Hyphaene thebaica* (L.) Mart.), common fig (*Ficus carica* L.), sycomore fig (*Ficus sycomorus* L.), Christ's thorn fruit (*Zizyphus spina-christi* (L.) Desf.) and coriander seed (*Co-*

riandrum sativum L.). Unintentional inclusions, such as weed seeds or fragments of plant foods in the vicinity of the brewing area but not deliberately added to the beer, cannot be excluded.

Only in one residue has a definite identification been made. This is a lump of cereal-based material in a jar from a Deir el-Medina tomb, now in the Musée du Louvre (E14617). It contains a seed gall from the sycomore fig. Sycomore figs are commonly found in ancient Egyptian tombs and other sites (see Chapter 24, this volume; Germer 1985: 25–7), and the symbolic importance of the sycomore fig tree is well-known (Chapter 24, this volume; Bleeker 1973: 35; Gerisch in press). It is thus likely to have been easily obtainable and abundant enough to add in sufficient volume to make a contribution to the flavour and character of ancient Egyptian beer. The distinctive appearance of the galls, and the single find in one residue alone, indicates that even if sycomore fig was a deliberate addition to this particular brew, it was not a standard ingredient of ancient Egyptian beer in general.

It has been reported that dates and grapes were identified in Predynastic brewing residues from Hierakonpolis (Geller 1992a: 21; Maksoud *et al.* 1994: 221; but on dates in beer see below and p. 556). No identification criteria for these fruits have been published. Other archaeobotanists who examined the residues distinguished only emmer grain and chaff and possibly a small amount of barley (Geller 1989: 47, 1992b: 110). Unfortunately, no comparable residues dating to periods between the Hierakonpolis remains and New Kingdom material have yet been examined.

Dates

Date fruits are widely thought to have been a main ingredient in ancient Egyptian beer (Faltings 1991: 110, 114; Helck 1971: 23, 32–3, 1975: 790). This is based on three strands of reasoning: the interpretation of the word *bnr* as dates; the appearance of *bnr* in two brewing scenes, those in a scene from the Sixth-Dynasty Saqqara tomb of Iynefert (now at Karlsruhe; see Faltings 1991: 110; Helck 1971: 29; Wiedemann and Pörtner 1906: 26–30, pls. 4–6) and in the Twelfth-Dynasty tomb of Intefiqer (TT60; see Davies and Gardiner 1920: 14–16, pls. 8–9A, 11–12A; Faltings 1991: 110; Helck 1971: 33; Wreszinski 1923: pls. 217, 220, 221); and documents listing *bnr* amongst commodities associated with or used for making beer, such as the Moscow Mathematical Papyrus, Papyrus Bulaq 18 and Papyrus Louvre 3326, amongst others (Helck 1971: 32–3; Nims 1958; Spalinger 1988: 258; Struve 1930; Wild 1966: 98). The function of dates is thought to have been both for flavour, and more importantly, to add sufficient sugar to the mash for fermentation to take place (Darby *et al.* 1977: 547; Faltings 1991: 110; Geller 1992b: 131; Lucas and Harris 1962: 15; Montet 1925: 250).

The tomb inscriptions may not refer to date fruits at all. There is some controversy about their meaning. Wild (1966: 97, n. 2), for example, suggests that in the tomb of Iynefert at Saqqara the word may not be related to activities but may be part of servants' names.

The archaeobotanical record does not support the widespread use of dates as a standard ingredient in ancient Egyptian beer, particularly in the earlier periods. If dates were always added to this staple food, there should be vast quantities of the highly durable, easily identifiable, large date stones produced as a by-product of brewing. Despite large gaps in the archaeobotanical record, on current evidence this is not the case. Far from the 'countless' finds of dates claimed by Darby *et al.* (1977: 724), the fruit and stones of the date prior to and throughout the Pharaonic period have been found in remarkably low numbers compared to other food resources, as demonstrated by Murray's tabulation in Chapter 24, this volume (see also de Vartavan and Asensi Amorós 1997: 193–9).

The low frequency of date stones in the Pharaonic period is particularly obvious at the site of Amarna. Here, systematic archaeobotanical recovery has been applied both to the New Kingdom Workmen's Village and to more recent excavations of a Late Antique monastery. Preservation is mainly by desiccation in both areas and therefore the archaeobotanical assemblages are directly comparable.

As a case study for food preparation in the New Kingdom, the Workmen's Village at Amarna was certainly an anomalous community, planned and supported by the state (Kemp 1987b: 43). Nevertheless, beer residues which have been recovered there, together with the tools for processing cereals and the enormous quantities of cereal chaff found in the village middens, indicate that the villagers prepared their own cereal foods, including beer. Plant remains have been recovered from across the site, in village houses, rubbish dumps, chapels and animal pens. Date stones were reasonably frequently found across the site, but were much less common than remains of dom palm fruits (Renfrew 1985: 184; and author's unpublished data). The evidence suggests that dates were certainly eaten but not in great abundance.

At the time of writing, analysis of the plant remains from the Amarna monastery is on-going. Preliminary results by Wendy Smith (pers. comm.) show that food plants make up an important part of the recovered remains. In sharp contrast to the Workmen's Village assemblage, at the Late Antique monastery date stones are ubiquitous, occur in large quantities, and have been recovered in caches of hundreds of stones.

Examination of ancient and modern date fruit tissue using the SEM has shown that they do not match any of the tissues in the New Kingdom beer residues from either the Workmen's Village at Amarna or Deir el-Medina. No pieces of date have been recovered from the large brewing masses rich in coarse chaff and grain fragments available from Deir el-Medina and elsewhere. If dates were a standard beer ingredient in New Kingdom times, fragments of fruit or stone would certainly be expected in at least some of these residues. The suggested need for dates in beer processing is discussed further on p. 556.

Beer processing

At the beginning of this chapter, a general definition for beer was suggested: a fermented beverage made from starchy ingredients. It is clear from residues of beer that the ancient Egyptians brewed from both barley and emmer wheat. As discussed in the section on fermentation (pp. 555–6), to ferment cereal foods the complex starch in the grain must be broken down into simple sugars which are digestible by yeast and lactic acid bacteria, and in addition, these sugars must be made accessible. The grain must therefore be broken up in some way and mixed with water. These two basic transformations, modification of starch into sugars and break up of grain, are discussed in the following sections. In order to describe how cereals can be manipulated to achieve these changes, the modern commercial Western brewing process is first presented as an example of known processes producing known results. Next, the archaeological evidence is discussed and used to suggest how New Kingdom Egyptians made beer.

Modern malting

Modern commercial brewers use the natural process of grain germination to convert starch into fermentable sugars. Most beer today is made of barley, but the process can be applied to any cereal. When a grain is exposed to adequate moisture, a cascade of biochemical reactions is initiated (Eskin 1990: 185–93; Palmer 1989: 93). Amongst these, enzymes stored mainly in the aleurone layer (Fig. 22.6) are released, and other enzymes are manufactured. Some of these break down the cell walls within the grain, while others degrade the protein matrix into amino acids (the building blocks of protein) and short amino acid chains. Another set of enzymes, called amylases, can then get access to the starch granules and cut up the long starch molecules. As the process continues, most of the starch is reduced to shorter molecules called dextrins, which in turn are mostly broken down into maltose and the simple sugar glucose, important for fermentation. In the normal sprouting grain, the amino acids and sugars are transported to the grain embryo. These nutrients are used by the young sprout until it is large enough to produce its own food by photosynthesis.

Brewers wish to maximise the quantity of sugars available to yeast by preventing the developing embryo from using up any nutrients. In practice, a small quantity is lost (Lewis and Young 1995: 36). Enzyme production is maximised by sprouting the grain with carefully controlled levels of moisture, temperature and other conditions (Briggs 1978: 526; Lewis and Young 1995: 51–8). Cell walls and much of the protein matrix are broken down while the concentration of amylases within each grain is raised as much as possible (MacLeod 1979: 222). The extent of amylase attack does not proceed very far. Then, the newly emerging sprout is killed by drying, usually by the application of gentle heat (Lewis and Young 1995: 83). The result is malt: slightly germinated grain in which much of the cell walls separating components has been removed, and which is rich in enzymes, partially broken down proteins and largely intact starch granules.

If the microstructure of malt is compared to raw grain (Fig. 22.8), considerable changes are evident (Dronzek *et al.* 1972; Palmer 1972; Pomeranz 1972). The cell walls which are clearly seen in raw grain are mostly gone in malt, as is much of the protein matrix. Most importantly for the identification of processing, the appearance of some starch granules has altered. The early action of enzymes on the granules causes a typical pattern of surface pitting. Where enzyme attack has been able to proceed further, the pits penetrate deeply into the granule and begin to extend to make interior channels. Most starch granules, though, are untouched by enzymatic action. The malt is friable because of the loss of binding materials – the cell walls and protein – which held the original grain firmly together.

Modern cooking

To produce large quantities of fermentable sugars from malt, modern brewers use a cooking process (Hough 1991: 58). Coarse grinding breaks up the malt into grist, which is composed of medium-textured fragments and large shreds of sheared chaff. This increases the surface area of each malt fragment, allowing better penetration of water and therefore more even and complete conversion of starch into sugar. The grist is then mixed with hot water and is held at 60–65 °C for about two hours. During this period, complex structural and biochemical changes occur. In the presence of water and at temperatures above 50 °C or so, starch granules begin to imbibe water, swell up, bend and twist. Eventually, in large amounts of water they rupture, dispersing the long starch chains into solution. At the same time in these elevated temperatures, the activity of amylases increases dramatically. The enzymes rapidly attack the dispersed starch molecules and freely floating starch granules, and almost completely break down the starch.

The excess quantities of water and the rapid changes which occur make it difficult to obtain samples of starch for microscopic analysis. Controlled experiments, however, show how starch granules progressively swell, dimple, bend and twist when heated in the presence of moisture, before merging together and, if water is present in excess, dispersing into solution (French 1973: 1055; Greenwood 1979: 132; Hoseney *et al.* 1977). The progressive action of enzymes on whole starch granules has also been separately documented (Palmer 1989). The outer surface of the granule may appear unchanged, with only a few pits visible. Inside, however, enzymes hollow out the

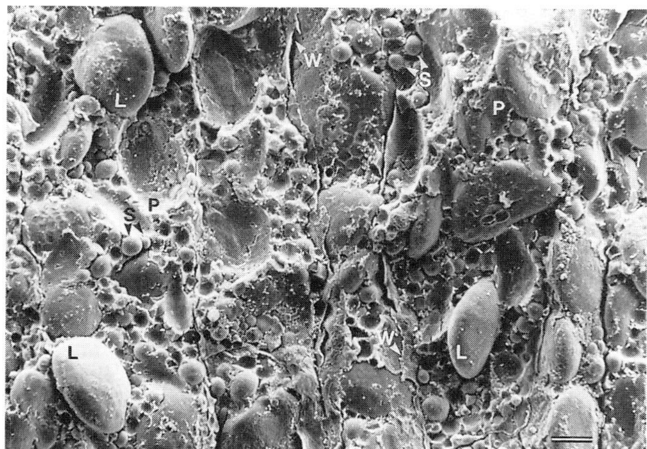

Figure 22.8a *Scanning electron micrograph of the starchy endosperm of a modern emmer grain. Large disk-shaped starch granules (L) and small spherical starch granules (S) are embedded in a protein matrix (P). These are contained within long cells; some cell walls (W) are visible here. Scale bar is 10 microns.*

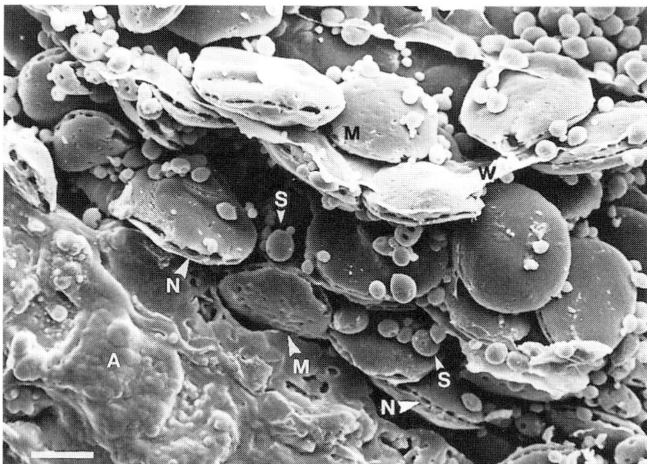

Figure 22.8b *Scanning electron micrograph of the starchy endosperm of a modern emmer grain which has been sprouted for 48 hours. In the lower left corner, part of the aleurone (A) layer can be seen. The marked changes which have occured in the starchy endosperm – compare to raw grain, Fig. 22.8a – are typical for sprouted grain, and are caused by the action of different enzymes upon the grain components. Fragments of cell wall (W) remain, but most has gone. Much of the protein has been broken down. Many of the large starch granules are pitted over most of their surfaces (M), or along their narrow edges (N). Some pitting is visible on the small starch granules (S), but this is less extensive than that of the large granules. The lack of uniform starch pitting is also typical, because some granules are more resistant to enzyme attack than others.*

granule in concentric layers until only a shell may remain. These interior concentric layers are highly distinctive.

Once most of the starch is converted into simple sugars by enzyme action, the temperature of the water is elevated still further to increase enzyme activity to the maximum, but in doing this, the enzymes are destroyed. Next, the cooked grist is usually transferred to another vessel, well stirred and the liquid drained off, naturally filtered by the shredded chaff. The liquid is called wort and is rich in maltose and glucose, amino acids and a complex mixture of flavour compounds from the cooked malt (Hough 1991: 92). Hops are added to the wort, the liquid is boiled and sterilised, and after cooling, yeast is mixed in and fermentation begins. From making grist to adding yeast, the brewing process normally takes a few hours. Fermentation proceeds over a few days, during which the yeast grows and gradually uses up the sugars, converting them to alcohol.

Ancient malting

Almost all the residues which have been examined using microscopy are very rich in starch. These residues include both large chaffy masses and thin coatings of residues from the two workmen's villages (Samuel 1996b, 1996c), as well as beer remains from wealthy Theban tombs (Grüss 1929a, 1929b, 1929c). The starch granules range from being slightly pitted to heavily pitted to completely hollow (Fig. 22.7). The pitting and channelling matches precisely the pattern observed in modern malt and malt-based foods. These observations of starch in many ancient beer remains leads to the conclusion that New Kingdom Egyptians certainly used malt for brewing.

The evidence for use of malt is borne out by a few archaeobotanical finds from rubbish deposits at the Amarna Workmen's Village (Fig. 22.9). One barley grain with delicate rootlets has been recovered. Two emmer grains were somewhat shrivelled, with deep furrows running along their backs. Such furrows are caused by the young shoot, which pushes between the tightly enclosing chaff and the soft, moist grain. Accidental germination of grain while the cereal crop is still growing in the field can occur in moist climates (Barnes 1989: 384, 389; Derera 1989; Meredith 1983). This can be ruled out for Egypt though, where the climate is too dry to allow grain to sprout in the ear. Ancient Egyptians would not have chosen to build their granaries on flood-prone land, so germination in store is highly unlikely. The sprouted grains at Amarna must have been exposed to plenty of moisture. The length of the rootlets and shoot furrows shows that this exposure must have been for a considerable period (i.e. at least three to four days). The only process which fits this evidence is deliberate malting.

It is not surprising that sprouted grains have not been found before in the archaeological record. Rootlets are delicate, very easily broken off and destroyed. The lack of sprouted grain in tombs only indicates that raw grain rather

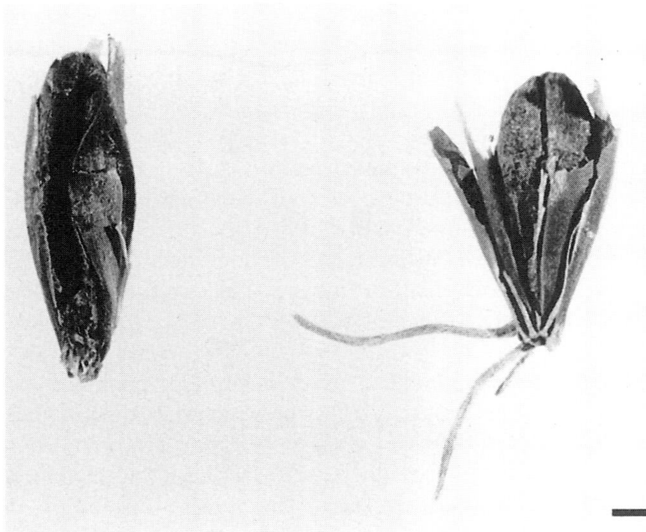

Figure 22.9 Two sprouted grains recovered from rubbish deposits at the Workmen's Village, Amarna. The barley grain on the right has three delicate rootlets still surviving. They are within the length range at which modern maltsters halt the sprouting of grain for optimal malt production. The emmer grain on the left has lost its rootlets. The deep channel down the centre of the back was formed by the shoot of the developing plant, and shows that the grain was encased in its tough chaff envelope during germination. Scale bar is 1 mm.

than malt was considered appropriate as food supplies for the after-life. Although storable, malt is a stage in food processing and therefore likely to have been a transitory product. Only large-scale archaeobotanical retrieval, as discussed by Murray (Chapter 21, this volume) will recover the low proportion of sprouted grain likely to be preserved. Since such comprehensive sampling is still rare on Egyptian archaeological sites, very little evidence of malted grain has been found.

The suggestion that malt was used for ancient Egyptian beer has been proposed before, based on lexicographical evidence. Nims (1950: 262) first suggested that the word *bšȝ* meant malt, based on its identity as some type of cereal and its close association with brewing. He later elaborated on and strengthened this proposal (Nims 1958: 61, 63). There has been some objection to this hypothesis because *bšȝ* is shown in the tomb of Ty as a cereal which seems to be destined for bread-making and is processed in various ways. The activity on the relief which most closely resembles malting (see p. 553) involves *swt*, another cereal, or cereal product, of uncertain meaning (Darby *et al.* 1977: 535; Wild 1966: 102). Faltings (1991: 114) proposes that *bšȝ* referred to malted wheat, and later reviews the evidence for *bšȝ* as malt (Faltings 1995). Helck (1971: 25, 37) accepts the meaning as malt, but points out that the word disappears in connection with New Kingdom brewing. Whether *bšȝ* is indeed malt cannot be confirmed from the available archaeological evidence. It is clear, however, that malt was a very important component of beer and it seems certain the Egyptians would have named it.

Since malt is produced from living grain, it must have been made from viable, intact and uncooked cereal. Malting would therefore have been an early step in the brewing process. The biology of barley and emmer shows that malting must have been done in the husk. The tightly adhering chaff of barley and the tough chaff of emmer make the husks difficult to remove (see Chapter 21, this volume). Large-scale dehusking treatment would damage the grain, particularly the vulnerable embryo. Without the embryo, the biochemical changes in the grain triggered by exposure to moisture will not take place. The deep furrows in the ancient sprouted emmer grains were caused by compression of the sprouts as they grew. Without the closely enfolding, rigid chaff, the elongating sprout would have curled away from the back of the grain. The observed morphology of the sprouted Amarna grains confirms that the chaff must still have been in place during germination.

It is difficult to estimate how long the ancient Egyptian malting process took, because the precise regimes of temperature, moisture, stirring, grain depth and other relevant factors (Palmer 1989: 129) are unknown. Also, little is known about emmer malting. Malt is best produced in shallow layers with good air flow. This encourages grain respiration and stops mould (Hough 1991: 21). Thin layers which are regularly turned prevent rootlets tangling and stimulate even germination. At least three days were probably needed to initiate germination in barley and perhaps a day or two longer for emmer, since the thick chaff would act as a barrier between water and the grain inside. If the length of rootlets and shoots observable on the germinated grains from Amarna are a good guide to general practice, then barley may have been sprouted from five to seven days and emmer from six to eight days.

The available evidence shows that, whatever the precise treatment, malting was a considerable investment in time and required adequate space to produce enough for the large quantities of beer brewed in ancient Egypt. Malt may have been made by being laid out on mats, in wide shallow bins or in shallow ceramic or wooden vats. Wild (1966: 101) suggests that malting took place in big jars placed on their sides; Ian Forrest of Scottish and Newcastle Breweries (pers. comm.) has described how this could be an efficient malting method. The side-turned jar would create a larger surface area on which to spread a layer of grain. The jar could then be regularly rolled to aerate the grain and prevent the roots tangling. If the grain was to be soaked in water, the jar could be turned upright again. Ian Forrest pointed out that such a system would allow evaporation through the porous ceramic fabric, and that this would help to maintain an even temperature, at a somewhat lower than ambient level.

A further advantage would be that, although damp and

sticky at this stage, the malt would have been easily handled and kept reasonably clean. Such a method would have been suitable for both large-scale and small household production, simply by varying the size and quantity of ceramic vessels in use. If this was indeed the ancient Egyptian system of malt production, it would be difficult to distinguish in the archaeological record, unless distinctive wear patterns were formed on the sides of large ceramic vessels.

As Wild (1966: 101) points out, such a side-turned big jar, into which a man is stretching his hand, may be seen in the baking and brewing scene depicted in the tomb of Ty at Saqqara (Épron and Daumas 1939: pl. 70, top right). The man with jar is accompanied by an inscription but unfortunately it has been damaged and the verb is missing (Montet 1925: 247). Two Middle Kingdom tomb models from Beni Hasan show large vessels which could well be malting jars. A model from the tomb of Nefery (BH116) shows a line of six jars lying on their sides in front of three brewers (Garstang 1907: 73, 76, figs. 61, 62; Wild 1966: 109). Even more convincing are two jars set at a slant with mesh clearly depicted covering their mouths (Garstang 1907: 94), in a model from the tomb of Khnumnakht (BH585). Wild (1966: 101, pl. 11) suggests that two baskets shown in a scene in the Eighteenth-Dynasty Theban tomb of Kenamun (TT93; Davies 1930: 51, pls. 7, 58; Wreszinski 1936: pl. 301) may also contain malt, although there is no accompanying inscription. Drawing a parallel with the side-turned jar in the tomb of Ty, he suggests a tilted jar below these baskets, into which a man is reaching, may also have served to produce malt. If these suggestions are correct, it indicates that the malting method remained essentially unchanged throughout much of Pharaonic history.

Until now, no malting installations have been recognised in the archaeological record. In smaller households, malting may have had no special equipment nor dedicated area. With the knowledge that malt was a major component of beer, it may now be possible to identify specific malting areas, if they existed, in larger households and in state breweries.

Although the precise details of malt production remain to be clarified, some comments can be made about the malt itself. The quality of malt from barley and emmer wheat would have been about the same. Modern comparative analyses show that free-threshing wheat malt matches barley malt in quality, including diastatic power, a crude measure of enzyme levels and activity (Briggs *et al.* 1981: 136, table 5.9). Singh *et al.* (1983) successfully malted emmer with good diastatic power and enzyme levels. An experiment with emmer wheat created a malt which matched well with barley in most respects (Samuel and Bolt 1995: 30). Its diastatic power was relatively low, but this was partly due to a much larger proportion of husk material. The good quality of the enzyme activity was demonstrated by the strong beer (6 per cent alcohol by volume) which was successfully brewed using a 1 : 1 mixture of this emmer malt and unmalted emmer. The beer was Tutankhamum Ale, made by Scottish Courage Brewers in 1996 to replicate ancient Egyptian brewing based on recent archaeological research.

Milling

Sprouting grain produces a packet of active enzymes and starch granules. The enzymes require water for their activity. The best way to allow enzymes good access to starch is to grind the malt into grist and then to mix the grist with water. By breaking up the grain, enzymes and starch can be released into solution, where the starch will be transformed into sugars, at a rate dependent on temperature.

There is good evidence that the ancient Egyptians milled their malt. The large fragments of grain and coarse shreds of husk in the loose chaffy residues were produced by a shearing rather than a crushing action. The friability of the malted grain would not have withstood pounding in a mortar without being reduced to fine particles before the chaff was appreciably affected. Therefore, the malt must have been broken up by grinding on a saddle quern. This stage must have been rapid, with each batch subjected to only a few strokes, for the chaffy residues have a very coarse texture.

Batch mixing

The evidence from the residues shows that ancient Egyptian brewing was different from that of modern commercial Western brewing. Many residues contain starch which has been so extensively modified that it is completely merged together, often losing any trace of individual granule boundaries. To cause this complete fusion, the coarsely milled grain or malt must have been well-heated in ample amounts of water. The evidence suggests this stage may have involved heating a thick porridge or gruel-like mass of broken grain and shredded chaff. Such a mixture would contain both fused and completely ruptured granules but few undistorted or partially distorted granules. The amounts of relatively unaffected granules produced with this procedure would depend on the length of heating and extent of mixing.

In the same ancient residues which contain fused, glassy-looking starch, there are starch granules which, whether pitted or unaffected by enzymes, are completely undistorted by heat. They sometimes even retain the little indentations on their surface caused by tight packing within the starchy endosperm. These granules are often adjacent to, or even embedded in, the fused starch (Fig. 22.10). In beer residues, partially distorted starch granules are quite rare.

There are two possible processing treatments which can explain the extreme classes of microstructure, unaffected and completely fused starch, in the residues. The ancient Egyptian brewing process may have involved both processes. The first feasible reason is that cereal may have been treated inefficiently so that during cooking, some starch

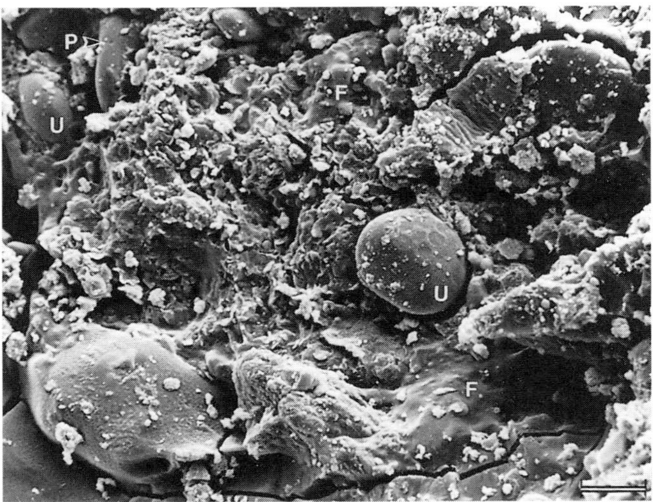

Figure 22.10 Scanning electron micrograph of desiccated beer residue from the Workmen's Village, Amarna (sample TAVR93–100). Whole, undistorted and unpitted starch granules (U) are embedded in completely fused starch (F). In the upper left corner, slight pitting (P) of one whole starch granule is visible. Such evidence supports an interpretation of a two-part process for ancient Egyptian brewing (see Fig. 22.2). Scale bar is 10 microns.

was completely fused while other granules were insulated from heat or water and were therefore unaffected. This is supported by some SEM views of residue microstructure, where there is a sharp transition between fused glassy starch and granules which completely retain their individual boundaries (Samuel 1996b: 9, fig. 7). The coarse texture of the large chaffy masses indicate that some granules were probably protected from water penetration and heat in the core of the grain fragments.

The very large quantities of fused starch, in which individual, undistorted starch granules are embedded, fits an alternative interpretation, however. The evidence fits well with the preparation of mixtures of two separately treated batches of grain (see Fig. 22.2). Some grain, perhaps all grain, destined for beer was malted. It appears that not all this malt was cooked; some was coarsely ground and set aside. It was then mixed with a batch of grain which had been well-cooked.

Although the ancient Egyptians would not have been aware of the biochemical basis for the success of such a method, this procedure is a very good way of converting starch to sugars without precise controls on volumes of ingredients and temperature. The batch of heated grain would contain very little amylase, because cooking would have destroyed the enzymes. If the cooked cereal was unsprouted, there would have been little amylase in any case. The starch, however, would be partially or completely dispersed out of the granules. Because the molecules of starch were no longer tightly packed together, they would be much more susceptible to enzyme attack (Hough 1991: 58).

The malt which was not heated, but only coarsely ground, would have all its amylases and other enzymes intact, with some of the starch granules just beginning to be affected by enzyme attack. Once mixed together in water, the amylases from the uncooked malt would rapidly and effectively attack and chemically cut up into sugars the dispersed starch from the heated grain. Attack would also proceed on the starch from the uncooked malt, but this would be much slower. Just as in the cooked malt, some starch would not be pitted at all, because it would be protected from enzyme breakdown within the larger fragments of grain produced during coarse milling. The result would be plenty of sugars available for yeast fermentation, but also starch which had not been affected by enzymes at all, or which had not been completely broken down.

The exact blending procedure used by the ancient Egyptians is difficult to define precisely. The cooked grain or malt and uncooked malt could not have been extensively heated during mixing or thereafter, otherwise there would be very few, if any, undistorted starch granules in the residues. If the fully cooked grain was added immediately after heating to the uncooked malt along with some water, the temperature of the whole mixture would probably have been warm enough to increase the rate of enzyme attack somewhat, without causing distortion of uncooked starch granules.

After mixing, the chaff was sieved out. The remains of brewed beer (i.e. thin, yeast-rich coatings) have only a few fine shreds of embedded chaff and bran. In contrast, since virtually none of the large chaffy masses with cracked grain fragments examined to date contains yeast, these could not be residues of the finished beer. These very chaffy, cereal-rich remains are well-explained as the material left in the sieve after the raw malt and cooked cereal had been mixed together.

Artistic depictions indicate the procedure. The cooked grain plus uncooked malt mixture was rinsed with water through a sieve into a large pottery vessel. This would wash through most of the soluble material and much of the free starch granules, while retaining most of the coarse chaff and large grain fragments. The squeezing stance of many depicted brewers suggests the effort made to remove as much water and soluble material as possible. The result was not bread loaves in the sieve as often suggested, but more-or-less fist-sized damp chaffy lumps.

For examples of models showing these little sausage-shaped chaffy masses around the edge of sieves see: the baking and brewing model from the Eleventh-Dynasty tomb of Meketra at Deir el-Bahari (Winlock 1955: 28–9, pl. 65 no. 5) now in the Metropolitan Museum of Art, New York (20.3.12); a model from the Sixth-Dynasty tomb of Niankhpepykem at Meir (Borchardt 1897: 129, upper figure no. 244, 132; 1911: 159, pl. 52.244) now in the Cairo Museum (CG244); and a model from the Twelfth-Dynasty tomb of Khety at Beni Hasan (BH366; see Bourriau 1988:

105–6; Garstang 1907: 126–8, fig. 124; Samuel 1994b: 9), now in the Fitzwilliam Museum, Cambridge (E.71d.1903).

That this squeezing method left behind fairly substantial quantities of palatable grain, starch and sugars is suggested by a scene from the Twelfth-Dynasty tomb of Intefiqer (TT60), in which a young child extends a bowl to the brewer working a mass over the sieve, and asks 'Give me some *srmt*; I am hungry' (Davies and Gardiner 1920: 15). The scene suggests that the word *srmt* might specify the chaffy mass produced at this stage. The large quantities of cooked grain left in many surviving chaffy residues bear out the idea that the first rinsing could leave behind a considerable quantity of edible cooked cereal. The cooked grain and malt may have given it a sweet caramel-like taste. At this stage, it would have contained no alcohol.

The cereal portion was likely to have been quite nutritious, but the large amounts of chaff would have made the whole mass indigestible (see p. 545). It may have been eaten, therefore, by chewing and sucking out the edible parts and spitting out the chewed fibrous debris. This is exactly analogous to the way that raw sugar cane is eaten as a snack in modern Egypt. Other fibrous foods are eaten like this in other parts of the world.

The liquid squeezed from the mixture of coarsely ground malt and cooked grain was the equivalent of modern wort. It would have been cloudy because it was full of suspended starch granules and small fragments of cereal tissue, as well as partially broken down starch and protein molecules. Amylases and other enzymes would still have been active, continuing to break down the starch, protein and other components into simple molecules.

One determinant of the strength of the beer would have been the quantity of water added at this stage. The more concentrated the sugar solution, the greater the final alcohol content would have been. If a strong beer was desired, limited water would have been used for rinsing, leaving relatively large quantities of whole and partially degraded starch behind. A weaker beer would have been made if more water was added. Perhaps warmed water was used to help rinse out as much starch and sugars as possible.

So rich in starch are some of the large chaffy residues that they would have been suitable for further rinsing to make a weaker beer. Such recycling was used in medieval and early modern English brewing, for example, to produce 'small beer', a thinner, less alcoholic beer (Sambrook 1996: 119–20). Recycling would explain some chaffy residues which have scarcely any starchy contents left; they may have been washed twice or even three times to make weaker beers. Documentary sources record beers of differing strength, although this relates to the quantity of starting cereal in relation to the volume of beer produced (e.g. Helck 1971: 43–52; 1975: 790–91; Kemp 1989: 124; Peet 1923: 112–21, 1931: 155–6).

In any case, the re-use of the first squeezings, either for further brews or for some other extraction of the residual pleasant-tasting cooked and malted starch, would explain some known aspects of *srmt*. Some jar labels from Amarna excavated by Petrie and examined by Griffith (1894: 34, pl. 24 nos. 69, 70, pl. 25 no. 97) show that *srmt* was stored. Indeed it could be used by the highest in the land; one inscription says 'good *srmt* of the queen'. Gardiner (1947: 234, no. 563) points out that in written sources, *srmt* is often associated with the adjective 'sweet', and that its determinative suggests the substance is grain-like or at least semi-solid when dry. All these observations fit very well with the preserved chaffy masses. Together, the evidence explains very satisfactorily why such material was placed in tombs; it was apparently a valued foodstuff.

Was bread a beer ingredient?

Unlike most descriptions of ancient Egyptian brewing, which state that beer was made from lightly baked bread (Fig. 22.1a), the foregoing discussion does not include well-leavened bread as a beer precursor (Fig. 22.2). The evidence refuting the use of bread in brewing is the morphology of starch in the beer residues. If the large quantities of fused starch in the residues came from bread, the dough must have been very moist to allow such extensive merging. Also, baking temperatures would need to be relatively high and reasonably prolonged. In such conditions, very few if any undistorted granules would have survived, and such a regime would have killed any yeast cells or lactic acid bacteria. In the presence of adequate moisture, starch begins to fuse at 60–65 °C (Banks and Greenwood 1975: 260; French 1973: 1055), but yeast begins to die at temperatures as low as 40 °C (Brown 1982: 71) and by about 67 °C, all the key sugar-converting enzymes in yeast are damaged or destroyed (Stear 1990: 541; van Dam 1986: 127). Thus, active yeast could not be present in any loaves cooked to produce the well-fused starch seen in the desiccated beer residues.

On the other hand, if bread had been baked lightly enough to preserve the viability of yeast and to leave a proportion of starch granules morphologically unchanged, very little fused starch could have been produced. It is not possible to produce bread with large quantities of fused starch, some completely undistorted starch granules and hardly any partially twisted granules. Yet this combination is what is seen in the residues. As on p. 564, in the section on ancient Egyptian dough mixing, desiccated loaves contain many partially twisted granules. Bread of the sort placed in tombs was therefore not used for brewing either.

Fermentation

The stage at which the fermentation step occurred can be deduced by the presence or absence of yeast in different residues. Virtually all the large chaffy masses contain unfused starch granules with no signs of amylase attack, undistorted granules with pitted surfaces and some interior channelling, as well as fused starch, but they do not seem to contain any yeast cells. This is consistent with the interpretation of this material as a mixture of cooked grain or malt with uncooked malt prior to fermentation. The high proportion of chaff shreds to grain fragments indicates that these residues are spent grain left from rinsing out the starch and sugars, while the lack of yeast indicates that fermentation took place later, in the resulting chaff-free but sugar- and amino acid-rich liquid.

There are a variety of possibilities for how fermentation was initiated, but no evidence has yet been found to suggest which is most likely. If the same vessels were always used for brewing and never washed, there would be plenty of the desirable yeasts and lactic acid bacteria left in the pores of the vessel walls to inoculate each new batch of 'wort'. This is common for traditional fermentation in many cultures (Djien 1982: 31; Platt 1964: 71; Wood 1994: 271). The need for constant supplies of beer would have meant frequent brewing, maintaining the right environment to encourage the micro-organisms. Another common inoculation method in traditional fermentation systems is to keep back a portion of the last brew and add it to the fresh liquid (Brown 1982: 58; Odunfa 1985: 171; Wood and Hodge 1985: 287). Again, this would provide a thriving population of desirable micro-organisms to begin growth and reproduction before any harmful microbes were able to get established. Leaving the vat of sugar-rich liquid open to the air would have allowed air-borne yeasts and bacteria to drop in, and could often have resulted in an acceptable brew. This technique is still used today to brew Belgian lambic beers (De Keersmaecker 1996). The method, however, is risky, since undesirable fungi, moulds and bacteria could also inoculate the liquid, producing an undrinkable result. Finally, a starter inoculum might have been prepared with ingredients which were rich in yeasts or likely to support active yeast growth, such as fruit whose skins often support a natural bloom of yeast cells. It is possible that inocula were freshly made for each batch of beer but these take time to prepare and are not always completely reliable sources of good fermentation micro-organisms. Given the quantities of beer required, it is likely that if used, such inocula were made from time to time as needed. All four methods may well have been applied under different circumstances and by different brewers.

The ecology of yeast-lactic acid bacteria systems is a subject of modern research and still fairly poorly understood (Wood and Hodge 1985: 287). Some systems evolve over time, with different species flourishing and then dying off as the metabolites of microbe activity change the acidity and available nutrients of the food (De Keersmaecker 1996: 60). Other systems are remarkably stable, the activities of the specific yeast and bacteria complementing each other to maintain good conditions for both, without allowing other, undesirable, species to thrive (Sugihara 1985: 251–3; Wood and Hodge 1985: 287). The nature of ancient Egyptian fermentation would, to some extent, depend on the ecology of the micro-organisms exploited, but there are no data available to draw any conclusions about this.

The type of fermentation and the species of micro-organisms involved would certainly have had an effect on the flavour of the beer. Lactic acid bacteria would have created a sharpness by fermenting sugars to lactic and other acids. This would be particularly desirable if other flavourings were not standard ingredients. Yeasts would have produced ethanol. Both micro-organisms generate other metabolites depending on the specific species and conditions (Brown 1993: 40; Prìhoda *et al.* 1993: 31). Somewhat different fermentation systems may well have been maintained by individual brewers, and in different geographical areas. The characteristics which might have distinguished these systems cannot now be fully investigated. As biomolecular analysis of archaeological materials progresses, the chemical constituents of beer residues may help to reconstruct more precisely the details of fermentation.

Were dates necessary?

The putative role for dates in ancient Egyptian brewing can now be reassessed. There is strong evidence that malt was an integral and major ingredient of New Kingdom beer. The evidence for the production of amylases during cereal germination, and the subsequent action of these enzymes on the cooked and uncooked starch, shows that more than adequate quantities of sugar were produced for conversion by yeast cells into alcohol. Furthermore, the amino acids and other components of malt would provide further nutrients for the growth of yeast. The addition of dates, or any other fruit or sweetener, was not necessary for successful fermentation.

It is possible that dates were an occasional flavouring for special beers, but as discussed above (see p. 549), there is no evidence for the use of date fruits in any New Kingdom beer residues examined so far. The sweet taste of dates, combined with the sweetish malty taste of the malted and cooked cereal, may not actually have been desirable in a beverage which was a staple and an important source of clean drinking liquid. A lightly acidic taste, possibly provided by lactic acid fermentation, was more likely to be refreshing and would have made the beer drinkable in large quantities. If inscriptions associated with brewing scenes in the Sixth-Dynasty tomb of Iynefert at Saqqara and of Intefiqer (TT60) of the Twelfth Dynasty at Thebes do indeed refer to date fruits (see p. 549), they may be references to the production of special, not everyday, beer, particularly as these depictions are from funerary contexts.

What of the interpretation of the word *bnr*? This is not the forum for a lexical investigation, and only a few comments can be made here. The word *bnr* has long been taken to mean date fruits; Wallert (1962: 40–1) reviews the evidence for this. She relies heavily on textual evidence which indicates the commodity was edible, sweet and closely associated with the palm tree. Date fruits do indeed possess

Figure 22.11 A mortar emplacement in house West Street 2/3 at the Workmen's Village, Amarna. In this emplacement, a limestone mortar is placed in a corner with the base slightly below floor level. The rim has been built up with mud brick and mud plaster. A soil sample taken from the floor adjacent to the emplacement was rich in emmer chaff (Samuel 1989: 280–86), showing this mortar had been used to process emmer spikelets. Another type of emplacement lacks the mud brick rim and the mortar is sunk so that the rim is level with the floor (e.g. Kemp 1987a: 30–32, figs. 3.1, 3.5). A similar limestone mortar to that shown here was used for emmer processing experiments (Samuel 1993, 1994a).

emmer in the spikelet was extensively processed by pounding at this village.

Numerous saddle querns have been recognised and recorded at Deir el-Medina by Bruyère (1939; e.g. 250 for house NE.V and 328 for house SW.V) and fewer at the Amarna village by Peet and Woolley (1923: 78–9, 88–9). The way in which they were used was recognised by Kemp (1986: 3, 1987a: 6) who has described the mud-brick box emplacements into which they were placed. The sloping upper surface of these emplacements allowed the rear part of the quern stone to be slightly raised (Fig. 22.12).

Prior to this, such instalments had been interpreted as kneading or mixing troughs (Bruyère 1939: 75–7; Sist 1987: 56) or some type of hearth or oven (Peet and Woolley 1923: e.g. 77). The interpretation of ovens arose because of frequent burn-marks on the walls against which these structures were placed. Miller (1987) has suggested that these were caused by deliberate controlled fires made to clean flour and grain-rich areas affected by insect infestations. He notes the wide use of ash as a traditional insecticide. No emplacement complete with saddle quern in place appears to have been found or published, but Peet (1921: 176, pl. 27 no. 2) shows a photograph of one such installation in house Gate Street 11, reasonably intact, with a clear impression for the stone quern to be set. The clarity of the impression for the quern suggests that the stone could be removed, which would have been an advantage for cleaning. Sketches of similar finds at the Amarna Workmen's Village (e.g. Peet and Woolley 1923: 77, fig. 11) indicate that removable querns may have been a feature of such quern emplacements in the Village and elsewhere.

Experimental reconstruction

To test the ancient Egyptian sequence of cereal processing, from removal from store of cereal still in the hull through to milled flour, a series of experiments was undertaken at Amarna (Samuel 1994a: 143–66). The experimental reconstruction was based on archaeological and archaeobotanical evidence, together with ethnographic information. Since the structure of each cereal differs, each will behave somewhat differently when processed in the same manner. It was therefore essential to work with authentic cereal species. To find out how the ancient tools functioned, modern emmer spikelets were used for processing experiments.

Tools Actual ancient tools were still robust enough to be used for these experiments. The tools were a limestone mortar, a quartzite saddle quern and a quartzite hand stone. Replica mortar and quern emplacements (Fig. 22.12) were constructed from mud brick and mud plaster, closely modelled on ancient examples found at the Amarna Workmen's Village (Samuel 1989: 262–3). A wooden pestle was closely modelled on an ancient pestle from house Main Street 6 of the Amarna Workmen's Village, published by Peet and Woolley (1923: 78, pl. XIX no. 1). Particular care was taken to replicate the curve of the lower, working end as precisely as possible (Samuel 1993: 280, fig. 5, 1994a: 147, fig. 5.12).

The ethnographic record indicates that sieving and winnowing tools would have been used in the dehusking sequence to separate chaff from grain. There is no precise archaeological information to show exactly what type of sieves or winnowing tools might have been used by the ancient Egyptians at this stage of processing. Sieves and winnowing fans and baskets have been recovered from various excavations, for example at Deir el-Medina (Gourlay 1981: e.g. 73–4 and pl. VI showing baskets, 129 and pl. IX showing sieves), but there is nothing to link them specifically to cereal dehusking. Replicas of these tools were therefore improvised for the purposes of experimentation.

Experiments Even when well-cleaned prior to storage, cereals processed in bulk during the harvest always contain various contaminants including small stones, clods of earth, pieces of straw, weed seeds and chaff. De Vartavan (1990: 478–9) found some of these types of items, as well as various main crops, in baskets of plant offerings from Tutankhamun's tomb. The first step in smaller-scale emmer spikelet processing is the removal of these contaminants. This was probably done by careful small-scale sieving and winnowing, but the last contaminants, of the same size, shape and mass as the spikelets, would have to have been picked out by hand. Such a hand-picking step

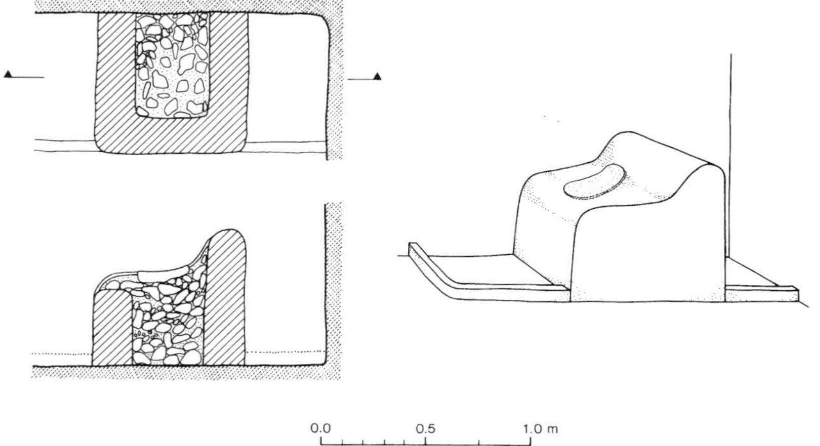

Figure 22.12 Drawing of an ancient Egyptian quern emplacement from house Gate Street 8, the Workmen's Village, Amarna. On the upper left is the emplacement plan, on the lower left, its elevation. On the right is a perspective reconstruction of the quern emplacement as it would have looked in use with the quern stone in position. The emplacement is a box of mud brick and mud plaster, with the back wall higher than the others. In this example, one side is made up by the house wall. The core is filled with rubble and sand. The top slopes, allowing the quern stone to be set at an angle. The upper surface and the basin in front is often coated with gypsum.

was carried out experimentally on a batch of modern emmer, and removed a wide range of inclusions.

To my knowledge, only one such action is portrayed in the artistic record. The baking and brewing scene from the Fifth-Dynasty tomb of Kaemrehu at Saqqara (D2), now in the Cairo Museum (CG1534; see Engelbach 1942: 157, fig. 33C; Mogensen 1930: 32, fig. 29; Saleh and Sourouzian 1987: no. 59), shows very clearly a figure, fifth from the right on the surviving block, delicately picking with thumb and forefinger from his cupped hand, with a heap on the table before him. This matches precisely the way in which small objects must be removed from the mass of spikelets or hulled barley grains. Helck (1971: 26) also draws attention to this scene of manual cleaning.

Ethnographic accounts show that dehusking hulled wheats is often done by pounding in a mortar with a pestle, and the finds of emmer spikelets and chaff around an ancient emplaced mortar indicate this was the case in ancient Egypt. Accordingly, the ancient limestone mortar was filled about one third full with whole emmer spikelets, and pounded with the replica wooden pestle. Without dampening, pounding caused most of the spikelets to fly out of the shallow mortar, while the remainder were smashed up. With the addition of a little water, however, dehusking was highly successful. The pounding action caused the spikelets to rub against each other without being crushed. The grains were released both because some chaff became thoroughly shredded, and because some dampened chaff became more flexible and allowed the grain to pop out of the whole, unshredded spikelet. Even with vigorous pounding, the great majority of the released emmer grains remained whole and, apart from a little rubbing of the bran and loss of many of the embryos, were unbroken.

Many accounts of emmer processing assert that parching is necessary to release the grain from the tough chaff (Moritz 1958: 25; Sallares 1995: 95; Spurr 1986: 11–12). These experiments clearly demonstrate that parching is not necessary to dehusk emmer spikelets with mortar and pestle (see also Nesbitt and Samuel 1996: 43–9 for a detailed discussion of hulled wheats and parching). Similar experiments with emmer dehusking in Germany support this conclusion (Meurers-Balke and Löning 1992: 349, 357). These experimenters found that parching rendered grain brittle and easily crushed. The key to dehusking with mortar and pestle is not heating, but dampening of the spikelets.

The result of pounding is a damp mass of shredded fine and heavy chaff and whole grain. This was spread out thinly in the sun to dry, which took about two hours in March. Once dry, the fine chaff was winnowed away by careful shaking with a basket, but in ancient times, winnowing with wind may have been used instead or as well. Completion of this stage left many large and small pieces of coarse chaff mixed together with whole grain.

Much of the large chaff could be separated from the grain by shaking with the winnowing basket so that grain settled at one side and empty spikelets at the other. A three-millimetre-mesh sieve retained the remaining large chaff pieces and let most of the grain and chaff fragments fall through (note that a three-millimetre-mesh sieve is roughly correct, given the size of emmer grain and chaff, see pp. 558–9). The last pieces of chaff were removed from the grain by hand picking, a step well attested in the ethnographic literature (e.g. Hillman 1984: 134). It was important to work with whole grain rather than cracked or crushed grain at this stage, otherwise the differences in density and size were not great enough to separate grain and chaff.

Overall, this cleaning phase was fairly tedious and time-consuming. The separation of chaff and grain was likely quite time consuming in ancient times as well, although it would have been more efficiently conducted by experienced people. In larger-scale operations, such as large households and temple bakeries, each step may have been carried out by one or a team of people, making the whole process more rapid. Such teams are suggested by the different people engaged in baking and brewing depicted in artistic scenes and models. On a small-scale domestic level, these jobs were probably carried out by several people, including children.

Once cleaned of chaff, the emmer grain was easily and efficiently milled on the ancient saddle quern (Fig. 22.13a). There was no need to add grit to the grain in order to obtain flour, as has sometimes been asserted (Fleming *et al.* 1980: 74; Leek 1972: 131; Smith 1986: 45; and see p. 565). The ancient Egyptians may first have cracked the whole grain in the mortar prior to milling, but such a step does not seem to be necessary.

The use of an emplacement to raise and angle the stone makes milling much less onerous than might be expected. Little force is needed to mill effectively, and no strain is placed on the back because the lower body is fully supported, leaving the upper body free to rock easily from the hips. The texture of the flour produced is entirely under the control of the miller. A few strokes of the hand stone rapidly reduces the whole grain to a medium-textured meal, while a few strokes more creates a very fine flour without the need for sieving (Fig. 22.13b). The limiting factor in the production of flour is the quantity of grain which can be placed on the saddle quern at one time: only a small handful will fit without grains rolling off the edges. Depending on the construction of the surround, however, it may well have been possible to fit a heap of grain behind the mill stone, which could then be pushed forward onto the quern as required.

Figure 22.13a The experimental quern emplacement in use. The emplacement is built with the same dimensions and of the same materials as the ancient excavated examples found at the Workmen's Village, Amarna, except the upper surface is made of mud plaster, not gypsum. The quern stone and hand stone are ancient excavated tools. The back of all excavated quern emplacements are situated about forty centimetres from a wall. This allows the miller to wedge between the house wall and the back of the emplacement, and to pivot back and forth at the hips over the quern stone. In the experimental set-up, flour was caught in a raised cloth-lined basket, but judging from artistic representations, the ancient millers allowed the flour to fall into the gypsum-lined compartment in front of the emplacement.

Figure 22.13b A close-up view of finely milled flour produced on the experimental quern emplacement. To the right is the hand stone. Some unground grains and bits of chaff not cleaned from the grain have fallen to the sides of the quern stone during milling.

Secondary processing: flour to baked loaves

Compared to the evidence for grain processing, there is much less archaeological information from domestic contexts to show how baking was carried out. There are, however, the invaluable preserved loaves themselves. Like the beer residues, they retain a record of processing techniques in the microstructure of the starch granules, as well as in their overall texture and composition. Ethnographic and archaeological data also give some indication of ancient Egyptian baking practice.

Shape and texture of ancient bread

Virtually all of the extant ancient loaves which I have examined were hand-formed. Only two (Louvre E.4084, from Eighteenth-Dynasty Deir el-Medina, and BM EA5346, possibly from New Kingdom Thebes) appear to have been made with moulds, which were small and cup-shaped. The remaining hand-formed loaves come in a great variety of shapes and sizes, from one in the form of a fish measuring nine centimetres in length, to heavy domed oval loaves sometimes over twenty centimetres in length. Both types can be found in the Turin Museum, from the Eighteenth-Dynasty tomb of Kha at Deir el-Medina (TT8; see Sist 1987: 58, fig. 61). Some of the loaves have been shaped into recognisable forms like the fish bread, or into human figures (Darby *et al.* 1977: fig. 12.17), while others are apparently abstract designs. Loaves can be decorated with slashes, pricked or indented holes, or bands of dough applied over the surfaces. For funerary occasions at least, making decorated loaves seems to have been common. They may have played a role in medicinal or magical belief, as bread in the form of a man is mentioned in at least one spell (Papyrus Chester Beatty VIII, BM EA10688, Rt. 3, 5–5, 3; see Gardiner 1935: 67–8).

Despite the enormous numbers of conical bread moulds found in New Kingdom times, especially in temple contexts (Jacquet-Gordon 1981: 19; Kemp 1979: 11; Kemp and Bomann 1984: 31; Rose 1987b: 119), there are few preserved conical loaves. I have observed three examples from Deir el-Medina now in the Dokki Museum, Cairo (inv. no. 4272) and illustrated in Darby *et al.* (1977: 520, fig. 12.12), the unprovenanced fig bread at the Boston Museum of Fine Arts (72.4757c; McDonald 1982: 113 and fig. 97, see p. 559) and an unpublished specimen of unknown provenance now in the National Museums of Scotland, Edinburgh (1971.113). All these were definitely shaped by hand. In the case of the Deir el-Medina examples, the dough was rolled out into a tapered strip, folded over and the seams pinched together. The large specimen in the National Museums of Scotland was built up out of several pieces and carefully smoothed together. A conical loaf is illustrated by Wittmack (1896: 71, fig. 3), but it is not possible to assess whether this too was made by hand or in a mould.

Shape is not an indicator of bread type. Similar forms such as triangles can be made according to different recipes. As far as can be assessed without microscopy, the diverse range of loaf forms found in the tomb of Kha (TT8) all seem to have been made from the same type of dough.

The texture of ancient bread varies a great deal. Although loaves can be remarkably full of chaff, this is rare. None of the shaped and baked loaves which I have seen, or for which a description has been published, are nearly as chaff-rich as the residues found in pottery vessels or in large, irregular loose lumps. The very coarse and chaffy 'bread loaves' examined by Ruffer (1920: 354; 1921: 288–9) are almost certainly beer residues (see p. 543, Fig. 22.5b). Most loaves have a few fragments of chaff, usually quite small, which are undoubtedly unintentional inclusions. The ancient Egyptians were capable of producing flour and bread which was very well-cleaned of chaff, for some loaves have no trace of husk material. It is very difficult to draw conclusions from the surviving funerary loaves about the quality of daily bread. Perhaps bread destined never to be eaten by the living was sometimes made with less care. The quality of bread may have varied from baker to baker, according to skill, experience and aptitude.

The texture of bread also provides an insight into milling practices. A few loaves are made of such well-ground flour that the type of cereal cannot be determined on simple observation alone. It is possible that such fine flour was produced by sieving. Experiments have shown, however, (see above and Fig. 22.13b) that very fine flour can be produced with the ancient Egyptian saddle quern and hand stone, while ethnographic evidence suggests that very fine flour may have been wet milled. Many loaves are made from flour which is slightly mealy, containing fragments of grain from approximately 0.5 to 1.5 millimetres in diameter. This suggests efficient but not extensive grinding.

Large pieces of cracked grain or whole emmer grains are common in the ancient loaves. The microscopy evidence suggests they were pre-cooked, or at least well-soaked, and then added to the dough. It has sometimes been stated that ancient Egyptian milling was crude and did not grind very effectively (e.g. Leek 1972: 129; Ruffer 1919: 45; Strouhal 1992: 125; Wilson 1988: 13). It is clear from the disjunctive size of flour fragments and the different treatment of the whole grain that this was not the case. Whole or cracked grain was deliberately added into finely- or medium-milled flour. The resulting texture is similar to the popular 'granary', 'harvest grain' or 'multi-grain' breads baked nowadays.

Microscopic evidence from ancient bread

Malt As with beer residues, the microstructure of ancient desiccated bread loaves preserves a record of past processing methods. In several ancient bread samples, heavily channelled starch granules make up part of the crumb. The typical concentric channels indicate that malt was an ingredient of these bread loaves. Because the action of heat has distorted much of the starch and because not all starch granules are affected by enzymes in sprouted grain, it is not possible to say whether these loaves were made entirely of malt or a mixture of malt and unsprouted grain.

Since embryos are damaged by dehusking (see p. 552), the malt for bread-making must have been prepared in the spikelet. Effective removal of the husk was important for bread-making and therefore the sprouted spikelets must have been thoroughly dried down, prior to preparation into flour according to the sequence which has been described for untreated spikelets (above and Fig. 22.3). If soaked emmer in the spikelet were dried by spreading in the sun, it would have taken considerably longer to dry than the shredded chaff and grain mixture, because much more moisture would have been absorbed. If malt was used for bread, it may have been necessary or desirable to heat it artificially. Different treatments, such as light warming or more intense roasting may have been applied and may have been a way of creating a variety of flavours, including a type of sweet malt suggested for brewing (see p. 556). The evidence for such a practice is not clear, however.

Dough mixing and moisture The overall microstructure of ancient bread can be quite variable within each loaf. Some areas contain starch granules with no discernible distortion, while other parts of the crumb are made up of almost fused starch. This suggests that the flour and water were not evenly mixed in the dough, and that kneading was not extensive. There would be no point in kneading emmer dough for long, since the purpose of kneading is to develop gluten into an elastic mass which creates a nicely risen, spongy loaf. The variable texture of many of the loaves would also prevent water from fully penetrating larger grain fragments. When heated, starch granules in the dough which were protected from moisture would not have distorted.

In areas where starch granules appear to be glassy, it is possible to observe many of the boundaries of the much-swollen granules (Samuel 1996c: 489, fig. 3). This indicates that the starch is not completely fused. On the inner surfaces of small air pockets, starch granules are only dimpled or swollen. These features show that the original dough was quite moist, but that water was still limited compared to the amounts which must have been used to cook coarsely ground malt or grain destined for beer. This observation reinforces the interpretation that bread was not an ingredient for beer-brewing. Few dimpled or swollen starch granules, common in ancient bread air pockets, have been found in the beer residues.

Grit Leek (1972) carried out investigations on thirteen ancient Egyptian loaves, to establish reasons for the heavy wear observed on ancient Egyptian teeth. He hypothesised that, since bread was a staple, its composition may have contributed to the distinctive tooth abrasion. He found that the bread samples contained variable amounts of inorganic particles embedded within the bread crumb, not just on the surface. Most such particles were rounded desert quartzitic sand grains but angular fragments and very fine inclusions were also present. Leek may not have observed that sometimes loaves contain remarkably large stone chunks, several millimetres in diameter. These must surely be fragments included through careless processing, perhaps because the bread in question was not intended for consumption by the living.

As Murray describes (Chapter 21, this volume), pre-storage grain-processing involved several sieving stages which removed inorganic fragments bigger than emmer spikelets, as well as finer sand, grit and dust. Experiments have firmly established that the addition of grit is unnecessary to mill flour of any desired texture.

There are therefore several possibilities for the source of grit in bread, most of which are discussed by Leek (1972: 131–2).

1) Spikelet-sized clods of earth attached to the harvested cereal crop were incorporated into the semi-cleaned grain and were not all removed during subsequent preparation stages. A mixture of angular and rounded mineral grains might be expected from this source.
2) Small particles were abraded off the quern during milling. This would certainly explain angular fragments and fine particles, but the rounded sand particles are perhaps more likely to have come from wind-blown sand. If quartzitic sandstone querns were composed of such rounded particles, however, the saddle quern may also have been the source. More work on the characterisation of saddle quern stone, compared to grit in bread, might help to answer this question.
3) Windblown grit may have contaminated bread during preparation. In a country surrounded by desert such as Egypt, this is a reasonable supposition. The extent to which this was common, however, is questionable, as it is not always windy in Egypt, villages were often located in the cultivation, not the desert, and the installations in ancient houses show that many processing steps were done indoors.
4) There is already good evidence to show that some funerary bread was made with little care. Grit in bread may be a further reflection of carelessness. A correlation between 'gritty' bread and other characteristics like unusually high chaff or weed content may support this hypothesis.

Baking methods

The archaeological evidence for baking during periods prior to the New Kingdom is still extremely limited (see p. 542). The main corpus of data at present is provided by the artistic evidence. This section therefore focuses on New Kingdom practice, which apparently differs in many respects from earlier baking methods. Tomb scenes indicate that prior to the New Kingdom, bread was baked in long, cylindrical moulds during the Middle Kingdom and in wider, much more robust moulds during the Old Kingdom (see also Jacquet-Gordon 1981). In addition, at least in the Middle Kingdom, hand-made loaves appear to have been baked on open hearths or griddles. Examples of preparing or baking such bread can be seen in the Beni Hasan tombs of Amenemhat (BH2; see Newberry 1893a: 30–1, pl. 12, register N) and Khnumhotep III (BH3; see Newberry 1893a: 68, pl. 29, register O). Währen (1960) provides a typology of oven types and baking methods over time based on artistic evidence.

Ethnographic evidence Emmer is used for human food on a small scale in parts of Europe (Perrino *et al.* 1996: 108–9), India (Bhatia 1938: 322; Howard and Howard 1909; Mithal and Kopper 1990: 201) and in Ethiopia (National Research Council 1996: 239). There are, however, very few detailed accounts of preparation and baking methods. Observations of traditional baking with other cereals are not necessarily good analogues, as different cereals can have quite different physico-chemical properties. Virtually nothing is known about emmer wheat baking characteristics, but the little information available (Le Clerc *et al.* 1918; Piergiovanni *et al.* 1996) indicates that emmer does not closely resemble other wheat species.

One feature of village houses at both Amarna and Deir el-Medina, as well as in larger Amarna city houses and temple bakeries, is the installation of cylindrical ovens (see below). These ancient ovens closely resemble the modern *tannour* which is widespread in the Near East and parts of North Africa (but not in Egypt), particularly in rural areas (Darby *et al.* 1977: 513, fig. 12.8b; McQuitty 1984: 261, figs. 3, 5; Samuel 1994a: 276; Währen 1961: 3). The *tannour* is constructed of mud brick or mud plaster, often with a thick wall of consolidated rubble. The interior is about fifty centimetres in diameter and is lined with a fine clay cylinder. The oven is heated with a fire built up inside, which is allowed to burn vigorously for about half an hour, making the inner clay lining very hot. At the same time, heat is absorbed by the thick outer oven wall. Then, the fire dies down to glowing embers in the base, while the baker quickly rinses soot from the internal walls with a wet brush or cloth. The baker forms flat discs of dough and rubs one side of each with milk or water before slapping them onto the hot inner wall. The discs adhere and bake in the stored heat of the oven lining and wall (Samuel 1989: 255, 1994a: 276–7). When ready, the loaves begin to peel away from the sides and are expertly caught and lifted out by the baker.

The round flat loaf baked in the *tannour* becomes distinctly curved in cross-section (Währen 1961: 3). Many ancient Egyptian disc-shaped loaves are similarly bowed (see Borchardt 1932: pl. 3, for example), suggesting they may have been baked in a similar fashion to modern *tannour* baking.

At least one tomb has depictions of the baking loaves within the oven, that of Rameses III (KV11; Darby *et al.* 1977: 523, fig. 12.14). Other scenes do not actually indicate the loaves baking on the oven walls, but suggest it by showing a person reaching inside while holding a disc of dough or baked bread in the other hand. One example, from the Eighteenth-Dynasty Theban tomb of Nebamun (TT17) is shown in Fig. 22.14, while others are to be found in the Eighteenth-Dynasty Theban tomb of Kenamun (TT93; see Davies 1930: 51, pl. 58; Wild 1966: pl. 11) and the Karnak Amarna-period *talatat* scene showing temple activities now in the Luxor Museum (Lauffray 1980: pl. 16, third register up, far right – second section, second zone).

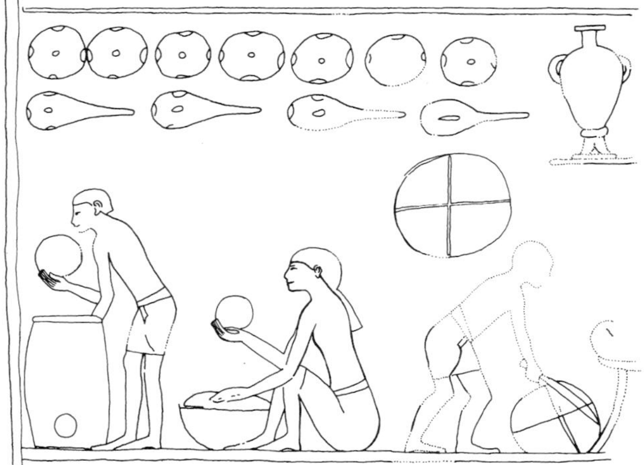

Figure 22.14 A baking scene from the Eighteenth-Dynasty tomb of Nebamun at Thebes (TT17). The figure on the right seems to be engaged in cutting a round object, possibly a loaf. The two left-hand figures are preparing disc-shaped and paddle-shaped loaves, baked in a cylindrical oven.

Such scenes have sometimes been misinterpreted. Klebs (1934: 175) and Vandier (1964: 310) suggest that the bread could only have been baked on the oven sides by being hung on little nails. No trace of such hooks have ever been found in excavated ancient cylindrical ovens, and ethnographic evidence shows that they are unnecessary. Borchardt (1916: 530), Erman (1894: 191), Ruffer (1919: 46) and Wilson (1988: 13) suggest bread was baked on the sloping outer walls of the oven. This is an impossible method, as clearly shown by an attempted reconstruction which is illustrated by Hepper (1992: 93). The ethnographic parallels explain what was being depicted: discs baked directly on the hot interior wall.

Archaeological evidence

I OVENS New Kingdom cylindrical ovens are made from a thick shell of mud brick and mud plaster. They are commonly situated in the corner of a room, the walls making up part of the shell. The interior is lined with a clay cylinder, about three centimetres thick. Sometimes the floor is also lined with clay. A few centimetres above floor level, a small hole about ten centimetres in diameter is pierced through the wall of the oven (Bruyère 1939: 72–4). Occasionally, the oven consists solely of the ceramic shell without the outer lining (Kemp 1987a: 71, fig. 6.1, unit [2810]).

Microscopy of a whitish deposit from the interior of a cylindrical oven in Chapel 556 of the Amarna Workmen's Village (unit [2810], Kemp 1987a: 71) has shown that it contains a few starch granules (Samuel 1994a: 299). This fits well with the technique of baking on the pre-heated oven wall as practised with the modern *tannour*. The evidence of the starch granules, the ubiquity of cylindrical ovens and the distinctive bowed shape of ancient disc-shaped bread loaves, all suggest that cylindrical ovens often functioned as the Middle Eastern *tannour* does today.

Other thicker loaves were too heavy to have been baked on the sides of ovens. They must have been placed on some sort of horizontal support, either the oven floor or something inserted into the oven. There is currently little which has been recognised in the archaeological record to suggest what such a removable support might have been. One possibility, ceramic bread platters, are discussed below (pp. 567–8).

II BREAD MOULDS Jacquet-Gordon (1981) has traced the evolution in bread-mould shape from the Old Kingdom through to the New Kingdom. The form evolved from enormous, thick-walled coarse cylinders of clay with a

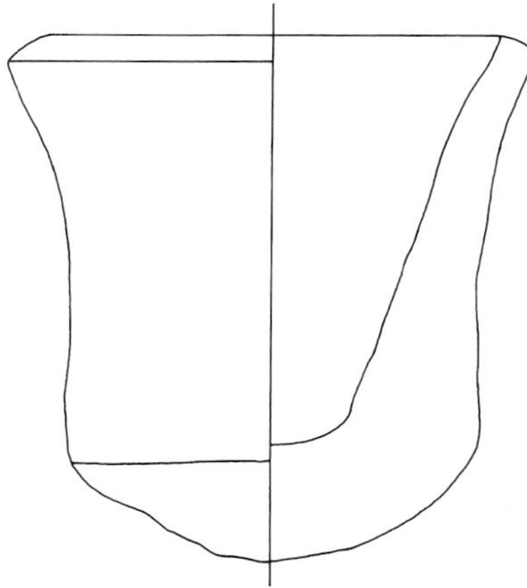

Figure 22.15a A type of Old Kingdom bread mould, from Nag el-Deir, dating to the Fourth or Fifth Dynasty. Like other Old Kingdom moulds of this type, it has a 'flower-pot' shape, slightly flaring walls and a thick, irregular, convex base. The maximum diameter of the mould is approximately 18 cm.

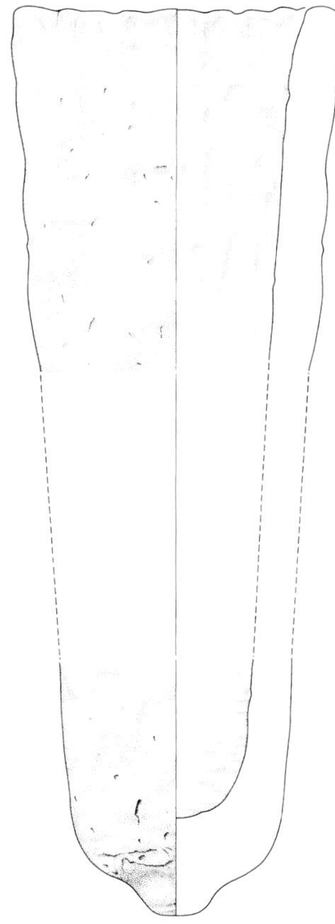

Figure 22.15b A reconstructed New Kingdom bread mould from Amarna. It is a typical conical shape, the base somewhat thicker than the sides. The base tapers to a point, a feature which is not always present on these bread moulds. Outer rim diameter is approximately 7.4 cm; height is 26.5 cm.

bowl-shaped interior (Fig. 22.15a), to coarsely and crudely made, but much smaller narrow cones in the New Kingdom (Fig. 22.15b). This type of vessel is identified as a bread mould on the basis of two observations (Jacquet-Gordon 1981: 12; Kemp 1979: 10). Firstly, many scenes of bread-baking which date throughout the Pharaonic era show precisely such vessels being used, and their form evolves in the depictions in tandem with the archaeological finds. Secondly, bread moulds are very frequently closely associated with ovens or cooking installations containing large amounts of charred material, for example at the New Kingdom sites of the Great Aten Temple of Amarna (Kemp 1979: 7–12), the treasury of Thutmose III at Karnak (Jacquet 1972: 154, plan 1, pls. 33–40, 1994a: 85–106, 1994b: pls. 36, 40, 46, for example) and at the Old Kingdom site of Giza (Lehner 1992: 3, 1993: 60).

At Amarna, the distribution of bread moulds near temples, chapels and altars suggests that, at this site, bread moulds were closely associated with specific ritual or official use. This is borne out by the lack of any known example of a preserved New Kingdom loaf which had been baked in a conical mould. In Old Kingdom times, however, baking in moulds appears to have been standard practice, since there are so many found in a wide range of contexts (Jacquet-Gordon 1981: 12). The use and significance of mould-baked bread seems to have evolved over time as baking technology changed, from widespread established practice, to specifically ritual production.

III BREAD PLATTERS One ceramic form which has been associated with baking is the platter or plate (Aston 1996: 13). Platters are roughly made, poorly fired and fragile (P. Rose pers. comm.). They are most often recovered only as fragments. Remains of these vessels appear throughout all Pharaonic levels and into the Greco-Roman period, with little apparent change. For examples of Old and Middle Kingdom platters see Arnold (1982: 28, fig. 4 no. 1; 51, fig. 14 no. 22), for New Kingdom forms see Nagel (1938: 152–3) and Figure 22.16, and for Late Period finds see French and Ghaly (1991: 116–17). The platter or plate continued to be made in Greco–Roman times; many platter sherds from these levels have been found at Buto (P. French pers. comm.). The best depiction of baking with what appears to be a platter is that

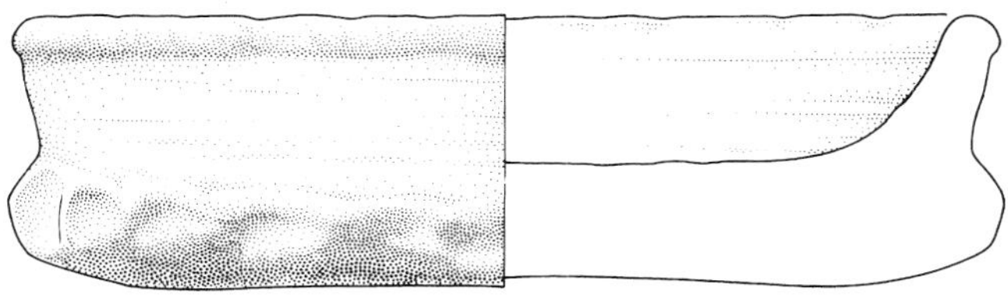

Figure 22.16 A New Kingdom 'bread platter' from house P46.33, Amarna. It is unslipped, measures 4.5 cm in height and the rim diameter is 18 cm. The outer edge is deeply moulded with finger indentations.

in the Twelfth-Dynasty tomb of Intefiqer at Thebes (TT60; Davies and Gardiner 1920: 14, pls. 8, 9, 9A).

Despite their longevity and ubiquity, platters have hardly been studied in a systematic manner. It is therefore difficult to draw any well-substantiated conclusions about them. The one notable variation appears to be that they change in size from the New Kingdom onwards, becoming larger over time (Redford 1994: 71). Judging from finds at Amarna, platters appear to come mainly from domestic areas, but at most sites little work has been done to link them to contexts or other vessel forms.

The Amarna platters are roughly formed from coarse silt clay with an untreated surface (Rose 1984: 136). They very rarely have a thin gypsum coating which may result from secondary reuse (Rose 1987a: 134). Occasional specimens have a simple design on the inner surface (Frankfort and Pendlebury 1933: pl. 54: type XXI.14). They have been found in close association with cylindrical ovens. One fragment was found inside such an oven (Peet 1921: 177). A few platter sherds were found in fill from the Kom el-Nana temple bakery at Amarna (P. Rose pers. comm.), but this association with a non-domestic context is unusual at Amarna.

In size and form, platters appear to be well-suited to baking loaves of a form too large and heavy to be baked on nearly vertical cylindrical oven walls. At Amarna, one of the largest recovered platters is about thirty centimetres in diameter (Rose 1987a: 134), and such a size could have accommodated the biggest of the ancient preserved loaves. The longest loaf that I have measured is thought to be Eighteenth-Dynasty in date, so it is broadly contemporary with Amarna. It is twenty-eight centimetres in length, a flat isosceles triangle-shaped bread now in the Egyptian Museum, Turin (no. 7019). The biggest loaves overall are over twenty centimetres in length, seventeen centimetres in width and ten centimetres high (Samuel 1994a: table 6.2), and could not possibly have been baked on the sides of cylindrical ovens.

The main reason that platters have been associated with ancient bread-making is the parallel with modern-day Egyptian vessels used for making *ʿeish shams*, or sun bread (Aston 1996: 13). Dough is put on these in order to rise. Peet and Woolley (1923: 64) and Woolley (1922: 58) describe how modern villagers living near Amarna baked with such platters, stating that dough is placed on unfired platters and both platter and bread baked together in the oven. Since baking is carried out by women in the villages, it may well be that the excavators did not see this procedure themselves and relied on descriptions by village men who did not themselves bake. On the several occasions I have been able to observe modern baking in the village near Amarna, platters were never used for the actual baking stage. A detailed account of modern Egyptian domestic bread baking is given by Rizqallah and Rizqallah (1978).

Despite the apparent modern parallel and the suitable shape of platters for baking bread, it is not at all clear exactly how the ancient platters might have been used. Bread made from emmer wheat does not rise like the spongy dough made from bread wheat (see p. 558), and thus an extended rising period does not seem likely. It is hard to imagine how such fragile platters, holding their heavy pieces of dough, could be placed in the bottom of very hot cylindrical ovens, often well over a metre in height. Even more mysterious is how the platters or the loaves were removed from the ovens when baking was complete. Unlike fired pots, they could not simply be left until the oven cooled because overexposure to heat would cause the bread either to burn or to be completely dried out. The upper surfaces and rims of these platters are better fired than the undersides, which does not suggest these platters were placed on hot embers. All the attention to manufacture has been concentrated on the interior and rim while the underside of the base was left rough and unfinished; it therefore seems impossible that they were turned upside down so that bread could be baked on the underside (P. Rose pers. comm.). Note, however, that the object depicted in the Twelfth-Dynasty tomb of Intefiqer (TT60; Davies and Gardiner 1920: pl. 9A), which appears to be a platter, is shown 'rim' side downwards, against the fire.

According to archive notes for the 1920s Amarna excavations, one platter was found scattered with bran. This may actually have been part of the abundant chaff temper which was not burnt out because of the low firing temperature (P. Rose pers. comm.). There are no loose fragments of bran adhering to the crust of any surviving loaves which I have examined, and in most loaves, only occasional pieces of chaff, which are stuck to both upper and lower surfaces rather than just the underside.

These observations suggest that the so-called bread platter may be misnamed. The longevity and ubiquity of the form, the close association with domestic contexts, and the occasional find in or close to ovens points to a domestic use, very possibly connected to cereal processing or food preparation. The link with bread-baking, however, seems rather tenuous on current evidence. More contextual work might help to resolve this problem. Meanwhile, the method by which large loaves were baked remains unknown.

Experimental evidence To date, only very small-scale experiments on ancient Egyptian baking have been carried out; much more remains to be done. A few useful insights have been obtained, however. As earlier work has established, emmer has a very high water absorption capacity. To make a dough, 82 per cent water was used in relation to emmer flour, compared to 69.5 per cent for bread wheat flour (Le Clerc *et al.* 1918: 216). When the normal bread wheat flour–water ratio is used for emmer flour, the resulting dough is so stiff and hard that it is nearly impossible to work (Samuel 1994a: 280), and certainly cannot be formed into the variety of shapes made by the ancient Egyptians. As is the case for rye flour (Prìhoda *et al.* 1993: 23), the high water absorption of emmer flour may be due to the molecular configuration of proteins and pentosans. The high uptake of water explains the considerable starch fusion seen in ancient emmer bread microstructure.

Experimental bread baked with sprouted emmer wheat resulted in a microstructure which most closely resembles that of the ancient loaves (author's unpublished data). When mixed with the same proportion of water, starch from emmer malt seems more susceptible to fusion than starch from unsprouted grain, under the same baking conditions. This may mean that the use of malt might have been more widespread than the evidence of heavily channelled starch granules currently indicates. There is very little modern comparative analysis of microstructural changes in bread made from malt, since any grain exposed to the least amount of germination is strenuously avoided in modern bakery, apart from a few speciality baked goods (Barnes 1989: 389; Pyler and Thomas 1991: 830). There are many details about ancient Egyptian baking which remain to be explored by experimental replication.

Comparison between ancient Egyptian baking and brewing technologies

The ancient Egyptians frequently depicted baking and brewing activities together. This is one reason why it has been thought that bread was a precursor to brewing beer. Bread- and beer-making were shown together because the same or similar technology was applied at many stages throughout the baking and brewing processes. In addition, the basic ingredients were the same. Bread and beer may well have been prepared in the same locations on large estates and in temple kitchens.

The first and most basic similarity between bread and beer is that they were made from the main agricultural produce, emmer wheat and barley. Although textual evidence suggests that barley was the predominant cereal in the Old and Middle Kingdoms while emmer was produced in greater quantities in the New Kingdom, to date there are not sufficient archaeobotanical data to test this hypothesis (see Chapter 21, this volume). At present there are also not enough data on the preserved foodstuffs to determine whether the cereals used to make bread and beer changed over time. Nearly all extant funerary loaves from the New Kingdom examined so far are made from emmer; there is little evidence that barley was ever an intentional addition. The few Middle Kingdom loaves which have been studied are also made of emmer wheat. There is no reason why barley could not have been a part or sole ingredient of bread, but it may be that barley was not considered appropriate for offerings. Until bread from domestic contexts is recovered, this question cannot be fully resolved. The surviving New Kingdom beer residues, on the other hand, show that beer was made from both cereals and sometimes a mixture of the two. Most residues examined to date are made from barley, but the sample size is too small to be certain that barley was more commonly brewed than emmer.

For brewing, and sometimes also for baking, cereals were malted. All examined beer residues contain evidence for the use of malt, but many of the loaves which have been studied have no evidence to show that they were made from sprouted grain. Again, the sample size is too small to establish whether malt bread was common, and whether it was eaten daily or reserved only for offerings.

Both bread- and beer-making involved milling. In the case of baking, this was preceded by dehusking so that only clean grain was ground to flour of varying textures. Both batches of cereal used for beer were coarsely ground, and the husk was included. Most of the chaff was removed by sieving later in the brewing sequence. Since grain milled for beer was only roughly broken up, grinding would have been rapid. The very fine texture of some loaves, in contrast, would have taken much longer to achieve. The cracked grain which was often added separately to bread dough may have been briefly ground on the saddle quern or perhaps was broken up with a few strokes of the pestle in the mortar.

Fermentation was a critical part of brewing, while at least some and perhaps all loaves were fermented. Microscopic examination shows that large colonies of yeast were actively growing in beer at the time of desiccation, and that lactic acid bacteria may well have been important for fermentation as well. The extent to which bread was fermented is not clear, but yeast was certainly an ingredient in at least some types of bread.

Heating and cooking played an important role in both baking and brewing. The methods which were used are not yet fully understood. There is good evidence to show that some flat breads were baked on the preheated sides of cylindrical ovens, but not all loaves could have been baked this way. Larger, thicker loaves may have been baked on clay platters, or in some other manner. Cereal for beer was not baked, but heated with sufficient water, perhaps to the consistency of a thick paste or porridge. Malt may sometimes or often have been heated when still damp to create caramel-type flavours. By the New Kingdom, heating may have been done in metal vessels, perhaps set over the mouth of cylindrical ovens. This method of cooking, not necessarily restricted to cereal foods, can be seen in several tomb scenes, for example in those of the Eighteenth-Dynasty Theban tomb of Rekhmira, (TT100; Davies 1943: 44, pl. 49; Wilkinson and Hill 1983: 89, 31.6.15, 31.6.30) and Kenamun (TT93; Davies 1930: 51, pl. 59).

Querns were thus certainly used for both baking and brewing, and cylindrical ovens probably were. Ceramic vessels were not always needed for bread-baking, and may not have been used to mix the dough either; mats or wooden containers might have served instead. Ceramic vessels were certainly used for brewing, as attested by the numerous examples with adhering residues of beer or beer precursors.

Vessels with residue have rarely been found on so-called beer jar forms of the New Kingdom. The identification of this particular ceramic type as a beer jar or beer bottle was made by Holthoer (1977: 86–7), for New Kingdom Sudanese Nubian pottery. He used this designation because these forms were often found together with what he called 'flower pots' and believed to be bread moulds, suggesting the two forms symbolically represented bread and beer as linked in a typical votive formula. There is no evidence to show such vessels were actually used for beer (Aston 1996: 13) although perhaps they may have been used for some stage of the brewing sequence. On the other hand, many other vessel forms, including amphorae, were certainly used for beer because beer residues have been found in them (e.g. Grüss 1929c; Winlock 1932: 32). There is some evidence which suggests that shallow bowls were used for drinking the final product. A number of such cup sherds from the Workmen's Village at Amarna contain classic beer residue with plenty of yeast. The shape – Group 5 in the modern Amarna corpus system, in the old system forms III.3, III.5 (Rose 1984: 135) – is common, and ideally suited to drinking.

There are still many areas of baking and brewing technology which are not yet understood. Various problems have been mentioned throughout this chapter. In particular, this discussion has focused primarily on New Kingdom practices. The development of beer- and bread-making over time remains to be properly investigated. The variations of bread and beer types according to region, class or occasion has hardly begun to be addressed. The whole range of tools and installations involved in brewing and baking has not yet been well established and sufficient archaeological evidence is still lacking or has not yet been fully examined. The suggestions which are presented here for ancient Egyptian brewing and baking technology, arising from the archaeological evidence, are not yet wholly applicable to the evidence from the artistic and documentary records. Adequate integration of all sources of evidence remains to be done. As a result, this chapter should not be seen as the last word on the subject. The study of brewing and baking throughout all Pharaonic periods is an active area of research which will continue to provide new insights into these key activities.

Acknowledgements

My research has been supported by the British Academy, the Egypt Exploration Society, the Natural Environment Research Council and Scottish and Newcastle Breweries. I am particularly grateful to the many museums who have permitted study and sampling. Warm thanks are due to Barry Kemp, Mark Nesbitt, Pamela Rose and Margaret Serpico for their helpful comments.

References

Angold, R.E. 1983. The structure of the cereal grain. In *Lipids in Cereal Technology* (ed. P.J. Barnes). London: Academic Press, pp. 1–10.

Arnold, D. 1982. Keramikbearbeitung in Dahschur 1976–1981. *MDAIK*, 38: 25–65.

Aston, D.A. 1996. *Egyptian Pottery of the Late New Kingdom and Third Intermediate Period (Twelfth–Seventh Centuries BC). Tentative Footsteps in a Forbidding Terrain.* Studien zur Archäologie und Geschichte Altägyptens 13. Heidelberg: Heidelberger Orientverlag.

Banks, W. and Greenwood, C.T. 1975. *Starch and its Components.* Edinburgh: Edinburgh University Press.

Barnes, P.J. 1989. Wheat in milling and baking. In *Cereal Science and Technology* (ed. G.H. Palmer). Aberdeen: Aberdeen University Press, pp. 376–411.

Barton-Wright, E.C., Booth, R.G. and Pringle, W.J.S. 1944. Analysis of barley from King Tuthankhamen's tomb. *Nature*, 153/3879: 288.

Bemment, D.W. 1985. Speciality malts. *The Brewer*, 71/854: 457–60.

Berry, D.R. 1982. *The Biology of Yeast.* Studies in Biology 140. London: Edward Arnold.

Bhatia, G.S. 1938. A new variety of 'Khapli emmer' wheat from India, and its bearing upon the place of origin of emmer wheats. *Journal of Genetics*, 35/3: 321–9.

Bircher, W.H. 1995. *The Date Palm: A Friend and Companion of Man.* Cairo: Elias Modern Press.

Bleeker, C.J. 1973. *Hathor and Thoth. Two Key Figures of the Ancient Egyptian Religion.* Studies in the history of religions (Supplements to *Numen*) 26. Leiden: E.J. Brill.

Blenkinsop, P. 1991. The manufacture, characteristics and uses of speciality malts. *Master Brewers Association of the Americas Technical Quarterly*, 28/4: 145–9.

Bonnet, E. 1902. Plantes antiques des nécropoles d'Antinoé. *Journal de Botanique*, 16: 314–19.

1905. Plantes antiques des nécropoles d'Antinoé (2e article). *Journal de Botanique*, 19/1: 5–12.

Bor, N.L. 1968. *Flora of Iraq. Volume 9: Gramineae.* Baghdad: Ministry of Agriculture, Republic of Iraq.

Borchardt, L. 1897. Die Dienerstatuen aus den Gräbern des alten Reiches. *ZÄS*, 35: 119–34.

1911. *Statuen und Statuetten von Königen und Privatleuten im Museum von Kairo, Nr. 1–1294. Teil 1. Text und Tafeln zu Nr. 1–380.* Berlin: Reichsdruckerei.

1916. Das altägyptische Wohnhaus im 14. Jahrhundert v. Chr. *Zeitschrift für Bauwesen*, 66/10–12: 510–58.

1932. Ein Brot. *ZÄS*, 68: 73–9.

Bourriau, J. 1988. *Pharaohs and Mortals: Egyptian Art in the Middle Kingdom.* Cambridge: CUP.

Bradbury, D., Cull, I. M. and MacMasters, M. M. 1956. Structure of the mature wheat kernel. I. Gross anatomy and relationships of parts. *Cereal Chemistry*, 33/6: 329–42.

Breasted, J.H. 1907. *Ancient Records of Egypt. Historical Documents from the Earliest Times to the Persian Conquest, Collected, Edited and Translated with Commentary. Volume 5. Index.* Ancient

Records Series. Chicago IL: University of Chicago Press.

1948. *Egyptian Servant Statues*. Washington DC: Pantheon Books.

Briggs, D.E. 1978. *Barley*. London: Chapman and Hall.

Briggs, D.E., Hough, J.S., Stevens, R. and Young, T.W. 1981. *Malting and Brewing Science. Volume 1. Malt and Sweet Wort*. 2nd edn. London: Chapman and Hall.

Brown, J. 1982. Yeast and fermentation. In *The Master Bakers' Book of Breadmaking* (ed. J. Brown). London: National Association of Master Bakers, pp. 58–77.

1993. Advances in breadmaking technology. In *Advances in Baking Technology* (eds. B.S. Kamel and C.E. Stauffer). Glasgow: Blackie Academic and Professional, pp. 38–87.

Brunton, G. and Caton-Thompson, G. 1928. *The Badarian Civilisation and Predynastic Remains near Badari*. BSAE and ERA 46. London: BSAE.

Bruyère, B. 1937. *Rapport sur les fouilles de Deir el Médineh (1934–1935). Deuxième partie: La nécropole de l'est*. Fouilles de l'Institut Français du Caire 15. Cairo: IFAO.

1939. *Rapport sur les fouilles de Deir el-Médineh (1934–1935). Troisième partie: Le village, les décharges publiques, la station de repos du col de la vallée des rois*. Fouilles de l'Institut Français du Caire 16. Cairo: IFAO.

Burckhardt, J.L. 1822. *Travels in Nubia*. 2nd edn. Association for Promoting the Discovery of the Interior Parts of Africa. London: John Murray.

Cooke, R.D., Twiddy, D.R. and Reilly, P.J.A. 1987. Lactic-acid fermentation as a low-cost means of food preservation in tropical countries. *FEMS Microbiology Reviews*, 46/3: 369–79.

Crawford, D.J. 1979. Food: tradition and change in Hellenistic Egypt. *WA*, 11/2: 136–46.

Curwen, E.C. 1937. Querns. *Antiquity*, 11/42: 133–51.

Darby, W.J., Ghalioungui, P. and Grivetti, L. 1977. *Food: The Gift of Osiris Volume 2*. London: Academic Press.

Davies, N. de G. 1902. *The Rock Tombs of Deir el-Gebrâwi II: Tomb of Zau and Tombs of the Northern Group*. Archaeological Survey of Egypt. London: EES.

1930. *The Tomb of Ken-Amun at Thebes*. The Metropolitan Museum of Art Egyptian Expedition. New York: MMA.

1943. *The Tomb of Rekh-mi-re at Thebes*. The Metropolitan Museum of Art Egyptian Expedition. New York: MMA.

Davies, N. de G. and Gardiner, A.H. 1920. *The Tomb of Antefoker, Vizier of Sesostris I, and of his Wife, Senet (No. 60)*. The Theban Tombs Series. London: George Allen and Unwin.

De Keersmaecker, J. 1996. The mystery of lambic beer. *Scientific American*, 275/2: 56–62.

Deák, T. 1991. Foodborne yeasts. *Advances in Applied Microbiology*, 36: 179–278.

Derera, N.F. 1989. *Preharvest Field Sprouting in Cereals*. Boca Raton FL: CRC Press.

Dickson, C. 1987. The identification of cereals from ancient bran fragments. *Circaea*, 4/2: 95–102.

Dirar, H.A. 1993. *Indigenous Fermented Foods of the Sudan: A Study in African Food and Nutrition*. Wallingford, UK: CAB International.

Djien, K.S. 1982. Indigenous fermented foods. In *Fermented Foods* (ed. A.H. Rose). Economic Microbiology 7. London: Academic Press, pp. 15–38.

Drenkhahn, R. 1975. Brot. *LÄ I*: 871.

Dronzek, B.L., Hwang, P. and Bushuk, W. 1972. Scanning electron microscopy of starch from sprouted wheat. *Cereal Chemistry*, 49/2: 232–9.

Duffy, J.C. (ed.) 1992. *Alcohol and Illness. The Epidemiological Viewpoint*. Health and society. Edinburgh: Edinburgh University Press.

Engelbach, R. 1942. Mechanical and technical processes, materials. In *The Legacy of Egypt* (ed. S.R.K. Glanville). Oxford: Clarendon Press, pp. 120–59.

Épron, L. and Daumas, F. 1939. *Le tombeau de Ti. Fascicule I. Les approches de la chapelle*. Mémoires publiés par les membres de l'Institut Français d'Archéologie Orientale du Caire 65. Cairo: IFAO.

Erman, A. 1894. *Life in Ancient Egypt*. [trans. H.M. Tirard], repr. 1971. New York: Dover.

Eskin, N.A.M. 1990. *Biochemistry of Foods*. 2nd edn. San Diego: Academic Press.

Faltings, D. 1991. Die Bierbrauerei im AR. *ZÄS*, 118: 104–16.

1995. *bš3* und *zwt* – zwei ungeklärte Begriffe der Getreidewirtschaft im AR. *GM*, 148: 35–44.

Firth, C.M. 1915. *The Archaeological Survey of Nubia Report for 1909–1910*. Cairo: Government Press.

Fleming, S., Fishman, B., O'Connor, D. and Silverman, D. 1980. *The Egyptian Mummy. Secrets and Science*. University Museum Handbook I. Philadelphia: The University Museum, University of Pennsylvania.

Forbes, R. J. 1954. Chemical, culinary, and cosmetic arts. In *A History of Technology Volume 1: From Early Times to Fall of Empires*. (eds. C. Singer, E.J. Holmyard and A.R. Hall). Oxford: Clarendon Press, pp. 238–98.

1965. *Studies in Ancient Technology, Volume 3*. 2nd edn. Leiden: E.J. Brill.

Frankfort, H. and Pendlebury, J.D.S. 1933. *The City of Akhenaten* II. London: EES.

French, D. 1973. Chemical and physical properties of starch. *Journal of Animal Science*, 37/4: 1048–61.

French, P. and Ghaly, H. 1991. Pottery chiefly of the Late Dynastic Period, from excavations by the Egyptian Antiquities Organisation at Saqqara, 1987. *CCE*, 2: 93–124.

Gardiner, A.H. 1906. A statuette of the high priest of Memphis, Ptahmose. *ZÄS*, 43: 55–9.

1935. *Hieratic Papyri in the British Museum. Third Series, Chester Beatty Gift, Volume I Text*. London: British Museum.

1947. *Ancient Egyptian Onomastica. Text, Volume 2*. Oxford: OUP.

Garstang, J. 1907. *The Burial Customs of Ancient Egypt as Illustrated by Tombs of the Middle Kingdom*. London: Archibald Constable.

Geller, J.R. 1989. Recent excavations at Hierakonpolis and their relevance to predynastic production and settlement. *CRIPEL*, 11: 41–52, pls. 4–6.

1992a. From prehistory to history: beer in Egypt. In *The Followers of Horus* (eds. R. Friedman and B. Adams). Egyptian Studies Association Publication 2. Oxford: Oxbow Books, pp. 19–26.

1992b. Predynastic Beer Production At Hierakonpolis, Upper Egypt: Archaeological Evidence and Anthropological Implications. PhD, Department of Anthropology, Washington University, USA.

Gerisch, R. in press. Die Baumgöttin als Lebensbaum. *Kemet*, 3.

Germer, R. 1985. *Flora des pharaonischen Ägypten*. Deutsches Archäologisches Institut, Abteilung Kairo, Sonderschrift 14. Mainz: von Zabern.

Glabau, C.A. and Goldman, P.F. 1938. Some physical and chemical properties of Egyptian bread. *Cereal Chemistry*, 15/3: 295–309.

Goering, K.J., Fritts, D.H. and Allen, K.G.D. 1974. A comparison of loss of birefringence with the percent gelatinization and viscosity on potato, wheat, rice, corn, cow cockle, and several barley starches. *Cereal Chemistry*, 51/6: 764–71.

Gourlay, Y.J.-L. 1981. *Les sparteries de Deir el-Médineh XVIIIe–XXe dynasties. II. Catalogue des objets de sparterie*. Cairo: IFAO.

Greenwood, C.T. 1979. Observations on the structure of the starch granule. In *Polysaccharides in Food* (eds. J.M.V. Blanshard and J.R. Mitchell). London: Butterworth, pp. 129–38.

Griffith, F. L. 1894. The jar inscriptions. In *Tell el-Amarna* (ed. W.M.F. Petrie). London: Methuen and Co., pp. 32–4.

Grüss, J. 1928. *Saccharomyces Winlocki*, die Hefe aus den Pharaonengräbern. *Tageszeitung für Brauerei*, 26/237: 1123–4.

1929a. *Saccharomyces Winlocki* die Hefe aus den Pharaonengräbern. *Tageszeitung für Brauerei*, 27/59: 275–8.

1929b. Weitere Hefenfunde aus den Pharaonengräbern II. *Tageszeitung für Brauerei*, 27/110: 517–20.

1929c. Weitere Hefenfunde in Trinkgefässen aus den Gräbern Alt-Aegyptens. *Tageszeitung für Brauerei*, 27/145: 679–81.

1932. Untersuchung von Broten aus der Ägyptischen Sammlung der Staatlichen Museen zu Berlin. *ZÄS*, 68: 79–80.

Gurr, E. 1953. *A Practical Manual of Medical and Biological Staining Techniques*. London: Leonard Hill.

Hallam, N.D. 1973. Fine structure of viable and non-viable rye and other embryos. In *Seed Ecology. Proceedings of the Nineteenth Easter School in Agricultural Science, University of Nottingham, 1972*. (ed. W. Heydecker). London, Butterworth, pp. 115–44.

Hansson, A.-M. 1996. Bread in Birka and on Björkö. *Laborativ Arkeologi. Journal of Nordic Archaeological Science*, 9: 61–78.

Hansson, A.-M. and Isaksson, S. 1994. Analyses of charred organic remains. *Laborativ Arkeologi. Journal of Nordic Archaeological Science*, 7: 21–9.

Harlan, J.R. 1967. A wild wheat harvest in Turkey. *Archaeology*, 20/3: 197–201.

Helck, W. 1961. *Materialien zur Wirtschaftsgeschichte des Neuen Reiches. Teil 1. Die Eigentümer. a. Die grossen Tempel*. Akademie der Wissenschaften und der Literatur. Abhandlungen der Geistes- und Sozialwissenschaftlichen Klasse Jahrgang 1960. Nr. 10. Mainz: Akademie der Wissenschaften und der Literatur.

1971. *Das Bier im Alten Ägypten*. Berlin: Gesellschaft für die Geschichte und Bibliographie des Brauwesens.

1975. Bier. *LÄ* I: 789–92.

Hepper, F.N. 1990. *Pharaoh's Flowers. The Botanical Treasures of Tutankhamun*. London: HMSO.

1992. *Illustrated Encyclopedia of Bible Plants*. Leicester: Inter Varsity Press.

Hillman, G.C. 1984. Traditional husbandry and processing of archaic cereals in modern times: Part I, the glume-wheats. *BSA*, 1: 114–52.

Hjelmqvist, H. 1984. Botanische Analyse einiger Brote. In *Birka II:1. Systematische Analysen der Gräberfunde* (ed. G. Arwidsson). Stockholm: Almqvist and Wiksell International, pp. 263–72.

1990. Über die Zusammensetzung einiger prähistorischer Brote. *Fornvännen. Tidskrift för Svensk Antikvarisk Forskning*, 85: 9–21.

Holden, T.G. 1986. Preliminary report on the detailed analyses of the macroscopic remains from the gut of Lindow man. In *Lindow Man: The Body in the Bog* (eds. I.M. Stead, J.B. Bourke and D. Brothwell). London: BMP, pp. 116–25.

Holthoer, R. 1977. *New Kingdom Pharaonic Sites: The Pottery*. Scandinavian Joint Expedition to Sudanese Nubia vol. 5:1. Stockholm: Scandinavian University Books.

Holzapfel, W.H., Geisen, R. and Schillinger, U. 1995. Biological preservation of foods with reference to protective cultures, bacteriocins and food-grade enzymes. *International Journal of Food Microbiology*, 24/3: 343–62.

Hoseney, R.C., Atwell, W.A. and Lineback, D.R. 1977. Scanning electron microscopy of starch isolated from baked products. *Cereal Foods World*, 22/2: 56–60.

Hough, J.S. 1991. *The Biotechnology of Malting and Brewing*. Cambridge Series in Biotechnology. Cambridge: CUP.

Howard, A. and Howard, G.L.C. 1909. *Wheat in India: Its Production, Varieties and Improvement*. Calcutta: Thacker, Spink and Co.

Hurley, J. and Horowitz, J. (eds.) 1990. *Alcohol and Health*. New York: Hemisphere.

Jackson, M. 1993. *Michael Jackson's Beer Companion*. London: Mitchell Beazley.

Jacquet, J. 1972. Fouilles de Karnak nord quatrième campagne 1971. *BIFAO*, 71: 151–60.

1994a. *Karnak-nord VII. Le trésor de Thoutmosis 1er. Installations antérieures ou postérieures au monument. Fascicule I. Texte*. Fouilles de l'Institut Français d'Archéologie Orientale du Caire 36/1. Cairo: IFAO.

1994b. *Karnak-nord VII. Le trésor de Thoutmosis 1er. Installations antérieures ou postérieures au monument. Fascicule II. Planches*. Fouilles de l'Institut Français d'Archéologie Orientale du Caire 36/2. Cairo: IFAO.

Jacquet-Gordon, H. 1981. A tentative typology of Egyptian bread moulds. In *Studien zur altägyptischen Keramik* (ed. D. Arnold). Mainz am Rhein: von Zabern, pp. 11–24.

Janssen, J.J. 1980. Absence from work by the necropolis workmen of Thebes. *SAK*, 8: 127–52.

Jensen, W.A. 1962. *Botanical Histochemistry*. San Francisco: W.H. Freeman.

Kamal, A.B. 1913. Le pain de nebaq des anciens égyptiens. *ASAE*, 12: 240–4.

Kemp, B.J. 1979. Preliminary report on the el-Amarna survey, 1978. *JEA*, 65: 5–12.

(ed.) 1984. *Amarna Reports* I. London: EES.

(ed.) 1985. *Amarna Reports* II. London: EES.

(ed.) 1986. *Amarna Reports* III. London: EES.

(ed.) 1987a. *Amarna Reports* IV. London: EES.

1987b. The Amarna Workmen's Village in retrospect. *JEA*, 73: 21–50.

1989. *Ancient Egypt. Anatomy of a Civilization*. London: Routledge.

Kemp, B. and Bomann, A. 1984. Report on the 1983 excavations. Chapel 561/450 (the 'main chapel'). In *Amarna Reports* I (ed. B.J. Kemp). London: EES, pp. 14–33.

Klebs, L. 1915. *Die Reliefs des alten Reiches (2980–2475 v. Chr.) Material zur ägyptischen Kulturgeschichte*. Abhandlungen der

Heidelberger Akademie der Wissenschaften 3. Heidelberg: Carl Winters Universität.

1922. *Die Reliefs und Malereien des mittleren Reiches (VII.-XVII. Dynastie ca 2475–1580 v. Chr.). Material zur ägyptischen Kulturgeschichte.* Abhandlungen der Heidelberger Akademie der Wissenschaften 6. Heidelberg: Carl Winters Universität.

1934. *Die Reliefs und Malereien des neuen Reiches (XVIII.–XX. Dynastie, ca 1580–1100 v. Chr.). Material zur ägyptischen Kulturgeschichte. Teil 1. Szenen aus dem Leben des Volkes.* Abhandlungen der Heidelberger Akademie der Wissenschaften 9. Heidelberg: Carl Winters Universität.

Körber-Grohne, U. and Piening, U. 1980. Microstructure of the surfaces of carbonized and non-carbonized grains of cereals as observed in scanning electron and light microscopes as an additional aid in determining prehistoric findings. *Flora*, 170: 189–228.

Larsen, H. 1936a. On baking in Egypt during the Middle Kingdom. *Acta Archaeologica (Copenhagen)*, 7: 51–7.

1936b. Vorbericht über die schwedischen Grabungen in Abu Ghâlib 1932/34. *MDAIK*, 6/1: 41–87.

Lauffray, J. 1979. *Karnak d'Égypte: domaine du divin*. Paris: CNRS.

1980. Les 'talatat' du IXe pylône de Karnak et le *Teny-Menou* (assemblage et première reconstruction d'une paroi du temple d'Aton dans le Musée de Louqsor). *Cahiers de Karnak, 1973–1977*, 7: 67–89, pls. 14–19.

Le Clerc, J.A., Bailey, L.H. and Wessling, H.L. 1918. Milling and baking tests of einkorn, emmer, spelt, and Polish wheat. *Journal of the American Society of Agronomy*, 10: 215–17.

Leek, F.F. 1972. Teeth and bread in ancient Egypt. *JEA*, 58: 126–32.

1973. Further studies concerning ancient Egyptian bread. *JEA*, 59: 199–204.

Lehner, M. 1992. Excavations at Giza 1988–1991: The location and importance of the pyramid settlement. *The Oriental Institute News and Notes*, 135(Fall): 1–9.

1993. Giza. In *The Oriental Institute 1991–1992 Annual Report* (ed. W.M. Sumner). Chicago IL: OIP, pp. 56–67.

Lewis, M. J. and Young, T.W. 1995. *Brewing*. London: Chapman and Hall.

Lucas, A. 1962. *Ancient Egyptian Materials and Industries*. 4th edn., rev. J.R. Harris. London: Edward Arnold.

Lutz, H.F. 1922. *Viticulture and Brewing in the Ancient Orient*. Leipzig: J.C. Hinrichs.

MacLeod, A.M. 1979. The physiology of malting. In *Brewing Science Volume* I (ed. J.R.A. Pollock). London: Academic Press, pp. 145–232.

Maksoud, S.A., El Hadidi, M.N. and Amer, W.M. 1994. Beer from the early dynasties (3500–3400 cal B.C.) of upper Egypt, detected by archaeochemical methods. *Vegetation History and Archaeobotany*, 3: 219–24.

Manniche, L. 1989. *An Ancient Egyptian Herbal*. Austin TX: University of Texas.

Mattern, P.J. 1991. Wheat. In *Handbook of Cereal Science and Technology* (eds. K.J. Lorenz and K. Kulp). New York: Marcel Dekker, pp. 1–53.

McDonald, J.K. 1982. Conical loaf of bread. In *Egypt's Golden Age: The Art of Living in the New Kingdom 1558–1085 BC*. (eds. E. Brovarski, S.K. Doll and R.E. Freed). Boston: MFA, pp. 113.

McQuitty, A. 1984. An ethnographic and archaeological study of clay ovens in Jordan. *Annual of the Department of Antiquities (Amman)*, 28: 259–67, pls. 53–4.

Megally, M. 1977. *Recherches sur l'économie, l'administration et la comptabilité égyptiennes à la XVIIIe dynastie d'après le Papyrus E.3226 du Louvre*. Cairo: IFAO.

Meredith, P. 1983. Aspects of field-sprouting of wheat. In *Progress in Cereal Chemistry and Technology. Part A. Proceedings of the VIIth World Cereal and Bread Congress, Prague, Czechoslovakia, June 28–July 2, 1982* (eds. J. Holas and J. Kratochvil). Developments in Food Science 5A. Amsterdam: Elsevier, pp. 127–32.

Meurers-Balke, J. and Lüning, J. 1992. Some aspects and experiments concerning the processing of glume wheats. In *Préhistoire de l'agriculture* (ed. P. C. Anderson). Monographie du Centre de Recherches Archéologiques 6. Paris: CNRS, pp. 341–62.

Miles, C.W., Kelsay, J.L. and Wong, N.P. 1988. Effect of dietary fiber on the metabolizable energy of human diets. *Journal of Nutrition*, 118/9: 1075–81.

Miller, R. 1987. Ash as an insecticide. In *Amarna Reports IV* (ed. B.J. Kemp). London: EES, pp. 14–15.

Mithal, S.K. and Kopper, M.N. 1990. Evaluation and conservation of wheat genetic resources in India. In *Wheat Genetic Resources: Meeting Diverse Needs* (eds. J.P. Srivastava and A.B. Damania). Chichester: John Wiley, pp. 201–9.

Mogensen, M. 1930. *La glyptothèque Ny Carlsberg: la collection égyptienne*. Copenhagen: Levin and Munksgaard.

Mohr, H.T. 1943. *The Mastaba of Hetep-Her-Akhti: Study on an Egyptian Tomb Chapel in the Museum of Antiquities, Leiden*. Leiden: E.J. Brill.

Mond, R. and Myers, O.H. 1937. *Cemeteries of Armant, Volume 1. Text*. London: EES.

Montet, P. 1925. *Scènes de la vie privée dans les tombeaux égyptiens de l'ancien empire*. Publications de la Faculté des Lettres de l'Université de Strasbourg 24. Strasbourg: Faculté des Lettres de l'Université de Strasbourg.

Morcos, S.R., Hegazi, S.M. and El-Damhougy, S.T. 1973. Fermented foods of common use in Egypt. II. The chemical composition of *bouza* and its ingredients. *Journal of the Science of Food and Agriculture*, 24: 1157–61.

Moritz, L.A. 1955. Husked and 'naked' grain. *Classical Quarterly*, New Series 5(3 and 4): 129–41.

1958. *Grain-Mills and Flour in Classical Antiquity*. Oxford: Clarendon Press.

Moussa, A.M., Altenmüller, H., Johannes, D. and Ruhm, W. 1977. *Das Grab des Nianchchnum und Chnumhotep*. Old Kingdom tombs at the causeway of King Unas at Saqqara. Mainz: von Zabern.

Nagel, G. 1938. *La ceramique du nouvel empire à Deir el-Médineh. Tome 1*. Documents de fouilles publié par les membres de l'Institut Français d'Archéologie Orientale du Caire 10. Cairo: IFAO.

National Research Council. 1996. *Lost Crops of Africa. 1. Grains*. Washington DC: National Academy Press.

Nesbitt, M. and Samuel, D. 1996. From staple crops to extinction? The archaeology and history of the hulled wheats. In *Hulled Wheats. Promoting the Conservation and Use of Underutilized and Neglected Crops. 4. Proceedings of the First International Workshop on Hulled Wheats, 21–22 July 1995, Castelvecchio*

Pascoli, Tuscany, Italy (eds. S. Padulosi, K. Hammer and J. Heller). Rome: International Plant Genetic Resources Institute, pp. 41–100.

Neve, R.A. 1991. *Hops*. London: Chapman and Hall.

Newberry, P.E. 1893a. *Beni Hasan I*. Archaeological Survey of Egypt. London: EEF.

1893b. *Beni Hasan II*. Archaeological Survey of Egypt. London: EEF.

Nims, C.F. 1950. Egyptian catalogues of things. A review article of A.H. Gardiner *Ancient Egyptian Onomastica*. *JNES*, 9: 253–62.

1958. The bread and beer problems of the Moscow Mathematical Papyrus. *JEA*, 44: 56–65.

Nout, M.J.R. and Rombouts, F.M. 1992. Fermentative preservation of plant foods. *Journal of Applied Bacteriology*, 73(Suppl.): 136S–47S.

Odunfa, S.A. 1985. African fermented foods. In *Microbiology of Fermented Foods. Volume 2* (ed. B.J.B. Wood). London: Elsevier Applied Science, pp. 155–91.

Palmer, G.H. 1972. Morphology of starch granules in cereal grains and malts. *Journal of the Institute of Brewing*, 78: 326–32.

1989. Cereals in malting and brewing. In *Cereal Science and Technology* (ed. G.H. Palmer). Aberdeen: Aberdeen University Press.

1995. Structure of ancient cereal grains. *Journal of the Institute of Brewing*, 101(March-April): 103–12.

Peet, T.E. 1914. *The Cemeteries of Abydos II: 1911–1912*. London: EEF.

1921. Excavations at Tell el-Amarna: A preliminary report. *JEA*, 7: 169–85.

1923. *The Rhind Mathematical Papyrus. British Museum 10057 and 10058*. London: Hodder and Stoughton.

1931. Review of Struve, W.W., Mathematischer Papyrus des Staatlichen Museums der Schönen Künste in Moskau. *JEA*, 17: 154–60.

Peet, T.E. and Loat, W.L.S. 1913. *The Cemeteries of Abydos III: 1912–1913*. London: EEF.

Peet, T.E. and Woolley, C.L. 1923. *The City of Akhenaten. Part I. Excavations of 1921 and 1922 at El-ʾAmarneh*. London: EES.

Peña-Chocarro, L. 1996. *In situ* conservation of hulled wheat species: the case of Spain. In *Hulled Wheats. Promoting The Conservation and Use of Underutilized and Neglected Crops. 4. Proceedings of the First International Workshop on Hulled Wheats, 21–22 July 1995, Castelvecchio Pascoli, Tuscany, Italy* (eds. S. Padulosi, K. Hammer and J. Heller). Rome: International Plant Genetic Resources Institute, pp. 129–46.

Perrino, P., Laghetti, G., D'Antuono, L.F., Al Ajlouni, M., Kanbertay, M., Szabó, A.T. and Hammer, K. 1996. Ecogeographical distribution of hulled wheat species. In *Hulled Wheats. Promoting the Conservation and Use of Underutilized and Neglected Crops. 4. Proceedings of the First International Workshop on Hulled Wheats, 21–22 July 1995, Castelvecchio Pascoli, Tuscany, Italy* (eds. S. Padulosi, K. Hammer and J. Heller). Rome: International Plant Genetic Resources Institute, pp. 101–19.

Petrie, W.M.F. 1901. *Diospolis Parva. The Cemeteries of Abadiyeh and Hu 1898–9*. Special extra publication of the Egypt Exploration Fund. London: EEF.

1907. *Gizeh and Rifeh*. London: BSAE.

1920. *Prehistoric Egypt*. London: BSAE.

Petrie, W.M.F. and Brunton, G. 1924. *Sedment I*. London: BSAE.

Piergiovanni, A.R., Laghetti, G. and Perrino, P. 1996. Characteristics of meal from hulled wheats (*Triticum dicoccon* Schrank and *T. spelta* L.): An evaluation of selected accessions. *Cereal Chemistry*, 73/61: 732–5.

Platt, B.S. 1964. Biological ennoblement: Improvement of the nutritive value of foods and dietary regimens by biological agencies. *Food Technology*, 18/5: 68–76.

Pomeranz, Y. 1972. Scanning electron microscopy of the endosperm of malted barley. *Cereal Chemistry*, 49/1: 5–19.

Ponte, J.G., Jr. and Reed, G. 1982. Bakery foods. In *Prescott and Dunn's Industrial Microbiology* (ed. G. Reed). Westport CT: AVI, pp. 246–92.

Prihoda, J., Holas, J. and Kratochvil, J. 1993. Rye flour, wholemeal breads, and rye breads. In *Advances in Baking Technology* (eds. B.S. Kamel and C.E. Stauffer). Glasgow: Blackie Academic and Professional, pp. 20–37.

Pyler, R.E. and Thomas, D.A. 1991. Malted cereals: Production and use. In *Handbook of Cereal Science and Technology* (eds. K. J. Lorenz and K. Kulp). New York: Marcel Dekker, pp. 815–32.

Ranhotra, G.S. 1991. Nutritional quality of cereals and cereal-based foods. In *Handbook of Cereal Science and Technology* (eds. K.J. Lorenz and K. Kulp). New York: Marcel Dekker, pp. 845–61.

Raven, P.H., Evert, R.F. and Curtis, H. 1981. *Biology of Plants*. 3rd edn. New York: Worth Publishers, Inc.

Redford, D. 1994. *The Akhenaten Temple Project. Volume 3: The Excavations of Kom El-Ahmar and Environs*. Aegypti Texta Propositaque II. Toronto: The Akhenaten Temple Project.

Renfrew, J.M. 1985. Preliminary report on the botanical remains. In *Amarna Reports II* (ed. B.J. Kemp). London: EES, pp. 175–90.

Richards, A.I. 1939. *Land, Labour and Diet in Northern Rhodesia: An Economic Study of the Bemba Tribe*. London: OUP.

Ridgely, B. 1994. African sorghum beer. *Zymurgy*, 17: 28–30.

Rizqallah, F. and Rizqallah, K. 1978. *La préparation du pain dans un village du delta égyptien (province de Charqia)*. Cairo: IFAO.

Robinson, D.M. and Graham, J.W. 1938. *Excavations at Olynthus. Part VIII. The Hellenic House. A Study of the Houses Found at Olynthus with a Detailed Account of Those Excavated in 1931 and 1934*. The Johns Hopkins University studies in archaeology 25. Baltimore MD: The Johns Hopkins Press.

Rooney, L.W., Kirleis, A.W. and Murty, D.S. 1986. Traditional foods from sorghum: their production, evaluation, and nutritional value. In *Advances in Cereal Science and Technology 8* (ed. Y. Pomeranz). St. Paul MN: American Association of Cereal Chemists, pp. 317–53.

Rose, P. 1984. The pottery distribution analysis. In *Amarna Reports I* (ed. B.J. Kemp). London: EES, pp. 133–53.

1987a. The pottery from Gate Street 8. In *Amarna Reports IV* (ed. B.J. Kemp). London: EES, pp. 132–43.

1987b. Report on the 1986 Amarna pottery survey. In *Amarna Reports IV* (ed. B.J. Kemp). London: EES, pp. 115–29.

1995. Report on the 1987 excavations. House P46.33: The pottery. In *Amarna Reports VI* (ed. B.J. Kemp). London: EES, pp. 137–45.

Ruffer, M.A. 1919. Food in Egypt. *Mémoires de l'Institute d'Égypte*, 1: 1–88.

1920. Study of abnormalities and pathology of ancient Egyptian teeth. *American Journal of Physical Anthropology*, 3: 335–82.

1921. *Studies in the Palaeopathology of Egypt*. Chicago IL: University of Chicago Press.

Runnels, C.N. and Murray, P.M. 1983. Milling in ancient Greece. *Archaeology*, 36: 62–3, 75.

Saleh, M. and Sourouzian, H. 1987. *Official Catalogue: The Egyptian Museum Cairo*. (trans. P. Der Manuelian and H. Jacquet-Gordon). Mainz: von Zabern.

Sallares, R. 1995. Molecular archaeology and ancient history. In *Food in Antiquity* (eds. J. Wilkins, D. Harvey and M. Dobson). Exeter: University of Exeter Press, pp. 87–100.

Sambrook, P. 1996. *Country House Brewing in England, 1500–1900*. London: The Hambledon Press.

Samuel, D. 1989. Their staff of life: initial investigations on ancient Egyptian bread baking. In *Amarna Reports V* (ed. B.J. Kemp). London: EES, pp. 253–90.

1993. Ancient Egyptian cereal processing: beyond the artistic record. *CAJ*, 3/2: 276–83.

1994a. An Archaeological Study of Baking and Bread in New Kingdom Egypt. PhD, Department of Archaeology, University of Cambridge, England.

1994b. A new look at bread and beer. *EA*, 4: 9–11.

1996a. Approaches to the archaeology of food. *Petits Propos Culinaires*, 54: 12–21.

1996b. Archaeology of ancient Egyptian beer. *Journal of the American Society of Brewing Chemists*, 54/1: 3–12.

1996c. Investigation of ancient Egyptian baking and brewing methods by correlative microscopy. *Science*, 273: 488–90.

Samuel, D. and Bolt, P. 1995. Rediscovering ancient Egyptian beer. *Brewers' Guardian*, 124/12: 26–31.

Säve-Söderbergh, T. 1957. *Private tombs at Thebes I: Four Eighteenth Dynasty Tombs*. Oxford: Griffith Institute.

Schön, W. and Holter, U. 1990. Grinding implements from the Neolithic and recent times in desert areas in Egypt and Sudan. *Beitrage zur Allgemeinen und Vergleichenden Archäologie*, 9–10: 359–79, pls. 96–97.

Schweinfurth, G. 1883. De la flore pharaonique. *BIE*, Deuxième serie 3: 51–76.

Schweizer, T.F. and Würsch, P. 1991. The physiological and nutritional importance of dietary fibre. *Experientia*, 47/2: 181–6.

Seibel, W. and Brümmer, J.-M. 1991. The sourdough process for bread in Germany. *Cereal Foods World*, 36/3: 299–304.

Shewry, P.R., Kirkman, M.A., Burgess, S.R., Festenstein, G.N. and Miflin, B.J. 1982. A comparison of the protein and amino acid composition of old and recent barley grain. *New Phytologist*, 90: 455–66.

Shewry, P.R., Tatham, A.S., Barro, F., Barcelo, P. and Lazzeri, P. 1995. Biotechnology of breadmaking: unraveling and manipulating the multi-protein gluten complex. *Biotechnology*, 13: 1185–90.

Singh, T., Maninder, K. and Bains, G.S. 1983. Malting of *Triticum dicoccum* (Khapli) wheat: response to gibberellic acid and use in baking in India. *Journal of Food Science*, 48/4: 1135–8.

Sist, L. 1987. Food production. In *Egyptian Civilization: Daily Life* (ed. A.M. Donadoni Roveri). Milan: Electa, pp. 46–75.

Smith, N.J.D. 1986. Dental pathology in an ancient Egyptian population. In *Science in Egyptology* (ed. R. A. David). Manchester: Manchester University Press, pp. 43–8.

Spalinger, A. 1986. Baking during the reign of Seti I. *BIFAO*, 86: 307–52.

1988. Dates in ancient Egypt. *SAK*, 15: 255–76.

Spurr, M.S. 1986. *Arable Cultivation in Roman Italy c. 200 BC–c. AD 100*. Journal of Roman Studies Monographs 3. London: Society for the Promotion of Roman Studies.

Stear, C.A. 1990. *Handbook of Breadmaking Technology*. London: Elsevier Applied Science.

Steinkraus, K.H. 1983. Lactic acid fermentation in the production of foods from vegetables, cereals and legumes. *Antonie van Leeuwenhoek*, 49: 337–48.

Strouhal, E. 1992. *Life in Ancient Egypt*. Cambridge: CUP.

Struve, W.W. 1930. *Mathematischer Papyrus des Staatlich Museums der Schönen Künste in Moskau*. Quellen und Studien zur Geschichte der Mathematik Abteilung A: Quellen; Band 1. Berlin: Julius Springer.

Sugihara, T.F. 1985. Microbiology of breadmaking. In *Microbiology of Fermented Foods I*. (ed. B.J.B. Wood). London: Elsevier Applied Science, pp. 249–61.

Täckholm, V. and Drar, M. 1950. *Flora of Egypt. Volume 2. Angiospermae, Part Monocotyledones: Cyperaceae – Juncaceae*. Cairo: Fouad I University Press.

Täckholm, V., Täckholm, G. and Drar, M. 1941. *Flora of Eygpt. Volume 1. Pteridophyta, Gymnospermae and Angiospermae, Part Monocotyledones: Typhaceae – Gramineae*. Bulletin of the Faculty of Science 17. Cairo: Fouad I University.

van Dam, H.W. 1986. The biotechnology of baker's yeast: Old or new business? In *Chemistry and Physics of Baking. Materials, Processes, and Products* (ed. J.M.V. Blanshard, P.J. Frazier and T. Galliard). London: Royal Society of Chemistry, pp. 117–31.

Vandier, J. 1964. *Manuel d'archéologie égyptienne IV: Bas-reliefs et peintures. Scènes de la vie quotidienne*. Paris: A. et J. Picard.

de Vartavan, C. 1990. Contaminated plant-foods from the tomb of Tutankhamun: a new interpretive system. *JAS*, 17: 473–94.

de Vartavan, C. and Asensi Amorós, M.V. 1997. *Codex of Ancient Egyptian Plant Remains. Codex des restes végétaux de l'Égypte ancienne*. London: Triade Exploration.

Währen, M. 1960. Die Backvorrichtungen des Altertums im Orient. *Brot und Gebäck*, 5: 86–96.

1961. Typologie der altägyptischen Brote und Gebäck. *Brot und Gebäck*, 6: 1–17.

1963. *Brot und Gebäck im Leben und Glauben der alten Ägypter*. Bern: Schweizerischer Bäcker-Konditorenmeister-Verband.

Wallert, I. 1962. *Die Palmen im alten Ägypten*. Münchner Ägyptologische Studien 1. Berlin: Bruno Hessling.

Whymper, R. 1913a. The influence of age on the vitality and chemical composition of the wheat berry. *Knowledge*, 36/536 (new series 10/3): 85–90.

1913b. The influence of age on the vitality and chemical composition of the wheat berry. *Knowledge*, 36/537 (new series 10/4): 135–8.

Wiedemann, A. and Pörtner, B. 1906. *Aegyptische Grabreliefs aus der grossherzoglichen Altertümer-Sammlung zu Karlsruhe*. Strassburg: von Schlesier and Schweikhardt.

Wild, H. 1966. Brasserie et panification au tombeau de Ti. *BIFAO*, 64: 95–120, pls. 9–11.

Wilkinson, C.K. and Hill, M. 1983. *Egyptian Wall Paintings*. The MMA's Collection of Facsimiles. New York: MMA.

Wilson, H. 1988. *Egyptian Food and Drink*. Aylesbury: Shire Egyptology.

1989. Pot-baked bread in ancient Egypt. *DE*, 13: 89–100.

Winlock, H.E. 1932. *The Tomb of Queen Meryet-Amun at Thebes.* Publications of the MMA Egyptian Expedition 6. New York: MMA.

1955. *Models of Daily Life in Ancient Egypt from the Tomb of Meket-Re at Thebes.* The MMA Egyptian Expedition. Cambridge MA: Harvard University Press.

Winton, A.L. and Winton, K.B. 1932. *The Structure and Composition of Foods I: Cereals, Starch, Oil Seeds, Nuts, Oils, Forage Plants.* New York: John Wiley.

Wittmack, L. 1896. Altägyptisches Brot. *Sitzungs-Bericht der Gesellschaft naturforschender Freunde zu Berlin,* 1896/5: 70–5.

1905. Our present knowledge of ancient plants. *Transactions of the Academy of Science of St. Louis,* 15: 1–15.

Wood, B.J.B. 1994. Technology transfer and indigenous fermented foods. *Food Research International,* 27: 269–80.

Wood, B.J.B. and Hodge, M.M. 1985. Yeast-lactic acid bacteria interactions and their contribution to fermented foodstuffs. In *Microbiology of Fermented Foods I* (ed. B.J.B. Wood). London: Elsevier Applied Science, pp. 263–93.

Woolley, C.L. 1922. Excavations at Tell el-Amarna. *JEA,* 8: 48–82.

Wreszinski, W. 1923. *Atlas zur altægyptischen kulturgeschichte.* Leipzig: J.C. Hinrichs.

1926. Bäckerei. *ZÄS,* 61: 1–15.

1936. *Atlas zur altägyptischen Kulturgeschichte. Teil III. Gräber des Alten Reiches.* Leipzig: J. C. Hinrichs.

Zeven, A.C. and de Wet, J.M.J. 1982. *Dictionary of Cultivated Plants and their Regions of Diversity; Excluding Most Ornamentals, Forest Trees and Lower Plants.* 2nd edn. Wageningen: Centre for Agricultural Publishing and Documentation.

Zohary, D. and Hopf, M. 1993. *Domestication of Plants in the Old World: The Origin and Spread of Cultivated Plants in West Asia, Europe, and the Nile Valley,* 2nd edn. Oxford: Clarendon Press.

23. Viticulture and wine production

MARY ANNE MURRAY [VITICULTURE AND WINE PRODUCTION] WITH
NEIL BOULTON AND CARL HERON [CHEMICAL DETECTION OF WINE]

Introduction

The history of wine in Egypt is an ancient one. The earliest Egyptian evidence for the grape, thus far, are seeds from the Predynastic settlements of Tell Ibrahim Awad and Tell el-Fara'in (Buto) in the Nile Delta, traditionally the prime wine-making region of ancient Egypt (Thanheiser 1991, 1992; de Roller 1992; also Table 24.1). Earlier still (~3150 BC) are numerous grape seeds from forty-seven storage jars, evidently imported from Palestine, recovered from the Predynastic cemetery of Umm el-Qaʿab at Abydos (Dreyer 1992, 1993; McGovern *et al.* 1997; McGovern 1998). While the presence of the grape does not necessarily indicate the practice of wine production, it is likely that between the simple possession of the easily fermented main ingredient and the strong Egyptian sun, the experience of basic wine-making was quickly realised. Indeed, the earliest indications, thus far, for ancient Egyptian wine itself are from the very start of the historic period, the beginning of the First Dynasty (*c.* 3000 BC). The first appearance of the hieroglyph of what is commonly identified as a possible wine press occurs at this time (see Fig. 23.1; Petrie, 1923: 102, 135; Emery 1961: 208; also see James 1995: 198, 200; and Pressing, p. 588) and the ancient Egyptian term for wine (*irp*) is known from the Second Dynasty onwards (e.g. Petrie 1927a: nos. 393–400; Emery and Saad 1938: pl. 64; Saad 1957; Kaplony 1963–4: III, 238–9). Large quantities of storage jars, often assumed to contain wine (although usually uninscribed), excavated from the tombs of Early Dynastic kings and nobles also suggest an early appreciation for wine, as well as providing an indication of its importance in the funerary context (e.g. Emery 1961; 1962; Dreyer 1992, 1993; Poo 1995: 5; McGovern *et al.* 1997; McGovern 1998).

It is primarily the many funerary uses of wine, i.e., the presence of wine jars in tombs, the regular offerings to the spirit of the dead by their *ka* (or spirit) servant, the inclusion of wine in offering lists, and particularly, from the Fourth Dynasty onwards, the illustrations of wine production on the walls of Pharaonic tomb-chapels, which have helped to preserve the record of ancient Egyptian viniculture that we have today (Fig. 23.2; Harpur 1987: 81–2; James 1995: 205; see also Poo 1995). To date, the bulk of information for Pharaonic wine production comes from the artistic and linguistic records of the New Kingdom, particularly from Thebes, although convincing evidence also exists from the earlier periods and other regions.

Figure 23.1 First-Dynasty seal impressions, with wine press in top right hand corner.

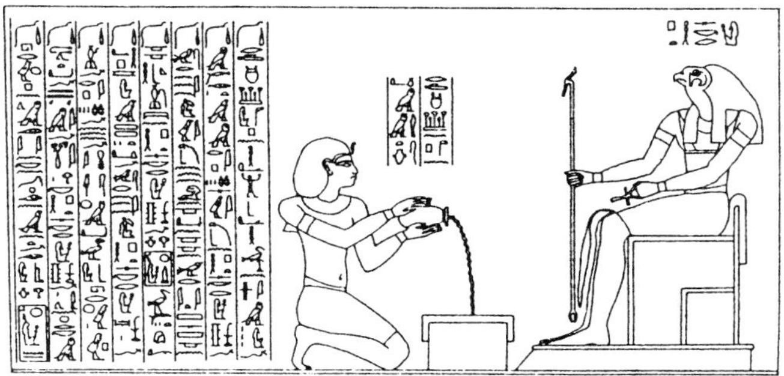

Figure 23.2 Wine offering liturgy at temple of Seti I, Abydos.

Where bread and beer were everyday commodities, wine, like meat, was not a staple although it may have been available, at least in small quantities at festivals and special occasions. Beer was brewed at the domestic level by most

Egyptians for daily use (see Chapter 22, this volume), whereas wine appears to have been largely produced for royalty, the upper classes and the funerary requirements of the élite (e.g. Poo 1995; Tallet 1998b). Wine was also considered to have divine qualities and was extensively used in religious rituals (e.g. Kitchen 1992; Poo 1995). The production of wine appears to have been more widespread by the New Kingdom than in earlier periods, and while its consumption still did not commonly extend to all levels of society, the textual record indicates that non-royal officials, and on special occasions, common people, also enjoyed wine (e.g. Jacquet-Gordon 1962; Lesko 1977, 1995; James 1995; Poo 1995; Tallet 1998b). However infrequently, the craftsmen of Deir el-Medina, for instance, were sometimes given bonuses of wine (Janssen 1975: 350–2) and a number of the wine jar labels were also recovered from the dumps associated with the Workmen's Village at Amarna (Leahy 1985) although it is unclear who in the hierarchy of the village would have consumed the wine.

The wine-making facilities themselves were primarily owned by the king or members of his family with little record, to date, of the private ownership of vineyards. Indeed, although wine-making scenes were frequently illustrated in private tombs, this was for the benefit of the deceased in the after-life and an involvement in this activity during the tomb owner's lifetime cannot be assumed (James 1995: 205). An exception may have been a Fourth-Dynasty official, Metjen, whose biographical details in his tomb at Saqqara (LS6) reveal that he was a landowner with a large vineyard (331 square metres) among his holdings (Sethe 1933: 4–5; Gödecken 1976; Lesko 1977: 11; Meeks 1993: 31; James 1995: 204). Poo (1995: 7, 15) notes that there are also several wine jars, from Malkata and Amarna, for example, which were labelled as coming from private vineyards and that it is possible that these vineyards may be under-represented in wine jar label assemblages since wines from royal premises were perhaps more likely to be labelled on a regular basis. Despite the aura of exclusivity surrounding wine in the Pharaonic period, the cultivation of grapes, along with the production, storage, trade, service and consumption of wine, would have touched a large proportion of the population to some degree (Lesko 1995: 230; McGovern *et al.* 1997: 8–9).

Various lines of investigation, including the artistic, textual and historical evidence for ancient Egyptian wine-making, converge to create a substantial picture of viticulture and wine production during the Pharaonic period. Many of the problems and possibilities associated with the basic lines of inquiry pertinent to the subject have been outlined in Chapter 21, in relation to the production and processing of cereals and the comments on the relative strengths and weaknesses of the evidence made there may be taken as a general guideline for this investigation as well.

The most accessible and, in many ways, the most informative, evidence on Egyptian wine-making is the substantial artistic record from private tomb-chapels which depict the many details of Pharaonic wine production. Twelve distinct elements can be distinguished from tomb-scenes although not all are found together in the same tomb nor in the same period, i.e. the Old, Middle and New Kingdoms (Lerstrup 1992: 65; see Table 23.1). According to Lerstrup (1992: 61), to date, wine-making scenes survive in twenty-nine tombs and one temple from the Old Kingdom, primarily from Giza and Saqqara, although several single tombs elsewhere also contain these scenes. Many of the illustrations are incomplete, but among the most informative are those from Saqqara, such as that of Niankhkhnum and Khnumhotep (Fifth Dynasty; Moussa and Altenmüller 1977) and Mereruka (Sixth Dynasty; Duell 1938). Lerstrup (1992: 61) notes that in the surviving record, there are eight Middle Kingdom tombs containing vintage scenes and all but two are from provincial tombs in Middle Egypt, including the Eleventh-Dynasty tombs of Bakt III (BH15) and Khety (BH17), and the early Twelfth-Dynasty tomb of Amenemhat (BH2) at Beni Hasan (see Newberry 1893). The comparatively sporadic artistic records from Old and Middle Kingdom tombs tend to be grouped together, although a coherent and convincing picture of wine production also emerges from each of these two periods (James 1995: 198).

For the New Kingdom, thus far, there are forty-two tombs in the Theban necropolis which illustrate the wine-making sequence (Lerstrup 1992: 61) and these not only provide a diverse record for Pharaonic wine production but also support the evidence from earlier periods (James 1995: 212). The highly stylised artistic record from the New Kingdom shows many elements of the wine-making process, including the grape harvest, the treading and pressing of the grapes, bottling, storage, serving, the consumption of wine, and even the results of excessive imbibing (Fig. 23.3; e.g. Lesko 1977, 1995). Major wine-making scenes from New Kingdom tombs include those from the Eighteenth-Dynasty tombs of Nakht (TT52; Davies 1917), Intef (TT155; Säve-Söderbergh 1957) and Khaemwaset (TT261). Lerstrup (1992: 61) notes that, thus far, only three Late Period tombs contain vintage scenes, as does a single tomb from the Greco-Roman period, that of Petosiris (Lefebvre 1923–4).

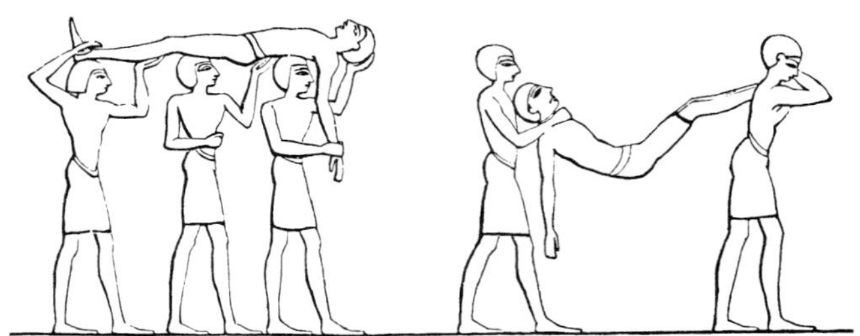

Figure 23.3 Scene showing the effects of excessive drinking, tomb of Senna at Thebes (TT169).

Obviously, additional tombs containing wine-making scenes may be uncovered at any time.

The artistic representations from tombs were never intended as a guide to a precise wine-making methodology and the frequent inattention to detail and lack of originality of many scenes, perhaps drawn without the artist ever actually witnessing the processes illustrated, casts doubt on their integrity as a realistic reflection of contemporary Pharaonic vineyards (e.g. James 1995: 205, 210). For example, it is apparent that processing scenes were often copied from tomb to tomb and while the purpose of each sequence may be clear, frequently its detail is not (James 1995: 205). Similarly, while certain major stages of the wine-making sequence are often shown consecutively, the more subtle intermediate stages may not be depicted at all, nor is there any indication of the time scale for or between each of these practices. Despite such shortcomings, these artistic representations not only illustrate the sequence and variation of the wine-making process throughout the Pharaonic period, but also show the importance that the ancient Egyptians placed on the production, religious significance and consumption of wine (Lesko 1995: 219).

The textual and lexicographic evidence from wine-jar sealings and labels, tomb texts and literary sources, add details to many wine related issues, such as its distribution, levies, and the location of vineyards, for example, which the artistic evidence does not. The Pyramid Texts in the Fifth-Dynasty pyramid of Unas (*c.* 2423 BC) at Saqqara, for instance, list five varieties of wine offered in remembrance of his name which then became standard features of later offering lists included within tombs and many interpretations have been suggested as to the exact nature of these wines (e.g. Meeks 1993; also see Barta 1963; Cheshire 1985; Meyer 1986: 6: col. 1172; Piankoff 1968: 66, 153–7; James 1995: 204; Poo 1995). From the New Kingdom, the textual evidence, for example, records such details as the offerings of wine by Rameses III to various temples, i.e. 22,566 jars of wine to temples at Thebes, 103,550 jars to the Heliopolitan temples, and 25,978 jars to the Memphite temples (e.g. Breasted 1906: 172).

Lexicographic data from wine-jar sealings and labels also provide a great variety of information. While seal impressions from Old Kingdom wine jars indicate that wine-making was well-established at that time, more detailed wine seals and labels, particularly those from the Eighteenth Dynasty onwards, e.g. from Malkata, Amarna, Deir el-Medina, the tomb of Tutankhamun (KV62), and the Ramesseum, identify much useful information, such as the date of the wine, the name of the wine maker and estate responsible for the wine, the location of the vineyard, and sometimes the quality of the wine therein, i.e. 'good', 'very good' or 'very, very good'. From these labels, it is clear that in antiquity the Egyptian wine-making regions were primarily in the Nile Delta and the chain of oases in the Western Desert. The known wines of ancient Egypt and their regions of origin is a vast subject in its own right and while it will be discussed briefly in the section on 'labelling', for further information see e.g. Speigelberg 1923; Gauthier 1927; Gardiner 1947; Hayes 1951; Cerny 1965; Darby *et al.* 1977: 597–607; Lesko 1977; 1995; Kitchen 1979: 673–96; 1992; Koenig 1980; Leahy 1978, 1985; Meeks 1993; Poo 1995; Tallet 1995, 1996, 1998a, 1998b.

Despite the curious denial of the existence of viticulture in Egypt by Herodotus (II, 77) (although he was writing during the Persian period and this may have been truer for that time) and a statement by Plutarch (I,353, 6, quoted in Darby *et al.* 1977: 553) that the Egyptians neither drank wine nor used it for libations prior to the time of the Twenty-sixth-Dynasty ruler Psamtek I (*c.* 664 BC), sources from the Greco–Roman period abound with references to Egyptian wines. Although wine and wine-making may have been rather different under the influences of the Classical period, these sources may provide many insightful details of native Egyptian practices during Pharaonic times. In general, Classical authors commented favourably on Egyptian wines. Several papyri from Greco–Roman period vineyard estates have also survived and describe the cultivation of grapes and other wine related matters (e.g. Rostovzeff 1922; Rathbone 1991).

The archaeological record provides a variety of relevant evidence, including wine jars and the important information inscribed on their seals and labels, as well as traces of the vineyards themselves, and the installations possibly associated with wine production (e.g. el-Fakharani 1983; Empereur 1993; Bietak 1985, 1986, 1996). While labelled storage jars provide an indication of contents, archaeological finds of uninscribed storage jars, particularly in large numbers, are sometimes assumed to have contained wine (e.g. Emery 1961). This often may have been the case, however, jar labels indicate that these vessels were also used to hold beer, meat, fat, honey, oil and a range of other commodities (e.g. Hayes 1951: 37). A number of sealed wine jars have been found (e.g. Emery 1962; Lesko 1977, 1995), although their contents have long since evaporated and in recent years, there has been an increase in the chemical analyses of the residues that these wines have left behind. Current research using the apparent presence of tartaric acid as a principal indicator of wine in ancient residues has been used at several sites throughout the Near East, including Egypt (e.g. McGovern and Michel 1995; McGovern *et al.* 1997; McGovern 1998; for other analyses see, e.g., Lucas 1962: 22; Badler *et al.* 1990, 1996; Biers and McGovern 1990; Heron and Pollard 1988; Heron and Evershed 1993; Formenti and Duthel 1995; Pollard and Heron 1996; see section on chemical detection of ancient wine, p. 599, this volume). It is important to note that for those storage jars without inscriptions; chemical analysis to determine contents; or the potential technique of correlating pottery shape and fabric with jar contents; (e.g. Serpico 1996; Serpico and White forthcoming; Serpico forthcoming; Chapter 18, this volume), the presence of stored wine cannot be assumed.

The archaeobotanical record of the grape from a range of thirty ancient Egyptian sites, dating from the Predynastic to the Islamic period, can be found in Table 24.1. While the remains of grapes clearly show the ancient history of the vine in Egypt (wood and pollen analysis may also indicate the presence of the vine), are we able to recognise the botanical residues of ancient wine-making in the archaeological record? The question is an important one and a variety of archaeobotanists and others have tried to determine its answer (e.g. Miller 1986, Marinval 1988; Rivera Núñez and Walker 1989; Sarpaki 1992; Palmer 1994; Buxo 1996; Zettler and Miller 1995; Mangafa and Kotsakis 1996; Murray 1998). Grape seeds found in storage jars are sometimes cited as evidence for the presence of wine, however, this would greatly depend on factors of deposition and the archaeological context. Other possibilities also must be considered, such as the storage of raisins. Palmer (1994: 18) has suggested that the lack of grape remains in storage vessels may provide a stronger argument for the presence of wine since even the simplest filtering methods would remove seeds, stems and skins. Indeed, an archaeobotanical assemblage including grape seeds, stalks and skins may be more likely to represent the residues of wine pressing. In areas of the Mediterranean, these residues are subsequently used as animal fodder or as fuel (e.g. Buxo 1996: 404) and therefore may be preserved by charring (see Chapter 21, for methods of plant preservation).

The ethnographic analysis of traditional Egyptian practices related to wine would undoubtedly add something to our understanding not only of the residues from wine-making at its various stages but also of other details relating to the many components of its production. Elements of wine-making practices similar to those described for ancient Egypt were observed in the Fayum in the seventeenth century AD (Vansleb 1678: 154–5), for instance, as well as in the early nineteenth century (Girard 1812: 608). An important link between the artistic, archaeological and ethnographic evidence would be the data retrieved from the experimental reconstruction of one or more of the various stages of ancient Egyptian wine-making. As yet, there has been no systematic experimental research related to the production of ancient Egyptian wines as there has been for beer (see Chapter 22) yet experimental evidence, together with the other lines of inquiry outlined above, may be the way forward, not only to appreciate the minutiae of the practice but to provide insight into many of the unresolved issues related to ancient Egyptian wine production.

This chapter is a brief overview of the process of wine production, from a description of the grape as the raw material to its cultivation, harvest and eventual storage as wine. For information on the post-storage stages of wine, such as its consumption, distribution, trade, taxation, association with religion, festivals, attitudes to wine drinking and other related subjects (see e.g. Lutz 1922; Montet 1925; Hayes 1951; Lucas 1962; Darby *et al.* 1977; Lesko 1977, 1995; Manniche 1989; Lerstrup 1992; Meeks 1993; Leonard 1995; Poo 1995; James 1995; Tallet 1995, 1996, 1998a, 1998b). The following discussion will follow the natural order of the production stages although this sequence is not always strictly followed in ancient Egyptian tomb scenes (e.g. Lerstrup 1992: 65).

Viticulture

*The grape (*Vitis vinifera*) [Vitaceae – Grape Family]*

The grape vine is a perennial woody climber with branched coiled tendrils arising opposite the lobed leaves and small densely clustered green flowers. The fruit is a fleshy, ovoid berry, 0.8–4 centimetres or more in length and up to 2.5 centimetres wide, which ranges in colour from dark purple to red, yellow or green and varies in taste, from sour to sweet, when ripe (Meikle 1977: 361; Polunin and Huxley 1987: 123; Zohary and Hopf 1994: 147, Olmo 1995b: 485). The cultivated grape vine contains both male and female flowers which precludes the need to supply male plants or to resort to artificial pollination, as is necessary with date and fig cultivation (Zohary 1995: 26). Grapes consist of 70–80 per cent water when fully ripe and this, together with sugar, acids and pectins, makes up most of the grape pulp. The primary sugars of the grape are glucose and fructose and these provide the basis for the alcohol content in the wine. Tartaric and malic acids are the principal acids of the fruit although others are also present (Unwin 1996: 34, 36) and it is tartaric acid which has been most commonly used thus far to indicate the presence of wine in ancient residues (e.g. McGovern and Michel 1995; McGovern *et al.* 1997, also see Chemical detection of wine, p. 599). Grapes are a commercial source for tartaric acid today (e.g. 'Cream of Tartar', used in baking, for example, is made from the tartaric acid crystals which form during fermentation) (Olmo 1995b: 485). The tannins in the grape are found primarily in the skins, stalks and seeds and affect the flavour, colour and body of the wine, i.e. excess tannins, from stalks and seeds crushed during pressing, will add a bitterness to the wine. The natural yeasts and bacteria that cause crushed grapes to ferment so easily are found on the skin of the grape (Unwin 1996: 36, 47; also see Chemical detection of wine, p. 599).

Apart from their use in wine-making, grapes can be eaten as fresh fruit, dried as raisins, or pressed for juice, which can be consumed fresh or also fermented into vinegar. Throughout history, the storability of wine and raisins have made the grape an important food source throughout the year (Singleton 1995: 73). Grapes can be dried into raisins by spreading them out in the sun, or alternatively – as in Spain, for example, high quality raisins can be made by cutting back the leaves and stalks to expose the grapes to the maximum amount of sunlight, thereby drying the grapes on the vine (Harrison *et al.* 1985: 90). The desiccated archaeobotanical evidence of grapes left as offerings in tombs, however, makes it unclear as to whether these had been placed in the tomb as fresh grapes or as dried raisins (e.g. Lauer *et al.* 1950: 133; Germer 1989; de Vartatvan 1990; Hepper 1990). In Pharaonic Egypt, raisins were also used medicinally as an ingredient in remedies for bladder disorders, 'a swollen belly' and other ailments (see Darby *et al.* 1977: 715–16, 577–9 and Manniche 1989: 81; Nunn 1996: 14). Wine, too, was an important medium for the consumption of medicines, although it was also taken on its own or applied externally (von Deines and Grapow 1957: 47–50; Darby *et al.* 1977: 577–9; Manniche 1989: 156; Nunn 1996: 14, 140). Wine was not only known to be an effective antiseptic in antiquity but was also considered to be nutritionally beneficial (see Gastineau *et al.* 1979 for nutritional benefits of wine). Hippocrates (*c.* 460–370 BC), for example, prescribed wine for this reason, as well as for the dressing of wounds, to quell fevers, as a purgative and a diuretic (Lucia 1963: 36).

History

The substantial finds of wild grapes from early Near Eastern sites clearly indicates their importance prior to domestication (Rivera Núñez and Walker 1989; Zohary and Hopf 1994: 143; Zohary 1995: 28). Although wild grapes are generally smaller and more sour than cultivated grapes, they are nevertheless suitable for wine-making (Zohary and Hopf 1994: 144; Olmo 1995b: 486; Singleton 1995: 72). The seed morphologies of wild and domesticated grape varieties (var. *sylvestris* and var. *vinifera*, respectively) overlap significantly, particularly if the seeds are preserved by charring. A number of criteria for distinguishing between wild and domesticated grapes have been discussed (e.g. Stummer 1911; Kislev 1988: 236–8; Rivera Núñez and Walker 1989; Smith and Jones 1990: 326; Sarpaki 1992: 70; Mangafa and Kotsakis 1996). The variability of grape seeds can be influenced by the state of maturation when harvested, the number of seeds per grape and other differences between grape varieties. Rivera Núñez and Walker (1989: 206) maintain that this variability may have more to do with local gene populations than with the selection of taxa for cultivation and note, for example, that the seeds of the famous domesticated Pinot Noir grape can have identical dimensions to wild grapes from Yugoslavia. The earliest archaeobotanical indications of grape cultivation come from archaeological sites which are outside the natural range of the wild grape, i.e. Jordan and Israel, in the Chalcolithic period (*c.* 3700–3200 BC) and the Early Bronze Age (*c.* 3200–1900 BC) (see Zohary and Hopf 1994: 149; Zohary 1995: 28). As the number of archaeobotanical finds of grape increase throughout the Bronze Age, so do artefacts related to wine production, such as wine presses, wine jars, wine labels, and artistic representations of both grapes and wine-making (e.g. Zohary 1995: 28; Powell 1995). Archaeobotanical finds of grape in Egypt are most likely to be of the domesticated variety, since Egypt lies outside the natural range of the wild grape, both in the present and most probably also in ancient times (Germer 1985: 116; Baum 1988; Zohary and Hopf 1994: 149).

The grape vine was among the first fruits associated with the beginnings of Old World horticulture, along with the date palm, fig and olive (Zohary and Spiegel-Roy 1975; Stager 1985; van Zeist 1991; Zohary and Hopf 1994; Chapter 24, this volume). The cultivated grape (*Vitis vinifera*) has a close genetic and morphological affinity with the entire wild and feral *Vitis* complex found in Western Asia and Europe. Wild forms of grape were once considered a separate species, (*V. sylvestris* C.C. Gmelin) but are now recognised by most botanists as the wild progenitor of the cultivar and are collectively known today as *Vitis vinifera* var. *sylvestris* (C.C. Gmelin) Berger (Meikle 1977: 361; Rivera Núñez and Walker 1989: 206–7; Zohary and Hopf 1994: 144; Zohary 1995: 24; Olmo 1995a: 32). As with the fig, the distinction between the wild and cultivated forms is obscured by a continuum of weedy forms, i.e. those propagated by seed, hybrid derivatives and feral escapees (Zohary and Hopf 1994: 144, 148; Zohary 1995: 25; Olmo 1995a: 32). Indeed many of these highly variable grape populations could be considered more as ecospecies than true biological types in their own right (Olmo 1995b: 486). Members of this wild grape complex are found from the Atlantic to the western Himalayas and appear to be native in the areas south of the Caspian Sea, southern Europe, the Near East and Africa (Zohary and Hopf 1994: 144). The region of Transcaucasia, e.g. Georgia and Armenia, is often considered to be where grapes were first cultivated (e.g. Vavilov 1951: 159–60; Levadoux 1956: 80; Olmo 1995a, 1995b). Although the area of the earliest grape domestication is not yet agreed upon (Meikle 1977: 361; Rivera Núñez and Walker 1989; Zohary and Hopf 1994; Olmo 1995a, 1995b; Unwin 1996) it seems most likely that the domesticated grape was introduced into Egypt from the Levant at least as early as the Predynastic period (Zohary and Spiegel-Roy 1975; Stager 1985; van Zeist 1991; Zohary and Hopf 1994: 143, 150). A large Predynastic assemblage of storage jars from Abydos (*c.* 3150 BC), reportedly containing the remains of wine from Palestine, suggest the early connection with the Levant (Dreyer 1993; McGovern *et al.* 1997).

As with other fruits, such as the date palm, fig and olive, the domestication of the grape signalled a change from sexual reproduction by seed, which bears unpredictably variable progeny, to the vegetative propagation of cuttings which are identical clones of the parent plant (Zohary and Hopf 1994: 143; Unwin 1996: 33; Chapter 24, this volume). With this method, desirable qualities, such as prolific fruit production, good flavour, high juice content, and berry colour, could be selected for and maintained, i.e. vineyards could be planted with genetically identical clones of the most favourable grape vines (Zohary and Hopf 1994: 143; Zohary 1995: 26; Unwin 1996: 33). For example, in wild grapes, red is the genetically dominant colour until an 'albino' or white mutation arises. The white variety must then be selected and maintained by the propagation of cuttings from the parent vine (Singleton 1995: 74). Traditional Old World viticulture was based on thousands of different clones. These varied widely in their habit, their requirements for soil type, climate and care, as well as in their shape, size, colour and sweetness of their fruits, thereby creating the widely variable quality of both table grapes and wine that we have today (Zohary and Hopf 1994: 143; Olmo 1976, 1995a: 40; also see Olmo 1995a: 39 for negative effects of clonal propagation). It has been estimated that there are presently as many as 10,000 genetically distinct grape cultivars in the world (Olmo 1995a: 40), and each member of a given population of cultivated clones may be genetically different from one another. The Pinot Noir grape, for example, is likely to be made up of a population of several hundred clones (Olmo 1995a: 40). By using DNA analysis, together with indicated rates of mutation, it may be possible to calculate the number of clones and seedling generations necessary to produce some of the older wine varieties, such as Cabernet Sauvignon, which is believed to have originated in Roman times (Singleton 1995: 74; also see Olmo 1995a: 41).

The archaeobotanical evidence for the grape vine in Egypt includes both charred and desiccated whole fruits or fruit fragments, grape seeds, stems (or peduncles), leaves and wood. As noted above, the earliest finds of grape seeds in Egypt, thus far, are from the Predynastic settlements of Tell Ibrahim Awad and Tell el-Faraʿin (Buto) in the Nile Delta (Thanheiser 1991, 1992; de Roller 1992; also Fig. 24.2) and also from Tomb U-j at Umm el-Qaʿab at Abydos (Dreyer 1993; McGovern *et al*. 1997). The many grape seeds from the latter site are the earliest from Egypt to date (3150 BC) although they were found within storage jars imported from Palestine which also reportedly showed traces of tartaric acid and therefore are believed to have contained wine (McGovern *et al.* 1997: 10). Other finds of grape remains include those from the First-Dynasty graves at Abydos and Nagada, from the Third-Dynasty Step Pyramid of Djoser at Saqqara (Täckholm 1961: 26, Lauer *et al.* 1950: 133; Germer 1985: 117), from Twelfth-Dynasty Kahun (Newberry 1890; Germer forthcoming), from Thirteenth-Dynasty Memphis (Murray forthcoming); and from Second Intermediate Period Tell el-Dabʿa (Thanheiser 1987; forthcoming). Several Eighteenth-Dynasty sites also have grape remains: these include Amarna (Renfrew 1985); Deir el-Medina (Bruyére 1939); Memphis (Murray forthcoming) and the tomb of Tutankhamun (Germer 1989; de Vartavan 1990; Hepper 1990). For post-Pharaonic finds of grape, see Table 24.1.

Vine cultivation

Under ideal conditions, the average yearly temperature for viticulture is approximately 15 °C, with a summer maximum of 22 °C and a winter minimum of 3 °C. High temperatures during the summer are necessary to encourage the setting of the fruit and ripening, while the cool temperatures allow the vine to lie dormant during the winter months (Unwin 1996: 42). The grape vine has a distinct annual cycle. During the winter dormancy, the sugar levels in the plant help to protect it against the frost and from temperatures as low as −18 °C for short periods. The vine remains dormant until the average daily temperature reaches about 10 °C. As the temperatures increase during the spring, the shoots of the vine grow rapidly for about eight weeks. Episodes of frosts in the spring are more damaging as temperatures of −4 °C can kill young leaves and −2 °C can damage the flower clusters. The clusters of flowers bloom about this time, usually when the average daily temperatures reach about 20 °C. After pollination and the fertilisation of the flowers, the fruit sets and the berries grow quickly at first and then more slowly until they reach the stage of ripening. Prior to full ripening, the rate of berry growth increases again, as does its sugar content, while its acidity decreases along with its chlorophyll, thereby fading the initial green colour and making the final colour of the grapes more evident (Unwin 1996: 33–4, 36). It is generally accepted that grapes are usually fully ripened and are ready for harvest about 100 days after flowering (Johnson 1974: 30; Unwin 1996: 34). This figure can vary, however, depending on the variety of vine grown, the number of days with average temperatures above 10 °C and the desired balance between the levels of sugar and acidity required for each type of wine (Unwin 1996: 34). The care and conditions during those 100 days can make the difference between a bad or good wine, and a good or great wine (Johnson 1974: 30; Palmer 1994: 15).

The variable quality of grapes and wine sometimes depends on climatic conditions, i.e. grapes grown in hot sunny climates generally ripen quickly and have a high sugar content with low acidity, whereas those grown in cooler environments tend to have higher levels of acidity, a richer colour and less sugar. Wines from hotter climates therefore tend to have a higher alcohol content, while those from cooler climates are usually fresher, more acidic wines (Unwin 1996: 43). The regions best suited for viticulture generally lie in the warm temperate zone between latitudes 50° and 30° North and South (Unwin 1996: 34). Egypt, with its hot and arid climate, lies outside this area, between latitudes 31° and 22° North and South (Baines and Málek 1984: 13) . Grapes are grown primarily in areas of the world which have an annual precipitation of between 400 and 800 millimetres (Unwin 1996: 43). On average, the annual rainfall in Egypt is about ten millimetres, and much of this falls along the Mediterranean coastal strip (Zahran and

Willis 1992: 308). For the large-scale cultivation of grapes in ancient Egypt, the irrigation of the vines would have been an important consideration of vineyard design.

Viticulture is frequently depicted in ancient Egyptian tombs (see Baum 1988: 137–40 for listings) and certain information on the tending of the vines and the vineyards themselves can be gleaned from this evidence. Vineyards were evidently thought of in terms closer to gardens and orchards than as purely agricultural lands. The ancient Egyptian term for vineyard (*k3mw/k3nw*), for example, is the same as that used for orchard or garden and the grape vine is illustrated in the same context as fruit trees and vegetable patches, and not in scenes depicting the production and processing of cereals and flax (Moens 1984; Baum 1988; Lerstrup 1992: 63; also see Abd er-Raziq 1979, 1988). Grape vines were an important element of formal gardens, and also were grown around ornamental pools (see Fig. 23.4; and see also Lutz 1922: 47; Lesko 1977: 15; Baum 1988; Hugonot 1989; Eyre 1994). Vineyards were evidently surrounded by walls which also tends to place them into the category of gardens and orchards (e.g. Abd er-Raziq 1979; Baum 1988; Lerstrup 1992: 63; Meeks 1993: 19). Among the evidence cited by Lerstrup (1992: 63–4) to demonstrate that vineyards were walled areas is the use of the determinative [⊏⊐] in the word for vineyard (*k3mw*) on New Kingdom wine jar labels. The Twentieth-Dynasty Papyrus Harris (I, 8.5 in Lerstrup 1992: 64) also provides some textual evidence for the practice: 'I made for you [name of a Delta vineyard] . . . surrounded with a wall all the way around'. Textual records also suggest that the Fourth-Dynasty private vineyard of Metjen at Saqqara (LS6), was probably surrounded by a wall (Gödecken 1976: 25). Archaeological excavations at Amarna and Qantir/Tell el-Dabʿa (dating to the Eighteenth and Nineteenth Dynasties respectively) have also uncovered walls connected with probable vineyards (Traunecker 1984; Bietak 1985). The watering of the vines by hand, as it is depicted in the artistic record, such as in the Eighteenth-Dynasty tomb-chapel of Khaemwaset (TT 261), also suggests a garden or orchard setting (Lerstrup 1992: 63) (see Table 23.1).

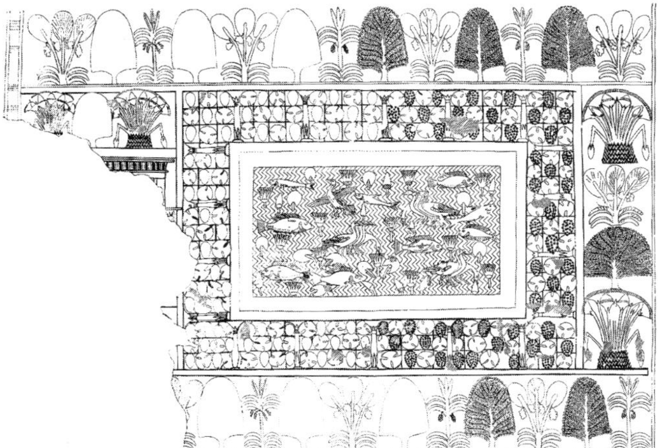

Figure 23.4 Scene from the Eighteenth-Dynasty tomb of Kenamun (TT93), showing a vineyard around a pool.

Table 23.1. *Elements of wine-making shown in tomb scenes (after Lerstrup 1992: 65).*

Element	Old Kingdom	Middle Kingdom	New Kingdom	Late Period
Tending the vine	2	—	5	—
Grape harvest	20	7	36	3
Transporting grapes	9	—	9	—
Treading vat	18	4	27	3
Beating the work rhythm	5	—	(5)	—
Sack press	17	6	4	2
Filling jars	14	4	17	2
Sealing jars	5	—	4	2
Jar registration	2	20	50	2
Fermentation	—	—	2	—
Transporting wine jars	1	—	3	—
Offering to Renenutet	—	—	14	—

NB – This is based on the limited and fragmentary archaeological evidence to date (Lerstrup 1992: 65).

The artistic record, particularly from the Old Kingdom, suggests that grape vines were grown on artificially raised areas, surrounded by earth or a small wall, or even grown in containers, as is indicated by the form of the hieroglyph used to determine the words for vine and grapes (Lutz 1922: 46–7; James 1995: 205). While growing vines in a small container would have helped to retain moisture, the practice would have ultimately cramped the roots of the vine which can spread and descend up to a depth of four to fifteen metres. While a deep root system is advantageous to the search for moisture, it is detrimental in areas with a high water table since it limits the aeration of the roots (Unwin 1996: 33). The structure of the soil can be more important to successful viticulture than its fertility or chemical composition, i.e. well-drained loams and gravels tend to be more suitable for vines than clays and silts (Unwin 1996: 44). It was no accident that the Nile Delta and the oases were the prime areas of ancient Egyptian viticulture since much of this land lay beyond the reach of the annual inundation with its deposition of fertile Nile silt, as highly fertile soil tends to produce a high yield of poor quality fruits. Some of the best European and Mediterranean vineyards, for example, are on lands considered unsuitable for other crops (Unwin 1996: 44; Sarpaki 1992: 70; Hanson 1992: 163; also Rostovtzeff 1922: 138 for Ptolemaic Egypt).

As the grape vine is a trailing or climbing plant, it is sometimes allowed to grow along the ground but is most commonly supported by training it over some type of trellis or arbour, and sometimes over trees (e.g. Foaden and Fletcher 1910: 589; Lutz 1922: 49–50; Darby *et al.* 1977: 556; Palmer 1994: 14; Unwin 1996: 33). Seals from the reign of the Second-Dynasty king Khasekhemwy indicate that grape vines were trailed over poles to create an arbour, a basic feature repeated in tomb scenes throughout the Pharaonic period (James 1995: 201). The artistic record shows five main ways of training vines over trellises through time (see Fig. 23.5). Lerstrup (1992: 62) points out that the differences in tomb scenes may either reflect a true progression of vine-trailing techniques or may be simply due to artistic conventions (also see Altenmüller 1982: 12–14). The latter possibility may explain scenes from the Fifth-Dynasty tomb of Niankhkhnum and Khnumhotep and that of Neferherenptah, for example, where the vineyard is illustrated twice and the vine is trellised differently in both cases (Lerstrup 1992: 62). Textual evidence provides other suggestions of vine trailing techniques. A statement in the Papyrus Harris (I, 8.5 in Erichsen: 10), for example, has led to speculation that grape vines might have been planted between olive trees with the vines trailed over the trees (Meyer 1986: 1173; Bietak 1985: 278; Abd er-Raziq 1979: 241). Lutz (1922: 50) also suggested that vines might have been trained over papyrus reeds. Early Ptolemaic period papyri mention the use of reed props on vineyards in the Fayum (Rostovtzeff 1922: 160), as do Roman texts related to a Fayum vineyard where these were collected from reed beds associated with the estate which were then constructed into trellises for the grape vines in January and February (Rathbone 1991: 248–250). A statement by Pliny (XVII, XXV, 185 quoted in Darby *et al.* 1977: 556) suggests that, at least in the Roman period, Egyptian vines were sometimes left trailing without support: 'the greater part of the world lets its vintage grapes lie on the ground inasmuch as this custom prevails both in Africa and in Egypt and in Syria'.

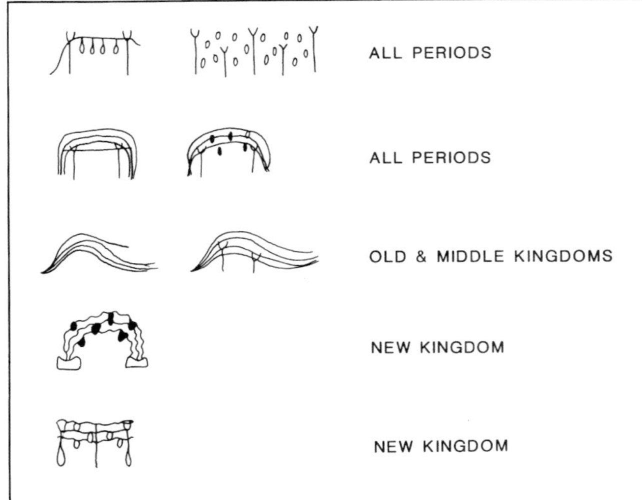

Figure 23.5 Grape trellis types.

Training vines on a trellis allows for maximum exposure to air and light and for a greater ease of not only the harvest but also the many jobs associated with viticulture, such as pruning, trenching, fertilising, weeding and irrigation (Palmer 1994: 14; Unwin 1996: 33). The methods used to train the vines also have an effect on the quality and quantity of grapes produced and are sometimes dependant on environmental conditions, i.e. if frost is a threat then grapes are often trained high, whereas vines can be trained low if the heat from the soil is required to help ripen the grapes (Unwin 1996: 33). Old Kingdom tomb scenes, such as those in the tomb of Ptahhotep (Davies 1900: pl. 21), show workers harvesting grapes by kneeling beneath the arbours suggesting that these were less than a few feet high (Fig. 23.6) (James 1995: 205). New Kingdom tomb scenes, particularly from Thebes, sometimes show an elaborate arrangement of trellises strengthened by rafters supported on painted and carved columns. These columns were far enough apart to form wide rows which facilitated work and communication but were narrow enough not to allow too much sunlight to evaporate moisture from the ground (Wilkinson 1878: 379; Lutz 1922: 49). Earlier this century in Egypt, the grape vine was generally trained over latticework trellises three to three and a half metres high, while allowing the vines to trail along the ground was rarely practised at that time (Foaden and Fletcher 1910: 586).

As with all aspects of agricultural production, the success of viticulture and the decisions related to it greatly depend on the location of the vineyard and the level of care, soil type, root stock, weather, and skill involved. Tending the vines can be a labour-intensive job, particular during the winter months. Grape vine cuttings are usually planted in February and March (Foaden and Fletcher 1910: 588; Ward 1993: 252, Olmo 1995b: 485). Prior to the demise of traditional flood basin irrigation in Egypt earlier this century, grapes were grown primarily around Alexandria and in the Fayum, where, in addition to the February/March planting, cuttings were reportedly also planted after the rise of the Nile, in August, although with less success (Foaden and Fletcher 1910: 588). Good cuttings are usually about a half a metre long and do best if planted at a slanting angle to encourage the growth of as many roots as possible and deep enough so that only two buds or eyes are left above the ground (Foaden and Fletcher 1910: 588). After two or three years, plants from cuttings or layering are usually transplanted in February while the vine is still dormant (Foaden and Fletcher 1910: 589). The quick growth and maturation of the species means that they will generally start to bear fruit about three years after planting (Wright 1938: 194; Zohary and Hopf 1994: 143; Singleton 1995: 73; see Hanson 1992; Amouretti 1992 for details on vine cultivation).

Figure 23.6 Wine-making scene in the Fifth-Dynasty tomb of Ptahhotep at Saqqara.

The important task of pruning the grape vine is to keep them manageable and to encourage the growth of new fruit bearing shoots rather than allowing the plant to put energy into its leaves or woody stem. This job takes place during the winter, usually in January to February, while the vine is in a dormant state (Foaden and Fletcher 1910: 589; Rathbone 1991: 251; Ward 1993: 251, Zohary and Hopf 1994: 143; Palmer 1994: 15; Olmo 1995b: 485; Unwin 1996: 33). Vines trained over latticework are best pruned back to two buds while those trailing on the ground should be pruned to resemble a bush (Foaden and Fletcher 1910: 589). Another important winter task is trenching or digging to deepen and enrich the soil around the roots of each vine by improving its contact with light, air, moisture and fertiliser. Roman texts concerning viticulture in the Fayum indicate that along with animal dung, rich silts were taken from the canals to be used as fertiliser for those vines growing under artificial irrigation (Rathbone 1991: 251–2). Earlier this century in Egypt, it was good practice to apply well-decomposed farmyard manure around the vines at least every second year (Foaden and Fletcher 1910: 589). Both pruning and trenching are essential to sustain prolific fruit production which is also improved by weeding, leaf thinning, fertilising and replacing old vines (Foaden and Fletcher 1910: 589; Wright 1938: 194–5; Hanson 1992; Palmer 1994: 15). A papyrus dated to 280 AD speaks of the many tasks associated with the tending of the vines, 'concerning the vineyard . . . layering as many vine shoots as are necessary, digging, scooping hollows round the vines and trenching . . . keeping the vines well tended, giving space to the growths, cutting back, needful thinning of foliage', (S.P., I, 18 in Darby *et al.* 1977: 713).

Wine production

Grape harvesting

The grape harvest is among the most commonly illustrated elements of vintage depicted in Pharaonic tomb scenes (Table 23.1). The exact timing of the harvest would have varied annually but would have usually occurred during the late summer months, for example, texts show that in Greco–Roman Egypt, this was usually during the month of August (Hepper 1990: 68; Rathbone 1991: 250; Unwin 1996: 187). This would have been after the cereal harvest and, as with that task, all available hands were probably used to complete it (Lutz 1922: 51). However, the harvesters in tomb scenes are primarily men, women or children being seldom depicted (see Lerstrup 1992: 66 for further details). As in tomb-scenes illustrating cereal fields, the important intermediate step of scaring away birds prior to the harvest is often in progress near to the vineyard but only once is this shown within the vineyard itself (Lerstrup 1992: 66). If the vines have been well cared for, i.e. the bunches properly thinned, then unlike figs or olives, grapes tend to ripen all about the same time (Wright 1938: 195; Palmer 1994: 15). As noted above, the grapes were harvested by workers standing or kneeling beneath vines trained over trellises (e.g. Figs. 23.6 and 23.7; James 1995: 205; Strudwick 1987). Tomb-scenes also suggest that grapes were harvested by hand without the use of a knife to cut them down (Lesko 1977: 17; Lerstrup 1992: 67; James 1995: 206).

The harvested grapes were placed into baskets which were then carried to the treading vat on the shoulder, head, or by means of a shoulder yoke. The same types of baskets appear to have been used for both the harvest and the transport of grapes (Lerstrup 1992: 67). Tomb scenes show groups of men walking in line with their baskets and the associated caption in the tomb of Ty at Saqqara (No. 60 [D22]), for example, reads 'the bringing of the grapes for pressing' (Lutz 1922: 51–2). Baskets of grapes are also shown covered with palm leaves or vines, presumably to protect them from the sun (Wilkinson 1978: 382; Lutz 1922: 52).

Figure 23.7 Grape harvest and treading scene in the Theban tomb-chapel of Nakht (TT52).

The end of the grape harvest is depicted in a Sixth-Dynasty tomb (No. 14 in Zawiyet el-Meitin) where the trellised vines have been stripped of their fruits and foliage by harvesters with filled baskets (Lutz 1922: 52). Other scenes allegedly show goats foraging on the vines after the harvest, as in the Twelfth-Dynasty tomb of Amenemhat at Beni Hasan (BH2; Newberry 1893). It seems doubtful, however, that livestock would be deliberately allowed to graze on viable grape vines (e.g. Rathbone 1991: 251; Olmo 1995a: 37; Singleton 1995: 73). It has also been noted that the bushes on which the goats are grazing in tomb scenes may not represent vines (Baum 1988; Lerstrup 1992: 66).

Treading

The treading of the grapes is also a commonly illustrated element in Pharaonic tomb scenes (Table 23.1; see Lerstrup 1992: 67). The harvested grapes were carried from the vineyard in baskets which were emptied directly into a large vat used to tread the juice from the grapes (see Duell 1938: 2: pl. 116). Throughout the Mediterranean and Near East, the traditional method used to crush grapes is to tread them underfoot (Lucas 1962: 17; Unwin 1996: 53), and tomb-scenes clearly illustrate that this method was also employed by the ancient Egyptians. The method is gentler than a modern wine press and is the most effective way to release the grape juice without also crushing large quantities of the seeds and stems which add unwanted tannins, astringency and colour to the juice (Lucas 1962: 17; Johnson 1974: 10). Other traditional methods of crushing grapes for wine include breaking up some of the harvest with a club and then relying on the heat of the day and the fermentation process to break open the remainder of the grapes (e.g. Johnson 1974: 10).

Several types of treading vat are illustrated during the Pharaonic period. In Old Kingdom scenes, the treading vat is very shallow and of an indeterminable shape (Fig. 23.6). At either end of the vat are upright poles, sometimes forked, which support a crossbar which the men treading the grapes hold onto for balance and more efficient treading. Between three and six men are shown. Lerstrup (1992: 68) has noted that there are an even number of men when they are facing each other, and an odd number of men when they are all facing forward in a row which may be an artistic convention not necessarily relevant to the treading process itself. From the Middle Kingdom, a similar type of vat is shown although the alignment of men appears less symmetrically rigid than in the Old Kingdom scenes (Fig. 23.8; see also Lerstrup 1992: 68).

Unlike the apparent continuity between the Old and Middle Kingdom treading scenes, three types of treading vat can be clearly distinguished in the New Kingdom depictions. The treaders also no longer hang onto the crossbar for support but rather from ropes hanging from it. The three types of treading vats are marked (a), (b) and (c) in Figure 23.8 and the distribution of these types in New Kingdom tombs is shown in Table 23.2, which indicates no closely defined time spans for their depiction (after Lerstrup 1992: 68). Treading vat type (a) is similar to the shallow vats of the Old and Middle Kingdoms and the manner of showing the men is also similar. Type (b) appears to be rounded and much deeper than the earlier forms and most examples have papyriform upright poles supporting the crossbar. Frequently, there is also a spout from which the extracted juice pours into a waiting container. Treading vat type (c) is more elaborate and appears to be raised on a platform, sometimes with steps leading up to it. The upright poles continue to support a cross bar or even a roof from which the support ropes hang down. Grapes and flowers sometimes decorate the poles and roof of the treading vat. Vats of this type also have a spout at their base from which the juice flows and an example in the tomb of Neferhotep has three spouts (TT49; Davis 1933: II: Pl. III; also see Lerstrup 1992: 68).

Although treading vats are commonly illustrated in Pharaonic tomb-scenes, there remains some dispute as to their shape and manufacture. James (1995: 206), for instance, suggests that a circular shape was most likely since the corners of a rectangular form would have been impractical in a treading vat. Lutz (1922: 53) also concludes that treading vats were rounded structures which were made of acacia wood, although he cites no evidence for this claim and other scholars regard this as an unlikely possibility (e.g. Montet 1958: 106; James 1995: 206). Lesko (1977: 17) suggests that baked mud or clay may have been used in their construction, perhaps plastered with gypsum, the latter having the effect of contributing an acidity to the wine which would have been lacking in grapes grown in such a warm climate. James (1995: 206) also notes that since durability from year to year was not of primary importance, the vats were perhaps made annually of sun-dried mud-brick, smoothed with Nile mud, then finished with a hard gesso plaster which would dry to the white colour of the vats depicted in the tomb-paintings. Montet (1958: 106) suggested that the vats must have been made of polished stone, since plaster, pottery or faience all would have added an unwanted aftertaste to the wine, while stone would have been watertight and easy to clean. Others (e.g. Darby *et al.* 1977: 557; James 1995: 206) have concluded that if these substantial artefacts were indeed made of stone, then examples would have been recovered by now, however, the heavy reuse of stone throughout Egyptian history may have obscured the original function of these artefacts. These issues have yet to be resolved, however, the presence of treading vats has been suggested in Nubia (Adams 1966) and it has also been suggested that a plastered stone vat (*c.* 1.5 × 0.5 metres) excavated from Tell el-Dabʿa in the Delta was used for grape crushing (Bietak 1985). Although the artefact is comparatively small in relation to the size indicated by the tomb-paintings, it was found near the re-

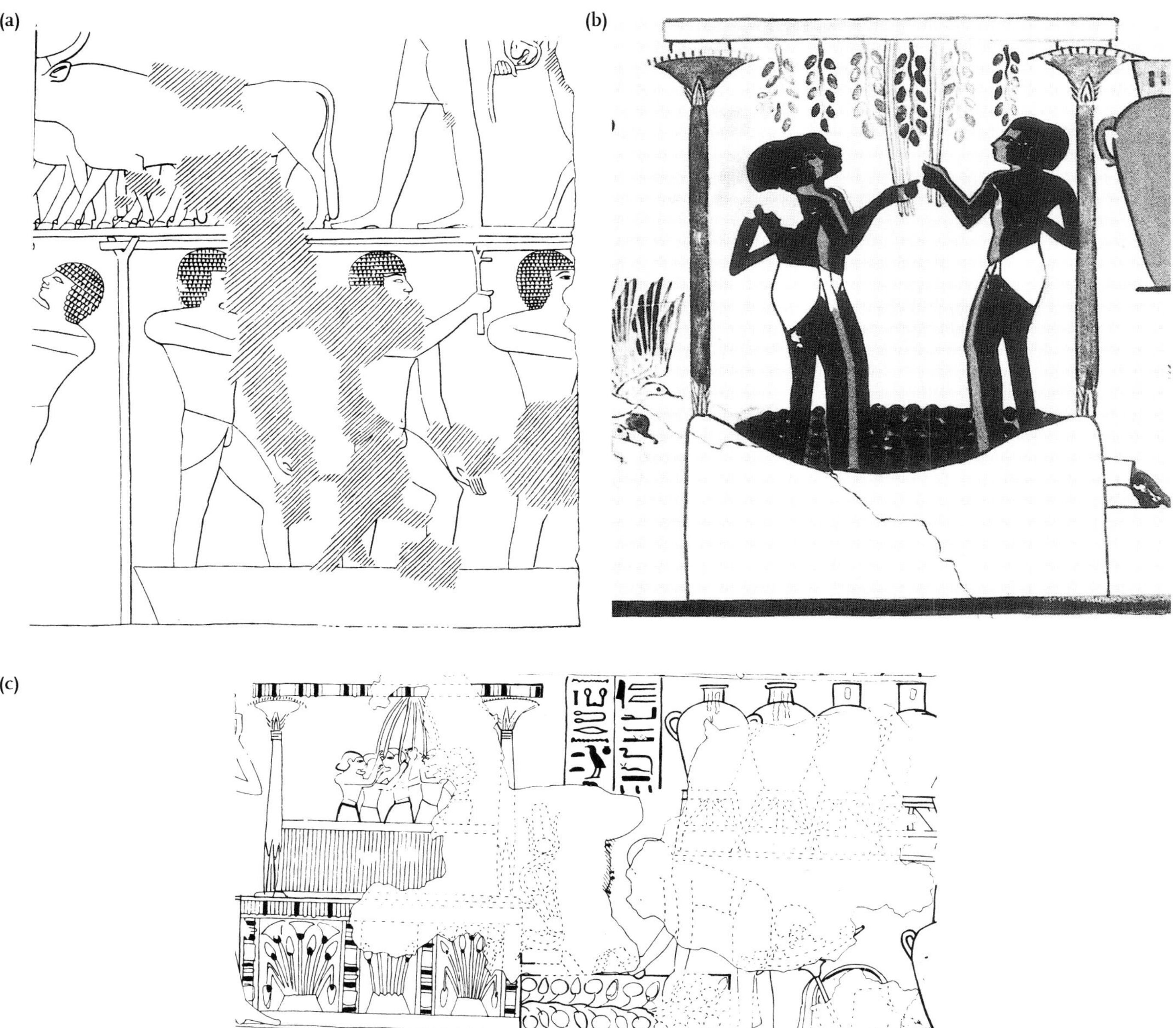

Figure 23.8 Treading vat types in the New Kingdom, as depicted in the tombs of (a) Puyemra (TT39), (b) Nakht (TT52) and (c) Nebamun (TT90).

mains of what appears to be a Second Intermediate Period vineyard (Bietak 1985). Indeed, in a study of probable treading vats from Bronze Age Crete, all were spouted vessels which ranged in height from 0.24 to 0.29 metres. and in width from 0.5 to 0.68 metres. All of the examples in the study, however, were associated with the small-scale production of wine at the household level and seventeen were made of terracotta and two were made of stone (see Palmer 1994: 18–22 for a detailed discussion).

The artistic evidence from Old Kingdom tombs indicates that the process of treading was sometimes accompanied by a rhythmic beat or music (Darby *et al.* 1977: 560; Lerstrup 1992: 70; Meeks 1993: 21; James 1995: 206). In the tombs of Mereruka and Neferherenptah (nos. 61 and D21) at Saqqara and in that of Senedjemib (Inty) at Giza (G 2370), the musicians beating a rhythm with clappers are sitting facing each other inside a circle or perhaps on a platform while in the Fifth-Dynasty tomb of Nefer and Kahay at Saqqara the two men are simply sitting next to each other with no suggestion of a platform (Lerstrup 1992: 70). By the New Kingdom, no musicians are depicted (Montet 1958: 106) but one of the men in the treading vat is sometimes shown singing, and a song to Renenutet, the harvest-goddess, is sometimes written above the workers

Table 23.2. *The distribution of treading vat types depicted in New Kingdom Theban tombs (after Lerstrup 1992: 81).*

Theban tomb number (TT#)	Tomb owner	Date	Type A	Type B	Type C
39	Puyemra	H-T3	x		
155	Intef	H-T3	x		
18	Baki	H-T3	x		
22	Wah	T3		x	
84	Amunedjeh	T3			x
127	Senemiah	T3	x		
	Paheri	T3	x		
79	Menkheper	T3–A2		x	
100	Rekhmira	T3–A2	x		
172	Mentiwyi	T3–A2		x	
56	Userhet	A2			x
92	Suemnut	A2			x
261	Khaemwaset	T4	x		
52	Nakht	T4		x	
77	Ptahemhet	T4			x
165	Nehemaway	T4			x
90	Nebamun	T4–A3			x
188	Parennefer	A3–A4		x	
49	Neferhotep	Ay			x
217	Ipuy	R2			x

H = Hatshepsut (Eighteenth Dynasty – 1473–1458 BC)
T3 = Thutmose III (Eighteenth Dynasty – 1479–1425 BC)
A2 = Amenhotep II (Eighteenth Dynasty – 1427–1401 BC)
T4 = Thutmose IV (Eighteenth Dynasty – 1401–1391 BC)
A3 = Amenhotep III (Eighteenth Dynasty – 1391–1353 BC)
A4 = Amenhotep IV (Eighteenth Dynasty – 1353–1335 BC)
Ay = Ay (Eighteenth Dynasty – 1323–1319 BC)
R2 = Rameses II (Nineteenth Dynasty 1290–1224 BC).

(e.g. TT100, Davies 1943: pl. XLV; TT155, Säve Söderbergh 1957: I: pl. XIV; see Lerstrup 1992: 70).

Pressing

It has been estimated that only about two-thirds of the juice from grapes can be extracted by treading (Palmer 1994: 16). Many tomb-scenes indicate that after this process, the remains of the grape, i.e. the crushed skins, stalks and seeds; could then be placed into a cloth or sack press, which was continually twisted until no further juice could be extracted. One Middle Kingdom scene, for example, describes the pressing process with the same word used to describe the process by which launderers 'wring out' linen (Montet 1925: 269; James 1995: 207; see Newberry 1894a: pls. 24, 31). The sacks used for the pressing might have been made of linen or perhaps some type of basketry (Lesko 1995: 217; see also Chapter 11, this volume). The techniques used for pressing wine were also used to extract oils or scent from various other plant materials, such as fruits, flowers, seeds or tubers. While depictions of presses are usually associated with wine production, a pressing scene from the Fifth-Dynasty tomb of Iymery at Giza is clearly illustrating oil extraction (Lepsius 1849–59: II, Bl. 49/53; see Chapter 17, this volume for a more detailed discussion of oil/wine pressing techniques). Wilkinson (1978: 384) and later Lutz (1922) noted that in Theban tombs, while the treading stage is commonly shown, the use of the sack press is rarely depicted. This may represent a change in the artistic genre of illustrating vintage scenes or may reflect other developments, such as the addition of spouts at the base of treading vats which would have ensured more efficient recovery of extracted grape juice (Tallet pers. comm.).

Three basic pressing techniques are illustrated for the Pharaonic period. Old Kingdom tomb scenes indicate that the crushed grapes were placed into a large cloth or sack, with poles attached to either end. The poles were then repeatedly twisted in opposite directions, like tourniquets, while the extracted juice was collected into a wide mouthed container (Fig. 23.9; see also Duell 1938: pl. 114; Davies 1900: pl. 21). This method usually involved a five-man team with two men twisting each pole and one who, by using both his hands and feet, maintained the tension on the poles by stretching out fully between them to keep them as far apart as possible. The job of the fifth man appears as an extraordinary act in the tomb-scenes and, as James (1995: 207) has noted, one which involves a range of movement untypical in Egyptian art (also see Klebs 1914: 25–6; Montet 1925: 269–70). James (1995: 207) also suggests the possibility that the artists themselves may have lacked first-hand knowledge of the wine-pressing procedure and that the successive copying of the scene made this part of the job look more unnatural than it actually was. In the Fifth-Dynasty tomb of Nefer and Kaha at Saqqara, it is, in fact, a baboon who is maintaining the tension on the poles (Moussa and Altenmüller 1971: 24, pls. 8, 12). It has been suggested this scene may represent a play on the ancient Egyptian words for both the animal and the sack or may relate somehow to the twisting process itself, since, in a boat-building scene from the same tomb, a baboon is also associated with the twisting of ropes (Moussa and Altenmüller 1971: 24, n. 137). A five-man team is usually involved in pressing scenes, although groups of as many as eight have been recorded, yet this may have more to do with artistic requirements than with the labour needed for the job (see Moussa and Altenmüller 1971: pl. 39.16). While this pressing technique is most closely associated with the Old Kingdom, it does sometimes occur in Middle and New Kingdom tombs. It is also illustrated in two tombs from the Late Period (see Lerstrup 1992: 71).

There are few pressing scenes from the Middle Kingdom but most informative are those from tombs at Beni Hasan. In some, such as that of Khety (BH17; Fig. 23.10),

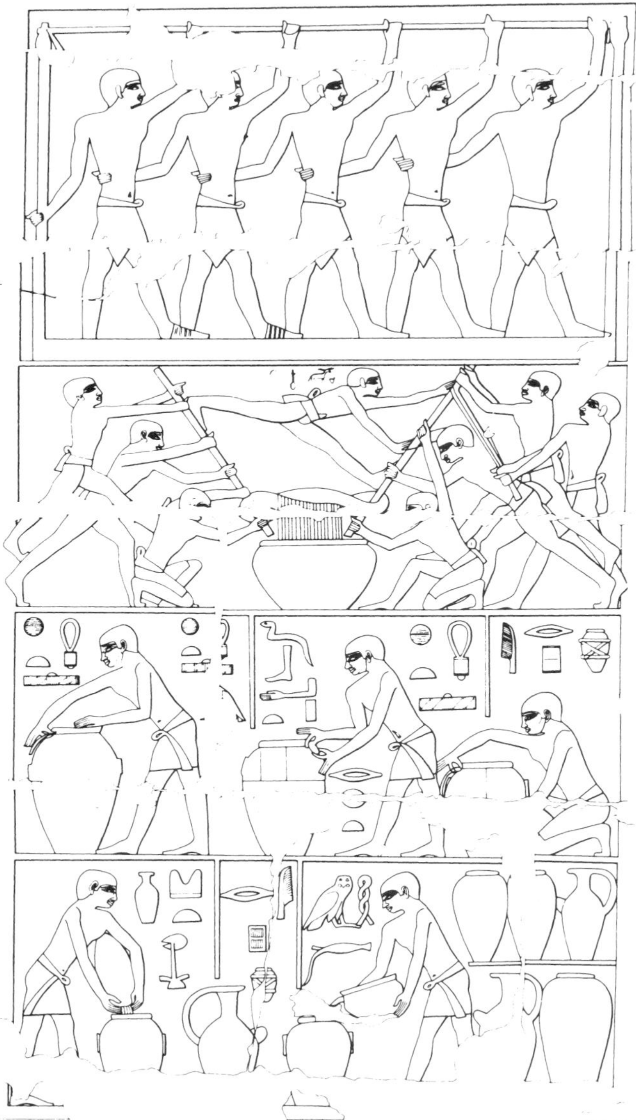

Figure 23.9 An Old Kingdom wine press, depicted in the Fifth-Dynasty tomb-chapel of Niankhkhnum and Khnumhotep at Saqqara.

where the Old Kingdom style press continues to be illustrated, James (1995: 212) notes that the overly simplistic depiction of the wine-making process suggests that the scene was copied without an understanding of either the sequence of events nor their purpose. Other Middle Kingdom scenes depict a new variation of the sack press, where the fixed post of a frame is used to secure one end of the sack while several men twist the free end. This type of press first appears in the Twelfth-Dynasty tomb of Bakt III (BH15) at Beni Hasan (Newberry 1894b: 48(2), pl. 6; see also Fig. 23.11). This unusual scene has been interpreted in many ways, such as portraying the intermediary stage of straining the grape juice between treading and pressing, as

Figure 23.10 Wine-making scene in the tomb-chapel of Khety at Beni Hasan (BH17).

Figure 23.11 Scene portraying the straining and pressing of grape juice, in the tomb-chapel of Bakt III at Beni Hasan (BH 15).

the cooking of wine, as preparing plants for oil extraction and as the production of grape syrup (Neuberger 1930: fig. 170; Lutz 1922: 56; Lucas 1962: 27; Tallet 1995; Chapter 17, this volume). The pressing method involving the twisting of only a single pole while the other end is attached was reportedly still used in the Fayum at the beginning of the nineteenth century AD (Girard 1812: 608; Lucas 1962: 17).

During the New Kingdom, a further variation of the sack press is depicted. Rather than the Old Kingdom technique of twisting both poles, or the Middle Kingdom variation of twisting one end while the other is attached to a fixed post, the New Kingdom version shows that either end of the sack could be attached to poles outside a frame (Fig. 23.12). With this technique, the bag was securely fixed in place while the poles at either end could be twisted using maximum leverage, for example, in the Eighteenth-Dynasty tomb of Intef (TT155; Säve-Söderbergh 1957: pl. 15).

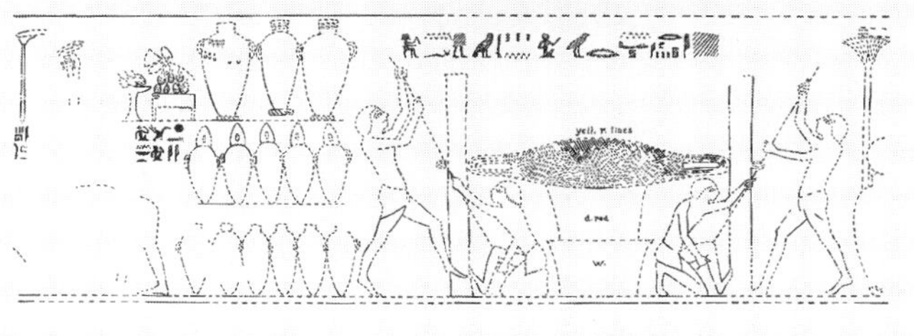

Figure 23.12 New Kingdom painting of a wine press from the Eighteenth-Dynasty tomb of Intef at Thebes (TT155).

The possibility that the presence of crushed grape skins, stalks and seeds in charred archaeobotanical assemblages may represent the remains of wine pressing, perhaps subsequently used as fuel and thus preserved, has been discussed by several authors working on Mediterranean sites (e.g. Py 1998; Buxo 1996; Mangafa and Kotsakis 1996; Murray 1998). As yet, although the presence of grape seeds has been cited frequently from Predynastic times onwards, the archaeobotanical remains of the pressing stage of wine-making have not been reported for the Pharaonic period. There may be several reasons for this, for example, relatively few sites have had systematic archaeobotanical recovery programs thus far. It is also possible that the separate elements of wine pressing remains may have not been recognised as a potentially meaningful assemblage in its own right and, in any case, perhaps the remains of wine-making would be less likely to be present in a typical village or sites outside the Delta and oases.

Fermentation

The fermentation process, which turns the extracted grape juice into wine, is simply the conversion of sugar into alcohol. This process quickly begins when the enzymes found in the sugar rich juice of the crushed grapes come into contact with the naturally occurring yeasts on the 'bloom' of the grape skins which are found primarily near the grape stalk and other yeasts can also be involved. The yeasts proceed to digest the grape sugar which is then converted into carbon dioxide and alcohol (Lucas 1962: 17; Johnson 1974: 11; Farkaš 1988: I: 171–237; Palmer 1994: 12; Singleton 1995: 72; Unwin 1996: 46–7). The level of alcohol produced depends on the amount of sugar present. When the alcohol level reaches between 13 and 16 per cent, the yeast cells are spent and the primary fermentation process eventually comes to an end (Lucas 1962: 18; Johnson 1974: 11; Palmer 1994: 12; Unwin 1996: 47). At this stage, any remaining unfermented sugar simply adds sweetness to the wine (Lucas 1962: 18; Johnson 1974: 11; Palmer 1994: 12; Singleton 1995: 73). After fermentation is complete, there is, on average, about 10 per cent alcohol in red wine and 11 per cent or so in white wine (Johnson 1974: 11). Although the basic tenets of the fermentation process are easily explained, i.e., that pressed grapes will ferment into wine and that wine exposed to the air will eventually turn to vinegar, it was not until the experiments of Louis Pasteur in the mid-nineteenth century that the many complexities and subtleties of the fermentation process began to be understood in scientific terms, as did the means to effectively control it (Pasteur 1866; Unwin 1996: 46; for more details on the fermentation process for wine see Unwin 1996, Farkaš 1988; Jackson 1994 and see Chapter 22 in this volume for a detailed discussion on how the fermentation process relates to beer).

The 'must' of wine is the juice that has been exposed to yeasts, and includes fresh juice, as well as the juice undergoing full fermentation. Different grades of must are produced during the various stages of pressing. 'Free-run must' is obtained prior to treading and pressing: it is the juice pressed out of the grapes simply by their own weight. Comparatively little of this is produced and if collected and fermented on its own, the result is a pure, sugar-rich, long-lived wine. Most of the juice used for wine comes from the next stage, the treading process, and this is known as 'first run must', while the excess juice extracted from the additional stage of pressing is the 'second run must' (Palmer 1994: 16). The level of impurities increases with the various grades of must, as does their potential to turn to acetic acid (vinegar) or lactic acid (Farkaš 1988: I: 208–14, 255; Palmer 1994: 17). While it seems clear from the tomb scenes that the juice extracted by treading and pressing were placed in open jars to continue fermentation, there is no evidence to indicate whether the juice from the two processes were eventually mixed together or whether they were fermented separately (Lucas 1962: 17). During the New Kingdom, at some stage prior to the final sealing of the wines, they were assessed, and their quality was often listed on the labels inscribed on wine jars. They were graded as 'good' (*nfr*), 'double good' (*nfr-nfr*) or even 'triple good' (*nfr-nfr-nfr*). It is possible that this grading system may reflect the variable qualities of must from the different levels of juice extraction (Lerstrup 1992: 72) or perhaps the blending of these types in various proportions.

The extracted grape juice may be transported just after its extraction, but the fermenting wine should not be moved until fully stabilised, i.e. until the fermentation process is complete (Palmer 1994: 17). The length of time that the juice is allowed to ferment, as well as the temperature of the fermentation greatly affects the final product. A short fermentation of one or two days produces a light wine, whereas heavy wines which are meant to be kept and matured may undergo long and hot fermentations for several weeks (Unwin 1996: 53). The high temperatures of the Egyptian summer would have promoted fermentation and it is likely that the process began immediately after the juice had been extracted. Indeed, wine jars may have been left in the sun to speed the fermentation process. It is not clear how long Egyptian wines would have been left to ferment although it is believed that perhaps after several days of primary fermentation in large mouthed jars, the contents was transferred to other containers or sealed in the original container (see section on Sealing p. 594; and see Lerstrup 1992: 75; Lucas 1962: 18). While the fermentation process is not explicitly shown in Old Kingdom tombs (James 1995: 207), it appears to be illustrated in the New Kingdom tombs of Amenemhat (TT82) and Nebamun (TT90; see Davies 1923a: pl. XXX; Davies and Gardiner 1915: pl. XXVI). Both tombs show a turbulent fermentation as the wine bubbles over the rim of the wine jars. A scene from the tomb of Amenemhat also shows wine jars being fanned, perhaps to cool them during the process (Lerstrup 1992: 75). Today, it is generally agreed that, particularly for white wines, a slow, cool fermentation produces a finer quality wine rather than a hot, turbulent process (Unwin 1996: 50). The possibility that ancient Egyptian wine-makers ever employed the slow, cool fermentation method cannot be ruled out. Two of the most important factors of the modern wine industry have been the large-scale introduction of cool fermentation and effective methods to stabilise wines before bottling (Unwin 1996: 45). For more on the fermentation within the wine jars, see section on Sealing, p. 594.

Wine colour and taste

The possible types of Egyptian wine produced, i.e. red, white, dry or sweet, would have been largely determined by factors related to the fermentation process. For example, two different qualities of wines would have been produced if the juice from treading and pressing were kept separate. The juice from pressing, which would have remained mixed with the stalks, seeds and skins of the grape for the longest period, thus would have acquired a richer colour and an added astringency than the juice from treading, particularly if red or 'black' grapes were used (Lucas 1962: 17). In contrast, if the juice taken directly from treading was immediately strained then a white wine was more likely to have been produced, even if red or 'black' grapes were used. With few exceptions, both white and black grapes produce a white juice although most wine today is made primarily from white grapes (Unwin 1996: 53–4) and red wine is produced by retaining the grape skins and seeds in the juice for a longer period (Lucas 1962: 17; Johnson 1974: 11). Wine colour, therefore, is determined not only by the colour of grape used, but also by the presence or absence of grape skins during the fermentation process.

While there is little explicit evidence of the colour of wine in Pharaonic Egypt, the artistic and textual records both suggest that red wine predominated. Indeed, it is a matter of speculation as to whether a white wine was ever made during this time. In tomb scenes, the colour of the grapes on the vine range from light green to blackish blue, while the juice extracted from the grapes varies from a light pink to dark red (Lesko 1977: 17, 1995: 219; James 1995: 205), although this range of colour may also have to do with the conventions of the genre and perhaps the whim of the individual artist (Darby *et al.* 1977: 556; Lesko 1977: 19). As noted above (in the section describing the grape, p. 580), red is the genetically dominant colour of wild grapes, and white grapes arise only from the appearance of an 'albino' or white mutation. If this is considered a desirable quality, then the characteristic must be maintained by planting cuttings of the parent plant (Singleton 1995: 74). Powell (1995: 113) has also noted that in texts from Bronze Age Mesopotamia, red was the only colour mentioned in relation to wine.

It has been suggested that a Middle Kingdom tomb scene from Deir el-Bersha may show the production of white wine, since the pressing scene directly follows the harvesting scene where greenish-coloured grapes are picked (Montet 1913: 117–18; Lucas 1962: 18). Lesko (1977: 18) argues, however, that there is no indication of the time spans between the two activities and that these badly damaged (and poorly recorded) paintings may have once illustrated the intermediate stages of treading and primary fermentation. Another piece of evidence used to suggest the making of Pharaonic white wine is a textual reference in a Middle Kingdom tomb at Meir (Blackman 1915: 30), although this refers to the term *3bš*, one of the five wines originally mentioned in the Pyramid Texts which is now thought to be a type of wine container rather than a type of wine itself (Meyer 1986: 6: col. 1172; Piankoff 1968: 66, 153–7; Lesko 1977: 17; Meeks 1977: 77.0616(W6 I, 179, 1), 1978: 78.0689). The first definite textual evidence for white wine in Egypt, thus far, dates to the third century AD, when Athenaeus (Deipnos. 7, 33, d–e quoted in Darby *et al.* 1977: 557) described Mareotic wine, from an area south of Alexandria, as 'excellent, white, pleasant, fragrant, easily assimilated, thin, not likely to go to the head and diuretic'.

Sweet wine

Among the twenty-six wine jars from the tomb of Tutankhamun (KV62), four of them were labelled *irp nḏm* ('sweet wine') (Cerny 1965; Hope 1993). Since the sweet wines were so clearly labelled, it has been suggested that perhaps the royal wines were generally dry (Lesko 1977: 22, 1995: 218, 225). Sweet wines usually have a higher alcohol content than dry wines and their high sugar content helps to preserve the wine for longer periods (Singleton 1995: 75; Unwin 1996: 54). The most effective way to create the sweetness of wine is to use either very ripe grapes or those which have been partially dried, since these contain a higher proportion of concentrated sugar. Both raisins and the wine must may also be added to increase the sugar content (Johnson 1974: 12; Singleton 1995: 75). At the Predynastic cemetery of Umm el-Qaʿab at Abydos, forty-seven probable wine jars, imported from Palestine, contained grape seeds (most contained between twenty and fifty each) and eleven vessels reportedly contained strings of sliced fig fruits which may have been used as a flavouring or as an added sweetener to the wine (McGovern *et al.* 1997: 10). While the addition of honey or fruits, would add sugar, they may also cause the wine to re-ferment (Singleton 1995: 75). The term for sweet wine *irp nḏm*, such as those found in Tutankhamun's tomb, is not the same as the *irp bnr*, a term cited in the medical texts, such as the Papyrus Ebers (28.9.16–28.10.2) which has been interpreted as either 'sweet wine' or 'date wine' (von Deines and Westendorf 1959; Lucas 1962: 23; Cerny 1965; Lesko 1995: 225).

Blended wines

Among the wine jar labels from the late Eighteenth-Dynasty palace site of Malkata, Hayes (1951: 89) found references to 'blended wines' (*irp sm3*), and there may be a reference to 'mixed wine' (*mdg/mtk*) in the *Sayings of Onchsheshonqy*, a wisdom text dating to the Ptolemaic period (Lichtheim 1980: 163; Johnson 1986; also see Quaegebeur 1990). It is not clear whether the blending of wines in ancient Egypt meant combining those from different years, vineyards, or types of grape, or perhaps even that the juice from treading was combined with that of pressing, or that wines were mixed with other fermented fruit juices or simply with water (Lesko 1977: 31; 1995: 219). A scene in the New Kingdom tomb of Kynebu (TT113) appears to illustrate the blending of wine, since the contents of different wine jars are shown being siphoned into another container (Fig. 23.13) (see Wilkinson 1878: II, 314). The fact that the final product here is not being siphoned into a storage jar, suggests that the process took place immediately prior to drinking. Darby *et al.* (1977: 567) broadly concluded that since blended wines were probably only mixed prior to consumption, then they were unlikely to be for distribution or sale, yet more information would be needed to make any firm conclusions on the nature of Egyptian blended wine.

Strabo (xvii: 1, 14) mentioned that Libyan wines were mixed with sea water, and Athenaeus (I: 33e) and Pliny (XIV: 9) also both mention the practice of diluting wines with water. While there is no evidence for the practice, to date, from Pharaonic Egypt, it has been suggested that if ancient wines were diluted, then perhaps the dilution of sweet wines was most likely since these are more concentrated and have a higher level of alcohol (Singleton 1995: 75). Rather than being used to diminish the potency of the wine, the practice of diluting was perhaps more likely to have been done as a means to improve the quality of the water. Wine has antiseptic properties which would have helped to kill microbial contaminants in water and this medicinal quality may have been a very practical reason why the drink was commonly among the rations of ancient armies on the move, such as the Roman legionaries (Singleton 1995: 75; also Unwin 1996: 179). In Egypt, for example, wine is mentioned as being among the provisions for armies during the reign of Thutmose II although it is unclear whether it was provisioned only for officials or if was meant for the troops as well (see Poo 1995: 32 for other possible examples). The detailed analysis of the textual evidence for wine in Mesopotamia found that while the blending of wines could be clearly demonstrated, no evidence could be found for the practice of diluting wine with water (Powell 1995: 112–13).

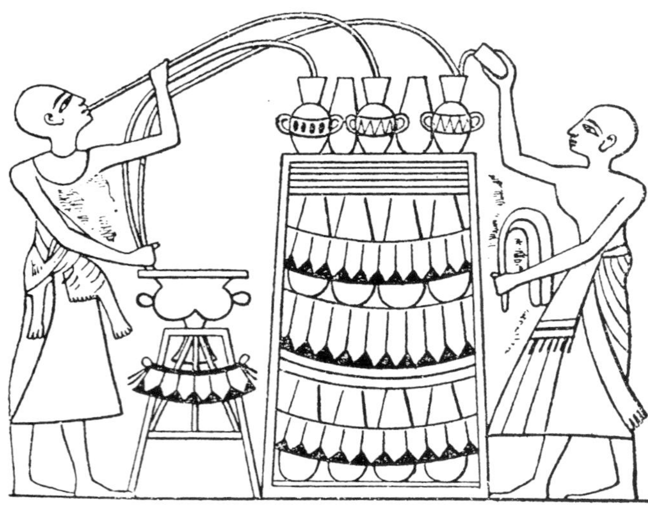

Figure 23.13 Scene from the Twentieth-Dynasty tomb of Kynebu at Thebes (TT113), showing the blending of different wines.

Other types of wine

Although the principal wines of ancient Egypt were made from grapes, there is evidence, primarily lexicographic, that wines were also made from other sweet fruits, such as pomegranate, date, palm, fig, and, according to Pliny writing in Roman times, the fruit of the Egyptian plum (*Cordia myxa*) (see Chapter 22, this volume). Although the exact methods used for making these wines are unknown, the basic tenets were probably similar to those used for grape wine. However, unlike the grape, which contains up to 30 per cent sugar (Johnson 1974: 10; Singleton 1995: 73), wines made from other fruits usually would have needed added sugars to complete the full fermentation process (Johnson 1974: 10).

The term *irp bnr*, has been interpreted as 'sweet wine' or 'date wine', derived from the pressing and fermentation of the fruits. It is attested from Egyptian texts as early as the Second Dynasty and is also cited in the medical texts (Saad 1957: 9; Täckholm and Drar 1950: 224; von Dienes and Westendorf 1959 IV: 121; Lucas 1962: 23; Darby *et al.* 1977: 614; Manniche 1989: 134; Hepper 1990: 62). Burckhardt (1819: 143) mentions a more recent type of date wine from Nubia made from fermenting the liquid of boiled dates, the practice is also noted in eastern Libya by Bates (1914: 26). The dearth of date remains in the archaeobotanical record prior to the New Kingdom, however, casts some doubt on the widespread availability of dates for use in the making of both beer and wine during much of the Pharaonic period. See Chapters 22 and 24, this volume for further discussion of this issue. In recent times, date wine was produced in Egypt but it was then distilled into a liqueur (Bircher 1995: 25) which is now prohibited (Fakhry 1973: 27).

Palm wine is derived, not from the date fruits but from the fermentation of the sap of the date palm (Wilkinson 1878: I, 397; Beadnell 1909: 218; Lucas 1962: 22; Bircher

1995). The extraction of the sap, however, by cutting the tree at the base of its fronds, significantly weakens the palm and is therefore best done with those trees well past their fruit-bearing years or with those male trees not required for pollination purposes (Wilkinson 1878: I, 397; Lucas 1962: 22; Darby *et al.* 1977: 614–15; Harrison *et al.* 1985: 106). Beadnell (1909: 218), however, states that palm sap can be extracted once or twice a month without harm and may even prove beneficial to unhealthy palms while Bircher (1995: 164) notes that the quality of male palm sap is thought to be inferior. Palm wine, or fermented *labgi,* was still being made in parts of Egypt in recent years (e.g. Wilkinson 1878: 397; Darby *et al.* 1977: 614–15; Bircher 1995: 164). According to the Classical authors, Diodorus and Herodotus, palm wine was also used to rinse bodies being prepared for mummification (Bauman 1960: 93; Fakhry 1973: 27; Darby *et al.* 1977: 615).

Another beverage, known as *šdḥ* was first mentioned in the New Kingdom and there have been a great variety of interpretations as to exactly what type of drink it may have been (e.g. Berlandini 1974). Evidence from the wine jar labels shows that *šdḥ* is always described as *nfr* or *nfr-nfr* – good to very good quality, including five labelled jars of *šdḥ* from the tomb of Tutankhamun (KV62) (Cerny 1965; Tallet 1995; Hope 1993) and it was evidently a more highly prized beverage than the typical Egyptian wine (e.g. Tallet 1995). It is commonly interpreted as a pomegranate juice or wine (e.g. Loret 1892; Lutz 1922; Pendlebury 1951; Fairman 1951; Lucas 1962; Leahy 1985; Lesko 1977, 1995) but also as a boiled or cooked wine (e.g. Derchain 1965; Charpentier 1981; Tallet 1995). A Nineteenth Dynasty letter concerning an estate which supplied wine to a mortuary temple is commonly used as evidence for the interpretation of *šdḥ* as pomegranate wine since included amongst its annual yield was 1,500 jars of wine, fifty jars of *šdḥ*, fifty jars of *p3–wr*, and 160 sacks and baskets of pomegranates and grapes (P. Anastasi IV, 6–7, quoted in Caminos 1954: 155; also see Aufrère 1987: 36–9). Tallet (1995) argues that it is unlikely that *šdḥ* is pomegranate wine but may be some form of cooked or treated wine. Textual evidence from post-Pharaonic Egypt refer to boiled wines (e.g. Rostovtzeff 1922: 175; Schnebel 1925: 290), although as yet this is not attested for the Pharaonic period.

'Bottling'

Wine was clearly both fermented and stored in jars. According to Lerstrup (1992: 72), tomb scenes indicate that wine jars were filled immediately after treading or pressing when only one of these stages is depicted, whereas, with few exceptions (e.g. tomb of Parennefer (TT188), the filling of these vessels follows the pressing scene when both procedures are illustrated. The wine must was decanted into large storage jars using smaller containers. The artistic record suggests that the latter were of various forms in the Old Kingdom, sometimes with a spout, while in the Middle Kingdom they were small rounded jars. The New Kingdom juglet depicted for this purpose was more oval in shape, either with or without a spout (Fig. 23.14; see also Lerstrup 1992: 72).

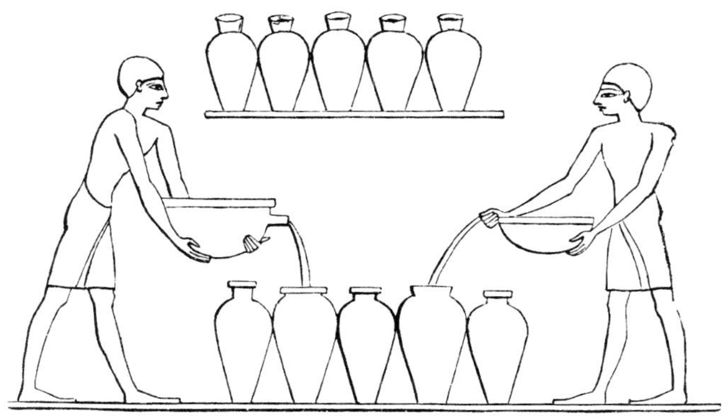

Figure 23.14 New Kingdom scene showing the pouring of wine.

The typical New Kingdom Egyptian storage jar frequently used for wine was a tall vessel with a tapered rounded or pointed base, not designed to remain upright without the support of a stand or frame or being twisted down into the sand (Fig. 23.15, e.g. Wilkinson 1878: 388; Lutz 1922: 58; Bourriau 1981: 73; Hope 1989; Lesko 1995: 220; Leonard 1995: 237–9). Evidence from the Ulu Burun shipwreck, as well as other archaeological examples of these storage vessels show that while they were commonly used for wine, they have also been found to hold a wide variety of other contents (e.g. Wood 1987: 76; Bass 1986: 277–9; Leonard 1995: 250–1; Serpico 1996; Serpico and White forthcoming; Bourriau 1997). Lesko (1995: 220) notes that the design was particularly well-suited to wine, i.e. for serving, transportation, the collection of the wine dregs in the tapered bottom, and for resisting of the build up of gases while the fermentation process was continuing within the jars. The porosity of the wine jars may have kept their contents cool in storage, but this feature also meant that the wines would not have remained drinkable for long periods, thus contributing to the perishable nature of the product (James 1995: 198; Hope 1989). Egyptian wine perhaps would not have preserved for more than five years, in any case (Tallet 1996).

It has been suggested that the insides of wine jars were coated with resin or bitumen to render them impermeable, to help preserve the wine or to add to its taste (Wilkinson 1878: 386; Lutz 1922: 56–7; Carter 1933: 148). Darby *et al.* (1977: 561) maintains that the practice is unlikely due to the size of the wine jars, the large amount of wine produced and the scarcity of sources for either bitumen or resin in Egypt (see Chapter 18, this volume). To date, the visual and chemical analyses of wine jar interiors from the Pharaonic period have found no trace of these added substances (e.g. Lucas 1962: 20; Heron and Pollard 1988; see Chapter 18,

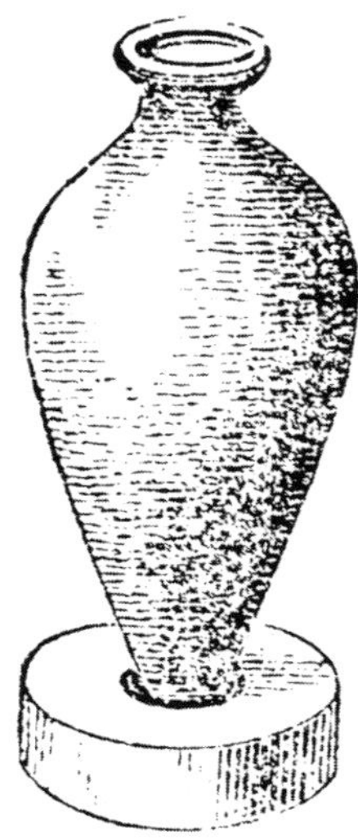

Figure 23.15 Stone ring wine stand, depicted in the Twentieth-Dynasty tomb of Ramose at Thebes (TT166).

this volume) and the practice of coating wine jar interiors or of adding resins to wine is thought to have been introduced into Egypt during the Ptolemaic period (Forbes 1965: 77; Lucas 1962: 20; Montet 1958: 88; Lerstrup 1992: 73; Heron and Pollard 1988; see Chapter 18, this volume). Recent chemical analysis of storage jars imported from Palestine found at the Predynastic site of Umm el-Qaʿab at Abydos, suggests the presence of both tartaric acid and its salt (probably wine) as well as traces of *Pistacia* resin in three of the vessels (McGovern *et al.* 1997: 10–11; McGovern 1998). There remains no indication at present, however, that adding resins to wine jars was a native Egyptian practice during the Pharaonic period.

Lesko (1995: 217) has suggested that three rows of wine jars in a scene from the early Eighteenth-Dynasty tomb of Intef (TT155) may represent two and perhaps three stages of wine bottling, even though the bottling process itself is not explicitly depicted (Fig. 23.16). The bottom row of wine jars are shown to be open, and are either empty or still fermenting, unlike the middle row of jars, which have their final mud seals in place. The top row of jars are without seals but unlike the bottom row, they are in ring stands and appear slightly different, perhaps representing jars partially sealed with secondary fermentation locks (below, see Säve-Söderbergh 1957: 17–18 and pls. 14–15).

Sealing

Wine jars would have had to be sealed within several days before acetous fermentation turned the wine into vinegar (see Fermentation, p. 590). Sealed wine jars are frequently depicted in tomb-scenes, such as in the Eighteenth Dynasty tombs of Nakht and Neferhotep (Fig. 23.7; Davies 1917: 70, pl. xxvi; 1933: pl. xlviii). While wine jar sealings have been recovered from several sites, much of the evidence of the practice comes from the New Kingdom assemblages from Malkata (Hope 1978), Amarna (Petrie 1894, Pendlebury 1951), Buhen (Smith 1976), the tomb of Tutankhamun (Hope 1993) and the Ramesseum (Spiegelberg 1898, 1923). After fermentation, the amphorae were frequently first sealed with a stopper consisting of reeds, straw, pottery or sometimes mud. The primary purpose of the stoppers was to prevent the wine from being contaminated by the mud from the final sealing which was to follow. These stoppers may also have served as a semi-permeable cover during the final stages of fermentation (Hope 1978: 6; 14). The remains of stoppers have survived intact, and samples analysed from the Eighteenth-Dynasty site of Malkata, for example, were found to be made primarily of sedge reed culms (*Cyperus* sp.), possibly those of papyrus (*Cyperus papyrus* L.). The reed stoppers varied from six to fifteen centimetres in diameter, and ranged from those which were woven, to a stopper made only of a tied bundle of reeds. Other stoppers made of organic remains included those made of leaves, chopped chaff mixed with an adhesive or mud and one of reeds wound into a ball (Hope 1978: 14, pls. I, II, IV; Hope 1993: 95). Small ceramic saucers, as well as broken fragments of pottery were also placed over the mouth of the jar for this purpose (Fig. 23.17; see also Hope 1978: 14, pl. IV b, d, 1993: 95). Mud stoppers were also occasionally used to close the neck of amphorae prior to the final sealing (Hope 1978: 14).

After the amphorae were stoppered, they were sealed with either hand- or mould-made sealings. Those made by hand simply consisted of placing an amount of dampened mud on the mouth of the jar and shaping it by hand before allowing it to dry in place. Hand-made sealings found at the Late Antique Monastery of Epiphanius, for example, were a mixture of black earth and chopped straw (Winlock and Crum 1926 I: 79). The archaeological evidence shows that the application of this final mud sealing often dislodged the stopper, pushing it into the neck of wine jar, although these were still seemingly effective at reducing contamination (Hope 1978: 14). Mould-made seals were more elaborate: they were made by either (1) filling an open-ended mould with mud and forcing it onto the neck of the amphorae in order to enclose it completely, down to the shoulders of the jar, or (2) covering the neck with mud, then applying the mould (Hope 1978: 7, 35). The necks of the amphorae were sometimes reinforced with a binding of rope, reed or leaves, prior to the sealing (Hope 1978: 7). The mould types can be described as cap-shaped, domed or cylindrical and while no one mould shape can be considered standard, the cylindrical sealings are the most common type found in the New Kingdom material thus far (Fig. 23.18; see also Hope 1978: 26–7, fig. 9; 1993: 91–4, fig. 1). The mud forced from the bottom of the mould was probably removed with a knife or other sharp object as the bottom of the mould sealing is

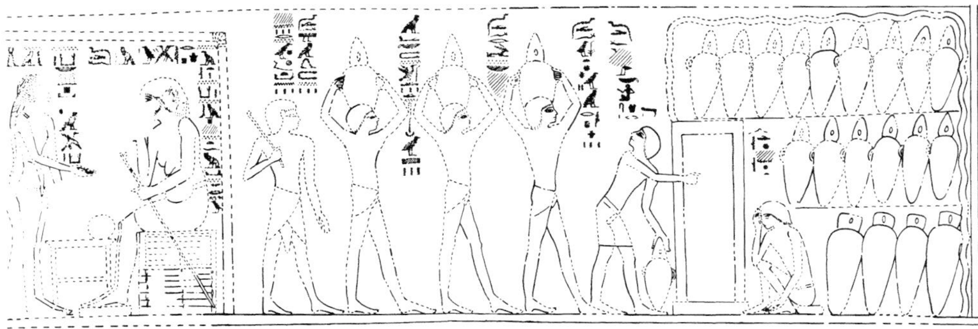

Figure 23.16 Wine storage, depicted in the Eighteenth-Dynasty tomb of Intef at Thebes (TT155).

usually evenly angled (Fig. 23.18; see also Hope 1978: 14, 29). Several mud sealings which had cracked during the drying process can be seen to have obviously been repaired with mud (Hope 1978: 6). Thirteen of the Malkata jar sealings were actually double sealings, each of which consisted of a small inner sealing completely encapsulated by a larger outer sealing which had been applied separately. Of the many possible explanations for this practice (Hope 1978: 7–8), the most probable may be that a second sealing was applied due to the cracking of the first during drying (Hope 1978: 8). Many of the Malkata wine jar sealings were also decorated (Hope 1978: 16–18, figs. 1–4).

Another reason for stoppering wine jars with a semi-permeable plug, such as a reed or straw bung, may have been the fact that it facilitated the release of the carbon dioxide gas which would have accumulated while fermentation continued within the jars (Hope 1978: 7). A small opening is occasionally found in wine jar sealings, such as those from the tomb of Tutankhamun (KV62) (Carter 1933: 148–9; Lesko 1977: 20), or in the neck of the wine jars themselves, as in two examples from the Late Antique Monastery of Epiphanius (Winlock and Crum 1926 I: 79). These are also usually interpreted as holes, perhaps kept open by the insertion of a hollow reed, for example, which would have allowed the release of the gases which would have accumulated after the wine jar had been sealed. These holes then could be easily closed after the secondary fermentation process was complete (e.g. Winlock and Crum 1926 I: 79; Carter 1933: 148–9; Lucas 1962: 19; James 1995: 198). This may not have been a common practice since comparatively few intact wine jars actually show this feature (Hope 1978: 7; Lerstrup 1992: 73), however, many wine jars are from a funerary context where the actual potability of the wine may not have been a prime concern. Of the fifteen complete wine jar sealings from the tomb of Tutankhamun, only four had these openings (out of twenty-four sealings in all), and none of the fifty-three Malkata sealings positively identified as being from wine jars, or the other twenty-four possible wine jar sealings, exhibited this feature (Černy 1965 II, 1–4; Hope 1978: 7) nor do any of the wine jar sealings recovered from Buhen (Smith 1976: 180). At Malkata, two of the sealings which did have these openings were for covering jars described as containing fat and two others provide no indication of contents and therefore could not necessarily be identified as belonging to wine jars (Hope 1978: 7).

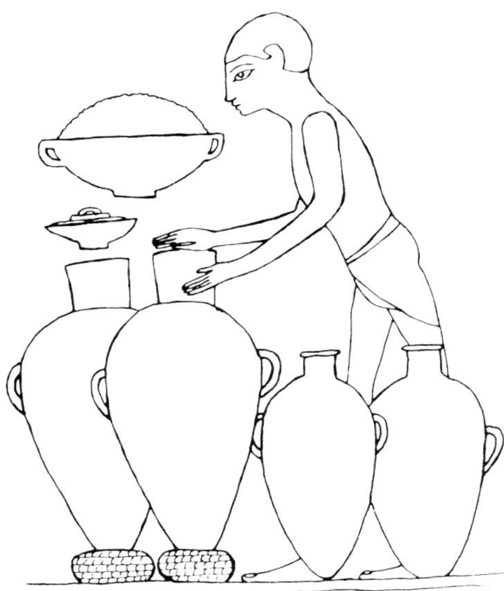

Figure 23.17 Wine jar sealing, depicted in the Eighteenth-Dynasty tomb of Khaemwaset at Thebes (TT261).

In the Eighteenth-Dynasty tomb of Tjanuni (TT74), perforations were found in the top of the sealings (Brack 1975: 68, 386, Taf. 47b), and Brack suggests that these were used to siphon wine, although none of the cited examples of wine jars with siphons have the sealing in place (Lerstrup 1992: 73). Lerstrup (1992: 73) notes that whatever the reason for these openings, they are unlikely to represent either attempts to cheat on measures or the theft of wine, since the sealings in Tutankhamun's tomb, for example, had later been closed and officially stamped (Černy 1965, nos. 1, 6, 11, 12). It has been suggested that due to the haste in which the tomb of the young king was prepared, perhaps the wines placed into the tomb of Tutankhamun had a particular need for a fermentation vent since the process may have been incomplete at the time of his burial (e.g. Lesko 1995). Indeed, it is believed that one of the wine jars found in Tutankhamun's tomb had been sealed prior the completion of fermentation and had burst open for this reason (Carter 1933: 148–9; Lucas 1962: 19; Hope 1978: 7; Lesko 1977: 21; 1995: 220). The majority of the wine jars from this tomb, however, are from the fourth and fifth years of his nine-year reign when surely the fermentation process would have been complete (Tallet 1996). James (1995: 198, 207) has noted that through experience the wine-maker would have known when the time was right to finally close the fermentation vent and store the wine jar safely.

The suggestion that the wine jars at Malkata had been reused was based primarily on the presence of more than one hieratic label on some wine jars (Hayes 1951: 39–40; see labelling). One piece of evidence that would seem to make this an infrequent practice is that wine jar sealings commonly also contain the necks of the wine jars themselves since it is clear that in order to get to the wine after the jar has been fully sealed, it was often necessary to break off not only the seal but the entire neck of the jar as well (Hope 1978: 8, 1989; 1993: 89; Leonard 1995: 252). Attempts to remove the sealings alone are apparent within the corpus of sealings from Malkata, i.e. pieces of sealings probably removed from the sides of the jar, as well as one seal which had had its top cut off (Hope 1978: 8). Leonard (1995: 252) notes an example of the reuse of Canaanite jars which perhaps had their tops broken off during the unsealing process, i.e. as the container attached to the *shaduf*, the device used to raise water for irrigation from the New Kingdom onwards, as depicted in the Nineteenth-Dynasty tomb of Ipuy (TT217; see Manniche 1989: 12; see Chapters 21 and 24, this volume).

It has been suggested that a scene from the Eighteenth-Dynasty tomb of Rekhmira (TT100) depicts the sealing of wine jars (Davies 1943: 43 pl. XLVIII) although the practice is more clearly illustrated in the tomb of Khaemwaset (TT261). A scene from the Eighteenth-Dynasty tomb of Parennefer (TT188) shows the dampening and then stamping of wine jar seals but probably not their manufacture (Davies 1923b: 136–45; Hope 1978: 33; Hope 1993: 94).

Labelling

After the wine jars were sealed, the official stamp was most likely to have been placed on them while the mud of the final sealing process was still soft. A scene from the above-mentioned tomb of Parennefer (Davies 1923b: 136–45) shows that the stamps were moistened prior to the application of the official stamp, perhaps to remove mud from previous sealings (Hope 1993: 96). Several examples of the carved official stamps used to label the mud sealings survive and show that they could have been made from faience, limestone, pottery and wood (e.g. Brunton 1948; Petrie 1896, 1927b; Smith 1976).

In the Old Kingdom, cylinder seals were used as official stamps for wine jars and those of the First Dynasty included the king's name in a *serekh* and depicted the god Horus who represented the king (see Fig. 23.1; see also Emery 1961: 209; Kaplony 1963–4; James 1995: 199). By the Second Dynasty, more information was added to seal impressions, such as the vine hieroglyph and the names of areas, such as 'White Walls', known to be Memphis, and Buto in the Delta which are presumed to be the places of origin for the wine and not its destination (Kaplony 1963–4: 3, figs. 310–11; James 1995: 199). Inscriptions were also sometimes hand-written on Old Kingdom wine jars which listed the king's regnal year but not his name (James 1995: 201). The quantities of surviving seal impressions, coupled with the artistic record and the wine jars themselves, suggests that wine-making was not uncommon in the Old Kingdom (James 1995: 199).

A seal impression dating to the reign of King Den, the fourth ruler of the First Dynasty (*c.* 2900 BC), which contains the hieroglyph of what appears to be a wine press, is often cited as the earliest evidence for wine-making in Egypt (Fig. 23.1; see Kaplony 1963–4: 3; pl. 67, figs 238–9). But James (1995: 200) notes that caution must be used in this interpretation since, as yet, there is no evidence for this type of framed press in Old Kingdom tomb scenes (see section on wine pressing, p. 588) and that the two-handled vessel shown below the press is not a ceramic shape associated with wine-making or indeed of a type yet found in excavations. In light of these observations, James (1995: 200) maintains that this early seal impression may represent an oil press instead. The evidence to date, however, indicates that the range of presses used for oil also could be used for wine (Chapter 17, this volume) and further investigation of this matter is required. Later seal impressions, i.e. those of the Second- and Third-Dynasty rulers Khasekhemwy and Djoser, contain hieroglyphs more convincingly related to wine-making, such as a vine growing from a pot and trellised on forked sticks, depictions which also appear in Old Kingdom tomb scenes (James 1995: 200–1; see Kaplony 1963–4: 3; pl. 82, nos. 309; pl. 84, nos. 316–18). There is a relative scarcity of archaeological evidence relating to the labelling of wine in the period *c.* 2600–1550 BC, i.e., between the seal impressions of the Early Dynastic period and the large number of detailed wine jar labels dating to the New Kingdom (James 1995: 201).

While many wine jar sealings were labelled with hieroglyphic stamps (e.g. Hayes 1951), from the late Eighteenth Dynasty onwards the surviving record includes numerous wine jars labelled directly onto the shoulder of the jar in hieratic script which included the regnal year, the name of the wine-maker, the name of the estate, the location of the vineyard and sometimes the quality of the wine, i.e. 'good', or 'very good' (for a detailed discussion, see Tallet 1998a). Hand-written wine jar labels would survive primarily in dry settlements and tombs and are most likely to be under-represented in the archaeological record compared to those inscriptions which are stamped or incised directly into the clay. The presence of both the hand-written labels on the shoulder of the jar and the stamped labels on the jar seals ensured that the jars could not be opened without damaging one or the other label, that the information could be easily read and that the jars could be stamped by workers who may not have been able to read or write themselves (Hayes 1951: 162; Hope 1993: 96). As with wine, the labelling of other commodities also became more common during the New Kingdom (e.g. Hayes 1951: 37), however, the evidence from several sites suggests that jars used for the storage and transport of wine appear to have been labelled more frequently than those used for other goods (Leahy 1985: 66; e.g. Hayes 1951; Smith 1975: 181–2; Leahy 1978: 2–3, 13; Koenig 1979, 1980; Hope 1993: 97). The evidence of the jar sealings and labels also provides some indication of the reuse of storage jars (e.g. Hayes 1951; Hope 1989; 1993: 131–2; Tallet 1998a).

While wine jar labels provide a range of valuable information, these assemblages are sometimes based on fortuitous finds of specific portions of vessels. Although some labels were more indelibly stamped, many were written on the vessels in temporary ink to describe the perishable contents within (Hayes 1951: 37). The surviving assemblages, therefore, may represent only a small portion of the wine actually consumed (Poo 1995: 28). The many variables associated with the production, distribution, use, discard, deposition and recovery of this class of information warns against their overinterpretation.

Wine jar labels have been found at various sites, although the main corpus of New Kingdom wine jar labels, thus far, are from five major assemblages: the royal, late Eighteenth-Dynasty sites of Malkata (e.g. Hayes 1951; Hope 1978; Leahy 1978), Amarna (e.g. Petrie 1894; Cerny 1964; Fairman 1951; Leahy 1985) and Tutankhamun's tomb (KV62) (Carter 1933; Černy 1965; Lesko 1977; Beinlich and Saleh 1989; Hope 1993; Tallet 1996), as well as the Nineteenth- and Twentieth-Dynasty sites of Deir el-Medina (Koenig 1979) and the Ramesseum (Spiegelberg 1898; 1923; Kitchen 1992). Lerstrup (1992: 75) has noted that the important procedure of labelling the jars is not actually depicted in the surviving tomb-scenes.

Wine jar labels suggest that the Nile Delta was a prime area of viticulture from the Early Dynastic period onwards. Early Dynastic labels indicate that there were vineyards in the Eastern and Western nomes of the Delta, particularly in Buto (Kaplony 1963 III: 238–9, 311–2, 318). The term 'wine of the north' (*irp mḥw*) from the Pyramid Texts probably

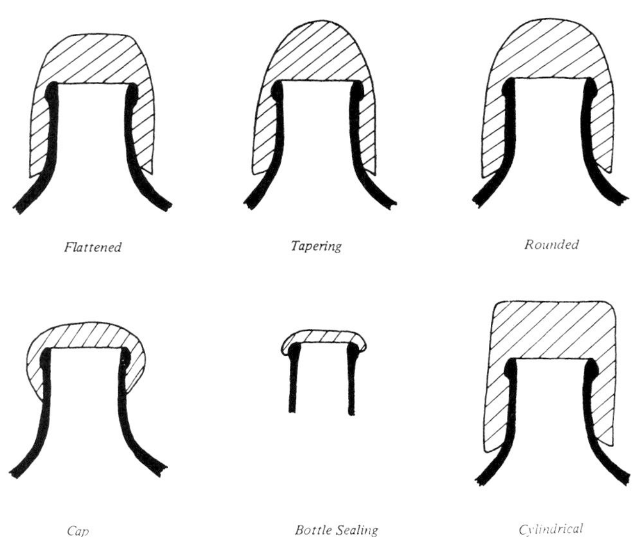

Figure 23.18 New Kingdom jar sealing types.

also refers to the Delta region. Many wine jar labels indicate that 'the Western River' was a prime wine-making region and this is thought to be the Canopic branch of the Nile (e.g. Gardiner 1947; Bietak 1975: 117–18; Poo 1995: 15–16 for other possible vineyard areas). The importance of the Delta as a wine growing area continued into the Greco–Roman period when Mareotic and Taeniotic wine from that region were well-regarded (e.g. Athenaeus I: 33, d–e). Wines were also made in the oases, such as Dakhla, although the oases' vineyards were perhaps at their most prosperous in the New Kingdom and later periods (Poo 1995: 19–20; also Breasted IV: 734, 992; Fakhry 1942; 1973; Giddy 1987; Tallet pers. comm.). Textual evidence also indicates that wines were made in Upper Egypt as well, such as at Elkab, for example (Kaplony 1963 III: 747, 748, 765) and the Papyrus Harris (I, 7, 10–12) notes that during the reign of Ramesses III, the Theban temples were given 433 vineyards although it is not clear if these were in Upper or Lower Egypt. As noted above, wine-making scenes from Theban tombs tend to show treading but not the use of the sack press, a detail which may have had some bearing on the variable quality between northern and southern wines. For details on the wine regions of Egypt, see e.g. Speigelberg 1923; Gauthier 1927; Gardiner 1947; Hayes 1951; Smith 1976; Cerny 1965; Darby *et al.* 1977: 597–607; Lesko 1977; 1995; Leahy 1978, 1985; Kitchen 1979: 673–96; Koenig 1979, 1980; Meeks 1993, Poo 1995; Tallet 1996, 1998a, 1998b).

The 285 wine jar labels from Malkata, the palace city of Amenhotep III (1391–1353 BC), were found in the magazines attached to palace buildings, discarded in rubbish heaps associated with these buildings, and in some of the houses in the workmen's village (Hayes 1951: 35–6,39;

Hope 1978: 3). Most of the labels are dated with the year of king's reign to indicate vintage and others name the chief vintner of the estate where the wines were produced. Most date to the last ten years of the reign of Amenhotep III (for more on this subject see Hayes 1951: 36–7, no. 14; also Fairman 1951: 152–7; Johnson 1993: 121–3; Vandersleyen 1995: 402–7; Murnane 1977: 123–69; von Beckerath 1984: 11–12; Tallet 1996: 371). Most of the inscribed wine-jar fragments date to the jubilee years of Amenhotep III's reign (30, 34 and 37) and many were labelled as special to the king's jubilee festival (*heb-sed*). The labels suggest the intense use of wine at the *heb-sed* (or perhaps an increase in wine labelling at the time) and may also indicate that the palace was used particularly for those festivities (see Hayes 1951: 36, 44, 82–3, fig. 4. no. 15). Since large numbers of jars of various commodities would have come into the palace every year, Hayes (1951: 83) notes that the Malkata finds may indicate that perhaps apart from those used during jubilee years, the majority of storage jars coming into Malkata were uninscribed or reused continually until the labels were obliterated. Most of the Malkata wines had come from the area of the 'Western River' (Hayes 1951: 88–9). Recent analysis of a residue from within a storage jar from the palace of Amenhotep III at Malkata reportedly showed traces of tartaric acid, suggesting the presence of wine (McGovern *et al.* 1996).

The 165 Amarna wine jar labels represent twenty-six different estates, most of these from the 'Western River' vineyards which bore the names of Akhenaten, members of his family, several temples of Aten and officials (Fig. 23.19). Most of the Amarna fragments were recovered from the area of the central palace. Other wines at Amarna came from the eastern Delta, from Memphis and three of the desert oases (Fairman 1951; Leahy 1985; Lesko 1995: 226; 1977: 28). It has been suggested that the comparatively small number of dated wine jars recovered from Amarna (165), the capital of Egypt for at least twelve years, may be an indication of how infrequent wine was consumed (or labelled) in most circumstances (Lesko 1995: 229) and may indicate that jars may have been returned for reuse (Leahy 1985: 66; Lesko 1977: 29; 1995: 226; Tallet 1998a).

In 1922, twenty-six labelled wine jars were recovered from the tomb of Tutankhamun (Carter 1933; Cerny 1965: 1–4, 21–4, pls. 1–5; Lesko 1977: 22–9, 1995: 220–5; Hope 1993). The wines were primarily from estates belonging to the Aten and Tutankhamun himself located along the 'Western River' while one wine came from the 'Southern Oasis' which refers to Dakhla in the south western desert and another from an uncertain location (Lesko 1995: 223; also see Sauneron and Yoyotte 1959; Černy 1965; Hope 1993; Tallet 1996). Lesko (1977: 23; 1995: 223) argues that if some of the best wines of Tutankhamun's reign had been buried with him, then the wines from his fourth, fifth and ninth years were among the best vintages of his

Figure 23.19 Akhenaten and his mother, Queen Tiye, drinking wine, in a scene from the tomb of Huya at Amarna (EA1).

short reign, as twenty-three of the twenty-six wine jars date to these three years. This would have meant that he had very young wines (from his ninth year) and 'old' four and five year vintages. It has been suggested, however, that wine probably would not have lasted much beyond that time in the storage vessels and, as old labels were not always erased, their inclusion may indicate the reuse of wine jars of earlier vintages (Hope 1989; 1993). Two older wine jars were also present in the tomb, including one dating to the thirty-first year of Amenhotep III. It has been argued that this jar had not been reused and may have been placed in the tomb for symbolic reasons (Hope 1993; Tallet pers. comm).

The Ramesseum, the Nineteenth-Dynasty mortuary temple of Ramsses II on the west bank at Thebes, offers the best evidence for wine jar labels for this period (Spiegelberg 1898; 1923: 25–6; Helck 1963 IV: 728–34; Kitchen 1979, 1992; Koenig 1994). This evidence shows that the Ramesseum owned at least eighteen vineyards and had dealings with many more (Kitchen 1992: 115, 120–1). While wines from the Eighteenth-Dynasty sites of Malkata and Amarna were primarily from the western ('Western River') and central areas of the Delta, most of the vineyards serving the Ramesseum were located nearer the Delta capital of Piramesse in the eastern Delta. Other wines came from vineyards as far south as the areas around Heliopolis, Meidum and Hermopolis (Kitchen 1992: 117–18). The designation of quality (*nfr, nfr-nfr*) on the wine jar labels attest to the generally high quality of the Ramesseum wines, particularly when compared to the lower proportion of vintages deemed *nfr-nfr* from the Workmen's Village at Deir el-Medina (Kitchen 1992: 119). During the Ramesside period, wine-making scenes had been largely replaced by funerary scenes and those of the hereafter and while, based on this evidence, it could not be assumed that wine-making itself had become less common, the large corpus of wine jar labels from the Ramesseum attests the continuation of wine production through the New Kingdom (Poo 1995: 11).

Wine jar labels from Buhen (Smith 1976), together with archaeobotanical remains of grape seeds from sites, such as those from Semna (van Zeist 1983), as well as other archaeological and textual evidence (e.g. Adams 1966) indicate that wine was traded from Egypt into Nubia during the New Kingdom and was also locally made. (For more on wine and Nubia, see Vercoutter 1959; Adams 1966, Meeks 1993; Kitchen 1993).

Storage

Tomb-scenes indicate that after sealing, the number of wine jars was recorded by a scribe sitting beside the jars and were then brought to the magazine for storage (Lerstrup 1992: 74–5). The regnal year or production date labelled on the wine jars would have been particularly important information at the storage stage due to the probable short-lived nature of Egyptian wines. Unfortunately, little is known of ancient Egyptian wine storage prior to the New Kingdom (James 1995: 207). As noted above (in the section on 'bottling'), due to its tapered base, the typical Egyptian wine jar was not designed to remain upright without some support and several Eighteenth-Dynasty tomb-scenes, such as that in the tomb of Intef (TT155), show wine jars leaning against each other (Figs. 23.12 and 23.16; see Säve-Söderbergh 1957: 2: pl. 15; Wilkinson 1878: 388; James 1995: 207; Lesko 1995: 220). Wine jars from some Early Dynastic tombs were also stored in this way (e.g. Emery 1961: pl. 20). Lesko (1995: 220) notes that the wine jars may have been designed for storage on their sides with the labels facing upwards. Placing these storage vessels upright or on their sides would have been a necessity due to their shape and the method of storing wine jars may not have been distinct from that of the storage of other commodities in this type of storage vessel.

Archaeological evidence also offers examples of wine storage in a funerary context and it is clear from some Early Dynastic tombs, such as the First Dynasty tomb 3504 at Saqqara, that the provisions of wine laid down for the after-life at that time were particularly vast (e.g. Emery 1961: 145, pls. 13, 20; Emery *et al.* 1954: 68; Spencer 1982; James 1995: 201–2). It has been argued that the contrast in provisions for the dead from these early tombs to those from the later periods in some cases may be due to the development of offering lists of necessary provisions within the tomb (Barta 1963; James 1995: 202). The inclusion of the offering list or stelae in the tomb served as a type of shorthand for what was needed in the after-life and therefore precluded the placement of large quantities of actual food and drink into the tomb. For example, the Second-Dynasty stele of Imti – one of the earliest private examples to clearly show an offering list – depicts a wine jar with a conical seal and the hieroglyphic sign for 1,000, thereby ensuring a plentiful supply of wine for the hereafter (James 1995: 202).

The chemical detection of ancient wine

[NEIL BOULTON AND CARL HERON]

Introduction

The identification of the plant and/or animal source of amorphous organic residues of archaeological interest is based upon matching the chemical composition of the residue (either the presence of a mixture of compounds or a specific compound often termed a 'biomarker') with that of a contemporary natural material (Evershed 1993; Heron and Evershed 1993). In the last decade, considerable advances have been made in the analysis and identification of organic deposits, either preserved on artefact surfaces or absorbed in permeable matrices, notably of ceramics. In particular, gas chromatography/mass spectrometry (GC/MS) provides very detailed information on the composition of organic residues. The range of ancient residues identified by this technique is testimony to its versatility and applicability to trace analysis of complex mixtures (see Chapters 17–19, this volume). The main obstacle to identification is the specificity of the 'biomarkers', since many organic compounds are distributed widely in the biosphere. Other issues include biomarker loss or degradation and sample contamination (Evershed 1993). Given the wide range of potential analytical tools available, the methodology developed should be rigorous such that the data generated should be sufficiently diagnostic to be able to answer the questions posed.

Summary of previous results

In his investigations of preserved amorphous deposits, Lucas (1962) made use of 'wet' chemical tests, in particular 'spot' tests, developed as a new field of analytical chemistry in the 1920s by Fritz Feigl (1966), as well as solubility and melting point determinations. These methods can provide useful information regarding chemical and physical properties of organic molecules, although many of the tests require relatively large (>1 mg) samples and have been replaced by a wide range of instrumental techniques of analysis. Lucas (1962: 22) briefly describes the analysis of three residues from wine jars; two from the tomb of Tutankhamun and one from the Monastery of St Simeon near Aswan. The identification of potassium carbonate and potassium tartrate demonstrated that 'the residues were those from wine'. Precise details of the tests used to identify these compounds are however not given in the book.

Wine is a complex mixture of several classes of organic compounds, including alcohols, aldehydes, acids, carbohydrates, esters, polyhydroxyphenols such as flavonols and anthocyanins, proteins, lipids and vitamins, as well as inorganic minerals (Jackson 1994; Farkaš 1988). Although there is a voluminous oenological literature on the ageing, deterioration and spoilage of wine, the analysis of putative wine residues in ceramic and glass containers has been motivated by archaeological curiosity. In the 1970s, Condamin and Formenti (1976, 1978; see also Formenti and Duthel 1995) identified wine residues in two intact and sealed Dressel 1 transport amphorae of Roman date recovered from the shipwreck of *La Madrague de Giens*. Subsequent tests were also reported on the contents of a sealed Lamboglia 2 amphora from the same wreck which contained both liquid (4.5 litres) and solid (50 cm^3) phases. (Formenti *et al.* 1978). Although sealed, the contents had been adulterated by at least some intrusion of sea water. Gas chromatography (GC) identified tartaric acid and various phenolic acid derivatives (tannin and anthocyanin degradation products) in both the residues and liquids. L(+)-Tartaric acid is found in nature almost exclusively in the genus *Vitis*, the grapevine (Singleton 1995, 67–9), and grape skins contain phenolic compounds (especially the anthocyanin pigments in red grapes). The data compared favourably with a modern wine sample (St Emilion) subjected to the same sample preparation.

In another study, the liquid contents of two of the fourteen intact bottles recovered during excavations of the 1749 wreck of the Dutch East Indiaman, the *Amsterdam* were extracted by tubes inserted through the corks. The almost pure wine was analysed by GC which identified the volatile and semi-volatile components and high performance liquid chromatography (HPLC) which enabled the identification of sugars, fruit acids and amino acids (Maarse and van den Berg 1985). The microbiological status of the wine testified to its healthy (i.e. drinkable) state.

These studies are interesting in their own right and represent an almost ideal scenario for a successful analysis. Yet the rarity of sealed vessels retaining their contents in a pristine condition limits the degree to which significant archaeological deductions can be made. For example, when and where did wine production begin, what kinds of vessels were used to prepare, store, transport and consume wine? To access this information, archaeologists must continue to rely on botanical remains, epigraphy and documentary evidence and deductions made from individual archaeological contexts (for example, presses or vessels stored on their sides).

However, interest in the detection of ancient wine has been enhanced considerably by recent work undertaken on the more common category of amorphous deposits found on the interior walls of open, unsealed ceramic containers or vessel fragments (e.g., Badler *et al.* 1990; 1996; Michel *et al.* 1992; 1993; McGovern *et al.* 1996; 1997; McGovern 1997). A methodology comprising chemical spot tests, infrared spectroscopy and more recently HPLC has been developed to characterise tartaric acid and tartrate salts in ancient samples. This approach is considered by its proponents to provide unambiguous proof of the detection of ancient wine residues in ceramic jars from the Near East. The studies have concentrated on very early samples from Iran, but deposits in Egyptian amphorae have also been studied, initially to provide a reference for the earlier material. These results provide the earliest evidence for the occurrence of wine in the archaeological record and inspired a symposium on the origins and ancient history of wine (McGovern *et al.* 1995; for a review see Samuel 1997). Badler *et al.* (1990) investigated a visible (deep burgundy in colour) deposit on the inner surface of a jar, excavated between 1967 and 1973 at the site of Godin Tepe, Iran (Period V, *c.* 3500–2900 BC) located in the central Zagros mountains of north-central Iran. Using a Feigl spot test, the residues emitted a green fluorescence ('a sign that they contained tartaric acid, a compound specific to grapes'). Contextual evidence suggested that the narrow-necked Godin Tepe jars had once been stoppered (Badler *et al.* 1990, 27–8) and stored on their sides, possibly to inhibit the wine from converting to vinegar. A funnel found with at least two jars in Room 2 (although lacking visible residues these vessels are thought to be 'empties' awaiting bottling) may have served to strain juice from the grapes. However, grape seeds are not known until the first millennium BC levels at the site.

More recently, positive results have been obtained on a sherd from a Neolithic jar (*c.* 5400–5000 BC) with a thin yellowish deposit from the site of Hajji Firuz Tepe, located some 200 miles north of Godin Tepe, in the Zagros mountains (McGovern *et al.* 1996) and on a spouted jar from Uruk (W 19604), dating to the late Uruk period (*c.* 3500–3100 BC; see Badler *et al.* 1996). The presence of plant resin considered to be *Pistacia atlantica* Desf. was also reported as a constituent of the Hajji Firuz Tepe deposit. The resin was interpreted as a preservative added deliberately to the wine. Positive results have been claimed with regard to the analysis of a resinous, dark-coloured deposit found on Byzantine amphora from Gebel Adda, a hilltop fortress in Nubia dating to the late fourth- to early sixth-century AD (Ballana-period cemetery 4, tomb 17; see Badler *et al.* 1990). These vessels are thought to have been imported from Upper Egypt and are considered to have been used for wine storage and transport. McGovern *et al.* (1996) also report a positive tartaric acid test on a deposit from an Egyptian amphora dating to the fourteenth century BC, from the palace of Amenhotep III at Malkata. McGovern (1997) details the analysis of nine wine ostraca and one 'ale' ostracon from Malkata. Finally, McGovern *et al.* (1997) report identification of tartaric acid, tartrate salts and *Pistacia* resin (terebinth) in residues taken from three imported jars excavated at Abydos dating to the late fourth millennium BC.

Analytical methodology

The methodology developed by McGovern and co-workers involves a Feigl spot test used to detect the presence of tartaric acid in the deposits. Any tartaric acid in the sample is converted, following addition of *β, β'-Dinaphthol* and concentrated sulphuric acid to a compound that exhibits green fluorescence under UV light. Diffuse-reflectance Fourier transform infrared spectroscopy (FT-IR) is undertaken on solid samples or solvent extracts of the deposits. It has been proposed that this technique identifies tartaric acid and, in particular, its insoluble salts in the deposits. An absorption band in the range 1700–1740 cm^{-1} corresponds to the carboxylic acid group of tartaric acid, and a maximum at 1600–1650 cm^{-1} results from the carboxylate group of a tartrate salt, possibly calcium tartrate, which would be expected to form from the acid in the basic, calcareous terrain of the sites. More recently, HPLC has been used to separate the principal constituents of the deposits (e.g. McGovern *et al.* 1996). Components eluting between 1.3–1.6 minutes are thought to include calcium tartrate and these results are considered to be closely comparable to a number of ancient and modern wine samples.

Collectively, these studies imply that, given the presence of surface deposits preserved by dry burial conditions, detection of ancient wine is a relatively routine procedure. However, some methodological refinement is necessary to reduce the ambiguities in the research undertaken to date. For example, the degree to which qualitative spot tests can be used with confidence in archaeological investigations is debatable. One problem is cross-reactivity leading to 'false positive' results. Although the spot test employed by McGovern and co-workers is claimed to be sensitive to 10 μg of tartaric acid, a possible cross-reaction is with malic acid (a common acid in many fruits), although it is reported to be a tenth as sensitive as tartaric acid (Eegriwe 1933, in Singleton 1995: 69). Feigl (1966) also reports that gluconic, glucuronic, dihydroxytartaric and tartronic acids cross-react but these may be inconsequential since their occurrence in ancient jars is unlikely. However, spot tests were not developed for the complexities of archaeological investigation, where a wide range of alteration products might be encountered. Spot tests at best fulfil a role in the preliminary screening of samples, although their utility even then is limited in comparison with established instrumental procedures (Boulton 1997).

The instrumental techniques of infrared (IR) and Fourier transform infrared (FT-IR) spectroscopy are very useful analytical tools for archaeological purposes yet there is a difficulty in using IR methods to trace individual molecules in potentially complex mixtures (see Heron and Evershed 1993: 262; Pollard and Heron 1996: 72–3). For example, many absorption bands are common to a vast range of organic molecules. IR and FT-IR have been used profitably as 'fingerprinting' techniques for certain organic substances, such as fossil and recent higher plant resins, beeswax and so on. However, combined separation and characterisation techniques (such as GC/MS) are preferred for detailed compositional analysis. Given the IR data published by McGovern and co-workers, it is possible that tartaric acid is represented as part of the composite spectrum, but it is difficult to be unequivocal. The use of alternative techniques will reduce the uncertainty.

High performance liquid chromatography (HPLC) is a highly sensitive and selective separation technique, although limited data have so far been presented in support of the claims made for ancient wine. Both reverse-phase and ion/ion-exchange approaches have been widely employed in oenology (see Boulton 1997; Singleton 1995) and work on ancient samples will surely follow. Coupling a liquid chromatograph to a mass spectrometer (LC/MS) would enable the generation of mass spectral data on each of the peaks separated and should confirm unambiguously the presence of tartaric acid as well as other components (such as phenolics) in the extracts of these deposits.

The presence of other organic substances (such as higher plant resins) in these residues must also be examined rigorously and interpreted cautiously. The suggestion that resin is used to flavour and preserve wine is only one possibility. However, this should not lead necessarily to the assumption that the identification of resin supports the presence of wine. Resins could have served as vessel sealants or as the bulk contents of ancient jars. It would appear that transport amphorae used for carrying wine (as well as a wide range of other organic commodities) were, from the Greco–Roman period onwards, often lined internally with resinous products, including wood tars, to prevent seepage of the liquid into the permeable ceramic matrix. The degree to which these substances served as flavourings is not easy to answer (Heron and Pollard, 1988; Koehler, 1995; see also Chapter 18, this volume).

Future developments

Aside from evolving the existing analytical approaches, a number of other developments are likely to be explored as improved or complementary methodologies are sought and as more sophisticated questions are posed. Singleton (1995) has proposed that syringic acid (3,5–dimethoxy-4–hydroxybenzoic acid), derived from the most common anthocyanin of *Vitis vinifera*, malvidin-3–glucoside could be a valuable biomarker at least for red wine. The distinction between wine and other grape products, such as must or vinegar merits consideration (see Samuel 1997). Although tartaric acid is present in significant quantities only in grape products, the conclusion that wine as opposed to other grape products is present should be supported by other evidence. Indeed, other biomarkers exist. In theory, wine can be distinguished from other grape products through the identification of biomarkers only present as a result of fermentation (such as butane-2,3–diol, succinic acid and so on). However, the solubility of some of these molecules might limit the degree to which they survive. Hitherto, success has only been achieved under very favourable conditions of preservation (e.g. Maarse and van den Berg 1985).

There is no doubt that biomolecular analysis of archaeological and historical samples is likely to play a major role in contributing to significant questions regarding the antiquity of ancient fermented beverages (McGovern *et al.* 1995). Hitherto, the analysis of wine residues in stoppered vessels containing liquid and solid deposits has provided definitive evidence for aged wine (tartaric acid and anthocyanins in the Roman amphorae and a range of compound classes, including volatile organic compounds in the wine bottles from the *Amsterdam*). Clearly, residues in unsealed or open vessels might not provide such favourable conditions for survival of a broad spectrum of compounds consistent with ancient grape products. There is a need for more rigour in the analysis of wine residues. For example, verification of the survival of biomarkers consistent with wine should be sought through the use of GC/MS and LC/MS. Spot tests and IR spectra are relatively cheap and simple to use (although are not always easy to interpret), yet these approaches are not the most appropriate for unambiguous characterisation of wine residues in the archaeological record. Ancient organic residues are, quite simply, bad and rather intractable samples; by definition residues are alteration products, modified by unobservable cultural practices, subjected to poorly understood degradation processes and often contaminated during burial through to recovery, storage and even analysis. Such challenges necessitate an appropriate response in the design and execution of archaeological research programmes.

Conclusions [MARY ANNE MURRAY]

Several authors have queried why the fermentation of barley for beer was more widespread in Egypt (and Mesopotamia) than the technically simpler process of fermenting grapes for wine, most common to the Mediterranean and Aegean (e.g. Palmer 1994: 12; Singleton 1995: 72). Unlike beer, grapes need only to have their skins broken to release their juice in order to start fermentation, particularly in the heat of the day. The process also would have been easier to understand and then repeat than the fermentation of barley for beer which requires several stages to complete (Singleton 1995: 72; Chapter 22, this volume). Due to its high sugar and acid content, wine stores more easily and for longer periods than beer, and also has a higher alcohol content (Singleton 1995: 72). In both Egypt and Mesopotamia, wine was largely reserved for the élite and for special occasions (e.g. Powell 1995; Poo 1995). For Mesopotamia, Powell (1995: 105) has shown the great expense of grapes and raisins as compared to barley or dates, and in Egypt, too, grapes were the higher priced commodity – as much as five to ten times more expensive than beer during the Ramesside period at Deir el-Medina, for example (Janssen 1975: 350–2). Palmer (1994: 12) has queried whether the population at large in Egypt and other parts of the Near East would have preferred wine to beer if they had had greater access to it. While there are many variables why beer production took precedence over wine production in ancient Egypt and Mesopotamia, the ultimate answer undoubtedly has much to do with the agricultural conditions necessary for large-scale, sustained wine production which were restricted to a limited number of areas in both Mesopotamia and Egypt in the Bronze Age (also see Powell 1995). While there is archaeobotanical (and possibly chemical) evidence for the grape from the earliest periods in both Egypt and Mesopotamia (e.g. Chapter 24, this volume; Zettler and Miller 1995), beer was made from barley, the ubiquitous cereal staple throughout the archaeological and cultural records of these two regions. In Egypt, the consumption of wine became more widespread during the Ptolemaic period due to the influx of a large Greek population and also the improvements in irrigation techniques at that time (e.g. Rostovzeff 1922: 93–103, 1941) although beer remained a daily staple for the Egyptian *fellahin* (Rostovzeff 1922: 94; Poo 1995: 29; Chapter 22, this volume).

Although it is clear that the ancient Egyptians produced wine from at least 3000 BC onwards, many questions relating to the process remain. Future archaeological excavations, for example, may uncover less fragmentary vintage scenes and perhaps offer additional, well-illustrated details on the intermediate stages of the wine-making process (Lerstrup 1992: 65). Similarly, the increasing evidence from the excavations of settlement sites in Egypt may perhaps offer some challenges to the current view that wine was largely exclusive to royalty and the élite class.

As yet, there has not been systematic experimental research concerning the production of ancient Egyptian wines, as there has been for beer (Chapter 22). This evidence, along with the archaeological data and ethnographic information on traditional Egyptian wine-making practices, would undoubtedly provide insight into several unresolved issues: e.g. what would have been the most practical type of treading vat to use out of the many suggestions offered? What would have been the relative time scale involved for each practice, for example, how soon can the fermenting wine be transferred to other containers? How soon can the final containers be sealed after secondary fermentation? Do the time scales required provide an indication as to why white wine was an apparently infrequent or non-existent commodity in the Pharaonic period? What other purposes might the openings found in the mud sealings serve, if not for the escape of fermentation gases? Is there any pragmatic reason for scenes in the artistic evidence which may not yet be explained?

The Egyptian archaeological record also provides a

great potential resource for the chemical analyses of ancient wine residues. Innovative techniques, such as gas chromatography, infrared spectroscopy and the potential correlation of pottery shape and fabric with jar contents are increasingly used to detect and identify ancient wine which may help to clarify the dates and distribution of its use in ancient Egypt (e.g. Badler *et al.* 1990, 1996; Biers and McGovern 1990; McGovern and Michel 1995; McGovern *et al.* 1997; Formenti and Duthel 1995; Serpico 1996; Serpico and White forthcoming; Serpico forthcoming; Chapter 18, this volume).

Today, the subject of ancient Egyptian wine clearly requires the expertise of a variety of specialists, including Egyptologists in general but particularly the skills of linguists, chemists, archaeologists, ceramicists, archaeobotanists, oenologists, geneticists and those with an expertise in the wine trade of the Bronze Age Mediterranean and Near East.

Acknowledgements

The author would like to thank those who kindly commented on an earlier version of the manuscript and who also offered much useful Egyptological advice; Janine Bourriau, Dr Colin Hope, Dr Stephen Quirke, Dr Pierre Tallet and Dr Margaret Serpico. Thanks too, to Dr Annette Lerstrup for the allowing me to include her research in Tables 23.1 and 23.2 and to Dr Colin Hope for the use of Figure 23.18.

References

Abd er-Raziq, M. 1979. Die altägyptischen Weingarten (*k3nw/k3mw*) bis zum Ende des Neuen Reiches. *MDAIK*, 35 (1970): 227–247.

1988. Bemerkungen zum Verhältnis des k3mw- und 't-nt-ḫt-Gartens. In *Karl-Richard Lepsius (1810–1884). Akten des Tagung anläßich seines 100. Toestages, 10.–12.7.1984 in Halle. Berlin, pp. 318–21.*

Adams, W.Y. 1966. The vintage of Kush. *Kush*, 14: 262–84.

Altenmüller, H. 1982. Arbeiten am Grab des Neferherenptah in Saqqara (1970–1975). *MDAIK*, 38: 1–16.

Amouretti, M-C. 1992. Oléiculture et viticulture dans la Grèce antique. In *Agriculture in Ancient Greece.* (ed. Berit Wells). Acta Instituti Atheniensis Regni Sueciae, Series in 4°, XLII. Stockholm: Paul Åstrom Förlag, pp 77–86.

Aufrère, S. 1987. Etudes de lexicologie et d'histoire naturelle. *BIFAO*, 87: 36–9.

Badler, V.R., McGovern, P.E., and Glusker, D.L. 1996. Chemical evidence for a wine residue from Warka (Uruk) inside a Late Uruk Period spouted jar. *Baghdader Mitteilungen*, 27: 39–43.

Badler, V.R., McGovern, P.E., and Michel, R.H. 1990. Drink and be merry!: Infrared spectroscopy and ancient Near Eastern wines. *Organic Contents of Ancient Vessels: Materials Analysis and Archaeological Investigation.* (eds. W.R. Biers and P.E. McGovern). MASCA Research Papers in Science and Archaeology 7. Philadelphia: MASCA, University Museum of Archaeology and Anthropology, pp. 25–36.

Baines, J and Málek, J. 1984. *Atlas of Ancient Egypt.* Oxford: Equinox.

Barta, W. 1963. *Die altägyptische Opferliste von der Frühzeit bis zur griechisch-romischen Epoche.* Berlin: B. Hessling.

Bass, G. 1986. The Bronze Age shipwreck at Ulu Burun (Kas): 1984 campaign. *AJA*, 90: 269–96.

Bates, O. 1914. *Eastern Libyans: An essay.* London: Macmillan.

Baum, N. 1988. *Arbres et arbustes d'Egypte ancienne.* Leuven: Departement Oriëntalistiek.

Bauman, B. 1960. The botanical aspects of Egyptian embalming and burial. *Economic Botany*, 14: 84–104.

Beadnell, H. 1909. *An Egyptian Oasis: An Account of the Oasis of Kharga in the Libyan Desert, with Special Reference to Its History, Physical Geography and Water-supply.* London: John Murray.

von Beckerath, J. 1984. Eine Bemerkung zu der vermuteten Koregenz Amenophis III und IV. *GM*, 83: 11–12.

Beinlich, H. and Saleh, M. 1989. *Corpus der hieroglyphischen Inschriften aus dem Grab des Tutanchamun.* Oxford: Griffith Institute.

Berlandini, J. 1974. Le dignitaire ramesside Ramsès-em-per-Rê. *BIFAO*, 74: 4.

Biers, W.R. and McGovern, P.E. 1990. *Organic Contents of Ancient Vessels: Materials Analysis and Archaeological Investigation.* MASCA Research Papers in Science and Archaeology 7. Philadelphia: MASCA, University Museum of Archaeology and Anthropology.

Bietak, M. 1975. *Tell el-Daba II.* Vienna: Verlag der Österreichischen Akademie der Wissenschaften.

1985. Ein altägyptische Weingarten in einem Tempelbezirk. *Anzeiger der Phil.-hist. Klasse der Österreichischen Akademie der Wissenschaften*, 122: 267–78.

1986. *Avaris and Piramesse: Archaeological Exploration in the Eastern Nile Delta.* Mortimer Wheeler Archaeological Lecture 1979. 2nd edn. Oxford: OUP.

1996. *Avaris: The Capital of the Hyksos. Recent Excavations at Tell el-Dab'a.* London: BMP.

Bircher, W. 1995. *The date palm: A friend and companion of man.* Cairo: Elias Modern Press.

Blackman, A.M. 1915. *The Rock Tombs of Meir* III. London: EEF.

Boulton, N.D. 1997. Ancient wine or modern myth? A critical evaluation of scientific claims for the identification of ancient wine in archaeology. Unpublished MA dissertation, University of Bradford, UK.

Bourriau, J. 1981. *Umm el-Ga'ab: Pottery from the Nile Valley before the Arab Conquest.* Cambridge: Fitzwilliam Museum and CUP.

1997. Before Avaris: the Second Intermediate Period in Egypt outside the eastern Delta. In *The Hyksos: New Historical and Archaeological Perspectives.* (ed. E.D. Oren). University Museum Symposium Series. Philadelphia: University Museum Press, pp. 159–82.

Brack, A. and Brack, A. 1975. Vorbericht uber Arbeiten in Grab des Tjanuni (PM 74) 1973–4. *MDAIK*, 31: 15–25.

Breasted, J.H. 1906. *Ancient Records of Egypt.* Chicago: University of Chicago Press.

Brunton, G. 1948. *Matmar.* London: Quaritch.

Bruyère, B. 1939. *Rapport sur les Fouilles de Deir el-Médineh.* (1934–

1935). 3ieme Partie: Le Village, Les Décharges Publiques, La Station de Repos du Col, de la Valée des Rois. Cairo: L'Institut Français d'Archéologie Orientale.

Burckhardt, J.L. 1819. *Travels in Nubia*. London.

Buxo, R. 1996. Evidence for vines and ancient cultivation from an urban area, Lattes (Hérault), southern France. *Antiquity*, 70: 393–407.

Carter, H. 1933. *The Tomb of Tut-ankh-amen III*. London: Cassell and Co.

Caminos, R. 1954. *Late Egyptian Miscellanies*. Brown Egyptological Studies 1. London: OUP.

Černy, J. 1964. Three regnal dates of the Eighteenth Dynasty. *JEA*, 50: 37–9.

1965. *Hieratic Inscriptions from the Tomb of Tutankhamun*. Tutankhamun's Tomb Series 2. Oxford: Griffith Institute.

Charpentier, G. 1981. *Receuil de matériaux epigraphiques relatifs à la botanique de l'Egypte antique*. 2 vols. Paris: Trismégiste.

Cheshire, W. 1985. Remarks on the names of Pelusium. *GM*, 84: 19–24.

Condamin, J. and Formenti, F. 1976. Recherche de traces d'huile d'olive et de vin dans les amphores antiques. *Figlina*, 1: 143–58.

1978. Detection du contenu d'amphores antiques (huiles,vin): etude methodologique. *Revue d'Archéometrie*, 2: 43–58.

Darby, W.J., Ghalioungui, P. and Grivetti, L. 1977. *Food: The Gift of Osiris* II. London: Academic Press.

Davies, N. de G. 1900. *The Mastaba of Ptahhetep and Akhethetep* I. London: EEF.

1905. *The Rock Tombs of el-Amarna* III. London: EEF, Quaritch and Kegan Paul, Trench and Trübner and Co.

1917. *The Tomb of Nakht at Thebes*. New York: MMA.

1923a. *The Tomb of Two Officials of Tuthmosis IV*. (Nos. 75 & 90). London: EES.

1923b. Akhenaten at Thebes. *JEA*, 9: 132–52.

1930. *The Tomb of Ken-Amun at Thebes*. The Metropolitan Museum of Art Egyptian Expedition. New York: MMA.

1933. *The Tomb of Nefer-hotep at Thebes*. vol. 1. Publication 9. New York: Metropolitan Museum of Art Egyptian Expedition.

1943. *The Tomb of Rekh-Mi-Re at Thebes*. 2 vols. New York: MMA.

1948. *Seven Private Tombs at Kurnah*, (ed. A.H. Gardiner). London: EES.

Davies N. de G. and Gardiner, A. 1915. *The Tomb of Amenemhet (No 82)*. London: EEF.

von Deines, H. and H. Grapow. 1959. *Wörterbuch der Ägyptischen Drogennamen. Grundriss der Medizen der Alten Aegypter* 6. Berlin: Akademie-Verlag.

Derchain, Ph. 1965. *Le Papyrus Salt 825: Ritual pour la conservation de la vie en Égypte*. Brussels: Palais de l'Academie.

Dreyer, G. 1992. Recent discoveries at Abydos cemetery U. In *The Nile Delta in Transition: 4th–3rd Millennium BC*. (ed. E. van der Brink). Tel Aviv: E. van der Brink, pp. 293–9.

1993. Umm el-Qaab; Nachuntersuchungen im frühzeitlichen Königsfriedhof, 5./6. Bericht. *MDAIK*, 49: 23–62.

Duell, P. 1938. *The Mastaba of Mereruka*. 2 vols. Chicago: OIP.

Emery, W.B. 1961. *Archaic Egypt*. Harmondsworth: Penguin.

1962. *A Funerary Repast in an Egyptian Tomb of the Archaic Period*. Leiden: Nederlands Institut voor het Nabije Oosten.

Emery, W.B. and Saad, Z.Y. 1938. *Excavations at Saqqara: The Tomb of Hemaka*. Cairo: Government Press.

Emery, W.B., James T.G.H., Klasens, A., Anderson, R., and Burney, C.A. 1954. *Great Tombs of the First Dynasty* II. London: EES.

Empereur, J.-Y. 1993. La production viticole dans dans l'Egypte ptolemaique et romaine. In *La production du vin et de l'huile en Mediterranée*. (eds. M.C. Amouretti and J.P. Brun). Bulletin de Correspondance Hellénique. Supplement XXVI. Athens: École Français d'Athenes, pp. 39–47.

Erichsen, W. 1993. *The Great Papyrus Harris I*. Bibl. Aeg. V: 10.

Evershed, R.P. 1993. Biomolecular archaeology and lipids. *WA*, 25/1: 74–93.

Eyre, C. 1994. The water regimes for orchards and plantations in Pharaonic Egypt. *JEA*, 80: 57–80.

Fairman, H.W. 1951. The inscriptions. In *The City of Akhenaten* III/1 (ed. J.D.S. Pendlebury). London: EES.

el-Fakharani, F. 1983. Recent excavations at Marea in Egypt. In *Das Römisch-Byzantinische Aegypten: Akten des internationalen Symposions 26–30 September 1978 in Trier*. (ed. E. Winter). Aegyptiaca Treverensia 2. Mainz: von Zabern.

Fakhry, A. 1942. *The Egyptian Deserts: Bahria Oasis*. Cairo: AUC.

1973. *Siwa Oasis*. Cairo: AUC.

Farkaš, J. 1988. *Technology and Biochemistry of Wine*. 2 vols. New York: Gordon and Breach.

Feigl, F. 1966. *Spot Tests in Organic Analysis*. 7th edn. New York: Elsevier.

Foaden, G., and Fletcher, F. 1910. *Textbook of Egyptian Agriculture* II. Cairo: F. Eimer.

Forbes, R.J. 1965. *Studies in Ancient Technology* III. Leiden: Brill.

Formenti, F. and Duthel, J.M. 1995. The analysis of wine and other organics inside amphoras of the Roman period. In *The Origins and Ancient History of Wine*. (eds. P. McGovern, S. Fleming and S. Katz). Luxembourg: Gordon and Breach, pp. 79–85.

Formenti, F., Hesnard, A. and Tchernia, A. 1978. Une amphore 'Lamboglia 2' contenant du vin dans l'épave de la Madrague de Giens. *Archaeonautica*, 2: 95–100.

Gardiner, A. 1947. *Ancient Egyptian Onomastica*. 2 vols. Oxford: OUP.

Gastineau, C.F., Darby, W.J. and Turner, T.B. (eds.). 1979. *Fermented Food Beverages in Nutrition*. New York: Academic Press.

Gauthier, H. 1927. *Dictionnaire des Nomes Geographiques Contenus dans les textes Hieroglyphiques*. 7 vols. Cairo: IFAO.

Germer, R. 1985 *Flora des Pharaonischen Agypten*. DAIK, Sonderschrift 14. Mainz: von Zabern.

1989. *Die Pflanzenmaterialien aus dem Grab des Tutanchamun*. Hildesheim: Gerstenberg.

forthcoming. The plant material found by Petrie at Lahun and some remarks on the problems of identifying Egyptian plant names. In *Lahun Studies*. (ed. S. Quirke). New Malden: SIA Publications.

Giddy, L. 1987. *Egyptian Oases*. Warminster: Aris and Philips.

Girard, P.S. 1812. *Description de l'Egypte, état moderne, II, Mémoire sur l'agriculture, l'industrie et le commerce de l'Egypte*. Paris.

Gödecken, K.B. 1976. *Eine Betrachtung der Inscriften des Meten im Rahmen der sozialen und rechtlichen Stellung von Privatleuten im ägyptischen Alten Reich*. Wiesbaden: Harrassowitz.

Hanson, V. 1992. Practical aspects of grape-growing and the ideology of Greek viticulture. In *Agriculture in Ancient Greece*. (ed. Berit Wells). Acta Instituti Atheniensis Regni Sueciae, Series in 4°, XLII. Stockholm: Paul Åstrom, pp. 161–6.

Harpur, Y. 1987. *Decoration in Egyptian Tombs of the Old Kingdom*. London: KPI.

Harrison, S.G., Masefield, G.B., Wallis, M., and Nicholson, B.E. 1985. *The Oxford Book of Food Plants*. London: Peerage Books.

Hayes, W.C. 1951. Inscriptions from the palace of Amenhotep III. *JNES*, 10: 35–56, 82–111, 157–83 and 231–42.

Helck, W. 1963. *Materialien zur Wirtschaftsgeschichte des Neuen Reiches IV*, Wiesbaden: F. Steiner.

Heron, C. and Pollard, A.M. 1988. The analysis of natural resinous materials from Roman amphoras. In *Science and Archaeology – Glasgow 1987. Proceedings of a Conference on the Application of Scientific Techniques to Archaeology* (eds. E.A. Slater and J.O. Tate) Oxford: BARS 196, pp. 429–46.

Heron, C. and Evershed, R. 1993. The analysis of organic residues and the study of pottery use. In *Archaeological Method and Theory* V. (ed. M.B. Schiffer). Arizona: University of Arizona Press, pp. 247–86.

Hepper, F. N. 1990. *Pharaoh's Flowers: The Botanical Treasures of Tutankhamun*. London: HMSO.

Hope, C. 1978. *Excavations at Malkata and the Birket Habu: Jar Sealings and Amphorae*. Warminster: Aris and Philips.

1989. Amphorae. *Pottery of the Egyptian New Kingdom: Three Studies*. Victoria: Victoria College Press.

1993. The jar sealings. In *Stone vessels, pottery and sealings from the tomb of Tutankhamun*. (ed. J. Baines). Oxford: Griffith Institute, pp. 87–138.

Hugonot, J.-C. 1989. *Le Jardin dans l'Egypte Ancienne*. Frankfurt: Peter Lang.

Jackson R. S. 1994. *Wine Science: Principles and Applications*. San Diego: Academic Press.

Jacquet-Gordon, H. 1962. *Les noms des domaines funéraires sous l'Ancien Empire égyptien*. Cairo: IFAO.

James, T.G.H. 1995. The earliest history of wine and its importance in ancient Egypt. In *The Origins and Ancient History of Wine* (eds. P. McGovern, S. Fleming and S. Katz). Luxembourg: Gordon and Breach, pp. 197–213.

Janssen, J. 1975. *Commodity Prices from the Ramesside Period: An Economic Study of the Village Necropolis Workmen at Thebes*. Leiden: E.J. Brill.

Johnson, H. 1974. *Wine*. London: Mitchell Beazley.

Johnson, J. H. 1986. *Thus Wrote Onchsheshonqy: An Introductory Grammar of Demotic*. Chicago: OIP.

Kaplony, P. 1963–4. *Die Inschriften der ägyptischen Fruhzeit*. 3 vols. and suppl. Wiesbaden: Harrassowitz.

Kislev, M. 1988. Fruit remains. In *The Egyptian Mining Temple at Timna* I (ed. B. Rothenberg). London: Institute of Archaeo-Metallurgical Studies, pp. 236–9.

Kitchen, K.A. 1979. *Ramesside Inscriptions. Historical and Biographical II*. Oxford: Blackwell.

1982. *Pharaoh Triumphant: The Life and Times of Ramesses II, King of Egypt*. Warminster: Aris and Philips.

1992. The vintage of the Ramesseum. In *Studies in Pharaonic Religion and Society in Honour of J. Gwyn Griffiths* (ed. A.B. Lloyd). London: EES, pp. 115–23.

1993. The land of Punt. In *The Archaeology of Africa: Food, Metals and Towns*. (eds. T. Shaw, P. Sinclair, B. Andah, and A. Okpoko). One World Archaeology. London: Routledge pp. 587–608.

Klebs. L. 1914. Die Tiefendimension in der Zeichnung des alten Reiches. *ZÄS* 52: 19–34.

Koehler, C. G. 1995. Wine amphoras in ancient Greek trade. In *The Origins and Ancient History of Wine*, (eds. P. E. McGovern, S. J. Fleming and S. H. Katz). Luxembourg: Gordon and Breach, pp. 323–37.

Koenig, Y. 1979. *Catalogue des etiquettes de jarres hieratiques de Deir el-Medineh*. Nos. 6000–6241. Fasicule I. Cairo: IFAO.

1980. *Catalogue des etiquettes de jarres hieratiques de Deir el-Medineh*. Nos. 6242–6497. Fasicule II. Cairo: IFAO.

1994. Nouveaux ostraca hieratiques trouves au Ramesseum. *Memnonia*, 4–5, 55–8.

Lauer, J.P., Täckholm, V., Laurent, V. and Aberg, E. 1950. Les plants découvertes dans les souterrains de l'enceinte du roi Zoser à Saqqarah (IIIe Dynastie). *BIE*, 32: 121–57.

Leahy, M.A. 1978. *Excavations at Malkata and the Birket Habu V: The Inscriptions*. Warminster: Aris and Philips.

1985 The hieratic labels. In *Amarna Reports* II (ed. B. Kemp). London: EES, pp. 65–109.

Lefebvre, G. 1923–4. Le tombeau de Petosiris. 3 vols. Cairo: IFAO.

Leonard, A. 1995. 'Canaanite jars' and the Late Bronze Age Aegeo-Levantine wine trade. In *The Origins and Ancient History of Wine* (eds. P. McGovern, S. Fleming, S. Katz). Luxembourg: Gordon and Breach, pp. 233–54.

Lepsius, K.R. 1849–59. *Denkmäler aus Ägypten und Äthiopien*. 6 pts in 12 vols. Leipzig: J.C. Hinrichs.

Lerstrup, A. 1992. The making of wine in Egypt. *GM*, 129: 61–82.

Lesko, L. 1977. *King Tut's Wine Cellar*. Berkeley: B.C. Scribe.

1995. Egyptian wine production during the New Kingdom. In *The Origins and Ancient History of Wine* (eds. P. McGovern, S. Fleming, S. Katz). Luxembourg: Gordon and Breach, pp. 215–30.

Levadoux, L. 1956. Les populations sauvages et cultivées de *Vitis vinifera* L. *L. Ann Amelior. Plantes* 1: 59–118.

Lichtheim, M. 1980. *Ancient Egyptian Literature III: The Late Period*. Berkeley CA: University of California Press.

Loret, V. 1892. *La Flore Pharaonique*. Paris: Ernest Leroux.

Lucas, A. 1962. *Ancient Egyptian Materials and Industries*. 4th edn., rev. J.R. Harris. London: Edward Arnold.

Lucia, S.P. 1963. *A history of wine as therapy*. Philadelphia: J.B. Lippincott.

Lutz, H.F. 1922. *Viticulture and Brewing in the Ancient Orient*. Leipzig: J.C. Hinrichs.

Maarse, H. and van den Berg, F. 1985. A study of an old wine by means of modern techniques. In *Amsterdam Project, Annual Report of the VOC-ship 'Amsterdam' Foundation 1985* (ed. J. H. G. Gawronski). Amsterdam: The Amsterdam Foundation, pp. 80–84.

McGovern, P. 1997. Wine of Egypt's golden age: an archaeological perspective. *JEA*, 83: 69–108.

1998. Wine for an eternity. *Archaeology*: 51/4.

McGovern, P. E., Fleming, S. J. and Katz, S. H. 1995. *The Origins and Ancient History of Wine*. Luxembourg: Gordon and Breach.

McGovern, P., and Michel, R. 1995. The analytical and archaeological challenge of detecting ancient wine: two case studies from the Near East. In *The Origins and Ancient History of Wine* (eds. P. McGovern, S. Fleming, and S. Katz). Luxembourg: Gordon and Breach, pp. 57–65.

McGovern, P. E., Glusker, D. L., Exner, L. J. and Voigt, M. M. 1996. Neolithic resinated wine. *Nature*, 381: 480–1.

McGovern, P., Hartung, U., Badler, V., Glusker, D. and Exner, L.J. 1997. The beginnings of winemaking and viniculture in the ancient Near East and Egypt. *Expedition*, 39/1: 3–21.

Mangafa, M. and Kotsakis, K. 1996. A new method for the identification of wild and cultivated charred grape seeds. *JAS*, 23: 409–18.

Manniche, L. 1989. *An Ancient Egyptian Herbal*. London: BMP.

Mariette, A. 1869. *Abydos* I. Paris: A. Franck.

Marinval, P. 1988. *L'alimentation vegetale en France du Mesolithique jusqu' a l'age du fer*. Paris: Editions du CNRS.

Meeks, D. 1977–8. *Année Lexicographique*. Paris: Margeride.

1993. La production de l'huile et du vin dans l'Égypte Pharaonique. In *La production du vin et de l'huile en Mediterranée* (eds. M.C. Amouretti and J.P. Brun). Bulletin de Correspondance Hellénique. Supplement XXVI. Athens: Ecole Français d'Athenes, pp. 3–38.

Meikle, R.D. 1977. *Flora of Cyprus*. Kew: Bentham-Moxon Trust.

Meyer, C. 1986. Wein. *LÄ* VI/8: 1169–82.

Michel, R. H., McGovern, P. E. and Badler, V. R. 1992. Chemical evidence for ancient beer. *Nature*, 360: 24.

1993. The first wine and beer: Chemical detection of ancient fermented beverages. *Analytical Chemistry*, 65/8: 408A–413A.

Miller, N. 1986. Vegetation and land use. In 'The Chicago Euphrates Archaeological Research Project 1980–1984: An Interim Report' *Anatolica*, 13: 37–148.

Moens, M-F. 1984. The ancient Egyptian garden in the New Kingdom: a study of representations. *Orientalia Lovaniensia Periodica*, 15: 11–53.

Montet, P. 1913. La fabrication du vin dans les tombeaux antérieurs au Nouvel Empire. *RT* 35: 117–24.

1925. *Scenes de la vie privée dans les tombeaux égyptiens de l'Ancien Empire*. Strasbourg: University of Strasbourg.

1958. *Everyday Life in Ancient Egypt*. Chatham: W. and J. Mackay.

Moussa, A.M. and Altenmüller, H. 1971. *The Tomb of Nefer and Ka-hay*. Archäologische Veroffentlichungen 5. Mainz: von Zabern.

1977. *Das Grab des Nianchchnum und Chnumhotep*. Mainz: von Zabern.

Murnane, W.J. 1977. *Ancient Egyptian Coregencies*. Chicago: OIP.

Murray, M. A. forthcoming. Agrarian practices at the ancient Egyptian settlements of Memphis, Abydos and Giza: an archaeobotanical perspective. Unpublished doctoral dissertation, Institute of Archaeology, University College London, England.

1988. Archaeobotanical report. In *Excavations at Kissonerga-Mosphilia, 1979–1992*. (ed. E. Peltenburg). Lemba Archaeological Project, Cyprus. Vol. II.1.B. Jonsered: P. Åström, pp. 215–23.

Neuburger, A. 1930. *Technical Arts and Sciences of the Ancients*. (trans. H.L. Brose). London: Methuen.

Newberry, P.E. 1890. The ancient botany. *Kahun, Gurob, and Hawara*. London: Kegan Paul, Trench, Trübner, pp. 46–50.

1893. *Beni Hassan* I. London: EEF.

1894a. *El-Bersheh* 1. London: EEF.

1894b. *Beni Hassan*. II. London: EEF.

Nunn, J.F. 1996. *Ancient Egyptian Medicine*. London: BMP.

Olmo, H. 1976. Grapes. In *Evolution of Crop Plants*. (ed. N. W. Simmonds). London: Longman, pp. 294–8.

1995a. The origin and domestication of the *Vinifera* grape. In *The Origins and Ancient History of Wine* (eds. P. McGovern, S. Fleming, S. Katz). Luxembourg: Gordon and Breach, pp. 31–43.

1995b. Grapes. In *Evolution of Crop Plants* (eds. J. Smartt and N. W. Simmonds). Harlow, Essex: Longham Scientific and Technical, pp. 485–90.

Palmer, R. 1994. Background to wine as an agricultural commodity. In *Wine in The Mycenean Palace Economy* (ed. R. Palmer). Aegaeum 10. Liège: Université de Liège, pp. 11–23.

Pasteur, L. 1866. *Etudes sur le vin, ses maladies, causes qui les provoquent, procédés nouveaux pour conserver et pour le vieller*. Paris: Imprimerie Impériale.

Pendlebury, J. 1951. *The City of Akhenaten* III. London: EES.

Petrie, W.M.F. 1896. Six temples at Thebes. London: Quaritch.

1894. *Tell el-Amarna*. London: EEF.

1923. *Social Life in Ancient Egypt*. London: Constable.

1927a. *Egyptian Hieroglyphs of the First and Second Dynasties*. London: Quaritch.

1927b. *Objects of Daily Use*. London: BSAE.

Piankoff, A. 1968. *The Pyramid of Unas*. Princeton: Princeton University Press.

Pollard, A.M. and Heron, C. 1996. *Archaeological Chemistry*. Cambridge: Royal Society of Chemistry.

Poo, M. 1995. *Wine and Wine Offering in the Religion of Ancient Egypt*. London: KPI.

Polunin, O. and Huxley, A. 1987. *Flowers of the Mediterranean*. London: Hogarth Press.

Powell, M.A. 1995. Wine and the vine in ancient Mesopotamia: the cuneiform evidence. In *The Origins and Ancient History of Wine* (eds. P. McGovern, S. Fleming and S. Katz). Luxembourg: Gordon and Breach, pp. 97–122.

Py, M. (ed.) 1992. Recherches sur l'économie vivrière des Lattarenses. *Lattara* 5.

Quaegebeur, J. 1990. Blended wines. *Ancient Society*, 21: 241–71.

Rathbone, D 1991. *Economic Rationalism and Rural Society in Third Century A.D. Egypt: The Heroninos Archive and the Appianus Estate*. Cambridge: CUP.

Renfrew, J. 1985. Preliminary reports on the botanical remains. *Amarna Reports* II (ed. B. J. Kemp). London: EES, pp. 175–90.

de Roller, G.J. 1992 . Archaeobotanical remains from Tell Ibrahim Awad, seasons 1988 and 1989. In *The Nile Delta in Transition: 4th–3rd Millennium BC*. (ed. E. van den Brink). Tel Aviv: E. van den Brink, pp. 111–16.

Rostovtzeff, M. 1922. *A Large Estate in Egypt in the Third Century B.C.: A Study in Economic History*. Madison: University of Wisconsin.

Rivera Núñez, D. and Walker, M.J. 1989. A review of palaeobotanical finds of early *Vitis* in the Mediterranean and of the origins of cultivated grape vines, with special reference to new pointers to prehistoric exploitation in western

Mediterranean. *Review of Palaeobotany and Palynology*, 61: 205–37.

Saad, Z. 1957. *Ceiling Stelae in the Second Dynasty Tombs*. Cairo: SAE.

Samuel, D. 1997. Review of P. E. McGovern, S. J. Fleming and S. H. Katz (eds.): 'The Origins and Ancient History of Wine'. *Antiquity*, 71: 236–7.

Sarpaki, A. 1992. The palaeoethnobotanical approach. The Mediterranean triad, or is it a quartet? In *Agriculture in Ancient Greece*. (ed. Berit Wells). Acta Instituti Atheniensis Regni Sueciae, Series in 4°, XLII. Stockholm: Paul Åstrom, pp. 61–76.

Sauneron, S. and Yoyotte, J. 1959. *La naissance du monde selon l'Egypte ancienne*, Sources Orientales 1. Paris: Aux Editions du Seuil.

Säve-Söderbergh, T. 1957. *Four Eighteenth Dynasty Tombs: Private Tombs at Thebes 1*. Oxford: Griffith Institute.

Schnebel, M. 1925. *Die Land Wirtschaft im hellenistischen Ägypten*. Munich: C.H. Bech'sche Verlagsbuchhandlung.

Serpico, M. 1996. Mediterranean resins in New Kingdom Egypt: A multi-disciplinary approach to trade and usage. Doctoral dissertation. Institute of Archaeology, University College London, England.

1999. New Kingdom Canaanite amphorae fragments from Buhen. In *Studies on Ancient Egypt in Honour of H. S. Smith* (eds. M. A. Leahy and W. J. Tait). London: EES.

Serpico, M. and White, R. forthcoming. The identification and use of varnishes on New Kingdom funerary equipment. In *Colour and Painting in Ancient Egypt* (ed. W.V. Davies). London: BMP.

Sethe, K. 1932. Urkunden des Alten Reiches. Leipzig: J.C. Hinrichs.

Singleton, V. 1995. An enologist's commentary on ancient wines. In *The Origins and Ancient History of Wine* (eds. P. McGovern, S. Fleming and S. Katz). Luxembourg: Gordon and Breach, pp. 67–77.

Smith, H.S. 1976. *The Fortress of Buhen II: The Inscriptions*. London: EES.

Smith, H., and Jones, G. 1990. Experiments on the effects of charring on cultivated grape seeds. *JAS*, 17: 317–27.

Spencer, A.J. 1982. *Death in ancient Egypt*. Harmondsworth: Penguin.

Spiegelberg, W. 1898. Hieratic Ostraca and Papyri found by J.E. Quibell in the Ramesseum. In *Ramesseum* (ed. J.E. Quibell). London: Quaritch.

1923. Bemerkungen zu den hieratischen Amphoreninschriften des Ramesseums. *ZÄS*, 58: 25–36.

Stager, L. 1985. The first fruits of civilization. In *Palestine in the Bronze and Iron Ages: Papers in Honour of Olga Tufnell* (ed. J.N. Tubb). Occasional Publication 11. London: Institute of Archaeology, pp. 172–87.

Strudwick, N. 1987. An Old Kingdom vintage scene. *BSEG*, 11: 111–17.

Stummer, A. 1911. Zur Urgeschichte der Rebe und des Weinbaues. *Mitteilungen der Anthropologischen Gesellschaft in Wien*, 41: 283–96.

Täckholm, V. 1961. Botanical identifications of the plants found at the Monastery of Phoebammon. In *Le Monastère de Phoebammon dans la Thébaïde – Tome III* (ed. C. Bachatly). Cairo: La société d'archéologie copte, pp. 1–38.

Täckholm, V., and Drar, M. 1950. *Flora of Egypt* II. Cairo: Fouad I University Press.

Tallet, P. 1995. Le shedeh, étude d'un procédé de vinification en Egypte ancienne. *BIFAO*, 95: 459–92.

1996. Une jarre de l'an 31 et une jarre de l'an 10 dans la tombe de Toutankhamon. *BIFAO*, 96: 369–83.

1998a. Les étiquettes de jarres à vin de Nouvel Empire. In *Proceedings of the Seventh International Congress of Egyptologists* (ed. C. Eyre). Leuven: Peeters.

1998b. Quelques aspects de l'economie du vin en Egypte ancienne, au nouvel empire. In *Le commerce en Egypte ancienne* (eds. N. Grimal and B. Menu). Cairo: IFAO.

Thanheiser, U. 1987. Untersuchungen zur ägyptischen Landwirtschaft in dynastischer Zeit an Hand von Pflanzenresten aus Tell el-Daba. Unpublished doctoral dissertation, University of Vienna.

1991. Untersuchungen zur Landwirtschaft der vor- und Frühdynastischen Zeit in Tell-el-Fara'in-Buto. *Ägypten und Levante* II. Vienna: Verlag der Österreichischen Akademie der Wissenschaften, pp. 39–45.

1992. Plant food at Tell Ibrahim Awad: preliminary report. In *The Nile Delta in Transition: 4th–3rd Millennium BC* (ed. E. van den Brink). Tel Aviv: E. van den Brink, pp. 117–22.

forthcoming. Ueber den Ackerbau in dynastischer Zeit. Ergebnisse der Untersuchungen von Pflanzenresten aus Tell el-Dab'a. *Tell el-Dab'a VIII: Interdisziplinaere Studien*. (eds M. Bietak, J. Dorner, J. Boessneck and A. van den Driesch, H. Egger, U. Thanheiser). Vienna: Austrian Academy of Sciences.

Traunecker, C. and F. 1984. Sur la salle dite 'du Couronnement' à Tell el-Amarna. *BSEG*, 9–10: 285–307.

Unwin, T. 1996. *Wine and the Vine: An Historical Geography of Viticulture and the Wine Trade*. London: Routledge.

Vandersleyen, Cl. 1995. *L'Egypte et la vallee du Nil* I. Paris.

Vansleb, R.D. 1678. The Present State of Egypt or a New Relation of a Late Voyage into That Kingdom (1672–1673). London: J. Starkey.

de Vartavan, C. 1990. Contaminated plant foods from the tomb of Tutankhamun: a new interpretative system. *JAS* 17: 473–94.

Vavilov, N.I. 1926. *Studies on the origins of cultivated plants*. Leningrad: Institut Botanique Appliqué et d'Amélioration des Plantes.

Vercoutter 1959. The God of Kush, *Kush*, 7: 120–54.

Ward, P.N. 1993. Systems of agricultural production in the Delta. In *The Agriculture of Egypt* (ed. G. M. Craig). Oxford: OUP, pp. 229–64.

Wilkinson, J.G. 1878. *The Manners and Customs of the Ancient Egyptians* I–III (ed. and revised by S. Birch). London: John Murray.

Winlock, H.E. and Crum, W.E. 1926. *The Monastery of Epiphanius at Thebes*, 2 vols. New York: Arno Press (repr. 1972, Warminster: Aris and Phillips).

Wood, B. 1987. Egyptian amphorae of the New Kingdom and Ramesside Periods. *Biblical Archaeologist*, 50: 75–83.

Wright, W. 1938, *Everyman's Encyclopedia of Gardening*. London: Dent and Sons.

Zahran, M.A., and Willis, A.J. 1992. *The Vegetation of Egypt*. London: Chapman and Hall.

van Zeist, W. 1983. Fruits in foundation deposits of two temples. *JAS*, 10: 351–4.

1991. Economic aspects. In *Progress in Old World Palaeoethnobotany* (eds. W. van Zeist, K. Wasylikowa, and K. Behre). Rotterdam: Balkema, pp. 109–30.

Zettler, R. and Miller, N. 1995. Searching for wine in the archaeological record of ancient Mesopotamia of the third and second millennia B.C. In *The Origins and Ancient History of Wine* (eds. P. McGovern, S. Fleming, and S. Katz). Luxembourg: Gordon and Breach, pp. 123–31.

Zohary, D. 1995. The domestication of the grapevine *Vitis vinifera* L. in the Near East. In *The Origins and Ancient History of Wine* (eds. P. McGovern, S. Fleming, and S. Katz). Luxembourg: Gordon and Breach, pp. 23–30.

Zohary, D., and Spiegel-Roy, P. 1975. Beginnings of fruit growing in the Old World. *Science*, 187: 319–27.

Zohary, D., and Hopf, M. 1994. *Domestication of Plants in the Old World: The Origin and Spread of Cultivated Plants in West Asia, Europe and the Nile Valley*. Oxford: Clarendon Press.

24. Fruits, vegetables, pulses and condiments

MARY ANNE MURRAY

Introduction

Due to the excellent preservational qualities of the arid Egyptian climate, the body of evidence indicating the many fruits and vegetables present in antiquity is comparatively vast. Traditionally, the recovery of the archaeological evidence for ancient foods outside of Egypt has been biased towards large and obvious food remains, primarily animal bones, with the result that early studies of ancient diet tended to confirm the once prevalent view that early societies subsisted primarily on meat. Due to the improved recovery of plant remains from archaeological sites, by using flotation and sieving techniques, however (see Chapter 21, this volume), a diverse array of plant foods is now known to have formed the major component of most farming and foraging cultures in the past. In contrast, based on the many lines of investigation available, the prevalence of plant foods in the ancient Egyptian diet has long been clearly established. The artistic evidence from tombs, the lexicographic data from texts, the archaeobotanical and artefactual evidence from the excavation of tombs and settlements, along with data from ethnographic and ethnohistoric observations have all indicated, not only the diversity of crops, but also information on crop husbandry and the agricultural history of many species. Current research on Pharaonic diet suggests that, together with bread and beer and some fish and fowl, fruits and vegetables were a predominate feature, while red meat was probably a relatively infrequent commodity to much of the ancient Egyptian population (Täckholm 1977: 272; Crawford 1979: 137; Strouhal 1992: 129; Chapter 25, this volume).

This chapter provides an overview of those fruits, vegetables, pulses and condiments most often cited, throughout both the popular and academic literature, as being used for food during the Pharaonic period (e.g. Darby *et al.* 1977; Sist 1987; Wilson 1988; Brewer *et al.* 1994, Zohary and Hopf 1994; Renfrew 1995). This is clearly not an exhaustive list but one which broaches many of the issues and assumptions associated with these species. For a full listing of the botanical species used as food in Pharaonic Egypt, see Germer 1985. For a full listing of all species recovered from Egyptian sites to date, see de Vartavan and Ansensi Amorós 1997. Although some discussion of the linguistic and artistic evidence is included, the emphasis of this chapter is on the direct archaeobotanical evidence for fruits and vegetables recovered from the excavations of Egyptian tombs and settlements.

The archaeobotanical record for each species discussed here, from thirty selected Egyptian sites, is shown in Table 24.1. These sites date from the Predynastic through to the Islamic period (*c.* 3000 BC–AD 1000) and illustrate the changes from, introductions of and the continuity within the Egyptian crop complex over time rather than simply showing the Pharaonic period evidence alone. The chosen sites include those with rich botanical assemblages, e.g. the tomb of Tutankhamun (KV62) and post-Pharaonic desert sites, and also those settlements where modern archaeobotanical methods of recovery have been used. The exceptional assemblage of Middle Kingdom plant remains from Kahun (Newberry 1890) have been included in this list even though there is some question as to whether at least some of this material might not date from a post-Pharaonic period (Germer forthcoming). The Kahun evidence offers the earliest known examples of certain species, such as the carob and the only Pharaonic example of others, such as the radish, and not to include this material would be inappropriate. The significance of the Kahun material is discussed for each species, where necessary. Predynastic and Pharaonic finds of each species are listed in the text and in Table 24.1, while post-Pharaonic finds are listed exclusively in Table 24.1. Tables 24.2–24.4 give a variety of details of the fruits, vegetables, pulses and condiments discussed here.

As outlined in Chapter 21 (this volume) in a discussion of Egyptian cereals, there are several reasons why caution must be taken when applying any single line of evidence to the subject of ancient food. For example, the artistic evidence preserved on the walls of Egyptian tombs illustrates countless representations of fruits and vegetables, especially in the form of food offerings (Fig. 24.1), yet the exact plant depicted is often unclear, particularly when distinguishing between members of the same botanical family or

Table 24.1. *Archaeobotanical evidence for fruit and vegetable species from selected ancient Egyptian sites.*

Period	Predynastic						OK				FIP		MK		SIP	NK				G-R		Roman			R/LA		LA		Islamic	
Sites	1	2	3	4	5	6	7	8	9	10	11	12	13	14	15	16	17	18	19	20	21	22	23	24	25	26	27	28	29	30
Phoenix dactylifera				✓	✓								✓	✓		✓	✓	✓	✓	✓	✓	✓	✓	✓	✓	✓	✓	✓	✓	✓
Hyphaene thebaica				✓	✓								✓			✓	✓	✓		✓	✓	✓	✓	✓	✓	✓		✓	✓	✓
Medemia argum													✓					✓												
Ficus sycomorus		o		✓				✓	✓			✓	✓	✓		✓	✓		✓	✓	✓	✓			✓		✓			□
Ficus carica			□				✓		✓			✓		✓	o			✓	✓			✓				✓	✓	✓		
Punica granatum																✓	✓	✓			✓	✓		✓	✓	✓	✓			
Mimusops laurifolia								✓					✓	✓		✓	✓		✓	✓	✓	✓			✓			✓		
Cordia myxa								✓										✓		✓	✓	✓	✓			✓	✓	✓		
Ceratonia siliqua													✓					✓		✓				✓		✓		✓		
Ziziphus spina-christi	✓			✓				✓					✓	✓			✓		✓	✓		✓	✓	✓		✓	✓	✓	✓	
Olea europaea														✓	✓	✓	✓		✓	✓	✓	✓	✓	✓	✓	✓	✓	✓		
Vitis vinifera		✓					✓	✓					✓	✓	✓	✓	✓	✓	✓		✓	✓	✓	✓	✓	✓	✓	✓	✓	
Allium cepa																✓		✓				✓		✓		✓	✓			✓
Allium ampeloprasum																														
Allium sativum																✓	✓	✓				✓		✓		✓			✓	✓
Lactuca sativa																						✓								
Apium graveolens																	✓					✓					✓			
Citrullus lanatus				o									✓			✓	✓	✓		✓		✓				✓				✓
Citrullus colocynthus	✓				✓	✓																✓	✓			✓		✓	✓	
Cucumis melo			□	✓												✓					✓	□			✓		o			
Cucumis sativus													✓					✓			✓	□				✓				□
Raphanus sativus													✓											✓				✓		
Cyperus esculentus												✓					✓	✓	✓									✓		
Lens culinaris		✓	✓			✓	✓	✓	✓		✓	✓		✓	✓	✓	✓		✓		✓	✓	✓			✓	✓	✓	✓	✓
Pisum sativum	✓				o	o	✓			✓			✓		✓	✓			✓		✓	✓								✓
Cicer arietinum																	✓	✓			✓	✓	✓	✓		✓			✓	
Vicia faba													✓								✓	✓	✓	✓		✓			✓	
Coriandrum sativum																✓	✓			✓	✓	✓	✓	✓		✓	✓		✓	✓
Cumin cyminum																		✓				✓				✓	✓			
Nigella sativa													✓				✓					✓								
Anethum graveolens																						✓				✓	✓			
Trigonella foenum-graecum																✓	✓					✓				✓			✓	

Predynastic: 1) KH3 and Naqada South Town (Wetterstrom 1986) CHARRED & DESICCATED/SETTLEMENT; 2) Tell Ibrahim Awad (van Zeist 1988, de Roller 1992; Thanheiser 1992) CHARRED/SETTLEMENT/TOMB; 3) Maadi (van Zeist and de Roller 1993) CHARRED & DESICCATED/SETTLEMENT; 4) Hierakonpolis (el-Hadidi 1982, Fahmy 1995, el-Hadidi *et al.* 1996) CHARRED & DESICCATED/SETTLEMENT; 5) el-Omari (Täckholm in Debono 1948; Barakat 1990) CHARRED/SETTLEMENT; 6) Armant (Litýnska 1994) CHARRED & DESICCATED/SETTLEMENT.

Old Kingdom: 7) Predynastic/Early Dynastic Buto (Thanheiser 1991) CHARRED/SETTLEMENT; 8) Third-Dynasty Tomb of Djoser (Lauer *et al.* 1950; Täckholm 1961:29) DESICCATED/TOMB; 9) Fourth-Dynasty Giza (Wetterstrom 1992, unpublished data; Murray forthcoming) CHARRED/SETTLEMENT; 10) Kom el-Hisn (Moens and Wetterstrom 1988) CHARRED/SETTLEMENT.

FIP: 11) First intermediate Period Tell el-Dabʿa (Thanheiser 1986; forthcoming) CHARRED/SETTLEMENT; 12) Fifth/Sixth-Dynasty Kom el-Sultan at Abydos (Murray forthcoming) CHARRED/SETTLEMENT.

Middle Kingdom: 13) Twelfth-Dynasty Kahun (Newberry 1890; Bienkowski and Southworth 1986:63; Germer forthcoming) DESICCATED/SETTLEMENT?; 14) Thirteenth-Dynasty Kom Rabiʿa at Memphis (Murray forthcoming) CHARRED/SETTLEMENT.

SIP: 15) Tell el-Dabʿa (Thanheiser 1986; forthcoming) CHARRED/SETTLEMENT.

New Kingdom: 16) Eighteenth-Dynasty Amarna (Renfrew 1985; Samuel pers. comm.) DESICCATED/SETTLEMENT;
17) Eighteenth-Dynasty tomb of Tutankhamun (Germer 1989; de Vartavan 1990; Hepper 1990)DESICCATED/TOMB;
18) Eighteenth-Dynasty Deir el-Medina (Bruyère 1937) DESICCATED/SETTLEMENT; 19) Eighteenth-/Nineteenth-Dynasty Kom Rabiaʾ at Memphis (Murray forthcoming) CHARRED/SETTLEMENT.

Greco–Roman: 20) el-Hiba (Wetterstrom 1984) DESICCATED/SETTLEMENT; 21) Hawara (Newberry 1889) DESICCATED/TOMB.
Roman: 22) Mons Claudianus (van der Veen 1996) DESICCATED/SETTLEMENT; 23) Quseir el-Qadim (Wetterstrom 1982) DESICCATED/SETTLEMENT; 24) Abu Shaʿar (el-Hadidi and Amer 1996) DESICCATED/SETTLEMENT.
Roman/Late Antique: 25) Douch (Barakat and Baum 1992) DESICCATED/TOMB; 26) Berenike (Cappers 1996, forthcoming) DESICCATED/SETTLEMENT.
Late Antique: 27) Kom el-Nana (Smith 1997) DESICCATED/SETTLEMENT; 28) Phoebamman (Täckholm 1961) DESICCATED/SETTLEMENT.
Islamic – AD 1000: 29) Quseir el-Qadim (Wetterstrom 1982) DESICCATED/SETTLEMENT; AD 1000 30) Qasr Ibrim (Rowley-Conwy 1989) DESICCATED/SETTLEMENT.

OK – Old Kingdom; **FIP** – First Intermediate period; **MK** – Middle Kingdom; **SIP** – Second Intermediate period; **NK** – New Kingdom; **G-R** – Greco–Roman; **R/LA** – Roman/Late Antique; **LA** – Late Antique.

✓ – present.
▯ – *cf.* or most closely resembles.
o – identified to genus only, i.e. *Ficus* sp. and not *F. sycomorus* or *F. carica*.

CHARRED – plant remains primarily preserved by charring.
DESICCATED – plant remains primarily preserved by desiccation (all settlement sites will also contain charred botanical remains).
TOMB – tomb site.
SETTLEMENT – settlement site.

N.B. – The first occurrence of a species in the table may not be its first occurrence in Egypt.
See text for other finds of these species from sites not included in this table.
See text for a discussion of those species with no finds listed in this table.
This is not a full listing of ancient plant remains from all Egyptian sites. For a full listing, see de Vartavan and Asensi Amorós 1997.

genus, e.g. the cucumber (*Cucumis sativus*) and the chate melon (*Cucumis melo* var. *chate.*) (Darby *et al.* 1977: 693, Germer 1985: 128–30; Manniche 1989: 95). Moreover, while the array of produce recorded in tomb-scenes and offering lists may provide insight into the diet of the upper strata of Egyptian society, the range of foods commonly available to most Egyptians may have been quite different, not only in terms of the potential choice but also in the quality and quantities of those foods (Crawford 1979: 138; Málek 1986: 44, Strouhal 1992: 133–4). Linguistically, many fruits and vegetables are seemingly well-documented for the Pharaonic period, although some are not and the terminology is often imprecise due to the variety of names and classifications given to these species through time and to the uncertainty of plant identifications (Janssen 1975; Darby *et al.* 1977; Charpentier 1981; Germer 1985, forthcoming; Baum 1988; Nunn 1996; de Vartavan and Asensi Amorós 1997). Ancient and modern (and cross-cultural) distinctions between what is a fruit and what is a vegetable may also cause some misunderstanding. The same pitfalls hold true for the later observations of Egyptian crops made by Classical authors, who had a very different classification

Figure 24.1 Scene showing offering bearers bringing fruits and vegetables in the Theban tomb of Nakht (TT52).

Table 24.2. *Ancient Egyptian fruits of the Pharaonic period.**

English name Latin name	*Family name* Arabic name	Probable Origin	First finds of seeds and fruits in Egypt	Found in *Tomb* Town	Frequency of finds (seeds, fruits)	*Habit* Height	*Seasonality* Harvest	Propagation method	Probable wild ancestor
Date palm	*Palmae*	Near East	Predynastics?,	*yes*	rare until MK,	*tree*	*evergreen*	rooting of basal	wild form(s) of *P.*
(*Phoenix dactylifera*)	balah/nahl		then MK	yes	occ. during NK	<25 m	autumn	offshoots	*dactylifera*
Dom palm	*Palmae*	Sudan/	Late	*yes*	more common	*tree*	*evergreen*	rooting of	wild form of
(*Hyphaene thebaica*)	dôm	Egypt?	Palaeolithic	yes	in Upper Egypt	<20 m	autumn/	basal offshoots	*H. thebaica?*
Argun palm	*palmae*	Sudan?	5th	*yes*	occasional	*tree*	*evergreen* spring	rooting of	*wild form of*
(*Medemia argun*)	'argoon		Dynasty	yes		<10 m		basal offshoots	*M. argun*
Sycamore fig	*Moraceae*	E. Africa	Predynastic	*yes*	common	*tree*	*evgrn/deciduous*	rooting of twigs	wild form of
(*Ficus sycomorus*)	gimmêz			yes		<30 m	3 crops a year		*F. sycomorus*
Common fig	*Moraceae*	Eastern	Predynastic	*yes*	occasional	*tree/shrub*	*deciduous*	rooting twigs or	wild form(s) of *F.*
(*Ficus carica*)	teen	Med.		yes		<4–7 m	summer	grafting	*carica*
Pomegranate	*Punicaceae*	S. Caspian/	12 Dynasty/	*yes*	occasional	*shrub/tree*	*evergn/deciduous*	offshoots/seeds/	wild form(s) of *P.*
(*Punica granatum*)	rummân	NE Turkey	SIP	yes		2–6m	autumn	grafting	*granatum*
Persea	*Sapotaceae*	East Africa	3rd	*yes*	occasional	*tree*	*evergreen*	offshoots/	wild form(s) of *Mimusops*
(*Mimusops laurifolia/ M. schimperi*)	lebbakh		Dynasty	yes		<20 m		seeds/grafting	
Egyptian plum	*Boraginaceae*	Tropical	Middle	*yes*	rare	*tree*	*evergreen*	offshoots/	Wild forms of *C. myxa*
(*Cordia myxa*)	mokheit	Asia?	Kingdom	no		<8 m	summer	seeds/grafting	
Carob	*Leguminosae*	Eastern	12th	*no*	rare	*tree*	*evergreen*	offshoots/	wild form of
(*Ceratonia siliqua*)	kharroub	med.	Dynasty#	yes		<10 m	autumn/winter	seeds/grafting	*C. siliqua*
Christ's Thorn	*Rhamnaceae*	East Africa?	Predynastic	*yes*	frequent	*shrub/tree*	*evergreen*	from seed or	wild form of
(*Ziziphus spina-christi*)	sidr/nabq	Near East?		yes		<20 m	autumn	grafting	*Z.spina-christi*
Grape ◇	*Vitaceae*	Trans-	Predynastic	*yes*	frequent	*woody*	*perennial*	rooting twigs or	*Vitis vinifera* var.
(*Vitis vinifera*)	'inab/zibîb	caucasia?		yes		*climber* <35 m	autumn	grafting	*sylvestris*
Olive ●	*Oleaceae*	Mediterr-	SIP, 13th	*yes*	rare until	*tree*	*evergreen*	offshoots/	*Olea europaea*
(*Olea europaea*)	zetoon	anean	Dynasty	yes	occasional from the 18th Dynasty	<10 m	autumn	cuttings/ grafting	subsp. *oleaster*

* Refers only to botanical finds until the end of the New Kingdon.
# The Twelfth-Dynasty find of radish is from Kahun and it has been suggested that the date of some of the plant remains from the site may be of a later date (Germer forthcoming).
◇ Grape is covered by Murray in Chapter 23
● Olive is covered by Serpico in Chapter 17.

system and terminology for the variety of species involved (e.g. Darby *et al.* 1977; French 1994). Indeed many of the Latin botanical names that we use today to ensure that the names of plants are universally understood to have changed numerous times throughout the nineteenth and twentieth centuries and are sometimes still cause for confusion. In any case, many fruit and vegetable species may have been used long before the written or pictorial record of their presence would suggest.

Archaeobotanical remains recovered from ancient tombs and towns provide direct evidence for the presence of individual genera or species. On most Near Eastern sites, plant remains are most commonly preserved by charring, however, in the arid conditions of Egypt, ancient plants are sometimes desiccated (or dried), and can be found in near perfect condition. Due to the elaborate Egyptian system of leaving food offerings for their dead, desiccated remains can be found in Pharaonic tombs and on dry sites in the Eastern and Western Deserts as well as at several Nile Valley settlements, such as Amarna (Renfrew 1985; Samuel 1989) and Hierakonpolis (el-Hadidi 1982; Fahmy 1995; see Chapter 21, this volume) (also Fig. 24.2 here). The assemblages of charred plant remains at most settlement sites are frequently well-suited to the study of cereal production and its associated weed flora due to the predominance of cereal processing residues and other debris which have been burned as fuel at these sites (see Chapter 21, this volume). The strength of the tomb evidence, however, is often the rich diversity of well-preserved finds of fruits and vegetables. Indeed, it is not uncommon for a particular species to be identified linguistically in texts from Mesopotamia or elsewhere, yet to be represented only by the archaeobotanical specimens recovered from Egyptian tombs (Stol 1987; Charles 1987; Stager 1985; Zohary and Hopf 1994; Germer forthcoming). Desiccated remains from settlement sites also tend to display a wider variety of species than samples

Table 24.3. *Ancient Egyptian vegetables of the Pharaonic period.**

English name Latin name	*Family name* Arabic name	Probable Origin	First finds of seeds and fruits in Egypt	Found in *Tomb* Town	Frequency of finds (seeds, fruits)	*Habit* Height	*Seasonality* Harvest	Propagation method	Probable wild ancestor
Onion (*Allium cepa*)	*Alliaceae* basal	Central Asia	13th Dyn.?, then 18th Dyn.	*yes* yes	rare	*erect herb* 30–120 cm	*ann/biennial* spring	seed	*A. vavilovii*
Leek/kurrat (*Allium ampeloprasum* var. *porrum*, var. *kurrat*)	*Alliaceae* kurrât rûmi/ *kurrât baladi*	Mediterranean basin/ *Near East*	date unknown date unknown	*yes/yes* no/no	*single find* single find	*erect herbs* 60cm–2m	*biennial* summer	seed	*Allium ampeloprasum*
Garlic (*Allium sativum*	*Alliaceae* tôm	C. Asia/ Near East	18th Dynasty	*yes* yes	rare	*erect herb* 13cm–1m	*perennial* winter/spring	cloves or bulbs	*Allium longicuspis?*
Lettuce (*Lactuca sativa*)	*Compositeae* hass	W. Asia/ Mediterranean	TIP/Ptolemaic/ Roman	– –	none	*erect herb* <1 m	annual winter/summer	seed	*Lactuca serriola*
Celery (*Apium graveolens*)	*Umbelliferae* karafs	S.W. Asia/ Europe	18th Dynasty	*yes* no	rare	*erect herb* 30 cm–1 m	*biennial* winter/spring	seed	wild forms
Water melon (*Citrullus lanatus*)	*Cucurbitaceae* batteekh/libb	N. Africa/ W. Asia	Predynastic	*yes* yes	occasional	*trailing herb* <5 m	*annual* summer	seed	*Citrullus colocynthis*
Colocynth (*Citrullus colocynthus*)	*Cucurbitaceae* handel	C. Asia/ Near East	Neolithic	*yes* yes	*Predyn-occ,* Dyn -rare	*trailing herb* <3 m	*perennial* summer	seed	wild form
Melon (*Cucumis melo*)	*Cucurbitaceae* shamman	Asia/ Africa	Predynastic	*yes* *yes*	rare	*trailing herb* <3 m	*annual* summer/autumn	seed	wild forms
Chate melon (*Cucumis melo* var. *chate*)	*Cucurbitaceae* khiar	Africa	Not distinguished from above	– –	Not distinguished from above	*trailing herb* <3 m	*annual* summer	seed	wild form
Cucumber (*Cucumis sativus*)	*Cucurbitaceae* khiâr qassa	N. India	none confirmed	– –	none confirmed	*trailing herb* <2 m	*annual* summer/autumn	seed	wild forms of *C. sativus*
Radish (*Raphanus sativus*)	*Brassicaceae* figl	Med/Asia/ Caspian Sea?	12th Dynasty#	*no* yes	single find	herb 20–90 cm	*ann/bienn* winter/spring	seeds	*R. caphinastrum*
Chufa, tiger nuts (*Cyperus esculentus*)	*Cyperaceae* su'd/habb el-aziz	Egypt?	Predynastic	*yes* yes	frequent	*erect herb* 30–90 cm	*perennial* *summer/autumn*	tubers	*Cyperus esculentus* var. *aureus*

* Refers only to botanical finds until the end of the New Kingdom.
# The Twelfth-dynasty find of radish is from Kahun and it has been suggested that the date of some of the plant remains from the site may be of a later date (Germer forthcoming).

of charred remains. This is due, in part, to the differential preservational qualities of charred and desiccated plants but other variables of plant use, such as deposition and recovery are also likely to influence each assemblage. For example, most fruits and vegetables (and their associated processing residues) are less likely to come into contact with fire or indeed survive the charring process than the residues of cereal processing which are commonly burned as fuel. In cases where the archaeobotanical evidence is lacking, how far can we rely on the artistic and textual records to demonstrate their presence?

The earliest archaeological evidence for food processing in Egypt is found in the archaeobotanical and artefactual records from the Late Palaeolithic site of Wadi Kubbaniya in Upper Egypt where the tubers of wild nut grass *Cyperus rotundus* were ground, probably not only to increase their digestibility but to decrease the toxic compounds present in this species (Wendorf, *et al.* 1989; Hillman *et al.* 1989; also see Stahl 1989). Other plants also would have needed processing for reasons of toxicity, i.e. faba beans, or palatability, i.e. dom and argun palm fruits. Drying, heating, grinding, pounding, grating, soaking, leaching and fermentation are among the many methods used to process food (e.g. Stahl 1989; Wiltshire 1995). Occasionally the remains of ancient food which have been made or flavoured with fruits or vegetables have been found, such as loaves of bread containing Christ's thorn fruits or sycomore figs (e.g. Kamal 1913; Chapter 22, this volume) and funerary meals prepared for the hereafter, including stewed figs or boiled lentils (Emery 1962; Schweinfurth 1885). For the most part, however, apart from basic information on how the foods might have been eaten, i.e. raw, cooked, dried; the exact methods used for food processing and preparation during the Pharaonic period are not yet fully understood. Some fruits or vegetables are usually consumed fresh soon after their harvest, such as lettuce, while others can be dried, ground, pickled, or pressed for long term storage, i.e. dates, figs, olives and grapes. In general, the potential for trade in these species will increase if they can be stored, especially for long periods of time; thereby extending the availability

Table 24.4. *Ancient Egyptian pulses and condiments of the Pharaonic period.**

English name Latin name	*Family name* Arabic name	Probable Origin	First finds of seeds and fruits in Egypt	Found in *Tomb* Town	Frequency of finds (seeds, fruits)	*Habit* Height	*Seasonality* Harvest	Propagation method	Probable wild ancestor
Lentils (*Lens culinaris*)	*Leguminaceae* ʻadz	Near East	Predynastic	*yes* yes	frequent	*erect herb* 15–75 cm	*annual* winter/spring	seed	*L. orientalis*
Pea (*Pisum sativum*)m	*Leguminaceae* bisilla	Med. basin/ Near East	Predynastic	*yes* yes	occasional	*erect herb* 25cm–2m	*annual* winter/spring	seed	*P. sativum* subsp. *humile*
Chick (*Cicer arietenum*)	*Leguminaceae* hummus	Near East	18th Dynasty	*yes* yes	rare	*erect herb* 25–50cm	*annual* spring	seed	*C. arietinum* subsp. *reticulatum*
Faba Bean (*Vicia faba* var. *minor*)	*Leguminaceae* fûl	Near East	5th Dynasty	*yes* yes	rare	*erect herb* <2 m	*annual* spring	seed	unknown
Coriander (*Coriandrum sativum*)	*Umbellifereae* kuzbarah	Near East/ East Med.	Predynastic, then 18th Dynasty	*yes* yes	rare	*erect herb* <1.3 m	*annual* winter/spring	seed	wild form of of *Coriandrum*
Cumin (*Cuminum cyminum*)	*Umbellifereae* kammoun	*C. Asia?*	18th Dynasty	*yes* no	*rare*	*erect herb* 5–40 cm	*annual* autumn	seed	wild form of *Cuminum*
Black cumin (*Nigella sativa*)	*Ranunculaceae*	Near East	18th Dynasty	*yes* no	single find	*erect herb* <70 m	*annual* winter/spring	seed	unknown
Dill (*Anethum graveolens*)	*Umbellifereae* shabath	Med. basin/ W. Asia	18th Dynasty	*yes* no	rare	*erect herb* 30–150 cm	*ann/bienn* summer	seed	wild forms of *Anethum*
Fenugreek (*Trigonella foenum-graecum*)	*Leguminosae* helba	Eastern Med./ Near East	Predynastic, then 18th Dynasty	*yes* yes	rare	*erect/spreading* 20–60 cm	*annual* summer/autumn	seed	unknown

* Refers only to botanical finds until the end of the New Kingdom

of crops beyond their natural season and, in some cases, their region of cultivation (e.g. Stager 1985; Halstead and O'Shea 1989; Haldane 1991, 1993; Forbes and Foxhall 1995: 77–8; Eyre 1994: 73; Chapter 19, this volume).

Due to the possibility of trade, the presence of certain species, particularly at a date earlier than previously assumed, makes it difficult to determine whether they might have been imported or grown locally. For example, until recently the documentary and archaeobotanical evidence for the olive (*Olea europaea*) pointed to its introduction in Egypt some time during the Eighteenth Dynasty (The olive is discussed in Chapter 17, this volume). Recent archaeobotanical research, however, has shown that the olive was present as early as the late Second Intermediate Period at Tell el-Dabʿa (Thanheiser 1986; forthcoming) and the Thirteenth Dynasty at Kom Rabiʿa Memphis (Giddy and Jeffreys 1991; Murray forthcoming) (see Table 24.2 and Chapter 17, this volume).

Oil- and resin-bearing species, such as olive, balanites, moringa, linseed, safflower, almond, pistacia and juniper are covered by Serpico in Chapters 17 and 18, this volume. Other oil crops which may also have served as important vegetables, including lettuce, radish and chufa tubers are discussed here but, to prevent overlap, certain aspects are considered in greater detail in Chapter 17, this volume. A discussion of the grape and viticulture are found in the section on wine (Chapter 23, this volume) although botanical information and archaeobotanical finds of grape can be found here in Tables 24.1 and 24.2. Many fruits and vegetables, such as the peach and pear, were introduced into Egypt during the Ptolemaic and Roman periods and are clearly outside the scope of this chapter (but for more information on these species and other late introductions, see e.g. Crawford 1979; Garnsey 1988; Zohary and Hopf 1994; Cappers 1996; van der Veen 1996, 1998, forthcoming; Smith 1997). The detailed analysis of the artistic, linguistic, and religious significance of the ancient Egyptian gardens and orchards themselves is a vast subject in its own right and will not be discussed here in any depth. For more information on these issues, see e.g. Wilkinson 1878; Loret 1892; Keimer 1924, 1984; Butzer 1976; Darby *et al.* 1977; Moens 1984; Germer 1985; Baum 1988; Hugonot 1989; Eyre 1994, 1995; van der Veen forthcoming. The subject of traditional flood basin and canal irrigation is covered in Chapter 21 in this volume and will be discussed here with regard to fruits and vegetables only briefly (e.g. Butzer 1976; Eyre 1994, 1995 for more information). All references to archaeobotanical finds refer to the seeds of the plant, unless stated otherwise. The nutritional statistics cited here from the FAO and other sources, are, for the

Figure 24.2 Typical garden layout in a scene decorating the Middle Kingdom tomb of Khnumhotep III at Beni Hasan (BH3).

most part, based on tests of modern, well fertilised specimens. For clarity, the nomenclature used for the species discussed is based on Zohary and Hopf 1994. (For more detailed botanical descriptions of species discussed here and for previous Latin botanical names, see Täckholm and Drar 1950, 1954; Polhill *et al.* 1949–94; Davis *et al.* 1965–88; M. Zohary 1966, 1972; Townsend and Guest 1966–1985; Feinbrun-Dothan 1978, 1986; Meikle 1977, 1985; Jansen 1981; Germer 1985, 1998; de Vartavan and Asensi Amorós 1997).

While the artistic and textual records of the Pharaonic period offer important information for the cultivation and processing of cereal crops (Chapter 21, this volume), the crop husbandry of fruits and vegetables is less well-documented. A brief discussion is included in each section on the methods commonly used to cultivate these crops under traditional flood basin and canal irrigation in the early twentieth century prior to the completion of the Aswan High Dam which effectively signalled the end of the annual inundation of the Nile (i.e. Foaden and Fletcher 1908, 1910). It is important to note that Egyptian agriculture has obviously changed profoundly since the Pharaonic period and this information should be used cautiously and not as a strict guide to the methodology of ancient Egyptian farmers. It is included in order to demonstrate the variability, the most likely areas of cultivation and the level of care required for each crop under these traditional irrigation regimes and to highlight the problems and possibilities associated with that now defunct system of agriculture. The main agrarian procedures of sowing, harvesting, threshing, winnowing, sieving and the tools used to carry them out are outlined with regard to cereal production in Chapter 21, this volume and many of the same principles and terminology apply to the cultivation of fruits, vegetables, pulses and condiments.

Irrigation

One of the primary differences between cereal cultivation and the farming of fruits and vegetables in Egypt was the need for a consistent water supply for the maintenance of gardens, orchards and vineyards (Fig. 24.3) (Butzer 1976: 48; Hugonot 1989: 170–4; Eyre 1994:). Under basin irrigation, the annual inundation flooded the Nile Valley during the summer months of July, August and into September and flood waters had generally receded by October and November when the winter crops, such as emmer wheat and barley, were sown (Chapter 21, this volume). Other crops also would have been sown at this time, including

Figure 24.3 Scene from the Fifth-Dynasty tomb of Niankhkhnum and Khnumhotep at Saqqara, thought to depict the cutting and watering of lettuce (Lactuca sativa).

the pulses – lentils, peas, chickpeas and faba beans; and vegetables, such as onions and garlic (Foaden and Fletcher 1910; Charles 1985: 43). A second vegetable crop, of melons, for example, might have been grown during the spring and early summer months although summer crops would have been more difficult to grow since the Nile would have been at its lowest level when these plants most needed regular watering. While this second harvest was theoretically possible, Butzer (1976: 47) has pointed out that there is no textual evidence for the planting of summer crops after the cereal harvest during the Dynastic period. There is also no record for crops being grown during the inundation period on high ground or on protected low ground which would have required further irrigation (Baer 1962, 1963; Butzer 1976: 47). The lack of textual evidence for growing out-of-season crops does not necessarily preclude its practice and Eyre (1994: 58) notes that vegetables and summer crops could have been planted on late draining low land near the river. Schenkel (1978: 58f), too, suggests that a second harvest was possible, based on records which indicate that a double rent was paid for certain fields from the New Kingdom onwards. The use of wells, cisterns and small ponds which tapped the water table also may have been a common feature in Pharaonic period gardens and orchards (Eyre 1994: 64–8). For the most part, however, the artistic evidence from tombs illustrates that the watering of fruits and vegetables would have consisted primarily of manually filling containers of water from the river and carrying them, sometimes by means of a shoulder yoke, to vegetable gardens and fruit trees (Fig. 24.3) (Butzer 1976: 46; Málek 1986: 43; Eyre 1994: 58, 62).

The *shaduf* was a simple pole and lever device which could lift a container of water from the river up to a metre or more in height (Chapter 21, this volume). The raised water then would be poured into small channels which fed the garden or orchard area to be irrigated and the process was repeated until this slow and arduous task was completed. The artistic and archaeological record of gardens, such as those from Amarna (Peet and Woolley 1923; Frankfort and Pendlebury 1933) indicate that they were square or rectangular features which had well delineated and highly effective compartments for retaining water. The water from the *shaduf* would not have been silt laden, therefore, animal dung, deposited silts dredged from canals, soils from rich middens (*sebakh*) and other types of fertilisers would have been used to enrich these artificially irrigated soils. The evidence to date, indicates that the *shaduf*, introduced during the Eighteenth Dynasty, was the only technical device used for irrigation prior to the Ptolemaic period (Erman 1894; Davies 1933; Butzer 1976; Eyre 1994, Fig. 21.6, this volume). The gradual expansion of the canal system during the Pharaonic period, for the efficient channelling and control of flood waters to areas previously unused for agriculture, was another innovation which, together with the *shaduf*, would have allowed for a greater emphasis on the growing of out-of-season crops (Eyre 1994: 78). The large scale, fully seasonal cultivation of gardens, orchards and vineyards, however, would have required a more continuous and controlled water source than the free-flooding annual inundation and the limited water lifting capability of the *shaduf*. This type of intensive agriculture would have been feasible only by using the *saqiya* or water wheel, not introduced until Ptolemaic times, and also the introduction of the *tanbour* or Archimedes screw which could provide a continuous flow of water on a large scale (Crawford 1971; Butzer 1976: 46; Watson 1983; Venit 1989; Eyre 1994: 80). Egyptian agriculture, in terms of the range of available crops and methods of crop husbandry, as well as the nature of land ownership and land tenure, changed radically during the Greco–Roman period, due, in large part, to the major improvements of the irrigation regime during that time (e.g. Rostovtzeff 1922; Schnebel 1925; Crawford 1971, 1979, Butzer 1976, Garnsey 1988; Bowman and Rathbone 1992; Ruf 1993; Rowlandson 1996).

Fruits

Fruit trees were an important element of ancient Egyptian food production and included, at various points through out the Pharaonic period, dates, figs, olives, grapes, persea, carob, Egyptian plum and Christ's thorn. Domestication for many of these species meant a change from sexual reproduction in the wild, i.e. propagation by seed, to vegetative propagation under cultivation, i.e. the planting of cuttings, rooting of twigs or offshoots from the parent tree. With this method, growers tended to select those trees exhibiting desirable characteristics such as large and abundant fruit production and were then able to propagate an identical clone of the desirable parent (Zohary and Spiegel-Roy 1975: 325; Zohary and Hopf 1994: 134). It is now clear that many of the fruits known from the Pharaonic period were introduced into Egypt from the Levant after the so-called 'Neolithic revolution' in Near Eastern agriculture (e.g. Zohary and Spiegel-Roy 1975; Stager 1985; Zohary 1992; Kislev 1992; Zohary and Hopf 1994). The success of the 'first wave' of Old World domesticated fruit trees, i.e. the date, fig, olive and grape undoubtedly had to do with their suitability for vegetative propagation. Other fruit trees, such as the apple, pear, plum and cherry were part of a 'second wave' of domestication, due to their need to be propagated primarily by grafting, as opposed to the simple vegetative propagation methods described above, and the art of grafting does not appear to have been practised until Greco–Roman times (Zohary and Hopf 1994: 136).

While cereals, pulses and vegetables are annual species requiring a short-term investment of time for a comparatively quick return, fruit trees are perennial species which not only need tending, but may not bear fruit until several

*Figure 24.4 Theban tomb-scene showing a garden pool surrounded by date palms (*Phoenix dactylifera*).*

years after planting (Zohary and Hopf 1994: 181). There is also a wide variation in fruit production. Depending on annual conditions, the variety grown and crop husbandry, an individual tree may have prolific fruit production one year and yield very little in the next (Charles 1987: 3). The textual and artistic records indicate that fruit trees were grown on high land along the river bank, around the edges of fields or in well-maintained gardens (Fig. 24.4) (Baum 1988; Hugonot 1989; Eyre 1994, 1995; Bietak 1996). Fruit trees also may have been grown on improved lands on the desert margins although this type of agriculture is not documented until the Greco–Roman period (Eyre 1994: 59–60).

*Date palm (*Phoenix dactylifera *L.) [Palmae – Palm family]*

The date palm is a tall unbranched, evergreen tree which can grow to a height of 25 m with a girth of about 75 cm. Its large pinnate leaves (two to three metres in length) have a strong midrib with many lateral leaflets (20–30 cm in length) (Greiss 1957: 33; Charles 1987: 2). New leaves emerge each spring and the characteristic rough markings on the trunk are the remains of previous leaf bases (Greiss 1957: 32; Harrison *et al.* 1985: 106; Charles 1987: 2; Hepper 1990: 62). The small white flowers of the tree usually appear between February and March and the sugary date fruit, a fleshy drupe, ripens from August to September (Täckholm and Drar 1950: 166). About twenty-five to thirty-five flowers, and eventually fruits, grow along each thin branchlet (or peduncle) of a large suspended branch which may consist of forty branchlets (Harrison *et al.* 1985: 106; Charles 1987: 2). Under modern conditions of cultivation, as much as forty kilograms of fruit per year can be obtained from the average date palm, while a very productive tree may yield more than double that figure (Wrigley 1995: 401; Zohary and Hopf 1994: 157). The date palm begins to produce fruit after four to seven years, with full production between eight and fifteen years after planting (Foaden and Fletcher 1910: 649; Harrison *et al.* 1985: 106; Zohary and Hopf 1994: 157; Wrigley 1995: 401). Fruit production generally begins to decline after thirty-five to forty seasons although the tree can continue to bear for between sixty and a hundred years (Foaden and Fletcher 1910: 649; Harrison *et al.* 1985: 106; Charles 1987: 2; Wrigley 1995: 401).

Date fruits are usually cylindrical in shape and contain a single large ventrally grooved stone. Depending on growing conditions, the date fruit can vary between 2 and 60 grams in weight, 2–11 cm in length and 1–3 cm in width (Wrigley 1995: 400). Thinning out the date bunches produces larger and better fruits which ripen more quickly than unthinned bunches (Foaden and Fletcher 1910: 649; Drar 1950: 183; Wrigley 1995: 401). Dates turn yellow or red while maturing and then amber or reddish brown to black when ripe (Foaden and Fletcher 1910: 650; el-Hadidi and Boulos 1988: 84). Birds, bats and hornets are common date fruit pests (Foaden and Fletcher 1910: 650; Drar 1950: 184). Depending on the variety, the intended use of the fruit and the time of harvest; harvesting can be done by hand-picking, by shaking the dates from the bunches or by cutting off an entire branchlet or bunch (Drar 1950: 185; Charles 1987: 3). In both modern and ancient specimens, date fruits show a wide diversity of size and quality, even those from the same branch, and therefore it is very difficult to distinguish between the many varieties of date palm on this basis (Foaden and Fletcher 1910: 464; Brown and Bohgot 1938: 46; Täckholm 1961: 9).

The date palm is a dioecious species, meaning that there are separate male and female trees (Foaden and Fletcher 1910: 649; Greiss 1957: 33; Zohary and Hopf 1994: 157) although hermaphrodite and monoecious flowers have been reported and a reversion of sex is not unknown (Täckholm and Drar 1950: 165). The species is naturally fertilised by the wind and perhaps by insects (Wrigley 1995: 401). It has been suggested that the ancient practice of artificially pollinating date palms by hand, first mentioned in the cuneiform texts of Ur (~2300 BC) (Zohary and Hopf 1994: 158; Wrigley 1995: 401), was probably introduced into Egypt during the Middle Kingdom (Täckholm and Drar 1950: 216; Täckholm 1961: 9). Under artificial pollination, a very small number of male date trees are necessary for pollination purposes, i.e. only a single male is required for the fertilisation of between twenty and fifty (Drar 1950: 179) or even up to a hundred female trees (Harrison *et al.* 1985: 106, Zohary and Hopf 1994: 158). Artificial pollination consists of collecting pollen from the male flowers and applying it with a brush, cloth, or by simply shaking it over the female flowers (Drar 1950: 179–80; Charles 1987: 2). Pollen also can be collected and stored until required (Foaden and Fletcher 1910: 649; Wrigley 1995: 401). If there are many male trees available, an entire male inflorescence may be placed near the opened female flowers (Harrison *et al.* 1985: 106; Charles 1987: 2), a procedure best carried out during the month of April in Egypt (Foaden and Fletcher 1910: 648). This method saves the cultivator repeated trips to the same tree (Charles 1987: 2), an important labour saving consideration since in Egypt, date palms often are not grown in plantations but are dotted across a landscape (Ward 1993: 251). The use of artificial pollination is also a resourceful use of water since the number of male trees necessary for the job is drastically reduced.

The date palm, together with the olive, grape and fig, was among the earliest cultivated fruit trees in the Old World (Zohary and Spiegel-Roy 1975; Zohary and Hopf 1994: 157). The wild progenitor of the domesticated date palm appears to be from a group of wild palms found in the Near East, northeastern Sahara and the deserts of northern Arabia (Zohary and Spiegel-Roy 1975: 323; Zohary and Hopf 1994: 158). These varieties are morphologically similar to the cultivated date, albeit with smaller, inferior fruits, and are fully interfertile with the domesticated date. Therefore, many botanists believe these should all be grouped taxonomically as *Phoenix dactylifera* (Zohary and Hopf 1994: 158; Wrigley 1995: 400). The date palm was probably domesticated in the region of the lower Mesopotamian basin, or in the oases of the southern limits of the Near Eastern arc (Zohary and Spiegel-Roy 1975: 323; Zohary and Hopf 1994: 162). The wild date is not present in Egypt today, only cultivated and feral date palms are to be found along the Nile, the Delta and in the desert oases (Täckholm and Drar 1950: 165; Boulos 1983: 140; Zahran and Willis 1992: 84, 101).

The date palm thrives in the hot, dry Egyptian climate and today the distribution of the species world-wide is in the arid to semi-arid zone between 35°N and 15°N latitude (Täckholm and Drar 1950: 166; Zohary and Hopf 1994: 157). The tree can tolerate temperatures upwards of 50°C although 35°C is considered optimal for pollination (Wrigley 1995: 400). The palm requires a sustained water supply from either high ground water or irrigation, although the tree suffers if ground water is more than two metres deep (Foaden and Fletcher 1910: 648; Wrigley 1995: 400). The date palm has a considerable tolerance for brackish water and saline conditions (Drar 1950: 171; Ward 1993: 251; Zohary and Hopf 1994: 157; Zahran and Willis 1992: 89–92, 279–81) although poor growth and fruit quality may result from excessive salt intake (Ward 1993: 251; Wrigley 1995: 400). The tree will also survive for long periods with its roots submerged in water (Drar 1950: 171). Indeed, the optimal growing conditions are illustrated by the Arabic expression of the palm 'It must have its feet in running water and its head in the fire of the sky' (el-Hadidi and Boulos 1988: 84; Wrigley 1995: 400). Providing that the date palm gets enough heat and water, it will grow in most types of soil although it grows best on a light sand with little organic material. While growth is slower on poor, non-rich soils, the fruit can be of a superior quality (Foaden and Fletcher 1910: 646). The great range of distribution and the diverse nature of the fruits and other botanical features indicate the successful adaptation of the date palm to a wide variety of local conditions (Wrigley 1995: 400). For this reason, the date palm has been an important food source to both the nomads and sedentary populations of many desert regions throughout history.

Although it is possible to grow dates from seed, fruit quality is more likely to be inferior and it may take many years to recognise the presence of the unproductive male trees (Foaden and Fletcher 1910: 647; Drar 1950: 171). In contrast, domesticated date palms are most successfully propagated by vegetative cloning, that is, the cutting and planting of offshoots or suckers found at the base of the parent tree (Foaden and Fletcher 1910: 647; Drar 1950: 171; Harrison *et al.* 1985: 106; Charles 1987: 2; Ward 1993: 251; Zohary and Hopf 1994: 157–8; Wrigley 1995: 400). The number of basal offshoots produced during the life span of a single tree is highly variable but it can be anywhere from six to twelve (Wrigley 1995: 401) to ten to thirty (Drar 1950: 173) although some trees produce none (Drar 1950: 173). These offshoots, which may weigh as much as forty kilograms when they are ready to be taken, are an important commodity in their own right and are removed from the parent with care prior to planting (Wrigley 1995: 401). August and September are considered good months for planting out the offshoots, especially in Upper Egypt, although they should not be removed until they are more than two years old (Drar 1950: 174) and are usually left for between three and five years (Foaden and Fletcher 1910: 647; Wrigley 1995: 402). Those trees exhibiting desirable qualities, such as the amount and quality of the fruit produced, salt tolerance and the ability of the tree to produce satisfactory and numerous basal offshoots, are most likely to be selected for clonal propagation. After many centuries of selecting trees with preferable characteristics, the date palm has been gradually modified and improved to suit local conditions (Ward 1993: 251; Wrigley 1995: 401).

Virtually every element of the many component parts of the date palm is utilised. The nutritious date fruits have considerable food value and although they can be eaten fresh, their high sugar content (70–80 per cent dry weight) inhibits bacterial decay which means that they can be stored for long periods of time (Hepper 1990: 62; Dagher 1991: 99; Wrigley 1995: 400). Based on textual evidence, *irp bnr*, has been interpreted as 'date wine' or 'sweet wine' which was evidently derived from the pressing and fermentation of date fruits from as early as the Second Dynasty (Täckholm and Drar 1950: 224; Lucas 1962: 23; Manniche 1989: 134; Hepper 1990: 62; however, see the discussion below and in Chapter 23, this volume for more on the presence of date fruits prior to the Middle Kingdom). In contrast, palm wine is derived from fermenting the sap of the tree (Wilkinson 1878: I, 397; Beadnell 1909: 218; Lucas 1962: 22; Manniche 1989: 133) although its extraction significantly weakens the palm and, therefore, is best done with those trees well past their fruit bearing years (Lucas 1962: 22; Harrison *et al.* 1985: 106; Bircher 1995: 164; Chapter 23, this volume). Many superstitions and religious beliefs have been associated with the date palm and during the Pharaonic period the tree was considered a symbol of femininity, just as the dom palm was a symbol of male strength (Täckholm and Drar 1950: 214; Täckholm 1977: 269). The fruits, seeds, timber, leaves, fibrous sheath, sap and other parts of the tree not only provided food, drink and shade but also supplied material for medicines, animal fodder, fuel, roofing, bedding, matting, furniture, fencing, water channels, *shadufs*, filters; brushes, brooms, rope, sandals, crates, cages, nets, fishing floats, and basketry (see Wilkinson 1878: 399–400; Foaden and Fletcher 1910: 650–1; Ruffer 1919: 60–1; Brown and Bohgot 1938; Täckholm and Drar 1950: 186–8, 223–37; Bauman 1960: 93; Osborn 1968: 175; Popenoe 1973; Bailey and Danin 1981: 155–7; Moens 1984; Germer 1985: 232–3; Charles 1987: 1; Lucas 1962: 444; Darby *et al.* 1977: 728–30; el-Hadidi and Boulos 1988: 84; Manniche 1989: 134; Hepper 1990: 62; Dagher 1991: 99; Zohary and Hopf 1994: 157; Bircher 1995: 156–65; Wrigley 1995: 400; Nunn 1996: 15; Chapters 10 and 15, this volume).

Much of the botanical evidence for date palm, prior to the Middle Kingdom, consists largely of leaves, fibre, and wood rather than date fruit. It has been argued that this is probably because artificial pollination was not practised in Egypt until sometime during the Middle Kingdom when the knowledge was introduced from Mesopotamia (Täckholm and Drar 1950: 216; Täckholm 1961: 9, 1977: 270), the source of the earliest finds of date outside Egypt (*c.* 4000 BC) (Zohary and Hopf 1994: 160). While unfertilised date flowers are capable of setting fruit without pollination, they usually are not as large nor is fruit production as prolific as from those trees improved by deliberate, artificial pollination (Harrison *et al.* 1985: 106; Wrigley 1995: 401). The only confirmed archaeobotanical finds of *Phoenix dactylifera* fruit prior to the Middle Kingdom, thus far, are a single date stone from Predynastic el-Omari (Debono 1948; Täckholm and Drar 1950: 218; also Geller 1992). Two other Predynastic finds are mentioned by Täckholm and Drar (1950: 219) who show that these were most probably modern intrusions. There appear to be no finds of date stones, thus far, recorded from the Old Kingdom. Based on the archaeobotanical evidence, it has been suggested that finds of date stones prior to the Middle Kingdom are probably the result of natural wind pollination (Täckholm and Drar 1950: 216). yet, even from the Middle Kingdom, finds of date stones are few in number and most are from the New Kingdom and post-Pharaonic periods.

It has been argued by Wallert (1962) and then by Germer (1985) that, based primarily on the artistic and linguistic evidence of the word for date (*bnr*), date fruits were plentiful from at least the Early Dynastic period (including the reference to date wine *irp bnr*,) and, therefore, artificial pollination must have been practised from that early time onwards. While the archaeobotanical evidence, thus far, does not support this theory, what is notable is not the presence of occasional Predynastic date stones but rather the comparatively few specimens known from the Middle and even the New Kingdom, especially considering the supposed importance of the fruit at that time. This may have to do, in part, with the relatively small number of sites from which archaeobotanical material has been systematically recovered, but even on well-sampled New Kingdom settlement sites, such as Kom Rabiʿa at Memphis (Murray forthcoming) and Amarna (Samuel pers comm. *contra* Renfrew 1985; Chapter 22, this volume), fewer date stones have been recovered than expected, particularly if they had been used in large numbers. The robust nature of their date stones may increase their likelihood of survival and their presence on settlements in large numbers would seem likely.

The issue becomes particularly relevant in relation to the widely accepted view, again based largely on the linguistic evidence, that dates were used extensively to flavour beer (e.g. Faltings 1991). While fragments of date fruit were reportedly found in beer remains from Hierakonpolis (Maksoud *et al.* 1994), the premise that dates were commonly used for this purpose, has been challenged by Samuel (1996, Chapter 22, this volume) who argues that since beer-making was an extremely frequent occurrence, done largely at the household level, then if dates were commonly used as a flavouring, one would expect to find the evidence for this on the settlements themselves. As yet, the archaeobotanical evidence does not indicate the large-scale use of date fruits but this and other issues concerning the many uses of the date palm should be investigated further on a site by site basis. It is also clear that a collaborative effort involving the latest archaeobotanical, linguistic and artistic evidence would undoubtedly help to clarify the importance of the date in the Pharaonic period.

Archaeobotanical finds of *P. dactylifera* stones or fruit are known from Middle Kingdom sites, such as the Eleventh-Dynasty tomb of Ani (Schweinfurth 1886), Twelfth-Dynasty Kahun (Bienkowski and Southworth 1986: 63; Germer forthcoming), Thirteenth-Dynasty Kom Rabiʿa at Memphis (Murray forthcoming) and Tell el-Dabʿa (Thanheiser forthcoming). The number of finds increases somewhat in the New Kingdom and they are known from the Eighteenth-Dynasty sites of Amarna (Renfrew 1985: 176), Kom Rabiʿa (Murray forthcoming), Deir el-Medina (Bruyère 1937) the tomb of Tutankhamun (Germer 1989: 45; de Vartavan 1990: 486; Hepper 1990: 62) and Twenty-first Dynasty Deir el-Bahari (Schweinfurth 1884) (see Täckholm and Drar 1950: 220–1 and de Vartavan and Asensi Amorós 1997: 193–6 for New Kingdom finds). Several stones from a

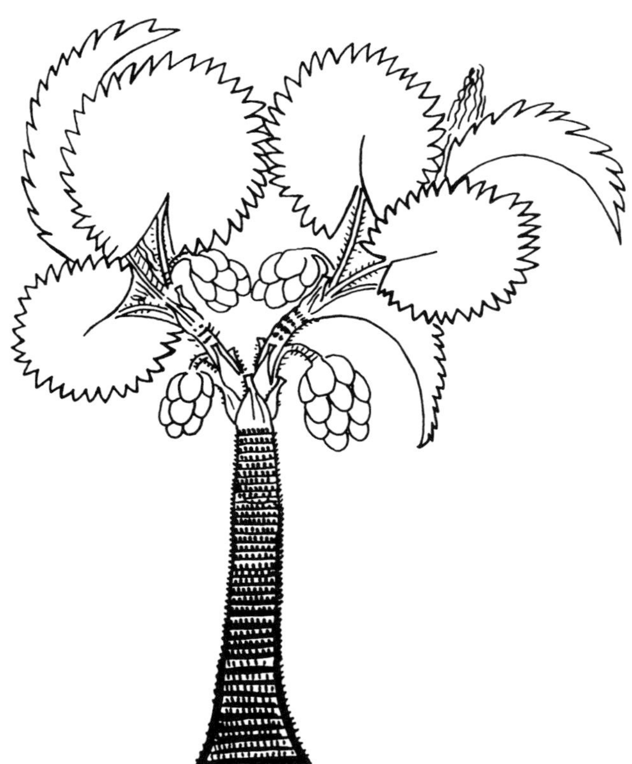

*Figure 24.5 Detail of a wall-painting in the Ramesside Theban tomb of Irinefer (TT290) showing a dom palm (*Hyphaene thebaica*).*

wild African date species (*P. reclinata*, previously identified as *P. sylvestris*) are known from an Upper Palaeolithic site at Kharga Oasis in Upper Egypt (Täckholm and Drar 1950: 209, 244; Caton-Thompson 1952: 84; Germer 1985: 232).

*Dom palm (*Hyphaene thebaica *(L.) Mart.) [Palmae – Palm family]*

The dom palm can grow to 20 m high with a girth of about 30 cm and, unlike the date palm, has a forked trunk. Anywhere from eight to forty fan-like palmate leaves form a terminal crown on each branch and the small, yellow flowers appear from February to April with the fruits ripening in eight to twelve months. Each branch can produce about forty shiny brown fruits, *c.* 7–8.5 cm long and 4–7 cm broad, whose shape can be described as a somewhat rounded square (Fig. 24.5). The fruits are produced between six and eight years after planting (Täckholm and Drar 1950: 273–4; Greiss 1957: 48; Täckholm 1961: 9; Darby *et al.* 1977: 730; Feinbrun-Dothan 1986: 329, FAO 1988: 333, 336; Hepper 1990: 60; Dagher 1991: 111). The dom palm is a dioecious species with separate male and female trees and, like the date palm, under artificial pollination a single male is sufficient to pollinate a large number of females in a wide radius (Täckholm and Drar 1950: 274). The tolerable temperature range for the species is 20 °C–35°/40 °C, although the tree is highly sensitive to moisture. Under hyper-arid conditions, for example, fruit size can be exceedingly small whereas moist conditions encourage a lush growth (Täckholm and Drar 1950: 275–6; FAO 1988: 336). The life-cycle of the dom palm is about sixty years (FAO 1988: 336).

Several species of dom palm are found throughout Africa, yet *Hyphaene thebaica* L. is largely restricted to Egypt and the Sudan (Täckholm and Drar 1950: 275; FAO 1988: 333; Hepper 1990: 60; Feinbrun-Dothan 1986: 329). In Egypt today, the tree is found primarily in the provinces of Qena and Aswan in Upper Egypt where it can form dense stands in valleys and depressions (Täckholm and Drar 1950: 274–5; Moens 1984: 32; FAO 1988: 36; Hepper 1990: 60; Zahran and Willis 1992: 110). The species is often distributed by nomadic peoples and by animals, such as baboons (FAO 1988: 336). Both wild and cultivated varieties of the dom palm occurred in the Pharaonic period (Täckholm 1977: 269) and archaeobotanical finds of the species are most common from Upper Egyptian sites, most likely reflecting its principal geographical distribution in antiquity.

As with the date palm, the various elements of dom palm have many uses. The strong, heavy timber of the tree is considered to be a superior building material to that of the date palm and is used for beams, doors, water pipes and in boat-building (Täckholm and Drar 1950: 276; Täckholm 1977: 270; FAO 1988: 336; Manniche 1989: 109) although to date, little, if any, dom palm wood has been identified from Pharaonic period sites (Chapter 15, this volume). Parts of the leaves, stalks and roots can be used for roofing, baskets, matting, sandals, bags, fibre for rope, nets, brushes and even paper (Täckholm and Drar 1950: 276–8; Darby *et al.* 1977: 730; Bailey and Danin 1981: 156; FAO 1988: 336; Chapter 10, this volume). Parts of the dom palm also can be used for the treatment of a number of medicinal complaints, the roots, for example, are taken for the relief of the common Egyptian ailment of bilharzia (or shistosomiasis) (Täckholm and Drar 1950: 277–8; Osborn 1968: 176; Darby *et al.* 1977: 733; Boulos 1983: 138; FAO 1988: 336). As yet, ancient Egyptian records from the Pharaonic period make no mention of medicinal uses of the dom palm (Manniche 1989: 109; Nunn 1996: 15). A black dye can be made from the edible mesocarp and small containers are fashioned from the underlying woody seed shell (FAO 1988: 336). When ripe, the hard, white kernel itself is used as a vegetable ivory to produce beads, buttons, rings and other small objects (Täckholm and Drar 1950: 277; Täckholm 1961: 9; Darby *et al.* 1977: 730; FAO 1988: 336; Dagher 1991: 111).

The dom palm fruit has a thin shiny brown covering enclosing the edible, fibrous, yet sugary mesocarp which smells and tastes of ginger bread. The mesocarp surrounds a woody endocarp containing a hard white seed, four centimetres long and two and a half centimetres broad (Täckholm and Drar 1950: 273–4; Täckholm 1961: 9; Darby *et al.* 1977: 730; Feinbrun-Dothan 1986: 329; FAO 1988: 334). There are many uses for the various components of the fruit which, if well-dried, can be stored for long periods of time (FAO 1988: 336). The primary food source is the fibrous mesocarp which can be eaten raw, yet is often soaked in water to soften it and make it more palatable (Täckholm and Drar 1950: 276, Darby *et al.* 1977: 730; Moens 1984: 32; Dagher 1991: 111). This tough pulp is rich in carbohydrates and is a good source of iron and niacin and can be ground into flour for cakes or made into a sweet carob-like syrup (FAO 1988: 335). Archaeobotanical finds include dom palm fruits which have had the edible mesocarp removed and those left as tomb offerings which remain intact (Täckholm 1961: 9). The kernel contains carbohydrate, protein and high levels of calcium and phosphorus (FAO 1988: 334) and prior to full ripening, can be eaten like coconut or can be pounded or ground to a pulp. These also can be sprouted and eaten as a vegetable. The heart of the palm is also edible, known as palm cabbage, although its procurement destroys the tree and this practice has become illegal in many countries (also Ruffer 1919: 60–1 for the date palm). A 'milk' can be extracted from unripe fruits which also can be boiled and eaten whole. The tree sap can be drunk fresh or fermented into a palm wine. The trunk, too, contains an edible, sago-like starch (FAO 1988: 334–5).

The dom palm is often depicted in the artistic record, such as in the Eighteenth-Dynasty Theban tomb of Rekhmira (TT100) and that of Ineni (TT81), who reputedly had 120 dom palms planted in his garden (Davies 1935, 1943; Wreszinski 1915 I, Pl. 60). The species also featured prominently in the 514 parks or sacred gardens which Rameses III donated to many temples during his reign (Täckholm and Drar 1950: 280–1). The textual record illustrates the importance of the dom palm as well, not only as a garden plant but as a sacred tree, known as a symbol of male strength (Täckholm and Drar 1950: 281; Täckholm 1977: 269). The dom palm is closely associated with the god of science, Thoth, who is often depicted as a baboon in Eighteenth-Dynasty Theban tombs. In the tomb of Rekhmira, they are shown greedily collecting the dom palm fruits (Davies 1935, 1943; Keimer 1939; Täckholm and Drar 1950: 282; Caminos 1954: 331–2). Funerary texts from this tomb also record an offering of 200 dom fruit cakes to the gods (Newberry 1900: 31).

Unlike the date, numerous dom palm fruits have been recovered from the earliest periods. The earliest remains of the fruits are from the Late Palaeolithic site of Wadi Kubbaniya (*c.* 18,000 BP) in Upper Egypt (Hillman *et al.* 1989: 198–201). Ancient finds from Predynastic times onwards have included the wood, leaves, fibre, inflorescence and fruits of the species (Täckholm and Drar 1950: 283–8; Täckholm 1961: 9; Germer 1985: 234–5). Other finds of dom palm fruits are known from Predynastic el-Badari (Brunton and Caton-Thompson 1928: 63), Twelfth-Dynasty Kahun (Newberry 1890: 49; Germer forthcoming), Eighteenth-Dynasty Deir el-Medina and Amarna (Bruyère 1937; Renfrew 1985: 176) and the Eighteenth-Dynasty tomb of Tutankhamun (Germer 1989: 47–8; Hepper 1990: 59).

Argun palm (Medemia argun *Württemb.) [Palmae – Palm family]*

The argun palm is a dioecious tree which can grow to a height of ten metres. It is straight and unbranched like the date palm, although its fan-like leaves more closely resemble those of the dom palm (Täckholm and Drar 1950: 296: Greiss 1957: 50). The comparatively unpalatable, violet to brown fruits of the argun palm are about four centimetres long and three centimetres broad although the species is most highly valued for its leaves which are used in the manufacture of mats and rope and its wood which is used as a construction material (Täckholm and Drar 1950: 297–8; Greiss 1957: 51; Täckholm 1977: 269; Germer 1985: 235).

Unlike the dom palm, the thick, fibrous mesocarp of the argun palm fruit is seemingly inedible and the reason for their presence in ancient tombs had been queried. In Nubia, however, the fruits are rendered palatable by burying them under ground for a period prior to consumption when the softened flesh acquires a taste similar to that of the coconut. Whether this process was practised in ancient Egypt, however, is not known (Täckholm and Drar 1950: 298; Moens 1984: 32). The argun palm was introduced into Egypt from Nubia and is thought to have been acclimatised to the area of Thebes by the Eighteenth Dynasty (Täckholm and Drar 1950: 300). The species was clearly more prevalent in ancient Egypt and Nubia than it is today although it was probably always a relative rarity in Egypt (Täckholm and Drar 1950: 297–301). The tree was considered a suitable garden specimen in the Pharaonic period, as artistic representations of the species can be found in the Eighteenth-Dynasty Theban tomb of Ineni (TT81) whose garden contained an argun palm tree (Loret 1892: 34; Täckholm and Drar 1950: 301; Germer 1985: 235; Wreszinski 1923 I, Pl. 60). In 1965, a field trip by Täckholm confirmed a report that a single specimen of the argun palm (with six juveniles growing at the base) was growing near the Dungul oases in the southwestern desert, the only remaining argun palms known in Egypt at that time (Zahran and Willis 1992: 108).

Modern specimens of the argun palm were first recognised in Nubia only after fruits of the species were recovered from ancient Egyptian tombs although, to date, comparatively few ancient argun fruits have been found. Archaeological finds include three fruits from an unnamed Fifth-Dynasty tomb at Saqqara (Täckholm and Drar 1950: 299; Greiss 1957: 50; Germer 1985: 235) and those from Eighteenth-Dynasty Deir el-Medina (Bruyère 1938: 108).

Small items carved out of argun palm nuts, such as knobs and handles, were also recovered from the Twelfth-Dynasty site of Kahun (Newberry 1890: 49, Germer forthcoming).

Sycomore fig (Ficus sycomorus *L.) [Moraceae – Mulberry family]*

Two species of fig were known to the ancient Egyptians, the sycomore fig (*Ficus sycomorus*) and the common fig (*Ficus carica*). The sycomore fig is taller, growing up to thirty metres in height, has a much wider canopy than the common fig tree and can live to a great age (M. Zohary 1982: 68; FAO 1988: 288; Hepper 1990: 59). The tree is an evergreen in hot climates and can be deciduous in cooler weather, thereby losing its large roughened ovate leaves (M. Zohary 1982: 68; el-Hadidi and Boulos 1988: 70; Hepper 1990: 58). The sycomore fig is found today in Egypt and wild and/or cultivated species are found elsewhere in the eastern Mediterranean basin, as well as in eastern Africa from the Sudan to South Africa and into the Yemen, yet the ancient cultivation of the species is considered to have been exclusively an Egyptian practice (Galil 1968; Zohary and Spiegel-Roy 1975: 324; FAO 1988: 288; Zohary and Hopf 1994: 156–7). It is a common feature of the savanna, although it grows best in areas with a high water table, such as the rich alluvial soils near streams or river beds (FAO 1988: 290; Zohary and Hopf 1994: 157).

In ancient Egypt the sycomore fig was highly valued for its fruits, or syconia, which grow in profusion on the trunk and branches of the tree and are generally smaller than the common fig, up to 3 cm in diameter, and not as sweet (see Fig. 15.6, this volume) (Galil and Eisikowitch 1968: 752; M. Zohary 1982: 69; FAO 1988: 288; Hepper 1990: 58). Sycomore figs have a high fibre content, are rich in minerals, iron and sugars, and contain moderate amounts of vitamins A, B and C. The leaves contain protein (6 per cent fresh weight), calcium, phosphorus and iron (FAO 1988: 289). The leaves, shoots and young plants can be eaten raw or as a cooked vegetable. The fruits are eaten when fresh or after they have been sun-dried and can be stored for several months. They also can be added to breads and cakes. They are still popular today, particularly in Lower Egypt, although they are generally not as highly appreciated outside of the country (Galil and Eisikowitch 1968: 745; Zohary and Hopf 1994: 157). In addition to being a valuable shade tree, they can be used to stabilise river and canal banks, can provide forage in the dry season and are a potential source of fuel (FAO 1988: 290; Zahran and Willis 1992: 333). The timber is used as a building material, and was used to make coffins and sarcophagi from at least the Fifth Dynasty onwards (Bauman 1960: 101; Galil 1968: 178; Hepper 1990: 58; Zohary and Hopf 1994: 156; W. V. Davies 1995, Chapter 15, this volume). An extract from the bark is useful for smoothing mud walls and its rough leaves can be used as a sandpaper (FAO 1988: 290). The species was widely used in Pharaonic medicine and is still used in folk medicine today (Manniche 1989: 103; Darby *et al.* 1977: 746, 748; FAO 1988: 290; Nunn 1996: 15). During the Pharaonic period, the sycomore fig tree was strongly associated with the goddess Hathor (Caminos 1954: 333–5; Galil 1968: 178; Täckholm 1977: 268–9; Darby *et al.* 1977: 745). The ancient Egyptians had a great affection and appreciation for the tree and its many uses and the species is one of the best represented from the Pharaonic period, in terms of the artistic, textual and archaeobotanical records (e.g. Loret 1892: 46; Darby *et al.* 1977: 745–6; Baum 1988: 18–85; W. V. Davies 1995; Chapter 15, this volume).

In its native habitat, the wild species reproduces sexually and is propagated by seed. Pollination, i.e. the setting of the seed, is dependent on the life-cycle of the symbiotic wasp, *Ceratosolen arabicus* Mayr. (Galil 1968: 178; Galil and Eisikowitch 1968: 747). The fig itself (or syconium) is a specialised inflorescence, unique to the *Ficus* genus. This is actually a flowering branch which develops into a hollow fruit, containing the tiny long- and short-styled flowers of the species (Zohary and Spiegel-Roy 1975: 324; Zohary and Hopf 1994: 151; Zohary 1995: 367). The *Ceratosolen* wasp enters the fig through a small hole (or ostiole) in the top of the syconium where it pollinates some of the flowers in the process of laying its eggs inside others. Due to the length of the ovipositor of the wasp, it can only deposit its eggs in the ovary of the short-styled flowers. While these flowers become insect galls, the long-styled flowers reach maturity, produce seed and therefore, edible fruits (Galil 1968: 178; Galil and Eisikowitch 1968: 747). In Egypt, however, the process is more complex since the *Ceratosolen* wasp either became extinct at a very early date in the country or, more probably, was never actually present in Egypt (or indeed Cyprus or Israel (Galil 1968: 179)), possibly due to an intolerance to the climate. Both the *Ceratosolen* wasp and the wild sycomore fig can still be found in the Sudan today (Zohary and Hopf 1994: 157).

Since antiquity, the life-cycle of two other wasp species, particularly *Sycophaga sycomori* L., have been synchronised with the life-cycle of the Egyptian sycomore fig (Galil 1968: 182). Unlike *Ceratosolen*, this wasp has the ability to lay its eggs in the long-styled flowers of the fruit which in turn, do not produce seeds but rather form empty galls where the seeds would have been (Galil 1968; Galil and Eisikowitch 1968; Täckholm 1977: 269; Smith 1997). Egyptian sycomore figs, therefore, produce no seeds. The antiquity of this phenomenon is not known but was reported by Theophrastus (372–287 BC) (4,2,1 in Darby *et al.* 1977: 746) and earlier archaeobotanical specimens also indicate this feature. Without seed production, the propagation of the species has been entirely dependent on human assistance i.e. it has been grown from cuttings, probably from the Neolithic onwards (Galil 1968: 178; Galil and Eisikowitch 1968: 746; Täckholm 1977: 269).

The ability of *Sycophaga sycomori* to create insect galls

rather than seeds may provide a clue as to the antiquity of the phenomenon since if left untreated, the wasp-infested fruit is rendered inedible (Galil 1968: 187). The ancient technique of 'gashing' or making a cut in the young fruits was once thought to be for the release of the wasps since gashed fruits were wasp-free. It is recognised now, however, that gashing shortens the ripening time by many weeks and thus curtails the life-cycle of the wasp in its entirety (Galil 1968: 188, 1976; Zohary and Hopf 1994: 157). In ancient Egypt, a special tool was used for the purpose of gashing sycomore fruits (Keimer 1928; Galil 1968: 179). Theophrastus (372–287 BC) witnessed this practice and correctly noted that after gashing, the syconia would ripen within four days (21, I, IV, 291 in Galil 1968: 179). The fig also grows about seven times in weight and volume after the gashing procedure (Galil 1968: 186). Archaeobotanical finds and artistic depictions of the sycomore fig fruits which have been intentionally gashed can be seen in tombs from the Twelfth Dynasty onwards, an indication of the antiquity of this crop husbandry practice (Täckholm 1977: 269; Germer 1985: 26). There are three main crops of these figs a year in Egypt but farmers generally only gash the fruit of the first two, in August–September (Galil 1968: 187). The gashing of sycomore fig fruits continues in Egypt, Israel and Cyprus today (Galil 1968: 179), however, due to the less labour-intensive husbandry associated with other fruit species, coupled with the numerous high quality fruits introduced from elsewhere, the tree is declining in numbers and importance in the Mediterranean, including Egypt (Galil 1968: 189).

Artistic representations of the tree are first known from the Old Kingdom and continue throughout the Pharaonic period (see Baum 1988 for listing). Finds of sycomore fig wood date from the Predynastic and are frequently found as objects from the Fifth Dynasty through to Roman times (Lucas 1962: 447; Chapter 15, this volume). While a basket of sycomore fig fruits was found in the tomb of Tutankhamun (KV62), as yet, none of the wood from the many objects in the tomb has been identified as *Ficus sycomorus* (Hepper 1990: 58; Waly 1996; Chapter 15, this volume). There is some difficulty distinguishing between the fruits of the common fig and sycomore fig in ancient material since desiccation can deform the fruit although the sycomore fig is generally smaller, more rounded, contains the empty insect galls and may also show signs of the incision made by gashing (Galil 1968: 180; Täckholm 1961: 10, 1977: 269; Smith 1997). It is possible that further archaeobotanical and palaeoentomological analysis will determine whether sycomore fig fruits in Egypt ever contained seeds or the male *Ceratosolen* wasp.

The first botanical evidence for sycomore fig fruit comes from Predynastic sites, such as el-Omari (Debono 1948) and the species is commonly found in tombs from the First Dynasty onwards (Germer 1985: 26; Hepper 1990: 58). Other finds include those from the Third Dynasty tomb of Djoser (Lauer *et al.* 1950: 130), Fourth-Dynasty Giza, First Intermediate Period Kom el-Sultan at Abydos, Thirteenth-Dynasty Kom Rabiʿa at Memphis (Murray forthcoming), Twelfth-Dynasty Kahun (Newberry 1890: 50) and Eighteenth-Dynasty Amarna (Renfrew 1985: 176).

*Common fig (*Ficus carica *L.) [Moraceae – Mulberry family]*

The common fig is a deciduous shrub or small tree which grows four to seven metres high with variably shaped leaves and bears abundant, pear-shaped fruits (Meikle 1985: 1467; Zohary 1995: 367). The common fig is one of the first domesticated fruits of the Old World and its cultivation is often closely associated with that of the olive and the grape vine (Zohary and Spiegel-Roy 1975: 324; Zohary and Hopf 1994: 155). The combined archaeobotanical and biological evidence indicates that the common fig was first cultivated in the eastern Mediterranean basin during the Chalcolithic period (~4000 BC) (Zohary 1995: 368). The wild ancestor of the cultivated fig is among the wild and weedy members of the species found primarily in the typical lowland *maquis* and *garrigue* areas of the Mediterranean. These are also regarded as *F. carica* since they all share close morphological, genetic and adaptive features with the cultivated fig (Zohary and Hopf 1994: 152; Zohary 1995: 367). A number of feral types which grow in man-made habitats, such as in ruins and old cisterns, can also be included in this group. The wild, feral, and cultivated varieties of *F. carica* found in the Mediterranean are also closely related and interfertile with similar non-Mediterranean types found to the south and east (Zohary and Hopf 1994: 152). Indeed, in experimental plots, the symbiotic wasp, *Blastophaga psenes*, needed for the pollination of the common fig, does not distinguish between the Mediterranean and non-Mediterranean types (Zohary and Spiegel-Roy 1975: 324; Zohary and Hopf 1994: 155; Zohary 1995: 368). It is the wild Mediterranean forms of the species, however, which are considered to be the original stock for the domesticated fig (Zohary and Hopf 1994: 156; Zohary 1995: 368).

The fig tree provides fresh fruit during the summer months which can be sun- or oven-dried and stored for use throughout the year (see Foaden and Fletcher 1910: 631). Several breads containing figs have survived from the Pharaonic period (Chapter 22, this volume). Dried figs are also an easily transportable commodity for trade (Foaden and Fletcher 1910: 627; Harrison *et al.* 1985: 94; Zohary 1995: 367). The fruits, leaves and wood ash can also be used for medicinal purposes (Boulos 1983: 134–5; Nunn 1996: 15). Fruit production in the fig usually starts three to four years after planting (Foaden and Fletcher 1910: 631; Zohary and Hopf 1994: 151) and the tree is at its productive best at between thirteen and fifteen years (Foaden and Fletcher 1910: 631). Fruiting ability is greatly affected by the intake of too much or too little water and the tree is best-suited to loosened alluvial soils or a well-manured friable loam (Foaden and Fletcher 1910: 628–30). Other species often are intercropped between fig trees in Egypt today, such as onions, garlic and berseem (e.g. Foaden and Fletcher 1910: 630).

The common fig is a dioecious species and wild populations reproduce sexually from seed (Foaden and Fletcher 1910: 629–30; Zohary and Spiegel-Roy 1975: 324; Zohary 1995: 367). As with the sycomore fig, the flowers of the species are housed inside the syconium, a fleshy branch which develops into a hollow chamber with a small opening (or ostiole) at its apex (Zohary and Spiegel-Roy 1975: 324; Zohary and Hopf 1994: 151; Zohary 1995: 367). The common fig is pollinated by the fig wasp *Blastophaga psenes*. Technically, the true fruit of the fig is not the entire syconium but rather the small seeds (or druplets) which form within the female flowers inside the syconium (Zohary 1995: 367). These contain long-styled flowers adapted to pollination and seed set. The caprifigs, on the other hand, contain pollen producing flowers and short-styled flowers. The caprifigs usually do not set seed but rather serve as a place to nurture the larvae of the fig wasp by turning into galls when the wasp eggs are deposited in them. The female wasps are the pollen carriers and after they hatch and emerge from the mature caprifigs, they enter the young female syconia of the true figs through the opening where, during pollination, they become trapped and eventually die. Since it is not possible for females to lay their eggs in the long-styled flowers of the true fig, this fruit never contains the larvae of the wasp (Galil and Neeman 1977; Zohary and Hopf 1994: 151). True figs produce a main crop in late summer while three crops of wasp infested caprifigs are produced annually and the life cycle of *Blastophaga* wasp continues along with the development of these three harvests (Zohary and Hopf 1994: 157; Zohary 1995: 367). An ancient practice, known from at least Greco-Roman times, of artificially pollinating the common fig, caprification, is sometimes also used. With this method, branches with mature wild caprifigs are attached to the true fig trees, thus bringing the fig wasp into closer contact with the female syconia (Zohary and Hopf 1994: 152; Zohary 1995: 367).

Sexual reproduction from seed bears unpredictably variable and therefore, economically useless progeny. Under cultivation, however, the species is propagated vegetatively by the rooting of twigs of the female fruit bearing clones in order to select for and maintain desirable genetic characteristics (Foaden and Fletcher 1910: 629–30; Zohary and Hopf 1994: 151, 156; Zohary 1995: 367–8). Most of the cultivars known today have been selected for their production of large, sweet fruits and for those clones which are able to fruit without pollination (Zohary and Hopf 1994: 151, 156; Zohary 1995: 367–8). It is impossible to distinguish between the seeds of the wild and domesticated fig in archaeological material (Zohary and Hopf 1994: 155) but Egypt lies outside the natural range of the wild species. Zohary and Hopf (1994: 151) argue that there may be a bias against the recovery of fig remains because the seeds are so small. On some Mediterranean sites, however, the species is clearly over-represented due to the enormous numbers of seeds in each fig (e.g. Murray 1998).

The common fig is frequently illustrated in tomb scenes, such as that of the Twelfth-Dynasty tomb of Khnumhotep III at Beni Hasan where baboons are harvesting fruits which are clearly the common fig and not the smaller, clustered sycomore fig (BH3; Täckholm 1961: 11; Germer 1985: 24). When the two fig types are shown together, such as on offering tables, the sycomore fig bears the incision of gashing to distinguish it from the common fig (Täckholm 1961: 11). From the Third Dynasty onwards common figs are also mentioned in the textual evidence, including the Fifth- and Sixth-Dynasty Pyramid Texts (Keimer 1926). Models of figs also have been found which probably date to the Middle Kingdom (Keimer 1929a; Darby *et al.* 1977: 708) and a schist vessel formed in the shape of a fig leaf from a Second-Dynasty tomb at Saqqara (Täckholm 1961: 11; Darby *et al.* 1977: 709) provides further evidence of the early knowledge of the species in Egypt.

Most of the archaeobotanical evidence for the *Ficus* genus in the Pharaonic period represents *F. sycomorus* and not *F. carica* (Täckholm 1961: 10: Darby *et al.* 1977: 708). Archaeobotanical finds of *F. carica* include whole figs and seeds, including finds from Predynastic Maadi (van Zeist and de Roller 1993: 3), Predynastic and Early Dynastic Buto (Thanheiser 1991: 45), Thirteenth- and Eighteenth-Dynasty Kom Rabiʿa in Memphis (Murray forthcoming), SIP Tell el-Dabʿa (Thanheiser forthcoming), and Eighteenth-Dynasty Deir el-Medina (Bruyère 1937: 108). The Predynastic finds from Maadi most closely resemble *F. carica*. Due to the overlap between the seeds of *F. carica* and *F. sycomorus*, however, and the uncertainty of the date at which the *Ceratosolen* wasp was present in Egypt to set seed in the sycomore fig, if ever, these early specimens have been labelled provisionally as *Ficus* (*carica*) (van Zeist and de Roller 1993: 8). It is interesting to note that no trace of *Ficus carica* was found in the rich remains from Eighteenth-Dynasty tomb of Tutankhamun (KV62) (Hepper 1990: 58).

*Pomegranate (*Punica granatum L.*) [Punicaceae – Pomegranate family]*

The pomegranate is a deciduous shrub or small tree which can grow from three to ten metres high. It has vivid red, orange or yellow flowers, either solitary or growing in small clusters, the sepals of which persist as a large crown calyx at the top of the fully formed fruit which varies greatly in size but is usually between 6 and 12 cm across. The many angular seeds, each enclosed in a sweet, slightly acidic juicy pulp, are found in several distinct compartments separated by pith (Foaden and Fletcher 1910: 614; Harrison *et al.* 1985: 94; FAO 1988: 420). The rounded fruit is covered with a smooth, leathery rind which, depending on ripeness, can be variously tinged with yellow, red or purple (Foaden and Fletcher 1910: 614; FAO 1988: 420). Its glossy oblong-lanceolate leaves are mostly opposite (Foaden and Fletcher 1910: 614; Harrison *et al.* 1985: 94; FAO 1988: 420) and the species is evergreen in a hot climate but loses its leaves in cooler areas (FAO 1988: 420). The tree flowers in the early summer and the fruits begin to ripen from early September and are usually at their best by October (Foaden and Fletcher 1910: 615). The pomegranate is a hardy plant, able to withstand poor soils, fairly high levels of salt and temperatures up to 45 °C while requiring less water than many other fruit tree species (Foaden and Fletcher 1910: 616; FAO 1988: 422). The tree grows best in a well-manured, well-drained sandy loam (Foaden and Fletcher 1910: 615).

The fruit pulp contains sugar, vitamin C, phosphorus and iron (FAO 1988: 421). It can be eaten fresh, pressed for its juice, used for syrup, jams, wine, and as the cordial 'grenadine' (Lucas 1962: 23; FAO 1988: 421; Dagher 1991: 106; see Chapter 23, this volume). The rind, bark, roots and seed oil of the pomegranate have medicinal properties, particularly for the treatment of stomach ailments and as a vermifuge (Boulos 1983: 149; Moens 1984: 28; FAO 1988: 422; Manniche 1989: 140; Nunn 1996: 15, 72). The rind is also used for tanning leather and as a dye (Pliny NH.XIII.XXXIV in Manniche 1989: 140; Foaden and Fletcher 1910: 617; Bailey and Danin 1981: 157; FAO 1988: 422; Hepper 1990: 64). The pomegranate has long been a symbol for fertility (Hepper 1990: 62) due to the prolific number of seeds borne by the species and is still considered a potent symbol in some areas of the eastern Mediterranean, including Cyprus where even in traditional weddings today, a pomegranate is thrown in the path of a newly-wed couple in order to release its many seeds (Georgiades 1985: 71).

The pomegranate, previously known as *Malum punicum* or apple of Carthage (Loret 1892: 76; Harrison *et al.* 1985: 94), was among the earliest cultivated fruit trees in the Old World and its wild forms can be found in several locations, including south of the Caspian Sea and northeastern Turkey (Zohary and Spiegel Roy 1975: 324; Zohary and Hopf 1994: 162). It is now cultivated in most parts of the warmer regions of the world, particularly in the subtropics (FAO 1988: 420). As with many other fruits, domestication included an increase in fruit size and a change from sexual reproduction to clonal propagation, i.e. the rooting of basal offshoots (FAO 1988: 423; Zohary and Hopf 1994: 162). The pomegranate can also be propagated by seed. Pomegranate trees take between four and eight years before regularly bearing fruit (FAO 1988: 423). If harvested prior to full ripeness, the fruit can be stored for five to six months where its quality will gradually improve (FAO 1988: 421).

The evidence for pomegranate comes from the artistic, textual and archaeobotanical records from Second Intermediate Period Tell el-Dabʿa (Thanheiser: forthcoming and the New Kingdom, including those from the Eighteenth-Dynasty settlement of Amarna (Renfrew 1985: 176) as well as a single, large desiccated pomegranate from the Eighteenth-Dynasty tomb of Djehuty (Hepper 1990: 64; Zohary and Hopf 1994: 162). The ancient Egyptian term *šdḥ* is commonly translated as pomegranate wine (e.g. Loret 1892; Lutz 1922; Lesko 1977; 1995), however, other interpretations have also been given (see Tallet 1995 for a full discussion). Several classes of artefact clearly represent the distinctive pomegranate shape, including ceramic vessels, jewellery and two silver and ivory vases, for example, found in the tomb of Tutankhamun (Hepper 1990: 62). Pomegranate leaves were also included in the king's lavish floral collar (Germer 1989: 11–15; Hepper 1990: 62). The earliest mention of the species in Egyptian texts is from the Eighteenth-Dynasty Theban tomb of Ani (TT168) describing the tree planted in his funerary park and the fruit is clearly shown in the Eighteenth-Dynasty temple of Thutmose III at Karnak (1450 BC) (Germer 1985: 42; Hepper 1990: 64).

Persea (Mimusops laurifolia *(forssk.) Friis)* (M. schimperi *Hochst.) [Sapotaceae – Sapote family]*

The persea tree can grow up to twenty metres high and has leathery, oval leaves, yellow flowers and fruits which are about 4 cm long, each containing two or three hard seeds (see Fig. 15.8, this volume) (Manniche 1989: 121; Hepper 1990: 15). Apart from a few specimens grown in recent years at the Egyptian Museum in Cairo from seeds imported from Arabia (Täckholm 1961: 27: Lucas 1962: 445), and its occasional presence as a garden tree, this species is uncommon in Egypt today (Täckholm 1961: 27; Hepper 1990: 15: Friis *et al.* 1986: 204). The persea species popular with the ancient Egyptians is from the Yemen and Ethiopia (Friis *et al.* 1986: 202; Hepper 1990: 15) where it continues to grow wild (Manniche 1989: 121). It has been shown, due to a re-examination of some ancient Egyptian specimens of persea leaves held at the Royal Botanic Gardens, Kew, that in light of additional botanical criteria and considerations of species distribution, these leaf specimens should now be categorised as *Mimusops laurifolia* (Forssk.) Friis (Friis *et al.* 1986: 202), however, the specific nature of the seeds and fruits are more difficult to determine and ancient specimens should be examined on a site by site basis (Friis *et al.* 1986: 204). Persea leaves were often used in the making of Pharaonic funeral garlands and since the leaves were folded and sewn into these garlands, they would have to have been fresh, thus indicating that the tree was grown locally (Hepper 1990: 15).

Several tomb-paintings from the Eighteenth Dynasty onwards depict this garden tree (Hepper 1990: 15), however there is some confusion between the illustrations of persea fruits and those of the mandrake (*Mandragora officinarum*)

(Germer 1985: 148; Manniche 1989: 121; Hepper 1990: 15). The many tomb finds of persea leaves and fruit indicate that the tree must have been widely cultivated in Pharaonic Egypt (Lauer *et al.* 1950: 129; Täckholm 1961: 27; Hepper 1990: 15). There is some evidence that persea was also appreciated for its medicinal qualities (Lucas 1962: 445; Manniche 1989: 122; although none cited by Nunn 1996: 15). During the Pharaonic period, persea was valued, not only for its fruits, leaves and wood but also for its deep association with Egyptian religion (Caminos 1954: 28; Täckholm 1961: 28; Hepper 1990: 15), principally its sacred status in relation to both Isis and Osiris (Darby *et al.* 1977: 740). The persea was completely extinct in Egypt by the seventeenth century AD and already may have been endangered as early as the Roman period when the cutting down of the persea tree was prohibited by law. Manniche (1989: 121) notes that only during the twentieth century has the tree been reintroduced into Egyptian gardens.

The earliest archaeobotanical finds of persea fruits are from the Third-Dynasty tomb of Djoser (Lauer *et al.* 1950: 129–30) and from the Fifth-Dynasty mortuary temple of Sahura at Abusir (Schweinfurth 1908). Other finds are known from Twelfth-Dynasty Kahun (Newberry 1890: 49); Eighteenth-Dynasty Amarna (Renfrew 1985: 176) and the Eighteenth-Dynasty tomb of Tutankhamun (Germer 1989: 11–18; de Vartavan 1990: 486; Hepper 1990: 15). Honey containing persea pollen was also recovered from a tomb dating to the Nineteenth Dynasty (Hepper 1990: 15). Theophrastus (IV: 2, 1, 5, 8 in Lucas 1962: 445) noted that objects, such as statues, beds and tables were made from persea wood, yet to date only a few wooden specimens have been identified as persea, including part of a Middle Kingdom coffin and a New Kingdom headrest (Lucas 1962: 445; Chapter 15, this volume). The leaves and twigs of persea have been found from the Twelfth Dynasty onwards and were often used in funeral garlands and bouquets, including those of Tutankhamun (Täckholm 1961: 27; Lucas 1962: 445; Friis *et al.* 1986: 202; Germer 1989: 20; Hepper 1990: 15; de Vartavan and Asensi Amorós 1997; Chapter 15 this volume).

*Egyptian plum, sebesten (*Cordia myxa *L.) [Boraginaceae – Borage Family]*

The Egyptian plum is actually a native of tropical Asia which grows up to eight metres tall and has white flowers and broad ovate leaves (Meikle 1985: 1120). It is cultivated in the oases and in the Mediterranean area of Egypt today. During the Classical period, Theophrastus (IV.2.10 in Darby *et al.* 1977: 707) gave a detailed description of the tree, calling it the Egyptian plum, and noted that the people of Upper Egypt harvested so many of its fruits at that time that they dried them, removed the stones and bruised the pulp in order to make cakes of them (Täckholm 1961: 29; Lucas 1962: 23; Darby *et al.* 1977: 707; Manniche 1989: 93). The fruits were used in medicine and Pliny mentioned that they were also fermented into wine (Täckholm 1961: 29; Lucas 1962: 23; Pliny (N.H., XIII, X, 51 in Darby *et al.* 1977: 707–8; Manniche 1989: 93; Chapter 23, this volume). The use of the fruit stones as beads is later seen in Greco–Roman tombs (Täckholm 1961: 30). Today, the sticky pulp of the fruit, sometimes mixed with honey, is used primarily for the making of bird lime which, when spread on tree branches, traps small birds (Täckholm 1961: 29, Meikle 1985: 1120; Kislev in press). The antiquity of the use of fruits for this purpose in Egypt is not known.

The sweet, orange fruits of the Egyptian plum were known from at least the Third Dynasty onwards, as suggested by the earliest archaeobotanical find of the species from the Step Pyramid of Djoser at Saqqara (Täckholm 1961: 29 although not noted in Lauer *et al.* 1950). A Middle Kingdom find from Thebes included leafy branches with attached fruits (Keimer 1924: 26), although unfortunately these were later destroyed in Berlin during the World War II (Täckholm 1961: 29). Fruit stones also were found at the Eighteenth-Dynasty site of Deir el-Medina (Täckholm 1961: 30; Germer 1985: 159).

*Carob (*Ceratonia siliqua *L.) – [Leguminosae – Pea Family]*

The carob, or locust bean tree, is an evergreen, growing up to ten metres in height with a broad canopy up to fourteen metres wide. It has small greenish flowers, oblong, leathery leaves and brown pods, 10–30 cm long and 1.5–3.5 cm wide, containing hard brown seeds (8–10 mm × 7–8 mm) (Meikle 1977: 590; Polunin and Huxley 1987: 91; Fig. 15.4, this volume). The carob is an eastern Mediterranean native of the *maquis* and *garrigue* environments of that area (Meikle 1977: 590). In Egypt today, it is found along the Mediterranean coastal strip and as a cultivated garden tree (Lucas 1962: 443; Darby *et al.* 1977: 701, Zahran and Willis 1992: 21; Chapter 15, this volume). Carob pods provide protein, starch and sugar and are used extensively as animal fodder and are also appreciated for their medicinal properties, particularly for the treatment of digestive disorders (Aykroyd *et al.* 1982: 88; Boulos 1983: 123; Le Houérou 1985: 131; Georgiades 1987: 26; Manniche 1989: 85–6; Dagher 1991: 104; Nunn 1996: 15). Carob pods are a popular food today in Egypt, especially during the month of Ramadan (Dagher 1991: 104). The tree also is cultivated extensively for its seeds and pods which are used to make a carob syrup and sweet gum extract which is used in other food products, such as a thickening agent and substitute for coffee and chocolate (Aykroyd *et al.* 1982: 88; Wetterstrom 1984: 62; Manniche 1989: 86; Dagher 1991: 104).

It has been noted that, in antiquity, carob pods were only fit for animal consumption due to their fibrous, unpalatable nature and that they became a suitable human food only after the development of improved modern varieties (Coit

1951), however, Wetterstrom (1984: 62) argues that the pods probably would not have been found as tomb offerings if they also had not been used as human food. Traditionally, carob pods are harvested in late summer and stone ground into a powder. The seeds are hard enough not to be ground in the process and are then separated from the carob pod powder which is later used to make a rich extract (Dagher 1991: 104). They may also have been included due to their medicinal properties. Although the tree was probably limited in its range and availability, carob pods may have been used as sweetener during the Pharaonic period. The hard seeds of the carob were the original carat, the standard measure of weight used by jewellers today (four grains) (Germer 1985: 95; Polunin and Huxley 1987: 91; Georgiades 1987: 26).

The earliest finds of carob fruit in Egypt are a single pod and six seeds found at the Twelfth-Dynasty site of Kahun (Newberry 1890: 50; Germer 1985: 95; forthcoming). Other finds of the Pharaonic period include those from Eighteenth-Dynasty Deir el-Medina (Bruyère 1937). Earlier claims for the presence of carob in Egypt are based on linguistic evidence, such as that of the First-Dynasty pottery inscriptions from the tomb of Hemaka at Saqqara (Saad 1938: 51). Carob wood makes a strong, sturdy building material (Willcox 1992: 9; Chapter 15, this volume), yet there are few archaeological examples of the carob tree from Egypt thus far, such as a carob wood bow dating from 1700 BC from Thebes (Lucas 1962: 443) and mummy-labels from the Roman period (Chapter 15, this volume).

*Christ's thorn (*Ziziphus spina-christi *(L.) Desf.) [Rhamnaceae family – Buckthorn family]*

Christ's thorn is a densely branched evergreen bush or tree which grows from four to twenty metres high. The rounded yellowish or reddish brown fruit, known as *nabk*, is 2 to 3 cm in diameter, is sweet and slightly astringent to the taste and is still popular today. The species has small yellow flowers and variable, ovate leaves with slightly toothed margins (see Fig. 15.11, this volume) (Meikle 1977: 358; M. Zohary 1982: 154–5, FAO 1988: 538; Hepper 1990: 68; Dagher 1991: 111). Christ's thorn gets it name from the sharp spines of varying lengths growing from the base of each leaf stalk which were reputedly used in the making of Jesus' crown of thorns (M. Zohary 1982: 154–5, Hepper 1990: 68). Christ's thorn is found in Egypt as well as other parts of north and east Africa, down to Tanzania, south Arabia and in the desert oases and rain fed areas of the Near East (FAO 1988: 538). Today the Christ's thorn tree, commonly known as *sidder*, is grown primarily for its shade throughout the Nile Valley but it was probably one of the original constituents of the wild flora of Egypt and continues to grow wild in Upper Egypt (Täckholm 1961: 25). The species is propagated by cuttings, or after the seed shell is cracked and soaked overnight in warm water, it can be more successfully propagated from seed (FAO 1988: 539).

The fruits contain carbohydrates, protein, vitamin C, some B vitamins, calcium and iron (FAO 1988: 538; Dagher 1991: 111). These are easily dried and stored (FAO 1988: 539) and acquire a soft date-like quality after a few weeks (Dagher 1991: 111). Pliny noted that the Egyptians ate the seeds as well as the fruit (NH.XIII.XXXIII, 111 in Darby *et al.* 1977: 703). The seeds are likely to be rich in protein and fat (FAO 1988: 538, although no published data are available) and this has been reported from other arid regions. The tree serves as an important windbreak, as an erosion control, as firewood and as browsing forage for livestock (FAO 1988: 539). Christ's thorn is still prized by bedouin and other desert peoples, not only for its fruits and shade but also for the spiritual qualities associated with the tree (Bailey and Danin 1981: 155; Hobbs 1989: 92). The tree held a religious significance for the ancient Egyptians as well (Hepper 1990: 68). The Papyrus Ebers indicates that Christ's thorn fruits and leaves were used frequently in ancient Egyptian medicine for a variety of ailments (Darby *et al.* 1977: 703; Nunn 1996: 15) and the species continues to be used in folk medicine today (Boulos 1983: 153; Manniche 1989: 158; Dagher 1991: 111). A wine can also be made from the fruits, as is still done by Coptic monks in desert monasteries (Strouhal 1992: 129) and *nabk* fruits were still used as an ingredient in Egyptian breads this century (Kamal 1913; Manniche 1989: 158; Chapter 22, this volume).

The tree has been appreciated for its fruit, timber and shade in Egypt since Predynastic times. The wood of the species has been found on many Egyptian sites where it was used to make dowels, coffins and other objects (Bauman 1960: 101; W. V. Davies 1995; Chapter 15, this volume). Among the oldest archaeobotanical finds of *nabk* fruits are from the Predynastic sites of KH3 and Naqada South Town (Wetterstrom 1986: Table 1) and Hierakonpolis (Fahmy 1995: 118), the First Dynasty tomb of Hemaka at Saqqara (Emery and Saad 1938) and from the Third-Dynasty tomb of Djoser at Saqqara where 700 Christ's thorn stones were recovered (Lauer *et al.* 1950: 131; Täckholm 1961: 26). Later finds are known from Twelfth-Dynasty Kahun (Newberry 1890: 50), Eighteenth- to Nineteenth-Dynasty Kom Rabiʿa and the Eighteenth-Dynasty tomb of Tutankhamun (KV62), which also included bread containing *Ziziphus* fruits (Germer 1989: 50–1; de Vartavan 1990: 486; Hepper 1990: 68). The continued importance of the fruit is evident from the many post-Pharaonic finds of the species (Table 24.1); de Vartavan and Asensi Amorós 1997).

Vegetables

The identification of the vegetables discussed in this section, using the linguistic, artistic and archaeobotanical records has been problematic in Egypt. For example, the confusion between leeks and kurrats, even among modern taxonomists (Havey 1995: 344) has an ancient history with regard to the artistic and linguistic record, while the lack of archaeobotanical evidence for these soft, leafy species, which also includes the lettuce, is another obvious complication. Cucumbers and melons, too, though they may seem dissimilar, are so alike botanically as to create uncertainty as to whether one or the other of these two is present on many sites or indeed known in Pharaonic Egypt at all. Another species discussed here, the radish, is found on only one Pharaonic period site, Twelfth-Dynasty Kahun (Newberry 1890), yet as previously noted, at least part of the Kahun material may actually date to the post-Pharaonic period (Germer forthcoming). The linguistic and artistic evidence for these species is sometimes still under debate, often serving to confuse these issues further, since it can be argued that ancient paintings and linguistic distinctions are not the most reliable criteria for demonstrating the existence of morphological traits and species identifications (e.g. Lindqvist 1960: 341; Germer forthcoming). A multidisciplinary approach, involving the archaeobotanical, linguistic and artistic records, will be the way forward to help clarify the presence, extent of use and other uncertainties associated with these species.

There is no textual evidence for the rotation of crops prior to the Ptolemaic period (Baer 1963: 6; Butzer 1976: 47). Nor is there any indication that the Pharaonic farmers intercropped their species, i.e. that vegetables or condiments were grown under fruit trees or together in the same plot, as is common in Egypt today. While crop rotation would require a consistent, perennial irrigation source, intercropping would not and the many benefits of the practice, including the optimal use of space and moisture, would seem to make it ideally suited to Pharaonic agriculture, particularly as the cultivation of summer crops would have been problematic (see irrigation, pp. 615–6). Eyre (1994: 62–3) has noted that tomb scenes depicting gardens and orchards may imply a type of intercropping, such as in the Twelfth-Dynasty tomb of Khnumhotep at Beni Hasan (BH3; Fig. 24.2), and concludes that, if practised at all, it was probably limited to domestic or pleasure gardens. It would seem unlikely, however, that the efficient practice of intercropping would not have been employed by the resourceful ancient Egyptian farmers. The detection of the practice in the archaeobotanical record may be possible, particularly if species were harvested and threshed together as is common today, but a detailed investigation of this issue is required.

In the Nile flood basins, the fertile silts deposited by the inundation, would have been well-suited to the cultivation of vegetables. If crops were grown in uninundated areas, during years of low floods, for example, then irrigation would have involved raising water from canals or the river, either manually or from the New Kingdom onwards, by using the *shaduf* (see irrigation, pp. 615–6 and Chapter 21, this volume). In these cases, the optimal soil type would have been a well-prepared friable, sandy loam as it is easily tilled, quickly workable after watering, warms up quickly in the spring and responds well to fertilisers, whereas soils which are too sandy or contain too much clay provide few nutrients and can be difficult to work when either wet or dry (Foaden and Fletcher 1910: 531; Arnon 1972: 430–1, 338–9). Vegetables need to grow quickly and continuously, otherwise the quality of their fruits can be poor. A high quality seed and good soil preparation are also important for their successful growth (e.g. Foaden and Fletcher 1910: 322–7, 531). Depending on the species grown and type of land, i.e. flood basin or canal irrigated land, soil preparation would have entailed varying degrees of ploughing, manuring, watering, and drainage which in turn would have benefited the soil through aeration, an increase in root extension, the addition and more effective use of nutrients, the reduction of weeds and crop pests, the retention of moisture, and ultimately a larger and better quality of produce (Foaden and Fletcher 1910: 531; Arnon 1972: 423, 430–1; Beshai 1993: 269). See Chapter 21, this volume for further discussion of these important factors. The methods of cultivation used under both flood basin and canal irrigation are discussed below for each taxon).

Onion (Allium cepa *L.) [Liliaceae – Lily family]*

The wild progenitor of the bulb onion, *Allium cepa*, is not yet recognised and the species most likely originates from Central Asia (Langer and Hill 1991: 33; Zohary and Hopf 1994: 185; Havey 1995: 345). The onion is an annual or biennial herb which grows from 60 to 120 cm in height. It has as many as 2,000 small, white to lilac flowers which

*Figure 24.6 Detail from a reconstructed wall of the Aten temple at East Karnak, showing a workman eating what appears to be onion (*Allium cepa*).*

form a rounded umbel between 4 and 9 cm in diameter and has two black angular seeds contained in each of the three locules of the fruit capsule. The edible bulb is composed of the thickened leaf bases attached to the underground stem (Täckholm and Drar 1954: 59, Meikle 1985: 1609; Langer and Hill 1991: 34). Although well-developed bulb onions are depicted in Egyptian tomb paintings, slender, long leafed spring onion with relatively small bulbs were also valued (also see section below on native Egyptian kurrats) (Fig. 24.6). These are a type of *A. cepa* which are harvested when young (Charles 1987: 11; Langer and Hill 1991: 36). The spring onion variety is still very popular in Egypt today and is often eaten raw with bread. Onions also can be fried, boiled or roasted for use in soups, sauces and stews. As with other *Allium* species the strong aroma of onion is due the presence of volatile oils and sulphur compounds (Täckholm and Drar 1954: 59; Havey 1995: 344). The juice of the onion has been extensively used in herbal medicine to treat coughs, colds, stomach ailments and other ills throughout antiquity (Täckholm and Drar 1954: 108–10; Darby *et al.* 1977: 662–3; Boulos 1983: 23; Manniche 1989: 69; Havey 1995: 344; Nunn 1996: 14). Onion skins produce a spectrum of yellow and brown dyes (Cannon and Cannon 1994: 84). The range of modern onion varieties vary enormously in size, shape, colour and taste (Täckholm and Drar 1954: 90; Harrison *et al.* 1985: 166; Charles 1987: 11; Havey 1995: 346).

The higher temperatures of Middle and Upper Egypt, particularly towards the end of the growing season, favour onion cultivation in those areas (Foaden and Fletcher 1910: 487; Beshai 1993: 269). Traditionally, onions are grown along the river bank and on the alluvial islands of Upper Egypt but can be grown on most soil types (Foaden and Fletcher 1910: 487). The onion is a winter crop and earlier this century, in both Upper and Lower Egypt, onion seed was usually sown in beds during September where the seedlings remained until they were eventually transplanted. The seedlings were well-watered prior to their removal from the beds and then exposed to the sun for a week or so to separate the weak from the strong. On the river bank or islands, the transplanting of seedlings would depend on when the floodwaters had receded although this was usually during November and December whereas under canal irrigation, transplanting occurred in December and January and could be as late as February (Foaden and Fletcher 1910: 490). No preparation of the soil or irrigation is necessary for onions grown on the river bank where, after the retreat of the Nile, the rich, moist alluvium was sufficient for the successful growth of the seedlings (Foaden and Fletcher 1910: 489).

In contrast, under canal irrigation the land was ploughed two or three times and then harrowed to create a fine, friable soil. Manure was usually broadcast onto dry soil but not mixed with it and the ground was then watered (Foaden and Fletcher 1910: 491). Ridges were created for the seedlings and irrigation water was allowed to fill the furrows below the crest of the ridges. Over-watering easily damages the plant by encouraging excessive leaf growth and inhibiting bulb development. About eight waterings are necessary during the growing season and no water is given at all during the twenty-five days or so prior to the harvest (Foaden and Fletcher 1910: 492). Harvesting takes place once most of the foliage has withered (Foaden and Fletcher 1910: 492; Charles 1987: 13; Langer and Hill 1991: 36) and although the timing of the harvest depends on soil type, climate and location, it usually takes place between four and five months after transplanting (Foaden and Fletcher 1910: 492). In Upper Egypt, onions are at their prime during April and are best in Lower Egypt in late April and May (Foaden and Fletcher 1910: 493). If onions are left unharvested for too long, the quality of the bulbs will decline since they tend to re-root themselves, particularly if exposed to high ground water or moisture just prior to harvest (Foaden and Fletcher 1910: 492). Onion losses due to sprouting or spoilage are also more likely in storage if they have been moistened at all before harvesting (Foaden and Fletcher 1910: 492; Langer and Hill 1991: 36). After the harvest, the onions are exposed to the sun for two days and then again for another day after their tops are cut off close to the bulb before being stored in a cool, dry place (Foaden and Fletcher 1910: 493).

Analysis of cuneiform texts from Mesopotamia suggests that the onion was grown there from the second millennium BC onwards (e.g. Stol 1987) although archaeobotanical evidence for the early presence of the species outside Egypt is slight (Charles 1987: 11; Zohary and Hopf 1994: 185). The onion was highly valued in Egypt from at least the Old Kingdom onwards where the tending of the species in gardens is depicted (Manniche 1989: 69). Early linguistic records for the onion come from the Fifth-Dynasty Pyramid Texts of Unas (*c.* 2420 BC) and Pepi II (*c.* 2200 BC) although these texts were probably already in use during the Third and Fourth Dynasties (Täckholm and Drar 1954: 98). Onions are a common feature on most offering tables from the Fourth Dynasty onwards, usually accompanied by bread, and they also appear to have been central to certain religious ceremonies, indeed, both Pliny (XIX, 1) and Juvenal (*Satire* XV, 9) derisively commented on the god-like status that the Egyptians bestowed on common garden vegetables, such as onions and garlic (Täckholm and Drar 1954: 98–9; Darby *et al.* 1977: 660–1). The avoidance of eating onions in Egypt, particularly by priests, was reported by Classical authors (Ruffer 1919: 75; Darby *et al.* 1977: 661–2)

There is some evidence that onions were used in the mummification process, i.e. placed in the body cavity of mummies as early as the Thirteenth Dynasty, and certainly from the Twenty-first Dynasty onwards, the species was often used in this way, including for the mummy of Ramses II (Ruffer 1919: 74–6; Täckholm and Drar 1954:

101–2, 105; Bauman 1960: 92). It has been suggested that this practice was believed to stimulate the dead to breathe again (Täckholm and Drar 1954: 102; Darby *et al.* 1977: 661; Strouhal 1992: 128). Although onions are represented in the artistic and textual records from the Old Kingdom onwards, the earliest archaeobotanical evidence for onions is reportedly from the aforementioned Thirteenth-Dynasty mummy (Ruffer 1919: 76; Täckholm and Drar 1954: 102). Several finds occur from the Eighteenth Dynasty onwards, including those from the Eighteenth-Dynasty settlements of Deir el-Medina (Bruyère 1937) and Amarna (Renfrew 1985: 176).

*Leeks and kurrats (*Allium ampeloprasum *var.* porrum *and var.* kurrat*) [Liliaceae – Lily family]*

There are two main varieties of leek in Egypt today; the common garden leek and the kurrat. The leek is a biennial herb which can grow up to one metre in height (Täckholm and Drar 1954: 84). The rounded inflorescence of purple flowers forms at the top of the round flowering stem. The garden leek is larger than the kurrat or *baladi* variety and is cultivated primarily for its bulbs while the kurrat develops only a small bulb and is grown principally for its fresh, elongated leaves. Leeks and kurrats are not known in the wild and the wild progenitor of both is thought to be *A. ampeloprasum*, a species common to the Mediterranean basin (Täckholm and Drar 1954: 84; Zohary and Hopf 1994: 183). There has been great confusion between the European garden leek (*A. porrum L.*) and the smaller, narrower leaved kurrat (*A. kurrat* Sfth and Krause) (Täckholm and Drar 1954: 103). The uncertainty over leek and kurrat arises from a 'confusion over what constitutes a distinct morphological character' between these two closely related plants (Havey 1995: 345) and consequently they have been recently reclassified as varieties of *A. ampeloprasum* (var. *porrum* and var. *kurrat*, respectively) rather than as separate species (Havey 1995: 344). The kurrat is not well-known outside of Egypt where it continues to be grown and is used as a raw vegetable and a seasoning (Täckholm 1977: 272; Havey 1995: 347). In Egypt today, the kurrat is known as *kurrat baladi* or local kurrat, whereas the leek is *kurrat rûmi* or foreign kurrat (Foaden and Fletcher 1910: 544; Täckholm and Drar 1954: 103).

Since both leeks and kurrats are in question here, the agricultural practices for both species will be discussed. Both are propagated by seed, which is broadcast sown in well manured plots of light loam in February or March. The common garden leek is then transplanted into earthen ridges in early July. The harvesting of the garden leek can usually commence three to three and a half months after it has been transplanted and may continue for two months or more, until the beginning of January (Foaden and Fletcher 1910: 544). For high quality leeks, the bulb itself is blanched, usually by planting the leeks in trenches or furrows and by covering them with soil for a fortnight prior to the harvest (Täckholm and Drar 1954: 84; Harrison *et al.* 1985: 168). In contrast, the kurrat can remain in the ground for up to two years although the harvest of leaves is much reduced during the second year. The quality of the harvest improves after the first two cuttings of the leaves and, depending on the amount of manure used, the leaves can be harvested more than twelve times a year (Foaden and Fletcher 1910: 544).

What evidence do we actually have for the cultivation of the leek in ancient Egypt? The artistic evidence is questionable since if modern taxonomists have difficulty determining distinctions between leeks and kurrats then it would seem unlikely that this can be done accurately from tomb paintings. An added complication may also be the pictorial similarity of not only leeks and kurrats but also of the long-leafed spring onion (Fig. 24.6). For the linguistic evidence, Loret (e.g. 1904) claimed that the earliest linguistic record for the leek (*ı͗ꜣkt*) is from the Sixth Dynasty, however, this has been disputed and it is also not clear if the Egyptian name refers to leeks or kurrats (Täckholm and Drar 1954: 95; Keimer 1984; Germer 1985: 193). The species denoted by the word *ı͗ꜣkt* in ancient Egypt was valued for its medicinal properties (Germer 1985: 194; Manniche 1989: 70; Nunn 1996: 14). Another problem of the leek/kurrat issue is the nature of the botanical evidence, since soft, leafy leeks and kurrats are less likely to preserve than many seeds, fruits or tubers, even under desiccated conditions. Thus far, a single specimen has been identified for both leek and kurrat for ancient Egypt (both of unknown date) (de Vartavan and Asensi Amorós 1997: 36). The presence of the leek in ancient Egypt, therefore, is based principally on linguistic grounds and a single identification. The continued investigation of the archaeobotanical and linguistic records of this taxa, as well as the native kurrat, may help to determine if and when the leek was ever present during the Pharaonic period.

*Garlic (*Allium sativum *L) [Liliaceae – Lily family]*

Garlic is often regarded as a flavouring or condiment rather than as a vegetable in its own right but will be treated as a vegetable in this discussion. The wild ancestry of cultivated garlic is not yet known although garlic has the closest morphological affinity to the wild species *Allium longicuspis* Regal, found in Central Asia, northern Iran and south eastern Turkey and this species is regarded by some botanists to be the likely wild progenitor (Charles 1987: 12; Langer and Hill 1991: 36; Zohary and Hopf 1994: 185). Garlic may have been cultivated originally in the northeastern fringe of the Near East (Zohary and Hopf 1994: 185).

Garlic is a perennial herb, growing up to a metre tall, which has white or pink flowers and flat, linear leaves. Garlic consists of an edible ovoid bulb made up of between six and ten bulblets or 'cloves', joined at the base and all encased in a papery sheath or tunic (Täckholm and Drar 1954: 87). The bulbs of the native Egyptian garlic (*Allium sativum* var. *minus*) are generally smaller than the common European type and the taste is not as strong, although there are a larger number of cloves (Foaden and Fletcher 1910: 542; Darby *et al.* 1977: 657). In the first century BC, Dioscorides (II, 152) described Egyptian garlic as being small, with a whole bulb not split into cloves and as having a purplish hue (Crawford 1973: 351; Darby *et al.* 1977: 657) and modern botanists, Täckholm and Drar (1954: 97), also have noted that specimens of this type may occasionally occur (also see Stol 1987). Archaeobotanical finds of garlic from the Pharaonic period all appear to be the cloved variety. In Egypt, garlic is most commonly used for seasoning and for the preservation of meat but the bulbs are also eaten raw or cooked and the species has been valued for the medicinal properties of its volatile oils since at least the New Kingdom onwards (Pliny N.H. XX, XXIII in Darby *et al.* 1977: 657; Täckholm and Drar 1954: 87, 112, Darby *et al.* 1977: 657; Boulos 1983: 25; Manniche 1989: 70; also see Nunn 1996: 14).

Garlic is a winter crop which grows best on a well-drained, well-manured, slightly acid loam (Foaden and Fletcher 1910: 542; Charles 1987: 13). For the most part, the species does not produce seed and therefore is propagated vegetatively by planting individual cloves or whole bulbs (Foaden and Fletcher 1910: 542; Täckholm and Drar 1954: 88; Charles 1987: 12; Havey 1995: 347). Hepper (1990: 55) has noted that the absence of garlic seeds indicates the 'long cultivation and uncertain ancestry' of the species. Planting can be done from the middle of August (Täckholm and Drar 1954: 88) although November is considered the optimal time (Foaden and Fletcher 1910: 542). Sowing also may be extended as late as December, after the annual floodwaters had receded from the basin lands in Upper Egypt (Foaden and Fletcher 1910: 542; Täckholm and Drar 1954: 88; Crawford 1973: 355). The species requires little water after the early stages of its development (Foaden and Fletcher 1910: 542; Charles 1987: 13) and a lack of water two weeks before the harvest encourages bulb formation. Weeding will benefit the crop as long as the shallow roots are not damaged (Foaden and Fletcher 1910: 542; Charles 1987: 13). The bulbs develop entirely underground and are harvested by uprooting about five to six months after planting (Foaden and Fletcher 1910: 542; Täckholm and Drar 1954: 88), usually after 10–25 per cent of the foliage has withered (Charles 1987: 13). Lease agreements from the Ptolemaic period suggest that January was the usual month for the garlic harvest (Crawford 1973: 355).

Traditionally, garlic bulbs are tied in bundles and dried before storage or selling (Foaden and Fletcher 1910: 542; Täckholm and Drar 1954: 88). The large scale cultivation of garlic, particularly in the area of the Fayum, was introduced to Egypt by the Greeks in the third century BC and many texts of the Greco–Roman period allude to various aspects of its cultivation (Crawford 1973). Aside from growing in the flood basins after the flood waters had receded, garlic may have been grown in small market gardens away from the basins and intercropped among other species, such as grape vines (Crawford 1973: 355).

Archaeological finds of white painted, unbaked clay models of what appear to be cloved garlic bulbs from the Predynastic sites of el-Mahasna, Naqada and the cemetery at Umm el Qaʿab at Abydos are considered to be the earliest-known record for garlic (Ayrton and Loat 1911; Petrie 1920: 43, pl. 46; Täckholm and Drar 1954: 102). The first archaeobotanical evidence for the species is from Eighteenth-Dynasty tomb finds while the first textual record for garlic in Egypt comes from the Twentieth Dynasty text, the Papyrus Harris (Loret 1904; Täckholm and Drar 1954: 94). Future analysis may fill in the gap between the two disparate pieces of evidence of the supposed Predynastic clay models of garlic and New Kingdom archaeobotanical and textual evidence for the species.

As noted above, the earliest archaeobotanical specimens are known from tomb finds from the Eighteenth Dynasty and later, including well-preserved examples from Deir el-Medina and the tomb of Tutankhamun (KV62) (Bruyère 1937; Täckholm and Drar 1954: 103; Germer 1989: 43–4; Hepper 1990: 55). Garlic was not only placed in tombs as an offering but was also used in the embalming process, perhaps due its valued properties as a preservative (Hepper 1990: 55). Specimens of garlic have also been found on the Eighteenth-Dynasty settlement site of Amarna (Renfrew 1985: 176).

*Lettuce (*Lactuca *sp. L.) [Compositae – Daisy family]*

The origins and taxonomy of the cultivated lettuce are complex and still much debated (see Chapter 19, this volume for full discussion). Members of the highly variable *sativa-serriola* complex found in the Mediterranean basin and elsewhere the Near East are interfertile and through selection, *Lactuca sativa* may have derived from *L. serriola* yet this remains an uncertainty (Lindqvist 1960: 340; Zohary and Hopf 1994: 186; Ryder and Whitaker 1995: 54). The first record ever of lettuce as a vegetable comes from Egyptian tomb-paintings from the Old Kingdom (e.g. Duell 1938, pl. 21) which illustrate the cultivation of a tall conical, form of lettuce with long overlapping leaves (fig. 24.3). It is also a common element in offering scenes of the Pharaonic period (Germer 1985: 185). Keimer (1924: 1) classified the ancient Egyptian form as *Lactuca sativa* var. *longifolia*, the Cos lettuce group (known as Romaine in the USA and France) (Lindqvist 1960: 340; Harlan 1986: 7; Manniche 1989: 112). Wild and primitive lettuce varieties were very different from the common lettuce types bought today, and are often characterised by their spiny, bitter tasting leaves (Harlan 1986: 7; Ryder and Whitaker 1995: 54). The hearted varieties of lettuce common today, for example, were not truly developed until the middle of the sixteenth century (Langer and Hill 1991: 163). A wild form of *Lactuca sativa* occurs in a semi-wild state in Egypt and is semi-cultivated for its leaves which can be eaten (el-Hadidi 1992: 324) and used as an animal fodder but is primarily valued for its oil bearing seed (Sickenberger 1901; Lindqvist 1960: 338; el-Hadidi 1992: 324).

It has been suggested that ancient Egyptian lettuce was grown primarily for the oil extracted from its seeds (Keimer 1924; Darby *et al.* 1977: 678; Harlan 1986: 7; Ryder and Whitaker 1995: 54). Oil-bearing varieties generally have bitter tasting leaves and are not commonly eaten as leafy vegetables (Harlan 1986: 7). The local Egyptian variety of lettuce grown today, prickly lettuce, *Lactuca scariola (=serriola)* var. *sativa*) is also a tall erect form whose heart is sweet and crisp but whose outer leaves are bitter and coarse. This species, too, closely resembles the Cos type lettuce, as does the form grown primarily for its oil-bearing seed *Lactuca scariola (=serriola)* var. *oleifera* (Foaden and Fletcher 1910: 562). If ancient Egyptian lettuce was valued for its seed, then the process of selecting those plants with the most desirable seed characteristics, e.g. large size, high oil content, may have taken precedence over the selection of plants for their leaf characteristics, e.g. large, good-tasting leaves. The possibility that lettuce was cultivated primarily for its oil bearing seeds in ancient Egypt, rather than as a leafy vegetable, certainly deserves further investigation.

The artistic record and historical accounts suggest that the lettuce of ancient Egypt was an upright variety, growing more than a metre in height, which exuded a white milky juice when broken. Keimer (1924) described an ancient Egyptian type lettuce growing in the Botanical Garden at Berlin-Dahlem as one and a half metres in height (also Harlan 1986: 7). In Egypt the lettuce became a symbol of fertility and had a strong association with the gods Min in the Old Kingdom and Amun in the New Kingdom (Keimer 1924; Caminos 1954: 341; Täckholm 1977: 272; Darby *et al.* 1977: 678; el-Hadidi 1992: 323). Min, the god of vegetation and procreation, is often shown throughout the Pharaonic period in what appears to be a stylised lettuce field, usually receiving a lettuce plant from Pharaoh, and the related text notes that the offering is to ask Min to perform the act of procreation (Darby *et al.* 1977: 678; el-Hadidi 1992: 323). Lettuce was thought to possess aphrodisiac qualities, while it has also been used extensively in folk medicine as a sedative (Darby *et al.* 1977: 678, 680; Boulos 1983: 67; Manniche 1989: 113). Today lettuce varieties contains more than 95 per cent water (Harrison *et al.* 1985: 150) and can be eaten raw, as a salad green or as a cooked vegetable. The oil extracted from the seeds is still used today (see Chapter 19, this volume).

Lettuce can be grown as a summer crop, although it grows well during the cooler weather on sandy or loamy soils (Harrison *et al.* 1985: 150). Two types of lettuce were grown in Egypt in recent years, garden lettuce from imported seed and local or prickly lettuce. The prickly lettuce seed is broadcast sown from the middle of September continuously until November and again in late February (Foaden and Fletcher 1910: 563). Seedlings are transplanted onto ridges about thirty to thirty-five days after sowing. Plenty of water and manure are necessary for a quick and continuous growth and it can be harvested two and a half to three months after transplanting (Foaden and Fletcher 1910: 563).

The archaeobotanical evidence for lettuce in ancient Egypt is slight and includes seeds from an unknown period housed in the Berlin Museum (Keimer 1924: 290), later destroyed during World War II, and lettuce seeds found inside Roman pottery now on exhibit in the Dokki Agricultural Museum in Cairo (Germer 1985: 185; Darby *et al.* 1977: 679). Lettuce seeds attributed to the Third Intermediate Period/Ptolemaic/Roman period have been found at Elephantine (Willerding and Wolf 1990); however, there is no secure archaeobotanical evidence for lettuce during the Pharaonic period and little from subsequent periods. The presence of lettuce in the Pharaonic period, therefore, is based exclusively on the artistic and linguistic records (For a debate on the linguistic evidence, see Keimer 1924: 126; Loret 1892: 69; Darby *et al.* 1977: 677–8).

*Celery (*Apium graveolens *L.) [Umbelliferae – Carrot family]*

Celery is sometimes mentioned in the list of vegetable species available during the Pharaonic period. Cultivated celery (*Apium graveolens* var. *dulce*), as we know it today, however, is a comparatively recent development (Harrison *et al.* 1985: 148; Riggs 1995: 482). The evidence to date, suggests that the species was only truly cultivated as a vegetable sometime during the fourteenth or fifteenth centuries in Italy (Riggs 1995: 482). Prior to that wild celery was used by the Greeks for medicinal purposes and, as was obviously the case in Egypt, as a pungent component in funeral wreaths (Riggs 1995: 482), including that of King Tutankhamun (Germer 1989: 8; Hepper 1990: 14). The Romans in Egypt also used celery as a medicinal herb (Nunn 1996: 14) and grew it on a small scale for use as a condiment, like parsley, rather than as a vegetable in its own right (Riggs 1995: 482).

To date, the only archaeobotanical evidence of celery from Pharaonic Egypt dates from towards the end of the New Kingdom and suggests that it was used, not as a vegetable but rather as an attractive addition to funeral garlands, where it was often alternated with petals of the blue lotus (*Nymphaea coerulea*), and as an ingredient in medicinal remedies used for a variety of diseases (Germer 1985: 137; Darby *et al.* 1977: 670; Boulos 1983: 180; Manniche 1989: 76). It also was a symbol of sorrow (Täckholm 1977: 273). The earliest direct evidence for the use of celery as food, is the use of celery seeds in the recipes of Apicius from the Roman period (Darby *et al.* 1977: 670). Archaeobotanical evidence of seeds from later periods suggests that celery may have been used more extensively, with finds from Greco–Roman Hawara (Newberry 1889: 53); Roman Mons Claudianus (van der Veen 1996: 139; 1998); and the Late Antique site of Kom el-Nana at Amarna (Smith 1997). More archaeobotanical data is needed to determine the extent and manner of use of the celery plant during the Pharaonic period but as yet, there is no evidence to show that celery was used as a vegetable or even a condiment at that time.

*Watermelon (*Citrullus lanatus *(Thunb.) Mansf.) [Cucurbitaceae – Melon family]*

The watermelon is native of tropical and subtropical Africa (Charles 1987: 6; Bates and Robinson 1995: 89). It is an annual spreading climber with hairy three- or five-lobed leaves and yellow flowers whose rounded, green fruits contain a juicy red, yellow or white flesh with many smooth, oval seeds scattered throughout (Fig. 24.7) (Charles 1987: 6; FAO 1988: 186–7; Ward 1993: 251). The leaves, fruit, flowers and seeds of the watermelon are edible. The fruits appear in the summer and contain 94 per cent water, carbohydrates and sugar (Langer and Hill 1991: 210). They can be eaten fresh and the nutritious roasted seeds are a popular food in Egypt today. The edible seeds contain protein (25–32 per cent), oil (20–45 per cent), vitamin E and fibre (Harrison *et al.* 1985: 120; FAO 1988: 188, Bates and Robinson 1995: 89). Foaden and Fletcher (1910: p. 664) observed that the oil was not extracted for use in Egypt at that time. In ancient Egypt, however, the watermelon may have been cultivated primarily for its seed (Täckholm 1961: 31; Germer 1985: 127–8), as is the case in many parts of Africa today (FAO 1988: 188). The young leaves, which contain vitamin A, and the fruits can be used as a vegetable, added to soups or used as a relish (FAO 1988: 188). Both the fruit and seeds occur in a number of prescriptions during the Pharaonic period (Manniche 1989: 92; Nunn 1996: 15) and are used in folk medicine today (FAO 1988: 189). The whole plant can be used for an animal forage and fodder (FAO 1988: 189).

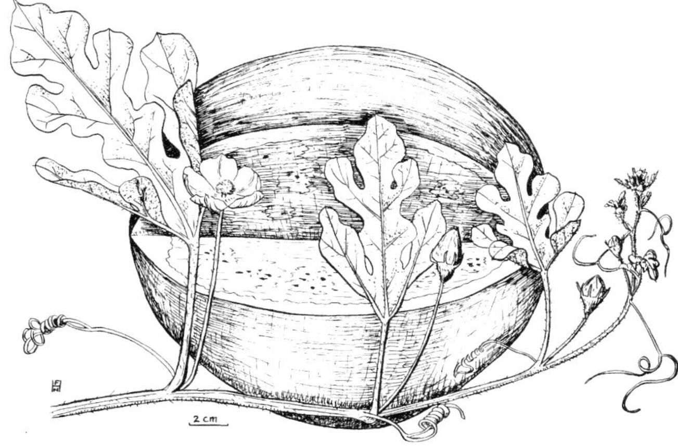

*Figure 24.7 Watermelon (*Citrullus lanatus*).*

Although requiring a ready water supply, watermelons are best-suited to a hot and dry climate (Charles 1987: 6). The species is propagated by seed and under basin irrigation earlier this century, watermelon was grown primarily along the river bank after the flood waters had retreated (Foaden and Fletcher 1910: 660). Watermelons will grow on a wide variety of soils but do best on a light sandy loam. Excessive moisture, nitrogen and depth of soil encourage the growth of inferior fruits. On the river bank, watermelon seed was soaked in water for twenty-four hours prior to being sown in rows. Holes were dug into the rows about two metres apart, then partially filled with bird or animal manure, and three to four seeds were sown into these, then covered with soil. These were later thinned to one or two seedlings. No additional watering was necessary after sowing. On other lands, two ploughings and a harrowing were sufficient land preparation prior to this process and frequent waterings were required for full fruit development (Foaden and Fletcher 1910: 662–3). If sown in March, the fruit generally begins to ripen three and a half to four and a half months later while those sown in July or August ripen in October or November. The plant continues to fruit for six weeks. The melon is ripe when it detaches easily from the vine, leaving a clean scar on the fruit (Foaden and Fletcher 1910: 664; FAO 1988: 189–90). If the desired product is the seed then fruits should be left in the field for another ten to fourteen days (FAO 1988: 190).

The wild progenitor of the watermelon is not yet fully recognised (Bates and Robinson 1995: 93), however, genetically the watermelon is most closely related to and is interfertile with the wild melon species Colocynth (*Citrullus colocynthis* (L.) Schrad.) and it is likely that the cultivated annual *Citrullus lanatus* originally derived from this perennial wild species (Zohary and Hopf 1994: 182; Bates and Robinson 1995: 94). Colocynth seeds have been found on several Predynastic sites, including KH3 and South Town at Naqada (Wetterstrom 1986: Table 1), el-Omari (Barakat 1990: 113) and Armant (Litynska 1994: 103) indicating that wild watermelon was used prior to its domestication (Zohary and Hopf 1994: 182). There appear to be few, if any, reported finds from the Pharaonic period (see Table 24.1). The fruits of the colocynth are notably smaller than those of the watermelon and bitter to the taste. When green, the colocynth can be an animal fodder and after prolonged processing, i.e. soaking in water, boiling or roasting, the seeds can be used as human food. The seeds are also used for their medicinal properties (Osborn 1968: 167; Bailey and Danin 1981: 151, Boulos 1983: 75; FAO 1988: 188; Bates and Robinson 1995: 89). Colocynth seeds also produce a useful oil and the species is discussed further in Chapter 17, this volume.

Watson (1983: 58) has argued that neither the botanical evidence of seeds or leaves, nor the artistic or linguistic evidence prove the existence of the watermelon (*Citrullus lanatus*) in pre-Islamic Egypt and that all proof points only to the presence of the colocynth (*Citrullus colocynthis*) instead. His evidence is based on a re-examination of the botanical material from the Cairo Agricultural Museum which allegedly showed that all pre-Islamic specimens were probably colocynth and not watermelon (Watson 1983: 175). Other grounds for the claim include the close resemblance of the colocynth to the watermelon in tomb-paintings and the similarities between the ancient Egyptian, Coptic and Arabic words which means melon in general although more specifically *Cucumis melo* (also see Darby *et al.* 1977: 718 for discussion of these terms). In any case, he argues that the watermelon species concerned was probably used more for its seed and cooked rind than its flesh since this would have been bitter and unpalatable prior to the development of improved varieties (Watson 1983: 59). While further investigation is needed to either refute or substantiate the argument that the cultivated watermelon in ancient Egypt actually may have been the gathered wild colocynth, botanists and archaeobotanists have long differentiated between the these two species in archaeological material reported (de Vartavan and Asensi Amorós 1997: 77–8).

Watermelon remains have been reported from Predynastic Hierakonpolis (Fahmy 1995: 115), the Fifth-Dynasty temple of Sahura at Abusir (Germer 1985: 128), Twelfth-Dynasty Kahun (Bienkowski and Southworth 1986: 63; Germer forthcoming), the Eighteenth-Dynasty settlement of Amarna (Renfrew 1985: 176), Eighteenth-Dynasty Deir el-Medina (Germer 1985: 128); two baskets of seeds from the Eighteenth-Dynasty tomb of Tutankhamun (Germer 1989: 127–8; de Vartavan 1990: 486; Hepper 1990: 56) and leaves from Deir el-Bahari (Darby *et al.* 1977: 718) as well as several post-Pharaonic sites (see Table 24.1).

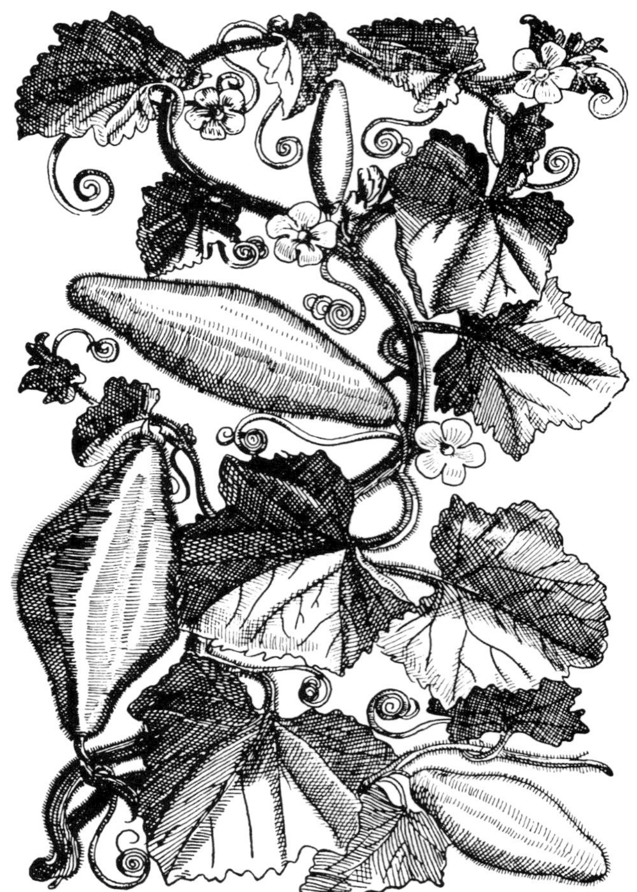

*Figure 24.8 Chate melon (*Cucumis melo *var.* chate).

*Melon (*Cucumis melo *L.) [Cucurbitaceae – Melon family]*

The melon, *Cucumis melo*, is an annual, trailing herb with yellow flowers, three- to seven-lobed, variable-toothed leaves with soft hairy, ridged stems and flattened, ovate seeds (Harrison *et al.* 1985: 118; FAO 1988: 228; Langer and Hill 1991: 211). The melon is one of the earliest cucurbits to be cultivated in the Old World and has a close affinity with a variable group of wild and weedy annual melons distributed over the subtropical and tropical parts of Asia and Africa. Other wild types are native to central Asia and the Mediterranean Basin (Zohary and Hopf 1994: 182; FAO 1988: 228; Bates and Robinson 1995: 92). The melon is a true polymorphic species meaning that it has a great diversity of cultivated forms and varieties and thus displays a wide range of colours, shapes, textures and sizes (Foaden and Fletcher 1910: 667; Langer and Hill 1991: 211; Charles 1987: 7; FAO 1988: 228; Bates and Robinson 1995: 93). *Cucumis melo* includes sweet melons, such as the musk melon, and also the non-sweet varieties, such as the green chate melon (*Cucumis melo* var. *chate*), which is comparatively rare today. Chate melons are oval in shape, often quite curved, with somewhat tapered ends and prominent longitudinal ridges, and thereby more closely resembling a cucumber than a typical rounded melon variety (Fig. 24.8) (Foaden and Fletcher 1910: 666–7; Darby *et al.* 1977: 694; Zohary and Hopf 1994: 182). Chate melons continue to grow in the Sudan.

Sweet melons are primarily eaten as a fresh fruit but also can be pickled or preserved and used in soups. They contain only 5 per cent sugar, half of that of an apple or pear, as well as vitamins A and C (Harrison *et al.* 1985: 118; FAO 1988: 229). Melons consist of up to 94 per cent water and continue to be an important water source in some areas of Africa today (FAO 1988: 229). The dry roasted seeds are a popular food in Egypt today (Harrison *et al.* 1985: 118; FAO 1988: 228–9; Bates and Robinson 1995: 89). The seed kernels contain 46 per cent edible oil and 36 per cent protein (FAO 1988: 229), although reportedly, earlier this century, the seeds were not usually processed for their oil in Egypt (Foaden and Fletcher 1910: 668). The chate melon is grown primarily for its seeds (Germer 1985). The leaves can be eaten as a vegetable (FAO 1988: 229) and they were used medicinally in mixtures taken for stomach ailments and other ills during the Pharaonic period and later in folk medicine (Boulos 1983: 75; Manniche 1989: 95; Nunn 1996: 14). The ash of the plant is rich in potassium, making it a good fertiliser (FAO 1988: 230).

Melons can be grown in the summer (Charles 1987: 9; Ward 1993: 251) yet when cultivated under basin irrigation earlier this century, melons were grown extensively on the alluvial bank of the Nile as soon as the flood water had retreated (Täckholm 1977: 272). Melons are propagated by seed and can be grown in a variety of ways depending on local conditions such as on level ground, ridges, hills or in pits. Melons prefer rich loamy soils and fruits ripen three to four months after planting (Harrison *et al.* 1985: 118; FAO 1988: 231). *Cucumis melo* var. *chate* is the earliest of all varieties grown, taking two and a half months to ripen (Foaden and Fletcher 1910: 666, 668).

From the Old Kingdom onwards, tomb scenes show offerings which appear to include the bent fruits of the chate melon. Faience models of the species have also been found although these are frequently interpreted as being cucumber (*Cucumis sativus*) (see Loret 1892; Keimer 1924: 14–17; Darby *et al.* 1977: 694; Germer 1985: 128–9). It has been suggested that the few archaeobotanical finds of cucumber type seeds also may well represent the small chate melon (Germer 1985: 128–9; Manniche 1989: 96; Hepper 1990: 56; van Zeist and de Roller 1993: 8). Finds of chate melon are known from Predynastic Maadi (van Zeist and de Roller 1993: 7–8) and *Cucumis melo* finds include those from Predynastic Hierakonpolis (Fahmy 1995: 115; el-Hadidi *et al.* 1996: 50) and Eighteenth-Dynasty Amarna (Renfrew 1985: 176).

*Cucumber (*Cucumis sativus* L.) [Cucurbitacae – Melon family]*

The cucumber is an annual species which trails or climbs by means of the tendrils found in the axis of the alternate leaves where the male and female yellow flowers are also found. The male flowers, often in clusters, open successively along the stem while the female flowers are usually solitary or in pairs and can be recognised by the presence of the inferior ovary at the base of the flower from which the cucumber fruit develops (Harrison *et al.* 1985: 116; Langer and Hill 1991: 213). The fruit is usually slightly curved, can be long or short and have longitudinal grooves (Charles 1987: 8) although modern varieties are highly diverse in characteristics, such as colour, size and shape (Bates and Robinson 1995: 92). The cucumber (*Cucumis sativus*) was probably first cultivated in India and introduced into the Near East comparatively late (Charles 1987: 7; Langer and Hill 1991: 212; Zohary and Hopf 1994: 183). Outside Egypt, the earliest archaeobotanical evidence for the species in the Near East are two seeds from 600 BC Nimrud in Iraq (Helbaek 1966). Cucumbers are usually eaten raw, but they can also be eaten as a cooked vegetable or pickled and are a popular vegetable in Egypt today (Foaden and Fletcher 1910: 675; Charles 1987: 7). The sugar and vitamin content provide the main food value of the species (Harrison *et al.* 1985: 116). The seeds are also edible and in some tropical areas, the cooked leaves are eaten (Charles 1987: 7).

The cucumber is propagated by seed (Foaden and Fletcher 1910: 575; Charles 1987: 9), usually into holes dug alongside shallow trenches which will be used later for the irrigation of the crop. In Egypt, a summer crop can be sown in March or earlier and harvested two to two and a half months after sowing, usually in May. A later flood crop is sown during July and August which ripens forty-five to fifty days later. The plant can continue to produce fruit for about thirty-five to forty days. The cucumber can be grown on many soil types but particularly thrives on well irrigated sandy loams, rich with manure, particularly pigeon dung (Foaden and Fletcher 1910: 575). The plants are usually harvested by snapping, rather than cutting the fruit off the vine (Charles 1987: 10). The timing of the harvest largely depends on the ultimate use of the vegetable, for example, if it is to be pickled or cooked, it can be picked quite early and if it is to be eaten raw or if the seeds are to be used, it should be left longer to mature (Charles 1987: 8).

Although the cucumber was known during the Greco–Roman period (Germer 1985: 130), was the cucumber a vegetable known to the Pharaonic Egyptians? As previously noted, there has been a confusion in interpretations of the artistic record between the cucumber (*Cucumis sativus*), the chate melon (*Cucumis melo* var. *chate*), fruits with a long or short, curved shape. The linguistic evidence for the cucumber also has been disputed (Loret 1892: 74, Keimer 1924: 132; Darby *et al.* 1977: 694; Hepper 1990: 56). From an archaeobotanical point of view, it is also very difficult to distinguish between the seeds of cucumber (*Cucumis sativus*) and melon (*Cucumis melo*) and they are often cited in the literature as *Cucumis sativus/melo*, e.g. Elephantine (Willerding and Wolf 1990: 266), Mons Claudianus (van der Veen 1996: 139). Archaeobotanical criteria required to distinguish these two species with certainty has been suggested (e.g. Frank and Stika 1988; van Zeist and de Roller 1993: 8; Vermeeren forthcoming) but as yet, their identification is not always possible in archaeological material. Germer (1985: 130; forthcoming) has noted that the identification of cucumber seeds, leaves and other parts from Pharaonic sites such as Twelfth-Dynasty Kahun (Newberry 1890: 50) and Eighteenth-Dynasty Deir el-Medina (Bruyère 1937) are more likely to represent the remains of the chate melon and that the cucumber probably was known only from Greco–Roman period. The close affinity between cucumber and the melon is not solely an archaeobotanical problem but extends to the understanding of the evolutionary relationship between the two species, a particularly important issue with regard to modern breeding and genetic research today (Bates and Robinson 1995: 90).

*Radish (*Raphanus sativus *L.) [Cruciferae – Cabbage family]*

The wild progenitor of the radish is not yet known. The greatest diversity of wild taxa occurs between the Mediterranean and the Caspian sea but wild types are also found in China and Japan (Crisp 1995: 87). The white, tapered edible root of the indigenous *baladi* radish (*Raphanus sativus* var. *aegyptiacus* Sick.) grows up to twenty centimetres in length and remains an important component of the Egyptian diet today where both the root and leaf are usually eaten raw (Foaden and Fletcher 1910: 540; Täckholm 1961: 14). It has been suggested that perhaps the radish was more highly prized in Pharaonic Egypt for the edible oil extracted from its seed than as a root vegetable but as yet there is not enough evidence to make this determination (Darby *et al.* 1977: 664, Strouhal 1992: 128; also see Chapter 19, this volume). The radish root contains calcium, phosphorus and provides a good source of vitamin C (FAO 1988: 425). Seeds contain 30–50 per cent edible oil and the leaves can also be eaten (FAO 1988: 425). Manniche (1989: 141) notes that in ancient Egypt the radish was used medicinally for the treatment of gallstones, kidney complaints and breathing disorders, however, Nunn (1996: 14) cites no medicinal use for the species. The whole plant also can be used for animal forage or fodder (FAO 1988: 426). Pliny commented that the Egyptian radish was sweet and that it was the most profitable crop in Egypt (NH. XIX.XXVI–LXXXVI in Manniche 1989: 141; Darby *et al.* 1977: 664). Apart from the indigenous white *baladi* radish (var. *aegyptiacus*) other radish varieties growing in Egypt today include the red topped variety (var. *radicula* DC.) and the Spanish black variety (var. *niger* Pers.) (Foaden and Fletcher 1910: 540; Täckholm 1961: 14; Darby *et al.* 1977: 664).

The species is propagated by seed and is usually broadcast sown at any time throughout the year, however, the autumn and winter months are considered best. Under good conditions, radishes grow very quickly and are usually ready for harvest after a month or so (Foaden and Fletcher 1910: 540). They grow best on a light, well-drained sandy friable soil, with good fertilisation and plenty of water to quicken growth (Foaden and Fletcher 1910: 540; Harrison *et al.* 1985: 170; FAO 1988: 427). Radish cultivation on heavy clay soils encourages abnormal root development (FAO 1988: 426).

The desiccated remains of the white Egyptian radish has been recovered from only one Pharaonic site to date, Twelfth-Dynasty Kahun (Newberry 1890: 50), however, Germer (forthcoming) is somewhat sceptical of this find since all subsequent finds of radish have been from post-Pharaonic sites and, as previously noted, there is a possibility that some of the desiccated botanical finds from Kahun may be of post-Pharaonic date. Other evidence for the radish from the Pharaonic period is based on the linguistic record (Darby *et al.* 1977: 664). For more details on the radish, see Chapter 19, this volume.

*Chufa or tiger nuts (*Cyperus esculentus *L.) [Cyperaceae – Sedge family]*

Chufa or yellow nut grass (*Cyperus esculentus*) is an upright perennial sedge, standing 30–90 cm high with long, narrow leaves, yellow to brown flowers and spikelets 1–1.5 cm long. The rhizomes end in a single rounded tuber about 5–20 mm long. This is unlike wild nut grass *C. rotundus* whose darker, unpleasant tasting tubers are formed in a chain (FAO 1988: 239; Täckholm and Drar 1950: 70). Chufa is distributed throughout the tropics, subtropics and warm temperate areas (FAO 1988: 239). Although it is a wet-loving species and is found along river and canal banks, it is also fairly tolerant of drought conditions and while it is salt tolerant, it cannot withstand shaded conditions (FAO 1988: 241). The wild variety of chufa is *Cyperus esculentus* var. *aureus* has smaller, more fibrous tubers and continues to grow in the Nile Valley today (Zohary and Hopf 1994: 186; Negbi 1992: 65). This variety and *C. rotundus* are also considered to be among the most persistent and troublesome weeds in the world (Holm *et al.* 1977; FAO 1988: 239; de Vries 1991; Negbi 1992: 64). It is maintained that chufa was first domesticated in Egypt (Negbi 1992: 65; Zohary and Hopf 1994: 186).

Chufa, known as *habb el-aziz* in Egypt today, is still cultivated for its nutritious tubers (or tiger nuts) which have a sweet, nutty flavour, similar to coconut (Fig. 24.9). These can be roasted, baked as a vegetable, ground into flour or eaten directly but are often soaked in water prior to consumption to render them more palatable (Täckholm and Drar 1950: 68; FAO 1988: 240). The tubers contain starch (20–30 per cent of dry weight) and oil (20–8 per cent of dry weight) and are a good source of phosphorus and iron. They also contain small amounts of protein (FAO 1988: 240). Theophrastus (372–287 BC) noted that the Egyptians boiled *C. esculentus* tubers in beer as an added flavouring (Täckholm and Drar 1950: 62; Negbi 1992: 65). Due to the find of chufa in a jar labelled (*wʿh*), it is now believed that a scene from the tomb of Rekhmira (TT100) also shows the preparation of a sweet made from ground chufa tubers mixed with honey (Davies 1943: 43–5, pl. 48–51; Edel 1970: 22; Negbi 1992: 64). In Egypt, a refreshing drink, *soubia*, is made from the tubers, as it is in Spain where it is known as *horchata di chufa* (Täckholm and Drar 1950: 68; FAO 1988: 240; Manniche 1989: 98). They are also commonly used in perfumery (Negbi 1992: 64; Chapter 19, this volume) and as an animal

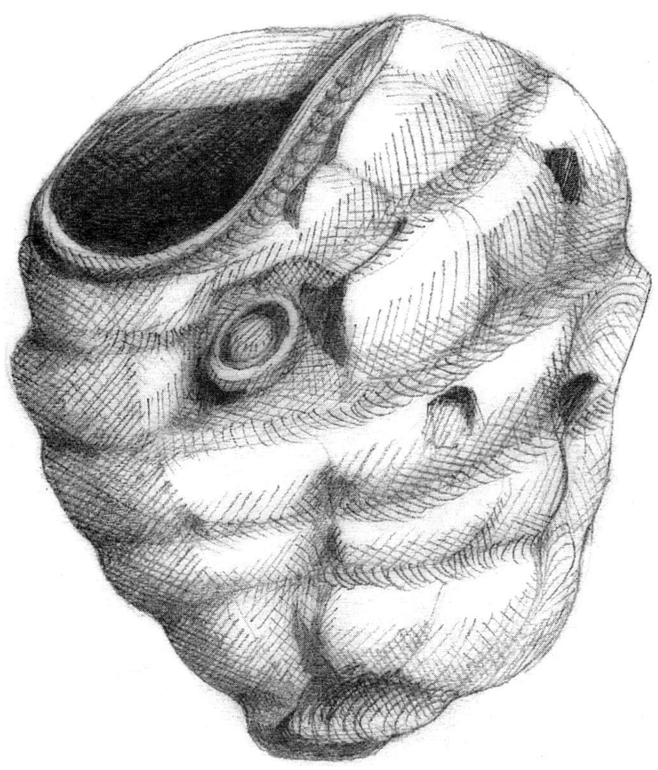

*Figure 24.9 Chufa or tiger nut (*Cyperus esculentus *L.).*

fodder (FAO 1988: 240). During the Pharaonic and later periods, chufa tubers were valued for their medicinal properties, including their use to increase lactation, as seen in the Papyrus Ebers and elsewhere (Täckholm and Drar 1950: 68; Boulos 1983: 80; Negbi 1992: 64; Nunn 1996: 14).

Chufa is propagated vegetatively by sowing the tubers from March to the middle of May. The tubers are soaked in water for twenty-four to thirty-six hours prior to sowing to encourage growth and their spacing is dependant on soil conditions, local preferences and the ultimate use of the crop (FAO 1988: 242). They are ready for harvest when the plant begins to wilt, between three to five months after sowing (Täckholm and Drar 1950: 68; FAO 1988: 242). Harvesting is done by digging up the tubers and most are found in the top 15 cm of soil. The tangle of tubers are then beaten with sticks to disengage them and free them of soil prior to their being washed and dried for one to three days before storage or sale (Täckholm and Drar 1950: 68; FAO 1988: 242). Chufa will keep in storage for long periods of time if well-dried or will keep in water, if it is changed daily, for up to ten days (FAO 1988: 240). For more on chufa as an oil-bearing species, see Chapter 19, this volume.

The edible tubers of the *Cyperus* genus are among the earliest foods known from ancient Egypt. The Late Palaeolithic finds of nut grass (*C. rotundus*) from Wadi Kubbaniya in Upper Egypt (Hillman *et al.* 1989) were probably the main source of carbohydrate for the inhabitants for at least part of the year (Wetterstrom 1993: 174). Other species of *Cyperus* tubers also have been recovered from Egyptian sites (see Täckholm and Drar 1950; Hillman *et al.* 1989; Hather 1995; de Vartavan and Asensi Amorós 1997: 94–102).

Archaeobotanical evidence of chufa (*Cyperus esculentus*) is known from several Predynastic sites (e.g. Brunton 1937: 90–1; Täckholm and Drar 1950: 62–3), from First-Dynasty Umm el-Qaʿab at Abydos (Täckholm and Drar 1950: 63), from the Eighth to Tenth Dynasties at Mostagedda (Brunton 1937: 111), the Eighteenth-Dynasty tomb of Kha (TT8; Täckholm and Drar 1950: 64), the Eighteenth-Dynasty tomb of Tutankhamun (de Vartavan 1990: 486), Eighteenth-Dynasty Deir el-Medina (Bruyère 1937), and Eighteenth-Dynasty Kom Rabiʿa at Memphis (Murray forthcoming). Due to the generally excellent conditions of preservation in Egypt these remains sometimes survive intact although when charred and fragmented, they may not be as readily recognised as they might be in desiccated material. Recent research, however, has now made it possible, with adequate reference material, to identify even very small fragments of the parenchymous tissue from ancient root and tuber specimens thus providing a valuable opportunity to further investigate this important, yet often overlooked, ancient food source (Hather 1991, 1993, 1995).

Pulses

If meat was not a regular item in the diet of most Egyptians, then pulses, such as lentils, peas, chickpeas, and faba beans, would have been an important and widely available source of protein for most of the population. Even in the Egyptian diet today, which often includes limited quantities of red meat (Alderman 1993: 117), pulses continue to play a major role. Cereal crops were invariably accompanied by pulses during the spread of Old World agriculture and these species are found together from the Neolithic onwards throughout the Near East (Zohary and Hopf 1994: 86). The proteins in legumes are rich in lysine but deficient in the sulphur containing amino acids, making them a good companion to the cereals (FAO 1988: 351; Dagher 1991: 35). Legumes also contain trypsin inhibitors, which makes some species difficult to digest without first processing them by various means, such as soaking, cooking or removing their seed coat (Aykroyd *et al.* 1982; Dagher 1991: 35: Shekib *et al.* 1992).

In Egypt, pulses are generally not found as tomb offerings, nor are they clearly depicted in tomb art, nor frequently mentioned in texts (Germer forthcoming). There is also limited archaeobotanical evidence for many of the legumes discussed here, particularly if the plant assemblage has been preserved by charring. Experimental evidence has also shown that legumes may not be recovered as efficiently as the seeds of cereal crops, for example, using some forms of flotation (Jones 1983: 31–8, tables 2.3, 2.6; Sarpaki 1992: 73). Key morphological features necessary for determining species often are obscured or missing in charred material and without them it may be impossible to distinguish between similar taxa or even between wild and domesticated forms. The separation of members of the Vicieae tribe, for example, can be very difficult due to the overlap of size, shape and other characteristics although using the high magnification of the scanning electron microscope (SEM) to analyse the micromorphology of the seed coat has proven a useful tool (Butler 1991). Some legumes are also prone to a type of crop mimicry where, due to selective pressure, a weedy vetch population, for example, can closely resemble an associated crop, especially the lentil. In this way, the weed may be unintentionally harvested and processed along with the lentil crop, thereby entering the archaeobotanical record (Barrett 1983: 264; Butler 1991: 61; Erskine *et al.* 1994: 327).

In addition to being a valuable food source, due to a symbiotic exchange with the root bacterium *Rhizobium*, pulses are able to fix atmospheric nitrogen and thus improve soil quality rather than deplete it (Langer and Hill 1991: 219; Zohary and Hopf 1994: 86). It is for this reason that the ancient practice of rotating cereal crops with a leguminous crop, which acts as a 'green manure', helps to ensure soil fertility. As previously noted, there is no textual evidence for crop rotation or intercropping before Ptolemaic times (Baer 1963: 6; Butzer 1976: 47; Eyre 1994: 61). It is not known whether the ancient Egyptian farmers recognised this valuable function of pulse crops which would have been largely unnecessary in the fertile flood basins but more useful on the uninundated lands irrigated by water taken from the canals.

Similarly, the antiquity of growing crops specifically for use as animal fodder in Egypt is not yet understood. The importance of a steady, reliable fodder supply cannot be overstressed in an arid country such as Egypt and the production of fodder would have been an integral part of the annual agricultural cycle and thus vital to the livelihood of the Egyptian farmer. Many small-seeded wild legumes, including those from the genera *Trifolium*, *Trigonella*, *Medicago*, and *Melilotus* are considered good forage and fodder plants. These small legumes are sometimes found in archaeobotanical samples containing animal dung used as fuel and indicate the use of these species as animal fodder (Chapter 21, this volume). While there is a tremendous morphological overlap between these species, recent techniques analysing the micromorphology of the seed coat by scanning electron microscopy can aid in the positive identification of these species (Butler 1991, 1996). There is archaeobotanical and textual evidence to demonstrate that certain legumes, such as berseem (*Trifolium alexandrium*), grass pea (*Lathyrus sativus*) and bitter vetch (*Vicia ervilia*) were grown deliberately as animal fodder since at least the Greco–Roman period in Egypt (e.g. Wetterstrom 1982: 367; Rowlandson 1996: 21–2) and similar analyses will help to determine the extent of their use for this purpose during the Pharaonic period as well.

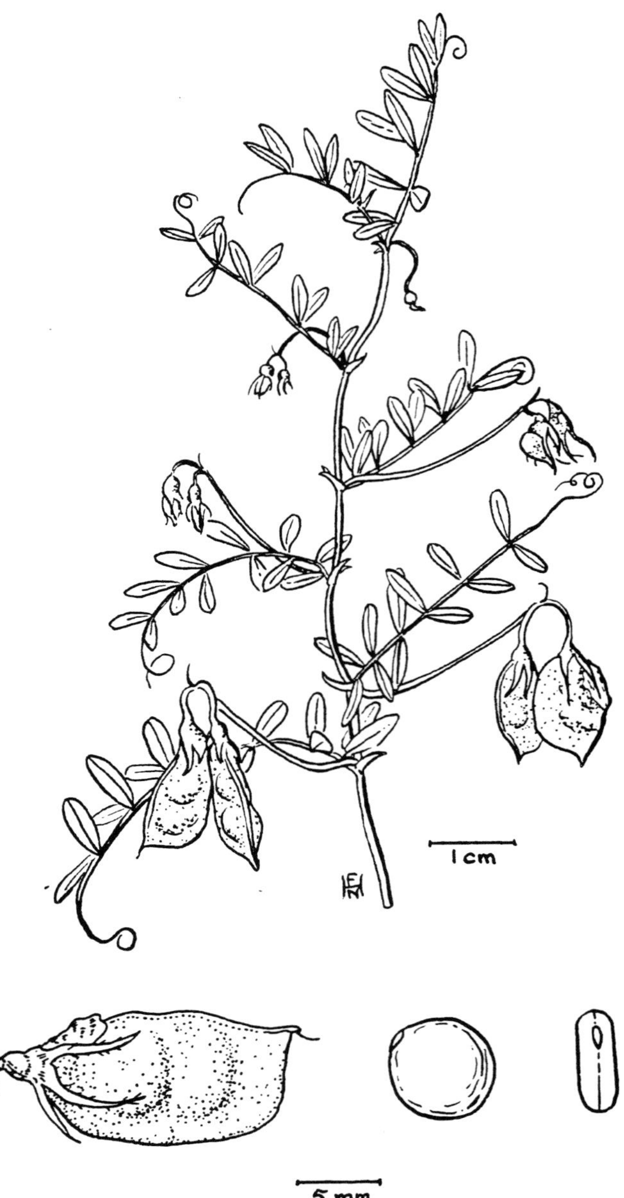

*Figure 24.10 Lentils (*Lens culinaris*).*

*Lentils (*Lens culinaris *Medik.) [Leguminosae – Pea family]*

The lentil is a much branched annual with thin, angular stems which can grow up to 15–75 cm high. The leaves are pinnate with four to seven pairs of oval leaflets. It has small blue or white paplionaceous flowers which are followed by pods containing one or two seeds whose shape gives the genus its name (Figure 24.10) (Harrison *et al.* 1985: 42, Hepper 1990: 61; FAO 1988: 350; Langer and Hill 1991: 260). Domesticated lentils fall into two basic categories: small seeded lentils (*L. culinaris* subsp. *microcarpa*) with seeds 3–6 mm in diameter and large seeded lentils (*L. culinaris* subsp. *macrocarpa*) with seeds 6–9 mm in diameter (FAO 1988: 350; Langer and Hill 1991: 260; Zohary and Hopf 1994: 88). Small-seeded lentils are found on Near Eastern sites throughout antiquity while the large-seeded subspecies is not known from Near Eastern archaeological sites prior to the first millennium BC (van Zeist 1985: 35; Zohary and Hopf 1994: 88). There is great overlap, however, between the domesticate and the various wild species, including the wild progenitor of the cultivated lentil, *Lens culinaris* subsp. *orientalis*, and this often creates uncertainty at early sites in areas where wild lentil species continue to grow (Zohary and Hopf 1994: 92). The question of domestication in these cases is an important one; however, Egypt lies outside the boundary of wild lentil populations, even on its Mediterranean coast, and it is likely that the same was true in antiquity.

Lentils are one of the principal components of the traditional Near Eastern crop complex and they are grown extensively in subtropical and warm temperate regions today (van Zeist 1985: 35; FAO 1988: 351; Zohary and Hopf 1994: 92). Lentils contain 25 per cent protein in a form more easily digestible than that from animal products and are considered an important meat substitute in many areas of the world (Harrison *et al.* 1985: 42; FAO 1988: 352; Langer and Hill 1991: 261; Zohary and Hopf 1994: 88). The seeds also provide carbohydrates, phosphorus, calcium, potassium, sodium, iron, the vitamins, A, some Bs, C, E, and K, along with some amino acids (FAO 1988: 351; Dagher 1991: 43). As a traditional Egyptian food today, lentils come second only to faba beans in consumption (Dagher 1991: 41). The seeds can be eaten raw or cooked, as a *dhal*, in soups, or salted and fried. Lentil flour can be mixed with cereal flour for breads and cakes and is frequently used as food for infants and invalids (Aykroyd *et al.* 1982: 92; FAO 1988: 352; Langer and Hill 1991: 261). The young pods can also be eaten as a vegetable (FAO 1988: 352). The plant is an effective green manure and forage plant and the threshed lentil straw is considered to be a more highly nutritious animal fodder than those of the pea, chickpea, or faba bean, particularly for milking stock (Foaden and Fletcher 1910: 460; Aykroyd *et al.* 1982: 92; FAO 1988: 352). Lentils are used in folk medicine for intestinal complaints and other ailments (FAO 1988: 352), although as yet there is no record of their use for medicinal purposes from the Pharaonic period (Manniche 1989: 115; Nunn 1996: 14).

Lentil is a winter crop, sown at the same time as wheat (Foaden and Fletcher 1910: 459; Beshai 1993: 269). The lentil crop is able to withstand four to twelve weeks of drought, and dry conditions are indeed preferable just before and during the harvest. The optimal temperature for high crop yields averages 24 °C (FAO 1988: 352). Although lentils may be relatively free from insect attack in the field (Foaden and Fletcher 1910: 460), over 10 per cent of stored lentils may be lost to damage from insects and rodents in traditional agricultural communities (FAO 1988: 352). The analysis of a cache of lentils dating from the early Ptolemaic period, for example, demonstrates the high level of infestation possible (Burleigh and Southgate 1975: 391–2).

Traditionally, lentils were grown under basin irrigation in Middle and Upper Egypt and to a lesser extent in Lower Egypt under canal irrigation (Foaden and Fletcher 1910: 459; Beshai 1993: 269). Lentils are a relatively recent, although highly successful crop in the Nile Delta (Ward 1993: 250). Earlier this century under basin irrigation, lentils were broadcast sown onto recently inundated fields, then covered and sometimes ploughed in after the ground had dried and hardened. In contrast, under canal irrigation, it was usually necessary to plough and harrow at least twice before broadcasting the seeds and then covering them with a harrow (Foaden and Fletcher 1910: 460). Weeding is essential since the plants are relatively slow growing and can easily become smothered by weeds, particularly by other weedy legumes, which greatly restrict their growth (Foaden and Fletcher 1910: 460; Erskine *et al.* 1994: 326). Under basin irrigation, no additional watering was necessary, while under canal irrigation, the crop was watered when sown, then two months later and again when flowering. Lentils are often intercropped with other species, such as wheat and barley, which support the trailing thin stems of the species. This increases the plant's exposure to air and light and has a positive effect on the subsequent yield when the plant is ready to be harvested five to five and a half months after sowing. The crop was harvested by uprooting and if grown with another crop, the two may have been harvested and threshed together (Foaden and Fletcher 1910: 460). The plants are often dried for seven to ten days after harvesting the pods in order to facilitate the threshing process (FAO 1988: 353).

The evidence for lentils throughout Egyptian history is substantial, including tomb finds from Predynastic Matmar (Brunton 1948), Predynastic and Early Dynastic Buto (Thanheiser 1991: 45), the Third-Dynasty tomb of Djoser (Lauer *et al.* 1950: 137–8) and the tomb of Tutankhamun (KV62; de Vartavan 1990: 486; Germer 1989: 34–5; Hepper 1990: 61). Finds from settlement sites include those from Predynastic Ma'adi (van Zeist and de Roller 1993: 3) Armant (Litynska 1994: 105) and Tell Ibrahim Awad (van Zeist 1988), Fourth Dynasty Giza (Wetterstrom 1992; Murray forthcoming), Fifth- to Sixth-Dynasty Kom el-Sultan at Abydos, Thirteenth- and Eighteenth-Dynasty Kom Rabi'a at Memphis (Murray forthcoming), Eighteenth-Dynasty Amarna (Renfrew 1985: 176) and First Intermediate Period and Second Intermediate Period Tell el-Dabʿa (Thanheiser 1986, forthcoming).

*Pea (*Pisum sativum L.*) [Leguminosae – Pea family]*

Domesticated peas exhibit a wide variation of morphological characteristics, such as height, flower colour and texture, as well as colour of the seed coat. In general, small-seeded varieties with coloured flowers and long vines are distinguished as field peas (var. *arvense*), while larger-seeded varieties with white flowers and shorter vines are regarded as garden peas (var. *sativum*) (Langer and Hill 1991: 269; Zohary and Hopf 1994: 95; D. R. Davies 1995: 295). Today, the garden pea is used most extensively as a human food while the field pea often is grown for fodder or for use as green manure although the seeds also can be used as split peas and pea meal (Harrison *et al.* 1985: 42). Dry pea seed contains 22 per cent crude protein (Langer and Hill 1991: 270). Foaden and Fletcher (1910: 674) noted that peas were not a particularly popular food in Egypt at that time. Peas have a wide distribution, particularly in regions with a cool and relatively humid climate (van Zeist 1985: 35; Zohary and Hopf 1994: 94; D. R. Davies 1995: 249). They are easily cultivated and are propagated by seed which is usually sown from October to mid-December in Egypt since they require cool temperatures to properly develop. Peas grow best if sown into holes dug within ridges of well manured, friable soil and receive frequent watering. The plant should be harvested before the seed coat becomes too hard and this usually begins two to three months after sowing and can last for another one to two months (Foaden and Fletcher 1910: 673–4).

The pea was among the founder species of the Near Eastern crop complex and the archaeobotanical evidence suggests that cultivation of the pea is almost as ancient as wheat or barley (Zohary and Hopf 1994: 99). *Pisum sativum* subsp. *humile* is the most likely wild progenitor of the cultivated pea and while this and other wild forms have roughly textured seed coat, domesticated peas have a smooth seed coat (van Zeist 1985: 35; Butler 1989: 395; Zohary and Hopf 1994: 96). In archaeological material, it is impossible to distinguish between the domesticated and wild varieties without the seed coat and this feature is often missing in charred remains. Similarly, it is often difficult to determine variety, i.e. between field peas and garden peas, in many archaeobotanical assemblages. Archaeological remains of the smooth coated, cultivated pea have been found at the Turkish sites of Çayönü at *c.* 6500 BC and Çatal Hüyük at 5850–5600 BC (Zohary and Hopf 1994: 99).

In Egypt, the earliest evidence of the species is from Merimda in the Delta, dating to *c.* 5000 BC (M. Hopf, unpublished data cited in Zohary and Hopf 1994: 101, 209) and from Naqada South Town in Upper Egypt dating from 3800–3400 BC (Wetterstrom 1986: table 1) and Predynastic and early Dynastic Buto (Thanheiser 1991: 45) although it is not clear whether these specimens are wild or domesticated. Specimens of *P. sativum* from Predynastic el-Omari are most likely to be wild (Barakat 1990: 111–12). Other finds include those from Old Kingdom Kom el-Hisn (Moens and Wetterstrom 1988: 163), Twelfth-Dynasty Kahun (Newberry 1890: 50; Germer forthcoming), and from Second Intermediate Period Tell el-Dabʿa (Thanheiser 1986, forthcoming) and Eighteenth-Dynasty Amarna (Renfrew 1985: 176).

*Figure 24.11 Chickpea (*Cicer arietinum*).*

*Chickpea (*Cicer arietinum L.*) [Leguminosae – Pea family]*

The chickpea is a much branched annual, growing 20–100 cm high. It has white to purplish solitary flowers, a pod

2 to 3.5 cm long and 1 to 2 cm broad with pinnate leaves of up to eight to seventeen leaflets each. Chickpea pods contain one or two seeds each (Fig. 24.11) (Foaden and Fletcher 1910: 501; Harrison *et al.* 1985: 38; FAO 1988: 175; Langer and Hill 1991: 255). The seeds are angularly rounded, between 5 and 10 mm in diameter, and have a distinctive protrusion of the embryo, a characteristic noted by the ancient Egyptians by their term for chickpea, *ḥr-bik,* which translates as 'falcon face' (Keimer 1929b: 47; Caminos 1954: 166; Darby *et al.* 1977: 685; Germer forthcoming). The species can show a wide range of variation in its seeds, leaves and flowers (Zohary and Hopf 1994: 101; FAO 1988: 175). As with the lentil and pea, the chickpea is considered one of the earliest Near Eastern domesticates yet it is reported less frequently from Near Eastern sites of Neolithic date (van Zeist 1985: 35; Zohary and Hopf 1994: 103; Ladizinsky 1995: 259). In 1974, the wild progenitor of the chickpea *Cicer arietinum* subsp. *reticulatum* was discovered in south eastern Turkey and the central part of the Near Eastern arc was probably the area of its first cultivation (Zohary and Hopf 1994: 103; Ladizinsky 1995: 259; Zohary 1996: 151). The earliest probable domesticates come from levels dating to the seventh millennium at several Near Eastern sites (Zohary and Hopf 1994: 103). The number of archaeological specimens of chickpea increases by the early Bronze Age but the finds are still comparatively few (Zohary and Hopf 1994: 105).

The seed has a protein content of between 12.4 and 31.5 per cent, is rich in starch and contains more oil (4–6 per cent) than most pulses (FAO 1988: 176; Langer and Hill 1991: 256; Ladizinsky 1995: 258). Today, chickpea ranks third in the world production of seed legumes (Zohary and Hopf 1994: 101). The species remains popular in Egypt and the eastern Mediterranean, where it is often, soaked, crushed and then mixed with spices and sesame paste to make *hummus.* The seed can also be consumed fresh or green, as a dry roasted bean, as a confection or ground into flour (FAO 1988: 176; Dagher 1991: 135). Foaden and Fletcher (1910: 503) noted that in Egypt steeping chickpeas in an infusion of wood ashes was traditionally practised in order to hasten their cooking time. The edible young leaves and shoots are high in protein, vitamin A and minerals (FAO 1988: 176). It is not known how the ancient Egyptians processed the chickpea for food and Pharaonic texts also make no mention of any medicinal qualities associated with the species (Manniche 1989: 87; Nunn 1996: 14). The Copts later used the species to encourage lactation (Manniche 1989: 87) and the leaves are still used in folk medicine for this purpose and for a variety of other ills (FAO 1988: 177). An indigo-like dye also can be extracted from the leaves of the plant (FAO 1988: 176). Traditionally, the chickpea was not used as a fodder crop in Egypt (Foaden and Fletcher 1910: 503).

The chickpea is tolerant of cool weather and in Egypt and the Mediterranean, it is grown during the coolest months. The plant can also tolerate a variety of soil types except those which are too sandy or too moist and particularly thrives on well-fertilised soils (Foaden and Fletcher 1910: 501; FAO 1988: 178; Langer and Hill 1991: 256). When sown in the flood basins earlier this century, the seed was broadcast onto the mud, then covered. On canal irrigated land, the field was usually ploughed only once and the seed was either broadcast or dropped behind the plough and covered with the harrow. The field was watered either before or after sowing. Sowing was usually done from the end of October until early December in Upper Egypt, and often later in Lower Egypt. The plant requires little attention after sowing. No additional water was necessary in the flood basins and on canal-fed lands the crop received only two waterings during the growing season. No manure was required at any time. The plants were harvested by uprooting about four months after sowing, towards the end of March, if the tender, green seeds were wanted, otherwise, harvesting usually took place about five and a half to six months after sowing (Foaden and Fletcher 1910: 502; also FAO 1988: 178). The crop was threshed either by beating with a stick, treading by animals or by the *norag* (see Chapter 21, this volume) (Foaden and Fletcher 1910: 503). The plant does not have many serious field pests, although losses in storage can be high (Aykroyd *et al.* 1982: 89; FAO 1988: 176). Small-scale farmers usually place chickpeas in baskets or bags since the crop is prone to insect infestation if stored in bulk. Coating stored seeds lightly with vegetable oil helps to reduce insect damage (FAO 1988: 176, also Panagiotakopulu *et al.* 1995: 706).

The evidence for the species in Egypt is limited and the general scarcity of finds might be partly because members of the pea family are less likely to be charred and therefore preserved or it simply may reflect a low incidence of use. It has also been suggested that the prominent beak of the species is often damaged or missing in charred material and the remaining badly charred seed then may not be as readily recognised (van Zeist and Bakker-Heeres 1982: 209; Ladizinsky 1995: 259). Chickpeas have been found at Eighteenth-Dynasty Deir el-Medina (Darby *et al.* 1977: 685–6; Germer 1985: 96) and a few specimens which were found mixed with cereals in a model granary from the Eighteenth-Dynasty tomb of Tutankhamun (KV62; Germer 1989: 36; de Vartavan 1990: 486; Hepper 1990: 55). There is also linguistic evidence for chickpea from the Eighteenth Dynasty onwards (Hepper 1990: 56) yet the earliest record for the species are small faience chickpea models, recovered from a Middle Kingdom tomb at Matariya (Keimer 1929a; Darby *et al.* 1977: 685).

Faba bean (= broad bean, horse bean) (Vicia faba *L. var.* minor) *[Leguminosae – Pea family]*

The faba bean is an erect, singly or sparsely branched annual, growing up to two metres high, with a characteristic four ribbed stem and compound leaves. It has white flowers, easily threshed pods and large seeds (Harrison *et al.* 1985: 40; Zohary and Hopf 1994: 107–8; Bond 1995: 312). The wild ancestor of the faba bean is not yet known with certainty but it has close morphological affinities to a group of wild vetches found in the Mediterranean and Near East (Zohary and Hopf 1994: 107; Bond 1995: 312). The archaeological evidence is as yet insufficient to show conclusively that *Vicia faba* was one of the original founder crops of the Old World (Bond 1995: 313; Zohary 1996: 144). Archaeobotanical finds of faba bean throughout the Near East, including Egypt, from Neolithic to Roman times are of the small-seeded variety (*Vicia faba* L. var. *minor*) (Täckholm 1977: 270; van Zeist 1985: 36; Harrison *et al.* 1985: 40; Zohary and Hopf 1994: 106). The species is cultivated widely throughout the world and a number of its botanical features show a great diversity due to its many adaptations to local conditions (Zohary and Hopf 1994: 107–8; Bond 1995: 314). Faba beans contain 20–5 per cent protein as well as phosphorous, iron, copper and potassium and they are one of the primary sources of food in the Nile Valley in both Egypt and the Sudan today (Foaden and Fletcher 1910: 573; Dagher 1991: 35; Zohary and Hopf 1994: 107–8). The young pod and seed are eaten raw and the seed is cooked in a variety of ways (Foaden and Fletcher 1910: 573), including *ful medammes*, a much beloved and nutritious national dish in Egypt, popular among rural and urban populations alike (Täckholm 1977: 272; Dagher 1991: 34; Alderman 1993: 118).

The consumption of faba beans and even the inhalation of faba bean pollen can cause a potentially lethal illness known as favism (Harrison *et al.* 1985: 40; Langer and Hill 1991: 273). Favism primarily affects males of eastern Mediterranean origin with a genetic deficiency in the G6PD enzyme, although faba beans are thought to offer those with a normal G6PD enzyme some protection against malaria (Aykroyd *et al.* 1982: 38; Langer and Hill 1991: 273; Jones and Halstead 1993: 104). In these cases, the consumption of faba beans can cause haemolytic anaemia, jaundice, high fever, sometimes resulting in death within twenty-four to forty-eight hours, particularly in children (Aykroyd *et al.* 1982: 37–8; Langer and Hill 1991: 273). The traditional processing of faba beans by cooking and removing the seed coat reduces the concentration of the anti-nutritional factors present in the species, a processing method which might also obscure its presence in the archaeobotanical record (also see Jones and Halstead 1993). During the Greco–Roman period, many restrictions and superstitions surrounded faba beans in parts of the Eastern Mediterranean, perhaps the best known example is that of Pythagoras who refused to eat faba beans and reputedly faced death at the hands of his pursuers rather than escape through a faba bean field (Arie 1959: 75). Several Classical authors have also noted that beans were a taboo or considered an unclean food in ancient Egypt, particularly by the priesthood (Ruffer 1919: 72–3; Darby *et al.* 1977: 683), but exactly which species were meant remains unclear as does the connection, if any, between the taboo and favism. Beans were reportedly used extensively in ancient Egyptian medicine (Nunn 1996: 14) but again, it is difficult to determine the exact species indicated. *Vicia faba* has spread widely from its probable Mediterranean and Near Eastern origin and at present there is not enough evidence to determine if the threat of favism would have limited its use in the Pharaonic period.

Beans are traditionally grown in Upper Egypt as the heavy loams and climate of the region are better suited to their cultivation (Foaden and Fletcher 1910: 456, 572; Beshai 1993: 269). Earlier this century, faba beans were sown from early September or as soon as the flood basins were emptying. Early sowing is critical to ensure that the seeds are hardened prior to the start of the relentless winds of the springtime *khamseen* which shrivel the pods and inhibit seed development (Foaden and Fletcher 1910: 456), although, if necessary, sowing could continue until late November (Foaden and Fletcher 1910: 572) The crop was sown by dropping three to four seeds into holes dug either into the ground or into prepared ridges at intervals of 30 to 35 cm apart (Foaden and Fletcher 1910: 456). In the flood basins, the crop received no further watering as its deep root system locates sufficient moisture on its own, while under canal irrigation, two to three waterings were given after sowing (Foaden and Fletcher 1910: 458). The green pods were ready for harvest three and a half to four months after sowing (Foaden and Fletcher 1910: 572), while the seed was ready for harvesting in four and a half to five months, which began in March in Upper Egypt. Harvesting was done by uprooting the plant or by cutting it with small hooks and generally occurred before the crop was fully ripened to prevent seed loss. After the harvest, the crop was left to dry for three to four days and was then threshed with a *norag*, winnowed and sieved (Foaden and Fletcher 1910: 458). Yield was enormously variable depending on the timing, and the extent of *khamseen* damage (Foaden and Fletcher 1910: 457). Faba bean straw was considered a poor, indigestible animal fodder and was used primarily as brick temper. The crushed seeds were used as a fodder for work animals, such as milking cattle and mules (Foaden and Fletcher 1910: 458). The parasitic plant broomrape (*Orabanche sp.*), some insects and the *khamseen* are the serious pests of the faba bean (Foaden and Fletcher 1910: 458).

Vicia faba type pollen was reportedly found exclusively in six samples dating from *c.* 3000 BC at the site of Mendes in Lower Egypt, from a possible storage, processing or disposal area for the species, and suggests an earlier presence for faba bean than the archaeobotanical evidence currently indicates (Ayyad and Krzywinski 1994: 30). The earliest archaeobotanical specimens in Egypt are from a Fifth-Dynasty tomb at Abusir (Germer 1985: 81) and the the Twelfth-Dynasty site of Kahun (Newberry 1890: 50; Germer, forthcoming).

Condiments

The condiments included here are among those commonly attributed to the Pharaonic period. For the most part, however, these species are known only by occasional finds, primarily from the New Kingdom period onwards (Table 24.4). Other, less well known species, such as *Trachyspermum copticum*, were probably also used to flavour foods as suggested by finds of the species at Amarna (Samuel 1995). Like so many of the other plants discussed here, these and other condiment species were not only used for food but were also used in ancient Egyptian medicine (e.g. Manniche 1989; Nunn 1996: 15).

*Coriander (*Coriandrum sativum *L.) [Umbelliferae – Parsley family]*

Coriander is an erect, annual herb which can grow up to 1.3 m high and has white and pinkish flowers forming a compound umbel, or umbrella-shaped flower head, which is characteristic of the family as a whole. The round, ribbed seeds are about 2.5 to 4.5 mm in diameter. It is a much-branched species with a solid stem, broad basal leaves and finely divided upper leaves which, together with its aromatic seeds, are a major condiment and seasoning of modern Egyptian cuisine (Fig. 24.12) (Jansen 1981: 58; M. Zohary 1982: 92; Meikle 1977: 778; Harrison *et al.* 1985: 138). They are used to spice meats, soups, and salads and the strong oil extracted from the seeds is used for flavouring foods and beverages and for medicinal purposes, such as a remedy for stomach ailments and coughs (Jansen 1981: 65; M. Zohary 1982: 92; Boulos 1983: 180; Germer 1985: 135; Manniche 1989: 94; Hepper 1990: 58; Nunn 1996: 15). Indeed, Pliny commented on the high quality of Egyptian coriander for its use as a medicine (N.H. XX, LXXXII, 216, 18 in Darby *et al.* 1977: 799; Manniche 1989: 94). Coriander was also used in antiquity as an effective insecticide in storage which has been suggested as a reason for the presence of the species in offerings in Tutankhamun's tomb (Panagiotakopulu *et al.* 1995: 706)

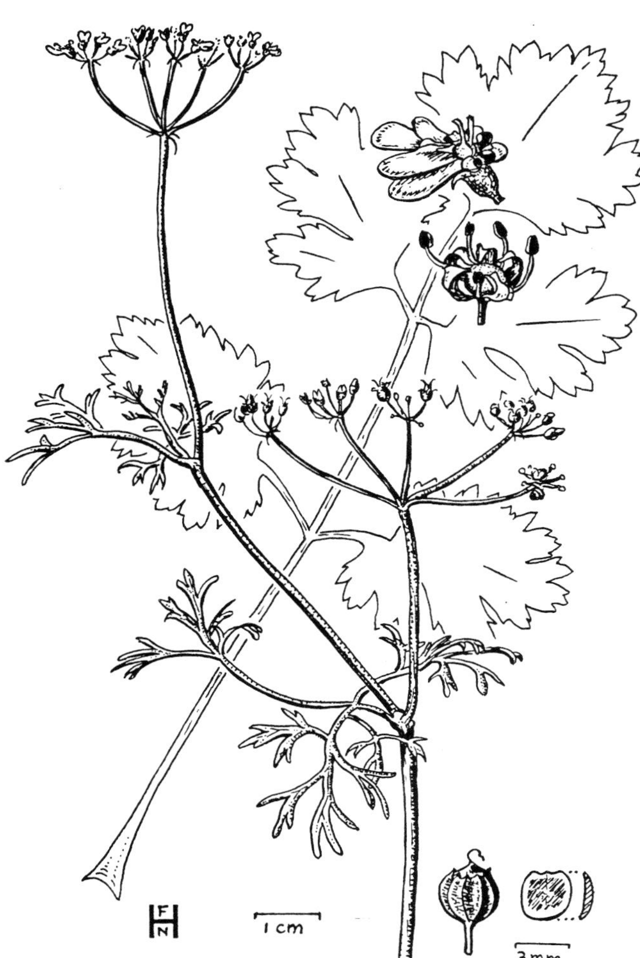

Figure 24.12 *Coriander (Coriandrum sativum* L.).

Coriander grows throughout the Near East and it is difficult to distinguish wild, weedy or naturalised varieties. The wild and domesticated forms of the species probably originated in the Near East and Eastern Mediterranean basin (Zohary and Hopf 1994: 188). Coriander is propagated by seed and can grow in diverse conditions, from the temperate zone to tropical areas. It is sometimes sown amongst other species, such as cereals (Jansen 1981: 62). The timing of germination, flowering and fruiting is variable depending on water availability. Harvest time, however, needs to be carefully chosen since unripe seeds have an unpleasant odour (Meikle 1977: 718; Jansen 1981: 63; Langer and Hill 1991: 152) while leaving the harvest too late can result in the loss of over ripe seeds. It is therefore best to harvest the entire plant in the early morning when it is least dry to minimise seed loss. For optimal results, after harvesting the plants are left to dry for a time prior to threshing by beating the plant with a stick. The threshed fruits are then thoroughly dried prior to storage. The yield of the crop varies greatly depending on water availability (Jansen 1981: 63).

The earliest ancient finds of this species, thus far, is a cache of coriander seeds from the Neolithic cave site of Nahal Hemar in Israel (Kislev 1988; Zohary and Hopf 1994: 188). Apart from a single Predynastic seed from Adaïma (de Vartavan and Asensi Amorós 1997: 85), the earliest finds of coriander from Egypt are much later and date from the Eighteenth-Dynasty tomb of Tutankhamun (Germer 1989: 60; de Vartavan 1990: 486; Hepper 1990: 58). Hepper (1990: 58) notes that the species may still have been a rarity in Egypt at that time. Other archaeobotanical finds include those from the Eighteenth-Dynasty settlement of Amarna (Renfrew 1985: 176), the Twenty-first Dynasty royal cache at Deir el-Bahari (Germer 1985: 135–6).

*Cumin (*Cuminum cyminum *L.) [Umbelliferae – Parsley family]*

Cumin is a branching erect or sub-erect annual herb, growing from 5 to 45 cm high with divided, alternate leaves and flowers that form umbels ranging in colour from white, pink to red (M. Zohary 1982: 88; Jansen 1981: 68–70; Harrison *et al.* 1985: 138). Wild forms of cumin are unknown in the Near East but occur in central Asia (Zohary and Hopf 1994: 189). The natural habitat of the species is near desert oases yet the plant cannot withstand extremes of either heat or moisture (Jansen 1981: 72). Cumin is used as a spice to flavour foods and breads, and is also prized for its medicinal qualities, particularly against stomach complaints and as an anti-spasmodic (Darby *et al.* 1977: 799; Jansen 1981: 75; M. Zohary 1982: 88; Boulos 1983: 183; Manniche 1989: 96; Nunn 1996: 15). Its oil is also used in perfumery (M. Zohary 1982: 88; Manniche 1989: 96).

Cumin is propagated from seed and when grown under irrigation, germination can occur after two weeks with flowering after six weeks. The fruits are ready to be harvested by uprooting when they turn yellow and the plant begins to whither, usually three to three and a half months after sowing. As with coriander and the other condiments discussed here, the seeds do not all mature all at once and therefore it is best to harvest the plant in the early morning to prevent seed loss. The harvested plants are then sun dried and threshing can be done by beating with sticks or trampling by animals (Jansen 1981: 72). Ethnographic observation in Ethiopia, for example, shows that cumin is grown primarily in small house gardens (Jansen 1981: 73).

The earliest evidence for the species in Egypt are several seeds from Eighteenth-Dynasty Deir el-Medina (Darby *et al.* 1977: 799; Germer 1985: 144).

*Black cumin (*Nigella sativa *L.) [Ranunculaceae – Buttercup family]*

The species is an erect annual herb, growing up to 70 cm high with a tough tap-root. It has whitish to pale blue solitary flowers and abundant, alternately arranged, finely divided leaves (Meikle 1977: 63; Jansen 1981: 77). After pollination, the ovary of the flower transforms into an enclosed capsule which houses the black trigonous seeds (Fig. 24.13) (M. Zohary 1982: 91; Jansen 1981: 78; Hepper 1990: 61). The evidence from the distribution of the species suggests that black cumin is a Near Eastern domesticate (Zohary and Hopf 1994: 189). The capsules are threshed with a stick to obtain the strongly aromatic seeds which are often used to flavour bread in Egypt and also can be processed for their oil (Jansen 1981: 83; Hepper 1990: 61; Zohary and Hopf 1994: 189). They have medicinal properties as well, and are used today for the relief of headaches and other ills, although, as yet, there is no evidence that the ancient Egyptians used them for this purpose (Jansen 1981: 83; Boulos 1983: 150; Manniche 1989: 125; Hepper 1990: 62).

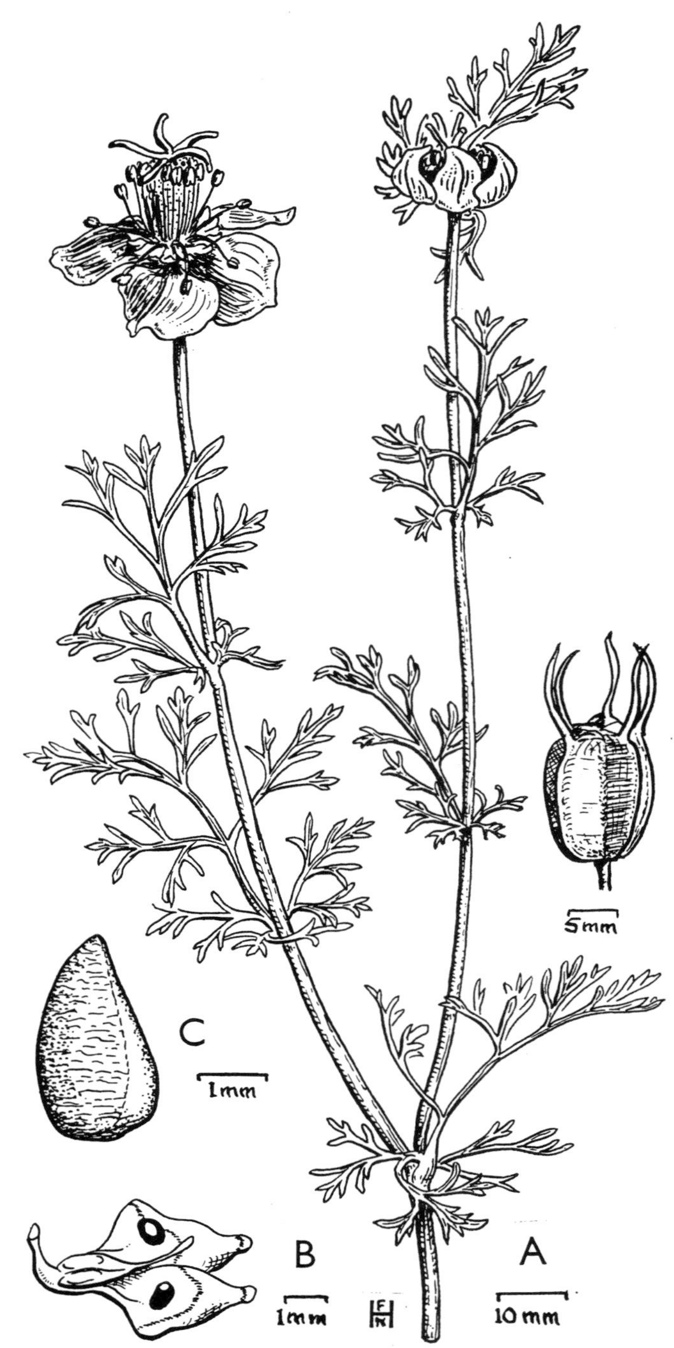

*Figure 24.13 Black cumin (*Nigella sativa*).*

Black cumin is propagated by seed and can grow on a wide variety of soil types, but seedlings are usually difficult to transplant. The seed is best broadcast on well prepared soil and in Ethiopia, for example, this is done after the first rains and therefore, sowing dates range from the beginning of July to September (Jansen 1981: 82). In Egypt, sowing may have taken place after the retreat of the flood waters in the late autumn to early winter months. Weeding and sometimes thinning of the crop are necessary. The plant can be harvested about 100–150 days after sowing, generally between November and March. The seed heads are easily threshed by beating and for this reason, harvesting is best conducted before the seeds completely dry out to minimise unintentional seed loss. They are thoroughly dried prior to storage to preserve their pungent quality, and can remain viable for up to two years. Black cumin is commonly intercropped with other species, particularly wheat or barley (Jansen 1981: 83).

There have been very few archaeobotanical finds of black cumin in Pharaonic Egypt, however, the earliest known are from the Twelfth-Dynasty Kahun (Bienkowski and Southworth 1986: 63; Germer forthcoming). Other specimens date to the New Kingdom, including those from the tomb of Tutankhamun (Germer 1989: 62; de Vartavan 1990: 486; Hepper 1990: 62; also see Germer 1985: 35). The only post-Pharaonic specimens recorded thus far are from Roman Mons Claudianus (van der Veen 1996: 139; 1998).

*Dill (*Anethum graveolens *L.) [Umbelliferae – Parsley family]*

Dill is a smooth stemmed, erect annual or biennial herb, with finely divided, alternate leaves which grows up to a height of 30–150 cm (Jansen 1981: 31; Harrison *et al.* 1985: 138). The flowers are yellow and the inflorescence is a typical compound umbel (Jansen 1981: 32). The fruit is slightly flattened and elliptical in shape (Harrison *et al.* 1985: 138). Today, this culinary herb is usually grown in gardens (M. Zohary 1982: 88; Jansen 1981: 31). Dill is easily propagated from seed, yet due to a large tap root, the transplantation of the seedlings often gives poor results. Like coriander and black cumin, dill is sometimes intercropped with other species, such as onions. If dill is grown for its leaves (dill weed) or for its essential oil, then the plant is best harvested before flowering while, as with the other condiments, if the fruits are desired (dill seed), then the plant is bested harvested in the morning when least dry. Observations in Ethiopia show that the seeds fully germinate in about a month, the plant flowers after two to three months and could be harvested after five to six months with yields of 500–700 kg/ha after threshing (Jansen 1981: 35).

Wild and weedy types of dill are widespread in the Mediterranean basin and western Asia (Zohary and Hopf 1994: 189). Its leaves are used to flavour soups and salads while its seeds flavour pickled foods, such as cucumbers and onions (Jansen 1981: 31). An essential oil can be extracted from the fruits (M. Zohary 1982: 88) from which a liqueur can be made and the pressed fruits can be used as animal fodder (Jansen 1981: 37). The plant has medicinal qualities, including the strong antiseptic properties of the extracted oil (Jansen 1981: 38; Boulos 1983: 175). In herbal medicine, dill seeds are considered a sedative, helpful to digestion and Papyrus Ebers (1534 BC) records the use of dill in ancient Egypt to relieve headaches (Keimer 1924: 37, 99; Darby *et al.* 1977: 800; Manniche 1989: 74; Nunn 1996: 15).

Eight stems of dill were found in the Eighteenth-Dynasty tomb of Amenhotep II (KV35)on the mummy of Merenptah (Darby *et al.* 1977: 800; Germer 1988: 10). Later finds of dill seed are known from the Greco-Roman period and the Late Antique period (Table 24.1).

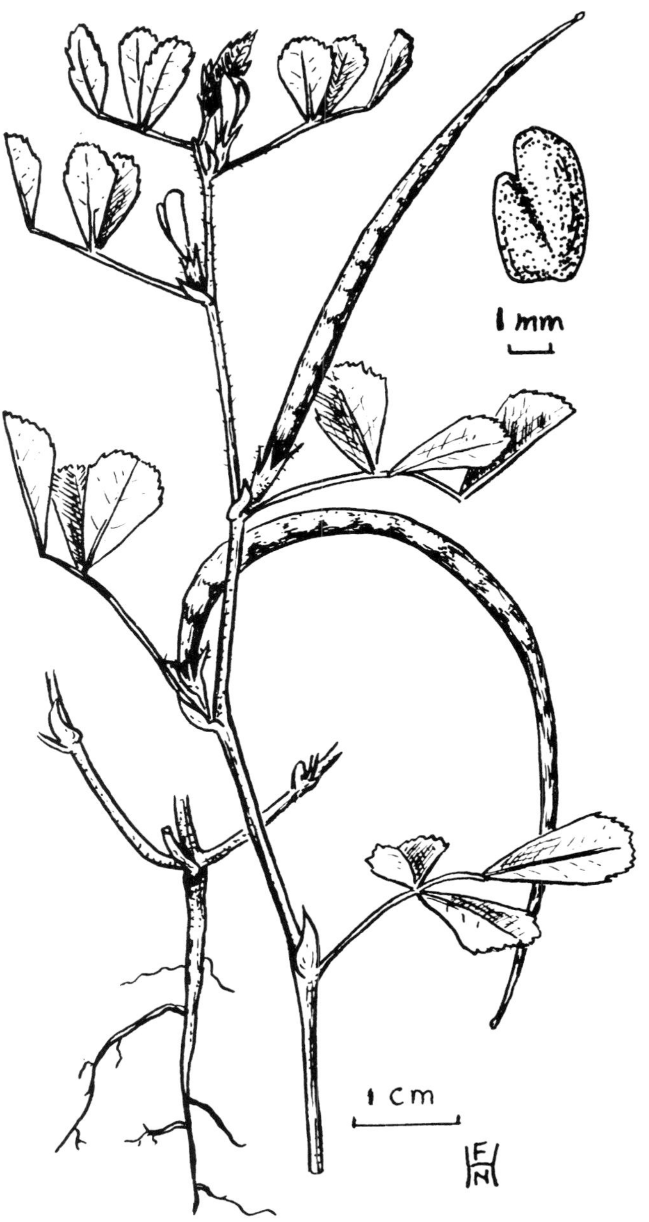

*Figure 24.14 Fenugreek (*Trigonella foenum-graecum*).*

*Fenugreek (*Trigonella foenum-graecum L.*) [Leguminosae – Pea family]*

Fenugreek is an erect or spreading annual which can grow up to 20 to 60 cm high and has the characteristic trifoliate leaves frequently found in the pea family (Leguminosae). Its solitary yellow to white flowers appear in March or April and ten to twenty rectangular seeds develop in beaked pods 7 to 15 cm in length (Fig. 24.14) (Meikle 1977: 408; FAO 1988: 493). The fenugreek plant grows best on deep, loamy, well drained soils and is fairly salt tolerant. When cultivated under basin agriculture earlier this century, fenugreek was sown after the Nile flood had receded around the end the of October or the beginning of November. In the Delta, it was sown in water after ploughing, similar to berseem (*Trifolium alexandrium*), and received additional waterings thereafter (Foaden and Fletcher 1910: 461). Under canal irrigation, deep ploughing and thorough harrowing are essential for optimal yield (FAO 1988: 496). In Upper Egypt, it was raised without water and was often intercropped with other species, such as berseem, vetches, beans and barley. If grown with other leguminous forage crops it was often treated as a green fodder to be grazed in the field. The growth of the plant is slower in Lower Egypt where it requires more weeding and here, the crop ripens about five months after sowing (Foaden and Fletcher 1910: 461). If fenugreek is intercropped with cereals, both are harvested and threshed together with the grain separated later on. On its own fenugreek straw is a poor quality fodder and is mostly fed to camels or used as a temper for brick making (Foaden and Fletcher 1910: 462). If well-dried, fenugreek leaves will store for up to one year and the seeds for up to two years (FAO 1988: 494).

Fenugreek is an eastern Mediterranean native and is grown today in Egypt and other countries, such as Yemen and India, as both an animal fodder and as a herb (Foaden and Fletcher 1910: 461; Harrison *et al.* 1985: 132; FAO 1988: 493). The leaves contain vitamin A, calcium, phosphorus and protein, and can be used as a cooked vegetable or as a salad green (Foaden and Fletcher 1910: 462; Harrison *et al.* 1985: 132; FAO 1988: 494; Manniche 1989: 151; Dagher 1991: 44). Fenugreek seeds are popular in Egypt today where they are eaten whole, either raw or cooked, are ground up to flavour breads and other foods, are used to make a hot beverage, or are used for their edible oil (Foaden and Fletcher 1910: 462; Darby *et al.* 1977: 802; FAO 1988: 494; Manniche 1989: 151; Hepper 1990: 65; Dagher 1991: 44; Alderman 1993: 115). The seeds are rich in protein, iron and many of the B vitamins, along with some amino acids and calcium (FAO 1988: 494). They are used medicinally to encourage lactation and as an ointment to heal inflammation and other ills (Meikle 1977: 408; Aykroyd *et al.* 1982: 99; Boulos 1983: 128; FAO 1988: 494, 496; Manniche 1989: 151; Hepper 1990: 65; Nunn 1996: 15). The shoots of sprouted fenugreek seeds are also consumed and contain about 30 per cent protein (Foaden and Fletcher 1910: 462; Darby *et al.* 1977: 802; Manniche 1989: 151; Dagher 1991: 44). Powdered fenugreek seeds also produce a yellow dye (FAO 1988: 495). The entire plant is also used as an effective insect repellent in grain storage (FAO 1988: 495; Secoy and Smith 1983: 36). It has been suggested that the presence of fenugreek seeds in the tomb of Tutankhamun (KV62) may have been used for this purpose (Panagiotakopulu *et al.* 1995: 708).

The earliest finds of fenugreek seeds from Egypt are from Predynastic contexts (*c.* 3000 BC) (Renfrew 1973: 188) but are not confirmed again until the Eighteenth Dynasty, in the tomb of Tutankhamun and the settlement of Amarna (Germer 1989: 151; de Vartavan 1990: 486; Hepper 1990: 64–5; Renfrew 1985: 176).

Future work

While the exceptionally well-preserved archaeobotanical record of ancient Egypt allows us to examine many issues concerning food which would otherwise be beyond our reach elsewhere, as yet there are wide temporal and geographical gaps in the information available. To date, the data have allowed us to test the relative merits of both charred and desiccated remains, often from the same site and clearly demonstrates the greater range of species preserved by desiccation (Table 24.1). Indeed, the majority of the plants discussed in this chapter have not yet been found in charred Pharaonic remains. There is a clear need for systematically recovered archaeobotanical data from a wider variety of well-dated and well-excavated Pharaonic period sites to fully address detailed comparisons between sites, periods and regions. For example, most desiccated remains date to the New Kingdom and later. What factors account for the increased numbers and range of species at this time, including possible luxury items, such as coriander, cumin and dill? Could it be the introduction of the *shaduf* and the expansion of the canal system? Are these species newly arrived into Egypt during a period characterised by the influx of new ideas, innovations and influences from elsewhere? Or is it simply the better preservation of desiccated material? Additional data from earlier Pharaonic settlements would also help to address this important question. Similarly, how do the selection of foods left as funerary offerings in tombs change through time. Moreover, how do archaeobotanical remains from funerary contexts compare with those found on settlements of the population at large? Why were some foods selected as offerings and perhaps not others? Can any pattern be detected involving regional differences in food availability, such as the preferable growing conditions found in Middle and Upper Egypt for the cultivation of the pulse crops and onions, for example, or for Lower Egypt as the primary area for the cultivation of the olive and the grape? With time, the careful sampling, recovery, analysis, quantification and interpretation of the Egyptian archaeobotanical record will gradually produce a clearer picture of fruit and vegetable distribution and use for the Pharaonic period.

Other important issues needing further investigation include evidence for agrarian practices, such as intercropping, the cultivation of animal fodder, and how clearly species were distinguished as garden crops and as field crops. In addition, based on the agricultural requirements of the fruits and vegetables discussed here, together with information on the system of flood basins, irrigation canals and other features, is it possible to create a realistic model of the agricultural landscape during the Pharaonic period? Other food related issues also need to be considered, such as the methods of food preparation and processing, not only for cooking but also to increase palatability or to decrease toxicity (e.g. Stahl 1989), different attitudes to foods through time and by region (e.g. Goody 1982) and also the important subjects of food avoidance and food taboos (e.g. Simoons 1994). Ethnographic parallels from Egypt for the cultivation, processing, preparation and storage of plant foods would greatly enrich our understanding of the uses of these species. A sound knowledge of the possible methods of food processing for the plants involved, coupled with a collaboration between linguists, and those familiar with the artistic record would undoubtedly also shed light on this subject.

Innovative techniques, such as gas chromatography, infrared spectroscopy and the extraction of DNA, are increasingly used to detect and identify less conspicuous or problematic remains of ancient food (Heron *et al.* 1991; Hillman *et al.* 1993; Evershed 1993; Brown *et al.* 1993, 1994; McLaren 1998). Similarly, the further investigation of plant-based foods and products, such as oils and resins will undoubtedly also provide clues of local production and foreign trade in these items (Heron and Pollard 1988; Mills and White 1989; Biers and McGovern 1990; Evans 1991; Knapp 1991; Haldane 1991, 1993; Heron and Evershed 1993; W. V. Davies 1995; Serpico and White 1996; Chapters 18 and 19, this volume). The methodology used in the search for the ancient gardens and orchards themselves is also improving and includes various chemical analyses of soil and the recovery of ancient plants, pollen, insects and molluscs by flotation or sieving and methods of careful excavation (e.g. Wilkinson 1988; Murphy and Scaife 1991; PACT 1994; Miller and Gleason 1994; Bietak 1996; de Moulins and Weir 1997: 40).

An increase in the analysis of desiccated wood and wood charcoals in recent years, ranging from the contents of hearths in settlements, to the wooden furniture in tombs can provide data on the use and distribution of those trees which were also valued for their fruits (Lucas 1962; Barakat 1995, W. V. Davies 1995, Chapter 15, this volume). The analysis of ancient insects will help to illuminate the poorly understood subjects of the pests and diseases of ancient fruit and vegetable crops in Egypt, the environmental requirements of these species and also the use of plants as insecticides and other issues concerning food storage (Secoy and Smith 1983; Kislev 1991; Levinson and Levinson 1994; Panagiotakopulu 1995 *et al.*, Panagiotakopulu and van der Veen 1997). The range of root and tuber species utilised during the Pharaonic period also is not yet fully recognised. New identification techniques using scanning electron microscopy offer the chance to determine the identity of these remains found on Egyptian settlements and will extend our knowledge of this potentially important food source (Hillman *et al.* 1989; Hather 1991, 1993, 1995).

While archaeobotanical reports understandably focus on the well-known cultivated cereal and fruit and vegetable crops, the diversity of wild species present at early sites, such as Wadi Kubbaniya, indicate the potential range of useful wild species in ancient Egypt (el-Hadidi 1985; Hillman *et al.* 1989, 1993; Wetterstrom 1993; Wasilykowa *et al.* 1995; Butler 1995). A continued reliance on wild plants during the Pharaonic period was likely, particularly by the poorer members of society and this valuable knowledge would have served the Nile dwellers well during times of poor floods and food scarcity. Pliny, for example, documents the extensive use of wild food species in Egypt during the Classical period, such as mallow and purslane (N.H. XXI, LII, 89. XXI, LVIII, 98 in Wilkinson 1878) and these plants were still described as important foods by Foaden and Fletcher (1910) and by the FAO (1988). Ethnobotanical analysis from Egypt and adjacent areas have shown the diverse array of wild plants valued for their seeds, fruits, leaves or tubers (e.g. Nicolaisen 1963; Bailey and Danin 1981; Goodman and Hobbs 1988; Hobbs 1989; Harlan 1989) and further ethnographic and ethnohistorical studies will undoubtedly provide a greater understanding of their potential use, not only as food and drink, but also as fodder, medicines, dyes, fuel, temper in pottery, plaster and mud brick, materials for matting, bedding, roofing and basketry.

Conclusions

In contrast to the large and varied archaeobotanical evidence and detailed textual records from the post-Pharaonic periods (e.g. Table 24.1), there is a clear need for further directed study of data from particular time spans and regions of Pharaonic Egypt in order to create a more substantial base from which well informed interpretations can be made. To date, much of what has been written about Pharaonic diet has been firmly based on the many common assumptions related to the subject yet, as this chapter has demonstrated, even the simple list of plant foods attributed to the period which are commonly cited throughout the literature clearly need to be reassessed, particularly in light of critical factors such as differential preservation of material and the type of sites from which that material is derived. The rich artistic representations from ancient Egyptian tombs has also undoubtedly created a sense that the information illustrated provides us with all we need to know about the food plants of the time, and the idea that the Pharaonic diet is so well understood as to see no further than a list of plant foods decribed in terms of how we know and use them today, is surely the truest danger of these previous assumptions.

Although comparisons between species is highly influenced by an array of variables, e.g. charred *vs.* desiccated; tomb *vs.* town; leafy vegetables *vs.* robust fruit stones; several general observations can be made of the archaeobotanical records of these species thus far. First, there is a great diversity of fruits and vegetables preserved from Pharaonic Egyptian sites and many species, such as the dom palm, the sycomore fig, Christ's thorn, chufa and lentils were clearly highly regarded and widely used from an early date. In some cases, however, the lack of evidence raises the question of whether certain other species commonly associated with the Pharaonic period were ever present during this time. As a leafy vegetable, the leek is less likely to survive than other species types; however, there is a single find of each (of unknown date) for the leek and the closely related native Egyptian kurrat. These two plants do not appear to be distinguished in the artistic and linguistic records and differentiating between these plants in modern material is problematic. The presence of the cucumber is also suspect. The linguistic evidence for the species is unclear and the artistic record of the cucumber is more likely to be a representation of the African native, the chate melon. It has been suggested that the archaeobotanical evidence for the cucumber is also most likely to represent the chate melon (Germer 1985: 129–30). The only examples of radish known from the Pharaonic period are from the Middle Kingdom site of Kahun (Newberry 1890) although there is some question as to whether at least some of this material might not date from a post-Pharaonic period (Germer forthcoming). While archaeobotanical remains of garlic are found from the Eighteenth Dynasty onwards, a Predynastic date for the presence of garlic in Egypt has been proposed due to several finds of clay models of what appear to be garlic bulbs (e.g. Aryton and Loat 1911). In light of the archaeobotanical and possible lexicographic evidence from a much later date, further investigation is necessary to establish the presence of this species during the Pharaonic period. In contrast, to these examples, the archaeobotanical record suggests that the argun palm, dom palm and persea were likely to have been more common in ancient Egypt than they are today.

Other plants, which we think of as vegetables today, may not have been used as such in the Pharaonic period. During this time, the melon and the watermelon were not likely to have been the sweet fleshy varieties that we currently recognise, instead these plants probably had bitter, unpalatable fruits, which may have been grown primarily for their nutritious seeds (Täckholm 1961: 31; Germer 1985: 127–8). It has been suggested that lettuce was cultivated primarily for its oil-bearing seed in the Pharaonic period (Keimer 1924) and such species are often not used as vegetables due to their prickly, bitter tasting leaves (e.g. Harlan 1986: 7). Unfortunately, there is no archaeobotanical record of the plant itself. While celery is known as a fragrant element of Pharaonic funeral garlands, there is no record that the plant was developed as a vegetable as such until sometime during the fourteenth or fifteenth centuries in Italy and the first record for the use of the seeds as a condiment is from the Roman period (Riggs 1995: 482). The increase in the systematic recovery of plant remains from ancient Egyptian sites, will undoubtedly help to fill the gaps in the current evidence that we have for many of the plants discussed here.

This chapter has been a brief overview of a vast subject which would greatly benefit from the variety of expertise which would be available with a truly multidisciplinary approach. Not only are the details of this subject important to archaeobotanists and anyone interested in daily life in ancient Egypt, but due to the superior preservation of plant material offered by the Egyptian climate, modern geneticists, too, look to Egypt with interest for evidence of the early presence and cultivation of many species (e.g. Zohary and Hopf 1994; Smartt and Simmonds 1995). The problems associated with the artistic, textual and archaeobotanical evidence have been discussed throughout this paper and it is hoped that future collaborations, particularly between archaeobotanists and linguists will significantly help to move the subject forward. Several studies applying linguistic and pictorial evidence to agrarian subjects have already been undertaken, thereby adding an important social context to the study of crops and crop husbandry (e.g. Crawford 1971, 1973, 1979; Janssen 1975; Charpentier 1981; Moens 1984; Moens and Wetterstrom 1988; Baum 1988, Hugonot 1989; Eyre 1994). Only by examining the many integrated facets relating to Pharaonic food production, processing and diet, will we be able to fully address the many unresolved questions concerning this vital component of Egyptian social and economic history.

Acknowledgements

Many thanks to those colleagues who commented on an earlier draft of this chapter including Drs Rene Cappers, Mike Charles, Frances McLaren, Dominique de Moulins, Mark Nesbitt, Delwen Samuel, Wendy Smith, Ursula Thanheiser, Marijke van der Veen and Wilma Wetterstrom. Special thanks to Renate Germer. Thanks too, to Nigel Hepper for allowing me to use many of his botanical drawings to illustrate the article, to Will Schenk for drawing Figure 24.9, and to Prof. Daniel Zohary for advice on tables 24.2–3.

References

Alderman, H. 1993. Food preferences and nutrition. In *The Agriculture of Egypt*. (ed. G. M. Craig). Oxford: OUP, pp. 114–27.

Alpin, P. 1980 (Reprinted text from 1581–1584). *Plantes d'Egypte.* Cairo: IFAO.

Arie, T.H.D. 1959. Pythagorus and beans. *Oxford Medical School Gazette* 2: 75.

Arnon, I. 1972. *Crop Production in Dry Regions 1: Background and Principles.* London: Leonard Hill.

Aykroyd, W.R., Doughty, J. and Walker, A. 1982. *Legumes in Human Nutrition.* FAO Food and Nutritrition Paper. No. 20. Rome: FAO.

Ayrton, E. and Loat, W. 1911. Predynastic cemetary at el-Mahasna. London: EES.

Ayyad, S., and Krzywinski, K. 1994. Archaeopalynological thoughts on *Vicia faba* type pollen from ancient Mendes (Tel el-Roba area, Egypt). *PACT Journal* 42: 20–33.

Baer, K. 1962. The low price of land in ancient Egypt. *JARCE.*, 1: 25–45.

1963. An 11th Dynasty farmer's letters to his family. *JAOS.*, 83: 1–19.

Bailey, C., and Danin, A. 1981. Bedouin plant utilisation in Sinai and the Negev. *Economic Botany* 35(2): 145–62.

Barakat, H.N. 1990. Plant remains from El Omari. In *El Omari: A Neolithic Settlement and Other Sites in the Vicinity of Wadi Hof, Helwan.* Appendix IV. (eds. F. Debono and B. Mortensen). Mainz: Deutsches Archaeologisches Institut, Abteilung, Kairo. pp. 109–13.

1995. Charcoals from Neolithic site at Nabta Playa (E–75–6), Egypt. *Acta Palaeobotanica* 35(1): 163–66.

Barakat, H.N., and Baum, N. 1992. *La Végétation Antique de Douch (Oasis de Kharga): Une Approche Macrobotanique.* Cairo: Institut Francais d'Archeologie Orientale du Caire.

Barrett, S. 1983. Crop mimicry in weeds. *Economic Botany* 37(3): 255–282.

Bates, D. and Robinson, R. 1995. Cucumbers, melons and watermelons. In *Evolution of Crop Plants.* (eds J. Smartt and N. M. Simmonds). Harlow, Essex: Longman Scientific and Technical, pp. 89–96.

Baum, N. 1988. *Arbres et Arbustes d'Egypt Ancienne.* Leuven: Departement Oriëntalistiek.

Bauman, B. 1960. The botanical aspects of Egyptian embalming and burial. *Economic Botany* 14: 84–104.

Beadnell, H. 1909. *An Egyptian Oasis: An Account of the Oasis of Kharga in the Libyan Desert, with Special Reference to its Physical Geography and Water Supply.* London.

Beshai, A.A. 1993. Systems of agricultural production in Middle and Upper Egypt. In *The Agriculture of Egypt.* (ed. G.M. Craig). Oxford: OUP, pp. 265–77.

Bienkowski, P. and Southworth, E. 1986. *Egyptian Antiquities in the Liverpool Museum* I. Warminster: Aris and Phillips, p. 63.

Biers, W.R. and McGovern, P.E. 1990. *Organic Contents of Ancient Vessels: Materials Analysis and Archaeological Investigation.* MASCA Research Papers in Science and Archaeology 7. Philadelphia: MASCA, University Museum of Archaeology and Anthropology.

Bietak, M. 1996. *Avaris: The Capital of the Hyksos. Recent Excavations at Tell el- Dab'a.* London: BMP.

Bircher, W. 1995. *The Date Palm: A Friend and Companion of Man.* Cairo: Elias Modern Press.

Bond, D.A. 1995. Faba bean. In *Evolution of Crop Plants.* (eds. J. Smartt and N.W. Simmonds). Harlow, Essex: Longman Scientific and Technical. pp, 312–16.

Boulos, L. 1983. *Medicinal Plants of North Africa.* Michigan: Reference Publications.

Bowman, A. and Rathbone, D. 1992. Cities and administration in Roman Egypt. *Journal of Roman Studies* 83: 107–27.

Brewer, D., Redford, D. and Redford, S. 1994. *Domestic Plants and Animals: The Egyptian Origins.* Warminster: Aris and Philips.

Brown, T. , and Bohgot, M. 1938. *Date Palm in Egypt.* Cairo: Ministry of Agriculture, Egypt.

Brown, T.A., Allaby, R.G., Brown, K.A. and Jones, M.K. 1993. Biomolecular archaeology of wheat: past, present and future. *World Archaeology.* 25: 64–73.

Brown, T.A., Allaby, R.G., Brown, K.A. 1994. DNA in wheat seeds from European archaeological sites. In *Conservation of Plant Genes II: Utilization of Ancient and Modern DNA.* (eds. R.P. Adams, J.S. Miller, E.M. Golenberg and J.E. Adams). Monographs in Systematic Botany 48. St. Louis, Missouri: Missouri Botanical Garden.

Brunton, G. 1937. *Mostagedda and the Tasian Culture.* British Museum Expedition to Middle Egypt, first and Second years 1928–29. London: BM.

1948. *Matmar.* London: Quaritch.

Brunton, G. and Caton-Thompson, G. 1928. *The Badarian Civilization.* London: British School of Archaeology in Egypt.

Bruyère, B. 1937. *Deir el-Médineh II: La Nécropole de l'Est.* (1934–1935). Cairo: Fouilles De L'Institut Français d'Archéologie Orientale Années.

Burleigh, R and Southgate, B.J. 1975. Insect infestation of stored Egyptian lentils in antiquity. *JAS,* 2: 391–392.

Butler, A. 1989. Cryptic anatomical characters as evidence of early cultivation in the grain legumes (pulses). *Foraging and Farming: The Evolution of Plant Exploitation* (eds. D. Harris and G. Hillman). London: Unwin and Hyman, pp. 390–407.

1991. The Vicieae: problems of identification. In *New Light on Early Farming.* (ed. J.M. Renfrew). Edinburgh: Edinburgh University Press, pp. 61–73.

1995. The role of small legumes as a resource in prehistory, with particular reference to temperate Africa. *Acta Palaeobotanica* 35 (1): 105–15.

1996. Trifolieae and related seeds from archaeological contexts: problems of identification. *Vegetation History and Archaeobotany* 5: 157–67.

Butzer, K. 1976. *Early hydraulic civilisation in Egypt: A study in cultural ecology.* Chicago: University of Chicago Press.

Caminos, R. 1954. *Late Egyptian Miscellanies.* London: Oxford University Press.

Cannon, J. and Cannon, M. 1994. *Dye plants and Dyeing.* Kew: Herbert Press and Royal Botanical Gardens.

Cappers, R. 1996. Archaeobotanical remains. In *Berenike 1995: Preliminary Report of the 1995 Excavations at Berenike (Egyptian Red Sea Coast) and the Survey of the Eastern Desert.* S. Sidebotham and W. Wendrich, eds. pp. 319–36. Leiden: Research School CNWS.

1998. Archaeobotanical remains. In *Berenike 1996: Preliminary Report of the 1995 Excavations at Berenike (Egyptian Red Sea Coast) and the Survey of the Eastern Desert.* S. Sidebotham and W. Wendrich, eds. Leiden: Research School CNWS, pp. 289–320.

Caton-Thompson, G. 1952. *Kharga Oasis in Prehistory.* London: University of London.

Charles, M. P. 1985. An introduction to the legume and oil plants of Mesopotamia. *BSA*. II: 39–61.

1987. Onions, cucumbers and the date palm. *BSA*. III: 1–22.

Charpentier, G. 1981. *Recueil de matériaux épigraphiques relatifs a la botanique de l'Égypte*. Paris: Trismégiste.

Coit, J. 1951. Carob or St. John's Bread. *Economic Botany* 5: 82–96.

Crawford, D. 1971. *Kerkeosiris: An Egyptian Village in the Ptolemaic Period*. Cambridge: CUP.

1973. Garlic growing and agricultural specialization in Graeco-Roman Egypt. *CdE* 96: 350–63.

1979. Food: tradition and change in Hellenistic Egypt. *World Archaeology* 11(2): 136–46.

Crisp, P. 1995. Radish. In *Evolution of Crop Plants*. (eds J. Smartt and N. M. Simmonds). Harlow, Essex: Longman Scientific and Technical, pp. 86–8.

Dagher, S.M. 1991. *Traditional foods in the Near East*. FAO Food and Nutrition Paper 50. Rome: FAO.

Darby, W.J., Ghalioungui, P. and Grivetti, L. 1977. *Food: The Gift of Osiris*. vol. 2. London: Academic Press.

Davies, N. de. G. 1933. *The Tomb of Nefer-hotep at Thebes*. vol. 1. Publication 9. New York: Metropolitan Museum of Art Egyptian Expedition.

1935. *Paintings from the Tomb of Rekh-Mi-Re* at Thebes. New: MMA.

1943. *The Tomb of Rekh-Mi-Re at Thebes*. 2 vols. New: MMA, Egyptian Expedition.

Davies, D. R. 1995. Peas. In *Evolution of Crop Plants*. (eds. J. Smartt and N. W. Simmonds). Harlow, Essex: Longman Scientific and Technical. pp. 294–6.

Davies, W. V. 1995. Ancient Egyptian timber imports: an analysis of wooden coffins in the British Museum. In *Egypt, the Aegean and the Levant*. (eds. W. V. Davies and L. Schofield). London: BMP, pp. 146–56.

Davis, P.H., Mill R. R. and Tan K. (eds.) 1965–88. *Flora of Turkey and the East Aegean Islands*. 10 Vols. Edinburgh: Edinburgh University Press.

Debono, F. 1948. El Omari (près d'Heloun), Exposée sommaire sur les campagnes des fouilles 1943–44 et 1948. *ASAE*. 48: 561–569.

Drar, M. 1950. Date palm in modern Egypt. In *Flora of Egypt*. Vol. II. (eds. V. Tackholm and M. Drar). Cairo: Fouad I University Press. pp. 167–203.

Duell, P. 1938. *The Mastaba of Mereruka*. 2 vols. Chicago: The Oriental Institute, University of Chicago.

Edel, E. 1970. *Die Felsengräber der Qubbet el-Hawa bei Assuan II.I.2 Text*. Wiesbaden: Otto Harrassowitz.

Emery, W.B. 1962. *A Funerary Repast in an Egyptian Tomb of the Archaic Period*. Leiden: Nederlands Institut voor het Nabije Oosten.

Emery, W.B. and Saad, Z.Y. 1938. *Excavations at Saqqara: The Tomb of Hemaka*. Cairo: Government Press.

Erman, A. 1894. *Life in Ancient Egypt*. London and New York: Macmillan and Company.

Erskine, W., Smartt, J. and Muehlbauer, F. 1994. Mimicry of lentil and the domestication of common vetch and grass pea. *Economic Botany* 48(3): 326–32.

Evans, J. 1991. Organic traces and their contribution to the understanding of trade. In *Bronze Age Trade in the Mediterranean*. (ed. N. H. Gale). Papers presented at the conference held at Rewley House, Oxford, in December 1989. Jonesered: P. Åström, pp. 289–94.

Evershed, R. 1993. Biomolecular archaeology and lipids. *World Archaeology* 25(1): 74–93.

Eyre, C.J. 1994. The water regimes for orchards and plantations in Pharaonic Egypt. *JEA*. 80: 57–80.

1995. The agricultural cycle, farming, and water management in the ancient Near East. In *Civilizations of the Ancient Near East* I. (ed. J.M. Sasson). New York: Scribner's, pp. 175–89.

Fahmy, A.G. 1995. *A historical flora of Egypt, preliminary survey*. Doctoral dissertation. Faculty of Science, Cairo University, Egypt.

Faltings, D. 1991. Die Bierbrauerei im AR. *ZÄS*. 118: 104–16.

FAO (Food and Agricultural Organization of the United Nations). 1988. *Traditional food plants: A resource book for promoting the exploitation and consumption of food plants in arid, semi-arid and sub-humid lands of Eastern Africa*. FAO Food and Nutrition Paper 42. Rome: FAO.

Feinbrun-Dothan, N. 1978, 1986. *Flora Palaestina*, vols. 3, 4. Jerusalem: Israel Academy of Sciences and Humanities.

Foaden, G., and Fletcher, F. 1908. *Textbook of Egyptian Agriculture*. vol. I. Cairo: National Printing Department.

1910. *Textbook of Egyptian Agriculture*. vol. II. Cairo: F. Eimer.

Forbes, H. and Foxhall, L. 1995. Ethnoarchaeology and storage in the ancient Mediterranean: beyond risk and survival. In *Food in Antiquity*. (eds J. Wilkins, D. Harvey, and M. Dobson). Exeter: University of Exeter Press, pp. 69–86.

Frank, K.S. and Stika, H.P. 1988. *Bearbeitung der makroskopischen Pflanzen-und einiger Tierreste des Römerkastells Sablonetum (Ellingen bei weissenburg in Bayern)*. Materialhefte zur bayerischen Vorgeschichte Reihe A, Bd. 61: Kallmunz/Opt.

Frankfort, H. and Pendlebury, J.D.S. 1933. *The City of Akhenaten II*. London: EES.

French, R. 1994. *Ancient Natural History*. London: Routledge.

Friis, I, Hepper, N. and Gasson, P. 1986. The botanical identity of the *Mimusops* in ancient Egyptian tombs. *JEA*. 72: 201–4.

Galil, J. 1968. An ancient technique for ripening sycamore fruits in Eastern Mediterranean countries. *Economic Botany* 22: 178–90.

Galil, J. and Eisikowitch, D. 1968. Flowering cycles and fruit types of *Ficus sycomorus* in Israel. *New Phytologist* 67: 745–758.

Galil J. and Neeman, G. 1977. Pollen transfer and pollination in the common fig (*Ficus carica* L.). *New Phytologist* 79: 163–71.

Garnsey, P. 1988. *Famine and Food Supply in the Graeco-Roman World*. Cambridge: CUP.

Geller, J.R. 1992. From prehistory to history: beer in Egypt. In *The followers of Horus*. (eds R. Friedman and B. Adams). Egyptian Studies Association Publication 2. Oxford: Oxbow Books, 19–26.

Georgiades, C. 1985. *Flowers of Cyprus: Plants of Medicine*. vol. I Nicosia: Ch. Georgiades.

1987. *Flowers of Cyprus: Plants of Medicine*. vol. II Nicosia: Ch. Georgiades.

Germer, R. 1985 *Flora des pharaonischen Ägypten*. Deutsches Archäologisches Institut, Abteilung Kairo, Sonderschrift 14. Mainz: Philipp von Zabern.

1988. *Katalog der Altägyptischen Pflanzenreste der Berliner Museen*. Wiesbaden: Otto Harrassowitz.

1989. *Die Pflanzenmaterialien aus dem Grab des Tutanchamun*. Hildesheim: Gerstenberg.

forthcoming. The plant material found by Petrie at Lahun and some remarks on the problems of identifying Egyptian plant names. In *Lahun Studies.* (ed. S. Quirke). New Malden: SIA Publications.

Giddy, L. and Jeffreys, D. 1991. Memphis 1990. *JEA.* 77: 1–6.

Goodman, S., and Hobbs, J. 1988. The ethnobotany of the Egyptian Eastern Desert: A comparison of common plant usage between two culturally distinct Bedouin groups. *Journal of Ethnopharmacology* 23: 73–89.

Goody, J. 1982. *Cooking, cuisine and class: A study in comparative sociology.* Cambridge: CUP.

Greiss, E.A.M. 1957. *Anatomical identification of some ancient Egyptian plant materials.* Mémoires de L'Institut d'Egypte 55. Cairo: Costa Tsoumas and Co.

el-Hadidi, M.N. 1982. The Predynastic flora of the Hierakonpolis region. In *The Predynastic of Hierakonpolis: An Interim Report.* (ed. M.A. Hoffman). Egyptian Studies Association Publication 1. Cairo: Cairo University Herbarium, pp. 102–9.

1985. Food plants of prehistoric and Predynastic Egypt. In *Plants for Arid Lands.* (eds. G. E. Wickens, J. R. Goodwin, and D. V. Field). Kew: Royal Botanical Gardens. pp. 87–92.

1992. Notes on Egyptian weeds of antiquity: 1. Min's lettuce and the Nagada plant. In *The Followers of Horus: Studies Dedicated to Michael Allen Hoffman 1944–1990.* Oxford: Oxbow Publications, pp. 322–6.

el-Hadidi, M.N and Amer, W. 1996. The Palaeoethnobotany of Abu Sha'ar site (AD 400–700), Red Sea Coast; Egypt. *Taeckholmia* 16: 31–44.

el-Hadidi, M.N., and Boulos, L. 1988. *The Street Trees of Cairo.* Cairo: American University in Cairo Press.

Haldane, C. 1991. Recovery and analysis of plant remains from some Mediterranean shipwreck sites. In *New Light on Early Farming: Recent Developments in Palaeoethnobotany.* (ed. J. Renfrew). Edinburgh: Edinburgh University Press, pp. 213–223.

1993. Direct evidence for organic cargoes in the Late Bronze Age. *World Archaeology* 24: 348–60.

Halstead, P. and O'Shea, J. 1989. *Bad Year Economics: Cultural Responses to Risk and Uncertainty.* Cambridge: CUP. pp. 123–26.

Harlan, J. R. 1986. Lettuce and the sycamore: sex and romance in ancient Egypt. *Economic Botany* 40: 4–15.

1989. Wild grass seed harvesting in the Sahara and the sub-Sahara of Africa. *Foraging and Farming: The Evolution of Plant Exploitation.* (eds. D. Harris and G. Hillman). London: Unwin and Hyman, pp. 11–26.

Harrison, S.G., Masefield, G.B., Wallis, M., and Nicholson, B.E. 1985. *The Oxford Book of Food Plants.* London: Peerage Books.

Hather, J. 1991. The identification of charred archaeological remains of vegetative parenchymous tissue. *JAS.* 18: 661–75.

1993. *An Archaeobotanical Guide to Root and Tuber Identification: Europe and South West Asia.* Oxford: Oxbow Monograph 28.

1995. Parenchymatous tissues from the early Neolithic site E–75–6 at Nabta Playa, Western Desert, south Egypt, preliminary report. *Acta Palaeobotanica* 35(1): 157–62.

Havey, M.J. 1995. Onions and other cultivated Alliums. In *Evolution of Crop Plants.* (eds. J. Smartt and N. W. Simmonds). Harlow, Essex: Longman Scientific and Technical, pp. 345–50.

Helbaek 1966. The plant remains from Nimrud. In *Nimrud and its remains.* (ed. M.E. Mallowan). Appendix I, vol 2. London: Collins, pp. 613–20.

Hepper, F. N. 1990. *Pharaoh's Flowers: The Botanical Treasures of Tutankhamun.* London: HMSO.

Heron, C. and Pollard, A. 1988. Analysis of natural resinous material for Roman amphorae. In *Science and Archaeology.* (eds. Slater, E.A. and Tate, J.O.) BAR 196. Glasgow: BAR, 429–47.

Heron, C. , Evershed, R.P. and Goad, L.J. 1991. Effects of migration of soil lipids on organic residues associated with buried pot sherds. *JAS.* 18: 641–59.

Heron, C. and Evershed, R.P. 1993. The analysis of organic residues and the study of pottery use. In *Archaeological Method and Theory V.* (ed. M.B. Schiffer). Arizona: University of Arizona Press, pp. 247–86.

Hillman, G. C., Madeyska, E. and Hather, J. 1989. Wild plant foods and diet at Late Palaeolithic Wadi Kubbaniya: the evidence from charred remains. In *Palaeoeconomy, Environment and Stratigraphy.* Vol. 2. (ed. A. Close). *The Prehistory of Wadi Kubbaniya.* Dallas: Southern Methodist University Press. pp. 162–242.

Hillman, G. C., Wales, S., McLaren, F., Evans, J. and Butler, A. 1993. Identifying problematic remains of ancient plant foods: a comparison of the role of chemical, histological and morphological criteria. *World Archaeology* 25(1): 94–121.

Hobbs, J. 1989. *Bedouin Life in the Egyptian Wilderness.* Cairo: American University Press.

Holm, L.G., Plucknett, D.L., Pancho, J.V., Herberger, J.P. 1977. *The World's Worst Weeds: Distribution and Biology.* Honolulu: Hawaii University Press.

Houérou Le, H.N. 1985. Forage and fuel plants in the arid zone of North Africa, the Near and Middle East. In *Plants for Arid Lands.* (eds. G. E. Wickens, J. R. Goodwin, and D. V. Field). Kew: Royal Botanical Gardens. pp. 117–41.

Hugonot, J.-C. 1989. *Le Jardin dans l'Egypte Ancienne.* Frankfort: Peter Lang.

Jansen, P.C.M. 1981. *Spices, condiments and medicinal plants in Ethiopia: their taxonomy and agricultural significance.* Wageningen: Centre for Agricultural Publishing and Documentation.

Janssen, J. 1975. *Commodity Prices from the Ramesside Period: An Economic Study of the Village Necropolis Workmen at Thebes.* Leiden: E.J. Brill.

Jones, G.E.M. 1983. The uses of ethnographic and ecological models in the interpretation of archaeological plant remains: case studies from Greece. Doctoral dissertation. Cambridge University, England.

Jones, G.E.M., and Halstead, P. 1993. An early find of 'fava' from Thebes. *The Annual Report of the British School at Athens* 88: 103–4.

Kamal, A.B. 1913. Le pain de nebaq des anciens Egyptiens. *ASAE.* 12: 240–4.

Keimer, L. 1924. *Die Gartenpflanzen im Alten Ägypten.* Mainz: Deutsches Archaologisches Institut, Abteilung Kairo.

1926. Agriculture in ancient Egypt. *American Journal of Semitic Languages and Literature* 42: 283–8.

1928. An ancient Egyptian knife in modern Egypt. *Ancient Egypt.* pp. 65–6.

1929a. Sur quelques petits fruits en faience emaillée datant du

moyen Empire. *BIFAO*. 28: 49–97.
1929b. Falcon face. *Ancient Egypt* 14 (2): 47–8.
1939. Pavian und Dum-Palme. *MDAIK*. 8: 42–5.
1984. Die Gartenpflanzen im alten Ägypten. Band II. *Sonderschrift* 13 (ed. R. Germer). Deutsches Archaologisches Institut, Abteilung Kairo. Mainz: von Zabern.
Kislev, M. 1988. Nahal Hemar Cave. Dessicated plant remains: an interim report. *Atiqot* 18: 76–81.
1991. Archaeobotany and storage archaeoentomology. In *New Light on Early Farming* (ed. J. Renfrew). Edinburgh: Edinburgh University Press, pp. 121–38.
1992. Agriculture in the Near East in the VIIth millennium. In *Préhistoire de L'Agriculture: Nouvelles Approches Expérimentales et Ethnographiques* (ed. P. Anderson). Monographie du Centre de Recherches Archéologiques 6. Paris: Éditions du CNRS, pp. 87–93.
in press. *Cordia myxa:* the birdlime tree of the Near East. In *Ashkelon I* (ed. L. Stager) Cambridge, MA.: Semitic Museum Harvard.
Knapp, A.B. 1991. Spice, drugs, grain and grog: Organic goods in Bronze Age East Mediteranean trade. *Bronze Age Trade in the Mediterranean.* (ed. N.H. Gale). Papers presented at the conference held at Rewley House, Oxford, in December 1989, Jonsered, 1991. P. Åström, pp. 21–68.
Ladizinsky, G. 1995. *Chick pea.* In *Evolution of Crop Plants.* (eds. J. Smartt and N. W. Simmonds). Harlow, Essex: Longman Scientific and Technical. pp. 258–60
Langer, R.H.M. and Hill, G.D. 1991. *Agricultural Plants.* 2nd edn. Cambridge: CUP.
Lauer, J.P., Täckholm, V., Laurent, V. and Aberg, E. 1950. Les plants découvertes dans les souterrains de l'enceinte du roi Zoser à Saqqarah (IIIe Dynastie). *BIE*. 32: 121–57.
Lesko, L. 1977. *King Tut's Wine Cellar.* Berkeley: B.C. Scribe.
1995. Egyptian wine production during the New Kingdom. In *The Origins and Ancient History of Wine* (eds. P. McGovern, S. Fleming, S. Katz). Luxembourg: Gordon and Breach, pp. 215–30.
Levinson, H. and Levinson, A. 1994. Origin of grain storage and insect species consuming desiccated food. *Anzeiger fär Schadlingskunde Pflanzenschutz* 67(3): 47–60.
Lindqvist, K. 1960. On the origin of cultivated lettuce. *Hereditas* 46: 319–350.
Litýnska, M. 1994. Remains of plants. In *Predynastic settlement near Armant.* (eds B. Gunter and J. Kozlowski). Studien zur Archäologie und Geschichte Altägyptens Band 6. Heidelberger Orientverlag. pp. 103–108.
Loret, V. 1892. *La Flore Pharaonique.* Paris: Ernest Leroux.
1904. L'ail chez les anciens Egyptiens. *Sphinx* 8: 135–47.
Lucas , A. 1962. *Ancient Egyptian Materials and Industries.* 4th edn. (rev. by J.R. Harris). London: Arnold.
Lutz, H.F. 1922. *Viticulture and Brewing in the Ancient Orient.* Leipzig: J.C. Hinrichs.
Maksoud, S. el-Hadidi, M.N. and Amer W.M. 1994. Beer from the early dynasties (3500–3400 cal BC) of Upper Egypt, detected by archaeochemical methods. *Vegetation History and Archaeobotany* 3: 219–24.
Málek, J. 1986 *In the Shadow of the Pyramids: Egypt during the Old Kingdom.* American University in Cairo Press.
Manniche, L. 1989. *An Ancient Egyptian Herbal.* London: BMP.
McLaren, F. 1998. Doura Cave, Syria: The botanical evidence from a Palaeolithic site in the arid zone. In *Life on the Edge: Human Settlement and Marginality.* (eds. C.M. Mills, and G. Coles). Symposium of the Association for Environmental Archaeology 13, pp. 179–87.
Meikle, R.D. 1977, 1985. *Flora of Cyprus.* Kew: Bentham-Moxon Trust.
Miller, N.F. and Gleason, K.L. (eds) 1994. *The Archaeology of Garden and Field.* Philadelphia: University of Pennsylvania Press.
Mills, J.S., and White, R. 1989. The identity of the resins from the late Bronze Age shipwreck at Ülü Bürün (Kas). *Archaeometry* 31: 37–44.
Moens, M.-F. 1984. The ancient Egyptian garden in the New Kingdom: A study of representations. *Orientalia Lovaniensia Periodica.* 15: 11–53.
Moens, M.-F., and Wetterstrom, W. 1988. The agricultural economy of an Old Kingdom town in Egypt's west Delta: insights from the plant remains. *JNES*. 47(3): 159–73.
de Moulins, D. and Weir, D. 1997. The potential and use of environmental techniques in gardens. *Journal of Garden History* 17(1): 40–6.
Murphy, P., and Scaife, R. 1991. The environmental archaeology of gardens. In *Garden Archaeology.* (ed. A.E. Brown). London: CBA Research Reports 78, 83–99.
Murray, M. A. forthcoming. Agrarian practices at the ancient Egyptian settlements of Memphis, Abydos and Giza: an archaeobotanical perspective. Doctoral dissertation. University College London.
1998. Archaeobotanical report. In *Excavations at Kissonerga-Mosphilia, 1979–1992.* (ed. E. Peltenburg). Lemba Archaeological Project, Cyprus. Vol. II.a. Jonsered: P Åström, pp. 215–23.
Negbi, M. 1992. A sweetmeat plant, a perfume plant and their weedy relatives: A chapter in the history of *Cyperus esculentus* L. and *C. rotundus* L. *Economic Botany* 46(1): 64–71.
Newberry, P. 1889. On the vegetable remains discovered in the cemetery of Hawara. *In Hawara, Biahmu and Arsinoe.* (ed. W. Petrie). London: Leadenhall Press, pp. 46–53.
1890. The ancient botany. In *Kahun, Gurob, and Hawara.* (ed. Petrie). London: Kegan Paul, Trench, Trübner. pp. 46–50.
1893. *Beni Hassan I.* London: Kegan Paul, Trench and Trübner.
1900. *The Life of Rekhmara.* London: Westminster.
Nicolaisen, J. 1963. *Ecology and Culture of the Pastoral Tuareg.* Nationalmuseets Skrifter Ethnografisk Raekke. IX. Copenhagen: National Museum of Copenhagen.
Nunn, J.F. 1996. *Ancient Egyptian Medicine.* London: BMP.
Osborn, D. 1968. Notes on medicinal and other uses of plants in Egypt. *Economic Botany* 22: 165–77.
PACT. 1994. *Garden History: Garden Plants, Species, Forms and Varieties from Pomeii to 1800.* (ed. Moe, D., Dickson, J. and Jorgensen, P.M.). Symposium at European University for Cultural Heritage, Ravello, June 1991. no. 42.
Panagiotakopulu, E., Buckland, P. and Day P. 1995. Natural insecticides and insect repellents in antiquity: a review of the evidence. *JAS*. 22: 705–10.
Panagiotakopulu, E. and van der Veen, M. 1997. Synanthropic insect faunas from Mons Claudianus, a Roman Quarry site in the Eastern Desert, Egypt. In *Studies in Quaternary Entomology – An Inordinate Fondness for Insects* (ed. a. Ashworth,

P. Buckland and J. Sadler). Chichester: Quaternary Proceeddings No. 5: John Wiley, pp. 199–205.

Peet, T.E. and Wooley, C.L. 1923. *The City of Akhenaten I. Excavations of 1921 and 1922 at el-Amarneh*. London: EES.

Petrie, W.M.F. 1920. *Prehistoric Egypt*. London: University College London.

Pliny, see Rackham 1968.

Polhill, R.M. *et al.* (eds.) 1949–94. in progress. *Flora of Tropical East Africa*. Rotterdam: Balkema.

Polunin, O. and Huxley, A. 1987. *Flowers of the Mediterranean*. London: Hogarth Press.

Popenoe, P.B. 1973. *The Date Palm*. Miami: Field Reseach Projects.

Rackham, H. (trans. and ed.) 1968. *Pliny (the Elder): Natural History*. 2nd edn. Cambridge MA: Loeb Classical Library, Harvard University Press.

Renfrew, J. 1973. *Palaeoethnobotany: The prehistoric food plants of the Near East and Europe*. London: Methuen.

1985. Preliminary reports on the botanical remains. *Amarna Reports* II: (ed. B. J. Kemp) London: EES, pp. 175–190.

1995. Vegetables in the ancient Near Eastern diet. In *Civilizations of the Ancient Near East I* (ed. J. M. Sasson). New York: Scribner's, pp. 191–202.

Riggs, T.J. 1995. Umbelliferous minor crops. In *Evolution of Crop Plants*. (eds. J. Smart and N. W. Simmonds). Harlow, Essex: Longham Scientific and Technical, pp. 481–485.

de Roller, G.J. 1992. Archaeobotanical remains from Tell Ibrahim Awad, seasons 1988 and 1989. In *The Nile Delta in Transition: 4th–3rd Millennium BC* (ed. E. van der Brink), Tel Aviv: Edwin van der Brink, pp. 111–16.

Rostovtzeff, M. 1922. *A Large Estate in Egypt in the Third Century B.C.: A Study in Economic History*. Madison: University of Wisconsin.

Rowlandson, J. 1996. *Land owners and tenants in Roman Egypt: The social relations of agriculture in the Oxyrhynchite nome*. Oxford: Clarendon Press.

Rowley-Conwy, P. 1989. Nubia AD 0–550 and the 'Islamic' agricultural revolution: preliminary botanical evidence from Qasr Ibrim, Egyptian Nubia. *Archéologie du Nil Moyen* 3: 131–8.

Ruf, T. 1993. The history of agricultural development. In *The Agriculture of Egypt*. (ed. G. M. Craig). Oxford: OUP.

Ruffer, M. 1919. Food in Egypt. *Mémoire Présenté à l'Institut Egyptien* 1. Cairo: IFAO.

Ryder, E. and Whitaker, T. 1995. Lettuce. In *Evolution of Crop Plants*. (eds. J. Smartt and N. M. Simmonds). Harlow, Essex: Longman Scientific and Technical, pp. 53–6.

Saad, Z.Y. 1938. The pottery: pot marks. In *Excavations at Saqqara: The Tomb of Hemaka* (ed. W.B. Emery). Cairo: Government Press, pp. 49–54.

Samuel, D. 1989. Their staff of life: initial investigations on ancient Egyptian bread baking. In *Amarna Reports* V, (ed. B.J. Kemp). London: EES. pp. 253–90.

1995. Umbellifer fruits (*Trachyspermum copticum* [L.] Link) from the Workmen's Village. *Amarna Reports* VI. (ed. B. Kemp). London: EES.

1996. Archaeology of ancient Egyptian beer. *Journal of the American Society of Brewing Chemists* 54(1): 3–12.

Sarpaki, A. 1992. The palaeoethnobotanical approach. The Mediterranean triad, or is it a quartet? *Agriculture in Ancient Greece*. Stockholm: Swedish Institute at Athens, pp. 61–76.

Schenkel, W. 1978. *Die Bewässerungsrevolution im Alten Ägypten*. Mainz/Rhein: Philipp von Zabern.

Schnebel, M. 1925. *Die Land wirtschaft im hellenistischen Ägypten*. Munich: C.H. Bech'sche Verlagsbuchhandlung.

Schweinfurth, G. 1885. Notice sur le restes de vegétaux de l'ancienne Egypte. Contenus dans une armoire du Musée de Boulaq. *Bulletin de l'Institut Egyptien* (*Année* 1884) 5: 3–10.

1886. Les dernieres découvertes botanique dans les anciens tombeaux de l'Egypte. *Bulletin de l'Institut Egyptien* (*Année* 1885) 6: 256–83.

1908. Über die Pflanzenreste aus mR29 and mR30 der Gräber des Mittleren Reiches zu Abusir. In *Priestergräber vom Totentempel des Ne-user-re* (ed. H. Schäfer). Leipzig, pp. 152–64.

Secoy, D., and Smith, A. 1983. Use of plants in control of agricultural and domestic pests. *Economic Botany* 37(1): 28–57.

Serpico, M. and White, R. 1996. A report on the analysis of the contents of a cache of jars from the tomb of Djer. In *Aspects of Early Egypt*. (ed. J. Spencer). London: BMP., pp. 128–39.

Shekib, L., el-Shimi, N. and el-Khodary, L. 1992. Effect of dehulling and cooking process on the nutritional quality of some Egyptian legume seeds. *Journal of Medicinal Research Institute* 13(3): 109–22.

Sickenberger, E. 1901. *Contributions a la Flore d'Egypte*. Cairo.

Simoons, F. 1994. *Eat not this flesh: Food avoidance in the Old World*. Madison: University of Wisconsin Press.

Sist, L. 1987. Food production. In *Egyptian Civilization: Daily Life*. (ed.) A.M. Donadoni Roveri. Milan: Electa, pp. 46–75.

Smartt, J. and Simmonds, N. M. (eds.). 1995. *Evolution of Crop Plants*. Harlow, Essex: Longman Scientific and Technical.

Smith, W. 1997. The agricultural practices and economy of an Egyptian Late Antique monastery: an archaeobotanical case study. Doctoral dissertation. University of Leicester, England.

Stager, L. 1985. The first fruits of civilization. *In Palestine in the Bronze and Iron Ages: Papers in Honour of Olga Tufnell*. (ed. J.N. Tubb). Occasional Publication 11. London: Institue of Archaeology, pp. 172–87.

Stahl, A. 1989. Plant food processing: implications for dietary quality. In *Foraging and Farming: The Evolution of Plant Exploitation*. (eds. D. Harris and G. Hillman). London: Unwin and Hyman, pp. 171–94.

Stol, M. 1987. Garlic, onion, leek. *BSA*. 3: 57–80.

Strouhal, E. 1992. *Life in Ancient Egypt*. Cambridge: CUP.

Täckholm, V. 1961. Botanical identifications of the plants found at the Monastery of Phoebammon. In *Le Monastère de Phoebammon dans la Thébaïde – Tome III*. (ed. C. Bachatly). Cairo: La Société d'Archéologie Copte, pp. 1–38.

1977. Flora. In *LÄ* Band II. Erntefest-Hordjedef (eds. W. Helck and E. Otto). Vol. 2. Wiesbaden: Otto Harrassowitz, pp. 267–75.

Täckholm, V., and Drar, M. 1950. *Flora of Egypt*. vol. II. Cairo: Fouad I University Press.

1954. *Flora of Egypt*. vol. III. Cairo: Fouad I University Press.

Tallet, P. 1995. Le shedeh, étude d'un procédé de vinification en Egypte ancienne. *BIFAO*, 95: 45992.

Thanheiser, U. 1986. *Investigation of the possibility of agrarian change under Asiatic influence at Avaris*. Unpublished M.Sc. dissertation. Institute of Archaeology. University College London.

1991. Untersuchungen zur Landwirtschaft der vor-und früh-dynastischen Zeit in Tell-el-Fara'in-Buto. *Agypten und Levante* II. Wein: Verlag der Osterreichischen A. de Wissenschaften, pp. 39–45.

1992. Plant food at Tell Ibrahim Awad: preliminary report. In *The Nile Delta in Transition: 4th–3rd Millennium BC* (ed. E. van der Brink). Tel Aviv: Edwin van der Brink, pp. 117–22.

forthcoming. Ueber den Ackerbau in dynastischer Zeit. Ergebnisse der Untersuchungen von Pflanzenresten aus Tell el-Dab'a. *Tell el-Dab'a VIII: Interdisziplinaere Studien.* (eds M. Bietak, J. Dorner, J. Boessneck and A. van den Driesch, H. Egger, U. Thanheiser). Vienna: Austrian Academy of Sciences.

Townsend, C.C. and Guest, E. (eds.) 1966–85. *Flora of Iraq* vols. 1, 2, 3, 4, 8, 9. (vol. 1 ed. by E. Guest). Baghdad: Ministry of Agriculture.

van der Veen, M. 1996. The plant remains from Mons Claudianus, a Roman quarry settlement in the Eastern Desert of Egypt - an interim report. *Vegetation History and Archaeobotany*, 5 (1–2): 137–41.

1998. A life of luxury in the desert? The food and fodder supply to Mons Claudianus. *Journal of Roman Archaeology* 11: 101–16.

forthcoming. *Life on the fringe – Living in the southern Egyptian deserts during the Roman and early Byzantine periods.* Leiden: CNWS.

van Zeist, W. 1985. Pulses and oil crops. *BSA*. II: 33–8.

1988. Plant remains from a First Dynasty burial at Tell Ibrahim Awad. In *The Archaeology of the Nile Delta: Problems and Priorities.* (ed. E. van der Brink). Amsterdam: NFARE, pp. 111–14.

van Zeist, W. and Bakker-Heeres, J. 1982. Archaeobotanical studies in the Levant 1. Neolithic sites in the Damascus Basin: Aswad, Ghoraife, Ramad. *Palaeohistoria* 24: 165–256.

van Zeist, W., and de Roller, G. 1993. Plant remains from Maadi, a Predynastic site in Lower Egypt. *Vegetation History and Archaeobotany* 2: 1–14.

de Vartavan, C. 1990. Contaminated plant foods from the tomb of Tutankhamun: a new interpretative system. *JAS*. 17: 473–94.

de Vartavan, C., and Asensi Amorós, V. 1997. *Codex of Ancient Egyptian Plant Remains.* London: Triade Exploration.

Venit, M.S. 1989. The painted tomb from Wardian and the antiquity of the *saqiya* in Egypt. *JARCE*. 26: 219–22.

Vermeeren, C. forthcoming. Identification criteria for distinguishing *Cucumis melo* and *C. sativus* seeds.

de Vries, F. 1991. Chufa (*Cyperus esculentus*, Cyperaceae): A weedy cultivar or a cultivated weed? *Economic Botany* 45(1): 27–37.

Wallert, I. 1962. *Die Palmen im Alten Ägyten.* Munchner Ägyptologische Studien 1. Berlin: Bruno Hessling.

Waly, N.W. 1996. Identified wood specimens from Tut Ankh Amon funerary furniture. *Taeckholmia* 16: 61–74.

Ward, P.N. 1993. Systems of agricultural production in the Delta. In *The Agriculture of Egypt.* (ed. G. M. Craig). Oxford: Oxford University Press, pp. 229–64.

Wasylikowa, K., Schild, R., Wendorf, F., Królik, H., Kubiak-Martens, L. and Harlan, J. 1995. Archaeobotany of the early Neolithic site E–75–6 at Nabta Playa, Western Desert, south Egypt. *Acta Palaeobotanica* 35(1): 133–55.

Watson, A. 1983. *Agricultural Innovation in the Early Islamic World: The Diffusion of Crops and Farming Techniques, 700–1100.* Cambridge: CUP.

Wendorf, F., Schild, R., (assemblers) and Close, A. (ed.). 1989. The Prehistory of Wadi Kubbaniya. vol. 2: Stratigraphy, Palaeoeconomy and Environment. Vol. 3: Late Palaeolithic Archaeology. Dallas: Southern Methodist University Press.

Wetterstrom, W. 1982. Plant remains. In *Quseir al Qadim 1980: Preliminary Report.* D. (eds D.Whitcomb and J. Johnson). Malibu: Undena Publications, pp. 355–77.

1984. The plant remains. In *Archaeological Investigations at El-Hibeh 1980: Preliminary report.* (ed. R. Wenke). Malibu: Undena Publications, pp. 50–77.

1986. *Ecology and agricultural intensification in Predynastic Egypt.* Unpublished final report to National Science Foundation. Washington, D. C.

1992. Plant remains from the Giza bakery/brewery. *Unpublished paper delivered to the Society for American Archaeology Annual Meeting.*

1993. Foraging and farming in Egypt: the transition from hunting and gathering to horticulture in the Nile valley. In *The Archaeology of Africa: Food, Metals and Towns.* (eds. P.S.T. Shaw, B. Andah, and A. Okpoko). One World Archaeology. London: Routledge. pp. 165–226.

Wilkinson, J.G. 1878. *The Manners and Customs of the Ancient Egyptians.* vols. I–III. London: John Murray.

Wilkinson, T.J. 1988. The archaeological component of agricultural soils in the Middle East: the effects of manuring in antiquity. In *Man-made Soils.* (eds. W. Groenman-van-Waateringe and M. Robinson). Oxford: OUP., pp. 93–114.

Willcox, G. 1992. Timber and trees: ancient exploitation in the Middle East: Evidence from plant remains. *BSA*. 6: 1–31.

Willerding, U. and Wolf, G. 1990. Paläeo-ethnobotanische Untersuchungen von Pflanzenresten aus dem 1. Jahr-tausend v. Chr. von Elephantine. *Mitteilungen des Deutschen Archäologischen Instituts*, 46: 263–7.

Wilson, H. 1988. *Egyptian food and drink.* Aylesbury: Shire Publications.

Wiltshire, P. 1995. The effect of food processing on the palatability of wild fruits with high tannin content. In *Res archaeobotanicae.* 9th Symposium IWGP. (eds H. Kroll and R. Pasternak). Kiel: Institut für Ur-und Frühgeschichte der Christian-Albrecht-Universität, pp. 49–68.

Wreszinski, W. 1915. *Atlas zur Altaegyptischen Kulturgeschichte.* Pt. 1. Leipzig: J.C. Hinrichs'sche Buchhandlung.

Wrigley, G. 1995. Date palm. In *Evolution of Crop Plants.* (eds J. Smartt and N. M. Simmonds). Harlow, Essex: Longman Scientific and Technical. pp. 399–403.

Zahran, M.A., and Willis, A.J. 1992. *The Vegetation of Egypt.* London: Chapman and Hall.

Zohary, D. 1992. Domestication of the Neolithic Near Eastern crop assemblage. In *Préhistoire de L'Agriculture: Nouvelles Approches Expérimentales et Ethnographiques* (ed. P. Anderson). Monographie du Centre de Recherches Archéologiques 6. Paris: Éditions du CNRS, pp. 81–86.

1995. Fig. In *Evolution of Crop Plants.* (eds. J. Smartt and N. M. Simmonds). Harlow, Essex: Longman Scientific and Technical. pp. 366–70.

1996. The mode of domestication of the founder crops of Southwest Asian agriculture. In *The Origins and Spread of Agriculture and Pastoralism in Eurasia.* (ed. D. Harris). London: UCL Press, pp. 142–58.

Zohary, D., and Hopf, M. 1994. *Domestication of Plants in the Old*

World: The Origin and Spread of Cultivated Plants in West Asia, Europe and the Nile Valley. 2nd edn. Oxford: Clarendon Press.

Zohary, D., and Speigel-Roy, P. 1975. Beginnings of fruit growing in the Old World. *Science* 187: 319–27.

Zohary, M. 1966, 1972. *Flora Palaestina*. vols. 1, 2. Jerusalem: Israel Academy of Sciences.

1982. *Plants of the Bible*. Cambridge: CUP.

25. Meat processing

SALIMA IKRAM

Introduction

Prior to animal domestication, the only access the Egyptians had to meat was through hunting, fowling, and fishing. Until the Old Kingdom this was relatively easy since the moister climate supported a large and diverse fauna in the area of the Nile Valley, as well as in the Red Sea Hills (Butzer 1976: 13). Many of these species are now locally extinct. It was from these wild animals that the Egyptians derived their main domesticates: sheep and goats, cattle, pigs, donkeys and poultry. In most cases domestication occurred before the Dynastic period. Some of the domesticated species of herd animals (sheep, goat, pig, possibly cattle) might have arrived in Egypt via Asia, and could have been bred with local stock to become regular agricultural staples (Butzer 1976: 8). Initially, however, it appears that the Egyptians did not limit their attempts at domestication to these animals, since tomb decoration shows 'wild' animals, such as hyena, oryx, addax and other types of antelope, being force-fed in a farming context (Smith 1969). Faunal remains from the Old Kingdom onwards corroborate this artistic evidence for such unusual food animals.

It is very difficult to establish the specific chronological points at which different animals became truly domesticated. Domestication implies human intervention in breeding animals by choosing them for specific traits that are beneficial to human kind (Clutton-Brock 1989), as opposed to a situation in which wild animals were tamed, eaten or used in some other manner. Thee would be very few obvious physical indications of this change. The only visible changes are those wrought upon bone structure and teeth; unless bones from Egyptian sites are extensively studied nothing can be determined about when animals were domesticated.

There has been much discussion as to the origins of most of the Egyptian domesticated animals. Some scholars believe that wild (long-horned) cattle arrived in Egypt via Asia in *c.* 6000–4000 BC, and were domesticated thereafter (Ghoneim 1977: 17; Epstein 1971: 554). Epstein (1971: 288) believes that the short-horned cattle came to Egypt from Asia towards the middle of the third millenium BC, and that the first archaeological evidence for them comes from Upper Egypt (e.g. Badari: Brunton and Caton-Thompson 1928: 38, 44) and the Fayum (Epstein 1971: 213; Caton-Thompson and Gardner 1934: 34). However, the evidence collected by Darby (1977: 90), supported by the study of fossils (Boessneck and von den Driesch 1982; Boessneck 1988: 13), dates the appearance of cattle in Egypt to the Pleistocene period. This is confirmed by the findings of Gautier (1980: 323, 1987: 433) who also has archaeological evidence of domestic cattle in Egypt dating from the late Palaeolithic onward (see also Wendorf *et al.* 1987: 447). Thus, the date of introduction of the earliest bovids in Egypt is disputed, although a very early date (perhaps sometime in the seventh millennium BC) seems feasible. It is probable that cattle were domesticated in Egypt independent of similar, and perhaps earlier, activities in Asia. It is generally agreed that ovicaprids (sheep and goats) were imported from Asia, via Syria, in the Neolithic, and then domesticated (Gautier 1980: 336).

Once the Egyptians had domesticated their 'staple' animals (sheep, goats, cattle, pigs and poultry), and had established places to keep them, they then had a fairly dependable source of protein at hand and were no longer entirely reliant on hunting. However, hunting, fishing and fowling all contributed not only to the meat supply but also to the diversification of the ancient Egyptian diet by the addition of wild animals such as antelopes, gazelles, hippopotami, hedgehogs, rabbits, fifty-six (or more) species of fish (Brewer and Friedman 1989) and innumerable species of birds.

Mammalian, piscian and avian meat (muscle tissue) would have been an important part of the ancient Egyptian diet. Meat consists of about 20 per cent protein, 20 per cent fat and 60 per cent water; it also contains a small percentage of the vitamins and minerals which are important for the nourishment and growth of the human body. These constituents differ depending on the type of animal, its age at slaughter, the type of feed it has eaten, the specific joint of meat and the leanness of the piece. The most important component of meat is protein, which provides the organic basis for structures such as muscle, cartilage, skin, tendons and hair. Protein also supplies amino acids necessary for the formation of new and depleted body protein, which not only builds, maintains and repairs tissue, but also provides 11 per cent of human energy intake. Although protein is obtainable from other sources, such as legumes, animal protein is recommended for humans as it is more efficiently absorbed by the human body than protein of vegetable origin. A deficiency of protein in any diet can result in poor muscle tone and posture, lowered resistance to disease, premature ageing, anaemia, stunted growth, tissue degeneration, oedema and slow recovery from illness or surgery.

Egyptian animal-slaughtering techniques

The first step towards consuming an animal is to kill it. All mammals, regardless of size, would have been butchered in the same way with some variations occurring for flaying and jointing, whereas birds and fish were killed in different ways. Evidence for ancient Egyptian methods of slaughtering animals comes not only from artistic and literary evidence, but also from cut-marks on bones found in archaeological contexts and from funerary offerings of food. Ethnographic and experimental studies further supplement the traditional sources of information and are especially useful in interpreting the artistic record.

Mammals

The first step in the sequence of killing a mammal is to bring it down to the ground. Large animals (antelopes, oxen) were brought down by lassooing and wrestling the animal to the ground which was then laid on its back with its feet trussed (Fig. 25.1). Smaller animals were merely wrestled to the ground and trussed or held still by the butcher's assistants during the subsequent operation.

Once the ox was laid trussed on its back, held by the butcher's assistants, the butcher would turn its throat to one side and cut it, severing the carotid artery, as is still done in Egypt today. Some scholars believe that an earlier custom entailed stupefying the victim by striking it on the head before slaughter (David 1973: 320; Otto 1950), but there is no evidence to support this claim (see Ikram 1996: 45–6). The painted reliefs in the Fifth-Dynasty tomb of Ptahhotep at Saqqara (Quibell 1898: 31, pl. 35) show that a *wʿb*-priest would often examine the animal for purity and health by testing its blood and entrails, much as is done by modern-day meat inspectors. After the throat was cut, the blood was drained from the body by pumping the foreleg of the animal, thereby forcing the blood to flow out from the severed veins and arteries of the neck. This helps explain why the foreleg is given so much attention even before it is cut off as an offering to the gods – it is a vital component of the 'pump' used to empty the body of blood, thus preventing spoilage of the meat. The head and foreleg could be severed from the body at this point, although this was not always the case.

After the animal was killed, it was flayed (see section on butchery in Chapter 12, this volume). There are no detailed scenes showing the process of flaying an animal, but ethnographic evidence aids in interpreting the probable sequence of subsequent events (Ikram 1996). The animal was skinned, starting with a cut made from its hind legs above the tarsals, which was carried down the inside of its legs along the belly, thus enabling the skin to be peeled away. In ancient Egypt (just as in modern times), this operation would have continued on the ground, if the animal was full-grown. However, if the animal was a young or small one, then the operation was performed with the carcass hanging on a tree from its hind legs. Once the skin had been removed it was put to one side, and the entrails were removed by making a slit from below the genitals all the way down to its belly, and pulling the viscera out of the body cavity.

In the tombs of Rameses III (KV35) and Ipuy (TT217) the entrails of the butchered animal are shown hanging on a line with other cuts of meat. Herodotus (II: 39–40; see Godley 1946: 321–4) states that the Egyptians left the entrails in the carcass, but this is most unlikely to have been the case, since, once the dead animal's intestines are cut, the visceral contents will rapidly infect the body cavity unless they are removed (J. Heath pers. comm. 1990). After the removal of the viscera the animal could be jointed and consumed or preserved.

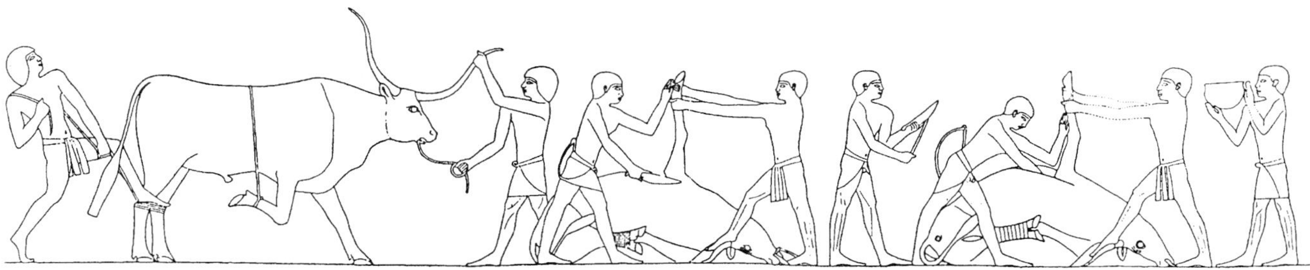

Figure 25.1 Scene of butchery in the Fifth-Dynasty tomb of Ty at Saqqara.

There are a number of unusual early representations of oryxes being slaughtered in a different manner. One of the scenes in the Fourth-Dynasty tomb of Nefermaat and Atet at Meidum shows a man seizing a standing oryx by its horns with one hand, while he cuts its throat with a knife held in the other hand. This representation is virtually unique to Meidum and to the oryx, although similar scenes of the slaughter of an oryx appear in the Luxor temple, dating to the reign of Amenhotep III, as well as some reliefs of the Late Period. These scenes are thought to have a complex symbolic meaning including the killing of the god Apophis and the provision of offerings for the king and gods (Derchain 1962: 27, 30–6). Modern butchers are unanimous in the view that such a method of slaughter was practically impossible, and that the closest one could get to killing such small standing animals (sheep, gazelle or goat) would be to straddle the body and grip it firmly between one's legs while holding the throat back by the horns or hair; although modern butchers deem this method of slaughter feasible, none of them actually recommend it. It is unclear whether there is any symbolic meaning attached to this particular mode of killing the oryx, or whether this was an initial way of slaughtering medium-sized animals (these tombs show smaller mammals such as goats being suspended from tree branches to aid in their despatching).

Poultry

In the case of poultry, representations in tomb-chapels show that birds, once captured by nets, throwsticks, or traps, were killed by strangulation, as they still are in many countries. This is despite the fact that such a technique of despatch would have caused the bird's arteries and veins to clog with blood, potentially encouraging disease. In modern Egypt, by contrast, the bird's throat is cut to make sure it bleeds, both out of respect for Islamic dietary law and fear of disease.

Non-bleeding is practiced today in many Western countries when game birds (including duck and geese) are either shot or strangled and then hung up to age and settle without being eviscerated. Modern butchers advise that mature game birds should be hung for up to six or seven days, and young birds for three or four days, although pigeons and quail are eaten fresh (Hume and Downes 1963: 254, 263). In some European countries, the viscera are left in the bird's body after it is dead, the neck is tied with string, and the body is beaten with sticks, thus releasing the enzymes and micro-organisms in the intestines which tenderise the meat and give it a distinct flavour; one or two days later, the viscera are removed from the body through a small slit in the ventral side of the bird, and the meat is consumed after being well-cooked (J. Heath pers. comm. 1990). The hanging of the birds without evisceration can be quite dangerous if they are not cleaned thoroughly or well-cooked prior to eating, as they can develop toxins (Montagné and Gottschalk 1961: 357).

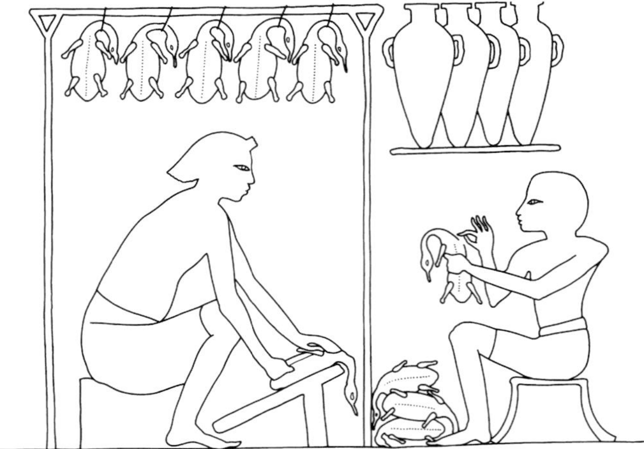

Figure 25.2 Scene of poultry processing in the Eighteenth-Dynasty tomb of Nakht at Thebes (TT52).

Ancient Egyptian poultry, however, did have their internal organs removed. When the birds are portrayed hanging up after being killed or placed on offering tables, they have slits in their ventral surfaces through which the viscera had been removed (see Fig. 25.2). Despite the artistic evidence mentioned above, it seems that the birds which were prepared as 'victual mummies' (ducks, geese and pigeons) were not strangled. Goodman (1987) studied the carcasses of such mummified birds and did not find any evidence of haematoma, a feature associated with strangulation; instead, he writes that in a few examples he found 'a considerable concentration of blood in the chest cavity, which . . . seems characteristic of slaughter by having the throat cut'. Thus, the physical data contradict the pictorial evidence from the tomb reliefs. It is possible that the ways in which the Egyptians dispatched poultry depended on how quickly they were to be consumed. The birds that were to be eaten immediately may have been strangled, while those that were to be preserved for later use might have had their throats cut and been bled.

After the neck of the bird was wrung, most reliefs show that it was plucked before being processed further. The head poulterer is depicted strangling and eviscerating the birds while an assistant sits nearby and plucks them (Fig. 25.2). The modern practice of immersing the feathered bird in a pot of boiling or hot water to facilitate plucking was either not practiced in the interest of preserving fuel, or was simply not depicted. After plucking, the feet, wing tips (and sometimes the heads) of the birds were frequently cut off. This was the case with the ancient birds which the author studied, but this was not an invariable rule, since two of the roasted spatch-cocked ducks from an unspecified Nineteenth-Dynasty worker's tomb at Deir el-Medina (Louvre E14551) still preserve their feet but are without their heads or wing tips. Such discrepancies can, however, be attributed to carelessness and a desire for the speedy procurement of funerary goods; in the ideal world of the after-life such omissions would not be expected to occur, since the birds' feet are always shown to be severed when depicted in the funerary reliefs and paintings.

Fish

Evidence for the methods used for catching and killing fish comes mainly from two-dimensional representations; these show that most fish, once caught in nets, traps, or on hooks, required little in the way of 'slaughtering'. They were generally pulled ashore or aboard the boat and left to die by asphixiation. Occasionally when a large fish was captured it was hit over the head to stun or kill it. A fine three-dimensional example illustrating this action appears in the boating model from the early Middle Kingdom tomb of Meketra at Deir el-Bahari (Metropolitan 20.3.6 and Cairo JE6085) and two-dimensional examples illustrating the same action can be seen in the Sixth-Dynasty *mastaba* of Kagemni and the Fifth-Dynasty *mastaba* of Idut at Saqqara (see Porter and Moss 1981: 618).

After the fish was caught, 'it was laid, belly down, on a block or a flat, sloped board. It was then cut in a downward stroke along the vertebral column, after which the viscera was removed . . . the head and vertebral column . . . was often left intact. In some cases the fish was opened from the belly instead of down the back' (Brewer and Friedman 1989: 12). The fish were left for further processing once they had been slit and emptied of their viscera. Frequently scenes showing the evisceration of fish include the removal and processing of the roes (mainly from *Mugil cephalus*) as part of the scene (see Fig. 25.3).

Figure 25.3 Scene of fish and roe processing in the Fifth-Dynasty tomb of Ty at Saqqara.

The fish do not appear to have been scaled, although this is difficult to determine from the representations. Certainly the dried fish which were found as funerary offerings in the tomb of Kha (TT8) at Deir el-Medina (Cairo JE315 and 44038; see Bruyère 1937: 107; Schiaparelli 1927: 159–60), as well as examples from other funerary contexts (e.g. BM EA36191), were unscaled, although they had been dried and perhaps salted. Given that fish scales have been found in middens and elsewhere on archaeological sites, it is likely that some fish were scaled but that this part of the processing did not figure in the representations.

Techniques of preservation

Introduction

After slaughtering any animal, a choice must usually be made between consuming it immediately or preserving it for later use. If consumption is immediate, then the animal is killed, jointed in the case of mammals, and eaten either directly or after the meat has been hung up for a few hours. The author has found experimentally that joints of meat can remain medically safe to eat for up to eight hours in the Egyptian climate in summer (if kept in a shaded area), and for twelve to sixteen hours in winter. The choice of storage-place greatly affects this 'safe' period and the overall quality of preservation. With poultry, the length of standing time depends on the species. In modern Egypt, geese and ducks are occasionally killed two to three hours before consumption, although this practice is uncommon, and never occurs in the case of chickens, since the bacteria breed in them more quickly than in other poultry. It should be noted, however, that there is scant evidence for chicken (*Gallus gallus*) in Egypt during the Dynastic period. There is no faunal evidence for it prior to the Ptolemaic period (see MacDonald and Edwards 1993) and the only clear pictorial representation in the Dynastic period is a New Kingdom ostracon from Thebes (BM EA68539).

If meat is not consumed immediately after slaughter, it has to be preserved in some way. Preserved meat provides a ready supply of protein in lean times or for travelling, as well as a means of storing any excess produced by the slaughter of an animal. A fattened ox, for example, will provide more meat than is immediately consumable in one meal by a family, therefore the excess would have to be somehow preserved in order to prevent spoilage. There were several methods of preserving meat available to the ancient Egyptians: drying, salting (dry and wet), smoking, a combination of any of these methods, pemmicaning, or curing with fat, beer or honey.

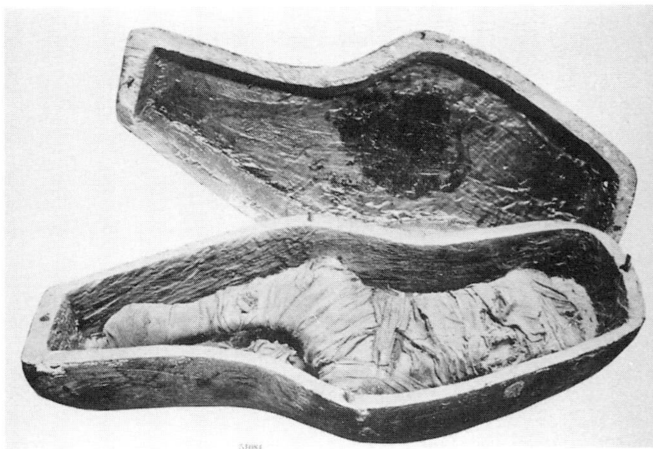

Figure 25.4 Victual mummy and coffinet (Cairo CG51084) from the tomb of Yuya and Tuyu (KV46).

Through the scientific study of archaeological evidence in the form of ancient meat samples and faunal remains, the critical examination of relevant representations, models, texts, and the comparison of such material with ethnographic, ethnohistoric and experimental evidence, we may reach tentative conclusions concerning specific meat preservation technologies utilised by the ancient Egyptians. The most valuable source of archaeological evidence available for the study of meat processing are 'victual mummies'. Although Bruyère (1937: 160) reports finding dried meat in small siltware vessels at the site of Deir el-Medina, he does not describe or test them, and, given that the meat disintegrated shortly after the excavation, there is little or no information to be derived from these findings.

The 'victual mummies' take a variety of shapes: entire joints, slabs (Fig. 25.4), strips, as well as poultry. Found exclusively in thirteen Theban tombs of the New Kingdom and Third Intermediate Period (KV34, KV35, KV36, KV43, KV46, KV60, KV62, QV46, QV51, TT358, the Twenty-first-Dynasty tomb of Istemkheb D at Deir el-Bahari, the burial of Henutmehyt, and the tomb of Amenemhat Q, the latter excavated by the Metropolitan Museum of Art in 1918–19). The only other possible examples are the offerings from the Middle Kingdom burial of Princess Nubhotepikhered at Dahshur, which consist of joints of meat or entire birds that are wrapped in bandages. Most of these bandaged meats were placed in individual sycamore-wood 'coffinets' shaped to the form and dimensions of the meat (Fig. 25.4). Some of the mummies are coloured brown; it is possible that a roasted appearance (browning) was given to victual mummies by the application of very hot resin on the wrapping which cooked the exterior surface of the mummy (Lortet and Gaillard 1905–9: I, 248). It is more likely, however, that the hot resin was applied to the 'coffinets' containing the mummies in order to firmly seal and waterproof them, and that this resin only accidently adhered to the bandaged joints causing them to be browned when they were placed inside the box. The browning can therefore be considered irrelevant to the actual process of meat preservation.

The following sections outline the basic methods of preservation available to the ancient Egyptians and evaluate their probable use in the context of the sources of evidence mentioned above.

Drying

Sun-and-air drying

Sun-and-air drying is the most common, quick, and straightforward way of preserving meat and is especially popular as the basic method of preservation in hot, dry countries, such as Egypt. The Plains Indians of the United States dry entire steers, including the viscera, cutting up a mature animal into pieces suitable for drying in five to six hours, (Weltfish 1965: 217); this is a technique which would have been available to the ancient Egyptians. Indeed, many representations of meat processing might be interpreted as showing sun-and-air dried meat (Fig. 25.5). The process of sun-and-air drying involves cutting off pieces of meat, preferably from a lean part of the animal, and then hanging them up in the sun and air to dry. Although the entire animal can be dried in this way, the cut of meat favoured for drying varies from culture to culture.

Depending on the temperature, humidity and thickness of the cut of meat involved, sun-drying takes from one to three weeks. Meat thus treated can last for up to two years, although consumption in the last few months of this period is not always medically safe (Dahl and Hjort 1976: 169). It is preferable for meat prepared in this way to be consumed within a year. The main problem with the process is that while the meat is drying, the outer parts of the cut dry first, trapping some internal water, and leaving a moist inner section which can cause the meat partially to spoil (Pyke 1970: 175; Dahl and Hjort 1976: 169; J. Heath pers. comm. 1990). If any of this internal liquid is contaminated by bacteria, the meat spoils completely and becomes inedible. This eventuality can be avoided, however, by careful regulation of the thickness of the cut to three to five centimetres, or by the addition of salt (see p. 663).

Pounding and drying

Pounding the meat before it is dried in order to thin it into even slices expels much of the water that is so damaging to the chances of successful preservation, and is a variation on simple drying. The meat is sliced, pounded thin with a stone, and hung up on a line to air-dry in the sun. As a further protection, salt can be rubbed into the meat before it is dried, although the thinner the meat, the less essential is this refinement.

Some reliefs, mainly from Old Kingdom Memphite *mastaba*-tombs, provide evidence for pounded-and-dried meat. They show a man near a butchery sequence beating an

Figure 25.5 Scene of butchery, the hanging of meat, and the processing of meat in Twelfth-Dynasty tomb of Intefiqer at Thebes (TT60).

unidentified object with a stone (Forbes 1965: 193; Klebs 1934: 91). This has also been interpreted either as a non-meat related activity, or as the hammering of meat to soften it before it is cooked (Klebs 1934: 91). Nearby there is often a line with hanging cuts of meat, although this appears more frequently in Middle Kingdom depictions. There are at least two representations from the Old Kingdom (MMA 08.201.1 and Petrie Museum UC14311) and one representation from the Middle Kingdom (*in situ* in Theban tomb TT60) which show meat being cut into thin pieces, pounded, and then hung up to dry.

Pounding and sun-and-air drying is a common way of preserving meat, still used by Africans and Native Americans (Weltfish 1965: 212–21) today. It is possible that the ancient Egyptian term *iwf dr*, which is usually translated simply as 'preserved meat', with the precise method of preservation being unknown (Hayes 1951: 91–2; Pendlebury 1951: 169–70; Leahy 1978: 16), may actually refer to meat thus processed. Pendlebury suggested that the word *dr* means pressed (1951: 169–70), giving the alternative translation of 'pressed meat'. Other translations of this word also support the idea that *iwf dr* is pounded or flattened meat, which would have been removed from the bone with the water already expelled from it; Faulkner (1976: 314–15) translates *dr* as to 'subdue' or 'repress', as well as to 'expel' or 'remove', meaning that water was expelled from the meat. Peet and Woolley (1923: 167) suggest that the term implies that the meat was removed from the bone before preservation, a theory supported by the butchery marks found on the bones from Malkata (Binford 1981; Ikram 1996: 145–6 and fig. 30). Furthermore, the storage jars with slightly carinated bodies and pointed bases, termed 'meat jars' by the excavators due to their being inscribed with the legend *iwf dr*, are of a shape and dimension that does not permit the insertion of a joint with a bone, but could have accommodated thin dried and flexible pieces of meat (their maximum meaurements are: sixty-six centimetres deep, and thirty centimetres wide; see Peet and Woolley 1923: pls. XLVIIII, XLIX, LIII; Frankfort and Pendlebury 1933: 112, type XII). It is possible that the jars contained meat that was preserved through some other or additional process, but all the jars were found empty and, as yet, no residue analysis has been performed on the sherds.

Boiling and drying

The last permutation of dried meat is that which results from boiling and drying, a process still used in Nigeria and China. Chunks of meat are first boiled in water, since heat and boiling are very effective in killing micro-organisms (pathogenic and putrefactive agents), especially surface micro-organisms. The meat is then put in an airy and sunny place to dry. In China, chopped-up pieces of meat are boiled with a variety of spices until the water evaporates, then the meat is deemed ready to be hung in a well-ventilated area and dried (A. Huang pers. comm. 1992). The method – which was also once used by the Plains Indians (Weltfish 1965: 217–21) – is most efficient (but not exclusively so) when small pieces of meat (about twenty centimetres long) are treated as they dry rapidly thereby giving fewer chances for microbial growth and infection. However, this method does extract the water-soluble protein and liquid fat from the meat, thereby lowering its nutritional value.

This boil-and-dry method of preservation may possibly have occurred in ancient Egypt, but the time required for boiling (depending on the amount and the thickness of the meat) would have been inefficient in terms of fuel. Stoves/fires with pots containing large joints with bones in them that appear in butchery scenes might argue for this method of preservation, but are not entirely convincing, as they could represent cooking for consumption in the near future, rather than long-term preservation. They might also depict brining rather than mere boiling (see p. 663).

Figure 25.6 Scene of dried duck in the Nineteenth-Dynasty tomb of Ipuy at Thebes (TT217).

Drying fish

Drying was (and still is) also the easiest way to preserve fish. All tomb representations of fish-processing can be interpreted as showing this process. Fish were first slit along the backbone, gutted, washed, and left in the open air and sun to dry (Fig. 25.3). Egyptians still clean out their fish in this manner; removing the intestines as soon as possible was the most important act of processing, as fish spoils faster than mammalian/avian meat, especially in the heat. Washing the fish was also a vital prelude to their safe consumption. Exposure to the sun not only removes surplus water, but exposes the fish to the antiseptic agency of ultraviolet light. It has also been suggested that fish were cut along their backs so that the thickest section would dry more easily (Keimer 1939: 228). In accordance with a majority of representations, fish could have easily been dried on the ground, although in some cases they are shown suspended on a line as in the case of meat (Fig. 25.5) and poultry (Fig. 25.6). The suspended method would have been optimal as air would circulate around the fish, thus ensuring that it dried evenly all over. Sometimes the fish were decapitated, but scales were normally left on dried fish. Herodotus (II: 92) mentions drying as the favoured method of preserving fish in ancient Egypt (Godley 1946: 379). Papyrus Anastasi IV (15, 7) includes reports of dried and preserved *buri, shena* and other fish that were to be found in the Egyptian Delta, and were distributed throughout Egypt and abroad (Caminos 1954: 200, 210–11; Hayes 1951: 160). The temple of Hathor at the Timna copper mines and the associated copper-smelting camps in the Negev region contained fish remains, including *Claridae*, the Nile catfish. Since Timna is located in the desert, any riverine fish found there must have had to be transported from some distance, and would therefore presumably have had to be dried (Rothenberg 1988: 244–5).

Many actual fish remains found in Egyptian tombs have been described as 'dried', but not all of these had been split open in the manner shown in representations. The fish found in the Theban tomb of Kha (TT8) were gutted and split, although not opened, and examples from the workmen's village at Deir el-Medina (Cairo JE 315 and 44038) were not even gutted, possibly having been salted whole rather than dried (see p. 663). However, other fish from Deir el-Medina must have been gutted and dried, since the ostraca and other textual sources from the site describe them as such (see Griffith 1898: 97). The dried fish in the collection of the British Museum (e.g. BM EA36191) are gutted but not split open. This splitting and drying of fish seems to be unique to the ancient Egyptians, as Radcliffe (1921: 355, n. 4) notes that Greeks and Copts 'rarely split their fish before packing them in large earthen pots'.

All representations of fish being consumed show fish which are closed, i.e. not spread open as they are when dried. This is not surprising, for dried fish were generally cooked or re-hydrated prior to consumption, both then and now, thus causing them to lose their splayed-out form. There is one exception to this, in the Eighteenth-Dynasty Memphite tomb of Horemheb (Martin 1989: pl. 33, 19–20), where people are shown consuming splayed-out dried fish.

Drying poultry

The Egyptians did not dry birds as they did fish and meat. The closest they came to drying birds was the case of the quail. According to Herodotus, quails, after migrating across the Mediterranean to Egypt, fell to the ground from exhaustion and were soon despatched. Some of them were hung, like joints of meat, and eaten shortly thereafter (Godley 1946: 365). It is more likely that these birds were hung up to improve the taste of their meat, since they were eaten raw (Lloyd 1976: 335). Indeed, all flesh improves in flavour if it is hung up temporarily as this allows the chemicals to reach equilibrium, rigor mortis to pass, and the meat to soften. This holds true both for mammalian and avian meat, and butchers and poulterers worldwide continue to suspend their meats. This would explain the presence of joints and birds hanging on lines over mammalian and avian processing sites in tomb representations (Figs. 25.2, 25.4–6). It should be noted, however, that there is no way of knowing whether raw birds or even raw fish were consumed during the Pharaonic period; the only references to the Egyptians' consumption of raw meat derive from the Greco–Roman period.

Only one tomb, that of Ipuy (TT217), contains painted decoration suggesting that birds were also dried (Fig. 25.6). The birds are shown hung up on lines and it has been suggested that they were 'either cured whole or cut in slices, which, after being hung up to dry on lines stretched between two posts, are potted in salt' (Davies 1927: 62). It is, however, by no means obvious that the strangely shaped objects on the line above the duck evisceration scene are

Figure 25.7 Scene of processing meat in the Eighteenth-Dynasty tomb of Thutnefer at Thebes (TT104).

indeed slices of drying duck. Unfortunately, no parallel to the scene exists, and contemporary ethnographic information, as well as information from butchers in the United States, Britain and the Middle East, provides no examples of the drying of fowl (see salting p. 663). Fowl flesh is unappetising when dry (with the exception of ostrich, which makes what is reputed to be 'delicious' biltong – see p. 665ff.); experiments show the results to be tough, inedible and very unpleasant. Rehydration or soaking the meat in a sauce might ameliorate the taste, but only to a limited extent. Furthermore, the chances of disease and pests in dried fowl flesh are much higher than in mammal or even fish meat, since poultry is denser, with a higher liquid content, and therefore does not dry thoroughly. This means that the meat has a propensity to spoil quickly and is particularly prone to bacterial infestation after death.

Paintings, reliefs and funerary models from tombs show that the practice of drying meat in ancient Egypt was prevalent; they often show pieces of meat and sometimes poultry strung up on a line, as well as gutted fish lying in the sun. In the case of beef or mutton, most scholars interpret these hanging pieces of meat on and off the bone as representations of the process of drying meat rather than the act of storing it when freshly butchered (e.g. Ghoneim 1977: 163–4). This might be the case with the triangular and long thin pieces of meat commonly featured in models and tombs (Fig. 25.7), but it is hard to believe that joints of meat containing tibias and femurs were being dried in this manner. It is possible to air-dry meat on the bone after boiling, although it is neither effective nor economical in terms of time and fuel. As mentioned above, Bruyère (1937: 160) describes finding dried meat in small silt vessels at Deir el-Medina, but he does not elaborate on the shape or chemical composition of the meat, so it remains uncertain if it was air-dried or salted and dried.

Wet and dry salt-curing

Salt curing is a very simple way of preserving meats of all kinds. Salt was widely available in ancient Egypt, as it is in Egypt today. It was found in the Wadi Natrun, the oases of Siwa, Kharga, Dakhla and Farafra, and the regions near Memphis, Thebes, Elkab and Lake Mareotis. In the coastal parts of the Delta region it was extracted from sea-water, while in areas further to the south it was taken from the marshes and even from the soil of the desert itself (Forbes 1965: 178). In addition, local deposits were scattered throughout Egypt. Salt sacks, cakes and bricks have all been found in tombs (Bruyère 1937: 152) and are mentioned in offering lists and as trade items (Janssen 1961: 83). We know that the Egyptians were capable of the process of salting meat, because both salt (NaCl) and natron (a form of salt) were frequently used in the preservation of formerly living organisms, including people and fish (Lucas 1962: 304; see also Chapter 16, this volume). There are two ways in which salt can be used for curing: the wet (brine) or the dry (salting) method. Wet-curing involves immersion in brine, and dry-curing entails packing in salt. Both wet- and dry salt-curing are used in modern times (Montagne and Gottschalk 1961: 358) and might easily have been used in ancient Egypt.

Wet salt-curing or brining

Meat brining/curing entails putting meat as chunks, fillets, or even cuts containing bone in a solution of salt and water, with occasionally a few other ingredients, and sealing it. This treatment is similar to that adopted for the curing of ham, or making salt beef. It takes several weeks, especially for larger pieces of meat, and meat thus cured lasts for one or more years depending on the amount of salt in the solution. Brining is most commonly used for preserving pork: salt improves the taste and is an effective agent against the harmful micro-organisms that find a good host in the pig.

According to Ingram (1962: 272), the basic modern brining recipe is:

20%	Salt (NaCl)
2%	Saltpetre/nitrate (KNi) [optional]
200 p.p.m.	Nitrite (NaNi) [optional]
1%	Sucrose (any sugar or honey will do)
77%	Water

This is the preferred modern method of meat preservation as salt and saltpetre prevent the activity of normal putrefactive bacteria in meat; only those very few organisms that are exceptionally tolerant of salt (or those that can obtain oxygen by reducing the nitrate or nitrite) will survive in a solution of brine (Ingram 1962: 272). The only health-related problem with brining is the fact that any disease (e.g. salmonella), if present in the meat or the brine, will be spread throughout the meat when there is insufficient salt. Brining also adversely affects the nutritive value and composition of the meat since 'when the salt penetrates the meat, [the] water and substances dissolved in it leave the meat. Among those substances are soluble protein, glucose and glucose phosphates, and lactic acid, derived from breakdown of muscle glycogen during rigor mortis in the carcass; probably small amounts of other sugars (e.g. ribose) and amino acids and pigments' (Ingram 1962: 272).

Herodotus (II: 77) writes that the Egyptians pickled birds in brine, stored them in large pots, and then consumed them raw (see Godley 1946: 365; Lloyd 1976: 335). In modern Egypt, no meat is eaten raw, and even salted meat is always cooked before consumption.

There is no record of salted birds in modern Egypt, but paintings in the Eighteenth-Dynasty Theban tomb of Nakht (TT52; Davies 1917: pls. XXII, XXIII) show birds being strangled, plucked, eviscerated and then put into large narrow-necked amphorae which possibly contained salt, either in a solid or a liquid state (see Fig. 25.2). Such an amphora containing preserved birds has been found in the tomb of Kha (TT8; Schiaparelli 1927: 159). The birds had been plucked, beheaded and eviscerated, and only some had their feet and wingtips removed. They had been preserved in salt, but it is unknown whether this was in solid or liquid form. It is more probable that they were brined; a solid salt would still be present unless the birds were brined, air-dried and then placed in the amphora. Birds found in squat pottery vessels from Balat (Mastaba V) were also preserved in salt, most probably in liquid form, due to the reasons mentioned above and the softness of their bones (Louis Chaix pers. comm. 1990). Although it is easy to see how birds could have been put into the amphorae when newly dead and malleable, how they were taken out when hardened and stiffened by salt is not so obvious. It is possible that the entire neck of the amphora was removed, thus giving easy access to the birds, and indeed Hope (1977: 48–58) notes that several of the large amphorae in the Eighteenth-Dynasty settlement at Malkata in western Thebes were found with their necks missing.

Herodotus also mentions the brining or pickling of fish (Lloyd 1976: 80), which involves immersing gutted fish in brine in a large vessel, such as an amphora, sealing it securely and leaving it for ten to twelve days. This is considered by some nutritionists to be the safest way of preserving fish (Dumont 1977: 136), but the higher the content of salt and water, the less protein can be derived from fish preserved in this way, due to being immersed in a solution (Proctor 1972: 146). Another problem with brined fish is that certain micro-organisms or even dermestid beetles reproduce and live in the liquid salt medium (Proctor 1972: 148). It is quite possible that the amphorae shown in the vicinity of the fish-processing scenes in several Old, Middle and New Kingdom tombs (see Ikram 1996: 304–5) were used for both wet and dry salting.

All salted and dried fish would have had to have been washed and soaked prior to consumption, and generally they would have been cooked as well. Although dried or dried-and-salted fish might have been consumed without cooking, this would have been inadvisable due to the presence of bacterial and pest infestation. Using brine in conjunction with other technologies is also popular today as a method of preservation. Partial drying (air-drying), for instance, can be combined with pickling in brine, again a technique favoured for pork (Pyke 1970: 175) as well as poultry. This method has the advantage of being quicker than simple brining and more efficient in eradicating bacteria. The excavations in the New Kingdom workmen's village at Deir el-Medina revealed ducks and pigeons which may have been salted and dried (Bruyère 1934: 156, 200–1), but none has ever been examined for traces of salt so it is unknown if they went through either or both of these processes.

Preserving poultry in brine is unusual, although one such method is used in modern China. After the duck has been slaughtered, eviscerated, and washed thoroughly, it is hung up to dry for two to three hours. Once dry, it is put into a squat jar which is filled with soy sauce (the salt element), sugar, alcohol and spices, and placed under a stone to insure its total and continual immersion. It is left to soak in this solution for three to seven days, after which it is removed and hung up to dry in a well ventilated place for ten days or more. It is ready for use after fifteen to twenty days, although the hanging period can be extended to one year without ill effects (A. Huang pers. comm. 1992). This technique of brining was available to the ancient Egyptians, though evidence for its use is minimal.

Another process involving brining followed by smoking and drying is also practised today, although this method is used more to achieve a particular flavour, rather than from any necessity of preservation, and is applied only to mammalian meat. Brine-cured meat is taken from its vessel and hung in a smoke house for three to five days or more so that it acquires the flavour of woodsmoke as it dries out.

Brining and boiling is yet another variation: instead of merely immersing the meat in salt and nitrate solution and sealing it, the meat is boiled in the brine. This is very effective in killing off almost all types of bacteria that could be expected to infect the meat while also preserving the protein content more effectively than other methods (Pyke 1970: 175), and it can also be combined with drying/smoking after the boiling is completed. Some Egyptologists consider this last method to have been commonly practised in ancient Egypt (Klebs 1922: 104).

Dry salt-curing (including production of biltong)

The basic element of dry-curing is salt, a compound that preserves the meat more thoroughly and effectively than air drying alone. The meat is cut into strips or chunks and massaged with salt before being hung up to dry or packed in salt in a vessel that is then sealed. Meat can be left on the bone to cure, although it is more likely to spoil if treated in this way. Through osmosis, salt draws out all the liquid in the meat, causing it to dry more evenly and efficiently than if it were merely sun-dried. The lack of water and other nutrients also makes the meat an inhospitable environment for micro-organisms, and the osmotic pressure within individual cells forces out bacteria. Salted and dried meat will definitely last for two years providing it is stored in a dry, protected place. In Europe sugar and nitrate/nitrite are added to the salt cure. The moisture from the meat is drawn out to form a brine and the curing ingredients are transported into the meat by diffusion. This procedure takes a few weeks and is similar to mummification. The joint/cut can be smoked thereafter for further protection or flavour (Pearson and Tauber 1984: 286).

Biltong is one of the best-known and common techniques of dry salt-curing and even today is used in Africa, North America, Britain, and parts of Australia and Asia. The term 'biltong' can refer to salted strips of meat, although it is more commonly asssociated with dried and spiced meat. Biltong is made from the meat of all types of domestic and wild animals. Spices do not just serve to mask undesirable flavours and smells (Niven, Jr. and Shesbro 1960: 310), but actually help the preservation process itself. Biltong is made by taking strips of meat (preferably fatless) between eight and thirteen centimetres thick, coating them in a mixture of spices (e.g. salt, celery, garlic, cumin and coriander, which were all available to the ancient Egyptians), and leaving them to dry in the sun. Honey, also present in ancient Egypt, is used on biltong (L. Susman pers. comm. 1992). Although it is possible to make biltong from broad, flat pieces of meat, in general long thin pieces are used. These can be cut from any area of the animal, although the rump and flanks are preferred (L. Susman pers. comm. 1992). Biltong in South Africa and Zimbabwe is made from the rump, whereas in other African countries it is taken from the flank. The Nunamiut Eskimos use the scapulae, lumbar vertebrae, humeri, metacarpals and phalanges (Binford 1978: 100, 428–31). The use of the metacarpal and phalanges is of interest as these elements seldom appear in Egypt as part of funerary offerings unless they are attached to the rest of the leg. The Nunamiut use of meat from the vertebrae is also of interest, given that vertebrae figure among Egyptian mummified offerings (Ikram 1996: 147, n. 2).

In Egypt, it would have taken seven to ten days to dry the meat thus treated, depending on the weather and the thickness of the cut. The author has made salted biltong in Egypt by massaging salt into two strips of meat from the metacarpal area of an ox. Piece A measured 16 × 5 centimetres and was 2 centimetres thick, while piece B measured 10 × 4.5 centimetres, with a thickness of 2.5 centimetres. The two pieces were tied with string and suspended on a sunny balcony in Cairo. They were completely desiccated in seven days, although they were left outside for twelve days, after which they were brought in and left in the kitchen. Their dimensions after desiccation (A: 14 × 2 × 0.8; B: 9 × 3.2 × 1) showed a considerable reduction in size. A portion of A was consumed raw with no ill-effects. After fifty-one days B was tested, and it too caused no health problems (see Ikram 1995).

Biltong lasts for a year or more under dry conditions, although it is best consumed before the end of the first year (L. Susman pers. comm. 1992). Even in particularly damp and humid conditions it can last for up to a year, although it does lose some of its flavour and becomes a trifle rancid. The author has also experimented on the longevity of biltong when stored under a variety of different conditions: pieces of biltong were kept in the bathroom, bedroom, kitchen, and drying closet (control) of a flat in Cambridge, England. Each area was characterised by different humidities and temperatures, the bathroom and kitchen being the most humid environments, although the whole appartment could be characterised as damp. After eight months, the biltong was examined. Apart from the drying-closet biltong, which was hard and very dry, the biltong stored in the bedroom was undoubtedly the best-preserved. It was stiff, had no mould and was edible and tasty, producing no ill-effects in the consumer. The biltong from the bathroom, however, was limp and grey, as a mould had settled on it. The mould was wiped away and the biltong was still edible; although definitely rancid tasting, no ill effects resulted from consuming it. The kitchen biltong had a faint dusting of mould, but it was stiffer and tastier with none of the sourness that was characteristic of the damp bathroom biltong. Thus it is apparent that even in damp, sunless conditions biltong can remain edible for eight months, if not more.

Among the funerary offerings found in the tomb of

Amenhotep II (KV35) and Thutmose III (KV34), Lortet and Gaillard (1905–9: I, 1–17) list long narrow pieces of meat that were salted and dried. Some of these, now in the Dokki Agricultural Museum, Cairo, have been examined by the author, although they have not been chemically tested. Varying from nine to twenty centimetres in length, they are shorter than strips of modern biltong, and also shorter than those pictured drying in tomb and temple reliefs (see Ikram 1996: 152), although – like their modern counterparts in the Siwa Oasis – they bear the impression of the string that was used to suspend them. It should be noted in addition that experiments with biltong show that the strips of meat reduce their size considerably as they dry. These pieces of meat from the tombs of Amenhotep II and Thutmose III could therefore have been a form of unspiced biltong. Under a hand-lens some of the meat fragments showed evidence of salt crystals, although no traces of spices were visible – it is quite likely that any trace of spices, less tenacious than salt crystals, would have crumbled away and disappeared. The samples examined were also odourless, although any scent indicative of spices could have evaporated over time, and it remains possible that the pieces of meat had, at one time, been impregnated with spices, such as cumin and coriander, which are known to have been available to the Egyptians.

Some steak-like and on-the-bone 'victual mummies' were tested to see if they contained any applied chemicals/elements which might have been used in the preserving process. The first test consisted of tasting all the joints from the Theban tomb of the Eighteenth-Dynasty prince Amenemhat Q (New York, MMA 1021), as well as several (approximately 90 per cent) of the joints from the Theban tomb of Ahmose Meritamun, who was probably the wife of Amenhotep I or II (TT358; see Wysocki 1984). These joints all tasted salty, while, in all but three or four instances, the bandages did not. Further tests consisted of microscopic examination of several of the joints, revealing white residues and crystals of what was probably salt. Only in two instances did the bandages show any sign of salt. A sample of the meat of one such 'steak' from the tomb of Amenhotep Q (American Museum of Natural History 95–3161) was obtained and its interior meat fibres were tested using a scanning electron microscope (SEM) hooked up to a LINK system and could identify the inorganic elements in the meat sample. The machine works as follows: the sample, coated with gold or a gold-palladium mixture is placed in a vaccum compartment and bombarded with electrons. These electrons agitate the sample and any inorganic elements or chemicals in it, which, in turn, emit electrons. These are interpreted in two ways. Firstly, they appear as an image on a screen which can be photographed (Figs 25.8 and 25.9), and secondly, the type of electrons given off can be analysed and their originating

Figure 25.9 Scanning electron micrograph: close-up of crystals on meat fibre.

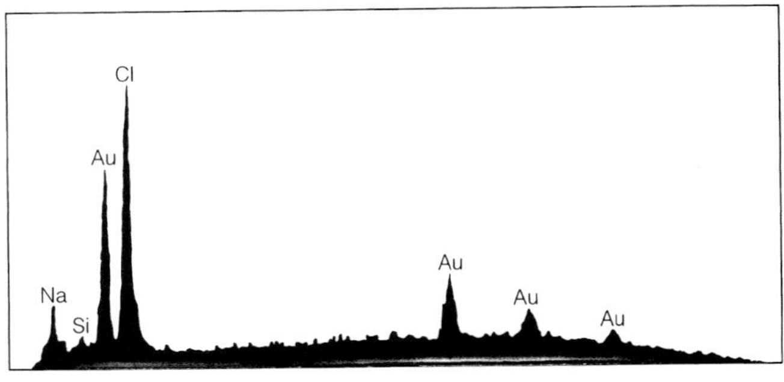

Figure 25.10 Graph showing the results of LINK analysis of those elements identified on meat fibre.

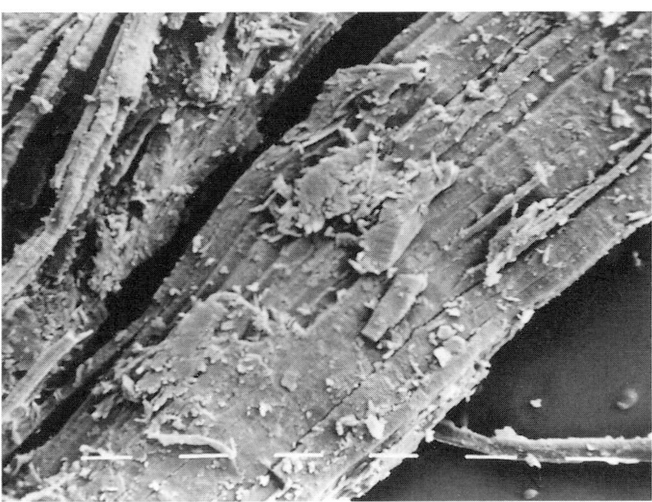

Figure 25.8 Scanning electron micrograph of meat fibre and attached crystals.

elements identified (Fig. 25.10). Figure 25.8 is a photograph of a meat fibre with an indication of crystals on it, and Figure 25.9 is a close-up of these crystals. Figure 25.10 shows the LINK analysis of the elements that were seen as crystals, conclusively demonstrating the presence of sodium and chloride, the two components of salt. While it cannot be proven incontrovertibly that this salt was deliberately added to the meat for preservation rather than merely being a precipitate from the ground water; the fact that the sample came from the interior of the joint, makes it less likely that the presence of salt was accidental. Furthermore, the meat was salty, whereas most of the bandages taste-tested were not salty.

Drying meat using salt is a common practice in contemporary Egypt: pieces of meat (chunks, joints, or strips, much like the 'victual mummies') have dry salt rubbed into them and are then hung in a windy place for two to three days, after which they remain safe to eat for three to five months. In Siwa Oasis, meat is cut into chunks, salted, and then threaded onto a string and hung out to dry (Fakhry 1973: 65). Unlike biltong, meat cured in this way is not eaten 'raw', but, as with salted fish, the salt is washed off and the meat cooked as if it had been fresh. This meat is known as *lahma mujfuf* or 'dried meat' (M. Khattab pers. comm. 1991).

Another method of meat preservation used in modern Egypt and Morocco is similar to that used in the production of pemmican. The word pemmican is used to describe a primarily North American Indian method of preservation that involves pounding mammalian meat, then mixing it with melted fat and berries (generally Sarvis berries, although grapes, plums and wild cherries are also used) to form a paste which is moulded into 'cakes'. Egyptians today chop up pieces of any meat, except chicken and fish, preferably boneless but from any part of the animal (M. Khattab pers. comm. 1991), and place them over a fire in a wide-mouthed cooking pot. Fat and salt are added, and after cooking for several hours the meat is cooled, put into a pottery container, sealed, and stored in as cool and dry a place as possible. When the time comes for the meat to be consumed, it is ladled out and cooked for a second time (M. Khattab pers. comm. 1991). The meat thus prepared, *lahma mahfooz*, or safe meat, lasts up to four months, sometimes more.

Dry-salt curing may also have been used to preserve fowl; this rare method of curing fowl is used in modern China, but only in the autumn and winter due to fear of spoilage (A. Huang pers. comm. 1992). After the bird is cleaned, washed and air-dried for an hour, salt (occasionally with added herbs and spices) is rubbed over the body cavity and skin of the bird. The bird is put into a jar and pressed down with a stone for three to four days, then it is hung for at least a week, after which it is ready to be eaten. Like brined fowl, birds cured in this way can be preserved for up to a year (A. Huang pers. comm. 1992).

Wet- and dry-salting fish

Since Egypt was famous for salted fish from Pharaonic times onwards, it seems almost certain that fish were being both wet- and dry-salted from an early date. Herodotus mentions the popularity of Egyptian salted fish in the fifth century BC, and about 400 years later Diodorus Siculus (Oldfather 1935) states that most fish were pickled in salt immediately after capture, and, slightly later, Julius Pollux records the export, in baskets or barrels, of Egyptian salt-fish, especially that from Canopus, to as far afield as Palestine (Radcliffe 1921: 355). It was a prosperous pickling industry that could export its products to Syria (Lloyd 1976: 80). Salted fish persisted into the Coptic period (Crum 1939: 44).

Either method using salt would have been the safest way of preserving fish, as salt not only kills micro-organisms but also protects it from insect attack (Green 1967: 331–4). Kenching (below) might have been a more effective way of safeguarding fish against pests and bacteria as more salt is applied to the fish, thereby rendering it more inhospitable to pests. The bacterial contamination in fish is not just determined by the method of preservation, but by the way in which it is caught (Shewan 1962: 170). If fish were caught in a net and dragged along the river floor through the mud, some would inevitably die in the process before reaching the surface, providing greater opportunity for bacterial infection to occur. The line, harpoon or trap would have been a preferable alternative as fish could be thus removed from bacterially rich environments before death.

With regard to fish, dry-salting might have involved a process known as kenching (rubbing the fish with salt after it had been gutted and washed) followed by hanging out to dry in the sun and air. It is quite possible that the drying fish shown in Egyptian tomb reliefs were also salted, since the procedure is identical except for the additional step of salting the fish before drying. Salt – whether solid or in solution – would definitely lengthen the 'shelf life' of fish as it expedites drying by drawing out water from the fish and killing bacteria with its antiseptic properties (Proctor 1972: 148). It is possible to smoke fish after salt-drying them as well as after sun-and-air drying, although it is doubtful that the Egyptians did this.

Another method of dry-salting fish was to leave the gutted or ungutted fish for several days between layers of salt in a large sealed vessel such as an amphora. Bulti and other fish from Lower Egypt appear to have been preserved in jars at the Eighteenth-Dynasty settlement of Malkata (see Hayes 1951: 104, 160), and fish preserved in this way also formed part of the food offerings of Kha at Deir el-Medina (TT8; Schiaparelli 1927: 159–60). The use of this method would explain the presence of amphorae in certain Egyptian fish-gutting scenes. The modern *faseekh* is made in this manner: fish are washed, gutted and rubbed with salt and then layered with dry salt in a pottery, metal or plastic container. Traditionally the last layer of salt is covered by heavy stones to weigh down the salt and fish, thus allowing the former to permeate the latter fully. The fish are left in the container for seven to ten days, after which the container is inverted and left for another week or so. During this time the bodily fluids drain away, and the salt solution penetrates the fish making it firm and fairly odoriforous. In Upper Egypt this preparation is called *melouha* (S. and I. Koraiem pers. comm. 1989).

Fish roe – one of the main byproducts of fish-gutting – is first attested in the in the painted reliefs on the walls of tombs at Saqqara dating to the Fifth Dynasty and later (Harpur 1987: 93; and see Fig. 25.3). The roe depicted in the tombs derives from the ovaries of the mullet (*Mugil cephalus* and *M. batarekh*), which is still an important source of food in modern Egypt (Darby and Ghaloungui 1977: 372). Egypt has been famed for mullet roe or *battarah* since at least 1657, and it was exported throughout the Middle East and even parts of Europe in the late nineteenth century (Keimer 1939: 234; Vandier 1964).

Battarah is made today by removing the ovaries (two oblong masses connected by a membrane), cutting the membrane, and washing the two separated masses with salt and water. It was common in the nineteenth century for the ovaries then to be pressed between planks to remove the salted water, but it is doubtful that this part of the procedure was performed in ancient Egypt; certainly roe-pressing with planks does not figure in any extant reliefs. The final step is to dry the *battarah* in the sun and air (Keimer 1939: 217). Battarah may also be smoked after salting, but again there is no evidence for this practice in ancient Egypt (de Morant 1973: 68).

Discussion

The evidence from ancient Egypt supports the argument for both wet and dry salt-curing of all types of meat. The funerary paintings and reliefs of the Pharaonic period, showing butchers, cooking pots and suspended lines of meat, might depict the process of boiling the meat in brine prior to subsequent drying (Fig. 25.5). The only disadvantage to this theory is the length of time and amount of fuel it would have taken to brine-boil the joints shown in such representations, since most are 'on the bone'. Unfortunately the surviving funerary models depicting meat processing do not clarify this process at all. However, given the ubiquity of salt and mummification in ancient Egypt, it seems likely that salt curing, whether brining or packing, was an established method of preserving meat.

Archaeological evidence from the late Eighteenth-Dynasty Workmen's Village at Amarna provides possible evidence for brining, in the form of salt crystals which were found adhering to a deposit of broken pottery vessels found close to buildings tentatively identified as pig butchery sites. The crystals were subsequently identified as pure salt, suggesting that pork was salted and cured here (Kemp 1986: 73–4). However, as our knowledge of the ground chemistry of this area is uncertain it is possible that the crystals derived from ground-water rather than from use, so there is no undisputed proof of brining.

The decision whether to use wet-salting, dry-salting or plain drying was largely dictated by the prosperity of the individual who was processing the meat, since any process involving salt would obviously have been more expensive than forms of sun-and-air drying. The amount of salt necessary for each recipe would also have been dictated by economic feasibility, and the vessels necessary for each preparation would also have contributed to the overall cost. Consequently, plain drying would have been both the cheapest and the most accessible of all the available methods, while a *faseekh*-type preparation would have been the most expensive. Between these extremes lay the option of brining.

Smoking

Smoking meat is a better method of preservation than drying (Dahl and Hjort 1976: 169), since the use of smoke kills any microbes that might be in and on the meat and simultaneously reduces the amount of water present, thereby improving the quality of preservation (Pyke 1970: 174). If meat is to be smoked, it must first be cut up into strips or large chunks, put on a frame and then placed over a fire preferably made with aromatic wood (e.g. hickory, cedar). If a fish or bird is to be smoked, then the entire animal is placed over the fire, preferably on a rack of some sort. To create smoke, the wood would either be slightly green or the fire would be covered by some damp organic material. This process is best-performed in an enclosed space in which the air allows smoke to circulate on all sides of the meat, unless the meat frame is stretched directly over the fire. It is necessary to guard against humidity in this process, but this would not have been a problem in ancient Egypt. If large joints of meat on the bone are being smoked, then a smoke house would be the only way of effectively smoking the joints. Three days of smoking per pound is the recommended length of time for this operation (Pearson and Tauber 1984: 286).

Despite its excellence as a method of preservation, there is little evidence for ancient Egyptian smoking or drying-and-smoking (the latter being more common ethnographically). There are a few paintings and reliefs, mainly dating to the Middle Kingdom, which show cuts of meat (and occasionally poultry) suspended on a line near a fire, and some scholars have suggested that these scenes show the smoking of meat for preservation, but this is improbable. Firstly, among the joints of meat depicted, some contain bones and would therefore certainly not be preserved by smoking as this would take several weeks to accomplish effectively (although if the meat were dried and smoked or salt-boiled and smoked this would be feasible: see section on brining, p. 663). Secondly, the scene includes a depiction of a pot on the fire, which severely limits the amount and direction of smoke available for the task. Thirdly, the joints are shown hung at some distance from the fire, although this might simply be the result of artistic convention.

As far as physical evidence for smoking is concerned, Bruyère (1937: 107) thought that some of the meat recovered from the tombs at Deir el-Medina might have been preserved by this method, but presented no convincing evidence of this for reasons already mentioned above. It should also be noted that Egypt was not rich in fuel, especially aromatic woods, therefore it is highly unlikely that, out of all the technologies available for preservation, the Egyptians would have favoured smoking, despite the fact that it was technically possible (Forbes 1965: 192). Meat is not smoked in modern Egypt, although it is common in areas with a more plentiful supply of fuel such as Palestine, other parts of the Near East and some parts of Africa.

Preservation using fat, honey and beer

The goose is a common source of fat in ancient Egypt , and it is possible that both geese and ducks were preserved in their own fat or some other source of fat. The method apparently used in ancient Egypt – whereby birds would be plucked, eviscerated and put into a fat-filled amphora, such as the one used in the tomb of Kha – is the same as that used in other parts of the world today (Montagne and Gottschalk 1961: 358). This would have been a likely alternative to salt-curing, especially since 'confit' of goose or duck can last for up to a year in a cool place, although a somewhat shorter period would have been possible in Egypt (Strang 1991: 36–9; G. Pinch pers. comm. 1992). Fat and salt are used together in modern Egypt in order to preserve mammalian meat (*lahma mahfooz*).

Honey is another method of preservation that has been suggested for ancient Egyptian poultry (D'Auria *et al.* 1988: 142); it has even been suggested that this was the means by which the body of Alexander the Great was mummified. Frequently used in curing food, especially hams, honey works well as a preservative because micro-organisms are unable to survive an environment with such a high sugar content (see the discussion of Chinese brining, p. 664). Preservation in honey does not deter moulds (J. Heath pers. comm. 1990) but they are are, however, less dangerous and can be washed or wiped off. The idea that the Egyptians used honey for curing and preserving is based on the example of the birds (ducks, geese and pigeons) found in the Eighteenth-Dynasty Theban tomb of Ahmose Meritamun, the wife of Amenhotep II (TT358). These were recently studied by Margaret Leveque of the conservation department of the Museum of Fine Arts, Boston, who suggests that 'the birds, which may have been cooked, were thinly wrapped in linen that had been saturated with an oily or resinous substance, perhaps even honey, intended to enhance both the preservation and the flavor of the food' (D'Auria *et al.* 1988: 142). Furthermore, as mentioned above (p. 665), biltong can also be made using honey.

Although honey was available in Egypt, and the Egyptians were undoubtedly aware of its preservative and curative powers, as is shown in several of the medical texts, there is absolutely no evidence that they used it with meats. Furthermore, as it was the only sweetening agent in ancient Egypt, and an expensive commodity, it is unlikely that it would have been used for the preservation of funerary offerings, the majority of which were preserved in salt (see pp. 665ff.). It is also questionable whether the ancient Egyptians would have mixed such extreme tastes since their food was generally simple, with little evidence for the mixing of ingredients. This holds true of contemporary Egyptian food which never mixes sweet, sour and salty foods. So far ancient poultry flesh has been unavailable for testing (for traces of sugar or salt) due to the paucity of available samples.

Bruyère (1937: 104) suggests that fish might have been preserved in beer (1937: 104), a hypothesis based on an item in Rekhmira's list of funerary offerings (in Theban tomb TT100) which he translates: 'curches de poissons (?) confits dans la bière, 2 amphores', but there is no real textual or practical reason to believe that this was an ancient Egyptian practice.

Conclusion

Meat – whether mammalian, avian or piscian – would have been available to most of the ancient Egyptian population at least once or twice a week. Poorer people would have obtained their meat by hunting, fishing or raising poultry, while the more wealthy would have consumed their 'small cattle' (sheep, goats, pigs) or even purchased meat from the temples when a surplus was available (see discussion of Papyrus Bulaq 11 in Peet 1934). The temples or the pharaoh would also have distributed meat (generally beef) on feast days, which would have added to the meat in the diet of most people.

The question of the existence of professional butchers and manufacturers of preserved meat remains unclear. Textual evidence from tombs provides the names of certain butchers (see Fischer 1960; Ikram 1996: 108–12), but most of these named individuals were either associated with the pharaoh or with a temple. It is possible that professional butchers only existed in conjunction with these two institutions, as they were responsible for the provision of most of the country's meat supply. Perhaps these butchers would have hired themselves out to individuals whenever they needed a butcher, as is done in Egypt today for all mammalian meat. Meat preservation was probably undertaken both by individuals in their own homes, and – on a much larger and more professional scale – by the pharaoh's household and the temples, since the two latter probably had to provide meat rations for a large part of the population of pharaonic Egypt.

Acknowledgements

I am grateful to Drs Schildkrout and Miller of the American Museum of Natural History for providing samples from the 'steaks' from the tomb of Amenhotep Q; to C. Putnis for the time and expertise spent on examining the samples with me; and to Dr D. Samuel for initiating me into SEM work. The depictions of meat in the Theban tomb of Amenmose (TT254) were kindly brought to my attention by Dr N. Strudwick.

References

Binford, L. 1978. *Nunamiut Ethnoarchaeology*. London: Academic Press.

1981. *Bones: Ancient Men and Modern Myths*. London: Academic Press.

Boessneck, J. 1988. *Die Tierwelt des Alten Ägypten*. Munich: C.H. Beck.

Boessneck, J. and von Driesch, A. 1982. *Studien an subfossilien Tiernochen aus Ägypten*. Munich and Berlin: MÄS.

Brewer, D. J. and Friedman, R.F. 1989. *Fish and Fishing in Ancient Egypt*. Warminster: Aris and Phillips.

Brunton, G. and Caton-Thompson, G. 1928. *Badarian Civilisation*. London: BSAE.

Bruyère, B. 1934. *Rapport sur les Fouilles de Deir el Médineh, 1931–32*. Cairo: IFAO.

1937. *Rapport sur les Fouilles de Deir el Médineh, 1934–35*. Cairo: IFAO.

Butzer, K.W. 1976. *Early Hydraulic Civilization in Egypt*. Chicago: University Press.

Caminos, R. 1954. *Late Egyptian Miscellanies*. Oxford: OUP.

Caton-Thompson, G. and Gardner, E. 1934. *Desert Fayum*, 2 vols. London: Royal Anthropological Institute of Great Britain and Ireland.

Clutton-Brock, J. (ed.) 1989 *The Walking Larder*. London: Unwin Hyman.

Crum, W.E. 1939. *Varia Coptica*. Aberdeen: Aberdeen University Press.

Dahl, G. and Hjort, A. 1976. *Having Herds*. Stockholm: University of Stockholm.

Darby, W.J. Ghalioungui, P. and Grivetti, L. 1977. *Food: the Gift of Osiris*, 2 vols. London: Academic Press.

D'Auria, S., Lacovara, P. and Roehrig, C.H. (eds.) 1988. *Mummies and Magic*. Boston: MFA.

David, R.A. 1973. *Religious Ritual at Abydos*. Warminster: Aris and Phillips.

Davies, N. de G. 1917. *The Tomb of Nakht at Thebes*. New York: MMA.

1920. *The Tomb of Antefoker, Vizier of Sesostris I, and of his Wife, Senet (no.60)*. London: EES.

1927. *Two Ramesside Tombs at Thebes*. New York: MMA.

1929. The town house in ancient Egypt. *Metropolitan Museum Studies*, 1: 232–55.

de Morant, H. 1973. L'Alimentation Chez les Egyptiens. *Archeologia*, 61: 64–71.

Derchain, P. 1962. Le rôle du roi d'Egypte dans le maintien de l'ordre cosmique. In *Le Pouvoir et le Sacré* (ed. L. de Heusch). Brussels: Université libre de Bruxelles, pp. 61–73.

Dumont, J. 1977. La Pèche dans le Fayoum hellenistique. *CdE*, 104: 125–55.

Epstein, H. 1971. *The Origin of the Domestic Animals of Africa*, 2 vols. New York: Africana Publishing Corporation.

Fakhry, A. 1973. *The Oases of Egypt* I. Cairo: American University.

Faulkner, R.O. 1976. *Concise Dictionary of Middle Egyptian*. Oxford: OUP.

Fischer, H.G. 1960. The butcher Ph-r-nfr. *Orientalia*, 29: 168–87.

Forbes, R.J. 1965. *Studies in Ancient Technology* III. Leiden: Brill.

Frankfort, H. and Pendlebury, J.D.S. 1933. *City of Akhenaten* II. London: EES.

Gautier, A. 1980. Contributions to the archaeozoology of Egypt. In *Prehistory of the Eastern Sahara* (eds. F. Wendorf and R. Schild). New York: Academic Press, pp. 317–44.

1987. Fishing, fowling and hunting in Late Palaeolithic times in the Nile Vally in Upper Egypt. In *Palaeoecology of Africa and Surrounding Islands* (ed. J. A. Coetzee) 18, pp. 429–40.

Ghoneim, W. 1977. *Die Ökonomische Bedeutung des Rindes im Alten Ägypten*. Bonn: Rudolf Habelt.

Godley, A.D. 1946. *Herodotus* I. London: Heinemann.

Goodman, S. 1987. Victual Egyptian bird mummies from a presumed late 17th or early 18th Dynasty tomb. *JSSEA*, 17/3: 67–77.

Green, A.A. 1967. The protection of dried sea-fish in South Arabia from infestation by dermestes frischii Kug. *Journal of Stored Products Research*, 2/4: 331–50.

Griffith, F. Ll. 1898. *Hieratic Papyri from Kahun and Gurob*. London: EES.

Harpur, Y. 1987. *Decoration in Egyptian Tombs of the Old Kingdom*. London: KPI.

Hayes, W.C. 1951. Inscriptions from the palace of Amenhotep III. *JNES*, 10: 35–56, 82–112, 156–83.

Hope, C. 1977. *Malkata: Jar Sealings and Amphorae*. Warminster: Aris and Phillips.

Hume, R. and Downes, M. 1963. *The Cordon Bleu Cookery Book*. Harmondsworth: Penguin.

Ikram, S. 1995. Did the ancient Egyptians eat biltong? *CAJ*, 5/2: 283–9.

1996. *Choice Cuts: Meat Production in Ancient Egypt*. Leuven: Peeters.

Ingram, M. 1962. The bacteriology of meat-curing brines. In *Recent Advances in Food Science* (eds. J. Hawthorn and M. Leitch). London: Butterworth.

Janssen, J. J. 1961. *Two Ancient Egyptian Ship's Logs*. Leiden: Brill.

Junker 1953. *Grabungen auf dem Friedhof des Alten Reiches bei den Pyramiden von Giza* 11. Vienna:

Keimer, L. 1939. La boutargue dans l'Egypte ancienne. *BIE*, 21: 215–43.

Kemp, B.J. (ed.) 1986. *Amarna Reports* III. London: EES.

Klebs, L. 1922. *Die Reliefs und Malereien des Mittleren Reiches*. Heidelberg: Carl Winters.

1934. *Die Reliefs und Malereien des Neuen Reiches*. Heidelberg: Carl Winters.

Leahy, M.A. 1978. *Excavations at Malkata and the Birket Habu 1971–74: the Inscriptions.* Warminster: Aris and Phillips.

Lloyd, A. 1976. *Herodotus: Book II, Commentary* I. Leiden: Brill.

Lortet, C. L. and Gaillard, C. 1905–9. *La Faune Momifiée de l'Ancienne Egypte.* Lyons: Libraire de la Faculté de Médecine et de la Faculté de Droit.

Lucas, A. 1962. *Ancient Egyptian Materials and Industries,* 4th edn., rev. J.R. Harris. London: Edward Arnold.

MacDonald, K.C. and Edwards, D.N. 1993. Chickens in Africa: the importance of Qasr Ibrim. *Antiquity,* 67: 584–90.

Martin, G.T. 1989. *The Memphite Tomb of Horemheb* I. London: EES.

Montagné, P. and Gottschalk P. 1961. *Larousse Gastronomique.* London: Paul Hamlyn.

Niven, Jr., C.F. and Shesbro, W.R. 1960. Meat preservation: chemicals and antibiotics. In *The Science of Meat and Meat Products* (ed. American Meat Institute Foundation). New York: American Meat Institute Foundation.

Oldfather, C.H. 1935. *Diodorus Siculus: The Library of History.* Loeb Classical Library. Cambridge MA and London: Harvard University Press and Heinemann.

Otto, E. 1950. An ancient Egyptian hunting ritual. *JNES,* 9: 164–77.

Pearson, A.M. and Tauber, F.W. 1984. *Processed Meats.* Westport CT: AVI.

Peet, T.E. 1934. The unit of value *š'ty* in Papyrus Bulaq 11. In *Mélanges Maspero* I. Cairo: IFAO, pp. 185–99.

Peet, T.E. and Woolley, C.L. 1923. *The City of Akhenaten* I. London: EES.

Pendlebury, J.D.S. 1951. *The City of Akhenaten* III, 2 vols. London: EES.

Porter, B. and Moss, R. 1981. *Topographical Bibliography of Ancient Egyptian Hieroglyphic Texts, Reliefs and Paintings* III. 2nd edn., rev. J. Malek. Oxford: Griffith Institute.

Proctor, D.L. 1972. The protection of smoke-dried fresh-water fish from insect damage during storage in Zambia. *Journal of Stored Product Research,* 8/2: 146–9.

Pyke, M. 1970. *Man and Food.* London: Weidenfeld and Nicolson.

Quibell, J.E. 1898. *The Ramesseum.* London: EES.

1908. *The Tomb of Yuaa and Thuiu.* Catalogue Generale. Cairo: IFAO.

Radcliffe, W. 1921. *Fishing from the Earliest Times.* London: John Murray.

Rothenberg, B. 1988. *The Egyptian Mining Temple at Timna.* London: Institute for Archaeo-Metallurgical Studies.

Schiaparelli, E. 1927. *Relazione sui Lavori della Missione Archeologica Italiana in Egitto II: La Tomba Intatta dell'Architetto Cha.* Turin: R. Museo di Antichita.

Shewan, J.M. 1962. The bacteriology of fresh and spoiling fish and some related chemical changes. In *Recent Advances in Food Science* (eds. J. Hawthorn and J. Leitch). London: Butterworth.

Smith, H.S. 1969. Animal domestication and animal cult in Dynastic Egypt. *The Domestication and Exploitation of Plants and Animals* (eds. P.J. Ucko and G. W. Dimbleby). London: Duckworth, pp. 307–14.

Strang, J. 1991. *Goose Fat and Garlic.* London: Kyle Cathie.

Vandier, J. 1964. Quelques remarques sur la preparation de la boutargue. *Kêmi,* 17: 26–34.

Weltfish, G. 1965. *The Lost Universe.* New York: Basic Books.

Wendorf, F. 1987. Early domestic cattle in the eastern Sahara. In *Palaeoecology of Africa and the Surrounding Islands (vol. 18)* (ed. J.A. Coetzee). Rotterdam: Balkema, pp. 441–8.

Wild, H. 1953–66. *Le Tombeau de Ti.* MIFAO LXV. Cairo: IFAO.

Wysocki, Z. 1984. The results of research, architectonic studies and protective work over the northern portico of the middle courtyard in the Hatshepsut temple at Deir el-Bahari. *MDAIK,* 40: 329–42.

Index

I General

For place names see also maps and their keys.

II Ancient Egyptian

N.B. A number of Egyptian words that are more commonly used (e.g. *shabti* and *serekh*) are included in the main index, with their more familiar anglicised spellings.

III Greek